WAYS OF READING

An Anthology for Writers

WAYS OF READING

An Anthology for Writers

Fourth Edition

David Bartholomae

UNIVERSITY OF PITTSBURGH

Anthony Petrosky

UNIVERSITY OF PITTSBURGH

BEDFORD BOOKS OF ST. MARTIN'S PRESS

Boston

For Bedford Books
President and Publisher: Charles H. Christensen
General Manager and Associate Publisher: Joan E. Feinberg
Managing Editor: Elizabeth M. Schaaf
Developmental Editor: Jane Betz
Editorial Assistant: Verity Winship
Production Editor: Lori Chong
Production Assistant: Christina Smith
Copyeditor: Cynthia Insolio Benn
Text Design: Anna Post-George
Cover Design: Night & Day Design
Cover Art: Summer (intaglio), 1987 by Jasper Johns. © 1996 Jasper Johns/Licensed
   by VAGA, New York, NY.

ACKNOWLEDGMENTS

Gloria Anzaldúa, "Entering into the Serpent" and "How to Tame a Wild Tongue." From *Borderlands/La
   frontera* by Gloria Anzaldúa. Copyright © 1987 by Gloria Anzaldúa. Reprinted by permission of
   Aunt Lute Books, (415) 558-8116.
John Berger, "Ways of Seeing." From *Ways of Seeing* by John Berger. Copyright © 1972 by Penguin Books
   Ltd. Used by permission of Viking Penguin, a division of Penguin Books USA Inc. Botticelli, *Venus
   and Mars;* Leonardo da Vinci, *Virgin of the Rocks* and *The Virgin and Child with St. Anne and St. John
   the Baptist.* Reproduced by courtesy of the Trustees, The National Gallery, London. Leonardo da
   Vinci, *Virgin of the Rocks.* Reprinted by permission of the Louvre Museum. Pierre Bourdieu and
   Alain Darbel, from *L'Amour de l'Art.* Reprinted by permission of Éditions de Minuit. Pieter Breughel
   the Elder, *The Procession to Calvary.* Reprinted by permission of Kunst Historisches Museum, Vienna. Frans Hals, *Regents of the Old Men's Alms House* and *Regentesses of the Old Men's Alms House.*
   Reprinted by permission of Frans Halsmuseum. Vincent van Gogh, *Wheatfield with Crows.* Vincent
   van Gogh Foundation/Van Gogh Museum, Amsterdam. Reprinted by permission of Stedelijk Museum. Jan Vermeer, *Woman Pouring Milk.* Reprinted by permission of Rijksmuseum-Stichting.
Joan Didion, "Sentimental Journeys." Reprinted with the permission of Simon & Schuster, Inc., from
   After Henry by Joan Didion. Copyright © 1992 by Joan Didion. Excerpt from William R. Taylor, "The
   Launching of a Commercial Culture," reprinted by permission of The Russell Sage Foundation.

*Acknowledgments and copyrights are continued at the back of the book on pages 852–53, which constitute an ex-
tension of the copyright page. It is a violation of the law to reproduce these selections by any means whatsoever
without the written permission of the copyright holder.*

Preface

Ways of Reading is designed for a course where students are given the opportunity to work on what they read, and to work on it by writing. When we began developing such courses, we realized the problems our students had when asked to write or talk about what they read were not "reading problems," at least not as these are strictly defined. Our students knew how to move from one page to the next. They could read sentences. They had, obviously, been able to carry out many of the versions of reading required for their education—skimming textbooks, cramming for tests, strip-mining books for term papers.

Our students, however, felt powerless in the face of serious writing, in the face of long and complicated texts—the kinds of texts we thought they should find interesting and challenging. We thought (as many teachers have thought) that if we just, finally, gave them something good to read—something rich and meaty—they would change forever their ways of thinking about English. It didn't work, of course. The issue is not only *what* students read, but what they can learn to *do* with what they read. We learned that the problems our students had lay not in the reading material (it was too hard) or in the students (they were poorly prepared) but in the classroom—in the ways we and they imagined what it meant to work on an essay.

There is no better place to work on reading than in a writing course, and this book is intended to provide occasions for readers to write. You will find a number of distinctive features in *Ways of Reading*. For one thing, it contains selections you don't usually see in a college reader: long, powerful, mysterious pieces like John Berger's "Ways of Seeing," Susan Griffin's "Our Secret," Adrienne Rich's "When We Dead Awaken: Writing as Re-Vision," Clifford Geertz's "Deep Play: Notes on the Balinese Cockfight," Mary Louise Pratt's "Arts of the Contact Zone," John Edgar Wideman's "Our Time," Michel Foucault's "Panopticism," and Joyce Carol Oates's "Theft." These are the sorts of readings we talk about when we talk with our colleagues. We have learned that we can talk about them with our students as well.

When we chose the essays and stories, we were looking for "readable" texts—that is, texts that leave some work for a reader to do. We wanted selections that invite students to be active, critical readers, that present powerful readings of common experience, that open up the familiar world and make it puzzling, rich, and problematic. We wanted to choose selections that invite students to be active readers and to take responsibility for their acts of interpretation. So we avoided the short set-pieces you find in so many anthologies. In a sense, those short selections misrepresent the act of reading. They can be read in a single sitting; they make arguments that can be easily paraphrased; they solve all the problems they raise; they wrap up Life and put it into a box; and so they turn reading into an act of appreciation, where the most that seems to be required is a nod of the head. And they suggest that a writer's job is to do just that, to write a piece that is similarly tight and neat and self-contained. We wanted to avoid pieces that were so plainly written or tightly bound that there was little for students to do but "get the point."

We learned that if our students had reading problems when faced with long and complex texts, the problems lay in the way they imagined a reader—the role a reader plays, what a reader does, why a reader reads (if not simply to satisfy the requirements of a course). When, for example, our students were puzzled by what they read, they took this as a sign of failure. ("It doesn't make any sense," they would say, as though the sense were supposed to be waiting on the page, ready for them the first time they read through.) And our students were haunted by the thought that they couldn't remember everything they had read (as though one could store all of Geertz's "Deep Play" in memory); or if they did remember bits and pieces, they felt that the fragmented text they possessed was evidence that they could not do what they were supposed to do. Our students were confronting the experience of reading, in other words, but they were taking the problems of reading—problems all readers face—and concluding that there was nothing for them to do but give up.

As expert readers, we have all learned what to do with a complex text. We know that we can go back to a text; we don't have to remember it—in fact, we've learned to mark up a text to ease that re-entry. We know that a reader is a person who puts together fragments. Those coherent readings we construct begin with confusion and puzzlement, and we construct those readings by writing and rewriting—by working on a text.

These are the lessons our students need to learn, and this is why a course in reading is also a course in writing. Our students need to learn that there is something they can do once they have first read through a complicated text; successful reading is not just a matter of "getting" an essay the first time. In a very real sense, you can't begin to feel the power a reader has until you realize the problems, until you realize that no one "gets" Geertz or Rich or Griffin or Wideman all at once. You work on what you read, and then what you have at the end is something that is yours, something you made. And this is what the teaching apparatus in *Ways of Reading* is designed to do. In a sense, it says to students, "OK, let's get to work on these essays; let's see what you can make of them."

This, then, is the second distinctive feature you will find in *Ways of Reading*: reading and writing assignments designed to give students access to the essays and stories. After each selection, for example, you will find "Questions for a Second Reading." We wanted to acknowledge that rereading is a natural way of carrying out the work of a reader, just as rewriting is a natural way of completing the work of a writer. It is not something done out of despair or as a punishment for not getting things right the first time. The questions we have written highlight what we see as central textual or interpretive problems. Geertz, for example, divides his essay into seven sections, each written in a different style. By going back through the essay with this in mind and by asking what Geertz is doing in each case (what his method is and what it enables him to accomplish), a student is in a position to see the essay as the enactment of a method and not just as a long argument with its point hidden away at the end. These questions might serve as preparations for class discussion or ways of directing students' work in journals. Whatever the case, they both honor and direct the work of rereading.

Each selection is also followed by two sets of writing assignments, "Assignments for Writing" and "Making Connections." The first set directs students back into the work they have just read. While the assignments vary, there are some basic principles behind them. They ask students to work on the essay by focusing on difficult or problematic moments in the text; they ask students to work on the author's examples, extending and testing his or her methods of analysis; or they ask students to apply the method of the essay (its way of seeing and understanding the world) to settings or experiences of their own. Students are asked, for example, to give a "Geertzian" reading to scenes from their own immediate culture (the behavior of people at a shopping mall, characteristic styles of dress) and they are asked to imagine that they are working alongside Geertz and making his project their own. Or they are asked to consider the key examples in Rich's "When We Dead Awaken" (poems from various points in her career) to see how as writers they might use the key terms of her argument ("structures of oppression," "renaming") in representing their own experience. The last assignments—

"Making Connections"—invite students to read one essay in the context of another, to see, for example, if Pratt's account of the "literate arts of the contact zone" can be used to frame a reading of Gloria Anzaldúa's prose, Harriet Jacobs's narrative, or Paulo Freire's account of education. In a sense, then, the essays are offered as models, but not as "prose models" in the strictest sense. What they model is a way of seeing or reading the world, of both imagining problems and imagining methods to make those problems available to a writer.

At the end of the book, we have included several longer assignment sequences and a goodly number of shorter sequences. In some cases these incorporate single assignments from earlier in the book; in most cases they involve students in projects that extend anywhere from two to three weeks for the shorter sequences to an entire semester's worth of work for the longer ones. Almost all the sequences include several of the stories or essays in the anthology and require a series of separate drafts and revisions. In academic life, readers seldom read single essays in isolation, as though one were "finished" with Geertz after a week or two. Rather, they read with a purpose—with a project in mind or a problem to solve. The assignment sequences are designed to give students a feel for the rhythm and texture of an extended academic project. They offer, that is, one more way of reading and writing. Because these sequences lead students through intellectual projects proceeding from one week to the next, they enable them to develop authority as specialists, to feel the difference between being an expert and being a "common" reader on a single subject. And, with the luxury of time available for self-reflection, students can look back on what they have done, not only to revise what they know, but also to take stock and comment on the value and direction of their work.

Because of their diversity, it is difficult to summarize the assignment sequences. Perhaps the best way to see what we have done is to turn to the back of the book and look at them. They are meant to frame a project for students but to leave open possibilities for new directions. You should feel free to add or drop readings, to mix sequences, and to revise the assignments to fit your course and your schedule.

You will also notice that there are few "glosses" appended to the essays. We have not added many editors' notes to define difficult words or to identify names or allusions to other authors or artists. We've omitted them because their presence suggests something we feel is false about reading. They suggest that good readers know all the words or pick up all the allusions or recognize every name that is mentioned. This is not true. Good readers do what they can and try their best to fill in the blanks; they ignore seemingly unimportant references and look up the important ones. There is no reason for students to feel they lack the knowledge necessary to complete a reading of these texts. We have translated foreign phrases and glossed some technical terms, but we have kept the selections as clean and open as possible.

Several of our reviewers asked us why we had included short stories in the collection. Perhaps the best answer is because we love to teach them. We think of them as having a status similar to that of the nonfiction narratives in the book: John Edgar Wideman's "Our Time," Ralph Ellison's "An Extravagance of Laughter," or Harriet Jacobs's "Incidents in the Life of a Slave Girl." They offer thick, readable slices of life—material rich enough for a reader's time and effort. We realize that we are ignoring traditional distinctions between fiction and nonfiction, but we are not sure that these are key distinctions in a course that presents reading as an action to be completed by writing. Students can work on Oates's story about Marya Knauer just as they can work on Wideman's representations of his brother, Robby.

We have also been asked on several occasions whether the readings aren't finally just too hard for students. The answer is no. Students will have to work on the selections, but that is the point of the course and the reason, as we said before, why a reading course is also a course in writing. College students want to believe that they can strike out on their own, make their mark, do something they have never done before. They want to *be* experts, not just hear from them. This is the great pleasure, as well as the great challenge, of undergraduate instruction. It is not hard to convince students they ought to be able to speak alongside of (or even speak back to) Clifford Geertz, Adrienne Rich, or Stephen Greenblatt. And, if a teacher is patient and forgiving— willing, that is, to let a student work out a reading of Percy, willing to keep from saying, "No, that's not it" and filling the silence with the "right" reading—then students can, with care and assistance, learn to speak for themselves. It takes a certain kind of classroom, to be sure. A teacher who teaches this book will have to be comfortable turning the essays over to the students, even with the knowledge that they will not do immediately on their own what a professional could do—at least not completely, or with the same grace and authority.

In our own teaching, we have learned that we do not have to be experts on every figure or every area of inquiry represented in this book. And, frankly, that has come as a great relief. We can have intelligent, responsible conversations about Geertz's "Deep Play" without being experts on Geertz or on anthropology or ethnography. We needed to prepare ourselves to engage and direct students as readers, but we did not have to prepare ourselves to lecture on Foucault or Rich, or post-structuralism, contemporary poetry, or American feminism. The classes we have been teaching, and they have been some of the most exciting we have ever taught, have been classes where students—together and with their instructors—work on what these essays might mean.

So here we are, imagining students working shoulder to shoulder with Geertz and Rich and Foucault, even talking back to them as the occasion arises. There is a wonderful Emersonian bravado in all this. But such is the case with strong and active readers. If we allow students to work on powerful texts, they will want to share the power. This is the heady fun of academic life, the real pleasure of thinking, reading, and writing. There is no reason to keep it secret from our students.

Note to the Fourth Edition. The fourth edition of *Ways of Reading* contains nine new selections: essays by Joan Didion, Susan Douglas, Ralph Ellison, Michel Foucault, Stephen Greenblatt, Susan Griffin, and Patricia J. Williams; a series of short stories by Lewis Nordan; and a long poem by Pulitzer Prize winner James Schuyler.

Our principle of selection remains the same—we were looking for "readable" texts, pieces that instructors and students would find challenging and compelling, pieces that offer powerful readings of ordinary experience, pieces worth extended work. Perhaps the most surprising addition is the poem. We have begun to use poetry more and more in our composition classes. We offer poems as ways of thinking and writing, just as we offer essays and stories and chapters from books, so their addition doesn't feel surprising to us. We have also used poetry, and Schuyler in particular, to direct students' attention to the sentence—to line, rhythm, and punctuation, for example.

We revised all of the assignment sequences, some to incorporate the new selections, others because, after teaching them again, we thought about them differently. The sequences that were most radically changed are: "The Aims of Education," "The Arts of the Contact Zone," "Reading Culture," and "Writing History." There are three new assignment sequences, all of them reflecting the ways we taught the new selections over the last two years. Two of them are the product of our increasing interest in autobiographical writing and the "personal" essay, "Autobiographical Explorations I and II." While there have always been assignments in *Ways of Reading* that ask students to use their experience as subject matter, this sequence looks critically and historically at the genre. The third new sequence also reflects a thread that has run through all of the editions of *Ways of Reading*. We have always had an eye for pieces of writing that challenge conventional forms and idioms, that complicate the usual ways of thinking about and representing knowledge and experience. And we have often asked students to write as though they too could participate in such revisionary projects. This kind of work is foregrounded in the new sequence, "Experimental Readings and Writings."

We continue to offer a number of shorter "minisequences." The shortest of these might engage a class for two to three weeks, the longest for a month or two. We wrote these minisequences at the request of instructors who wanted more flexibility and a wider range of projects to offer their students.

We've also updated and expanded *Resources for Teaching* WAYS OF READING, with a long interview with our colleague Jean Carr, on having students work with archival materials, and essays by graduate students on problems specific to teaching the materials in *Ways of Reading*. These essays offer advice on how to work with the book. They stand as examples of the kinds of papers graduate students might write when they use *Ways of Reading* in conjunction with a teaching seminar. They stand best, however, as examples of graduate students speaking frankly to other graduate students about teaching and about this book.

With our colleagues, we have taught every selection in this book, including the new ones. Several of us worked together to prepare the new assignment sequences; these, too, have been tested in class. As we have traveled around giving talks, we've met many people who have used *Ways of Reading*. We have been delighted to hear them talk about how it has served their teaching, and we have learned much from their advice and example. It is an unusual and exciting experience to see our course turned into a text, to see our work read, critiqued, revised, and expanded. We have many people to thank. The list that follows can't begin to name all those to whom we owe a debt. And it can't begin to express our gratitude.

Acknowledgments. We owe much to the friendship and wisdom of the people with whom we have worked at Pitt, particularly Jonathan Arac, Ellen Bishop, Jean Ferguson Carr, Steve Carr, Nick Coles, Joe Harris, Paul Kameen, Margaret Marshall, Mariolina Salvatori, Jim Seitz, Phil Smith, Kathleen Welsch, and Matt Willen; Donna Dunbar-Odom, Bianca Falbo, Angie Farkas, Gwen Gorzelsky, Jean Grace, Linda Huff, Linda Jordan, Julia Sawyer, Steve Sutherland, and Daniel Wild. Several of our graduate students worked on the new selections and assignment sequences: We thank especially Robert Atkins and Steve Sutherland. Ellen Bishop did a fine job drafting headnotes and working with assignments and assignment sequences for this edition. Richard Miller made wonderful suggestions at every stage of the project and gave a close and careful reading to drafts of the manuscript. He is a terrific teacher and a great reader.

We owe much to colleagues at other schools who have followed our work with interest and offered their support and criticism, particularly Connie Aloise, Bette-B Bauer, Margaret Bayless, Patricia Bizzell, Pamelyn Dane, Kathryn Flannery, Bruce Herzberg, Sue Ellen Holbrook, Donald McQuade, Gordon Pradl, Thomas Recchio, Mike Rose, Mary Rosner, James Slevin, Nancy Sommers, Kurt Spellmeyer, Eileen Thompson, and Lynn Bastida Tullis.

We were fortunate to have a number of outstanding reviewers on the project. We would first like to thank those who did in-depth reviews of the third edition: Jean Ferguson Carr, University of Pittsburgh; Jim Crosswhite, University of Oregon; Hugh English, Rutgers University; Judith Goleman, University of Massachusetts–Boston; Cecile Gray, Ohio Dominican College; Alfred Guy, New York University; Sue Ellen Holbrook, Southern Connecticut State University; Margaret J. Marshall, University of Pittsburgh; Robert S. Newman, State University of New York at Buffalo; Thomas Recchio, University of Connecticut; Fred Siegal, Drexel University; and Jim Seitz, University of Pittsburgh. And we would like to thank those who reviewed the new selections: Jean Ferguson Carr, University of Pittsburgh; Alfred Guy, New York University; Richard Miller, Rutgers University; and Thomas Recchio, University of Connecticut.

We would also like to thank those who responded to our questionnaire:

Miriam Amster, Cleveland State University; Martina Anderson, University of Minnesota; Jennifer Ashton, Johns Hopkins University; Nancy A. Barta-Smith, Drake University; Bette-B Bauer, University of Oregon; Margaret Bayless, Lane Community College; Pamela Beal, State University of New York at Buffalo; Daniel Berardinelli, Kent State University; Linda S. Bergmann, Illinois Institute of Technology; Neal Bruss, University of Massachusetts–Boston; William Burgos, Yale University; Michelle Burnham, State University of New York at Buffalo; Melissa Capers, University of Richmond; Susan Carlton, University of Michigan; Susie Chin, State University of New York at Buffalo; Sarah H. Collins, Rochester Institute of Technology; Glenda Conway, University of Louisville; Dulce M. Cruz, George Mason University; Wendy Judith Cutler, Portland Community College; Eric Daffron, State University of New York at Buffalo; Pamelyn Dane, Lane Community College; Jared D'Onofrio, University of Pittsburgh; Rachel Dresbeck, University of Oregon; Jane Dugan, Cleveland State University; Brenton Faber, University of Utah; Kathryn Flannery, Indiana University; Barry J. Foulk, University of Illinois; Sharon S. Gibson, Towson State University; Geraldine Griffin, University of Massachusetts–Boston; Matthew Hartman, State University of New York at Buffalo; Sally Peltier Harvey, Butte College; Carol P. Haviland, California State University at San Bernardino; Karen Cubie Henck, University of Connecticut; Bruce Horner, Drake University; Richard Howard, University of Florida; Noreen Hyde, Virginia Polytechnic Institute and State University; Kelly Hynes, University of Utah; Robert Johnson, Midwestern State University; Allan Johnston, Illinois Institute of Technology; M. Rocle Kallarud, State University of New York at Buffalo; Peter D. Kittle, University of Oregon; Kathleen Kolijian, University of Connecticut; Barry Laga, Purdue University; Don Langford, Ohio State University; Josephine Lee, Smith College; Jessica Levine, University of California at Berkeley; Thomas Loebel, State University of New York at Buffalo; Jane Maher, State University of New York at Purchase; John Maitino, California State Polytechnic University; Cheryl Marsh, Simpson College; Tomasz Mazur, University of Florida; Michael F. McClure, Oglethorpe University; Bernard P. McDonnell, Jr., University of Massachusetts–Boston; Richard McLamore, University of Connecticut; Paige B. McThenia, Boston University; Lorraine Mercer, Portland State University; E. A. Miller, Wabash College; Barbara J. Molette, Eastern Connecticut State University; Daniel G. Newell, University of Utah; Kristen Nystrom, University of Massachusetts–Boston; Diane Raptosh, Albertson College of Idaho; Poulson Reed, University of Utah; Deborah L. Repplier, University of Massachusetts–Boston; Bethany L. Reynders, Allegheny College; Georgia Rhoades, Kentucky State University; Cheryl Ruggiero, Virginia Polytechnic Institute and State University; Connie Ruzich, Malone College; Jeanne C. Ryan, Cleveland State University; Roger Sale, University of Washington; Julia Sawyer, University of Pittsburgh; Cynthia Scheinberg, Mills College; Meryl Schwartz, University of Hartford; Myra Seaman, Portland Community College; Michael Sexson, Montana State University; David Sherman, Lane Community College; Rich Sides, University of Pittsburgh; M. Simonton, Albertson College of Idaho; Bill Siverly, Portland Community College; Paul Slodky, Augusta College; Valerie A. Smith, University of Connecticut; John Spurlock, Seton Hall College; Margaret Shaw, Kent State University; Deborah Starr, University of Michigan; Joseph H. Stodder, California State Polytechnic University; Patti Capel Swartz, Georgia Southern University; Craig Thompson, Mira Costa College; Stuart R. Thompson, Seton Hall College; Howard Tinberg, Bristol Community College; Vivian Wagner, University of Illinois; Elizabeth Walden, University of Minnesota; Margaret D. Watson, Malone College; Brian Whaley, University of Oregon; Elizabeth Zanichkowsky, University of Wisconsin–Waukesha Center; Da Zheng, Boston University; and Gail Zwirn, Community College of Allegheny County.

Chuck Christensen of Bedford Books remains the best in the business. Joan Feinberg helped to shape this project from its very beginnings. She is a fine and thoughtful friend as well as a fine and thoughtful editor. Jane Betz took over with the fourth edition. It was a treat to work with her. She helped greatly in thinking through possible selections; she is a fine reader and guided us past deadlines with grace and good humor. We would not have this book without her. Verity Winship helped to locate books and readings, handled permissions, and kept a careful eye on the manuscript and our schedule. Lori Chong guided the manuscript through production. She, too, made crucial suggestions about both design and content. Cynthia Benn was an excellent copyeditor, sensitive to the quirks of our prose and with an amazing memory for pattern and detail.

And, finally, we are grateful to Joyce and Ellen, and to Jesse, Dan, Kate, Matthew, and Ben, for their love and support.

Contents

CONTENTS

CONTENTS

CONTENTS

Assignments

SEQUENCE FOURTEEN   *Writing and "Real" Life*   845

Assignments

WAYS OF READING

An Anthology for Writers

Introduction:
Ways of Reading

Making a Mark

*R*EADING involves a fair measure of push and shove. You make your mark on a book and it makes its mark on you. Reading is not simply a matter of hanging back and waiting for a piece, or its author, to tell you what the writing has to say. In fact, one of the difficult things about reading is that the pages before you will begin to speak only when the authors are silent and you begin to speak in their place, sometimes for them—doing their work, continuing their projects—and sometimes for yourself, following your own agenda.

This is an unusual way to talk about reading, we know. We have not mentioned finding information or locating an author's purpose or identifying main ideas, useful though these skills are, because the purpose of our book is to offer you occasions to imagine other ways of reading. We think of reading as a social interaction—sometimes peaceful and polite, sometimes not so peaceful and polite.

We'd like you to imagine that when you read the works we've collected here, somebody is saying something to you, and we'd like you to imagine that you are in a position to speak back, to say something of your own in

1

turn. In other words, we are not presenting our book as a miniature library (a place to find information) and we do not think of you, the reader, as a term-paper writer (a person looking for information to write down on three-by-five cards).

When you read, you hear an author's voice as you move along; you believe a person with something to say is talking to you. You pay attention, even when you don't completely understand what is being said, trusting that it will all make sense in the end, relating what the author says to what you already know or expect to hear or learn. Even if you don't quite grasp everything you are reading at every moment (and you won't), and even if you don't remember everything you've read (no reader does—at least not in long, complex pieces), you begin to see the outlines of the author's project, the patterns and rhythms of that particular way of seeing and interpreting the world.

When you stop to talk or write about what you've read, the author is silent; you take over—it is your turn to write, to begin to respond to what the author said. At that point this author and his or her text become something you construct out of what you remember or what you notice as you go back through the text a second time, working from passages or examples but filtering them through your own predisposition to see or read in particular ways.

In "The Achievement of Desire," one of the essays in this book, Richard Rodriguez tells the story of his education, of how he was drawn to imitate his teachers because of his desire to think and speak like them. His is not a simple story of hard work and success, however. In a sense, Rodriguez's education gave him what he wanted—status, knowledge, a way of understanding himself and his position in the world. At the same time, his education made it difficult to talk to his parents, to share their point of view; and to a degree, he felt himself becoming consumed by the powerful ways of seeing and understanding represented by his reading and his education. The essay can be seen as Rodriguez's attempt to weigh what he had gained against what he had lost.

If ten of us read his essay, each would begin with the same words on the page, but when we discuss the chapter (or write about it), each will retell and interpret Rodriguez's story differently; we will emphasize different sections—some, for instance, might want to discuss the strange way Rodriguez learned to read, others might be taken by his difficult and changing relations to his teachers, and still others might want to think about Rodriguez's remarks about his mother and father.

Each of us will come to his or her own sense of what is significant, of what the point is, and the odds are good that what each of us makes of the essay will vary from one to another. Each of us will understand Rodriguez's story in his or her own way, even though we read the same piece. At the same time, if we are working with Rodriguez's essay (and not putting it aside or ignoring its peculiar way of thinking about education), we will be working within a framework he has established, one that makes education stand, metaphorically, for a complicated interplay between permanence and change, imitation and freedom, loss and achievement.

In "The Achievement of Desire," Rodriguez tells of reading a book by Richard Hoggart, *The Uses of Literacy*. He was captivated by a section of this book in which Hoggart defines a particular kind of student, the "scholarship boy." Here is what Rodriguez says:

> Then one day, leafing through Richard Hoggart's *The Uses of Literacy*, I found, in his description of the scholarship boy, myself. For the first time I realized that there were other students like me, and so I was able to frame the meaning of my academic success, its consequent price—the loss.

For Rodriguez, this phrase, "scholarship boy," became the focus of Hoggart's book. Other people, to be sure, would read that book and take different phrases or sections as the key to what Hoggart has to say. Some might argue that Rodriguez misread the book, that it is really about something else, about British culture, for example, or about the class system in England. The power and value of Rodriguez's reading, however, are represented by what he was able to *do* with what he read, and what he was able to do was not record information or summarize main ideas but, as he says, "frame the meaning of my academic success." Hoggart provided a frame, a way for Rodriguez to think and talk about his own history as a student. As he goes on in his essay, Rodriguez not only uses this frame to talk about his experience, but he resists it, argues with it. He casts his experience in Hoggart's terms but then makes those terms work for him by seeing both what they can and what they cannot do. This combination of reading, thinking, and writing is what we mean by *strong reading*, a way of reading we like to encourage in our students.

When we have taught "The Achievement of Desire" to our students, it has been almost impossible for them not to see themselves in Rodriguez's description of the scholarship boy (and this was true of students who were not minority students and not literally on scholarships). They, too, have found a way of framing (even inventing) their own lives as students—students whose histories involve both success and loss. When we have asked our students to write about this essay, however, some students have argued, and quite convincingly, that Rodriguez had either to abandon his family and culture or to remain ignorant. Other students have argued equally convincingly that Rodriguez's anguish was destructive and self-serving, that he was trapped into seeing his situation in terms that he might have replaced with others. He did not necessarily have to turn his back on his family. Some have contended that Rodriguez's problems with his family had nothing to do with what he says about education, that he himself shows how imitation need not blindly lead a person away from his culture, and these student essays, too, have been convincing.

Reading, in other words, can be the occasion for you to put things together, to notice this idea or theme rather than that one, to follow a writer's announced or secret ends while simultaneously following your own. When this happens, when you forge a reading of a story or an essay, you make your mark on it, casting it in your terms. But the story makes its mark on you as well, teaching you not only about a subject (Rodriguez's struggles with his teachers and his parents, for example) but about a way of seeing and under-standing a subject. The text provides the opportunity for you to see through someone else's powerful language, to imagine your own familiar settings through the images, metaphors, and ideas of others. Rodriguez's essay, in other words, can make its mark on readers, but they, too, if they are strong, active readers, can make theirs on it.

Readers learn to put things together by writing. It is not something you can do, at least not to any degree, while you are reading. It requires that you work on what you have read, and that work best takes shape when you sit down to write. We will have more to say about this kind of thinking in a later section of the introduction, but for now let us say that writing gives you a way of going to work on the text you have read. To write about a story or essay, you go back to what you have read to find phrases or passages that de-fine what for you are the key moments, that help you interpret sections that seem difficult or troublesome or mysterious. If you are writing an essay of your own, the work that you are doing gives a purpose and a structure to that rereading.

Writing also, however, gives you a way of going back to work on the text of your own reading. It allows you to be self-critical. You can revise not just to make your essay neat or tight or tidy but to see what kind of reader you have been, to examine the pattern and consequences in the choices you have made. Revision, in other words, gives you the chance to work on your essay, but it also gives you an opportunity to work on your reading—to qualify or extend or question your interpretation of, say, "The Achievement of Desire."

We can describe this process of "re-vision," or re-seeing, fairly simply. You should not expect to read "The Achievement of Desire" once and com-pletely understand the essay or know what you want to say. You will work out what you have to say while you write. And once you have constructed a reading—once you have completed a draft of your essay, in other words—you can step back, see what you have done, and go back to work on it. Through this activity—writing and rewriting—we have seen our students become strong, active, and critical readers.

Not everything a reader reads is worth that kind of effort. The pieces we have chosen for this book all provide, we feel, powerful ways of seeing (or framing) our common experience. The selections cannot be quickly summa-rized. They are striking, surprising, sometimes troubling in how they chal-lenge common ways of seeing the world. Some of them (we're thinking of pieces by Michel Foucault, Clifford Geertz, Adrienne Rich, and Virginia

4

Woolf) have captured and altered the way our culture sees and understands daily experience. The essays have changed the ways people think and write. In fact, every selection in the book is one that has given us, our students, and colleagues that dramatic experience, almost like a discovery, when we suddenly saw things as we had never seen them before and, as a consequence, we had to work hard to understand what had happened and how our thinking had changed.

If we recall, for example, the first time we read Susan Griffin's "Our Secret" or John Edgar Wideman's "Our Time," we know that they have radically shaped our thinking. We carry these essays with us in our minds, mulling over them, working through them, hearing Griffin and Wideman in sentences we write or sentences we read; we introduce the essays in classes we teach whenever we can; we are surprised, reading them for the third or fourth time, to find things we didn't see before. It's not that we failed to "get" these essays the first time around. In fact, we're not sure we have captured them yet, at least not in any final sense, and we disagree in basic ways about what Griffin and Wideman are saying or about how these essays might best be used. Essays like these are not the sort that you can "get" like a loaf of bread at the store. We're each convinced that the essays are ours in that we know best what's going on in them, and yet we have also become theirs, creatures of these essays, because of the ways they have come to dominate our seeing, talking, reading, and writing. This captivity is something we welcome, yet it is also something we resist.

Our experience with these texts is a remarkable one and certainly hard to provide for others, but the challenges and surprises are reasons we read—we hope to be taken and changed in just these ways. Or, to be more accurate, it is why we read outside the daily requirements to keep up with the news or conduct our business. And it is why we bring reading into our writing courses.

Ways of Reading

Before explaining how we organized this book, we would like to say more about the purpose and place of the kind of strong, aggressive, labor-intensive reading we've been referring to.

Readers face many kinds of experiences, and certain texts are written with specific situations in mind and invite specific ways of reading. Some texts, for instance, serve very practical purposes—they give directions or information. Others, like the short descriptive essays often used in English textbooks and anthologies, celebrate common ways of seeing and thinking and ask primarily to be admired. These texts seem self-contained; they announce their own meanings with little effort and ask little from the reader, making it clear how they want to be read and what they have to say. They ask only for a nod of the head or for the reader to take notes and give a sigh of admiration ("yes, that was very well said"). They are clear and direct. It is as though the authors could anticipate all the questions their essays might raise and solve all the problems a reader might imagine. There is not much work for a reader to do, in other words, except, perhaps, to take notes and, in the case of textbooks, to work step-by-step, trying to remember as much as possible.

This is how assigned readings are often presented in university classrooms. Introductory textbooks (in biology or business, for instance) are good examples of books that ask little of readers outside of note-taking and memorization. In these texts the writers are experts and your job, as novice, is to digest what they have to say. And, appropriately, the task set before you is to summarize—so you can speak again what the author said, so you can better remember what you read. Essay tests are an example of the writing tasks that often follow this kind of reading. You might, for instance, study the human nervous system through textbook readings and lectures and then be asked to write a summary of what you know from both sources. Or a teacher might ask you during a class discussion to paraphrase a paragraph from a textbook describing chemical cell communication to see if you understand what you've read.

Another typical classroom form of reading is reading for main ideas. With this kind of reading you are expected to figure out what most people (or most people within a certain specialized group of readers) would take as the main idea of a selection. There are good reasons to read for main ideas. For one, it is a way to learn how to imagine and anticipate the values and habits of a particular group—test-makers or, if you're studying business, Keynesian economists, perhaps. If you are studying business, to continue this example, you must learn to notice what Keynesian economists notice—for instance, when they analyze the problems of growing government debt—to share key terms, to know the theoretical positions they take, and to adopt for yourself their common examples and interpretations, their jargon, and their established findings.

There is certainly nothing wrong with reading for information or reading to learn what experts have to say about their fields of inquiry. These are not, however, the only ways to read, although they are the ones most often taught. Perhaps because we think of ourselves as writing teachers, we are concerned with presenting other ways of reading in the college and university curriculum.

A danger arises in assuming that reading is only a search for information or main ideas. There are ways of thinking through problems and working with written texts which are essential to academic life, but which are not represented by summary and paraphrase or by note-taking and essay exams.

Student readers, for example, can take responsibility for determining the meaning of the text. They can work as though they were doing something other than finding ideas already there on the page and they can be guided by their own impressions or questions as they read. We are not, now, talking about finding hidden meanings. If such things as hidden meanings can be said to exist, they are hidden by readers' habits and prejudices (by readers' assumptions that what they read should tell them what they already know), or by readers' timidity and passivity (by their unwillingness to take the responsibility to speak their minds and say what they notice).

Reading to locate meaning in the text places a premium on memory, yet a strong reader is not necessarily a person with a good memory. This point may seem minor, but we have seen too many students haunted because they could not remember everything they read or retain a complete essay in their minds. A reader could set herself the task of remembering as much as she could from Walker Percy's "The Loss of the Creature," an essay filled with stories about tourists at the Grand Canyon and students in a biology class, but a reader could also do other things with that essay; a reader might figure out, for example, how both students and tourists might be said to have a common problem seeing what they want to see. Students who read Percy's essay as a memory test end up worrying about bits and pieces (bits and pieces they could go back and find if they had to) and turn their attention away from the more pressing problem of how to make sense of a difficult and often ambiguous essay.

A reader who needs to have access to something in the essay can use simple memory aids. A reader can go back and scan, for one thing, to find passages or examples that might be worth reconsidering. Or a reader can construct a personal index, making marks in the margin or underlining passages that seem interesting or mysterious or difficult. A mark is a way of saying, "This is something I might want to work on later." If you mark the selections in this book as you read them, you will give yourself a working record of what, at the first moment of reading, you felt might be worth a second reading.

If Percy's essay presents problems for a reader, they are problems of a different order from summary and recall. The essay is not the sort that tells you what it says. You would have difficulty finding one sentence that sums up or announces, in a loud and clear voice, what Percy is talking about. At the point you think Percy is about to summarize, he turns to one more example that complicates the picture, as though what he is discussing defies his attempts to sum things up. Percy is talking about tourists and students, about such things as individual "sovereignty" and our media culture's "symbolic packages," but if he has a point to make, it cannot be stated in a sentence or two.

In fact, Percy's essay is challenging reading in part because it does not have a single, easily identifiable main idea. A reader could infer that it has several points to make, none of which can be said easily and some of which, perhaps, are contradictory. To search for information, or to ignore the rough edges in search of a single, paraphrasable idea, is to divert attention from the task at hand, which is not to remember what Percy says but to speak about the essay and what it means to you, the reader. In this sense, the Percy essay is not the sum of its individual parts; it is, more accurately, what its readers make of it.

A reader could go to an expert on Percy to solve the problem of what to make of the essay—perhaps to a teacher, perhaps to a book in the library. And if the reader pays attention, he could remember what the expert said or she could put down notes on paper. But in doing either, the reader only rehearses what he or she has been told, abandoning the responsibility to make the essay meaningful. There are ways of reading, in other words, in which Percy's essay, "The Loss of the Creature," is not what it means to the experts but what it means to you as a reader willing to take the chance to construct a reading. You can be the authority on Percy; you don't have to turn to others. The meaning of the essay, then, is something you develop as you go along, something for which you must take final responsibility. The meaning is forged from reading the essay, to be sure, but it is determined by what you do with the essay, by the connections you can make and your explanation of why those connections are important, and by your account of what Percy might mean when he talks about "symbolic packages" or a "loss of sovereignty" (phrases Percy uses as key terms in the essay). This version of Percy's essay will finally be yours; it will not be exactly what Percy said. (Only his words in the order he wrote them would say exactly what he said.) You will choose the path to take through his essay and support it as you can with arguments, explanations, examples, and commentary.

If an essay or story is not the sum of its parts but something you as a reader create by putting together those parts that seem to matter personally, then the way to begin, once you have read a selection in this collection, is by reviewing what you recall, by going back to those places that stick in your memory—or, perhaps, to those sections you marked with checks or notes in the margins. You begin by seeing what you can make of these memories and notes. You should realize that with essays as long and complex as those we've included in this book, you will never feel, after a single reading, as though you have command of everything you read. This is not a problem. After four or five readings (should you give any single essay that much attention), you may still feel that there are parts you missed or don't understand. This sense of incompleteness is part of the experience of reading, at least the experience of reading serious work. And it is part of the experience of a strong reader. No reader could retain one of these essays in her mind, no matter how proficient her memory or how experienced she might be. No reader, at least no reader we would trust, would admit that he understood everything that Michel Foucault or Adrienne Rich or Patricia J. Williams had to say. What strong readers know is that they have to begin, and they have to begin regardless of their doubts or hesitations. What you have after your first reading of an essay is a starting place, and you begin with your marked passages or examples or notes, with questions to answer, or with problems to solve. Strong readings, in other words, put a premium on individual acts of attention and composition.

Strong Readers, Strong Texts

We chose pieces for this book that invite strong readings. Our selections require more attention (or a different form of attention) than a written summary, a reduction to gist, or a recitation of main ideas. They are not "easy" reading. The challenges they present, however, do not make them inaccessible to college students. The essays are not specialized studies; they have interested, pleased, or piqued general and specialist audiences alike. To say that they are challenging is to say, then, that they leave some work for a reader to do. They are designed to teach a reader new ways to read (or to step outside habitual ways of reading), and they anticipate readers willing to take the time to learn. These readers need not be experts on the subject matter. Perhaps the most difficult problem for students is to believe that this is true.

You do not need experts to explain these stories and essays, although you could probably go to the library and find an expert guide to most of the selections we've included. Let's take, for example, Adrienne Rich's "When We Dead Awaken: Writing as Re-Vision." This essay looks at the history of women's writing (and at Rich's development as a poet). It argues that women have been trapped within a patriarchal culture—speaking in men's voices and telling stories prepared by men—and, as a consequence, according to Rich, "We need to know the writing of the past, and know it differently than we have ever known it; not to pass on a tradition but to break its hold over us."

You could go to the library to find out how Rich is regarded by experts, by literary critics or feminist scholars, for example; you could learn how her work fits into an established body of work on women's writing and the representation of women in modern culture. You could see what others have said about the writers she cites: Virginia Woolf, Jane Austen, and Elizabeth Bishop. You could see how others have read and made use of Rich's essay. You could see how others have interpreted the poems she includes as part of her argument. You could look for standard definitions of key terms like "patriarchy" or "formalism."

Though it is often important to seek out other texts and to know what other people are saying or have said, it is often necessary and even desirable to begin on your own. Rich can also be read outside any official system of interpretation. She is talking, after all, about our daily experience. And when she addresses the reader, she addresses a person—not a term-paper writer. When she says, "We need to know the writing of the past, and know it differently than we have ever known it," she means us and what we know and how we know what we know. (Actually the "we" of her essay refers most accurately to women readers, leading men to feel the kind of exclusion women must feel when the reader is always "he." But it is us, the men who are in the act of reading this essay, who feel and respond to this pressure.)

The question, then, is not what Rich's words might mean to a literary critic, or generally to those who study contemporary American culture. The question is what you, the reader, can make of those words given your own experience, your goals, and the work you do with what she has written. In this sense, "When We Dead Awaken" is not what it means to others (those who have already decided what it means) but what it means to you, and this meaning is something you compose when you write about the essay; it is your account of what Rich says and how what she says might be said to make sense.

A teacher, poet, and critic we admire, I. A. Richards, once said, "Read as though it made sense and perhaps it will." To take command of complex material like the selections in this book, you need not subordinate yourself to experts; you can assume the authority to provide such a reading on your own. This means you must allow yourself a certain tentativeness and recognize your limits. You should not assume that it is your job to solve the problems between men and women. You can speak with authority while still acknowledging that complex issues *are* complex.

There is a paradox here. On the one hand, the essays are rich, magnificent, too big for anyone to completely grasp all at once, and before them, as before inspiring spectacles, it seems appropriate to stand humbly, admiringly. And yet, on the other hand, a reader must speak with authority.

In "The American Scholar," Ralph Waldo Emerson says, "Meek young men grow up in libraries, believing it their duty to accept the views, which Cicero, which Locke, which Bacon, have given, forgetful that Cicero, Locke, and Bacon were only young men in libraries when they wrote these books." What Emerson offers here is not a fact but an attitude. There is creative reading, he says, as well as creative writing. It is up to you to treat authors as your equals, as people who will allow you to speak too. At the same time, you must respect the difficulty and complexity of their texts and of the issues and questions they examine. Little is to be gained, in other words, by turning Rich's essay into a message that would fit on a poster in a dorm room: "Be Yourself" or "Stand on Your Own Two Feet."

Reading with and against the Grain

Reading, then, requires a difficult mix of authority and humility. On the one hand, a reader takes charge of a text; on the other, a reader gives generous attention to someone else's (a writer's) key terms and methods, commits his time to her examples, tries to think in her language, imagines that this strange work is important, compelling, at least for the moment.

Most of the questions in *Ways of Reading* will have you moving back and forth in these two modes, reading with and against the grain of a text, repro-

ducing an author's methods, questioning his or her direction and authority.
With the essay "When We Dead Awaken," for example, we have asked students to give a more complete and detailed reading of Rich's poems (the poems included in the essay) than she does, to put her terms to work, to extend her essay by extending the discussion of her examples. We have asked students to give themselves over to her essay—recognizing that this is not necessarily an easy thing to do. Or, again in Rich's name, we have asked students to tell a story of their own experience, a story similar to the one she tells, one that can be used as an example of the ways a person is positioned by a dominant culture. Here we are saying, in effect, read your world in Rich's terms. Notice what she would notice. Ask the questions she would ask. Try out her conclusions.

To read generously, to work inside someone else's system, to see your world in someone else's terms—we call this "reading with the grain." It is a way of working *with* a writer's ideas, in conjunction with someone else's text. As a way of reading, it can take different forms. In the reading and writing assignments that follow the selections in this book, you will sometimes be asked to summarize and paraphrase, to put others' ideas into your terms, to provide your account of what they are saying. This is a way of getting a tentative or provisional hold on a text, its examples and ideas; it allows you a place to begin to work. And sometimes you will be asked to extend a writer's project—to add your examples to someone else's argument, to read your experience through the frame of another's text, to try out the key terms and interpretive schemes in another writer's work. In the assignments that follow the Rich essay, for example, students are asked both to reproduce her argument and to extend her terms to examples from their own experience.

We have also asked students to read against the grain, to read critically, to turn back, for example, *against* Rich's project, to ask questions they believe might come as a surprise, to look for the limits of her vision, to provide alternate readings of her examples, to find examples that challenge her argument, to engage her, in other words, in dialogue. How might her poems be read to counter what she wants to say about them? If her essay argues for a new language for women, how is this language represented in the final poem or the final paragraphs, when the poem seems unreadable and the final paragraph sounds familiarly like the usual political rhetoric? If Rich is arguing for a collective movement, a "we" represented by the "we" of her essay, who is included and who is excluded by the terms and strategies of her writing? To what degree might you say that this is a conscious or necessary strategy?

Many of the essays in this book provide examples of writers working against the grain of common sense or everyday language. This is true of John Berger, for example, who redefines the "art museum" against the way it is usually understood. It is true of John Edgar Wideman, who reads against his own text while he writes it—asking questions that disturb the story as it emerges on the page. It is true of Harriet Jacobs, Patricia J. Williams, and Virginia Woolf, whose writings show the signs of their efforts to work against the grain of the standard essay, habitual ways of representing what it means to know something, to be somebody, to speak before others.

This, we've found, is the most difficult work for students to do, this work against the grain. For good reasons and bad, students typically define their skill by reproducing rather than questioning or revising the work of their teachers (or the work of those their teachers ask them to read). It is important to read generously and carefully and to learn to submit to projects that others have begun. But it is also important to know what you are doing—to understand where this work comes from, whose interests it serves, how and where it is kept together by will rather than desire, and what it might have to do with you. To fail to ask the fundamental questions—Where am I in this? How can I make my mark? Whose interests are represented? What can I learn by reading with or against the grain?—to fail to ask these questions is to mistake skill for understanding, and it is to misunderstand the goals of a liberal education. All of the essays in this book, we would argue, ask to be read, not simply reproduced; they ask to be read and to be read with a difference. Our goal is to make that difference possible.

Reading and Writing:
The Questions and Assignments

Strong readers, we've said, remake what they have read to serve their own ends, putting things together, figuring out how ideas and examples relate, explaining as best they can material that is difficult or problematic, translating phrases like Richard Rodriguez's "scholarship boy" into their own terms. At these moments, it is hard to distinguish the act of reading from the act of writing. In fact, the connection between reading and writing can be seen as almost a literal one, since the best way you can show your reading of a rich and dense essay like "The Achievement of Desire" is by writing down your thoughts, placing one idea against another, commenting on what you've done, taking examples into account, looking back at where you began, perhaps changing your mind, and moving on.

Readers, however, seldom read a single essay in isolation, as though their only job were to arrive at some sense of what an essay has to say. Although we couldn't begin to provide examples of all the various uses of reading in academic life, it is often the case that readings provide information and direction for investigative projects, whether they are philosophical or scientific in nature. The reading and writing assignments that follow each selection in this book are designed to point you in certain directions, to give you ideas and projects to work with, and to challenge you to see one writer's ideas through another's.

Strong readers often read critically, weighing, for example, an author's claims and interpretations against evidence—evidence provided by the author in the text, evidence drawn from other sources, or the evidence that is assumed to be part of a reader's own knowledge and experience. Critical reading can produce results as far-reaching as a biochemist publicly challenging the findings and interpretations in an article on cancer research in the *New England Journal of Medicine* or as quiet as a student offering a personal interpretation of a story in class discussion.

You will find that the questions we have included in our reading and writing assignments often direct you to test what you think an author is saying by measuring it against your own experience. Paulo Freire, for example, in "The 'Banking' Concept of Education" talks about the experience of the student, and one way for you to develop or test your reading of his essay is to place what he says in the context of your own experience, searching for examples that are similar to his and examples that differ from his. If the writers in this book are urging you to give strong readings of your common experience, you have access to what they say because they are talking not only to you but about you. Freire has a method that he employs when he talks about the classroom—one that compares "banking" education with "problem-posing" education. You can try out his method and his terms on examples of your own, continuing his argument as though you were working with him on a common project. Or you can test his argument as though you want to see not only where and how it will work but where and how it will not.

You will also find questions that ask you to extend the argument of the essay by looking in detail at some of the essay's own examples. John Berger, for example, gives a detailed analysis of two paintings by Frans Hals in "Ways of Seeing." Other paintings in the essay he refers to only briefly. One way of working on his essay is to look at the other examples, trying to do with them what he has done for you earlier.

Readers, as we have said, seldom read an essay in isolation, as though, having once worked out a reading of Virginia Woolf's "A Room of One's Own," they could go on to something else, something unrelated. It is unusual for anyone, at least in an academic setting, to read in so random a fashion. Readers read most often because they have a project in hand—a question they are working on or a problem they are trying to solve. For example, if as a result of reading Woolf's essay you become interested in the difference between women's writing and men's writing, and you begin to notice things you would not have noticed before, then you can read other essays in the book through this frame. If you have a project in mind, that project will help determine how you read these other essays. Sections of an essay that might otherwise seem unimportant suddenly become important—Gloria Anzaldúa's unusual prose style, Rich's references to Woolf, the moments when Harriet Jacobs addresses the "women of the North." Woolf may enable you to read Jacobs's narrative differently. Jacobs may spur you to rethink Woolf.

In a sense, then, you do have the chance to become an expert reader, a reader with a project in hand, one who has already done some reading, who has watched others at work, and who has begun to develop a method of analysis and a set of key terms. You might read Jacobs's narrative "Incidents in the Life of a Slave Girl," for example, in the context of Mary Louise Pratt's discussion of "autoethnography," or you might read the selections by Gloria Anzaldúa, Ralph Ellison, John Edgar Wideman, and Patricia J. Williams as offering differing accounts of racism in America. Imagining yourself operating alongside some of the major figures in contemporary thought can be great fun and heady work—particularly when you have the occasion to speak back to them.

In every case, then, the material we provide to direct your work on the essay, story, or poem will have you constructing a reading, but then doing something with what you have read—using the selection as a frame through which you can understand (through which you can "read") your own experience, the examples of others, or the ideas and methods of other writers.

You may find that you have to alter your sense of who a writer is and what a writer does as you work on your own writing. Writers are often told that they need to begin with a clear sense of what they want to do and what they want to say. The writing assignments we've written, we believe, give you a sense of what you want (or need) to do. We define a problem for you to work on, and the problem will frame the task for you. You will have to decide where you will go in the texts you have read to find materials to work with, the primary materials that will give you a place to begin as you work on your essay. It would be best, however, if you did not feel that you need to have a clear sense of what you want to say before you begin. You may begin to develop a sense of what you want to say while you are writing—as you begin, for example, to examine how and why Anzaldúa's prose could be said to be difficult to read, and what that difficulty might enable you to say about what Anzaldúa expects of a reader. It may also be the case, however, that the subjects you will be writing about are too big for you to assume that you need to have all the answers or that it is up to you to have the final word or to solve the problems once and for all. When you work on your essays, you should cast yourself in the role of one who is exploring a question, examining what might be said, and speculating on possible rather than certain conclusions. If you consider your responses to be provisional, examples of what might be said by a bright and serious student at this point in time, you will be in a position to learn more, as will those who read what you write. Think of yourself, then, as a writer intent on opening a subject up rather than closing one down.

Let us turn briefly now to the three categories of reading and writing assignments you will find in the book.

Questions for a Second Reading

Immediately following each selection are questions designed to guide your second reading. You may, as we've said, prefer to follow your own instincts as you search for the materials to build your understanding of the essay or story. These questions are meant to assist that process or develop those instincts. Most of the essays and stories in the book are longer and more difficult than those you may be accustomed to reading. They are difficult enough that any reader would have to reread them and work to understand them; these questions are meant to suggest ways of beginning that work.

The second reading questions characteristically ask you to consider the relations between ideas and examples in what you have read or to test specific statements in the essays against your own experience (so that you can get a sense of the author's habit of mind, his or her way of thinking about subjects that are available to you, too). Some turn your attention to what we take to be key terms or concepts, asking you to define these terms by observing how the writer uses them throughout the essay.

These are the questions that seemed "natural" to us; they reflect our habitual way of reading and, we believe, the general habits of mind of the academic community. These questions have no simple answers; you will not find a correct answer hidden somewhere in the selection. In short, they are not the sorts of questions asked on SAT or ACT exams. They are real questions, questions that ask about the basic methods of an essay or about the issues the essay raises. They pose problems for interpretation or indicate sections where, to our minds, there is some interesting work for a reader to do. They are meant to reveal possible ways of reading the text, not to indicate that there is only one correct way, and that we have it.

You may find it useful to take notes as you read through each selection a second time, perhaps in a journal you can keep as a sourcebook for more formal written work.

Assignments for Writing

This book actually offers three different kinds of writing assignments; assignments that ask you to write about a single essay or story; assignments that ask you to read one selection through the frame of another; and longer sequences of assignments that define a project within which three or four of the selections serve as primary sources. All of these assignments serve a dual purpose. Like the second reading questions, they suggest a way for you to reconsider the stories or essays; they give you access from a different perspective. The assignments also encourage you to be a strong reader and actively interpret what you have read. In one way or another, they all invite you to use a story or an essay as a way of framing experience, as a source of terms and methods to enable you to interpret something else—some other text, events and objects around you, or your own memories and experience. The assignment sequences can be found at the end of the book. The others (titled "Assignments for Writing" and "Making Connections") come immediately after each selection.

"Assignments for Writing" ask you to write about a single selection. Although some of these assignments call for you to paraphrase or reconstruct difficult passages, most ask you to interpret what you have read with a specific purpose in mind. The work you are to do is generally of two sorts. For most of the essays, one question asks you to interpret a moment from your own experience through the frame of the essay. This, you will remember, is the use that Rodriguez made of Richard Hoggart's *The Uses of Literacy*.

Other assignments, however, ask you to turn an essay back on itself or to extend the conclusions of the essay by reconsidering the examples the writer has used to make his or her case. Adrienne Rich's essay, "When We Dead Awaken: Writing as Re-Vision," is built around a series of poems she wrote at various stages in her career. She says that the development represented by these poems reflects her growing understanding of the problems women in a patriarchal society have in finding a language for their own experience. She presents the poems as examples but offers little detailed discussion of them. One of the assignments, then, asks you to describe the key differences in these poems. It next asks you to comment on the development of her work and to compare your account of that development with hers.

In her essay, Rich also says that writing is "renaming." This is an interesting and, one senses, a potentially powerful term. For it to be useful, however, a reader must put it to work, to see what results when you accept the challenge of the essay and think about writing as renaming. Another assignment, then, asks you to apply this term to one of her poems and to discuss the poem as an act of renaming. The purpose of this assignment is not primarily to develop your skill as a reader of poems but to develop your sense of the method and key terms of Rich's argument.

A note on the writing assignments: When we talk with teachers and students using *Ways of Reading*, we are often asked about the wording of these assignments. The assignments are long. The wording is often unusual, unexpected. The assignments contain many questions, not simply one. The directions seem indirect, confusing. "Why?" we're asked. "How should we work with these?" When we write assignments, our goal is to point students toward a project, to provide a frame for their reading, a motive for writing, a way of asking certain kinds of questions. In that sense, the assignments should not be read as a set of directions to be followed literally. In fact, they are written to resist that reading, to forestall a writer's desire to simplify, to be efficient, to settle for the first clear line toward the finish. We want to provide a context to suggest how readers and writers might take time, be thoughtful. And we want the projects students work on to become their own. We hope to provoke varied responses, to leave the final decisions to the students. So the assignments try to be open and suggestive rather than narrow and direct. We ask lots of questions, but students don't need to answer them all (or any of them) once they begin to write. Our questions are meant to suggest ways of questioning, starting points. "What do you want?" Our own students ask this question. We want writers to make the most they can of what they read, including our questions and assignments.

Making Connections

The connections questions will have you work with two or more readings at a time. These are not so much questions that ask you to compare or contrast the essays or stories as they are directions on how you might use one text as the context for interpreting another. Mary Louise Pratt, for example, in "Arts of the Contact Zone" looks at the work of a South American native, an Inca named Guaman Poma, writing in the seventeenth century to King Philip III of Spain. His work, she argues, can be read as a moment of contact, one in which different cultures and positions of power come together in a single text—in which a conquered person responds to the ways he is represented in the mind and the language of the conqueror. Pratt's reading of Guaman Poma's letter to King Philip, and the terms she uses to describe the way she reads it, provides a powerful context for a reader looking at essays by other writers, like Harriet Jacobs or Gloria Anzaldúa or Patricia J. Williams, for whom the "normal" or "standard" language of American culture is difficult, troubling, unsatisfactory, or incomplete. There are, then, assignments that ask you both to extend and to test Pratt's reading through your reading of alternative texts. In another assignment, you are asked to consider different ways of writing "history," writing about the past, by looking at the work of two very different writers: John Edgar Wideman, a fiction writer who turns his hand to "real life" when he writes about his brother and his family, and Patricia Nelson Limerick, a professional historian who writes not only about the American West but also about the writing of the American West, about how the American West has been written into popular culture and the popular imagination.

The purpose of all these assignments is to demonstrate how the work of one author can be used as a frame for reading and interpreting the work of another. This can be exciting work, and it demonstrates a basic principle of liberal arts education: students should be given the opportunity to adopt different points of view, including those of scholars and writers who have helped to shape modern thought. These kinds of assignments give you the chance, even as a novice, to try your hand at the work of professionals.

The Assignment Sequences

The assignment sequences are more broad-ranging versions of the making connections assignments; in the sequences, several reading and writing assignments are linked and directed toward a single goal. They allow you to work on projects that require more time and incorporate more readings than would be possible in a single assignment. And they encourage you to develop your own point of view in concert with those of the professionals who wrote the essays and stories you are reading.

The assignments in a sequence build on one another, each relying on the ones before. A sequence will usually make use of three or four reading selections. The first is used to introduce an area of study or inquiry as well as to establish a frame of reference, a way of thinking about the subject. In the sequence titled "The Aims of Education," you begin with an essay by Paulo Freire. Freire, a Marxist educator, takes a standard account of education (in which students are said to be "given" knowledge by a teacher) and, as he says, "problematizes" that account, opens it up to question, by arguing that such classrooms only reproduce the powerlessness students will face in the larger society. The goal of the sequence is to provide a point for you to work from, one that you can open up to question. Subsequent assignments ask you to develop examples from your own schooling as you work through other accounts of education in, for example, Adrienne Rich's "When We Dead Awaken," Mary Louise Pratt's "Arts of the Contact Zone," or Susan Griffin's "Our Secret."

The sequences allow you to participate in an extended academic project, one in which you take a position, revise it, look at a new example, hear what someone else has to say, revise it again, and see what conclusions you can draw about your subject. These projects always take time—they go through stages and revisions as a writer develops a command over his or her material, pushing against habitual ways of thinking, learning to examine an issue from different angles, rejecting quick conclusions, seeing the power of understanding that comes from repeated effort, and feeling the pleasure writers take when they find their own place in the context of others whose work they admire. This is the closest approximation we can give you of the rhythm and texture of academic life, and we offer our book as an introduction to its characteristic ways of reading, thinking, and writing.

The Readings

GLORIA
ANZALDÚA

G LORIA ANZALDÚA *grew up in southwest Texas, the physical and cultural borderland between the United States and Mexico, an area she has called* "una herida abierta," *an open wound, "where the Third World grates against the first and bleeds." Defining herself as lesbian, feminist, Chicana—a representative of the new* mestiza—*she has dramatically revised the usual narrative of American autobiography. "I am a border woman," she says. "I grew up between two cultures, the Mexican (with a heavy Indian influence) and the Anglo (as a member of a colonized people in our own territory). I have been straddling that* tejas-*Mexican border, and others, all my life." Cultural, physical, spiritual, sexual, linguistic—the borderlands defined by Anzaldúa extend beyond geography. "In fact," she says, "the Borderlands are present where two or more cultures edge each other, where people of different races occupy the same territory, where under, lower, middle, and upper classes touch, where the space between two individuals shrinks with intimacy." In a sense, her writing argues against the concept of an "authentic," unified, homogeneous culture, the pure "Mexican experience," a nostalgia that underlies much of the current interest in "ethnic" literature.*

In the following selections, which represent two chapters from her book Border-lands/La frontera *(1987), Anzaldúa mixes genres, moving between poetry and prose, weaving stories with sections that resemble the work of a cultural or political theorist. She tells us a story about her childhood, her culture, and her people that is at once both myth and history. Her prose, too, is mixed, shifting among Anglo-American English, Castilian Spanish, Tex-Mex, Northern Mexican dialect, and Nahuatl (Aztec), speaking to us in the particular mix that represents her linguistic heritage: "Presently this infant language, this bastard language, Chicano Spanish, is not approved by any society. But we Chicanos no longer feel that we need to beg entrance, that we need always to make the first overture—to translate to Anglos, Mexicans, and Latinos, apology blurting out of our mouths with every step. Today we ask to be met halfway. This book is our invitation to you." The book is an invitation, but not always an easy one. The chapters that follow make a variety of demands on the reader. The shifting styles, genres, and languages can be confusing or disturbing, but this is part of the effect of Anzaldúa's prose, part of the experience you are invited to share.*

In a chapter from the book that is not included here, Anzaldúa gives this account of her writing:

> *In looking at this book that I'm almost finished writing, I see a mosaic pattern (Aztec-like) emerging, a weaving pattern, thin here, thick there. I see a preoccupation with the deep structure, the underlying structure, with the gesso underpainting that is red earth, black earth. . . . This almost finished product seems an assemblage, a montage, a beaded work with several leitmotifs and with a central core, now appearing, now disappearing in a crazy dance. The whole thing has had a mind of its own, escaping me and insisting on putting together the pieces of its own puzzle with minimal direction from my will.*

Beyond her prose, she sees the competing values of more traditionally organized narratives, "art typical of Western European cultures, [which] attempts to manage the energies of its own internal system. . . . It is dedicated to the validation of itself. Its task is to move humans by means of achieving mastery in content, technique, feeling. Western art is always whole and always 'in power.'"

Anzaldúa's prose puts you, as a reader, on the borderland; in a way, it re-creates the position of the mestiza. *As you read, you will need to meet this prose halfway, generously, learning to read a text that announces its difference.*

In addition to Borderlands/La Frontera, *Anzaldúa has edited* Haciendo Caras: Making Face/Making Soul *(1990) and coedited an anthology,* This Bridge Called My Back: Writings by Radical Women of Color *(1983).*

Entering into the Serpent

*Sueño con serpientes, con serpientes del mar,
Con cierto mar, ay de serpientes sueño yo.
Largas, transparentes, en sus barrigas llevan
Lo que puedan arebatarle al amor.*

22

Oh, oh, oh, la mató y aparese una mayor.
Oh, con mucho más infierno en digestión.

I dream of serpents, serpents of the sea,
A certain sea, oh, of serpents I dream.
Long, transparent, in their bellies they carry
All that they can snatch away from love.
Oh, oh, oh, I kill one and a larger one appears.
Oh, with more hellfire burning inside!
— SILVIO RODRÍGUES,
Sueño con serpientes"[1]

In the predawn orange haze, the sleepy crowing of roosters atop the trees. *No vayas al escusado en lo oscuro.* Don't go to the outhouse at night, Prieta, my mother would say. *No se te vaya a meter algo pour allá.* A snake will crawl into your *nalgas,*[2] make you pregnant. They seek warmth in the cold. *Dicen que las culebras* like to suck *chiches,*[3] can draw milk out of you.

En el escusado in the half-light spiders hang like gliders. Under my bare buttocks and the rough planks the deep yawning tugs at me. I can see my legs fly up to my face as my body falls through the round hole into the sheen of swarming maggots below. Avoiding the snakes under the porch I walk back into the kitchen, step on a big black one slithering across the floor.

Ella tiene su tono[4]

Once we were chopping cotton in the fields of Jesus Maria Ranch. All around us the woods. *Quelite*[5] towered above me, choking the stubby cotton that had outlived the deer's teeth.

I swung *el azadón*[6] hard. *El quelite* barely shook, showered nettles on my arms and face. When I heard the rattle the world froze.

I barely felt its fangs. Boot got all the *veneno.*[7] My mother came shrieking, swinging her hoe high, cutting the earth, the writhing body.

I stood still, the sun beat down. Afterwards I smelled where fear had been: back of neck, under arms, between my legs, I felt its heat slide down my body. I swallowed the rock it had hardened into.

When Mama had gone down the row and was out of sight, I took out my pocketknife. I made an X over each prick. My body followed the blood, fell onto the soft ground. I put my mouth over the red and sucked and spit between the rows of cotton.

I picked up the pieces, placed them end on end. *Culebra de cascabel.*[8] I counted the rattlers: twelve. It would shed no more. I buried the pieces between the rows of cotton.

That night I watched the window sill, watched the moon dry the blood on the tail, dreamed rattler fangs filled my mouth, scales covered my body. In the morning I saw through snake eyes, felt snake blood course through my body. The serpent, *mi tono*, my animal counterpart. I was immune to its venom. Forever immune.

Snakes, *víboras:* since that day I've sought and shunned them. Always when they cross my path, fear and elation flood my body. I know things older than Freud, older than gender. She—that's how I think of *la Víbora*, Snake Woman. Like the ancient Olmecs, I know Earth is a coiled Serpent. Forty years it's taken me to enter into the Serpent, to acknowledge that I have a body, that I am a body and to assimilate the animal body, the animal soul.

Coatlalopeuh, She Who Has Dominion over Serpents

Mi mamagrande Ramona toda su vida mantuvo un altar pequeño en la esquina del comedor. Siempre tenía las velas prendidas. Allí hacía promesas a la Virgen de Guadalupe. My family, like most Chicanos, did not practice Roman Catholicism but a folk Catholicism with many pagan elements. *La Virgen de Guadalupe's* Indian name is *Coatlalopeuh.* She is the central deity connecting us to our Indian ancestry.

Coatlalopeuh is descended from, or is an aspect of, earlier Mesoamerican fertility and Earth goddesses. The earliest is *Coatlicue,* or "Serpent Skirt." She had a human skull or serpent for a head, a necklace of human hearts, a skirt of twisted serpents, and taloned feet. As creator goddess, she was mother of the celestial deities, and of *Huitzilopochtli* and his sister, *Coyolxauhqui,* She with Golden Bells, Goddess of the Moon, who was decapitated by her brother. Another aspect of *Coatlicue* is *Tonantsi.*[9] The Totonacs, tired of the Aztec human sacrifices to the male god, *Huitzilopochtli,* renewed their reverence for *Tonantsi* who preferred the sacrifice of birds and small animals.[10]

The male-dominated Azteca-Mexica culture drove the powerful female deities underground by giving them monstrous attributes and by substituting male deities in their place, thus splitting the female Self and the female deities. They divided her who had been complete, who possessed both upper (light) and underworld (dark) aspects. *Coatlicue,* the Serpent goddess, and her more sinister aspects, *Tlazolteotl* and *Cihuacoatl,* were "darkened" and disempowered much in the same manner as the Indian *Kali.*

Tonantsi—split from her dark guises, *Coatlicue, Tlazolteotl,* and *Cihuacoatl*—became the good mother. The Nahuas, through ritual and prayer, sought to oblige *Tonantsi* to ensure their health and the growth of their crops. It was she who gave *México* the cactus plant to provide her people with milk and pulque. It was she who defended her children against the wrath of the Christian God by challenging God, her son, to produce mother's milk (as she had done) to prove that his benevolence equalled his disciplinary harshness.[11]

After the Conquest, the Spaniards and their Church continued to split *Tonantsi/Guadalupe*. They desexed *Guadalupe*, taking *Coatlalopeuh*, the serpent/sexuality, out of her. They completed the split begun by the Nahuas by making *la Virgen de Guadalupe/Virgen María* into chaste virgins and *Tlazolteotl/Coatlicue/la Chingada* into *putas*; into the Beauties and the Beasts. They went even further; they made all Indian deities and religious practices the work of the devil.

Thus *Tonantsi* became *Guadalupe*, the chaste protective mother, the defender of the Mexican people.

> *El nueve de diciembre del año 1531*
> *a las cuatro de la madrugada*
> *un pobre indio que se llamaba Juan Diego*
> *iba cruzando el cerro de Tepeyác*
> *cuando oyó un cantó de pájaro.*
> *Alzó al cabeza vío que en la cima del cerro*
> *estaba cubierta con una brillante nube blanca.*
> *Parada en frente del sol*
> *sobre una luna creciente*
> *sostenida por un ángel*
> *estaba una azteca*
> *vestida en ropa de india.*
> *Nuestra Señora María de Coatlalopeuh*
> *se le apareció.*
> *"Juan Diegito, El-que-habla-como-un-águila,"*
> *la Virgen le dijo en el lenguaje azteca.*
> *"Para hacer mi altar este cerro eligo.*
> *Dile a tu gente que yo soy la madre de Dios,*
> *a los indios yo les ayudaré.*
> *Estó se lo contó a Juan Zumarraga*
> *pero el obispo no le creyo.*
> *Juan Diego volvió, lleño su tilma[12]*
> *con rosas de castilla*
> *creciendo milagrosamiente en la nieve.*
> *Se las llevó al obispo,*
> *y cuando abrío su tilma*
> *el retrato de la Virgen*
> *ahí estaba pintado.*

Guadalupe appeared on December 9, 1531, on the spot where the Aztec goddess, *Tonantsi* ("Our Lady Mother"), had been worshiped by the Nahuas and where a temple to her had stood. Speaking Nahua, she told Juan Diego, a poor Indian crossing Tepeyac Hill, whose Indian name was *Cuautlaohuac* and who belonged to the *mazehual* class, the humblest within the Chichimeca tribe, that her name was *María Coatlalopeuh*. *Coatl* is the Nahuatl word for serpent. *Lopeuh* means "the one who has dominion over serpents." I interpret this as "the one who is at one with the beasts." Some spell her name *Coatlaxopeuh* (pronounced *"Cuatlashupe"* in Nahuatl) and say that *"xopeuh"* means "crushed or stepped on with disdain." Some say it means "she who crushed the serpent," with the serpent as the symbol of the indigenous religion, meaning that her religion was to take the place of the Aztec religion.[13] Because *Coatlalopeuh* was homophonous to the Spanish *Guadalupe*, the Spanish identified her with the dark Virgin, *Guadalupe*, patroness of West Central Spain.[14]

From that meeting, Juan Diego walked away with the image of *la Virgen* painted on his cloak. Soon after, Mexico ceased to belong to Spain, and *la Virgen de Guadalupe* began to eclipse all the other male and female religious figures in Mexico, Central America, and parts of the U.S. Southwest. *"Desde entonces para el mexicano ser Guadalupano es algo esencial/*Since then for the Mexican, to be a *Guadalupano* is something essential."[15]

Mi Virgen Morena	My brown virgin
Mi Virgen Ranchera	my country virgin
Eres nuestra Reina	you are our queen
México es tu tierra	Mexico is your land
Y tú su bandera.	and you its flag.
	– "La Virgen Ranchera"[16]

In 1660 the Roman Catholic Church named her Mother of God, considering her synonymous with *la Virgen María;* she became *la Santa Patrona de los mexicanos.* The role of defender (or patron) has traditionally been assigned to male gods. During the Mexican Revolution, Emiliano Zapata and Miguel Hidalgo used her image to move *el pueblo mexicano* toward freedom. During the 1965 grape strike in Delano, California, and in subsequent Chicano farmworkers' marches in Texas and other parts of the Southwest, her image on banners heralded and united the farmworkers. *Pachucos* (zoot suiters) tattoo her image on their bodies. Today, in Texas and Mexico she is more venerated than Jesus or God the Father. In the Lower Rio Grande Valley of south Texas it is *la Virgen de San Juan de los Lagos* (an aspect of *Guadalupe*) that is worshiped by thousands every day at her shrine in San Juan. In Texas she is considered the patron saint of Chicanos. *Cuando Carito, mi hermanito,* was missing in action and, later, wounded in Viet Nam, *mi mamá* got on her knees *y le prometío a Ella que si su hijito volvía vivo* she would crawl on her knees and light novenas in her honor.

Today, *la Virgen de Guadalupe* is the single most potent religious, political, and cultural image of the Chicano/*mexicano.* She, like my race, is a synthesis of the old world and the new, of the religion and culture of the two races in our psyche, the conquerors and the conquered. She is the symbol of the *mestizo* true to his or her Indian values. *La cultura chicana* identifies with the mother (Indian) rather than with the father (Spanish). Our faith is rooted in indigenous attributes, images, symbols, magic, and myth. Because *Guadalupe* took upon herself the psychological and physical devastation of the conquered and oppressed *indio*, she is our spiritual, political, and psychological symbol. As a symbol of hope and faith, she sustains and insures our survival. The Indian, despite extreme despair, suffering, and near genocide, has survived. To Mexicans on both sides of the border, *Guadalupe* is the symbol of our rebellion against the rich, upper and middle class; against their subjugation of the poor and the *indio*.

Guadalupe unites people of different races, religions, languages: Chicano protestants, American Indians, and whites. "*Nuestra abogada siempre serás/*Our mediatrix you will always be." She mediates between the Spanish and the Indian cultures (or three cultures as in the case of *mexicanos* of African or other ancestry) and between Chicanos and the white world. She mediates between humans and the divine, between this reality and the reality of spirit entities. *La Virgen de Guadalupe* is the symbol of ethnic identity and of the tolerance for ambiguity that Chicanos-*mexicanos*, people of mixed race, people who have Indian blood, people who cross cultures, by necessity possess.

La gente Chicana tiene tres madres. All three are mediators: *Guadalupe*, the virgin mother who has not abandoned us, *la Chingada (Malinche)*, the raped mother whom we have abandoned, and *la Llorona*, the mother who seeks her lost children and is a combination of the other two.

Ambiguity surrounds the symbols of these three "Our Mothers." *Guadalupe* has been used by the Church to mete out institutionalized oppression: to placate the Indians and *mexicanos* and Chicanos. In part, the true identity of all three has been subverted—*Guadalupe* to make us docile and enduring; *la Chingada* to make us ashamed of our Indian side, and *la Llorona* to make us long-suffering people. This obscuring has encouraged the *virgen/puta* (whore) dichotomy.

Yet we have not all embraced this dichotomy. In the U.S. Southwest, Mexico, Central and South America the *indio* and the *mestizo* continue to worship the old spirit entities (including *Guadalupe*) and their supernatural power, under the guise of Christian saints.[17]

> *Las invoco diosas mías, ustedes las indias*
> *sumergidas en mi carne que son mis sombras.*
> *Ustedes que persisten mudas en sus cuevas.*
> *Ustedes Señoras que ahora, como yo,*
> *están en desgracia.*

For Waging War Is My Cosmic Duty: The Loss of the Balanced Oppositions and the Change to Male Dominance

Therefore I decided to leave
The country [Aztlán],
Therefore I have come as one charged with a special duty,
Because I have been given arrows and shields,

27

For waging war is my duty,
And on my expeditions I
Shall see all the lands,
I shall wait for the people and meet them
In all four quarters and I shall give them
Food to eat and drinks to quench their thirst,
For here I shall unite all the different peoples!
                                    — HUITZILOPOCHTLI
                        speaking to the Azteca-Mexica[18]

Before the Aztecs became a militaristic, bureaucratic state where male predatory warfare and conquest were based on patrilineal nobility, the principle of balanced opposition between the sexes existed.[19] The people worshiped the Lord and Lady of Duality, *Ometecuhtli* and *Omecihuatl*. Before the change to male dominance, *Coatlicue*, Lady of the Serpent Skirt, contained and balanced the dualities of male and female, light and dark, life and death.

The changes that led to the loss of the balanced oppositions began when the Azteca, one of the twenty Toltec tribes, made the last pilgrimage from a place called Aztlán. The migration south began about the year A.D. 820. Three hundred years later the advance guard arrived near Tula, the capital of the declining Toltec empire. By the eleventh century, they had joined with the Chichimec tribe of Mexitin (afterwards called Mexica) into one religious and administrative organization within Aztlán, the Aztec territory. The Mexitin, with their tribal god *Tetzauhteotl Huitzilopochtli* (Magnificent Humming Bird on the Left), gained control of the religious system.[20] (In some stories *Huitzilopochtli* killed his sister, the moon goddess *Malinalxoch,* who used her supernatural power over animals to control the tribe rather than wage war.)

Huitzilopochtli assigned the Azteca-Mexica the task of keeping the human race (the present cosmic age called the Fifth Sun, *El Quinto Sol*) alive. They were to guarantee the harmonious preservation of the human race by unifying all the people on earth into one social, religious, and administrative organ. The Aztec people considered themselves in charge of regulating all earthly matters.[21] Their instrument: controlled or regulated war to gain and exercise power.

After 100 years in the central plateau, the Azteca-Mexica went to Chapultepec, where they settled in 1248 (the present site of the park on the outskirts of Mexico City). There, in 1345, the Aztec-Mexica chose the site of their capital, Tenochtitlan.[22] By 1428, they dominated the Central Mexican lake area.

The Aztec ruler, *Itzcoatl*, destroyed all the painted documents (books called codices) and rewrote a mythology that validated the wars of conquest and thus continued the shift from a tribe based on clans to one based on classes. From 1429 to 1440, the Aztecs emerged as a militaristic state that preyed on neighboring tribes for tribute and captives.[23] The "wars of flowers" were encounters between local armies with a fixed number of warriors, operating within the Aztec World, and, according to set rules, fighting ritual battles at fixed times and on predetermined battlefields. The religious purpose of these wars was to procure prisoners of war who could be sacrificed to the deities of the capturing party. For if one "fed" the gods, the human race would be saved from total extinction. The social purpose was to enable males of noble families and warriors of low descent to win honor, fame, and administrative offices, and to prevent social and cultural decadence of the elite. The Aztec people were free to have their own religious faith, provided it did not conflict too much with the three fundamental principles of state ideology: to fulfill the special duty set forth by *Huitzilopochtli* of unifying all peoples, to participate in the wars of flowers, and to bring ritual offerings and do penance for the purpose of preventing decadence.[24]

Matrilineal descent characterized the Toltecs and perhaps early Aztec society. Women possessed property, and were curers as well as priestesses. According to the codices, women in former times had the supreme power in Tula, and in the beginning of the Aztec dynasty, the royal blood ran through the female line. A council of elders of the Calpul headed by a supreme leader, or *tlactlo,* called the father and mother of the people, governed the tribe. The supreme leader's vice-emperor occupied the position of "Snake Woman" or *Cihuacoatl,* a goddess.[25] Although the high posts were occupied by men, the terms referred to females, evidence of the exalted role of women before the Aztec nation became centralized. The final break with the democratic Calpul came when the four Aztec lords of royal lineage picked the king's successor from his siblings or male descendants.[26]

La Llorona's wailing in the night for her lost children has an echoing note in the wailing or mourning rites performed by women as they bid their sons, brothers, and husbands good-bye before they left to go to the "flowery wars." Wailing is the Indian, Mexican, and Chicana woman's feeble protest when she has no other recourse. These collective wailing rites may have been a sign of resistance in a society which glorified the warrior and war and for whom the women of the conquered tribes were booty.[27]

In defiance of the Aztec rulers, the *macehuales* (the common people) continued to worship fertility, nourishment, and agricultural female deities, those of crops and rain. They venerated *Chalchiuhtlicue* (goddess of sweet or inland water), *Chicomecoatl* (goddess of food), and *Huixtocihuatl* (goddess of salt).

Nevertheless, it took less than three centuries for Aztec society to change from the balanced duality of their earlier times and from the egalitarian traditions of a wandering tribe to those of a predatory state. The nobility kept the tribute, the commoner got nothing, resulting in a class split. The conquered tribes hated the Aztecs because of the rape of their women and the heavy taxes levied on them. The *Tlaxcalans* were the Aztec's bitter enemies and it was they who helped the Spanish defeat the Aztec rulers, who were by this time so unpopular with their own common people that they could not even mobilize the populace to defend the city. Thus the Aztec nation fell not because *Malinali (la Chingada)* interpreted for and slept with Cortés, but because the ruling elite had subverted the solidarity between men and women and between noble and commoner.[28]

Sueño con serpientes

Coatl. In pre-Columbian America the most notable symbol was the serpent. The Olmecs associated womanhood with the Serpent's mouth which was guarded by rows of dangerous teeth, a sort of *vagina dentate*. They considered it the most sacred place on earth, a place of refuge, the creative womb from which all things were born and to which all things returned. Snake people had holes, entrances to the body of the Earth Serpent; they followed the Serpent's way, identified with the Serpent deity, with the mouth, both the eater and the eaten. The destiny of humankind is to be devoured by the Serpent.[29]

> Dead,
> the doctor by the operating table said.
> I passed between the two fangs,
> the flickering tongue.
> Having come through the mouth of the serpent,
> swallowed,
> I found myself suddenly in the dark,
> sliding down a smooth wet surface
> down down into an even darker darkness.
> Having crossed the portal, the raised hinged mouth,
> having entered the serpent's belly,
> now there was no looking back, no going back.
>
> Why do I cast no shadow?
> Are there lights from all sides shining on me?
> Ahead, ahead.
> curled up inside the serpent's coils,
> the damp breath of death on my face.
> I knew at that instant; something must change
> or I'd die.
> *Algo tenía que cambiar.*

After each of my four bouts with death I'd catch glimpses of an otherworld Serpent. Once, in my bedroom, I saw a cobra the size of the room, her hood expanding over me. When I blinked she was gone. I realized she was, in my psyche, the mental picture and symbol of the instinctual in its collective impersonal, prehuman. She, the symbol of the dark sexual drive, the chthonic (underworld), the feminine, the serpentine movement of sexuality, of creativity, the basis of all energy and life.

The Presences

She appeared in white, garbed in white,
standing white, pure white.
— BERNARDINO DE SAHAGÚN[30]

On the gulf where I was raised, *en el Valle del Río Grande* in South Texas—that triangular piece of land wedged between the river *y el golfo* which serves as the Texas-U.S./Mexican border—is a Mexican *pueblito* called Hargill (at one time in the history of this one-grocery-store, two-service-stations town there were thirteen churches and thirteen *cantinas*). Down the road, a little ways from our house, was a deserted church. It was known among the *mexicanos* that if you walked down the road late at night you would see a woman dressed in white floating about, peering out the church window. She would follow those who had done something bad or who were afraid. *Los mexicanos* called her *la Jila*. Some thought she was *la Llorona*. She was, I think, *Cihuacoatl*, Serpent Woman, ancient Aztec goddess of the earth, of war and birth, patron of midwives, and antecedent of *la Llorona*. Covered with chalk, *Cihuacoatl* wears a white dress with a decoration half red and half black. Her hair forms two little horns (which the Aztecs depicted as knives) crossed on her forehead. The lower part of her face is a bare jawbone, signifying death. On her back she carries a cradle, the knife of sacrifice swaddled as if it were her papoose, her child.[31] Like *la Llorona*, *Cihuacoatl* howls and weeps in the night, screams as if demented. She brings mental depression and sorrow. Long before it takes place, she is the first to predict something is to happen.

Back then, I, an unbeliever, scoffed at these Mexican superstitions as I was taught in Anglo school. Now, I wonder if this story and similar ones were the culture's attempts to "protect" members of the family, especially girls, from "wandering." Stories of the devil luring young girls away and having his way with them discouraged us from going out. There's an ancient Indian tradition of burying the umbilical cord of an infant girl under the house so she will never stray from it and her domestic role.

A mis ancas caen los cueros de culebra,
cuatro veces por año los arrastro,
me tropiezo y me caigo
y cada vez que miro una culebra le pregunto
¿Qué traes conmigo?

Four years ago a red snake crossed my path as I walked through the woods. The direction of its movement, its pace, its colors, the "mood" of the trees and the wind and the snake—they all "spoke" to me, told me things. I look for omens everywhere, everywhere catch glimpses of the patterns and cycles of my life. Stones "speak" to Luisah Teish, a Santera; trees whisper their secrets to Chrystos, a Native American. I remember listening to the voices of the wind as a child and understanding its messages. *Los espíritus* that ride the back of the south wind. I remember their exhalation blowing in through the slits in the door during those hot Texas afternoons. A gust of wind raising the linoleum under my feet, buffeting the house. Everything trembling.

We're not supposed to remember such otherworldly events. We're supposed to ignore, forget, kill those fleeting images of the soul's presence and of the spirit's presence. We've been taught that the spirit is outside our bodies or above our heads somewhere up in the sky with God. We're supposed to forget that every cell in our bodies, every bone and bird and worm has spirit in it.

Like many Indians and Mexicans, I did not deem my psychic experiences real. I denied their occurrences and let my inner senses atrophy. I allowed white rationality to tell me that the existence of the "other world" was mere pagan superstition. I accepted their reality, the "official" reality of the rational, reasoning mode which is connected with external reality, the upper world, and is considered the most developed consciousness—the consciousness of duality.

The other mode of consciousness facilitates images from the soul and the unconscious through dreams and the imagination. Its work is labeled "fiction," make-believe, wish-fulfillment. White anthropologists claim that Indians have "primitive" and therefore deficient minds, that we cannot think in the higher mode of consciousness—rationality. They are fascinated by what they call the "magical" mind, the "savage" mind, the *participation mystique* of the mind that says the world of the imagination—the world of the soul—and of the spirit is just as real as physical reality.[32] In trying to become "objective," Western culture made "objects" of things and people when it distanced itself from them, thereby losing "touch" with them. This dichotomy is the root of all violence.

Not only was the brain split into two functions but so was reality. Thus people who inhabit both realities are forced to live in the interface between the two, forced to become adept at switching modes. Such is the case with the *india* and the *mestiza*.

Institutionalized religion fears trafficking with the spirit world and stigmatizes it as witchcraft. It has strict taboos against this kind of inner knowledge. It fears what Jung calls the Shadow, the unsavory aspects of ourselves. But even more it fears the suprahuman, the god in ourselves.

"The purpose of any established religion . . . is to glorify, sanction, and bless with a superpersonal meaning all personal and interpersonal activities. This occurs through the 'sacraments,' and indeed through most religious rites."[33] But it sanctions only its own sacraments and rites. Voodoo, Santeria, Shamanism, and other native religions are called cults and their beliefs are called mythologies. In my own life, the Catholic Church fails to give meaning to my daily acts, to my continuing encounters with the "other world." It and other institutionalized religions impoverish all life, beauty, pleasure.

The Catholic and Protestant religions encourage fear and distrust of life and of the body; they encourage a split between the body and the spirit and totally ignore the soul; they encourage us to kill off parts of ourselves. We are taught that the body is an ignorant animal; intelligence dwells only in the head. But the body is smart. It does not discern between external stimuli and stimuli from the imagination. It reacts equally viscerally to events from the imagination as it does to "real" events.

So I grew up in the interface trying not to give countenance to *el mal aigre*,[34] evil nonhuman, noncorporeal entities riding the wind, that could come in through the window, through my nose with my breath. I was not supposed to believe in *susto*, a sudden shock or fall that frightens the soul out of the body. And growing up between such opposing spiritualities how could I reconcile the two, the pagan and the Christian?

No matter to what use my people put the supranatural world, it is evident to me now that the spirit world, whose existence the whites are so adamant in denying, does in fact exist. This very minute I sense the presence of the spirits of my ancestors in my room. And I think *la Jila* is *Cihuacoatl*, Snake Woman; she is *la Llorona*, Daughter of Night, traveling the dark terrains of the unknown searching for the lost parts of herself. I remember *la Jila* following me once, remember her eerie lament. I'd like to think that she was crying for her lost children, *los* Chicanos/*mexicanos*.

La facultad

La facultad is the capacity to see in surface phenomena the meaning of deeper realities, to see the deep structure below the surface. It is an instant "sensing," a quick perception arrived at without conscious reasoning. It is an acute awareness mediated by the part of the psyche that does not speak, that communicates in images and symbols which are the faces of feelings, that is, behind which feelings reside/hide. The one possessing this sensitivity is excruciatingly alive to the world.

Those who are pushed out of the tribe for being different are likely to become more sensitized (when not brutalized into insensitivity). Those who do not feel psychologically or physically safe in the world are more apt to develop this sense. Those who are pounced on the most have it the strongest—the females, the homosexuals of all races, the darkskinned, the outcast, the persecuted, the marginalized, the foreign.

When we're up against the wall, when we have all sorts of oppressions coming at us, we are forced to develop this faculty so that we'll know when the next person is going to slap us or lock us away. We'll sense the rapist when he's five blocks down the street. Pain makes us acutely anxious to avoid more of it, so we hone that radar. It's a kind of survival tactic that people, caught between the worlds, unknowingly cultivate. It is latent in all of us.

I walk into a house and I know whether it is empty or occupied. I feel the lingering charge in the air of a recent fight or lovemaking or depression. I sense the emotions someone near is emitting—whether friendly or threatening. Hate and fear—the more intense the emotion, the greater my reception of it. I feel a tingling on my skin when someone is staring at me or thinking about me. I can tell how others feel by the way they smell, where others are by the air pressure on my skin. I can spot the love or greed or generosity lodged in the tissues of another. Often I sense the direction of and my distance from people or objects—in the dark, or with my eyes closed, without looking. It must be a vestige of a proximity sense, a sixth sense that's lain dormant from long-ago times.

Fear develops the proximity sense aspect of *la facultad*. But there is a deeper sensing that is another aspect of this faculty. It is anything that breaks into one's everyday mode of perception, that causes a break in one's defenses and resistance, anything that takes one from one's habitual grounding, causes the depths to open up, causes a shift in perception. This shift in perception deepens the way we see concrete objects and people; the senses become so acute and piercing that we can see through things, view events in depth, a piercing that reaches the underworld (the realm of the soul). As we plunge vertically, the break, with its accompanying new seeing, makes us pay attention to the soul, and we are thus carried into awareness—an experiencing of soul (Self).

We lose something in this mode of initiation, something is taken from us: our innocence, our unknowing ways, our safe and easy ignorance. There is a prejudice and a fear of the dark, chthonic (underworld), material such as depression, illness, death, and the violations that can bring on this break. Confronting anything that tears the fabric of our everyday mode of consciousness and that thrusts us into a less literal and more psychic sense of reality increases awareness and *la facultad*.

NOTES

[1] From the song *"Sueño con serpientes"* by Silvio Rodrígues, from the album *Días y flores.* Translated by Barbara Dane with the collaboration of Rina Benmauor and Juan Flores.

[2] *Nalgas:* vagina, buttocks.

[3] *Dicen que las culebras like to suck chiches:* they say snakes like to suck women's teats.

[4] *Ella tiene su tono:* she has supernatural power from her animal soul, the *tono.*

[5] *Quelite:* weed.

[6] *Ázadón:* hoe.

[7] *Veneno:* venom, poison.

[8] *Culebra de cascabel:* rattlesnake.

[9] In some Nahuatl dialects *Tonantsi* is called *Tonatzin*, literally "Our Holy Mother." *"Tonan* was a name given in Nahuatl to several mountains, these being the congelations of the Earth Mother at spots convenient for her worship." The Mexica considered the mountain mass southwest of Chapultepec to be their mother. Burr Cartwright Brundage, *The Fifth Sun: Aztec Gods, Aztec World* (Austin, TX: University of Texas Press, 1979), 154, 242.

[10] Ena Campbell, "The Virgin of Guadalupe and the Female Self-image: A Mexican

Case History," *Mother Worship: Themes and Variations,* James J. Preston, ed. (Chapel Hill, NC: University of North Carolina Press, 1982), 22.

[11] Alan R. Sandstrom, "The Tonantsi Cult of the Eastern Nahuas," *Mother Worship: Themes and Variations,* James J. Preston, ed.

[12] *Una tela tejida con asperas fibras de agave.* It is an oblong cloth that hangs over the back and ties together across the shoulders.

[13] Andres Gonzales Guerrero, Jr., *The Significance of Nuestra Señora de Guadalupe and La Raza Cósmica in the Development of a Chicano Theology of Liberation* (Ann Arbor, MI: University Microfilms International, 1984), 122.

[14] *Algunos dicen que Guadalupe es una palabra derivada del lenguaje arabe que significa "Río Oculto."* Tomie de Paola, *The Lady of Guadalupe* (New York, NY: Holiday House, 1980), 44.

[15] *"Desde el cielo una hermosa mañana,"* from *Propios de la misa de Nuestra Señora de Guadalupe,* Guerrero, 124.

[16] From *"La Virgen Ranchera,"* Guerrero, 127.

[17] *La Virgin María* is often equated with the Aztec *Teleoinam,* the Maya *Ixchel,* the Inca *Mamacocha,* and the Yoruba *Yemayá.*

[18] Geoffrey Parrinder, ed., *World Religions: From Ancient History to the Present* (New York, NY: Facts on File Publications, 1971), 72.

[19] Lévi-Strauss's paradigm which opposes nature to culture and female to male has no such validity in the early history of our Indian forebears. June Nash, "The Aztecs and the Ideology of Male Dominance," *Signs* (Winter, 1978), 349.

[20] Parrinder, 72.

[21] Parrinder, 77.

[22] Nash, 352.

[23] Nash, 350, 355.

[24] Parrinder, 355.

[25] Jacques Soustelle, *The Daily Life of the Aztecs on the Eve of the Spanish Conquest* (New York, NY: Macmillan Publishing Company, 1962). Soustelle and most other historians got their information from the Franciscan father, Bernardino de Sahagún, chief chronicler of Indian religious life.

[26] Nash, 252–253.

[27] Nash, 358.

[28] Nash, 361–362.

[29] Karl W. Luckert, *Olmec Religion: A Key to Middle America and Beyond* (Norman, OK: University of Oklahoma Press, 1976), 68, 69, 87, 109.

[30] Bernardino de Sahagún, *General History of the Things of New Spain* (Florentine Codex), Vol. I Revised, trans. Arthur Anderson and Charles Dibble (Sante Fe, NM: School of American Research, 1950), 11.

[31] The Aztecs muted Snake Woman's patronage of childbirth and vegetation by placing a sacrificial knife in the empty cradle she carried on her back (signifying a child who died in childbirth), thereby making her a devourer of sacrificial victims. Snake Woman had the ability to change herself into a serpent or into a lovely young woman to entice young men, who withered away and died after intercourse with her. She was known as a witch and a shape-shifter. Brundage, 168–171.

[32] Anthropologist Lucien Levy-Bruhl coined the word *participation mystique.* According to Jung, "It denotes a peculiar kind of psychological connection . . . [in which] the subject cannot clearly distinguish himself from the object but is bound to it by a direct relationship which amounts to partial identity." Carl Jung, "Definitions," in *Psychological Types, The Collected Works of C. G. Jung,* Vol. 6 (Princeton, NJ: Princeton University Press, 1953), par. 781.

[33] I have lost the source of this quote. If anyone knows what it is, please let the publisher know. [Author's note]

[34] Some *mexicanos* and Chicanos distinguish between *aire,* air, and *mal aigre,* the evil spirits which reside in the air.

How to Tame a Wild Tongue

"We're going to have to control your tongue," the dentist says, pulling out all the metal from my mouth. Silver bits plop and tinkle into the basin. My mouth is a motherlode.

The dentist is cleaning out my roots. I get a whiff of the stench when I gasp. "I can't cap that tooth yet, you're still draining," he says.

"We're going to have to do something about your tongue," I hear the anger rising in his voice. My tongue keeps pushing out the wads of cotton, pushing back the drills, the long thin needles. "I've never seen anything as strong or as stubborn," he says. And I think, how do you tame a wild tongue, train it to be quiet, how do you bridle and saddle it? How do you make it lie down?

> Who is to say that robbing a people of
> its language is less violent than war?
>
> — RAY GWYN SMITH[1]

I remember being caught speaking Spanish at recess—that was good for three licks on the knuckles with a sharp ruler. I remember being sent to the corner of the classroom for "talking back" to the Anglo teacher when all I was trying to do was tell her how to pronounce my name. "If you want to be American, speak 'American.' If you don't like it, go back to Mexico where you belong."

"I want you to speak English. Pa' hallar buen trabajo tienes que saber hablar el inglés bien. Qué vale toda tu educación si todavía hablas inglés con un 'accent,'" my mother would say, mortified that I spoke English like a Mexican. At Pan American University, I and all Chicano students were required to take two speech classes. Their purpose: to get rid of our accents.

Attacks on one's form of expression with the intent to censor are a violation of the First Amendment. El Anglo con cara de inocente nos arrancó la lengua. Wild tongues can't be tamed, they can only be cut out.

Overcoming the Tradition of Silence

> Ahogadas, escupimos el oscuro.
> Peleando con nuestra propia sombra
> el silencio nos sepulta.

En boca cerrada no entran moscas. "Flies don't enter a closed mouth" is a saying I kept hearing when I was a child. Ser habladora was to be a gossip and a liar, to talk too much. Muchachitas bien criadas, well-bred girls don't answer back. Es una falta de respeto to talk back to one's mother or father. I remember one of the sins I'd recite to the priest in the confession box the few times I went to confession: talking back to my mother, *hablar pa' 'tras, repelar. Hocio-cona, repelona, chismosa,* having a big mouth, questioning, carrying tales are all signs of being *mal criada.* In my culture they are all words that are derogatory if applied to women—I've never heard them applied to men.

The first time I heard two women, a Puerto Rican and a Cuban, say the word *"nosotras,"* I was shocked. I had not known the word existed. Chicanas use *nosotros* whether we're male or female. We are robbed of our female being by the masculine plural. Language is a male discourse.

> And our tongues have become
> dry   the wilderness has
> dried out our tongues   and
> we have forgotten speech.
>   — IRENA KLEPFISZ[2]

Even our own people, other Spanish speakers *nos quieren poner candados en la boca.* They would hold us back with their bag of *reglas de academia.*

Oyé como ladra: el lenguaje de la frontera

Quien tiene boca se equivoca.
— Mexican saying

"Pocho, cultural traitor, you're speaking the oppressor's language by speaking English, you're ruining the Spanish language," I have been accused by various Latinos and Latinas. Chicano Spanish is considered by the purist and by most Latinos deficient, a mutilation of Spanish.

But Chicano Spanish is a border tongue which developed naturally. Change, *evolución, enriquecimiento de palabras nuevas por invención o adopción* have created variants of Chicano Spanish, *un nuevo lenguaje. Un lenguaje que corresponde a un modo de vivir.* Chicano Spanish is not incorrect, it is a living language.

For a people who are neither Spanish nor live in a country in which Spanish is the first language; for a people who live in a country in which English is the reigning tongue but who are not Anglo; for a people who cannot entirely identify with either standard (formal, Castilian) Spanish nor standard English, what recourse is left to them but to create their own language? A language which they can connect their identity to, one capable of communicating the realities and values true to themselves—a language with terms that are neither *español ni inglés,* but both. We speak a patois, a forked tongue, a variation of two languages.

Chicano Spanish sprang out of the Chicanos' need to identify ourselves as a distinct people. We needed a language with which we could communicate with ourselves, a secret language. For some of us, language is a homeland closer than the Southwest—for many Chicanos today live in the Midwest and the East. And because we are a complex, heterogeneous people, we speak many languages. Some of the languages we speak are

1. Standard English
2. Working class and slang English
3. Standard Spanish
4. Standard Mexican Spanish
5. North Mexican Spanish dialect
6. Chicano Spanish (Texas, New Mexico, Arizona, and California have regional variations)
7. Tex-Mex
8. *Pachuco* (called *caló*)

My "home" tongues are the languages I speak with my sister and brothers, with my friends. They are the last five listed, with 6 and 7 being closest to my heart. From school, the media, and job situations, I've picked up standard and working class English. From Mamagrande Locha and from reading Spanish and Mexican literature, I've picked up Standard Spanish and Standard Mexican Spanish. From *los recién llegados*, Mexican immigrants, and *braceros*, I learned the North Mexican dialect. With Mexicans I'll try to speak either Standard Mexican Spanish or the North Mexican dialect. From my parents and Chicanos living in the Valley, I picked up Chicano Texas Spanish, and I speak it with my mom, younger brother (who married a Mexican and who rarely mixes Spanish with English), aunts, and older relatives.

With Chicanas from *Nuevo México* or *Arizona* I will speak Chicano Spanish a little, but often they don't understand what I'm saying. With most California Chicanas I speak entirely in English (unless I forget). When I first moved to San Francisco, I'd rattle off something in Spanish, unintentionally embarrassing them. Often it is only with another Chicana *tejano* that I can talk freely.

Words distorted by English are known as anglicisms or *pochismos*. The *pocho* is an anglicized Mexican or American of Mexican origin who speaks Spanish with an accent characteristic of North Americans and who distorts and reconstructs the language according to the influence of English.[3] Tex-Mex, or Spanglish, comes most naturally to me. I may switch back and forth from English to Spanish in the same sentence or in the same word. With my sister and my brother Nune and with Chicano *tejano* contemporaries I speak in Tex-Mex.

From kids and people my own age I picked up *Pachuco*. *Pachuco* (the language of the zoot suiters) is a language of rebellion, both against Standard Spanish and Standard English. It is a secret language. Adults of the culture and outsiders cannot understand it. It is made up of slang words from both English and Spanish. *Ruca* means girl or woman, *vato* means guy or dude, *chale* means no, *simón* means yes, *churro* is sure, talk is *periquiar, pigionear* means petting, *que gacho* means how nerdy, *ponte águila* means watch out, death is called *la pelona*. Through lack of practice and not having others who can speak it, I've lost most of the *Pachuco* tongue.

Chicano Spanish

Chicanos, after 250 years of Spanish/Anglo colonization, have developed significant differences in the Spanish we speak. We collapse two adjacent vowels into a single syllable and sometimes shift the stress in certain words such as *maíz/maiz, cohete/cuete*. We leave out certain consonants when they appear between vowels: *lado/lao, mojado/mojao*. Chicanos from South Texas pronounce *f* as *j* as in *jue (fue)*. Chicanos use "archaisms," words that are no longer in the Spanish language, words that have been evolved out. We say *semos, truje, haiga, ansina,* and *naiden*. We retain the "archaic" *j*, as in *jalar*, that derives from an earlier *h* (the French *halar* or the Germanic *halon* which was lost to standard Spanish in the sixteenth century), but which is still found in several regional dialects such as the one spoken in South Texas. (Due to geography, Chicanos from the Valley of South Texas were cut off linguistically from other Spanish speakers. We tend to use words that the Spaniards brought over from Medieval Spain. The majority of the Spanish colonizers in Mexico and the Southwest came from Extremadura—Hernán Cortés was one of them—and Andalucía. Andalucians pronounce *ll* like a *y*, and their *d*'s tend to be absorbed by adjacent vowels: *tirado* becomes *tirao*. They brought *el lenguaje popular, dialectos y regionalismos*.)[4]

Chicanos and other Spanish speakers also shift *ll* to *y* and *z* to *s*.[5] We leave out initial syllables, saying *tar* for *estar, toy* for *estoy, hora* for *ahora* (*cubanos* and *puertorriqueños* also leave out initial letters of some words). We also leave out the final syllable such as *pa* for *para*. The intervocalic *y*, the *ll* as in *tortilla, ella, botella*, gets replaced by *tortia* or *toriya, ea, botea*. We add an additional syllable at the beginning of certain words: *atocar* for *tocar, agastar* for *gastar*. Sometimes we'll say *lavaste las vacijas*, other times *lavates* (substituting the *ates* verb endings for the *aste*).

We use anglicisms, words borrowed from English: *bola* from ball, *carpeta* from carpet, *máchina de lavar* (instead of *lavadora*) from washing machine. Tex-Mex argot, created by adding a Spanish sound at the beginning or end of an English word such as *cookiar* for cook, *watchar* for watch, *parkiar* for park, and *rapiar* for rape, is the result of the pressures on Spanish speakers to adapt to English.

We don't use the word *vosotros/as* or its accompanying verb form. We don't say *claro* (to mean yes), *imagínate*, or *me emociona*, unless we picked up Spanish from Latinas, out of a book, or in a classroom. Other Spanish-speaking groups are going through the same, or similar, development in their Spanish.

Linguistic Terrorism

Deslenguadas. Somos los del español deficiente. We are your linguistic nightmare, your linguistic aberration, your linguistic *mestisaje*, the subject of your *burla*. Because we speak with tongues of fire we are culturally crucified. Racially, culturally, and linguistically *somos huérfanos*—we speak an orphan tongue.

Chicanas who grew up speaking Chicano Spanish have internalized the belief that we speak poor Spanish. It is illegitimate, a bastard language. And because we internalize how our language has been used against us by the dominant culture, we use our language differences against each other.

Chicana feminists often skirt around each other with suspicion and hesitation. For the longest time I couldn't figure it out. Then it dawned on me. To be close to another Chicana is like looking into the mirror. We are afraid of what we'll see there. *Pena.* Shame. Low estimation of self. In childhood we are told that our language is wrong. Repeated attacks on our native tongue diminish our sense of self. The attacks continue throughout our lives.

Chicanas feel uncomfortable talking in Spanish to Latinas, afraid of their censure. Their language was not outlawed in their countries. They had a whole lifetime of being immersed in their native tongue; generations, centuries in which Spanish was a first language, taught in school, heard on radio and TV, and read in the newspaper.

If a person, Chicana or Latina, has a low estimation of my native tongue, she also has a low estimation of me. Often with *mexicanas y latinas* we'll speak English as a neutral language. Even among Chicanas we tend to speak English at parties or conferences. Yet, at the same time, we're afraid the other will think we're *agringadas* because we don't speak Chicano Spanish. We oppress each other trying to out-Chicano each other, vying to be the "real" Chicanas, to speak like Chicanos. There is no one Chicano language just as there is no one Chicano experience. A monolingual Chicana whose first language is English or Spanish is just as much a Chicana as one who speaks several variants of Spanish. A Chicana from Michigan or Chicago or Detroit is just as much a Chicana as one from the Southwest. Chicano Spanish is as diverse linguistically as it is regionally.

By the end of this century, Spanish speakers will comprise the biggest minority group in the United States, a country where students in high schools and colleges are encouraged to take French classes because French is considered more "cultured." But for a language to remain alive it must be used.[6] By the end of this century English, and not Spanish, will be the mother tongue of most Chicanos and Latinos.

So, if you want to really hurt me, talk badly about my language. Ethnic identity is twin skin to linguistic identity—I am my language. Until I can take pride in my language, I cannot take pride in myself. Until I can accept as legitimate Chicano Texas Spanish, Tex-Mex, and all the other languages I speak, I cannot accept the legitimacy of myself. Until I am free to write bilingually and to switch codes without having always to translate, while I still have to speak English or Spanish when I would rather speak Spanglish, and as long as I have to accommodate the English speaker rather than having them accommodate me, my tongue will be illegitimate.

I will no longer be made to feel ashamed of existing. I will have my voice: Indian, Spanish, white. I will have my serpent's tongue—my woman's voice, my sexual voice, my poet's voice. I will overcome the tradition of silence.

> My fingers
> move sly against your palm
> Like women everywhere, we speak in code. . . .
> — MELANIE KAYE/KANTROWITZ[7]

"Vistas," corridos, y comida: My Native Tongue

In the 1960s, I read my first Chicano novel. It was *City of Night* by John Rechy, a gay Texan, son of a Scottish father and a Mexican mother. For days I walked around in stunned amazement that a Chicano could write and could get published. When I read *I Am Joaquín*[8] I was surprised to see a bilingual book by a Chicano in print. When I saw poetry written in Tex-Mex for the first time, a feeling of pure joy flashed through me. I felt like we really existed as a people. In 1971, when I started teaching High School English to Chicano students, I tried to supplement the required texts with works by Chicanos, only to be reprimanded and forbidden to do so by the principal. He claimed that I was supposed to teach "American" and English literature. At the risk of being fired, I swore my students to secrecy and slipped in Chicano short stories, poems, a play. In graduate school, while working toward a Ph.D., I had to "argue" with one adviser after the other, semester after semester, before I was allowed to make Chicano literature an area of focus.

Even before I read books by Chicanos or Mexicans, it was the Mexican movies I saw at the drive-in—the Thursday night special of $1.00 a carload—that gave me a sense of belonging. "*Vámonos a las vistas,*" my mother would call out and we'd all—grandmother, brothers, sister, and cousins—squeeze into the car. We'd wolf down cheese and bologna white bread sandwiches while watching Pedro Infante in melodramatic tearjerkers like *Nosotros los pobres*, the first "real" Mexican movie (that was not an imitation of European movies). I remember seeing *Cuando los hijos se van* and surmising that all Mexican movies played up the love a mother has for her children and what ungrateful sons and daughters suffer when they are not devoted to their mothers. I remember the singing-type "westerns" of Jorge Negrete and Miquel Aceves Mejía. When watching Mexican movies, I felt a sense of homecoming as well as alienation. People who were to amount to something didn't go to Mexican movies, or *bailes*, or tune their radios to *bolero, rancherita*, and *corrido* music.

The whole time I was growing up, there was *norteño* music sometimes called North Mexican border music, or Tex-Mex music, or Chicano music, or *cantina* (bar) music. I grew up listening to *conjuntos*, three- or four-piece bands made up of folk musicians playing guitar, *bajo sexto*, drums, and button accordion, which Chicanos had borrowed from the German immigrants who had come to Central Texas and Mexico to farm and build breweries. In the Rio Grande Valley, Steven Jordan and Little Joe Hernández were popular, and Flaco Jiménez was the accordion king. The rhythms of Tex-Mex music are those of the polka, also adapted from the Germans, who in turn had borrowed the polka from the Czechs and Bohemians.

I remember the hot, sultry evenings when *corridos*—song of love and death on the Texas-Mexican borderlands—reverberated out of cheap amplifiers from the local *cantinas* and wafted in through my bedroom window. *Corridos* first became widely used along the South Texas/Mexican border during the early conflict between Chicanos and Anglos. The *corridos* are usually about Mexican heroes who do valiant deeds against the Anglo oppressors. Pancho Villa's song, *"La cucaracha,"* is the most famous one. *Corridos* of John F. Kennedy and his death are still very popular in the Valley. Older Chicanos remember Lydia Mendoza, one of the great border *corrido* singers who was called *la Gloria de Tejas*. Her *"El tango negro,"* sung during the Great Depression, made her a singer of the people. The ever-present *corridos* narrated one hundred years of border history, bringing news of events as well as entertaining. These folk musicians and folk songs are our chief cultural mythmakers, and they made our hard lives seem bearable.

I grew up feeling ambivalent about our music. Country-western and rock-and-roll had more status. In the fifties and sixties, for the slightly educated and *agringado* Chicanos, there existed a sense of shame at being caught listening to our music. Yet I couldn't stop my feet from thumping to the music, could not stop humming the words, nor hide from myself the exhilaration I felt when I heard it.

There are more subtle ways that we internalize identification, especially in the forms of images and emotions. For me food and certain smells are tied to my identity, to my homeland. Woodsmoke curling up to an immense blue sky; woodsmoke perfuming my grandmother's clothes, her skin. The stench of cow manure and the yellow patches on the ground; the crack of a .22 rifle and the reek of cordite. Homemade white cheese sizzling in a pan, melting inside a folded *tortilla*. My sister Hilda's hot, spicy *menudo, chile colorado* making it deep red, pieces of *panza* and hominy floating on top. My brother Carito barbequing *fajitas* in the backyard. Even now and 3,000 miles away, I can see my mother spicing the ground beef, pork, and venison with *chile*. My mouth salivates at the thought of the hot steaming *tamales* I would be eating if I were home.

Si le preguntas a mi mamá, "¿Qué eres?"

> Identity is the essential core of who
> we are as individuals, the conscious
> experience of the self inside.
> — GERSHEN KAUFMAN[9]

Nosotros los Chicanos straddle the borderlands. On one side of us, we are constantly exposed to the Spanish of the Mexicans, on the other side we hear the Anglos' incessant clamoring so that we forget our language. Among ourselves we don't say *nosotros los americanos, o nosotros los españoles, o nosotros los hispanos*. We say *nosotros los mexicanos* (by *mexicanos* we do not mean citizens of Mexico; we do not mean a national identity, but a racial one). We distinguish between *mexicanos del otro lado* and *mexicanos de este lado*. Deep in our hearts we believe that being Mexican has nothing to do with which country one lives in. Being Mexican is a state of soul—not one of mind, not one of citizenship. Neither eagle nor serpent, but both. And like the ocean, neither animal respects borders.

> *Dime con quien andas y te diré quien eres.*
> (Tell me who your friends are and I'll tell you who you are.)
> — Mexican saying

Si le preguntas a mi mamá, "¿Qué eres?" te dirá, "Soy mexicana." My brothers and sister say the same. I sometimes will answer *"soy mexicana"* and at others will say *"soy Chicana" o "soy tejana."* But I identified as *"Raza"* before I ever identified as *"mexicana"* or "Chicana."

As a culture, we call ourselves Spanish when referring to ourselves as a linguistic group and when copping out. It is then that we forget our predominant Indian genes. We are 70–80 percent Indian.[10] We call ourselves Hispanic[11] or Spanish-American or Latin American or Latin when linking ourselves to other Spanish-speaking peoples of the Western hemisphere and when copping out. We call ourselves Mexican-American[12] to signify we are neither Mexican nor American, but more the noun "American" than the adjective "Mexican" (and when copping out).

Chicanos and other people of color suffer economically for not acculturating. This voluntary (yet forced) alienation makes for psychological conflict, a kind of dual identity—we don't identify with the Anglo-American cultural values and we don't totally identify with the Mexican cultural values. We are a synergy of two cultures with various degrees of Mexicanness or Angloness. I have so internalized the borderland conflict that sometimes I feel like one cancels out the other and we are zero, nothing, no one. *A veces no soy nada ni nadie. Pero hasta cuando no lo soy, lo soy.*

When not copping out, when we know we are more than nothing, we call ourselves Mexican, referring to race and ancestry; *mestizo* when affirming both our Indian and Spanish (but we hardly ever own our Black) ancestry; Chicano when referring to a politically aware people born and/or raised in the United States; *Raza* when referring to Chicanos; *tejanos* when we are Chicanos from Texas.

Chicanos did not know we were a people until 1965 when Cesar Chavez and the farmworkers united and *I Am Joaquín* was published and *la Raza Unida* party was formed in Texas. With that recognition, we became a distinct people. Something momentous happened to the Chicano soul—we became aware of our reality and acquired a name and a language (Chicano Spanish) that reflected that reality. Now that we had a name, some of the fragmented pieces began to fall together—who we were, what we were, how we had evolved. We began to get glimpses of what we might eventually become.

Yet the struggle of identities continues, the struggle of borders is our reality still. One day the inner struggle will cease and a true integration take place. In the meantime, *tenémos que hacer la lucha. ¿Quién está protegiendo los ranchos de mi gente? ¿Quién está tratando de cerrar la fisura entre la india y el blanco en nuestra sangre? El Chicano, si, el Chicano que anda como un ladrón en su propia casa.*

Los Chicanos, how patient we seem, how very patient. There is the quiet of the Indian about us.[13] We know how to survive. When other races have given up their tongue we've kept ours. We know what it is to live under the hammer blow of the dominant *norteamericano* culture. But more than we count the blows, we count the days the weeks the years the centuries the aeons until the white laws and commerce and customs will rot in the deserts they've created, lie bleached. *Humildes* yet proud, *quietos* yet wild, *nosotros los mexicanos-Chicanos* will walk by the crumbling ashes as we go about our business. Stubborn, persevering, impenetrable as stone, yet possessing a malleability that renders us unbreakable, we, the *mestizas* and *mestizos*, will remain.

NOTES

[1] Ray Gwyn Smith, *Moorland Is Cold Country,* unpublished book.

[2] Irena Klepfisz, *"Di rayze aheym*/The Journey Home," in *The Tribe of Dina: A Jewish Women's Anthology,* Melanie Kaye/Kantrowitz and Irena Klepfisz, eds. (Montpelier, VT: Sinister Wisdom Books, 1986), 49.

[3] R. C. Ortega, *Dialectología Del Barrio,* trans. Hortencia S. Alwan (Los Angeles, CA: R. C. Ortega Publisher & Bookseller, 1977), 132.

[4] Eduardo Hernández-Chávez, Andrew D. Cohen, and Anthony F. Beltramo, *El Lenguaje de los Chicanos: Regional and Social Characteristics of Language Used by Mexican Americans* (Arlington, VA: Center for Applied Linguistics, 1975), 39.

[5] Hernandéz-Chávez, xvii.

[6] Irena Klepfisz, "Secular Jewish Identity: Yidishkayt in America," in *The Tribe of Dina,* Kaye/Kantrowitz and Klepfisz, eds., 43.

[7] Melanie Kaye/Kantrowitz, "Sign," in *We Speak in Code: Poems and Other Writings* (Pittsburgh, PA: Motheroot Publications, Inc., 1980), 85.

[8] Rodolfo Gonzales, *I Am Joaquín/Yo Soy Joaquín* (New York, NY: Bantam Books, 1972). It was first published in 1967.

[9] Gershen Kaufman, *Shame: The Power of Caring* (Cambridge, MA: Schenkman Books, Inc., 1980), 68.

[10] John R. Chávez, *The Lost Land: The Chicano Images of the Southwest* (Albuquerque, NM: University of New Mexico Press, 1984), 88–90.

[11] "Hispanic" is derived from *Hispanis* (*España*, a name given to the Iberian Peninsula in ancient times when it was a part of the Roman Empire) and is a term designated by the U.S. government to make it easier to handle us on paper.

[12] The Treaty of Guadalupe Hidalgo created the Mexican-American in 1848.

[13] Anglos, in order to alleviate their guilt for dispossessing the Chicano, stressed the Spanish part of us and perpetrated the myth of the Spanish Southwest. We have accepted the fiction that we are Hispanic, that is Spanish, in order to accommodate ourselves to the dominant culture and its abhorrence of Indians. Chávez, 88–91.

•   •   •   •   •   •   •   •   •   •   •   •   •

QUESTIONS FOR A SECOND READING

1. The most immediate challenge to many readers of these chapters will be the sections that are written in Spanish. Part of the point of a text that mixes languages is to give non-Spanish-speaking readers the feeling of being lost, excluded, left out. What is a reader to do with this prose? One could learn Spanish and come back to reread, but this is not a quick solution and, according to Anzaldúa, not even a completely satisfactory one, since some of her Spanish is drawn from communities of speakers not represented in textbooks and classes.

   So how do you read this text if you don't read Spanish? Do you ignore the words? sound them out? improvise? Anzaldúa gives translations of some words or phrases, but not all. Which ones does she translate? Why? Reread these chapters with the goal of explaining how you handled Anzaldúa's polyglot style.

2. These chapters are made up of shorter sections written in a variety of styles (some as prose poems, some with endnotes, some as stories). And, while the sections are obviously ordered, the order is not a conventional argumentative one. The text is, as Anzaldúa says elsewhere in her book, "an assemblage, a montage, a beaded work, . . . a crazy dance":

   > In looking at this book that I'm almost finished writing, I see a mosaic pattern (Aztec-like) emerging, a weaving pattern, thin here, thick there. . . . This almost finished product seems an assemblage, a montage, a beaded work with several leitmotifs and with a central core, now appearing, now disappearing in a crazy dance. The whole thing has had a mind of its own, escaping me and insisting on putting together the pieces of its own puzzle with minimal direction from my will. It is a rebellious, willful entity, a precocious girl-child forced to grow up too quickly, rough, unyielding, with pieces of feather sticking out here and there, fur, twigs, clay. My child, but not for much longer.

> This female being is angry, sad, joyful, is Coatlicue, dove, horse, serpent, cactus. Though it is a flawed thing—clumsy, complex, groping, blind thing, for me it is alive, infused with spirit. I talk to it; it talks to me.

This is not, in other words, a conventional text; it makes unexpected demands on a reader. As you reread, mark sections you could use to talk about how, through the text, Anzaldúa invents a reader and/or a way of reading. Who is Anzaldúa's ideal reader? What does he or she need to be able to do?

3. Although Anzaldúa's text is not a conventional one, it makes an argument and proposes terms and examples for its readers to negotiate. How might you summarize Anzaldúa's argument in these two chapters? How do the individual chapters mark stages or parts of her argument? How might you explain the connections between the chapters? As you reread this selection, mark those passages where Anzaldúa seems to you to be creating a case or argument. What are its key terms? its key examples? What are its conclusions?

ASSIGNMENTS FOR WRITING

1. Anzaldúa has described her text as a kind of crazy dance (see the second "Question for a Second Reading"); it is, she says, a text with a mind of its own, "putting together the pieces of its own puzzle with minimal direction from my will." Hers is a prose full of variety and seeming contradictions; it is a writing that could be said to represent the cultural "crossroads" which is her experience/sensibility.

   As an experiment whose goal is the development of an alternate (in Anzaldúa's terms, a mixed or *mestiza*) understanding, write an autobiographical text whose shape and motives could be described in her terms: a mosaic, woven, with numerous overlays; a montage, a beaded work, a crazy dance, drawing upon the various ways of thinking, speaking, understanding that might be said to be part of your own mixed cultural position, your own mixed sensibility.

   To prepare for this essay, think about the different positions you could be said to occupy, the different voices that are part of your background or present, the competing ways of thinking that make up your points of view. Imagine that your goal is to present your world and your experience to those who are not necessarily prepared to be sympathetic or to understand. And, following Anzaldúa, you should work to construct a mixed text, not a single unified one. This will be hard, since you will be writing what might be called a "forbidden" text, one you have not been prepared to write.

2. In *"La conciencia de la mestiza*/Towards a New Consciousness," the last essay-like chapter in her book (the remaining chapters are made up of poems), Anzaldúa steps forward to define her role as writer and yours as reader. She says, among other things,

   > Many women and men of color do not want to have any dealings with white people. . . . Many feel that whites should help their own people rid themselves of race hatred and fear first. I, for one, choose to use some of my energy to serve as mediator. I think we need to allow

whites to be our allies. Through our literature, art, *corridos*, and folk-tales we must share our history with them so when they set up committees to help Big Mountain Navajos or the Chicano farmworkers or *los Nicaragüenses* they won't turn people away because of their racial fears and ignorances. They will come to see that they are not helping us but following our lead.

Individually, but also as a racial entity, we need to voice our needs. We need to say to white society: We need you to accept the fact that Chicanos are different, to acknowledge your rejection and negation of us. We need you to own the fact that you looked upon us as less than human, that you stole our lands, our personhood, our self-respect. We need you to make public restitution: to say that, to compensate for your own sense of defectiveness, you strive for power over us, you erase our history and our experience because it makes you feel guilty—you'd rather forget your brutish acts. To say you've split yourself from minority groups, that you disown us, that your dual consciousness splits off parts of yourself, transferring the "negative" parts onto us. . . . To say that you are afraid of us, that to put distance between us, you wear the mask of contempt. Admit that Mexico is your double, that she exists in the shadow of this country, that we are irrevocably tied to her. Gringo, accept the doppelganger in your psyche. By taking back your collective shadow the intracultural split will heal. And finally, tell us what you need from us.

This is only a part of the text—one of the ways it defines the roles of reader and writer—but it is one that asks to be taken account of, with its insistent list of what a white reader must do and say. (Of course not every reader is white, and not all white readers are the same. What Anzaldúa is defining here is a "white" way of reading.)

Write an essay in which you tell a story of reading, the story of your work with the two chapters of *Borderlands/La Frontera* reprinted here. Think about where you felt at home with the text and where you felt lost, where you knew what you were doing and where you needed help; think about the position (or positions) you have taken as a reader and how it measures up against the ways Anzaldúa has figured you in the text, the ways she has anticipated a response, imagined who you are and how you habitually think and read.

3. In "How to Tame a Wild Tongue" (p. 36), Anzaldúa says, "I will no longer be made to feel ashamed of existing. I will have my voice: Indian, Spanish, white. I will have my serpent's tongue—my woman's voice, my sexual voice, my poet's voice." Anzaldúa speaks almost casually about "having her voice," not a single, "authentic" voice, but one she names in these terms: Indian, Spanish, white; woman, lesbian, poet. What is "voice" as defined by these chapters? Where does it come from? What does it have to do with the act of writing or the writer?

As you reread these chapters, mark those passages that you think best represent Anzaldúa's voices. Using these passages as examples, write an essay in which you discuss how these voices are different—both different from one another and different from a "standard" voice (as a "standard" voice is imagined by Anzaldúa). What do these voices represent? How do they figure in your reading? in her writing?

4. Anzaldúa's writing is difficult to categorize as an essay or a story or a poem; it has all of these within it. The writing may appear to have been just put together, but it is more likely that it was carefully crafted to represent the various voices Anzaldúa understands to be a part of her. She speaks directly about her voices—her woman's voice, her sexual voice, her poet's voice; her Indian, Spanish, and white voices on page 41 of "How to Tame a Wild Tongue."

   Following Anzaldúa, write an argument of your own, one that requires you to use a variety of voices, in which you carefully present the various voices that you feel are a part of you or a part of the argument.

   When you have completed this assignment, write a two-page essay in which you explain why the argument you made might be worth a reader's attention.

MAKING CONNECTIONS

1. In "Arts of the Contact Zone" (p. 528), Mary Louise Pratt talks about the "autoethnographic" text, "a text in which people undertake to describe themselves in ways that engage with representations others have made of them," and about "transculturation," the "processes whereby members of subordinated or marginal groups select and invent from materials transmitted by a dominant or metropolitan culture."

   Write an essay in which you present a reading of these two chapters as an example of an autoethnographic and/or transcultural text. You should imagine that you are writing to someone who is not familiar with either Pratt's argument or Anzaldúa's book. Part of your work, then, is to present Anzaldúa's text to readers who don't have it in front of them. You have the example of Pratt's reading of Guaman Poma's *New Chronicle and Good Government*. And you have her discussion of the "literate arts of the contact zone." Think about how Anzaldúa's text might be similarly read, and about how her text does and doesn't fit Pratt's description. Your goal should be to add an example to Pratt's discussion and to qualify it, to give her discussion a new twist or spin now that you have had a chance to look at an additional example.

2. Both Adrienne Rich in "When We Dead Awaken: Writing as Re-Vision" (p. 549) and Gloria Anzaldúa in these two chapters could be said to be writing about the same issues—writing, identity, gender, history. Both texts contain an argument; both, in their peculiar styles, enact an argument—they demonstrate how and why one might need to revise the usual ways of writing. Identify what you understand to be the key points, the key terms, and the key examples in each selection.

   Beginning with the passages you have identified, write an essay in which you examine the similarities and differences in these two texts. Look particularly for the differences, since they are harder to find and harder to explain. Consider the selections as marking different positions on writing, identity, politics, history. How might you account for these differences (if they represent more than the fact that different people are likely to differ)? How are these differences significant?

JOHN
BERGER

*J*OHN BERGER *(b. 1926), like few other art critics, elicits strong and contradic-*
tory reactions to his writing. He has been called (and sometimes in the same re-
view) "preposterous" as well as "stimulating," "pompous" yet "exciting." He has
been accused of falling prey to "ideological excesses" and of being a victim of his own
"lack of objectivity," but he has been praised for his "scrupulous" and "cogent" ob-
servations on art and culture. He is one of Europe's most influential Marxist critics,
yet his work has been heralded and damned by leftists and conservatives alike. Al-
though Berger's work speaks powerfully, its tone is quiet, thoughtful, measured. Ac-
cording to the poet and critic Peter Schjeldahl, "The most mysterious element in Mr.
Berger's criticism has always been the personality of the critic himself, a man of
strenuous conviction so loath to bully that even his most provocative arguments sit
feather-light on the mind."

The following selection is the first chapter from Ways of Seeing, *a book which*
began as a series on BBC television. In fact, the show was a forerunner of those ency-
clopedic television series later popular on public television stations in the United
States: Civilization, The Ascent of Man, Cosmos. *Berger's show was less glittery*
and ambitious, but in its way it was more serious in its claims to be educational. As
you watched the screen, you saw a series of images (like those in the following text).
These were sometimes presented with commentary, but sometimes in silence, so that

you constantly saw one image in the context of another—for example, classic presentations of women in oil paintings interspersed with images of women from contemporary art, advertising, movies, and "men's magazines." The goal of the exercise, according to Berger, was to "start a process of questioning," to focus his viewer's attention not on a single painting in isolation but on "ways of seeing" in general, on the ways we have learned to look at and understand the images that surround us, and on the culture that teaches us to see things as we do. The method of Ways of Seeing, a book of art history, was used by Berger in another book, A Seventh Man, to document the situation of the migrant worker in Europe.

Berger has written poems, novels, essays, and film scripts, including G, A Fortunate Man, The Success and Failure of Picasso, and About Looking. He lived and worked in England for years, but he currently lives in Quincy, a small peasant village in Haute-Savoie, France, where he has, for the past few years, been writing a trilogy of books on peasant life, titled Into Their Labours. The first book in the series, Pig Earth, is a collection of essays, poems, and stories set in Haute-Savoie. The second, Once in Europa, consists of five peasant tales that take love as their subject. The third and final book in the trilogy, Lilac and Flag: An Old Wives' Tale of the City, published in 1990, is a novel about the migration of peasants to the city. His most recent book is Corker's Freedom: A Novel, published in 1993.

Ways of Seeing

Seeing comes before words. The child looks and recognizes before it can speak.

But there is also another sense in which seeing comes before words. It is seeing which establishes our place in the surrounding world; we explain that world with words, but words can never undo the fact that we are surrounded by it. The relation between what we see and what we know is never settled. Each evening we *see* the sun set. We *know* that the earth is turning away from it. Yet the knowledge, the explanation, never quite fits the sight. The Surrealist painter Magritte commented on this always-present gap between words and seeing in a painting called *The Key of Dreams*.

The way we see things is affected by what we know or what we believe. In the Middle Ages when men believed in the physical existence of Hell the sight of fire must have meant something different from what it means today. Nevertheless their idea of Hell owed a lot to the sight of fire consuming and the ashes remaining—as well as to their experience of the pain of burns.

When in love, the sight of the beloved has a completeness which no

The Key of Dreams by Magritte 1898–1967

words and no embrace can match: a completeness which only the act of making love can temporarily accommodate.

Yet this seeing which comes before words, and can never be quite covered by them, is not a question of mechanically reacting to stimuli. (It can only be thought of in this way if one isolates the small part of the process which concerns the eye's retina.) We only see what we look at. To look is an act of choice. As a result of this act, what we see is brought within our reach—though not necessarily within arm's reach. To touch something is to situate oneself in relation to it. (Close your eyes, move round the room and notice how the faculty of touch is like a static, limited form of sight.) We never look at just one thing; we are always looking at the relation between things and ourselves. Our vision is continually active, continually moving, continually holding things in a circle around itself, constituting what is present to us as we are.

Soon after we can see, we are aware that we can also be seen. The eye of the other combines with our own eye to make it fully credible that we are part of the visible world.

If we accept that we can see that hill over there, we propose that from that hill we can be seen. The reciprocal nature of vision is more fundamental than that of spoken dialogue. And often dialogue is an attempt to verbalize this—an attempt to explain how, either metaphorically or literally, "you see things," and an attempt to discover how "he sees things."

In the sense in which we use the word in this book, all images are man-made [see above]. An image is a sight which has been recreated or reproduced. It is an appearance, or a set of appearances, which has been detached from the place and time in which it first made its appearance and preserved—for a few moments or a few centuries. Every image embodies a way of seeing. Even a photograph. For photographs are not, as is often assumed, a mechanical record. Every time we look at a photograph, we are aware, however slightly, of the photographer selecting that sight from an infinity of other possible sights. This is true even in the most casual family snapshot. The photographer's way of seeing is reflected in his choice of subject. The painter's way of seeing is reconstituted by the marks he makes on the canvas or paper. Yet, although every image embodies a way of seeing, our perception or appreciation of an image depends also upon our own way of seeing. (It may be, for example, that Sheila is one figure among twenty; but for our own reasons she is the one we have eyes for.)

Images were first made to conjure up the appearance of something that was absent. Gradually it became evident that an image could outlast what it represented; it then showed how something or somebody had once looked—and thus by implication how the subject had once been seen by other people. Later still the specific vision of the image-maker was also recognized as part of the record. An image became a record of how X had seen Y. This was the result of an increasing consciousness of individuality, accompanying an in-

52

creasing awareness of history. It would be rash to try to date this last development precisely. But certainly in Europe such consciousness has existed since the beginning of the Renaissance.

No other kind of relic or text from the past can offer such a direct testimony about the world which surrounded other people at other times. In this respect images are more precise and richer than literature. To say this is not to deny the expressive or imaginative quality of art, treating it as mere documentary evidence; the more imaginative the work, the more profoundly it allows us to share the artist's experience of the visible.

Yet when an image is presented as a work of art, the way people look at it is affected by a whole series of learnt assumptions about art. Assumptions concerning:

> Beauty
> Truth
> Genius
> Civilization
> Form
> Status
> Taste, etc.

Many of these assumptions no longer accord with the world as it is. (The world-as-it-is is more than pure objective fact, it includes consciousness.) Out of true with the present, these assumptions obscure the past. They mystify rather than clarify. The past is never there waiting to be discovered, to be recognized for exactly what it is. History always constitutes the relation between a present and its past. Consequently fear of the present leads to mystification of the past. The past is not for living in; it is a well of conclusions from which we draw in order to act. Cultural mystification of the past entails a double loss. Works of art are made unnecessarily remote. And the past offers us fewer conclusions to complete in action.

When we "see" a landscape, we situate ourselves in it. If we "saw" the art of the past, we would situate ourselves in history. When we are prevented from seeing it, we are being deprived of the history which belongs to us. Who benefits from this deprivation? In the end, the art of the past is being mystified because a privileged minority is striving to invent a history which can retrospectively justify the role of the ruling classes, and such a justification can no longer make sense in modern terms. And so, inevitably, it mystifies.

Let us consider a typical example of such mystification. A two-volume study was recently published on Frans Hals.[1] It is the authoritative work to date on this painter. As a book of specialized art history it is no better and no worse than the average.

The last two great paintings by Frans Hals [p. 54] portray the Governors and the Governesses of an Alms House for old paupers in the Dutch

Regents of the Old Men's Alms House by Hals 1580–1666

Regentesses of the Old Men's Alms House by Hals 1580–1666

seventeenth-century city of Haarlem. They were officially commissioned portraits. Hals, an old man of over eighty, was destitute. Most of his life he had been in debt. During the winter of 1664, the year he began painting these pictures, he obtained three loads of peat on public charity, otherwise he would have frozen to death. Those who now sat for him were administrators of such public charity.

The author records these facts and then explicitly says that it would be incorrect to read into the paintings any criticism of the sitters. There is no evidence, he says, that Hals painted them in a spirit of bitterness. The author considers them, however, remarkable works of art and explains why. Here he writes of the Regentesses:

> Each woman speaks to us of the human condition with equal importance. Each woman stands out with equal clarity against the *enormous* dark surface, yet they are linked by a firm rhythmical arrangement and the subdued diagonal pattern formed by their heads and hands. Subtle modulations of the *deep,* glowing blacks contribute to the *harmonious fusion* of the whole and form an *unforgettable contrast* with the *powerful* whites and vivid flesh tones where the detached strokes reach *a peak of breadth and strength.* [Berger's italics]

The compositional unity of a painting contributes fundamentally to the power of its image. It is reasonable to consider a painting's composition. But here the composition is written about as though it were in itself the emotional charge of the painting. Terms like *harmonious fusion, unforgettable contrast,* reaching *a peak of breadth and strength* transfer the emotion provoked by the image from the plane of lived experience, to that of disinterested "art appreciation." All conflict disappears. One is left with the unchanging "human condition," and the painting considered as a marvellously made object.

Very little is known about Hals or the Regents who commissioned him. It is not possible to produce circumstantial evidence to establish what their relations were. But there is the evidence of the paintings themselves: the evidence of a group of men and a group of women as seen by another man, the painter. Study this evidence and judge for yourself.

The art historian fears such direct judgement:

> As in so many other pictures by Hals, the penetrating characterizations almost seduce us into believing that we know the personality traits and even the habits of the men and women portrayed.

What is this "seduction" he writes of? It is nothing less than the paintings working upon us. They work upon us because we accept the way Hals saw his sitters. We do not accept this innocently. We accept it in so far as it corresponds to our own observation of people, gestures, faces, institutions. This is possible because we still live in a society of comparable social relations and moral values. And it is precisely this which gives the paintings their psychological and social urgency. It is this—not the painter's skill as a "seducer"—which convinces us that we *can* know the people portrayed. The author continues:

> In the case of some critics the seduction has been a total success. It has, for example, been asserted that the Regent in the tipped slouch hat, which hardly covers any of his long, lank hair, and whose curiously set eyes do not focus, was shown in a drunken state. [below]

This, he suggests, is a libel. He argues that it was a fashion at that time to wear hats on the side of the head. He cites medical opinion to prove that the Regent's expression could well be the result of a facial paralysis. He insists that the painting would have been unacceptable to the Regents if one of them

had been portrayed drunk. One might go on discussing each of these points for pages. (Men in seventeenth-century Holland wore their hats on the side of their heads in order to be thought of as adventurous and pleasure-loving. Heavy drinking was an approved practice. Etcetera.) But such a discussion would take us even farther away from the only confrontation which matters and which the author is determined to evade.

In this confrontation the Regents and Regentesses stare at Hals, a destitute old painter who has lost his reputation and lives off public charity; he examines them through the eyes of a pauper who must nevertheless try to be objective; i.e., must try to surmount the way he sees as a pauper. This is the drama of these paintings. A drama of an "unforgettable contrast."

Mystification has little to do with the vocabulary used. Mystification is the process of explaining away what might otherwise be evident. Hals was the first portraitist to paint the new characters and expressions created by capitalism. He did in pictorial terms what Balzac did two centuries later in literature. Yet the author of the authoritative work on these paintings sums up the artist's achievement by referring to

> Hals's unwavering commitment to his personal vision, which
> enriches our consciousness of our fellow men and heightens
> our awe for the ever-increasing power of the mighty impulses
> that enabled him to give us a close view of life's vital forces.

That is mystification.

In order to avoid mystifying the past (which can equally well suffer pseudo-Marxist mystification) let us now examine the particular relation which now exists, so far as pictorial images are concerned, between the present and the past. If we can see the present clearly enough, we shall ask the right questions of the past.

Today we see the art of the past as nobody saw it before. We actually perceive it in a different way.

This difference can be illustrated in terms of what was thought of as perspective. The convention of perspective, which is unique to European art and which was first established in the early Renaissance, centres everything on the eye of the beholder. It is like a beam from a lighthouse—only instead of light travelling outwards, appearances travel in. The conventions called those appearances *reality*. Perspective makes the single eye the centre of the visible world. Everything converges on to the eye as to the vanishing point of infinity. The visible world is arranged for the spectator as the universe was once thought to be arranged for God.

According to the convention of perspective there is no visual reciprocity. There is no need for God to situate himself in relation to others: he is himself the situation. The inherent contradiction in perspective was that it structured all images of reality to address a single spectator who, unlike God, could only be in one place at a time.

After the invention of the camera this contradiction gradually became apparent.

> I'm an eye. A mechanical eye. I, the machine, show you a world the way only I can see it. I free myself for today and forever from human immobility. I'm in constant movement. I approach and pull away from objects. I creep under them. I move alongside a running horse's mouth. I fall and rise with the falling and rising bodies. This is I, the machine, manoeuvring in the chaotic movements, recording one movement after another in the most complex combinations.
>
> Freed from the boundaries of time and space, I coordinate any and all points of the universe, wherever I want them to be. My way leads towards the creation of a fresh perception of the world. Thus I explain in a new way the world unknown to you.[2]

The camera isolated momentary appearances and in so doing destroyed the idea that images were timeless. Or, to put it another way, the camera showed that the notion of time passing was inseparable from the experience of the vi-

Still from *Man with a Movie Camera* by Vertov

sual (except in paintings). What you saw depended upon where you were when. What you saw was relative to your position in time and space. It was no longer possible to imagine everything converging on the human eye as on the vanishing point of infinity.

This is not to say that before the invention of the camera men believed that everyone could see everything. But perspective organized the visual field as though that were indeed the ideal. Every drawing or painting that used perspective proposed to the spectator that he was the unique centre of the world. The camera—and more particularly the movie camera—demonstrated that there was no centre.

The invention of the camera changed the way men saw. The visible came to mean something different to them. This was immediately reflected in painting.

For the Impressionists the visible no longer presented itself to man in order to be seen. On the contrary, the visible, in continual flux, became fugitive. For the Cubists the visible was no longer what confronted the single eye, but the totality of possible views taken from points all round the object (or person) being depicted [below].

The invention of the camera also changed the way in which men saw paintings painted long before the camera was invented. Originally paintings were an integral part of the building for which they were designed. Sometimes in an early Renaissance church or chapel one has the feeling that the images on the wall are records of the building's interior life, that together they make up the building's memory—so much are they part of the particularity of the building [p. 60, top].

Still Life with Wicker Chair by Picasso 1881–1973

Church of St. Francis at Assisi

The uniqueness of every painting was once part of the uniqueness of the place where it resided. Sometimes the painting was transportable. But it could never be seen in two places at the same time. When the camera reproduces a painting, it destroys the uniqueness of its image. As a result its meaning changes. Or, more exactly, its meaning multiplies and fragments into many meanings.

This is vividly illustrated by what happens when a painting is shown on a television screen. The painting enters each viewer's house. There it is surrounded by his wallpaper, his furniture, his mementos. It enters the atmos-

phere of his family. It becomes their talking point. It lends its meaning to their meaning. At the same time it enters a million other houses and, in each of them, is seen in a different context. Because of the camera, the painting now travels to the spectator rather than the spectator to the painting. In its travels, its meaning is diversified.

One might argue that all reproductions more or less distort, and that therefore the original painting is still in a sense unique. Here [below] is a reproduction of the *Virgin of the Rocks* by Leonardo da Vinci.

Having seen this reproduction, one can go to the National Gallery to look at the original and there discover what the reproduction lacks. Alternatively one can forget about the quality of the reproduction and simply be reminded, when one sees the original, that it is a famous painting of which somewhere one has already seen a reproduction. But in either case the uniqueness of the original now lies in it being *the original of a reproduction*. It is no longer what its image shows that strikes one as unique; its first meaning is no longer to be found in what it says, but in what it is.

This new status of the original work is the perfectly rational consequence of the new means of reproduction. But it is at this point that a process of mystification again enters. The meaning of the original work no longer lies in what it uniquely says but in what it uniquely is. How is its unique existence evaluated and defined in our present culture? It is defined

Virgin of the Rocks by Leonardo da Vinci 1452–1519. Reproduced by courtesy of the Trustees, The National Gallery, London

as an object whose value depends upon its rarity. This market is affirmed and gauged by the price it fetches on the market. But because it is nevertheless "a work of art"—and art is thought to be greater than commerce—its market price is said to be a reflection of its spiritual value. Yet the spiritual value of an object, as distinct from a message or an example, can only be explained in terms of magic or religion. And since in modern society neither of these is a living force, the art object, the "work of art," is enveloped in an atmosphere of entirely bogus religiosity. Works of art are discussed and presented as though they were holy relics: relics which are first and foremost evidence of their own survival. The past in which they originated is studied in order to prove their survival genuine. They are declared art when their line of descent can be certified.

Before the *Virgin of the Rocks* the visitor to the National Gallery would be encouraged by nearly everything he might have heard and read about the painting to feel something like this: "I am in front of it. I can see it. This painting by Leonardo is unlike any other in the world. The National Gallery has the real one. If I look at this painting hard enough, I should somehow be able

Virgin of the Rocks by Leonardo da Vinci 1452–1519.
Louvre Museum

to feel its authenticity. The *Virgin of the Rocks* by Leonardo da Vinci: it is authentic and therefore it is beautiful."

To dismiss such feelings as naive would be quite wrong. They accord perfectly with the sophisticated culture of art experts for whom the National Gallery catalogue is written. The entry on the *Virgin of the Rocks* is one of the longest entries. It consists of fourteen closely printed pages. They do not deal with the meaning of the image. They deal with who commissioned the painting, legal squabbles, who owned it, its likely date, the families of its owners. Behind this information lie years of research. The aim of the research is to prove beyond any shadow of doubt that the painting is a genuine Leonardo. The secondary aim is to prove that an almost identical painting in the Louvre is a replica of the National Gallery version.

French art historians try to prove the opposite [see p. 62].

The National Gallery sells more reproductions of Leonardo's cartoon of *The Virgin and Child with St. Anne and St. John the Baptist* [below] than any other picture in their collection. A few years ago it was known only to scholars. It became famous because an American wanted to buy it for two and a half million pounds.

Now it hangs in a room by itself. The room is like a chapel. The drawing is behind bullet-proof perspex. It has acquired a new kind of impressiveness. Not because of what it shows—not because of the meaning of its image. It has become impressive, mysterious, because of its market value.

The Virgin and Child with St. Anne and St. John the Baptist
by Leonardo da Vinci 1452–1519. Reproduced by courtesy of the
Trustees, The National Gallery, London.

• • •

The bogus religiosity which now surrounds original works of art, and which is ultimately dependent upon their market value, has become the substitute for what paintings lost when the camera made them reproducible. Its function is nostalgic. It is the final empty claim for the continuing values of an oligarchic, undemocratic culture. If the image is no longer unique and exclusive, the art object, the thing, must be made mysteriously so.

The majority of the population do not visit art museums. The following table shows how closely an interest in art is related to privileged education.

National proportion of art museum visitors according to level of education:
Percentage of each educational category who visit art museums

	Greece	Poland	France	Holland		Greece	Poland	France	Holland
With no educational qualification	0.02	0.12	0.15	—	Only secondary education	10.5	10.4	10	20
Only primary education	0.30	1.50	0.45	0.50	Further and higher education	11.5	11.7	12.5	17.3

Source: Pierre Bourdieu and Alain Darbel, *L'Amour de l'art*, Editions de Minuit, Paris 1969, Appendix 5, table 4

The majority take it as axiomatic that the museums are full of holy relics which refer to a mystery which excludes them: the mystery of unaccountable wealth. Or, to put this another way, they believe that original masterpieces belong to the preserve (both materially and spiritually) of the rich. Another table indicates what the idea of an art gallery suggests to each social class.

Of the places listed below which does a museum remind you of most?

	Manual workers	Skilled and white collar workers	Professional and upper managerial
	%	%	%
Church	66	45	30.5
Library	9	34	28
Lecture hall	—	4	4.5
Department store or entrance hall in public building	—	7	2
Church and library	9	2	4.5
Church and lecture hall	4	2	—
Library and lecture hall	—	—	2
None of these	4	2	19.5
No reply	8	4	9
	100 (n = 53)	100 (n = 98)	100 (n =99)

Source: as above, Appendix 4, table 8

In the age of pictorial reproduction the meaning of paintings is no longer attached to them; their meaning becomes transmittable: that is to say it becomes information of a sort, and, like all information, it is either put to use or ignored; information carries no special authority within itself. When a painting is put to use, its meaning is either modified or totally changed. One should be quite clear about what this involves. It is not a question of reproduction failing to reproduce certain aspects of an image faithfully; it is a question of reproduction making it possible, even inevitable, that an image will be used for many different purposes and that the reproduced image, unlike an original work, can lend itself to them all. Let us examine some of the ways in which the reproduced image lends itself to such usage.

Reproduction isolates a detail of a painting from the whole. The detail is transformed. An allegorical figure becomes a portrait of a girl.

Venus and Mars by Botticelli 1445–1510. Reproduced by courtesy of the Trustees, The National Gallery, London

When a painting is reproduced by a film camera it inevitably becomes material for the film-maker's argument.

A film which reproduces images of a painting leads the spectator, through the painting, to the film-maker's own conclusions. The painting lends authority to the film-maker. This is because a film unfolds in time and a painting does not. In a film the way one image follows another, their succession, constructs an argument which becomes irreversible. In a painting all its elements are there to be seen simultaneously. The spectator may need time to examine each element of the painting but whenever he reaches a conclusion, the simultaneity of the whole painting is there to reverse or qualify his conclusion. The painting maintains its own authority [below]. Paintings are often reproduced with words around them [p. 67, top].

Procession to Calvary by Breughel 1525–1569

This is a landscape of a cornfield with birds flying out of it. Look at it for a moment [below]. Then turn the page [p. 68, top].

It is hard to define exactly how the words have changed the image but undoubtedly they have. The image now illustrates the sentence.

In this essay each image reproduced has become part of an argument which has little or nothing to do with the painting's original independent meaning. The words have quoted the paintings to confirm their own verbal authority. . . .

Wheatfield with Crows by Van Gogh 1853–1890

This is the last picture that Van Gogh painted before he killed himself.

Reproduced paintings, like all information, have to hold their own against all the other information being continually transmitted [below].

Consequently a reproduction, as well as making its own references to the image of its original, becomes itself the reference point for other images. The meaning of an image is changed according to what one sees immediately beside it or what comes immediately after it. Such authority as it retains, is distributed over the whole context in which it appears [see p. 69].

Because works of art are reproducible, they can, theoretically, be used by anybody. Yet mostly—in art books, magazines, films, or within gilt frames in living-rooms—reproductions are still used to bolster the illusion that nothing has changed, that art, with its unique undiminished authority, justifies most other forms of authority, that art makes inequality seem noble and hierarchies seem thrilling. For example, the whole concept of the National Cultural

Subject and significance in Titian's Death of Actaeon

If women knew then... what they know now.

Heritage exploits the authority of art to glorify the present social system and
its priorities.

The means of reproduction are used politically and commercially to disguise or deny what their existence makes possible. But sometimes individuals use them differently [p. 70].

Adults and children sometimes have boards in their bedrooms or living-
rooms on which they pin pieces of paper: letters, snapshots, reproductions of
paintings, newspaper cuttings, original drawings, postcards. On each board
all the images belong to the same language and all are more or less equal
within it, because they have been chosen in a highly personal way to match
and express the experience of the room's inhabitant. Logically, these boards
should replace museums.

What are we saying by that? Let us first be sure about what we are not
saying.

We are not saying that there is nothing left to experience before original
works of art except a sense of awe because they have survived. The way original works of art are usually approached—through museum catalogues,
guides, hired cassettes, etc.—is not the only way they might be approached.
When the art of the past ceases to be viewed nostalgically, the works will

69

cease to be holy relics—although they will never re-become what they were before the age of reproduction. We are not saying original works of art are now useless.

Original paintings are silent and still in a sense that information never is. Even a reproduction hung on a wall is not comparable in this respect for in the original the silence and stillness permeate the actual material, the paint, in which one follows the traces of the painter's immediate gestures. This has the effect of closing the distance in time between the painting of the picture and one's own act of looking at it. In this special sense all paintings are contemporary. Hence the immediacy of their testimony. Their historical moment is literally there before our eyes. Cézanne made a similar observation from the painter's point of view. "A minute in the world's life passes! To paint it in its reality, and forget everything for that! To become that minute, to be the sensitive plate . . . give the image of what we see, forgetting everything that has appeared before our time . . ." What we make of that painted moment when it is before our eyes depends upon what we expect of art, and that in turn depends today upon how we have already experienced the meaning of paintings through reproductions.

Nor are we saying that all art can be understood spontaneously. We are not claiming that to cut out a magazine reproduction of an archaic Greek head, because it is reminiscent of some personal experience, and to pin it to a board beside other disparate images, is to come to terms with the full meaning of that head.

The idea of innocence faces two ways. By refusing to enter a conspiracy, one remains innocent of that conspiracy. But to remain innocent may also be to remain ignorant. The issue is not between innocence and knowledge (or between the natural and the cultural) but between a total approach to art which attempts to relate it to every aspect of experience and the esoteric approach of a few specialized experts who are the clerks of the nostalgia of a ruling class in decline. (In decline, not before the proletariat, but before the new power of the corporation and the state.) The real question is: to whom does the meaning of the art of the past properly belong? to those who can apply it to their own lives, or to a cultural hierarchy of relic specialists?

The visual arts have always existed within a certain preserve; originally this preserve was magical or sacred. But it was also physical: it was the place, the cave, the building, in which, or for which, the work was made. The experience of art, which at first was the experience of ritual, was set apart from the rest of life—precisely in order to be able to exercise power over it. Later the preserve of art became a social one. It entered the culture of the ruling class, whilst physically it was set apart and isolated in their palaces and houses. During all this history the authority of art was inseparable from the particular authority of the preserve.

What the modern means of reproduction have done is to destroy the authority of art and to remove it—or, rather, to remove its images which they reproduce—from any preserve. For the first time ever, images of art have be-

Woman Pouring Milk by Vermeer 1632–1675

come ephemeral, ubiquitous, insubstantial, available, valueless, free. They surround us in the same way as a language surrounds us. They have entered the mainstream of life over which they no longer, in themselves, have power.

Yet very few people are aware of what has happened because the means of reproduction are used nearly all the time to promote the illusion that nothing has changed except that the masses, thanks to reproductions, can now begin to appreciate art as the cultured minority once did. Understandably, the masses remain uninterested and sceptical.

If the new language of images were used differently, it would, through its use, confer a new kind of power. Within it we could begin to define our experiences more precisely in areas where words are inadequate. (Seeing comes from words.) Not only personal experience, but also the essential historical experience of our relation to the past: that is to say the experience of seeking to give meaning to our lives, of trying to understand the history of which we can become the active agents.

The art of the past no longer exists as it once did. Its authority is lost. In its place there is a language of images. What matters now is who uses that language for what purpose. This touches upon questions of copyright for reproduction, the ownership of art presses and publishers, the total policy of public art galleries and museums. As usually presented, these are narrow professional matters. One of the aims of this essay has been to show that what is really at stake is much larger. A people or a class which is cut off from its own past is far less free to choose and to act as a people or class than one that has been able to situate itself in history. This is why—and this is the only reason why—the entire art of the past has now become a political issue.

Many of the ideas in the preceding essay have been taken from another, written over forty years ago by the German critic and philosopher Walter Benjamin.

His essay was entitled The Work of Art in the Age of Mechanical Reproduction. *This essay is available in English in a collection called* Illuminations *(Cape, London, 1970).*

NOTES
[1] Seymour Slive, *Frans Hals* (Phaidon, London).
[2] This quotation is from an article written in 1923 by Dziga Vertov, the revolutionary Soviet film director.

•   •   •   •   •   •   •   •   •   •   •

QUESTIONS FOR A SECOND READING

1. Berger says, "The past is never there waiting to be discovered, to be recognized for exactly what it is. History always constitutes the relation between a present and its past" (p. 53). And he says, "If we 'saw' the art of the past, we would situate ourselves in history. When we are prevented from seeing it, we are being deprived of the history which belongs to us" (p. 53). As you reread this essay, pay particular attention to Berger's uses of the word "history." What does it stand for? What does it have to do with looking at pictures? How might you define the term if your definition were based on its use in this essay?

   You might take Berger's discussion of the Hals paintings as a case in point. What is the relation Berger establishes between the past and the present? If he has not "discovered" the past or recognized it for exactly what it is, what has Berger done in writing about these paintings? What might it mean to say that he has "situated" us in history or has returned a history that belongs to us? And in what way might this be said to be a political act?

2. Berger argues forcefully that the account of the Hals painting offered by the unnamed art historian is a case of "mystification." How would you characterize Berger's account of that same painting? Would you say that he sees what is "really" there? If so, why wasn't it self-evident? Why does it take an expert to see "clearly"? As you read back over the essay, look for passages you could use to characterize the way Berger looks at images or paintings. If, as he says, "The way we see things is affected by what we know or what we believe," what does he know and what does he believe?

ASSIGNMENTS FOR WRITING

1. Berger says that the real question is this: "To whom does the meaning of the art of the past properly belong?" Let's say, in Berger's spirit, that it belongs to you. Look again at the painting by Vermeer, *Woman Pouring Milk*, that is included in the essay (p. 71). Berger includes the painting but without much discussion, as though he were, in fact, leaving it for you. Write an essay that shows others how they might best understand that painting. You should offer this lesson in the spirit of John Berger. Imagine that you are doing this work for him, perhaps as his apprentice.

2.   Original paintings are silent and still in a sense that information never
     is. Even a reproduction hung on a wall is not comparable in this respect
     for in the original the silence and stillness permeate the actual material,
     the paint, in which one follows the traces of the painter's immediate
     gestures. This has the effect of closing the distance in the time between
     the painting of the picture and one's own act of looking at it. . . . What
     we make of that painted moment when it is before our eyes depends
     upon what we expect of art, and that in turn depends today upon how
     we have already experienced the meaning of paintings through repro-
     ductions. (pp. 70–71)

While Berger describes original paintings as silent in this passage, it is
clear that these paintings begin to speak if one approaches them properly, if
one learns to ask "the right questions of the past." Berger demonstrates one
route of approach, for example, in his reading of the Hals paintings, where
he asks questions about the people and objects and their relationships to the
painter and the viewer. What the paintings might be made to say, however,
depends upon the viewer's expectations, his or her sense of the questions
that seem appropriate or possible. Berger argues that, because of the way art
is currently displayed, discussed, and reproduced, the viewer expects only to
be mystified.

For this paper, imagine that you are working against the silence and
mystification Berger describes. Go to a museum—or, if that is not possible,
to a large-format book of reproductions in the library (or, if that is not possible, to the reproductions in this essay)—and select a painting that seems
silent and still, yet invites conversation. Your job is to figure out what sorts
of questions to ask, to interrogate the painting, to get it to speak, to engage
with the past in some form of dialogue. Write an essay in which you record
this process and what you have learned from it. Somewhere in your paper,
perhaps at the end, turn back to Berger's essay and speak to it about
how this process has or hasn't confirmed what you take to be Berger's
expectations.

Note: If possible, include with your essay a reproduction of the painting
you select. (Check the postcards at the museum gift shop.) In any event, you
want to make sure that you describe the painting in sufficient detail for your
readers to follow what you say.

MAKING CONNECTIONS

1. Walker Percy, in "The Loss of the Creature" (p. 511), like Berger in "Ways of
   Seeing," talks about the problems people have seeing things. "How can the
   sightseer recover the Grand Canyon?" Percy asks. "He can recover it in any
   number of ways, all sharing in common the strategem of avoiding the approved confrontation of the tour and the Park Service." There is a way in
   which Berger also tells a story about tourists—tourists going to a museum to
   see paintings, to buy postcards, gallery guides, reprints, and T-shirts featuring
   the image of the Mona Lisa. "The way original works of art are usually approached—through museum catalogues, guides, hired cassettes, etc.—is not
   the only way they might be approached. When the art of the past ceases to be

viewed nostalgically, the works will cease to be holy relics—although they will never re-become what they were before the age of reproduction" (p. 70).

Write an essay in which you describe possible "approaches" to a painting in a museum, approaches that could provide for a better understanding or a more complete "recovery" of that painting than would be possible to a casual viewer, to someone who just wandered in, for example, with no strategy in mind. You should think of your essay as providing real advice to a real person. (You might, if you can, work with a particular painting in a particular museum.) What should that person do? How should that person prepare? What would the consequences be?

At least one of your approaches should reflect Percy's best advice to a viewer who wanted to develop a successful strategy, and at least one should represent the best you feel Berger would have to offer. When you've finished explaining these approaches, go on in your essay to examine the differences between those you associate with Percy and those you associate with Berger. What are the key differences? And what do they say about the different ways these two thinkers approach the problem of why we do or do not see that which lies before us?

2. Both John Berger in "Ways of Seeing" and Michel Foucault in "Panopticism" (p. 178) discuss what Foucault calls "power relations." Berger claims that "the entire art of the past has now become a political issue," and he makes a case for the evolution of a "new language of images" that could "confer a new kind of power" if people were to understand history in art. Foucault argues that the Panopticon signals an "inspired" change in power relations. "It is," he says, "an important mechanism, for it automatizes and disindividualizes power. Power has its principle not so much in a person as in a certain concerted distribution of bodies, surfaces, lights, gazes; in an arrangement whose internal mechanisms produce the relation in which individuals are caught up" (p. 185).

Both Berger and Foucault create arguments about power and its methods and goals. As you read through their essays, mark passages you might use to explain how each author thinks about power—where it comes from, who has it, how it works, where you look for it, how you know it when you see it, what it does, where it goes. You should reread the essays as a pair, as part of a single project in which you are seeking to explain theories of power.

Write an essay in which you present and explain "Ways of Seeing" and "Panopticism" as examples of Berger's and Foucault's theories of power and vision. Both Berger and Foucault are arguing against usual understandings of power and knowledge and history. In this sense, their projects are similar. You should be sure, however, to look for differences as well as similarities.

3. Clifford Geertz, in "Deep Play: Notes on the Balinese Cockfight" (p. 228), argues that the cockfights are a "Balinese reading of Balinese experience; a story they tell themselves about themselves." They are not, then, just cockfights. Or, as Geertz says, the cockfights can be seen as texts "saying something of something." Berger's essay, "Ways of Seeing," offers a view of our culture and, in particular, of the way our culture reproduces and uses images from the past. They are placed in museums, on bulletin boards, on T-shirts, and in advertisements. They are described by experts in certain predictable

tones or phrases. It is interesting to look at our use of those images as a story we tell ourselves about ourselves, as a practice that says something about something else.

Geertz's analysis of the cockfight demonstrates this way of seeing and interpreting a feature of a culture. Write an essay in which you use Geertz's methods to interpret the examples that Berger provides of the ways our culture reproduces and uses images from the past. If these practices say something about something else, what do they say, and about what do they say it? What story might we be telling ourselves about ourselves?

Note: For this assignment, you should avoid rushing to the conclusion Berger draws—that the story told here is a story about the ruling class and its conspiracy against the proletariat. You should see, that is, what other interpretation you can provide. You may, if you choose, return to Berger's conclusions in your paper, but only after you have worked on some of your own.

JOAN
DIDION

*J*OAN DIDION (b. 1934) began her career as a writer in 1956, winning Vogue
*magazine's "Prix de Paris" Award and a job writing for the magazine. As an
undergraduate at the University of California at Berkeley, she majored in English literature. In an essay titled "Why I Write," she reflects on her training in college. She
says, "During the years when I was an undergraduate at Berkeley, I tried, with a
kind of hopeless late adolescent energy, to buy some temporary visa into the world of
ideas, to forge for myself a mind that could deal with the abstract." And, she says, she
failed.*

> *My attention veered inexorably back to the specific, to the tangible, to
> what was generally considered by everyone I knew then and for that
> matter have known since, the peripheral. . . . I would try to read lin-
> guistic theory and would find myself wondering instead if the lights
> were on in the bevatron up the hill. When I say that I was wondering
> if the lights were on in the bevatron you might immediately suspect, if
> you deal in ideas at all, that I was registering the bevatron as a politi-
> cal symbol, thinking in shorthand about the military-industrial com-
> plex and its role in the university community, but you would be
> wrong. I was only wondering if the lights were on in the bevatron,
> and how they looked. A physical fact.*

From this, she concludes, she learned what she was, which was a writer, "a per-son whose most absorbed and passionate hours are spent arranging words on pieces of paper." A writer, according to Didion, is not a person without ideas; it is a person who takes a different route to ideas, who makes a different use of them. "Had I been blessed with even limited access to my own mind," she said, "there would have been no reason to write. I write entirely to find out what I'm thinking, what I'm looking at, what I see and what it means. What I want and what I fear. . . . Why have the night lights in the bevatron burned in my mind for twenty years?"

Didion has been a prolific and influential writer. She has written four novels. Her first, Run River *(1964), focused on power and politics in a small California town about to be taken over by developers. Her second and most well known,* Play It As It Lays *(1970), deals with the life of a fragile, middle-class woman whose life is busy, fast, and empty. It has been compared with T. S. Eliot's "The Waste Land" for its representation of "images of alienation and desolation, fragments of banal conver-sations, the minutiae of everyday life joined in a mosaic of nothingness." This book was followed by two screenplays, in collaboration with her husband, John Gregory Dunne, for the films* Panic in Needle Park *(1971) and* A Star Is Born *(1976). Her next novel,* A Book of Common Prayer *(1977), chronicles the life and death of a middle-class housewife whose daughter is revealed to be a political terrorist. And in 1984 she published* Democracy, *a novel that traces the life of a politician and his wife as he makes his way to the top. Although clearly fictional,* Democracy *also in-cludes Didion in recognizable scenes of her own life as well as characters named for "real" people, thus blurring the borders between fiction and fact and raising difficult questions about the relations between narrative and history, between stories and the ways things are.*

This attention to "real" people, to current events—to the "idea" of America and the meaning of the news—came as no surprise to those following Didion's career. She is equally known (perhaps even more well known) for her work as a reporter and essayist, writing on contemporary cultural and political life. Her first collection of essays, Slouching Towards Bethlehem *(1968), explored in nonfictional form the social politics of the California that figured as landscape in* Run River. *This was fol-lowed by three other collections—*Telling Stories *(1978),* The White Album *(1979), and* True Confessions *(1981)—all of which announced a more general con-cern with national issues. In 1983 she published* Salvador, *her controversial first-hand account of the effects of American foreign policy in Latin America, which of-fered a stinging criticism of the circular logic that enabled millions of dollars to be funneled into a country notorious for human rights abuses.* Salvador *was followed in 1987 by* Miami, *a collection of essays that looks at the city in terms of the uneasy racial balances between Anglos, African Americans, and Cubans.*

The following piece, titled "Sentimental Journeys," is taken from her latest col-lection of essays, After Henry *(1992). It marks something of a departure for Didion, since it is not so much a piece of investigative reporting as it is an essay about re-porting and the effects of the media, particularly print media, in determining the con-sciousness of a city and defining the stories New Yorkers tell themselves about them-selves. In this sense, her work in this essay is much like that of a literary critic,*

78

reading texts and thinking about what they say and how they work. She asks you to think about a news story as a "story," as more than a simple or objective account of the facts; she asks you to think of the story itself as a form of interpretation or imagination. As you read this essay, you will recall a difficult period in New York City's recent history and you will see how its details were organized into ideas, shaped to serve the public's desire for all events to make sense.

Sentimental Journeys

1

We know her story, and some of us, although not all of us, which was to become one of the story's several equivocal aspects, know her name. She was a twenty-nine-year-old unmarried white woman who worked as an investment banker in the corporate finance department at Salomon Brothers in downtown Manhattan, the energy and natural resources group. She was said by one of the principals in a Texas oil stock offering on which she had collaborated as a member of the Salomon team to have done "top-notch" work. She lived alone in an apartment on East 83rd Street, between York and East End, a sublet cooperative she was thinking about buying. She often worked late and when she got home she would change into jogging clothes and at eight-thirty or nine-thirty in the evening would go running, six or seven miles through Central Park, north on the East Drive, west on the less traveled road connecting the East and West Drives at approximately 102nd Street, and south on the West Drive. The wisdom of this was later questioned by some, by those who were accustomed to thinking of the park as a place to avoid after dark, and defended by others, the more adroit of whom spoke of the citizen's absolute right to public access ("That park belongs to us and this time nobody is going to take it from us," Ronnie Eldridge, at the time a Democratic candidate for the City Council of New York, declared on the op-ed page of the *New York Times*), others of whom spoke of "running" as a preemptive right. "Runners have Type A controlled personalities and they don't like their schedules interrupted," one runner, a securities trader, told the *Times* to this point. "When people run is a function of their life-style," another runner said. "I am personally very angry," a third said, "because women should have the right to run any time."

For this woman in this instance these notional rights did not prevail. She was found, with her clothes torn off, not far from the 102nd Street connecting road at one-thirty on the morning of April 20, 1989. She was taken near death to Metropolitan Hospital on East 97th Street. She had lost 75 percent of her blood. Her skull had been crushed, her left eyeball pushed back through its socket, the characteristic surface wrinkles of her brain flattened. Dirt and twigs were found in her vagina, suggesting rape. By May 2, when she first woke from coma, six black and Hispanic teenagers, four of whom had made videotaped statements concerning their roles in the attack and another of whom had described his role in an unsigned verbal statement, had been charged with her assault and rape and she had become, unwilling and unwitting, a sacrificial player in the sentimental narrative that is New York public life.

NIGHTMARE IN CENTRAL PARK, the headlines and display type read. *Teen Wolfpack Beats and Rapes Wall Street Exec on Jogging Path. Central Park Horror. Wolf Pack's Prey. Female Jogger Near Death After Savage Attack by Roving Gang. Rape Rampage. Park Marauders Call It 'Wilding,' Street Slang for Going Berserk. Rape Suspect: 'It Was Fun.' Rape Suspect's Jailhouse Boast: 'She Wasn't Nothing.' The teenagers were back in the holding cell, the confessions gory and complete. One shouted "hit the beat" and they all started rapping to "Wild Thing." The Jogger and the Wolf Pack. An Outrage and a Prayer.* And, on the Monday morning after the attack, on the front page of the *New York Post,* with a photograph of Governor Mario Cuomo and the headline NONE OF US IS SAFE, this italic text: "A visibly shaken Governor Cuomo spoke out yesterday on the vicious Central Park rape: 'The people are angry and frightened—my mother is, my family is. To me, as a person who's lived in this city all of his life, this is the ultimate shriek of alarm.' "

Later it would be recalled that 3,254 other rapes were reported that year, including one the following week involving the near decapitation of a black woman in Fort Tryon Park and one two weeks later involving a black woman in Brooklyn who was robbed, raped, sodomized, and thrown down the air shaft of a four-story building, but the point was rhetorical, since crimes are universally understood to be news to the extent that they offer, however erroneously, a story, a lesson, a high concept. In the 1986 Central Park death of Jennifer Levin, then eighteen, at the hands of Robert Chambers, then nineteen, the "story," extrapolated more or less from thin air but left largely uncorrected, had to do not with people living wretchedly and marginally on the underside of where they wanted to be, not with the Dreiserian pursuit of "respectability" that marked the revealed details (Robert Chambers's mother was a private-duty nurse who worked twelve-hour night shifts to enroll her son in private schools and the Knickerbocker Greys), but with "preppies," and the familiar "too much too soon."

Susan Brownmiller, during a year spent monitoring newspaper coverage of rape as part of her research for *Against Our Will: Men, Women and Rape,* found, not surprisingly, that "although New York City police statistics showed that black women were more frequent victims of rape than white women, the favored victim in the tabloid headline . . . was young, white, middle-class, and 'attractive.' " In its quite extensive coverage of rape-murders during the year 1971, according to Ms. Brownmiller, the *Daily News* published in its four-star final edition only two stories in which the victim was not described in the lead paragraph as "attractive": one of these stories involved an eight-year-old child, the other was a second-day follow-up on a first-day story which had in fact described the victim as "attractive." The *Times*, she found, covered rapes only infrequently that year, but what coverage they did "concerned victims who had some kind of middle-class status, such as 'nurse,' 'dancer,' or 'teacher,' and with a favored setting of Central Park."

As a news story, "Jogger" was understood to turn on the demonstrable "difference" between the victim and her accused assailants, four of whom lived in Schomburg Plaza, a federally subsidized apartment complex at the northeast corner of Fifth Avenue and 110th Street in East Harlem, and the rest of whom lived in the projects and rehabilitated tenements just to the north and west of Schomburg Plaza. Some twenty-five teenagers were brought in for questioning; eight were held. The six who were finally indicted ranged in age from fourteen to sixteen. That none of the six had a previous police record passed, in this context, for achievement; beyond that, one was recalled by his classmates to have taken pride in his expensive basketball shoes, another to have been "a follower." *I'm a smooth type of fellow, cool, calm, and mellow,* one of the six, Yusef Salaam, would say in the rap he presented as part of his statement before sentencing.

> I'm kind of laid back, but now I'm speaking so that you know
> I got used and abused and even was put on the news. . . .
> I'm not dissing them all, but the some that I called
> They tried to dis me like I was an inch small, like a midget,
> a mouse, something less than a man.

The victim, by contrast, was a leader, part of what the *Times* would describe as "the wave of young professionals who took over New York in the 1980s," one of those who were "handsome and pretty and educated and white," who, according to the *Times*, not only "believed they owned the world" but "had reason to." She was from a Pittsburgh suburb, Upper St. Clair, the daughter of a retired Westinghouse senior manager. She had been Phi Beta Kappa at Wellesley, a graduate of the Yale School of Management, a congressional intern, nominated for a Rhodes scholarship, remembered by the chairman of her department at Wellesley as "probably one of the top four or five students of the decade." She was reported to be a vegetarian, and "fun-loving," although only "when time permitted," and also to have had (these were the *Times*'s details) "concerns about the ethics of the American business world."

In other words she was wrenched, even as she hung between death and life and later between insentience and sentience, into New York's ideal sister, daughter, Bachrach bride: a young woman of conventional middle-class privilege and promise whose situation was such that many people tended to overlook the fact that the state's case against the accused was not invulnerable. The state could implicate most of the defendants in the assault and rape in their own videotaped words, but had none of the incontrovertible forensic evidence—no matching semen, no matching fingernail scrapings, no matching blood—commonly produced in this kind of case. Despite the fact that jurors in the second trial would eventually mention physical evidence as having been crucial in their bringing guilty verdicts against one defendant, Kevin Richardson, there was not actually much physical evidence at hand. Fragments of hair "similar [to] and consistent" with that of the victim were found on Kevin Richardson's clothing and underwear, but the state's own criminologist had testified that hair samples were necessarily inconclusive since, unlike fingerprints, they could not be traced to a single person. Dirt samples found on the defendants' clothing were, again, similar to dirt found in the part of the park where the attack took place, but the state's criminologist allowed that the samples were also similar to dirt found in other uncultivated areas of the park. To suggest, however, that this minimal physical evidence could open the case to an aggressive defense—to, say, the kind of defense that such celebrated New York criminal lawyers as Jack Litman and Barry Slotnick typically present—would come to be construed, during the weeks and months to come, as a further attack on the victim.

She would be Lady Courage to the *New York Post*, she would be A Profile in Courage to the *Daily News* and *New York Newsday*. She would become for Anna Quindlen in the *New York Times* the figure of "New York rising above the dirt, the New Yorker who has known the best, and the worst, and has stayed on, living somewhere in the middle." She would become for David Dinkins, the first black mayor of New York, the emblem of his apparently fragile hopes for the city itself: "I hope the city will be able to learn a lesson from this event and be inspired by the young woman who was assaulted in the case," he said. "Despite tremendous odds, she is rebuilding her life. What a human life can do, a human society can do as well." She was even then for John Gutfreund, the chairman and chief executive officer of Salomon Brothers, the personification of "what makes this city so vibrant and so great," now "struck down by a side of our city that is as awful and terrifying as the creative side is wonderful." It was precisely in this conflation of victim and city, this confusion of personal woe with public distress, that the crime's "story" would be found, its lesson, its encouraging promise of narrative resolution.

One reason the victim in this case could be so readily abstracted, and her situation so readily made to stand for that of the city itself, was that she remained, as a victim of rape, unnamed in most press reports. Although the American and English press convention of not naming victims of rape (adult rape victims are named in French papers) derives from the understandable wish to protect the victim, the rationalization of this special protection rests on a number of doubtful, even magical, assumptions. The convention assumes, by providing a protection for victims of rape not afforded victims of other assaults, that rape involves a violation absent from other kinds of assault. The convention assumes that this violation is of a nature best kept secret, that the rape victim feels, and would feel still more strongly were she identified, a shame and self-loathing unique to this form of assault; in other words that she has been in an unspecified way party to her own assault, that a special contract exists between this one kind of victim and her assailant.

The convention assumes, finally, that the victim would be, were this special contract revealed, the natural object of prurient interest; that the act of male penetration involves such potent mysteries that the woman so penetrated (as opposed, say, to having her face crushed with a brick or her brain penetrated with a length of pipe) is permanently marked, "different," even— especially if there is a perceived racial or social "difference" between victim and assailant, as in nineteenth-century stories featuring white women taken by Indians—"ruined."

These quite specifically masculine assumptions (women do not want to be raped, nor do they want to have their brains smashed, but very few mystify the difference between the two) tend in general to be self-fulfilling, guiding the victim to define her assault as her protectors do. "Ultimately we're doing women a disservice by separating rape from other violent crimes," Deni Elliott, the director of Dartmouth's Ethics Institute, suggested in a discussion of this custom in *Time*. "We are participating in the stigma of rape by treating victims of this crime differently." Geneva Overholser, the editor of the Des Moines *Register*, said about her decision to publish in February 1990 a five-part piece about a rape victim who agreed to be named. "When we as a society refuse to talk openly about rape, I think we weaken our ability to deal with it." Susan Estrich, a professor of criminal law at Harvard Law School and the manager of Michael Dukakis's 1988 presidential campaign, discussed, in *Real Rape*, the conflicting emotions that followed her own 1974 rape:

> At first, being raped is something you simply don't talk about. Then it occurs to you that people whose houses are broken into or who are mugged in Central Park talk about it *all* the time. . . . If it isn't my fault, why am I supposed to be ashamed? If I'm not ashamed, if it wasn't "personal," why look askance when I mentioned it?

There were, in the 1989 Central Park attack, specific circumstances that reinforced the conviction that the victim should not be named. She had clearly been, according to the doctors who examined her at Metropolitan Hospital and to the statements made by the suspects (she herself remembered neither the attack nor anything that happened during the next six weeks), raped by one or more assailants. She had also been beaten so brutally that fifteen months later she could not focus her eyes or walk unaided. She had lost all sense of smell. She could not read without experiencing double vision. She was believed at the time to have permanently lost function in some areas of her brain.

Given these circumstances, the fact that neither the victim's family nor, later, the victim herself wanted her name known struck an immediate chord of sympathy, seemed a belated way to protect her as she had not been protected in Central Park. Yet there was in this case a special emotional undertow that derived in part from the deep and allusive associations and taboos attaching, in American black history, to the idea of the rape of white women. Rape remained, in the collective memory of many blacks, the very core of their victimization. Black men were accused of raping white women, even as black women were, Malcolm X wrote in *The Autobiography of Malcolm X*, "raped by the slavemaster white man until there had begun to emerge a homemade, handmade, brainwashed race that was no longer even of its true color, that no longer even knew its true family names." The very frequency of sexual contact between white men and black women increased the potency of the taboo on any such contact between black men and white women. The abolition of slavery, W. J. Cash wrote in *The Mind of the South,*

> in destroying the rigid fixity of the black at the bottom of the scale, in throwing open to him at least the legal opportunity to advance, had inevitably opened up to the mind of every Southerner a vista at the end of which stood the overthrow of this taboo. If it was given to the black to advance at all, who could say (once more the logic of the doctrine of his inherent inferiority would not hold) that he would not one day advance the whole way and lay claim to complete equality, including, specifically, the ever crucial right of marriage?
>
> What Southerners felt, therefore, was that any assertion of any kind on the part of the Negro constituted in a perfectly real manner an attack on the Southern woman. What they saw, more or less consciously, in the conditions of Reconstruction was a passage toward a condition for her as degrading, in their view, as rape itself. And a condition, moreover, which, logic or no logic, they infallibly thought of as being as absolutely forced upon her as rape, and hence a condition for which the term "rape" stood as truly as for the *de facto* deed.

Nor was the idea of rape the only potentially treacherous undercurrent in this case. There has historically been, for American blacks, an entire complex of loaded references around the question of "naming": slave names, masters' names, African names, call me by my rightful name, nobody knows my name; stories, in which the specific gravity of naming locked directly into that of rape, of black men whipped for addressing white women by their given names.

That in this case just such an interlocking of references could work to fuel resentments and inchoate hatreds seemed clear, and it seemed equally clear that some of what ultimately occurred—the repeated references to lynchings, the identification of the defendants with the Scottsboro boys, the insistently provocative repetition of the victim's name, the weird and self-defeating insistence that no rape had taken place and little harm been done the victim—derived momentum from this historical freight. "Years ago, if a white woman said a Black man looked at her lustfully, he could be hung higher than a magnolia tree in bloom, while a white mob watched joyfully sipping tea and eating cookies," Yusef Salaam's mother reminded readers of the *Amsterdam News*. "The first thing you do in the United States of America when a white woman is raped is round up a bunch of black youths, and I think that's what happened here," the Reverend Calvin O. Butts III of the Abyssinian Baptist Church in Harlem told the *New York Times*. "You going to arrest me now 'cause I said the jogger's name?" Gary Byrd asked rhetorically on his WLIB show, and was quoted by Edwin Diamond in *New York* magazine:

> I mean, she's obviously a public figure, and a very mysterious one, I might add. Well, it's a funny place we live in called America, and should we be surprised that they're up to their usual tricks? It was a trick that got us here in the first place.

This reflected one of the problems with not naming this victim: she was in fact named all the time. Everyone in the courthouse, everyone who worked for a paper or a television station or who followed the case for whatever professional reason, knew her name. She was referred to by name in all court records and in all court proceedings. She was named, in the days immediately following the attack, on local television stations. She was also routinely named—and this was part of the difficulty, part of what led to a damaging self-righteousness among those who did not name her and to an equally damaging embattlement among those who did—in Manhattan's black-owned newspapers, the *Amsterdam News* and the *City Sun*, and she was named as well on WLIB, the Manhattan radio station owned by a black partnership which included Percy Sutton and, until 1985 when he transferred his stock to his son, Mayor Dinkins.

That the victim in this case was identified on Centre Street and north of 96th Street but not in between made for a certain cognitive dissonance, especially since the names of even the juvenile suspects had been released by the police and the press before any suspect had even been arraigned, let alone indicted. "The police normally withhold the names of minors who are accused of crimes," the *Times* explained (actually, the police normally withhold the names of accused "juveniles," or minors under age sixteen, but not of minors sixteen or seventeen), "but officials said they made public the names of the youths charged in the attack on the woman because of the seriousness of the incident." There seemed a debatable point here, the question of whether "the seriousness of the incident" might not have in fact seemed a compelling reason to avoid any appearance of a rush to judgment by preserving the anonymity of a juvenile suspect; one of the names released by the police and published in the *Times* was of a fourteen-year-old who was ultimately not indicted.

There were, early on, certain aspects of this case that seemed not well handled by the police and prosecutors, and others that seemed not well handled by the press. It would seem to have been tactically unwise, since New York state law requires that a parent or guardian be present when children under sixteen are questioned, for police to continue the interrogation of Yusef Salaam, then fifteen, on the grounds that his Transit Authority bus pass said he was sixteen, while his mother was kept waiting outside. It would seem to have been unwise for Linda Fairstein, the assistant district attorney in charge of Manhattan sex crimes, to ignore, at the precinct house, the mother's assertion that the son was fifteen, and later to suggest, in open court, that the boy's age had been unclear to her because the mother had used the word "minor."

It would also seem to have been unwise for Linda Fairstein to tell David Nocenti, the assistant U.S. attorney who was paired with Yusef Salaam in a "Big Brother" program and who had come to the precinct house at the mother's request, that he had "no legal standing" there and that she would file a complaint with his supervisors. It would seem in this volatile a case imprudent of the police to follow their normal procedure by presenting Raymond Santana's initial statement in their own words, cop phrases that would predictably seem to some in the courtroom, as the expression of a fourteen-year-old held overnight and into the next afternoon for interrogation, unconvincing:

> On April 19, 1989, at approximately 20:30 hours, I was at the Taft Projects in the vicinity of 113th St. and Madison Avenue. I was there with numerous friends. . . . At approximately 21:00 hours, we all (myself and approximately 15 others) walked south on Madison Avenue to E. 110th Street, then walked westbound to Fifth Avenue. At Fifth Avenue and 110th Street, we met up with an additional group of approximately 15 other males, who also entered Central Park with us at that location with the intent to rob cyclists and joggers. . . .

In a case in which most of the defendants had made videotaped statements admitting at least some role in the assault and rape, this less than meticulous attitude toward the gathering and dissemination of information seemed peculiar and self-defeating, the kind of pressured or unthinking standard procedure that could not only exacerbate the fears and angers and suspicions of conspiracy shared by many blacks but conceivably open what seemed, on the basis of the confessions, a conclusive case to the kind of doubt that would eventually keep juries out, in the trial of the first three defendants, ten days, and, in the trial of the next two defendants, twelve days. One of the reasons the jury in the first trial could not agree, *Manhattan Lawyer* reported in its October 1990 issue, was that one juror, Ronald Gold, remained "deeply troubled by the discrepancies between the story [Antron] McCray tells on his videotaped statement and the prosecution scenario":

> Why did McCray place the rape at the reservoir, Gold demanded, when all evidence indicated it happened at the 102 Street crossdrive? Why did McCray say the jogger was raped where she fell, when the prosecution said she'd been dragged 300 feet into the woods first? Why did McCray talk about having to hold her arms down, if she was found bound and gagged?
>
> The debate raged for the last two days, with jurors dropping in and out of Gold's acquittal [for McCray] camp....
>
> After the jurors watched McCray's video for the fifth time, Miranda [Rafael Miranda, another juror] knew it well enough to cite the time-code numbers imprinted at the bottom of the videotape as he rebuffed Gold's arguments with specific statements from McCray's own lips. [McCray, on the videotape, after admitting that he had held the victim by her left arm as her clothes were pulled off, volunteered that he had "got on top" of her, and said that he had rubbed against her without an erection "so everybody would ... just know I did it."] The pressure on Gold was mounting. Three jurors agree that it was evident Gold, worn down perhaps by his own displays of temper as much as anything else, capitulated out of exhaustion. While a bitter Gold told other jurors he felt terrible about ultimately giving in, Brueland [Harold Brueland, another juror who had for a time favored acquittal for McCray] believes it was all part of the process.
>
> "I'd like to tell Ronnie some day that nervous exhaustion is an element built into the court system. They know that," Brueland says of court officials. "They know we're only going to be able to take it for so long. It's just a matter of, you know, who's got the guts to stick with it."

So fixed were the emotions provoked by this case that the idea that there could have been, for even one juror, even a moment's doubt in the state's case, let alone the kind of doubt that could be sustained over ten days or twelve, seemed, to many in the city, bewildering, almost unthinkable: the attack of the jogger had by then passed into narrative, and the narrative was about confrontation, about what Governor Cuomo had called "the ultimate shriek of alarm," about what was wrong with the city and about its solution. What was wrong with the city had been identified, and its names were Raymond Santana, Yusef Salaam, Antron McCray, Kharey Wise, Kevin Richardson, and Steve Lopez. "They never could have thought of it as they raged through Central Park, tormenting and ruining people," Bob Herbert wrote in the *News* after the verdicts came in on the first three defendants.

There was no way it could have crossed their vicious minds. Running with the pack, they would have scoffed at the very idea. They would have laughed.

And yet it happened. In the end, Yusef Salaam, Antron Mc-Cray, and Raymond Santana were nailed by a woman.

Elizabeth Lederer stood in the courtroom and watched Saturday night as the three were hauled off to jail.... At times during the trial, she looked about half the height of the long and lanky Salaam, who sneered at her from the witness stand.

Salaam was apparently too dumb to realize that Lederer—this petite, soft-spoken, curly-haired prosecutor—was the jogger's avenger....

You could tell that her thoughts were elsewhere, that she was thinking about the jogger.

You could tell that she was thinking: I did it.

I did it for you.

Do this in remembrance of me: the solution, then, or so such pervasive fantasies suggested, was to partake of the symbolic body and blood of The Jogger, whose idealization was by this point complete, and was rendered, significantly, in details stressing her "difference," or superior class. The Jogger was someone who wore, according to *Newsday,* "a light gold chain around her slender neck" as well as, according to the *News,* a "modest" gold ring and "a thin sheen" of lipstick. The Jogger was someone who would not, according to the *Post,* "even dignify her alleged attackers with a glance." The Jogger was someone who spoke, according to the *News,* in accents "suited to boardrooms," accents that might therefore seem "foreign to many native New Yorkers." In her first appearance on the witness stand she had been subjected, the *Times* noted, "to questions that most people do not have to answer publicly during their lifetimes," principally about her use of a diaphragm on the Sunday preceding the attack, and had answered these questions, according to an editorial in the *News,* with an "indomitable dignity" that had taught the city a lesson "about courage and class."

This emphasis on perceived refinements of character and of manner and of taste tended to distort and to flatten, and ultimately to suggest not the actual victim of an actual crime but a fictional character of a slightly earlier period, the well-brought-up maiden who briefly graces the city with her presence and receives in turn a taste of "real life." The defendants, by contrast, were seen as incapable of appreciating these marginal distinctions, ignorant of both the norms and accoutrements of middle-class life. "Did you have jogging clothes on?" Elizabeth Lederer asked Yusef Salaam, by way of trying to discredit his statement that he had gone into the park that night only to "walk around." Did he have "jogging clothes," did he have "sports equipment," did he have "a bicycle." A pernicious nostalgia had come to permeate the case, a longing for the New York that had seemed for a while to be about "sports equipment," about getting and spending rather than about having and not having: the reason that this victim must not be named was so that she could go unrecognized, it was astonishingly said, by Jerry Nachman, the editor of the *New York Post*, and then by others who seemed to find in this a particular resonance, to Bloomingdale's.

Some New York stories involving young middle-class white women do not make it to the editorial pages, or even necessarily to the front pages. In April 1990, a young middle-class white woman named Laurie Sue Rosenthal, raised in an Orthodox Jewish household and at age twenty-nine still living with her parents in Jamaica, Queens, happened to die according to the coroner's report from the accidental toxicity of Darvocet in combination with alcohol, in an apartment at 36 East 68th Street in Manhattan. The apartment belonged to the man she had been, according to her parents, seeing for about a year, a minor assistant city commissioner named Peter Franconeri. Peter Franconeri, who was at the time in charge of elevator and boiler inspections for the Buildings Department and married to someone else, wrapped Laurie Sue Rosenthal's body in a blanket; placed it, along with her handbag and ID, outside the building with the trash; and went to his office at 60 Hudson Street. At some point an anonymous call was made to 911. Franconeri was identified only after her parents gave the police his beeper number, which they found in her address book. According to *Newsday*, which covered the story more extensively than the *News*, the *Post*, or the *Times*,

> initial police reports indicated that there were no visible wounds on Rosenthal's body. But Rosenthal's mother, Ceil, said yesterday that the family was told the autopsy revealed two "unexplained bruises" on her daughter's body.
>
> Larry and Ceil Rosenthal said those findings seemed to support their suspicions that their daughter was upset because they received a call from their daughter at 3 A.M. Thursday "saying that he had beaten her up." The family reported the conversation to police.
>
> "I told her to get into a cab and get home," Larry Rosenthal said yesterday. "The next I heard was two detectives telling me terrible things."
>
> "The ME [medical examiner] said the bruises did not constitute a beating but they were going to examine them further," Ceil Rosenthal said.

"There were some minor bruises," a spokeswoman for the office of the chief medical examiner told *Newsday* a few days later, but the bruises "did not in any way contribute to her death." This is worth rerunning: a young woman calls her parents at three in the morning, "distraught." She says that she has been beaten up. A few hours later, on East 68th Street between Madison and Park avenues, a few steps from Porthault and Pratesi and Armani and Saint Laurent and the Westbury Hotel, at a time of day in this part of New York 10021 when Jim Buck's dog trainers are assembling their morning packs and Henry Kravis's Bentley is idling outside his Park Avenue apartment and the construction crews are clocking in over near the Frick at the multimillion-dollar houses under reconstruction for Bill Cosby and for the owner of The Limited, this young middle-class white woman's body, showing bruises, gets put out with the trash.

"Everybody got upside down because of who he was," an unidentified police officer later told Jim Dwyer of *Newsday*, referring to the man who put the young woman out with the trash. "If it had happened to anyone else, nothing would have come of it. A summons would have been issued and that would have been the end of it." In fact nothing did come of the death of Laurie Sue Rosenthal, which might have seemed a natural tabloid story but failed, on several levels, to catch the local imagination. For one thing, she could not be trimmed into the role of the preferred tabloid victim, who is conventionally presented as fate's random choice (Laurie Sue Rosenthal had, for whatever reason, taken the Darvocet instead of a taxi home, her parents reported treatment for a previous Valium dependency, she could be presumed to have known over the course of a year that Franconeri was married and yet continued to see him); for another, she seemed not to have attended an expensive school or to have been employed in a glamour industry (no Ivy Grad, no Wall Street Exec), which made it hard to cast her as part of "what makes this city so vibrant and so great."

In August 1990, Peter Franconeri pleaded guilty to a misdemeanor, the unlawful removal of a body, and was sentenced by Criminal Court Judge Peter Benitez to seventy-five hours of community service. This was neither surprising nor much of a story (only twenty-three lines even in *Newsday*, on page twenty-nine of the city edition), and the case's resolution was for many people a kind of relief. The district attorney's office had asked for "some incarceration," the amount usually described as a touch, but no one wanted, it was said, to crucify the guy: Peter Franconeri was somebody who knew a lot of people, understood how to live in the city, who had for example not only the apartment on East 68th Street between Madison and Park but a house in Southampton and who also understood that putting a body outside with the trash was nothing to get upside down about, if it was handled right. Such understandings may in fact have been the city's true "ultimate shriek of alarm," but it was not a shriek the city wanted to recognize.

2

Perhaps the most arresting collateral news to surface during the first few days after the attack on the Central Park jogger was that a significant number of New Yorkers apparently believed the city sufficiently well ordered to incorporate Central Park into their evening fitness schedules. "Prudence" was defined, even after the attack, as "staying south of 90th Street," or having "an awareness that you need to think about planning your routes," or, in the case of one woman interviewed by the *Times,* deciding to quit her daytime job (she was a lawyer) because she was "tired of being stuck out there, running later and later at night." "I don't think there's a runner who couldn't describe the silky, gliding feeling you get running at night," an editor of *Runner's World* told the *Times.* "You see less of what's around you and you become centered on your running."

The notion that Central Park at night might be a good place to "see less of what's around you" was recent. There were two reasons why Frederick Law Olmsted and Calvert Vaux, when they devised their winning entry in the 1858 competition for a Central Park design, decided to sink the transverse roads below grade level. One reason, the most often cited, was aesthetic, a recognition on the part of the designers that the four crossings specified by the terms of the competition, at 65th, 79th, 85th, and 97th streets, would intersect the sweep of the landscape, be "at variance with those agreeable sentiments which we should wish the park to inspire." The other reason, which appears to have been equally compelling, had to do with security. The problem with grade-level crossings, Olmsted and Vaux wrote in their "Greensward" plan, would be this:

> The transverse roads will . . . have to be kept open, while the park proper will be useless for any good purpose after dusk; for experience has shown that even in London, with its admirable police arrangements, the public cannot be assured safe transit through large open spaces of ground after nightfall.
>
> These public thoroughfares will then require to be well lighted at the sides, and, to restrain marauders pursued by the police from escaping into the obscurity of the park, strong fences or walls, six or eight feet high, will be necessary.

The park, in other words, was seen from its conception as intrinsically dangerous after dark, a place of "obscurity," "useless for any good purpose," a refuge only for "marauders." The parks of Europe closed at nightfall, Olmsted noted in his 1882 pamphlet *The Spoils of the Park: With a Few Leaves from the Deep-laden Note-books of "A Wholly Unpractical Man,"* "but one surface road is kept open across Hyde Park, and the superintendent of the Metropolitan Police told me that a man's chances of being garrotted or robbed were, because of the facilities for concealment to be found in the Park, greater in passing at night along this road than anywhere else in London."

In the high pitch of the initial "jogger" coverage, suggesting as it did a city overtaken by animals, this pragmatic approach to urban living gave way to a more ideal construct, one in which New York either had once been or should be "safe," and now, as in Governor Cuomo's "none of us is safe," was not. It was time, accordingly, to "take it back," time to "say no"; time, as David Dinkins would put it during his campaign for the mayoralty in the summer of 1989, to "draw the line." What the line was to be drawn against was "crime," as abstract, a free-floating specter that could be dispelled by certain acts of personal affirmation, by the kind of moral rearmament which later figured in Mayor Dinkins's plan to revitalize the city by initiating weekly "Tuesday Night Out Against Crime" rallies.

By going into the park at night, Tom Wicker wrote in the *Times*, the victim in this case had "affirmed the primacy of freedom over fear." A week after the assault, Susan Chace suggested on the op-ed page of the *Times* that readers walk into the park at night and join hands. "A woman can't run in the park at an offbeat time," she wrote. "Accept it, you say. I can't. It shouldn't be like this in New York City, in 1989, in spring." Ronnie Eldridge also suggested that readers walk into the park at night, but to light candles. "Who are we that we allow ourselves to be chased out of the most magnificent part of our city?" she asked, and also: "If we give up the park, what are we supposed to do: fall back to Columbus Avenue and plant grass?" This was interesting, suggesting as it did that the city's not inconsiderable problems could be solved by the willingness of its citizens to hold or draw some line, to "say no"; in other words, that a reliance on certain magical gestures could affect the city's fate.

The insistent sentimentalization of experience, which is to say the encouragement of such reliance, is not new in New York. A preference for broad strokes, for the distortion and flattening of character, and for the reduction of events to narrative has been for well over a hundred years the heart of the way the city presents itself: Lady Liberty, huddled masses, ticker-tape parades, heroes, gutters, bright lights, broken hearts, eight million stories in the naked city; eight million stories and all the same story, each devised to obscure not only the city's actual tensions of race and class but also, more significantly, the civic and commercial arrangements that rendered those tensions irreconcilable.

Central Park itself was such a "story," an artificial pastoral in the nineteenth-century English romantic tradition, conceived, during a decade when the population of Manhattan would increase by 58 percent, as a civic project that would allow the letting of contracts and the employment of voters on a scale rarely before undertaken in New York. Ten million cartloads of dirt would need to be shifted during the twenty years of its construction. Four to five million trees and plants would need to be planted, half a million cubic yards of topsoil imported, 114 miles of ceramic pipe laid.

Nor need the completion of the park mean the end of the possibilities: in 1870, once William Marcy Tweed had revised the city charter and invented his Department of Public Parks, new roads could be built whenever jobs were needed. Trees could be dug up and replanted. Crews could be set loose to prune, to clear, to hack at will. Frederick Law Olmsted, when he objected, could be overridden, and finally eased out. "A 'delegation' from a great political organization called on me by appointment," Olmsted wrote in *The Spoils of the Park*, recalling the conditions under which he had worked:

After introductions and handshakings, a circle was formed, and a gentleman stepped before me, and said, "We know how much pressed you must be . . . but at your convenience our association would like to have you determine what share of your patronage we can expect, and make suitable arrangements for our using it. We will take the liberty to suggest, sir, that there could be no more convenient way than that you should send us our due quota of tickets, if you please, sir, in this form, *leaving us to fill in the name.*" Here a pack of printed tickets was produced, from which I took one at random. It was a blank appointment and bore the signature of Mr. Tweed. . . .

As superintendent of the Park, I once received in six days more than seven thousand letters of advice as to appointments, nearly all from men in office. . . . I have heard a candidate for a magisterial office in the city addressing from my doorsteps a crowd of such advice-bearers, telling them that I was bound to give them employment, and suggesting plainly, that, if I was slow about it, a rope round my neck might serve to lessen my reluctance to take good counsel. I have had a dozen men force their way into my house before I had risen from bed on a Sunday morning, and some break into my drawing-room in their eagerness to deliver letters of advice.

Central Park, then, for its underwriters if not for Olmsted, was about contracts and concrete and kickbacks, about pork, but the sentimentalization that worked to obscure the pork, the "story," had to do with certain dramatic contrasts, or extremes, that were believed to characterize life in this as in no other city. These "contrasts," which have since become the very spine of the New York narrative, appeared early on: Philip Hone, the mayor of New York in 1826 and 1827, spoke in 1843 of a city "overwhelmed with population, and where the two extremes of costly luxury in living, expensive establishments and improvident wastes are presented in daily and hourly contrast with squalid mixing and hapless destruction." Given this narrative, Central Park could be and ultimately would be seen the way Olmsted himself saw it, as an essay in democracy, a social experiment meant to socialize a new immigrant population and to ameliorate the perilous separation of rich and poor. It was the duty and the interest of the city's privileged class, Olmsted had suggested some years before he designed Central Park, to "get up parks, gardens, music, dancing schools, reunions which will be so attractive as to force into contact the good and the bad, the gentleman and the rowdy."

The notion that the interests of the "gentleman" and the "rowdy" might be at odds did not intrude: then as now, the preferred narrative worked to veil actual conflict, to cloud the extent to which the condition of being rich was predicated upon the continued neediness of a working class; to confirm the responsible stewardship of "the gentleman" and to forestall the possibility of a self-conscious, or politicized, proletariat. Social and economic phenomena, in this narrative, were personalized. Politics were exclusively electoral. Problems were best addressed by the emergence and election of "leaders," who could in turn inspire the individual citizen to "participate," or "make a difference." "Will you help?" Mayor Dinkins asked New Yorkers, in a September address from St. Patrick's Cathedral intended as a response to the "New York crime wave" stories then leading the news. "Do you care? Are you ready to become part of the solution?"

"Stay," Governor Cuomo urged the same New Yorkers. "Believe. Participate. Don't give up." Manhattan Borough President Ruth Messinger, at the dedication of a school flagpole, mentioned the importance of "getting involved" and "participating," or "pitching in to put the shine back on the Big Apple." In a discussion of the popular "New York" stories written between 1902 and 1910 by William Sidney Porter, or "O. Henry," William R. Taylor of the State University of New York at Stony Brook spoke of the way in which these stories, with their "focus on individuals' plights," their "absence of social or political implications" and "ideological neutrality," provided "a miraculous form of social glue":

> These sentimental accounts of relations between classes in the city have a specific historical meaning: empathy without political compassion. They reduce the scale of human suffering to what atomized individuals endure as their plucky, sad lives were recounted week after week for almost a decade. . . . Their sentimental reading of oppression, class differences, human suffering, and affection helped create a new language for interpreting the city's complex society, a language that began to replace the threadbare moralism that New Yorkers inherited from nineteenth-century readings of the city. This language localized suffering in particular moments and confined it to particular occasions; it smoothed over differences because it could be read almost the same way from either end of the social scale.[1]

Stories in which terrible crimes are inflicted on innocent victims, offering as they do a similarly sentimental reading of class differences and human suffering, a reading that promises both resolution and retribution, have long performed as the city's endorphins, a built-in source of natural morphine working to blur the edges of real and to a great extent insoluble problems. What is singular about New York, and remains virtually incomprehensible to people who live in less rigidly organized parts of the country, is the minimal level of comfort and opportunity its citizens have come to accept. The romantic capitalist pursuit of privacy and security and individual freedom, so taken for granted nationally, plays, locally, not much role. A city where virtually every impulse has been to stifle rather than to encourage normal competi-

---

[1]William R. Taylor, "The Launching of a Commercial Culture: New York City, 1860–1930," in John Hull Mollenkopf's *Power, Culture, and Place: Essays on New York City* (Russell Sage Foundation, 1988), pp. 107–133.

tion, New York works, when it does work, not on a market economy but on little deals, payoffs, accommodations, baksheesh, arrangements that circumvent the direct exchange of goods and services and prevent what would be, in a competitive economy, the normal ascendance of the superior product.

There were in the five boroughs in 1990 only 581 supermarkets (a supermarket, as defined by the trade magazine *Progressive Grocer,* is a market that does an annual volume of two million dollars), or, assuming a population of eight million, one supermarket for every 13,769 citizens. Groceries, costing more than they should because of this absence of competition and also because of the proliferation of payoffs required to ensure this absence of competition (produce, we have come to understand, belongs to the Gambinos, and fish to the Lucheses and the Genoveses, and a piece of the construction of the market to each of the above, but keeping the door open belongs finally to the inspector here, the inspector there), are carried home or delivered, as if in Jakarta, by pushcart.

It has historically taken, in New York as if in Mexico City, ten years to process and specify and bid and contract and construct a new school; twenty or thirty years to build or, in the cases of Bruckner Boulevard and the West Side Highway, to not quite build a highway. A recent public scandal revealed that a batch of city-ordered Pap smears had gone unread for more than a year (in the developed world the Pap smear, a test for cervical cancer, is commonly read within a few days); what did not become a public scandal, what is still accepted as the way things are, is that even Pap smears ordered by Park Avenue gynecologists can go unread for several weeks.

Such resemblances to cities of the Third World are in no way casual, or based on the "color" of a polyglot population: these are all cities arranged primarily not to improve the lives of their citizens but to be labor-intensive, to accommodate, ideally at the subsistence level, since it is at the subsistence level that the work force is most apt to be captive and loyalty assured, a Third World population. In some ways New York's very attractiveness, its promises of opportunity and improved wages, its commitments as a city in the developed world, were what seemed destined to render it ultimately unworkable. Where the vitality of such cities in the less developed world had depended on their ability to guarantee low-cost labor and an absence of regulation, New York had historically depended instead on the constant welling up of new businesses, of new employers to replace those phased out, like the New York garment manufacturers who found it cheaper to make their clothes in Hong Kong or Kuala Lumpur or Taipei, by rising local costs.

It had been the old pattern of New York, supported by an expanding national economy, to lose one kind of business and gain another. It was the more recent error of New York to misconstrue this history of turnover as an indestructible resource, there to be taxed at will, there to be regulated whenever a dollar could be seen in doing so, there for the taking. By 1977, New York had lost some 600,000 jobs, most of them in manufacturing and in the kinds of small businesses that could no longer maintain their narrow profit margins inside the city. During the "recovery" years, from 1977 until 1988, most of these jobs were indeed replaced, but in a potentially perilous way: of the 500,000 new jobs created, most were in the area most vulnerable to a downturn, that of financial and business services, and many of the rest in an area not only equally vulnerable to bad times but dispiriting to the city even in good, that of tourist and restaurant services.

The demonstration that many kinds of businesses were finding New York expendable had failed to prompt real efforts to make the city more competitive. Taxes grew still more punitive, regulation more byzantine. Forty-nine thousand new jobs were created in New York's city agencies between 1983 and 1990, even as the services provided by those agencies were widely perceived to decline. Attempts at "reform" typically tended to create more jobs: in 1988, in response to the length of time it was taking to build or repair a school, a new agency, the School Construction Authority, was formed. A New York City school, it was said, would now take only five years to build. The head of the School Construction Authority was to receive $145,000 a year and each of the three vice-presidents $110,000 a year. An executive gym, with Nautilus equipment, was contemplated for the top floor of the agency's new headquarters at the International Design Center in Long Island City. Two years into this reform, the backlog on repairs to existing schools stood at 33,000 outstanding requests. "To relieve the charity of friends of the support of a half-blind and half-witted man by employing him at the public expense as an inspector of cement may not be practical with reference to the permanent firmness of a wall," Olmsted noted after his Central Park experience, "while it is perfectly so with reference to the triumph of sound doctrine at an election."

In fact the highest per capita taxes of any city in the United States (and, as anyone running a small business knows, the widest variety of taxes) provide, in New York, unless the citizen is prepared to cut a side deal here and there, only the continuing multiplication of regulations designed to benefit the contractors and agencies and unions with whom the regulators have cut their own deals. A kitchen appliance accepted throughout the rest of the United States as a basic postwar amenity, the in-sink garbage disposal unit, is for example illegal in New York. Disposals, a city employee advised me, not only encourage rats and "bacteria," presumably in a way that bags of garbage sitting on the sidewalk do not ("because it is," I was told when I asked how this could be), but also encourage people "to put their babies down them."

On the one hand this illustrates how a familiar urban principle, that of patronage (the more garbage there is to be collected, the more garbage collectors can be employed), can be reduced, in the bureaucratic wilderness that is any Third World city, to voodoo; on the other it reflects this particular city's underlying criminal ethic, its acceptance of graft and grift as the bedrock of every transaction. "Garbage costs are outrageous," an executive of Supermarkets General, which owns Pathmark, recently told City Limits about why the chains preferred to locate in the suburbs. "Every time you need to hire a contractor, it's a problem." The problem, however, is one from which not only the contractor but everyone with whom the contractor does business—a chain of direct or indirect patronage extending deep into the fabric of the day—stands to derive one or another benefit, which was one reason the death of the young middle-class white woman in the East 68th Street apartment of the assistant commissioner in charge of boiler and elevator inspections flickered so feebly on the local attention span.

It was only within the transforming narrative of "contrasts" that both the essential criminality of the city and its related absence of civility could become points of pride, evidence of "energy": if you could make it here you could make it anywhere, hello sucker, get smart. Those who did not get the deal, who bought retail, who did not know what it took to get their electrical work signed off, were dismissed as provincials, bridge-and-tunnels, out-of-towners who did not have what it took not to get taken. "Every tourist's nightmare became a reality for a Maryland couple over the weekend when the husband was beaten and robbed on Fifth Avenue in front of Trump Tower," began a story in the *New York Post* this summer. "Where do you think we're from, Iowa?" the prosecutor who took Robert Chambers's statement said on videotape by way of indicating that he doubted Chambers's version of Jennifer Levin's death. "They go after poor people like you from out of town, they prey on the tourists," a clerk explained last spring in the West 46th Street computer store where my husband and I had taken refuge to escape three muggers. My husband said that we lived in New York. "That's why they didn't get you," the clerk said, effortlessly incorporating this change in the data. "That's how you could move fast."

The narrative comforts us, in other words, with the assurance that the world is knowable, even flat, and New York its center, its motor, its dangerous but vital "energy." FAMILY IN FATAL MUGGING LOVED NEW YORK was the *Times* headline on a story following the September murder, in the Seventh Avenue IND station, of a twenty-two-year-old tourist from Utah. The young man, his parents, his brother, and his sister-in-law had attended the U.S. Open and were reportedly on their way to dinner at a Moroccan restaurant downtown. "New York, to them, was the greatest place in the world," a family friend from Utah was quoted as having said. Since the narrative requires that the rest of the country provide a dramatic contrast to New York, the family's hometown in Utah was characterized by the *Times* as a place where "life revolves around the orderly rhythms of Brigham Young University" and "there is only about one murder a year." The town was in fact Provo, where Gary Gilmore shot the motel manager, both in life and in *The Executioner's Song*. "She loved New York, she just loved it," a friend of the assaulted jogger told the *Times* after the attack. "I think she liked the fast pace, the competitiveness."

New York, the *Times* concluded, "invigorated" the jogger, "matched her energy level." At a time when the city lay virtually inert, when forty thousand jobs had been wiped out in the financial markets and former traders were selling shirts at Bergdorf Goodman for Men, when the rate of mortgage delinquencies had doubled, when fifty or sixty million square feet of office space remained unrented (sixty million square feet of unrented office space is the equivalent of fifteen darkened World Trade Towers) and even prime commercial blocks on Madison Avenue in the Seventies were boarded up, empty; at a time when the money had dropped out of all the markets and the Europeans who had lent the city their élan and their capital during the eighties had moved on, vanished to more cheerful venues, this notion of the city's "energy" was sedative, as was the commandeering of "crime" as the city's central problem.

3

The extent to which the October 1987 crash of the New York financial markets damaged the illusions of infinite recovery and growth on which the city had operated during the 1980s had been at first hard to apprehend. "Ours is a time of New York ascendant," the New York City Commission on the Year 2000, created during the mayoralty of Ed Koch to reflect the best thinking of the city's various business and institutional establishments, had declared in its 1987 report. "The city's economy is stronger than it has been in decades, and is driven both by its own resilience and by the national economy; New York is more than ever the international capital of finance, and the gateway to the American economy. . . ."

And then, its citizens had come gradually to understand, it was not. This perception that something was "wrong" in New York had been insidious, a slow-onset illness at first noticeable only in periods of temporary remission. Losses that might have seemed someone else's problem (or even comeuppance) as the markets were in their initial 1987 free fall, and that might have seemed more remote still as the markets regained the appearance of strength, had come imperceptibly but inexorably to alter the tone of daily life. By April 1990, people who lived in and around New York were expressing, in interviews with the *Times,* considerable anguish and fear that they did so: "I feel very resentful that I've lost a lot of flexibility in my life," one said. "I often wonder, 'Am I crazy for coming here?' " "People feel a sense of impending doom about what may happen to them," a clinical psychologist said. People were "frustrated," "feeling absolutely desolate," "trapped," "angry," "terrified," and "on the verge of panic."

It was a panic that seemed in many ways specific to New York, and inexplicable outside it. Even now, when the troubles of New York are a common theme, Americans from less depressed venues have difficulty comprehending the nature of those troubles, and tend to attribute them, as New Yorkers themselves have come to do, to "crime." ESCAPE FROM NEW YORK was the headline on the front page of the *New York Post* on September 10, 1990. RAMPAGING CRIME WAVE HAS 59 PERCENT OF RESIDENTS TERRIFIED. MOST WOULD GET OUT OF THE

CITY, SAYS TIME/CNN POLL. This poll appeared in the edition of *Time* dated September 17, 1990, which carried the cover legend THE ROTTING OF THE BIG APPLE. "Reason: a surge of drugs and violent crime that government officials seem utterly unable to combat," the story inside explained. Columnists referred, locally, to "this sewer of a city." The *Times* ran a plaintive piece about the snatching of Elizabeth Rohatyn's Hermès handbag outside Arcadia, a restaurant on East 62nd Street that had for a while seemed the very heart of the New York everyone now missed, the New York where getting and spending could take place without undue reference to having and not having, the duty-free New York; that this had occurred to the wife of Felix Rohatyn, who was widely perceived as having saved the city from its fiscal crisis in the midseventies, seemed to many a clarion irony.

This question of crime was tricky. There were in fact eight American cities with higher homicide rates, and twelve with higher overall crime rates. Crime had long been taken for granted in the less affluent parts of the city, and had become in the midseventies, as both unemployment and the costs of maintaining property rose and what had once been functioning neighborhoods were abandoned and burned and left to whoever claimed them, endemic. "In some poor neighborhoods, crime became almost a way of life," Jim Sleeper, an editor at *Newsday* and the author of *The Closest of Strangers: Liberalism and the Politics of Race in New York,* noted in his discussion of the social disintegration that occurred during this period:

> . . . a subculture of violence with complex bonds of utility and affection within families and the larger, "law-abiding" community. Struggling merchants might "fence" stolen goods, for example, thus providing quick cover and additional incentive for burglaries and robberies; the drug economy became more vigorous, reshaping criminal life-styles and tormenting the loyalties of families and friends. A walk down even a reasonably busy street in a poor, minority neighborhood at high noon could become an unnerving journey into a landscape eerie and grim.

What seemed markedly different a decade later, what made crime a "story," was that the more privileged, and especially the more privileged white, citizens of New York had begun to feel unnerved at high noon in even their own neighborhoods. Although New York City Police Department statistics suggested that white New Yorkers were not actually in increased mortal danger (the increase in homicides between 1977 and 1989, from 1,557 to 1,903, was entirely in what the NYPD classified as Hispanic, Asian, and black victims; the number of white murder victims had steadily declined, from 361 in 1977 to 227 in 1984 and 190 in 1989), the apprehension of such danger, exacerbated by street snatches and muggings and the quite useful sense that the youth in the hooded sweatshirt with his hands jammed in his pockets might well be a predator, had become general. These more privileged New Yorkers now felt unnerved not only on the street, where the necessity for evasive strategies had become an exhausting constant, but even in the most insulated and protected apartment buildings. As the residents of such buildings, the owners of twelve- and sixteen- and twenty-four-room apartments, watched the potted ficus trees disappear from outside their doors and the graffiti appear on their limestone walls and the smashed safety glass from car windows get swept off their sidewalks, it had become increasingly easy to imagine the outcome of a confrontation between, say, the relief night doorman and six dropouts from Julia Richman High School on East 67th Street.

And yet those New Yorkers who had spoken to the *Times* in April of 1990 about their loss of flexibility, about their panic, their desolation, their anger, and their sense of impending doom, had not been talking about drugs, or crime, or any of the city's more publicized and to some extent inflated ills. These were people who did not for the most part have twelve- and sixteen-room apartments and doormen and the luxury of projected fears. These people were talking instead about an immediate fear, about money, about the vertiginous plunge in the value of their houses and apartments and condominiums, about the possibility or probability of foreclosure and loss; about, implicitly, their fear of being left, like so many they saw every day, below the line, out in the cold, on the street.

This was a climate in which many of the questions that had seized the city's attention in 1987 and 1988, for example that of whether Mortimer Zuckerman should be "allowed" to build two fifty-nine-story office towers on the site of what is now the Coliseum, seemed in retrospect wistful, the baroque concerns of better times. "There's no way anyone would make a sane judgment to go into the ground now," a vice-president at Cushman and Wakefield told the *New York Observer* about the delay in the Coliseum project, which had in fact lost its projected major tenant, Salomon Brothers, shortly after Black Monday, in 1987. "It would be suicide. You're better off sitting in a tub of water and opening your wrists." Such fears were, for a number of reasons, less easy to incorporate into the narrative than the fear of crime.

The imposition of a sentimental, or false, narrative on the disparate and often random experience that constitutes the life of a city or a country means, necessarily, that much of what happens in that city or country will be rendered merely illustrative, a series of set pieces, or performance opportunities. Mayor Dinkins could, in such a symbolic substitute for civic life, "break the boycott" (the Flatbush boycott organized to mobilize resentment of Korean merchants in black neighborhoods) by purchasing a few dollars' worth of produce from a Korean grocer on Church Avenue. Governor Cuomo could "declare war on crime" by calling for five thousand additional police; Mayor Dinkins could "up the ante" by calling for sixty-five hundred. "White slut comes into the park looking for the African man," a black woman could say, her voice loud but still conversational, in the corridor outside the courtroom where, during the summer of 1990, the first three defendants in the Central Park attack, Antron McCray, Yusef Salaam, and Raymond Santana, were tried on charges of attempted murder, assault, sodomy, and rape. "Boyfriend beats shit out of her, they blame it on our boys," the woman could continue, and then, referring to a young man with whom the victim had at one time split the cost of an apartment: "How about the roommate, anybody test his semen? No. He's white. They don't do it to each other."

Glances could then flicker among those reporters and producers and courtroom sketch artists and photographers and cameramen and techs and summer interns who assembled daily at 111 Centre Street. Cellular phones could be picked up, a show of indifference. Small talk could be exchanged with the marshals, a show of solidarity. The woman could then raise her voice: "White folk, all of them are devils, even those that haven't been born yet, they are *devils. Little demons.* I don't understand these devils, I guess they think this is *their court."* The reporters could gaze beyond her, faces blank, no eye contact, a more correct form of hostility and also more lethal. The woman could hold her ground but avert her eyes, letting her gaze fall on another black, in this instance a black *Daily News* columnist, Bob Herbert. "You," she could say. "You are a *disgrace.* Go ahead. Line up there. Line up with the white folk. Look at them, lining up for their first-class seats while *my* people are downstairs behind *barricades* . . . kept behind barricades like *cattle* . . . not even allowed in the room to see their sons lynched . . . is that an *African* I see in that line? Or is that a *negro?* Oh, oh, sorry, shush, white folk didn't know, he was *passing.* . . ."

In a city in which grave and disrupting problems had become general— problems of not having, problems of not making it, problems that demonstrably existed, among the mad and the ill and the underequipped and the overwhelmed, with decreasing reference to color—the case of the Central Park jogger provided more than just a safe, or structured, setting in which various and sometimes only marginally related rages could be vented. "This trial," the *Daily News* announced on its editorial page one morning in July 1990, midway through the trial of the first three defendants, "is about more than the rape and brutalization of a single woman. It is about the rape and the brutalization of a city. The jogger is a symbol of all that's wrong here. And all that's right, because she is nothing less than an inspiration."

The *News* did not define the ways in which "the rape and brutalization of the city" manifested itself, nor was definition necessary: this was a city in which the threat or the fear of brutalization had become so immediate that citizens were urged to take up their own defense, to form citizen patrols or militia, as in Beirut. This was a city in which between twenty and thirty neighborhoods had already given over their protection, which was to say the right to determine who belonged in the neighborhood and who did not and what should be done about it, to the Guardian Angels. This was a city in which a Brooklyn vigilante group, which called itself "Crack Busters" and was said to be trying to rid its Bedford-Stuyvesant neighborhood of drugs, would before September was out "settle an argument" by dousing with gasoline and setting on fire an abandoned van and the three homeless citizens inside. This was a city in which the *Times* would soon perceive, in the failing economy, "a bright side for the city at large," the bright side being that while there was believed to have been an increase in the number of middle-income and upper-income families who wanted to leave the city, "the slumping market is keeping many of those families in New York."

In this city rapidly vanishing into the chasm between its actual life and its preferred narratives, what people said when they talked about the case of the Central Park jogger came to seem a kind of poetry, a way of expressing, without directly stating, different but equally volatile and similarly occult visions of the same disaster. One vision, shared by those who had seized upon the attack on the jogger as an exact representation of what was wrong with the city, was of a city systematically ruined, violated, raped by its underclass. The opposing vision, shared by those who had seized upon the arrest of the defendants as an exact representation of their own victimization, was of a city in which the powerless had been systematically ruined, violated, raped by the powerful. For so long as this case held the city's febrile attention, then, it offered a narrative for the city's distress, a frame in which the actual social and economic forces wrenching the city could be personalized and ultimately obscured.

Or rather it offered two narratives, mutually exclusive. Among a number of blacks, particularly those whose experience with or distrust of the criminal justice system was such that they tended to discount the fact that five of six defendants had to varying degrees admitted taking part in the attack, and to focus instead on the absence of any supporting forensic evidence incontrovertibly linking this victim to these defendants, the case could be read as a confirmation not only of their victimization but of the white conspiracy they saw at the heart of that victimization. For the *Amsterdam News*, which did not veer automatically to the radical analysis (a typical recent issue lauded the FBI for its minority recruiting and the Harlem National Guard for its high morale and readiness to go to the Gulf), the defendants could in this light be seen as victims of "a political trial," of a "legal lynching," of a case "rigged from the very beginning" by the decision of "the white press" that "whoever was arrested and charged in this case of the attempted murder, rape and sodomy of a well-connected, bright, beautiful and promising white woman was guilty, pure and simple."

For Alton H. Maddox, Jr., the message to be drawn from the case was that the American criminal justice system, which was under any circumstances "inherently and unabashedly racist," failed "to function equitably at any level when a Black male is accused of raping a white female." For others the message was more general, and worked to reinforce the fragile but functional mythology of a heroic black past, the narrative in which European domination could be explained as a direct and vengeful response to African superiority. "Today the white man is faced head on with what is happening on the Black Continent, Africa," Malcolm X wrote.

> Look at the artifacts being discovered there, that are proving over and over again, how the black man had great, fine, sensitive civilizations before the white man was out of the caves. Below the Sahara, in the places where most of America's Negroes' foreparents were kidnapped, there is being unearthed some of the finest craftsmanship, sculpture and other objects, that has ever been seen by modern man. Some of these things now are on view in such places as New York City's Museum of Modern Art. Gold work of such fine tolerance and workmanship that it has no rival. Ancient objects produced by black hands . . . refined by those black hands with results that no human hand today can equal.
>
> History has been so "whitened" by the white man that even the black professors have known little more than the most ignorant black man about the talents and rich civilizations and cultures of the black man of millenniums ago. . . .

"Our proud African queen," the Reverend Al Sharpton had said of Tawana Brawley's mother, Glenda Brawley: "She stepped out of anonymity, stepped out of obscurity, and walked into history." It was said in the corridors of the courthouse where Yusef Salaam was tried that he carried himself "like an African king."

"It makes no difference anymore whether the attack on Tawana happened," William Kunstler had told *New York Newsday* when the alleged rape and torture of Tawana Brawley by a varying number of white police officers seemed, as an actual prosecutable crime if not as a window on what people needed to believe, to have dematerialized. "If her story was a concoction to prevent her parents from punishing her for staying out all night, that doesn't disguise the fact that a lot of young black women are treated the way she said she was treated." The importance of whether or not the crime had occurred was, in this view, entirely resident in the crime's "description," which was defined by Stanley Diamond in *The Nation* as "a crime that did not occur" but was "described with skill and controlled hysteria by the black actors as the epitome of degradation, a repellent model of what actually happens to too many black women."

A good deal of what got said around the edges of the jogger case, in the corridors and on the call-in shows, seemed to derive exclusively from the suspicions of conspiracy increasingly entrenched among those who believe themselves powerless. A poll conducted in June 1990 by the *New York Times* and WCBS-TV News determined that 77 percent of blacks polled believed that it was either "true" or "might possibly be true" (as opposed to "almost certainly not true") that the government of the United States "singles out and investigates black elected officials in order to discredit them in a way it doesn't do with white officials." Sixty percent believed that it was true or might possibly be true that the government "deliberately makes sure that drugs are easily available in poor black neighborhoods in order to harm black people." Twenty-nine percent believed that it was true or might possibly be true that "the virus which causes AIDS was deliberately created in a laboratory in order to infect black people." In each case, the alternative response to "true" or "might possibly be true" was "almost certainly not true," which might have seemed in itself to reflect a less than ringing belief in the absence of conspiracy. "The conspiracy to destroy Black boys is very complex and interwoven," Jawanza Kunjufu, a Chicago educational consultant, wrote in his *Countering the Conspiracy to Destroy Black Boys,* a 1982 pamphlet which has since been extended to three volumes.

> There are many contributors to the conspiracy, ranging from the very visible who are more obvious, to the less visible and silent partners who are more difficult to recognize.
>
> Those people who adhere to the doctrine of white racism, imperialism, and white male supremacy are easier to recognize. Those people who actively promote drugs and gang violence are active conspirators, and easier to identify. What makes the conspiracy more complex are those people who do not plot together to destroy Black boys, but, through their indifference, perpetuate it. This passive group of conspirators consists of parents, educators, and white liberals who deny being racists, but through their silence allow institutional racism to continue.

For those who proceeded from the conviction that there was under way a conspiracy to destroy blacks, particularly black boys, a belief in the innocence of these defendants, a conviction that even their own statements had been rigged against them or wrenched from them, followed logically. It was in the corridors and on the call-in shows that the conspiracy got sketched in, in a series of fantasy details that conflicted not only with known facts but even with each other. It was said that the prosecution was withholding evidence that the victim had gone to the park to meet a drug dealer. It was said, alternately or concurrently, that the prosecution was withholding evidence that the victim had gone to the park to take part in a satanic ritual. It was said that the forensic photographs showing her battered body were not "real" photographs, that "they," the prosecution, had "brought in some corpse for the pictures." It was said that the young woman who appeared on the witness stand and identified herself as the victim was not the "real" victim, that "they" had in this case brought in an actress.

What was being expressed in each instance was the sense that secrets must be in play, that "they," the people who had power in the courtroom, were in possession of information systematically withheld—since information itself was power—from those who did not have power. On the day the first three defendants were sentenced, C. Vernon Mason, who had formally entered the case in the penalty phase as Antron McCray's attorney, filed a brief which included the bewildering and untrue assertion that the victim's boyfriend, who had not at that time been called to testify, was black. That some whites jumped to engage this assertion on its own terms (the *Daily News* columnist Gail Collins referred to it as Mason's "slimiest argument of the hour—an announcement that the jogger had a black lover") tended only to reinforce the sense of racial estrangement that was the intended subtext of the assertion, which was without meaning or significance except in that emotional deep where whites are seen as conspiring in secret to sink blacks in misery. "Just answer me, who got addicted?" I recall one black spectator asking another as they left the courtroom. "I'll tell you who got addicted, the inner city got addicted." He had with him a pamphlet that laid out a scenario in which the government had conspired to exterminate blacks by flooding their neighborhoods with drugs, a scenario touching all the familiar points, Laos, Cambodia, the Golden Triangle, the CIA, more secrets, more poetry.

"From the beginning I have insisted that this was not a racial case," Robert Morgenthau, the Manhattan district attorney, said after the verdicts came in on the first jogger trial. He spoke of those who, in his view, wanted "to divide the races and advance their own private agendas," and of how the city was "ill-served" by those who had so "sought to exploit" this case. "We had hoped that the racial tensions surrounding the jogger trial would begin to dissipate soon after the jury arrived at a verdict," a *Post* editorial began a few days later. The editorial spoke of an "ugly claque of 'activists,'" of the "divisive atmosphere" they had created, and of the anticipation with which the city's citizens had waited for "mainstream black leaders" to step forward with praise for the way in which the verdicts had brought New York "back from the brink of criminal chaos":

> Alas, in the jogger case, the wait was in vain. Instead of praise for a verdict which demonstrated that sometimes criminals are caught and punished, New Yorkers heard charlatans like the Rev. Al Sharpton claim the case was fixed. They heard that C. Vernon Mason, one of the engineers of the Tawana Brawley hoax—the attorney who thinks Mayor Dinkins wears "too many yarmulkes"—was planning to appeal the verdicts. . . .

To those whose preferred view of the city was of an inherently dynamic and productive community ordered by the natural play of its conflicting elements, enriched, as in Mayor Dinkins's "gorgeous mosaic," by its very "contrasts," this case offered a number of useful elements. There was the confirmation of "crime" as the canker corroding the life of the city. There was, in the random and feral evening described by the East Harlem attackers and the clear innocence of and damage done to the Upper East Side and Wall Street victim, an eerily exact and conveniently personalized representation of what the *Daily News* had called "the rape and the brutalization of a city." Among the reporters on this case, whose own narrative conventions involved "hero cops" and "brave prosecutors" going hand to hand against "crime" (the SE-CRET AGONY OF JOGGER D.A., we learned in the *Post* a few days after the verdicts in the first trial, was that "Brave Prosecutor's Marriage Failed as She Put Rapists Away"), there seemed an unflagging enthusiasm for the repetition and reinforcement of these elements, and an equally unflagging resistance, even hostility, to exploring the point of view of the defendants' families and friends and personal or political allies (or, as they were called in news reports, the "supporters") who gathered daily at the other end of the corridor from the courtroom.

This was curious. Criminal cases are widely regarded by American reporters as windows on the city or culture in which they take place, opportunities to enter not only households but parts of the culture normally closed, and yet this was a case in which indifference to the world of the defendants extended even to the reporting of names and occupations. Yusef Salaam's mother, who happened to be young and photogenic and to have European features, was pictured so regularly that she and her son became the instantly recognizable "images" of Jogger One, but even then no one got her name quite right. For a while in the papers she was "Cheroney," or sometimes "Cheron*a*y," McEllhonor; then she became Cheroney McEllhonor Salaam. After she testified the spelling of her first name was corrected to "Sharonne," although, since the byline on a piece she wrote for the *Amsterdam News* spelled it differently, "Sharrone," this may have been another misunderstanding. Her occupation was frequently given as "designer" (later, after her son's conviction, she went to work as a paralegal for William Kunstler), but no one seemed to take this seriously enough to say what she designed or for whom; not until after she testified, when *Newsday* reported her testimony that on the evening of her son's arrest she had arrived at the precinct house late because she was an instructor at the Parsons School of Design, did the notion of "designer" seem sufficiently concrete to suggest an actual occupation.

The Jogger One defendants were referred to repeatedly in the news columns of the *Post* as "thugs." The defendants and their families were often said by reporters to be "sneering." (The reporters, in turn, were said at the other end of the corridor to be "smirking.") "We don't have nearly so strong a question as to the guilt or innocence of the defendants as we did at Bensonhurst," a *Newsday* reporter covering the first jogger trial said to the *New York Observer*, well before the closing arguments, by way of explaining why *Newsday*'s coverage may have seemed less extensive on this trial than on the Bensonhurst trials. "There is not a big question as to what happened in Central Park that night. Some details are missing, but it's fairly clear who did what to whom."

In fact this came close to the heart of it: that it seemed, on the basis of the videotaped statements, fairly clear who had done what to whom was precisely the case's liberating aspect, the circumstance that enabled many of the city's citizens to say and think what they might otherwise have left unexpressed. Unlike other recent high-visibility cases in New York, unlike Bensonhurst and unlike Howard Beach and unlike Bernhard Goetz, here was a case in which the issue not exactly of race but of an increasingly visible underclass could be confronted by the middle class, both white and black, without guilt. Here was a case which gave this middle class a way to transfer and express what had clearly become a growing and previously inadmissible rage with the city's disorder, with the entire range of ills and uneasy guilts that came to mind in a city where entire families slept in the discarded boxes in which new Sub-Zero refrigerators were delivered, at twenty-six hundred per, to more affluent families. Here was also a case, most significantly, in which even that transferred rage could be transferred still further, veiled, personalized: a case in which the city's distress could be seen to derive not precisely from its underclass but instead from certain identifiable individuals who claimed to speak for this underclass, individuals who, in Robert Morgenthau's words, "sought to exploit" this case, to "advance their own private agendas"; individuals who wished even to "divide the races."

If the city's problems could be seen as deliberate disruptions of a naturally cohesive and harmonious community, a community in which, undisrupted, "contrasts" generated a perhaps dangerous but vital "energy," then those problems were tractable, and could be addressed, like "crime," by the call for "better leadership." Considerable comfort could be obtained, given this story line, through the demonization of the Reverend Al Sharpton, whose presence on the edges of certain criminal cases that interested him had a polarizing effect that tended to reinforce the narratives. Jim Sleeper, in *The Closest of Strangers,* described one of the fifteen marches Sharpton led through Bensonhurst after the 1989 killing of an East New York sixteen-year-old, Yusuf Hawkins, who had come into Bensonhurst and been set upon, with baseball bats and ultimately with bullets, by a group of young whites.

> An August 27, 1989, *Daily News* photo of the Reverend Al Sharpton and a claque of black teenagers marching in Bensonhurst to protest Hawkins's death shows that they are not really "marching." They are stumbling along, huddled together, heads bowed under the storm of hatred breaking over them, eyes wide, hanging on to one another and to Sharpton, scared out of their wits. They, too, are innocents—or were until that day, which they will always remember. And because Sharpton is with them, his head bowed, his face showing that he knows what they're feeling, he is in the hearts of black people all over New York.
>
> Yet something is wrong with this picture. Sharpton did not invite or coordinate with Bensonhurst community leaders who wanted to join the march. Without the time for organizing which these leaders should have been given in order to rein in the punks who stood waving watermelons; without an effort

by black leaders more reputable than Sharpton to recruit whites citywide and swell the march, Sharpton was assured that the punks would carry the day. At several points he even baited them by blowing kisses. . . .

"I knew that Bensonhurst would clarify whether it had been a racial incident or not," Sharpton said by way of explaining, on a recent *Frontline* documentary, his strategy in Bensonhurst. "The fact that I was so controversial to Bensonhurst helped them forget that the cameras were there," he said. "So I decided to help them . . . I would throw kisses to them, and they would go nuts." *Question,* began a joke often told in the aftermath of the first jogger trial. *You're in a room with Hitler, Saddam Hussein, and Al Sharpton. You have only two bullets. Who do you shoot? Answer: Al Sharpton. Twice.* Sharpton did not exactly fit the roles New York traditionally assigns, for maximum audience comfort, to prominent blacks. He seemed in many ways a phantasm, someone whose instinct for the connections between religion and politics and show business was so innate that he had been all his life the vessel for other people's hopes and fears. He had given his first sermon at age four. He was touring with Mahalia Jackson at eleven. As a teenager, according to Robert D. McFadden, Ralph Blumenthal, M. A. Farber, E. R. Shipp, Charles Strum, and Craig Wolff, the *New York Times* reporters and editors who collaborated on *Outrage: The Story Behind the Tawana Brawley Hoax,* Sharpton was tutored first by Adam Clayton Powell, Jr. ("You got to know when to hit it and you got to know when to quit it and when it's quittin' time, don't push it," Powell told him), then by the Reverend Jesse Jackson ("Once you turn on the gas, you got to cook or burn 'em up," Jackson told him), and eventually, after obtaining a grant from Bayard Rustin and campaigning for Shirley Chisholm, by James Brown. "Once, he trailed Brown down a corridor, through a door, and, to his astonishment, onto a stage flooded with spotlights," the authors of *Outrage* reported. "He immediately went into a wiggle and dance."

It was perhaps this talent for seizing the spotlight and the moment, this fatal bent for the wiggle and the dance, that most clearly disqualified Sharpton from casting as the Good Negro, the credit to the race, the exemplary if often imagined figure whose refined manners and good grammar could be stressed and who could be seen to lay, as Jimmy Walker said of Joe Louis, "a rose on the grave of Abraham Lincoln." It was left, then, to cast Sharpton, and for Sharpton to cast himself, as the Outrageous Nigger, the familiar role—assigned sixty years ago to Father Divine and thirty years later to Adam Clayton Powell—of the essentially manageable fraud whose first concern is his own well-being. It was for example repeatedly mentioned, during the ten days the jury was out on the first jogger trial, that Sharpton had chosen to wait out the verdict not at 111 Centre Street but "in the air-conditioned comfort" of C. Vernon Mason's office, from which he could be summoned by beeper.

Sharpton, it was frequently said by whites and also by some blacks, "represented nobody," was "self-appointed" and "self-promoting." He was an "exploiter" of blacks, someone who "did them more harm than good." It was pointed out that he had been indicted by the state of New York in June of 1989 on charges of grand larceny. (He was ultimately acquitted.) It was pointed out that *New York Newsday*, working on information that appeared to have been supplied by federal law enforcement agencies, had in January 1988 named him as a federal informant, and that he himself admitted to having let the government tap his phone in a drug-enforcement effort. It was routinely said, most tellingly of all in a narrative based on the magical ability of "leaders" to improve the common weal, that he was "not the right leader," "not at all the leader the black community needs." His clothes and his demeanor were ridiculed (my husband was asked by *Esquire* to do a piece predicated on interviewing Sharpton while he was having his hair processed), his motives derided, and his tactics, which were those of an extremely sophisticated player who counted being widely despised among his stronger cards, not very well understood.

Whites tended to believe, and to say, that Sharpton was "using" the racial issue—which, in the sense that all political action is based on "using" one issue or another, he clearly was. Whites also tended to see him as destructive and irresponsible, indifferent to the truth or to the sensibilities of whites—which, most notoriously in the nurturing of the Tawana Brawley case, a primal fantasy in which white men were accused of a crime Sharpton may well have known to be a fabrication, he also clearly was. What seemed not at all understood was that for Sharpton, who had no interest in making the problem appear more tractable ("The question is, do you want to 'ease' it or do you want to 'heal' it," he had said when asked if his marches had not worked against "easing tension" in Bensonhurst), the fact that blacks and whites could sometimes be shown to have divergent interests by no means suggested the need for an ameliorative solution. Such divergent interests were instead a lucky break, a ready-made organizing tool, a dramatic illustration of who had the power and who did not, who was making it and who was falling below the line; a metaphor for the sense of victimization felt not only by blacks but by all those Sharpton called "the left-out opposition." *We got the power*, the chants go on "Sharpton and Fulani in Babylon: volume 1 the battle of New York City," a tape of the speeches of Sharpton and of Leonora Fulani, a leader of the New Alliance party. *We are the chosen people. Out of the pain. We that can't even talk together. Have learned to walk together.*

"I'm no longer sure what I thought about Al Sharpton a year or two ago still applies," Jerry Nachman, the editor of the *New York Post*, who had frequently criticized Sharpton, told Howard Kurtz of the *Washington Post* in September 1990. "I spent a lot of time on the street. There's a lot of anger, a lot of frustration. Rightly or wrongly, he may be articulating a great deal more of what typical attitudes are than some of us thought." Wilbert Tatum, the editor and publisher of the *Amsterdam News*, tried to explain to Kurtz how, in his view, Sharpton had been cast as "a caricature of black leadership":

> He was fat. He wore jogging suits. He wore a medallion and gold chains. And the unforgivable of unforgivables, he had processed hair. The white media, perhaps not consciously, said, "We're going to promote this guy because we can point up the ridiculousness and paucity of black leadership."
>
> Al understood precisely what they were doing, precisely. Al is probably the most brilliant tactician this country has ever produced. . . .

Whites often mentioned, as a clinching argument, that Sharpton paid his demonstrators to appear; the figure usually mentioned was five dollars, but the figure floated by a prosecutor on the jogger case was four dollars (by November 1990, when Sharpton was fielding demonstrators to protest the killing of a black woman alleged to have grabbed a police nightstick in the aftermath of a domestic dispute, a police source quoted in the *Post* had jumped the payment to twenty dollars). This seemed on many levels a misunderstanding, or an estrangement, or as blacks would say, a disrespect, too deep to address, but on its simplest level it served to suggest what value was placed by whites on what they thought of as black time.

In the fall of 1990, the fourth and fifth of the six defendants in the Central Park attack, Kevin Richardson and Kharey Wise, went on trial. Since this particular narrative had achieved full resolution, or catharsis, with the conviction of the first three defendants, the city's interest in the case had by then largely waned. Those "charlatans" who had sought to "exploit" the case had been whisked, until they could next prove useful, into the wings. Even the verdicts in this second trial, coinciding as they did with the most recent arrest of John (the Dapper Don) Gotti, a reliable favorite on the New York stage, did not lead the local news. It was in fact the economy itself that had come center stage in the city's new, and yet familiar, narrative work: a work in which the vital yet beleaguered city would or would not weather yet another "crisis" (the answer was a resounding yes); a work, or a dreamwork, that emphasized not only the cyclical nature of such "crises" but the regenerative power of the city's "contrasts." "With its migratory population, its diversity of cultures and institutions, and its vast resources of infrastructure, capital, and intellect, New York has been the quintessential modern city for more than a century, constantly reinventing itself," Michael Stone concluded in his *New York* magazine cover story, "Hard Times." "Though the process may be long and painful, there's no reason to believe it won't happen again."

These were points commonly made in support of a narrative that tended, with its dramatic line of "crisis" and resolution, or recovery, only to obscure further the economic and historical groundwork for the situation in which the city found itself: that long unindictable conspiracy of criminal and semi-criminal civic and commercial arrangements, deals, negotiations, gimmes and getmes, graft and grift, pipe, topsoil, concrete, garbage; the conspiracy of those in the know, those with a connection, those with a friend at the Department of Sanitation or the Buildings Department or the School Construction Authority or Foley Square, the conspiracy of those who believed everybody got upside down because of who it was, it happened to anybody else, a summons gets issued, and that's the end of it. On November 12, 1990, in its page-one analysis of the city's troubles, the *New York Times* went so far as to locate, in "public spending," not the drain on the city's vitality and resources it had historically been but "an important positive factor":

> Not in decades has so much money gone for public works in the area—airports, highways, bridges, sewers, subways and other projects. Roughly $12 billion will be spent in the metropolitan region in the current fiscal year. Such government outlays are a healthy counterforce to a 43 percent decline since 1987 in the value of new private construction, a decline related to the sharp drop in real estate prices.... While nearly every industry in the private sector has been reducing payrolls since spring, government hiring has risen, maintaining an annual growth rate of 20,000 people since 1987....

That there might well be, in a city in which the proliferation of and increase in taxes were already driving private-sector payrolls out of town, hardly anyone left to tax for such public works and public-sector jobs was a point not too many people wished seriously to address: among the citizens of a New York come to grief on the sentimental stories told in defense of its own lazy criminality, the city's inevitability remained the given, the heart, the first and last word on which all the stories rested. We love New York, the narrative promises, because it matches our energy level.

•   •   •   •   •   •   •   •   •   •   •   •

QUESTIONS FOR A SECOND READING

1. Among the key terms of Didion's essay are *story* and *narrative*. The piece begins, "We know her story," the story of the jogger raped in Central Park, and Didion moves quickly to think about the victim as an unwitting and unwilling "character" in the "sentimental narrative that is New York public life." When Didion talks about stories and narratives, she yanks those terms from their usual contexts (where there is a sharp dividing line between a bedtime story and a news story, between fiction and fact, between entertainment and

work, imagination and the "real" world). As you reread, pay close attention to how and where Didion talks about story and narrative. How might the horrible events of Central Park be thought of as a fiction, a story, a "sentimental narrative"? What is a narrative, in Didion's view? Where does it come from and who is its author? How does it work? Who reads it and why? Why call it "sentimental"?

2. Didion asks a reader to think about the newspaper and media accounts in "Sentimental Journeys" as stories, as narratives with stock characters and predictable outcomes. She assumes that they are standard fare in the American imaginary. As you reread, see if you can get a handle on these narratives as common or predictable. How would you describe these stories? What title would you give them? Who are the stock characters? How are they expected to behave? What are the predictable outcomes? What lessons are these stories meant to teach? Where have you heard them?

ASSIGNMENTS FOR WRITING

1. "Sentimental Journeys" can be taken as a lesson in how to read the news. The essay can be read, that is, as an exemplary project in cultural analysis. Didion follows a news story, reads its key accounts closely (looking for the master narrative giving them shape and meaning), and she reads it against other stories, stories that become "meaningless" or back-page material in the face of the dominance of the key story. Didion shows a reader how to read the news as a text, she shows how to read the news as more than just "the news," and she shows how to write out such readings. Her essay provides a fine example of how a writer takes large blocks of texts (the block quotations in this essay) and works with them through the medium of the paragraph.

For this assignment, follow Didion's lead and provide a similar reading of a local or national news story. You should look for a "front-page" story of some duration—one, that is, that stayed in the news for several weeks. You will need to present the event and its accounts so that a reader can follow both the story as it evolves in the media and the story as it serves your line of thinking. Following Didion, you will need to read those accounts for evidence of the master narrative they represent (perhaps a "sentimental" narrative), and you will need to think about whose interests are served in its production and reception.

Note: It would probably be useful to work with a relatively recent story. Your library will have back issues of local and national newspapers. You will need a current or breaking story. (It would be a different assignment and a different challenge to deal with a "historical" event.)

2. Didion titled her essay "Sentimental Journeys" to make a certain point about the culture and politics of New York City in the late 1980s. As you reread the essay, mark two or three sections where Didion is speaking directly about the life of New York, about the city and its desire to sentimentalize public events. What might Didion mean by "sentimentalize"? What makes a narra-

tive "sentimental"? And what is at stake here? Who is doing what to whom? What, you might ask, is the author's purpose, where the author in question is not Didion but the "author" of "the sentimental narratives that is New York public life"?

Write an essay in which you explain Didion's account of the relationship between "sentimental narrative" and "New York public life" in the 1980s. Your goal should be to move from the specific case of New York to a more general discussion of "narrative and public life," one where you not only represent Didion's argument but also engage with it. Where and how does her argument make sense to you (or not make sense to you)? You should assume that your reader has not read Didion's essay.

MAKING CONNECTIONS

1. According to Didion, one of the narratives that structured the account of the Central Park jogger was a narrative about race, about black and white in America. As you work back through the essay, look particularly at the accounts she gives of the way assumptions about race determine the plot and characters in the narrative of crime in New York. What, according to these accounts, were the stories people told themselves about race and racial difference?

   Patricia J. Williams, in "And We Are Not Married (p. 694)," is also concerned with how "raciality is socially constructed," with the sources and effects of the stories we tell about African Americans. Like Didion, she writes about the media (and about the case of Tawana Brawley) but she also writes more generally about American thought and American culture.

   Write an essay in which you imagine Williams's essay as a black intellectual's account of (and response to) the argument in "Sentimental Journeys." You should imagine that your readers are familiar with both essays, but that they don't have the texts in front of them. You will need to provide the kind of presentation that can allow a reader a way back into each essay.

2. Stephen Greenblatt, in "Marvelous Possessions" (p. 268), looks at the ways the "New World" was written into narratives by European writers for European audiences. He says, for example,

   > We can demonstrate that, in the face of the unknown, Europeans used their conventional intellectual and organizational structures, fashioned over centuries of mediated contact with other cultures, and that these structures greatly impeded a clear grasp of the radical otherness of the American lands and peoples. (p. 270)

   Joan Didion, in "Sentimental Journeys," similarly looks at the ways the media write New York City into what she calls "sentimental narratives":

   > The imposition of a sentimental, or false, narrative on the disparate and often random experience that constitutes the life of a city or a country means, necessarily, that much of what happens in that city or country will be rendered merely illustrative, a series of set pieces or performance opportunities. (p. 100)

Are Didion and Greenblatt talking about the same thing? Does writing serve the same purposes in the 1990s that it did in the 1490s? If so, how would you show this to be the case? If not, where do you find differences and how might you account for them?

Write an essay in which you examine the relationship between writing and experience (or language and the "real") as it is worked out by Greenblatt in his discussion of narratives of discovery and by Didion in her discussion of narratives of New York. You should assume that your reader is familiar with the issues and questions involved in these pieces but that your reader does not have these essays at hand.

3. In "Our Secret" (p. 319), Susan Griffin tells sets of interrelated stories representing the life of Heinrich Himmler, the development of rockets in World War II Germany, cell RNA and DNA, the lives of World War II survivors, and aspects of her own life and upbringing. She makes use of an unusual method of presenting her stories, placing them next to each other rather than in a logical or hierarchical relation (where they might serve as examples of a predetermined thesis or steps toward a conclusion). In a real sense, she redefines the work of reading.

Like Griffin, Didion works with stories. Like Griffin, she writes with some urgency about stories and imaginative life, about violence and how it is part of who we are, how we think, and how we are made.

Write an essay in which you explore the ways Griffin and Didion imagine the role of stories and the work of reading. How do stories work? What is their relation to history? to public life? What does it mean to be a reader? How do Griffin and Didion define in their writing (and not just in their arguments) a position on how and why we might work on reading and writing?

SUSAN
DOUGLAS

S *USAN DOUGLAS (b. 1950) is a professor of media and American studies at* Hampshire College in Massachusetts. She is also the media critic for the Progres-*sive and has written for the* Village Voice, *the* Nation, *and* In These Times. *Her first book,* Inventing American Broadcasting, 1899–1922, *was published in 1986.*

In the introduction to her second book, Where the Girls Are *(1994), Susan Douglas introduces herself as "one of those people the* Wall Street Journal, CBS News, *and* Spy *magazine love to make fun of . . . a professor of Media Studies." She suggests that this caricature of her profession is part of the media's program to protect themselves from close scrutiny, to deflect attention away from their power and influence, to encourage the belief that we are free, independent consumers of images and products. The questions Douglas raises are questions at the center of national debates about the power of the media. Should we be concerned about the movie industry, about TV and radio? How does popular culture affect behavior? What, if anything, does it teach? Does it direct or determine the ways we think and act? And, if so, how? "If it was important enough for them to spend hundreds of thousands of dollars to bring us* Mr. Ed, Enjoli *perfume ('I can bring home the bacon, fry it up in the pan, and never, ever let you forget you're a man'), and* Dallas," *Douglas says, "then it's important enough for us to figure out why."*

In Where the Girls Are, *Douglas uses her own skeptical and humorous critique of mass media to focus on representations of teenage girls and women since the 1950s. She asks how millions of baby-boom girls, like herself, who were "slaves" to the media as young adolescents, "went from singing 'I Want to Be Bobby's Girl' to 'I Am Woman, Hear Me Roar.'" She examines the contradictory images of women from* Bewitched *in the 1960s to Hillary Rodham Clinton in the 1992 presidential election. She argues:*

> American women today are a bundle of contradictions because much of the media imagery we grew up with was itself filled with mixed messages about what women should and should not do, what women could and could not be. This was true in the 1960s, and it is true today. The media, of course, urged us to be pliant, cute, sexually available, thin, blond, poreless, wrinkle-free, and deferential to men. But it is easy to forget that the media also suggested we could be rebellious, tough, enterprising, and shrewd. And much of what we watched was porous, allowing us to accept and rebel against what we saw and how it was presented.

And she concludes:

> The mass consumption of that culture . . . actually encouraged many of us to embrace feminism in some form. For throughout this process, we have found ourselves pinioned between two voices, one insisting we were equal, the other insisting we were subordinate. After a while, the tension became unbearable, and millions of women found they were no longer willing to tolerate the gap between the promises of equality and the reality of inequality.

But in the history Douglas charts, there is never a simple victory of feminism over the interests of those who would manipulate images of women to produce a desire to buy and consume. In the chapter reprinted here, "Narcissism as Liberation," Douglas looks at advertising's attempts to capture the "liberated" woman's consumer dollars since the 1970s by exploiting feminism. She notes advertising's clumsy initial attempts at this exploitation by reminding readers of the Virginia Slims campaign, "You've Come a Long Way, Baby," which "equated liberation with the freedom to give yourself lung cancer." She argues that "by the 1980s, advertis[ers] had figured out how to make feminism—and antifeminism—work for them," producing a struggle that reflects, reinforces, and exaggerates our culture's ambivalence about women's roles.

Douglas's prose is witty and sharply pointed. She speaks at times as a cultural historian, generalizing about movements in American thought and popular culture, at times for women of her generation, the "baby boomers," and at times from the position of her own experience, remembering herself as a young woman watching TV or thinking in the present about the things she buys and the way advertising produces desire.

Narcissism as Liberation

"I'm worth it," insists Cybill Shepherd in her brattiest, na-na-na-poo-poo voice as she swirls her blond hair in my face. Since I have to be restrained, physically, from hatcheting my television set to death whenever this ad appears (and every woman I know has the same reaction), it is amazing to think it actually sells hair dye. But it must, since this campaign has been harassing us for nearly a decade. "I'm worth it" became the motto for the 1980s woman we saw in television and magazine ads. Endless images of women lounging on tiled verandas, or snuggling with their white angora cats while wearing white silk pajamas, exhorted us to be self-indulgent, self-centered, private, hedonistic. In stark contrast to the selfless wife and mom of *The Feminine Mystique*, not to mention those hideous, loudmouthed feminists who thought sisterhood and political activism mattered, women of the 1980s were urged to take care of themselves, and to do so *for* themselves. An ad for Charles of the Ritz, featuring a gorgeous model dripping with pearls and staring off into space, summed up women's recent history. "I'm not the girl I used to be. Now I want to surround myself with beautiful things. And I want to look beautiful too. I've discovered that it's easier to face the world when I like what I see in the mirror."

By the 1980s, advertising agencies had figured out how to make feminism—and antifeminism—work for them. There had been a few clumsy starts in the 1970s, like the Virginia Slims "You've Come a Long Way, Baby" campaign, which equated liberation with the freedom to give yourself lung cancer. And feminine hygiene sprays like Massengill's pictured the product with a political button reading "Freedom Now" and touted the crotch rot in the can as "The Freedom Spray." But the approaches got more subtle and certainly more invidious as America's multibazillion-dollar cosmetics industry realized that all those kids who once bought Clearasil and Stri-Dex were now getting something even worse than acne—wrinkles. Here was an enormous market—women who grew up with, who in fact made possible, a youth culture—now getting old. You could almost hear the skin cream moguls in their boardrooms yelling yippie-kiyo-kiyay.

The appropriation of feminist desires and feminist rhetoric by Revlon, Lancôme, and other major corporations was nothing short of spectacular. Women's liberation metamorphosed into female narcissism unchained as political concepts and goals like liberation and equality were collapsed into distinctly personal, private desires. Women's liberation became equated with women's ability to do whatever they wanted for themselves, whenever they wanted, no matter what the expense. These ads were geared to the woman who had made it in a man's world, or who hoped she would, and the message was Reward yourself, you deserve it. There was enormous emphasis on luxury, and on separating oneself from the less enlightened, less privileged

THE CELLULITE SOLUTION.

BIOTHERM 10 Day Body Contouring Treatment.

Now you can reduce the appearance of cellulite in a mere 10 days. Suddenly, ripples are diminished. Your skin looks remarkably toned and taut.

Creme Contour Suractive 10 Jours dramatically improves the biomechanical properties of the skin while measurably reducing distortion at the affected area.

It's been proven at the famous Biotherm spa in Deauville. Now prove it to yourself. What you'll discover is a sleeker, firmer, more beautiful you. With regular use, you can even have a slimmer appearance.

Clinical studies have shown that the degree of results will depend upon your skin's condition. For the maximum achievable benefit, use daily.

10 Day Body Contouring Treatment. From now on, Biotherm. Simply beautiful skin.

BIOTHERM

PARIS • MONACO • DEAUVILLE

The cosmetics industry invented "cellulite" in the 1970s to describe that portion of the female body between the knee and the waist. To achieve the "buns of steel" that the upscale female workaholic was supposed to have, you could either spend half your life in a health club or slop some Biotherm on your thighs. *(Collection of the author.)*

herd. The ability to spend time and money on one's appearance was a sign of personal success and of breaking away from the old roles and rules that had held women down in the past. Break free from those old conventions, the ads urged, and get *truly* liberated: put yourself first.

Narcissism was more in for women than ever, and the ability to indulge oneself, pamper oneself, and focus at length on oneself without having to listen to the needy voices of others was the mark of upscale female achievement. These were the years when we were supposed to put the naive, idealistic, antimaterialistic 1960s behind us and, instead, go to polo matches and wash our hair with bottled water from the Alps. Ralph Lauren, in his ads for sheets and oxford cloth shirts, used manor houses, antique furniture, riding boots, and safari gear to make us long for the days when the sun never set on the British Empire, when natives (and women) knew their place, and robber barons ran America. Huge museum exhibits celebrated England's "Treasure Houses" and the gowns favored by Marie Antoinette and her pals, each of which represented the work of 213 starving peasant seamstresses.[1] *The Big Chill* suggested that even radical baby boomers had sold out to Wall Street, a move portrayed as inevitable and perfectly understandable.

For women in the age of Reagan, elitism and narcissism merged in a perfect appeal to forget the political already, and get back to the personal, which you might be able to do something about. But let's not forget the most ubiquitous and oppressive anatomical symbol of the new woman's achievement that came into its own in the 1980s: the perfectly sculpted, dimple-free upper thigh and buttock. A tour through the land of smooth faces and even smoother buttocks and thighs makes one appreciate why the women of the 1980s who had reason to feel pride in their accomplishments still felt like worthless losers when they looked in the mirror or, horror of horrors, put on a bathing suit. Of course, these feelings were hardly confined to baby boomers. Nor are they confined to the past. Though I write about what emerged in the 1980s in the past tense, I feel awkward about doing so, because the ad strategies established then are still in high gear, and we watch their effects with sorrow, anger, and empathy. When I go to any number of college or university swimming pools, I see women twenty years younger than I, at their physical peak, healthy and trim, walk out to the pool with towels wrapped around their waists so their thighs will be exposed to the world only for the few nanoseconds it takes to drop the towel and dive into the pool. I have *never* seen a young man do this. Then they go back to the locker room and slather their sweet, twenty-year-old faces with Oil of Olay so they can fight getting old "every step of the way."

Advertisers in the 1980s, especially those targeting women, apparently had a new bible: Christopher Lasch's 1979 best-seller, *The Culture of Narcissism.* Lasch identified what he saw as a new trend, the emergence of people who seemed self-centered and self-satisfied but were really deeply anxious about what others thought of them. Americans were becoming increasingly self-absorbed, he wrote, but not because they were conceited. On the contrary, Americans were desperately insecure, consumed by self-doubt and self-loathing, and totally obsessed with competing with other people for approval and acclaim. The "narcissistic personality," according to Lasch, was compulsively "other-directed" and consumed by self-doubt, even self-hatred. As a result, the narcissist craved approval and fantasized about adulation. Any sense of self-esteem was fleeting, hinging on things like whether someone looked at you funny or laughed at one of your jokes. This obsessive need for admiration prompted the narcissist to become skilled at managing impressions, at assuming different roles, and at developing a magnetic personality. Narcissists were always measuring themselves against others; being envied, for example, had become infinitely more important than being admired or respected. Narcissists had a strong belief in their right to be gratified and were constantly searching for heightened emotional experiences, for instant gratification, to stave off the fear that life is unreal, artificial, and meaningless. Narcissists were especially terrified of aging and death. Lasch particularly emphasized how the messages and ploys of American advertising had cultivated such narcissistic personalities.

When I read this book, I was struck by two things. First, Lasch kept using the pronoun *he* to talk about the narcissist, and this helped make the trend he was describing seem new. But for women, this wasn't so new, this was the story of our lives, of how we had been socialized since childhood. Second, it was in ads geared specifically to women, especially ads for cosmetics and other personal care items, that we saw advertisers applying, with a vengeance, the various insights of Lasch's book. Under the guise of addressing our purported new confidence and self-love, these ads really reinforced how we failed to measure up to others. Hanes, for example, in a classic campaign, skillfully resolved the tensions surrounding new womanhood in its series of ads titled "Reflections On . . ." A woman was pictured sitting across the arms of a leather chair, or in a wicker patio lounger, with her legs prominently displayed. She was usually dressed up in a glittery cocktail dress, exchanging smiles with a man in a tux. She was always white. In one ad, the admiring male voice said, "She messes up the punch line of every joke; can tell a Burgundy from a Bordeaux; and her legs . . . Oh yes, Joanna's legs." In another version, the copy read: "She does this flawless imitation of Groucho Marx; recites the most astonishing passages from Hemingway; ahh, and her legs . . . Emily's legs."

Joanna's and Emily's nonanatomical achievements were impressive—they knew things only elite men used to know, like how to select a wine, and their favorite writer wasn't Edith Wharton or Alice Walker, it was Mr. Macho himself. They didn't imitate Mae West (too threatening), they imitated a constantly lecherous man. They had cracked the male code, but, because of Hanes, they were still ladies. These women were huge successes at managing the impressions they gave to others, coming across as distinctive, nonconformist women who nonetheless conform perfectly to dominant standards of beauty. They were self-satisfied and self-assured, yet their value came from male admiration and approval. The ads suggested that without inner confidence, and a core self that is assured and discriminating (made possible, one can infer, by feminism), these women would not be the charmers they are today. But without male approval and admiration, they would not have the acclaim on which narcissistic self-esteem rests. It was in campaigns such as this that the appearance of female self-love and achievement was used to reinforce female dependence on male approval. If you wore Hanes, in other words, you would feel the contradictions between feminism and prefeminism thread together smoothly as you pulled them up over your legs and hips and then strode confidently out into the world.

The cult of narcissism Lasch saw in the 1970s exploded in the 1980s, nurtured by Reagan's me-first-and-to-hell-with-everyone-else political and moral philosophies. Under the guise of telling women, "You're worth it," advertisers suggested we weren't worth it at all but could feel we were, for a moment, if we bought the right product. Here we were again, same as it ever was, bombarded by the message that approval from others, especially men, means everything, and without it you are nothing, an outcast, unworthy and unloved. We were right back to Tinker Bell and Cinderella, urged to be narcissistic yet ridiculed if it was discovered that we were.

The narcissism as liberation campaign found its happiest home in certain television ads, such as those that sponsored shows like *Dynasty*, and in women's magazines like *Vogue, Harper's Bazaar, Mademoiselle, Glamour, Cosmopolitan*, and the aptly named *Self*. These magazines, with their emphasis on clothes, makeup, and dieting, were much more hospitable than *Ladies' Home Journal* or *McCall's*, which acknowledged that women couldn't be completely self-indulgent since they still were the ones responsible for pureeing bananas for the baby and getting dinner on the table at night. *Vogue* et al. didn't contaminate their pages with such gritty reminders of reality, thank God. Instead, they created a narcissistic paradise, a luxurious daydream, in which women focused on themselves and their appearance, and in which any change was possible, as long as it was personal.

Now, before I get on my high horse about cures for what the fashion magazines call "orange peel skin" and subdermal rehydrating systems, let me be perfectly honest about my own vulnerability to these really preposterous ploys. Like a lot of women, I look at ads for things like Elizabeth Arden's Ceramide Time Complex Capsules, little gelatinous spheres that look like a cross between a diaphragm and a UFO, which claim to—get this—"boost [the] skin's hydration level over 450% after one hour" because they are "supercharged with HCA, a unique alpha-hydroxy complex," and I think—or sometimes yell—would you puleeze get real here. I know that in 1987 the FDA had cracked down on cosmetics ads then in print because they were, to put it euphemistically, inflated in their claims. I know that putting collagen on your skin does nothing. Nevertheless, there's this perfectly airbrushed model, young, beautiful, and carefree, her eyebrows the only lines on her face, and I sigh a longing sigh. Even when we are fully able to deconstruct these pseudoscientific sales pitches which would make any self-respecting snake oil salesman blush, there we are, a part of us still wanting to believe that we can look younger and that it's desirable to do so. I don't "read" *Vogue* or *Glamour*; if you'll pardon the masculine metaphor, I enter them. I escape in to them, into a world where I have nothing more stressful to do than smooth on some skin cream, polish my toenails, and lie on the beach. But despite these soft spots, I'm here to say that deconstruction can make us strong, so let's be on with it.

In ads for personal care products in the 1980s, especially skin creams, makeup, and perfume, we confronted our ideal selves, eternally young, flawless, confident, assured of the envy of others, yet insulated from the needs of others. The Lutèce Bath, for example, created "your private world of luxury." In these ads, the contradictions that we'd lived with all our lives, the tensions between the need to be passive and the need to be active, were subtly and brilliantly resolved. Usually the women pictured were enjoying leisure moments, or what *Glamour* called "private time." They were sitting alone on their enormous porches, or reclining in beds of satin sheets, or soaking in bubble baths, sometimes with their eyes closed, in a state of relaxation and escape. In one of my favorites, an ad for something called Terme di Montecatini, we saw the profile of a woman at a spa, covered from forehead to rib cage with a kind of mud we assumed would make her even more beautiful while she just rested. Women like this are passive, inactive, supine. Yet make no mistake about it, these women are in complete control: they are dependent on no one, their time is their own, they are beyond the cares of the world, they long for nothing they don't already have. Those symbols of wealth—a huge veranda, the Riviera, art objects, unusual breeds of dogs, the omnipresent glass of white wine—convey comfort, luxury, insulation from the masses, and control.

It wasn't enough to put some Lubriderm on your face—my God!—that was like consigning your skin to the soup kitchens of moisturizers. No, you had to spend money, and plenty of it, to be a discriminating, knowledgeable, accomplished woman. An ad for a product called Oligo-Major lectured, "No woman can afford to be without it." The cosmetics industry employed three main strategies to get women to buy the high-priced spreads for their faces instead of using the cheap shit, Pond's or Nivea—the building construction approach, the haute cuisine approach, and the high-tech approach, all intended to flatter the "new woman." They were designed to convey one basic message: you get what you pay for, and if you scrimp on skin-care products, you get what you deserve—crow's-feet, eye bags, turkey neck, the worst. Fail to spend $42.50 on one-thirty-second of an ounce of skin cream and the next time you look in the mirror, you'll see Lyndon Johnson in drag.

The building construction approach was best represented by a fabulous new product, Line Fill, a kind of Silly Putty for the face. Line Fill was also called skin Spackle—now we were supposed to think of ourselves as a slab of drywall—and was best used to "fill those character lines we can all do without." In the same age when "character," particularly for male politicians, became an obsession, women didn't dare look like they had any character at all. Chanel's Lift Sérum Anti-Wrinkle Complex relied on Plastoderm, which, despite its name, operated as a kind of hydraulic jack for sagging skin. "Wrinkles," informed the ad, "are 'lifted' by gentle upward pressure." The haute cuisine approach reached its apotheosis with "skin caviar," an "intensive concentration of vitamins, humectants, emollients, and plant naturals." The assumption here was that aging skin was merely malnourished; so in a gesture reminiscent of our new heroine, Marie Antoinette, the truly discriminating woman should say, "Let it eat caviar."

But without doubt the most prevalent approach was the high-tech approach, the one that introduced us to "delivery systems," "collagen," and lots of words starting with *micro-* and *lipo-*. What women's liberation really meant was that now the labs of America would turn to our real concerns: our crow's-feet. Science and technology, those onetime villains that had brought us napalm, the bomb, Three Mile Island, Love Canal, and the Dalkon Shield, were themselves given a face-lift for women. They were rehabilitated as our allies and our minions. Science and technology were the most effective agents of luxurious narcissism, and the various forms of white goop that we slopped on our faces had amazing names that cloaked the products in mystery while keeping supposedly technophobic and techno-dumbo females engaged and credulous.

Here we see another clever twist on feminism. The women's health movement of the 1970s, as embodied in *Our Bodies, Ourselves,* insisted that doctors not treat women like morons but that they talk to us as adults, provide us with information and choices, and give us more control over our bodies. Advertisers said OK, you want technical, medical information, we'll give it to you. They got to have it both ways—they flattered the "new woman" with all this pseudoscientific jargon, suggesting that this was the kind of information she wanted, needed, and could easily understand, and they got to make the goop they were selling sound as if it had been developed at Cal Tech.

In the 1980s, in nearly every cosmetic ad we saw, science and technology were women's servants, and servants not just to expedite domestic chores (as in the bad, selfless old days) but through which women could remake themselves, conquer time, and conquer nature by overcoming their genetic heritage. Here women's desires for more control over and more autonomy in their lives were shrewdly co-opted. Naomi Wolf argues that the high-tech approach sought to speak to women whose work was increasingly dominated by computers and the microchip.[2] The words *performance, precision,* and *control* were used repeatedly, and products such as Swiss Performing Extract or Niosôme Système Anti-Age performed on you (you are passive) while performing for you (you are in command). One product's slogan was, simply, "The Victory of Science over Time." This product, like so many, contained "patented liposomes," which, in case you needed an explanation, were "micro-capsules of select ingredients of natural origin which fuse with the membrane restoring fluidity, promoting reactivation of cells in your skin." Niosôme produced "an exclusive action, 'Biomimitism.'" This was not supposed to make you think of conjugating spirogyra; it was supposed to make you feel privy to the world of the scientist. It was very important to feature microscopes, women in white lab jackets, and lots of footnotes about patents pending to suggest the weight of a scientific abstract.

As we read other ads for competing products (and there was no shortage of them), a pattern started to emerge. Nearly all the cosmetics companies referred to their products as "systems." These systems "penetrate" the "intercellular structure" of the skin, increasing "microcirculation." Using only the most advanced "delivery systems," presumably inspired by NASA, the Pentagon, and Star Wars, these creams and lotions deployed "advanced microcarriers" or "active anti-age agents," presumably trained by the CIA to terminate wrinkles with extreme prejudice. So cosmetics actually became weapons, and the word *defense* began to proliferate in ads at the same time, interestingly, that the Pentagon's budget was going through the roof.

In copy sounding as if it had been written by Alexander Haig, our skin was put in a bunker or, better yet, behind Reagan's version of Star Wars, as "protective barriers" and "invisible shields" deflected "external aggressors."

These muscular products relied on the same high-tech weaponry we saw in *The Empire Strikes Back* and had straightforward names like Defense Cream and Skin Defender. You could almost see Luke Skywalker, backed up by the Green Berets, zapping those wrinkles back to kingdom come. Turning on its head the feminist argument that the emphasis on beauty undermines women's ability to be taken seriously and to gain control over their lives, advertisers now assured women that control *comes* from cosmetics. Cosmetics were sold as newly engineered tools, precision instruments you could use on yourself to gain more control than ever over the various masks and identities you as a woman must present to the world.

But lest all this high-tech talk alienate women, cosmetics firms also made sure to give their products European-, and especially French-sounding names. System was usually spelled *système*; concentrated became *concentré*. Accent signs became essential, as did the pronoun *Le*. Several product names simply went for broke, as in this little gem, Crème Multi Modelanté bio-suractivée, or Lift Extrême Nutri-Collagène Concentré. What were brilliantly brought together were the seemingly opposite worlds of advanced, ever-changing, American engineering technology and laboratory science (traditionally the province of men) and the preindustrialist, timeless, beauty-oriented cultural authority of Europe (which caters to women). For new beauty products to sell, it seems, the ads had to refer to and unite recent scientific breakthroughs and the language of engineering with references to France, Switzerland, or Italy. The words *extract, serum,* and *molecular* suggested both the lab *and* elements found in nature. Thus Niosôme, from Lancôme, is an antiaging "system" with a French-sounding name that "recreates the structure of a young skin." Cosmetics ads straddled the Atlantic, linking American technology with European culture, and the traditions of the old world with the futurism of the new.

With the union of science and aesthetics, women now could draw from the achievements of men in a world in which science and technology did what we always wished they would do—slow the passage of time, provide us with cost-free luxury and convenience, and allow us to remake ourselves. It was through the female form, and the idealized female face in particular, that science and technology were made to seem altruistic, progressive, relevant to everyday needs, and responsive to women's desires. They were made humane and romantic, and allied with the realms of art, nature, and tradition.

At the same time, the pseudoscientific language not only legitimated cosmetic companies' claims but also assured women that these products were for discriminating, upscale consumers. The new woman was now sophisticated enough and privileged enough to benefit from a scientific enterprise designed specifically for elite white women. The linking of American science and technology with European cultural authority served to unite narcissism with elitism, to make elitism seem natural, legitimate, and inevitable, and to suggest that if you truly loved yourself, you had to aspire to the privileged, idle, self-indulgent world of the rich, who were the rightful beneficiaries of technology, and the true arbiters of high art. Here we had a new kind of magic. How could products that relied on herbal treatments, molecular biology, and chemistry fail to transform us into newer, better selves?

Of course, if you'd been derelict in your moisturizing duties, there were more heroic methods to combat the signs of aging. Article after article touted plastic surgery, so that no woman would ever have to go out in public again looking like Eleanor Roosevelt, Simone de Beauvoir, or Margaret Mead did in their later years. Experts from skin-care labs, their names trailed by twenty-eight initials signifying their degrees and affiliations, happily agreed to interviews for *Harper's Bazaar* and elsewhere, promoting the knife. They always said these really informative and logical things, like that the first part of the body people usually look at is the face, which is why you shouldn't have any lines on yours. So what if, after a few tucks, you were laid up for six weeks and looked like you'd gone eighteen rounds with George Foreman? It was true, some women did experience a little facial paralysis after a lift, and you might not look as Occidental as you used to or have enough skin to smile in quite the same way, but these concerns were all picky, picky, picky. Did you want to look like Cher, or not?

The other intermediate step was promoted in full-page ads by the Collagen Corporation. Here we met Sunny Griffin, "mother, building contractor, and former TV correspondent and model." Already I felt pretty inferior, but it quickly got worse. Sunny was ten years older than I and easily looked ten years younger. Sunny, it turned out, "didn't like those 'little commas' at the corners of her mouth, her crow's-feet, or the lines on her forehead. So she did something about them." But, unlike me, she was a woman of action. She went to a doctor who stuck needles in her face, filling in those hideous lines with "injectable Zyderm© and Zyplast© Collagen." Now those wrinkles were "mere memories." Here were prefeminism and feminism beautifully reconciled in Sunny Griffin, Collagen poster girl. As a feminist, this superwoman had tackled male jobs and female jobs and combined them successfully with motherhood. This gave her permission to indulge her prefeminist side, the one still obsessed with little commas and crow's-feet, especially if she took decisive medical action to take control of her face and herself.

In the collagen ad, it was the beautiful, rich, and successful Sunny Griffin versus the rest of us. And that was the other important thrust of the narcissism as liberation campaign, the continuation of the cat-fight, the war between women. In all these ads, sisterhood was out, competitive individualism was in. It got worse if you actually fell for these ads (hey, I was in my thirties, what did I know?) and went out to buy some skin defender. If you've ever bought anything at a Clinique, Lancôme, or other such counter, you know what I mean. The saleswoman's face is made up like a Kabuki mask to put you off balance right away. And, clearly, all these women were trained wherever that awful, secret place is that they train used car salesmen.

Using a combination of intimidation, pressure, and highly uncharitable as-sessments of your existing skin-care regimen, these women sought to shame you into buying everything they had, which could come to the equivalent of a monthly car payment. The worst, and I mean the worst, thing you could say to one of these women was that you mixed products—you know, used a cleanser from one company and moisturizer from another. Then they'd nearly croak from exasperation at your stupidity and your self-destructive tendencies. Didn't you know, these cosmetic lines were *integrated* systems; each component worked with the other components as a unit. Mixing prod-ucts was akin to putting a Chevy carburetor inside a Porsche engine and ex-pecting the car to run. You'd wreck your face by mixing products; you had to buy into the entire system or risk waking up one morning to discover your face turning into melting wax.

The notion of sisterhood being powerful seemed a real joke under this on-slaught. Fisticuffs seemed more appropriate. It took work to remember that the salesclerks needed these jobs, that many of them were supporting kids with their salaries, and that while we squared off against each other across the glass-cased counter, the big boys upstairs who didn't need face cream were getting ready for their three-martini lunches and their affairs with women twenty years younger than they.

Tensions between technology and nature, between feminism and anti-feminism, and between self-love and self-doubt were played out not only on the terrain of the flawless female face. Everywhere we looked, in the in-cessant "get-back-in-shape" TV ads and magazine articles, on billboards, in the catalogs that jammed our mailboxes, and in the endless diet soda and ce-real ads on the airwaves, the perfectly smooth, toned buttocks and thighs of models and actresses accosted the women of America. They jutted out at us from the new, high-cut, split-'em-in-two bathing suits and exercise outfits, challenging us and humbling us, reminding all women that nothing in the world is more repulsive and shameful than "orange peel skin," a.k.a. "cel-lulite." They provided women, whether black or white, rich or poor, with a universal standard of achievement and success. They insisted that the rest of us should feel only one thing when we put on a bathing suit: profound mortification.

It's true that we also started seeing more female biceps, and every few months *The New York Times* asserted that breasts were back "in." But, still, it was the slim, dimple-free buttock and thigh that became, in the 1980s and the 1990s, the ultimate signifier of female fitness, beauty, and character. To make sure you couldn't hide them, the fashion industry gave us bathing suits with legs cut up to just below the armpit. Trim, smug models were positioned with their knees bent or their bodies curled so that their superhuman hindquarters were front and center. And not just in *Vogue* or *Cosmo*, either: even in *The Village Voice*, between the exposés on racism and government malfeasance, ads appeared for products like the videotape *Buns of Steel*, which promised, "Now you can have the buns you've always wanted."

Saddlebag-busting products like Biotherm appeared, which actually suggested that if you just rubbed some cream on your buttocks, the dimples would go into remission.

Why this part of the body? Why were we suddenly but constantly confronted by these perfectly sculpted rumps? During the mammary mania of the 1950s and '60s, bust creams, exercisers, and padded bras suggested that women could compensate for what nature forgot. Yet while less-endowed women might buy such products, and bemoan their lack of voluptuousness, there was also a basic understanding that, short of surgery, there was little a woman could do to actually change the size of her breasts. The thigh was different: this body part could be yoked to another pathology of the 1980s, the yuppie work ethic. Thin thighs and dimple-free buttocks became instant, automatic evidence of discipline, self-denial, and control. You, too, the message went, can achieve perfect thighs through dieting and exercise. As Jane Fonda put it, "Discipline Is Liberation."[3]

Emphasis on the thigh, which still harasses us, stems from the fitness craze of the past fifteen years, when increasing numbers of women discovered the physical and psychic benefits of exercise. I learned in graduate school, for example, that if I swam sixty-seven laps in the pool I was less likely to strangle the pompous white male professors making my life miserable, and I'd also sort out some problem with my own work as well. Plus, for inspiration to get off your butt, there were women like Billie Jean King, one of my heroes, a fabulous athlete and a feminist, and the first woman athlete to earn more than $100,000 a year. When she beat the living crap out of Bobby Riggs in the much touted "Battle of the Sexes" in 1973, as women like me screamed with delight in our living rooms, she not only vindicated female athletes and feminism but also inspired many of us to get in shape—not because it would make us beautiful but because it would make us strong and healthy.

What too many of us forget is that the fitness movement began as a radical reaction against the degradation of food by huge conglomerates, and against the work routines and convenience technologies that encouraged us to be passive and sedentary. The organic health food movement was, initially, at its core, anticapitalist. The women's fitness movement, too, was a site of resistance, as women sought to break into sports previously restricted to men and other women simply sought to get strong. But one of capitalism's great strengths—perhaps its greatest—is its ability to co-opt and domesticate opposition, to transubstantiate criticism into a host of new, marketable products. And so it was with fitness.

Corporations saw immediately that there was gold in them thar thighs. The key to huge profits was to emphasize beauty over health, sexuality over fitness, and to equate thin thighs with wealth and status. What had worked so well in the past was to set up standards of perfection that were cast as unattainable yet somehow within reach if only the right product were purchased. So we got a new, even narrower ideal of beauty that continues to bombard us from every media outlet and serves the needs of a host of corporations.

Yet there was much more going on here than just the media capitalizing on a trend or the standard let's-make-'em-feel-inferior-so-they'll-buy-our-product routine. The flawless rump became *the* most important female body part of the 1980s because its cultivation and display fit in so well with the great myth of Reaganism: that superficial appearances really can be equated with a person's deepest character strengths and weaknesses. The emphasis on streamlined rumps allowed for a dramatic reshaping of feminist urgings that women take control of their bodies and their health. All we had to do was listen to Cher in those health spa ads, she'd tell us: thin thighs and dimple-free buttocks meant you worked hard, took yourself seriously, and were ready to compete with anyone. They were indicators of a woman's potential for success. Any woman, so the message went, could achieve perfect thighs through concentrated effort, self-denial, and deferred gratification, the basic tenets of the work ethic. All she had to do was apply herself, and, of course, be a discriminating, upscale consumer. "You don't get this far by accident," proclaimed one sneaker ad displaying a tight, toned rump; "you've worked hard." Another magazine ad, this one for a spa, also spotlighted a machine-tooled hindquarter, intoning, "When you work at it, it shows." Meaning, if you've been slacking off, that will show too. Only "new women" had buns of steel; out-of-date women who had failed to have their consciousnesses raised didn't.

It didn't matter if you were healthy, exercised regularly, and weren't overweight. If wearing one of the new, ultrahigh-cut bathing suits would reveal too much roundness, a little fat (what the cosmetics industry christened "cellulite" in the 1970s), you would be dismissed as slothful and lacking moral fiber and self-respect, not to mention lazy, self-indulgent, insufficiently vigorous, lacking control, sedentary, and old. (The only acceptable sedentary indulgence was to lie on a chaise longue, slathered from head to toe in sludge, à la Terme di Montecatini.) No matter that the female hip area is naturally more fatty than the male (a function of reproduction), or that most women's jobs require constant sitting, two factors that tend to work against developing buns of steel. Over and again we were told that a real woman, whatever her age, would get off her butt and, by overcoming her sloth, not just get in shape but conquer genetics and history. Her buns of steel would instantly identify her as someone who subscribed to the new yuppie ethic that insisted that even in leisure hours, the truly tough, the truly deserving, never stopped working. The sleek, smooth, tight butt was—and is—a badge, a medal asserting that anal compulsiveness is an unalloyed virtue.

Perfect thighs, in other words, were an achievement, a product, and one to be admired and envied. They demonstrated that the woman had made something of herself, that she had character and class, that she was the master of her body and, thus, of her fate. If she had conquered her own adipose tissue, she could conquer anything. She was a new woman, liberated and in control. She had made her buttocks less fatty, more muscular, more, well . . . like a man's. So here we have one of the media's most popular—and pernicious—distortions of feminism: that ambitious women want, or should want, to be just like men. The woman whose upper thigh best approximated a fat-free male hindquarter was the woman most entitled to enjoy the same privileges as men. Orange-peel skin should be a source of shame, not only because it's "ugly," but also because it's inherently female. It indicates that, as a woman, you aren't working hard enough, aren't really taking responsibility for your own life. You aren't really liberated because you haven't overcome being a woman. A desirable woman doesn't look like a real woman looks; thus, one of the basic physical markers of femaleness is cast as hideous.

Yet well-toned, machine-tooled thighs suggested that women could compete with men while increasing their own desirability. Thighs, rather than breasts, became the focus in the 1980s because presumably everyone, the flat-chested and the stacked, men as well as women, could work toward buns of steel. Women could develop the same anatomical zones that men did, giving their muscles new definition, a definition meant to serve simultaneously as a warning and an enticement to men. Buns of steel marked a woman as a desirable piece of ass, and as someone who could kick ass when necessary.

What made these thighs desirable was that, while they were fat-free, like men's, they also resembled the thighs of adolescent girls. The ideal rump bore none of the marks of age, responsibility, work, or motherhood. And the crotch-splitting, cut-up-to-the-waistline, impossible-to-swim-in bathing suits featured in such publications as the loathsome *Sports Illustrated* swimsuit issue could never reveal that other marker of adulthood, pubic hair. So, under the guise of female fitness and empowerment, of control over her own body, was an idealized image that infantilized women, an image that kept women in their place.

The upper thigh thus became freighted with meaning. The work ethic, the ethos of production and achievement, self-denial and deferred gratification was united there with egoism, vanity, self-absorption, and other-directedness. With the work ethic moved from the workplace to the private sphere, the greatest female achievement became, ironically, her body, her self. The message was that women were capable of remaking themselves and that this remaking required not only intelligent consumption but also hard work. Thus could women be, simultaneously, self-indulgent consumers, buying high-priced exercise shoes and spa memberships, and self-denying producers who were working hard to remake something—their bodies. They could be active subjects in control of their own images and passive objects judged by those images. They could be prefeminists and new women at the same time.

By the middle of the 1980s, these buttocks and thighs were making me and all the other women I knew really hostile and defensive. Their sleek, seemingly healthy surfaces really demanded that we all be pathological:

compulsive, filled with self-hate, and schizophrenic, and we were already schizophrenic enough, thank you very much. Aside from the impossible standards of perfection they imposed, these buns of steel urged women to never stop and to be all things to all people: to be both competitive work-aholics *and* sex objects, to be active workers in control of their bodies *and* pas-sive ornaments for the pleasure of men, to be hard-as-nails superwomen *and* vulnerable, unthreatening, teenage beach bunnies. Straddling such contra-dictions, even on toned, fat-free, muscular legs is, in real life, impossible. And buns of steel were meant to separate the truly classy, deserving women from the rest of the lumpy female proletariat. Buns of steel, like a Pierre Cardin label, were a mark of well-earned exclusivity. Lumpy thighs were K mart thighs, not the thighs of Rodeo Drive.

The 1980s are over, but buns of steel are very much with us, in Diet Pepsi ads, Victoria's Secret catalogs, and women's magazines. A 1993 survey re-ported that while 6 percent of women wished their breasts were either bigger or smaller, a whopping 72 percent wished they had "better thighs."[4] That same year, the cover of *Glamour* promised, in a two-inch headline, "A Better Butt, Fast!" The cover also promised to explain "Why 15 Million Women Own Guns."[5] I figure it's to shoot everyone involved in the campaign to make us think we need buns of steel. The article inside, titled euphoniously enough "The World-Class Butt," accompanied by exercise instructions and an enor-mous photo of a smooth, sixteen-year-old butt in white eyelet short shorts, lec-tured, "A toned, firm bottom has plenty to recommend it, as the photo on the right confirms." I also learned that the "flat bottom featured in those beach-blanket movies" was really out. "Now women want a defined, sculpted look with higher, rounder cheeks." Yep, this has been an overarching goal I've wanted to devote a lot of time to in the 1990s. But there's the same old hitch: "You have to work hard to firm them up. So get busy." No need to repeat which expletives I use when reading an exhortation such as this.

So where do these buttocks and thighs leave the rest of us, the real women of America who sit at desks or stand at sinks, who are over sixteen, and who don't have the time, money, personal trainer, or surgical team to help us forge our own buns of steel? Even nonoverweight women, and women who do and should know better, have been worked over so well that whenever we look at ourselves in the mirror, or, worse, have to be seen in public in a bathing suit, all we can feel is disgust and shame. But it isn't just shame of our bodies. Buns of steel have taught us to be ashamed of the way we live our day-to-day lives; of the fact that whatever we're doing, we aren't working hard enough; that we don't have that badge of entitlement; that we don't really have enough self-respect and dignity; that we aren't enough like men; and worst of all, that we're adult females in a culture that still prefers, by and large, little girls. All it takes is the slightest roundness, the smallest dimple, to mark a woman as a lazy, and therefore worthless, unattractive person whose thighs obliterate whatever other admirable traits or impressive accomplishments she might possess.

I'm tired of being told never to stop, and that some physical exertion, like pumping a Nautilus machine, is more valuable than some other exertion, such as chasing a two-year-old. I'm tired of Cher's rump, Christie Brinkley's thighs, and countless starved, airbrushed, surgically enhanced hindquarters being shoved in my face. I'm tired of being told that if I just exercise a lot more and eat a lot less, I, too, can conquer biology, make my thighs less female, and thus not be eyed with derision. I'm *real* tired of the Marquis de Sade "bathing suits" foisted on us by the fashion industry. Most of all, I'm tired of the endless self-flagellation we women subject ourselves to because of the way this latest, unattainable, physical ideal has been combined with the yuppie work ethic.

And I'm not alone. Backlash works two ways, and women, especially cranky women my age, are really getting the fed-up-skis with advertisers' obsession with machine-tooled faces and thighs. I think that catalogs like Lands' End must be making a fortune on this backlash against buns of steel. They sell bathing suits that fit and that you can actually swim in. If you make the mistake of waiting until late June to order one, they're out of stock because furious women all over the country now refuse to try on a glorified G-string under fluorescent lights that make you look like a very fat dead person.

At the same time that we can't exorcise such long-standing inferiority complexes about our bodies, we see women trying to reclaim the fitness movement from Kellogg's, Diet Pepsi, Biotherm, and all the rest of the buttocks and thighs cartel. Women know, in their heads if not their hearts, that buns of steel are not about fitness: they are about pretending that some anorexic, unnatural, corporate-constructed ideal is really a norm. Buns of steel are designed to humiliate women, and to make us complicit in our own degradation, and most women know this too. Silly as they may seem, buns of steel are worth being angry about because of the eating disorders they promote among young women and the general sexism they reinforce in society. So the next time some curled-up rump is forced into your field of vision, view it not with envy but with contempt. For it doesn't reflect hard work or entitlement so much as mindless narcissism, unproductive self-absorption, and the media's ongoing distortion of feminism to further their own misogynistic, profit-maximizing ends. Buns of steel are just another media Trojan horse, pretending to advance feminism but harboring antifeminist weaponry.

Narcissism as liberation gutted many of the underlying principles of the women's movement. Instead of group action, we got escapist solitude. Instead of solidarity, we got female competition over men. And, most important, instead of seeing personal disappointment, frustrations, and failures as symptoms of an inequitable and patriarchal society, we saw these, just as in the 1950s, as personal failures, for which we should blame ourselves. Smooth, toned thighs and buttocks obstruct any vision of social change and tell us that, as women, personal change, physical change, is our last, best, and most realistic hope. Women are to take control of their bodies not for political or health reasons but to make them aesthetically pleasing. The "new woman" of the 1980s, then, perpetuated and legitimated the most crass, selfish aspects of consumer capitalism and thus served to distort and deny the most basic and revolutionary principles of feminism. Narcissism as liberation is liberation repackaged, deferred, and denied. Again women felt pinioned, trapped in a web of warring messages. We were supposed to work harder than ever; in fact, the mark of success was having no time for your friends, your family, or yourself. But we were also supposed to indulge ourselves, and to know when and how to kick back, and to do so with style.

Let's take, for example, the politics of the face-lift. Baby boomers with sufficient discretionary income are starting to confront this one, and with the explosion in celebrity journalism, stars' face-lifts and other nips and tucks have become headline news, serving as an enticement and a warning. Cosmetic surgery is being presented as a perfectly natural, affordable, routine procedure, and increasing numbers of women are heeding the call. Cosmetic surgery is growing at a faster rate than any other medical specialty and grosses approximately $300 million a year.[6] The decision to get a face-lift or not is, inescapably, a political decision. Getting one means you're acquiescing to our country's sick norms about beauty, youth, and being "worth it." Not getting one means you're gonna tough it out, be baggy-faced, and take the heat. Actresses and models have no choice. The rest of American women are pulled between these nodes.

But here's what doesn't come out in the war against wrinkles and cellulite: women are as conflicted about aging as they are about other aspects of their lives. For example, when I was twenty and had streaked blond hair, walking down pretty much any street was a nightmare. The incessant yells of "Hey, baby," and other more anatomically graphic remarks, the whistles and other simianlike sounds some men seem to spend an inordinate amount of time perfecting, all these infuriated me and kept me constantly on the defensive. Now that doesn't happen anymore—and I love it. I can walk—no comments; I can jog—no comments; I can walk along the beach—no leers. My eye bags and my "cellulite" are now my friends, my protectors, my armor, and I love them for that. At the same time, part of me will always want to sandpaper them off.

Then there's the love-hate relationship with the eye bags. No woman wants to look like George Shultz after a bad night, but a woman's facial lines are the story of her life. I got mine from pulling too many all-nighters in college, from smoking pot, from drinking tequila with my brother and champagne with my husband, from baking way too long in the sun, from putting in sixty-hour workweeks, from having a child unfamiliar with the concept of sleep, and, of course, from growing older. They've tracked my joys and sorrows, my failures and successes, and I'm supposed to want to chop them off so I can look like an empty vessel, a bimbette? Besides, my husband, who hates it when his favorite actresses get face-lifts and don't look like themselves anymore, likes them. They go with his; they're a team.

So here's the question, girls. And it's one you guys should consider too as Grecian Formula, Clinique, and Soloflex eye your sagging faces and bodies greedily. What if every woman in America woke up tomorrow and simply decided that she was happy with the way she looked? She might exercise to keep herself healthy, and get some Vaseline Intensive Care from CVS to soothe her dry skin, but, basically, that would be the extent of it. Think of the entire multibillion-dollar industries that would crumble. This is one of the reasons lesbians are so vilified—many of them have already made this choice, thereby costing the beauty industry millions. If women decided in the war between feminism and antifeminism being waged in skin-care and diet soda ads that antifeminism had way too big an advantage, women might decide to shift the odds a bit. For example, they might decide to take the $42.50 for skin caviar or skin Spackle and send it, instead, to the Fund for the Feminist Majority, the International Red Cross, the Children's Defense Fund, or some other organization that works for the benefit of women and children.

The reason this won't happen is that advertising, women's magazines, movies, and TV shows have been especially effective in alienating women from their faces and bodies. Women of all ages, who are perfectly capable of denouncing sexist news coverage, or making their own empowering and subversive meanings out of TV shows and films, find it extremely difficult to resist the basic tenet that a face with lines or a thigh with dimples means you are worthless. The media's relentlessly coercive deployment of perfect faces and bodies, and the psychologically, politically, and economically punitive measures taken against women who fail to be young, thin, and beautiful, have intersected seamlessly with age-old American ideals about the work ethic, being productive, and being deserving of rewards. The "I'm Worth It" campaign and all its allies and imitators co-opt the feminist effort to promote female self-esteem to reassure women that, deep down, they aren't worth it at all. The same women who have been able to find feminist empowerment in the most unlikely places—from Harry Reasoner's editorials to Krystle and Alexis's cat-fights—find nothing but self-hatred and disempowerment here. Of all the disfigurements of feminism, this, perhaps, has been the most effective.

NOTES

[1] For a funny and very smart discussion of elite culture in the 1980s see Debora Silverman, *Selling Culture: Bloomingdale's, Diana Vreeland and the New Aristocracy of Taste in Reagan's America* (New York: Pantheon, 1986).

[2] Naomi Wolf, *The Beauty Myth* (New York: Doubleday, 1991), p. 109.

[3] Ibid., p. 99.

[4] Melissa Stanton, "Looking After Your Looks," *Glamour,* August 1993, p. 233.

[5] "A Better Butt, Fast!" and "Why 15 Million Women Own Guns" in *Glamour,* May 1993, p. 270ff and p. 260ff.

[6] Wolf, *The Beauty Myth,* p. 232.

. . . .

QUESTIONS FOR A SECOND READING

1. Susan Douglas's text can be fun to read. She's witty and irreverent, especially when she writes about advertisements, and she likes to make satirical comments in her critiques of the industry and its creation of "endless images of women" (p. 117). As you reread, take notes on the images of women she presents as a part of her critique. What, you might ask, are the underlying assumptions about what might be considered "womanly" in the images she values? in the images she disparages?

2. Douglas's text can be fun to read. It is also an exercise in a form of analysis that requires some technical sophistication. She is not simply venting; she is also doing a kind of work on advertising that is related to other efforts in the analysis of culture, including the analysis of literature, film, fashion, sports, art, and architecture. Her prose is written to reach and please (and affect) a large audience; even so, behind it is a fairly specialized training. You can see traces of this in her vocabulary (references to "the male code," to "sites of resistance," to "deconstruction," to "capitalism" and its ability to "co-opt and domesticate opposition"). And you can see it in her essay's larger ambitions, connecting ads in "women's magazines" to American history and American political life (to the 1980s, the 1990s and the "age of Reagan").

   As you reread, look for traces of this training, for the terms and interpretive strategies (the lingo and the moves) that define Douglas's project. What are the key terms and assumptions? Who or what is responsible for determining the meaning of women's bodies? What is at stake?

ASSIGNMENTS FOR WRITING

1. Susan Douglas's chapter begins immediately with a quotation from a television advertisement featuring Cybill Shepherd, who speaks, Douglas writes, "in her brattiest, na-na-na-poo-poo voice as she swirls her blond hair. . . ." From the beginning, Douglas presents her readers with material she has gathered from her sources. She works closely with sources throughout the chapter. On almost every page she presents her reader with examples of how she gathers materials, thinks them through, and recasts them.

   As you read through "Narcissism as Liberation" for a second time, look for two or three examples of what you might call Douglas's methods. How would you explain what she is doing? How would you describe and name her methods?

   After you have read through "Narcissism as Liberation" and taken notes, write an essay in which you present and explain two or three examples which you think represent Douglas's most powerful or important methods of working with her materials. What do the methods allow her to do or accomplish? How do they constrain her work?

2. Susan Douglas critiques numerous advertisements directed toward women throughout "Narcissism as Liberation." During the course of these critiques she draws conclusions about the advertisements, the ways they "work" on women, and she builds an argument centered on a notion of narcissism she borrows from Christopher Lasch.

   Her argument seems full and persuasive. What would it take to open it to question? Or how might a reader, how might you, enter into conversation or dialogue with Douglas? (*Questioning, conversation,* and *dialogue* are key terms here. It is not hard to imagine the position of someone who wanted simply to dismiss Douglas's argument or to take the opposite point of view. A writer would have to work carefully, however, to engage Douglas on her own terms or with and through her own materials.)

   Write an essay in which you respond to "Narcissism as Liberation." You should imagine you are writing for someone who may have read the essay but who doesn't have the text at hand or a clear memory of its details. And, as you work on your essay (perhaps in revision), find how and where you can begin to establish your position as someone who has thought about these issues, studied ads, and carefully considered the arguments.

3. For this assignment, imagine that you are accepting the challenge of Douglas's essay (or following in her footsteps). Write an essay in which you extend her project to a set of related advertisements of your choosing. (Don't choose ads that are essentially the same as Douglas's.) These could be ads directed at men—or, for that matter, at any representative group. (Photo or clip the ads and include them with your essay.)

   Your goal should be to begin with and to test (to engage with, perhaps to argue with) Douglas's critical frame. You will need to "read" and present your ads closely and carefully, as she does, and to use them to think about the forces of power and influence in American popular culture. You should, that is, find yourself moving to make statements about the second half of the 1990s.

MAKING CONNECTIONS

1. Douglas's prose is written to reach and please a large audience; even so, behind it is a fairly specialized training. You can see traces of this in her vocabulary (references to "the male code," to "sites of resistance," to "deconstruction," to "capitalism" and its ability to "co-opt and domesticate opposition"). And you can see it in her essay's larger ambitions, connecting ads in "women's magazines" to American history and American political life (to the 1980s, the 1990s, and the "age of Reagan").

   Douglas is both making an argument about the effects of popular culture and offering her readers a lesson in how to read—in particular, a lesson in how to read materials, like magazine advertisements, that seem to be so naturally and inevitably a part of the cultural landscape that they don't need to be "read at all." "Ads are ads," we can imagine ourselves saying, "so what's the fuss? What else is there to say?" Plenty, if we take Douglas as a guide.

Douglas's work, like John Berger's in *Ways of Seeing* (p. 50) is designed to make the obvious seem strange and arbitrary, part of a design that has been hidden from us. So what is this design? Who is the designer? According to Douglas, who is doing what to whom, and why? And what about John Berger—is his argument similar or different? Both Douglas and Berger are interested in correcting the way images are read. Both are concerned with the ways images serve the interests of power and money. Both are writing to get the attention of a general audience and to teach readers how and why they should pay a different kind of attention to the images around them.

Write an essay in which you consider the two essays as examples of an ongoing project. Berger's essay precedes Douglas's by at least a quarter of a century. If you look closely at one or two of their examples, and if you look at the larger concerns in their arguments, are they saying the same thing? doing the same work? If so, why? Why is such work still necessary? If not, how do their projects differ? And how might you account for those differences?

2 Both Susan Douglas's "Narcissism as Liberation" and Ralph Ellison's "an Extravagance of Laughter" (p. 140) provoke laughter from readers, yet they are quite different pieces of writing. As you reread the selections, identify two moments in each that you think represent the kind of humor that is particular to each of these writers. Then write an essay that explains the ways in which these humorous moments "work," both for a reader (i.e., you) and for the writer (i.e., Douglas).

3. In "The Loss of the Creature" (p. 511), Walker Percy charts several routes to the Grand Canyon. You can take the packaged tour, you can get off the beaten track, you can wait for a disaster, you can follow the "dialectical movement which brings one back to the beaten track but at a level above it." This last path (or strategem), he says, is for the complex traveler. The other routes are, he says, common approaches. As you reread "The Loss of the Creature," imagine that Susan Douglas, as she writes in "Narcissism as Liberation," is an explorer in the realm of advertising. According to your reading of Percy, what kind of explorer might she be? Do her critiques of advertisements, that is, allow you to think of them as common or complex approaches to "reading" the ads she critiques?

For this assignment, write an essay in which you use Percy's distinctions between common and complex approaches to "reading" to identify and explain Douglas's approach to advertisements. What tourist stories seem to portray Douglas's methods and purposes in her critiques? How would you use one or two of these tourist stories to explain Douglas's approach to ads?

RALPH
ELLISON

"*A*N EXTRAVAGANCE OF LAUGHTER" *was written toward the end of Ralph Ellison's career, when he was seventy-one, for the collection of essays titled* Going to the Territory. *It tells the story of an event in the 1930s, when Ellison visited New York, met Richard Wright and other African American artists and intellectuals, and first began to imagine his career as a writer. Ellison grew up in Oklahoma City, where his parents had migrated in hopes of a greater freedom than they could find in the Deep South. "Going to the territory"—that is, going to the Indian territories, including those in Oklahoma—was a phrase used earlier by escaped slaves to describe the hope for a greater freedom. While the conditions of black life were different in the West, Oklahoma City was racially segregated. Ellison's father died there when he was three. He lived with his mother and brother in relative poverty, but always with the belief that he could overcome the limits imposed by economic insecurity and racial prejudice. (His father had named him after Ralph Waldo Emerson; Ellison would later argue for the importance of Emersonian self-determination and self-reliance, sometimes in ways that made him suspect among black and Left intellectuals, who felt that he was ignoring the determining factors of poverty, racism, and oppression.)*

As a child growing up in Oklahoma City, Ellison fell in love with African American music, particularly jazz. He played the trumpet, taught himself Louis

Armstrong solos, and traded yard work for private lessons from the conductor of the Oklahoma City Orchestra. Ellison went to Tuskegee as a music major. His dream was to write a symphony that would bring the blues into classical form. It is at this point that Ellison made his first trip to New York. He was looking to make money to support his education and he was hoping to meet Richard Wright. He later returned and, with Richard Wright's aid, began to work with the Federal Writers Project. In 1952 he published Invisible Man, one of the most widely read and most influential novels of the twentieth century. It won the National Book Award and was immediately a best-seller.

For the rest of his career, Ellison was much in the public eye. In the 1960s and 1970s, he was often represented as an "Uncle Tom," as too enamored of white European culture and values, as too uncommitted to black causes to serve an emerging and militant African American counterculture. He was also criticized for not joining Martin Luther King, Jr.'s opposition to the Vietnam War and for not stepping forward as a spokesman for the civil rights movement.

In a famous exchange in the early 1960s, one that captured the attention of readers both inside and outside the academy, literary critic Irving Howe criticized the optimism of Invisible Man and accused Ellison (and James Baldwin) of abandoning the harsh truths of American racism portrayed in Richard Wright's Native Son. Howe wrote of Ellison's novel,

> Nor is one easily persuaded by the hero's discovery that "my world had become one of infinite possibilities," by his refusal to be the "invisible man" whose body is manipulated by various social groups. Though the unqualified assertion of self-liberation was a favorite strategy among American literary people in the fifties, it is also vapid and insubstantial. It violates the reality of social life, the interplay between external conditions and personal will. . . . The unfortunate fact remains that to define one's individuality is to stumble upon social barriers which stand in the way, all too much in the way, of "infinite possibilities."

Here is part of Ellison's response to Howe:

> Evidently Howe feels that unrelieved suffering is the only "real" Negro experience, and that the true Negro writer must be ferocious.
>
> But there is also an American Negro tradition which teaches one to deflect racial provocation and to master and contain pain. It is a tradition which abhors as obscene any trading on one's own anguish for gain or sympathy; which springs not from a desire to deny the harshness of existence but from a will to deal with it as men at their best have always done. It takes fortitude to be a man and no less to be an artist. Perhaps it takes even more if the black man would be an artist. If so, there are no exemptions. It would seem to me, therefore, that the question of how the "sociology of his existence" presses upon a Negro writer's work depends upon how much of his life the individual writer is able to transform into art. What moves a writer to eloquence is less meaningful than what he makes of it. How much, by the way, do we know of Sophocles' wounds?

> *One unfamiliar with what Howe stands for would get the impression that when he looks at a Negro he sees not a human being but an abstract embodiment of living hell.*

In his book Heroism and the Black Intellectual: Ralph Ellison, Politics, and Afro-American Intellectual Life *(1994), Jerry Watts makes the point that Ellison was not arguing against political involvement. Ellison, rather, was arguing that art is a form of political engagement. In his essays, Ellison looks at jazz, at the blues, at novels and poems, at the African American church, and in "An Extravagance of Laughter," at jokes and stories as forms of artistic production.*

"An Extravagance of Laughter" thus stands as the writer's way of thinking back to a moment in a theater in New York. Since it was written at the end of Ellison's career, it can also be read as a way of thinking back over a lifetime as a public figure, not only living out but standing for key moments in our country's history and its racial politics. In his Los Angeles Times *review of* Going to the Territory, *David Bradley said,*

> *These essays never fail to be elegantly written, beautifully composed, and intellectually sophisticated. The personality that emerges from the pages is witty, literate, endearingly modest, delightfully puckish. So much so that, while one cannot completely forgive Ellison for not writing that novel we've all been waiting for, one does start to wonder if we have not been waiting for the wrong thing.*

Ellison himself offers "An Extravagance of Laughter" as an "autobiographical investigation." It ranges wide in its thinking, well beyond the episode in a Broadway theater, and offers a wonderful example of how writing can serve as an instrument of inquiry. As an essay, it moves by indirection; it takes its time; its movements are both surprising and subtle—in fact, the structure might be described in relation to Ellison's passion for jazz. The writer begins by stating a theme, improvises, follows this thread and then that, and then returns to the theme at the end. In his 1986 New York Times *review, John Edgar Wideman says, "What captures the reader . . . are the subtle jazz-like changes Mr. Ellison rings against the steady back-beat of his abiding concerns as an artist and critic." In an essay published in 1945, Ellison offered this definition of the blues: "As a form, the blues is an autobiographical chronicle of personal catastrophe expressed lyrically." And the attraction of the blues, he said,*

> *lies in this, that they at once express both the agony of life and the possibility of conquering it through sheer toughness of spirit. They fall short of tragedy only in that they provide no solution, offer no scapegoat but the self.*

Ralph Ellison (1914–1994) published three books. The novel, Invisible Man *(1952), and two collections of essays,* Shadow and Act *(1964) and* Going to the

Territory *(1986). When he died in 1994, he was still at work on his second novel. El-lison taught at Bard College, at the University of Chicago, and in 1970 was named the Albert Schweitzer Professor of the Humanities at New York University, where he taught until his retirement.*

An Extravagance
of Laughter

In December 1983 the good news that Erskine Caldwell had reached his eightieth birthday reminded me that although I have had the pleasure of see-ing him on and off for some twenty years, I have never been able to offer him an apology for an offense of which I was guilty back in the 1930s. Perhaps I failed because my offense took the form of laughter—or, to be more precise, of a particular quality and an *extravagance* of laughter; which, since it came at the expense of Caldwell's most famous work of comedy, may explain both my confusion and my reluctance. And since the work in question was *de-signed* and intended to evoke laughter, any account of why I should term my particular laughter "offensive" will require a bit of autobiographical explo-ration which may well enable me both to understand my failure to apologize and to clarify the role which that troublesome moment of laughter was to play in my emotional and intellectual development.

Charles Baudelaire observed that "the wise man never laughs but that he trembles." Therefore, for the moment let it suffice to say that being both far from wise and totally unaware of Baudelaire's warning, I not only laughed ex-travagantly but trembled even *as* I laughed; and thus I found myself utterly unprepared for the Caldwell-inspired wisdom which erupted from that incon-gruous juxtaposition of mirth and quaking. This is no excuse, however, be-cause Aesop and Uncle Remus have taught us that comedy is a disguised form of philosophical instruction; and especially when it allows us to glimpse the animal instincts operating beneath the surface of our civilized affectations. For by allowing us to laugh at that which is normally *un*laughable, comedy provides an otherwise unavailable clarification of vision that calms that clammy trembling which ensues whenever we pierce the veil of conventions that guard us from the basic absurdity of the human condition. During such moments the world of appearances is turned upside down, and in my case Caldwell's comedy plunged me quite unexpectedly into the deepest levels of a most American realm of the absurd while providing me with the magical wings with which to ascend back to a world which, for all his having knocked it quite out of kilter, I then found more rational. Caldwell had no way of knowing what I was experiencing, but even though I caused unforeseen trouble, he was a wise and skillful guide, and thus it is that I offer him both my apologies and, for reasons to be made clear a bit later, my heartfelt thanks.

It all began in 1936, a few weeks after my arrival in New York, when I was lucky enough to be invited by an old hero and new-found friend, Langston Hughes, to be his guest at what would be my introduction to Broadway theater. I was so delighted and grateful for the invitation that I failed to ask my host the title of the play, and it was not until we arrived at the theater that I learned that it would be Jack Kirkland's dramatization of Erskine Caldwell's famous novel *Tobacco Road*. No less successful than in its original form, the play was well on its way to a record-breaking seven-year run in the theater, and that alone was enough to increase my expectations. And so much so that I failed to note the irony of circumstance that would have as my introduction to New York theater a play with a Southern setting and characters that were based upon a type and class of whites whom I had spent the last three years trying to avoid. Had I been more alert, it might have occurred to me that somehow a group of white Alabama farm folk had learned of my presence in New York, thrown together a theatrical troupe, and flown north to haunt me. But being dazzled by the lights, the theatrical atmosphere, the babble of the playgoing crowd, it didn't. And yet that irony arose precisely from the mixture of motives—practical, educational, and romantic—that had brought me to the North in the first place.

Among these was my desire to enjoy a summer free of the South and its problems while meeting the challenge of being on my own for the first time in a great Northern city. Fresh out of Alabama, with my junior year at Tuskegee Institute behind me, I was also in New York seeking funds with which to complete my final year as a music major—a goal at which I was having less success than I had hoped. However, there had been compensations. For between working in the Harlem YMCA cafeteria as a substitute for vacationing waiters and countermen and searching for a more profitable job, I had used my free time exploring the city's many cultural possibilities, making new acquaintances, and enjoying the many forms of social freedom that were unavailable to me in Alabama. The very idea of being in New York was dreamlike, for like many young Negroes of the time, I thought of it as the freest of American cities and considered Harlem as the site and symbol of Afro-American progress and hope. Indeed, I was both young and bookish enough to think of Manhattan as my substitute for Paris and of Harlem as a place of Left Bank excitement. So now that I was there in its glamorous scene, I meant to make the most of its opportunities.

Yes, but I had discovered, much to my chagrin, that while I was physically out of the South, I was restrained—sometimes consciously, sometimes not—by certain internalized thou-shalt-nots that had structured my public conduct in Alabama. It was as though I had come to the Eden of American culture and found myself indecisive as to which of its fruits were free for my picking. Thus, for all my bright expectations, my explorations had taken on certain aspects of an unanticipated and amorphous rite of initiation in which the celebrant—if indeed one existed—remained mute and beyond my range of ear and vision. Therefore, I found myself forced to act as my own guide and instructor, and had to enact, touch-and-go, the archetypical American role of pioneer in what was our most sophisticated and densely populated city. And in the process I found myself being compelled, as it were, to improvise a makeshift map of the city's racially determined do's-and-don'ts and impose it upon the objective scene by dealing consciously with such complications of character and custom as might materialize in the course of my explorations.

I missed, in brief, a sense of certainty which the South imposed in the forms of signs and symbols that marked the dividing lines of racial segregation. This was an embarrassing discovery, so given what I assumed would be the shortness of my visit, I tried to deal with it and remained quite eager to take the risks necessary to achieve New York's promises. After certain disappointments, however, I had been going about it in the manner of one learning to walk again upon a recently mended leg that still felt strange without the protective restraint of a plaster cast now left happily behind. So there were moments when I reminded myself of the hero of the old Negro folktale who, after arriving mistakenly in heaven and being issued a pair of wings, was surprised to learn that there were certain earthlike restrictions which required people of his complexion to fly with one wing strapped to their sides. But, while surprised, the new arrival came to the philosophical conclusion that even in heaven, that place of unearthly perfection, there had to be rules and regulations. And since rules were usually intended to make one think, no less than to provide guidance, he decided to forgo complaint and get on with the task of mastering the challenge of one-wing flying. As a result, he soon became so proficient at the art that by the time he was cast out of heaven for violating its traffic regulations, he could declare (and so truthfully that not even Saint Peter could say him nay) that he was the most skillful one-winged flyer ever to have been grounded by heavenly decision.

So, following the example of my legendary ancestor, I determined to master my own equivalent of one-winged flying in such a manner as to do the least violence to myself or to such arcane rules of New York's racial arrangements as I might encounter. Which meant that I would have to mask myself and confront its mysteries with a combination of uncertainty and daring. Thus it was that by the time I stumbled onto *Tobacco Road*, I had been nibbling steadily at the "Big Apple"—which even in those days was the Harlemite's fond name for the city—and in the process had discovered more than an ambiguous worm or two. Nevertheless, it should be remembered that worms teach small earthly truths even as serpents teach theology.

Beyond the borders of Harlem's brier patch—which seemed familiar because of my racial and cultural identification with the majority of its people and the lingering spell that had been cast nationwide by the music, dance, and literature of the so-called Harlem Renaissance—I viewed New Yorkers through the overlay of my Alabama experience. Contrasting the whites I encountered with those I had observed in the South, I weighed class against class and compared Southern styles with their Northern counterparts. I listened to diction and noted dress, and searched for attitudes in inflections, carriage, and manners. And in pursuing this aspect of my extracurricular education, I explored the landscape.

I crossed Manhattan back and forth from river to river and up, down, and around again, from Spuyten Duyvil Creek to the Battery, looking and listening and gadding about; rode streetcar and el, subway and bus; took a hint from Edna Millay and spent an evening riding back and forth on the Staten Island Ferry. For given my Oklahoma-Alabama perspective, even New York's forms of transportation were unexpected sources of education. From the elevated trains I saw my first penthouses with green trees growing atop tall buildings, caught remote glimpses of homes, businesses, and factories while moving above the teeming streets, and felt a sense of quiet tranquility despite the bang and clatter. Yes, but the subways were something else again.

In fact, the subways were utterly confusing to my Southern-bred idea of good manners, and especially the absence of a certain gallantry that men were expected to extend toward women. Subway cars appeared to be underground arenas in which Northern social equality took the form of an endless shoving match in which the usual rules of etiquette were turned upside down—or so I concluded after watching a five-o'clock foot race in a crowded car.

The contest was between a huge white woman who carried an armful of bundles, and a small Negro man who lugged a large suitcase. At the time I was standing against the track-side door, and when the train stopped at a downtown station I saw the two come charging through the opening doors like race horses leaving the starting gate at Belmont. And as they spied and dashed for the single empty seat, the outcome appeared up for grabs, but it was the woman, thanks to a bustling, more ruthless stride (and more subway know-how) who won—though but by a hip and a hair. For just as they reached the seat she swung a well-padded hip and knocked the man off stride, thus causing him to lose his balance as she turned, slipped beneath his reeling body, and plopped into the seat. It was a maneuver which produced a startling effect—at least on me.

For as she banged into the seat it caused the man to spin and land smack-dab into her lap—in which massive and heaving center of gravity he froze, stared into her face nose-tip to nose, and then performed a springlike leap to his feet as from a red-hot stove. It was but the briefest conjunction, and then, as he reached down and fumbled for his suitcase, the woman began adjusting her bundles, and with an elegant toss of her head she looked up into his face with the most ladylike and triumphant of smiles.

I had no idea of what to expect next, but to her sign of good sportswomanship the man let out with an exasperated "Hell, you can have it, I don't want it!" A response which evoked a phrase from an old forgotten ditty to which my startled mind added the unstated line—"Sleeping in the bed with your hand right on it"—and shook me with visions of the train screech-ing to a stop and a race riot beginning . . .

But not at all. For while the defeated man pushed his way to another part of the car the crowd of passengers simply looked on and laughed. The interracial aspects of the incident with its evocation of the naughty lyric left me shaken, but I was learning something of the truth of what Henry James meant by the arduousness of being an American. And that went double for a Tuskegee stu-dent who was trying to adjust to the New York underground. I never knew what to expect, because there appeared to be no agreed-upon rules of conduct. Indeed, in the subways the operating slogan appeared to be "Every Man and Woman for Themselves." Or perhaps it was "Hurray for Me and Phoo-phoo on You!" But *whatever* its operating principle, whenever I rode the subway trains something I had never seen before seemed fated to happen.

As during a trip in another crowded car when I found myself standing beside a Negro man who stood just in front of a seat that was about to be va-cated—when suddenly from on his other side a woman decided to challenge him for its possession. This time, however, it was the man who won. For in a flash the man folded his arms, dropped into the posture of a Cossack dancer, and was in the seat before the woman could make her move. Then, as she grabbed a handhold and glared down into his face, he restored something of my sense of reality by saying, "Madam, all you had to do was risk the slight possibility that I just *might* be a gentleman. Because if you had, I would have been *compelled* to step aside."

And then, opening a copy of *The Wall Street Journal,* he proceeded to read.

But for all their noise and tension, it was not the subways that most in-trigued me. For although a pleasant way to explore the city, my rides in New York buses soon aroused questions about matters that I had hoped to leave behind. And yet the very fact that I encountered little on Northern buses that was distressing allowed me to face up to a problem which had puzzled me down South: the relationship between Southern buses and racial status. In the South you occupied the back of the bus, and nowhere *but* the back, or so help you God. So being in the North and encouraged by my anonymity, I ex-perimented by riding all *over* New York buses, excluding only the driver's seat—front end, back end, right side, left side, sitting or standing as the route and flow of passengers demanded. *And,* since those were the glorious days of double-deckers, both enclosed and open, I even rode *top* side.

Thus having convinced myself that no questions of racial status would be raised by where I chose to ride, I asked myself whether a seat at the back of the bus wasn't actually more desirable than one at the front. For not only did it provide more leg room, it offered a more inclusive perspective on both the interior and exterior scenes. I found the answer obvious and quite amusing, but then, as though to raise to consciousness more serious ques-tions that I had too long ignored, the buses forced a more troubling contra-diction upon my attention. Now that I was no longer forced by law and compelled by custom to ride at the back and to surrender my seat to any white who demanded it, what was more desirable—the possibility of exercising what was routinely accepted in the North as an abstract, highly symbolic (even trivial) form of democratic freedom, or the creature comfort which was to be had by occupying a spot from which more of the passing scene could be observed? And in my own personal terms, what was more important—my own individual comfort, or the exercise of the democratic right to be squeezed and jostled by strangers? The highly questionable privilege of being touched by anonymous whites—not to mention reds, browns, blacks, and yellows—or the minor pleasure afforded by having a maximum of breathing space? Such questions were akin to that of whether you lived in a Negro neighborhood because you were forced to do so, or because you preferred living among those of your own background. Which was easy to answer, because having experienced life in mixed neighborhoods as a child, I preferred to live where people spoke my own version of the American language, and where misreadings of tone or gesture were less likely to ignite lethal conflict. Segregation laws aside, this was a matter of personal choice, for even though class and cultural differences existed among Negroes, it was far easier to deal with hostilities arising between yourself and your own people than with, say, Jeeter Lester or, more realistically, Lester Maddox. And that even though I would have found it far better to be Lestered by Jeeter than mattock-handled by Maddox, that most improbable governor of a state that I had often visited!

But my interrogation by the New York scene (for that is what it had become) was not to stop there, for once my mind got rolling on buses, it was difficult to stop and get off. So I became preoccupied with defining the difference between Northern and Southern buses. Of the two, New York buses were simpler, if only for being earthbound. They were merely a form of transportation, an inflated version of a taxicab or passenger car which one took to get from one locality to another. And as far as one's destination and motives were concerned they were neutral. But this was far from true of Southern buses. For when compared with its New York counterparts, even the most dilapidated of Southern buses seemed (from my New York perspective) to be a haunted form of transportation.

A Southern bus was a contraption contrived by laying the South's social pyramid on its side, knocking out a few strategic holes, and rendering it vehicular through the addition of engine, windows, and wheels. Thus converted, with the sharp apex of the pyramid blunted and equipped with fare box and steering gear, and its sprawling base curtailed severely and narrowly aligned (and arrayed with jim-crow signs), a ride in such a vehicle became, at least for Negroes, as unpredictable as a trip in a spaceship doomed to be caught in the time warp of history—that man-made "fourth dimension" which ever confounds our American grasp of "real," or *actual*, time or duration.

For blacks and whites alike, Southern buses were places of hallucination, but especially for Negroes. Because once inside, their journey ended even before the engine fired and the wheels got rolling. Then, as with a "painted ship upon a painted ocean," the engine chugged, the tires scuffed, and the scenery outside flashed and flickered, but they themselves remained, like Zeno's arrow, ever in the same old place. Thus the motorized mobility of the social pyramid did little to advance the Negroes' effort toward equality. Because although they were allowed to enter the section that had been—in its vertical configuration—its top, any semblance of upward mobility ended at the fare box—from whence, once their fares were deposited, they were sent, forthwith, straight to the rear, or horizontalized bottom. And along the way almost *anything* could happen, from push to shove, assaults on hats, heads, or aching corns, to unprovoked tongue-lashings from the driver or from any white passenger, drunk or sober, who took exception to their looks, attitude, or mere existence. Nor did the perils of this haunted, gauntletlike passage end at the back of the bus. For often it was so crowded that there was little breathing space, and since the segregated passengers were culturally as "Southern" as the whites, the newcomer might well encounter a few contentious Negroes who would join in the assault—if only because he appeared uneasy in his command of the life-preserving "cool" which protected not only the individual Negro but each member of the group in his defenseless, nonindividualized status. In brief, all were faceless nobodies caught up in an endless trip to nowhere—or so it seemed to me in my Northern sanctuary.

For even as the phantomized bus went lurching and fuming along its treadmill of a trajectory, the struggle within scuffled and raged in fitful retrograde. Thus, as it moved without moving, those trapped inside played out their roles like figures in dreams—with one group ever forcing the other to the backmost part, and the other ever watching and waiting as they bowed to force and clung to sanity. And indeed the time would come when such bus en-scened pantomime would erupt in a sound and fury of action that would engulf the South and change American society. And most surprising and yet most fittingly, it would begin when a single tired Negro woman refused to go on with what had now become an unbearable farce. Then would come fire and gunshot, cattle prods and attack dogs, but the enchantment would end, and at last the haunted bus would shift gears and move on to the road of reality and toward the future. . . .

But of this I had no way of knowing at the time. I only knew that Southern bus rides had the power to haunt and confuse my New York passage. Moreover, they were raising the even more troublesome question of to what extent had I failed to grasp a certain degree of freedom that had always existed in my group's state of unfreedom? Of what had I neglected to avail myself through fear or lack of interest while sitting silently behind jim-crow signs? For after all, a broad freedom of expression within restrictions could be heard in jazz and seen in sports, and that freedom was made movingly manifest in religious worship. There was an Afro-American dimension in Southern culture, and the lives of many black Southerners possessed a certain verve and self-possessed fullness—so to what extent had I overlooked similar opportunities for self-discovery while accepting a definition of possibility laid down by those who would deny me freedom?

Thus, while I enjoyed my summer, such New York-provoked questions made for a certain unease which I tried to ignore. Nevertheless, they made me aware that whatever its true shape turned out to be, Northern freedom could be grasped only by my running the risk of the unknown and by acting in the face of uncertainty. Which meant that I would have to keep moving into racially uncharted areas. Otherwise I would remain physically in Harlem and psychologically in Alabama—neither of which was acceptable. Harlem was "Harlem," a dream place of glamour and excitement—what with its music, its dance, its style. But it was all of this because it was a part of (and apart *from*) the larger city. Harlem, I came to feel, was the shining transcendence of a national negative, and it took its fullest meaning from that which it was not, and without which I would have regarded it as less interesting than, say, Kansas City, Missouri—or South Side Chicago. Harlem, whose ironic inhabitants described it a thousand times a day as being "nowhere," took much of its meaning from the larger metropolis; so I could only achieve the fullest measure of its attractions by experiencing that which it was not. Which meant, in the broadest sense, that I would have to use Harlem as a base and standard of measurement from which to pursue, in all its plenitude, that which was denied me in the South. In brief, if I were to grasp American freedom, I was compelled to continue my explorations of downtown Manhattan.

Yes, but as I say, my explorations of the city were rendered uncertain by the ongoing conflict between the past and the present as they existed within me: between the dream in my head and the murky, seek-and-find-it shiftings of the New York scene; between the confounding complexity of America's racial arrangements as they coincided and differed according to the customs, laws, and values fostered by both North and South. I still clung to the Southern Negro's conception of New York as the freest of American cities, but although now far removed from the geographical region where old-time things are defiantly not forgotten, I was learning that even here, where memories of the past were deliberately repressed, if not forgotten, the past itself continued to shape perceptions and attitudes. And it appeared that for some New Yorkers, I *myself* constituted a living symbol of that complexity of American experience which they had never known, and a disquieting reminder of their involvement in certain unsavory aspects of America's social reality that they preferred to ignore.

And yet, given my persistent questing, how could they? For I, who was an unwilling and not always conscious embodiment of that historical complexity, and a symbol of the Civil War's sacrificial bloodshed, kept showing up in areas of culture where few of my people were to be seen. Thus, in my dark singularity I often appeared to be perceived more as a symbol than as an individual, more as a threatening sign (a dark cloud no larger than a human hand, but somehow threatening) than as a disinterested seeker after culture. This made for problems because I had no way of anticipating the response to my presence.

Prior to stumbling onto *Tobacco Road*—at which I shall presently arrive—I had already encountered some of the complexity evoked by my probings. As the guest of a white female friend who reported musical events for a magazine, I had occupied a seat in the orchestra section of Carnegie Hall without inciting protest. But shortly thereafter I had been denied admission to a West Side cinema house that featured European movies. Then I had learned that while one midtown restaurant would make you welcome, in another (located in Greenwich Village, Harlem's twin symbol of Manhattan's freedom), the waiters would go through the polite motions of seating you but then fill your food with salt. And to make certain that you got the message, they would enact a rite of exorcism in which the glasses and crockery, now considered hopelessly contaminated by your touch, were enfolded in the tablecloth and smithereened in the fireplace.

Or again, upon arriving at a Central Park West apartment building to deliver a music manuscript for the Tuskegee composer William L. Dawson, you encountered a doorman with a European accent who was so rude that you were tempted to break his nose. Fortunately, you didn't, for after you refused to use the servant's elevator he rang up the tenant into whose hands alone you were instructed to make the delivery, Jacques Gordon of the Gordon String Quartet, who hurried down and invited you up to his apartment. Where, to your surprise and delight, he talked with you without condescension about his recordings, questioned you sympathetically about your musical background, and encouraged you in your ambitions to become a composer. So if you weren't always welcome to break bread in public places, an interest in the arts *could* break down social distance and allow for communication that was uninhibited by questions of race—or so it seemed.

As on a Madison Avenue bus when an enthusiastic, bright-eyed little old Jewish lady, fresh from an art exhibition with color catalogue in hand, would engage you in conversation and describe knowingly the styles and intentions of French painters of whom you'd never heard.

"Then you must go to galleries," she insisted.

"Stir yourself and go to museums," she demanded.

"This is one of the world's great centers of art, so learn about them! Why are you waiting? Enough already!" she exhorted.

And eventually, God bless her, I did.

But then, on another bus ride, a beautifully groomed and expensively dressed woman would become offended when you retrieved and attempted to return the section of a newspaper that she had dropped when preparing to depart, apparently mistaking what was intended as an act of politeness for a reprimand from a social inferior. So it appeared that in New York one had to choose the time, place, and person even when exercising one's Southern good manners.

On the other hand, it soon became clear that one could learn the subtleties of New York's racial manners only by being vulnerable and undiscriminating oneself; an attitude which the vast anonymity of the great metropolis encouraged. Here the claustrophobic provincialism which marked, say, Montgomery, Alabama, of that period, was absent, but one had to be on guard because reminders of the South could spring up from behind the most unlikely of façades.

Shopping for a work of T. S. Eliot's in a 59th Street bookstore, I struck up a conversation with a young City College student who turned out to share my literary interests, and in recounting an incident of minor embarrassment having to do with my misinterpretation of a poetic trope, I used the old cliché "And was my face red"—whereupon, between the utterance and the reality, the idea I intended to convey and my stereotype phrase, there fell the shadow of things I sought to forget.

"What do you mean by 'red,'" he said, impaling me upon the points of his smirking stare, "what you *really* mean is 'ashes of roses'!"

And suddenly I was slapped into a conscious awareness of certain details of his presence that my eyes had registered but to which, in the context of our exchange, my brain had attached no special significance. Intent upon sharing his ideas of Eliot, I had seen only that which I wished to see, but now, out of the eyes of my past I saw that our differences of background and religion were imprinted upon his face no less indelibly than mine upon my own. And in my Southern-trained ear the echo of his trace of accent became amplified, the slight kink in his hair sprang into focus, and his nose evoked superimposed images of the Holy Land and Cyrano.

I didn't like it, but there it was—I had been hit in midflight; and so, brought down to earth, I joined in his laughter. But while he laughed in bright major chords I responded darkly in minor-sevenths and flatted-fifths, and I doubted that he was attuned to the deeper source of our inharmonic harmony. For how could he know that when a child in Oklahoma, I had played with members of his far-flung tribe and thus learned in friendly games of mutual insult the hoary formulae with which to make him squirm. But why bother? Out of some obscure need a stranger had chosen to define to his own advantage that which was at best a fleeting relationship. Perhaps because I had left an opening that was irresistible. Or perhaps he saw my interest in poetry as an invasion of his special turf, which had to be repelled with a reminder of my racial status. For what right had *I* to be interested in Eliot, even though the great poet had written of himself as having been "a small boy with a nigger drawl"?

Or was he implying that I was trying verbally to pass for white? But if so, wasn't that to confuse words with reality and a metaphor with the thing or condition it named? And didn't he realize that there might be as much of irony in one of his background embracing Eliot as he seemed to find in my doing so? And how take poetry seriously if he himself would limit the range of metaphor, that indispensable linguistic device for making unities of diversities?

That chance encounter left me a bit disenchanted, but also consciously aware of certain vague assumptions which I held concerning racial relations that I'd find in the North. I had hoped that in New York there would exist generally a type of understanding which obtained in the South between certain individual whites and Negroes. This was a type of Southern honor that did little to alter the general system of inequity, but it allowed individual whites to make exceptions in exerting the usual gestures of white supremacy. Such individuals refused to use racial epithets and tried, within the limitations of the system, to treat Negroes fairly. This was a saving grace and a balm to the aches and pains of the South's endless racial contention.

Thus I had assumed that in the North there would exist a general understanding between outsiders of whatever color or background, and that all would observe a truce or convention through which they would shun insults that focused on race, religion, or physical appearance; entities that were inherited and about which all were powerless to modify or change. (At that time I was unaware that there were whites who passed themselves off as being of other backgrounds.) And yet I realized that except for those rare Southern examples, there was no firm base for my expectations. For I knew that from the days of the minstrel shows to the musicals and movies then current, many non-Negro outsiders had reaped fame and fortune by assuming the stereotyped mask of blackness. I knew also that our forms of popular culture, from movies to comic strips, were a source of a national mythology in which Negroes were the chief scapegoats, and that the function of that mythology was to allow whites a more secure place (if only symbolically) in American society. Only years later would I learn that during periods of intense social unrest, even sensitive intellectuals who had themselves been victims of discrimination would find it irresistible to use their well-deserved elevation to the upper levels of their professions as platforms from which, in the name of the most abstract—and fashionable—of philosophical ideas, to reduce Negroes to stereotypes that were no less reductive and demeaning than those employed by the most ignorant and bigoted of white Southerners. Fortunately, that knowledge was still in the future, and so, doing unto another as I would have had him do unto me, I dismissed my chance acquaintance as an insecure individual, and not the representative of a group or general attitude. But he did serve as a warning that if I wished to communicate with New Yorkers, I must watch my metaphors, for here one man's cliché was another man's facile opportunity for victimage.

So I was learning that exploring New York was a journey without a map, Baedeker or Henry James, and that how one was received by the natives depended more upon how one presented oneself than upon any ironclad rule of exclusion. Here the portals to many places of interest were guarded by hired help, and if you approached with uncertain mien, you were likely to be turned away by anyone from doormen to waiters to ticket agents. However, if you acted as though you were in fact a New Yorker exercising a routine freedom, chances were that you'd be accepted. Which is to say that in many instances I found that my air and attitude could offset the inescapable fact of my color. For it seemed that in the hustle and bustle of the most theatrical of American cities, one was accepted on the basis of what one *appeared* to be. This involved risks to one's self-esteem, not to mention the discipline demanded by a constant state of wariness.

But W. B. Yeats had reminded us that "there is a relation between personal discipline and the theatrical sense [and that] if we cannot imagine ourselves as different from what we are and assume the second self, we cannot impose a discipline upon ourselves, though we may accept one from others." And he advised us that "active virtue, as distinct from the passive acceptance of a current code, is the wearing of a mask."

At the time I was unaware of Yeats's observation, but if I had been so fortunate, I would have applied it to my own situation by changing his "we" to "an Afro-American," his "what we are" to "what many whites assume an American Negro to be," and his "current code" to "prevailing racial attitudes." But with his contention that the assertion of a second self is to assume a mask, and that to do so is "the condition of an arduous full life," I would have agreed wholeheartedly. For in effect, I was attempting to act out a self-elected role and to improvise into being a "second self" that I strongly felt but vaguely visualized. And although I was finding life far from full, I was certainly finding it arduous.

For in Yeats's sense, "masking" is more than the adoption of a disguise. Rather, it is a playing upon possibility, a strategy through which the individual projects a self-elected identity and makes of himself a "work of art." And in my case it was a means of discovering the dimensions and cost of Northern freedom. In his critical biography *Yeats: The Man & the Masks*, Richard Ellman notes that the great Irish poet was writing of himself, but his theory applies, nevertheless, to the problematic nature of American identity. For while all human societies are "dramatic"—at least to the extent that, as Kenneth Burke points out, the members of all societies "enact roles . . . change roles . . . participate . . . [and] develop modes of social appeal"—the semi-open structure of American society, with its many opportunities for individual self-transformation, intensifies the dramatic element by increasing the possibilities for both cooperation and conflict. It is a swiftly changing society in which traditional values are ever under attack, even as they are exploited by individuals and group alike. And with its upward—yes, and *downward*—mobility and its great geographical space, masking (which includes speech, and costume as well as pose and posture) serves the individual as a means for projecting that aspect of his social self which seems useful in a given situation.

Such a state of affairs encourages hope and confidence in those who are not assigned and restricted to predesignated roles in the hierarchal drama of

RALPH ELLISON

American society. Melville has great fun with the comic aspects of this situation in *The Confidence Man.* To an extent, and for an endless variety of motives—benign or malignant, competitive or cooperative, creative and/or destructive—the "American" is a self-confident man or woman who is engaged in projecting a second self and dealing with the second selves of others. The American creed of democratic equality encourages the belief in a second chance that is to be achieved by being born again—and not simply in the afterlife, but here and now, on earth. Change your name and increase your chances. Create by an act of immaculate self-conception an autobiography like that which transformed James Gatz into "Jay Gatsby." Alter the shape of your nose, tint of skin, or texture of hair. Change your sexual identity by dress or by surgery. "Get thee to boutique and barbershop and *Unisex* thyself," the ads exhort us—for anything is possible in pursuit of the second self. It sounds fantastic, but the second self's hope for a second chance has now been extended even beyond the limits of physical death, thanks to the ability of medical science to transplant hearts, lungs, and kidneys. Are you dissatisfied with your inherited self? Your social status? Then have a change of heart and associate with those of a different kidney!

> College boy, thy courage muster,
> Shave off that Fuzzy
> Cookie duster—
> Use Burma Shave!

So, to enjoy the wonders of New York, I assumed a mask which I conceived as that of a "New Yorker," and decided to leave it to those whites who might object to seek out the questioning Tuskegeian who was hidden behind the mask. But a famous poet had invited me to see *Tobacco Road,* and suddenly, there in the darkness of a Broadway theater, I was snatched back to rural Alabama, and before I realized what was happening, I had blown my cover.

Nor was it that the likes of Jeeter Lester and his family were new to me. As a Tuskegee student I had often seen them in Macon County, Alabama; but in that setting their capacity for racial violence would have been far more overwhelming than their comical wrong-headedness. Indeed, in look, gesture, and deed they had crowded me so continuously that I had been tempted to armor myself against their threat by denying them *their* humanity as they sought to deny me mine. And so in my mind I assigned them to a limbo beneath the threshold of basic humanity.

Which was one of the Southern Negroes' strategies for dealing with poor whites, and an attitude given expression in the child's jingle:

> My name is Ran,
> I work in the sand, but
> I'd rather be a *nigger*
> Than a poor white man . . .

152

But while such boasting brags—and there were others (*These white folks think they so fine / But their raggedy drawers / Stink just like mine* is another)—provided a release of steam, they were not only childish but ultimately frustrating. For if such sentiments were addressed directly, their intended targets could prove dangerous. Thus the necessity for keeping one's negative opinions of whites within one's own group became a life-preserving discipline. One countered racial provocation by cloaking one's feelings in that psychologically inadequate equivalent of a plaster cast—or bullet-proof vest—known as "cool." I had read Hemingway's definition, but for Negroes, "grace under pressure" was far less a gauge of courage than of good common sense. The provocative words of whites were intended to goad one *beyond* words and into the area of physical violence. But while sticks and stones broke bones, mere words could be dismissed by considering their source and keeping a cool eye on the odds arrayed against one. So when racial epithets flew, we reminded ourselves that our mission was not that of proving our courage to any mouthy white who sought to provoke us, but to stay alive and pursue our education. Coolness helped to keep our values warm, and racial hostility stoked our fires of inspiration. But even for students protected by a famous campus, this was an arduous discipline, and one which obviated any superstitious overevaluation of whiteness. Nevertheless, I tried, as I say, to avoid the class of whites from which Erskine Caldwell drew the characters of *Tobacco Road*.

For during the summer of 1933, while hoboing to Tuskegee, I had been hustled off a freight train by railroad detectives in the rail yards of Decatur, Alabama. This was at a time when the town and the surrounding countrysides were undergoing a siege of lynch-fever stirred up by the famous trial in which the Scottsboro boys were charged with the rape of two white girls on a freight train. I escaped unharmed, but the incident returned to mind whenever I went traveling. Therefore, I gave Jeeter Lester types a wide berth but found it impossible to avoid them entirely—because many were law-enforcement officers who served on the highway patrols with a violent zeal like that which Negro slave narratives ascribed to the "paterollers" who had guarded the roads during slavery. (As I say, Southern buses were haunted, and so, in a sense, were Southern roads and highways.) And that was especially true of a section of the route between Tuskegee and Columbus, Georgia. I traveled it frequently, both as a member of a jazz orchestra and when on pleasure trips to Columbus. And it was on such travels that I was apt to relive my Decatur experience.

By a fateful circumstance of geography the forty-mile route passed through Phenix City, Alabama, then a brawling speed-trap of a town through which it was impossible to drive either slow enough or fast enough to satisfy the demands of its traffic policemen. No one, black or white, escaped their scrutiny, but since Tuskegee students were regarded as on their way to becoming "uppity educated nigras," we were especially vulnerable

The police lay in wait for us, clocked our speed by a standard known only to themselves, and used any excuse to delay and harass us. Usually they limited themselves to fines and verbal abuse, but I was told that the year before I arrived the police had committed an act that had caused great indignation on campus and become the inspiration of much bull-session yarn-spinning.

On that occasion, I was told, two Phenix City policemen had stopped a carload of Tuskegee students and learned during the course of routine questioning that one of the group, a very black-skinned young man, bore the surname of "Whyte"—and then, as one of my informants said, "It was shame on him!"

For when Whyte uttered his name the cops stared, exchanged looks of mock disbelief, and became red-faced with manic inspiration.

"Damn, boy," one of them said, "y'all been drinking?"

"No, sir," Whyte said.

"Well now, I don't know about that," the cop said, "'cause you sho sound drunk to *me*."

"No, sir," Whyte said. "Because I don't drink."

"You sho?"

"Yes, sir!"

So then the cop turns to his buddy and says, "What you think, Lonzo? Is he drunk, or am I mistaken?"

"Well now, if you want my opinion," the other cop said, "he's either drunk or something very serious is wrong with him. Yes, suh, something *seerious* is wrong with this boy."

"And why is that, Lonzo," the first cop said.

"'Cause it stands to reason that there's no way in the *world* for a nigra as black as that to pretend that his name is 'White.' Not unless he's blind-staggers drunk or else plum out of his nappy-headed cotton-pickin' mind!"

"That's *my* exact opinion," the first cop said. "But anyway, lets us give 'im another chance. So now once agin, boy—what is your last name?"

"Officer, it's Whyte," Whyte said. "That's the truth and I'll swear to it."

So that's when the other cop, ol' Lonzo, *he* takes over. He frowns at Whyte and shakes his head like he's dealing with a *very* sad case. And naturally, he's a big potbellied mother who chews Brown Mule tobacco.

"Damn, boy," he says (in what proved to be a long-range prediction of then unimaginable things to come), "if we let you git away with a damn lie like that, next thing we know that ol' Ramblin' Wreck over at Georgia Tech'll have a goddamn nigra *engineer*! Now, you think about that and let's have that name agin!"

"But, Officer," Whyte said, "Whyte's the only last name I have."

And then, gentlemen, my informant, a sergeant in the ROTC and student of veterinary medicine, said, "the battle was *on!*" He then described how with simulated indignation the policemen forced Whyte to pronounce his name again and again while insisting that they simply couldn't believe that such a gross misnaming was possible—especially in the South—and gave a detailed account of the policemen's reactions.

"Man," he said, "they went after Whyte like he had insulted their mammas! And when he still wouldn't deny his name, they came down on him like he was responsible for all the fuckup [meaning the genetic untidiness and confusion of black and white nomenclature] of Southern history!"

"So, then, man," another informant broke in, "those crackers got so damn disgusted with ol' Whyte that every time he said his name, the ignorant bastards tried to dot where they thought an 'i' should have been by pounding his head with their blackjacks. They did everything but shoot that cat!"

"That's right, cousin," someone else said, "they made him whisper his name and they made him shout it. They made him write it down on a pad and then they made him spell it out—and I mean out *loud!* And when he spelled it with a 'y' instead of an 'i' they swore he was lying and trying to be smart, and really went up side his head!"

"Yeah, man," my original informant said, "and when Whyte still wouldn't change his statement, they made him give the names of his mother and father, his granddaddys and grandmammas on both sides and their origins in slavery, present whereabouts, police records, and occupations—"

"That's right, cousin, and since ol' Whyte came from a very, *very* large family and the cops were putting all that pressure on him, the poor cat sounded like a country preacher scatting out the 'begats' from the Book of Genesis—Damn!"

And then it was back to Whyte's offensive surname, and the head-whipping sounded, in the words of another informant—a music major and notorious prevaricator—"like somebody beating out the *Anvil Chorus* on a coconut!"

"Yeah, cousin, but what really made the bastards mad was that ol' Whyte wouldn't let some crackers beat him out of his name!"

"Oh, yes, and you have to give it to him. That Whyte was a damn good man!"

Finally, tired of the hazing and defeated in their effort to make Whyte deny his heritage, the cops knocked him senseless and ordered his friends to place him in the car and get out of town. . . .

Although obviously exaggerated in the telling, it was a nasty incident. However, my point is not its violence, but the contradiction between its ineffectiveness as intimidation while serving as a theme for a tall-tale improvisation. Thus was violence transcended with cruel but homeopathic laughter, and racial cruelty transformed by a traditional form of folk art. It did nothing to change the Phenix City police, and probably wouldn't have even if they heard the recitation. They continued to make life so uncertain that each time we reached Columbus and returned safely to Tuskegee, it was as though we'd passed through fire and emerged, like the mythical phoenix bird (after which, presumably, the town was named), from the flames. Still we continued to risk the danger, for such was our eagerness for the social life of Columbus—the pleasure of parties, dances, and picnics in the company of pretty girls—that we continued to run the gauntlet.

But it didn't cancel out the unpleasantness or humiliation. Thus, back on campus we were compelled to buffer the pain and negate the humiliation by making grotesque comedy out of the extremes to which whites would go to keep us in what they considered to be our "place." Once safe at Tuskegee, we'd become fairly hysterical as we recounted our adventures and laughed as much at ourselves as at the cops. We mocked their modes of speech and styles of intimidation, and teased one another as we parodied our various modes of feigning fear when telling them who we were and where we were headed. It was a wild, he-man, schoolboy silliness but the only way we knew for dealing with the inescapable conjunction of laughter and pain. My problem was that I couldn't completely dismiss such experiences with laughter. I brooded and tried to make sense of it beyond that provided by our ancestral wisdom. That a head with a few knots on it was preferable to a heart with bullets through it was obviously true. And if the philosopher's observation that absolute power corrupts absolutely was also true, then an absolute power based on mere whiteness made for a deification of madness. Depending on the circumstance, whiteness might well be a sign of evil, of a "motiveless malignancy" which was to be avoided as strange dogs in rabid weather.

But you were surrounded by whiteness, and it was far from secure in its power. It thrived on violence and sought endlessly for victims, and in its hunger to enforce racial discrimination, it was most indiscriminating as to its victims. It didn't care whether its victims were guilty or innocent, for guilt lay not in individual acts of wrong-doing but in non-whiteness, in Negroness. Whiteness was a form of manifest destiny which designated Negroes as its territory and challenge. Whiteness struck at signs, at coloration, hair texture, and speech idiom, and thus denied you individuality. How then avoid it, when history and geography brought it ever in juxtaposition with blackness? How escape it when it asserted itself in law, in the layout of towns, the inflections of voices, the nuances of manners, the quality of mercy, justice, and charity? When it raged at interracial sex, but then violated its own values in the manner of Senator Bilbo (the name means "shackle"), who was said to find sexual satisfaction only with Negro prostitutes? How escape it when it violated its own most sacred principles, both in spirit and in law, while converting the principles of democracy by which we sought to live into their opposites?

Considered soberly and without the consolation of laughter, it was mad, surreal, and further complicated by the fact that not all whites abhorred Negroes. The evil expressed itself most virulently in the mass and appeared to be regional, a condition of place, of climate, since most whites who supported the school were Northerners who appeared for a few days in spring and then departed. And since not even all white Southerners were hostile, you had ever to make fine distinctions between individuals just as you had to distinguish between the scenes and circumstances in which you encountered them. Your safety demanded a careful attention as to detail and mood of social scene, because you had to avoid even friendly whites when they were in the company of their fellows. Because it was in crowds that the hate, fear, and blood-madness took over. And when it did it could transform otherwise friendly whites into mindless members of mobs. Most of all, you must avoid them when women of their group were present. For when a Negro male came into view, the homeliest white woman became a goddess, a cult figure deified in the mystique of whiteness, a being from whom a shout or cry or expression of hand or eye could unleash a rage for human sacrifice. And when the ignorant, torch-bearing armies assembled by night, black men burned in the fire of white men's passions.

If all of this seems long ago and far away, it is worth remembering that the past, as William Faulkner warned, is never past. Nor are its social and political consequences guaranteed to be limited to a single geographical area. The past emerges no less in the themes and techniques of art than in the contentions of politics, and since art (and especially the art of the Depression period) is apt to be influenced by politics, it is necessary at this point to take a backward glance at my Tuskegee student's perception, admittedly immature and subjective, of Southern society as it influenced my reaction to *Tobacco Road.*

In the South of that day the bottom rung of the social ladder was reserved for that class of whites who were looked down upon as "poor white trash," and the area immediately beneath them and below the threshold of upward social mobility was assigned to Negroes, whether educated or ignorant, prosperous or poor. But although they were barely below the poor whites in economic status (and were sometimes better off), it was the Negroes who were designated the South's untouchable caste. As such they were perceived as barely controllable creatures of untamed instincts and a group against whom all whites were obligated to join in the effort required for keeping them within their assigned place. This mindless but widely held perception was given doctrinal credibility through oppressive laws and an endless rhetorical reiteration of anti-Negro stereotypes. Negroes were seen as ignorant, cowardly, thieving, lying, hypocritical and superstitious in their religious beliefs and practices, morally loose, drunken, filthy of personal habit, sexually animalistic, rude, crude, and disgusting in their public conduct, and aesthetically just plain unpleasant. And if a few were not, it was due to the presence of "white" blood, a violation of the Southern racial code which rendered mixed-bloods especially dangerous and repugnant.

In brief, Negroes were considered guilty of all the seven deadly sins except the sin of pride, and were seen as a sometimes comic but nevertheless threatening negative to the whites' idealized image of themselves. Most Negroes were characterized—in the jargon of sociology—by a "high visibility" of pigmentation which made the group easily distinguishable from other citizens and therefore easy to keep in line and politically powerless. That powerlessness was justified and reinforced by the stereotypes, which denied blacks individuality and allowed any Negro to be interchangeable with any other. Thus, as far as many whites were concerned, not only were blacks faceless, but that facelessness made the idea of mistaken identity meaningless, and the democratic assumption that Negro citizens should share the individual's recognized responsibility for the welfare of society was regarded as subversive.

In this denial of personality (sponsored by both law and custom) anti-Negro stereotypes served as an efficient and easily manipulated instrument of governance. Moreover, they prepared Negroes for the role of sacrificial scapegoat in the ritual drama of Southern society, and helped bind the poor whites to the middle and upper classes with whom they shared ethnic identity. Being uncomfortably close to the Negroes in economic status, the poor whites clung to the stereotypes as to a life raft in turbulent waters, and politicians were able to use their fear and antipathy toward blacks as a sure-fire source of power. Because not only were the stability of social order and the health of business seen as depending upon white dominance, but the sanctity of the *moral* order as well. For whether denied or admitted, in this area religion was in the service of politics.

Thus, by pitting the interests of the poor whites against those of the Negroes, Southern congressmen countered the South's Civil War defeat by using its carefully nurtured racial conflict as a means for amassing great political power in Washington. Being representatives of what were, in effect, one-party states, enabled them to advance to the chairmanship of powerful governmental committees, and through the political horse-trading which keeps the national government functioning, that power was used to foil the progress of Negroes in areas far from the geopolitical center of white supremacy. Here, however, it should be noted that Negroes owe much of their progress since the Second World War to presidents who were of Southern background and heritage. People change, but as Faulkner has pointed out, "was" is never "was," it is "now," and in the South a concern with preserving the "wasness" of slavocracy was an obsession which found facile expression in word and in deed. Their memories of the War Between the States, of Reconstruction, and the difficult times that followed the Hayes-Tilden Compromise had long been mythologized both as a means for keeping Negroes powerless and for ensuring the loyalty of poor whites in keeping them so. Thus it is ironic that even though the condition of blacks became a national standard by which many whites, both North and South, measured their social advancement, Negroes themselves remained at the bottom of society and the most anti-Negro of whites remained with them. It was Booker T. Washington who had warned that it is impossible to keep another man in a ditch without remaining with him, but unfortunately, that advice came from a powerful Southern leader who was also an ex-slave.

More and more, through depression and war, America lived up to its claim of being the land of opportunity whose rewards were available to the individual through the assertion of a second self; but for many poor and un-ambitious Southern whites the challenge of such an assertion was far less inviting than clinging to the conviction that they by the mere fact of race, color, and tradition alone were superior to the black masses below them. And yet, in their own way, they were proud idealists to whom the South's racial arrangement was sacred beyond most benefits made possible by social change. Therefore, they continued to wrestle with the stereotype of Negro in-feriority much as Brer Rabbit kept clinging to Tar Baby's stickiness. And they were so eager to maintain their grip on the status quo and to ignore its costs and contradictions that they willingly used anything, including physical vio-lence, to do so. For in rationalizing their condition, they required victims, real or symbolic, and in the daily rituals which gave support to their cherished myth of white supremacy, anti-Negro stereotypes and epithets served as symbolic substitutes for that primitive blood-rite of human sacrifice to which they resorted in times of racial tension—but which, for a complexity of rea-sons, political, economic, and humane, were rejected by their more respon-sible leaders. So it was fortunate, both for Afro-Americans and for the nation as a whole, that the Southern rituals of race were usually confined to the realm of the symbolic. Anti-Negro stereotypes were the currency through which the myth of white supremacy was kept alive, while the awe-inspiring enactment of the myth took the form of a rite in which a human victim was sacrificed. In then became a ritual drama that was usually enacted in a prese-lected scene (such as a clearing in the woods or in the courthouse square) in an atmosphere of high excitement and led by a masked celebrant dressed in a garish costume who manipulated the numinous objects (lynch ropes, the American flag, shotgun, gasoline, and whiskey jugs) associated with the rite as he inspired and instructed the actors in their gory task. This was the anthropological meaning of lynching, a blood-rite that ended in the death of a scapegoat whose obliteration was seen as necessary to the restoration of social order. Thus it served to affirm white goals and was enacted to ter-rorize Negroes.

Normally, the individual dies his own death, but because lynch mobs are driven by a passionate need to destroy the distinction between the actual and the symbolic, its victim is forced to undergo death for all his group. Nor is he sacrificed to ensure its fertility or save its soul, but to fill its members with an unreasoning fear of whiteness.

For the lynch mob, blackness is a sign of satanic evil given human form. It is the dark consubstantial shadow which symbolizes all that its opponents re-ject in social change and in democracy. And thus it does not matter if its sac-rificial victim be guilty or innocent, because the lynch mob's object is to pro-pitiate its insatiable god of whiteness, that myth-figure worshipped as the true source of all things bright and beautiful, by destroying the human attrib-utes of its god's antagonist which they perceive as the power of blackness. In action, racial discrimination is as nondiscriminating as a car bomb detonated in a crowded public square—because both car bomb and lynch rope are savagely efficient ways of destroying distinctions between the members of a hated group while rendering quite meaningless any moral questioning that might arise regarding the method used. For the ultimate goal of lynchers is that of achieving ritual purification through destroying the lynchers' identification with the basic *humanity* of their victims. Hence their deafness to cries of pain, their stoniness before the sight and stench of burning flesh, their exhilarated and grotesque self-righteousness. And hence our horror at the idea of supposedly civilized men destroying—and in the name of their ideal conception of the human—an aspect of their own humanity. Yes, but for the group thus victimized, such sacrifices are the source of emotions that move far beyond the tragic conception of pity and terror and down into the abysmal levels of conflict and folly from which arise our famous American humor. Brother, the blackness of *Afro-American* "black humor" is not black, it is tragically human and finds its source and object in the notion of "whiteness". . .

But let me not overstate beyond the point necessary for conveying an idea of my state of mind prior to my unanticipated stumble onto *Tobacco Road*. The threat, real or imagined, of being the subject of such victimization was offset by that hopeful attitude that is typical of youth and necessary for dealing with life everywhere. So while racial danger was always with me, I lived with it as with threats of natural disaster or acts of God. And just as Henry James felt it prudent to warn Americans against a "superstitious evaluation of Europe," Negro folklore with its array of survival strategies warned me against an overevaluation of white pretensions. And despite their dominance and low opinion of Negro intelligence, whites suspected the presence of profound reservations even when Negroes were far less assertive than they are today. This made for a constant struggle over the nature of reality, in which each group probed and sparred as they tried to determine the other's true motives and opinions. A poignant instance of such struggle appears in Faulkner's *The Sound and the Fury* when Quentin Compson gives Deacon, a raffish Negro mythomaniac who does odd jobs around Harvard, an important letter to be delivered to Quentin's roommate the following afternoon. But when Deacon notes that the envelope is sealed, he suspects that he is being sent on a fool's errand such as whites delighted in sending Negroes down South. This causes him to drop his Northern mask for that of an old inarticulate "darkey," a pose which reminds Quentin of a Negro retainer whom he'd known as a child. Deacon then asks if a joke is being played on him; which Quentin denies. But then, appealing for that flattering reassurance that Southern whites were accustomed to exacting from Negroes, he asks Deacon if any Southerner had ever played a joke on him. Deacon's reply, as was often true of such exchanges, is ambiguous.

"You're right," he says, "they're fine folks. But you can't live with them."

Then, looking through Deacon into his own hopeless despair, Quentin asks, "Did you ever try?"

But the answer is not forthcoming. For in a flash the transplanted black

Southerner had retired behind one of the many trickster's masks which his second self had assumed upon coming north and agrees briskly to deliver the letter. Ironically, however, there *is* a fool's errand involved, but it isn't Deacon's. For the letter conveys Quentin's intention to drown himself. Thus Deacon, who has rejected the role assigned him by his native South, ends up playing not the traditional black fool but, all unknowingly, the death-messenger for a pathetic Southern aristocrat who is driven to self-destruction by the same prideful confusion of values from which, as Southerners, both suffered. Having tried to live in the South, both had come north dragging the past behind them; but while Deacon used his Southern craftiness to play upon life's possibilities, the past-haunted Quentin destroyed himself because he was unable to reconcile the mythical South he loved with that which had sent Deacon packing.

As Deacon said, many white Southerners were "fine folks," and that was the problem. Whites both hostile and friendly were part of my college scene, and thus a good part of my extracurricular education consisted in learning to live with them while retaining my self-esteem. Negro folklore taught the preservation of one's humanity by masking one's motives and emotions, just as it prepared one to be unsurprised at anything that whites might do, because a concern with race could negate all human bonds, including those of shared blood and experience.

So I tried to observe such ancestral wisdom as I awaited the day when I could leave the South. The catch here was that even the roads that led *away* from the South were also haunted; a circumstance which I should have learned, but did not, from numerous lyrics that were sung to the blues. And so, full of great expectations, I went north. And where uneducated Deacon assumed the mask of a former Harvard divinity student, I took on that of a sophisticated New Yorker.

In *Tobacco Road*, Erskine Caldwell appears to have taken a carefully screened assemblage of anti-Negro stereotypes and turned them against the very class in which they found their most fervent proponents—and what he did with them was most outrageous. Indeed, he turned things around in such a manner that it was as though Whyte, the Tuskegee victim of the Phenix City hazing, had read Mark Twain, George Washington Harris, Rabelais, Groucho Marx, and Voltaire, learned to write, and then, passing for "white" in order to achieve a more intimate knowledge of his characters, had proceeded to embody the most outrageous stereotypes in the Jeeter Lester family, in-laws, and friends. (Caldwell, I hasten to add, is a Georgia-born Anglo-Saxon.)

Nevertheless, Caldwell presents Jeeter Lester as an ignorant, impoverished, Depression-ruined poor white who urges Ellie May, his sixteen-year-old younger daughter, to seduce her older sister's husband so that he, Lester, may steal the equally impoverished young man's only food, a bag of turnips. The father of other mature children who now live in the city, he is a slothful farmer whose run-down farm is in such neglect that even the rats have abandoned the corncrib, and a criminally negligent son whose aged mother must forage for food in the woods, where, by the play's end, she dies alone and neglected. And yet Caldwell keeps Jeeter within the range of the human by having him be so utterly himself. He makes him a poor-white version of the "great sinner" on the order of Dostoevsky's elder Karamazov, and with a similar vitality and willfulness. He is a lecher who has fathered children by his neighbor's wife, and has incestuous inclinations toward one of his married daughters. But it is his stubborn refusal to bow before the economic and ecological developments that have rendered his type of farming no longer possible which gives the play its movement. Jeeter is a symbol of human willfulness reduced to its illogical essence.

Ada, Mrs. Lester, is an ineffectual wife and mother who has no control over either her husband or their children. Half starved and worn-out from childbearing, she exerts what physical and moral strength she has in trying to save Pearl, her pride and joy through a casual affair with a stranger, from the decay of Tobacco Road.

Pearl, whom Jeeter married off at the age of twelve, is the wife of Lov, a struggling young workman with whom she refuses either to sleep or talk—a situation utterly baffling for Lov, and annoying to Jeeter because it has become a subject for local Negro laughter.

Ellie May, the younger daughter, is harelipped, and so helplessly frustrated sexually that Jeeter tries to persuade Lov to exchange her for Pearl and take her away from Tobacco Road before, as he says, the Negroes get her. But if in Ellie May the Lester sex drive has gotten quite out of hand, in her brother Dude it is unawakened.

Dude, the adolescent son (who opens the play with a mindless bouncing of a ball against the house), is sadistic, disdainful of parental authority, and utterly disrespectful of life and death. And if Jeeter is a comic embodiment of selfish wrong-headedness, Dude (who takes more than his share of Jeeter's stolen turnips by physical force), is the embodiment of his father's character gone to violence. He is also the agent of his mother's death.

In brief, the Lester family is as seedy as the house in which they live. They have plunged through the fragile floor of civilized humanity, and even the religion which had once given a semblance of order to their lives had become as superstitious as that which the stereotypes attribute to Negroes.

That superstition is exploited by Sister Bessie Rice, a dowdy itinerant preacher of no known denomination who sees sin in even the most innocent of human actions and uses prayer as a magical incantation through which to manipulate her listener's residue of religious belief to her own advantage. She is a confidence woman who promises for small contributions to cure all ills through the magic of prayer.

Homely and gregarious in manner, Sister Bessie is a widow in search of a mate, both as husband and as a preaching partner with whom she can be more efficient in spreading her version of religion. Her unlikely choice toward this goal is teen-age Dude. But while Jeeter is quite agreeable to such a union of April and December, Dude is uninterested. Until, that is, Sister Bessie promises to use the money left by her deceased husband to purchase a new automobile. This does the trick. With Dude in tow, Sister Bessie buys first a marriage license and then the car; whereupon they speed back to the Lester farm. There Sister Bessie loses no time in performing her own marriage ceremony. And this accomplished, she rushes Dude to their wedding chamber—outside of which Jeeter stands on a chair in an effort to watch her initiate Dude into the sexual mysteries of wedlock.

As it turns out, however, Dude is less interested in connubial pleasure than in driving the new car—which, blowing its horn idiotically and speeding, he does, so recklessly that he runs into a loaded wagon and wrecks the car. Later he backs the car over his mother and kills her. Thus, not even the wedding of modern technology with sex and religion can restore Tobacco Road to a state of fertility. The sex instinct remained out of control, religious values corrupted, the laws guiding the relations between parents and children destroyed, and the words and rituals that once imposed religious and political ideals upon human conduct were used to justify greed, incest, sloth, and theft. In brief, the economic Depression, abetted by Jeeter's sloth and wrong-headedness, has deprived the family not only of its livelihood but denuded them of civilized humanity. Ultimately it was Ada's efforts to save Pearl from further humiliation and Jeeter's dogged will to survive the imbalance of nature and the bank's foreclosure on his farm that redeemed the family from a total fall into bestiality.

And yet, Caldwell's handling of such material does not produce a response of disgust and hopelessness in the audience. Instead it is swept by a wave of cathartic laughter which leaves it optimistic. Perhaps, as it has been noted in Cleanth Brooks, R. W. B. Lewis, and Robert Penn Warren's *American Literature: The Makers and the Making,* the Lesters' "lack of any burden of guilt and their ability to dispense with most of the contrivances of civilization gave a sense of release to a great many people."

I would add that during the Depression days of the play's great success, there was such great need for relief, both economic and spiritual, that the grotesque nature of its comedy was fully justified. Perhaps its viewers laughed, and then in retrospect grasped the interplay of social and economic forces upon which the play is focused, and trembled. Which, given Caldwell's anger over the despoilation of the South, must have been his intention.

According to Kenneth Burke, "Comedy should enable us to be observers of ourselves while acting. Its ultimate end would not be passiveness but maximum consciousness. [It should allow] one to 'transcend' himself by noting his own foibles . . . [and should] provide a rationale for locating the irrational and the non-rational."

To follow the action of a comedy is to react through its actors, and to identify either with them or with the values with which they struggle. For as David Daziel Duncan has written, "the difference between symbolic and social drama is the difference between imaginary and real obstacles, but to produce effects on audiences, symbolic drama must reflect the real obstacles of social drama. Conflict must be resolved in the symbolic realm by the expression of attitudes which make conformity possible. All such expression, like prayer, is an exhortation to the self and to others. It is a preparation for social action, an investment of the self with confidence and strength." Duncan is speaking of the drama of everyday life in which all successful stage plays are rooted, and when we consider the popularity of *Tobacco Road*, it suggests that during the Great Depression it was most successful in providing its viewers with a rationale for locating the irrational both in themselves and in their society.

The greater the stress within society the stronger the comic antidote required. And in this instance the stress imposed by the extreme dislocations of American society was so strong and chaotic that it called for a comedy of the grotesque. Jeeter Lester, the poor white as fool, was made to act the clown in order to save his audience's sanity. Here it is instructive to use the Southern Negroes' handling of stress for comparison. For since such stress was an enforced norm of their lives, Negroes struggled with the role assigned them for the same ends that Shakespeare juxtaposed the Fool with Lear—which was to maintain a measure of common sense before the extreme assertions of Lear's kingly pride. In the Lear-like drama of white supremacy Negroes were designated both clowns and fools, but they "fooled" by way of maintaining their own sense of rational order, no matter how they were perceived by whites. For it was far better to be looked down upon as "niggers" than to lose themselves in a world rendered surreal through an excess of racial pride. Their challenge was to endure while imposing their claims upon America's conscience and consciousness, just as they had imposed their style upon its culture. Forced to be wary observers, they recognized that American life is of a whole, and that what happens to blacks will accrue eventually, one way or another, to the nation as a whole. This is their dark-visioned version of the broader "American Joke." Like Faulkner, Caldwell appears to have recognized its existence, for in responding to the imbalance which was shaking American social hierarchy from its apex to its base, he placed the yokelike anti-Negro stereotypes upon the necks of whites, and thus his audience reacted with a shock of recognition. Caldwell was answering a deeply felt need, and it is interesting that it was during the period of *Tobacco Road*'s record-breaking run that the Museum of Modern Art's presentation of its famous exhibit of Dadaist art was widely successful.

For me the shock of Caldwell's art began when Ellie May and Lov were swept up by a forbidden sexual attraction so strong that, uttering sounds of animal passion, they went floundering and skittering back-to-back across the stage in the startling action which father Jeeter, that randy Adam in an Eden gone to weed, named "horsing." For when the two went into their bizarre choreography of sexual "frustrabation" I was reduced to such helpless laughter that I distracted the entire balcony and embarrassed both myself and my host. It was a terrible moment, for before I could regain control, more attention was being directed toward me than at the action unfolding on the stage.

Then it was as though I had been stripped naked, kicked out of a low-flying plane onto an Alabama road, and ordered to laugh for my life. I laughed and laughed, bending and straightening in a virtual uncontrollable cloud-and-dam-burst of laughter, a self-immolation of laughter over which I had no control. And yet I was hypersensitive to what was happening around me, a fact which left me all the more embarrassed.

Seeing an expression of shocked disbelief on the face of my host, I imagined him saying, "Damn, if I'd known this would be his reaction I would have picked a theater with laughing-barrels!"

And suddenly, in addition to my soul-wracking agony of embarrassment, I was being devastated by an old in-group joke which played upon the themes of racial conflict, social freedom, and the blackness of Negro laughter; a joke whose setting was some small Southern town in which Negro freedom of expression was so restricted that its public square was marked by a series of huge whitewashed barrels labeled FOR COLORED, and into which any Negro who felt a laugh coming on was forced—*pro bono publico*—to thrust his boisterous head.

The joke was used by Tuskegee students, who considered themselves more sophisticated to kid freshmen from small Southern towns, but although I had heard it many times, it now flashed in my mind with implications that had hitherto escaped me. And as it played a counterpoint between my agony of laughter and the action taking place on the stage set of *Tobacco Road* below, it was as though Erskine Caldwell had snared me as an offstage instrument for extending the range of his outrageous plotting—and I mean with a cacophony of minor thirds and flatted-fifths voiced fortissimo by braying gut-bucket brasses!

For now, in my hypersubjective state, viewers around me in the balcony were no longer following the action unfolding on the stage; they were getting to their feet to gawk at me. It was as though I had plunged into a nightmare in which my personality was split in twain, with the lucid side looking on in wonder while the manic side convulsed my body as though a drunken accordionist was using it to belt out the "Beer Barrel Polka." And while I wheezed and choked with laughter, my disgusted lucid self dramatized its cool detachment by noting that things were getting so out of control that Northern white folk in balcony and loge were now catching fire and beginning to howl and cheer the disgraceful loss of self-control being exhibited by a young Negro who had become deranged by the shock wave of comedy set in motion by a troupe of professional actors who were doing nothing more extraordinary than portraying the outrageous antics of a group of Southern whites who were totally imaginary; a young man who was so gross as to demonstrate his social unacceptability by violating a whole *encyclopedia* of codes that regulated proper conduct no less in the theater than in society at large.

In my distorted consciousness the theater was rapidly becoming the scene of a virtual orgy of disgraceful conduct, with everyone getting into the scene-stealing action. And so much so, that now the lucid side of me noted with despair that Jeeter Lester (played by Will Geer) and the other Lesters were now shading their eyes and peering open-mouthed toward the balcony—as if to say "What the hell's happening? Who's upstaging the stage and turning *Tobacco Road* upside down?" Or perhaps, in shock and dismay, they too were thinking of laughing-barrels.

For in the joke the barrels were considered a civic necessity and had been improvised as a means of protecting the sensibilities of whites from a peculiar form of insanity suffered exclusively by Negroes, who in light of their social status and past condition of servitude were regarded as having absolutely *nothing* in their daily experience which could possibly inspire *rational* laughter. And yet Negroes continued—much as one side of me was doing—to laugh.

They laughed even when overcome by mirth while negotiating the public square, an area graced by its proud military statue, its Civil War cannon and pyramid of cannon balls, which was especially off-limits to all forms of Negro profanation. Thus, since any but the most inaudible Negro laughter was forbidden in public, Negroes who were wise—or at least fast on their feet—took off *posthaste* for a laughing-barrel. (Just as I, in my present predicament, would gladly have done.) For despite their eccentric risibility, the local Negroes bowed to public pressure and cooperated—at least to the extent that they were physically able.

But now as I continued to roar at the weird play-without-a-play in which part of me was involved, my sober self marked the fact that the entire audience was being torn in twain. Most of the audience was white, but now many who occupied seats down in the orchestra section were beginning to protest the unscheduled disruption taking place above them. Leaping to their feet, they were shaking their fists at those in the balcony, and they in turn were shouting their disdain for those so lacking in an appreciation for the impromptu broadening of the expected comedy. And as they raged at one another in what was rapidly becoming a Grangerford-Shepherdson feud of expletives, I recalled a similar conflict which took place in the laughing-barrel town and cracked up again.

For there, too, certain citizens had assumed their democratic right of dissent to oppose the barrels as an *ipso jure* form of reverse discrimination. Why not, they argued, force Negroes to control themselves at their *own* expense, as did everyone else. An argument which fell on deaf ears, because it ignored the self-evident fact that Negro self-control was the very *last* thing in the world that they really wanted—whether in this or in any other area of Negro lives. Therefore, these passionate quodlibetarians and their objections to quotas were ignored because the great majority of the citizenry regarded their unique form of public accommodation as bestowing a dual blessing upon their town. And to an extent, that blessing included the Negroes. For not only did the laughing-barrels save many a black a sore behind (and the under-staffed police force, energy sorely needed in other areas), they performed the far more important function of providing whites a means of saving face before the confounding, persistent, and embarrassing mystery of black laughter.

Unfortunately, it was generally agreed that the barrels were by no means an *elegant* solution of what whites regarded as a most grievous and inelegant problem. For after all, having to observe the posture of a Negro stuck halfway into a laughing-barrel (or rising and falling helplessly in a theater balcony) was far from an aesthetic experience. Nor was that all, for often when seen laughing with their heads stuck in a barrel and standing, as it were, upside down upon the turbulent air, Negroes appeared to be taken over by a form of schizophrenia which left them even more psychically frazzled than whites regarded them as being by nature.

But while the phenomenon was widely discussed, not even the wisest of whites could come up with a satisfactory explanation. All they knew was that when such an incident occurred, instead of sobering up, as any white man in a similar situation would have done, a Negro might well take off and laugh all the harder (as I in my barrelless state was doing). For it appeared that in addition to reacting to whatever ignorant, harebrained notion had set him off in the first place, the Negro was apt to double up with a second gale of laughter—and that triggered, apparently, by his own mental image of himself laughing at himself laughing upside down. It was, all whites agreed, another of the many Negro mysteries with which it was their lot to contend; and *whatever* its true cause, it was most disturbing to a white observer.

And especially on Market Day, a time when the public square teemed with whites and blacks seeking in their separate-but-equal fashions to combine business with pleasure while taking advantage of the square's holiday atmosphere. For on Market Days, thanks to the great influx of Negroes, the uproar from laughing-barrels could become so loud and raucous that it not only disturbed the serenity of the entire square, but shook up the whites' fierce faith in the stability of their most cherished traditions. For on such occasions the uproar from the laughing-barrels could become so contagious and irresistible that any whites who were so unfortunate as to be caught near the explosions of laughter would find themselves compelled to join in—and this included even such important figures as the mayor, lawyer, cotton broker, Baptist minister, and brewers of prime "white-lightning" whiskey. It was an appalling state of affairs, for despite their sternest resistance, even such distinguished whites literally cracked up and roared! And although it was recognized that it sprang from the *unnatural* and corrupting blackness of Negro laughter, it was a fact of Southern life, and thus it was that from time to time even the most dignified and tradition-bound whites found themselves joining in. (As, much to the discomfort of my somber balcony-trapped self, the whites around me were doing).

Nor did it help that many of the town's whites suspected that when a Negro had his head thrust into a laughing-barrel he became endowed with a strange form of extrasensory perception—or second sight—which allowed him to respond, and uproariously, to their unwilling participation. For it was clear that given a black laugher's own uncouth uproar, he could not possibly *hear* its infectious damage to them. And when such reversals occurred the whites assumed that in some mysterious fashion the Negro involved was not only laughing at *himself* laughing, but was also laughing at *them* laughing at his laughing against their own most determined wills. And if such was the truth, it suggested that somehow a Negro (and this meant *any* Negro) could become with a single hoot-and-cackle both the source and master of an outrageous and untenable situation. So it was viewed as a most aggravating problem, and, indeed, the most vicious of vicious circles ever to be imposed upon the long-suffering South by the white man's burden.

For since it was an undisputed fact that whites and blacks were of different species, it followed that they could by no means be expected to laugh at the same things. Therefore, when whites found themselves joining in with the coarse merriment issuing from the laughing-barrels, they suffered the double embarrassment of laughing against their own God-given nature while being unsure of exactly why, or at what, specifically, they were laughing. Which meant that somehow the Negro in the barrel had them *over* a barrel.

This, then, was the crux of the town's dilemma: efforts to control Negro laughter with laughing-barrels was as futile as attaining Christian grace by returning to the womb, because a Negro laughing in a laughing-barrel simply turned the world upside down and inside out. And in so doing, he *in*-verted (and thus *sub*-verted) tradition and thus the preordained and cherished scheme of Southern racial relationships was blasted asunder. Therefore, it was feared that if such unhappy instances of interracial laughter occurred with any frequency, it would create a crisis in which social order would be fatally undermined by something as unpolitical as a bunch of Negroes with their laughing heads stuck into the interiors of a batch of old whitewashed whiskey barrels.

The outrageous absurdity of this state of affairs was as vexing to the town as that in which I found myself as the old joke banged and shuddered through my memory. For despite the fact that the whites had done everything they could think of to control the blackness of Negro laughter, the Negroes continued to laugh. And the disapproval of the general public notwithstanding, they were even *bursting* barrels all over the public square, and thus adding to the high cost of maintaining public order. *And* since this was (in more ways than one!) at white expense, the whites were faced with a Hobson's choice between getting rid of the Negroes and suffering the economic loss of their labor, or living with the commotion in the laughing-barrels. (Yes, but they had at least a ghost of a choice, while by now it was as though I had been taken over by embattled Siamese twins who couldn't agree for disagreeing, and neither of whom could exit the scene, thanks to the detachment of one and the mirth-wracked state of the other.)

In the town, however, great argument raged on both sides of the question. All agreed that the laughing-barrels were an economic burden, but the proponents of the "Barrel Act," as it was known, justified their position with philosophical arguments to the effect that while it was true that the unique public facilities were costly, they served not only as a form of noise-pollution control, but the higher—and more spiritual—purpose of making it unnecessary for white folks to suffer the indignity of having to observe the confounding and degrading spectacle of a bunch of uncultivated Negroes knocking themselves out with a form of laughter that had no apparent motivation or discernible target . . .

What a terrible time and place to be ambushed by such an irreverent joke! By now my eyes were so full of tears that I could no longer see Hughes or anyone else, but at least the moisture had the effect of calming me down. Then, as the unruly world of *Tobacco Road* finally returned, my divided selves were made one again by a sense of catharsis. Yes, but at the expense of undergoing what a humiliating, body-wracking conflict of emotions! Embarrassment, self-anger, ethnic scorn, and at last a feeling of comic relief. And all because Erskine Caldwell compelled me to laugh at his symbolic, and therefore nonthreatening, Southern whites, and thus he shocked me into recognizing certain absurd aspects of our common humanity. Kenneth Burke would probably have said that I had been hit with a "perspective by incongruity," leading to a reversal of expectations in which the juxtaposition of past and present, comic Southland and quasi-illusory New York, had set up vibrations that routed my self-composure. It was as though I had plunged through the wacky mirrors of a fun house, to discover on the other side a weird distortion of perspective which made for a painful but redeeming rectification of vision. And in a flash, time was telescoped and the imaginary assumed the lineaments of past experiences through which Jeeter Lester's comic essence became a recognizable property of characters and events that I had known in the past.

Because, thanks to Governor "Alfalfa Bill" Murray's Jeeter Lesterish appeal to the bias of Oklahoma's farm vote, hadn't I seen the state capitol's grounds a-wave with grain "as high as an elephant's eye" (which proved to be a foreshadowing of events which led, years later, to the adoption of Rodgers and Hammerstein's "Oklahoma" as the state's official song)? And a bit later, hadn't I seen those same graciously landscaped grounds splattered with far more oil rigs than there were holes dug by Ty Ty in his futile search for gold in Caldwell's *God's Little Acre*? I had indeed, and the main difference was that the oil rigs produced oil; otherwise, Alfalfa Bill might have stepped out of a Caldwell novel. Thus I now recognized that there was much more of Jeeter Lester's outrageousness in my past than I had ever imagined, and quite a bit of it showed up on my side of the color line.

There were uneducated men whose attitudes and bearing ripped through the usual stereotypes like a Brahma bull goring the paper image displayed on Bull Durham Tobacco Company billboards. Their violence was usually directed against their own kind, but they were known to go after whites as well, and were no more respectful of what most people considered civilized conduct than Jeeter Lester. I had known the type in Oklahoma and admired a few for insisting upon being themselves. Often they were of vernacular folk culture but with active minds and were absolutely unrestrained in attacking any subject that caught their attention. Once while working as a barbershop shoeshine boy I had heard such a group engage in a long discussion of Mr. John D. Rockefeller Senior's relations with the women whom they assumed it natural for such a powerful man to have. They took it for granted that he had no less than a "stable full" and speculated as to how much he paid for their favors, and concluded that he rewarded them with trunks full of brand-new dimes.

Then they discussed the brands of brandy and whiskey which they assumed Mr. Rockefeller drank, and argued over the designs and costs of the silk underwear worn by his favorite fancy women, and then almost came to blows when estimating the number of "yard chillun" he had scattered around the country and abroad.

Poor old John D., he didn't know it, but they put him through the windmill of their fantasies with gusto. And what's more, he emerged enhanced in their sight as an even more exceptional man among such exceptional men as themselves—thanks to their having endowed him with a sexual potency and an utter disregard for genteel conduct that would have blown that gentleman's mind.

Before they were done they had the founder of Standard Oil shooting pool, playing strip poker, and engaging in a barbecue-eating contest with J. P. Morgan and Henry Ford—from which, naturally, he emerged the winner. Only when they put him through a Charleston contest with "Tickle-toes from Tulsa," a famous Negro dancer, did he fall below their exacting standards. Nevertheless he remained the mighty Rockefeller, though so magnified that he was far more "John Henry" than John Davidson. And in working him over, they created such an uproar of laughter that the owner had to ask them to leave the barbershop. But by that time, both to my bewilderment and to my delight, they had touched one of the most powerful men of the nation with the tarbrush of their comic imaginations, Afro-Americanized him, and claimed him as one of their very own.

It was amazing how consistently they sought (like Jeeter Lester) to make the world conform to the narrow compass of their own hopes and dreams. And there were still others who in pursuing their self-reliant wrongheadedness had given me a glimpse of the "tragic."

For had not I seen a good part of my community, including teen-age boys, reduced to despair over the terrible death of a self-taught genius of an automobile mechanic, who after burning his fingers while working with the electrical system of a Model T Ford had cut out the offending flesh with his pocketknife—an act of ignorant pride which resulted in his death by lock-jaw? In those days any boy who could lay hands on a coil from a Model T and the hand-cranked magneto from a discontinued telephone would rig it as a device for shocking his unsuspecting friends, but now to our dismay, death was revealed to be lurking within our rare electrical toys.

But even closer to my immediate experience, wasn't Ellie May's and Lov's "horsing" all over the stage of *Tobacco Road* embarrassingly symbolic of my own frustration as a healthy young man whose sexual outlet was limited (for the most part) to "belly-rubbing" with girls met casually at public dances? It was and it wasn't, depending upon my willingness to make or withhold a human identification. Actually, I had no choice but to identify, for Caldwell's art had seen to that.

Thus, for all its intentional outrageousness, the comedy of *Tobacco Road* was deeply rooted in the crazy-quilt life I knew. And Caldwell had me both coming and going, black side, white side, and straight down my improvised American middle. On one side of my mind I had thought of my life as being of a whole, segregated but in many ways superior to that of the Lesters. On the other side, I thought of the Lester type as being, in the Negro folk phrase, "a heap of whiteness gone to waste" and therefore a gross caricature of anything that was viable in the idea of white superiority. But now Caldwell had highlighted the warp and woof of my own ragtag American pattern. And so, laughing hysterically, I felt like the fat man whom I'd seen slip and fall on the icy sidewalk and who lay there laughing while passers-by looked on in bewilderment—until he got to his feet still laughing and punched the one man who had joined in his laughter square in the mouth. In my case, however, there was no one to punch, because I embodied both fat man and the passer-by who was so rash as to ignore Baudelaire's warning. Therefore I laughed and I trembled, and gained thereby a certain wisdom.

I couldn't have put it into words at the time, but by forcing me to see the comedy in Jeeter Lester's condition and allowing me to react to it in an interracial situation without the threat of physical violence, Caldwell told me something important about who I was. And by easing the conflict that I was having with my Southern experience (yes, and with my South-Southwestern identity), helped initiate me into becoming, if not a "New Yorker," at least a more tolerant American. I suppose such preposterous comedy is an indispensable agency for dealing with American experience precisely because it allows for redeeming perspectives on our rampant incongruities. Given my background and yearnings, there was no question but that I needed such redemption, and for that I am eternally grateful to Erskine Caldwell—Southerner, American humorist, and mighty destroyer of laughing-barrels.

. . . .

QUESTIONS FOR A SECOND READING

1. From the opening pages, Ellison works with a theory of laughter, one represented early in the text through references to Baudelaire, Aesop, and Uncle Remus. The terms of this discussion appear again and again as points of reference for Ellison when he is talking about humor or the uses of humor or when he is telling stories of jokes and reversals. As you work back through the text, be prepared to write out a quick paraphrase of the argument available to Ellison through these and later references to the "idea" of laughter— to what it is that laughter could be said to represent. And look to see how, as Ellison works with them, these ideas can be used (or altered) to think about African American experience especially in the long (and strange) section on the "laughing-barrels."

2. In the middle of the essay, Ellison cites W. B. Yeats, the Irish poet, on "masks" in a passage that concludes with the (perhaps surprising) assertion that "active virtue . . . is the wearing of a mask." And then, to make Yeats's words work for him, Ellison has to imagine a revision of the passage, adapting it as a concept that can be used to think about African American experience. As you reread, let the opening of the essay lead you to that passage. Then, when you get there, take a moment to work out the Ellison revision of Yeats: What does it say once the substitutions are made? And, from that, how do you read the rest of the essay? What is Ellison saying about "active virtue"? And to whom is he speaking?

3. "An Extravagance of Laughter" is an essay that works by indirection. It takes a long time and several turns to get from the opening reference to *Tobacco Road* to the story of what happened at the performance. And even then, the conclusions, if there are any, are difficult and subtle. This is how Ellison, the writer, works; this is how readers work (or learn to work) as they give themselves over to the text. As you reread, think about how you would describe and chart this essay as a project or as a piece of work. What are its stages and strategies? What is its design? What are its characteristic methods? Ellison refers to the essay as an "autobiographical exploration." From your perspective, what is this genre? If you had to write such an exploration (or help others to write one), what instructions could you provide?

ASSIGNMENTS FOR WRITING

1. It is interesting that Ellison feels the need to apologize to Erskine Caldwell and not Langston Hughes. Caldwell was not present in the theater; Hughes was present and thereby implicated in the scene in a way that Caldwell was not. He had reason to be embarrassed by his young friend, newly arrived from the South.

   One way of thinking about this is to assume that Hughes needed no explanation. As an African American, there are things he would know and understand that Caldwell, who was white, would not. In this sense, the essay is very much an attempt to explain to a white audience the particular experience of an African American. If you think about the essay this way, Ellison's concluding comment, "Caldwell told me something important about who I was," refers to how the play, and his response, allowed Ellison to understand who he was in relation to America's complicated regional and racial geography, where it is important not only to think about race, but to think about race in relation to Oklahoma, Alabama, and New York. So what *does* Ellison come to understand? Why was this situation hard to understand, and why is it hard to explain? That is, why doesn't Ellison just say what he has to say on the first page and be done with it?

Ellison refers to "An Extravagance of Laughter" as an autobiographical exploration, a way of thinking things through. So what are his conclusions? Write an essay in which you explain what it is that Ellison represents as the end of that exploration. What is the end? Where does he arrive? How does he get there? How does he represent the difficulty of exploring and explaining his "emotional and intellectual" development? You should assume that your readers know something about Ralph Ellison but that they have never read this piece.

2. For most readers, one of the strangest and most difficult moments in the essay comes toward the end, when Ellison introduces the "old in-group joke" of the laughing-barrels and then uses them as a point of reference in thinking about humor, about the South, and about the relations between blacks and whites.

What can you make of this section of "An Extravagance of Laughter"? Write an essay, one directed at other readers of this piece, ideally your colleagues in this class, showing how you read this section of the essay, explaining what you can make of the text. What is Ellison doing? What is he getting at? What does this section have to do with the rest of the essay—that is, how does the rest of the essay prepare you to read the example of the laughing-barrels? Or how does the example of the laughing-barrels prepare you to read (or to reflect on) the rest of the essay?

3. Ellison refers to "An Extravagance of Laughter" as an "autobiographical exploration." An earlier assignment asks students to think about this in relation to content—what does Ellison learn? You could also use the phrase "autobiographical exploration" to name a *way* of writing, a method, one that combines autobiography with a desire to analyze and to explore (to think about experience, not just recount it) and, at least in Ellison's case, to think broadly about ideas and issues (about W. B. Yeats and masks, about humor, about race relations in the North and South in the 1930s).

As you prepare to write this assignment, read through the essay again to think about it as a way of doing one's work, as a project, as a way of writing. What are its key features? What is its shape or design? How does Ellison the writer do what he does? And you might ask: What would it take to learn to write like this? How is this writing related to the writing taught in school? Where and how might it serve you as a student? (The third "Question for a Second Reading" is designed to prompt this kind of reflection.)

Once you have developed a sense of Ellison's method, write an autobiographical exploration of your own, one that has the rhythm and the moves, the shape and the design of "An Extravagance of Laughter." As far as subject matter is concerned, consider Ellison's text an invitation to you to write about race or difference or region or travel or difficult moments, but don't feel compelled to follow his lead. You can write about anything you want. The key is to follow the essay as an example of a *way* of writing—moving slowly, turning this way and that, combining stories and reflection, working outside of a rigid structure of thesis and proof.

MAKING CONNECTIONS

1. One of the obvious questions that a reader might ask of Ralph Ellison's essay "An Extravagance of Laughter" has to do with his methods of writing, thinking, and working. What, one might ask, are his characteristic ways of gathering materials, of thinking them through, of presenting them to readers? As you work through Ellison's essay, think about the writing as an example of method and intention. You also might ask yourself, for instance, questions about the kinds of readers his work requires: What does he assume of his readers? How does he teach his readers to read?

   The same questions can be asked of Susan Griffin's essay "Our Secret" (p. 319) (or of the selections by Gloria Anzaldúa, p. 22, or of the excerpt from Virginia Woolf's "A Room of One's Own," p. 719). What, you might ask, are her characteristic ways of gathering materials, of thinking them through, and of presenting them to a reader? How would you describe her method? What are its key features? What would you say she is doing, for example, in the first two paragraphs? What happens next? What is an "autobiographical exploration" as it is represented in this text? And what does she assume of her readers? Who *is* the audience and how does she teach her readers to read?

   Write an essay in which you use the selections by Ellison and Griffin (or those by Anzaldúa or Woolf) to talk about writers, their methods, and the writerly project of "autobiographical explorations." Be sure to work closely with examples from each reading. Be sure to look for differences as well as similarities. And see, in your essay, if you can move beyond your discussion of their examples to think more generally about the problems of writing. About oneself? You might ask, what is it that adults work on when they work on their writing? What is it that younger writers need to learn? What might a writer learn from these two examples? Where and how might the lessons learned serve in the academy or outside?

2. Both Ralph Ellison, in "An Extravagance of Laughter," and John Edgar Wideman, in "Our Time" (p. 652), write about the experience of growing up, and of growing up black in the United States. Wideman and Ellison are major figures in American cultural life. And the selections you are reading were written at about the same time, in the mideighties (Wideman's in 1984, Ellison's in 1985). They write about different moments in American history, however, and they speak from different generations of experience.

Wideman was not yet alive when Ellison met Langston Hughes in New York and attended the performance of *Tobacco Road*.

Write an essay in which you discuss the differences in the experience *and* the point of view of each writer. How were their lives different? How do they see things differently? What differences are there in their points of reference—in the way they imagine the difficulties in doing what they do as writers and in the resources they draw on to do their work?

MICHEL
FOUCAULT

*M*ICHEL FOUCAULT *(1926–1984) stands at the end of the twentieth century as one of the world's leading intellectuals. He was trained as a philosopher, but much of his work, like that presented in* Discipline and Punish: The Birth of the Prison *(1975), traces the presence of certain ideas across European history. So he could also be thought of as a historian, but a historian whose goal is to revise the usual understanding of history—not as a progressive sequence but as a series of repetitions governed by powerful ideas, terms, and figures. Foucault was also a public intellectual, involved in prominent issues such as prison reform. He wrote frequently for French newspapers and reviews. His death from AIDS was front-page news in* Le Monde, *the French equivalent of the* New York Times. *He taught at several French universities and in 1970 was appointed to a professorship at the College de France, the highest position in the French system. He traveled widely, lecturing and visiting at universities throughout the world.*

Foucault's work is central to much current work in the humanities and the social sciences. In fact, it is hard to imagine any area of the academy that has not been influenced by his writing. There is a certain irony in all this, since Foucault argued persuasively that we need to give up thinking about knowledge as individually produced; we have to stop thinking the way we do about the "author" or the "genius," about individuality or creativity; we have to stop thinking as though there were truths that stand beyond the interests of a given moment. It is both dangerous and wrong, he argued, to assume that knowledge is disinterested. Edward Said had this to say of Foucault:

> *His great critical contribution was to dissolve the anthropological models of identity and subjecthood underlying research in the humanistic and social sciences. Instead of seeing everything in culture and society as ultimately emanating from either a sort of unchanging Cartesian ego or a heroic solitary artist, Foucault proposed the much juster notion that all work, like social life itself, is collective. The principal task therefore is to circumvent or break down the ideological biases that prevent us from saying that what enables a doctor to practice medicine or a historian to write history is not mainly a set of individual gifts, but an ability to follow rules that are taken for granted as an unconscious a priori by all professionals. More than anyone before him, Foucault specified rules for those rules, and even more impressively, he showed how over long periods of time the rules became epistemological enforcers of what (as well as of how) people thought, lived, and spoke.*

These rules, these unconscious enforcers, are visible in "discourse"—ways of thinking and speaking and acting that we take for granted as naturally or inevitably there but that are constructed over time and preserved by those who act without question, without stepping outside the discourse and thinking critically. But, says Foucault, there is no place "outside" the discourse, no free, clear space. There is always only another discursive position. A person in thinking, living, and speaking expresses not merely himself or herself but the thoughts and roles and phrases governed by the available ways of thinking and speaking. The key questions to ask, then, according to Foucault, are not Who said this? or Is it original? or Is it true? or Is it authentic? but Who talks this way? or What unspoken rules govern this way of speaking? or Where is this discourse used? Who gets to use it? when? and to what end?

The following selection is the third chapter of Discipline and Punish: The Birth of the Prison *(translated from the French by Alan Sheridan). In this book, Foucault is concerned with the relationships between knowledge and power, arguing that knowledge is not pure and abstract but is implicated in networks of power relations. Or, as he puts it elsewhere, people govern themselves "through the production of truth." This includes the "truths" that determine how we imagine and manage the boundaries between the "normal" and the transgressive, the lawful and the delinquent. In a characteristic move, Foucault reverses our intuitive sense of how things are. He argues, for example, that it is not the case that prisons serve the courts and a system of justice but that the courts are the products, the servants of "the prison," the prison as an idea, as the central figure in a way of thinking about transgression, order, and the body, a way of thinking that is persistent and general, present, for example, through all efforts to produce the normal or "disciplined individual": "in the central position that [the prison] occupies, it is not alone, but linked to a whole series*

of 'carceral' mechanisms which seem distinct enough—since they are intended to alleviate pain, to cure, to comfort—but which all tend, like the prison, to exercise a
power of normalization." Knowledge stands in an antagonistic role in Discipline
and Punish; it is part of a problem, not a route to a solution.

You will find "Panopticism" difficult reading. All readers find Foucault's prose
tough going. It helps to realize that it is necessarily difficult. Foucault, remember, is
trying to work outside of, or in spite of, the usual ways of thinking and writing. He is
trying not to reproduce the standard discourse but to point to what it cannot or will
not say. He is trying to make gestures beyond what is ordinarily, normally said. So
his prose struggles with its own situation. Again, as Edward Said says, "What [Fou-
cault] was interested in . . . was 'the more' that can be discovered lurking in signs
and discourses but that is irreducible to language and speech; 'it is this "more,"' he
said, 'that we must reveal and describe.' Such a concern appears to be both devious
and obscure, yet it accounts for a lot that is specially unsettling in Foucault's writing. There is no such thing as being at home in his writing, neither for reader nor for
writer." While readers find Foucault difficult, he is widely read and widely cited. His
books include The Birth of the Clinic: An Archaeology of Medical Perception
(1963), The Order of Things: An Archaeology of the Human Sciences (1966),
The Archaeology of Knowledge (1969), Madness and Civilization (1971), and
the three-volume History of Sexuality (1976, 1979, 1984).

Panopticism

The following, according to an order published at the end of the seventeenth century, were the measures to be taken when the plague appeared in a
town.[1]

First, a strict spatial partitioning: the closing of the town and its outlying
districts, a prohibition to leave the town on pain of death, the killing of all
stray animals; the division of the town into distinct quarters, each governed
by an intendant. Each street is placed under the authority of a syndic, who
keeps it under surveillance; if he leaves the street, he will be condemned to
death. On the appointed day, everyone is ordered to stay indoors: it is forbidden to leave on pain of death. The syndic himself comes to lock the door of
each house from the outside; he takes the key with him and hands it over to
the intendant of the quarter; the intendant keeps it until the end of the quarantine. Each family will have made its own provisions; but, for bread and
wine, small wooden canals are set up between the street and the interior of
the houses, thus allowing each person to receive his ration without communicating with the suppliers and other residents; meat, fish, and herbs will be
hoisted up into the houses with pulleys and baskets. If it is absolutely necessary to leave the house, it will be done in turn, avoiding any meeting. Only

the intendants, syndics, and guards will move about the streets and also, between the infected houses, from one corpse to another, the "crows," who can be left to die: these are "people of little substance who carry the sick, bury the dead, clean, and do many vile and abject offices." It is a segmented, immobile, frozen space. Each individual is fixed in his place. And, if he moves, he does so at the risk of his life, contagion, or punishment.

Inspection functions ceaselessly. The gaze is alert everywhere: "A considerable body of militia, commanded by good officers and men of substance," guards at the gates, at the town hall, and in every quarter to ensure the prompt obedience of the people and the most absolute authority of the magistrates, "as also to observe all disorder, theft and extortion." At each of the town gates there will be an observation post; at the end of each street sentinels. Every day, the intendant visits the quarter in his charge, inquires whether the syndics have carried out their tasks, whether the inhabitants have anything to complain of; they "observe their actions." Every day, too, the syndic goes into the street for which he is responsible; stops before each house: gets all the inhabitants to appear at the windows (those who live overlooking the courtyard will be allocated a window looking onto the street at which no one but they may show themselves); he calls each of them by name; informs himself as to the state of each and every one of them—"in which respect the inhabitants will be compelled to speak the truth under pain of death"; if someone does not appear at the window, the syndic must ask why: "In this way he will find out easily enough whether dead or sick are being concealed." Everyone locked up in his cage, everyone at his window, answering to his name and showing himself when asked—it is the great review of the living and the dead.

This surveillance is based on a system of permanent registration: reports from the syndics to the intendants, from the intendants to the magistrates or mayor. At the beginning of the "lock up," the role of each of the inhabitants present in the town is laid down, one by one; this document bears "the name, age, sex of everyone, notwithstanding his condition": a copy is sent to the intendant of the quarter, another to the office of the town hall, another to enable the syndic to make his daily roll call. Everything that may be observed during the course of the visits—deaths, illnesses, complaints, irregularities— is noted down and transmitted to the intendants and magistrates. The magistrates have complete control over medical treatment; they have appointed a physician in charge; no other practitioner may treat, no apothecary prepare medicine, no confessor visit a sick person without having received from him a written note "to prevent anyone from concealing and dealing with those sick of the contagion, unknown to the magistrates." The registration of the pathological must be constantly centralized. The relation of each individual to his disease and to his death passes through the representatives of power, the registration they make of it, the decisions they take on it.

Five or six days after the beginning of the quarantine, the process of purifying the houses one by one is begun. All the inhabitants are made to leave;

in each room "the furniture and goods" are raised from the ground or suspended from the air; perfume is poured around the room; after carefully sealing the windows, doors, and even the keyholes with wax, the perfume is set alight. Finally, the entire house is closed while the perfume is consumed; those who have carried out the work are searched, as they were on entry, "in the presence of the residents of the house, to see that they did not have something on their persons as they left that they did not have on entering." Four hours later, the residents are allowed to reenter their homes.

This enclosed, segmented space, observed at every point, in which the individuals are inserted in a fixed place, in which the slightest movements are supervised, in which all events are recorded, in which an uninterrupted work of writing links the center and periphery, in which power is exercised without division, according to a continuous hierarchical figure, in which each individual is constantly located, examined, and distributed among the living beings, the sick, and the dead—all this constitutes a compact model of the disciplinary mechanism. The plague is met by order; its function is to sort out every possible confusion: that of the disease, which is transmitted when bodies are mixed together; that of the evil, which is increased when fear and death overcome prohibitions. It lays down for each individual his place, his body, his disease, and his death, his well-being, by means of an omnipresent and omniscient power that subdivides itself in a regular, uninterrupted way even to the ultimate determination of the individual, of what characterizes him, of what belongs to him, of what happens to him. Against the plague, which is a mixture, discipline brings into play its power, which is one of analysis. A whole literary fiction of the festival grew up around the plague: suspended laws, lifted prohibitions, the frenzy of passing time, bodies mingling together without respect, individuals unmasked, abandoning their statutory identity and the figure under which they had been recognized, allowing a quite different truth to appear. But there was also a political dream of the plague, which was exactly its reverse: not the collective festival, but strict divisions; not laws transgressed, but the penetration of regulation into even the smallest details of everyday life through the mediation of the complete hierarchy that assured the capillary functioning of power; not masks that were put on and taken off, but the assignment to each individual of his "true" name, his "true" place, his "true" body, his "true" disease. The plague as a form, at once real and imaginary, of disorder had as its medical and political correlative discipline. Behind the disciplinary mechanisms can be read the haunting memory of "contagions," of the plague, of rebellions, crimes, vagabondage, desertions, people who appear and disappear, live and die in disorder.

If it is true that the leper gave rise to rituals of exclusion, which to a certain extent provided the model for and general form of the great Confinement, then the plague gave rise to disciplinary projects. Rather than the massive, binary division between one set of people and another, it called for multiple separations, individualizing distributions, an organization in depth of surveillance and control, an intensification and a ramification of power. The leper was caught up in a practice of rejection, of exile-enclosure; he was left to his doom in a mass among which it was useless to differentiate; those sick of the plague were caught up in a meticulous tactical partitioning in which individual differentiations were the constricting effects of a power that multiplied, articulated, and subdivided itself; the great confinement on the one hand; the correct training on the other. The leper and his separation; the plague and its segmentations. The first is marked; the second analyzed and distributed. The exile of the leper and the arrest of the plague do not bring with them the same political dream. The first is that of a pure community, the second that of a disciplined society. Two ways of exercising power over men, of controling their relations, of separating out their dangerous mixtures. The plague-stricken town, traversed throughout with hierarchy, surveillance, observation, writing; the town immobilized by the functioning of an extensive power that bears in a distinct way over all individual bodies—this is the utopia of the perfectly governed city. The plague (envisaged as a possibility at least) is the trial in the course of which one may define ideally the exercise of disciplinary power. In order to make rights and laws function according to pure theory, the jurists place themselves in imagination in the state of nature; in order to see perfect disciplines functioning, rulers dreamed of the state of plague. Underlying disciplinary projects the image of the plague stands for all forms of confusion and disorder; just as the image of the leper, cut off from all human contact, underlies projects of exclusion.

They are different projects, then, but not incompatible ones. We see them coming slowly together, and it is the peculiarity of the nineteenth century that it applied to the space of exclusion of which the leper was the symbolic inhabitant (beggars, vagabonds, madmen, and the disorderly formed the real population) the technique of power proper to disciplinary partitioning. Treat "lepers" as "plague victims," project the subtle segmentations of discipline onto the confused space of internment, combine it with the methods of analytical distribution proper to power, individualize the excluded, but use procedures of individualization to mark exclusion—this is what was operated regularly by disciplinary power from the beginning of the nineteenth century in the psychiatric asylum, the penitentiary, the reformatory, the approved school, and to some extent, the hospital. Generally speaking, all the authorities exercising individual control function according to a double mode; that of binary division and branding (mad/sane; dangerous/harmless; normal/abnormal); and that of coercive assignment, of differential distribution (who he is; where he must be; how he is to be characterized; how he is to be recognized; how a constant surveillance is to be exercised over him in an individual way, etc.). On the one hand, the lepers are treated as plague victims; the tactics of individualizing disciplines are imposed on the excluded; and, on the other hand, the universality of disciplinary controls makes it possible to brand the "leper" and to bring into play against him the dualistic mechanisms of exclusion. The constant division between the normal and the abnormal, to which every individual is subjected, brings us back to our own time, by applying the binary branding and exile of the leper to quite different objects; the existence of a whole set of techniques and institutions for measuring, supervising, and correcting the abnormal brings into play the disciplinary mechanisms to which the fear of the plague gave rise. All the mechanisms of power which, even today, are disposed around the abnormal individual, to brand him and to alter him, are composed of those two forms from which they distantly derive.

Bentham's *Panopticon* is the architectural figure of this composition. We know the principle on which it was based: at the periphery, an annular building; at the center, a tower; this tower is pierced with wide windows that open onto the inner side of the ring; the peripheric building is divided into cells, each of which extends the whole width of the building; they have two windows, one on the inside, corresponding to the windows of the tower; the other, on the outside, allows the light to cross the cell from one end to the other. All that is needed, then, is to place a supervisor in a central tower and to shut up in each cell a madman, a patient, a condemned man, a worker, or a schoolboy. By the effect of backlighting, one can observe from the tower, standing out precisely against the light, the small captive shadows in the cells of the periphery. They are like so many cages, so many small theaters, in which each actor is alone, perfectly individualized and constantly visible. The panoptic mechanism arranges spatial unities that make it possible to see constantly and to recognize immediately. In short, it reverses the principle of the dungeon; or rather of its three functions—to enclose, to deprive of light, and to hide—it preserves only the first and eliminates the other two. Full lighting and the eye of a supervisor capture better than darkness, which ultimately protected. Visibility is a trap.

To begin with, this made it possible—as a negative effect—to avoid those compact, swarming, howling masses that were to be found in places of confinement, those painted by Goya or described by Howard. Each individual, in his place, is securely confined to a cell from which he is seen from the front by the supervisor; but the side walls prevent him from coming into contact with his companions. He is seen, but he does not see; he is the object of information, never a subject in communication. The arrangement of his room, opposite the central tower, imposes on him an axial visibility; but the divisions of the ring, those separated cells, imply a lateral invisibility. And this invisibility is a guarantee of order. If the inmates are convicts, there is no danger of a plot, an attempt at collective escape, the planning of new crimes for the future, bad reciprocal influences; if they are patients, there is no danger of contagion; if they are madmen, there is no risk of their committing violence upon one another; if they are schoolchildren, there is no copying, no noise, no chatter, no waste of time; if they are workers, there are no disorders, no theft, no coalitions, none of those distractions that slow down the rate of work, make it less perfect, or cause accidents. The crowd, a compact mass, a locus of multiple exchanges, individualities merging together, a collective effect, is abolished and replaced by a collection of separated individualities. From the point of view of the guardian, it is replaced by a multiplicity that can be numbered and supervised; from the point of view of the inmates, by a sequestered and observed solitude (Bentham 60–64).

Hence the major effect of the Panopticon: to induce in the inmate a state of conscious and permanent visibility that assures the automatic functioning of power. So to arrange things that the surveillance is permanent in its effects even if it is discontinuous in its action; that the perfection of power should tend to render its actual exercise unnecessary; that this architectural apparatus should be a machine for creating and sustaining a power relation independent of the person who exercises it; in short, that the inmates should be caught up in a power situation of which they are themselves the bearers. To achieve this, it is at once too much and too little that the prisoner should be constantly observed by an inspector: too little, for what matters is that he knows himself to be observed; too much, because he has no need in fact of

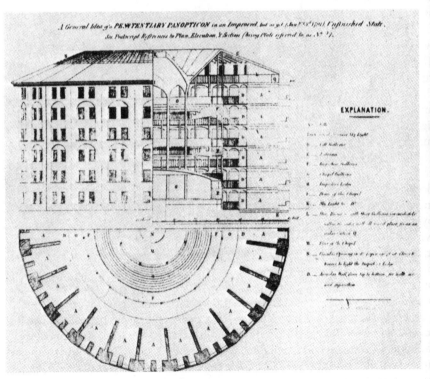

Plan of the Panopticon by J. Bentham (*The Works of Jeremy Bentham*, ed. Bowring, vol. IV, 1843, 172–73)

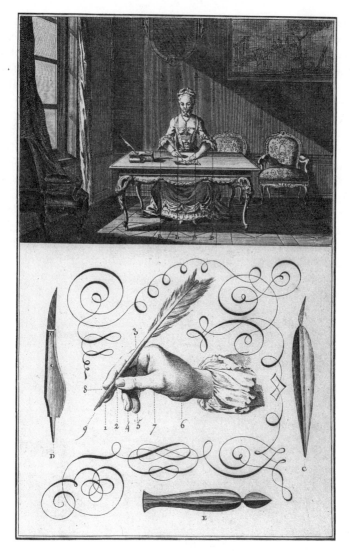

Handwriting model. *Collections historiques de l'I.N.R.D.P.*

being so. In view of this, Bentham laid down the principle that power should be visible and unverifiable. Visible: the inmate will constantly have before his eyes the tall outline of the central tower from which he is spied upon. Unverifiable: the inmate must never know whether he is being looked at at any one moment; but he must be sure that he may always be so. In order to make the presence or absence of the inspector unverifiable, so that the prisoners, in their cells, cannot even see a shadow, Bentham envisaged not only venetian

Interior of the penitentiary at Stateville, United States, twentieth century

blinds on the windows of the central observation hall, but, on the inside, partitions that intersected the hall at right angles and, in order to pass from one quarter to the other, not doors but zigzag openings; for the slightest noise, a gleam of light, a brightness in a half-opened door would betray the presence of the guardian.[2] The Panopticon is a machine for dissociating the see/being seen dyad: in the peripheric ring, one is totally seen, without ever seeing; in the central tower, one sees everything without ever being seen.[3]

It is an important mechanism, for it automatizes and disindividualizes power. Power has its principle not so much in a person as in a certain concerted distribution of bodies, surfaces, lights, gazes; in an arrangement whose internal mechanisms produce the relation in which individuals are caught up. The ceremonies, the rituals, the marks by which the sovereign's surplus power was manifested are useless. There is a machinery that assures dissymmetry, disequilibrium, difference. Consequently, it does not matter who exercises power. Any individual, taken almost at random, can operate the machine: in the absence of the director, his family, his friends, his visitors, even his servants (Bentham 45). Similarly, it does not matter what motive an-

Lecture on the evils of alcoholism in the auditorium of Fresnes prison

imates him: the curiosity of the indiscreet, the malice of a child, the thirst for knowledge of a philosopher who wishes to visit this museum of human nature, or the perversity of those who take pleasure in spying and punishing. The more numerous those anonymous and temporary observers are, the greater the risk for the inmate of being surprised and the greater his anxious awareness of being observed. The Panopticon is a marvelous machine which, whatever use one may wish to put it to, produces homogeneous effects of power.

A real subjection is born mechanically from a fictitious relation. So it is not necessary to use force to constrain the convict to good behavior, the mad-mad to calm, the worker to work, the schoolboy to application, the patient to the observation of the regulations. Bentham was surprised that panoptic in-stitutions could be so light: there were no more bars, no more chains, no more heavy locks; all that was needed was that the separations should be clear and the openings well arranged. The heaviness of the old "houses of se-curity," with their fortresslike architecture, could be replaced by the simple, economic geometry of a "house of certainty." The efficiency of power, its constraining force have, in a sense, passed over to the other side—to the side of its surface of application. He who is subjected to a field of visibility, and who knows it, assumes responsibility for the constraints of power; he makes them play spontaneously upon himself; he inscribes in himself the power re-lation in which he simultaneously plays both roles; he becomes the principle of his own subjection. By this very fact, the external power may throw off its physical weight; it tends to the noncorporal; and, the more it approaches this limit, the more constant, profound, and permanent are its effects: it is a per-petual victory that avoids any physical confrontation and which is always decided in advance.

Bentham does not say whether he was inspired, in his project, by Le Vaux's menagerie at Versailles: the first menagerie in which the different ele-ments are not, as they traditionally were, distributed in a park (Loisel 104–7). At the center was an octagonal pavilion which, on the first floor, consisted of only a single room, the king's *salon;* on every side large windows looked out onto seven cages (the eighth side was reserved for the entrance), containing different species of animals. By Bentham's time, this menagerie had disap-peared. But one finds in the program of the Panopticon a similar concern with individualizing observation, with characterization and classification, with the analytical arrangement of space. The Panopticon is a royal menagerie; the animal is replaced by man, individual distribution by specific grouping, and the king by the machinery of a furtive power. With this excep-tion, the Panopticon also does the work of a naturalist. It makes it possible to draw up differences: among patients, to observe the symptoms of each indi-vidual, without the proximity of beds, the circulation of miasmas, the effects of contagion confusing the clinical tables; among schoolchildren, it makes it possible to observe performances (without there being any imitation or copy-ing), to map aptitudes, to assess characters, to draw up rigorous classifica-tions, and in relation to normal development, to distinguish "laziness and stubbornness" from "incurable imbecility"; among workers, it makes it pos-sible to note the aptitudes of each worker, compare the time he takes to perform a task, and if they are paid by the day, to calculate their wages (Bentham 60–64).

So much for the question of observation. But the Panopticon was also a laboratory; it could be used as a machine to carry out experiments, to alter behavior, to train or correct individuals. To experiment with medicines and monitor their effects. To try out different punishments on prisoners, according to their crimes and character, and to seek the most effective ones. To teach different techniques simultaneously to the workers, to decide which is the best. To try out pedagogical experiments—and in particular to take up once again the well-debated problem of secluded education, by using orphans. One would see what would happen when, in their sixteenth or eighteenth year, they were presented with other boys or girls; one could verify whether, as Helvetius thought, anyone could learn anything; one would follow "the genealogy of every observable idea"; one could bring up different children according to different systems of thought, making certain children believe that two and two do not make four or that the moon is a cheese, then put them together when they are twenty or twenty-five years old; one would then have discussions that would be worth a great deal more than the sermons or lectures on which so much money is spent; one would have at least an opportunity of making discoveries in the domain of metaphysics. The Panopticon is a privileged place for experiments on men, and for analyzing with complete certainty the transformations that may be obtained from them. The Panopticon may even provide an apparatus for supervising its own mechanisms. In this central tower, the director may spy on all the employees that he has under his orders: nurses, doctors, foremen, teachers, warders; he will be able to judge them continuously, alter their behavior, impose upon them the methods he thinks best; and it will even be possible to observe the director himself. An inspector arriving unexpectedly at the center of the Panopticon will be able to judge at a glance, without anything being concealed from him, how the entire establishment is functioning. And, in any case, enclosed as he is in the middle of this architectural mechanism, is not the director's own fate entirely bound up with it? The incompetent physician who has allowed contagion to spread, the incompetent prison governor or workshop manager will be the first victims of an epidemic or a revolt. "'By every tie I could devise,' said the master of the Panopticon, 'my own fate had been bound up by me with theirs'" (Bentham 177). The Panopticon functions as a kind of laboratory of power. Thanks to its mechanisms of observation, it gains in efficiency and in the ability to penetrate into men's behavior; knowledge follows the advances of power, discovering new objects of knowledge over all the surfaces on which power is exercised.

The plague-stricken town, the panoptic establishment—the differences are important. They mark, at a distance of a century and a half, the transformations of the disciplinary program. In the first case, there is an exceptional situation: against an extraordinary evil, power is mobilized; it makes itself everywhere present and visible; it invents new mechanisms; it separates, it immobilizes, it partitions; it constructs for a time what is both a counter-city and the perfect society; it imposes an ideal functioning, but one that is reduced, in the final analysis, like the evil that it combats, to a simple dualism of life and death: that which moves brings death, and one kills that which moves. The Panopticon, on the other hand, must be understood as a generalizable model of functioning; a way of defining power relations in terms of the everyday life of men. No doubt Bentham presents it as a particular institution, closed in upon itself. Utopias, perfectly closed in upon themselves, are common enough. As opposed to the ruined prisons, littered with mechanisms of torture, to be seen in Piranese's engravings, the Panopticon presents a cruel, ingenious cage. The fact that it should have given rise, even in our own time, to so many variations, projected or realized, is evidence of the imaginary intensity that it has possessed for almost two hundred years. But the Panopticon must not be understood as a dream building: it is the diagram of a mechanism of power reduced to its ideal form; its functioning, abstracted from any obstacle, resistance, or friction, must be represented as a pure architectural and optical system: it is in fact a figure of political technology that may and must be detached from any specific use.

It is polyvalent in its applications; it serves to reform prisoners, but also to treat patients, to instruct schoolchildren, to confine the insane, to supervise workers, to put beggars and idlers to work. It is a type of location of bodies in space, of distribution of individuals in relation to one another, of hierarchical organization, of disposition of centers and channels of power, of definition of the instruments and modes of intervention of power, which can be implemented in hospitals, workshops, schools, prisons. Whenever one is dealing with a multiplicity of individuals on whom a task or a particular form of behavior must be imposed, the panoptic schema may be used. It is—necessary modifications apart—applicable "to all establishments whatsoever, in which, within a space not too large to be covered or commanded by buildings, a number of persons are meant to be kept under inspection" (Bentham 40; although Bentham takes the penitentiary house as his prime example, it is because it has many different functions to fulfill—safe custody, confinement, solitude, forced labor, and instruction).

In each of its applications, it makes it possible to perfect the exercise of power. It does this in several ways: because it can reduce the number of those who exercise it, while increasing the number of those on whom it is exercised. Because it is possible to intervene at any moment and because the constant pressure acts even before the offenses, mistakes, or crimes have been committed. Because, in these conditions, its strength is that it never intervenes, it is exercised spontaneously and without noise, it constitutes a mechanism whose effects follow from one another. Because, without any physical instrument other than architecture and geometry, it acts directly on individuals; it gives "power of mind over mind." The panoptic schema makes any apparatus of power more intense: it assures its economy (in material, in personnel, in time); it assures its efficacity by its preventative character, its continuous functioning and its automatic mechanisms. It is a way of obtaining from power "in hitherto unexampled quantity," "a great and new instrument of government . . . ; its great excellence consists in the great strength it is capable of giving to *any* institution it may be thought proper to apply it to" (Bentham 66).

It's a case of "it's easy once you've thought of it" in the political sphere. It can in fact be integrated into any function (education, medical treatment, production, punishment); it can increase the effect of this function, by being linked closely with it; it can constitute a mixed mechanism in which relations of power (and of knowledge) may be precisely adjusted, in the smallest detail, to the processes that are to be supervised; it can establish a direct proportion between "surplus power" and "surplus production." In short, it arranges things in such a way that the exercise of power is not added on from the outside, like a rigid, heavy constraint, to the functions it invests, but is so subtly present in them as to increase their efficiency by itself increasing its own points of contact. The panoptic mechanism is not simply a hinge, a point of exchange between a mechanism of power and a function; it is a way of making power relations function in a function, and of making a function function through these power relations. Bentham's preface to *Panopticon* opens with a list of the benefits to be obtained from his "inspection-house": "*Morals reformed—health preserved—industry invigorated—instruction diffused— public burthens lightened*—Economy seated, as it were, upon a rock—the gordian knot of the Poor-Laws not cut, but untied—all by a simple idea in architecture!" (Bentham 39).

Furthermore, the arrangement of this machine is such that its enclosed nature does not preclude a permanent presence from the outside: we have seen that anyone may come and exercise in the central tower the functions of surveillance, and that, this being the case, he can gain a clear idea of the way in which the surveillance is practiced. In fact, any panoptic institution, even if it is as rigorously closed as a penitentiary, may without difficulty be subjected to such irregular and constant inspections: and not only by the appointed inspectors, but also by the public; any member of society will have the right to come and see with his own eyes how the schools, hospitals, factories, prisons function. There is no risk, therefore, that the increase of power created by the panoptic machine may degenerate into tyranny; the disciplinary mechanism will be democratically controlled, since it will be constantly accessible "to the great tribunal committee of the world."[4] This Panopticon, subtly arranged so that an observer may observe, at a glance, so many different individuals, also enables everyone to come and observe any of the observers. The seeing machine was once a sort of dark room into which individuals spied; it has become a transparent building in which the exercise of power may be supervised by society as a whole.

The panoptic schema, without disappearing as such or losing any of its properties, was destined to spread throughout the social body; its vocation was to become a generalized function. The plague-stricken town provided an exceptional disciplinary model: perfect, but absolutely violent; to the disease that brought death, power opposed its perpetual threat of death; life inside it was reduced to its simplest expression; it was, against the power of death, the meticulous exercise of the right of the sword. The Panopticon, on the other hand, has a role of amplification; although it arranges power, although it is intended to make it more economic and more effective, it does so not for power itself, nor for the immediate salvation of a threatened society: its aim is to strengthen the social forces—to increase production, to develop the economy, spread education, raise the level of public morality; to increase and multiply.

How is power to be strengthened in such a way that, far from impeding progress, far from weighing upon it with its rules and regulations, it actually facilitates such progress? What intensificator of power will be able at the same time to be a multiplicator of production? How will power, by increasing its forces, be able to increase those of society instead of confiscating them or impeding them? The Panopticon's solution to this problem is that the productive increase of power can be assured only if, on the one hand, it can be exercised continuously in the very foundations of society, in the subtlest possible way, and if, on the other hand, it functions outside these sudden, violent, discontinuous forms that are bound up with the exercise of sovereignty. The body of the king, with its strange material and physical presence, with the force that he himself deploys or transmits to some few others, is at the opposite extreme of this new physics of power represented by panopticism; the domain of panopticism is, on the contrary, that whole lower region, that region of irregular bodies, with their details, their multiple movements, their heterogeneous forces, their spatial relations; what are required are mechanisms that analyze distributions, gaps, series, combinations, and which use instruments that render visible, record, differentiate, and compare: a physics of a relational and multiple power, which has its maximum intensity not in the person of the king, but in the bodies that can be individualized by these relations. At the theoretical level, Bentham defines another way of analyzing the social body and the power relations that traverse it; in terms of practice, he defines a procedure of subordination of bodies and forces that must increase the utility of power while practicing the economy of the prince. Panopticism is the general principle of a new "political anatomy" whose object and end are not the relations of sovereignty but the relations of discipline.

The celebrated, transparent, circular cage, with its high tower, powerful and knowing, may have been for Bentham a project of a perfect disciplinary institution; but he also set out to show how one may "unlock" the disciplines and get them to function in a diffused, multiple, polyvalent way throughout the whole social body. These disciplines, which the classical age had elaborated in specific, relatively enclosed places—barracks, schools, workshops—and whose total implementation had been imagined only at the limited and temporary scale of a plague-stricken town, Bentham dreamed of transforming into a network of mechanisms that would be everywhere and always alert, running through society without interruption in space or in time. The panoptic arrangement provides the formula for this generalization. It programs, at the level of an elementary and easily transferable mechanism, the basic functioning of a society penetrated through and through with disciplinary mechanisms.

There are two images, then, of discipline. At one extreme, the discipline-blockade, the enclosed institution, established on the edges of society, turned inwards towards negative functions: arresting evil, breaking communications, suspending time. At the other extreme, with panopticism, is the discipline-mechanism: a functional mechanism that must improve the exercise of power by making it lighter, more rapid, more effective, a design of subtle coercion for a society to come. The movement from one project to the other, from a schema of exceptional discipline to one of a generalized surveillance, rests on a historical transformation: the gradual extension of the mechanisms of discipline throughout the seventeenth and eighteenth centuries, their spread throughout the whole social body, the formation of what might be called in general the disciplinary society.

A whole disciplinary generalization—the Benthamite physics of power represents an acknowledgment of this—had operated throughout the classical age. The spread of disciplinary institutions, whose network was beginning to cover an ever larger surface and occupying above all a less and less marginal position, testifies to this: what was an islet, a privileged place, a circumstantial measure, or a singular model, became a general formula; the regulations characteristic of the Protestant and pious armies of William of Orange or of Gustavus Adolphus were transformed into regulations for all the armies of Europe; the model colleges of the Jesuits, or the schools of Batencour or Demia, following the example set by Sturm, provided the outlines for the general forms of educational discipline; the ordering of the naval and military hospitals provided the model for the entire reorganization of hospitals in the eighteenth century.

But this extension of the disciplinary institutions was no doubt only the most visible aspect of various, more profound processes.

1. *The functional inversion of the disciplines.* At first, they were expected to neutralize dangers, to fix useless or disturbed populations, to avoid the inconveniences of over-large assemblies; now they were being asked to play a positive role, for they were becoming able to do so, to increase the possible utility of individuals. Military discipline is no longer a mere means of preventing looting, desertion, or failure to obey orders among the troops; it has become a basic technique to enable the army to exist, not as an assembled crowd, but as a unity that derives from this very unity an increase in its forces; discipline increases the skill of each individual, coordinates these skills, accelerates movements, increases fire power, broadens the fronts of attack without reducing their vigor, increases the capacity for resistance, etc. The discipline of the workshop, while remaining a way of enforcing respect for the regulations and authorities, of

preventing thefts or losses, tends to increase aptitudes, speeds, output, and therefore profits; it still exerts a moral influence over behavior, but more and more it treats actions in terms of their results, introduces bodies into a machinery, forces into an economy. When, in the seventeenth century, the provincial schools or the Christian elementary schools were founded, the justifications given for them were above all negative: those poor who were unable to bring up their children left them "in ignorance of their obligations: given the difficulties they have in earning a living, and themselves having been badly brought up, they are unable to communicate a sound upbringing that they themselves never had"; this involves three major inconveniences: ignorance of God, idleness (with its consequent drunkenness, impurity, larceny, brigandage), and the formation of those gangs of beggars, always ready to stir up public disorder and "virtually to exhaust the funds of the Hôtel-Dieu" (Demia 60–61). Now, at the beginning of the Revolution, the end laid down for primary education was to be, among other things, to "fortify," to "develop the body," to prepare the child "for a future in some mechanical work," to give him "an observant eye, a sure hand and prompt habits" (Talleyrand's Report to the Constituent Assembly, 10 September 1791, quoted by Léon 106). The disciplines function increasingly as techniques for making useful individuals. Hence their emergence from a marginal position on the confines of society, and detachment from the forms of exclusion or expiation, confinement, or retreat. Hence the slow loosening of their kinship with religious regularities and enclosures. Hence also their rooting in the most important, most central, and most productive sectors of society. They become attached to some of the great essential functions: factory production, the transmission of knowledge, the diffusion of aptitudes and skills, the war-machine. Hence, too, the double tendency one sees developing throughout the eighteenth century to increase the number of disciplinary institutions and to discipline the existing apparatuses.

2. *The swarming of disciplinary mechanisms.* While, on the one hand, the disciplinary establishments increase, their mechanisms have a certain tendency to become "deinstitutionalized," to emerge from the closed fortresses in which they once functioned and to circulate in a "free" state; the massive, compact disciplines are broken down into flexible methods of control, which may be transferred and adapted. Sometimes the closed apparatuses add to their internal and specific function a role of external surveillance, developing around themselves a whole margin of lateral controls. Thus the Christian School must not simply train docile children; it must also make it possible to supervise the parents, to gain information as to their way of life, their resources, their piety, their morals. The school tends to constitute minute social observatories that penetrate even to the adults and exercise regular supervision over them: the bad behavior of the child, or his absence, is a legitimate pretext, according to Demia, for one to go and question the neighbors, especially if there is any reason to believe that the family will not tell the truth; one can then go and question the parents themselves, to find out whether they know their catechism and the prayers, whether they are determined to

root out the vices of their children, how many beds there are in the house and what the sleeping arrangements are; the visit may end with the giving of alms, the present of a religious picture, or the provision of additional beds (Demia 39–40). Similarly, the hospital is increasingly conceived of as a base for the medical observation of the population outside; after the burning down of the Hôtel-Dieu in 1772, there were several demands that the large buildings, so heavy and so disordered, should be replaced by a series of smaller hospitals; their function would be to take in the sick of the quarter, but also to gather information, to be alert to any endemic or epidemic phenomena, to open dispensaries, to give advice to the inhabitants, and to keep the authorities informed of the sanitary state of the region.[5]

One also sees the spread of disciplinary procedures, not in the form of enclosed institutions, but as centers of observation disseminated throughout society. Religious groups and charity organizations had long played this role of "disciplining" the population. From the Counter-Reformation to the philanthropy of the July monarchy, initiatives of this type continued to increase; their aims were religious (conversion and moralization), economic (aid and encouragement to work), or political (the struggle against discontent or agitation). One has only to cite by way of example the regulations for the charity associations in the Paris parishes. The territory to be covered was divided into quarters and cantons and the members of the associations divided themselves up along the same lines. These members had to visit their respective areas regularly. "They will strive to eradicate places of ill-repute, tobacco shops, life-classes, gaming house, public scandals, blasphemy, impiety, and any other disorders that may come to their knowledge." They will also have to make individual visits to the poor; and the information to be obtained is laid down in regulations: the stability of the lodging, knowledge of prayers, attendance at the sacraments, knowledge of a trade, morality (and "whether they have not fallen into poverty through their own fault"); lastly, "one must learn by skillful questioning in what way they behave at home. Whether there is peace between them and their neighbors, whether they are careful to bring up their children in the fear of God . . . , whether they do not have their older children of different sexes sleeping together and with them, whether they do not allow licentiousness and cajolery in their families, especially in their older daughters. If one has any doubts as to whether they are married, one must ask to see their marriage certificate."[6]

3. *The state-control of the mechanisms of the discipline.* In England, it was private religious groups that carried out, for a long time, the functions of social discipline (cf. Radzinovitz 203–14); in France, although a part of this role remained in the hands of parish guilds or charity associations, another—and no doubt the most important part—was very soon taken over by the police apparatus.

The organization of a centralized police had long been regarded, even by contemporaries, as the most direct expression of royal absolutism; the sovereign had wished to have "his own magistrate to whom he might directly entrust his orders, his commissions, intentions, and who was entrusted with the execution of orders and orders under the King's private seal" (a note by Duval, first secretary at the police magistrature, quoted in Funck-Brentano I). In effect, in taking over a number of preexisting functions—the search for criminals, urban surveillance, economic and political supervision—the police magistratures and the magistrature-general that presided over them in Paris transposed them into a single, strict, administrative machine: "All the radiations of force and information that spread from the circumference culminate in the magistrate-general. . . . It is he who operates all the wheels that together produce order and harmony. The effects of his administration cannot be better compared than to the movement of the celestial bodies" (Des Essarts 344, 528).

But, although the police as an institution were certainly organized in the form of a state apparatus, and although this was certainly linked directly to the center of political sovereignty, the type of power that it exercises, the mechanisms it operates, and the elements to which it applies them are specific. It is an apparatus that must be coextensive with the entire social body and not only by the extreme limits that it embraces, but by the minuteness of the details it is concerned with. Police power must bear "over everything": it is not, however, the totality of the state nor of the kingdom as visible and invisible body of the monarch; it is the dust of events, actions, behavior, opinions—"everything that happens";[7] the police are concerned with "those things of every moment," those "unimportant things," of which Catherine II spoke in her Great Instruction (Supplement to the *Instruction for the Drawing Up of a New Code,* 1769, article 535). With the police, one is in the indefinite world of a supervision that seeks ideally to reach the most elementary particle, the most passing phenomenon of the social body: "The ministry of the magistrates and police officers is of the greatest importance; the objects that it embraces are in a sense definite, one may perceive them only by a sufficiently detailed examination" (Delamare, unnumbered preface): the infinitely small of political power.

And, in order to be exercised, this power had to be given the instrument of permanent, exhaustive, omnipresent surveillance, capable of making all visible, as long as it could itself remain invisible. It had to be like a faceless gaze that transformed the whole social body into a field of perception: thousands of eyes posted everywhere, mobile attentions ever on the alert, a long, hierarchized network which, according to Le Maire, comprised for Paris the forty-eight *commissaires,* the twenty *inspecteurs,* then the "observers," who were paid regularly, the *"basses mouches,"* or secret agents, who were paid by the day, then the informers, paid according to the job done, and finally the prostitutes. And this unceasing observation had to be accumulated in a series of reports and registers; throughout the eighteenth century, an immense police text increasingly covered society by means of a complex documentary organization (on the police registers in the eighteenth century, cf. Chassaigne). And, unlike the methods of judicial or administrative writing, what was registered in this way were forms of behavior, attitudes, possibilities, suspicions—a permanent account of individuals' behavior.

Now, it should be noted that, although this police supervision was entirely "in the hands of the king," it did not function in a single direction. It was in fact a double-entry system: it had to correspond, by manipulating the machinery of justice, to the immediate wishes of the king, but it was also capable of responding to solicitations from below; the celebrated *lettres de cachet,* or orders under the king's private seal, which were long the symbol of arbitrary royal rule and which brought detention into disrepute on political grounds, were in fact demanded by families, masters, local notables, neighbors, parish priests; and their function was to punish by confinement a whole infrapenality, that of disorder, agitation, disobedience, bad conduct; those things that Ledoux wanted to exclude from his architecturally perfect city and which he called "offenses of nonsurveillance." In short, the eighteenth-century police added a disciplinary function to its role as the auxiliary of justice in the pursuit of criminals and as an instrument for the political supervision of plots, opposition movements, or revolts. It was a complex function since it linked the absolute power of the monarch to the lowest levels of power disseminated in society; since, between these different, enclosed institutions of discipline (workshops, armies, schools), it extended an intermediary network, acting where they could not intervene, disciplining the nondisciplinary spaces; but it filled in the gaps, linked them together, guaranteed with its armed force an interstitial discipline and a metadiscipline. "By means of a wise police, the sovereign accustoms the people to order and obedience" (Vattel 162).

The organization of the police apparatus in the eighteenth century sanctioned a generalization of the disciplines that became coextensive with the state itself. Although it was linked in the most explicit way with everything in the royal power that exceeded the exercise of regular justice, it is understandable why the police offered such slight resistance to the rearrangement of the judicial power; and why it has not ceased to impose its prerogatives upon it, with ever-increasing weight, right up to the present day; this is no doubt because it is the secular arm of the judiciary; but it is also because, to a far greater degree than the judicial institution, it is identified, by reason of its extent and mechanisms, with a society of the disciplinary type. Yet it would be wrong to believe that the disciplinary functions were confiscated and absorbed once and for all by a state apparatus.

"Discipline" may be identified neither with an institution nor with an apparatus; it is a type of power, a modality for its exercise, comprising a whole set of instruments, techniques, procedures, levels of application, targets; it is a "physics" or an "anatomy" of power, a technology. And it may be taken over either by "specialized" institutions (the penitentiaries or "houses of correction" of the nineteenth century), or by institutions that use it as an essential instrument for a particular end (schools, hospitals), or by preexisting authorities that find in it a means of reinforcing or reorganizing their internal mechanisms of power (one day we should show how intrafamilial relations, essentially in the parents-children cell, have become "disciplined," absorbing since the classical age external schemata, first educational and military, then medical, psychiatric, psychological, which have made the family the privileged locus of emergence for the disciplinary question of the normal and the abnormal), or by apparatuses that have made discipline their principle of internal functioning (the disciplinarization of the administrative apparatus from the Napoleonic period), or finally by state apparatuses whose major, if not exclusive, function is to assure that discipline reigns over society as a whole (the police).

On the whole, therefore, one can speak of the formation of a disciplinary society in this movement that stretches from the enclosed disciplines, a sort of social "quarantine," to an indefinitely generalizable mechanism of "panopticism." Not because the disciplinary modality of power has replaced all the others; but because it has infiltrated the others, sometimes undermining them, but serving as an intermediary between them, linking them together, extending them, and above all making it possible to bring the effects of power to the most minute and distant elements. It assures an infinitesimal distribution of the power relations.

A few years after Bentham, Julius gave this society its birth certificate (Julius 384–86). Speaking of the panoptic principle, he said that there was much more there than architectural ingenuity: it was an event in the "history of the human mind." In appearance, it is merely the solution of a technical problem; but, through it, a whole type of society emerges. Antiquity had been a civilization of spectacle. "To render accessible to a multitude of men the inspection of a small number of objects": this was the problem to which the architecture of temples, theaters, and circuses responded. With spectacle, there was a predominance of public life, the intensity of festivals, sensual proximity. In these rituals in which blood flowed, society found new vigor and formed for a moment a single great body. The modern age poses the opposite problem: "To procure for a small number, or even for a single individual, the instantaneous view of a great multitude." In a society in which the principal elements are no longer the community and public life, but, on the one hand, private individuals and, on the other, the state, relations can be regulated only in a form that is the exact reverse of the spectacle: "It was to the modern age, to the ever-growing influence of the state, to its ever more profound intervention in all the details and all the relations of social life, that was reserved the task of increasing and perfecting its guarantees, by using and directing towards that great aim the building and distribution of buildings intended to observe a great multitude of men at the same time."

Julius saw as a fulfilled historical process that which Bentham had described as a technical program. Our society is one not of spectacle, but of surveillance; under the surface of images, one invests bodies in depth; behind the great abstraction of exchange, there continues the meticulous, concrete training of useful forces; the circuits of communication are the supports of an accumulation and a centralization of knowledge; the play of signs defines the anchorages of power; it is not that the beautiful totality of the individual is amputated, repressed, altered by our social order, it is rather that the individual is carefully fabricated in it, according to a whole technique of forces and bodies. We are much less Greeks than we believe. We are neither in the amphitheater, nor on the stage, but in the panoptic machine, invested by its effects of power, which we bring to ourselves since we are part of its mechanism. The importance, in historical mythology, of the Napoleonic character probably derives from the fact that it is at the point of junction of the monarchical, ritual exercise of sovereignty and the hierarchical, permanent exercise of indefinite discipline. He is the individual who looms over everything with a single gaze which no detail, however minute, can escape: "You may consider that no part of the Empire is without surveillance, no crime, no offense, no contravention that remains unpunished, and that the eye of the genius who can enlighten all embraces the whole of this vast machine, without, however, the slightest detail escaping his attention" (Treilhard 14). At the moment of its full blossoming, the disciplinary society still assumes with the Emperor the old aspect of the power of spectacle. As a monarch who is at one and the same time a usurper of the ancient throne and the organizer of the new state, he combined into a single symbolic, ultimate figure the whole of the long process by which the pomp of sovereignty, the necessarily spectacular manifestations of power, were extinguished one by one in the daily exercise of surveillance, in a panopticism in which the vigilance of intersecting gazes was soon to render useless both the eagle and the sun.

The formation of the disciplinary society is connected with a number of broad historical processes—economic, juridico-political, and lastly, scientific—of which it forms part.

1. Generally speaking, it might be said that the disciplines are techniques for assuring the ordering of human multiplicities. It is true that there is nothing exceptional or even characteristic in this: every system of power is presented with the same problem. But the peculiarity of the disciplines is that they try to define in relation to the multiplicities a tactics of power that fulfills three criteria: firstly, to obtain the exercise of power at the lowest possible cost (economically, by the low expenditure it involves; politically, by its discretion, its low exteriorization, its relative invisibility, the little resistance it arouses); secondly, to bring the effects of this social power to their maximum intensity and to extend them as far as possible, without either failure or interval; thirdly, to link this "economic" growth of power with the output of the apparatuses (educational, military, industrial, or medical) within which it is exercised; in short, to increase both the docility and the utility of all the elements of the system. This triple objective of the disciplines corresponds to a well-known historical conjuncture. One aspect of this conjuncture was the large demographic thrust of the eighteenth century; an increase in the floating population (one of the primary objects of discipline is to fix; it is an anti-nomadic technique); a change of quantitative scale in the groups to be super-

vised or manipulated (from the beginning of the seventeenth century to the eve of the French Revolution, the school population had been increasing rapidly, as had no doubt the hospital population; by the end of the eighteenth century, the peacetime army exceeded 200,000 men). The other aspect of the conjuncture was the growth in the apparatus of production, which was becoming more and more extended and complex; it was also becoming more costly and its profitability had to be increased. The development of the disciplinary methods corresponded to these two processes, or rather, no doubt, to the new need to adjust their correlation. Neither the residual forms of feudal power nor the structures of the administrative monarchy, nor the local mechanisms of supervision, nor the unstable, tangled mass they all formed together could carry out this role: they were hindered from doing so by the irregular and inadequate extension of their network, by their often conflicting functioning, but above all by the "costly" nature of the power that was exercised in them. It was costly in several senses: because directly it cost a great deal to the Treasury; because the system of corrupt offices and farmed-out taxes weighed indirectly, but very heavily, on the population; because the resistance it encountered forced it into a cycle of perpetual reinforcement; because it proceeded essentially by levying (levying on money or products by royal, seigniorial, ecclesiastical taxation; levying on men or time by *corvées* of press-ganging, by locking up or banishing vagabonds). The development of the disciplines marks the appearance of elementary techniques belonging to a quite different economy: mechanisms of power which, instead of proceeding by deduction, are integrated into the productive efficiency of the apparatuses from within, into the growth of this efficiency and into the use of what it produces. For the old principle of "levying-violence," which governed the economy of power, the disciplines substitute the principle of "mildness-production-profit." These are the techniques that make it possible to adjust the multiplicity of men and the multiplication of the apparatuses of production (and this means not only "production" in the strict sense, but also the production of knowledge and skills in the school, the production of health in the hospitals, the production of destructive force in the army).

In this task of adjustment, discipline had to solve a number of problems for which the old economy of power was not sufficiently equipped. It could reduce the inefficiency of mass phenomena: reduce what, in a multiplicity, makes it much less manageable than a unity; reduce what is opposed to the use of each of its elements and of their sum; reduce everything that may counter the advantages of number. That is why discipline fixes; it arrests or regulates movements; it clears up confusion; it dissipates compact groupings of individuals wandering about the country in unpredictable ways; it establishes calculated distributions. It must also master all the forces that are formed from the very constitution of an organized multiplicity; it must neutralize the effects of counterpower that spring from them and which form a resistance to the power that wishes to dominate it: agitations, revolts, spontaneous organizations, coalitions—anything that may establish horizontal conjunctions. Hence the fact that the disciplines use procedures of partitioning and verticality, that they introduce, between the different elements at the same level, as solid separations as possible, that they define compact hierarchical networks, in short, that they oppose to the intrinsic, adverse force of multiplicity the technique of the continuous, individualizing pyramid. They must also increase the particular utility of each element of the multiplicity, but by means that are the most rapid and the least costly, that is to say, by using the multiplicity itself as an instrument of this growth. Hence, in order to extract from bodies the maximum time and force, the use of those overall methods known as timetables, collective training, exercises, total and detailed surveillance. Furthermore, the disciplines must increase the effect of utility proper to the multiplicities, so that each is made more useful than the simple sum of its elements: it is in order to increase the utilizable effects of the multiple that the disciplines define tactics of distribution, reciprocal adjustment of bodies, gestures, and rhythms, differentiation of capacities, reciprocal coordination in relation to apparatuses or tasks. Lastly, the disciplines have to bring into play the power relations, not above but inside the very texture of the multiplicity, as discreetly as possible, as well articulated on the other functions of these multiplicities and also in the least expensive way possible: to this correspond anonymous instruments of power, coextensive with the multiplicity that they regiment, such as hierarchical surveillance, continuous registration, perpetual assessment, and classification. In short, to substitute for a power that is manifested through the brilliance of those who exercise it, a power that insidiously objectifies those on whom it is applied; to form a body of knowledge about these individuals, rather than to deploy the ostentatious signs of sovereignty. In a word, the disciplines are the ensemble of minute technical inventions that made it possible to increase the useful size of multiplicities by decreasing the inconveniences of the power which, in order to make them useful, must control them. A multiplicity, whether in a workshop or a nation, an army or a school, reaches the threshold of a discipline when the relation of the one to the other becomes favorable.

If the economic take-off of the West began with the techniques that made possible the accumulation of capital, it might perhaps be said that the methods for administering the accumulation of men made possible a political take-off in relation to the traditional, ritual, costly, violent forms of power, which soon fell into disuse and were superseded by a subtle, calculated technology of subjection. In fact, the two processes—the accumulation of men and the accumulation of capital—cannot be separated; it would not have been possible to solve the problem of the accumulation of men without the growth of an apparatus of production capable of both sustaining them and using them; conversely, the techniques that made the cumulative multiplicity of men useful accelerated the accumulation of capital. At a less general level, the technological mutations of the apparatus of production, the division of labor and the elaboration of the disciplinary techniques sustained an ensemble of very close relations (cf. Marx, *Capital*, vol. I, chapter XIII and the very interesting analysis in Guerry and Deleule). Each makes the other possible and necessary; each provides a model for the other. The disciplinary pyramid constituted the small cell of power within which the separation, co-ordination, and supervision of tasks was imposed and made efficient; and analytical partitioning of time, gestures, and bodily forces constituted an operational schema that could easily be transferred from the groups to be subjected to the mechanisms of production; the massive projection of military methods onto industrial organization was an example of this modeling of the division of labor following the model laid down by the schemata of power. But, on the other hand, the technical analysis of the process of production, its "mechanical" breaking-down, were projected onto the labor force whose task it was to implement it: the constitution of those disciplinary machines in which the individual forces that they bring together are composed into a whole and therefore increased is the effect of this projection. Let us say that discipline is the unitary technique by which the body is reduced as a "political" force at the least cost and maximized as a useful force. The growth of a capitalist economy gave rise to the specific modality of disciplinary power, whose general formulas, techniques of submitting forces and bodies, in short, "political anatomy," could be operated in the most diverse political regimes, apparatuses, or institutions.

2. The panoptic modality of power—at the elementary, technical, merely physical level at which it is situated—is not under the immediate dependence or a direct extension of the great juridico-political structures of a society; it is nonetheless not absolutely independent. Historically, the process by which the bourgeoisie became in the course of the eighteenth century the politically dominant class was masked by the establishment of an explicit, coded, and formally egalitarian juridical framework, made possible by the organization of a parliamentary, representative regime. But the development and generalization of disciplinary mechanisms constituted the other, dark side of these processes. The general juridical form that guaranteed a system of rights that were egalitarian in principle was supported by these tiny, everyday, physical mechanisms, by all those systems of micropower that are essentially nonegalitarian and asymmetrical that we call the disciplines. And although, in a formal way, the representative regime makes it possible, directly or indirectly, with or without relays, for the will of all to form the fundamental authority of sovereignty, the disciplines provide, at the base, a guarantee of the submission of forces and bodies. The real, corporal disciplines constituted the foundation of the formal, juridical liberties. The contract may have been regarded as the ideal foundation of law and political power; panopticism constituted the technique, universally widespread, of coercion. It continued to work in depth on the juridical structures of society, in order to make the effective mechanisms of power function in opposition to the formal framework that it had acquired. The "Enlightenment," which discovered the liberties, also invented the disciplines.

In appearance, the disciplines constitute nothing more than an infralaw.

They seem to extend the general forms defined by law to the infinitesimal level of individual lives; or they appear as methods of training that enable individuals to become integrated into these general demands. They seem to constitute the same type of law on a different scale, thereby making it more meticulous and more indulgent. The disciplines should be regarded as a sort of counterlaw. They have the precise role of introducing insuperable asymmetries and excluding reciprocities. First, because discipline creates between individuals a "private" link, which is a relation of constraints entirely different from contractual obligation; the acceptance of a discipline may be underwritten by contract; the way in which it is imposed, the mechanisms it brings into play, the nonreversible subordination of one group of people by another, the "surplus" power that is always fixed on the same side, the inequality of position of the different "partners" in relation to the common regulation, all these distinguish the disciplinary link from the contractual link, and make it possible to distort the contractual link systematically from the moment it has as its content a mechanism of discipline. We know, for example, how many real procedures undermine the legal fiction of the work contract: workshop discipline is not the least important. Moreover, whereas the juridical systems define juridical subjects according to universal norms, the disciplines characterize, classify, specialize; they distribute along a scale, around a norm, hierarchize individuals in relation to one another and, if necessary, disqualify and invalidate. In any case, in the space and during the time in which they exercise their control and bring into play the asymmetries of their power, they effect a suspension of the law that is never total, but is never annulled either. Regular and institutional as it may be, the discipline, in its mechanism, is a "counterlaw." And, although the universal juridicism of modern society seems to fix limits on the exercise of power, its universally widespread panopticism enables it to operate, on the underside of the law, a machinery that is both immense and minute, which supports, reinforces, multiplies the asymmetry of power and undermines the limits that are traced around the law. The minute disciplines, the panopticisms of every day may well be below the level of emergence of the great apparatuses and the great political struggles. But, in the genealogy of modern society, they have been, with the class domination that traverses it, the political counterpart of the juridical norms according to which power was redistributed. Hence, no doubt, the importance that has been given for so long to the small techniques of discipline, to those apparently insignificant tricks that it has invented, and even to those "sciences" that give it a respectable face; hence the fear of abandoning them if one cannot find any substitute; hence the affirmation that they are at the very foundation of society, and an element in its equilibrium, whereas they are a series of mechanisms for unbalancing power relations definitively and everywhere; hence the persistence in regarding them as the humble, but concrete form of every morality, whereas they are a set of physico-political techniques.

To return to the problem of legal punishments, the prison with all the corrective technology at its disposal is to be resituated at the point where the codified power to punish turns into a disciplinary power to observe; at the point where the universal punishments of the law are applied selectively to certain individuals and always the same ones; at the point where the redefinition of the juridical subject by the penalty becomes a useful training of the criminal; at the point where the law is inverted and passes outside itself, and where the counterlaw becomes the effective and institutionalized content of the juridical forms. What generalizes the power to punish, then, is not the universal consciousness of the law in each juridical subject; it is the regular extension, the infinitely minute web of panoptic techniques.

3. Taken one by one, most of these techniques have a long history behind them. But what was new, in the eighteenth century, was that, by being combined and generalized, they attained a level at which the formation of knowledge and the increase of power regularly reinforce one another in a circular process. At this point, the disciplines crossed the "technological" threshold. First the hospital, then the school, then, later, the workshop were not simply "reordered" by the disciplines; they became, thanks to them, apparatuses such that any mechanism of objectification could be used in them as an instrument of subjection, and any growth of power could give rise in them to possible branches of knowledge; it was this link, proper to the technological systems, that made possible within the disciplinary element the formation of clinical medicine, psychiatry, child psychology, educational psychology, the rationalization of labor. It is a double process, then: an epistemological "thaw" through a refinement of power relations; a multiplication of the effects of power through the formation and accumulation of new forms of knowledge.

The extension of the disciplinary methods is inscribed in a broad historical process: the development at about the same time of many other technologies—agronomical, industrial, economic. But it must be recognized that, compared with the mining industries, the emerging chemical industries or methods of national accountancy, compared with the blast furnaces or the steam engine, panopticism has received little attention. It is regarded as not much more than a bizarre little utopia, a perverse dream—rather as though Bentham had been the Fourier of a police society, and the Phalanstery had taken on the form of the Panopticon. And yet this represented the abstract formula of a very real technology, that of individuals. There were many reasons why it received little praise; the most obvious is that the discourses to which it gave rise rarely acquired, except in the academic classifications, the status of sciences; but the real reason is no doubt that the power that it operates and which it augments is a direct, physical power that men exercise upon one another. An inglorious culmination had an origin that could be only grudgingly acknowledged. But it would be unjust to compare the disciplinary techniques with such inventions as the steam engine or Amici's microscope. They are much less; and yet, in a way, they are much more. If a historical equivalent or at least a point of comparison had to be found for them, it would be rather in the "inquisitorial" technique.

The eighteenth century invented the techniques of discipline and the examination, rather as the Middle Ages invented the judicial investigation. But it did so by quite different means. The investigation procedure, an old fiscal and administrative technique, had developed above all with the reorganization of the Church and the increase of the princely states in the twelfth and thirteenth centuries. At this time it permeated to a very large degree the jurisprudence first of the ecclesiastical courts, then of the lay courts. The investigation as an authoritarian search for a truth observed or attested was thus opposed to the old procedures of the oath, the ordeal, the judicial duel, the judgment of God, or even of the transaction between private individuals. The investigation was the sovereign power arrogating to itself the right to establish the truth by a number of regulated techniques. Now, although the investigation has since then been an integral part of Western justice (even up to our own day), one must not forget either its political origin, its link with the birth of the states and of monarchical sovereignty, or its later extension and its role in the formation of knowledge. In fact, the investigation has been the no doubt crude, but fundamental element in the constitution of the empirical sciences; it has been the juridico-political matrix of this experimental knowledge, which, as we know, was very rapidly released at the end of the Middle Ages. It is perhaps true to say that, in Greece, mathematics were born from techniques of measurement; the sciences of nature, in any case, were born, to some extent, at the end of the Middle Ages, from the practices of investigation. The great empirical knowledge that covered the things of the world and transcribed them into the ordering of an indefinite discourse that observes, describes, and establishes the "facts" (at a time when the Western world was beginning the economic and political conquest of this same world) had its operating model no doubt in the Inquisition—that immense invention that our recent mildness has placed in the dark recesses of our memory. But what this politico-juridical, administrative, and criminal, religious and lay, investigation was to the sciences of nature, disciplinary analysis has been to the sciences of man. These sciences, which have so delighted our "humanity" for over a century, have their technical matrix in the petty, malicious minutiae of the disciplines and their investigations. These investigations are perhaps to psychology, psychiatry, pedagogy, criminology, and so many other strange sciences, what the terrible power of investigation was to the calm knowledge of the animals, the plants, or the earth. Another power, another knowledge. On the threshold of the classical age, Bacon, lawyer and statesman, tried to develop a methodology of investigation for the empirical sciences. What Great Observer will produce the methodology of examination for the human sciences? Unless, of course, such a thing is not possible. For, although it is true that, in becoming a technique for the empirical sciences, the investigation has detached itself from the inquisitorial procedure, in which it was historically rooted, the examination has remained extremely close to the disciplinary power that shaped it. It has always been and still is an intrinsic element of the disciplines. Of course it seems to have undergone a speculative purification by integrating itself with such sciences as psychology and psychiatry. And, in effect, its appearance in the form of tests, interviews, interrogations, and consultations is apparently in order to rectify the mechanisms of discipline: educational psychology is supposed to correct the rigors of the school, just as the medical or psychiatric interview is supposed to rectify the effects of the discipline of work. But we must not be misled; these techniques merely refer individuals from one disciplinary authority to another, and they reproduce, in a concentrated or formalized form, the schema of power-knowledge proper to each discipline (on this subject, cf. Tort). The great investigation that gave rise to the sciences of nature has become detached from its politico-juridical model; the examination, on the other hand, is still caught up in disciplinary technology.

In the Middle Ages, the procedure of investigation gradually superseded the old accusatory justice, by a process initiated from above; the disciplinary technique, on the other hand, insidiously and as if from below, has invaded a penal justice that is still, in principle, inquisitorial. All the great movements of extension that characterize modern penality—the problematization of the criminal behind his crime, the concern with a punishment that is a correction, a therapy, a normalization, the division of the act of judgment between various authorities that are supposed to measure, assess, diagnose, cure, transform individuals—all this betrays the penetration of the disciplinary examination into the judicial inquisition.

What is now imposed on penal justice as its point of application, its "useful" object, will no longer be the body of the guilty man set up against the body of the king; nor will it be the juridical subject of an ideal contract; it will be the disciplinary individual. The extreme point of penal justice under the Ancien Régime was the infinite segmentation of the body of the regicide: a manifestation of the strongest power over the body of the greatest criminal, whose total destruction made the crime explode into its truth. The ideal point of penality today would be an indefinite discipline: an interrogation without end, an investigation that would be extended without limit to a meticulous and ever more analytical observation, a judgment that would at the same time be the constitution of a file that was never closed, the calculated leniency of a penalty that would be interlaced with the ruthless curiosity of an examination, a procedure that would be at the same time the permanent measure of a gap in relation to an inaccessible norm and the asymptotic movement that strives to meet in infinity. The public execution was the logical culmination of a procedure governed by the Inquisition. The practice of placing individuals under "observation" is a natural extension of a justice imbued with disciplinary methods and examination procedures. Is it surprising that the cellular prison, with its regular chronologies, forced labor, its authorities of surveillance and registration, its experts in normality, who continue and multiply the functions of the judge, should have become the modern instrument of penality? Is it surprising that prisons resemble factories, schools, barracks, hospitals, which all resemble prisons?

NOTES

[1] Archives militaires de Vincennes, A 1,516 91 sc. Pièce. This regulation is broadly similar to a whole series of others that date from the same period and earlier.

[2] In the *Postscript to the Panopticon*, 1791, Bentham adds dark inspection galleries painted in black around the inspector's lodge, each making it possible to observe two stories of cells.

[3] In his first version of the *Panopticon*, Bentham had also imagined an acoustic surveillance, operated by means of pipes leading from the cells to the central tower. In the *Postscript* he abandoned the idea, perhaps because he could not introduce into it the principle of dissymmetry and prevent the prisoners from hearing the inspector as well as the inspector hearing them. Julius tried to develop a system of dissymmetrical listening (Julius 18).

[4] Imagining this continuous flow of visitors entering the central tower by an underground passage and then observing the circular landscape of the Panopticon, was Bentham aware of the Panoramas that Barker was constructing at exactly the same period (the first seems to have dated from 1787) and in which the visitors, occupying the central place, saw unfolding around them a landscape, a city, or a battle. The visitors occupied exactly the place of the sovereign gaze.

[5] In the second half of the eighteenth century, it was often suggested that the army should be used for the surveillance and general partitioning of the population. The army, as yet to undergo discipline in the seventeenth century, was regarded as a force capable of instilling it. Cf., for example, Servan, *Le Soldat citoyen*, 1780.

[6] Arsenal, MS. 2565. Under this number, one also finds regulations for charity associations of the seventeenth and eighteenth centuries.

[7] Le Maire in a memorandum written at the request of Sartine, in answer to sixteen questions posed by Joseph II on the Parisian police. This memorandum was published by Gazier in 1879.

BIBLIOGRAPHY

Archives militaires de Vincennes, A 1,516 91 sc.

Bentham, J., *Works*, ed. Bowring, IV, 1843.

Chassaigne, M., *La Lieutenance générale de police*, 1906.

Delamare, N., *Traité de police*, 1705.

Demia, C., *Règlement pour les écoles de la ville de Lyon*, 1716.

Des Essarts, T. N., *Dictionnaire universel de police*, 1787.

Funck-Brentano, F., *Catalogue des manuscrits de la bibliothèque de l'Arsenal*, IX.

Guerry, F., and Deleule, D., *Le Corps productif*, 1973.

Julius, N. H., *Leçons sur les prisons*, I, 1831 (Fr. trans.).

Léon, A., *La Révolution française et l'éducation technique*, 1968.

Loisel, G., *Histoire des ménageries*, II, 1912.

Marx, Karl, *Capital*, vol. I, ed. 1970.

Radzinovitz, L., *The English Criminal Law*, II, 1956.

Servan, J., *Le Soldat citoyen*, 1780.

Tort, Michel, *Q.I.*, 1974.

Treilhard, J. B., *Motifs du code d'instruction criminelle*, 1808.

Vattel, E. de, *Le Droit des gens*, 1768.

. . . .

QUESTIONS FOR A SECOND READING

1. Foucault's text begins with an account of a system enacted in the seventeenth century to control the spread of plague. After describing this system of surveillance, he compares it to the "rituals of exclusion" used to control lepers. He says, "The exile of the leper and the arrest of the plague do not bring with them the same political dream" (p. 181). At many points he sets up similar pairings, all in an attempt to understand the relations of power and knowledge in modern public life.

   As you reread, mark the various points at which Foucault works out the differences between a prior and the current "political dream" of order. What are the techniques or instruments that belong to each? What moments in history are defined by each? How and where are they visible in public life?

2. Toward the end of the chapter Foucault says, "The extension of the disciplinary methods is inscribed in a broad historical process." Foucault writes a difficult kind of history (at one point he calls it a genealogy), since it does not make use of the usual form of historical narrative—with characters, plots, scenes, and action. As you reread, take notes that will allow you to trace time, place, and sequence (and, if you can, agents and agency) in Foucault's account of the formation of the disciplinary society based on technologies of surveillance. Why do you think he avoids a narrative mode of presentation?

3. As you reread Foucault's text, bring forward the stages in his presentation (or the development of his argument). Mark those moments that you consider key or central to the working out of his argument concerning the panopticon. What sentences of his would you use to represent key moments in the text? The text at times turns to numbered sections. How, for example, do they function? Describe the beginning, middle, and end of the essay. Describe the skeleton or understructure of the chapter. What are its various stages or steps? How do they relate to each other?

ASSIGNMENTS FOR WRITING

1. About three-quarters of the way into this chapter, Foucault says,

   > Our society is one not of spectacle, but of surveillance; under the surface of images, one invests bodies in depth; behind the great abstraction of exchange, there continues the meticulous, concrete training of useful forces; the circuits of communication are the supports of an accumulation and a centralization of knowledge; the play of signs defines the anchorages of power; it is not that the beautiful totality of the individual is amputated, repressed, altered by our social order, it is rather that the individual is carefully fabricated in it, according to a whole technique of forces and bodies. (pp. 197–98)

This prose is eloquent and insists on its importance to our moment and our society; it is also very hard to read or to paraphrase. Who is doing what to whom? How do we think about the individual's being carefully fabricated in the social order?

Take this chapter as a problem to solve. What is it about? What are its key arguments? its examples and conclusions? Write an essay that summarizes "Panopticism." Imagine that you are writing for readers who have read the chapter (although they won't have the pages in front of them). You will need to take time to present and discuss examples from the text. Your job is to help your readers figure out what it says. You get the chance to take the lead and be the teacher. You should feel free to acknowledge that you don't understand certain sections even as you write about them.

So, how do you write about something you don't completely understand? Here's a suggestion. When you have completed your summary, read it over and treat it as a draft. Ask questions like these: What have I left out? What was I tempted to ignore or finesse? Go back to those sections of the chapter that you ignored and bring them into your essay. Revise by adding discussions of some of the very sections you don't understand. You can write about what you think Foucault *might* be saying—you can, that is, be cautious and tentative; you can admit that the text is what it is, hard to read. You don't have to master this text. You do, however, need to see what you can make of it.

2. About a third of the way through his text, Foucault asserts, "The Panopticon is a marvelous machine which, whatever use one may wish to put it to, produces homogeneous effects of power." Write an essay in which you explain the machinery of the panopticon as a mechanism of power. Paraphrase Foucault and, where it seems appropriate, use his words. Present Foucault's account as you understand it. As part of your essay, and in order to explain what he is getting at, turn to two examples—one of his, perhaps, and then one of your own.

3. Perhaps the most surprising thing about Foucault's argument in "Panopticism" is the way it equates prisons with schools, hospitals, and workplaces, sites we are accustomed to imagining as very different from a prison. Foucault argues against our commonly accepted understanding of such things.

At the end of the chapter Foucault asks two questions. These are rhetorical questions, strategically placed at the end. Presumably we are prepared to feel their force and to think of possible answers.

> Is it surprising that the cellular prison, with its regular chronologies, forced labor, its authorities of surveillance and registration, its experts in normality, who continue and multiply the functions of the judge, should have become the modern instrument of penality? Is it surprising that prisons resemble factories, schools, barracks, hospitals, which all resemble prisons? (pp. 205–06)

For this assignment, take the invitation of Foucault's conclusion. No, you want to respond, it is not surprising that "experts in normality, who continue and multiply the functions of the judge, should have become the modern instrument of penality." No, it is not surprising that "prisons resemble factories, schools, barracks, hospitals, which all resemble prisons." Why isn't it surprising? Or, why isn't it surprising if you are thinking along with Foucault?

Write an essay in which you explore one of these possible resemblances. You may, if you choose, cite Foucault. You can certainly pick up some of his key terms or examples and put them into play. You should imagine, however, that it is your turn. With your work on Foucault behind you, you are writing to a general audience about "experts in normality" and the key sites of surveillance and control.

MAKING CONNECTIONS

1. Both John Berger in "Ways of Seeing" (p. 50) and Foucault in "Panopticism" discuss what Foucault calls "power relations." Berger claims that "the entire art of the past has now become a political issue," and he makes a case for the evolution of a "new language of images" which could "confer a new kind of power" if people were to understand history in art. Foucault argues that the Panopticon signals an "inspired" change in power relations. "It is," he says,

> an important mechanism, for it automatizes and disindividualizes power. Power has its principle not so much in a person as in a certain concerted distribution of bodies, surfaces, lights, gazes; in an arrangement whose internal mechanisms produce the relation in which individuals are caught up. (p. 185)

Both Berger and Foucault create arguments about power, its methods and goals. As you read through their essays, mark passages you might use to explain how each author thinks about power—where it comes from, who has it, how it works, where you look for it, how you know when you see it, what it does, where it goes. You should reread the essays as a pair, as part of a single project in which you are looking to explain theories of power.

Write an essay in which you present and explain "Ways of Seeing" and "Panopticism" as examples of Berger's and Foucault's theories of power. Both Berger and Foucault are arguing against usual understandings of power and knowledge and history. In this sense, their projects are similar. You should be sure, however, to look for differences as well as similarities.

2. Both "And We Are Not Married" (p. 694) by Patricia J. Williams and "Panopticism" by Michel Foucault present difficulties to their readers. Let's assume that these essays are deliberately difficult, that they are difficult for all readers, not just for college students, and that the difficulty is necessary, strategic, not just an error in judgment or evidence of a writer's failure to be clear.

Go to each selection and, as you review it, look for sections or examples you could use to define the peculiar difficulties each presents to its readers—or to you as its reader. Think about the different demands the two essays make. And begin to think about how you would explain the experience of reading these to someone getting ready to work on them for the first time.

What demands do they make of a reader? How do they ask to be read? Why would anyone want to read (or to write) this way? What have you learned about reading by having worked on these texts?

Write an essay in which you use these two selections as examples of the kinds of reading demanded at the university. What makes this material hard to read? How might one value (rather than regret) the work of reading as it is defined in these cases? What advice would you give to students who follow you, who might also be asked to read these selections?

PAULO
FREIRE

*P*aulo Freire (pronounce it "Fr-air-ah" unless you can make a Portuguese "r") is
*one of the most influential radical educators of our world. A native of Recife,
Brazil, he spent most of his early career working in poverty-stricken areas of his
homeland, developing methods for teaching illiterate adults to read and write and (as
he would say) to think critically and, thereby, to take power over their own lives. Because he has created a classroom where teachers and students have equal power and
equal dignity, his work has stood as a model for educators around the world. It led
also to sixteen years of exile after the military coup in Brazil in 1964. During that
time he taught in Europe and in the United States and worked for the Allende government in Chile, training the teachers whose job it would be to bring modern agricultural methods to the peasants.*

*Freire was born in 1921. He has worked with the adult education programs of
UNESCO, the Chilean Institute of Agrarian Reform, and the World Council of
Churches. He is now professor of educational philosophy at the Catholic University
of São Paulo. He is the author of* Education for Critical Consciousness, The Politics of Education, The Pedagogy of the Oppressed *(from which the following
essay is drawn), and* Learning to Question: A Pedagogy of Liberation *(with Antonio Faundez).*

For Freire, education is not an objective process, if by objective we mean "neutral" or "without bias or prejudice." Because teachers could be said to have something that their students lack, it is impossible to have a "neutral" classroom; and when teachers present a subject to their students they also present a point of view on that subject. The choice, according to Freire, is fairly simple: teachers either work "for the liberation of the people—their humanization—or for their domestication, their domination." The practice of teaching, however, is anything but simple. According to Freire, a teacher's most crucial skill is his or her ability to assist students' struggle to gain control over the conditions of their lives, and this means helping them not only to know but "to know that they know."

Recently, Freire edited, along with Henry A. Giroux of Miami University in Ohio, a series of books on education and teaching. In Literacy: Reading the Word and the World, *a book for the series, Freire describes the interrelationship between reading the written word and understanding the world that surrounds us.*

> *My parents introduced me to reading the word at a certain moment in this rich experience of understanding my immediate world. Deciphering the word flowed naturally from reading my particular world; it was not something superimposed on it. I learned to read and write on the grounds of the backyard of my house, in the shade of the mango trees, with words from my world rather than from the wider world of my parents. The earth was my blackboard, the sticks my chalk.*

For Freire, reading the written word involves understanding a text in its very particular social and historical context. Thus reading always involves "critical perception, interpretation, and rewriting of what is read."

The "Banking" Concept of Education

A careful analysis of the teacher-student relationship at any level, inside or outside the school, reveals its fundamentally *narrative* character. This relationship involves a narrating Subject (the teacher) and patient, listening objects (the students). The contents, whether values or empirical dimensions of reality, tend in the process of being narrated to become lifeless and petrified. Education is suffering from narration sickness.

The teacher talks about reality as if it were motionless, static, compartmentalized, and predictable. Or else he expounds on a topic completely alien to the existential experience of the students. His task is to "fill" the students with the contents of his narration—contents which are detached from reality, disconnected from the totality that engendered them and could give them significance. Words are emptied of their concreteness and become a hollow, alienated, and alienating verbosity.

The outstanding characteristic of this narrative education, then, is the sonority of words, not their transforming power. "Four times four is sixteen; the capital of Pará is Belém." The student records, memorizes, and repeats these phrases without perceiving what four times four really means, or realizing the true significance of "capital" in the affirmation "the capital of Pará is Belém," that is, what Belém means for Pará and what Pará means for Brazil.

Narration (with the teacher as narrator) leads the students to memorize mechanically the narrated content. Worse yet, it turns them into "containers," into "receptacles" to be "filled" by the teacher. The more completely he fills the receptacles, the better a teacher he is. The more meekly the receptacles permit themselves to be filled, the better students they are.

Education thus becomes an act of depositing, in which the students are the depositories and the teacher is the depositor. Instead of communicating, the teacher issues communiqués and makes deposits which the students patiently receive, memorize, and repeat. This is the "banking" concept of education, in which the scope of action allowed to the students extends only as far as receiving, filing, and storing the deposits. They do, it is true, have the opportunity to become collectors or cataloguers of the things they store. But in the last analysis, it is men themselves who are filed away through the lack of creativity, transformation, and knowledge in this (at best) misguided system. For apart from inquiry, apart from the praxis, men cannot be truly human. Knowledge emerges only through invention and reinvention, through the restless, impatient, continuing, hopeful inquiry men pursue in the world, with the world, and with each other.

In the banking concept of education, knowledge is a gift bestowed by those who consider themselves knowledgeable upon those whom they consider to know nothing. Projecting an absolute ignorance onto others, a characteristic of the ideology of oppression, negates education and knowledge as processes of inquiry. The teacher presents himself to his students as their necessary opposite; by considering their ignorance absolute, he justifies his own existence. The students, alienated like the slave in the Hegelian dialectic, accept their ignorance as justifying the teacher's existence—but, unlike the slave, they never discover that they educate the teacher.

The *raison d'être* of libertarian education, on the other hand, lies in its drive towards reconciliation. Education must begin with the solution of the teacher-student contradiction, by reconciling the poles of the contradiction so that both are simultaneously teachers *and* students.

This solution is not (nor can it be) found in the banking concept. On the contrary, banking education maintains and even stimulates the contradiction through the following attitudes and practices, which mirror oppressive society as a whole:

a. the teacher teaches and the students are taught;
b. the teacher knows everything and the students know nothing;

c. the teacher thinks and the students are thought about;

d. the teacher talks and the students listen—meekly;

e. the teacher disciplines and the students are disciplined;

f. the teacher chooses and enforces his choice, and the students comply;

g. the teacher acts and the students have the illusion of acting through the action of the teacher;

h. the teacher chooses the program content, and the students (who were not consulted) adapt to it;

i. the teacher confuses the authority of knowledge with his own professional authority, which he sets in opposition to the freedom of the students;

j. the teacher is the Subject of the learning process, while the pupils are mere objects.

It is not surprising that the banking concept of education regards men as adaptable, manageable beings. The more students work at storing the deposits entrusted to them, the less they develop the critical consciousness which would result from their intervention in the world as transformers of that world. The more completely they accept the passive role imposed on them, the more they tend simply to adapt to the world as it is and to the fragmented view of reality deposited in them.

The capability of banking education to minimize or annul the students' creative power and to stimulate their credulity serves the interests of the oppressors, who care neither to have the world revealed nor to see it transformed. The oppressors use their "humanitarianism" to preserve a profitable situation. Thus they react almost instinctively against any experiment in education which stimulates the critical faculties and is not content with a partial view of reality but always seeks out the ties which link one point to another and one problem to another.

Indeed, the interests of the oppressors lie in "changing the consciousness of the oppressed, not the situation which oppresses them,"[1] for the more the oppressed can be led to adapt to that situation, the more easily they can be dominated. To achieve this end, the oppressors use the banking concept of education in conjunction with a paternalistic social action apparatus, within which the oppressed receive the euphemistic title of "welfare recipients." They are treated as individual cases, as marginal men who deviate from the general configuration of a "good, organized, and just" society. The oppressed are regarded as the pathology of the healthy society, which must therefore adjust these "incompetent and lazy" folk to its own patterns by changing their mentality. These marginals need to be "integrated," "incorporated" into the healthy society that they have "forsaken."

The truth is, however, that the oppressed are not "marginals," are not men living "outside" society. They have always been "inside"—inside the structure which made them "beings for others." The solution is not to "integrate" them into the structure of oppression, but to transform that structure so that they can become "beings for themselves." Such transformation, of course, would undermine the oppressors' purposes; hence their utilization of the banking concept of education to avoid the threat of student *conscientização*.°

The banking approach to adult education, for example, will never propose to students that they critically consider reality. It will deal instead with such vital questions as whether Roger gave green grass to the goat, and insist upon the importance of learning that, on the contrary, Roger gave green grass to the rabbit. The "humanism" of the banking approach masks the effort to turn men into automatons—the very negation of their ontological vocation to be more fully human.

Those who use the banking approach, knowingly or unknowingly (for there are innumerable well-intentioned bank-clerk teachers who do not realize that they are serving only to dehumanize), fail to perceive that the deposits themselves contain contradictions about reality. But, sooner or later, these contradictions may lead formerly passive students to turn against their domestication and the attempt to domesticate reality. They may discover through existential experience that their present way of life is irreconcilable with their vocation to become fully human. They may perceive through their relations with reality that reality is really a *process*, undergoing constant transformation. If men are searchers and their ontological vocation is humanization, sooner or later they may perceive the contradiction in which banking education seeks to maintain them, and then engage themselves in the struggle for their liberation.

But the humanist, revolutionary educator cannot wait for this possibility to materialize. From the outset, his efforts must coincide with those of the students to engage in critical thinking and the quest for mutual humanization. His efforts must be imbued with a profound trust in men and their creative power. To achieve this, he must be a partner of the students in his relations with them.

The banking concept does not admit to such partnership—and necessarily so. To resolve the teacher-student contradiction, to exchange the role of depositor, prescriber, domesticator for the role of student among students would be to undermine the power of oppression and serve the cause of liberation.

Implicit in the banking concept is the assumption of a dichotomy between man and the world: man is merely *in* the world, not *with* the world or with others; man is spectator, not re-creator. In this view, man is not a conscious being *(corpo consciente)*; he is rather the possessor of *a* consciousness: an empty "mind" passively open to the reception of deposits of reality from

---

conscientização According to Freire's translator, "The term *conscientização* refers to learning to perceive social, political, and economic contradictions, and to take action against the oppressive elements of reality."

the world outside. For example, my desk, my books, my coffee cup, all the objects before me—as bits of the world which surrounds me—would be "inside" me, exactly as I am inside my study right now. This view makes no distinction between being accessible to consciousness and entering consciousness. The distinction, however, is essential: the objects which surround me are simply accessible to my consciousness, not located within it. I am aware of them, but they are not inside me.

It follows logically from the banking notion of consciousness that the educator's role is to regulate the way the world "enters into" the students. His task is to organize a process which already occurs spontaneously, to "fill" the students by making deposits of information which he considers to constitute true knowledge.[2] And since men "receive" the world as passive entities, education should make them more passive still, and adapt them to the world. The educated man is the adapted man, because he is better "fit" for the world. Translated into practice, this concept is well suited to the purposes of the oppressors, whose tranquillity rests on how well men fit the world the oppressors have created, and how little they question it.

The more completely the majority adapt to the purposes which the dominant minority prescribe for them (thereby depriving them of the right to their own purposes), the more easily the minority can continue to prescribe. The theory and practice of banking education serve this end quite efficiently. Verbalistic lessons, reading requirements,[3] the methods for evaluating "knowledge," the distance between the teacher and the taught, the criteria for promotion: everything in this ready-to-wear approach serves to obviate thinking.

The bank-clerk educator does not realize that there is no true security in his hypertrophied role, that one must seek to live *with* others in solidarity. One cannot impose oneself, nor even merely coexist with one's students. Solidarity requires true communication, and the concept by which such an educator is guided fears and proscribes communication.

Yet only through communication can human life hold meaning. The teacher's thinking is authenticated only by the authenticity of the students' thinking. The teacher cannot think for his students, nor can he impose his thought on them. Authentic thinking, thinking that is concerned about *reality*, does not take place in ivory tower isolation, but only in communication. If it is true that thought has meaning only when generated by action upon the world, the subordination of students to teachers becomes impossible.

Because banking education begins with a false understanding of men as objects, it cannot promote the development of what Fromm calls "biophily," but instead produces its opposite: "necrophily."

> While life is characterized by growth in a structured, functional manner, the necrophilous person loves all that does not grow, all that is mechanical. The necrophilous person is driven by the

216

> desire to transform the organic into the inorganic, to approach life mechanically, as if all living persons were things. . . . Memory, rather than experience; having, rather than being, is what counts. The necrophilous person can relate to an object—a flower or a person—only if he possesses it; hence a threat to his possession is a threat to himself; if he loses possession he loses contact with the world. . . . He loves control, and in the act of controlling he kills life.[4]

Oppression—overwhelming control—is necrophilic; it is nourished by love of death, not life. The banking concept of education, which serves the interests of oppression, is also necrophilic. Based on a mechanistic, static, naturalistic, spatialized view of consciousness, it transforms students into receiving objects. It attempts to control thinking and action, leads men to adjust to the world, and inhibits their creative power.

When their efforts to act responsibly are frustrated, when they find themselves unable to use their faculties, men suffer. "The suffering due to impotence is rooted in the very fact that the human equilibrium has been disturbed."[5] But the inability to act which causes men's anguish also causes them to reject their impotence, by attempting

> to restore [their] capacity to act. But can [they], and how? One way is to submit to and identify with a person or group having power. By this symbolic participation in another person's life, [men have] the illusion of acting, when in reality [they] only submit to and become part of those who act.[6]

Populist manifestations perhaps best exemplify this type of behavior by the oppressed, who, by identifying with charismatic leaders, come to feel that they themselves are active and effective. The rebellion they express as they emerge in the historical process is motivated by that desire to act effectively. The dominant elites consider the remedy to be more domination and repression, carried out in the name of freedom, order, and social peace (that is, the peace of the elites). Thus they can condemn—logically, from their point of view—"the violence of a strike by workers and [can] call upon the state in the same breath to use violence in putting down the strike."[7]

Education as the exercise of domination stimulates the credulity of students, with the ideological intent (often not perceived by educators) of indoctrinating them to adapt to the world of oppression. This accusation is not made in the naive hope that the dominant elites will thereby simply abandon the practice. Its objective is to call the attention of true humanists to the fact that they cannot use banking educational methods in the pursuit of liberation, for they would only negate that very pursuit. Nor may a revolutionary society inherit these methods from an oppressor society. The revolutionary society which practices banking education is either misguided or mistrusting of men. In either event, it is threatened by the specter of reaction.

Unfortunately, those who espouse the cause of liberation are themselves surrounded and influenced by the climate which generates the banking concept, and often do not perceive its true significance or its dehumanizing power. Paradoxically, then, they utilize this same instrument of alienation in what they consider an effort to liberate. Indeed, some "revolutionaries" brand as "innocents," "dreamers," or even "reactionaries" those who would challenge this educational practice. But one does not liberate men by alienating them. Authentic liberation—the process of humanization—is not another deposit to be made in men. Liberation is a praxis: the action and reflection of men upon their world in order to transform it. Those truly committed to the cause of liberation can accept neither the mechanistic concept of consciousness as an empty vessel to be filled, nor the use of banking methods of domination (propaganda, slogans—deposits) in the name of the liberation.

Those truly committed to liberation must reject the banking concept in its entirety, adopting instead a concept of men as conscious beings, and consciousness as consciousness intent upon the world. They must abandon the educational goal of deposit-making and replace it with the posing of the problems of men in their relations with the world. "Problem-posing" education, responding to the essence of consciousness—*intentionality*—rejects communiqués and embodies communications. It epitomizes the special characteristic of consciousness: being *conscious of*, not only as intent on objects but as turned in upon itself in a Jasperian "split"—consciousness as consciousness *of* consciousness.

Liberating education consists in acts of cognition, not transferrals of information. It is a learning situation in which the cognizable object (far from being the end of the cognitive act) intermediates the cognitive actors—teacher on the one hand and students on the other. Accordingly, the practice of problem-posing education entails at the outset that the teacher-student contradiction be resolved. Dialogical relations—indispensable to the capacity of cognitive actors to cooperate in perceiving the same cognizable object—are otherwise impossible.

Indeed, problem-posing education, which breaks with the vertical patterns characteristic of banking education, can fulfill its function as the practice of freedom only if it can overcome the above contradiction. Through dialogue, the teacher-of-the-students and the students-of-the-teacher cease to exist and a new term emerges: teacher-students with students-teacher. The teacher is no longer merely the-one-who-teaches, but one who is himself taught in dialogue with the students, who in turn while being taught also teach. They become jointly responsible for a process in which all grow. In this process, arguments based on "authority" are no longer valid; in order to function, authority must be *on the side of* freedom, not *against* it. Here, no one teaches another, nor is anyone self-taught. Men teach each other, mediated by the world, by the cognizable objects which in banking education are "owned" by the teacher.

The banking concept (with its tendency to dichotomize everything) distinguishes two stages in the action of the educator. During the first he cognizes a cognizable object while he prepares his lessons in his study or his laboratory; during the second, he expounds to his students about that object. The students are not called upon to know, but to memorize the contents narrated by the teacher. Nor do the students practice any act of cognition, since the object towards which that act should be directed is the property of the teacher rather than a medium evoking the critical reflection of both teacher and students. Hence in the name of the "preservation of culture and knowledge" we have a system which achieves neither true knowledge nor true culture.

The problem-posing method does not dichotomize the activity of the teacher-student: he is not "cognitive" at one point and "narrative" at another. He is always "cognitive," whether preparing a project or engaging in dialogue with the students. He does not regard cognizable objects as his private property, but as the object of reflection by himself and the students. In this way, the problem-posing educator constantly re-forms his reflections in the reflection of the students. The students—no longer docile listeners—are now critical coinvestigators in dialogue with the teacher. The teacher presents the material to the students for their consideration, and reconsiders his earlier considerations as the students express their own. The role of the problem-posing educator is to create, together with the students, the conditions under which knowledge at the level of the *doxa* is superseded by true knowledge, at the level of the *logos*.

Whereas banking education anesthetizes and inhibits creative power, problem-posing education involves a constant unveiling of reality. The former attempts to maintain the *submersion* of consciousness; the latter strives for the *emergence* of consciousness and *critical intervention* in reality.

Students, as they are increasingly posed with problems relating to themselves in the world and with the world, will feel increasingly challenged and obliged to respond to that challenge. Because they apprehend the challenge as interrelated to other problems within a total context, not as a theoretical question, the resulting comprehension tends to be increasingly critical and thus constantly less alienated. Their response to the challenge evokes new challenges, followed by new understandings: and gradually the students come to regard themselves as committed.

Education as the practice of freedom—as opposed to education as the practice of domination—denies that man is abstract, isolated, independent, and unattached to the world; it also denies that the world exists as a reality apart from men. Authentic reflection considers neither abstract man nor the world without men, but men in their relations with the world. In these relations consciousness and world are simultaneous: consciousness neither precedes the world nor follows it.

> La conscience et le monde sont donnés d'un même coup: extérieur par essence à la conscience, le monde est, par essence relatif à elle.[8]

In one of our culture circles in Chile, the group was discussing . . . the anthropological concept of culture. In the midst of the discussion, a peasant who by banking standards was completely ignorant said: "Now I see that without man there is no world." When the educator responded: "Let's say, for the sake of argument, that all the men on earth were to die, but that the earth itself remained, together with trees, birds, animals, rivers, seas, the stars . . . wouldn't all this be a world?"

"Oh, no," the peasant replied emphatically. "There would be no one to say: 'This is a world.'"

The peasant wished to express the idea that there would be lacking the consciousness of the world which necessarily implies the world of consciousness. *I* cannot exist without a *not-I*. In turn, the *not-I* depends on that existence. The world which brings consciousness into existence becomes the world of that consciousness. Hence, the previously cited affirmation of Sartre: "*La conscience et le monde sont donnés d'un même coup.*"

As men, simultaneously reflecting on themselves and on the world, increase the scope of their perception, they begin to direct their observations towards previously inconspicuous phenomena:

> In perception properly so-called, as an explicit awareness [*Gewahren*], I am turned towards the object, to the paper, for instance. I apprehend it as being this here and now. The apprehension is a singling out, every object having a background in experience. Around and about the paper lie books, pencils, inkwell, and so forth, and these in a certain sense are also "perceived," perceptually there, in the "field of intuition"; but whilst I was turned towards the paper there was no turning in their direction, nor any apprehending of them, not even in a secondary sense. They appeared and yet were not singled out, were not posited on their own account. Every perception of a thing has such a zone of background intuitions or background awareness, if "intuiting" already includes the state of being turned towards, and this also is a "conscious experience," or more briefly a "consciousness of" all indeed that in point of fact lies in the co-perceived objective background.[9]

That which had existed objectively but had not been perceived in its deeper implications (if indeed it was perceived at all) begins to "stand out," assuming the character of a problem and therefore of challenge. Thus, men begin to single out elements from their "background awarenesses" and to reflect upon them. These elements are now objects of men's consideration, and, as such, objects of their action and cognition.

In problem-posing education, men develop their power to perceive critically *the way they exist* in the world *with which* and *in which* they find themselves; they come to see the world not as a static reality, but as a reality in process, in transformation. Although the dialectical relations of men with the world exist independently of how these relations are perceived (or whether or not they are perceived at all), it is also true that the form of action men adopt is to a large extent a function of how they perceive themselves in the world. Hence, the teacher-students and the students-teacher reflect simultaneously on themselves and the world without dichotomizing this reflection from action, and thus establish an authentic form of thought and action.

Once again, the two educational concepts and practices under analysis come into conflict. Banking education (for obvious reasons) attempts, by mythicizing reality, to conceal certain facts which explain the way men exist in the world; problem-posing education sets itself the task of demythologizing. Banking education resists dialogue; problem-posing education regards dialogue as indispensable to the act of cognition which unveils reality. Banking education treats students as objects of assistance; problem-posing education makes them critical thinkers. Banking education inhibits creativity and domesticates (although it cannot completely destroy) the *intentionality* of consciousness by isolating consciousness from the world, thereby denying men their ontological and historical vocation of becoming more fully human. Problem-posing education bases itself on creativity and stimulates true reflection and action upon reality, thereby responding to the vocation of men as beings who are authentic only when engaged in inquiry and creative transformation. In sum: banking theory and practice, as immobilizing and fixating forces, fail to acknowledge men as historical beings; problem-posing theory and practice take man's historicity as their starting point.

Problem-posing education affirms men as beings in the process of *becoming*—as unfinished, uncompleted beings in and with a likewise unfinished reality. Indeed, in contrast to other animals who are unfinished, but not historical, men know themselves to be unfinished; they are aware of their incompletion. In this incompletion and this awareness lie the very roots of education as an exclusively human manifestation. The unfinished character of men and the transformational character of reality necessitate that education be an ongoing activity.

Education is thus constantly remade in the praxis. In order to *be*, it must *become*. Its "duration" (in the Bergsonian meaning of the word) is found in the interplay of the opposites *permanence* and *change*. The banking method emphasizes permanence and becomes reactionary; problem-posing education—which accepts neither a "well-behaved" present nor a predetermined future—roots itself in the dynamic present and becomes revolutionary.

Problem-posing education is revolutionary futurity. Hence, it is prophetic (and, as such, hopeful). Hence, it corresponds to the historical nature of man. Hence, it affirms men as beings who transcend themselves, who move forward and look ahead, for whom immobility represents a fatal threat, for whom looking at the past must only be a means of understanding more clearly what and who they are so that they can more wisely build a future.

Hence, it identifies with the movement which engages men as beings aware of their incompletion—an historical movement which has its point of departure, its Subjects, and its objective.

The point of departure of the movement lies in men themselves. But since men do not exist apart from the world, apart from reality, the movement must begin with the men-world relationship. Accordingly, the point of departure must always be with men in the "here and now," which constitutes the situation within which they are submerged, from which they emerge, and in which they intervene. Only by starting from this situation—which determines their perception of it—can they begin to move. To do this authentically they must perceive their state not as fated and unalterable, but merely as limiting—and therefore challenging.

Whereas the banking method directly or indirectly reinforces men's fatalistic perception of their situation, the problem-posing method presents this very situation to them as a problem. As the situation becomes the object of their cognition, the naive or magical perception which produced their fatalism gives way to perception which is able to perceive itself even as it perceives reality, and can thus be critically objective about that reality.

A deepened consciousness of their situation leads men to apprehend that situation as an historical reality susceptible of transformation. Resignation gives way to the drive for transformation and inquiry, over which men feel themselves to be in control. If men, as historical beings necessarily engaged with other men in a movement of inquiry, did not control that movement, it would be (and is) a violation of men's humanity. Any situation in which some men prevent others from engaging in the process of inquiry is one of violence. The means used are not important; to alienate men from their own decision-making is to change them into objects.

This movement of inquiry must be directed towards humanization—man's historical vocation. The pursuit of full humanity, however, cannot be carried out in isolation or individualism, but only in fellowship and solidarity; therefore it cannot unfold in the antagonistic relations between oppressors and oppressed. No one can be authentically human while he prevents others from being so. Attempting *to be more* human, individualistically, leads to *having more*, egotistically: a form of dehumanization. Not that it is not fundamental to *have* in order *to be* human. Precisely because it *is* necessary, some men's *having*, must not be allowed to constitute an obstacle to others' *having*, must not consolidate the power of the former to crush the latter.

Problem-posing education, as a humanist and liberating praxis, posits as fundamental that men subjected to domination must fight for their emancipation. To that end, it enables teachers and students to become Subjects of the educational process by overcoming authoritarianism and an alienating intellectualism; it also enables men to overcome their false perception of reality. The world—no longer something to be described with deceptive words—becomes the object of that transforming action by men which results in their humanization.

Problem-posing education does not and cannot serve the interests of the oppressor. No oppressive order could permit the oppressed to begin to question: why? While only a revolutionary society can carry out this education in systematic terms, the revolutionary leaders need not take full power before they can employ the method. In the revolutionary process, the leaders cannot utilize the banking method as an interim measure, justified on grounds of expediency, with the intention of *later* behaving in a genuinely revolutionary fashion. They must be revolutionary—that is to say, dialogical—from the outset.

NOTES

[1] Simone de Beauvoir, *La pensée de droite, aujourd'hui* (Paris); ST, *El pensamiento político de la derecha* (Buenos Aires, 1963), p. 34.

[2] This concept corresponds to what Sartre calls the "digestive" or "nutritive" concept of education, in which knowledge is "fed" by the teacher to the students to "fill them out." See Jean-Paul Sartre, "Une idée fundamentale de la phénomenologie de Husserl: L'intentional-ité," *Situations* I (Paris, 1947).

[3] For example, some professors specify in their reading lists that a book should be read from pages 10 to 15—and do this to "help" their students!

[4] Eric Fromm, *The Heart of Man* (New York, 1966), p. 41.

[5] Ibid., p. 31.

[6] Ibid.

[7] Reinhold Niebuhr, *Moral Man and Immoral Society* (New York, 1960), p. 130.

[8] Sartre, op. cit., p. 32. [The passage is obscure but could be read as "Consciousness and the world are given at one and the same time: the exterior world as it enters consciousness is relative to our ways of seeing and understanding that world."—Editors' note]

[9] Edmund Husserl, *Ideas—General Introduction to Pure Phenomenology* (London, 1969), pp. 105–106.

•   •   •   •   •   •   •   •   •   •

QUESTIONS FOR A SECOND READING

1. While Freire speaks powerfully about the politics of the classroom, he provides few examples of actual classroom situations. As you go back through the essay, try to ground (or to test) what he says with examples of your own. What would take place in a "problem-posing" class in English, history, psychology, or math? What is an "authentic form of thought and action"? How might you describe what Freire refers to as "reflection"? What, really, might teachers be expected to learn from their students? What example can you give of a time when you were "conscious of consciousness" and it made a difference to you with your school work?

   You might also look for moments when Freire does provide examples of his own. On pages 215–16, for example, Freire makes the distinction between a student's role as a "spectator" and as "re-creator" by referring to his own relationship to the objects on his desk. How might you explain this distinction? Or, how might you use the example of his books and coffee cup to explain the distinction he makes between "being accessible to consciousness" and "entering consciousness"?

2. Freire uses two terms drawn from Marxist literature: *praxis* and *alienation*. From the way these words are used in the essay, how would you define them? And how might they be applied to the study of education?

3. A writer can be thought of as a teacher and a reader as a student. If you think of Freire as your teacher in this essay, does he enact his own principles? Does he speak to you as though he were making deposits in a bank? Or is there a way in which the essay allows for dialogue? Look for sections in the essay you could use to talk about the role Freire casts you in as a reader.

ASSIGNMENTS FOR WRITING

1. Surely all of us, anyone who has made it through twelve years of formal education, can think of a class, or an occasion outside of class, to serve as a quick example of what Freire calls the "banking" concept of education, where students were turned into "containers" to be "filled" by their teachers. If Freire is to be useful to you, however, he must do more than enable you to call up quick examples. He should allow you to say more than that a teacher once treated you like a container or that a teacher once gave you your freedom.

Write an essay that focuses on a rich and illustrative incident from your own educational experience and read it (that is, interpret it) as Freire would. You will need to provide careful detail: things that were said and done, perhaps the exact wording of an assignment, a textbook, or a teacher's comments. And you will need to turn to the language of Freire's argument, to take key phrases and passages and see how they might be used to investigate your case.

To do this you will need to read your account as not simply the story of you and your teacher, since Freire is not writing about individual personalities (an innocent student and a mean teacher, a rude teacher, or a thoughtless teacher) but about the roles we are cast in, whether we choose to be or not, by our culture and its institutions. The key question, then, is not who you were or who your teacher was but what roles you played and how those roles can lead you to better understand the larger narrative or drama of Education (an organized attempt to "regulate the way the world 'enters into' the students," p. 216).

Freire would not want you to work passively or mechanically, however, as though you were following orders. He would want you to make your own mark on the work he has begun. Use your example, in other words, as a way of testing and examining what Freire says, *particularly those passages that you find difficult or obscure.*

2. Problem-posing education, according to Freire, "sets itself the task of demythologizing"; it "stimulates true reflection and action"; it allows students

to be "engaged in inquiry and creative transformation." These are grand and powerful phrases, and it is interesting to consider what they might mean if applied to the work of a course in reading and writing.

If the object for study were Freire's essay, "The 'Banking' Concept of Education," what would Freire (or a teacher determined to adapt his practices) ask students to *do* with the essay? What writing assignment might he set for his students? Prepare that assignment, or a set of questions or guidelines or instructions (or whatever) that Freire might prepare for his class.

Once you've prepared the writing assignment, write the essay that you think would best fulfill it. And, once you've completed the essay, go on, finally, to write the teacher's comments on it—to write what you think Freire, or a teacher following his example, might write on a piece of student work.

MAKING CONNECTIONS

1. Freire says,

> Students, as they are increasingly posed with problems relating to themselves in the world and with the world, will feel increasingly challenged and obliged to respond to that challenge. Because they apprehend the challenge as interrelated to other problems within a total context, not as a theoretical question, the resulting comprehension tends to be increasingly critical and thus constantly less alienated. (p. 219)

Students learn to respond, Freire says, through dialogue with their teachers. Freire could be said to serve as your first teacher here. He has raised the issue for you and given you some language you can use to frame questions and to imagine the possibilities of response.

Using one of the essays in this book as a starting point, pose a problem that challenges you and makes you feel obliged to respond, a problem that, in Freire's terms, relates to you "in the world and with the world." This is a chance for you, in other words, to pose a Freirean question and then to write a Freirean essay, all as an exercise in the practice of freedom.

When you are done, you might reread what you have written to see how it resembles or differs from what you are used to writing. What are the indications that you are working with greater freedom? If you find evidence of alienation or "domination," to what would you attribute it and what, then, might you do to overcome it?

2. Freire writes about the distribution of power and authority in the classroom and argues that education too often alienates individuals from their own historical situation. Richard Rodriguez, in "The Achievement of Desire" (p. 567), writes about his education as a process of difficult but necessary alienation from his home, his childhood, and his family. And he writes about power—about the power that he gained and lost as he became increasingly successful as a student.

But Freire and Rodriguez write about education as a central event in the shaping of an adult life. It is interesting to imagine what they might have to say to each other. Write a dialogue between the two in which they discuss what Rodriguez has written in "The Achievement of Desire." What would they say to each other? What questions would they ask? How would they respond to each other in the give-and-take of conversation?

Note: This should be a dialogue, not a debate. Your speakers are trying to learn something about each other and about education. They are not trying to win points or convince a jury.

CLIFFORD
GEERTZ

*C*LIFFORD GEERTZ *was born in San Francisco in 1926. After two years in the U.S. Navy Reserve, he earned a B.A. from Antioch College and a Ph.D. from Harvard. A Fellow of the National Academy of Science, the American Academy of Arts and Sciences, and the American Philosophical Society, Geertz has been a professor in the department of social science of the Institute for Advanced Study in Princeton, New Jersey, since 1970. He has written several books (mostly anthropological studies of Third World cultures) and published two collections of essays,* Interpretation of Cultures *(1977) and* Local Knowledge *(1985).* Interpretation of Cultures, *from which the following essay is drawn, became a classic and won for Geertz the rare distinction of being an academic whose scholarly work is eagerly read by people outside his academic discipline, even outside the academic community altogether. His book* Works and Lives: The Anthropologist as Author *(1989) won the* National Book Critics Circle Award for Criticism. *Geertz's most recent work,* After the Fact: Two Countries, Four Decades, One Anthropologist, *is a collection of essays from his 1995 Jerusalem-Harvard lectures.*

"Deep Play" was first presented at a Paris conference organized by Geertz, the literary critic Paul de Man, and the American Academy of Arts and Sciences. The purpose of the conference was to bring together scholars from various academic departments (in the humanities, the social sciences, and the natural sciences) to see if

they could find a way of talking to each other and, in doing so, find a common ground to their work. The conference planners believed that there was a common ground, that all of these scholars were bound together by their participation in what they called "systematic study of meaningful forms." This is a grand phrase, but Geertz's essay clearly demonstrates what work of this sort requires of an anthropologist. The essay begins with a story, an anecdote, and the story Geertz tells is as open to your interpretation as it is to anyone's else's. What follow, however, are Geertz's attempts to interpret the story he has told, first this way and then that. As you watch him work—finding patterns, making comparisons, drawing on the theories of experts, proposing theories of his own—you are offered a demonstration of how he finds meaningful forms and then sets out to study them systematically.

"Deep Play," in fact, was sent out as a model for all prospective conference participants, since it was a paper that showed not only what its author knew about his subject (cockfights in Bali) but what the knew about the methods and procedures that gave him access to his subject. It is a witty and sometimes dazzling essay with a wonderful story to tell—a story of both a Balinese cockfight and an anthropologist trying to write about and understand people whose culture seems, at first, so very different from his own.

Deep Play: Notes on the Balinese Cockfight

The Raid

Early in April of 1958, my wife and I arrived, malarial and diffident, in a Balinese village we intended, as anthropologists, to study. A small place, about five hundred people, and relatively remote, it was its own world. We were intruders, professional ones, and the villagers dealt with us as Balinese seem always to deal with people not part of their life who yet press themselves upon them: as though we were not there. For them, and to a degree for ourselves, we were nonpersons, specters, invisible men.

We moved into an extended family compound (that had been arranged before through the provincial government) belonging to one of the four major factions in village life. But except for our landlord and the village chief, whose cousin and brother-in-law he was, everyone ignored us in a way only a Balinese can do. As we wandered around, uncertain, wistful, eager to please, people seemed to look right through us with a gaze focused several yards behind us on some more actual stone or tree. Almost nobody greeted us; but nobody scowled or said anything unpleasant to us either, which would have been almost as satisfactory. If we ventured to approach someone (something one is powerfully inhibited from doing in such an atmosphere), he moved, negligently but definitively, away. If, seated or leaning against a wall, we had him trapped, he said nothing at all, or mumbled what for the Balinese is the ultimate nonword—"yes." The indifference, of course, was studied; the villagers were watching every move we made and they had an enormous amount of quite accurate information about who we were and what we were going to be doing. But they acted as if we simply did not exist, which, in fact, as this behavior was designed to inform us, we did not, or anyway not yet.

This is, as I say, general in Bali. Everywhere else I have been in Indonesia, and more latterly in Morocco, when I have gone into a new village people have poured out from all sides to take a very close look at me, and, often, an all-too-probing feel as well. In Balinese villages, at least those away from the tourist circuit, nothing happens at all. People go on pounding, chatting, making offerings, staring into space, carrying baskets about while one drifts around feeling vaguely disembodied. And the same thing is true on the individual level. When you first meet a Balinese, he seems virtually not to relate to you at all; he is, in the term Gregory Bateson and Margaret Mead made famous, "away."[1] Then—in a day, a week, a month (with some people the magic moment never comes)—he decides, for reasons I have never been quite able to fathom, that you *are* real, and then he becomes a warm, gay, sensitive, sympathetic, though, being Balinese, always precisely controlled person. You have crossed, somehow, some moral or metaphysical shadow line. Though you are not exactly taken as a Balinese (one has to be born to that), you are at least regarded as a human being rather than a cloud or a gust of wind. The whole complexion of your relationship dramatically changes to, in the majority of cases, a gentle, almost affectionate one—a low-keyed, rather playful, rather mannered, rather bemused geniality.

My wife and I were still very much in the gust of wind stage, a most frustrating, and even, as you soon begin to doubt whether you are really real after all, unnerving one, when, ten days or so after our arrival, a large cockfight was held in the public square to raise money for a new school.

Now, a few special occasions aside, cockfights are illegal in Bali under the Republic (as, for not altogether unrelated reasons, they were under the Dutch), largely as a result of the pretensions to puritanism radical nationalism tends to bring with it. The elite, which is not itself so very puritan, worries about the poor, ignorant peasant gambling all his money away, about what foreigners will think, about the waste of time better devoted to building up the country. It sees cockfighting as "primitive," "backward," "unprogressive," and generally unbecoming an ambitious nation. And, as with those other embarrassments—opium smoking, begging, or uncovered breasts—it seeks, rather unsystematically, to put a stop to it.

Of course, like drinking during prohibition or, today, smoking marihuana, cockfights, being a part of "The Balinese Way of Life," nonetheless go on happening, and with extraordinary frequency. And, like prohibition or marihuana, from time to time the police (who, in 1958 at least, were almost all not Balinese but Javanese) feel called upon to make a raid, confiscate the cocks and spurs, fine a few people, and even now and then expose some of them in the tropical sun for a day as object lessons which never, somehow, get learned, even though occasionally, quite occasionally, the object dies.

As a result, the fights are usually held in a secluded corner of a village in semisecrecy, a fact which tends to slow the action a little—not very much, but the Balinese do not care to have it slowed at all. In this case, however, perhaps because they were raising money for a school that the government was unable to give them, perhaps because raids had been few recently, perhaps, as I gathered from subsequent discussion, there was a notion that the necessary bribes had been paid, they thought they could take a chance on the central square and draw a larger and more enthusiastic crowd without attracting the attention of the law.

They were wrong. In the midst of the third match, with hundreds of people, including, still transparent, myself and my wife, fused into a single body around the ring, a superorganism in the literal sense, a truck full of policemen armed with machine guns roared up. Amid great screeching cries of "pulisi! pulisi!" from the crowd, the policemen jumped out, and, springing into the center of the ring, began to swing their guns around like gangsters in a motion picture, though not going so far as actually to fire them. The superorganism came instantly apart as its components scattered in all directions. People raced down the road, disappeared head first over walls, scrambled under platforms, folded themselves behind wicker screens, scuttled up coconut trees. Cocks armed with steel spurs sharp enough to cut off a finger or run a hole through a foot were running wildly around. Everything was dust and panic.

On the established anthropological principle, When in Rome, my wife and I decided, only slightly less instantaneously than everyone else, that the thing to do was run too. We ran down the main village street, northward, away from where we were living, for we were on that side of the ring. About halfway down another fugitive ducked suddenly into a compound—his own, it turned out—and we, seeing nothing ahead of us but rice fields, open country, and a very high volcano, followed him. As the three of us came tumbling into the courtyard, his wife, who had apparently been through this sort of thing before, whipped out a table, a tablecloth, three chairs, and three cups of tea, and we all, without any explicit communication whatsoever, sat down, commenced to sip tea, and sought to compose ourselves.

A few moments later, one of the policemen marched importantly into the yard, looking for the village chief. (The chief had not only been at the fight, he had arranged it. When the truck drove up he ran to the river, stripped off his sarong, and plunged in so he could say, when at length they found him sitting there pouring water over his head, that he had been away bathing when the whole affair had occurred and was ignorant of it. They did not believe him and fined him three hundred rupiah, which the village raised collectively.) Seeing my wife and I, "White Men," there in the yard, the policeman performed a classic double take. When he found his voice again he asked, approximately, what in the devil did we think we were doing there. Our host of five minutes leaped instantly to our defense, producing an impassioned description of who and what we were, so detailed and so accurate that it was my turn, having barely communicated with a living human being save my landlord and the village chief for more than a week, to be astonished. We had a perfect right to be there, he said, looking the Javanese upstart in the eye. We were American professors; the government had cleared us; we were there to study culture; we were going to write a book to tell Americans about Bali. And we had all been there drinking tea and talking about cultural matters all afternoon and did not know anything about any cockfight. Moreover, we had not seen the village chief all day, he must have gone to town. The policeman retreated in rather total disarray. And, after a decent interval, bewildered but relieved to have survived and stayed out of jail, so did we.

The next morning the village was a completely different world for us. Not only were we no longer invisible, we were suddenly the center of all attention, the object of a great outpouring of warmth, interest, and, most especially, amusement. Everyone in the village knew we had fled like everyone else. They asked us about it again and again (I must have told the story, small detail by small detail, fifty times by the end of the day), gently, affectionately, but quite insistently teasing us: "Why didn't you just stand there and tell the police who you were?" "Why didn't you just say you were only watching and not betting?" "Were you really afraid of those little guns?" As always, kinesthetically minded and, even when fleeing for their lives (or, as happened eight years later, surrendering them), the world's most poised people, they gleefully mimicked, also over and over again, our graceless style of running and what they claimed were our panic-stricken facial expressions. But above all, everyone was extremely pleased and even more surprised that we had not simply "pulled out our papers" (they knew about those too) and asserted our Distinguished Visitor status, but had instead demonstrated our solidarity with what were now our covillagers. (What we had actually demonstrated was our cowardice, but there is fellowship in that too.) Even the Brahmana priest, an old, grave, halfway-to-Heaven type who because of its associations with the underworld would never be involved, even distantly, in a cockfight, and was difficult to approach even to other Balinese, had us called into his courtyard to ask us about what had happened, chuckling happily at the sheer extraordinariness of it all.

In Bali, to be teased is to be accepted. It was the turning point so far as our relationship to the community was concerned, and we were quite literally "in." The whole village opened up to us, probably more than it ever would have otherwise (I might actually never have gotten to that priest, and our accidental host became one of my best informants), and certainly very much faster. Getting caught, or almost caught, in a vice raid is perhaps not a very generalizable recipe for achieving that mysterious necessity of anthropological field work, rapport, but for me it worked very well. It led to a sudden and unusually complete acceptance into a society extremely difficult for outsiders to penetrate. It gave me the kind of immediate, inside-view grasp of an aspect of "peasant mentality" that anthropologists not fortunate enough to flee headlong with their subjects from armed authorities normally do not get. And, perhaps most important of all, for the other things might have come in other ways, it put me very quickly on to a combination emotional explosion, status war, and philosophical drama of central significance to the society whose inner nature I desired to understand. By the time I left I had spent about as much time looking into cockfights as into witchcraft, irrigation, caste, or marriage.

Of Cocks and Men

Bali, mainly because it is Bali, is a well-studied place. Its mythology, art, ritual, social organization, patterns of child rearing, forms of law, even styles of trance, have all been microscopically examined for traces of that elusive substance Jane Belo called "The Balinese Temper."[2] But, aside from a few passing remarks, the cockfight has barely been noticed, although as a popular obsession of consuming power it is at least as important a revelation of what being a Balinese "is really like" as these more celebrated phenomena.[3] As much of America surfaces in a ball park, on a golf links, at a race track, or around a poker table, much of Bali surfaces in a cock ring. For it is only apparently cocks that are fighting there. Actually, it is men.

To anyone who has been in Bali any length of time, the deep psychological identification of Balinese men with their cocks is unmistakable. The double entendre here is deliberate. It works in exactly the same way in Balinese as it does in English, even to producing the same tired jokes, strained puns, and uninventive obscenities. Bateson and Mead have even suggested that, in line with the Balinese conception of the body as a set of separately animated parts, cocks are viewed as detachable, self-operating penises, ambulant genitals with a life of their own.[4] And while I do not have the kind of unconscious material either to confirm or disconfirm this intriguing notion, the fact that they are masculine symbols *par excellence* is about as indubitable, and to the Balinese about as evident, as the fact that water runs downhill.

The language of everyday moralism is shot through, on the male side of it, with roosterish imagery. *Sabung,* the word for cock (and one which appears in inscriptions as early as A.D. 922), is used metaphorically to mean "hero," "warrior," "champion," "man of parts," "political candidate," "bachelor," "dandy," "lady-killer," or "tough guy." A pompous man whose behavior presumes above his station is compared to a tailless cock who struts about as though he had a large, spectacular one. A desperate man who makes a last, irrational effort to extricate himself from an impossible situation is likened to a dying cock who makes one final lunge at his tormentor to drag him along to a common destruction. A stingy man, who promises much, gives little, and begrudges that is compared to a cock which, held by the tail, leaps at another without in fact engaging him. A marriageable young man still shy with the opposite sex or someone in a new job anxious to make a good impression is called "a fighting cock caged for the first time."[5] Court trials, wars, political contests, inheritance disputes, and street arguments are all compared to cockfights.[6] Even the very island itself is perceived from its shape as a small, proud cock, poised, neck extended, back taut, tail raised, in eternal challenge to large, feckless, shapeless Java.[7]

But the intimacy of men with their cocks is more than metaphorical. Balinese men, or anyway a large majority of Balinese men, spend an enormous amount of time with their favorites, grooming them, feeding them, discussing them, trying them out against one another, or just gazing at them with a mixture of rapt admiration and dreamy self-absorption. Whenever you see a group of Balinese men squatting idly in the council shed or along the road in their hips down, shoulders forward, knees up fashion, half or more of them will have a rooster in his hands, holding it between his thighs, bouncing it gently up and down to strengthen its legs, ruffling its feathers with abstract sensuality, pushing it out against a neighbor's rooster to rouse its spirit, withdrawing it toward his loins to calm it again. Now and then, to get a feel for another bird, a man will fiddle this way with someone else's cock for a while, but usually by moving around to squat in place behind it, rather than just having it passed across to him as though it were merely an animal.

In the houseyard, the high-walled enclosures where the people live, fighting cocks are kept in wicker cages, moved frequently about so as to maintain the optimum balance of sun and shade. They are fed a special diet, which varies somewhat according to individual theories but which is mostly maize, sifted for impurities with far more care than it is when mere humans are going to eat it and offered to the animal kernel by kernel. Red pepper is stuffed down their beaks and up their anuses to give them spirit. They are bathed in the same ceremonial preparation of tepid water, medicinal herbs, flowers, and onions in which infants are bathed, and for a prize cock just about as often. Their combs are cropped, their plumage dressed, their spurs trimmed, their legs massaged, and they are inspected for flaws with the squinted concentration of a diamond merchant. A man who has a passion for cocks, an enthusiast in the literal sense of the term, can spend most of his life with them, and even those, the overwhelming majority, whose passion though intense has not entirely run away with them, can and do spend what seems not only to an outsider, but also to themselves, an inordinate amount of time with them. "I am cock crazy," my landlord, a quite ordinary *afficionado* by Balinese standards, used to moan as he went to move another cage, give another bath, or conduct another feeding. "We're all cock crazy."

The madness has some less visible dimensions, however, because although it is true that cocks are symbolic expressions or magnifications of their owner's self, the narcissistic male ego writ out in Aesopian terms, they are also expressions—and rather more immediate ones—of what the Balinese regard as the direct inversion, aesthetically, morally, and metaphysically, of human status: animality.

The Balinese revulsion against any behavior regarded as animal-like can hardly be overstressed. Babies are not allowed to crawl for that reason. Incest, though hardly approved, is a much less horrifying crime than bestiality. (The appropriate punishment for the second is death by drowning, for the first being forced to live like an animal.)[8] Most demons are represented—in sculpture, dance, ritual, myth—in some real or fantastic animal form. The main puberty rite consists in filing the child's teeth so they will not look like animal fangs. Not only defecation but eating is regarded as a disgusting, almost obscene activity, to be conducted hurriedly and privately, because of its association with animality. Even falling down or any form of clumsiness is considered to be bad for these reasons. Aside from cocks and a few domestic animals—oxen, ducks—of no emotional significance, the Balinese are aversive to animals, and treat their large number of dogs not merely callously but with a phobic cruelty. In identifying with his cock, the Balinese man is identifying not just with his ideal self, or even his penis, but also, and at the same time, with what he most fears, hates, and ambivalence being what it is, is fascinated by—The Powers of Darkness.

The connection of cocks and cockfighting with such Powers, with the animalistic demons that threaten constantly to invade the small, cleared off space in which the Balinese have so carefully built their lives and devour its inhabitants, is quite explicit. A cockfight, any cockfight, is in the first instance a blood sacrifice offered, with the appropriate chants and oblations, to the demons in order to pacify their ravenous, cannibal hunger. No temple festival should be conducted until one is made. (If it is omitted someone will inevitably fall into a trance and command with the voice of an angered spirit that the oversight be immediately corrected.) Collective responses to natural evils—illness, crop failure, volcanic eruptions—almost always involve them. And that famous holiday in Bali, The Day of Silence (*Njepi*), when everyone sits silent and immobile all day long in order to avoid contact with a sudden influx of demons chased momentarily out of hell, is preceded the previous day by large-scale cockfights (in this case legal) in almost every village on the island.

In the cockfight, man and beast, good and evil, ego and id, the creative power of aroused masculinity and the destructive power of loosened animality fuse in a bloody drama of hatred, cruelty, violence, and death. It is little wonder that when, as is the invariable rule, the owner of the winning cock takes the carcass of the loser—often torn limb from limb by its enraged owner—home to eat, he does so with a mixture of social embarrassment, moral satisfaction, aesthetic disgust, and cannibal joy. Or that a man who has lost an important fight is sometimes driven to wreck his family shrines and curse the gods, an act of metaphysical (and social) suicide. Or that in seeking earthly analogues for heaven and hell the Balinese compare the former to the mood of a man whose cock has just won, the latter to that of a man whose cock has just lost.

The Fight

Cockfights (*tetadjen; sabungan*) are held in a ring about fifty feet square. Usually they begin toward late afternoon and run three or four hours until sunset. About nine or ten separate matches (*sehet*) comprise a program. Each match is precisely like the others in general pattern: there is no main match, no connection between individual matches, no variation in their format, and each is arranged on a completely ad hoc basis. After a fight has ended and the emotional debris is cleaned away—the bets paid, the curses cursed, the carcasses possessed—seven, eight, perhaps even a dozen men slop negligently into the ring with a cock and seek to find there a logical opponent for it. This process, which rarely takes less than ten minutes and often a good deal longer, is conducted in a very subdued, oblique, even dissembling manner. Those not immediately involved give it at best but disguised, sidelong attention; those who, embarrassedly, are, attempt to pretend somehow that the whole thing is not really happening.

A match made, the other hopefuls retire with the same deliberate indifference, and the selected cocks have their spurs (*tadji*) affixed—razor-sharp, pointed steel swords, four or five inches long. This is a delicate job which only a small portion of men, a half-dozen or so in most villages, know how to do properly. The man who attaches the spurs also provides them, and if the rooster he assists wins its owner awards him the spur-leg of the victim. The spurs are affixed by winding a long length of string around the foot of the spur and the leg of the cock. For reasons I shall come to presently, it is done somewhat differently from case to case, and is an obsessively deliberate affair. The lore about spurs is extensive—they are sharpened only at eclipses and the dark of the moon, should be kept out of the sight of women, and so forth. And they are handled, both in use and out, with the same curious combination of fussiness and sensuality the Balinese direct toward ritual objects generally.

The spurs affixed, the two cocks are placed by their handlers (who may or may not be their owners) facing one another in the center of the ring.[9] A coconut pierced with a small hole is placed in a pail of water, in which it takes about twenty-one seconds to sink, a period known as a *tjeng* and marked at beginning and end by the beating of a slit gong. During these twenty-one seconds the handlers (*pengangkeb*) are not permitted to touch their roosters. If, as sometimes happens, the animals have not fought during this time, they are picked up, fluffed, pulled, prodded, and otherwise insulted, and put back in the center of the ring and the process begins again. Sometimes they refuse to fight at all, or one keeps running away, in which case they are imprisoned together under a wicker cage, which usually gets them engaged.

Most of the time, in any case, the cocks fly almost immediately at one another in a wing-beating, head-thrusting, leg-kicking explosion of animal fury so pure, so absolute, and in its own way so beautiful, as to be almost abstract, a Platonic concept of hate. Within moments one or the other drives home a solid blow with his spur. The handler whose cock has delivered the blow immediately picks it up so that it will not get a return blow, for if he does not the match is likely to end in a mutually mortal tie as the two birds wildly hack each other to pieces. This is particularly true if, as often happens, the spur sticks in its victim's body, for then the aggressor is at the mercy of his wounded foe.

With the birds again in the hands of their handlers, the coconut is now sunk three times after which the cock which has landed the blow must be set down to show that he is firm, a fact he demonstrates by wandering idly around the ring for a coconut sink. The coconut is then sunk twice more and the fight must recommence.

During this interval, slightly over two minutes, the handler of the wounded cock has been working frantically over it, like a trainer patching a mauled boxer between rounds, to get it in shape for a last, desperate try for victory. He blows in its mouth, putting the whole chicken head in his own mouth and sucking and blowing, fluffs it, stuffs its wounds with various sorts of medicines, and generally tries anything he can think of to arouse the last ounce of spirit which may be hidden somewhere within it. By the time he is forced to put it back down he is usually drenched in chicken blood, but, as in prize fighting, a good handler is worth his weight in gold. Some of them can virtually make the dead walk, at least long enough for the second and final round.

In the climactic battle (if there is one; sometimes the wounded cock simply expires in the handler's hands or immediately as it is placed down again), the cock who landed the first blow usually proceeds to finish off his weakened opponent. But this is far from an inevitable outcome, for if a cock can walk he can fight, and if he can fight, he can kill, and what counts is which cock expires first. If the wounded one can get a stab in and stagger on until the other drops, he is the official winner, even if he himself topples over an instant later.

Surrounding all this melodrama—which the crowd packed tight around the ring follows in near silence, moving their bodies in kinesthetic sympathy with the movement of the animals, cheering their champions on with wordless hand motions, shiftings of the shoulders, turnings of the head, falling back *en masse* as the cock with the murderous spurs careens toward one side of the ring (it is said that spectators sometimes lose eyes and fingers from being too attentive), surging forward again as they glance off toward another—is a vast body of extraordinarily elaborate and precisely detailed rules.

These rules, together with the developed lore of cocks and cockfighting which accompanies them, are written down in palm leaf manuscripts (*lontar;*

rontal), passed on from generation to generation as part of the general legal and cultural tradition of the villages. At a fight, the umpire (*saja komong; djuru kembar*)—the man who manages the coconut—is in charge of their application and his authority is absolute. I have never seen an umpire's judgment questioned on any subject, even by the more despondent losers, nor have I ever heard, even in private, a charge of unfairness directed against one, or, for that matter, complaints about umpires in general. Only exceptionally well-trusted, solid, and, given the complexity of the code, knowledgeable citizens perform this job, and in fact men will bring their cocks only to fights presided over by such men. It is also the umpire to whom accusations of cheating, which, though rare in the extreme, occasionally arise, are referred; and it is he who in the not infrequent cases where the cocks expire virtually together decides which (if either, for, though the Balinese do not care for such an outcome, there can be ties) went first. Likened to a judge, a king, a priest, and a policeman, he is all of these, and under his assured direction the animal passion of the fight proceeds within the civic certainty of the law. In the dozens of cockfights I saw in Bali, I never once saw an altercation about rules. Indeed, I never saw an open altercation, other than those between cocks, at all.

This crosswise doubleness of an event which, taken as a fact of nature, is rage untrammeled and, taken as a fact of culture, is form perfected, defines the cockfight as a sociological entity. A cockfight is what, searching for a name for something not vertebrate enough to be called a group and not structureless enough to be called a crowd, Erving Goffman has called a "focused gathering"—a set of persons engrossed in a common flow of activity and relating to one another in terms of that flow.[10] Such gatherings meet and disperse; the participants in them fluctuate; the activity that focuses them is discreet—a particulate process that reoccurs rather than a continuous one that endures. They take their form from the situation that evokes them, the floor on which they are placed, as Goffman puts it; but it is a form, and an articulate one, nonetheless. For the situation, the floor is itself created, in jury deliberations, surgical operations, block meetings, sit-ins, cockfights, by the cultural preoccupations—here, as we shall see, the celebration of status rivalry—which not only specify the focus but, assembling actors and arranging scenery, bring it actually into being.

In classical times (that is to say, prior to the Dutch invasion of 1908), when there were no bureaucrats around to improve popular morality, the staging of a cockfight was an explicitly societal matter. Bringing a cock to an important fight was, for an adult male, a compulsory duty of citizenship; taxation of fights, which were usually held on market day, was a major source of public revenue; patronage of the art was a stated responsibility of princes; and the cock ring, or *wantilan,* stood in the center of the village near those other monuments of Balinese civility—the council house, the origin temple, the marketplace, the signal tower, and the banyan tree. Today, a few special occasions aside, the newer rectitude makes so open a statement of the connection between the excitements of collective life and those of blood sport impossible, but, less directly expressed, the connection itself remains intimate and intact. To expose it, however, it is necessary to turn to the aspect of cockfighting around which all the others pivot, and through which they exercise their force, an aspect I have thus far studiously ignored. I mean, of course, the gambling.

Odds and Even Money

The Balinese never do anything in a simple way that they can contrive to do in a complicated one, and to this generalization cockfight wagering is no exception.

In the first place, there are two sorts of bets, or *toh*.[11] There is the single axial bet on the center between the principals (*toh ketengah*), and there is the cloud of peripheral ones around the ring between members of the audience (*toh kesasi*). The first is typically large; the second typically small. The first is collective, involving coalitions of bettors clustering around the owner; the second is individual, man to man. The first is a matter of deliberate, very quiet, almost furtive arrangement by the coalition members and the umpire huddled like conspirators in the center of the ring; the second is a matter of impulsive shouting, public offers, and public acceptances by the excited throng around its edges. And most curiously, and as we shall see most revealingly, *where the first is always, without exception, even money, the second, equally without exception, is never such.* What is a fair coin in the center is a biased one on the side.

The center bet is the official one, hedged in again with a webwork of rules, and is made between the two cock owners, with the umpire as overseer and public witness.[12] This bet, which, as I say, is always relatively and sometimes very large, is never raised simply by the owner in whose name it is made, but by him together with four or five, sometimes seven or eight, allies—kin, village mates, neighbors, close friends. He may, if he is not especially well-to-do, not even be the major contributor, though, if only to show that he is not involved in any chicanery, he must be a significant one.

Of the fifty-seven matches for which I have exact and reliable data on the center bet, the range is from fifteen ringgits to five hundred, with a mean at eighty-five and with the distribution being rather noticeably tri-modal: small fights (15 ringgits either side of 35) accounting for about 45 percent of the total number; medium ones (20 ringgits either side of 70) for about 25 percent; and large (75 ringgits either side of 175) for about 20 percent, with a few very small and very large ones out at the extremes. In a society where the normal daily wage of a manual laborer—a brickmaker, an ordinary farmworker, a market porter—was about three ringgits a day, and considering the fact that fights were held on the average about every two-and-a-half days in the immediate area I studied, this is clearly serious gambling, even if the bets are pooled rather than individual efforts.

The side bets are, however, something else altogether. Rather than the solemn, legalistic pactmaking of the center, wagering takes place rather in the fashion in which the stock exchange used to work when it was out on the curb. There is a fixed and known odds paradigm which runs in a continuous series from ten-to-nine at the short end to two-to-one at the long: 10-9, 9-8, 8-7, 7-6, 6-5, 5-4, 4-3, 3-2, 2-1. The man who wishes to back the *underdog cock* (leaving aside how favorites, *kebut,* and underdogs, *ngai,* are established for the moment) shouts the short-side number indicating the odds he wants *to be given.* That is, if he shouts *gasal,* "five," he wants the underdog at five-to-four (or, for him, four-to-five); if he shouts "four," he wants it at four-to-three (again, he putting up the "three"), if "nine," at nine-to-eight, and so on. A man backing the favorite, and thus considering giving odds if he can get them short enough, indicates the fact by crying out the color-type of that cock—"brown," "speckled," or whatever.[13]

As odds-takers (backers of the underdog) and odds-givers (backers of the favorite) sweep the crowd with their shouts, they begin to focus in on one another as potential betting pairs, often from far across the ring. The taker tries to shout the giver into longer odds, the giver to shout the taker into shorter ones.[14] The taker, who is the wooer in this situation, will signal how large a bet he wishes to make at the odds he is shouting by holding a number of fingers up in front of his face and vigorously waving them. If the giver, the wooed, replies in kind, the bet is made; if he does not, they unlock gazes and the search goes on.

The side betting, which takes place after the center bet has been made and its size announced, consists then in a rising crescendo of shouts as backers of the underdog offer their propositions to anyone who will accept them, while those who are backing the favorite but do not like the price being offered, shout equally frenetically the color of the cock to show they too are desperate to bet but want shorter odds.

Almost always odds-calling, which tends to be very consensual in that at any one time almost all callers are calling the same thing, starts off toward the long end of the range—five-to-four or four-to-three—and then moves, also consensually, toward the short end with greater or lesser speed and to a greater or lesser degree. Men crying "five" and finding themselves answered only with cries of "brown" start crying "six," either drawing the other callers fairly quickly with them or retiring from the scene as their too-generous offers are snapped up. If the change is made and partners are still scarce, the procedure is repeated in a move to "seven," and so on, only rarely, and in the very largest fights, reaching the ultimate "nine" or "ten" levels. Occasionally, if the cocks are clearly mismatched, there may be no upward movement at all, or even a movement down the scale to four-to-three, three-to-two, very, very rarely two-to-one, a shift which is accompanied by a declining number of bets as a shift upward is accompanied by an increasing number. But the general pattern is for the betting to move a shorter or longer distance up the scale toward the, for sidebets, nonexistent pole of even money, with the overwhelming majority of bets falling in the four-to-three to eight-to-seven range.[15]

As the moment for the release of the cocks by the handlers approaches, the screaming, at least in a match where the center bet is large, reaches almost frenzied proportions as the remaining unfulfilled bettors try desperately to find a last minute partner at a price they can live with. (Where the center bet is small, the opposite tends to occur: betting dies off, trailing into silence, as odds lengthen and people lose interest.) In a large-bet, well-made match—the kind of match the Balinese regard as "real cockfighting"—the mob scene quality, the sense that sheer chaos is about to break loose, with all those waving, shouting, pushing, clambering men is quite strong, an effect which is only heightened by the intense stillness that falls with instant suddenness, rather as if someone had turned off the current, when the slit gong sounds, the cocks are put down, and the battle begins.

When it ends, anywhere from fifteen seconds to five minutes later, *all bets are immediately paid.* There are absolutely no IOU's, at least to a betting opponent. One may, of course, borrow from a friend before offering or accepting a wager, but to offer or accept it you must have the money already in hand and, if you lose, you must pay it on the spot, before the next match begins. This is an iron rule, and as I have never heard of a disputed umpire's decision (though doubtless there must sometimes be some), I have also never heard of a welshed bet, perhaps because in a worked-up cockfight crowd the consequences might be, as they are reported to be sometimes for cheaters, drastic and immediate.

It is, in any case, this formal asymmetry between balanced center bets and unbalanced side ones that poses the critical analytical problem for a theory which sees cockfight wagering as the link connecting the fight to the wider world of Balinese culture. It also suggests the way to go about solving it and demonstrating the link.

The first point that needs to be made in this connection is that the higher the center bet, the more likely the match will in actual fact be an even one. Simple considerations of rationality suggest that. If you are betting fifteen ringgits on a cock, you might be willing to go along with even money even if you feel your animal somewhat the less promising. But if you are betting five hundred you are very, very likely to be loath to do so. Thus, in large-bet fights, which of course involve the better animals, tremendous care is taken to see that the cocks are about as evenly matched as to size, general condition, pugnacity, and so on as is humanly possible. The different ways of adjusting the spurs of the animals are often employed to secure this. If one cock seems stronger, an agreement will be made to position his spur at a slightly less advantageous angle—a kind of handicapping, at which spur affixers are, so it is said, extremely skilled. More care will be taken, too, to employ skillful handlers and to match them exactly as to abilities.

In short, in a large-bet fight the pressure to make the match a genuinely fifty-fifty proposition is enormous, and is consciously felt as such. For medium fights the pressure is somewhat less, and for small ones less yet, though there is always an effort to make things at least approximately equal, for even at fifteen ringgits (five days' work) no one wants to make an even money bet in a clearly unfavorable situation. And, again, what statistics I have tend to bear this out. In my fifty-seven matches, the favorite won thirty-three times overall, the underdog twenty-four, a 1.4 to 1 ratio. But if one splits the figures at sixty ringgits center bets, the ratios turn out to be 1.1 to 1 (twelve favorites, eleven underdogs) for those above this line, and 1.6 to 1 (twenty-one and thirteen) for those below it. Or, if you take the extremes, for very large fights, those with center bets over a hundred ringgits the ratio is 1 to 1 (seven and seven); for very small fights, those under forty ringgits, it is 1.9 to 1 (nineteen and ten).[16]

Now, from this proposition—that the higher the center bet the more exactly a fifty-fifty proposition the cockfight is—two things more or less immediately follow: (1) the higher the center bet, the greater is the pull on the side betting toward the short-odds end of the wagering spectrum and vice versa; (2) the higher the center bet, the greater the volume of side betting and vice versa.

The logic is similar in both cases. The closer the fight is in fact to even money, the less attractive the long end of the odds will appear and, therefore, the shorter it must be if there are to be takers. That this is the case is apparent from mere inspection, from the Balinese's own analysis of the matter, and from what more systematic observations I was able to collect. Given the difficulty of making precise and complete recordings of side betting, this argument is hard to cast in numerical form, but in all my cases the odds-giver, odds-taker consensual point, a quite pronounced minimax saddle where the bulk (at a guess, two-thirds to three-quarters in most cases) of the bets are actually made, was three or four points further along the scale toward the shorter end for the large-center-bet fights than for the small ones, with medium ones generally in between. In detail, the fit is not, of course, exact, but the general pattern is quite consistent: the power of the center bet to pull the side bets toward its own even-money pattern is directly proportional to its size, because its size is directly proportional to the degree to which the cocks are in fact evenly matched. As for the volume question, total wagering is greater in large-center-bet fights because such fights are considered more "interesting" not only in the sense that they are less predictable, but, more crucially, that more is at stake in them—in terms of money, in terms of the quality of the cocks, and consequently, as we shall see, in terms of social prestige.[17]

The paradox of fair coin in the middle, biased coin on the outside is thus a merely apparent one. The two betting systems, though formally incongruent, are not really contradictory to one another, but part of a single larger system in which the center bet is, so to speak, the "center of gravity," drawing, the larger it is the more so, the outside bets toward the short-odds end of the scale. The center bet thus "makes the game," or perhaps better, defines it, signals what, following a notion of Jeremy Bentham's, I am going to call its "depth."

The Balinese attempt to create an interesting, if you will, "deep," match by making the center bet as large as possible so that the cocks matched will be as equal and as fine as possible, and the outcome, thus, as unpredictable as possible. They do not always succeed. Nearly half the matches are relatively trivial, relatively uninteresting—in my borrowed terminology, "shallow"—affairs. But that fact no more argues against my interpretation than the fact that most painters, poets, and playwrights are mediocre argues against the view that artistic effort is directed toward profundity and, with a certain frequency, approximates it. The image of artistic technique is indeed exact: the center bet is a means, a device, for creating "interesting," "deep" matches, *not* the reason, at least not the main reason, *why* they are interesting, the source of their fascination, the substance of their depth. The question why such matches are interesting—indeed, for the Balinese, exquisitely absorbing—takes us out of the realm of formal concerns into more broadly sociological and social-psychological ones, and to a less purely economic idea of what "depth" in gaming amounts to.[18]

Playing with Fire

Bentham's concept of "deep play" is found in his *The Theory of Legislation*.[19] By it he means play in which the stakes are so high that it is, from his utilitarian standpoint, irrational for men to engage in it at all. If a man whose fortune is a thousand pounds (or ringgits) wages five hundred of it on an even bet, the marginal utility of the pound he stands to win is clearly less than the marginal disutility of the one he stands to lose. In genuine deep play, this is the case for both parties. They are both in over their heads. Having come together in search of pleasure they have entered into a relationship which will bring the participants, considered collectively, net pain rather than net pleasure. Bentham's conclusion was, therefore, that deep play was immoral from the first principles and, a typical step for him, should be prevented legally.

But more interesting than the ethical problem, at least for our concerns here, is that despite the logical force of Bentham's analysis men do engage in such play, both passionately and often, and even in the face of law's revenge. For Bentham and those who think as he does (nowadays mainly lawyers, economists, and a few psychiatrists), the explanation is, as I have said, that such men are irrational—addicts, fetishists, children, fools, savages, who need only to be protected against themselves. But for the Balinese, though naturally they do not formulate it in so many words, the explanation lies in the fact that in such play money is less a measure of utility, had or expected, than it is a symbol of moral import, perceived or imposed.

It is, in fact, in shallow games, ones in which smaller amounts of money are involved, that increments and decrements of cash are more nearly synonyms for utility and disutility, in the ordinary, unexpanded sense—for pleasure and pain, happiness and unhappiness. In deep ones, where the amounts of money are great, much more is at stake than material gain: namely esteem, honor, dignity, respect—in a word, though in Bali a profoundly freighted word, status.[20] It is at stake symbolically, for (a few cases of ruined addict gamblers aside) no one's status is actually altered by the outcome of a cockfight; it is only, and that momentarily, affirmed or insulted. But for the Balinese, for whom nothing is more pleasurable than an affront obliquely delivered or more painful than one obliquely received—particularly when mutual acquaintances, undeceived by surfaces, are watching—such appraisive drama is deep indeed.

This, I must stress immediately, is *not* to say that the money does not matter, or that the Balinese is no more concerned about losing five hundred ringgits than fifteen. Such a conclusion would be absurd. It is because money *does,* in this hardly unmaterialistic society, matter and matter very much that the more of it one risks the more of a lot of other things, such as one's pride, one's poise, one's dispassion, one's masculinity, one also risks, again only momentarily but again very publicly as well. In deep cockfights an owner and his collaborators, and, as we shall see, to a lesser but still quite real extent also their backers on the outside, put their money where their status is.

It is in large part *because* the marginal disutility of loss is so great at the higher levels of betting that to engage in such betting is to lay one's public self, allusively and metaphorically, through the medium of one's cock, on the line. And though to a Benthamite this might seem merely to increase the irrationality of the enterprise that much further, to the Balinese what it mainly increases is the meaningfulness of it all. And as (to follow Weber rather than Bentham) the imposition of meaning on life is the major end and primary condition of human existence, that access of significance more than compensates for the economic costs involved.[21] Actually, given the even-money quality of the larger matches, important changes in material fortune among those who regularly participate in them seem virtually nonexistent, because matters more or less even out over the long run. It is, actually, in the smaller, shallow fights, where one finds the handful of more pure, addict-type gamblers involved—those who *are* in it mainly for the money—that "real" changes in social position, largely downward, are affected. Men of this sort, plungers, are highly dispraised by "true cockfighters" as fools who do not understand what the sport is all about, vulgarians who simply miss the point of it all. They are, these addicts, regarded as fair game for the genuine enthusiasts, those who do understand, to take a little money away from, something that is easy enough to do by luring them, through the force of their greed, into irrational bets on mismatched cocks. Most of them do indeed manage to ruin themselves in a remarkably short time, but there always seem to be one or two of them around, pawning their land and selling their clothes in order to bet, at any particular time.[22]

This graduated correlation of "status gambling" with deeper fights and, inversely, "money gambling" with shallower ones is in fact quite general. Bettors themselves form a sociomoral hierarchy in these terms. As noted earlier, at most cockfights there are, around the very edges of the cockfight area, a large number of mindless, sheer-chance type gambling games (roulette, dice throw, coin-spin, pea-under-the-shell) operated by concessionaires. Only women, children, adolescents, and various other sorts of people who do not (or not yet) fight cocks—the extremely poor, the socially despised, the personally idiosyncratic—play at these games, at, of course, penny ante levels. Cockfighting men would be ashamed to go anywhere near them. Slightly above these people in standing are those who, though they do not themselves fight cocks, bet on the smaller matches around the edges. Next, there are those who fight cocks in small, or occasionally medium matches, but have not the status to join in the large ones, though they may bet from time to time on the side in those. And finally, there are those, the really substantial members of the community, the solid citizenry around whom local life revolves, who fight in the larger fights and bet on them around the side. The focusing element in these focused gatherings, these men generally dominate and define the sport as they dominate and define the society. When a Balinese male talks, in that almost venerative way, about "the true cockfighter," the *bebatoh* ("bettor") or *djuru kurung* ("cage keeper"), it is this sort of person, not those who bring the mentality of the pea-and-shell game into the quite different, inappropriate context of the cockfight, the driven gambler (*potét*, a word which has the secondary meaning of thief or reprobate), and the wistful hanger-on, that they mean. For such a man, what is really going on in a match is something rather close to an *affaire d'honneur* (though, with the Balinese talent for practical fantasy, the blood that is spilled is only figuratively human) than to the stupid, mechanical crank of a slot machine.

What makes Balinese cockfighting deep is thus not money in itself, but what, the more of it that is involved the more so, money causes to happen: the migration of the Balinese status hierarchy into the body of the cockfight. Psychologically an Aesopian representation of the ideal/demonic, rather narcissistic, male self, sociologically it is an equally Aesopian representation of the complex fields of tension set up by the controlled, muted, ceremonial, but for all that deeply felt, interaction of those selves in the context of everyday life. The cocks may be surrogates for their owners' personalities, animal mirrors of psychic form, but the cockfight is—or more exactly, deliberately is made to be—a simulation of the social matrix, the involved system of crosscutting, overlapping, highly corporate groups—villages, kingroups, irrigation societies, temple congregations, "castes"—in which its devotees live.[23] And as prestige, the necessity to affirm it, defend it, celebrate it, justify it, and just plain bask in it (but not, given the strongly ascriptive character of Balinese stratification, to seek it), is perhaps the central driving force in the society, so also—ambulant penises, blood sacrifices, and monetary exchanges aside—is it of the cockfight. This apparent amusement and seeming sport is, to take another phrase from Erving Goffman, "a status bloodbath."[24]

The easiest way to make this clear, and at least to some degree to demonstrate it, is to invoke the village whose cockfighting activities I observed the closest—the one in which the raid occurred and from which my statistical data are taken.

As all Balinese villages, this one—Tihingan, in the Klungkung region of southeast Bali—is intricately organized, a labyrinth of alliances and oppositions. But, unlike many, two sorts of corporate groups, which are also status groups, particularly stand out, and we may concentrate on them, in a part-for-whole way, without undue distortion.

First, the village is dominated by four large, patrilineal, partly endogamous descent groups which are constantly vying with one another and form the major factions in the village. Sometimes they group two and two, or rather the two larger ones versus the two smaller ones plus all the unaffiliated people; sometimes they operate independently. There are also subfactions within them, subfactions within the subfactions, and so on to rather fine levels of distinction. And second, there is the village itself, almost entirely endogamous, which is opposed to all the other villages round about in its cockfight circuit (which, as explained, is the market region), but which also forms alliances with certain of these neighbors against certain others in various supravillage political and social contexts. The exact situation is thus, as everywhere in Bali, quite distinctive; but the general pattern of a tiered hierarchy of status rivalries between highly corporate but various based groupings (and, thus, between the members of them) is entirely general.

Consider, then, as support of the general thesis that the cockfight, and especially the deep cockfight, is fundamentally a dramatization of status concerns, the following facts, which to avoid extended ethnographic description I will simply pronounce to be facts—though the concrete evidence—examples, statements, and numbers that could be brought to bear in support of them is both extensive and unmistakable:

1. A man virtually never bets against a cock owned by a member of his own kingroup. Usually he will feel obliged to bet for it, the more so the closer the kin tie and the deeper the fight. If he is certain in his mind that it will not win, he may just not bet at all, particularly if it is only a second cousin's bird or if the fight is a shallow one. But as a rule he will feel he must support it and, in deep games, nearly always does. Thus the great majority of the people calling "five" or "speckled" so demonstratively are expressing their allegiance to their kinsman, not their evaluation of his bird, their understanding of probability theory, or even their hopes of unearned income.

2. This principle is extended logically. If your kingroup is not involved you will support an allied kingroup against an unallied one in the same way, and so on through the very involved networks of alliances which, as I say, make up this, as any other, Balinese village.

3. So, too, for the village as a whole. If an outsider cock is fighting any cock

from your village, you will tend to support the local one. If, what is a rare circumstance but occurs every now and then, a cock from outside your cockfight circuit is fighting one inside it you will also tend to support the "home bird."

4. Cocks which come from any distance are almost always favorites, for the theory is the man would not have dared to bring it if it was not a good cock, the more so the further he has come. His followers are, of course, obliged to support him, and when the more grand-scale legal cockfights are held (on holidays, and so on) the people of the village take what they regard to be the best cocks in the village, regardless of ownership, and go off to support them, although they will almost certainly have to give odds on them and to make large bets to show that they are not a cheapskate village. Actually, such "away games," though infrequent, tend to mend the ruptures between village members that the constantly occurring "home games," where village factions are opposed rather than united, exacerbate.

5. Almost all matches are sociologically relevant. You seldom get two outsider cocks fighting, or two cocks with no particular group backing, or with group backing which is mutually unrelated in any clear way. When you do get them, the game is very shallow, betting very slow, and the whole thing very dull, with no one save the immediate principals and an addict gambler or two at all interested.

6. By the same token, you rarely get two cocks from the same group, even more rarely from the same subfaction, and virtually never from the same sub-subfaction (which would be in most cases one extended family) fighting. Similarly, in outside village fights two members of the village will rarely fight against one another, even though, as bitter rivals, they would do so with enthusiasm on their home grounds.

7. On the individual level, people involved in an institutionalized hostility relationship, called *puik,* in which they do not speak or otherwise have anything to do with each other (the causes of this formal breaking of relations are many: wife-capture, inheritance arguments, political differences) will bet very heavily, sometimes almost maniacally, against one another in what is a frank and direct attack on the very masculinity, the ultimate ground of his status, of the opponent.

8. The center bet coalition is, in all but the shallowest games, *always* made up by structural allies—no "outside money" is involved. What is "outside" depends upon the context, of course, but given it, no outside money is mixed in with the main bet; if the principals cannot raise it, it is not made. The center bet, again especially in deeper games, is thus the most direct and open expression of social opposition, which is one of the reasons why both it and match making are surrounded by such an air of unease, furtiveness, embarrassment, and so on.

9. The rule about borrowing money—that you may borrow *for* a bet but not *in* one—stems (and the Balinese are quite conscious of this) from similar

considerations: you are never at the *economic* mercy of your enemy that way. Gambling debts, which can get quite large on a rather short-term basis, are always to friends, never to enemies, structurally speaking.

10. When two cocks are structurally irrelevant or neutral so far as *you* are concerned (though, as mentioned, they almost never are to each other) you do not even ask a relative or a friend whom he is betting on, because if you know how he is betting and he knows you know, and you go the other way, it will lead to strain. This rule is explicit and rigid; fairly elaborate, even rather artificial precautions are taken to avoid breaking it. At the very least you must pretend not to notice what he is doing, and he what you are doing.

11. There is a special word for betting against the grain, which is also the word for "pardon me" (*mpura*). It is considered a bad thing to do, though if the center bet is small it is sometimes all right as long as you do not do it too often. But the larger the bet and the more frequently you do it, the more the "pardon me" tack will lead to social disruption.

12. In fact, the institutionalized hostility relation, *puik*, is often formally initiated (though its causes always lie elsewhere) by such a "pardon me" bet in a deep fight, putting the symbolic fat in the fire. Similarly, the end of such a relationship and resumption of normal social intercourse is often signaled (but, again, not actually brought about) by one or the other of the enemies supporting the other's bird.

13. In sticky, cross-loyalty situations, of which in this extraordinarily complex social system there are of course many, where a man is caught between two more or less equally balanced loyalties, he tends to wander off for a cup of coffee or something to avoid having to bet, a form of behavior reminiscent of that of American voters in similar situations.[25]

14. The people involved in the center bet are, especially in deep fights, virtually always leading members of their group—kinship, village, or whatever. Further, those who bet on the side (including these people) are, as I have already remarked, the more established members of the village—the solid citizens. Cockfighting is for those who are involved in the everyday politics of prestige as well, not for youth, women, subordinates, and so forth.

15. So far as money is concerned, the explicitly expressed attitude toward it is that it is a secondary matter. It is not, as I have said, of no importance; Balinese are no happier to lose several weeks' income than anyone else. But they mainly look on the monetary aspects of the cockfight as self-balancing, a matter of just moving money around, circulating it among a fairly well-defined group of serious cockfighters. The really important wins and losses are seen mostly in other terms, and the general attitude toward wagering is not any hope of cleaning up, of making a killing (addict gamblers again excepted), but that of the horseplayer's prayer: "O, God, please let me break even." In prestige terms, however, you do not want to break even, but, in a momentary, punctuate sort of way, win

utterly. The talk (which goes on all the time) is about fights against such-and-such a cock of So-and-So which your cock demolished, not on how much you won, a fact people, even for large bets, rarely remember for any length of time, though they will remember the day they did in Pan Loh's finest cock for years.

16. You must bet on cocks of your own group aside from mere loyalty considerations, for if you do not people generally will say, "What! Is he too proud for the likes of us? Does he have to go to Java or Den Pasar [the capital town] to bet, he is such an important man?" Thus there is a general pressure to bet not only to show that you are important locally, but that you are not so important that you look down on everyone else as unfit even to be rivals. Similarly, home team people must bet against outside cocks or the outsiders will accuse it—a serious charge—of just collecting entry fees and not really being interested in cockfighting, as well as again being arrogant and insulting.

17. Finally, the Balinese peasants themselves are quite aware of all this and can and, at least to an ethnographer, do state most of it in approximately the same terms as I have. Fighting cocks, almost every Balinese I have ever discussed the subject with has said, is like playing with fire only not getting burned. You activate village and kingroup rivalries and hostilities, but in "play" form, coming dangerously and entrancingly close to the expression of open and direct interpersonal and intergroup aggression (something which, again, almost never happens in the normal course of ordinary life), but not quite, because, after all, it is "only a cock-fight."

More observations of this sort could be advanced, but perhaps the general point is, if not made, at least well-delineated, and the whole argument thus far can be usefully summarized in a formal paradigm:

THE MORE A MATCH IS . . .

1. Between near status equals (and/or personal enemies)
2. Between high status individuals

THE DEEPER THE MATCH.

THE DEEPER THE MATCH . . .

1. The closer the identification of cock and man (or: more properly, the deeper the match the more the man will advance his best, most closely-identified-with cock).
2. The finer the cocks involved and the more exactly they will be matched.
3. The greater the emotion that will be involved and the more the general absorption in the match.

4. The higher the individual bets center and outside, the shorter the outside bet odds will tend to be, and the more betting there will be overall.
5. The less an "economic" and the more a "status" view of gaming will be involved, and the "solider" the citizens who will be gaming.[26]

Inverse arguments hold for the shallower the fight, culminating, in a reversed-signs sense, in the coin-spinning and dice-throwing amusements. For deep fights there are no absolute upper limits, though there are of course practical ones, and there are a great many legendlike tales of great Duel-in-the-Sun combats between lords and princes in classical times (for cockfighting has always been as much an elite concern as a popular one), far deeper than anything anyone, even aristocrats, could produce today anywhere in Bali.

Indeed, one of the great culture heroes of Bali is a prince, called after his passion for the sport, "The Cockfighter," who happened to be away at a very deep cockfight with a neighboring prince when the whole of his family—father, brothers, wives, sisters—were assassinated by commoner usurpers. Thus spared, he returned to dispatch the upstarts, regain the throne, reconstitute the Balinese high tradition, and build its most powerful, glorious, and prosperous state. Along with everything else that the Balinese see in fighting cocks—themselves, their social order, abstract hatred, masculinity, demonic power—they also see the archetype of status virtue, the arrogant, resolute, honor-mad player with real fire, the *ksatria* prince.[27]

Feathers, Blood, Crowds, and Money

"Poetry makes nothing happen," Auden says in his elegy of Yeats, "it survives in the valley of its saying . . . a way of happening, a mouth." The cockfight too, in this colloquial sense, makes nothing happen. Men go on allegorically humiliating one another and being allegorically humiliated by one another, day after day, glorying quietly in the experience if they have triumphed, crushed only slightly more openly by it if they have not. *But no one's status really changes.* You cannot ascend the status ladder by winning cockfights; you cannot, as an individual, really ascend it at all. Nor can you descend it that way.[28] All you can do is enjoy and savor, or suffer and withstand, the concocted sensation of drastic and momentary movement along an aesthetic semblance of that ladder, and kind of behind-the-mirror status jump which has the look of mobility without its actuality.

As any art form—for that, finally, is what we are dealing with—the cockfight renders ordinary, everyday experience comprehensible by presenting it in terms of acts and objects which have had their practical consequences removed and been reduced (or, if you prefer, raised) to the level of sheer appearances, where their meaning can be more powerfully articulated and more exactly perceived. The cockfight is "really real" only to the cocks—it does not kill anyone, castrate anyone, reduce anyone to animal status, alter the hierarchical relations among people, nor refashion the hierarchy; it does not even redistribute income in any significant way. What it does is what, for other peoples with other temperaments and other conventions, *Lear* and *Crime and Punishment* do; it catches up these themes—death, masculinity, rage, pride, loss, beneficence, chance—and, ordering them into an encompassing structure, presents them in such a way as to throw into relief a particular view of their essential nature. It puts a construction on them, makes them, to those historically positioned to appreciate the construction, meaningful—visible, tangible, graspable—"real," in an ideational sense. An image, fiction, a model, a metaphor, the cockfight is a means of expression; its function is neither to assuage social passions nor to heighten them (though, in its play-with-fire way, it does a bit of both), but, in a medium of feathers, blood, crowds, and money, to display them.

The question of how it is that we perceive qualities in things—paintings, books, melodies, plays—that we do not feel we can assert literally to be there has come, in recent years, into the very center of aesthetic theory.[29] Neither the sentiments of the artist, which remain his, nor those of the audience, which remain theirs, can account for the agitation of one painting or the serenity of another. We attribute grandeur, wit, despair, exuberance to strings of sounds; lightness, energy, violence, fluidity to blocks of stone. Novels are said to have strength, buildings eloquence, plays momentum, ballets repose. In this realm of eccentric predicates, to say that the cockfight, in its perfected cases at least, is "disquietful" does not seem at all unnatural, merely, as I have just denied it practical consequence, somewhat puzzling.

The disquietfulness arises, "somehow," out of a conjunction of three attributes of the fight: its immediate dramatic shape; its metaphoric content; and its social context. A cultural figure against a social ground, the fight is at once a convulsive surge of animal hatred, a mock war of symbolical selves, and a formal simulation of status tensions, and its aesthetic power derives from its capacity to force together these diverse realities. The reason it is disquietful is not that it has material effects (it has some, but they are minor); the reason that it is disquietful is that, joining pride to selfhood, selfhood to cocks, and cocks to destruction, it brings to imaginative realization a dimension of Balinese experience normally well-obscured from view. The transfer of a sense of gravity into what is in itself a rather blank and unvarious spectacle, a commotion of beating wings and throbbing legs, is effected by interpreting it as expressive of something unsettling in the way its authors and audience live, or, even more ominously, what they are.

As a dramatic shape, the fight displays a characteristic that does not seem so remarkable until one realizes that it does not have to be there: a radically atomistical structure.[30] Each match is a world unto itself, a particulate burst of form. There is the match making, there is the betting, there is the fight, there is the result—utter triumph and utter defeat—and there is the hurried, embarrassed passing of money. The loser is not consoled. People drift away from him, look through him, leave him to assimilate his momentary descent into nonbeing, reset his face, and return, scarless and intact, to the fray. Nor are winners congratulated, or events rehashed; once a match is ended the crowd's attention turns totally to the next, with no looking back. A shadow of the experience no doubt remains with the principals, perhaps even with some of the witnesses, of a deep fight, as it remains with us when we leave the theater after seeing a powerful play well-performed; but it quite soon fades to become at most a schematic memory—a diffuse glow or an abstract shudder—and usually not even that. Any expressive form lives only in its own present—the one it itself creates. But, here, that present is severed into a string of flashes, some more bright than others, but all of them disconnected, aesthetic quanta. Whatever the cockfight says, it says in spurts.

But, as I have argued lengthily elsewhere, the Balinese live in spurts.[31] Their life, as they arrange it and perceive it, is less a flow, a directional movement out of the past, through the present, toward the future than an on-off pulsation of meaning and vacuity, an arhythmic alternation of short periods when "something" (that is, something significant) is happening and equally short ones where "nothing" (that is, nothing much) is—between what they themselves call "full" and "empty" times, or, in another idiom, "junctures" and "holes." In focusing activity down to a burning-glass dot, the cockfight is merely being Balinese in the same way in which everything from the monadic encounters of everyday life, through the changing pointillism of *gamelan* music, to the visiting-day-of-the-gods temple celebrations are. It is not an imitation of the punctuateness of Balinese social life, nor a depiction of it, nor even an expression of it; it is an example of it, carefully prepared.[32]

If one dimension of the cockfight's structure, its lack of temporal directionality, makes it seem a typical segment of the general social life, however, the other, its flat-out, head-to-head (or spur-to-spur) aggressiveness, makes it seem a contradiction, a reversal, even a subversion of it. In the normal course of things, the Balinese are shy to the point of obsessiveness of open conflict. Oblique, cautious, subdued, controlled, masters of indirection and dissimulation—what they call *alus*, "polished," "smooth"—they rarely face what they can turn away from, rarely resist what they can evade. But here they portray themselves as wild and murderous, manic explosions of instinctual cruelty. A powerful rendering of life as the Balinese most deeply do not want it (to adapt a phrase Frye has used of Gloucester's blinding) is set in the context of a sample of it as they do in fact have it.[33] And, because the context suggests that the rendering, if less than a straightforward description is nonetheless more than an idle fancy, it is here that the disquietfulness—the disquietfulness of the *fight*, not (or, anyway, not necessarily) its patrons, who seem in fact rather thoroughly to enjoy it—emerges. The slaughter in the cock ring is not a depiction of how things literally are among men, but, what is almost worse, of how, from a particular angle, they imaginatively are.[34]

The angle, of course, is stratificatory. What, as we have already seen, the cockfight talks most forcibly about is status relationships, and what it says about them is that they are matters of life and death. That prestige is a profoundly serious business is apparent everywhere one looks in Bali—in the village, the family, the economy, the state. A peculiar fusion of Polynesian title ranks and Hindu castes, the hierarchy of pride is the moral backbone of the society. But only in the cockfight are the sentiments upon which that hierarchy rests revealed in their natural colors. Enveloped elsewhere in a haze of etiquette, a thick cloud of euphemism and ceremony, gesture and allusion, they are here expressed in only the thinnest disguise of an animal mask, a mask which in fact demonstrates them far more effectively than it conceals them. Jealousy is as much a part of Bali as poise, envy as grace, brutality as charm; but without the cockfight the Balinese would have a much less certain understanding of them, which is, presumably, why they value it so highly.

Any expressive form works (when it works) by disarranging semantic contexts in such a way that properties conventionally ascribed to certain things are unconventionally ascribed to others, which are then seen actually to possess them. To call the wind a cripple, as Stevens does, to fix tone and manipulate timbre, as Schoenberg does, or, closer to our case, to picture an art critic as a dissolute bear, as Hogarth does, is to cross conceptual wires; the established conjunctions between objects and their qualities are altered and phenomena—fall weather, melodic shape, or cultural journalism—are clothed in signifiers which normally point to other referents.[35] Similarly, to connect—and connect, and connect—the collision of roosters with the divisiveness of status is to invite a transfer of perceptions from the former to the latter, a transfer which is at once a description and a judgment. (Logically, the transfer could, of course, as well go the other way; but, like most of the rest of us, the Balinese are a great deal more interested in understanding men than they are in understanding cocks.)

What sets the cockfight apart from the ordinary course of life, lifts it from the realm of everyday practical affairs, and surrounds it with an aura of enlarged importance is not, as functionalist sociology would have it, that it reinforces status discriminations (such reinforcement is hardly necessary in a society where every act proclaims them), but that it provides a metasocial commentary upon the whole matter of assorting human beings into fixed hierarchical ranks and then organizing the major part of collective existence around that assortment. Its function, if you want to call it that, is interpretive: it is a Balinese reading of Balinese experience; a story they tell themselves about themselves.

Saying Something of Something

To put the matter this way is to engage in a bit of metaphorical refocusing of one's own, for it shifts the analysis of cultural forms from an endeavor in general parallel to dissecting an organism, diagnosing a symptom, deciphering a code, or ordering a system—the dominant analogies in contemporary anthropology—to one in general parallel with penetrating a literary text. If one takes the cockfight, or any other collectively sustained symbolic structure, as a means of "saying something of something" (to invoke a famous Aristotelian tag), then one is faced with a problem not in social mechanics but social semantics.[36] For the anthropologist, whose concern is with formulating sociological principles, not with promoting or appreciating cockfights, the question is, what does one learn about such principles from examining culture as an assemblage of texts?

Such an extension of the notion of a text beyond written material, and even beyond verbal, is, though metaphorical, not, of course, all that novel. The *interpretatio naturae* tradition of the Middle Ages, which, culminating in Spinoza, attempted to read nature as Scripture, the Nietzschean effort to treat value systems as glosses on the will to power (or the Marxian one to treat them as glosses on property relations), and the Freudian replacement of the enigmatic text of the manifest dream with the plain one of the latent, all offer precedents, if not equally recommendable ones.[37] But the idea remains theoretically undeveloped; and the more profound corollary, so far as anthropology is concerned, that cultural forms can be treated as texts, as imaginative works built out of social materials, has yet to be systematically exploited.[38]

In the case at hand, to treat the cockfight as a text is to bring out a feature of it (in my opinion, the central feature of it) that treating it as a rite or a pastime, the two most obvious alternatives, would tend to obscure: its use of emotion for cognitive ends. What the cockfight says it says in a vocabulary of sentiment—the thrill of risk, the despair of loss, the pleasure of triumph. Yet what it says is not merely that risk is exciting, loss depressing, or triumph gratifying, banal tautologies of affect, but that it is of these emotions, thus exampled, that society is built and individuals put together. Attending cockfights and participating in them is, for the Balinese, a kind of sentimental education. What he learns there is what his culture's ethos and his private sensibility (or, anyway, certain aspects of them) look like when spelled out externally in a collective text; that the two are near enough alike to be articulated in the symbolics of a single such text; and—the disquieting part—that the text in which this revelation is accomplished consists of a chicken hacking another mindlessly to bits.

Every people, the proverb has it, loves its own form of violence. The cockfight is the Balinese reflection on theirs: on its look, its uses, its force, its fascination. Drawing on almost every level of Balinese experience, it brings together themes—animal savagery, male narcissism, opponent gambling, status rivalry, mass excitement, blood sacrifice—whose main connection is their involvement with rage and the fear of rage, and, binding them into a set of rules which at once contains them and allows them play, builds a symbolic structure in which, over and over again, the reality of their inner affiliation can be intelligibly felt. If, to quote Northrop Frye again, we go to see *Macbeth* to learn what a man feels like after he has gained a kingdom and lost his soul,

Balinese go to cockfights to find out what a man, usually composed, aloof, almost obsessively self-absorbed, a kind of moral autocosm, feels like when, attacked, tormented, challenged, insulted, and driven in result to the extremes of fury, he has totally triumphed or been brought totally low. The whole passage, as it takes us back to Aristotle (though to the *Poetics* rather than the *Hermeneutics*), is worth quotation:

> But the poet [as opposed to the historian], Aristotle says, never makes any real statements at all, certainly no particular or specific ones. The poet's job is not to tell you what happened, but what happens: not what did take place, but the kind of thing that always does take place. He gives you the typical, recurring, or what Aristotle calls universal event. You wouldn't go to *Macbeth* to learn about the history of Scotland—you go to it to learn what man feels like after he's gained a kingdom and lost his soul. When you meet such a character as Micawber in Dickens, you don't feel that there must have been a man Dickens knew who was exactly like this: you feel that there's a bit of Micawber in almost everybody you know, including yourself. Our impressions of human life are picked up one by one, and remain for most of us loose and disorganized. But we constantly find things in literature that suddenly coordinate and bring into focus a great many such impressions, and this is part of what Aristotle means by the typical or universal human event.[39]

It is this kind of bringing of assorted experiences of everyday life to focus that the cockfight, set aside from that life as "only a game" and reconnected to it as "more than a game," accomplishes, and so creates what, better than typical or universal, could be called a paradigmatic human event—that is, one that tells us less what happens than the kind of thing that would happen if, as is not the case, life were art and could be as freely shaped by styles of feeling as *Macbeth* and *David Copperfield* are.

Enacted and reenacted, so far without end, the cockfight enables the Balinese, as, read and reread, *Macbeth* enables us, to see a dimension of his own subjectivity. As he watches fight after fight, with the active watching of an owner and a bettor (for cockfighting has no more interest as a pure spectator sport than croquet or dog racing do), he grows familiar with it and what it has to say to him, much as the attentive listener to string quartets or the absorbed viewer of still lifes grows slowly more familiar with them in a way which opens his subjectivity to himself.[40]

Yet, because—in another of those paradoxes, along with painted feelings and unconsequenced acts, which haunt aesthetics—that subjectivity does not properly exist until it is thus organized, art forms generate and regenerate the very subjectivity they pretend only to display. Quartets, still lifes, and cockfights are not merely reflections of a preexisting sensibility analogically represented; they are positive agents in the creation and maintenance of such a sensibility. If we see ourselves as a pack of Micawbers it is from reading too much Dickens (if we see ourselves as unillusioned realists, it is from reading too little); and similarly for Balinese, cocks, and cockfights. It is in such a way, coloring experience with the light they cast it in, rather than through whatever material effects they may have, that the arts play their role, as arts, in social life.[41]

In the cockfight, then, the Balinese forms and discovers his temperament and his society's temper at the same time. Or, more exactly, he forms and discovers a particular face of them. Not only are there a great many other cultural texts providing commentaries on status hierarchy and self-regard in Bali, but there are a great many other critical sectors of Balinese life besides the stratificatory and the agonistic that receive such commentary. The ceremony consecrating a Brahmana priest, a matter of breath control, postural immobility, and vacant concentration upon the depths of being, displays a radically different, but to the Balinese equally real, property of social hierarchy—its reach toward the numinous transcendent. Set not in the matrix of the kinetic emotionality of animals, but in that of the static passionlessness of divine mentality, it expresses tranquillity not disquiet. The mass festivals at the village temples, which mobilize the whole local population in elaborate hostings of visiting gods—songs, dances, compliments, gifts—assert the spiritual unity of village mates against their status inequality and project a mood of amity and trust.[42] The cockfight is not the master key to Balinese life, any more than bullfighting is to Spanish. What it says about that life is not unqualified nor even unchallenged by what other equally eloquent cultural statements say about it. But there is nothing more surprising in this than in the fact that Racine and Molière were contemporaries, or that the same people who arrange chrysanthemums cast swords.[43]

The culture of a people is an ensemble of texts, themselves ensembles, which the anthropologist strains to read over the shoulders of those to whom they properly belong. There are enormous difficulties in such an enterprise, methodological pitfalls to make a Freudian quake, and some moral perplexities as well. Nor is it the only way that symbolic forms can be sociologically handled. Functionalism lives, and so does psychologism. But to regard such forms as "saying something of something," and saying it to somebody, is at least to open up the possibility of an analysis which attends to their substance rather than to reductive formulas professing to account for them.

As in more familiar exercises in close reading, one can start anywhere in a culture's repertoire of forms and end up anywhere else. One can stay, as I have here, within a single, more or less bounded form and circle steadily within it. One can move between forms in search of broader unities or informing contrasts. One can even compare forms from different cultures to define their character in reciprocal relief. But whatever the level at which one operates, and however intricately, the guiding principle is the same: societies, like lives, contain their own interpretations. One has only to learn how to gain access to them.

CLIFFORD GEERTZ

REFERENCES

[1] Gregory Bateson and Margaret Mead, *Balinese Character: A Photographic Analysis* (New York: New York Academy of Sciences, 1942), p. 68.

[2] Jane Belo, "The Balinese Temper," in Jane Belo, ed., *Traditional Balinese Culture* (New York: Columbia University Press, 1970; originally published in 1935), pp. 85–110.

[3] The best discussion of cockfighting is again Bateson and Mead's (*Balinese Character*, pp. 24–25, 140), but it, too, is general and abbreviated.

[4] Ibid., pp. 25–26. The cockfight is unusual within Balinese culture in being a single-sex public activity from which the other sex is totally and expressly excluded. Sexual differentiation is culturally extremely played down in Bali and most activities, formal and informal, involve the participation of men and women on equal ground, commonly as linked couples. From religion, to politics, to economics, to kinship, to dress, Bali is a rather "unisex" society, a fact both its customs and its symbolism clearly express. Even in contexts where women do not in fact play much of a role—music, painting, certain agricultural activities—their absence, which is only relative in any case, is more a mere matter of fact than socially enforced. To this general pattern, the cockfight, entirely of, by, and for men (women—at least *Balinese* women—do not even watch), is the most striking exception.

[5] Christiaan Hooykass, *The Lay of the Jaya Prana* (London, 1958), p. 39. The lay has a stanza (no. 17) with the reluctant bridegroom use. Jaya Prana, the subject of a Balinese Uriah myth, responds to the lord who has offered him the loveliest of six hundred servant girls: "Godly King, my Lord and Master / I beg you, give me leave to go / such things are not yet in my mind; / like a fighting cock encaged / indeed I am on my mettle / I am alone / as yet the flame has not been fanned."

[6] For these, see V. E. Korn, *Het Adatrecht van Bali*, 2d ed. ('S-Gravenhage: G. Naeff, 1932), index under *toh*.

[7] There is indeed a legend to the effect that the separation of Java and Bali is due to the action of a powerful Javanese religious figure who wished to protect himself against a Balinese culture hero (the ancestor of two Ksatria castes) who was a passionate cockfighting gambler. See Christiaan Hooykass, *Agama Tirtha* (Amsterdam: Noord-Hollandsche, 1964), p. 184.

[8] An incestuous couple is forced to wear pig yokes over their necks and crawl to a pig trough and eat with their mouths there. On this, see Jane Belo, "Customs Pertaining to Twins in Bali," in Belo, ed., *Traditional Balinese Culture*, p. 49; on the abhorrence of animality generally, Bateson and Mead, *Balinese Character*, p. 22.

[9] Except for unimportant, small-bet fights (on the question of fight "importance," see below) spur affixing is usually done by someone other than the owner. Whether the owner handles his own cock or not more or less depends on how skilled he is at it, a consideration whose importance is again relative to the importance of the fight. When spur affixers and cock handlers are someone other than the owner, they are almost always a close relative—a brother or cousin—or a very intimate friend of his. They are thus almost extensions of his personality, as the fact that all three will refer to the cock as "mine," say "I" fought So-and-So, and so on, demonstrates. Also, owner-handler-affixer triads tend to be fairly fixed, though individuals may participate in several and often exchange roles within a given one.

[10] Erving Goffman, *Encounters: Two Studies in the Sociology of Interaction* (Indianapolis: Bobbs-Merrill, 1961), pp. 9–10.

[11] This word, which literally means an indelible stain or mark, as in a birthmark or a vein in a stone, is used as well for a deposit in a court case, for a pawn, for security offered in a loan, for a stand-in for someone else in a legal or ceremonial context, for an earnest advanced in a business deal, for a sign placed in a field to indicate its ownership is in dispute, and for the status of an unfaithful wife from whose lover her husband must gain satisfaction or surrender her to him. See Korn, *Het Adatrecht van Bali*; Theodoor Pigeaud, *Javaans-Nederlands Handwoordenbock* (Groningen: Wolters, 1938); H. H. Juynboll, *Oudjavaansche-Nederlandsche Woordenlijst* (Leiden: Brill, 1923).

[12] The center bet must be advanced in cash by both parties prior to the actual fight. The umpire holds the stakes until the decision is rendered and then awards them to the winner, avoiding, among other things, the intense embarrassment both winner and loser would feel if the latter had to pay off personally following his defeat. About 10 percent of the winner's receipts are subtracted for the umpire's share and that of the fight sponsors.

[13] Actually, the typing of cocks, which is extremely elaborate (I have collected more than twenty classes, certainly not a complete list), is not based on color alone, but on a series of independent, interacting, dimensions, which include, beside color, size, bone thickness, plumage, and temperament. (But *not* pedigree. The Balinese do not breed cocks to any significant extent, nor, so far as I have been able to discover, have they ever done so. The *asil*, or jungle cock, which is the basic fighting strain everywhere the sport is found, is native to southern Asia, and one can buy a good example in the chicken section of almost any Balinese market for anywhere from four or five ringgits up to fifty or more.) The color element is merely the one normally used as the type name, except when the two cocks of different types—as on principle they must be—have the same color, in which case a secondary indication from one of the other dimensions ("large speckled" v. "small speckled," etc.) is added. The types are coordinated with various cosmological ideas which help shape the making of matches, so that, for example, you fight a small, headstrong, speckled brown-on-white cock with flat-lying feathers and thin legs from the east side of the ring on a certain day of the complex Balinese calendar, and a large, cautious, all-black cock with tufted feathers and stubby legs from the north side on another day, and so on. All this is again recorded in palm-leaf manuscripts and endlessly discussed by the Balinese (who do not all have identical systems), and full-scale componential-cum-symbolic analysis of cock classifications would be extremely valuable both as an adjunct to the description of the cockfight and in itself. But my data on the subject, though extensive and varied, do not seem to be complete and systematic enough to attempt such an analysis here. For Balinese cosmological ideas more generally see Belo, ed., *Traditional Balinese Culture*, and J. L. Swellengrebel, ed., *Bali: Studies in Life, Thought, and Ritual* (The Hague: W. van Hoeve, 1960); for calendrical ones, Clifford Geertz, *Person, Time, and Conduct in Bali: An Essay in Cultural Analysis* (New Haven: Southeast Asia Studies, Yale University, 1966), pp. 45–53.

[14] For purposes of ethnographic completeness, it should be noted that it is possible for the man backing the favorite—the odds-giver—to make a bet in which he wins if his cock wins or there is a tie, a slight shortening of the odds (I do not have enough cases to be exact, but ties seem to occur about once every fifteen or twenty matches.) He indicates his wish to do this by shouting *sapih* ("tie") rather than the cock-type, but such bets are in fact infrequent.

[15] The precise dynamics of the movement of the betting is one of the most intriguing, most complicated, and, given the heroic conditions under which it occurs, most difficult to study, aspects of the fight. Motion picture recording plus multiple observers would probably be necessary to deal with it effectively. Even impressionistically—the only approach open to a lone ethnographer caught in the middle of all this—it is clear that certain men lead both in determining the favorite (that is, making the opening cock-type calls which always initiate the process) and in directing the movement of the odds, these "opinion leaders" being the more accomplished cockfighters-cum-solid-citizens to be discussed below. If these men begin to change their calls, others follow; if they begin to make bets, so do others and—though there is always a large number of frustrated bettors crying for shorter or longer odds to the end—the movement more or less ceases. But a detailed understanding of the whole process awaits what, alas, it is not very likely ever to get: a decision theorist armed with precise observations of individual behavior.

[16] Assuming only binominal variability, the departure from a fifty-fifty expectation in the sixty ringgits and below case is 1.38 standard deviations, or (in a one-direction test) an eight in one hundred possibility by chance alone; for the below forty ringgits case it is 1.65

standard deviations, or about five in one hundred. The fact that these departures though real are not extreme merely indicates, again, that even in the smaller fights the tendency to match cocks at least reasonably evenly persists. It is a matter of relative relaxation of the pressures toward equalization, not their elimination. The tendency for high-bet contests to be coin-flip propositions is, of course, even more striking, and suggests the Balinese know quite well what they are about.

[17] The reduction in wagering in smaller fights (which, of course, feeds on itself; one of the reasons people find small fights uninteresting is that there is less wagering in them, and contrariwise for large ones) takes place in three mutually reinforcing ways. First, there is a simple withdrawal of interest as people wander off to have a cup of coffee or chat with a friend. Second, the Balinese do not mathematically reduce odds, but bet directly in terms of stated odds as such. Thus, for a nine-to-eight bet, one man wagers nine ringgits, the other eight; for five-to-four, one wagers five, the other four. For any given currency unit, like the ringgit, therefore, 6.3 times as much money is involved in a ten-to-nine bet as in a two-to-one bet, for example, and, as noted, in small fights betting settles toward the longer end. Finally, the bets which are made tend to be one- rather than two-, three-, or in some of the very largest fights, four- or five-finger ones. (The fingers indicate the *multiples* of the stated bet odds at issue, not absolute figures. Two fingers in a six-to-five situation means a man wants to wager ten ringgits on the underdog against twelve, three in an eight-to-seven situation, twenty-one against twenty-four, and so on.)

[18] Besides wagering there are other economic aspects of the cockfight, especially its very close connection with the local market system which, though secondary both to its motivation and to its function, are not without importance. Cockfights are open events to which anyone who wishes may come, sometimes from quite distant areas, but well over 90 percent, probably over 95, are very local affairs, and the locality concerned is defined not by the village, nor even by the administrative district, but by the rural market system. Bali has a three-day market week with familiar "solar-system" type rotation. Though the markets themselves have never been very highly developed, small morning affairs in a village square, it is the microregion such rotation rather generally marks out—ten or twenty square miles, seven or eight neighboring villages (which in contemporary Bali is usually going to mean anywhere from five to ten to eleven thousand people) from which the core of any cockfight audience, indeed virtually all of it, will come. Most of the fights are in fact organized and sponsored by small combines of petty rural merchants under the general premise, very strongly held by them and indeed by all Balinese, that cockfights are good for trade because "they get money out of the house, they make it circulate." Stalls selling various sorts of things as well as assorted sheer-chance gambling games (see below) are set up around the edge of the area so that this even takes on the quality of a small fair. This connection of cockfighting with markets and market sellers is very old, as, among other things, their conjunction in inscriptions (Roelof Goris, *Prasasti Bali*, 2 vols. [Bandung: N. V. Masa Baru, 1954]) indicates. Trade has followed the cock for centuries in rural Bali and the sport has been one of the main agencies of the island's monetization.

[19] The phrase is found in the Hildreth translation, International Library of Psychology, 1931, note to p. 106; see L. L. Fuller, *The Morality of Law* (New Haven: Yale University Press, 1964), pp. 6ff.

[20] Of course, even in Bentham, utility is not normally confined as a concept to monetary losses and gains, and my argument here might be more carefully put in terms of a denial that for the Balinese, as for any people, utility (pleasure, happiness . . .) is merely identifiable with wealth. But such terminological problems are in any case secondary to the essential point: the cockfight is not roulette.

[21] Max Weber, *The Sociology of Religion* (Boston: Beacon Press, 1963). There is nothing specifically Balinese, of course, about deepening significance with money, as Whyte's description of corner boys in a working-class district of Boston demonstrates: "Gambling plays an important role in the lives of Cornerville people. Whatever game the corner boys play, they nearly always bet on the outcome. When there is nothing at stake, the game is not

considered a real contest. This does not mean that the financial element is all-important. I have frequently heard men say that the honor of winning was much more important than the money at stake. The corner boys consider playing for money the real test of skill and, unless a man performs well when money is at stake, he is not considered a good competitor." W. F. Whyte, *Street Corner Society*, 2d ed. (Chicago: University of Chicago Press, 1955), p. 140.

[22] The extreme to which this madness is conceived on occasion to go—and the fact that it is considered madness—is demonstrated by the Balinese folktale *I Tuhung Kuning*. A gambler becomes so deranged by his passion that, leaving on a trip, he orders his pregnant wife to take care of the prospective newborn if it is a boy but to feed it as meat to his fighting cocks if it is a girl. The mother gives birth to a girl, but rather than giving the child to the cocks she gives them a large rat and conceals the girl with her own mother. When the husband returns the cocks, crowing a jingle, inform him of the deception and, furious, he sets out to kill the child. A goddess descends from heaven and takes the girl up to the skies with her. The cocks die from the food given them, the owner's sanity is restored, the goddess brings the girl back to the father and reunites him with his wife. The story is given as "Geel Komkommertje" in Jacoba Hooykaas-van Leeuwen Boomkamp, *Sprookjes en Verhalen van Bali* ('S-Gravenhage: Van Hoeve, 1956), pp. 19–25.

[23] For a fuller description of Balinese rural social structure, see Clifford Geertz, "Form and Variation in Balinese Village Structure," *American Anthropologist*, 61 (1959), 94–108; "Tihingan, A Balinese Village," in R. M. Koentjaraningrat, *Villages in Indonesia* (Ithaca: Cornell University Press, 1967), pp. 210–243; and, though it is a bit off the norm as Balinese villages go, V. E. Korn, *De Dorpsrepubliek tnganan Pagringsingan* (Santpoort [Netherlands]: C. A. Mees, 1933).

[24] Goffman, *Encounters*, p. 78.

[25] B. R. Berelson, P. F. Lazersfeld, and W. N. McPhee, *Voting: A Study of Opinion Formation in a Presidential Campaign* (Chicago: University of Chicago Press, 1954).

[26] As this is a formal paradigm, it is intended to display the logical, not the casual, structure of cockfighting. Just which of these considerations leads to which, in what order, and by what mechanisms, is another matter—one I have attempted to shed some light on in the general discussion.

[27] In another of Hooykaas-van Leeuwen Boomkamp's folk tales ("De Gast," *Sprookjes en Verhalen van Bali*, pp. 172–180), a low caste *Sudra*, a generous, pious, and carefree man who is also an accomplished cockfighter, loses, despite his accomplishment, fight after fight until he is not only out of money but down to his last cock. He does not despair, however—"I bet," he says, "upon the Unseen World."

His wife, a good and hard-working woman, knowing how much he enjoys cockfighting, gives him her last "rainy day" money to go and bet. But, filled with misgivings due to his run of ill luck, he leaves his own cock at home and bets merely on the side. He soon loses all but a coin or two and repairs to a food stand for a snack, where he meets a decrepit, odorous, and generally unappetizing older beggar leaning on a staff. The old man asks for food, and the hero spends his last coins to buy him some. The old man then asks to pass the night with the hero, which the hero gladly invites him to do. As there is no food in the house, however, the hero tells his wife to kill the last cock for dinner. When the old man discovers this fact, he tells the hero he has three cocks in his own mountain hut and says the hero may have one of them for fighting. He also asks for the hero's son to accompany him as a servant, and, after the son agrees, this is done.

The old man turns out to be Siva and, thus, to live in a great palace in the sky, though the hero does not know this. In time, the hero decides to visit his son and collect the promised cock. Lifted up into Siva's presence, he is given the choice of three cocks. The first crows: "I have beaten fifteen opponents." The second crows, "I have beaten twenty-five opponents." The third crows, "I have beaten the King." "That one, the third, is my choice," says the hero, and returns with it to earth.

When he arrives at the cockfight, he is asked for an entry fee and replies, "I have no money; I will pay after my cock has won." As he is known never to win, he is let in because the king, who is there fighting, dislikes him and hopes to enslave him when he loses and cannot pay off. In order to insure that this happens, the king matches his finest cock against the hero's. When the cocks are placed down, the hero's flees, and the crowd, led by the arrogant king, hoots in laughter. The hero's cock then flies at the king himself, killing him with a spur stab in the throat. The hero flees. His house is encircled by the king's men. The cock changes into a Garuda, the great mythic bird of Indic legend, and carries the hero and his wife to safety in the heavens.

When the people see this, they make the hero king and his wife queen and they return as such to earth. Later his son, released by Siva, also returns and the hero-king announces his intention to enter a hermitage. ("I will fight no more cockfights. I have bet on the Unseen and won.") He enters the hermitage and his son becomes king.

[28] Addict gamblers are really less declassed (for their status is, as everyone else's, inherited) than merely impoverished and personally disgraced. The most prominent addict gambler in my cockfight circuit was actually a very high caste *satria* who sold off most of his considerable lands to support his habit. Though everyone privately regarded him as a fool and worse (some, more charitable, regarded him as sick), he was publicly treated with the elaborate deference and politeness due his rank. On the independence of personal reputation and public status in Bali, see Geertz, *Person, Time, and Conduct*, pp. 28–35.

[29] For four, somewhat variant treatments, see Susanne Langer, *Feeling and Form* (New York: Scribner's, 1953); Richard Wollheim, *Art and Its Objects* (New York: Harper and Row, 1968); Nelson Goodman, *Languages of Art* (Indianapolis: Bobbs-Merrill, 1968); Maurice Merleau-Ponty, "The Eye and the Mind," in his, *The Primacy of Perception* (Evanston: Northwestern University Press, 1964), pp. 159–190.

[30] British cockfights (the sport was banned there in 1840) indeed seem to have lacked it, and to have generated, therefore, a quite different family of shapes. Most British fights were "mains," in which a preagreed number of cocks were aligned into two teams and fought serially. Score was kept and wagering took place both on the individual matches and on the main as a whole. There were also "battle Royales," both in England and on the Continent, in which a large number of cocks were let loose at once with the one left standing at the end the victor. And in Wales, the so-called "Welsh main" followed an elimination pattern, along the lines of a present-day tennis tournament, winners proceeding to the next round. As a genre, the cockfight has perhaps less compositional flexibility than, say, Latin comedy, but it is not entirely without any. On cockfighting more generally, see Arch Ruport, *The Art of Cockfighting* (New York: Devin-Adair, 1949); G. R. Scott, *History of Cockfighting* (1957); and Lawrence Fitz-Barnard, *Fighting Sports* (London: Odhams Press, 1921).

[31] *Person, Time, and Conduct*, esp. pp. 42ff. I am, however, not the first person to have argued it: see G. Bateson, "Bali, the Value System of a Steady State," and "An Old Temple and a New Myth," in Belo, ed., *Traditional Balinese Culture*, pp. 384–402 and 111–136.

[32] For the necessity of distinguishing among "description," "representation," "exemplification," and "expression" (and the irrelevance of "imitation" to all of them), as modes of symbolic reference, see Goodman, *Languages of Art*, pp. 6–10, 45–91, 225–241.

[33] Northrop Frye, *The Educated Imagination* (Bloomington: University of Indiana Press, 1964), p. 99.

[34] There are two other Balinese values and disvalues which, connected with punctuate temporality on the one hand and unbridled aggressiveness on the other, reinforce the sense that the cockfight is at once continuous with ordinary social life and a direct negation of it: what the Balinese call *ramé*, and what they call *paling*. *Ramé* means crowded, noisy, and active, and is a highly sought after social state: crowded markets, mass festivals, busy streets are all *ramé*, as of course, is, in the extreme, a cockfight. *Ramé* is what happens in the "full" times (its opposite, *sepi*, "quiet," is what happens in the "empty" ones.) *Paling* is social vertigo, the dizzy, disoriented, lost, turned around feeling one gets when one's place in the coordinates of social space is not clear, and it is a tremendously disfavored, immensely anxiety-producing state. Balinese regard the exact maintenance of spatial orientation ("not

to know where north is" is to be crazy), balance, decorum, status relationships, and so forth, as fundamental to ordered life (*krama*) and *paling*, the sort of whirling confusion of position the scrambling cocks exemplify as its profoundest enemy and contradiction. On *ramé*, see Bateson and Mead, *Balinese Character*, pp. 3, 64; on *paling*, ibid., p. 11, and Belo, ed., *Traditional Balinese Culture*, pp. 90ff.

[35] The Stevens reference is to his "The Motive for Metaphor" ("You like it under the trees in autumn, / Because everything is half dead. / The wind moves like a cripple among the leaves / And repeats words without meaning"); the Schoenberg reference is to the third of his *Five Orchestral Pieces* (Opus 16), and is borrowed from H. H. Drager, "The Concept of 'Tonal Body,'" in Susanne Langer, ed., *Reflections of Art* (New York: Oxford University Press, 1961), p. 174. On Hogarth, and on this whole problem—there called "multiple matrix matching"—see E. H. Gombrich, "The Use of Art for the Study of Symbols," in James Hogg, ed., *Psychology and the Visual Arts* (Baltimore: Penguin Books, 1969), pp. 149–170. The more usual term for this sort of semantic alchemy is "metaphorical transfer," and good technical discussions of it can be found in M. Black, *Models and Metaphors* (Ithaca: Cornell University Press, 1962), pp. 25ff; Goodman, *Languages of Art*, pp. 44ff; and W. Percy, "Metaphor as Mistake," *Sewanee Review*, 66 (1958), 78–99.

[36] The tag is from the second book of the *Organon, On Interpretation*. For a discussion of it, and for the whole argument for freeing "the notion of text . . . from the notion of scripture or writing," and constructing, thus, a general hermeneutics, see Paul Ricoeur, *Freud and Philosophy* (New Haven: Yale University Press, 1970), pp. 20ff.

[37] Ibid.

[38] Lévi-Strauss's "structuralism" might seem an exception. But it is only an apparent one, for, rather than taking myths, totem rites, marriage rules, or whatever as texts to interpret, Lévi-Strauss takes them as ciphers to solve, which is very much not the same thing. He does not seek to understand symbolic forms in terms of how they function in concrete situations to organize perceptions (meanings, emotions, concepts, attitudes); he seeks to understand them entirely in terms of their internal structure, *indépendent de tout sujet, de tout objet, et de toute contexte*. For my own view of this approach—that is suggestive and indefensible—see Clifford Geertz, "The Cerebral Savage: On the Work of Lévi-Strauss," *Encounter*, 48 (1967), 25–32.

[39] Frye, *The Educated Imagination*, pp. 63–64.

[40] The use of the, to Europeans, "natural" visual idiom for perception—"see," "watches," and so forth—is more than usually misleading here, for the fact that, as mentioned earlier, Balinese follow the progress of the fight as much (perhaps, as fighting cocks are actually rather hard to see except as blurs of motion, more) with their bodies as with their eyes, moving their limbs, heads, and trunks in gestural mimicry of the cocks' maneuvers, means that much of the individual's experience of the fight is kinesthetic rather than visual. If ever there was an example of Kenneth Burke's definition of a symbolic act as "the dancing of an attitude" (*The Philosophy of Literary Form*, rev. ed. [New York: Vintage Books, 1957], p. 9) the cockfight is it. On the enormous role of kinesthetic perception in Balinese life, [see] Bateson and Mead, *Balinese Character*, pp. 84–88; on the active nature of aesthetic perception in general, [see] Goodman, *Languages of Art*, pp. 241–244.

[41] All this coupling of the occidental great with the oriental lowly will doubtless disturb certain sorts of aestheticians as the earlier effort of anthropologists to speak of Christianity and totemism in the same breath disturbed certain sorts of theologians. But as ontological questions are (or should be) bracketed in the sociology of religion, judgmental ones are (or should be) bracketed in the sociology of art. In any case, the attempt to deprovincialize the concept of art is but part of the general anthropological conspiracy to deprovincialize all important social concepts—marriage, religion, law, rationality—and though this is a threat to aesthetic theories which regard certain works of art as beyond the reach of sociological analysis, it is no threat to the conviction, for which Robert Graves claims to have been reprimanded at his Cambridge tripos, that some poems are better than others.

[42] For the consecration ceremony, see V. E. Korn, "The Consecration of the Priest," in

Swellengrebel, ed., *Bali*, pp. 131–154; for (somewhat exaggerated) village communion, Roelof Goris, "The Religious Character of the Balinese Village," ibid., pp. 79–100.

[43] That what the cockfight has to say about Bali is not altogether without perception and the disquiet it expresses about the general pattern of Balinese life is not wholly without reason is attested by the fact that in two weeks of December 1965, during the upheavals following the unsuccessful coup in Djakarta, between forty and eighty thousand Balinese (in a population of about two million) were killed, largely by one another—the worst outburst in the country. (John Hughes, *Indonesian Upheaval* [New York: McKay, 1967], pp. 173–183. Hughes's figures are, of course, rather casual estimates, but they are not the most extreme.) This is not to say, of course, that the killings were caused by the cockfight, could have been predicted on the basis of it, or were some sort of enlarged version of it with real people in the place of the cocks—all of which is nonsense. It is merely to say that if one looks at Bali not just through the medium of its dances, its shadowplays, its sculpture, and its girls, but—as the Balinese themselves do—also through the medium of its cockfight, the fact that the massacre occurred seems, if no less appealing, less like a contradiction to the laws of nature. As more than one real Gloucester has discovered, sometimes people actually get life precisely as they most deeply do not want it.

• • • • • • • • • • • •

QUESTIONS FOR A SECOND READING

1. Geertz says that the cockfight provides a "commentary upon the whole matter of sorting human beings into fixed hierarchical ranks and then organizing the major parts of collective existence around that assortment." The cockfights don't reinforce the patterns of Balinese life; they comment on them. Perhaps the first question to ask as you go back to the essay is "What is that commentary?" What do the cockfights say? And what don't they say?

2. "Deep Play: Notes on the Balinese Cockfight" is divided into seven sections. As you reread the essay, pay attention to the connections between these sections and the differences in the ways they are written. For each, think about what they propose to do (some, for example, tell stories, some use numbers, some have more footnotes than others).

   What is the logic or system that makes one section follow another? Do you see the subtitles as seven headings on a topic outline?

   If you look at the differences in the style or method of each section, what might they be said to represent? If each is evidence of something Geertz, as an anthropologist, knows how to do, what, in each case, is he doing? What is his expertise? And why, in each case, would it require this particular style of writing? The last two sections are perhaps the most difficult to read and understand. They also make repeated reference to literary texts. Why? What is Geertz doing here?

3. Throughout the essay Geertz is working very hard to *do* something with what he observed in Bali. (There are "enormous difficulties in such an enterprise," he says.) He is also, however, working hard *not* to do some things.

(He doesn't want to be a "formalist," for example.) As you read the essay for the second time, look for passages that help you specifically define what it is Geertz wants to do and what it is he wants to be sure not to do.

4. It could be argued that "Deep Play" tells again the story of how white Western men have taken possession of the Third World, here with Geertz performing an act of intellectual colonization. In the opening section, for example, Geertz (as author) quickly turns both his wife and the Balinese people into stock characters, characters in a story designed to make him a hero. And, in the service of this story, he pushes aside the difficult political realities of Bali—the later killing of Balinese by the police is put in parentheses (so as not to disturb the flow of the happy story of how an anthropologist wins his way into the community). The remaining sections turn Balinese culture into numbers and theories, reducing the irreducible detail of people's lives into material for the production of goods (an essay furthering his career). And, one could argue, the piece ends by turning to Shakespeare and Dickens to "explain" the Balinese, completing the displacement of Balinese culture by Western culture.

   This, anyway, is how such an argument might be constructed. As you reread the essay, mark passages you could use, as the author, to argue both for and against Geertz and his relationship to this story of colonization. To what extent can one say that Geertz is, finally, one more white man taking possession of the Third World? And to what extent can one argue that Geertz, as a writer, is struggling against this dominant, conventional narrative, working to revise it or to distance himself from it?

ASSIGNMENTS FOR WRITING

1. If this essay were your only evidence, how might you describe the work of an anthropologist? What do anthropologists do and how do they do it? Write an essay in which you look at "Deep Play" section by section, including the references, describing on the basis of each what it is that an anthropologist must be able to do. In each case, you have the chance to watch Geertz at work. (Your essay, then, might well have sections that correspond to Geertz's.) When you have worked through them all, write a final section that discusses how these various skills or arts fit together to define the expertise of someone like Geertz.

2. Geertz says that "the culture of a people is an ensemble of texts, themselves ensembles, which the anthropologist strains to read over the shoulders of those to whom they properly belong." Anthropologists are expert at "reading" in this way. One of the interesting things about being a student is that you get to (or you have to) act like an expert, even though, properly speaking, you are not. Write an essay in which you prepare a Geertzian "reading" of some part of our culture you know well. Ideally, you should go out and observe the behavior you are studying, examining it and taking notes with your project in mind. You should imagine that you are working in Geertz's

spirit, imitating his method and style and carrying out work that he has begun.

3. This is really a variation on the first assignment. This assignment, however, invites you to read against the grain of Geertz's essay. Imagine that someone has made the argument outlined briefly in the fourth "Question for a Second Reading"—that "Deep Play" is just one more version of a familiar story, a story of a white man taking possession of everything that is not already made in his own image. If you were going to respond to this argument—to extend it or to answer it—to what in the essay would you turn for evidence? And what might you say about what you find?

Write an essay, then, in which you respond to the argument that says "Deep Play" is one more version of the familiar story of a white man taking possession of that which is not his.

MAKING CONNECTIONS

1. Susan Douglas in "Narcissism as Liberation" (p. 117), Jane Tompkins in "Indians" (p. 618), and Susan Griffin in "Our Secret" (p. 319) could all be said to take an "anthropological" view of the people and practices they study. The worlds they describe are familiar (at least compared with Bali), and yet, as writers, they distance themselves from those worlds, make the familiar seem exotic, look at the people involved as "natives" whose behavior they choose to read as a strange and arbitrary text.

Choose one of these selections—by Douglas, Tompkins, or Griffin—and read it along with Geertz's. Both read cultural patterns and cultural artifacts. Look at characteristic examples of their ways of reading. What might you say about their methods? Do they look for the same things?

Write an essay in which you explore and describe the different methods of the two writers. As researchers, what do they notice? What do they do with what they notice? Do they seek the same *kinds* of conclusions? How do they gather their materials, weight them, think them through? How, that is, do they do their work? And what might you conclude about the possibilities and limitations of each writer's project?

2. In "The Loss of the Creature" (p. 511), Walker Percy writes about tourists (actually several different kinds of tourists) and the difficulty they have seeing what lies before them. Properly speaking, anthropologists are not tourists. There is a scholarly purpose to their travel, and presumably they have learned or developed the strategies necessary to get beyond the preformed "symbolic complexes" which would keep them from seeing the place or the people they have traveled to study. Geertz is an expert, in other words, not just any "layman seer of sights."

In his travels to Bali, Geertz seems to get just what he wants. He gets both the authentic experience and a complex understanding of that experience. If you read "Deep Play" from the perspective of Percy's essay, however, it is interesting to ask whether Percy would say that this was the case, and to ask how Percy would characterize the "strategies" that define Geertz's approach to his subject.

Write an essay in which you place Geertz in the context of Percy's tourists—not all of them, but the two or three whose stories seem most interesting when placed alongside Geertz's. The purpose of your essay should be to determine whether or not Geertz has solved the problem Percy defines for the tourist in "The Loss of the Creature."

STEPHEN
GREENBLATT

S TEPHEN GREENBLATT was born in 1943 in Cambridge, Massachusetts. He studied at Yale and Cambridge. Since 1969 he has taught at the University of California at Berkeley, where he currently holds an endowed chair. His books in-clude: Sir Walter Raleigh: The Renaissance Man and His Roles *(1973),* Alle-gory and Representation *(1979),* Renaissance Self-fashioning: From More to Shakespeare *(1980),* Representing the English Renaissance *(1988),* Shake-spearean Negotiations *(1988), and* Learning to Curse *(1990). He is also the edi-tor of* Representations, *a scholarly journal.*

Greenblatt is one of the most influential, provocative, and widely read figures in an area of literary criticism known as the "new historicism." The new historicists have been concerned to read literary texts in relation to their historical moment—to acknowledge, for example, references to the French Revolution and the rise of the American women's rights movement in The Scarlet Letter, *even though the novel is set in Puritan New England, and to think about how that novel served as part of a larger cultural project (teaching mid-nineteenth-century American readers how to think about women's independence and the consequences of revolt).*

And the new historicists have turned the tools and habits of literary analysis, in-cluding close reading, to historical documents. In the case of the essay that follows, Greenblatt thinks about Christopher Columbus, not as a discoverer or an adventurer, but as a writer. According to Greenblatt, it has become common to say that as Europe took physical possession of the lands and bodies in the New World, that action was accompanied by, even enabled by, writing. Like Michel Foucault, whose work was important to the new historicists, Greenblatt is interested in the technologies of power. For the Europeans who first ventured to the New World, these technologies included not only navigational instruments, effective armor, gunpowder, and highly lethal weapons, but also writing.

"Marvelous Possessions" is the middle chapter in a book of the same name (Marvelous Possessions: The Wonder of the New World, 1991). *The book began in 1988 as a series of lectures, given first at Oxford University in England and later at the University of Chicago. In a brief introduction to the book, Greenblatt says that as a child, his favorite books were* The Arabian Nights *and Richard Halliburton's* Book of Marvels. *The former was filled with marvelous stories presented as stories; the latter with marvelous stories presented as "real." And, Greenblatt says, "I suppose that my suburban soul, constricted by the conventionality of the Eisenhower 1950s, eagerly embraced the relief that Halliburton offered, the sense that the real world was full of wonder, the wide-eyed account of exotic travels—Igassu Falls, Chichén Itzá, the Golden Gate Bridge." Later, he says,*

> *I passed from the naive to what Schiller calls the sentimental—that is, I stopped reading books of marvels and began reading ethnographies and novels—but my childhood interests have survived in a passionate curiosity about other cultures and a fascination with tales. It will not escape anyone who reads this book that my chapters are constructed largely around anecdotes, what the French call* petites histoires, *as distinct from the* grand récit *of totalizing, integrated, progressive history, a history that knows where it is going. As is appropriate for voyagers who thought that they knew where they were going and ended up in a place whose existence they had never imagined, the discourse of travel in the late Middle Ages and the Renaissance is rarely if ever interesting at the level of sustained narrative and teleological design, but gripping at the level of anecdote.*

If Greenblatt's reading passed from the naive to the sentimental, as a scholar and theorist he also learned how and why to read as a skeptic, to question and not simply receive accounts of the past. In reading the early anecdotes representing the New World, he says, "we find ourselves groping uneasily among the mass of textual traces, instances of brazen bad faith jostling homely (and often equally misleading) attempts to tell the truth." And, he says,

> *In the chapters that follow I have tried less to distinguish between true and false representations than to look attentively at the nature of the representational practices that the Europeans carried with them to America and deployed when they tried to describe to their fellow countrymen what they saw and did. I have been very wary of taking anything Europeans wrote or drew as an accurate and reliable account of the nature of the New World lands and its peoples. It is*

*almost impossible, I find, to make this skepticism an absolute and un-
wavering principle—I catch myself constantly straining to read into
the European traces an account of what the American natives were
"really" like—but I have resisted as much as I can the temptation to
speak for or about the native cultures as if the mediation of European
representations were an incidental consideration, easily corrected
for. . . . We can be certain only that European representations of the
New World tell us something about the European practice of representation: this seems like a modest enough claim, but I hope this book
will show that it rewards exploration.*

Marvelous Possessions

Let us begin at the most famous of beginnings:

As I know that you will be pleased at the great victory with
which Our Lord has crowned my voyage, I write this to you,
from which you will learn how in thirty-three days, I passed
from the Canary Islands to the Indies with the fleet which the
most illustrious king and queen, our sovereigns, gave to me.
And there I found very many islands filled with people innumerable, and of them all I have taken possession for their highnesses, by proclamation made and with the royal standard un-
furled, and no opposition was offered to me. To the first island
which I found, I gave the name *San Salvador,* in remembrance
of the Divine Majesty, Who has marvelously bestowed all this;
the Indians call it "Guanahani." To the second, I gave the name
Isla de Santa Maria de Concepción; to the third, *Fernandina;* to the
fourth, *Isabella;* to the fifth, *Isla Juana,* and so to each one I gave
a new name.[1]

Thus begins Columbus's celebrated account, in a letter to Luis de Santangel, of his first voyage.[2] The moment, of course, has become fixed in the popular imagination: the great adventurer on the beach, unfurling the royal standard and taking possession of the New World. Columbus's words are filled
out by what we know to have followed: other voyages, widening discoveries,
the dawning realization that classical geography was wrong and that a whole
new hemisphere had been discovered, the violent encounter of civilizations,
the missionary enterprise, mass enslavement and death, the immense project
of colonization.

Apart from the determination to return, Columbus could not have known
or anticipated any of this subsequent history; what from this distance is striking is how little he could grasp in 1492 where he was or what he was initiating. His words then, like the words of the Articles of Agreement with which

he set sail, were in some important sense written as empty placeholders for uncharted lands and unimaginable future events—*todo esto*, "all this," as he puts it, with an expansive gesture that prudently avoids any specification of what "all this" amounts to. And yet Columbus's letter does seem to anticipate and to promote the mythic sense with which time has invested his account. We can sense his myth-making already in the flourish with which he proclaims "*la gran vitoria*," a phrase more appropriate in 1492 to the conquest of Granada than to landfall in the Caribbean,[3] and in the term used to describe God's bestowal of the discovered islands: "marvelously" (*maravillosamente*). I shall argue that Columbus had a highly self-conscious interest in the marvelous.

Why did Columbus, who was carrying a passport and royal letters, think to take possession of anything, if he actually believed that he had reached the outlying regions of the Indies? It did not, after all, occur to Marco Polo in the late thirteenth century to claim for the Venetians any territorial rights in the East or to rename any of the countries; nor in the fourteenth century did Sir John Mandeville unfurl a banner on behalf of a European monarch. Indeed, . . . in the climactic moment of Mandeville's account the knight and his companions piously refuse to pick up the gold and precious stones that litter the valley through which they pass. Columbus, who almost certainly had carefully read the travel accounts of both Marco Polo and Mandeville, behaved startlingly differently.

The difference may be traced of course to the fact that, unlike Marco Polo or Mandeville, Columbus was neither a merchant nor a pilgrim: he was on a state-sponsored mission from a nation caught up in the enterprise of the *Reconquista*. But the objective of this mission has been notoriously difficult to determine. Columbus's passport appears to suggest that he is to proceed to a known place—the Indies—on business concerning the orthodox faith.[4] The original of his *Diario* or logbook has disappeared, but the transcription by his contemporary Las Casas indicates that Columbus was charged to go to the city of Quinsay—that is, Hangzhou—"to give Your Highnesses' letters to the Grand Khan, and to ask for, and to come with, a reply."[5] At the same time, the grant that Columbus received from Ferdinand and Isabella speaks of Columbus as "going by our command, with certain vessels of ours and with our subjects, to discover and to gain certain islands and mainland in the Ocean Sea" (lxxii). This language—"descobrir é ganar"—suggests something more than a diplomatic or commercial voyage, but neither the sailors nor the ships of the first expedition were appropriate for a serious military campaign, so that it is difficult to envisage what kind of "gaining" the monarchs had in mind.[6] I have no solution to these famous enigmas, but I propose that we look carefully at the action Columbus reports and that we consider the extraordinary extent to which that action is *discursive*.

The claim of a "great victory" and the unfurling of the royal standard suggest that we are about to hear an account of a battle, but what we get instead is an account of a series of speech acts: a proclamation (*pregón*) by which Columbus takes possession of the islands followed by the giving of new names. These speech acts—*he tomado posesión, puse nombre*—are so familiar to us that it is difficult to find anything in them worth remarking, but we would do well to look at them more closely.[7] Here, and throughout the early discourse of the New World, the reassuring signs of administrative order—bureaucratic formulas already well established in a very large number of earlier military, diplomatic, and juridical encounters in Europe and Africa—are deceptive; consciously or unconsciously, they draw us away from a sense of all that is unsettling, unique, and terrible in the first European contacts with the peoples of America.

It is important, I think, to resist the drift toward normalizing what was *not* normal. We can demonstrate that, in the face of the unknown, Europeans used their conventional intellectual and organizational structures, fashioned over centuries of mediated contact with other cultures, and that these structures greatly impeded a clear grasp of the radical otherness of the American lands and peoples. What else would we expect? But such demonstrations do not—or should not—efface the incommensurability, the astonishing singularity, of the contact initiated on October 12, 1492. Virtually all prior recorded encounters between Europeans and other cultures took place across boundaries that were to some degree, however small, porous; this means that all prior encounters had been to some degree, however small, anticipated. To be sure, there were many earlier occasions on which European voyagers experienced the shock of extreme cultural difference: "And so on the third day after leaving Soldaia," writes William of Rubruck in the thirteenth century, "we came across the Tartars; when I came among them it seemed indeed to me as if I were stepping into some other world."[8] But however strange the Tartars seemed to William, there had been a sporadic history of contact; William expected them to be there and knew roughly where to find them. Moreover, they were reached by a series of small stages that took William gradually away from his familiar world and toward the strange. Prior to Columbus there had been nothing comparable to the absolute break brought about by the exceptionally long ocean crossing, a break that effaced the process of acclimatization on the margins, the incremental signs of growing distance and difference that characterized earlier travel.[9] Alexander the Great managed to lead his army into India, but, as Arrian's biography makes clear, the advance consisted of innumerable smaller acts of reconnaissance, negotiation, and conflict. And this was the pattern for almost all episodes of expansion and warfare.

The European landfall in the Caribbean in 1492 was drastically different—the extreme length of the voyage, the invaders' total unfamiliarity with the land, and their absolute ignorance of its inhabitants' cultures, languages, sociopolitical organizations, and beliefs made it so. In consequence, all of the familiar procedures had, from the beginning, a quality of displacement. Detached from the world in which they had long functioned coherently (or at least routinely) and dropped into an entirely alien world, they have the odd air of quotations. Our initial interpretive move, I think, must be not to sweep away these quotations—the formularies and stereotypical gestures—but to realize how extremely strange they are or rather how strange they become in this unprecedented situation. Even if every detail is based on some precedent or other, each is destabilized, defamiliarized, uprooted. There are real bodies and real consequences, but the very conventions used to demarcate the real (in denoting sovereignty and legitimate possession) seem in the peculiar light of 1492 to be signs as much of the imaginary as of the real.

The display of the royal standard in the first moments after Columbus's landfall marks the formality of the occasion and officially designates the sovereign on whose behalf his speech acts are performed; what we are witnessing is a legal ritual observed by men whose culture takes both ceremony and judicial formalities extremely seriously. Columbus's journal entry for October 12 provides some of the details of the ritual: "The Admiral called to the two captains and to the others who had jumped ashore and to Rodrigo Descobedo, the *escrivano* of the whole fleet, and to Rodrigo Sánchez de Segovia; and he said that they should be witnesses that, in the presence of all, he would take, as in fact he did take, possession of the said island for the king and for the queen his lords, making the declarations that were required, and which at more length are contained in the testimonials made there in writing."[10] About twenty years later, in a royal instruction to Juan Díaz de Solís (a Portuguese navigator in the employ of the Crown of Castille), we get a more detailed account of the formal acts by which the Crown's representatives took possession of "new" lands:

> The manner that you must have in the taking of possession of the lands and parts which you shall have discovered is to be that, being in the land or part that you shall have discovered, you shall make before a notary public and the greatest possible number of witnesses, and the best known ones, an act of possession in our name, cutting trees and boughs, and digging or making, if there be an opportunity, some small building [*edificio*], which should be in a part where there is some marked hill or a large tree, and you shall say how many leagues it is from the sea, a little more or less, and in which part, and what signs it has, and you shall make a gallows there, and have somebody bring a complaint before you, and as our captain and judge you shall pronounce upon and determine it, so that, in all, you shall take the said possession; which is to be for that part where you shall take it, and for all its district [*partido*] and province or island, and you shall bring testimony thereof signed by the said notary in a manner to make faith.[11]

As the phrase "if there be an opportunity" suggests, this is less a description of actual Spanish practice than an ideal type, a compact anthology of legitimating gestures: actual presence in the land (mere sighting from shipboard does not suffice), the mechanism of legal recording (requiring a notary and witnesses), the physical alteration or marking of the land, the construction of an edifice on a distinctive site that is mapped (and hence can be verified and reoccupied), the formal exercise of justice. From other documents in the period one can expand the list of common symbolic acts: placing stones, cutting grass, raising mounds or pillars, erecting crosses, even drinking water. Captains would in effect select from the repertory and, within its generic limits, improvise a formal ceremony. Cortés, we are told, "moved walking on the said land from one part to another, and throwing sand from one part to another, and with his sword he struck certain trees that were there, and he commanded to the people who were there that they should have him for governor of His Majesty of those said lands, and did other acts of possession."[12] Pedro de Guzmán "delegated his authority to a seaman who swam ashore and there erected a cross, cut down boughs of trees, and took possession of the island, his acts being witnessed by two other seamen who had swum ashore with him and whose testimony formed the basis of the formal notarial act that was subsequently drawn up on board the ship."[13] Columbus's version is more simple and abstract; he makes no mention of cutting boughs or throwing sand, let alone constructing a house or gallows. There are no attempts in the initial landfall to inscribe the Spanish presence on the land, to leave even an ephemeral mark such as a gash in a tree or a cleared patch of grass.[14] His actions are performed entirely *for a world elsewhere*.

For Columbus taking possession is principally the performance of a set of linguistic acts: declaring, witnessing, recording. The acts are public and official: the admiral speaks as a representative of the king and queen, and his speech must be heard and understood by competent, named witnesses, witnesses who may subsequently be called upon to testify to the fact that the unfurling of the banner and the "declarations that are required" took place as alleged. At issue is not only the Crown's claim to sovereignty but Columbus's own status; after months of difficult negotiation, he had obtained, in the Capitulations of April 17, 1492, appointment as Admiral, Viceroy, and Governor-General over all islands and mainland "which by his labor and industry shall be discovered or acquired."[15] He was also granted one-tenth of all the treasure and merchandise produced or obtained in these domains, free of all taxes. In a further, extraordinary concession, the Crown agreed that Columbus's title and prerogatives would be enjoyed by his heirs and successors "perpetually." On October 12 then Columbus is not only the medium through which the Crown could claim possession; he also enacts the ritual of possession on his own behalf and on behalf of his descendants.

And because Columbus's culture does not entirely trust verbal testimony, because its judicial procedures require written proofs, he makes certain to perform his speech acts in the presence of the fleet's recorder (for a fleet which had no priest had a recorder), hence ensuring that everything would be written down and consequently have a greater authority. The papers are carefully sealed, preserved, carried back across thousands of leagues of ocean to officials who in turn countersign and process them according to the procedural rules; the notarized documents are a token of the truth of the encounter and hence of the legality of the claim. Or rather they help to produce "truth" and "legality," ensuring that the words Columbus speaks do not disappear as soon as their sounds fade, ensuring that the memory of the encounter is fixed, ensuring that there are not competing versions of what happened on the beach on October 12. A priest may be said to facilitate a transaction with eternity, but an *escrivano* facilitates a transaction with a more immediately useful form of temporality, the institutional form secured by writing.

A distinction between peoples who have writing and peoples who do not will, as we have seen, become crucial in the discourse of the New World, but in the initial moments with which we are concerned Columbus does not know enough about those he has encountered to make such a distinction. He evidently does not feel the need to know anything about them at this moment, and we should note that the instruction to De Solis similarly does not include any provision for recognition of the cultural level, rights, or even the existence of the natives. Columbus's journal mentions that naked people were sighted on shore before the Spanish landed, but it is not altogether clear that the ritual of possession took place within earshot of these people who subsequently approached in large numbers.[16] Ceremonies take the place of cultural contacts; rituals of possession stand in for negotiated contracts. Columbus acts entirely within what Michel de Certeau calls "the scriptural operation"[17] of his own culture, an operation that leads him not simply to pronounce certain words or alternatively to write them down but rather to perform them orally in the presence of the fleet's named and officially sanctioned recorder. Writing here fixes a set of public linguistic acts, gives them official standing, makes them "historical" events. But what are these linguistic acts? For whom and by what right are they being performed? Why are they assumed to be efficacious?

In part the answer may lie in the odd phrase in his letter to Santangel, "y no me fué contradicho"—not, as the English translation renders it, "and no opposition was offered to me," but rather "and I was not contradicted." This presumably refers not to the Spanish—who were called upon to bear witness and who would scarcely object[18]—but to the natives. But what can such a phrase mean? It is possible, I suppose, to imagine it as either a cynical sneer or a skeptical joke. In the former case, Columbus would be laughing at the impossibility of the natives contradicting something they are deliberately kept from understanding or, alternatively, at their impotence to contradict a seizure of their lands even if they were to understand the proclamation perfectly. In the latter case, Columbus would be laughing at the natives' hopeless ignorance: "if the horse had anything to say, he would speak up." But rarely if ever in his writings does Columbus seem either cynical or skeptical, least of all here, when he is recounting the crucial event of the entire voyage. We must assume that he is writing in earnest and that he takes seriously the "fact" that he was not contradicted.

The absence of "contradiction" had a specific force: such a fact would be important in establishing for the Spanish Crown a legal claim to the newly discovered lands by the "voluntary choice" of the original inhabitants.[19] That is, if those inhabitants actually wished to transfer title to their lands and possessions to the Spanish, they should be allowed to do so. The legal basis for such a transaction is found in Roman law where, according to Justinian's *Institutes*, "there is nothing so natural as that the intent of the owner to transfer his property to another should have effect given to it."[20] In the *Digest* of Justinian Ulpian writes that "We say that a person possesses by stealth who has entered into possession without the knowledge of him who, he suspects, would oppose his taking [*quem sibi controuersiam facturum suspicabatur*]. . . . No one acquires possession by stealth who takes possession with the knowledge or consent [*sciente aut uolente*] of the thing's owner."[21] And in his important midthirteenth-century gloss on this passage, Accursius adds the phrase "*et non contradicente.*"[22] From this phrase would seem to derive Columbus's declaration "and I was not contradicted," or in the Latin translation of his letter, "*contradicente nemine possessionem accepi.*"[23]

But how should such a principle be thought to apply in this case? The problem is not simply opposing interests—the natives' desire to retain possession of their land against the Spanish desire to appropriate it—but incommensurable positions.[24] The Arawak are not simply denied the opportunity to dispute the Spanish claim; they are not in the same universe of discourse. Even if one discounts the incompatibility of a bureaucratic system based on legal title and a way of life that does not conceive of the land as alienable "real estate," the abyss between the two parties remains so overwhelming that Columbus's claim that he was not contradicted seems absurd.[25] Why should words spoken in a language the native inhabitants had obviously never before heard be thought to constitute a valid speech act, transferring their lands to those whose utterly incomprehensible visual signs—a cross, two crowns, the letters F and Y—were printed on the Spanish banners? Why should the natives be thought capable, under the circumstances, of assenting or offering a contradiction?[26]

The answer, I think, may lie in the extreme formalism of Columbus's linguistic acts. That is, Columbus is observing a form—the journal, let us recall, spoke of making the "required declarations"—and that form evidently calls for the possibility of a contradiction, a counterdeclaration to the one by which possession is claimed. It is this formal occasion that must be observed rather than the contingency for which the formal occasion must originally have been conceived. Fulfilling the forms is enough: what we would be tempted to dismiss as *mere* form is for Columbus and for the Spanish whom he serves the heart of the matter. Hence Columbus does not write, "the natives did not contradict me," but rather, "I was not contradicted." He is not concerned with a particular subjective consciousness responding to the proclamation and hence with consent as an inner act of volition but with the formal absence of an objection to his words. *Why* there was no objection is of no consequence; all that matters is that there was none. The formalism of Columbus's proclamation derives not only from the fact that it represents the scrupulous observance of a preconceived form (hence is not spontaneous or aleatory) but also from its complete indifference to the consciousness of the other. The words are a closed system, closed in such a way as to silence those whose objection might challenge or negate the proclamation which formally, but only formally, envisages the possibility of contradiction.

According to medieval concepts of natural law, uninhabited territories become the possession of the first to discover them.[27] We might say that Columbus's formalism tries to make the new lands uninhabited—*terrae nullius*—by emptying out the category of the other. The other exists only as an empty sign, a cipher. Hence there can be no contradiction to the proclamation from anyone on the islands themselves, because only linguistic competence, the ability to understand and to speak, would enable one to fill in the sign. There is, of course, a whole multinational culture—the Europe from which Columbus has come—that has this competence and could both understand and dispute the claimed possession, but then this culture is not in the right place at the right time. When the moment arrived to contradict the proclamation, those who could contradict it were absent, and all subsequent claims will be forever belated and thus invalid. When, almost immediately after his return, Columbus's letter is published in several languages all over Europe, in effect it promulgates the Spanish claim and affirms that the moment for contradiction has irrevocably passed. The ritual of possession, though it is apparently directed toward the natives, has its full meaning then in relation to other European powers when they come to hear of the discovery. It is as if from the instant of landfall Columbus imagines that everything he sees is already the possession of one of the monarchies he has offered to serve—Portuguese, English, Spanish—and he proceeds to establish the correct claim by the proper formal speech act. I said at the outset that Columbus's words—"And there I found very many islands filled with people innumerable, and of them all I have taken possession for their highnesses"—were empty placeholders for the unknown and unimaginable. We could call this quality of the words their *open formalism,* since it is precisely their formal vacancy (a set of blanks that have not yet been filled in) that makes possible the imperial indeterminacy of the claim to possession. But now we find that this openness is itself the effect of an underlying *closed formalism,* since the ritual of possession itself precludes the intervention (or even the understanding) of those who, the ceremony implicitly acknowledges, are most likely to object. Formalism then has the virtue of at once inviting and precluding contradiction both in the present and in the future: "Speak now or forever hold your peace."[28]

The formalism I have described is generally important in the functioning of legal and religious rituals, but it is by no means limited to these discourses. The letter to Santangel, after all, is not a legal document but a narrative.[29] Narrative is a comfortable home for the discursive strategy I have been describing because the pressure of linked events and the assumed coherence of the tale help to pull the reader past the awkwardness of incommensurable positions and silenced voices. It is one of the principal powers of narrative to gesture toward what is not in fact expressed, to create the illusion of presences that are in reality absent. For this reason, the formal acknowledgment of beings who are at the same time rendered silent is less discordant in Columbus's narrative, less obviously anomalous, than it is in juridical or theological discourse where it soon provoked eloquent and sustained protest.

If we recognize that formalism in the letter to Santangel functions as the discursive agent of Columbus's power, I think we should resist the notion that formalism has a necessary and inherent politics, and that this politics is colonialist. For in the next generation a comparable formalism led Francisco de Vitoria (c. 1492–1546) to argue from the tenets of natural law that the indigenous peoples had not had their rights respected, and to challenge the basis for the whole Spanish claim to the Indies. Thus, for example, Vitoria quickly dispatches the claim to sovereignty through the right of discovery. There is a title, he writes in *De indiis,*

> which can be set up, namely, by right of discovery; and no other title was originally set up, and it was in virtue of this title alone that Columbus the Genoan first set sail. And this seems to be an adequate title because those regions which are deserted become, by the law of nations and the natural law, the property of the first occupant [*Institutes* 2. 1. 12]. Therefore, as the Spaniards were the first to discover and occupy the provinces in question, they are in lawful possession thereof, just as if they had discovered some lonely and thitherto uninhabited region.
>
> Not much, however, need be said about this . . . title of ours, because, as proved above, the barbarians were true owners, both from the public and from the private standpoint. Now the rule of the law of nations is that what belongs to nobody is granted to the first occupant, as is expressly laid down in the aforementioned passage of the *Institutes.* And so, as the object in question was not without an owner, it does not fall under the title which we are discussing. . . . In and by itself [this title] gives no support to a seizure of the aborigines any more than if it had been they who had discovered us.[30]

It could be demonstrated then, on purely formal grounds, that Columbus's ritual of possession was not valid.[31] Conversely, a theoretical position quite opposed to formalism could be used to support the Spanish claim. Thus, from the perspective of an antiformalist historicism, Gonzalo Fernandez de Oviedo, the official chronicler for Charles V, in effect discounts the paramount importance of Columbus's formal acts. To be sure, Oviedo celebrates the voyage for its visionary daring, its unprecedented use of navigational instruments, its geopolitical significance, but then he carefully collects stories designed to show that Columbus learned his route from a dying pilot, that others had been there before, that the alleged discovery is in reality a rediscovery. Above all, Oviedo proves to his own satisfaction at least that the Indies are identical to the Hesperides. And on the principle that "provinces and kingdoms in olden days took the name of the princes or lords who founded, conquered, settled or fell heir to them," he concludes that the Hesperides were named for Hesperus, twelfth king of Spain in descent from Tubal Cain, and hence that "it has now been 3193 years that Spain and Hesperus, her king, have held dominion over these islands." "So, with such very ancient right," he declares, "God returned this domain to Spain after so many centuries."[32]

Oviedo's argument was not a quaint expression of historical curiosity; it was a sophisticated intervention in the long legal battle, the *pleitos de Colón*, between the Crown and Columbus's heirs over the latter's claim to hereditary rights in the New World. Those rights had been granted for any lands that Columbus had "discovered or gained"; if there was no authentic discovery but only a restoration of rights, then the position of the heirs would be substantially weakened. A further function of Oviedo's historicizing claim was to weaken the link between Spanish sovereignty in the New World and the "donation" of the Indies to Spain by Pope Alexander VI in 1493. Papal bulls granted to Ferdinand and Isabella dominion over all the lands inhabited by non-Christians that they might discover in the Atlantic. But, as Anthony Pagden notes, this donation "rested on the two claims which Spanish jurists and theologians found hardest to accept: the claims that the papacy possessed temporal as well as spiritual authority and that it could exercise this authority over pagans as well as Christians."[33] Moreover, when the Catholic Church began to play a more independent role in Spain's American possessions and to dispute certain of its policies, especially its treatment of the Indians, the Crown sought to create some distance between the papal donation and its own "right of possession," now revealed to be of great antiquity. Hence a Spanish jurist of the late seventeenth century, Diego Andrés Rocha, maintains that from a theological perspective Spain's claim to the New World derives from God's providential design to propagate the true faith through the agency of the Spanish, but that from a juridical perspective it derives from the *derecho de reversion*, the right of restitution, whereby lands are returned to their legitimate possessors.[34] We should add that comparable "historical" arguments—claims to prior migrations and possession by ancient rulers—were made for other European peoples, including the Portuguese, the Frisians, and the Welsh.[35] But obviously the further we get from actual power, the more idle (in a sense, the more "merely formal") these claims become: even if all of Europe had freely granted that there was a strong resemblance between Nahuatl, the Aztec language, and Welsh, the Spanish crown was not about to cede its territorial claims in Mexico.

Should we not say then that the words do not matter, that the discursive tactics are interchangeable, that language is a mere screen for the brutal reality of power? There is a flood of words about the New World in the generations after Columbus, there are serious debates in Salamanca and elsewhere about the legitimacy of the Spanish rule, there are denunciations of atrocities and passionate defenses of the necessity of military sternness—but what difference does any of it make? Isn't the whole miserable story, the story of an absolute denial of consent, already written in the first Spanish sneeze, with its millions of invisible bullets? Isn't the fate of the natives sealed in the first innocently drawn blood: "I showed them swords and they took them by the edge and through ignorance cut themselves" (*Diario*, 67). This "ignorance"— the first glimpse of a decisive imbalance in military technology, carefully noted at the initial encounter—would, in conjunction with vulnerability to European disease, doom the natives of the Caribbean and fatally weaken the great Indian empires that the Spaniards were shortly to encounter. One should perhaps add another brute physical fact: the horrible misfortune that the earth of the New World harbored gold and that many of the native peoples worked this gold into ornaments and hence carried it on their bodies for the Spanish to see. No doubt the weapons and microbes would have reached the New World peoples anyway, but without the gold the destructive forces would have come more slowly, and there might have been time for a defense.

From this vantage point, words seem like mere covers for Spanish actions and the physical consequences of those actions. The webs of discourse should be stripped away and discarded in order to face unflinchingly the terrible meaning of the 1492 and its aftermath: swords and bullets pierce naked flesh and microbes kill bodies that lack sufficient immunities. I am a teacher of literature, and so by training and impulse hostile to such an argument, but I find it very difficult to dismiss. Words in the New World seem always to be trailing after events that pursue a terrible logic quite other than the fragile meanings that they construct.

But if we are thus forced to abandon the dream of linguistic omnipotence, the fantasy that to understand the discourse is to understand the event, we are not at the same time compelled or even permitted to discard words altogether. For if microbes lie altogether beyond the grasp of Renaissance discourse, the other forces that we have cited as brute facts should under no circumstances be naturalized. The possession of weapons and the will to use them on defenseless people are cultural matters that are intimately bound up with discourse: with the stories that a culture tells itself, its conceptions of personal boundary and liability, its whole collective system of rules. And if gold is a natural phenomenon, the all-consuming craving for gold most assuredly is not.

The *unnaturalness* of the desire for gold is one of the great themes of the fifteenth and sixteenth centuries, a theme tirelessly rehearsed by poets, playwrights, and moralists and frequently illustrated by tales of European behavior in the New World. One of the most famous images of the Spanish in America depicts a group of Indians punishing a *conquistador* for his insatiable thirst for gold by pouring the molten metal down his throat.[36] In part such images, which drew upon ancient polemics against greed, reflected sectarian hostilities—here Protestant against Catholic—but in part they reflected a more ecumenical uneasiness in the face of the growth of a money economy and an uncertainty about the status of gold.

Moreover, if certain crucial aspects of the European encounter with the New World were beyond words (and beyond the comprehension of any of the participants), the Europeans themselves struggled to bring as much of their experience as possible under the control of discourse. How could they—or, for that matter, how could we—do otherwise?[37] And it is not only as a futile attempt to comprehend the unimaginable that this discourse may interest us but as both an instrument of empire and an expression, however constrained and half-hearted, of resistance.

Hence, to return to Columbus's initial proclamation, if the declaration that he was not contradicted is absurd, it is also a sign—one of the few signs that we have from this first voyage—of an ethical reservation, a sense that the wishes of the native inhabitants should be respected. The reservation is not direct, it may not have been conscious, and it was certainly not effective, but it nevertheless exists, so deeply entrenched in the language of the judicial procedure that it could not be simply forgotten or eliminated. The procedure was directed, I have observed, to other Europeans, in order to record and legitimate the Spanish claim, but legitimation necessarily included an acknowledgment of the existence of the natives and a recognition of values other than superior force. And though it is important to recognize the practical emptiness of this acknowledgment and to understand how it was emptied out, there seems to me nothing to be gained from a contemptuous dismissal of the discourse in which the acknowledgment is embedded. Where else do we get our own ragged sense that there is something other than force, our own craving for justice? In a dark time (or for that matter an expansive time filled with a sense of infinite possibility and an indifference to the human cost), the awareness of a "contradiction" is carried precisely in the small textual resistances—a kind of imagined possibility, a dream of equity—that Columbus had to contrive to overcome.

The overcoming in this case is made possible by formalism. If there is no theoretical necessity to his formalism, no innate politics, and no determining power, there are none the less strategic reasons for its presence as a shaping force in his discourse. It enables him, as we have seen, to stage a legal ritual that depends upon the formal possibility of contradiction without actually permitting such contradiction; that is, it enables him to empty out the existence of the natives, while at the same time officially acknowledging that they exist. But does this paradox not simply empty out the legal ritual itself? Does it not make a mockery of the basis on which Columbus is grounding the Spanish claim to the Indies? Columbus's founding speech act in the New World is spectacularly "infelicitous" in virtually every one of the senses detailed by Austin in *How to Do Things with Words:* it is misfire, a misinvocation, a misapplication, and a misexecution.[38] And it is difficult to believe that Columbus is unaware of these infelicities, for he knows very well that these are *not* uninhabited territories; indeed he notes that they have an immense population—*gente sin número.* It might have been possible to argue that these numberless people were so barbarous that they had no rights—the argument was made repeatedly in the sixteenth century and beyond—but Columbus does not do so and would probably have resisted the suggestion, since he wishes to believe that he has arrived in the "Indies" and hence he must assume that he is in the outlying regions of a great empire, ultimately under the control of the Grand Khan.[39] And he recognizes almost at once that even here, on these small islands with their naked inhabitants living in tiny hamlets and appearing to share everything, there is a political and social order of some kind.

Indeed in the logbook Columbus describes communities characterized not by savage confusion but by an admirable orderliness. He admires the "wonderful dignity" of the native "king" whose people "all obey him so that it is a marvel." "All of these lords," he goes on to note, "are of few words and of very attractive customs; and their commands are for the most part carried out by hand signs so soon understood that it is a marvel" (*Diario*, 275). Columbus makes no mention of this indigenous social order in the opening sentences of the letter to Santangel—evidently he did not consider it relevant to the ceremony of possession—but he subsequently refers to their "chief or king" who is given as many as twenty wives, while common men have only one.[40]

The recognition of a hierarchical society returns us to the question, how is it possible to "take possession" of such a place in the presence of those who inhabit it? For Francisco de Vitoria, such a recognition should invalidate the Spanish claim; the Indians manifestly are rational human agents, "because there is a certain method in their affairs, for they have polities which are orderly and arranged and they have definite marriage and magistrates, overlords, laws, and workshops, and a system of exchange, all of which call for the use of reason."[41] The territory of people who live in such polities cannot justly be appropriated, even if the people are pagans and hence in a state of mortal sin. The juridical problem does not arise if the lands are uninhabited—for under the law of nations and natural law, deserted regions become the property of the first occupant—nor does it arise, at least in the same terms, if one is conquering a recognized enemy. In his account of the third voyage (1498–1500), Columbus, responding to attacks upon his conduct, attempts to recast his role. "At home," he writes to Doña Juana, governess to the Infante D. Juan, "they judge me as a governor sent to Sicily or to a city or two under settled government, and where the laws can be fully maintained, without fear of all being lost." Such a perspective on the situation, he argues, is wholly inappropriate: "I ought to be judged as a captain who went from Spain to the Indies to conquer a people, warlike and numerous, and with customs and beliefs very different from ours, a people, living in highlands and mountains, having no settled dwellings, and apart from us; and where, by the will of God, I have brought under the dominion of the king and queen, our sovereigns, another world, whereby Spain, which was called poor, is now most rich."[42]

The first letter is careful to indicate that the formal rites of legality had been observed; this letter by contrast insists that such observation would be wholly inappropriate, a kind of theoretical fastidiousness that ends by losing everything. By 1498 both Columbus's personal circumstances and the institutional context in which he was operating had changed profoundly. In 1493 Pope Alexander VI had issued the bull *Inter caetera*, donating the newly discovered lands, out of "mere liberality, certain science, and apostolic authority," to the sovereigns of Spain and Portugal.[43] The Indians in Columbus's account can now be assigned the marks of outlaws or rebels; they are people who live on the margins—"*sierras y montes, syn pueblo asentado, ni nosotros.*" This marginal existence, the lives of those who are "not us," marks their distance from civility. The "infinity of small hamlets" mentioned in the first letter have disappeared, and the Indians have been assimilated to a conception of nomadic barbarism as old as ancient Greece. They are the people who live outside of all just order, apart from settled human community and hence from the very condition of the virtuous life. "He who is unable to live in society, or who has no need because he is sufficient for himself," Aristotle wrote, "must be either a beast or a god."[44] The Indians were clearly not gods and hence could in this light be regarded as beasts.

Their unsettled life, in Columbus's self-justifying account, not only reveals their bestial nature but also marks the difficulty of pacifying or containing them. For European authority in the early modern period was the authority of the plain, of walled towns that could if necessary be besieged and starved into submission; the central authorities feared and hated the mountains. And, of course, for Columbus the natives of the New World are not merely like the untamed dwellers of the European wastelands; from the first days he suspects something worse, and the suspicion hardens into a certainty that many of the islands are inhabited by cannibals.[45]

But in 1492 Columbus goes out of his way to present a very different picture of all of the natives whom he actually encounters. These natives do not, to be sure, live in towns or villages, but they inhabit small hamlets (*pequeñas poblaciones*), and they are utterly harmless: "They have no iron or steel or weapons, nor are they fitted to use them, not because they are not well-built men and of handsome stature, but because they are very marvelously timorous [*muy temerosos á maravilla*]" (i. 6). What makes their timorousness marvelous? They flee at the approach of the Spaniards, Columbus explains,

Communication and cultural difference: the Tupinamba greeting
ritual copied by a Frenchman. From Jean de Léry, *Histoire d'un voyage
fait en la terre du Brésil, dite Amerique* (Geneva: Vignon, 1600).
Bancroft Library, University of California Berkeley

"even a father not waiting for his son" (i. 8). The example assumes a norm of natural courage, the courage that instinctively arises in all men to defend their offspring, or, more precisely, their male offspring. And this creatural instinct is inexplicably absent in the timorous natives, inexplicably not only in relation to a father's natural care for his son but in relation to the entirely friendly and generous deportment of the Spanish.

It is odd: Columbus has just unilaterally taken possession of everything he sees on behalf of the king and queen of Spain; he declares moreover that "as soon as I arrived in the Indies, in the first island which I found, I took by force some of them, in order that they might learn and give me information" (i. 10).[46] Yet this armed invader who seizes lands and people regards his own intentions as impeccably generous: "at every point where I have been and have been able to have speech, I have given to them of all that I had, such as cloth and many other things, without receiving anything for it" (i. 8). It is characteristic of Columbus's discourse that it yokes together actions, attitudes, or perceptions that would seem ethically incompatible, here seizing everything on the one hand and giving everything on the other. The two are clearly related in some way, but they do not directly impinge on one another, just as there is an unexpressed, unacknowledged relation between the fact that the natives do not understand his language and the fact that no one contradicts his proclamation. It would, I suppose, be possible to term this hypocrisy, but the term suggests a staging of moral attitudes that are not actually felt in the deep recesses of the heart, a theatrical self-consciousness, that seems to me quite alien to Columbus's ardent faith. I think rather that we are encountering an important aspect of Columbus's discursive economy, a characteristic rhetorical feature of what we may call his Christian imperialism.

This discursive economy brings opposites into the closest conjunction with one another and yet leaves the heart of their relation a mystery. Columbus takes absolute possession on behalf of the Spanish Crown in order to make an absolute gift; he seeks earthly gain in order to serve a divine purpose; the Indians must lose everything in order to receive everything; the innocent natives will give away their gold for trash, but they will receive a treasure far more precious than gold; the wicked natives (the "cannibals") will be enslaved in order to be freed from their own bestiality. Empowering these paradoxes is an ancient Christian rhetoric that has its most famous Renaissance English expression in the Holy Sonnets of John Donne:

> That I may rise, and stand, o'erthrow mee, and bend
>   Your force, to break, blowe, burn, and make me new . . .
>   Take me to you, imprison me, for I
>   Except you'enthrall mee, never shall be free,
>   Nor ever chast, except you ravish me.

Columbus's version of this rhetoric is at once less histrionic and more paradoxical, since it is cast neither in a prayer nor in a poem but in a report establishing secular authority over newly discovered lands and peoples:

Quitlauhtique

The go-between: Doña Marina interprets for Cortés. From *Lienzo de Tlaxcala* (original drawing by an Aztec artist). Photograph from Alfredo Chavero, *Antigüedades Mexicanas*, 1892. Bancroft Library, University of California, Berkeley

imperialism is by no means the opposite of Christianity but neither is it simply identical with it. For like the legal formalism at which we have glanced, Christian faith could empower radically opposed positions: if in the name of Christianity, Queen Isabella could decree the use of force against the Indians "whenever conversion to the holy Catholic Faith and allegiance to the Crown were not immediately forthcoming,"[47] so too in the name of Christianity, Bartolomé de Las Casas could bitterly condemn the entire Spanish enterprise.

From the first moments, the encounter with the New World mobilizes in Columbus cravings for power and status and wealth, cravings that sit in an uneasy relation to his Franciscan religiosity, his appetite to convert and save, his apocalyptic dreams. It would be a mistake to think of these simply as opposed desires—a spiritual side of Columbus at war with his carnal side—for the whole achievement of the discourse of Christian imperialism is to represent desires as *convertible* and in a constant process of exchange. Were these desires actually identical, Columbus would have no need to articulate all of the ways in which they are cross-coupled; were they actually opposed, he would not be able to exchange one for the other. The possibility of such an exchange, rooted perhaps in his experience of Italian merchant life, haunts his writing: "Genoese, Venetians, and all who have pearls, precious stones, and other things of value, all carry them to the end of the world in order to exchange them, to turn [*convertir*] them into gold. Gold is most excellent. Gold constitutes treasure, and he who possesses it may do what he will in the world, and may so attain as to bring souls to Paradise" (ii. 102–04). In this rhapsodic moment, from his account of the fourth voyage, the conversion of commodities into gold slides liquidly into the conversion and hence salvation of souls. If it seems strange, we might recall that in the Spanish of the Middle Ages and Renaissance, the Crusade to the Holy Land was called not the *cruzada*—that word referred to the special papal concessions granted to the Spanish crown to fight against the infidel within its own territory—but rather the *empresa* or *negocio*, terms in which the mercantile and the religious are intertwined.[48]

The rhetorical task of Christian imperialism then is to bring together commodity conversion and spiritual conversion.[49] Most often these are simply juxtaposed by Columbus, as if the energies of the one would naturally spill over into the other but, on occasion, their interchange is articulated more directly: "You shall say to their highnesses," writes Columbus to his agent Antonio de Torres in 1494,

> that the welfare of the souls of the said cannibals [the natives whom the Spanish have enslaved and shipped back to Spain], and also of those here, has induced the idea that the more that may be sent over, the better it will be, and in this their highnesses may be served in the following way. That, having seen how necessary cattle and beasts of burden are here, for the support of the people who have to be here, and indeed for all these islands, their highnesses might give licence and a permit for a sufficient number of caravels to come here every year and to carry the said cattle and other supplies and things for the colonization of the country and the development of the land, and this at reasonable prices at the cost of those who transport them. Payment for these things could be made to them in slaves, from among these cannibals, a people very savage and suitable for the purpose, and well made and of very good intelligence. We believe that they, having abandoned that inhumanity, will be better than any other slaves, and their inhumanity they will immediately lose when they are out of their own land. (i. 90–92)

Beasts of burden will be exchanged for beasts of burden: so many Indians for so many cattle. Columbus cannot be content, however, with a purely mercantile transaction, nor is this his overriding interest. He cannot allow himself, for reasons both tactical and more deeply spiritual, to say simply,

"We need cattle; we have slaves; let us trade one for the other." The exchange must be presented as undertaken in the interests of the enslaved. We might call this enslavement with a human face, or rather, liberating enslavement. For the exchange Columbus envisions would put into practice the religious rhetoric that we glimpsed in Donne: at its core is not an economic transaction but a dream of marvelous transformation. Those Indians identified as cannibals will be hunted down, seized, torn from their lands and their culture, loaded onto ships still stinking of the animals for whom they are being exchanged, and sent into slavery. But the economic transaction as Columbus conceives it will be undertaken for the welfare of the souls of the enslaved: the Indians are exchanged for beasts in order to convert them into humans. This transformation will not enfranchise them; it will only make them into excellent slaves.[50] But they will have gained their spiritual freedom. At the heart of the transaction is not wealth or convenience, though these are welcome, but a metamorphosis from inhumanity into humanity. The Crown, we might note, evidently had doubts, on legal and religious grounds, about the legitimacy of the proposed exchange: Isabella intervened and stopped the sale of the slaves.[51]

The occult relation between apparent opposites in the Christian discourse of John Donne draws the reader toward contemplation of the mysterious nature of the Incarnation; the occult relation between apparent opposites in the Christian imperialist discourse of Columbus draws the reader toward contemplation of the "marvelous" nature of the New World and its inhabitants. The wonder aroused by the cannibals is twofold; it lies in the uncanny conjunction of native intelligence and inhumanity, and again in the uncanny power of enslavement to humanize. But, as we have already observed, it is not only the warlike cannibals who awaken wonder. In the letter of 1500 Columbus wishes his readers to think of the Indians as warlike; in the letter of 1492 he wishes that they be thought timid, indeed marvelously timid.[52] The term "marvelous," which we have already seen Columbus use in the first sentence of the first letter, obviously appeals to readerly expectations about the genre of travel literature. But timidity in this context is a peculiar marvel, and Columbus intensifies its peculiarity by stressing that the natives are "well-built men and of handsome stature." We are not dealing here with a strange race of creatures that do not bear arms because they literally do not have arms, or legs, or heads on their shoulders. Columbus's readers would be well-prepared for the monstrous. What they might not expect to find is the marvelous in human timidity. In urging them to do so, and by thus relocating the marvelous from the grotesque to the ordinary, Columbus induces his readers to join him in what we may call an act of ideological forgetting. If one clearly remembered the actions Columbus has just described—the sudden arrival of armed and armored strangers, kidnapping, and expropriation of lands—it would be more difficult to find the natives' panic fear all that marvelous.

Columbus does not use the discourse of the marvelous in order to create a momentary amnesia about his actions; he induces a momentary amnesia about his actions in order to create the discourse of the marvelous. Indeed the production of a sense of the marvelous in the New World is at the very center of virtually all of Columbus's writings about his discoveries, though the meaning of that sense shifts over the years.[53] His constant insistence on the marvelous is generally treated as if it were a simple record of what he and his companions felt, as if Columbus's discourse were perfectly transparent and his feelings those "naturally" evoked by his experiences. (Alternatively, it is possible to argue—incorrectly, I think—that Columbus had such an impoverished vocabulary that he could think of no other word to describe his experiences.)[54] But we may take Columbus himself in testimony to the special significance of the experience of wonder. In his official report to Ferdinand and Isabella on the third voyage, Columbus writes that in response to "the defaming and disparagement of the undertaking that had been begun" in the New World, because he "had not immediately sent caravels laden with gold," he "decided to come to Your Highnesses, and to cause you to wonder at everything, and to show you the reason that I had for all [*y maravillarme de todo, y mostrarles la razón que en todo avía*]" (ii. 4–6).[55] There is by the third voyage a specific political and rhetorical reason for the performance and production of wonder: the marvelous is precisely the sense that will confirm the power and validity of Columbus's claims against those cavilling skeptics who want more tangible signs of gain. Not to manifest and arouse wonder is to succumb to the attacks against him. The marvelous stands for the missing caravels laden with gold; it is—like the ritual of possession itself—a word pregnant with what is imagined, desired, promised.

The production of wonder then is not only an expression of the effect that the voyage had upon Columbus but a calculated rhetorical strategy, the evocation of an aesthetic response in the service of a legitimation process. It is possible that the *explicit* calculation marks the frustration of Columbus's early hopes and the darkening of his situation, and that his constant expressions of wonder in the earlier voyages are a more spontaneous response to the innocence, beauty, and freshness of the Caribbean islands and their peoples. But we should recall that Columbus's first use of the marvelous refers not to the land itself but to its possession—Columbus gives thanks to the "Divine Majesty, Who has marvelously bestowed all this." If the use of wonder as a rhetorical strategy becomes explicit in the third voyage, when an increasingly embattled Columbus is forced to articulate his purposes, its place in the legitimation process is already at work, as we have seen, in the first voyage.

Wonder, however, does not inherently legitimate a claim to possession. Indeed, as we have seen in *Mandeville's Travels*, in the Middle Ages the experience of marvels seems to lead precisely to a sense of dispossession, a disclaimer of dogmatic certainty, a self-estrangement in the face of the strangeness, diversity, and opacity of the world. The medieval sense of the marvelous, Jacques Le Goff has suggested, expressed perceptions of nature potentially or actually inimical to the transcendental being and providential authority of the Christian God and His servant the Church.[56] It stood then for all that could not be securely held, all that resisted appropriation. Why should Columbus, whose interests are diametrically opposed to dispossession and self-estrangement, continually invoke wonder? In part, he may do so because the marvelous is closely linked in classical and Christian rhetoric to heroic enterprise. The voyages of Odysseus in particular were for centuries the occasion for aesthetic and philosophical speculations on the relation between heroism and the arousal of wonder through a representation of marvels. In part, he may do so to associate his discoveries with a specifically "Christian marvelous" that, in opposition to all that is irregular and heterodox in the experience of wonder, identifies spiritual authenticity with the proper evocation of marvels.[57] And, most simply and directly, Columbus may strive to arouse wonder because marvels are inseparably bound up in rhetorical and pictorial tradition with voyages to the Indies. To affirm the "marvelous" nature of the discoveries is, even without the lucrative shipments yet on board, to make good on the claim to have reached the fabled realms of gold and spices. This is the significance, I think, of Columbus's mention in the first letter of a province in Cuba that the Indians call "Avan" where "the people are born with tails";[58] such prodigies were a virtual requirement for travelers to the Indies. That he singles out Cuba in particular as the probable site of the authenticating wonders of the East is probably a reflection of the hope Columbus recorded in the logbook that this island— toward which the natives seemed to be directing him—was Japan, or "Cipango" as Marco Polo called it. "And I believe so," Columbus writes with a blind conviction born of wish-fulfillment, "because I believe that it is so according to the signs that all the Indians of these islands and those that I have with me make (because I do not understand them through speech) [and] that it is the island of Cipango of which marvelous things [*cosas maravillosas*] are told" (*Diario*, 113).

Yet the observations that he records to create the effect of the marvelous are for the most part strikingly unlike the marvels conventionally recorded in travelers' tales. Once, off the coast of Haiti, Columbus sighted "three mermaids [*serenas*] who came quite high out of the water," but his logbook description of these prodigies—in all likelihood, Caribbean manatees or sea cows—tellingly suggests a resistance to the traditional iconography: they "were not as pretty as they are depicted, for somehow in the face they look like men" (*Diario*, 321).[59] In his logbook entry for November 4, 1492, Columbus notes apparent native confirmation of marvels about which he must have been inquiring: "far from there," the natives supposedly inform him, "there were one-eyed men, and others, with snouts of dogs, who ate men, and that as soon as one was taken they cut his throat and drank his blood and cut off his genitals" (*Diario*, 133). (The display of signs that Columbus must have made to elicit this information may help to explain why the natives, as he notes in the same entry, were "very timid.") But by the time he writes the first letter, he seems far more skeptical: "In these islands I have so far found no human monstrosities, as many expected, but on the contrary the whole population is very well-formed" (i. 14). He appears to be distinguishing then between monstrosities and marvels: the former are vivid, physical violations of universal norms, the latter are physical impressions that arouse wonder. Columbus is not willing to rule out the possibility of the monstrous, but he is scrupulous in limiting his claims to have personally witnessed monstrosities; the marvelous, by contrast, he notes at firsthand again and again.

The marvelous functions for Columbus as the agent of conversion: a fluid mediator between outside and inside, spiritual and carnal, the realm of objects and the subjective impressions made by those objects, the recalcitrant otherness of a new world and the emotional effect aroused by that otherness. More precisely it registers the presence of Columbus's fears and desires in the very objects he perceives and conversely the presence in his discourse of a world of objects that exceed his understanding of the probable and the familiar. Hence, for example, he writes that he "saw many trees very different from ours, and among them many which had branches of many kinds, and all on one trunk. And one little branch is of one kind, and another of another, and so different that it is the greatest wonder in the world [*la mayor maravilla del mundo*]" (*Diario*, 89). "Here the fish are so different from ours," he notes in the same logbook entry for October 16, "that it is a marvel. There are some shaped like dories, of the finest colors in the world: blues, yellows, reds, and of all colors; and others colored in a thousand ways. And the colors are so fine that there is no man who would not marvel and take great delight in seeing them" (*Diario*, 89–91). As such passages suggest, it is not simply the recognition of the unusual that constitutes a marvel but a certain excess, a hyperbolic intensity, a sense of awed delight.[60]

The marvelous for Columbus usually involves then a surpassing of the measure but not in the direction of the monstrous or grotesque; rather, a heightening of impressions until they reach a kind of perfection. Española, he writes in the first letter, is "very fertile to a limitless degree"; its harbors are "beyond comparison with others which I know in Christendom," it has many good and large rivers "which is marvelous" (*que es maravilla*); and its mountains are "beyond comparison with the island of Teneriffe" (i. 4).[61] These mountains, however, are not forbidding; "all are most beautiful, of a thousand shapes, and all are accessible and filled with trees of a thousand kinds and tall, and they seem to touch the sky" (i. 4–6). The trees, Columbus is told, never lose their foliage, and he believes what is told, "for I saw them as green and as lovely as they are in Spain in May. . . . And the nightingale was singing and other birds of a thousand kinds in the month of November" (i. 6). Large numbers, particularly "a thousand," are repeated as conventional talismans of wonder, though even much smaller figures will do: "There are six or eight kinds of palm, which are a wonder to behold [*ques es admiración verlas*] on account of their beautiful variety," and there are "marvelous pine groves [*pinares á maravilla*]." The marvelous, as can be seen here, has little or nothing to do with the grotesque or outlandish. It denotes, to be sure, some departure, displacement, or surpassing of the normal or the probable, but in the direction of delicious variety and loveliness.

This loveliness extends in the first letter to the natives. When they overcame their "marvelous timorousness," the natives "all brought something to eat and drink, which they gave with extraordinary affection [*con un amor maravilloso*]" (i. 10). The logbook entries are even more explicit: "they brought us all that they had in the world and knew that the Admiral wanted; and all so bigheartedly [*con un Coraçon tan largo*] and so happily that it was a wonder [*maravilla*]" (*Diario*, 255).[62] Columbus's response to this marvelous generosity is revealing: "The Admiral gave them glass beads and brass rings and bells: not because they asked for something, but because it seemed to him that it was right; and above all, says the Admiral, because he already considers them as Christians and as more the subjects of the sovereigns of Castile than the Castilians. And he says that nothing is lacking except to know the language and to give them orders, because everything they are ordered to do they will do without any opposition [*sin contradiçion algua*]" (*Diario*, 259). The spirit of the gift-giving, as Columbus understands it, is not reciprocal: the Indians give out of an unconstrained openness of heart that is a marvel; the Spanish in return give out of a sense of what is right, a sense of obligation bound up with the conviction that the Indians have *already* become the Christian subjects of the sovereigns of Castile.[63] They are easily imagined as subjects because they are so easily imagined as already subjected, inhabitants of lands appropriated without contradiction (*y no me fué contradicho*) on the day of the initial encounter. "They should," Columbus writes in the logbook entry for that day, "be good and intelligent servants" (*Diario*, 67–69).

Columbus does not imagine that the Indians could have anything like a comparable thought about the Spanish. Their extraordinary affection, Columbus implies, is powered by their conviction that he, with his ships and men, have come from heaven;[64] that is, for the Indians, who had never before seen large ships or clothed men, the Spanish too are a marvel. But this recognition of a reverse wonderment does not qualify Columbus's own perceptions or render the marvelous a mere sign of unfamiliarity or *naiveté*. The natives do not make their mistake because they are stupid; they possess, he says, a very acute intelligence, "so that it is amazing [*es maravilla*] how good an account they give of everything" (i. 10).[65] All of his delighted impressions cohere for Columbus in a single overwhelming perception: "*la Española es maravilla*" (i. 7).[66]

In such a phrase the marvelous has been detached altogether from the enumeration of bizarre particulars and has been broadened in scope to characterize an entire place, a place of surprising and intense beauty. To look (*mirar*) at such a place is to wonder (*maravillar*). This characterization associates the discoveries with a long tradition of poems evoking the *locus amoenus*, the landscape of delight. Again and again Columbus's logbook records the intense pleasure of looking:

[October 14:] And later [I noticed], near the said islet, groves of trees, the most beautiful that I saw and with their leaves as green as those of Castile in the months of April and May. (*Diario*, 75–77)

[October 17:] In this time I also walked among those trees, which were more beautiful to see than any other thing that has ever been seen, seeing as much verdure and in such degree as in the month of May in Andalusia. (*Diario*, 93)

[October 19:] [T]he island [is] the most beautiful thing that I have seen. For if the others are very beautiful this one is more so. It is an island of many very green and very large trees. . . . I do not know where to go first; nor do my eyes grow tired of seeing such beautiful verdure and so different from ours. (*Diario*, 99–101)

[October 21:] [If the other islands] already seen are very beautiful and green and fertile, this one is much more so and with large and very green groves of trees. Here there are some big lakes and over and around them the groves are marvelous. And here and in all of the island the groves are all green and the verdure like that in April in Andalusia. And the singing of the small birds [is so marvelous] that it seems that a man would never want to leave this place. And [there are] flocks of parrots that obscure the sun; and birds of so many kinds and sizes, and so different from ours, that it is a marvel. (*Diario*, 105)

"It seems that a man would never want to leave this place." If the dream of marvelous possession in such passages is tinged with an undertone of loss, it is not only because Columbus feels the urgent compulsion to pass on to other islands—"I am not taking pains to see much in detail because I could not do it in 50 years and because I want to see and explore as much as I can so I can return to Your Highnesses in April" (*Diario*, 103)—but also because in Christian poetry the *locus amoenus* at its most intense is always touched with remembrance of paradise lost. In the years that follow, the location of the Earthly Paradise interests Columbus with increasing intensity and becomes intertwined with other dreams: the discourse of enraptured looking is shaped by a longing at once erotic and infantile, by the gaze, marveling and forever unsatisfied, of love poetry.

The world is not perfectly round, he writes in a letter sent from Hispaniola in 1498, during his third voyage, but rather has the shape of a pear or of a ball on which is placed "something like a woman's nipple" (ii. 30). The nipple of the world is the newly discovered land and all signs point to the location at its center of the Earthly Paradise.[67] And if these signs—above all the great streams of fresh water that emanate from the land—do not point to Eden, if the water does not come from paradise, it seems, Columbus writes, "to be a still greater marvel (*pareçe aun mayor maravilla*), for I do not believe that there is known in the world a river so great and so deep" (ii. 38). The no-tion of a marvel greater than paradise is startling, but it arises from the only other hypothesis Columbus can posit for his observations: "And I say that if it be not from the earthly paradise that this river comes, it originates from a vast land, lying to the south, of which hitherto no knowledge has been ob-tained" (ii. 42). Faced with such a staggering thought—the idea, in effect, of South America—Columbus retreats to the safer ground of the land of Eden: "But I am much more convinced in my own mind that there where I have said is the earthly paradise."

An actual recovery of the earthly paradise would partake of the miracu-lous, but Columbus stops short of such a claim, as he does throughout most of his writings.[68] In effect, the marvelous takes the place of the miraculous, absorbing some of its force but avoiding the theological and evidentiary problems inherent in directly asserting a miracle. Instead of a theological claim, the term *maravilla* as Columbus uses it makes a different kind of claim, one that combines religious and erotic longings in a vision of surpassing beauty. That marvelous vision had since late antiquity played a crucial role in European aesthetics, a role that intensified in the Middle Ages and was ex-haustively theorized in the generations after Columbus. "No one can be called a poet," writes the influential Italian critic Minturno in the 1550s, "who does not excel in the power of arousing wonder."[69] For Aristotelians wonder is associated with pleasure as the end of poetry; in the *Poetics* Aristotle exam-ines the strategies by which tragedians and epic poets employ the marvelous to arouse pleasurable wonder. For the Platonists too wonder is an essential element in art, for it is one of the principal effects of beauty. In the words of Plotinus, "This is the effect that Beauty must ever induce, wonderment and a pleasant astonishment, longing and love and a dread that is pleasurable."[70] In the sixteenth century, the Neoplatonist Francesco Patrizi defines the poet as a "maker of the marvelous," and the marvelous is found, as he puts it, when men "are astounded, ravished in ecstasy." Patrizi goes so far as to posit marveling as a special faculty of the mind, a faculty which in effect mediates between the capacity to think and the capacity to feel.[71]

The aesthetic theory of the marvelous sidesteps the miraculous but does not altogether resolve questions of credibility. Indeed for the Aristotelian Francesco Robortelli, the marvelous and the credible are in conflict, a conflict that may be masked by a variety of poetic devices but cannot be altogether eliminated.[72] But other poets and theorists saw the two as working in con-junction to produce pleasure. Lodovico Castelvetro wrote that the poet "must above all seek credibility or verisimilitude in combination with the marvelous: credibility so that the unimaginative audience will believe, the marvelous so that it will find pleasure in the uncommon and the extraordi-nary";[73] "we find some true things more marvelous than the false," argued Jacopo Mazzoni, "not merely in natural things . . . but also in human his-tory";[74] and Tasso elaborated a theory of the Christian marvelous in which verisimilitude is conferred by faith: "One and the same action may therefore be both marvelous and verisimilar: marvelous if one consider it in itself and hemmed in by natural limitations, verisimilar if one consider it separated from such limitations with respect to its cause, which is a supernatural force capable of and accustomed to producing such marvels."[75]

In Renaissance aesthetic theory wonder is associated with the overcoming of great difficulties and with a strange blend of chance and human intention (Castelvetro); or with the spectacle of the unexpected and the extraordinary (Robortelli); or with passions, reversals, and discoveries (Vettori); or with the reconciliation of unity and variety (Tasso); or with novel and surprising twists of narrative (Denores, Talentoni), or with the effects of awe and wonder associated with religious feelings and hence with sublimity and high gravity (Patrizi).[76] Virtually all of these aesthetic categories are implicit in Columbus's insistent use of the marvelous, not, of course, because he is deliberately alluding to them—they are, for the most part, fully articulated only after his time—but because they emerged from the same cultural matrix that shaped his language and perceptions.

We are now perhaps in a position to understand why the term is so important to him and how it bears on the formal legal ritual by which he claims Spanish possession of the Indies.[77] That ritual had at its center, as we have seen, a defect, an absurdity, a tragicomic invocation of the possibility of a refusal that could not in fact conceivably occur: *y no me fué contradicho*. The legal declaration could take place in the spirit of a radical formalism, but that formalism leaves in its wake an emotional and intellectual vacancy, a hole, that threatens to draw the reader of Columbus's discourse toward laughter or tears and toward a questioning of the legitimacy of the Spanish claim.[78] Columbus tries to draw the reader toward wonder, a sense of the marvelous that in effect fills up the emptiness at the center of the maimed rite of possession. Immediately after describing that rite, let us recall, Columbus declares that "To the first island which I found, I gave the name *San Salvador*, in remembrance of the Divine Majesty, Who has marvelously bestowed all this." The marvel of the divine gift here is at once a legitimation and a transcendence of the legal act. Roman law procedures dictate the principal gesture of appropriation, but they are supplemented by an incommensurable and marvelous assurance, the assurance in effect of the biblical promise: "If you diligently keep all these commandments that I now charge you to observe, by loving the Lord your God, by conforming to his ways and by holding fast to him, the Lord will drive out all these nations before you and you shall occupy the territory of nations greater and more powerful than you. Every place where you set the soles of your feet shall be yours" (Deut. 11: 22–24).

By itself a sense of the marvelous cannot confer title; on the contrary, it is associated with longing, and you long precisely for what you do not have. Columbus's whole life is marked by a craving for something that continually eluded him, for the kingdom or the paradise or the Jerusalem that he could not reach, and his expressions of the marvelous, insofar as they articulate this craving, continue the medieval sense that wonder and secure temporal possession are mutually exclusive. But something happens to the discourse of the marvelous when it is linked to the discourse of the law: the inadequacy of the legal ritual to confer title and the incapacity of the marvelous to confer possession cancel each other out, and both the claim and the emotion are intensified by the conjunction. Neither discourse is freestanding and autonomous; on the contrary, each—like individual words themselves—takes its meaning from its conjunction with other motifs, tropes, and speech acts, and from the situation in which it is inserted. And there is a further motive for the conjunction: under the actual circumstances of the first encounter, there was no discourse adequate to the occasion. In the unprecedented, volatile state of emergence and emergency in which Columbus finds himself, anything he says or does will be defective. His response is to conjoin the most resonant legal ritual he can summon up with the most resonant emotion.

In a remarkable passage to which I have already alluded, Aquinas's teacher, Albertus Magnus, attempts in his *Commentary on the Metaphysics of Aristotle* to provide a convincing account of the internal dynamics of wonder:

> wonder is defined as a constriction and suspension of the heart caused by amazement at the sensible appearance of something so portentous, great, and unusual, that the heart suffers a systole. Hence wonder is something like fear in its effect on the heart. This effect of wonder, then, this constriction and systole of the heart, springs from an unfulfilled but felt desire to know the cause of that which appears portentous and unusual: so it was in the beginning when men, up to that time unskilled, began to philosophize. . . . Now the man who is puzzled and wonders apparently does not know. Hence wonder is the movement of the man who does not know on his way to finding out, to get at the bottom of that at which he wonders and to determine its cause. . . . Such is the origin of philosophy.[79]

Wonder here is not a steady state; it is inherently unstable, a shifter, not only the sign but the principal instigator of movement. For Albertus Magnus the movement driven by the marvelous is from the blankness of ignorance to the fullness of philosophical understanding.[80] Obviously, wonder does not lead Columbus toward philosophy, but it does, in response to God's portentous and unusual gift, lead him toward an act that is closely linked in the Middle Ages and Renaissance to philosophy: the act of naming. That naming, to be sure, has much to do with the manifestation of power through eponymous titles—hence Fernandina, Isabella, and Isla Juana (for Prince Juan, islands traditionally having feminine endings). Moreover, the legal act of possession customarily involved naming, since Crown lawyers "believed that no one could well lay claim to a nameless city, and that a province without a name was hardly a province at all."[81] But more than legal formality is involved here. The first two names—San Salvador and Isla de Santa María de Concepcíon—suggest once again that the assertion of possession is bound up for Christian imperialism with the giving of a precious gift. And the giving of the gift is in turn bound up with superior knowledge, and knowledge of the truth.

When in Genesis 2:19 Adam names the animals, medieval commentators understood this to be an act of marvelous *understanding.* Martin Luther is following a long exegetical tradition when he glosses the verse as follows:

> Here again we are reminded of the superior knowledge and wisdom of Adam, who was created in innocence and right- eousness. Without any new enlightenment, solely because of the excellence of his nature, he views all the animals and thus arrives at such a knowledge of their nature that he can give each one a suitable name that harmonizes with its nature.[82]

Such understanding, Luther continues, is linked with power: "From this enlightenment there also followed, of course, the rule over all the animals, something which is also pointed out here, since they were named in accordance with Adam's will. Therefore by one single word he was able to compel lions, bears, boars, tigers, and whatever else there is among the most outstanding animals to carry out whatever suited their nature" (119–20). As

A Jerusalem-centered world: T-O map from Isidore of Seville *Etymologiae* (Augsburg, 1472). The first world map to be issued from the printing press in Europe. Newberry Library

The marvels of the East: from a Spanish edition of *Mandeville's Travels* (*Libro de las Maravillas del mundo llamado Selva deleytosa* [Alcala, 1547]). Houghton Library, Harvard University

Francis Bacon puts it, when man "shall be able to call the creatures by their true names he shall again command them."[83]

Columbus may have thought that he was near to Paradise, but he also knew that he was the inheritor of Adam's sin through which, as Luther remarks, we lost Paradise as well as this power to bestow primal names and to compel through naming. In his letter, moreover, Columbus makes it clear that he is encountering not a world that has never before been named but rather a world of alien names: "the Indians call it 'Guanahaní.'" His act then is a cancellation of an existing name.[84] But why should Columbus, unlike Marco Polo or Mandeville, think to rename the lands he has encountered? Why should he confer on each island *"una nombre nuevo"*? In order, he says, to commemorate the Savior's marvelous gift. The founding action of Christian imperialism is a christening.[85] Such a christening entails the cancellation of the native name—the erasure of the alien, perhaps demonic, identity—and hence a kind of making new; it is at once an exorcism, an appropriation, and a gift. Christening then is the culminating instance of the marvelous speech act: in the wonder of the proper name, the movement from ignorance to knowledge, the taking of possession, the conferral of identity are fused in a moment of pure linguistic formalism.

Signs of possession: Athore shows Laudonnière the marker-column set up by Ribault and now worshiped by the Indians. From Theodor de Bry, *America*, Part I (1591), pl. VIII. Bancroft Library, University of California, Berkeley

In the first encounter, Columbus had seized several of the natives to use them as informants and interpreters. Six of these survived the voyage back to Spain and in a remarkable ceremony, with Ferdinand, Isabella, and the Infante acting as godparents, were baptized.[86] The cleverest of the natives, the one most serviceable to the Spanish, was given Columbus's own surname and the Christian name of his first-born child: he was christened Don Diego Colón. The magic of renaming extended to Columbus himself: after the Discovery, in place of Cristóbal, he began to sign his letters Christoferens, the Christ-bearer.[87] And according to the cosmographer Sebastian Münster, the king of Spain said that Columbus should be called not *Almirante,* the admiral, but *Admirans,* the one who wonders.[88] This playful christening conveys in tiny compass the trajectory we have been following: from legal ritual through the experience of the marvelous to the mystical understanding and appropriative power of naming. The claim of possession is grounded in the power of wonder.

As Columbus's vision darkened over the years, he seems to have invested more and more of his hopes for possession in the marvelous power of the name. Looking back on his years of fruitless searching for royal support, he

Indi Hifpanis aurum fitientibus, aurum lique- **XX.**
factum infundunt.

The Spanish "thirst" for gold quenched: Indians pouring molten gold in the mouth of a captive. From Theodor de Bry, *America*, Part IV (1592), pl. XX. Bancroft Library, University of California, Berkeley

declares that he never gave up hope, because God "spake so clearly of these lands by the mouth of Isaiah, in many places of his Book, affirming that from Spain His holy name should be proclaimed to them" (ii. 4). Columbus's first act of naming then—San Salvador for Guanahaní—is the fulfillment of a biblical prophecy.[89] Making new is paradoxically the realization of the old. If the act of naming makes the world conform to the word, Columbus believes at the same time that the word is conforming at last to the world.[90] In the words of Scripture, "As his name is, so is he" (1 Samuel 25: 25).

On his last voyage to the New World, in despair, surrounded by hostile natives, "utterly alone, in a high fever and in a state of great exhaustion," Columbus falls asleep and hears a "compassionate voice" that speaks to him about his own name:

> O fool and slow to believe and to serve thy God, the God of all! What more did He for Moses or for His servant David? Since thou wast born, ever has he had thee in His most watchful care.

Travel as folly. Anonymous map based on one by Ortelius, enclosed within the visor of a fool's cap. c. 1600. Douce Portfolio 142 (92). Bodleian Library, Oxford

> When He saw thee of an age with which He was content, He caused thy name to sound marvelously in the land [*maravillosamente hizo sonar tu nombre en la tierra*].

Now it is not the divine name but Columbus's own that is the heart of the wonder. And now, in Columbus's mind and in his text, the conjunction of the land, the marvelous, and the name produces an absolute possession, not for the king and queen of Spain but for himself alone. "The Indies, which are so rich a part of the world," the mysterious voice continues,

> He gave thee for thine own; thou hast divided them as it pleased thee, and He enabled thee to do this. Of the barriers of the Ocean sea, which were closed with such mighty chains, He gave thee the keys; and thou wast obeyed in many lands and among Christians thou hast gained an honorable fame. What did He more for the people of Israel when He brought them out of Egypt? Or for David, whom from a shepherd He made to be king in Judaea?[91]

For a moment at least—a moment at once of perfect wonder and of possessive madness—Columbus has become king of the Promised Land.

The gift of trifles: Algonquian child holding an English doll. Watercolor by John White.
British Library

The gift of necessities: Inhabitants of Guiana bringing food to Sir Walter Raleigh.
From Theodor de Bry, *America,* Part VII/VIII (1599). Bancroft Library,
University of California, Berkeley

Die figur anzaigt vns das voleī vnd insel die gefunden ist durch den cristenlichen Künig zū Portigal oder von seinen vnterthonen. Die leūt sind also nacket hübsch. braun wolgestalt von leib. ir he häls. aren. scham. füß. frawen vnd mann ain wenig mit federn bedeckt. Auch haben die mann in iren angesichten vnd brust vil edel gestain. Es hat auch nyemants nichts sunder sind alle ding ge Vnd die mann habend weyber welche in gefallen. es sey mütter. schwester oder freūndte. darinn haben sy kain vnterschayd. Sy essen auch mit einander. Sy streyten auch mit einander. Sy essen auch ainander selbs die ere werden. vnd henckan das selbig fl: isch in den rauch. Sy werden alt hundert vnd fünzig iar. Vnd haben kain regiment.

A very early German woodcut (Augsburg or Nuremburg c. 1505), ostensibly illustrating the Tupinambas of coastal Brazil. Note the conjunction of domesticity and horror. The Spencer Collection, New York Public Library, Astor, Lenox, and Tilden Foundations

NOTES

[1] *Select Documents Illustrating the Four Voyages of Columbus,* trans. and ed. Cecil Jane, 2 vols. (London: Hakluyt Society, 1930), i. 2. "Señor, porque sé que avréis plazer de la gran vitoria que Nuestro Señor me ha dado en mi viaje, vos escrivo esta, por la qual sabréys como en .xxxiii. días pasé de las islas de Canaria á las Indias con la armada que los ilustrísimos rey é reyna nuestros señores me dieron, donde yo fallé muy muchas islas pobladas con gente sin número; y d'ellas todas he tomado posesión por Sus Altezas con pregón y vandera real estendida, y no me fué contradicho. á la primera que yo fallé puse nombre "San Salvador," á comemoración de Su Alta Magestad, el qual maravillosamente todo esto ha dado; los Indios la llaman "Guanahaní"; á la segunda puse nombre "la isla de Santa María de Concepción"; á la tercera "Fernandina"; á la quarta "la Ysabela"; á la quinta "la isla Juana," é así á cada una nombre nuevo." Quotations from Columbus's letters, unless otherwise noted, will be from this edition.

[2] Santangel, the *escribano de ración,* had helped Columbus find the money to finance his voyage. Santangel was a member of a family of *conversos.* A copy of the letter was also sent to Gabriel Sanchez, the treasurer of Aragon and also from a family of *conversos.*

[3] Over whom does Columbus imagine that he has achieved a victory: over the Indians? over the destructive power of the sea? over his detractors in Europe? over the classical geographers and indeed the whole classical world? At the close of the letter, Columbus returns to the language of victory. He speaks of "the eternal God, our Lord, Who gives to all those who walk in His way triumph [*victoria*] over things which appear to be impossible," and he urges all of Christendom to share this sense of triumph: "So that, since Our Redeemer has

given this victory to our most illustrious king and queen, and to their renowned kingdoms, in so great a matter, for this all Christendom ought to feel delight and make great feast and give solemn thanks to the Holy Trinity with many solemn prayers for the great exaltation which they shall have, in the turning of so many peoples to our holy faith, and afterwards for temporal benefits, for not only Spain but all Christians will have hence refreshment and gain" (Jane, i. 18).

Theodore J. Cachey, Jr. points out that the Latin translation of Columbus's letter, by Leandro de Cosco (a chancellor in the Roman Curia, an Aragonese at the court of Alexander VI), omits Columbus's martial rhetoric. Instead of *"la gran victoria,"* the Latin renders the sentence, "Since I know that it will please you that I have carried to completion the duty which I assumed. . . ." ("The Earliest Literary Response of Renaissance Italy to the New World Encounter," in *Columbus,* ed. Anne Paolucci and Henry Paolucci [New York: Griffin House for the Council on National Literatures, 1989], 28). Cachey calls attention to the recurrence of the verbal motif of the *victoria* at the close of the letter (so that the motif, in effect, frames the narrative): "since, thus Our Redeemer has given this victory to our most illustrious King and Queen. . . ." "The martially connotated language of Columbus's *exordium,"* Cachey writes, "is based upon the link in Columbus's mind (established explicitly in the dedicatory letter to the *Diario*) between his Discovery and the "victoria" at Granada, the final act of the Reconquest" (p. 28).

[4]"Mittimus in presenciarum nobilem virum Christoforum Colon cum tribus caravelis armatis per maria oceania ad partes Indie pro aliquibus causis et negotiis seruicium Dei ac fidem ortodoxe concernentibus" (Jane, p. lxx).

[5]*The "Diario" of Christopher Columbus's First Voyage to America, 1492–1493,* transcribed and trans. by Oliver Dunn and James E. Kelley, Jr. (Norman: University of Oklahoma Press, 1989), 109.

[6]An often-repeated modern theory is that no one had really thought ahead of time about the difficulties. "Surely, the reader will ask, you do not suppose that Ferdinand and Isabella (and Henry VII) were so simple as to suppose that three small vessels (or one still smaller) with ninety (or eighteen) men could sail into a harbor of Japan or China and simply take over? The answer is, yes, they were as simple as that" (Samuel Eliot Morison, *Admiral of the Ocean Sea: A Life of Christopher Columbus* [Boston: Little, Brown, 1942], 106–107). This view is supported by the recent study of Spanish practices before 1492: In the Spanish invasion of Majorca, we are told, "A pattern was established which remained influential throughout the history of the expansion of the Crown of Aragon—indeed, in some respects, throughout the history of western Mediterranean expansion generally. The problems were not considered in advance" (Felipe Fernández-Armesto, *Before Columbus: Exploration and Colonization from the Mediterranean to the Atlantic, 1229–1492* [Philadelphia: University of Pennsylvania Press, 1987], 18). I might add that in his letter to Santangel, Columbus supplements the language of legal possession with the language of occupation.

[7]In an important unpublished paper, Patricia Seed suggests that the Spanish term *tomar posesión* (and the Portuguese *tomar posse*) did not have the same meaning as the English "to take possession." "Possession" in Elizabethan royal patents such as that granted to Sir Humphrey Gilbert and Sir Walter Raleigh means to "have, hold, occupy and enjoy," and to wield over the territory so held "full power to dispose thereof . . . according to the lawes of England." In Spanish usage, Seed argues, the phrase *"tomar posesión"* referred to the repertory of symbolic actions and formulaic pronouncements. The difference is reflected in Elizabeth's response to Spanish complaints against Francis Drake. According to William Camden, the queen denied that the Spanish had established "possession": Spaniards, she said, "had touched here and there upon the Coasts, built Cottages, and given Names to a River or Cape which does not entitle them to ownership; . . . Prescription without possession is worth little [*cum praescriptio sine possessione haud valeat*]" (William Camden, *Rerum Anglicarvm et hibernicarvm Annales regnante Elisabetha* [London: Ludwig Batarorvm, 1639], 328). The actions that Elizabeth characterizes as mere "prescription" are precisely what the Spanish seem to have meant by "taking possession."

[8] Christopher Dawson (ed.), *The Mongol Mission: Narratives and Letters of the Franciscan Missionaries in Mongolia and China in the Thirteenth and Fourteenth Centuries* (London: Sheed & Ward, 1955), 93.

[9] The Sahara is in some way a similar obstacle, but there had been, of course, many contacts over the centuries, esp. along the coasts of Africa.

[10] *Diario* 63–65. Morison translates *escrivano* as "secretary"; other translations render it "ship's clerk," "recorder," and "purser." The *escrivano* was also an "officer of the court"; as such, his testimony was equal to that of three other witnesses (see Stanley S. Jados, *Consulate of the Sea and Related Documents* [Tuscaloosa: University of Alabama Press, 1975], art. 330).

[11] Quoted in Arthur S. Keller, Oliver J. Lissitzyn, Frederick J. Mann, *Creation of Rights of Sovereignty through Symbolic Acts, 1400–1800* (New York: Columbia University Press, 1938), 39–40. For the Spanish text, see "Instrución que dió el Rey á Juan Diaz de Solís para el viage expresado," 24 de Nov., 1514, in Don Martin Fernandez de Navarrete (ed.), *Colección de los viages y descubrimientos que hicieron por mar los Españoles*, 5 vols. (Buenos Aires: Editorial Guarania, 1945; orig. pub. 1825), iii. 149–50.

[12] Keller et al. 41.

[13] Ibid. 35.

[14] On Hispaniola, on December 12, Columbus had his men raise "a large cross at the western side of the entrance to the harbor on a conspicuous height, as a sign, he says, that Your Highnesses claim the land as your own, and chiefly as a sign of Jesus Christ Our Lord and in honor of Christianity" (*Diario*, 219).

[15] *Journals and Other Documents on the Life and Voyages of Christopher Columbus*, trans. and ed. Samuel Eliot Morison (New York: Heritage Press, 1963), 27.

[16] After describing the ritual, the logbook entry goes on to say, "Soon many people of the island gathered there" (*Diario*, 65). Given the Arawaks' timidity, it is possible that they kept their distance at this point.

[17] Michel de Certeau, *The Writing of History*, trans. Tom Conley (New York: Columbia University Press, 1988), 212.

[18] It is remotely conceivable that the phrase was intended to include the Spanish as well as the natives, since it was certainly possible for Columbus to imagine a Spaniard who would dispute his authority. But the principal reference must be to the inhabitants of the land whose possession is being claimed.

[19] For a useful collection of legal texts bearing on the possession of Indian lands in North America, see Charles M. Haar and Lance Liebman, *Property and Law* (Boston: Little, Brown, 1977).

[20] *Institutes* II. i. 40. This passage is cited by Francisco de Vitoria in his brilliant review of the Spanish (and, more generally, the European) claims to the Indies. See James Brown Scott, *The Spanish Origin of International Law: Francisco de Vitoria and His Law of Nations* (Oxford: Clarendon Press, 1934), p. xxxiii.

[21] *Digest* 41. 2. 6.

[22] Accursius, *Glossa ordinaria*, on *Digest* 41.2.6. I am indebted for this reference to Laurent Mayali.

[23] *The Letter of Columbus on the Discovery of America* (New York: Lenox Library, 1892), 19.

[24] This is an instance of the situation Jean-François Lyotard has called the "differend": "the case where the plaintiff is divested of the means to argue and becomes for that reason a victim" (*The Differend: Phrases in Dispute*, trans. Georges Van Den Abbeele [Minneapolis: University of Minnesota Press, 1988], 9). A differend—rather than simply a difference—between two parties takes place, Lyotard explains, "when the 'regulation' of the conflict that opposes them is done in the idiom of one of the parties while the wrong suffered by the other is not signified in that idiom" (p. 9). Columbus and the Arawak are an extreme version of such a case. But it would not necessarily have been better had Columbus recognized the incommensurability of Spanish and native cultural constructions of reality. For such a recognition was in the early sixteenth century precisely the argument of those who sought

to deny the natives any right to have rights. Thus, as Anthony Pagden points out, the jurist Palacios Rubios had argued in 1513 that a society that did not possess property relations (and hence did not live within a legitimate civil community) could not for that reason claim on behalf of any of its individuals *dominium rerum* when confronted by invaders attempting to seize their lands. In other words, a full recognition of the profound disparity between the indigenous culture and that of the invaders would not necessarily lead to what we regard as equity: on the contrary, it could lead to a justification for seizure. See, similarly, the argument made in 1550 by Juan Ginés de Sepúlveda that "since no Indian society had had a monetary economy, no Indian could be said to have exercised any rights over any precious metal. These were, therefore, still a common part of Adam's patrimony, to which the Spaniards had a high moral claim by having traded metals which had been useless in the ancient Indian world for such useful things as iron, European agricultural techniques, horses, donkeys, goats, pigs, sheep, and so on" (Anthony Pagden, "Dispossessing the Barbarian: the Language of Spanish Thomism and the Debate over the Property Rights of the American Indians," in *The Languages of Political Theory in Early-Modern Europe*, ed. Anthony Pagden [Cambridge: Cambridge University Press, 1987], 81, 92).

[25] For an illuminating discussion of the problem of cultural incompatibility, see Don F. McKenzie, "The Sociology of a Text: Oral Culture, Literacy and Print in Early New England," *The Social History of Language*, ed. Peter Burke and Roy Porter (Cambridge: Cambridge University Press, 1987), 161–96.

[26] Vitoria's refutation of the claim in the 1530s is worth quoting:

This title, too, is insufficient. This appears, in the first place, because fear and ignorance, which vitiate every choice, ought to be absent. But they were markedly operative in the cases of choice and acceptance under consideration, for the Indians did not know what they were doing; nay, they may not have understood what the Spaniards were seeking. Further, we find the Spaniards seeking it in armed array from an unwarlike and timid crowd. Further, inasmuch as the aborigines, as said above, had real lords and princes, the populace could not procure new lords without other reasonable cause, this being to the hurt of their former lords. Further, on the other hand, these lords themselves could not appoint a new prince without the assent of the populace. Seeing, then, that in such cases of choice and acceptance as these there are not present all the requisite elements of a valid choice, the title under review is utterly inadequate and unlawful for seizing and retaining the provinces in question. (xxxiii–xxxiv)

[27] See Richard Epstein, "Possession as the Root of Title," in *Georgia Law Review* 13 (1979), 1221–43; Carol M. Rose, "Possession as the Origin of Property," *University of Chicago Law Review* 51 (1985), 73 ff.

[28] Closed formalism is in fact one step beyond the marriage ritual whose formulaic phrases after all are actually spoken in the presence of those who could, if they wished, "speak now." Columbus's required declarations are presumably made in the present tense, but their actual orientation is the future perfect: they are directed to those who will have heard that they were already made. The future perfect tense is a highly serviceable, if often unacknowledged, device in legal ritual.

[29] "Narrative," writes Lyotard, "is perhaps the genre of discourse within which the heterogeneity of phrase regimens, and even the heterogeneity of genres of discourse, have the easiest time passing unnoticed. . . . The narrative function is redeeming in itself. It acts as if the occurrence, with its potentiality of differends, could come to completion, or as if there were a last word" (*The Differend*, 151).

[30] Francisco de Vitoria, in *The Spanish Origin of International Law*, ed. Scott, pp. xxiv–xxv.

[31] See Anthony Pagden, *The Fall of Natural Man: The American Indian and the Origins of Comparative Ethnology* (Cambridge: Cambridge University Press, 1982). Pagden's remarkable book makes it clear that the most sustained and intellectually coherent challenge to the

Spanish claim to possession was mounted on formal principles by Spanish jurists and theologians.

[32]Gonzalo Fernandez de Oviedo y Valdes, *General and Natural History of the Indies,* trans. Earl Raymond Hewitt and Theodor Terrones, 2 vols. (Madrid: Royal Academy of History, 1851), i. 36–40 [I. I. I. iii].

[33]Pagden, *The Fall of Natural Man,* 30.

[34]Giuliano Gliozzi, *Adamo e il nuovo mondo. La nascita dell'antropologia come ideologia coloniale: dalle genealogie bibliche alle teorie razziali (1500–1700)* (Florence: La nuova Italia editrice, 1976), 47. "O the profound wisdom and knowledge of the Most High," writes Rocha, "that after so many centuries ordained that these islands would be returned by Columbus to the Spanish crown."

[35]See ibid. 15–48. The evidence for the Welsh claim includes Montezuma's testimony that he and his people are descended from foreigners, along with what seemed to a Welsh observer the obvious linguistic parallels. (Cf. *New American World, A Documentary History of North America to 1612,* ed. David Beers Quinn, 5 vols. [New York: Arno Press and Hector Bye, 1979], i. 66–68.)

[36]Montezuma is said to have asked Cortés why the strangers had such a hunger for gold, and Cortés is said to have replied that Spaniards had a disease about the heart, for which the only cure was gold.

[37]The drive to bring experience under discursive control is inseparable from the task of ethical justification and legitimation. The disastrous epidemic diseases that afflicted the Indians may ultimately have proved a more decisive historical factor than the Spanish atrocities, but the ethically compelling concern is an inner account of what guides actions, that is, an account of intentions. I should add that sixteenth-century observers attempted to moralize the epidemic diseases in a variety of ways: as God's punishment of pagan unbelief, for example, or as the horrible consequence of Spanish cruelty. These moralizations may be understood as attempts to understand and hence imaginatively control the natural. Post-Enlightenment strategies for achieving such control have centered on science rather than religious polemic and have characteristically involved searching for cures (or at least medical causes) on the one hand and searching for means to inflict disease (through biological agents) on the other.

[38]J. L. Austin, *How to Do Things with Words,* ed. J. O. Urmson and Marina Sbisà (Cambridge, Mass.: Harvard University Press, 1975). See also the remarks of John Searle about the conditions that must be met for a declaration, proclamation or any speech act that involves a "double direction of fit" (the world to the word and the word to the world) to be valid (John Searle and Daniel Vanderverken, *Foundations of Illocutionary Logic* [Cambridge: Cambridge University Press, 1985], 52 ff.)

[39]It is not entirely clear whom the Spanish imagined the Grand Khan to be or how they conceived of his rule, but it is clear that they imagined that there was some kind of empire with a centralized authority structure.

[40]*Select Documents,* ed. Jane, i. 14 (*su mayoral ó rey*). Men, Columbus writes, appear generally to be content with one woman, but the chief is given as many as twenty wives. And these wives, he implies, have economic value: "It appears to me that the women work more than the men." Columbus is uncertain, however, if this social arrangement entails a notion of private property: "I have not been able to learn if they hold private property [*bienes propios*]; what seemed to me to appear was that, in that which one had, all took a share, especially of eatable things" (i. 14).

[41]Quoted in Etienne Grisel, "The Beginnings of International Law and General Public Law Doctrine: Francisco de Vitoria's *De Indiis prior,*" in *First Images of America: The Impact of the New World on the Old,* ed. Fredi Chiappelli, 2 vols. (Berkeley: University of California Press, 1976), I. 309. See also Pagden, for a wonderfully detailed and intelligent discussion of the categories at issue here.

[42]*Select Documents,* ed. Jane, ii. 66.

[43] For the texts of the two drafts of this famous papal bull, see *Bullarum diplomatum et privilegiorum sanctorum romanorum pontificum* (Rome: Franco and Henrico Dalmazzo, 1858).

[44] *Politics*, 1253a, 28–29.

[45] In the letter to Santangel, Columbus mentions an island he calls "Quaris," which is inhabited "by a people who are regarded in all the islands as very fierce and who eat human flesh" (i. 14). On Columbus's perceptions of cannibalism, see the remarkable book by Peter Hulme, *Colonial Encounters: Europe and the Native Caribbean, 1492–1797* (London: Methuen, 1986); Michael Palencia-Roth, "Cannibalism and the New Man of Latin America in the fifteenth- and sixteenth-century European Imagination," in *Comparative Civilizations Review* 12 (1985), 1–27.

[46] Earlier in the letter he casually mentions that he "understood sufficiently from other Indians, *whom I had already taken,* that this land was nothing but an island" (i. 4) (emphasis added). And in his journal entry for October 12, 1492, he writes, "Our Lord pleasing, at the time of my departure I will take six of them from here to Your Highnesses that they may learn to speak" (*Diario,* 69). . . .

[47] See Bartolomé de Las Casas, *History of the Indies,* trans. Andrée M. Collard (New York: Harper & Row, 1971), 127.

[48] See Alain Milhou, *Colón y su mentalidad mesianica,* 289: "El 'negocio' o la 'negociación' de las Indias tiene, como la palabra 'empresa,' unas connotactiones dobles: una mercantil, la del mundo de los 'negocios' en que se crió Colón, pero también otra religiosa, la del *negotium crucis* de los cruzados as cual equiparaba su 'negocio' ultramarino. . . ."

[49] For the paradoxicality of Christian imperialism, see the letter on the third voyage: "I came with the mission to your royal presence, as being the most exalted of Christian princes and so ardently devoted to the Faith and to its increase. . . . On this matter I spent six or seven years of deep anxiety, expounding, as well as I could, how great service might in this be rendered to the Lord, by proclaiming abroad His holy name and His faith to so many peoples, which was all a thing of so great excellence and for the fair fame of great princes and for a notable memorial for them. It was needful also to speak of the temporal gain therein. . . ." (ii. I). It is possible, of course, to see such passages as evidence not of paradox but of unresolved tension, comparable to the class tension explored with great intelligence by David Quint in "The Boat of Romance and Renaissance Epic" (*Romance: Generic Transformation from Chrétien de Troyes to Cervantes,* ed. Kevin and Marina Brownlee [Hanover, NH: University Press of New England, 1985], 178–202). Quint argues that the central contradiction was between an aristocratic account of the voyages of discovery and a "bourgeois" account; the former allied itself with epic, the latter with romance. Columbus seems to me to combine both with a reckless disregard for literary decorum.

[50] Claude Lévi-Strauss quotes (or paraphrases) the finding of the commission of the monks of the Order of St. Jerome in 1517: the Indian "is better off as a slave, among men, than as an animal on his own" (*Tristes Tropiques,* trans. John Russell [New York: Atheneum, 1961; orig. pub. 1955], 80).

[51] "Because we wish to be informed by civil lawyers, canonists and theologians whether we may, with a good conscience, sell these Indians or not" (Pagden, *Fall of Natural Man,* 31). Pagden notes that one year later the queen "ordered all the Indian slaves in Seville to be taken from their masters and sent back to their former homes."

[52] In his logbook entry for October 12, Columbus also emphasizes that the Indians were friendly, so friendly in fact "that it was a marvel" [*quedarō tanto nro(s?) q̄ era maravilla*] (*Diario,* 64–65).

[53] There are obviously some parallels between the role of the marvelous in the early literature of discovery and the stylistic feature of contemporary Latin American writing, known as the *"real maravilloso."* See J. Edgardo Rivera Martínez, "La literatura geografica del siglo xvi en Francia como antecedente de lo real maravilloso," in *Revista de Critica Litteraria Latinoamericana* 5/9 (1979), 7–19. But my aim is to insist on the very specific purposes served by the marvelous in late fifteenth- and early sixteenth-century writing.

[54]Columbus appears to have been fluent in Castilian (all of his surviving writings, including letters he wrote to Italian correspondents, are in Castilian), and he had what by our standards would be reasonably impressive linguistic gifts. See Pauline Watts, "Prophecy and Discovery": "Columbus did not have the advanced, specialized education of a professional academic. But he did read and annotate works composed in Latin (for example, d'Ailly's *Imago mundi* and Pius II's *Historia*), Castilian (Alfonso de Palencia's translation of Plutarch's *Lives*), and Italian (Cristoforo Landino's translation of Pliny's *Naturalis historia*)," 75. See likewise V. I. Milani, *The Written Language of Christopher Columbus* (Buffalo: State University of New York at Buffalo [for *Forum Italicum*], 1973) and Paolo Emilia Taviani, *Christopher Columbus: The Grand Design,* trans. Taviani and William Weaver (London: Orbis, 1985). It is very unlikely that Columbus could not, if he had wished, have found a synonym for "marvelous."

[55]Jane's rendering of *"maravillarme"* as "to cause you to wonder" may be misleading. The phrase appears to mean "to show or perform my wonder."

[56]Jacques Le Goff, *L'Imaginaire médiéval* (Paris: Gallimard, 1985), 17–39.

[57]See esp. Baxter Hathaway, *Marvels and Commonplaces: Renaissance Literary Criticism* (New York: Random House, 1968), 133–51. See also Hathaway's *The Age of Criticism: The Late Renaissance in Italy* (Ithaca, NY: Cornell University Press, 1962). Le Goff, however, denies the ultimate compatibility of Christianity and the marvelous: "Si je simplifiais ma réflexion sur le merveilleux dans l'Occident médiéval jusqu'à la caricature, je dirais qu'en définitive il n'y a pas de merveilleux chrétien et que le christianisme, en tout case le christianisme médiéval, est allergique au merveilleux" (*L'Imaginaire médiéval,* 37).

[58]i. 12; cf. the skeptical remark by Andrés Bernáldez, who believes that these stories are told by some Indians in mockery of others who wear clothing (i. 128).

[59]Samuel Eliot Morison's translation of this passage (*Admiral of the Ocean Sea: A Life of Christopher Columbus* [Boston: Little, Brown, 1942], 309–10) is rather more flattering to men: the mermaids "were not as beautiful as they are painted, although to some extent they have a human appearance in the face."

[60]In the *Diario,* Columbus repeatedly uses the term *"maravilla"* and its variants to characterize the natural features of the world he has discovered: the trees and fish (Oct. 16), the groves and the birdsong, and the diversity, size, and difference of the birds (Oct. 21), the sheer number of islands (Nov. 14), the harbors (Nov. 26), the fields and the general beauty of the lands and the trees (Nov. 27), the beauty of a harbor (Dec. 6), the beauty of a river (Dec. 7), the valleys, rivers, and good water (Dec. 16), the green mountains (Dec. 21), the green and cultivated mountains (Jan. 9).

[61]In fact the highest peak on Teneriffe is considerably higher than the highest peak on Hispaniola.

[62]Columbus (or, alternatively, Las Casas) evidently regards the point as worth repeating. In the same entry, he writes, "all or most of the Indians began to run to the town, which must have been near, to bring him more food and parrots and other things of those that they had, with such open hearts that it was a marvel" (*Diario,* 259).

[63]There is at least a latent polemical irony in this passage that makes one suspect that Las Casas is exercising a more active, shaping presence in the transcription than he admits, but in the absence of the original text there is no way of confirming the suspicion.

[64]Several logbook entries record this Indian belief and thereby seem to indicate that Columbus had some curiosity about the native view of the encounter. On Oct. 21, Columbus notes that "it is true that any little thing given to them, as well as our coming, they considered great marvels; and they believed that we had come from the heavens" (*Diario,* 109). Columbus does not quite put the two observations together and reflect that they might well treasure even almost worthless articles—bits of broken crockery, cheap cloth, rusted nails—if they believe that the givers come from the heavens. Why doesn't he put them together? Perhaps because it would have led to the ironic self-recognition so characteristic of Mandeville—just as we collect the relics (bits of wood supposedly from the cross, nails, shriv-

eled pieces of skin, and so forth) associated with those we regard as sanctified, so do these people collect relics from us.

On Nov. 5, Columbus notes similarly, "The Indians touched them and kissed their hands and feet, marveling [*maravillandose*] and believing that the Spaniards came from the heavens, and so they gave them to understand" (*Diario*, 137). The last phrase, in Las Casas's transcription, is ambiguous, but it would seem to mean that the Spanish gave the Indians to understand that they, the Spanish, came from the heavens; if so, we are dealing not with a naive misapprehension on the part of the natives but with an improvisatory lie.

In an important article on Cabeza de Vaca's *Naufragios* (in *Representations* 33 [1991], 163–99), Rolena Adorno suggests that the misapprehension was Spanish rather than Indian. She observes that the "interpreters of Columbus's text, from Las Casas to Don Hernando Colón and Hernán Perez de Oliva, all claim that the natives meant that the Spaniards "came down from heaven.'" But she notes that in a phrase dropped from later editions Cabeza de Vaca offers a more plausible gloss; he writes that "Among all these peoples, it was held for very certain that we came from the sky, because about all the things that they do not understand nor have information regarding their origins, they say that such phenomena come from the sky" (183).

[65]Columbus does not seem greatly interested in disabusing the natives of their mistaken beliefs about the Spanish, though he does tell them that he comes from another kingdom and not from heaven. When, on the second voyage, he explains to an Indian cacique that he serves the rulers of that kingdom, the cacique is surprised: "And the Indian, greatly marvelling [*muy maravillado*], replied to the interpreter, saying: 'How? Has this admiral another lord, and does he yield obedience?' And the Indian interpreter said: 'To the king and to the queen of Castile, who are the greatest sovereigns in the world.' And forthwith he recounted to the cacique and to the old man and to all the other Indians the things which he had seen in Castile and the marvels of Spain, and told them of the great cities and fortresses and churches, and of the people and horses and animals, and of the great nobility and wealth of the sovereigns and great lords, and of the kinds of food, and of the festivals and tournaments which he had seen, and of bull-fighting, and of that which he had learned of the wars" (i. 154). It is possible that Columbus regarded the arousal of wonder in the Indians as a potential source of power. Other writers in the period anticipate that such an arousal would lead to domination: see, for example, Hieronymus Müntzer's letter to D. Joao II (1493): "O what glory you would gain, if you made the habitable Orient known to the Occident, and what profits would its commerce give you, for you would make those islands of the Orient tributaries, and their kings amazed [*sus reyes maravillados*] would quietly submit to your sovereignty!" (in Morison, *Admiral of the Ocean Sea*, 77).

[66]We can also cite Andrés Bernáldez, with whom Columbus stayed on his return from the second voyage, and to whom he supplied information about the discoveries. Bernáldez notes that the Spanish saw "more than a million and a half cormorants" all together in the sky and were amazed (*obieron por maravilla*) (i. 148). See, likewise, the "marvelous" pastoral scene by the fountain (i. 132).

[67]On Columbus and the location of Paradise, see Alain Milhou, *Colón y su mentalidad mesianica*, 407 ff.

[68]Vitoria considers the possibility of a Spanish title to the Indies based upon a "special grant from God." He concludes that "it would be hazardous to give credence to one who asserts a prophecy against the common law and against the rules of scripture, unless his doctrine were confirmed by miracles." Columbus, of course, explicitly claims that the discovery of the Indies had been prophesied by Isaiah and others, but he seems wary of claiming miraculous confirmation. Vitoria does not believe anyone has made the latter claim: "Now, no such [miracles] are adduced by prophets of this type" (p. xxxiv). See Etienne Grisel, "The Beginnings of International Law," in *First Images of America*, i. 312.

Las Casas does, however, quote Columbus as saying, upon the discovery of Trinidad, that God's "exalted power guides me, and in such manner that He receives much service and your highnesses much pleasure, since it is certain that the discovery of this land in this place was as great a miracle as the discovery of land on the first voyage" (Jane, ii. 13n.). In Spanish writing of the period, however, *"maravilla"* could on occasion function as the equivalent of miracle. See, for example, the anti-Semitic passage by the Franciscan Juan de Pineda: "Llegado a Jerusalén, restaurará el templo de Salomón, en el cual . . . se sentará blasfemando de la divinidad del Redentor; y con esto se le darán los judios sus parientes muy obedientes, y habiendo él destruido los lugares sanctos, donde nuestro Redentor hizo sus maravillas, enviará sus mensajeros por el mundo . . ." (quoted in Milhou, 446).

[69] Quoted in J. V. Cunningham, *Woe or Wonder: The Emotional Effect of Shakespearean Tragedy* (Denver: Denver University Press, 1951), 82.

[70] *Enneades,* I. 6. 4, quoted in Cunningham, 67.

[71] Hathaway, 66–69. Hathaway's account of Patrizi is taken largely from Bernard Weinberg, *A History of Literary Criticism in the Italian Renaissance,* 2 vols. (Chicago: University of Chicago Press, 1961). See Francesco Patrizi, *Della poetica,* ed. Danilo Aguzzi Barbagli (Florence, Istituto nazionale di studi sul Rinascimento, 1969–71), vol. ii. For Patrizi, the poet is not only a *"factore del mirabile"* but also a *"mirabile facitore"* (Weinberg, ii. 773).

[72] For Robortelli, Weinberg writes, "in the last analysis, the poet is virtually permitted to discard all concern for credibility in order to exploit all the available means of achieving the marvelous and the pleasure connected with it" (Weinberg, i. 397–98).

[73] *Poetica d'Aristotele vulgarizzata et sposta* (1570), quoted in Weinberg, i. 69. Castelvetro's theory, like that of many of his contemporaries, is centrally concerned with the problem of obtaining the credence of the audience—this rhetorical motive is what makes their analysis so interesting in the context of the New World discourse, concerned as it was with a comparable problem and willing to alter the truth to achieve its effect: "In all such considerations of historical truth or natural probability or necessity and verisimilitude, the primary aim is not the imitation of nature for the sake of making the poem resemble nature but rather the resemblance to nature for the sake of obtaining the credence of the audience" (ibid., i. 58).

[74] *Discorso in difesa della 'Commedia' del divino poeta Dante* (1572), in Allan H. Gilbert, *Literary Criticism: Plato to Dryden* (Detroit: Wayne State University Press, 1962), 371. Cf. Lorenzo Giacomini: tragedy "pleases through the marvelous, demonstrating that a thing not believed can readily come to pass" (*Sopra la purgazione della tragedia* [1586]), in Weinberg, i. 628.

[75] *Discorsi del poema heroico* (c. 1575–80), in Weinberg, i. 341. Tasso, Weinberg writes, "thinks of the marvelous as consisting of those events which do not enter into natural probability. How, then, can they be credible and acceptable in the poem? The answer is in the beliefs, even the faith, of the audience. For Christians believe the miracles of the Bible, know them to be true even though they are improbable. This is the only kind of credibility which the poet seeks" (i. 630). One might note, for a pagan precedent, Aristotle's remark that "there is a probability of things happening also against probability" (*Poetics* 25. 1461^{b}15).

[76] All of these positions may be found in Hathaway, passim.

[77] It is important to recognize that this use of the term "marvelous" is not Columbus's individual signature; it is the mark of a shared emotional effect and a common rhetoric. Hence, for example, Dr. Chanca who accompanied Columbus on the second voyage notes that the natives "have many tools, such as hatchets and axes, made of stone, so handsome and so fashioned, that it is marvelous how they are able to make them without iron" (i. 68). Even when Chanca expresses distaste for the natives, he does so in the idiom of the marvelous. "These people," he writes, "are so degraded (*tan bestial*) that they have not intelligence enough to seek out a suitable place in which to live. As for those who live on the shore, it is marvelous how barbarously they build [*es maravilla cuan bestialmente edifcan*]" (i. 52). It is striking, however, how infrequently Columbus uses the language of the marvelous to express, as Chanca does here, his disapproval or disdain.

[78] In the years that followed, both were in fact called forth: the tears of Las Casas, on the one hand; the laughter of those stories of Indians declaring that the Pope was drunk or mad to think that he could give away what was not his.

[79] Albertus Magnus, trans. in J. V. Cunningham, *Woe and Wonder* (Denver: Denver Uni-

versity Press, 1951), 79–80. I am greatly indebted to Cunningham's account of wonder. The intensity of the experience Albertus Magnus is attempting to define seems to me somewhat greater in the original:

> Nam omnes homines qui nunc in nostro tempore et primum ante nostra tempora philosophati sunt, non sunt moti ad philosophandum nisi admirative. Admirationem autem vocamus agoniam et suspensionem cordis in stuporem prodigii magni in sensum apparentis, ita quod cor systolem patitur. Proper quod etiam admiratio aliquid simile habet timori in motus cordis, qui est ex suspensione. Hujus igitur motus admirationis in agonia et systole cordis est ex suspensione desiderii ad cognoscendam causam entis quod apparet prodigii: et ideo a principio cum adhuc rudes philosophari inceperunt, mirantes erant quaedam dubitabilium quae paratiora erant ad solvendum, sicut Pythagorici de numerorum passionibus, est de pari et impari, et perfecto et abundanti et diminuto numero. . . . Qui autem dubitant et admiratus, ignorans videtur: est enim admiratio motus ignorantis procedentis ad inquirendum, ut sciat causam ejus de quo miratus: cujus signum est, quia ipse Philomithes secundum hunc modum Philosophus est: quia fabula sua construitur ab ipso ex mirandis. (vi. 30)

(In Albertus Magnus, *Opera Omnia,* ed. Augustus Borgnet, 20 vols. [Paris: Ludovicus Vives, 1890] vi. 39 [I Metaphysicorum, tract. II, caput vi].)

[80] In a response to the version of this chapter that I delivered at the University of Chicago, Professor Arnold Davidson suggested that it is important not to confound the theology of the marvelous in Albertus Magnus with the aesthetics of the marvelous that I have earlier discussed. For the poet, the arousal of wonder is one of the ends of art; for Albertus wonder is used up and vanishes when the mind actually comes to understand those phenomena by which it has been seized. The distinction seems to me significant, but I have argued here that it is deconstructed by the actual historical circumstances in which Columbus found himself. We may, in effect, take the vanishing of wonder to be a model for the way in which legal title absorbs the potentially disruptive power of the marvelous, a power that in these extraordinary circumstances legal formality none the less needs in order to make up for the deficiency at its center.

[81] George R. Stewart, *Names on the Land: A Historical Account of Place-Naming in the United States,* rev. edn. (Boston: Houghton Mifflin, 1958), 12. Stewart cites the "Instrucción dada por el Rey à Pedrarias Dávila": "Arrived here by good providence, first of all you must give a name to the country as a whole, and to the cities, towns, and places."

[82] *Luther's Works,* vol. i: "Lectures on Genesis," chaps. 1–5, ed. Jaroslav Pelikan (St. Louis: Concordia Publishing House, 1958), 119.

[83] Francis Bacon, in *A Selection of His Works,* ed. Sidney Warhaft (New York: Odyssey, 1965), 21.

[84] It is then a renaming such as the renaming of Jacob after his struggle with the mysterious man. "He said to Jacob, 'What is your name?' and he answered, 'Jacob.' The man said, 'Your name shall no longer be Jacob, but Israel, because you strove with God and with men, and prevailed'" (Gen. 32:27–29). Such a context would place Columbus in the position of the messenger of God.

[85] See Rudolf Schnackenburg, *Baptism in the Thought of St. Paul,* trans. G. R. Beasley-Murray (New York: Herder & Herder, 1964), 20: "The naming of a person had the meaning of attaching the baptized to this person so that the baptized belonged to him. This is confirmed by exegesis; for the consequence and effect of baptism 'in the name' of Christ may be gathered from a consideration of Paul's assertion, 'you belong to Christ.'" (I owe this reference to Michael Ragussis.)

[86] Morison, *Admiral,* 360.

[87] See Paolo Emilio Taviani, *Christopher Columbus* (Paris, 1980), 38–40. Columbus's son Ferdinand wrote about the 'mystery' of his father's name and linked that mystery to the original baptism: "If we consider the common surname of his forebears, we may say that he

was truly Columbus or Dove, because he carried the grace of the Holy Ghost to that New World which he discovered, showing those people who knew Him not Who was God's beloved son, as the Holy Ghost did in the figure of a dove when St. John baptized Christ; and because over the waters of the ocean, like the dove of Noah's ark, he bore the olive branch and oil of baptism, to signify that those people who had been shut up in the ark of darkness and confusion were to enjoy peace and union with the Church" (quoted in Pauline Moffitt Watts, "Prophecy and Discovery," 101).

[88] *First Images,* ii. 619.

[89] See Columbus's *Libro de las profecías,* in *Raccolta di documenti e studi pubblicati dalla R. Commissione Colombiana pel quarto centenario dalla scoperta dell'America* (Rome: Ministero Sella pubblica istruzione, 1894), pt. I, vol. ii, *Scritti di Cristoforo Colombo,* ed. C. de Lollis, 76–160. In the unfinished letter to the Catholic monarchs with which he intended to introduce the *Book of Prophecies,* Columbus says that his decision to sail westward was inspired by the Holy Ghost:

> Animated by a heavenly fire, I came to your highnesses: all who heard of my enterprise mocked at it; all the sciences I had acquired profited me nothing; seven years did I pass in your royal court, disputing the case with persons of great authority and learned in all the arts, and in the end they decided that all was vain. In your highnesses alone remained faith and constancy. Who will doubt that this light was from the Holy Scriptures, illuminating you as well as myself with rays of marvelous brightness? [*con rrayos de claridad maravillosos*]

(Trans. in John Leddy Phelan, *The Millennial Kingdom of the Franciscans in the New World,* 2nd rev. edn. [Berkeley: University of California Press, 1970], 20. For the original see *Raccolta di Documenti,* 79–80.)

On Columbus and prophecy, see Pauline Moffitt Watts, "Prophecy and Discovery," 73–102; Marjorie Reeves, *Joachim di Fiore and the Prophetic Future* (London: SPCK, 1976), 128–29. On his deathbed, Columbus took the habit of a Franciscan.

[90] For the notion of the land "conforming" to the name, see Columbus's relation of his third voyage: "I called this place there *Jardines,* for it corresponded to that name [*porque así conforman por el nombre*]" (Jane, ii. 24). See, similarly, the naming of Trinidad (ii. 12). There is, of course, in such naming an element both of magical hope and of tactical cunning. For a candid glimpse of the latter, see Lopez Vaz (1586), in Purchas xii. 292: "The discoverer of these islands named them the Isles of Solomon, to the end that the Spaniards supposing them to be those Isles from whence Solomon fetched Gold to adorne the Temple at Jerusalem, might be the more desirous to goe and inhabit the same."

[91] ii. 90–92. The reference to the keys is paraphrased from Seneca's *Medea.* On Columbus and the figure of David there is a substantial literature, including a long-standing debate about the status of Judaism in Columbus's thought. See Alain Milhou, *Colón y su mentalidad mesianica,* esp. 230–51; Juan Gil, *Colón y la Casa Santa,* "Historiografía y Bibliografía Americanistas," E.E.H.A., 21 (1977), 125–35.

•   •   •   •   •   •   •   •   •   •   •

QUESTIONS FOR A SECOND READING

1. At a key point in the essay, Greenblatt acknowledges that of course the Europeans took possession of the New World by means of bullets and swords and microbes. These were "brute physical facts." But, Greenblatt says, he is a teacher of literature, and so also prepared to think about how language was

used to understand, to represent and to take possession of a "new" world that stood in a difficult relationship to European ways of thinking, speaking, and writing. He says,

> Moreover, if certain crucial aspects of the European encounter with the New World were beyond words (and beyond the comprehension of any of the participants), the Europeans themselves struggled to bring as much of their experience as possible under the control of discourse. How could they—or, for that matter, how could we—do otherwise? And it is not only as a futile attempt to comprehend the unimaginable that this discourse may interest us but as both an instrument of empire and an expression, however constrained and half-hearted, of resistance. (p. 279)

Greenblatt has an interesting and unusual way of talking about language: language as action, language as instrument. He refers not only to language but to "discourse," and in a later phrase, "discursive economy."

As you reread, pay close attention to how Greenblatt does what he does with the passages from Columbus's letters and journals. You will need, at some point, to be able to put a word like "discourse" to work in sentences of your own. You will need to talk about writing as discursive action—as a way of doing something and not simply reporting the "facts" of the world. You need to get a feel for how Greenblatt uses "discourse" and what it comes to mean for him. What *are* the discourses within which Columbus writes the story of the New World? Where do they come from? How do others, writers from Columbus's time and later, make use of them?

2. Greenblatt combines a historian's knowledge of the past (and of the texts that bring us the past) with a literary critic's skill in close reading and interpretation. The essay "Marvelous Possessions" offers a lesson in how to *write* a close reading of a text. You can see this in the way Greenblatt uses quotations—in the ways he prepares for them, sets them up, works them into his paragraphs, shows us (in a sense) how to read them, and follows with a discussion that refines or focuses our sense of what we have just read. He teaches us how to read, and he does this by writing us into a close encounter with passages he has chosen from the writing that is his subject. As you reread, pay particular attention to how Greenblatt uses quotations (both block quotations and intralinear quotations). See if you can derive from them a set of principles, strategies, or guidelines that you could use for your work as a writer.

3. You have the text of Greenblatt's essay to study. You also have its subtext or after-text, the endnotes—ninety-one of them! Take time to read through the notes as a text—that is, to read them from beginning to end. What story do they tell about a scholar and his work, his resources, and his interests? What work do notes *do* beyond the mere citing of page, title, and publication date? What can you learn from this example about the academy, its habits and values?

ASSIGNMENTS FOR WRITING

1. Greenblatt offers a powerful lesson in how to read the past. You can feel this in his command of the material and in the range of examples available to

him. You can also feel it in the demonstrations he provides, in the careful, close readings of long passages from Columbus's letters and journals (and from the texts that surround this work). He is arguing that Europeans took possession of the New World through acts of language, through writing. He shows how to read a text that seems at first glance to be "normal," to be transparent; he shows how to read that text as both strange or noteworthy and as a discursive act, as a complex way of working on the world.

Go back to the essay to look closely at both the ways Greenblatt talks about language and at one or two examples of his work with the passages that he cites. (The first two "Questions for a Second Reading" might be useful for this.) Then, to see if you can make a similar (or a contradictory) argument by performing a similar kind of reading, write an essay in which you take as your primary text one of the following:

a. Any text, including a recent one, that stands as an attempt by someone (or some group) to bring experience under the control of discourse (perhaps to "grasp the radical otherness" of people and/or places).

b. The following section of Columbus's journals:

> Sunday, Oct. 21st [1492]. At 10 o'clock, we arrived at a cape of the island, and anchored, the other vessels in company. After having dispatched a meal, I went ashore, and found no habitation save a single house, and that without an occupant; we had no doubt that the people had fled in terror at our approach, as the house was completely furnished. I suffered nothing to be touched, and went with my captains and some of the crew to view the country. This island even exceeds the others in beauty and fertility. Groves of lofty and flourishing trees are abundant, and also large lakes, surrounded and overhung by foliage, in a most enchanting manner. Everything looked as green as in April in Andalusia. The melody of the birds was so exquisite that one was never willing to part from the spot, and the flocks of parrots obscured the heavens. The diversity in the appearance of the feathered tribe from those of our country is extremely curious. A thousand different sorts of trees, with their fruit were to be met with, and of a wonderfully delicious odour. It was a great affliction to me to be ignorant of their natures, for I am very certain they are all valuable; specimens of them and of the plants I have preserved. Going round one of these lakes, I saw a snake, which we killed, and I have kept the skin for your Highnesses; upon being discovered he took to the water; whither we followed him, as it was not deep, and dispatched him with our lances; he was seven spans in length; I think there are many more such about here. I discovered also the aloe tree, and am determined to take on board the ship to-morrow, ten quintals of it, as I am told it is valuable. While we were in search of some good water, we came upon a village of the natives about half a league from the place where the ships lay; the inhabitants on discovering us abandoned their houses, and took to flight, carrying off their goods to the mountain. I ordered that nothing which they had left should be taken, not even the value of a pin. Presently we saw several of the natives advancing towards our party, and one of them came up to us, to whom we gave some hawk's bells and glass beads, with which he was delighted. We asked him in return, for water, and after I had gone on board the ship, the natives came down to the shore with their calabashes full, and showed great pleasure in presenting us with it. I ordered more glass beads to be given them, and they promised to return the next day. It is my wish to fill

all the water casks of the ships at this place, which being executed, I shall depart immediately, if the weather serve, and sail round the island, till I succeed in meeting with the king, in order to see if I can acquire any of the gold, which I hear he possesses. Afterwards I shall set sail for another very large island which I believe to be *Cipango*, according to the indications I receive from the Indians on board. They call the Island *Colba*, and say there are many large ships, and sailors there. This other island they name *Bosio*, and inform me that it is very large; the others which lie in our course, I shall examine on the passage, and according as I find gold or spices in abundance, I shall determine what to do; at all events I am determined to proceed on to the continent, and visit the city of *Guisay* where I shall deliver the letters of your Highnesses to the *Great Can*, and demand an answer, with which I shall return.

– from The Heath Anthology of American Literature,
ed. Paul Lauter et al. (1990), 1:70–71

c. The following essay, written by a college student when asked to write about other people and other places:

A few summers ago, I accompanied my church youth group on a mission trip to St. Croix, in the Virgin Islands. We were to clean up damage from a hurricane which passed through the summer before. To tell you the truth, I really wasn't looking forward to working, but rather I was excited to visit the Virgin Islands. But, by the end of my trip, I would not have traded my experience for anything in the world.

Our group flew from Philadelphia to Puerto Rico, and then to St. Croix. After arriving from a long plane trip we were driven to the place which for the next couple of weeks we would call home. We stayed on an old plantation which was located in the lower class part of St. Croix. The plantation was surrounded by a 15-foot-high stone wall, but on the other side of the wall were the slums. As we entered the driveway leading to the plantation, adults as well as children lined up. They all watched carefully, probably trying to figure out why we were on their island.

On the first day of our journey, we started by picking up trash and tree limbs which had fallen to the ground from the hurricane the year before. It was so incredible how much damage was done and how it appeared that the hurricane had just passed. This task took several days to accomplish, even in a small area. There were just so many things covering the ground it was just unbelievable.

From day to day, we came in contact with lots of people who had lived on the island for many years. Quickly, we learned how many of the islanders felt about people from the "States." Once, while we were working, a group of islanders approached us and inquired why we were there. They asked why we were intruding on their land when we had a land of our own which was better. It was almost as if they were afraid that we were trying to take their island from them. I could tell by their voice of inquiry that they felt threatened. Even after we tried to explain that we were trying to help them in a time of need, they still wanted to know what we expected in return. At this point in time, I felt shut out. They would not accept that the only reason that we were there was to help them.

Over the weeks we accomplished several tasks. These tasks included digging up 5-foot-diameter tree stumps, rebuilding roofs of homes which were blown off, picking up trash, and helping run a coffee shop for the homeless and less fortunate. All of these tasks were time-consuming and entailed much work. As we went to the different locations, I found the chance to talk to a lot of the islanders. They seemed very anxious to know my reasons for helping them. I explained that all my work was volunteer and that I liked to help others. Slowly they started to accept the fact that I, as well as the others, just wanted to befriend them. I witnessed their feelings starting to change toward us and soon they appreciated the work we had done.

As our time of service came to an end, I looked back on the huge difference which we had made on the island. After these several weeks, the islanders came to realize that we did not expect anything in return for our work, except their friendship. In the beginning, this concept was hard for them to understand, but as they watched the changes occur, they learned to appreciate our help. In fact, by the end, the many people who at one time had questioned our existence were the ones to tell us how sad they were to see us leave. They graciously thanked us over and over for our help. Their appreciation was unbelievable. They just constantly asked how they could pay us back. They praised the work which we had done and expressed their undying gratitude.

This change in our position in such a short amount of time was incredible. We went from being the unacceptable in their community to the heroes of the community. We were once looked down and frowned upon, but after working hard to prove our position we were more than accepted. Our efforts proved to change our position in that particular society and we became well-respected guests on the island.

2. Greenblatt argues that Europeans used conventional intellectual and organization structures to take possession of the New World. He writes at length about the "discourse of the marvelous." What is this discourse? What are its interests and its effects? Who uses it—when, why, and to what end?

But what about Greenblatt and, through him, us? What is he doing to Columbus and the New World in this text? In what ways might you define and locate his writing as discursive action? Has he made Columbus's logbook entries into something "marvelous"? Has he taken possession of them? Are they written into the narratives of discovery or commerce?

Write an essay in which you explain Greenblatt's account of the discourse of the marvelous. You should assume that you are writing to someone who has read "Marvelous Possessions," but not recently, and who does not have the text close at hand. And see if you can use this discussion of the "marvelous" as a way of thinking back on this text and its aims and intentions, on Greenblatt as a writer, and on the discourse, or discourses, at play in this genre of criticism.

MAKING CONNECTIONS

1. Stephen Greenblatt, in "Marvelous Possessions," looks at the ways the New World was written into narratives by European writers for European audiences. He says, for example,

> We can demonstrate that, in the face of the unknown, Europeans used their conventional intellectual and organizational structures, fashioned over centuries of mediated contact with other cultures, and that these structures greatly impeded a clear grasp of the radical otherness of the American lands and peoples. (p. 270)

Joan Didion, in "Sentimental Journeys" (p. 79), similarly looks at the ways the media write New York City into what she calls "sentimental narratives":

> The imposition of a sentimental, or false, narrative on the disparate and often random experience that constitutes the life of a city or a country means, necessarily, that much of what happens in that city or country will be rendered merely illustrative, a series of set pieces, or performance opportunities. (p. 100)

Are Didion and Greenblatt talking about the same thing? If so, how would you show this to be the case? (Does writing serve the same purposes in the 1990s that it did in the 1490s?) If not, what examples from the text might you use to make your case? How might you explain the difference between the "marvelous" and the "sentimental"?

Write an essay in which you examine the relationship between writing and experience (or language and the "real") as it is worked out by Greenblatt in his discussion of narratives of discovery and Didion in her discussion of narratives of New York. You should imagine that your reader is familiar with the issues and questions involved in these pieces but that your reader has not read these essays.

2. While Mary Louise Pratt does not write about Columbus in "Arts of the Contact Zone" (p. 528), she writes about moments of contact between Europe and the New World. And she offers a theoretical account of how writing functions at those moments. Her interest is in the writing produced from the other side, from the side of the natives or those who are put into a subordinate position in relationship to a dominant culture. (If the native Americans had written about or to Columbus, she would be interested in those documents.)

Stephen Greenblatt, in "Marvelous Possessions," is interested in texts written by Europeans about the New World and its inhabitants. And, in a sense, he also charts the "literate arts of the contact zone." Using Pratt's theory (of contact zones) and her terms (like "autoethnography") as points of reference, write an essay in which you discuss one or two of the long passages quoted in Greenblatt (or perhaps some of the images included in his chapter). What are the "literate arts" of the conquerers? How might you describe their characteristic practices? What connections can you make between the literate arts of the conquerors and those of the conquered?

SUSAN

GRIFFIN

*S*USAN GRIFFIN *(b. 1943) is a well-known and respected feminist writer, poet,*
essayist, lecturer, teacher, playwright, and filmmaker. She has published more
than twenty books, including an Emmy Award–winning play, Voices, *with a pref-*
ace by Adrienne Rich (1975); two books of poetry, Like the Iris of an Eye *(1976)*
and Unremembered Country *(1987); and four books of nonfiction that have be-*
come key feminist texts, Women and Nature: The Roaring inside Her *(1978),*
Rape: The Power of Consciousness *(1979),* Pornography and Silence: Culture's Revenge against Nature *(1981), and* A Chorus of Stones: The Private
Life of War *(1992).*

"Our Secret" is a chapter from Susan Griffin's moving and powerful book A
Chorus of Stones, *winner of the Bay Area Book Reviewers Association Award and*
a finalist for the Pulitzer Prize in nonfiction. The book explores the connections be-
tween present and past, public life and private life, an individual life and the lives of
others. Griffin writes, for example, "I do not see my life as separate from history. In
my mind my family secrets mingle with the secrets of statesmen and bombers." In
one section of the book she writes of her mother's alcoholism and her father's response
to it. In another she writes of her paternal grandmother, who was banished from the
family for reasons never spoken. Next to these she thinks about Heinrich Himmler,
head of the Nazi secret police, or Hugh Trenchard of the British Royal Air Force, who

introduced the saturation bombing of cities and civilians to modern warfare, or Wernher von Braun and the development of rockets and rocketry. "As I held these [figures and scenes] in my mind," she writes, "a certain energy was generated between them. There were two subjects but one theme: denying and bearing witness."

A Chorus of Stones combines the skills of a careful researcher working with the documentary records of war, the imaginative powers of a novelist entering the lives and experiences of those long dead, and a poet's attention to language. It is a remarkable piece of writing, producing in its form and style the very experience of surprise and connectedness that Griffin presents as the product of her research. "It's not a historian's history," she once told an interviewer. "What's in it is true, but I think of it as a book that verges on myth and legend, because those are the ways we find the deepest meanings and significance of events."

Griffin's history is not a historian's history; her sociology is not a sociologist's; her psychology is not written in conventional forms or registers. She is actively engaged in the key research projects of our time, providing new knowledge and new ways of thinking and seeing, but she works outside the usual forms and boundaries of the academic disciplines. There are other ways of thinking about this, she seems to say. There are other ways to do this work. Her book on rape, for example, ends with a collage of women's voices, excerpts from public documents, and bits and pieces from the academy.

"Our Secret" has its own peculiar structure and features—the sections in italics, for example. As a piece of writing, it proceeds with a design that is not concerned to move quickly or efficiently from introduction to conclusion. It is, rather, a kind of collage or collection of stories, sketches, anecdotes, fragments. While the sections in the essay are presented as fragments, the essay is not, however, deeply confusing or disorienting. The pleasure of the text, in fact, is moving from here to there, feeling a thread of connection at one point, being surprised by a new direction at another. The writing is careful, thoughtful, controlled, even if this is not the kind of essay that announces its thesis and then collects examples for support. It takes a different attitude toward examples—and toward the kind of thinking one might bring to bear in gathering them and thinking them through. As Griffin says, "the telling and hearing of a story is not a simple act." It is not simple and, as her writing teaches us, it is not straightforward. As you read this essay, think of it as a lesson in reading, writing, and thinking. Think of it as a lesson in working differently. And you might ask why it is that this kind of writing is seldom taught in school.

Our Secret

The nucleus of the cell derives its name from the Latin nux, *meaning nut. Like the stone in a cherry, it is found in the center of the cell, and like this stone, keeps its precious kernel in a shell.*

She is across the room from me. I am in a chair facing her. We sit together in the late darkness of a summer night. As she speaks the space between us grows larger. She has entered her past. She is speaking of her childhood. Her father. The war. Did I know her father fought in the Battle of the Bulge? What was it for him, this great and terrible battle? She cannot say. He never spoke of it at home. They knew so little, her mother, her brothers, herself. Outside, the sea has disappeared. One finds the water now only by the city lights that cease to shine at its edges. California. She moved here with her family when her father became the commander of a military base. There were nuclear missiles standing just blocks from where she lived. But her father never spoke about them. Only after many years away from home did she learn what these weapons were.

The first guided missile is developed in Germany, during World War II. It is known as the Vergeltungswaffe, *or the Vengeance weapon. Later, it will be called the V-1 rocket.*

She is speaking of another life, another way of living. I give her the name Laura here. She speaks of the time after the war, when the cold war was just beginning. The way we are talking now, Laura tells me, was not possible in her family. I nod in recognition. Certain questions were never answered. She learned what not to ask. She begins to tell me a story. Once when she was six years old she went out with her father on a long trip. It was not even a year since the war ended. They were living in Germany.

They drove for miles and miles. Finally they turned into a small road at the edge of a village and drove through a wide gate in a high wall. The survivors were all gone. But there were other signs of this event beyond and yet still within her comprehension. Shoes in great piles. Bones. Women's hair, clothes, stains, a terrible odor. She began to cry a child's frightened tears and then to scream. She had no words for what she saw. Her father admonished her to be still. Only years later, and in a classroom, did she find out the name of this place and what had happened here.

The shell surrounding the nucleus is not hard and rigid; it is a porous membrane. These pores allow only some substances to pass through them, mediating the movement of materials in and out of the nucleus.

• • •

Often I have looked back into my past with a new insight only to find that some old, hardly recollected feeling fits into a larger pattern of meaning. Time can be measured in many ways. We see time as moving forward and hope that by our efforts this motion is toward improvement. When the atomic bomb exploded, many who survived the blast say time stopped with the flash of light and was held suspended until the ash began to descend. Now, in my mind, I can feel myself moving backward in time. I am as if on a train. And the train pushes into history. This history seems to exist somewhere, waiting, a foreign country behind a border and, perhaps, also inside me. From the windows of my train, I can see what those outside do not see. They do not see each other, or the whole landscape through which the track is laid. This is a straight track, but still there are bends to fit the shape of the earth. There are even circles. And returns.

The missile is guided by a programmed mechanism. There is no electronic device that can be jammed. Once it is fired it cannot stop.

It is 1945 and a film is released in Germany. This film has been made for other nations to see. On the screen a train pulls into a station. The train is full of children. A man in a uniform greets the children warmly as they step off the train. Then the camera cuts to boys and girls who are swimming. The boys and girls race to see who can reach the other side of the pool first. Then a woman goes to a post office. A man goes to a bank. Men and women sit drinking coffee at a cafe. The film is called *The Führer Presents the Jews with a City*. It has been made at Terezin concentration camp.

Through the pores of the nuclear membrane a steady stream of ribonucleic acid, RNA, the basic material from which the cell is made, flows out.

It is wartime and a woman is writing a letter. *Everyone is on the brink of starvation*, she says. In the right-hand corner of the page she has written *Nordhausen, Germany 1944*. She is writing to Hans. *Do you remember*, she asks, the day this war was declared? The beauty of the place. The beauty of the sea. *And I bathed in it that day, for the last time.*

In the same year, someone else is also writing a letter. In the right-hand corner he has put his name followed by a title. *Heinrich Himmler. Reichsführer, SS. Make no mention of the special treatment of the Jews*, he says, use only the words Transportation of the Jews toward the Russian East.

A few months later this man will deliver a speech to a secret meeting of leaders in the district of Posen. *Now you know all about it, and you will keep quiet*, he will tell them. Now we share a secret and *we should take our secret to our graves.*

• • •

The missile flies from three to four thousand feet above the earth and this makes it difficult to attack from the ground.

The woman who writes of starvation is a painter in her seventy-seventh year. She has lost one grandchild to this war. And a son to the war before. Both boys were named Peter. Among the drawings she makes which have already become famous: a terrified mother grasps a child, *Death Seizes Children;* an old man curls over the bent body of an old woman, *Parents;* a thin face emerges white from charcoal, *Beggars.*

A small but critical part of the RNA flowing out of the pores holds most of the knowledge issued by the nucleus. These threads of RNA act as messengers.

Encountering such images, one is grateful to be spared. But is one ever really free of the fate of others? I was born in 1943, in the midst of this war. And I sense now that my life is still bound up with the lives of those who lived and died in this time. Even with Heinrich Himmler. All the details of his existence, his birth, childhood, adult years, death, still resonate here on earth.

The V-1 rocket is a winged plane powered by a duct motor with a pulsating flow of fuel.

It is April 1943, Heinrich Himmler, Reichsführer SS, has gained control of the production of rockets for the Third Reich. The SS Totenkampf stand guard with machine guns trained at the entrance to a long tunnel, two miles deep, fourteen yards wide and ten yards high, sequestered in the Harz Mountains near Nordhausen. Once an old mining shaft, this tunnel serves now as a secret factory for the manufacture of V-1 and V-2 missiles. The guards aim their machine guns at the factory workers who are inmates of concentration camp Dora.

Most of the RNA flowing out of the cell is destined for the construction of a substance needed to compensate for the continual wearing away of the cell.

It is 1925. Heinrich Himmler, who is now twenty-five years old, has been hired as a secretary by the chief of the Nazi Party in Landshut. He sits behind a small desk in a room overcrowded with party records, correspondence, and newspaper files. On the wall facing him he can see a portrait of Adolf Hitler. He hopes one day to meet the Führer. In anticipation of that day, while he believes no one watches, he practices speaking to this portrait.

It is 1922. Heinrich visits friends who have a three-year-old child. Before going to bed this child is allowed to run about naked. And this disturbs Heinrich. He writes in his diary, *One should teach a child a sense of shame.*

It is the summer of 1910. Heinrich begins his first diary. He is ten years old. He has just completed elementary school. His father tells him his childhood is over now. In the fall he will enter Wilhelms Gymnasium. There the grades he earns will determine his prospects for the future. From now on he must learn to take himself seriously.

Eight out of ten of the guided missiles will land within eight miles of their targets.

His father Gebhard is a schoolmaster. He knows the requirements. He provides the boy with pen and ink. Gebhard was once a tutor for Prince Heinrich of Wittelsbach. He has named his son Heinrich after this prince. He is grateful that the prince consented to be Heinrich's godparent. Heinrich is to write in his diary every day. Gebhard writes the first entry in his son's diary, to show the boy how it is to be done.

July 13 Departed at 11:50 and arrive safely on the bus in L. We have a very pretty house. In the afternoon we drink coffee at the coffee house.

I open the cover of the journal I began to keep just as I started my work on this book. I want to see what is on the first page. *It is here I begin a new life,* I wrote. Suffering many losses at once, I was alone and lonely. Yet suddenly I felt a new responsibility for myself. *The very act of keeping a journal,* I sensed, would help me into this life that would now be my own.

Inside the nucleus is the nucleolus where the synthesis of RNA takes place. Each nucleolus is filled with a small jungle of fern-like structures all of whose fronds and stalks move and rotate in perfect synchrony.

It is 1910. The twenty-second of July. Gebhard adds the words *first swim* to his son's brief entry, *thirteenth wedding anniversary of my dear parents.* 1911. Over several entries Heinrich lists each of thirty-seven times he takes a swim, in chronological order. *11:37 A.M. Departed for Lindau.* He does not write of his feelings. *August 8, Walk in the park.* Or dreams. *August 10, Bad weather.*

In the last few years I have been searching, though for what precisely I cannot say. Something still hidden which lies in the direction of Heinrich Himmler's life. I have been to Berlin and Munich on this search, and I have walked over the gravel at Dachau. Now as I sit here I read once again the fragments from Heinrich's boyhood diary that exist in English. I have begun to think of these words as ciphers. Repeat them to myself, hoping to find a door into the mind of this man, even as his character first forms so that I might learn how it is he becomes himself.

The task is not easy. The earliest entries in this diary betray so little. Like the words of a schoolboy commanded to write what the teacher requires of him, they are wooden and stiff. The stamp of his father's character is so heavy on this language that I catch not even a breath of a self here. It is easy to see how this would be true. One simply has to imagine Gebhard standing behind Heinrich and tapping his foot.

His father must have loomed large to him. Did Gebhard lay his hand on Heinrich's shoulder? The weight of that hand would not be comforting. It would be a warning. A reminder. Heinrich must straighten up now and be still. Yet perhaps he turns his head. Maybe there is a sound outside. A bird. Or his brother Gebhard's voice. But from the dark form behind him he hears a name pronounced. This is his name, *Heinrich.* The sound rolls sharply off his father's tongue. He turns his head back. He does not know what to write. He wants to turn to this form and beseech him, but this man who is his father is more silent than stone. And now when Heinrich can feel impatience all around him, he wants to ask, *What should I write?* The edge of his father's voice has gotten sharper. *Why can't you remember?* Just write what happened yesterday. And make sure you get the date right. *Don't you remember?* We took a walk in the park together and we ran into the duchess. Be certain you spell her name correctly. And look here, you must get the title right. That is extremely important. Cross it out. Do it again. *The title.*

The boy is relieved. His mind has not been working. His thoughts were like paralyzed limbs, immobile. Now he is in motion again. He writes the sentences as they are dictated to him. *The park.* He crosses out the name. He writes it again. Spelling it right. *The duchess.* And his father makes one more correction. The boy has not put down the correct time for their walk in the park.

And who is the man standing behind? In a photograph I have before me of the aging Professor and Frau Himmler, as they pose before a wall carefully composed with paintings and family portraits, Frau Himmler adorned with a demure lace collar, both she and the professor smiling kindly from behind steel-rimmed glasses, the professor somewhat rounded with age, in a dark three-piece suit and polka-dot tie, looks so ordinary.

The missile carries a warhead weighing 1, 870 pounds. It has three different fuses to insure detonation.

Ordinary. What an astonishing array of images hide behind this word. The ordinary is of course never ordinary. I think of it now as a kind of mask, not an animated mask that expresses the essence of an inner truth, but a mask that falls like dead weight over the human face, making flesh a stationary object. One has difficulty penetrating the heavy mask that Gebhard and his family wore, difficulty piercing through to the creatures behind.

It must not have been an easy task to create this mask. One detects the dimensions of the struggle in the advice of German child-rearing experts from this and the last century. *Crush the will,* they write. *Establish dominance. Permit no disobedience. Suppress everything in the child.*

I have seen illustrations from the books of one of these experts, perhaps the most famous of these pedagogues, Dr. Daniel Gottlieb Moritz Schreber. At first glance these pictures recall images of torture. But they are instead pictures of children whose posture or behavior is being corrected. A brace up the spine, a belt tied to a waist and the hair at the back of the neck so the child will be discouraged from slumping, a metal plate at the edge of a desk keeping the child from curling over her work, a child tied to a bed to prevent poor sleeping posture or masturbation. And there are other methods recommended in the text. An enema to be given before bedtime. The child immersed in ice-cold water up to the hips, before sleep.

The nightmare images of the German child-rearing practices that one discovers in this book call to mind the catastrophic events of recent German history. I first encountered this pedagogy in the writing of Alice Miller. At one time a psychoanalyst, she was haunted by the question, *What could make a person conceive the plan of gassing millions of human beings to death?* In her work, she traces the origins of this violence to childhood.

Of course there cannot be one answer to such a monumental riddle, nor does any event in history have a single cause. Rather a field exists, like a field of gravity that is created by the movements of many bodies. Each life is influenced and it in turn becomes an influence. Whatever is a cause is also an effect. Childhood experience is just one element in the determining field.

As a man who made history, Heinrich Himmler shaped many childhoods, including, in the most subtle of ways, my own. And an earlier history, a history of governments, of wars, of social customs, an idea of gender, the history of a religion leading to the idea of original sin, shaped Heinrich Himmler's childhood as certainly as any philosophy of child raising. One can take for instance any formative condition of his private life, the fact that he was a frail child, for example, favored by his mother, who could not meet masculine standards, and show that this circumstance derived its real meaning from a larger social system that gave inordinate significance to masculinity.

Yet to enter history through childhood experience shifts one's perspective not away from history but instead to an earlier time just before history has finally shaped us. Is there a child who existed before the conventional history that we tell of ourselves, one who, though invisible to us, still shapes events, even through this absence? How does our sense of history change when we consider childhood, and perhaps more important, why is it that until now we have chosen to ignore this point of origination, the birthplace and womb of ourselves, in our consideration of public events?

In the silence that reverberates around this question, an image is born in my mind. I can see a child's body, small, curled into itself, knees bent toward the chest, head bending softly into pillows and blankets, in a posture thought unhealthy by Dr. Schreber, hand raised to the face, delicate mouth making a circle around the thumb. There is comfort as well as sadness in this image. It is a kind of a self-portrait, drawn both from memory and from a feeling that is still inside me. As I dwell for a moment with this image I can imagine Heinrich in this posture, silent, curled, fetal, giving comfort to himself.

But now, alongside this earlier image, another is born. It is as if these two images were twins, always traveling in the world of thought together. One does not come to mind without the other. In this second portrait, which is also made of feeling and memory, a child's hands are tied into mittens. And by a string extending from one of the mittens, her hand is tied to the bars of her crib. She is not supposed to be putting her finger in her mouth. And she is crying out in rage while she yanks her hand violently trying to free herself of her bonds.

To most of existence there is an inner and an outer world. Skin, bark, surface of the ocean open to reveal other realities. What is inside shapes and sustains what appears. So it is too with human consciousness. And yet the mind rarely has a simple connection to the inner life. At a certain age we begin to define ourselves, to choose an image of who we are. I am this and not that, we say, attempting thus to erase whatever is within us that does not fit our idea of who we should be. In time we forget our earliest selves and replace that memory with the image we have constructed at the bidding of others.

One can see this process occur in the language of Heinrich's diaries. If in the earliest entries, except for the wooden style of a boy who obeys authority, Heinrich's character is hardly apparent, over time this stilted style becomes his own. As one reads on, one no longer thinks of a boy who is forced to the task, but of a prudish and rigid young man.

In Heinrich's boyhood diaries no one has been able to find any record of rage or of events that inspire such rage. Yet one cannot assume from this evidence that such did not exist. His father would have permitted neither anger nor even the memory of it to enter these pages. That there must be no visible trace of resentment toward the parent was the pedagogy of the age. Dr. Schreber believed that children should learn to be grateful. The pain and humiliation children endure are meant to benefit them. The parent is only trying to save the child's soul.

Now, for different reasons, I too find myself on the track of a child's soul. The dimensions of Heinrich Himmler's life have put me on this track. I am trying to grasp the inner state of his being. For a time the soul ceased to exist in the modern mind. One thought of a human being as a kind of machine, or as a cog in the greater mechanism of society, operating within another machine, the earth, which itself operates within the greater mechanical design of the universe.

When I was in Berlin, I spoke to a rabbi who had, it seemed to me, lost his faith. When I asked him if he still believed in God, he simply shook his head and widened his eyes as if to say, *How is this possible?* He had been telling me about his congregation: older people, many of Polish origin, survivors of the holocaust who were not able to leave Germany after the war because they were too ill to travel. He was poised in this painful place by choice. He had come to lead this congregation only temporarily but, once feeling the condition of his people, decided to stay. Still, despite his answer, and as much as the holocaust made a terrible argument for the death of the spirit, talking in that small study with this man, I could feel from him the light of something surviving.

The religious tradition that shaped Heinrich's childhood argues that the soul is not part of flesh but is instead a prisoner of the body. But suppose the soul is meant to live in and through the body and to know itself in the heart of earthly existence?

Then the soul is an integral part of the child's whole being, and its growth is thus part of the child's growth. It is, for example, like a seed planted underground in the soil, naturally moving toward the light. And it comes into its fullest manifestation thus only when seen, especially when self meeting self returns a gaze.

What then occurs if the soul in its small beginnings is forced to take on a secret life? A boy learns, for instance, to hide his thoughts from his father simply by failing to record them in his journals. He harbors his secrets in fear and guilt, confessing them to no one until in time the voice of his father chastising him becomes his own. A small war is waged in his mind. Daily implosions take place under his skin, by which in increments something in him seems to disappear. Gradually his father's voice subsumes the vitality of all his desires and even his rage, so that now what he wants most passionately is his own obedience, and his rage is aimed at his own failures. As over time his secrets fade from memory, he ceases to tell them, even to himself, so that finally a day arrives when he believes the image he has made of himself in his diaries is true.

The child, Dr. Schreber advised, *should be permeated by the impossibility of locking something in his heart.* The doctor who gave this advice had a son who was hospitalized for disabling schizophrenia. Another of his children committed suicide. But this was not taken as a warning against his approach. His methods of educating children were so much a part of the canon of everyday life in Germany that they were introduced into the state school system.

That this philosophy was taught in school gives me an interior view of the catastrophe to follow. It adds a certain dimension to my image of these events to know that a nation of citizens learned that no part of themselves could be safe from the scrutiny of authority, nothing locked in the heart, and at the same time to discover that the head of the secret police of this nation was the son of a schoolmaster. It was this man, after all, Heinrich Himmler, Reichsführer SS, who was later to say, speaking of the mass arrests of Jews, *Protective custody is an act of care.*

• • •

The polite manner of young Heinrich's diaries reminds me of life in my grandmother's home. Not the grandmother I lost and later found, but the one who, for many years, raised me. She was my mother's mother. The family would assemble in the living room together, sitting with a certain reserve, afraid to soil the surfaces. What was it that by accident might have been made visible?

All our family photographs were posed. We stood together in groups of three or four and squinted into the sun. My grandmother directed us to smile. I have carried one of these photographs with me for years without acknowledging to myself that in it my mother has the look she always had when she drank too much. In another photograph, taken near the time of my parents' divorce, I can see that my father is almost crying, though I could not see this earlier. I must have felt obliged to see only what my grandmother wanted us to see. Tranquil, domestic scenes.

In the matrix of the mitochondria all the processes of transformation join together in a central vortex.

We were not comfortable with ourselves as a family. There was a great shared suffering and yet we never wept together, except for my mother, who would alternately weep and then rage when she was drunk. Together, under my grandmother's tutelage, we kept up appearances. Her effort was ceaseless.

When at the age of six I went to live with her, my grandmother worked to reshape me. I learned what she thought was correct grammar. The manners she had studied in books of etiquette were passed on to me, not by casual example but through anxious memorization and drill. Napkin to be lifted by the corner and swept onto the lap. Hand to be clasped firmly but not too firmly.

We were not to the manner born. On one side my great-grandfather was a farmer, and on the other a butcher newly emigrated from Ireland, who still spoke with a brogue. Both great-grandfathers drank too much, the one in public houses, the other more quietly at home. The great-grandfather who farmed was my grandmother's father. He was not wealthy but he aspired to gentility. My grandmother inherited both his aspiration and his failure.

We considered ourselves finer than the neighbors to our left with their chaotic household. But when certain visitors came, we were as if driven by an inward, secret panic that who we really were might be discovered. Inadvertently, by some careless gesture, we might reveal to these visitors who were our betters that we did not belong with them, that we were not real. Though of course we never spoke of this, to anyone, not even ourselves.

Gebhard Himmler's family was newly risen from poverty. Just as in my family, the Himmlers' gentility was a thinly laid surface, maintained no doubt only with great effort. Gebhard's father had come from a family of peasants and small artisans. Such a living etched from the soil, and by one's hands, is tenuous and hard. As is frequently the case with young men born to poverty, Johann became a soldier. And, like many young soldiers, he got himself into trouble more than once for brawling and general mischief. On one occasion he was reproved for what was called *immoral behavior with a low woman*. But nothing of this history survived in his son's version of him. By the time Gebhard was born, Johann was fifty-six years old and had reformed his ways. Having joined the royal police force of Bavaria, over the years he rose to the rank of sergeant. He was a respectable man, with a respectable position.

Perhaps Gebhard never learned of his father's less than respectable past. He was only three years old when Johann died. If he had the slightest notion, he did not breathe a word to his own children. Johann became the icon of the Himmler family, the heroic soldier who single-handedly brought his family from the obscurity of poverty into the warm light of the favored. Yet obscure histories have a way of casting a shadow over the present. Those who are born to propriety have a sense of entitlement, and this affords them some ease as they execute the correct mannerisms of their class. More recent members of the elect are less certain of themselves; around the edges of newly minted refinement one discerns a certain fearfulness, expressed perhaps as uncertainty, or as its opposite, rigidity.

One can sense that rigidity in Gebhard's face as a younger man. In a photograph of the Himmler family, Gebhard, who towers in the background, seems severe. He has the face of one who looks for mistakes. He is vigilant. Heinrich's mother looks very small next to him, almost as if she is cowering. She has that look I have seen many times on my father's face, which one can only describe as ameliorating. Heinrich is very small. He stands closest to the camera, shimmering in a white dress. His face is pretty, even delicate.

I am looking now at the etching called *Poverty*, made in 1897. Near the center, calling my attention, a woman holds her head in her hands. She stares through her hands into the face of a sleeping infant. Though the infant and the sheet and pillow around are filled with light, one recognizes that the child is dying. In a darker corner, two worried figures huddle, a father and another child. Room, mother, father, child exist in lines, a multitude of lines, and each line is filled with a rare intelligence.

Just as the physicist's scrutiny changes the object of perception, so does art transmute experience. One cannot look upon what Käthe Kollwitz has drawn without feeling. The lines around the child are bleak with unreason. Never have I seen so clearly that what we call poverty is simply a raw exposure to the terror and fragility of life. But there is more in this image. There is meaning in the frame. One can feel the artist's eyes. Her gaze is in one place soft, in another intense. Like the light around the infant, her attention interrupts the shadow that falls across the room.

The artist's choice of subject and the way she saw it were both radical departures, not only from certain acceptable assumptions in the world of art, but also from established social ideas because the poor were thought of as less than human. The death of a child to a poor parent was supposed to be a less painful event. In her depiction, the artist told a different story.

Heinrich is entering a new school now, and so his father makes a list of all his future classmates. Beside the name of each child he writes the child's father's name, what this father does for a living, and his social position. Heinrich must be careful, Gebhard tells him, to choose whom he befriends. In his diaries the boy seldom mentions his friends by name. Instead he writes that he played, for instance, with the landlord's child.

There is so much for Heinrich to learn. Gebhard must teach him the right way to bow. The proper forms of greeting. The history of his family; the history of his nation. Its heroes. His grandfather's illustrious military past. There is an order in the world and Heinrich has a place in this order which he must be trained to fill. His life is strictly scheduled. At this hour a walk in the woods so that he can appreciate nature. After that a game of chess to develop his mind. And after that piano, so that he will be cultured.

If a part of himself has vanished, that part of the self that feels and wants, and from which hence a coherent life might be shaped, Heinrich is not at sea yet. He has no time to drift or feel lost. Each moment has been spoken for, every move prescribed. He has only to carry out his father's plans for him.

But everything in his life is not as it should be. He is not popular among his classmates. Should it surprise us to learn that he has a penchant for listening to the secrets of his companions, and that afterward he repeats these secrets to his father, the schoolmaster? There is perhaps a secret he would like to learn and one he would like to tell, but this has long since been forgotten. Whatever he learns now he must tell his father. He must not keep anything from him. He must keep his father's good will at all costs. For, without his father, he does not exist.

And there is another reason Heinrich is not accepted by his classmates. He is frail. As an infant, stricken by influenza, he came close to perishing and his body still retains the mark of that illness. He is not strong. He is not good at the games the other boys play. At school he tries over and over to raise himself on the crossbars, unsuccessfully. He covets the popularity of his stronger, more masculine brother, Gebhard. But he cannot keep up with his brother. One day, when they go out for a simple bicycle ride together, Heinrich falls into the mud and returns with his clothes torn.

It is 1914. A war begins. There are parades. Young men marching in uniform. Tearful ceremonies at the railway station. Songs. Decorations. Heinrich is enthusiastic. The war has given him a sense of purpose in life. Like other boys, he plays at soldiering. He follows the war closely, writing in his diary of the progress of armies, *This time with 40 Army Corps and Russia and France against Germany*. The entries he makes do not seem so listless now; they have a new vigor. As the war continues, a new ambition gradually takes the shape of determination. Is this the way he will finally prove himself? Heinrich wants to be a soldier. And above all he wants a uniform.

It is 1915. In her journal Käthe Kollwitz records a disturbing sight. The night before at the opera she found herself sitting next to a young soldier. He was blinded. He sat *without stirring, his hands on his knees, his head erect.* She could not stop looking at him, and the memory of him, she writes now, *cuts her to the quick.*

It is 1916. As Heinrich comes of age he implores his father to help him find a regiment. He has many heated opinions about the war. But his thoughts are like the thoughts and feelings of many adolescents; what he expresses has no steady line of reason. His opinions are filled with contradictions, and he lacks that awareness of self which can turn ambivalence into an inner dialogue. Yet, beneath this amorphous bravado, there is a pattern. As if he were trying on different attitudes, Heinrich swings from harshness to compassion. In one place he writes, *The Russian prisoners multiply like vermin.* (Should I write here that this is a word he will one day use for Jews?) But later he is sympathetic to the same prisoners because they are so far away from home. Writing once of *the silly old women and petty bourgeois . . . who so dislike war,* in another entry, he remembers the young men he has seen depart on trains and he asks, *How many are alive today?*

Is the direction of any life inevitable? Or are there crossroads, points at which the direction might be changed? I am looking again at the Himmler family. Heinrich's infant face resembles the face of his mother. His face is soft. And his mother? In the photograph she is a fading presence. She occupied the same position as did most women in German families, secondary and obedient to the undisputed power of her husband. She has a slight smile which for some reason reminds me of the smile of a child I saw in a photograph from an album made by the SS. This child's image was captured as she stood on the platform at Auschwitz. In the photograph she emanates a certain frailty. Her smile is a very feminine smile. Asking, or perhaps pleading, *Don't hurt me.*

Is it possible that Heinrich, looking into that child's face, might have seen himself there? What is it in a life that makes one able to see oneself in others? Such affinities do not stop with obvious resemblance. There is a sense in which we all enter the lives of others.

It is 1917, and a boy who will be named Heinz is born to Catholic parents living in Vienna. Heinz's father bears a certain resemblance to Heinrich's father. He is a civil servant and, also like Gebhard, he is pedantic and correct in all he does. Heinrich will never meet this boy. And yet their paths will cross.

Early in the same year as Heinz's birth, Heinrich's father has finally succeeded in getting him into a regiment. As the war continues for one more year, Heinrich comes close to achieving his dream. He will be a soldier. He is sent to officer's training. Yet he is not entirely happy. *The food is bad,* he writes to his mother, *and there is not enough of it. It is cold. There are bedbugs. The room is barren.* Can she send him food? A blanket? Why doesn't she write him more often? Has she forgotten him? They are calling up troops. Suppose he should be called to the front and die?

But something turns in him. Does he sit on the edge of a neat, narrow military bunk bed as he writes in his diary that he does not want to be like a boy who whines to his mother? Now, he writes a different letter: *I am once more a soldier body and soul.* He loves his uniform; the oath he has learned to write; the first inspection he passes. He signs his letters now, *Miles Heinrich.* Soldier Heinrich.

I am looking at another photograph. It is of two boys. They are both in military uniform. Gebhard, Heinrich's older brother, is thicker and taller. Next to him Heinrich is still diminutive. But his face has become harder, and his smile, though faint like his mother's smile, has gained a new quality, harsh and stiff like the little collar he wears.

Most men can remember a time in their lives when they were not so different from girls, and they also remember when that time ended. In ancient Greece a young boy lived with his mother, practicing a feminine life in her household, until the day he was taken from her into the camp of men. From this day forward the life that had been soft and graceful became rigorous and hard, as the older boy was prepared for the life of a soldier.

My grandfather on my mother's side was a contemporary of Heinrich Himmler. He was the youngest boy in the family and an especially pretty child. Like Heinrich and all small boys in this period, he was dressed in a lace gown. His hair was long and curled about his face. Like Heinrich, he was his mother's favorite. She wanted to keep him in his finery. He was so beautiful in it, and he was her last child. My great-grandmother Sarah had a dreamy, artistic nature, and in his early years my grandfather took after her. But all of this made him seem girlish. And his father and older brothers teased him mercilessly. Life improved for him only when he graduated to long pants. With them he lost his dreamy nature too.

The soul is often imagined to be feminine. All those qualities thought of as soulful, a dreaminess or artistic sensibility, are supposed to come more naturally to women. Ephemeral, half seen, half present, nearly ghostly, with only the vaguest relation to the practical world of physical law, the soul appears to us as lost. The hero, with his more masculine virtues, must go in search of her. But there is another, older story of the soul. In this story she is firmly planted on the earth. She is incarnate and visible everywhere. Neither is she faint of heart, nor fading in her resolve. It is she, in fact, who goes bravely in search of desire.

1918. Suddenly the war is over. Germany has lost. Heinrich has failed to win his commission. He has not fought in a single battle. Prince Heinrich, his namesake, has died. The prince will be decorated for heroism, after his death. Heinrich returns home, not an officer or even a soldier any longer. He returns to school, completing his studies at the gymnasium and then the university. But he is adrift. Purposeless. And like the world he belongs to, dissatisfied. Neither man nor boy, he does not know what he wants.

Until now he could rely on a strict regimen provided by his father. Nothing was left uncertain or undefined for long in his father's house. The thoroughness of Gebhard's hold over his family comes alive for me through this procedure: every package, letter or money order to pass through the door was by Gebhard's command to be duly recorded. And I begin to grasp a sense of Gebhard's priorities when I read that Heinrich, on one of his leaves home during the war, assisted his mother in this task. The shadow of his father's habits will stretch out over history. They will fall over an office in Berlin through which the SS, and the entire network of concentration camps, are administered. Every single piece of paper issued with regard to this office will pass over Heinrich's desk, and to each page he will add his own initials. Schedules for trains. Orders for building supplies. Adjustments in salaries. No detail will escape his surmise or fail to be recorded.

But at this moment in his life Heinrich is facing a void. I remember a similar void, when a long and intimate relationship ended. What I felt then was fear. And at times panic. In a journal I kept after this separation, I wrote, *Direct knowledge of the illusory nature of panic. The feeling that I had let everything go out of control.* I could turn in only one direction: inward. Each day I abated my fears for a time by observing myself. But what exists in that direction for Heinrich? He has not been allowed to inhabit that terrain. His inner life has been sealed off both from his father and himself.

I am not certain what I am working for, he writes, and then, not able to let this uncertainty remain, he adds, *I work because it is my duty.* He spends long hours in his room, seldom leaving the house at all. He is at sea. Still somewhat the adolescent, unformed, not knowing what face he should put on when going out into the world, in his journal he confesses that he still lacks that *naturally superior kind of manner that he would dearly like to possess.*

Is it any wonder then that he is so eager to rejoin the army? The army gave purpose and order to his life. He wants his uniform again. In his uniform he knows who he is. But his frailty haunts him. Over and over he shows up at recruiting stations throughout Bavaria only to be turned away each time, with the single word, *Untauglich.* Unfit. At night the echo of this word keeps him awake.

When he tries to recover his pride, he suffers another failure of a similar kind. A student of agriculture at the university, now he dreams of becoming a farmer. He believes he can take strength and vitality from the soil. After all his own applications are rejected, his father finds him a position in the countryside. He rides toward his new life on his motorcycle and is pelted by torrents of rain. Though he is cold and hungry, he is also exuberant. He has defeated his own weakness. But after only a few weeks his body fails him again. He returns home ill with typhus and must face the void once more.

What Germany needs now is a man of iron. How easy it is to hear the irony of these words Heinrich records in his journal. But at this moment in history, he is hearing another kind of echo. There are so many others who agree with him. The treaty of Versailles is taken as a humiliation. An unforgivable weakness, it is argued, has been allowed to invade the nation.

1920. 1922. 1923. Heinrich is twenty, twenty-two, twenty-three. He is growing up with the century. And he starts to adopt certain opinions popular at this time. As I imagine myself in his frame of mind, facing a void, cast into unknown waters, these opinions appear like rescue ships on the horizon, a promise of *terra firma*, the known.

It is for instance fashionable to argue that the emergence of female equality has drained the nation of its strength. At social gatherings Heinrich likes to discuss the differences between men and women. That twilight area between the certainties of gender, homosexuality, horrifies him. A man should be a man and a woman a woman. Sexually explicit illustrations in a book by Oscar Wilde horrify him. Uncomfortable with the opposite sex, so much so that one of his female friends believes he hates women, he has strong feelings about how men and women ought to relate. *A real man,* he sets down in his diary, *should love a woman as a child who must be admonished perhaps even punished, when she is foolish, though she must also be protected and looked after because she is so weak.*

As I try to enter Heinrich's experience, the feeling I sense behind these words is of immense comfort. I know who I am. My role in life, what I am to feel, what I am to be, has been made clear. I am a man. I am the strong protector. And what's more, I am needed. There is one who is weak. One who is weaker than I am. And I am the one who must protect her.

And yet behind the apparent calm of my present mood, there is an uneasiness. Who is this one that I protect? Does she tell me the truth about herself? I am beginning to suspect that she hides herself from me. There is something secretive in her nature. She is an unknown, even dangerous, territory.

The year is 1924. And Heinrich is still fascinated with secrets. He discovers that his brother's fiancée has committed one or maybe even two indiscretions. At his urging, Gebhard breaks off the engagement. But Heinrich is still not satisfied. He writes a friend who lives near his brother's former fiancée, *Do you know of any other shameful stories?* After this, he hires a private detective to look into her past.

Is it any coincidence that in the same year he writes in his diary that he has met a *great man, genuine and pure?* This man, he notes, may be the new leader Germany is seeking. He finds he shares a certain drift of thought with this man. He is discovering who he is now, partly by affinity and partly by negation. In his picture of himself, a profile begins to emerge cast in light and shadow. He knows now who he is and who he is not. He is not Jewish.

And increasingly he becomes obsessed with who he is not. In this pursuit, his curiosity is fed by best-selling books, posters, films, journals; he is part of a larger social movement, and this no doubt gives him comfort, and one cannot, in studying the landscape of his mind as set against the landscape of the social body, discover where he ends and the milieu of this time begins. He is perhaps like a particle in a wave, a wave which has only the most elusive relationship with the physical world, existing as an afterimage in the mind.

I can imagine him sitting at a small desk in his bedroom, still in his father's home. Is it the same desk where he was required to record some desultory sentences in his diary every day? He is bent over a book. It is evening. The light is on, shining on the pages of the book. Which book among the books he has listed in his journal does he read now? Is it *Das Liebnest* (*The Lovenest*), telling the story of a liaison between a Jewish man and a gentile woman? *Rasse?* Explaining the concept of racial superiority? Or is it *Judas Schuldsbach* (*The Book of Jewish Guilt*). Or *Die Sünde wider das Blut* (*The Sin Against the Blood*).

One can follow somewhat his train of thought here and there where he makes comments on what he reads in his journal. When he reads *Tscheka*, for instance, a history of the secret police in Russia, he says he is disappointed. *Everyone knows,* he writes, that the Jews control the secret police in Russia. But nowhere in the pages of this book does he find a mention of this "fact."

His mind has begun to take a definite shape, even a predictable pattern. Everywhere he casts his eyes he will discover a certain word. Wherever his thoughts wander he brings them back to this word. *Jew. Jude. Jew.* With this word he is on firm ground again. In the sound of the word, a box is closed, a box with all the necessary documents, with all the papers in order.

My grandfather was an anti-Semite. He had a long list of enemies that he liked to recite. Blacks were among them. And Catholics. And the English. He was Protestant and Irish. Because of his drinking he retired early (though we never discussed the cause). In my childhood I often found him sitting alone in the living room that was darkened by closed venetian blinds which kept all our colors from fading. Lonely myself, I would try to speak with him. His repertoire was small. When I was younger he would tell me stories of his childhood, and I loved those stories. He talked about the dog named Blackie that was his then. A ceramic statue of a small black dog resembling him stood near the fireplace. He loved this dog in a way that was almost painful to hear. But he could never enter that intricate world of expressed emotion in which the shadings of one's life as it is felt and experienced become articulated. This way of speaking was left to the women of our family. As I grew older and he could no longer tell me the story of his dog, he would talk to me about politics. It was then that, with a passion he revealed nowhere else, he would recite to me his long list filled with everyone he hated.

I did not like to listen to my grandfather speak this way. His face would get red, and his voice took on a grating tone that seemed to abrade not only the ears but some other slower, calmer velocity within the body of the room. His eyes, no longer looking at me, blazed with a kind of blindness. There was no reaching him at these moments. He was beyond any kind of touch or remembering. Even so, reciting the long list of those he hated, he came temporarily alive. Then, once out of this frame of mind, he lapsed into a kind of fog which we called, in the family, his retirement.

There was another part of my grandfather's mind that also disturbed me. But this passion was veiled. I stood at the borders of it occasionally catching glimpses. He had a stack of magazines by the chair he always occupied. They were devoted to the subject of crime, and the crimes were always grisly, involving photographs of women or girls uncovered in ditches, hacked to pieces or otherwise mutilated. I was never supposed to look in these magazines, but I did. What I saw there could not be reconciled with the other experience I had of my grandfather, fond of me, gentle, almost anachronistically protective.

Heinrich Himmler was also fascinated with crime. Along with books about Jews, he read avidly on the subjects of police work, espionage, torture. Despite his high ideals regarding chastity, he was drawn to torrid, even pornographic fiction, including *Ein Sadist im Priesterrock* (*A Sadist in Priestly Attire*) which he read quickly, noting in his journal that it was a book *about the corruption of women and girls . . . in Paris.*

Entering the odd and often inconsistent maze of his opinions, I feel a certain queasiness. I cannot find a balance point. I search in vain for some center, that place which is in us all, and is perhaps even beyond nationality, or even gender, the felt core of existence, which seems to be at the same time the most real. In Heinrich's morass of thought there are no connecting threads, no integrated whole. I find only the opinions themselves, standing in an odd relation to gravity, as if hastily formed, a rickety, perilous structure.

I am looking at a photograph. It was taken in 1925. Or perhaps 1926. A group of men pose before a doorway in Landshut. Over this doorway is a wreathed swastika. Nearly all the men are in uniform. Some wear shiny black boots. Heinrich is among them. He is the slightest, very thin. Heinrich Himmler. He is near the front. At the far left there is the blurred figure of a man who has been caught in motion as he rushes to join the other men. Of course I know his feeling. The desire to partake, and even to be part of memory.

Photographs are strange creations. They are depictions of a moment that is always passing; after the shutter closes, the subject moves out of the frame and begins to change outwardly or inwardly. One ages. One shifts to a different state of consciousness. Subtle changes can take place in an instant, perhaps one does not even feel them—but they are perceptible to the camera.

The idea we have of reality as a fixed quantity is an illusion. Everything moves. And the process of knowing oneself is in constant motion too, because the self is always changing. Nowhere is this so evident as in the process of art which takes one at once into the self and into *terra incognita,* the land of the unknown. *I am groping in the dark,* the artist Käthe Kollwitz writes in her journal. Here, I imagine she is not so much uttering a cry of despair as making a simple statement. A sense of emptiness always precedes creation.

Now, as I imagine Himmler, dressed in his neat uniform, seated behind his desk at party headquarters, I can feel the void he feared begin to recede. In every way his life has taken on definition. He has a purpose and a schedule. Even the place left by the cessation of his father's lessons has now been filled. He is surrounded by men whose ideas he begins to adopt. From Alfred Rosenberg he learns about the history of Aryan blood, a line Rosenberg traces back to thousands of years before Christ. From Walther Darré he learns that the countryside is a source of Nordic strength. (And that Jews gravitate toward cities.)

Yet I do not find the calmness of a man who has found himself in the descriptions I have encountered of Heinrich Himmler. Rather, he is filled with an anxious ambivalence. If there was once someone in him who felt strongly one way or the other, this one has long ago vanished. In a room filled with other leaders, he seems to fade into the woodwork, his manner obsequious, his effect inconsequential. He cannot make a decision alone. He is known to seek the advice of other men for even the smallest decisions. In the years to come it will be whispered that he is being led by his own assistant, Reinhard Heydrich. He has made only one decision on his own with a consistent resolve. Following Hitler with unwavering loyalty, he is known as *der treuer Heinrich,* true Heinrich. He describes himself as an instrument of the Führer's will.

But still he has something of his own. Something hidden. And this will make him powerful. He is a gatherer of secrets. As he supervises the sale of advertising space for the Nazi newspaper, *Der Völkischer Beobachter,* he instructs the members of his staff to gather information, not only on the party enemies, the socialists and the communists, but on Nazi Party members themselves. In his small office he sits surrounded by voluminous files that are filled with secrets. From this he will build his secret police. By 1925, with an order from Adolf Hitler, the Schutzstaffel, or SS, has become an official institution.

His life is moving now. Yet in this motion one has the feeling not of a flow, as in the flow of water in a cell, nor as the flow of rivers toward an ocean, but of an engine, a locomotive moving at high speed, or even a missile, traveling above the ground. History has an uncanny way of creating its own metaphors. In 1930, months after Himmler is elected to the Reichstag,

Wernher von Braun begins his experiments with liquid fuel missiles that will one day soon lead to the development of the V-2 rocket.

The successful journey of a missile depends upon the study of ballistics. Gravitational fields vary at different heights. The relationship of a projectile to the earth's surface will determine its trajectory. The missile may give the illusion of liberation from the earth, or even abandon. Young men dreaming of space often invest the missile with these qualities. Yet, paradoxically, one is more free of the consideration of gravity while traveling the surface of the earth on foot. There is no necessity for mathematical calculation for each step, nor does one need to apply Newton's laws to take a walk. But the missile has in a sense been forced away from its own presence; the wisdom that is part of its own weight has been transgressed. It finds itself thus careening in a space devoid of memory, always on the verge of falling, but not falling and hence like one who is constantly afraid of illusion, gripped by an anxiety that cannot be resolved even by a fate that threatens catastrophe.

The catastrophes which came to pass after Heinrich Himmler's astonishing ascent to power did not occur in his own life, but came to rest in the lives of others, distant from him, and out of the context of his daily world. It is 1931. Heinz, the boy born in Vienna to Catholic parents, has just turned sixteen, and he is beginning to learn something about himself. All around him his school friends are falling in love with girls. But when he searches inside himself, he finds no such feelings. He is pulled in a different direction. He finds that he is still drawn to another boy. He does not yet know, or even guess, that these feelings will one day place him in the territory of a target.

It is 1933. Heinrich Himmler, Reichsführer SS, has become President of the Bavarian police. In this capacity he begins a campaign against *subversive elements.* Opposition journalists, Jewish business owners, Social Democrats, Communists—names culled from a list compiled on index cards by Himmler's deputy, Reinhard Heydrich—are rounded up and arrested. When the prisons become too crowded, Himmler builds temporary camps. Then, on March 22, the Reichsführer opens the first official and permanent concentration camp at Dachau.

It is 1934. Himmler's power and prestige in the Reich are growing. Yet someone stands in his way. Within the hierarchy of the state police forces, Ernst Röhm, Commandant of the SA, stands over him. But Himmler has made an alliance with Hermann Göring, who as President Minister of Prussia controls the Prussian police, known as the Gestapo. Through a telephone-tapping technique Göring has uncovered evidence of a seditious plot planned by Röhm against the Führer, and he brings this evidence to Himmler. The Führer, having his own reasons to proceed against Röhm, a notorious homosexual and a socialist, empowers the SS and the Gestapo to form an execution committee. This committee will assassinate Röhm, along with the other leaders of the SA. And in the same year, Göring transfers control of the Gestapo to the SS.

But something else less easy to conquer stands in the way of his dreams for himself. It is his own body. I can see him now as he struggles. He is on a playing field in Berlin. And he has broken out in a sweat. He has been trying once again to earn the Reich's sports badge, an honor whose requirements he himself established but cannot seem to fulfill. For three years he has exercised and practiced. On one day he will lift the required weights or run the required laps, but at every trial he fails to throw the discus far enough. His attempt is always a few centimeters short.

And once he is Reichsführer, he will set certain other standards for superiority that, no matter how heroic his efforts, he will never be able to meet. A sign of the *Übermensch*, he says, is blondness, but he himself is dark. He says he is careful to weed out any applicant for the SS who shows traces of a mongolian ancestry, but he himself has the narrow eyes he takes as a sign of such a descent. *I have refused to accept any man whose size was below six feet because I know only men of a certain size have the necessary quality of blood,* he declares, standing just five foot seven behind the podium.

It is the same year, and Heinz, who is certain now that he is a homosexual, has decided to end the silence which he feels to be a burden to him. From the earliest years of his childhood he has trusted his mother with all of his secrets. Now he will tell her another secret, the secret of whom he loves. *My dear child,* she tells him, *it is your life and you must live it.*

It is 1936. Though he does not know it, Himmler is moving into the sphere of Heinz's life now. He has organized a special section of the Gestapo to deal with homosexuality and abortion. On October 11, he declares in a public speech, *Germany's forebears knew what to do with homosexuals. They drowned them in bogs.* This was not punishment, he argues, but *the extermination of unnatural existence.*

As I read these words from Himmler's speech, they call to mind an image from a more recent past, an event I nearly witnessed. On my return from Berlin and after my search for my grandmother, I spent a few days in Maine, close to the city of Bangor. This is a quiet town, not much used to violence. But just days before I arrived a young man had been murdered there. He was a homosexual. He wore an earring in one ear. While he walked home one evening with another man, three boys stopped him on the street. They threw him to the ground and began to kick him. He had trouble catching his breath. He was asthmatic. They picked him up and carried him to a railing of a nearby bridge. He told them he could not swim. Yet still, they threw him over the railing of the bridge into the stream, and he drowned. I saw a picture of him printed in the newspaper. That kind of beauty only very graceful children possess shined through his adult features. It was said that he had come to New England to live with his lover. But the love had failed, and before he died he was piecing his life back together.

When Himmler heard that one of his heroes, Frederick the Great, was a homosexual, he refused to believe his ears. I remember the year when my sister announced to my family that she was a lesbian. I can still recall the chill of fear that went up my spine at the sound of the word "queer." We came of age in the fifties; this was a decade of conformity, awash with mood both public and private, bearing on the life of the body and the body politic. Day after day my grandfather would sit in front of the television set watching as Joseph McCarthy interrogated witnesses about their loyalty to the flag. At the same time, a strict definition of what a woman or a man is had returned to capture the shared imagination. In school I was taught sewing and cooking, and I learned to carry my books in front of my chest to strengthen the muscles which held up my breasts.

I was not happy to hear that my sister was a homosexual. Moved from one member of my family to another, I did not feel secure in the love of others. As the child of divorce I was already different. *Where are your mother and father? Why don't you live with them?* I dreaded these questions. Now my sister, whom I adored and in many ways had patterned myself after, had become an outcast, moved even further out of the circle than I.

It is March 1938. Germany has invaded Austria. Himmler has put on a field-gray uniform for the occasion. Two hand grenades dangle from his Sam Browne belt. Accompanied by a special command unit of twenty-eight men armed with tommy guns and light machine guns, he proceeds to Vienna. Here he will set up Gestapo headquarters in the Hotel Metropole before he returns to Berlin.

It is a Friday, in March of 1939. Heinz, who is twenty-two years old now, and a university student, has received a summons. He is to appear for questioning at the Hotel Metropole. Telling his mother it can't be anything serious, he leaves. He enters a room and stands before a desk. The man behind the desk does not raise his head to nod. He continues to write. When he puts his pen down and looks up at the young man, he tells him, *You are a queer, homosexual, admit it.* Heinz tries to deny this. But the man behind the desk pulls out a photograph. He sees two faces here he knows. His own face and the face of his lover. He begins to weep.

I have come to believe that every life bears in some way on every other. The motion of cause and effect is like the motion of a wave in water, continuous, within and not without the matrix of being, so that all consequences, whether we know them or not, are intimately embedded in our experience.

But the missile, as it hurls toward its target, has lost its context. It has been driven farther than the eye can see. How can one speak of direction any longer? Nothing in the space the missile passes through can seem familiar. In the process of flight, alienated by terror, this motion has become estranged from life, has fallen out of the natural rhythm of events.

I am imagining Himmler as he sits behind his desk in January of 1940. The procedures of introduction into the concentration camps have all been outlined or authorized by Himmler himself. He supervises every detail of these operations. Following his father's penchant for order, he makes many very explicit rules, and requires that reports be filed continually. Train schedules, orders for food supplies, descriptions of punishments all pass over his desk. He sits behind a massive door of carved wood, in his office, paneled in light, unvarnished oak, behind a desk that is normally empty, and clean, except for the bust of Hitler he displays at one end, and a little drummer boy at the other, between which he reads, considers and initials countless pieces of paper.

One should teach a child a sense of shame. These words of Himmler's journals come back to me as I imagine Heinz now standing naked in the snow. The weather is below zero. After a while he is taken to a cold shower, and then issued an ill-fitting uniform. Now he is ordered to stand with the other prisoners once more out in the cold while the commandant reads the rules. All the prisoners in these barracks are homosexuals. There are pink triangles sewn to their uniforms. They must sleep with the light on, they are told, and with their hands outside their blankets. This is a rule made especially for homosexual men. Any man caught with his hands under his blankets will be taken outside into the icy night where several bowls of water will be poured over him, and where he will he made to stand for an hour.

Except for the fact that this punishment usually led to death from cold and exposure, this practice reminds me of Dr. Schreber's procedure for curing children of masturbation. Just a few nights ago I woke up with this thought: *Was Dr. Schreber afraid of children?* Or the child he once was? Fear is often just beneath the tyrant's fury, a fear that must grow with the trajectory of his flight from himself. At Dachau I went inside a barrack. It was a standard design, similar in many camps. The plan of the camps too was standard, and resembled, so I was told by a German friend, the camp sites designed for the Hitler Youth. This seemed to me significant, not as a clue in an analysis, but more like a gesture that colors and changes a speaker's words.

It is the summer of 1940. After working for nearly a decade on liquid fuel rockets, Wernher von Braun begins to design a missile that can be used in the war. He is part of a team trying to meet certain military specifications. The missile must be carried through railway tunnels. It must cover a range of 275 kilometers and carry a warhead weighing one metric ton. The engineers have determined that the motor of this rocket, a prototype of the V-2, will need to be fueled by a pump, and now a pump has been made. Von Braun is free to turn his attention to the turbine drive.

When I think of this missile, or of men sleeping in a barrack, hands exposed, lying on top of worn blankets, an image of Himmler's hands comes to me. Those who remember him say that as he conducted a conversation, discussing a plan, for example, or giving a new order, his hands would lie on top of his desk, limp and inert. He did not like to witness the consequences of his commands. His plans were launched toward distant targets and blind to the consequences of flesh.

After a few months, in one of countless orders which mystify him, coming from a nameless source, and with no explanation, but which he must obey, Heinz is transferred from Sachsenhausen to Flossenbürg. The regime at this camp is the same, but here the commandant, unlike Himmler, does not choose to distance himself from the suffering of others. He is instead drawn to it. He will have a man flogged for the slightest infraction of the rules, and then stand to watch as this punishment is inflicted. The man who is flogged is made to call out the number of lashes as he is lashed, creating in him, no doubt, the feeling that he is causing his own pain. As the man's skin bursts open and he cries out in pain, the commandant's eyes grow excited. His face turns red. His hand slips into his trousers, and he begins to handle himself.

Was the commandant in this moment in any way an extension of the Reichsführer, living out a hidden aspect of this man, one who takes pleasure in the pain of others? This explanation must shed some light, except perhaps as it is intended through the category of an inexplicable perversity to put the crimes Himmler committed at a distance from any understanding of ourselves. The Reichsführer's sexuality is so commonplace. He was remarkable only for the extent of his prudery as a young man. Later, like so many men, he has a wife, who dominates him, and a mistress, younger, more docile, adoring, whom he in turn adores. It has been suggested that he takes pleasure in seeing the naked bodies of boys and young men. If he has a sexual fetish it is certainly this, the worship of physical perfection in the male body. And this worship has its sadistic aspects: his efforts to control reproduction, to force SS men to procreate with many women, the kidnapping from occupied countries of children deemed worthy. Under the veneer of his worship, an earlier rage must haunt him. The subject of cruel insults from other boys with hardier bodies, and the torturous methods his father used to raise him, does he not feel rage toward his persecutors, a rage that, in the course of time, enters history? Yet this is an essential part of the picture: he is dulled to rage. So many of his feelings are inaccessible to him. Like the concentration camps he commands, in many ways he remains absent to himself. And in this he is not so different from the civilization that produced him.

• • •

Writing this, I have tried to find my own rage. The memory is immediate. I am a child, almost nine years old. I sit on the cold pavement of a winter day in Los Angeles. My grandmother has angered me. There is a terrible injustice. A punishment that has enraged me. As I sit picking blades of grass and arranging them into piles, I am torturing her in my mind. I have tied her up and I am shouting at her. Threatening her. Striking her. I batter her, batter her as if with each blow, each landing of my hand against her flesh, I can force my way into her, I can be inside her, I can grab hold of someone inside her, someone who feels, who feels as I do, who feels the hurt I feel, the wound I feel, who feels pain as I feel pain. I am forcing her to feel what I feel. I am forcing her to know me. And as I strike her, blow after blow, a shudder of weeping is released in me, and I become utterly myself, the weeping in me becoming rage, the rage turning to tears, all the time my heart beating, all the time uttering a soundless, bitter, passionate cry, a cry of vengeance and of love.

Is this what is in the torturer's heart? With each blow of his whip does he want to make the tortured one feel as he himself has felt? The desire to know and be known is strong in all of us. Many years after the day I imagined myself as my grandmother's torturer I came to understand that, just as I had wanted my grandmother to feel what I had felt, she wanted me to feel as she had felt. Not what she felt as a woman, but what she had felt long ago as a child. Her childhood was lost to her, the feelings no longer remembered. One way or another, through punishment, severity, or even ridicule, she could goad me into fury and then tears. I expressed for her all she had held inside for so long.

One day, the commandant at Flossenbürg encounters a victim who will not cry and Heinz is a witness to this meeting. As usual this prisoner must count out the number of blows assigned to him. The beating commences. And the prisoner counts out the numbers. But otherwise he is silent. Except for the numbers, not a cry, not a sound, passes his lips. And this puts the commandant in a rage. He orders the guard to strike harder with the lash; he increases the number of lashes; he orders the prisoner to begin counting from zero again. Finally, the beating shall continue *until the swine starts screaming,* he shouts. And now, when the prisoner's blood is flowing to the ground, he starts to howl. And with this, the commandant's face grows red, and his hands slip into his trousers again.

A connection between violence and sexuality threads its way through many histories. As we sit in the living room together, looking out over the water, Laura's stories move in and out of the world of her family, and of our shared world, its habits, its wars. She is telling me another story about her father, the general. They were living on the missile base. She had been out late baby-sitting. When she returned home the house was dark. She had no key. It was raining hard. She rang. There was no answer. Then she began to pound on the door. Suddenly the door opened. The hallway was dark. She was yanked into this darkness by her father. He was standing naked. Without speaking to her he began to slap her hard across the face, again and again, and did not stop until her mother, appearing in the stairs in a bathrobe, stood between them. *I knew,* she told me, *they had been making love.*

What was the source of his rage? Did it come from childhood, or battle, or both, the battle awakening the panic of an earlier abuse? The training a soldier receives is to wreak his anger on others. Anyone near receives it. I have heard stories of a man waking at night screaming in terror, reaching for a gun hidden under the pillow, and pointing it or even firing at his own family. In a play about Heracles by Euripides, the great warrior, who has just returned from the underworld, thinking that he has vanquished death, is claimed by madness. He believes himself to be in the home of his enemy. But he is in his own home and, finding his own children, mistakes them for the children of his enemy, clubs one to death and then kills the other two with arrows.

But it is not only warriors who wreak vengeance on their own children. Suffering is passed on from parent to child unto many generations. Did I know as a child that my grandmother's unclaimed fury had made its way into my mother's psyche too? With all her will my mother tried not to repeat against her own children the crimes that had battered her. Where my grandmother was tyrannical, my mother was tolerant and gave free reign. Where my grandmother goaded with critical remarks, my mother was encouraging, and even elaborately praising. But, like my grandfather, my mother drank too much. It was a way of life for her. Sooner or later the long nights would come. Every time I returned home, either to live with her or to visit, I prayed she would not drink again, while I braced myself for what I knew to be inevitable. The evening would begin with a few beers at home, followed by an endless tour of several bars. Either I went along and waited in cars, or I waited at home. In the early morning she would return, her eyes wandering like moths in their sockets. We would sit in two chairs opposite each other, as if these were prearranged places, marked out for us on the stage by a powerful but invisible director. She would start by joking with me. She was marvelously witty when she was drunk. All her natural intelligence was released then and allowed to bloom. But this performance was brief. Her humor turned by dark degrees to meanness. What must have daily constricted her, a kind of sea monster, feeding beneath the waters of her consciousness, and strong, would rise up to stop her glee and mine. Then she would strike. If I was not in my chair to receive her words, she would come and get me. What she said was viperous to me, sank like venom into my veins, and burned a path inside me. Even today I can remember very few of the words she used. She said that my laugh was too loud, or ugly. That I was incapable of loving. I am thankful now that, because she was not in her right mind, I knew at least in a part of myself that these accusations were unfounded. Yet they

343

produced a doubt in me, a lingering shadow, the sense that perhaps I deserved whatever suffering befell me, and that shadow lingers.

Even if a feeling has been made secret, even if it has vanished from memory, can it have disappeared altogether? A weapon is lifted with the force of a forgotten memory. The memory has no words, only the insistence of a pain that has turned into fury. A body, tender in its childhood or its nakedness, lies under this weapon. And this body takes up the rage, the pain, the disowned memory with each blow.

1893. *Self-portrait at Table.* An etching and aquatint, the first in a long series of self-portraits that span the artist's life. A single lamp illuminates her face, the upper part of the body and the table where she sits. Everything else is in darkness. At first glance one thinks of loneliness. But after a moment it is solitude one sees. And a single moment in that solitude, as if one note of music, resonant and deep, played uninterrupted, echoing from every surface, coming to full consciousness in this woman, who in this instant looks out to those who will return her gaze with a face that has taken in and is expressing the music in the air about her. Solemnly and with a quiet patience, her hands pause over the etching she makes, a form she is bringing into being, the one she recognizes as herself.

Who are we? The answer is not easy. There are so many strands to the story, and one must trace every strand. I begin to suspect each thread goes out infinitely and touches everything, everyone. I read these words from an ancient gnostic text, words that have been lost to us for a long time: *For I am the first and the last.* Though in another account we have heard the beginning of this speech spoken by Jesus, here these words come to us in the voice of the goddess. *I am the honored one and scorned one,* the older text goes on. *I am the whore and the holy one. I am the wife and the virgin. I am the barren one, and many are her sons.* These words take on a new meaning for me, as I remember them now. *I am the silence that is incomprehensible,* the text reads, and ends, *I am the utterance of my name.*

Were you to trace any life, and study even the minute consequences, the effect, for instance, of a three-minute walk over a patch of grass, of words said casually to a stranger who happens to sit nearby in a public place, the range of that life would extend way beyond the territory we imagine it to inhabit. This is of course less difficult to understand when imagining the boundaries of a life such as Heinrich Himmler had.

After my visit to Dachau, I went to Paris where, in the fourteenth arrondissement, in the Métro station, I met Hélène. She stopped to help me read my map. We found we were going in the same direction, and thus it was on our way there that we began to speak. Something told me she had survived a concentration camp. And she had. She too fell into the circle of Himmler's life and its consequences. Himmler never went to Paris. At the time of the first mass arrests there he was taking a group of high Nazi officials on a tour of Auschwitz. During the tour, by his orders, the prisoners were made to stand at attention for six hours under the hot sun, but that is another story. Under his command, the Gestapo in Paris began to prepare for the mass arrests of Jews.

Paris had fallen to the German armies in July 1940. By September of that year a notice went up in all the neighborhoods. *Avis aux Israélites,* it read. *Notice to Israelites. By the demand of the occupying authorities, Israelites must present themselves, by October 2, without delay, equipped with identification papers, to the office of the Censor, to complete an identity card.* The notice was signed by the mayor and threatened the most severe punishment for the failure to comply. Through this process vital information was recorded about each Jewish family. Names, ages, addresses, occupations, places of work. An index card was made up for each person. And each card was then duplicated and sent to the offices of the Gestapo on Avenue Foch. There, the cards were duplicated several more times so that the names could be filed by several categories, alphabetically by surname, by address, by arrondissement, occupation, and nationality. At this point in history, work that would be done by computer now was painstakingly completed by countless men and women. Their labor continued feverishly almost until the hour of the first mass arrests, the *rafles,* two years later.

One can trace every death to an order signed by Himmler, yet these arrests could never have taken place on such a massive scale without this vast system of information. What did they think, those who were enlisted for this work? They were civilians. French. There were of course Nazi collaborators, among them, those who shared the same philosophy, or who simply obeyed and profited from whoever might be in power. But among the men and women who did this work, my suspicion is, there were many who tried to keep from themselves the knowledge of what they did. Of course, the final purpose of their labors was never revealed to those who prepared the machinery of arrest. If a man allowed his imagination to stray in the direction of this purpose, he could no doubt comfort himself with the argument that he was only handling pieces of paper. He could tell himself that matters were simply being set in order. The men and women who manufacture the trigger mechanisms for nuclear bombs do not tell themselves they are making weapons. They say simply that they are metal forgers.

There are many ways we have of standing outside ourselves in ignorance. Those who have learned as children to become strangers to themselves do not find this a difficult task. Habit has made it natural not to feel. To ignore the consequences of what one does in the world becomes ordinary. And this tendency is encouraged by a social structure that makes fragments of real events. One is never allowed to see the effects of what one does. But this ignorance is not entirely passive. For some, blindness becomes a kind of refuge, a way of life that is chosen, even with stubborn volition, and does not yield easily even to visible evidence.

The arrests were accompanied by an elaborate procedure, needed on some level, no doubt, for practical reasons, but also serving another purpose. They garbed this violence in the cloak of legality. A mind separated from the depths of itself cannot easily tell right from wrong. To this mind, the outward signs of law and order signify righteousness. That Himmler had such a mind was not unique in his generation, nor, I suspect, in ours.

In a museum in Paris I found a mimeographed sheet giving instructions to the Parisian police on how to arrest Jews. They must always carry red pencils, the sheet admonished, because all records regarding the arrests of Jews must be written in red. And the instructions went on to specify that, regarding the arrests of Jews, all records must be made in triplicate. Finally, the sheet of instructions included a way to categorize those Jews arrested. I could not make any sense of the categories. I only knew them to be crucial. That they might determine life and death for a woman, or man, or child. And that in the mind that invented these categories they had to have had some hidden significance, standing, like the crudely shaped characters of a medieval play, for shades of feeling, hidden states of being, secret knowledge.

For the most part, the men who designed the first missiles were not interested in weapons so much as flight. In his account of the early work at Peenemünde laboratories, Wernher von Braun explains that the scientists there had discovered a way to fund their research by making rockets appeal to the military. Colonel Dornberger told the other scientists that they could not hope to continue if all they created were experimental rockets. All Wernher von Braun wanted was to design vehicles that would travel to the moon. In the early fifties, in a book he wrote with two other scientists, he speaks of the reasons for such a flight. Yes, he says, curiosity and adventure play a part. But the primary reason is *to increase man's knowledge of the universe.*

To tell a story, or to hear a story told, is not a simple transmission of information. Something else in the telling is given too, so that, once hearing, what one has heard becomes a part of oneself. Hélène and I went to the museum in Paris together. There, among photographs of the first mass arrests and the concentration camp at Drancy, she told me this story. Reading the notice signed by the mayor, she presented herself immediately at the office of the censor. She waited with others, patiently. But when her turn in line came, the censor looked at her carefully. She was blond and had blue eyes. *Are you really Jewish?* he asked her.

The question of who was and who was not Jewish was pivotal to the Nazi mind and much legal controversy hung in the balance of this debate. For a few years, anyone with three Jewish grandparents was considered Jewish. An ancestor who belonged to the faith, but was not of Jewish blood would be

Jewish. One who did not belong to the faith, but was of Jewish blood, was also Jewish. At the heart of this controversy, I hear the whisper of ambivalence, and perhaps the smallest beginning of compassion. For, to this mind, the one who is not Jewish becomes recognizable as like oneself.

Yes, I am Jewish, she said. *But your mother*, he asked again. *Can you be certain? Yes*, she said. *Ask her, go home and ask her*, he said, putting his stamp away. *But my mother is dead*, she protested. Then, he said, keeping his stamp in the drawer, *Your father. Your father must not be Jewish. Go home and ask him. I know he is Jewish*, Hélène answered. *There is no doubt that he is Jewish. He has always been Jewish, and I am Jewish too.* Then the man was silent, he shook his head. And, looking past her, said, *Perhaps your father was not really your father. Have you thought of that? Perhaps he was not your father?* She was young. *Of course he's my father. How can you say that? Certainly he is my father*, she insisted. *He is Jewish and so am I.* And she demanded that her papers be stamped.

What was in this man's mind as he questioned her? Did he say to himself, Perhaps here is someone I can save? Did he have what Pierre Sauvage has called *a moment of goodness?* What we know as goodness is not a static quality but arrives through a series of choices, some imperceptible, which are continually presented to us.

It is 1941. And Heinrich Himmler pays a visit to the Russian front. He has been put in charge of organizing the *Einsatzgruppen*, moving groups of men who carry out the killing of civilians and partisans. He watches as a deep pit is dug by the captured men and women. Then, suddenly, a young man catches his eye. He is struck by some quality the man possesses. He takes a liking to him. He has the commandant of the *Einsatzgruppen* bring the young man to him. *Who was your father?* he asks. *Your mother? Your grandparents? Do you have at least one grandparent who was not Jewish?* He is trying to save the young man. But he answers no to all the questions. So Himmler, strictly following the letter of the law, watches as the young man is put to death.

The captured men, women, and children are ordered to remove their clothing then. Naked, they stand before the pit they have dug. Some scream. Some attempt escape. The young men in uniform place their rifles against their shoulders and fire into the naked bodies. They do not fall silently. There are cries. There are open wounds. There are faces blown apart. Stomachs opened up. The dying groan. Weep. Flutter. Open their mouths.

There is no photograph of the particular moment when Heinrich Himmler stares into the face of death. What does he look like? Is he pale? He is stricken, the accounts tell us, and more than he thought he would be. He has imagined something quieter, more efficient, like the even rows of numbers, the alphabetical lists of names he likes to put in his files. Something he might be able to understand and contain. But one cannot contain death so easily.

●　●　●

Death with Girl in Her Lap. One of many studies the artist did of death. A girl is drawn, her body dead or almost dead, in that suspended state where the breath is almost gone. There is no movement. No will. The lines the artist has drawn are simple. She has not rendered the natural form of head, arm, buttock, thigh exactly. But all these lines hold the feeling of a body in them. And as my eyes rest on this image, I can feel my own fear of death, and also, the largeness of grief, how grief will not let you remain insulated from your own feelings, or from life itself. It is as if I knew this girl. And death, too, appears to know her, cradling the fragile body with tenderness; she seems to understand the sorrow of dying. Perhaps this figure has taken into herself all the deaths she has witnessed. And in this way, she has become merciful.

Because Himmler finds it so difficult to witness these deaths, the commandant makes an appeal to him. If it is hard for you, he says, think what it must be for these young men who must carry out these executions, day after day. Shaken by what he has seen and heard, Himmler returns to Berlin resolved to ease the pain of these men. He will consult an engineer and set him to work immediately on new designs. Before the year has ended, he presents the *Einsatzgruppen* with a mobile killing truck. Now the young men will not have to witness death day after day. A hose from the exhaust pipe funnels fumes into a chamber built on the bed of a covered truck, which has a red cross painted on its side so its passengers will not be alarmed as they enter it.

To a certain kind of mind, what is hidden away ceases to exist.

Himmler does not like to watch the suffering of his prisoners. In this sense he does not witness the consequences of his own commands. But the mind is like a landscape in which nothing really ever disappears. What seems to have vanished has only transmuted to another form. Not wishing to witness what he has set in motion, still, in a silent part of himself, he must imagine what takes place. So, just as the child is made to live out the unclaimed imagination of the parent, others under Himmler's power were made to bear witness for him. Homosexuals were forced to witness and sometimes take part in the punishment of other homosexuals, Poles of other Poles, Jews of Jews. And as far as possible, the hands of the men of the SS were protected from the touch of death. Other prisoners were required to bury the bodies, or burn them in the ovens.

Hélène was turned in by a Jewish man who was trying, no doubt, to save his own life, and she was put under arrest by another Jewish man, an inmate of the same camp to which she was taken. She was grateful that she herself had not been forced to do harm. But something haunted her. A death that came to stand in place of her own death. As we walked through the streets of Paris she told me this story.

By the time of her arrest she was married and had a young son. Her husband was taken from their apartment during one of the mass arrests that began in July of 1942. Hélène was out at the time with her son. For some time she wandered the streets of Paris. She would sleep at night at the homes of various friends and acquaintances, leaving in the early morning so that she would not arouse suspicion among the neighbors. This was the hardest time, she told me, because there was so little food, even less than she was to have at Drancy. She had no ration card or any way of earning money. Her whole existence was illegal. She had to be as if invisible. She collected scraps from the street. It was on the street that she told me this story, as we walked from the fourth arrondissement to the fifth, crossing the bridge near Notre Dame, making our way toward the Boulevard St. Michel.

Her husband was a citizen of a neutral country and for this reason legally destined for another camp. From this camp he would not be deported. Instead he was taken to the French concentration camp at Drancy. After his arrest, hoping to help him, Hélène managed to take his papers to the Swiss Consulate. But the papers remained there. After her own arrest she was taken with her son to Drancy, where she was reunited with her husband. He told her that her efforts were useless. But still again and again she found ways to smuggle out letters to friends asking them to take her husband's papers from the Swiss Consulate to the camp at Drancy. One of these letters was to save their lives.

After a few months, preparations began to send Hélène and her family to Auschwitz. Along with many other women, she was taken to have her hair cut short, though those consigned to that task decided she should keep her long, blond hair. Still, she was herded along with the others to the train station and packed into the cars. Then, just two hours before the train was scheduled to leave, Hélène, her son, and her husband were pulled from the train. Her husband's papers had been brought by the Swiss consul to the camp. The Commandant, by assuming Hélène shared the same nationality with her husband, had made a fortuitous mistake.

But the train had to have a specific number of passengers before it could leave. In Hélène's place the guards brought a young man. She would never forget his face, she told me, or his name. Later she tried to find out whether he had lived or died but could learn nothing.

Himmler did not partake in the actual preparations for what he called "the final solution." Nor did he attend the Wannsee Conference where the decision to annihilate millions of human beings was made. He sent his assistant Heydrich. Yet Heydrich, who was there, did not count himself entirely present. He could say that each decision he made was at the bequest of Heinrich Himmler. In this way an odd system of insulation was created. These crimes, these murders of millions, were all carried out in absentia, as if by no one in particular.

This ghostlike quality, the strange absence of a knowing conscience, as if the living creature had abandoned the shell, was spread throughout the entire chain of command. So a French bureaucrat writing a letter in 1942 speaks in detail of the mass arrests that he himself supervised as if he had no other part in these murders except as a kind of spiritless cog in a vast machine whose force compelled him from without. *The German authorities have set aside especially for that purpose enough trains to transport 30,000 Jews,* he writes. *It is therefore necessary that the arrests made should correspond to the capacity of the trains.*

It is August 23, 1943. The first inmates of concentration camp Dora have arrived. Is there some reason why an unusually high percentage of prisoners ordered to work in this camp are homosexuals? They are set to work immediately, working with few tools, often with bare hands, to convert long tunnels carved into the Harz Mountains into a factory for the manufacture of missiles. They work for eighteen hours each day. Six of these hours are set aside for formal procedures, roll calls, official rituals of the camp. For six hours they must try to sleep in the tunnels, on the damp earth, in the same area where the machines, pickaxes, explosions, and drills are making a continually deafening noise, twenty-four hours of every day. They are fed very little. They see the daylight only once a week, at the Sunday roll call. The tunnels themselves are illuminated with faint light bulbs. The production of missiles has been moved here because the factories at Peenemünde were bombed. Because the secret work at Peenemünde had been revealed to the Allies by an informer, after the bombing the Reichsführer SS proposed that the factories should be installed in a concentration camp. Here, he argued, security could be more easily enforced; only the guards had any freedom, and they were subject to the harsh discipline of the SS. The labor itself could be hidden under the soil of the Harz Mountains.

Memory can be like a long, half-lit tunnel, a tunnel where one is likely to encounter phantoms of a self, long concealed, no longer nourished with the force of consciousness, existing in a tortured state between life and death. In his account of his years at Peenemünde, Wernher von Braun never mentions concentration camp Dora. Yet he was seen there more than once by inmates who remembered him. As the designing engineer, he had to supervise many details of production. Conditions at camp Dora could not have escaped his attention. Dora did not have its own crematorium. And so many men and women died in the course of a day that the bodies waiting to be picked up by trucks and taken to the ovens of Buchenwald were piled high next to the entrance to the tunnels.

Perhaps von Braun told himself that what went on in those tunnels had nothing to do with him. He had not wished for these events, had not wanted them. The orders came from someone who had power over him. In the course of this writing I remembered a childhood incident that made me disown myself in the same way. My best friend, who was my neighbor, had a mean streak and because of this had a kind of power over the rest of us who played with her. For a year I left my grandmother's house to live with my mother again. On my return I had been replaced by another little girl, and the two of them excluded me. But finally my chance arrived. My friend had a quarrel with her new friend and enlisted me in an act of revenge. Together we cornered her at the back of a yard, pushing her into the garbage cans, yelling nasty words at her, throwing things at her.

My friend led the attack, inventing the strategies and the words which were hurled. With part of myself I knew what it was to be the object of this kind of assault. But I also knew this was the way to regain my place with my friend. Later I disowned my acts, as if I had not committed them. Because I was under the sway of my friend's power, I told myself that what I did was really her doing. And in this way became unreal to myself. It was as if my voice threatening her, my own anger, and my voice calling names, had never existed.

I was told this story by a woman who survived the holocaust. The war had not yet begun. Nor the exiles. Nor the mass arrests. But history was on the point of these events, tipping over, ready to fall into the relentless path of consequences. She was then just a child, playing games in the street. And one day she found herself part of a circle of other children. They had surrounded a little boy and were calling him names because he was Jewish. He was her friend. But she thought if she left this circle, or came to his defense, she herself would lose her standing among the others. Then, suddenly, in an angry voice her mother called her in from the street. As soon as the door shut behind her, her mother began to shout, words incomprehensible to her, and slapped her across the face. *Your father*, her mother finally said, after crying, and in a quieter voice, *was Jewish.* Her father had been dead for three years. Soon after this day her mother too would die. As the danger grew worse her gentile relatives would not harbor her any longer, and she joined the fate of those who tried to live in the margins, as if invisible, as if mere shadows, terrified of a direct glance, of recognition, existing at the unsteady boundary of consciousness.

In disowning the effects we have on others, we disown ourselves. My father watched the suffering of my childhood and did nothing. He was aware of my mother's alcoholism and the state of her mind when she drank. He knew my grandmother to be tyrannical. We could speak together of these things almost dispassionately, as if both of us were disinterested witnesses to a fascinating social drama. But after a day's visit with him, spent at the park, or riding horses, or at the movies, he would send me back into that world of suffering we had discussed so dispassionately.

His disinterest in my condition was not heartless. It reflected the distance he kept from his own experience. One could sense his suffering but he never expressed it directly. He was absent to a part of himself. He was closer to tears than many men, but he never shed those tears. If I cried he would fall into a frightened silence. And because of this, though I spent a great deal of time with him, he was always in a certain sense an absent father. Unknowingly I responded in kind, for years, feeling a vaguely defined anger that would neither let me love nor hate him.

My father learned his disinterest under the guise of masculinity. Boys don't cry. There are whole disciplines, institutions, rubrics in our culture which serve as categories of denial.

Science is such a category. The torture and death that Heinrich Himmler found disturbing to witness became acceptable to him when it fell under this rubric. He liked to watch the scientific experiments in the concentration camps. And then there is the rubric of military order. I am looking at a photograph. It was taken in 1941 in the Ukraine. The men of an *Einstazgruppen* are assembled in a group pose. In front of them their rifles rest in ceremonial order, composed into tripods. They stand straight and tall. They are clean-shaven and their uniforms are immaculate, in *apple-pie order,* as we would say in America.

It is not surprising that cleanliness in a profession that sheds blood would become a compulsion. Blood would evidence guilt and fear to a mind trying to escape the consequence of its decisions. It is late in the night when Laura tells me one more story. Her father is about to be sent to Europe, where he will fight in the Battle of the Bulge and become a general. For weeks her mother has prepared a party. The guests begin to arrive in formal dress and sparkling uniforms. The white-gloved junior officers stand to open the doors. Her mother, regal in satin and jewels, starts to descend the staircase. Laura sits on the top stair watching, dressed in her pajamas. Then suddenly a pool of blood appears at her mother's feet, her mother falls to the floor, and almost as quickly, without a word uttered, a junior officer sweeps up the stairs, removes her mother into a waiting car, while another one cleans up the blood. No one tells Laura that her mother has had a miscarriage, and the party continues as if no event had taken place, no small or large death, as if no death were about to take place, nor any blood be spilled.

But the nature of the material world frustrates our efforts to remain free of the suffering of others. The mobile killing van that Himmler summoned into being had some defects. Gas from the exhaust pipes leaked into the cabin where the drivers sat and made them ill. When they went to remove the bodies from the van they were covered with blood and excrement, and their faces bore expressions of anguish. Himmler's engineers fixed the leak, increased the flow of gas so the deaths would be quicker, and built in a drain to collect the bodily fluids that are part of death.

There are times when no engineers can contain death. Over this same landscape through which the mobile killing vans traveled, an invisible cloud would one day spread, and from it would descend a toxic substance that would work its way into the soil and the water, the plants and the bodies of animals, and into human cells, not only in this landscape of the Ukraine, but in the fjords of Norway, the fields of Italy and France, and even here, in the far reaches of California, bringing a death that recalled, more than forty years later, those earlier hidden deaths.

You can see pictures of them. Whole families, whole communities. The fabric on their backs almost worn through. Bodies as if ebbing away before your eyes. Poised on an edge. The cold visible around the thin joints of arms and knees. A bed made in a doorway. Moving then, over time, deeper and deeper into the shadows. Off the streets. Into back rooms, and then to the attics or the cellars. Windows blackened. Given less and less to eat. Moving into smaller and smaller spaces. Sequestered away like forbidden thoughts, or secrets.

Could he have seen in these images of those he had forced into hiding and suffering, into agony and death, an image of the outer reaches of his own consciousness? It is only now that I can begin to see he has become part of them. Those whose fate he sealed. Heinrich Himmler. A part of Jewish history. Remembered by those who fell into the net of his unclaimed life. Claimed as a facet of the wound, part of the tissue of the scar. A mark on the body of our minds, both those of us who know this history and those who do not.

For there is a sense in which we are all witnesses. Hunger, desperation, pain, loneliness, these are all visible in the streets about us. The way of life we live, a life we have never really chosen, forces us to walk past what we see. And out at the edge, beyond what we see or hear, we can feel a greater suffering, cries from a present or past starvation, a present or past torture, cries of those we have never met, coming to us in our dreams, and even if these cries do not survive in our waking knowledge, still, they live on in the part of ourselves we have ceased to know.

I think now of the missile again and how it came into being. Scientific inventions do not spring whole like Athena from the head of Zeus from the analytic implications of scientific discoveries. Technological advance takes shape slowly in the womb of society and is influenced and fed by our shared imagination. What we create thus mirrors the recesses of our own minds, and perhaps also hidden capacities. Television mimics the ability to see in the mind's eye. And the rocket? Perhaps the night flight of the soul, that ability celebrated in witches to send our thoughts as if through the air to those distant from us, to send images of ourselves, and even our secret feelings, out into an atmosphere beyond ourselves, to see worlds far flung from and strange to us becomes manifest in a sinister fashion in the missile.

Self-portrait in charcoal. Since the earliest rendering she made of her own image, much time has passed. The viewer here has moved closer. Now the

SUSAN GRIFFIN

artist's head fills the frame. She is much older in years and her features have taken on that androgyny which she thought necessary to the work of an artist. Her hair is white on the paper where the charcoal has not touched it. She is in profile and facing a definite direction. Her eyes look in that direction. But they do not focus on anyone or anything. The portrait is soft, the charcoal rubbed almost gently over the surface, here light, here dark. Her posture is one not so much of resolution as resignation. The portrait was drawn just after the First World War, the war in which her son Peter died. I have seen these eyes in the faces of those who grieve, eyes that are looking but not focused, seeing perhaps what is no longer visible.

After the war, German scientists who developed the V-1 and V-2 rocket immigrate to the United States where they continue to work on rocketry. Using the Vengeance weapon as a prototype, they develop the first ICBM missiles.

On the twenty-third of May 1945, as the war in Europe comes to an end, Heinrich Himmler is taken prisoner by the Allied command. He has removed the military insignia from his clothing, and he wears a patch over one eye. Disguised in this manner, and carrying the identity papers of a man he had condemned to death, he attempts to cross over the border at Bremervörde. No one at the checkpoint suspects him of being the Reichsführer SS. But once under the scrutiny of the guards, all his courage fails him. Like a trembling schoolboy, he blurts out the truth. Now he will be taken to a center for interrogation, stripped of his clothing and searched. He will refuse to wear the uniform of the enemy, so he will be given a blanket to wrap over his underclothing. Taken to a second center for interrogation, he will be forced to remove this blanket and his underclothes. The interrogators, wishing to make certain he has no poison hidden anywhere, no means by which to end his life and hence avoid giving testimony, will surround his naked body. They will ask him to open his mouth. But just as one of them sees a black capsule wedged between his teeth, he will jerk his head away and swallow. All attempts to save his life will fail. He will not survive to tell his own story. His secrets will die with him.

There were many who lived through those years who did not wish to speak of what they saw or did. None of the German rocket engineers bore witness to what they saw at concentration camp Dora. Common rank and file members of the Nazi Party, those without whose efforts or silent support the machinery could not have gone on, fell almost as a mass into silence. In Berlin and Munich I spoke to many men and women, in my generation or younger, who were the children of soldiers, or party members, or SS men, or generals, or simply believers. Their parents would not speak to them of what had happened. The atmosphere in both cities was as if a pall had been placed over memory. And thus the shared mind of this nation has no roots, no continuous link with what keeps life in a pattern of meaning.

Lately I have come to believe that an as yet undiscovered human need and even a property of matter is the desire for revelation. The truth within us has a way of coming out despite all conscious efforts to conceal it. I have heard stories from those in the generation after the war, all speaking of the same struggle to ferret truth from the silence of their parents so that they themselves could begin to live. One born the year the war ended was never told a word about concentration camps, at home or in school. She began to wake in the early morning hours with nightmares which mirrored down to fine and accurate detail the conditions of the camps. Another woman searching casually through some trunks in the attic of her home found a series of pamphlets, virulently and cruelly anti-Semitic, which had been written by her grandfather, a high Nazi official. Still another pieced together the truth of her father's life, a member of the Gestapo, a man she remembered as playful by contrast to her stern mother. He died in the war. Only over time could she put certain pieces together. How he had had a man working under him beaten. And then, how he had beaten her.

Many of those who survived the holocaust could not bear the memories of what happened to them and, trying to bury the past, they too fell into silence. Others continue to speak as they are able. The manner of speech varies. At an artist's retreat in the Santa Cruz Mountains I met a woman who survived Bergen Belsen and Auschwitz. She inscribes the number eight in many of her paintings. And the number two. This is the story she is telling with those numbers. It was raining the night she arrived with her mother, six brothers and sisters at Auschwitz. It fell very hard, she told me. We were walking in the early evening up a hill brown in the California fall. The path was strewn with yellow leaves illuminated by the sun in its descent. They had endured the long trip from Hungary to Poland, without food or water. They were very tired. Now the sky seemed very black but the platform, lit up with stadium lights, was blinding after the darkness of the train. She would never, she told me, forget the shouting. It is as if she still cannot get the sound out of her ears. The Gestapo gave one shrill order after another, in a language she did not yet understand. They were herded in confusion, blows coming down on them randomly from the guards, past a tall man in a cape. This was Dr. Mengele. He made a single gesture toward all her family and continued it toward her but in a different direction. For days, weeks, months after she had learned what their fate had been she kept walking in the direction of their parting and beyond toward the vanishing point of her vision of them.

There were seven from her family who died there that night. The eighth to die was her father. He was sent to a different camp and died on the day of liberation. Only two lived, she and one brother. The story of one life cannot be told separately from the story of other lives. Who are we? The question is not simple. What we call the self is part of a larger matrix of relationship and society. Had we been born to a different family, in a different time, to a different world, we would not be the same. All the lives that surround us are in us.

On the first day that I met Lenke she asked a question that stays with me still. Why do some inflict on others the suffering they have endured? What is it in a life that makes one choose to do this, or not? It is a question I cannot answer. Not even after several years pondering this question in the light of Heinrich Himmler's soul. Two years after my conversation with Lenke, as if there had been a very long pause in our dialogue, I was given a glimpse in the direction of an answer. Leo told me his story; it sounded back over time, offering not so much solution as response.

The nucleus of every cell in the human body contains the genetic plan for the whole organism.

We sat together in a large and noisy restaurant, light pouring through the windows, the present clamoring for our attention, even as we moved into the past. Leo was nine years old when the war entered his life. He remembers standing in a crowd, he told me, watching as a partisan was flogged and executed by the Germans. *What do you think I felt?* he asked me, the irony detectable in his voice. What he told me fell into his narration as part of a larger picture. The capture, the roughness, the laceration of flesh, the sight of death, all this excited him.

Violence was not new to him. Through bits and pieces surrounding the central line of his story I came to some idea of what his childhood must have been. His father was a cold man, given to rages over small errors. Leo was beaten often. Such attacks had already forced his older half brother out of the house. It was to this brother that Leo bonded and gave his love.

Leo remembered a party before the war. The room was lively with talk until his older brother arrived. Then a silence fell over everyone. The older men were afraid of this young man, even his father. And to Leo, his brother, with his air of power and command, was a hero. He could scarcely understand the roots of this power, moored in a political system of terror so effective, few even spoke of it. Leo's brother was a young member of Stalin's secret police. Cast into the streets while still a boy, he learned the arts of survival. Eventually he was arrested for assaulting and robbing a man. It was under this circumstance that he offered himself to the NKVD, the forerunner of the KGB, as an interrogator. He learned to torture men and women suspected of treason or of harboring secrets.

He wore high black leather boots and a black leather jacket, which impressed Leo. Leo followed him about, and they would take long walks together, his brother telling him the stories he could tell no one else. How he had tortured a woman. How he had made blood flow from the nipples of her breasts.

Everything he heard from his brother he took into himself. Such love as Leo had for his brother can be a forceful teacher. He did not see his brother often, nor was his intimacy with him great enough to create familiarity. What he had was a continual taste awakening hunger. Never did he know the daily presence of the beloved, or all his imperfections, the real person dwelling behind the mask of the ideal, the shiny and impervious leather. To fill the nearly perpetual absence of his brother he clung to this ideal. An appearance of strength. A certain arrogance in the face of violence, promising an even greater violence. Love always seeks a resting place.

I knew a similar attachment to my sister. Separated when I was six and she was thirteen, the experience of love I knew with her was longing, and over time this bonded me to longing itself. And to the books she brought me to read, the poems she read to me, worlds she pointed me toward.

And the German occupation of the Ukraine? The accident at Chernobyl had taken place just weeks before we met. But long before this event, the same land suffered other wounds. As the Soviet army retreated, they burned crops and killed livestock. Even before the German invasion, the land was charred and black for miles around. Then when the German army came, the executions began. And the deportations. Many were taken away to forced labor camps. Leo was among them.

His father was an agronomist with some knowledge of how to increase crop yields. The whole family was transported to Germany, but at the scientist's camp Leo was transported in another direction. His father watched him go, Leo told me, with no protest, not even the protestation of tears.

What was it like for him in the labor camp to which he was sent? His telling of the past existed in a framework of meaning he had built slowly over the years, and with great pain, forced to this understanding by events that he himself had brought into being, later in his life.

It is a question of passion, he told me. While he was in the camps, he began to worship the uniformed members of the SS and the SA, just as he had loved his brother. Their strength, their ideals, their willingness to do violence, to live for something beyond themselves, the black leather they wore, the way they were clean and polished and tall. He saw those who, like himself, were imprisoned as small and demeaned, caught in the ugliness of survival, lacking any heroism, cowardly, petty. Even now, as he looked back himself with another eye, his disdain for those who suffered persisted in a phantom form, in the timbre of his voice.

The punishment of the guards did not embitter him. In his mind he believed he himself was always justly punished. Once, against the rules, he stole food, honey, while he was working. He did not accept his own hunger as an argument for kindness. He admired the strength with which he was hit.

Even the intimacy of the blows gave him a certain pride in himself. Loving the arms that hit him, he could think of this power as his own.

But there were two assaults which he could not forgive. They humiliated him. Now as I write I can see that to him his attackers must have been unworthy of his admiration. He was on a work detail in the neighboring village when a boy his own age slapped him. And later an old woman spat in his face.

This was all he told me of his time of imprisonment. After the liberation, he went into Germany to search for his family. Did he believe that perhaps, even now, something outside of the circle drawn by what he had suffered existed for him? Was there a seed of hope, a wish that made him, thin, weak, on shaking legs, travel the hundreds of miles, sleeping in trains and train stations, to search? He was exhausted, I can imagine, past that edge of weariness in which whatever is real ceases entirely to matter and existence itself is just a gesture, not aimed any longer at outcome, but just a simple expression of what remains and so can seem even brighter. He was making a kind of pilgrimage.

It is in this way, coldness beyond cold, frailty beyond endurance, that sorrow becomes a power. A light begins to shine past the fire of ovens, yet from them, as if stars, or turning leaves, falling and trapped in their fall, nevertheless kept their brilliance, and this brilliance a beacon, like a code, flashes out the precise language of human suffering. Then we know that what we suffer is not going to pass by without meaning.

Self-portrait, 1923. The artist's face is drawn of lines left white on the page which seem as if they were carved out of night. We are very close to her. It is only her face we see. Eye to eye, she looks directly at us. But her eyes are unfocused and weary with that kind of tiredness that has accumulated over so much time we think of it as aging. Her mouth, wide and frank, does not resist gravity any longer. This mouth smiles with an extraordinary subtlety. We can almost laugh with this mouth, drawn with lines which, like all the lines on the lines on the page, resemble scars, or tears in a fabric.

A story is told as much by silence as by speech. Like the white spaces in an etching, such silences render form. But unlike an etching in which the whole is grasped at once, the silence of a story must be understood over time. Leo described to me what his life was like after he found his parents, but he did not describe the moment, or even the day or week, when he found them. Only now as I write these words does the absence of joy in this reunion begin to speak to me. And in the space of this absence I can feel the kind of cold that can extinguish the most intense of fires.

Leo was soon streetwise. His family was near starvation. He worked the black market. Older men buying his goods would ask him for women, and he began to procure for them. He kept his family alive. His father, he told me, never acknowledged his effort. When they moved to America a few years later and Leo reminded him that his work had fed him, his father exclaimed, in a voice of shock and disparagement, *And what you did!*

In 1957, the Soviet Union develops the SS-6, a surface-to-surface missile. It is launched with thirty-two engines. Failing as a weapon, this device is used to launch the first satellite into space. In 1961, the Soviet Union develops the SS-7. These missiles carry nuclear warheads. They are launched from hardened silos to protect them from attack.

In America he was sent to high school. But he did not know how to be an ordinary boy among boys. He became a street fighter. Together with a group of boys among whom he was the toughest, he would look for something to happen. More than once they devised a trap for homosexual men. They would place the prettiest boy among them on a park bench and wait behind the trees and bushes. Usually a man would pull up in his car and go to sit on the bench next to the boy. When this man made any gesture of seduction, or suggested the boy leave with him, the boys would suddenly appear and, surrounding him, beat him and take his money.

I am thinking of these boys as one after another they forced the weight of their bodies into another man's body and tried to hurt him, to bloody him, to defeat him. I know it is possible to be a stranger to one's feelings. For the years after I was separated from my mother, I forgot that I missed her. My feeling was driven so deep, it was imperceptible, so much a part of me, I would not have called it grief. It is said that when boys or young men attack a man they find effeminate or believe to be homosexual they are trying to put at a distance all traces of homosexuality in themselves. But what does this mean? What is the central passion in this issue of manhood, proven or disproven? In my imagination I witness again the scene that Leo described to me. It is a passionate scene, edged by a love the boys feel for each other, and by something more, by a kind of grief, raging because it is buried so deep inside. Do they rage against this man's body because of what has been withheld from them, held back, like the food of intimacy, imprisoned and guarded in the bodies of older men, in the bodies of fathers? Is it this rage that fires the mettle of what we call manhood?

Yet, are we not all affected by this that is withheld in men? Are we not all forged in the same inferno? It was never said directly, but I know my greatgrandfather beat my grandfather, and lectured him, drunkenly, humiliating and shaming him. I am told that as adults they quarreled violently over politics. No one in my family can remember the substance of the disagreement, only the red faces, the angry voices. Now, as I look back to imagine my grandfather passionately reciting the list of those he hated, our black neighbors, the Jews, the Communists, I follow the path of his staring eyes and begin to make out a figure. It is my great-grandfather Colvin, receiving even

SUSAN GRIFFIN

after his death too indifferently the ardent and raging pleas of his son. And hearing that voice again, I hear an echo from my grandfather's daughter, my mother, whose voice when she had been drinking too much had the same quality, as of the anguish of feeling held back for so long it has become monstrous, the furies inside her unleashed against me.

Leo's telling had a slightly bitter edge, a style which felt like the remnant of an older harshness. He kept looking at me as if to protect himself from any sign of shock in my face. Now he was not certain he would tell me the rest of his story. But he did.

Just after he graduated from high school, the Korean War began. He was drafted, and sent directly to Korea. Was he in combat? Leo shook his head. He was assigned to an intelligence unit. He spoke Russian. And he was directed to interrogate Russian prisoners who were captured behind enemy lines. He told me this story. He was given two men to question. With the first man he made every kind of threat. But he carried nothing out. The man was resolutely silent. And Leo learned nothing from him. He left the room with all his secrets. *You can never,* Leo told me later, *let any man get the better of you.* With the second man he was determined not to fail. He would get him to tell whatever he knew. He made the same threats again, and again met silence. Then, suddenly, using his thumb and finger, he put out the man's eye. And as the man was screaming and bleeding, he told him he would die one way or the other. He was going to be shot. But he had the choice now of seeing his executioners or not, of dying in agony or not. And then the man told him his secrets.

Self-portrait, 1927. She has drawn herself in charcoal again, and in profile. And she still looks out but now her eyes are focused. She is looking at something visible, distant, but perhaps coming slowly closer. Her mouth still turns down, and this must be a characteristic expression because her face is lined in that direction. The form of her face is drawn with soft strokes, blended into the page, as one life blends into another life, or a body into earth. There is something in the quality of her attention, fine lines sketched over her eyebrow. A deeper black circle under her eye. With a resolute, unhappy awareness, she recognizes what is before her.

The life plan of the body is encoded in the DNA molecule, a substance that has the ability to hold information and to replicate itself.

Self-portrait, 1934. As I look now I see in her face that whatever it was she saw before has now arrived. She looks directly at us again and we are even closer to her than before. One finger at the edge of the frame pulls against her eyebrow, against lines drawn there earlier, as if to relieve pain. All the lines lead downward, like rain. Her eyes are open but black, at once impenetrable

360

and infinite. There is a weariness here again, the kind from which one never recovers. And grief? It is that grief I have spoken of earlier, no longer apart from the flesh and bone of her face.

After many years of silence, my mother and I were able to speak of what happened between us and in our family. It was healing for us, to hear and speak the truth, and made for a closeness we had not felt before. Both of us knew we were going to speak before we did.

Before a secret is told one can often feel the weight of it in the atmosphere. Leo gazed at me for a long moment. There was more he wanted to tell me and that I wanted to hear. The rest of his story was elsewhere, in the air, in our hands, the traffic on the street, felt. He shook his head again before he began. The war was over, but he had started in a certain direction and now he could not stop. He befriended a young man from the army. This man looked up to him the way he had to his brother. He wanted to teach the younger man what he knew. He had already committed several robberies, and he wanted an accomplice. They went out together, looking for an easy target for the young man to practice on. They found someone who was easy. He was old, and black. Leo showed his friend how to hold his gun, up close to the temple, pointing down. The boy did this. But the old man, terrified, simply ran. As Leo directed him, the younger man held the gun out in front of him to shoot and he pulled the trigger. But the cartridge of the bullet stuck in the chamber. So the man, still alive, kept running. Then, as Leo urged him on, his friend ran after the old man and, jumping on his back, began to hit him on the head with the butt of his pistol. The moment overtook him. Fear, and exhilaration at mastering fear, a deeper rage, all made a fuel for his fury. He hit and hit again and again. He drew blood. Then the man ceased to cry out, ceased to struggle. He lay still. And the younger man kept on hitting, so that the moment of the older man's death was lost in a frenzy of blows. Then finally there was silence. The young man, knowing he had caused a death, stood up shaking and walked away. He was stunned, as if he himself had been beaten. And Leo, who had been calling and shouting to encourage his friend, who had been laughing, he said, so hard he had to hold himself, was silent too. He went to stand by the body of the old man. Blood poured profusely from the wounds on his head. He stared into the face of this dead man. And now in his telling of the story he was crying. He paused. What was it there in that face for him, broken, afraid, shattered, flesh and bone past repair, past any effort, any strength? *I could see,* he told me, *that this man was just like me.*

In 1963 America develops a new missile, the Titan II. It has a larger range, a larger carrying capacity, a new guidance system, and an improved vehicle for re-entry. These missiles are still being deployed.

1938. *Self-portrait.* The artist is once again in profile. But now she faces another direction. The bones of her cheeks, mouth, nose, eyes are still all in shadow. Her eyebrows arch in tired anticipation. She has drawn herself with the simplest of strokes. Charcoal blending softly downward, all the strokes moving downward. This is old age. Not a single line drawn for vanity, or for the sake of pretense, protects us from her age. She is facing toward death.

We knew, both Leo and I, that now he was telling me what was most crucial to him. In the telling, some subtle change passed through him. Something unknown was taking shape here, both of us witnesses, both of us part of the event. This that he lived through was what I was seeking to understand. What he saw in the face of the dead man did not leave him. For a long time he was afraid of his own dreams. Every night, the same images returned to him, but images in motion, belonging to a longer narration. He dreamed that he entered a park and began to dig up a grave there. Each night he would plunge his hands in the earth and find the body buried there. But each night the body he found was more and more eroded. This erosion filled him with horror. He could not sleep alone. Every night he would find a different woman to sleep with him. Every night he would drink himself into insensibility. But the images of dreams began to come to him even in his waking hours. And so he began to drink ceaselessly. Finally he could not go on as before. Two months after the death he had witnessed he confessed his part in it.

For many reasons his sentence was light. Both he and his friend were young. They had been soldiers. He knew that, had the man he helped to kill not been black, his sentence would have been longer; or he may himself have been put to death. He said nothing of his years of imprisonment. Except that these years served to quiet the dreams that had haunted him. His wit, his air of toughness, all he had seen make him good at the work he does now with boys who have come into conflict with society, a work which must in some way be intended as restitution.

Yet, as he spoke, I began to see that he believed some part of his soul would never be retrieved. *There is a circle of humanity,* he told me, *and I can feel its warmth. But I am forever outside.*

I made no attempt to soften these words. What he said was true. A silence between us held what had been spoken. Then gradually we began to make small movements. Hands reaching for a key, a cigarette. By a quiet agreement, his story was over, and we were in the present again.

The telling and the hearing of a story is not a simple act. The one who tells must reach down into deeper layers of the self, reviving old feelings, reviewing the past. Whatever is retrieved is reworked into a new form, one that narrates events and gives the listener a path through these events that leads to some fragment of wisdom. The one who hears takes the story in, even to a place not visible or conscious to the mind, yet there. In this inner place a story from another life suffers a subtle change. As it enters the memory of the listener it is augmented by reflection, by other memories, and even the body hearing and responding in the moment of the telling. By such transmissions, consciousness is woven.

Over a year has passed now since I heard Leo's story. In my mind's eye, I see the events of his life as if they were carved out in woodblock prints, like the ones Käthe Kollwitz did. Of all her work, these most resemble Expressionist art. Was it intended that the form be so heavy, as if drawn centuries back into a mute untold history? Her work, and the work of the Expressionist movement, was called degenerate by the Nazis. These images, images of tumultuous inner feelings, or of suffering caused and hidden by social circumstance, were removed from the walls of museums and galleries.

When I was in Munich, a German friend told me that her generation has been deprived of German culture. What existed before the Third Reich was used in Nazi propaganda, and so has become as if dyed with the stain of that history. The artists and writers of the early twentieth century were silenced; they went into exile or perished. The link with the past was broken. Yet, even unremembered, the past never disappears. It exists still and continues under a mantle of silence, invisibly shaping lives.

The DNA molecule is made of long, fine, paired strands. These strands are helically coiled.

What is buried in the past of one generation falls to the next to claim. The children of Nazis and survivors alike have inherited a struggle between silence and speech.

The night I met Hélène at a Métro station in Paris I was returning from dinner with a friend. Ten years older than I, Jewish, French, in 1942, the year before my own birth, Natalie's life was put in danger. She was given false papers and shepherded with other children out of Paris through an underground movement. She lived out the duration of war in the countryside in the home of an ambassador who had diplomatic immunity. A woman who has remained one of her closest friends to this day was with her in this hiding place. The night we had dinner Natalie told me a story about her. This friend, she said, grew up determined to shed her past. She made Natalie promise never to reveal who she was or what had happened to her. She changed her name, denied that she was Jewish, and raised her children as gentiles. Then, opening her hands in a characteristic gesture, Natalie smiled at me. The story was to take a gently ironic turn. The past was to return. This summer, she told me, she had held one end of a bridal canopy, what in a Jewish wedding is called a chuppa, at the wedding of her friend's daughter. This girl was marrying the son of an Orthodox rabbi. And her son too, knowing nothing of his mother's past, had gravitated toward Judaism.

In 1975 the SS-19 missile is deployed in the Soviet Union. It carries several warheads, each with a different target. A computer within it controls and detects deviations from its programmed course.

One can find traces of every life in each life. There is a story from my own family history that urges its way onto the page here. Sometime in the eighteenth century three brothers migrated from Scotland to the United States. They came from Aberdeen and bore the name Marks, a name common in that city to Jewish families who had immigrated from Germany to escape the pogroms. Jacob Marks, who descended from these brothers, was my great-great-grandfather. The family story was that he was descended from Huguenots. In our family, only my sister and I speak of the possibility that he could have been Jewish. Jacob married Rosa and they gave birth to a daughter whom they named Sarah. She married Thomas Colvin, and their last son was Ernest Marks Colvin, my grandfather, the same grandfather who would recite to me his furious list of those he hated, including Jews.

Who would my grandfather, I wonder now, have been if he had known his own history. Could he then have seen the shape of his life as part of a larger configuration? Wasn't he without this knowledge like the missile, or the neutron torn away from gravity, the matrix that sustains and makes sense of experience?

In any given cell only a small fraction of the genes are active. Messages to awaken these genes are transmitted by the surrounding cytoplasm, messages from other cells, or from outside substances.

I cannot say for certain what our family history was. I know only that I did gravitate myself toward what seemed missing or lost in me. In my first years of high school I lived alone with my father. He was often gone, at work or staying with his girlfriend. I adopted the family of a school friend, spending hours with them, baby-sitting their younger children, helping with household tasks, sharing meals, spending an evening speaking of art or politics. Then one evening, as I returned home, I saw a strange man standing near my door. He had come to tell me my father was dead, struck by an automobile while he was crossing the street in the light of dusk. I turned for solace and finally shelter to my adopted family. In the short time we lived together, out of my love for them, I took on their gestures, the manner and rhythm of their thought, ways of cooking, cadences, a sprinkling of Yiddish vocabulary. I became in some ways Jewish.

In the late seventies the United States develops a circuitry for the Minuteman rocket which allows for a target to be changed in the midst of flight.

• • •

Is there any one of us who can count ourselves outside the circle circumscribed by our common past? Whether or not I was trying to reweave threads severed from my family history, a shared heritage of despair and hope, of destruction and sustenance, was within me. What I received from my adopted family helped me to continue my life. My suffering had been placed, even wordlessly, in a larger stream of suffering, and as if wrapped and held by a culture that had grown up to meet suffering, to retell the tales and place them in a larger context by which all life continues.

L'chayim. Life. Held to even at the worst times. The dream of a better world. The schoolbook, tattered, pages flying loose, gripped in the hands of a young student, his coat open at the shoulder and along the front where the fabric was worn. The ghetto of Slonim. 1938. The Passover cup, fashioned secretly by inmates at Terezin, the Passover plate, the menorah, made at the risk of death from purloined materials. Pictures drawn by those who were there. Despair, the attrition of pain, daily cold, hunger somehow entering the mark of pencil or brush. Butterflies painted by children who all later perished. Stitches made across Lenke's drawings, reminding us of the stitches she sustained in one operation after another, after her liberation, when she was stricken with tuberculosis of the spine. The prisoner forced to pick up discarded clothing of those sent to the gas chambers, who said that among this clothing, as he gathered it, he saw *Stars of David like a drift of yellow flowers.*

As the fertilized egg cell starts to divide, all the daughter cells have identical DNA, but the cells soon cease to look alike, and in a few weeks, a number different kinds of cells can be recognized in the embryo.

I am thinking again of a child's body. Curled and small. Innocent. The skin soft like velvet to the touch. Eyes open and staring without reserve or calculation, quite simply, into the eyes of whoever appears in this field of vision. Without secrets. Arms open, ready to receive or give, just in the transpiration of flesh, sharing the sound of the heartbeat, the breath, the warmth of body on body.

In 1977 the Soviet Union puts the SS-NX-17 and SS N-18 into service. These are ballistic missiles to be launched from submarines. In 1978 the United States perfects the underwater launch system of the Tomahawk missile.

I could not, in the end, for some blessed reason, turn away from myself. Not at least in this place. The place of desire. I think now of the small lines etching themselves near the eyes of a woman's face I loved. And how, seeing these lines, I wanted to stroke her face. To lean myself, my body, my skin into her. A part of me unravels as I think of this, and I am taken toward longing, and beyond, into another region, past the walls of this house, or all I can see, stretching farther than the horizon where right now sea and sky blend. It is as if my cells are moving in a larger wave, a wave that takes in every history, every story.

At the end of nine months a multitude of different cells make up the newborn infant's body, including nerve cells, muscle cells, skin cells, retinal cells, liver cells, brain cells, cells of the heart that beats, cells of the mouth that opens, cells of the throat that cries . . .

When I think of that young man now, who died in the river near the island of my father's birth, died because he loved another man, I like to imagine his body bathed in the pleasure of that love. To believe that the hands that touched this young man's thighs, his buttocks, his penis, the mouth that felt its way over his body, the man who lay himself between his legs, or over, around his body did this lovingly, and that then the young man felt inside his flesh what radiated from his childlike beauty. Part angel. Bathed in a passionate sweetness. Tasting life at its youngest, most original center, the place of reason, where one is whole again as at birth.

In the last decade the Soviet Union improves its antiballistic missiles to make them maneuverable and capable of hovering in midair. The United States continues to develop and test the MX missile, with advanced inertial guidance, capable of delivering ten prearmed electronically guided warheads, each with maneuverability, possessing the power and accuracy to penetrate hardened silos. And the Soviet Union begins to design a series of smaller one-warhead mobile missiles, the SS-25, to be driven around by truck, and the SS-X-24, to be drawn on railroad tracks. And the United States develops a new warhead for the Trident missile carrying fourteen smaller warheads that can be released in a barrage along a track or a road.

A train is making its way through Germany. All along its route those who are in the cars can look out and see those who are outside the cars. And those who are outside can see those who are inside. Sometimes words are exchanged. Sometimes there is a plea for water. And sometimes, at the risk of life, water is given. Sometimes names are called out, or curses are spoken, under the breath. And sometimes there is only silence.

Who are those on the inside and where are they going? There are rumors. It is best not to ask. There are potatoes to buy with the last of the rations. There is a pot boiling on the stove. And, at any rate, the train has gone; the people have vanished. You did not know them. You will not see them again. Except perhaps in your dreams. But what do those images mean? Images of strangers. Agony that is not yours. A face that does not belong to you. And so in the daylight you try to erase what you have encountered and to forget those tracks that are laid even as if someplace in your body, even as part of yourself.

. . . .

QUESTIONS FOR A SECOND READING

1. One of the challenges a reader faces with Griffin's text is knowing what to make of it. It's a long piece, but the reading is not difficult. The sections are short and straightforward. While the essay is made up of fragments, the arrangement is not deeply confusing or disorienting. Still, the piece has no single controlling idea; it does not move from thesis to conclusion. One way of reading the essay is to see what one can make of it, what it might add up to. In this sense, the work of reading is to find an idea, passage, image, or metaphor—something in the text—and use this to organize the essay.

   As you prepare to work back through the text, think about the point of reference you could use to organize your reading. Is the essay "about" Himmler? secrets? fascism? art? Germany? the United Sates? families and child-rearing? gay and lesbian sexuality? Can one of the brief sections be taken as a key to the text? What about the italicized sections—how are they to be used?

   You should not assume that one of these is the right way to read. Assume, rather, that one way of working with the text is to organize it around a single point of reference, something you could say that Griffin "put there" for you to notice and to use.

   Or you might want to do this in your name rather than Griffin's. That is, you might, as you reread, chart the connections *you* make, connections that you feel belong to you (to your past, your interests, your way of reading), and think about where and how you are drawn into the text (and with what you take to be Griffin's interests and desires). You might want to be prepared to talk about why you sum things up the way you do.

2. Although this is not the kind of prose you would expect to find in a textbook for a history course, and although the project is not what we usually think of as a "research" project, Griffin is a careful researcher. The project is serious and deliberate; it is "about" history, both family history and world history. Griffin knows what she is doing. So what *is* Griffin's project? As you reread, look to those sections where Griffin seems to be speaking to her readers about her work—about how she reads and how she writes, about how she gathers her materials and how she studies them. What is she doing? What is at stake in adopting such methods? How and why might you teach someone to do this work?

ASSIGNMENTS FOR WRITING

1. Griffin's text gathers together related fragments and works on them, but does so without yoking examples to a single, predetermined argument or thesis. In this sense, it is a kind of antiessay. One of the difficulties readers of this text face is in its retelling. If someone says to you, "Well, what was it about?," the answer is not easy or obvious. The text is so far-reaching, so

carefully composed of interrelated stories and reflections, and so suggestive in its implications and in the connections it enables that it is difficult to summarize without violence, without seriously reducing the text.

But, imagine that somebody asks, "Well, what was it about?" Write an essay in which you present your reading of "Our Secret." You want to give your reader a sense of what the text is like (or what it is like to read the text), and you want to make clear that the account you are giving is your reading, your way of working it through. You might, in fact, want to suggest what you leave out or put to the side. (The first "Question for a Second Reading" might help you prepare for this.)

2. At several points in her essay, Griffin argues that we—all of us, especially all of us who read her essay—are part of a complex web of connections. At one point she says,

> Who are we? The question is not simple. What we call the self is part of a larger matrix of relationship and society. Had we been born to a different family, in a different time, to a different world, we would not be the same. All the lives that surround us are in us. (pp. 355–56)

At another point she asks, "Is there any one of us who can count ourselves outside the circle circumscribed by our common past?" (p. 365). She speaks of a "field,"

> like a field of gravity that is created by the movements of many bodies. Each life is influenced and it in turn becomes an influence. Whatever is a cause is also an effect. Childhood experience is just one element in the determining field. (p. 324)

One way of thinking about this concept of the self (and of interrelatedness), at least under Griffin's guidance, is to work on the connections that she implies and asserts. As you reread the selection, look for powerful and surprising juxtapositions, fragments that stand together in interesting and suggestive ways. Think about the arguments represented by the blank space between those sections. (And look for Griffin's written statements about "relatedness.") Look for connections that seem important to the text (and to you) and representative of Griffin's thinking (and yours). Then, write an essay in which you use these examples to think through your understanding of Griffin's claims for this "larger matrix," the "determining field," or our "common past."

3. It is useful to think of Griffin's prose as experimental. She is trying to do something that she can't do in the "usual" essay form. She wants to make a different kind of argument or engage her reader in a different manner. And so she mixes personal and academic writing. She assembles fragments and puts seemingly unrelated material into surprising and suggestive relationships. She breaks the "plane" of the page with italicized inter-sections. She organizes her material, but not in the usual mode of thesis-example-conclusion. The arrangement is not nearly so linear. At one point, when she seems to be prepared to argue that German child-rearing practices produced the Holocaust, she quickly says:

> Of course there cannot be one answer to such a monumental riddle, nor does any event in history have a single cause. Rather a field exists, like a field of gravity that is created by the movements of many bodies.

Each life is influenced and it in turn becomes an influence. Whatever is
a cause is also an effect. Childhood experience is just one element in the
determining field." (p. 325)

Her prose serves to create a "field," one where many bodies are set in relationship.

It is useful, then, to think about Griffin's prose as the enactment of a
method, as a way of doing a certain kind of intellectual work. One way to
study this, to feel its effects, is to imitate it, to take it as a model. For this assignment, write a Griffin-like essay, one similar in its methods of organization and argument. You will need to think about the stories you might tell,
about the stories and texts you might gather (stories and texts not your own).
As you write, you will want to think carefully about arrangement and about
commentary (about where, that is, you will speak to your reader *as* the writer
of the piece). You should not feel bound to Griffin's subject matter, but you
should feel that you are working in her spirit.

MAKING CONNECTIONS

1.   Is it surprising that prisons resemble factories, schools, bar-
      racks, hospitals, which all resemble prisons? (p. 206)

                                              – MICHEL FOUCAULT
                                                Panopticism

      The child, Dr. Schreber advised, *should be permeated by the im-*
      possibility of locking something in his heart. . . . That this philoso-
      phy was taught in school gives me an interior view of the cata-
      strophe to follow. It adds a certain dimension to my image of
      these events to know that a nation of citizens learned that no
      part of themselves could be safe from the scrutiny of authority,
      nothing locked in the heart, and at the same time to discover
      that the head of the secret police of this nation was the son of a
      schoolmaster. It was this man, after all, Heinrich Himmler,
      Reichsführer SS, who was later to say, speaking of the mass ar-
      rests of Jews, *Protective custody is an act of care.* (p. 326)

                                              – SUSAN GRIFFIN
                                                Our Secret

Both Griffin and Foucault write about the "fabrication" of human life and desire within the operations of history and of specific social institutions—the
family, the school, the military, the factory, the hospital. Both are concerned
with the relationship between forces that are hidden, secret, and those that
are obvious, exposed. Both write with an urgent concern for the history of
the present, for the ways our current condition is tied to history, politics, and
culture.

And yet these are very different pieces to read. They are written differently—that is, they differently invite a reader's participation and understanding. They take different examples from history. They offer different

accounts of the technologies of order and control. It can even be said that they do their work differently and that they work toward different ends.

Write an essay in which you use one of the essays to explain and to investigate the other—where you use Griffin as a way of thinking about Foucault or Foucault as a way of thinking about Griffin. "To explain," "to investigate"— perhaps you would prefer to think of this encounter as a dialogue or a conversation, a way of bringing the two texts together. You should imagine that your readers are familiar with both texts, but have not yet thought of the two together. You should imagine that your readers do not have the texts in front of them, that you will need to do the work of presentation and summary.

2. Both Gloria Anzaldúa in the two chapters reprinted here from her book *Borderlands/La frontera* (p. 22) and Susan Griffin in "Our Secret" write mixed texts, or what might be called "montages." Neither of their pieces proceeds as simply a story or an essay, although both have elements of fiction and nonfiction in them (and, in Anzaldúa's case, poetry). They both can be said to be making arguments and to be telling stories. Anzaldúa, in her chapters, is directly concerned with matters of identity and the ways identity is represented through sexuality, religion, and culture. Griffin is concerned with the "self" as "part of a larger matrix of relationship and society."

   Write an essay in which you present and explain Anzaldúa's and Griffin's key arguments about the relation of identity, history, culture, and society. What terms and examples do they provide? What arguments or concerns? What different positions do they take? And what about their writing styles? How might their concerns be reflected in the ways they write?

3. At one point in her essay, Susan Griffin refers to masks:

   > Ordinary. What an astonishing array of images hide behind this word. The ordinary is of course never ordinary. I think of it now as a kind of mask, not an animated mask that expresses the essence of an inner truth, but an mask that falls like dead weight over the human face, making flesh a stationary object. One has difficulty penetrating the heavy mask that Gebhard [Himmler] and his family wore, difficulty piercing through to the creatures behind. (p. 323)

   Ralph Ellison, in "An Extravagance of Laughter" (p. 140), also speaks about masks, although to a very different end, as he thinks about the relations between black Americans and white Americans in the 1930s. He, too, thinks about how the ordinary was never ordinary and about the difficulty of piercing through to the creatures behind.

   Write an essay in which you bring Ellison's essay—the stories he tells but also his way of understanding those stories—into play with Griffin's essay. If, for example, she were to turn her attention to race relations in this country by weaving Ellison and his example into her work, what might she notice and what might she say? Or, if you would like to work in the other direction, if you take Ellison as a starting point, what can you learn from his way of thinking about, of reviewing and using the past, that you could use to take a position on Griffin and her work, her sense of how and why we might search out and listen to other people's stories?

4. One of the obvious questions that a reader might ask of Susan Griffin's essay, "Our Secret," has to do with her methods of writing, thinking, and

working. What, one might ask, are her characteristic ways of gathering materials, of thinking them through, of presenting them to readers? As you work back through her essay, think about the writing as an example of method and intention. You also might ask yourself, for instance, questions about the kinds of readers her work requires. What does she assume about her readers? How does she teach her readers to read?

The same questions can be asked of Ralph Ellison's essay, "An Extravagance of Laughter" (p. 140). What, you might ask, are his characteristic ways of gathering materials, of thinking them through, and of presenting them to a reader? How would you describe his method? What are its key features? What would you say he is doing, for example, in the first two paragraphs? Then what happens? What is an "autobiographical exploration" as it is represented in this text? And what does he assume of his readers? Who *is* the audience and how does he teach his readers to read?

Write an essay in which you use Griffin and Ellison to talk about writers and their methods. Be sure to work closely with examples from each. Be sure to look for differences as well as similarities. And see, in your essay, if you can move beyond your discussion of their examples to think more generally about the problems of writing. You might ask, what is it experienced writers work on when they work on their writing? What is it that writers need to learn? What might a writer learn from these two examples? Where and how might it serve in the academy? outside?

HARRIET
JACOBS

*H*arriet Jacobs was born in North Carolina in or around 1815. The selection *that follows reproduces the opening chapters of her autobiography,* Incidents in the Life of a Slave Girl, *and tells the story of her life from childhood to early adulthood, through the birth of her first child. In these chapters Jacobs describes how she came to understand her identity as men's property—as a slave and as a woman—as that identity was determined by her particular situation (her appearance, her education, the psychology of her owner, the values of her family) and by the codes governing slavery in the South.*

In the remaining chapters of her book, Jacobs tells of the birth of a second child, of her escape from her owner, Dr. Flint, and of seven years spent hiding in a crawl space under the roof of her grandmother's house. The father of her children, Mr. Sands, did not, as she thought he might, purchase and free her, although he eventually did purchase her children and allow them to live with her grandmother. He did not free the children, and they never bore his name.

Around 1842 Jacobs fled to New York, where she made contact with her children and found work as a nursemaid in the family of Nathaniel P. Willis, a magazine editor who with his wife helped hide Jacobs from southern slaveholders and eventually purchased Jacobs and her children and gave them their freedom.

This is the end of Jacobs's story as it is reported in Incidents. *Recent research, however, enables us to tell the story of the production of this autobiography, the text that represents its author's early life. Through her contact with the Willises, Jacobs met both black and white abolitionists and became active in the antislavery movement. She told her story to Amy Post, a feminist and abolitionist, and Post encouraged her to record it, which she did by writing in the evenings between 1853 and 1858. After unsuccessfully seeking publication in England, and with the help of the white abolitionist writer L. Maria Child, who read the manuscript and served as an editor (by rearranging sections and suggesting that certain incidents be expanded into chapters), Jacobs published* Incidents *in Boston in 1861 under the pseudonym "Linda Brent," along with Child's introduction, which is also reproduced here. During the Civil War, Jacobs left the Willises to be a nurse for black troops. She remained active, working with freed slaves for the next thirty years, and died in Washington, D.C., in 1897.*

For years scholars questioned the authenticity of this autobiography, arguing that it seemed too skillful to have been written by a slave, and that more likely it had been written by white abolitionists as propaganda for their cause. The recent discovery, however, of a cache of letters and the research of Jean Fagan Yellin have established Jacobs's authorship and demonstrated that Child made only minor changes and assisted primarily by helping Jacobs find a publisher and an audience.

Still, the issue of authorship remains a complicated one, even if we can be confident that the writing belongs to Jacobs and records her struggles and achievements. The issue of authorship becomes complicated if we think of the dilemma facing Jacobs as a writer, telling a story that defied description to an audience who could never completely understand. There is, finally, a precarious relationship between the story of a slave's life, the story Jacobs had to tell, and the stories available to her and to her readers as models—stories of privileged, white, middle-class life: conventional narratives of family and childhood, love and marriage.

Houston Baker, one of our leading scholars of black culture, has described the situation of the slave narrator this way:

> *But the slave narrator must also accomplish the almost unthinkable (since thought and language are inseparable) task of transmuting an authentic, unwritten self—a self that exists outside the conventional literary discourse structures of a white reading public—into a literary representation. . . . The voice of the unwritten self, once it is subjected to the linguistic codes, literary conventions, and audience expectations of a literate population, is perhaps never again the authentic voice of black American slavery. It is, rather, the voice of a self transformed by an autobiographical act into a sharer in the general public discourse about slavery.*

The author of Incidents *could be said to stand outside "the general public discourse," both because she was a slave and because she was a woman. The story she has to tell does not fit easily into the usual stories of courtship and marriage or the dominant attitudes toward sexuality and female "virtue." When you read Jacobs's concerns about her "competence," about her status as a woman or as a writer,*

concerns that seem strange in the face of this powerful text; when you hear her ad-
dressing her readers, sometimes instructing them, sometimes apologizing, trying to
bridge the gap between her experience and theirs, you should think not only of the
trials she faced as a woman and a mother but also of her work as a writer. Here, too,
she is struggling to take possession of her life.

Incidents in the Life of a Slave Girl

Written by Herself

Northerners know nothing at all about Slavery. They think it is
perpetual bondage only. They have no conception of the depth
of *degradation* involved in that word, SLAVERY; if they had, they
would never cease their efforts until so horrible a system was
overthrown.

— A WOMAN OF NORTH CAROLINA

Rise up, ye women that are at ease! Hear my voice, ye careless
daughters! Give ear unto my speech.

— *Isaiah xxxii.9*

Preface by the Author

Linda Brent

Reader, be assured this narrative is no fiction. I am aware that some of
my adventures may seem incredible; but they are, nevertheless, strictly true.
I have not exaggerated the wrongs inflicted by Slavery; on the contrary, my
descriptions fall far short of the facts. I have concealed the names of places,
and given persons fictitious names. I had no motive for secrecy on my own
account, but I deemed it kind and considerate towards others to pursue this
course.

I wish I were more competent to the task I have undertaken. But I trust
my readers will excuse deficiencies in consideration of circumstances. I was
born and reared in Slavery; and I remained in a Slave State twenty-seven
years. Since I have been at the North, it has been necessary for me to work
diligently for my own support, and the education of my children. This has
not left me much leisure to make up for the loss of early opportunities to improve myself; and it has compelled me to write these pages at irregular intervals, whenever I could snatch an hour from household duties.

When I first arrived in Philadelphia, Bishop Paine advised me to publish a
sketch of my life, but I told him I was altogether incompetent to such an undertaking. Though I have improved my mind somewhat since that time, I still re-

main of the same opinion; but I trust my motives will excuse what might otherwise seem presumptuous. I have not written my experiences in order to attract attention to myself; on the contrary, it would have been more pleasant to me to have been silent about my own history. Neither do I care to excite sympathy for my own sufferings. But I do earnestly desire to arouse the women of the North to a realizing sense of the condition of two millions of women at the South, still in bondage, suffering what I suffered, and most of them far worse. I want to add my testimony to that of abler pens to convince the people of the Free States what Slavery really is. Only by experience can any one realize how deep, and dark, and foul is that pit of abominations. May the blessing of God rest on this imperfect effort in behalf of my persecuted people!

Introduction by the Editor

L. Maria Child

The author of the following autobiography is personally known to me, and her conversation and manners inspire me with confidence. During the last seventeen years, she has lived the greater part of the time with a distinguished family in New York, and has so deported herself as to be highly esteemed by them. This fact is sufficient, without further credentials of her character. I believe those who know her will not be disposed to doubt her veracity, though some incidents in her story are more romantic than fiction.

At her request, I have revised her manuscript; but such changes as I have made have been mainly for purposes of condensation and orderly arrangement. I have not added any thing to the incidents, or changed the import of her very pertinent remarks. With trifling exceptions, both the ideas and the language are her own. I pruned excrescences a little, but otherwise I had no reason for changing her lively and dramatic way of telling her own story. The names of both persons and places are known to me; but for good reasons I suppress them.

It will naturally excite surprise that a woman reared in Slavery should be able to write so well. But circumstances will explain this. In the first place, nature endowed her with quick perceptions. Secondly, the mistress, with whom she lived till she was twelve years old, was a kind, considerate friend, who taught her to read and spell. Thirdly, she was placed in favorable circumstances after she came to the North; having frequent intercourse with intelligent persons, who felt a friendly interest in her welfare, and were disposed to give her opportunities for self-improvement.

I am well aware that many will accuse me of indecorum for presenting these pages to the public; for the experiences of this intelligent and much-injured woman belong to a class which some call delicate subjects, and others indelicate. This peculiar phase of Slavery has generally been kept veiled; but the public ought to be made acquainted with its monstrous features, and I willingly take the responsibility of presenting them with the veil withdrawn.

I do this for the sake of my sisters in bondage, who are suffering wrongs so foul, that our ears are too delicate to listen to them. I do it with the hope of arousing conscientious and reflecting women at the North to a sense of their duty in the exertion of moral influence on the question of Slavery, on all possible occasions. I do it with the hope that every man who reads this narrative will swear solemnly before God that, so far as he has power to prevent it, no fugitive from Slavery shall ever be sent back to suffer in that loathsome den of corruption and cruelty.

Incidents in the Life of a Slave Girl, Seven Years Concealed

I
Childhood

I was born a slave; but I never knew it till six years of happy childhood had passed away. My father was a carpenter, and considered so intelligent and skilful in his trade, that, when buildings out of the common line were to be erected, he was sent for from long distances, to be head workman. On condition of paying his mistress two hundred dollars a year, and supporting himself, he was allowed to work at his trade, and manage his own affairs. His strongest wish was to purchase his children; but, though he several times offered his hard earnings for that purpose, he never succeeded. In complexion my parents were a light shade of brownish yellow, and were termed mulattoes. They lived together in a comfortable home; and, though we were all slaves, I was so fondly shielded that I never dreamed I was a piece of merchandise, trusted to them for safe keeping, and liable to be demanded of them at any moment. I had one brother, William, who was two years younger than myself—a bright, affectionate child. I had also a great treasure in my maternal grandmother, who was a remarkable woman in many respects. She was the daughter of a planter in South Carolina, who, at his death, left her mother and his three children free, with money to go to St. Augustine, where they had relatives. It was during the Revolutionary War; and they were captured on their passage, carried back, and sold to different purchasers. Such was the story my grandmother used to tell me; but I do not remember all the particulars. She was a little girl when she was captured and sold to the keeper of a large hotel. I have often heard her tell how hard she fared during childhood. But as she grew older she evinced so much intelligence, and was so faithful, that her master and mistress could not help seeing it was for their interest to take care of such a valuable piece of property. She became an indispensable personage in the household, officiating in all capacities, from cook and wet nurse to seamstress. She was much praised for her cooking; and her nice crackers became so famous in the neighborhood that many people were desirous of obtaining them. In consequence of numerous requests of this kind, she asked permission of her mistress to bake crackers at night, after all the household work was done; and she obtained leave to do it, provided she would clothe herself and her children from the profits. Upon these terms, after working hard all day for her mistress, she began her midnight bakings, assisted by her two oldest children. The business proved profitable; and each year she laid by a little, which was saved for a fund to purchase her children. Her master died, and the property was divided among his heirs. The widow had her dower in the hotel, which she continued to keep open. My grandmother remained in her service as a slave; but her children were divided among her master's children. As she had five, Benjamin, the youngest one, was sold, in order that each heir might have an equal portion of dollars and cents. There was so little difference in our ages that he seemed more like my brother than my uncle. He was a bright, handsome lad, nearly white; for he inherited the complexion my grandmother had derived from Anglo-Saxon ancestors. Though only ten years old, seven hundred and twenty dollars were paid for him. His sale was a terrible blow to my grandmother; but she was naturally hopeful, and she went to work with renewed energy, trusting in time to be able to purchase some of her children. She had laid up three hundred dollars, which her mistress one day begged as a loan, promising to pay her soon. The reader probably knows that no promise or writing given to a slave is legally binding; for, according to Southern laws, a slave, *being* property, can *hold* no property. When my grandmother lent her hard earnings to her mistress, she trusted solely to her honor. The honor of a slaveholder to a slave!

To this good grandmother I was indebted for many comforts. My brother Willie and I often received portions of the crackers, cakes, and preserves she made to sell; and after we ceased to be children we were indebted to her for many more important services.

Such were the unusually fortunate circumstances of my early childhood. When I was six years old, my mother died; and then, for the first time, I learned, by the talk around me, that I was a slave. My mother's mistress was the daughter of my grandmother's mistress. She was the foster sister of my mother; they were both nourished at my grandmother's breast. In fact, my mother had been weaned at three months old, that the babe of the mistress might obtain sufficient food. They played together as children; and, when they became women, my mother was a most faithful servant to her whiter foster sister. On her death-bed her mistress promised that her children should never suffer for any thing; and during her lifetime she kept her word. They all spoke kindly of my dead mother, who had been a slave merely in name, but in nature was noble and womanly. I grieved for her, and my young mind was troubled with the thought who would now take care of me and my little brother. I was told that my home was now to be with her mistress; and I found it a happy one. No toilsome or disagreeable duties were imposed upon me. My mistress was so kind to me that I was always glad to do her bidding, and proud to labor for her as much as my young years would permit. I would sit by her side for hours, sewing diligently, with a heart as free from care as that of any free-born white child. When she thought I was tired, she would send me out to run and jump; and away I bounded, to gather berries or flowers to decorate her room. Those were happy days—too happy to last. The slave child had no thought for the morrow; but there came that blight, which too surely waits on every human being born to be a chattel.

When I was nearly twelve years old, my kind mistress sickened and died. As I saw the cheek grow paler, and the eye more glassy, how earnestly I prayed in my heart that she might live! I loved her; for she had been almost like a mother to me. My prayers were not answered. She died, and they buried her in the little churchyard, where, day after day, my tears fell upon her grave.

I was sent to spend a week with my grandmother. I was now old enough to begin to think of the future; and again and again I asked myself what they would do with me. I felt sure I should never find another mistress so kind as the one who was gone. She had promised my dying mother that her children should never suffer for any thing; and when I remembered that, and recalled her many proofs of attachment to me, I could not help having some hopes that she had left me free. My friends were almost certain it would be so. They thought she would be sure to do it, on account of my mother's love and faithful service. But, alas! we all know that the memory of a faithful slave does not avail much to save her children from the auction block.

After a brief period of suspense, the will of my mistress was read, and we learned that she had bequeathed me to her sister's daughter, a child of five years old. So vanished our hopes. My mistress had taught me the precepts of God's Word: "Thou shalt love thy neighbor as thyself." "Whatsoever ye would that men should do unto you, do ye even so unto them." But I was her slave, and I suppose she did not recognize me as her neighbor. I would give much to blot out from my memory that one great wrong. As a child, I loved my mistress; and, looking back on the happy days I spent with her, I try to think with less bitterness of this act of injustice. While I was with her, she taught me to read and spell; and for this privilege, which so rarely falls to the lot of a slave, I bless her memory.

She possessed but few slaves; and at her death those were all distributed among her relatives. Five of them were my grandmother's children, and had shared the same milk that nourished her mother's children. Notwithstanding my grandmother's long and faithful service to her owners, not one of her children escaped the auction block. These God-breathing machines are no more, in the sight of their masters, than the cotton they plant, or the horses they tend.

II
The New Master and Mistress

Dr. Flint, a physician in the neighborhood, had married the sister of my mistress, and I was now the property of their little daughter. It was not without murmuring that I prepared for my new home; and what added to my unhappiness, was the fact that my brother William was purchased by the same family. My father, by his nature, as well as by the habit of transacting business as a skilful mechanic, had more of the feelings of a freeman than is common among slaves. My brother was a spirited boy; and being brought up under such influences, he early detested the name of master and mistress. One day, when his father and his mistress both happened to call him at the same time, he hesitated between the two; being perplexed to know which had the strongest claim upon his obedience. He finally concluded to go to his mistress. When my father reproved him for it, he said, "You both called me, and I didn't know which I ought to go to first."

"You are *my* child," replied our father, "and when I call you, you should come immediately, if you have to pass through fire and water."

Poor Willie! He was now to learn his first lesson of obedience to a master. Grandmother tried to cheer us with hopeful words, and they found an echo in the credulous hearts of youth.

When we entered our new home we encountered cold looks, cold words, and cold treatment. We were glad when the night came. On my narrow bed I moaned and wept, I felt so desolate and alone.

I had been there nearly a year, when a dear little friend of mine was buried. I heard her mother sob, as the clods fell on the coffin of her only child, and I turned away from the grave, feeling thankful that I still had something left to love. I met my grandmother, who said, "Come with me, Linda"; and from her tone I knew that something sad had happened. She led me apart from the people, and then said, "My child, your father is dead." Dead! How could I believe it? He had died so suddenly I had not even heard that he was sick. I went home with my grandmother. My heart rebelled against God, who had taken from me mother, father, mistress, and friend. The good grandmother tried to comfort me. "Who knows the ways of God?" said she. "Perhaps they have been kindly taken from the evil days to come." Years afterwards I often thought of this. She promised to be a mother to her grandchildren, so far as she might be permitted to do so; and strengthened by her love, I returned to my master's. I thought I should be allowed to go to my father's house the next morning; but I was ordered to go for flowers, that my mistress's house might be decorated for an evening party. I spent the day gathering flowers and weaving them into festoons, while the dead body of my father was lying within a mile of me. What cared my owners for that? he was merely a piece of property. Moreover, they thought he had spoiled his children, by teaching them to feel that they were human beings. This was blasphemous doctrine for a slave to teach; presumptuous in him, and dangerous to the masters.

The next day I followed his remains to a humble grave beside that of my dear mother. There were those who knew my father's worth, and respected his memory.

My home now seemed more dreary than ever. The laugh of the little slave-children sounded harsh and cruel. It was selfish to feel so about the joy of others. My brother moved about with a very grave face. I tried to comfort him, by saying, "Take courage, Willie; brighter days will come by and by."

"You don't know any thing about it, Linda," he replied. "We shall have to stay here all our days; we shall never be free."

I argued that we were growing older and stronger, and that perhaps we might, before long, be allowed to hire our own time, and then we could earn money to buy our freedom. William declared this was much easier to say than to do; moreover, he did not intend to *buy* his freedom. We held daily controversies upon this subject.

Little attention was paid to the slaves' meals in Dr. Flint's house. If they could catch a bit of food while it was going, well and good. I gave myself no trouble on that score, for on my various errands I passed my grandmother's house, where there was always something to spare for me. I was frequently threatened with punishment if I stopped there; and my grandmother, to avoid detaining me, often stood at the gate with something for my breakfast or dinner. I was indebted to *her* for all my comforts, spiritual or temporal. It was *her* labor that supplied my scanty wardrobe. I have a vivid recollection of the linsey-woolsey dress given me every winter by Mrs. Flint. How I hated it! It was one of the badges of slavery.

While my grandmother was thus helping to support me from her hard earnings, the three hundred dollars she had lent her mistress was never re-paid. When her mistress died, her son-in-law, Dr. Flint, was appointed executor. When grandmother applied to him for payment, he said the estate was insolvent, and the law prohibited payment. It did not, however, prohibit him from retaining the silver candelabra, which had been purchased with that money. I presume they will be handed down in the family, from generation to generation.

My grandmother's mistress had always promised her that, at her death, she should be free; and it was said that in her will she made good the promise. But when the estate was settled, Dr. Flint told the faithful old servant that, under existing circumstances, it was necessary she should be sold.

On the appointed day, the customary advertisement was posted up, proclaiming that there would be a "public sale of negroes, horses, &c." Dr. Flint called to tell my grandmother that he was unwilling to wound her feelings by putting her up at auction, and that he would prefer to dispose of her at private sale. My grandmother saw through his hypocrisy; she understood very well that he was ashamed of the job. She was a very spirited woman, and if he was base enough to sell her, when her mistress intended she should be free, she was determined the public should know it. She had for a long time supplied many families with crackers and preserves; consequently, "Aunt Marthy," as she was called, was generally known, and every body who knew her respected her intelligence and good character. Her long and faithful service in the family was also well known, and the intention of her mistress to leave her free. When the day of sale came, she took her place among the chattels, and at the first call she sprang upon the auction-block. Many voices called out, "Shame! Shame! Who is going to sell *you*, Marthy? Don't stand there! That is no place for *you*." Without saying a word she quietly awaited her fate. No one bid for her. At last, a feeble voice, said, "Fifty dollars." It came from a maiden lady, seventy years old, the sister of my grandmother's deceased mistress. She had lived forty years under the same roof with my grandmother; she knew how faithfully she had served her owners, and how cruelly she had been defrauded of her rights; and she resolved to protect her. The auctioneer waited for a higher bid; but her wishes were respected; no one bid above her. She could neither read nor write; and when the bill of sale was made out, she signed it with a cross. But what consequence was that, when she had a big heart overflowing with human kindness? She gave the old servant her freedom.

At that time, my grandmother was just fifty years old. Laborious years had passed since then; and now my brother and I were slaves to the man who had defrauded her of her money, and tried to defraud her of her freedom. One of my mother's sisters, called Aunt Nancy, was also a slave in his family. She was a kind, good aunt to me; and supplied the place of both housekeeper and waiting maid to her mistress. She was, in fact, at the beginning and end of every thing.

Mrs. Flint, like many southern women, was totally deficient in energy. She had not strength to superintend her household affairs; but her nerves were so strong, that she could sit in her easy chair and see a woman whipped, till the blood trickled from every stroke of the lash. She was a member of the church; but partaking of the Lord's supper did not seem to put her in a Christian frame of mind. If dinner was not served at the exact time on that particular Sunday, she would station herself in the kitchen, and wait till it was dished, and then spit in all the kettles and pans that had been used for cooking. She did this to prevent the cook and her children from eking out their meagre fare with the remains of the gravy and other scrapings. The slaves could get nothing to eat except what she chose to give them. Provisions were weighed out by the pound and ounce, three times a day. I can assure you she gave them no chance to eat wheat bread from her flour barrel. She knew how many biscuits a quart of flour would make, and exactly what size they ought to be.

Dr. Flint was an epicure. The cook never sent a dinner to his table without fear and trembling; for if there happened to be a dish not to his liking, he would either order her to be whipped, or compel her to eat every mouthful of it in his presence. The poor, hungry creature might not have objected to eating it; but she did object to having her master cram it down her throat till she choked.

They had a pet dog, that was a nuisance in the house. The cook was ordered to make some Indian mush for him. He refused to eat, and when his head was held over it, the froth flowed from his mouth into the basin. He died a few minutes after. When Dr. Flint came in, he said the mush had not been well cooked, and that was the reason the animal would not eat it. He sent for the cook, and compelled her to eat it. He thought that the woman's stomach was stronger than the dog's; but her sufferings afterwards proved that he was mistaken. This poor woman endured many cruelties from her master and mistress; sometimes she was locked up, away from her nursing baby, for a whole day and night.

When I had been in the family a few weeks, one of the plantation slaves was brought to town, by order of his master. It was near night when he arrived, and Dr. Flint ordered him to be taken to the work house, and tied up to the joist, so that his feet would just escape the ground. In that situation he was to wait till the doctor had taken his tea. I shall never forget that night. Never before, in my life, had I heard hundreds of blows fall, in succession, on a human being. His piteous groans, and his "O, pray don't, massa," rang in my ear for months afterwards. There were many conjectures as to the cause of this terrible punishment. Some said master accused him of stealing corn; others said the slave had quarrelled with his wife, in presence of the overseer, and had accused his master of being the father of her child. They were both black, and the child was very fair.

I went into the work house next morning, and saw the cowhide still wet with blood, and the boards all covered with gore. The poor man lived, and continued to quarrel with his wife. A few months afterwards Dr. Flint handed them both over to a slave-trader. The guilty man put their value into his pocket, and had the satisfaction of knowing that they were out of sight and hearing. When the mother was delivered into the trader's hands, she said, "You *promised* to treat me well." To which he replied, "You have let your tongue run too far; damn you!" She had forgotten that it was a crime for a slave to tell who was the father of her child.

From others than the master persecution also comes in such cases. I once saw a young slave girl dying soon after the birth of a child nearly white. In her agony she cried out, "O Lord, come and take me!" Her mistress stood by, and mocked at her like an incarnate fiend. "You suffer, do you?" she exclaimed. "I am glad of it. You deserve it all, and more too."

The girl's mother said, "The baby is dead, thank God; and I hope my poor child will soon be in heaven, too."

"Heaven!" retorted the mistress. "There is no such place for the like of her and her bastard."

The poor mother turned away, sobbing. Her dying daughter called her, feebly, and as she bent over her, I heard her say, "Don't grieve so, mother; God knows all about it; and HE will have mercy upon me."

Her sufferings, afterwards, became so intense, that her mistress felt unable to stay; but when she left the room, the scornful smile was still on her lips. Seven children called her mother. The poor black woman had but the one child, whose eyes she saw closing in death, while she thanked God for taking her away from the greater bitterness of life.

III
The Slaves' New Year's Day

Dr. Flint owned a fine residence in town, several farms, and about fifty slaves, besides hiring a number by the year.

Hiring-day at the south takes place on the 1st of January. On the 2d, the slaves are expected to go to their new masters. On a farm, they work until the corn and cotton are laid. They then have two holidays. Some masters give them a good dinner under the trees. This over, they work until Christmas eve. If no heavy charges are meantime brought against them, they are given four or five holidays, whichever the master or overseer may think proper. Then comes New Year's eve; and they gather together their little alls, or more properly speaking, their little nothings, and wait anxiously for the dawning of day. At the appointed hour the grounds are thronged with men, women, and children, waiting, like criminals, to hear their doom pronounced. The slave is sure to know who is the most humane, or cruel master, within forty miles of him.

It is easy to find out, on that day, who clothes and feeds his slaves well; for he is surrounded by a crowd, begging, "Please, massa, hire me this year. I will work *very* hard, massa."

If a slave is unwilling to go with his new master, he is whipped, or locked up in jail, until he consents to go, and promises not to run away during the year. Should he chance to change his mind, thinking it justifiable to violate an extorted promise, woe unto him if he is caught! The whip is used till the blood flows at his feet; and his stiffened limbs are put in chains, to be dragged in the field for days and days!

If he lives until the next year, perhaps the same man will hire him again, without even giving him an opportunity of going to the hiring-ground. After those for hire are disposed of, those for sale are called up.

O, you happy free women, contrast *your* New Year's day with that of the poor bond-woman! With you it is a pleasant season, and the light of the day is blessed. Friendly wishes meet you every where, and gifts are showered upon you. Even hearts that have been estranged from you soften at this season, and lips that have been silent echo back, "I wish you a happy New Year." Children bring their little offerings, and raise their rosy lips for a caress. They are your own, and no hand but that of death can take them from you.

But to the slave mother New Year's day comes laden with peculiar sorrows. She sits on her cold cabin floor, watching the children who may all be torn from her the next morning; and often does she wish that she and they might die before the day dawns. She may be an ignorant creature, degraded by the system that has brutalized her from childhood; but she has a mother's instincts, and is capable of feeling a mother's agonies.

On one of these sale days, I saw a mother lead seven children to the auction-block. She knew that *some* of them would be taken from her; but they took *all*. The children were sold to a slave-trader, and their mother was bought by a man in her own town. Before night her children were all far away. She begged the trader to tell her where he intended to take them; this he refused to do. How *could* he, when he knew he would sell them, one by one, wherever he could command the highest price? I met that mother in the street, and her wild, haggard face lives to-day in my mind. She wrung her hands in anguish, and exclaimed, "Gone! All gone! Why *don't* God kill me?" I had no words wherewith to comfort her. Instances of this kind are of daily, yea, of hourly occurrence.

Slaveholders have a method, peculiar to their institution, of getting rid of *old* slaves, whose lives have been worn out in their service. I knew an old woman, who for seventy years faithfully served her master. She had become almost helpless, from hard labor and disease. Her owners moved to Alabama, and the old black woman was left to be sold to any body who would give twenty dollars for her.

IV
The Slave Who Dared to Feel Like a Man

Two years had passed since I entered Dr. Flint's family, and those years had brought much of the knowledge that comes from experience, though they had afforded little opportunity for any other kinds of knowledge.

My grandmother had, as much as possible, been a mother to her orphan grandchildren. By perseverance and unwearied industry, she was now mistress of a snug little home, surrounded with the necessaries of life. She would have been happy could her children have shared them with her. There remained but three children and two grandchildren, all slaves. Most earnestly did she strive to make us feel that it was the will of God: that He had seen fit to place us under such circumstances; and though it seemed hard, we ought to pray for contentment.

It was a beautiful faith, coming from a mother who could not call her children her own. But I, and Benjamin, her youngest boy, condemned it. We reasoned that it was much more the will of God that we should be situated as she was. We longed for a home like hers. There we always found sweet balsam for our troubles. She was so loving, so sympathizing! She always met us with a smile, and listened with patience to all our sorrows. She spoke so hopefully, that unconsciously the clouds gave place to sunshine. There was a grand big oven there, too, that baked bread and nice things for the town, and we knew there was always a choice bit in store for us.

But, alas! even the charms of the old oven failed to reconcile us to our hard lot. Benjamin was now a tall, handsome lad, strongly and gracefully made, and with a spirit too bold and daring for a slave. My brother William, now twelve years old, had the same aversion to the word master that he had when he was an urchin of seven years. I was his confidant. He came to me with all his troubles. I remember one instance in particular. It was on a lovely spring morning, and when I marked the sunlight dancing here and there, its beauty seemed to mock my sadness. For my master, whose restless, craving, vicious nature roved about day and night, seeking whom to devour, had just left me, with stinging, scorching words; words that scathed ear and brain like fire. O, how I despised him! I thought how glad I should be, if some day when he walked the earth, it would open and swallow him up, and disencumber the world of a plague.

When he told me that I was made for his use, made to obey his command in *every* thing; that I was nothing but a slave, whose will must and should surrender to his, never before had my puny arm felt half so strong.

So deeply was I absorbed in painful reflections afterwards, that I neither saw nor heard the entrance of any one, till the voice of William sounded close beside me. "Linda," said he, "what makes you look so sad? I love you. O, Linda, isn't this a bad world? Every body seems so cross and unhappy. I wish I had died when poor father did."

I told him that every body was *not* cross, or unhappy; that those who had pleasant homes, and kind friends, and who were not afraid to love them, were happy. But we, who were slave-children, without father or mother, could not expect to be happy. We must be good; perhaps that would bring us contentment.

"Yes," he said, "I try to be good; but what's the use? They are all the time troubling me." Then he proceeded to relate his afternoon's difficulty with young master Nicholas. It seemed that the brother of master Nicholas had pleased himself with making up stories about William. Master Nicholas said he should be flogged, and he would do it. Whereupon he went to work; but William fought bravely, and the young master, finding he was getting the better of him, undertook to tie his hands behind him. He failed in that likewise. By dint of kicking and fisting, William came out of the skirmish none the worse for a few scratches.

He continued to discourse on his young master's *meanness;* how he whipped the *little* boys, but was a perfect coward when a tussle ensued between him and white boys of his own size. On such occasions he always took to his legs. William had other charges to make against him. One was his rubbing up pennies with quicksilver, and passing them off for quarters of a dollar on an old man who kept a fruit stall. William was often sent to buy fruit, and he earnestly inquired of me what he ought to do under such circumstances. I told him it was certainly wrong to deceive the old man, and that it was his duty to tell him of the impositions practised by his young master. I assured him the old man would not be slow to comprehend the whole, and there the matter would end. William thought it might with the old man, but not with *him*. He said he did not mind the smart of the whip, but he did not like the *idea* of being whipped.

While I advised him to be good and forgiving I was not unconscious of the beam in my own eye. It was the very knowledge of my own shortcomings that urged me to retain, if possible, some sparks of my brother's God-given nature. I had not lived fourteen years in slavery for nothing. I had felt, seen, and heard enough, to read the characters, and question the motives, of those around me. The war of my life had begun; and though one of God's most powerless creatures, I resolved never to be conquered. Alas, for me!

If there was one pure, sunny spot for me, I believed it to be in Benjamin's heart, and in another's, whom I loved with all the ardor of a girl's first love. My owner knew of it, and sought in every way to render me miserable. He did not resort to corporal punishment, but to all the petty, tyrannical ways that human ingenuity could devise.

I remember the first time I was punished. It was in the month of February. My grandmother had taken my old shoes, and replaced them with a new pair. I needed them; for several inches of snow had fallen, and it still continued to fall. When I walked through Mrs. Flint's room, their creaking grated harshly on her refined nerves. She called me to her, and asked what I had about me that made such a horrid noise. I told her it was my new shoes. "Take them off," said she; "and if you put them on again, I'll throw them into the fire."

I took them off, and my stockings also. She then sent me a long distance, on an errand. As I went through the snow, my bare feet tingled. That night I was very hoarse; and I went to bed thinking the next day would find me sick, perhaps dead. What was my grief on waking to find myself quite well!

I had imagined if I died, or was laid up for some time, that my mistress would feel a twinge of remorse that she had so hated "the little imp," as she styled me. It was my ignorance of that mistress that gave rise to such extravagant imaginings.

Dr. Flint occasionally had high prices offered for me; but he always said, "She don't belong to me. She is my daughter's property, and I have no right to sell her." Good, honest man! My young mistress was still a child, and I could look for no protection from her. I loved her, and she returned my affection. I once heard her father allude to her attachment to me; and his wife promptly replied that it proceeded from fear. This put unpleasant doubts into my mind. Did the child feign what she did not feel? or was her mother jealous of the mite of love she bestowed on me? I concluded it must be the latter. I said to myself, "Surely, little children are true."

One afternoon I sat at my sewing, feeling unusual depression of spirits. My mistress had been accusing me of an offence, of which I assured her I was perfectly innocent; but I saw, by the contemptuous curl of her lip, that she believed I was telling a lie.

I wondered for what wise purpose God was leading me through such thorny paths, and whether still darker days were in store for me. As I sat musing thus, the door opened softly, and William came in. "Well, brother," said I, "what is the matter this time?"

"O Linda, Ben and his master have had a dreadful time!" said he.

386

My first thought was that Benjamin was killed. "Don't be frightened, Linda," said William; "I will tell you all about it."

It appeared that Benjamin's master had sent for him, and he did not immediately obey the summons. When he did, his master was angry, and began to whip him. He resisted. Master and slave fought, and finally the master was thrown. Benjamin had cause to tremble; for he had thrown to the ground his master—one of the richest men in town. I anxiously awaited the result.

That night I stole to my grandmother's house, and Benjamin also stole thither from his master's. My grandmother had gone to spend a day or two with an old friend living in the country.

"I have come," said Benjamin, "to tell you good by. I am going away."

I inquired where.

"To the north," he replied.

I looked at him to see whether he was in earnest. I saw it all in his firm, set mouth. I implored him not to go, but he paid no heed to my words. He said he was no longer a boy, and every day made his yoke more galling. He had raised his hand against his master, and was to be publicly whipped for the offence. I reminded him of the poverty and hardships he must encounter among strangers. I told him he might be caught and brought back; and that was terrible to think of.

He grew vexed, and asked if poverty and hardships with freedom, were not preferable to our treatment in slavery. "Linda," he continued, "we are dogs here; foot-balls, cattle, every thing that's mean. No, I will not stay. Let them bring me back. We don't die but once."

He was right; but it was hard to give him up. "Go," said I, "and break your mother's heart."

I repented of my words ere they were out.

"Linda," said he, speaking as I had not heard him speak that evening, "how *could* you say that? Poor mother! be kind to her, Linda; and you, too, cousin Fanny."

Cousin Fanny was a friend who had lived some years with us.

Farewells were exchanged, and the bright, kind boy, endeared to us by so many acts of love, vanished from our sight.

It is not necessary to state how he made his escape. Suffice it to say, he was on his way to New York when a violent storm overtook the vessel. The captain said he must put into the nearest port. This alarmed Benjamin, who was aware that he would be advertised in every port near his own town. His embarrassment was noticed by the captain. To port they went. There the advertisement met the captain's eye. Benjamin so exactly answered its description, that the captain laid hold on him, and bound him in chains. The storm passed, and they proceeded to New York. Before reaching that port Benjamin managed to get off his chains and throw them overboard. He escaped from the vessel, but was pursued, captured, and carried back to his master.

When my grandmother returned home and found her youngest child had fled, great was her sorrow; but, with characteristic piety, she said, "God's will be done." Each morning, she inquired if any news had been heard from her boy. Yes, news *was* heard. The master was rejoicing over a letter, announcing the capture of his human chattel.

That day seems but as yesterday, so well do I remember it. I saw him led through the streets in chains, to jail. His face was ghastly pale, yet full of determination. He had begged one of the sailors to go to his mother's house and ask her not to meet him. He said the sight of her distress would take from him all self-control. She yearned to see him, and she went; but she screened herself in the crowd, that it might be as her child had said.

We were not allowed to visit him; but we had known the jailer for years, and he was a kind-hearted man. At midnight he opened the jail door for my grandmother and myself to enter, in disguise. When we entered the cell not a sound broke the stillness. "Benjamin, Benjamin!" whispered my grandmother. No answer. "Benjamin!" she again faltered. There was a jingle of chains. The moon had just risen, and cast an uncertain light through the bars of the window. We knelt down and took Benjamin's cold hands in ours. We did not speak. Sobs were heard, and Benjamin's lips were unsealed; for his mother was weeping on his neck. How vividly does memory bring back that sad night! Mother and son talked together. He asked her pardon for the suffering he had caused her. She said she had nothing to forgive; she could not blame his desire for freedom. He told her that when he was captured, he broke away, and was about casting himself into the river, when thoughts of *her* came over him, and he desisted. She asked if he did not also think of God. I fancied I saw his face grow fierce in the moonlight. He answered, "No, I did not think of him. When a man is hunted like a wild beast he forgets there is a God, a heaven. He forgets every thing in his struggle to get beyond the reach of the bloodhounds."

"Don't talk so, Benjamin," said she. "Put your trust in God. Be humble, my child, and your master will forgive you."

"Forgive me for *what*, mother? For not letting him treat me like a dog? No! I will never humble myself to him. I have worked for him for nothing all my life, and I am repaid with stripes and imprisonment. Here I will stay till I die, or till he sells me."

The poor mother shuddered at his words. I think he felt it; for when he next spoke, his voice was calmer. "Don't fret about me, mother. I ain't worth it," said he. "I wish I had some of your goodness. You bear every thing patiently, just as though you thought it was all right. I wish I could."

She told him she had not always been so; once, she was like him; but when sore troubles came upon her, and she had no arm to lean upon, she learned to call on God, and he lightened her burdens. She besought him to do likewise.

We overstaid our time, and were obliged to hurry from the jail.

Benjamin had been imprisoned three weeks, when my grandmother went to intercede for him with his master. He was immovable. He said Benjamin should serve as an example to the rest of his slaves; he should be kept in jail till he was subdued, or be sold if he got but one dollar for him. However, he afterwards relented in some degree. The chains were taken off, and we were allowed to visit him.

As his food was of the coarsest kind, we carried him as often as possible a warm supper, accompanied with some little luxury for the jailer.

Three months elapsed, and there was no prospect of release or of a purchaser. One day he was heard to sing and laugh. This piece of indecorum was told to his master, and the overseer was ordered to re-chain him. He was now confined in an apartment with other prisoners, who were covered with filthy rags. Benjamin was chained near them, and was soon covered with vermin. He worked at his chains till he succeeded in getting out of them. He passed them through the bars of the window, with a request that they should be taken to his master, and he should be informed that he was covered with vermin.

This audacity was punished with heavier chains, and prohibition of our visits.

My grandmother continued to send him fresh changes of clothes. The old ones were burned up. The last night we saw him in jail his mother still begged him to send for his master, and beg his pardon. Neither persuasion nor argument could turn him from his purpose. He calmly answered, "I am waiting his time."

Those chains were mournful to hear.

Another three months passed, and Benjamin left his prison walls. We that loved him waited to bid him a long and last farewell. A slave-trader had bought him. You remember, I told you what price he brought when ten years of age. Now he was more than twenty years old, and sold for three hundred dollars. The master had been blind to his own interest. Long confinement had made his face too pale, his form too thin; moreover, the trader had heard something of his character, and it did not strike him as suitable for a slave. He said he would give any price if the handsome lad was a girl. We thanked God that he was not.

Could you have seen that mother clinging to her child, when they fastened the irons upon his wrists; could you have heard her heart-rending groans, and seen her bloodshot eyes wander wildly from face to face, vainly pleading for mercy; could you have witnessed that scene as I saw it, you would exclaim, *Slavery is damnable!*

Benjamin, her youngest, her pet, was forever gone! She could not realize it. She had had an interview with the trader for the purpose of ascertaining if Benjamin could be purchased. She was told it was impossible, as he had given bonds not to sell him till he was out of the state. He promised that he would not sell him till he reached New Orleans.

With a strong arm and unvaried trust, my grandmother began her work of love. Benjamin must be free. If she succeeded, she knew they would still be separated; but the sacrifice was not too great. Day and night she labored. The trader's price would treble that he gave; but she was not discouraged.

She employed a lawyer to write to a gentleman, whom she knew, in New Orleans. She begged him to interest himself for Benjamin, and he willingly favored her request. When he saw Benjamin, and stated his business, he thanked him; but said he preferred to wait a while before making the trader an offer. He knew he had tried to obtain a high price for him, and had invariably failed. This encouraged him to make another effort for freedom. So one morning, long before day, Benjamin was missing. He was riding over the blue billows, bound for Baltimore.

For once his white face did him a kindly service. They had no suspicion that it belonged to a slave; otherwise, the law would have been followed out to the letter, and the *thing* rendered back to slavery. The brightest skies are often overshadowed by the darkest clouds. Benjamin was taken sick, and compelled to remain in Baltimore three weeks. His strength was slow in returning; and his desire to continue his journey seemed to retard his recovery. How could he get strength without air and exercise? He resolved to venture on a short walk. A by-street was selected, where he thought himself secure of not being met by any one that knew him; but a voice called out, "Halloo, Ben, my boy! what are you doing *here*?"

His first impulse was to run; but his legs trembled so that he could not stir. He turned to confront his antagonist, and behold, there stood his old master's next door neighbor! He thought it was all over with him now; but it proved otherwise. That man was a miracle. He possessed a goodly number of slaves, and yet was not quite deaf to that mystic clock, whose ticking is rarely heard in the slaveholder's breast.

"Ben, you are sick," said he. "Why, you look like a ghost. I guess I gave you something of a start. Never mind, Ben, I am not going to touch you. You had a pretty tough time of it, and you may go on your way rejoicing for all men. But I would advise you to get out of this place plaguy quick, for there are several gentlemen here from our town." He described the nearest and safest route to New York, and added, "I shall be glad to tell your mother I have seen you. Good by, Ben."

Benjamin turned away, filled with gratitude, and surprised that the town he hated contained such a gem—a gem worthy of a purer setting.

This gentleman was a Northerner by birth, and had married a southern lady. On his return, he told my grandmother that he had seen her son, and of the service he had rendered him.

Benjamin reached New York safely, and concluded to stop there until he had gained strength enough to proceed further. It happened that my grandmother's only remaining son had sailed for the same city on business for his mistress. Through God's providence, the brothers met. You may be sure it was a happy meeting. "O Phil," exclaimed Benjamin, "I am here at last." Then he told him how near he came to dying, almost in sight of free land, and how he prayed that he might live to get one breath of free air. He said life was worth something now, and it would be hard to die. In the old jail he had not valued it; once, he was tempted to destroy it; but something, he did not know what, had prevented him; perhaps it was fear. He had heard those who profess to be religious declare there was no heaven for self-murderers; and as his life had been pretty hot here, he did not desire a continuation of the same in another world. "If I die now," he exclaimed, "thank God, I shall die a freeman!"

He begged my uncle Phillip not to return south; but stay and work with him, till they earned enough to buy those at home. His brother told him it would kill their mother if he deserted her in her trouble. She had pledged her house, and with difficulty had raised money to buy him. Would he be bought?

"No, never!" he replied. "Do you suppose, Phil, when I have got so far out of their clutches, I will give them one red cent? No! And do you suppose I would turn mother out of her home in her old age? That I would let her pay all those hard-earned dollars for me, and never to see me? For you know she will stay south as long as her other children are slaves. What a good mother! Tell her to buy *you*, Phil. You have been a comfort to her, and I have been a trouble. And Linda, poor Linda; what'll become of her? Phil, you don't know what a life they lead her. She has told me something about it, and I wish old Flint was dead, or a better man. When I was in jail, he asked her if she didn't want *him* to ask my master to forgive me, and take me home again. She told him, No; that I didn't want to go back. He got mad, and said we were all alike. I never despised my own master half as much as I do that man. There is many a worse slaveholder than my master; but for all that I would not be his slave."

While Benjamin was sick, he had parted with nearly all his clothes to pay necessary expenses. But he did not part with a little pin I fastened in his bosom when we parted. It was the most valuable thing I owned, and I thought none more worthy to wear it. He had it still.

His brother furnished him with clothes, and gave him what money he had.

They parted with moistened eyes; and as Benjamin turned away, he said, "Phil, I part with all my kindred." And so it proved. We never heard from him again.

Uncle Phillip came home; and the first words he uttered when he entered the house were, "Mother, Ben is free! I have seen him in New York." She stood looking at him with a bewildered air. "Mother, don't you believe it?" he said, laying his hand softly upon her shoulder. She raised her hands, and exclaimed, "God be praised! Let us thank him." She dropped on her knees, and poured forth her heart in prayer. Then Phillip must sit down and repeat to her every word Benjamin had said. He told her all; only he forbore to mention how sick and pale her darling looked. Why should he distress her when she could do him no good?

The brave old woman still toiled on, hoping to rescue some of her other children. After a while she succeeded in buying Phillip. She paid eight hundred dollars, and came home with the precious document that secured his freedom. The happy mother and son sat together by the old hearthstone that night, telling how proud they were of each other, and how they would prove to the world that they could take care of themselves, as they had long taken care of others. We all concluded by saying, "He that is *willing* to be a slave, let him be a slave."

V
The Trials of Girlhood

During the first years of my service in Dr. Flint's family, I was accustomed to share some indulgences with the children of my mistress. Though this seemed to me no more than right, I was grateful for it, and tried to merit the kindness by the faithful discharge of my duties. But I now entered on my fifteenth year—a sad epoch in the life of a slave girl. My master began to whisper foul words in my ear. Young as I was, I could not remain ignorant of their import. I tried to treat them with indifference or contempt. The master's age, my extreme youth, and the fear that his conduct would be reported to my grandmother, made me bear this treatment for many months. He was a crafty man, and resorted to many means to accomplish his purposes. Sometimes he had stormy, terrific ways, that made his victims tremble; sometimes he assumed a gentleness that he thought must surely subdue. Of the two, I preferred his stormy moods, although they left me trembling. He tried his utmost to corrupt the pure principles my grandmother had instilled. He peopled my young mind with unclean images, such as only a vile monster could think of. I turned from him with disgust and hatred. But he was my master. I was compelled to live under the same roof with him—where I saw a man forty years my senior daily violating the most sacred commandments of nature. He told me I was his property; that I must be subject to his will in all things. My soul revolted against the mean tyranny. But where could I turn for protection? No matter whether the slave girl be as black as ebony or as fair as her mistress. In either case, there is no shadow of law to protect her from insult, from violence, or even from death; all these are inflicted by fiends who bear the shape of men. The mistress, who ought to protect the helpless victim, has no other feelings towards her but those of jealousy and rage. The degradation, the wrongs, the vices, that grow out of slavery, are more than I can describe. They are greater than you would willingly believe. Surely, if you credited one half the truths that are told you concerning the helpless millions suffering in this cruel bondage, you at the north would not help to tighten the yoke. You surely would refuse to do for the master, on your own soil, the mean and cruel work which trained bloodhounds and the lowest class of whites do for him at the south.

Every where the years bring to all enough of sin and sorrow; but in slavery the very dawn of life is darkened by these shadows. Even the little child, who is accustomed to wait on her mistress and her children, will learn, before she is twelve years old, why it is that her mistress hates such and such a one among the slaves. Perhaps the child's own mother is among those hated ones. She listens to violent outbreaks of jealous passion, and cannot help understanding what is the cause. She will become prematurely knowing in evil things. Soon she will learn to tremble when she hears her master's footfall. She will be compelled to realize that she is no longer a child. If God has bestowed beauty upon her, it will prove her greatest curse. That which commands admiration in the white woman only hastens the degradation of the female slave. I know that some are too much brutalized by slavery to feel the humiliation of their position; but many slaves feel it most acutely, and shrink from the memory of it. I cannot tell how much I suffered in the presence of these wrongs, nor how I am still pained by the retrospect. My master met me at every turn, reminding me that I belonged to him, and swearing by heaven and earth that he would compel me to submit to him. If I went out for a breath of fresh air, after a day of unwearied toil, his footsteps dogged me. If I knelt by my mother's grave, his dark shadow fell on me even there. The light heart which nature had given me became heavy with sad forebodings. The other slaves in my master's house noticed the change. Many of them pitied me; but none dared to ask the cause. They had no need to inquire. They knew too well the guilty practices under that roof; and they were aware that to speak of them was an offence that never went unpunished.

I longed for some one to confide in. I would have given the world to have laid my head on my grandmother's faithful bosom, and told her all my troubles. But Dr. Flint swore he would kill me, if I was not as silent as the grave. Then, although my grandmother was all in all to me, I feared her as well as loved her. I had been accustomed to look up to her with a respect bordering upon awe. I was very young, and felt shamefaced about telling her such impure things, especially as I knew her to be very strict on such subjects. Moreover, she was a woman of a high spirit. She was usually very quiet in her demeanor; but if her indignation was once roused, it was not very easily quelled. I had been told that she once chased a white gentleman with a loaded pistol, because he insulted one of her daughters. I dreaded the consequences of a violent outbreak; and both pride and fear kept me silent. But though I did not confide in my grandmother, and even evaded her vigilant watchfulness and inquiry, her presence in the neighborhood was some protection to me. Though she had been a slave, Dr. Flint was afraid of her. He dreaded her scorching rebukes. Moreover, she was known and patronized by many people; and he did not wish to have his villany made public. It was lucky for me that I did not live on a distant plantation, but in a town not so large that the inhabitants were ignorant of each other's affairs. Bad as are the laws and customs in a slaveholding community, the doctor, as a professional man, deemed it prudent to keep up some outward show of decency.

O, what days and nights of fear and sorrow that man caused me! Reader, it is not to awaken sympathy for myself that I am telling you truthfully what I suffered in slavery. I do it to kindle a flame of compassion in your hearts for my sisters who are still in bondage, suffering as I once suffered.

I once saw two beautiful children playing together. One was a fair white child; the other was her slave, and also her sister. When I saw them embracing each other, and heard their joyous laughter, I turned sadly away from the lovely sight. I foresaw the inevitable blight that would fall on the little slave's heart. I knew how soon her laughter would be changed to sighs. The fair child grew up to be a still fairer woman. From childhood to womanhood her pathway was blooming with flowers, and overarched by a sunny sky. Scarcely one day of her life had been clouded when the sun rose on her happy bridal morning.

How had those years dealt with her slave sister, the little playmate of her childhood? She, also, was very beautiful; but the flowers and sunshine of love were not for her. She drank the cup of sin, and shame, and misery, whereof her persecuted race are compelled to drink.

In view of these things, why are ye silent, ye free men and women of the north? Why do your tongues falter in maintenance of the right? Would that I had more ability! But my heart is so full, and my pen is so weak! There are noble men and women who plead for us, striving to help those who cannot help themselves. God bless them! God give them strength and courage to go on! God bless those, every where, who are laboring to advance the cause of humanity!

VI
The Jealous Mistress

I would ten thousand times rather that my children should be the half-starved paupers of Ireland than to be the most pampered among the slaves of America. I would rather drudge out my life on a cotton plantation, till the grave opened to give me rest, than to live with an unprincipled master and a jealous mistress. The felon's home in a penitentiary is preferable. He may repent, and turn from the error of his ways, and so find peace; but it is not so with a favorite slave. She is not allowed to have any pride of character. It is deemed a crime in her to wish to be virtuous.

Mrs. Flint possessed the key to her husband's character before I was born. She might have used this knowledge to counsel and to screen the young and the innocent among her slaves; but for them she had no sympathy. They were the objects of her constant suspicion and malevolence. She watched her husband with unceasing vigilance; but he was well practiced in means to evade it. What he could not find opportunity to say in words he manifested in signs. He invented more than were ever thought of in a deaf and dumb asylum. I let them pass, as if I did not understand what he meant; and many were the curses and threats bestowed on me for my stupidity. One day he caught me teaching myself to write. He frowned, as if he was not well pleased; but I suppose he came to the conclusion that such an accomplishment might help to advance his favorite scheme. Before long, notes were often slipped into my hand. I would return them, saying, "I can't read them, sir." "Can't you?" he replied; "then I must read them to you." He always finished the reading by asking, "Do you understand?" Sometimes he would complain of the heat of the tea room, and order his supper to be placed on a small table in the piazza. He would seat himself there with a well-satisfied smile, and tell me to stand by and brush away the flies. He would eat very slowly, pausing between the mouthfuls. These intervals were employed in describing the happiness I was so foolishly throwing away, and in threatening me with the penalty that finally awaited my stubborn disobedience. He boasted much of the forbearance he had exercised towards me, and reminded me that there was a limit to his patience. When I succeeded in avoiding opportunities for him to talk to me at home, I was ordered to come to his office, to do some errand. When there, I was obliged to stand and listen to such language as he saw fit to address to me. Sometimes I so openly expressed my contempt for him that he would become violently enraged, and I wondered why he did not strike me. Circumstanced as he was, he probably thought it was better policy to be forbearing. But the state of things grew worse and worse daily. In desperation I told him that I must and would apply to my grandmother for protection. He threatened me with death, and worse than death, if I made any complaint to her. Strange to say, I did not despair. I was naturally of a buoyant disposition, and always I had a hope of somehow getting out of his clutches. Like many a poor, simple slave before me, I trusted that some threads of joy would yet be woven into my dark destiny.

I had entered my sixteenth year, and every day it became more apparent that my presence was intolerable to Mrs. Flint. Angry words frequently passed between her and her husband. He had never punished me himself, and he would not allow any body else to punish me. In that respect, she was never satisfied; but, in her angry moods, no terms were too vile for her to bestow upon me. Yet I, whom she detested so bitterly, had far more pity for her than he had, whose duty it was to make her life happy. I never wronged her, or wished to wrong her; and one word of kindness from her would have brought me to her feet.

After repeated quarrels between the doctor and his wife, he announced his intention to take his youngest daughter, then four years old, to sleep in his apartment. It was necessary that a servant should sleep in the same room, to be on hand if the child stirred. I was selected for that office, and informed for what purpose that arrangement had been made. By managing to keep within sight of people, as much as possible, during the day time, I had hitherto succeeded in eluding my master, though a [razor] was often held to my throat to force me to change this line of policy. At night I slept by the side of my great aunt, where I felt safe. He was too prudent to come into her room. She was an old woman, and had been in the family many years. Moreover, as a married man, and a professional man, he deemed it necessary to save appearances in some degree. But he resolved to remove the obstacle in the way of his scheme; and he thought he had planned it so that he should evade suspicion. He was well aware how much I prized my refuge by the side of my old aunt, and he determined to dispossess me of it. The first night the doctor had the little child in his room alone. The next morning, I was ordered to take my station as nurse the following night. A kind Providence interposed in my favor. During the day Mrs. Flint heard of this new arrangement, and a storm followed. I rejoiced to hear it rage.

After a while my mistress sent for me to come to her room. Her first question was, "Did you know you were to sleep in the doctor's room?"

"Yes, ma'am."

"Who told you?"

"My master."

"Will you answer truly all the questions I ask?"

"Yes, ma'am."

"Tell me, then, as you hope to be forgiven, are you innocent of what I have accused you?"

"I am."

She handed me a Bible, and said, "Lay your hand on your heart, kiss this holy book, and swear before God that you tell me the truth."

I took the oath she required, and I did it with a clear conscience.

"You have taken God's holy word to testify your innocence," said she. "If you have deceived me, beware! Now take this stool, sit down, look me directly in the face, and tell me all that has passed between your master and you."

I did as she ordered. As I went on with my account her color changed frequently, she wept, and sometimes groaned. She spoke in tones so sad, that I was touched by her grief. The tears came to my eyes; but I was soon convinced that her emotions arose from anger and wounded pride. She felt that her marriage vows were desecrated, her dignity insulted; but she had no compassion for the poor victim of her husband's perfidy. She pitied herself as a martyr; but she was incapable of feeling for the condition of shame and misery in which her unfortunate, helpless slave was placed.

Yet perhaps she had some touch of feeling for me; for when the conference was ended, she spoke kindly, and promised to protect me. I should have been much comforted by this assurance if I could have had confidence in it; but my experiences in slavery had filled me with distrust. She was not a very refined woman, and had not much control over her passions. I was an object of her jealousy, and, consequently, of her hatred; and I knew I could not expect kindness or confidence from her under the circumstances in which I was placed. I could not blame her. Slaveholders' wives feel as other women would under similar circumstances. The fire of her temper kindled from small sparks, and now the flame became so intense that the doctor was obliged to give up his intended arrangement.

I knew I had ignited the torch, and I expected to suffer for it afterwards; but I felt too thankful to my mistress for the timely aid she rendered me to care much about that. She now took me to sleep in a room adjoining her own. There I was an object of her especial care, though not of her especial comfort, for she spent many a sleepless night to watch over me. Sometimes I woke up, and found her bending over me. At other times she whispered in my ear, as though it was her husband who was speaking to me, and listened to hear what I would answer. If she startled me, on such occasions, she would glide stealthily away; and the next morning she would tell me I had been talking in my sleep, and ask who I was talking to. At last, I began to be fearful for my life. It had been often threatened; and you can imagine, better than I can describe, what an unpleasant sensation it must produce to wake up in the dead of night and find a jealous woman bending over you. Terrible as this experience was, I had fears that it would give place to one more terrible.

My mistress grew weary of her vigils; they did not prove satisfactory. She changed her tactics. She now tried the trick of accusing my master of crime, in my presence, and gave my name as the author of the accusation. To my utter astonishment, he replied, "I don't believe it; but if she did acknowledge it, you tortured her into exposing me." Tortured into exposing him! Truly, Satan had no difficulty in distinguishing the color of his soul! I understood his object in making this false representation. It was to show me that I gained nothing by seeking the protection of my mistress; that the power was still all in his own hands. I pitied Mrs. Flint. She was a second wife, many years the junior of her husband; and the hoary-headed miscreant was enough to try the patience of a wiser and better woman. She was completely foiled, and knew not how to proceed. She would gladly have had me flogged for my supposed false oath; but, as I have already stated, the doctor never allowed any one to whip me. The old sinner was politic. The application of the lash might have led to remarks that would have exposed him in the eyes of his children and grandchildren. How often did I rejoice that I lived in a town where all the inhabitants knew each other! If I had been on a remote plantation, or lost among the multitude of a crowded city, I should not be a living woman at this day.

The secrets of slavery are concealed like those of the Inquisition. My master was, to my knowledge, the father of eleven slaves. But did the mothers dare to tell who was the father of their children? Did the other slaves dare to allude to it, except in whispers among themselves? No, indeed! They knew too well the terrible consequences.

My grandmother could not avoid seeing things which excited her suspicions. She was uneasy about me, and tried various ways to buy me; but the never-changing answer was always repeated: "Linda does not belong to *me*. She is my daughter's property, and I have no legal right to sell her." The conscientious man! He was too scrupulous to *sell* me; but he had no scruples whatever about committing a much greater wrong against the helpless young girl placed under his guardianship, as his daughter's property. Sometimes my persecutor would ask me whether I would like to be sold. I told him I would rather be sold to any body than to lead such a life as I did. On such occasions he would assume the air of a very injured individual, and reproach me for my ingratitude. "Did I not take you into the house, and make you the companion of my own children?" he would say. "Have I ever treated you like a negro? I have never allowed you to be punished, not even to please your mistress. And this is the recompense I get, you ungrateful girl!" I answered that he had reasons of his own for screening me from punishment, and that the course he pursued made my mistress hate me and persecute me. If I wept, he would say, "Poor child! Don't cry! don't cry! I will make peace for you with your mistress. Only let me arrange matters in my own way. Poor, foolish girl! you don't know what is for your own good. I would cherish you. I would make a lady of you. Now go, and think of all I have promised you."

I did think of it.

Reader, I draw no imaginary pictures of southern homes. I am telling you the plain truth. Yet when victims make their escape from this wild beast of Slavery, northerners consent to act the part of bloodhounds, and hunt the poor fugitive back into his den, "full of dead men's bones, and all uncleanness." Nay, more, they are not only willing, but proud, to give their daughters in marriage to slaveholders. The poor girls have romantic notions of a sunny clime, and of the flowering vines that all the year round shade a happy home. To what disappointments are they destined! The young wife soon learns that the husband in whose hands she has placed her happiness pays no regard to his marriage vows. Children of every shade of complexion play with her own fair babies, and too well she knows that they are born unto him of his own household. Jealousy and hatred enter the flowery home, and it is ravaged of its loveliness.

Southern women often marry a man knowing that he is the father of many little slaves. They do not trouble themselves about it. They regard such children as property, as marketable as the pigs on the plantation; and it is seldom that they do not make them aware of this by passing them into the slave-trader's hands as soon as possible, and thus getting them out of their sight. I am glad to say there are some honorable exceptions.

I have myself known two southern wives who exhorted their husbands to free those slaves towards whom they stood in a "parental relation"; and their request was granted. These husbands blushed before the superior nobleness of their wives' natures. Though they had only counselled them to do that which it was their duty to do, it commanded their respect, and rendered their conduct more exemplary. Concealment was at an end, and confidence took the place of distrust.

Though this bad institution deadens the moral sense, even in white women, to a fearful extent, it is not altogether extinct. I have heard southern ladies say of Mr. Such a one, "He not only thinks it no disgrace to be the father of those little niggers, but he is not ashamed to call himself their master. I declare, such things ought not to be tolerated, in any decent society!"

VII
The Lover

Why does the slave ever love? Why allow the tendrils of the heart to twine around objects which may at any moment be wrenched away by the hand of violence? When separations come by the hand of death, the pious soul can bow in resignation, and say, "Not my will, but thine be done, O Lord!" But when the ruthless hand of man strikes the blow, regardless of the misery he causes, it is hard to be submissive. I did not reason thus when I was a young girl. Youth will be youth. I loved, and I indulged the hope that the dark clouds around me would turn out a bright lining. I forgot that in the land of my birth the shadows are too dense for light to penetrate. A land

> Where laughter is not mirth; nor thought the mind;
> Nor words a language; nor e'en men mankind.
> Where cries reply to curses, shrieks to blows,
> And each is tortured in his separate hell.

There was in the neighborhood a young colored carpenter; a free-born man. We had been well acquainted in childhood, and frequently met together afterwards. We became mutually attached, and he proposed to marry me. I loved him with all the ardor of a young girl's first love. But when I reflected that I was a slave, and that the laws gave no sanction to the marriage of such, my heart sank within me. My lover wanted to buy me; but I knew that Dr. Flint was too wilful and arbitrary a man to consent to that arrangement. From him, I was sure of experiencing all sorts of opposition, and I had nothing to hope from my mistress. She would have been delighted to have got rid of me, but not in that way. It would have relieved her mind of a burden if she could have seen me sold to some distant state, but if I was married near home I should be just as much in her husband's power as I had previously been,—for the husband of a slave has no power to protect her. Moreover, my mistress, like many others, seemed to think that slaves had no right to any family ties of their own; that they were created merely to wait upon the family of the mistress. I once heard her abuse a young slave girl, who told her that a colored man wanted to make her his wife. "I will have you peeled and pickled, my lady," said she, "if I ever hear you mention that subject again. Do you suppose that I will have you tending *my* children with the children of that nigger?" The girl to whom she said this had a mulatto child, of course not acknowledged by its father. The poor black man who loved her would have been proud to acknowledge his helpless offspring.

Many and anxious were the thoughts I revolved in my mind. I was at a loss what to do. Above all things, I was desirous to spare my lover the insults that had cut so deeply into my own soul. I talked with my grandmother about it, and partly told her my fears. I did not dare to tell her the worst. She had long suspected all was not right, and if I confirmed her suspicions I knew a storm would rise that would prove the overthrow of all my hopes.

This love-dream had been my support through many trials; and I could not bear to run the risk of having it suddenly dissipated. There was a lady in the neighborhood, a particular friend of Dr. Flint's, who often visited the house. I had a great respect for her, and she had always manifested a friendly interest in me. Grandmother thought she would have great influence with the doctor. I went to this lady, and told her my story. I told her I was aware that my lover's being a free-born man would prove a great objection; but he wanted to buy me; and if Dr. Flint would consent to that arrangement, I felt sure he would be willing to pay any reasonable price. She knew that Mrs. Flint disliked me; therefore, I ventured to suggest that perhaps my mistress would approve of my being sold, as that would rid her of me. The lady listened with kindly sympathy, and promised to do her utmost to promote my wishes. She had an interview with the doctor, and I believe she pleaded my cause earnestly; but it was all to no purpose.

How I dreaded my master now! Every minute I expected to be summoned to his presence; but the day passed, and I heard nothing from him. The next morning, a message was brought to me: "Master wants you in his study." I found the door ajar, and I stood a moment gazing at the hateful man who claimed a right to rule me, body and soul. I entered, and tried to appear calm. I did not want him to know how my heart was bleeding. He looked fixedly at me, with an expression which seemed to say, "I have half a mind to kill you on the spot." At last he broke the silence, and that was a relief to both of us.

"So you want to be married, do you?" said he, "and to a free nigger."

"Yes, sir."

"Well, I'll soon convince you whether I am your master, or the nigger fellow you honor so highly. If you *must* have a husband, you may take up with one of my slaves."

What a situation I should be in, as the wife of one of *his* slaves, even if my heart had been interested!

I replied, "Don't you suppose, sir, that a slave can have some preference about marrying? Do you suppose that all men are alike to her?"

"Do you love this nigger?" said he, abruptly.

"Yes, sir."

"How dare you tell me so!" he exclaimed, in great wrath. After a slight pause, he added, "I supposed you thought more of yourself; that you felt above the insults of such puppies."

I replied, "If he is a puppy I am a puppy, for we are both of the negro race. It is right and honorable for us to love each other. The man you call a puppy never insulted me, sir; and he would not love me if he did not believe me to be a virtuous woman."

He sprang upon me like a tiger, and gave me a stunning blow. It was the first time he had ever struck me; and fear did not enable me to control my anger. When I had recovered a little from the effects, I exclaimed, "You have struck me for answering you honestly. How I despise you!"

There was silence for some minutes. Perhaps he was deciding what should be my punishment; or, perhaps, he wanted to give me time to reflect on what I had said, and to whom I had said it. Finally, he asked, "Do you know what you have said?"

"Yes, sir; but your treatment drove me to it."

"Do you know that I have a right to do as I like with you,—that I can kill you, if I please?"

"You have tried to kill me, and I wish you had; but you have no right to do as you like with me."

"Silence!" he exclaimed, in a thundering voice. "By heavens, girl, you forget yourself too far! Are you mad? If you are, I will soon bring you to your senses. Do you think any other master would bear what I have borne from you this morning? Many masters would have killed you on the spot. How would you like to be sent to jail for your insolence?"

"I know I have been disrespectful, sir," I replied; "but you drove me to it; I couldn't help it. As for the jail, there would be more peace for me there than there is here."

"You deserve to go there," said he, "and to be under such treatment, that you would forget the meaning of the word *peace.* It would do you good. It would take some of your high notions out of you. But I am not ready to send you there yet, notwithstanding your ingratitude for all my kindness and forbearance. You have been the plague of my life. I have wanted to make you happy, and I have been repaid with the basest ingratitude; but though you have proved yourself incapable of appreciating my kindness, I will be lenient towards you, Linda. I will give you one more chance to redeem your character. If you behave yourself and do as I require, I will forgive you and treat you as I always have done; but if you disobey me, I will punish you as I would the meanest slave on my plantation. Never let me hear that fellow's name mentioned again. If I ever know of your speaking to him, I will cowhide you both; and if I catch him lurking about my premises, I will shoot him as soon as I would a dog. Do you hear what I say? I'll teach you a lesson about marriage and free niggers! Now go, and let this be the last time I have occasion to speak to you on this subject."

Reader, did you ever hate? I hope not. I never did but once; and I trust I never shall again. Somebody has called it "the atmosphere of hell"; and I believe it is so.

For a fortnight the doctor did not speak to me. He thought to mortify me; to make me feel that I had disgraced myself by receiving the honorable addresses of a respectable colored man, in preference to the base proposals of a white man. But though his lips disdained to address me, his eyes were very loquacious. No animal ever watched its prey more narrowly than he watched me. He knew that I could write, though he had failed to make me read his letters; and he was now troubled lest I should exchange letters with another man. After a while he became weary of silence; and I was sorry for it. One morning, as he passed through the hall, to leave the house, he contrived to thrust a note into my hand. I thought I had better read it, and spare myself the vexation of having him read it to me. It expressed regret for the blow he had given me, and reminded me that I myself was wholly to blame for it. He hoped I had become convinced of the injury I was doing myself by incurring his displeasure. He wrote that he had made up his mind to go to Louisiana; that he should take several slaves with him, and intended I should be one of the number. My mistress would remain where she was; therefore I should have nothing to fear from that quarter. If I merited kindness from him, he assured me that it would be lavishly bestowed. He begged me to think over the matter, and answer the following day.

The next morning I was called to carry a pair of scissors to his room. I laid them on the table, with the letter beside them. He thought it was my answer, and did not call me back. I went as usual to attend my young mistress to and from school. He met me in the street, and ordered me to stop at his office on my way back. When I entered, he showed me his letter, and asked me why I had not answered it. I replied, "I am your daughter's property, and it is in your power to send me, or take me, wherever you please." He said he was very glad to find me so willing to go, and that we should start early in the autumn. He had a large practice in the town, and I rather thought he had made up the story merely to frighten me. However that might be, I was determined that I would never go to Louisiana with him.

Summer passed away, and early in the autumn Dr. Flint's eldest son was sent to Louisiana to examine the country, with a view to emigrating. That news did not disturb me. I knew very well that I should not be sent with *him*. That I had not been taken to the plantation before this time, was owing to the fact that his son was there. He was jealous of his son; and jealousy of the overseer had kept him from punishing me by sending me into the fields to work. Is it strange that I was not proud of these protectors? As for the overseer, he was a man for whom I had less respect than I had for a bloodhound.

Young Mr. Flint did not bring back a favorable report of Louisiana, and I heard no more of that scheme. Soon after this, my lover met me at the corner of the street, and I stopped to speak to him. Looking up, I saw my master watching us from his window. I hurried home, trembling with fear. I was sent for, immediately, to go to his room. He met me with a blow. "When is mistress to be married?" said he, in a sneering tone. A shower of oaths and imprecations followed. How thankful I was that my lover was a free man! that my tyrant had no power to flog him for speaking to me in the street!

Again and again I revolved in my mind how all this would end. There was no hope that the doctor would consent to sell me on any terms. He had an iron will, and was determined to keep me, and to conquer me. My lover was an intelligent and religious man. Even if he could have obtained permission to marry me while I was a slave, the marriage would give him no power to protect me from my master. It would have made him miserable to witness the insults I should have been subjected to. And then, if we had children, I knew they must "follow the condition of the mother." What a terrible blight that would be on the heart of a free, intelligent father! For *his* sake, I felt that I ought not to link his fate with my own unhappy destiny. He was going to Savannah to see about a little property left him by an uncle; and hard as it was to bring my feelings to it, I earnestly entreated him not to come back. I advised him to go to the Free States, where his tongue would not be tied, and where his intelligence would be of more avail to him. He left me, still hoping the day would come when I could be bought. With me the lamp of hope had gone out. The dream of my girlhood was over. I felt lonely and desolate.

Still I was not stripped of all. I still had my good grandmother, and my affectionate brother. When he put his arms round my neck, and looked into my eyes, as if to read there the troubles I dared not tell, I felt that I still had something to love. But even that pleasant emotion was chilled by the reflection that he might be torn from me at any moment, by some sudden freak of my master. If he had known how we loved each other, I think he would have exulted in separating us. We often planned together how we could get to the north. But, as William remarked, such things are easier said than done. My movements were very closely watched, and we had no means of getting any money to defray our expenses. As for grandmother, she was strongly opposed to her children's undertaking any such project. She had not forgotten poor Benjamin's sufferings, and she was afraid that if another child tried to escape, he would have a similar or a worse fate. To me, nothing seemed more dreadful than my present life. I said to myself, "William *must* be free. He shall go to the north, and I will follow him." Many a slave sister has formed the same plans. . . .

X
A Perilous Passage in the Slave Girl's Life

After my lover went away, Dr. Flint contrived a new plan. He seemed to have an idea that my fear of my mistress was his greatest obstacle. In the blandest tones, he told me that he was going to build a small house for me, in a secluded place, four miles away from the town. I shuddered; but I was constrained to listen, while he talked of his intention to give me a home of my own, and to make a lady of me. Hitherto, I had escaped my dreaded fate, by being in the midst of people. My grandmother had already had high words with my master about me. She had told him pretty plainly what she thought of his character, and there was considerable gossip in the neighborhood about our affairs, to which the open-mouthed jealousy of Mrs. Flint contributed not a little. When my master said he was going to build a house for me, and that he could do it with little trouble and expense, I was in hopes something would happen to frustrate his scheme; but I soon heard that the house was actually begun. I vowed before my Maker that I would never enter it. I had rather toil on the plantation from dawn till dark; I had rather live and die in jail, than drag on, from day to day, through such a living death. I was determined that the master, whom I so hated and loathed, who had blighted the prospects of my youth, and made my life a desert, should not, after my long struggle with him, succeed at last in trampling his victim under his feet. I would do any thing, every thing, for the sake of defeating him. What *could* I do? I thought and thought, till I became desperate, and made a plunge into the abyss.

And now, reader, I come to a period in my unhappy life, which I would gladly forget if I could. The remembrance fills me with sorrow and shame. It pains me to tell you of it; but I have promised to tell you the truth, and I will do it honestly, let it cost me what it may. I will not try to screen myself behind the plea of compulsion from a master; for it was not so. Neither can I plead ignorance or thoughtlessness. For years, my master had done his utmost to pollute my mind with foul images, and to destroy the pure principles inculcated by my grandmother, and the good mistress of my childhood. The influences of slavery had had the same effect on me that they had on other young girls; they had made me prematurely knowing, concerning the evil ways of the world. I knew what I did, and I did it with deliberate calculation.

But, O, ye happy women, whose purity has been sheltered from childhood, who have been free to choose the objects of your affection, whose homes are protected by law, do not judge the poor desolate slave girl too severely! If slavery had been abolished, I, also, could have married the man of my choice; I could have had a home shielded by the laws; and I should have been spared the painful task of confessing what I am now about to relate; but all my prospects had been blighted by slavery. I wanted to keep myself pure; and, under the most adverse circumstances, I tried hard to preserve my self-respect; but I was struggling alone in the powerful grasp of the demon Slavery; and the monster proved too strong for me. I felt as if I was forsaken by God and man; as if all my efforts must be frustrated; and I became reckless in my despair.

I have told you that Dr. Flint's persecutions and his wife's jealousy had given rise to some gossip in the neighborhood. Among others, it chanced that a white unmarried gentleman had obtained some knowledge of the circumstances in which I was placed. He knew my grandmother, and often spoke to me in the street. He became interested for me, and asked questions about my master, which I answered in part. He expressed a great deal of sympathy, and a wish to aid me. He constantly sought opportunities to see me, and wrote to me frequently. I was a poor slave girl, only fifteen years old.

So much attention from a superior person was, of course, flattering; for human nature is the same in all. I also felt grateful for his sympathy, and encouraged by his kind words. It seemed to me a great thing to have such a friend. By degrees, a more tender feeling crept into my heart. He was an educated and eloquent gentleman; too eloquent, alas, for the poor slave girl who trusted in him. Of course I saw whither all this was tending. I knew the impassable gulf between us; but to be an object of interest to a man who is not married, and who is not her master, is agreeable to the pride and feelings of a slave, if her miserable situation has left her any pride or sentiment. It seems less degrading to give one's self, than to submit to compulsion. There is something akin to freedom in having a lover who has no control over you, except that which he gains by kindness and attachment. A master may treat you as rudely as he pleases, and you dare not speak; moreover, the wrong does not seem so great with an unmarried man, as with one who has a wife to be made unhappy. There may be sophistry in all this; but the condition of a slave confuses all principles of morality, and, in fact, renders the practice of them impossible.

When I found that my master had actually begun to build the lonely cottage, other feelings mixed with those I have described. Revenge, and calculations of interest, were added to flattered vanity and sincere gratitude for kindness. I knew nothing would enrage Dr. Flint so much as to know that I favored another; and it was something to triumph over my tyrant even in that small way. I thought he would revenge himself by selling me, and I was sure my friend, Mr. Sands, would buy me. He was a man of more generosity and feeling than my master, and I thought my freedom could be easily obtained from him. The crisis of my fate now came so near that I was desperate. I shuddered to think of being the mother of children that should be owned by my old tyrant. I knew that as soon as a new fancy took him, his victims were sold far off to get rid of them; especially if they had children. I had seen several women sold, with his babies at the breast. He never allowed his offspring by slaves to remain long in sight of himself and his wife. Of a man who was not my master I could ask to have my children well supported; and in this case, I felt confident I should obtain the boon. I also felt quite sure that they would be made free. With all these thoughts revolving in my mind, and seeing no other way of escaping the doom I so much dreaded, I made a headlong plunge. Pity me, and pardon me, O virtuous reader! You never knew what it is to be a slave; to be entirely unprotected by law or custom; to have the laws reduce you to the condition of a chattel, entirely subject to the will of another. You never exhausted your ingenuity in avoiding the snares, and eluding the power of a hated tyrant; you never shuddered at the sound of his footsteps, and trembled within hearing of his voice. I know I did wrong. No one can feel it more sensibly than I do. The painful and humiliating memory will haunt me to my dying day. Still, in looking back, calmly, on the events of my life, I feel that the slave woman ought not to be judged by the same standard as others.

The months passed on. I had many unhappy hours. I secretly mourned over the sorrow I was bringing on my grandmother, who had so tried to shield me from harm. I knew that I was the greatest comfort of her old age, and that it was a source of pride to her that I had not degraded myself, like most of the slaves. I wanted to confess to her that I was no longer worthy of her love; but I could not utter the dreaded words.

As for Dr. Flint, I had a feeling of satisfaction and triumph in the thought of telling *him*. From time to time he told me of his intended arrangements, and I was silent. At last, he came and told me the cottage was completed, and ordered me to go to it. I told him I would never enter it. He said, "I have heard enough of such talk as that. You shall go, if you are carried by force; and you shall remain there."

I replied, "I will never go there. In a few months I shall be a mother."

He stood and looked at me in dumb amazement, and left the house without a word. I thought I should be happy in my triumph over him. But now that the truth was out, and my relatives would hear of it, I felt wretched. Humble as were their circumstances, they had pride in my good character. Now, how could I look them in the face? My self-respect was gone! I had resolved that I would be virtuous, though I was a slave. I had said, "Let the storm beat! I will brave it till I die." And now, how humiliated I felt!

I went to my grandmother. My lips moved to make confession, but the words stuck in my throat. I sat down in the shade of a tree at her door and began to sew. I think she saw something unusual was the matter with me. The mother of slaves is very watchful. She knows there is no security for her children. After they have entered their teens she lives in daily expectation of trouble. This leads to many questions. If the girl is of a sensitive nature, timidity keeps her from answering truthfully, and this well-meant course has a tendency to drive her from maternal counsels. Presently, in came my mistress, like a mad woman, and accused me concerning her husband. My grandmother, whose suspicions had been previously awakened, believed what she said. She exclaimed, "O Linda! has it come to this? I had rather see you dead than to see you as you now are. You are a disgrace to your dead mother." She tore from my fingers my mother's wedding ring and her silver thimble. "Go away!" she exclaimed, "and never come to my house again." Her reproaches fell so hot and heavy, that they left me no chance to answer. Bitter tears, such as the eyes never shed but once, were my only answer. I rose from my seat, but fell back again, sobbing. She did not speak to me; but the tears were running down her furrowed cheeks, and they scorched me like fire. She had always been so kind to me! *So* kind! How I longed to throw myself at her feet, and tell her all the truth! But she had ordered me to go, and never to come there again. After a few minutes, I mustered strength, and started to obey her. With what feelings did I now close that little gate, which I used to open with such an eager hand in my childhood! It closed upon me with a sound I never heard before.

Where could I go? I was afraid to return to my master's. I walked on recklessly, not caring where I went, or what would become of me. When I had gone four or five miles, fatigue compelled me to stop. I sat down on the stump of an old tree. The stars were shining through the boughs above me. How they mocked me, with their bright, calm light! The hours passed by, and as I sat there alone a chilliness and deadly sickness came over me. I sank on the ground. My mind was full of horrid thoughts. I prayed to die; but the prayer was not answered. At last, with great effort I roused myself, and walked some distance further, to the house of a woman who had been a friend of my mother. When I told her why I was there, she spoke soothingly to me; but I could not be comforted. I thought I could bear my shame if I could only be reconciled to my grandmother. I longed to open my heart to her. I thought if she could know the real state of the case, and all I had been bearing for years, she would perhaps judge me less harshly. My friend advised me to send for her. I did so; but days of agonizing suspense passed before she came. Had she utterly forsaken me? No. She came at last. I knelt before her, and told her the things that had poisoned my life; how long I had been persecuted; that I saw no way of escape; and in an hour of extremity I had become desperate. She listened in silence. I told her I would bear any thing and do any thing, if in time I had hopes of obtaining her forgiveness. I begged of her to pity me, for my dead mother's sake. And she did pity me. She did not say, "I forgive you"; but she looked at me lovingly, with her eyes full of tears. She laid her old hand gently on my head, and murmured, "Poor child! Poor child!"

XI
The New Tie to Life

I returned to my good grandmother's house. She had an interview with Mr. Sands. When she asked him why he could not have left her one ewe lamb,—whether there were not plenty of slaves who did not care about character,—he made no answer; but he spoke kind and encouraging words. He promised to care for my child, and to buy me, be the conditions what they might.

I had not seen Dr. Flint for five days. I had never seen him since I made the avowal to him. He talked of the disgrace I had brought on myself; how I had sinned against my master, and mortified my old grandmother. He intimated that if I had accepted his proposals, he, as a physician, could have saved me from exposure. He even condescended to pity me. Could he have offered wormwood more bitter? He, whose persecutions had been the cause of my sin!

"Linda," said he, "though you have been criminal towards me, I feel for you, and I can pardon you if you obey my wishes. Tell me whether the fellow you wanted to marry is the father of your child. If you deceive me, you shall feel the fires of hell."

I did not feel as proud as I had done. My strongest weapon with him was gone. I was lowered in my own estimation, and had resolved to bear his abuse in silence. But when he spoke contemptuously of the lover who had always treated me honorably; when I remembered that but for *him* I might have been a virtuous, free, and happy wife, I lost my patience. "I have sinned against God and myself," I replied; "but not against you."

He clinched his teeth, and muttered, "Curse you!" He came towards me, with ill-suppressed rage, and exclaimed, "You obstinate girl! I could grind your bones to powder! You have thrown yourself away on some worthless rascal. You are weak-minded, and have been easily persuaded by those who don't care a straw for you. The future will settle accounts between us. You are blinded now; but hereafter you will be convinced that your master was your best friend. My lenity towards you is a proof of it. I might have punished you in many ways. I might have had you whipped till you fell dead under the lash. But I wanted you to live; I would have bettered your condition. Others cannot do it. You are my slave. Your mistress, disgusted by your conduct, forbids you to return to the house; therefore I leave you here for the present; but I shall see you often. I will call tomorrow."

He came with frowning brows, that showed a dissatisfied state of mind. After asking about my health, he inquired whether my board was paid, and who visited me. He then went on to say that he had neglected his duty; that as a physician there were certain things that he ought to have explained to me. Then followed talk such as would have made the most shameless blush. He ordered me to stand up before him. I obeyed. "I command you," said he, "to tell me whether the father of your child is white or black." I hesitated. "Answer me this instant!" he exclaimed. I did answer. He sprang upon me like a wolf, and grabbed my arm as if he would have broken it. "Do you love him?" said he, in a hissing tone.

"I am thankful that I do not despise him," I replied.

He raised his hand to strike me; but it fell again. I don't know what arrested the blow. He sat down, with lips tightly compressed. At last he spoke. "I came here," said he, "to make you a friendly proposition; but your ingratitude chafes me beyond endurance. You turn aside all my good intentions towards you. I don't know what it is that keeps me from killing you." Again he rose, as if he had a mind to strike me.

But he resumed. "On one condition I will forgive your insolence and crime. You must henceforth have no communication of any kind with the father of your child. You must not ask any thing from him, or receive any thing from him. I will take care of you and your child. You had better promise this at once, and not wait till you are deserted by him. This is the last act of mercy I shall show towards you."

I said something about being unwilling to have my child supported by a man who had cursed it and me also. He rejoined, that a woman who had sunk to my level had no right to expect any thing else. He asked, for the last time, would I accept his kindness? I answered that I would not.

"Very well," said he; "then take the consequences of your wayward course. Never look to me for help. You are my slave, and shall always be my slave. I will never sell you, that you may depend upon."

Hope died away in my heart as he closed the door after him. I had calculated that in his rage he would sell me to a slave-trader; and I knew the father of my child was on the watch to buy me.

About this time my uncle Phillip was expected to return from a voyage. The day before his departure I had officiated as bridesmaid to a young friend. My heart was then ill at ease, but my smiling countenance did not betray it. Only a year had passed; but what fearful changes it had wrought! My heart had grown gray in misery. Lives that flash in sunshine, and lives that are born in tears, receive their hue from circumstances. None of us know what a year may bring forth.

I felt no joy when they told me my uncle had come. He wanted to see me, though he knew what had happened. I shrank from him at first; but at last consented that he should come to my room. He received me as he always had done. O, how my heart smote me when I felt his tears on my burning cheeks! The words of my grandmother came to my mind,—"Perhaps your mother and father are taken from the evil days to come." My disappointed heart could now praise God that it was so. But why, thought I, did my relatives ever cherish hopes for me? What was there to save me from the usual fate of slave girls? Many more beautiful and more intelligent than I had experienced a similar fate, or a far worse one. How could they hope that I should escape?

My uncle's stay was short, and I was not sorry for it. I was too ill in mind and body to enjoy my friends as I had done. For some weeks I was unable to leave my bed. I could not have any doctor but my master, and I would not have him sent for. At last, alarmed by my increasing illness, they sent for him. I was very weak and nervous; and as soon as he entered the room, I began to scream. They told him my state was very critical. He had no wish to hasten me out of the world, and he withdrew.

When my babe was born, they said it was premature. It weighed only four pounds; but God let it live. I heard the doctor say I could not survive till morning. I had often prayed for death; but now I did not want to die, unless my child could die too. Many weeks passed before I was able to leave my bed. I was a mere wreck of my former self. For a year there was scarcely a day when I was free from chills and fever. My babe also was sickly. His little limbs were often racked with pain. Dr. Flint continued his visits, to look after my health; and he did not fail to remind me that my child was an addition to his stock of slaves.

I felt too feeble to dispute with him, and listened to his remarks in silence. His visits were less frequent; but his busy spirit could not remain quiet. He employed my brother in his office, and he was made the medium of frequent notes and messages to me. William was a bright lad, and of much use to the doctor. He had learned to put up medicines, to leech, cup, and bleed. He had taught himself to read and spell. I was proud of my brother; and the old doctor suspected as much. One day, when I had not seen him for several weeks, I heard his steps approaching the door. I dreaded the encounter, and hid myself. He inquired for me, of course; but I was nowhere to be found. He went to his office, and despatched William with a note. The color mounted to my brother's face when he gave it to me; and he said, "Don't you hate me, Linda, for bringing you these things?" I told him I could not blame him; he was a slave, and obliged to obey his master's will. The note ordered me to come to his office. I went. He demanded to know where I was when he called. I told him I was at home. He flew into a passion, and said he knew better. Then he launched out upon his usual themes,—my crimes against him, and my ingratitude for his forbearance. The laws were laid down to me anew, and I was dismissed. I felt humiliated that my brother should stand by, and listen to such language as would be addressed only to a slave. Poor boy! He was powerless to defend me; but I saw the tears, which he vainly strove to keep back. This manifestation of feeling irritated the doctor. William could do nothing to please him. One morning he did not arrive at the office so early as usual; and that circumstance afforded his master an opportunity to vent his spleen. He was put in jail. The next day my brother sent a trader to the doctor, with a request to be sold. His master was greatly incensed at what he called his insolence. He said he had put him there to reflect upon his bad conduct, and he certainly was not giving any evidence of repentance. For two days he harassed himself to find somebody to do his office work; but every thing went wrong without William. He was released, and ordered to take his old stand, with many threats, if he was not careful about his future behavior.

As the months passed on, my boy improved in health. When he was a year old, they called him beautiful. The little vine was taking deep root in my existence, though its clinging fondness excited a mixture of love and pain. When I was most sorely oppressed I found a solace in his smiles. I loved to watch his infant slumbers; but always there was a dark cloud over my enjoyment. I could never forget that he was a slave. Sometimes I wished that he might die in infancy. God tried me. My darling became very ill. The bright eyes grew dull, and the little feet and hands were so icy cold that I thought death had already touched them. I had prayed for his death, but never so earnestly as I now prayed for his life; and my prayer was heard. Alas, what mockery it is for a slave mother to try to pray back her dying child to life! Death is better than slavery. It was a sad thought that I had no name to give my child. His father caressed him and treated him kindly, whenever he had a chance to see him. He was not unwilling that he should bear his name; but he had no legal claim to it; and if I had bestowed it upon him, my master would have regarded it as a new crime, a new piece of insolence, and would, perhaps, revenge it on the boy. O, the serpent of Slavery has many and poisonous fangs!

. . . .

QUESTIONS FOR A SECOND READING

1. This text makes it difficult to say what we are prepared to say: that slaves were illiterate, uneducated, simple in their speech and thought. Jacobs's situation was not typical, to be sure, but she challenges the assumptions we

bring to our imagination of this country's past and its people. This text has to be read carefully or it becomes familiar, a product of what we think we already know.

As you reread, mark sentences or phrases or paragraphs you might use to illustrate Jacobs's characteristic style or skill as a writer. And mark those features of the text you might use to identify this text as the work of a woman held in slavery. Where and how is doing this difficult? surprising? a problem?

2. In her preface, Jacobs says that she doesn't care to excite sympathy for her suffering but to "arouse the women of the North to a realizing sense of the condition of two millions of women at the South." As you reread this selection, pay attention to the ways Jacobs addresses (and tries to influence) her readers. Why would she be suspicious of sympathy? What do you suppose she might have meant by "a realizing sense"? What kind of reader does she want? Why does she address women?

   Be sure to mark those sections that address the reader directly, and also those that seem to give evidence of Jacobs as a writer, working on the material, highlighting some incidents and passing over others (why do we get "incidents" and not the full story?), organizing our experience of the text, shaping scenes and sentences, organizing chapters. What is Jacobs doing in this text? What might her work as a writer have to do with her position (as a female slave) in relation to the world of her readers?

3. The emotional and family relations between people are difficult to chart in this selection, partly because they defy easy categorization. Can we, for example, assume that blacks and whites lived separately? that blacks were in bondage and whites were free? that family lines and color lines were distinct markers? that lovers were lovers and enemies were enemies? As you reread, pay close attention to the ways people are organized by family, love, community, and color. See what you can determine about the codes that govern relations in this representation of slave culture. And ask where and how Jacobs places herself in these various networks.

ASSIGNMENTS FOR WRITING

1. In the preface to her edition of *Incidents in the Life of a Slave Girl*, Jean Fagin Yellin says the following about Jacobs's narrative:

   > Contrasting literary styles express the contradictory thrusts of the story. Presenting herself as a heroic slave mother, Jacobs's narrator includes clear detail, uses straightforward language, and when addressing the reader directly, utilizes standard abolitionist rhetoric to lament the inadequacy of her descriptions and to urge her audience to involve themselves in antislavery efforts. But she treats her sexual experiences obliquely, and when addressing the reader concerning her sexual behavior, pleads for forgiveness in the overwrought style of popular fiction. These melodramatic confessions are, however, subsumed within the text. What finally dominates is a new voice. It is the voice of a woman who, although she cannot discuss her sexual past without ex-

pressing deep conflict, nevertheless addresses this painful personal subject in order to politicize it, to insist that the forbidden topic of the sexual abuse of slave women be included in public discussions of the slavery question. By creating a narrator who presents her private sexual history as a subject of public political concern, Jacobs moves her book out of the world of conventional nineteenth-century polite discourse. In and through her creation of Linda Brent, who yokes her success story as a heroic slave mother to her confession as a woman who mourns that she is not a storybook heroine, Jacobs articulates her struggle to assert her womanhood and projects a new kind of female hero.

Yellin's account of the "voice" in Jacobs's text gives us a way to foreground the difference between life and narrative, a person (Harriet Jacobs) and a person rendered on the page ("Linda Brent," the "I" of the narrative), between the experience of slavery and the conventional ways of telling the story of slavery, between experience and the ways in which experience is shaped by a writer, readers, and a culture. It is interesting, in this sense, to read Yellin's account of *Incidents* along with Houston Baker's more general account of the "voice of the Southern slave" (quoted at length on p. 373). Baker, you may recall, said: "The voice of the unwritten self, once it is subjected to the linguistic codes, literary conventions, and audience expectations of a literate population, is perhaps never again the authentic voice of black American slavery. It is, rather, the voice of a self transformed by an autobiographical act into a sharer in the general public discourse about slavery."

Jacobs's situation as a writer could be said to reproduce her position as a slave, cast as a member of the community but not as a person. Write an essay in which you examine Jacobs's work as a writer. Consider the ways she works on her reader (a figure she both imagines and constructs) and also the ways she works on her material (a set of experiences, a language, and the conventional ways of telling the story of one's life). To do this, you will need to reread the text as something constructed (see the second "Question for a Second Reading").

2. We can take these opening chapters of *Incidents in the Life of a Slave Girl* as an account of a girl's coming of age, particularly in the sense that coming of age is a cultural (and not simply a biological) process. The chapters represent the ways in which Jacobs comes to be positioned as a woman in the community, and they represent her understanding of that process (and the necessary limits to her understanding, since no person can stand completely outside her culture and what it desires her to believe or to take as natural).

Read back through "Incidents," paying particular attention to what Jacobs sees as the imposed structure of slave culture and what she takes as part of human nature. Remember that there are different ways of reading the codes that govern human relations. What Jacobs takes to be unnatural may well seem natural to Dr. Flint. Jacobs could be said to be reading "against" what Flint, or the Slave Owner as a generic type, would understand as naturally there.

Now read through again, this time reading against Jacobs, to see how her view of relationships could be said to be shaped also by a set of beliefs and interests. Look for a system governing Jacobs's understanding. You might ask, for instance, what system leads her to see Dr. Flint and Mr. Sands as different, since they could also be said to be similar—both slave owners, both after the same thing. How does Jacobs place herself in relation to other slaves? other blacks? Jacobs is light skinned. How does she fit into a system governed by color? Both Mrs. Flint and her grandmother react strongly to Jacobs. What system governs Jacobs's sense of the difference between these two women?

Write an essay in which you try to explain the codes that govern the relations between people in slave culture, at least as that culture is represented in "Incidents."

MAKING CONNECTIONS

1. Alice Walker's reading of the history of African American women in her essay, "In Search of Our Mothers' Gardens" (p. 639), pays particular attention to the "creative spirit" of these women in the face of oppressive working and living conditions. Of her mother, Walker writes:

   > Her face, as she prepares the Art that is her gift, is a legacy of respect
   > she leaves to me, for all that illuminates and cherishes life. She has
   > handed down respect for the possibilities—and the will to grasp them.
   > (p. 646)

   And to the poet Phillis Wheatley she writes: "It is not so much what you sang, as that you kept alive, in so many of our ancestors, *the notion of song*" (p. 643).

   Although Walker does not include Harriet Jacobs in her essay, one could imagine ways in which Jacobs's work as a writer is appropriate to Walker's discussion of African American women's creativity. As you reread Jacobs's selection, note the choices she makes as a writer: her language, her selection of incidents and details, her method of addressing an audience, the ways in which she negotiates a white literary tradition. Where, for instance, do you see her writing purposely negotiating a literary tradition that is not hers? Who does she imagine as her audience? How does she use language differently for different purposes? Why?

   How would you say that the writerly choices Jacobs makes and enacts allow her to express a creativity that otherwise would have been stifled? What type of legacy does she create in her narrative to pass on to her descendants? And, as Walker writes in honor of her mother and Wheatley, what might Walker or you write in honor of Jacobs?

   Write an essay in which you extend Walker's project by considering where and how Jacobs's work as a writer and artist would complement Walker's argument for the "creative spirit" of African American women in the face of oppressive conditions.

2. In "When We Dead Awaken: Writing as Re-Vision" (p. 549), Adrienne Rich says, "Re-vision—the act of looking back, of seeing with fresh eyes, of entering an old text from a new critical direction—is for women more than a chapter in cultural history: it is an act of survival. Until we can understand the

assumptions in which we are drenched we cannot know ourselves" (p. 550).

Let's imagine that one of the difficulties we have in reading "Incidents" is that we approach it drenched in assumptions; we look with old eyes (or the wrong eyes). In honor of the challenge Rich sets for a reader—or, for that matter, in honor of Harriet Jacobs and the challenge she sets for a reader— write an essay in which you show what it would mean to revise your reading (or what you take to be most people's reading, the "common" reading) of "Incidents." You will want to show both how the text would be read from this new critical direction and what effort (or method) would be involved in pushing against the old ways of reading.

3. Here, from "Arts of the Contact Zone" (p. 528), is Mary Louise Pratt on the "autoethnographic" text:

> Guaman Poma's *New Chronicle* is an instance of what I have proposed to call an *autoethnographic* text, by which I mean a text in which people undertake to describe themselves in ways that engage with representations others have made of them. Thus if ethnographic texts are those in which European metropolitan subjects represent to themselves their others (usually their conquered others), autoethnographic texts are representations that the so-defined others construct *in response to* or in dialogue with those texts. . . . [T]hey involve a selective collaboration with and appropriation of idioms of the metropolis or the conqueror. These are merged or infiltrated to varying degrees with indigenous idioms to create self-representations intended to intervene in metropolitan modes of understanding. . . . Such texts often constitute a marginalized group's point of entry into the dominant circuits of print culture. It is interesting to think, for example, of American slave autobiography in its autoethnographic dimensions, which in some respects distinguish it from Euramerican autobiographical tradition. (pp. 531–32)

Reread Jacobs's "Incidents in the Life of a Slave Girl" after reading Pratt's essay. Using the example of Pratt's work with the *New Chronicle,* write an essay in which you present a reading of Jacobs's text as an example of an autoethnographic and/or transcultural text. You should imagine that you are working to put Pratt's ideas to the test, but also to see what you can say on your own about "Incidents" as a text, as something written and read.

PATRICIA NELSON
LIMERICK

*

*P*ATRICIA NELSON LIMERICK (b. 1951) is one of this country's most influential historians. She is certainly one of the most visible, with appearances on national radio and television, a regular column in USA Today, even a profile in
People magazine. Limerick is a revisionist historian, revising the usual stories we
tell of the American West (stories of open spaces, cowboys and Indians, the frontier,
progress, the spread of civilization). These stories, she says, have a persistent power
over the American imagination, affecting everything from movies and books to federal land management and American foreign policy. Generations of Americans, she
says in a characteristically memorable formulation, grew up playing cowboys and Indians, while it was impossible to play master and slave. And the reason, she argues,
is that southern historians did their job well and western historians did not. The
West was not an empty place but a meeting ground. The movement west was not a
simple story of progress but a complicated story of conquest and negotiation.

   Limerick did her undergraduate work at the University of California at Santa
Cruz and received her M.A. and Ph.D. from Yale University. She taught at Harvard
before moving to her current position as Professor of History at the University of
Colorado at Boulder. Her major work is her book The Legacy of Conquest: The
Unbroken Past of the American West (1987), from which the following selection
is taken. Her first book was Desert Passages: Encounters with the American

Deserts (1985). She is coeditor of A Society to Match the Scenery (1991) and Trails: Toward a New Western History (1991). Limerick also wrote the text for Sweet Medicine: Sites of Indian Massacres, Battlefields, and Treaties (photographs by Drex Brooks, 1995). In 1995, she was named a Fellow by the MacArthur Foundation.

"Empire of Innocence" is the first chapter of The Legacy of Conquest. Here, Limerick looks at the problems of historical understanding as writing problems, problems related to the work of any writer attempting to represent others and the past. In this sense, the selection is particularly useful for an undergraduate writing course.

As a historian, Limerick is redirecting her profession's attention to the American West and changing the terms that govern their conception of its history. Her ambitions, however, extend beyond the academy. Her work is "popular" in a way that much of the work of academic historians is not, and it is directed at changing the way Americans think—not only about the past but in the present. And, unlike that of many contemporary intellectuals, Limerick's thinking is hopeful, utopian. This is the final paragraph of The Legacy of Conquest:

> When Anglo-Americans look across the Mexican border or into an Indian reservation, they are more likely to see stereotypes than recognizable individuals or particular groups; the same distortion of vision no doubt works the other way too. The unitary character known as "the white man" has never existed, nor has "the Indian." Yet the phrases receive constant use, as if they carried necessary meaning. Indians, Hispanics, Asians, Blacks, Anglos, businesspeople, workers, politicians, bureaucrats, natives, and newcomers, we share the same region and its history, but we wait to be introduced. The serious exploration of the historical process that made us neighbors provides that introduction.

The "serious exploration of the historical process" for Limerick, as you will see, involves a serious attention to reading and writing. We need to read carefully but also differently; we need, for example, to read not only Anglo-American accounts of Native American history but also Native American accounts of that history, including Native American accounts of the early contacts with European settlers. And we need to write in ways that allow us to represent, rather than erase, experiences and points of view that lie outside the standard narrative. As Limerick says, "One skill essential to the writing of Western American history is a capacity to deal with multiple points of view. It is as if one were a lawyer at a trial designed on the principle of the Mad Hatter's tea party—as soon as one begins to understand and empathize with the plaintiff's case, it is time to move over and empathize with the defendant." Yet it is even more complicated than this, for "seldom are there only two parties or only two points of view." Part of the pleasure of reading Limerick's prose is the opportunity it provides to hear, in brief, a variety of representative anecdotes from the American West, and part of the pleasure is the opportunity it provides to witness her judgment. There is more at work here, in other words, than "empathy." It is interesting to ask what else enables Limerick to do the work she does and to think, through her *examples, about what it might mean to "deal" as a reader or writer with multiple points of view.*

Empire of Innocence

I

When academic territories were parceled out in the early twentieth century, anthropology got the tellers of tales and history got the keepers of written records. As anthropology and history diverged, human differences that hinged on literacy assumed an undeserved significance. Working with oral, preindustrial, prestate societies, anthropologists acknowledged the power of culture and of a received worldview; they knew that the folk conception of the world was not narrowly tied to proof and evidence. But with the disciplinary boundary overdrawn, it was easy for historians to assume that literacy, the modern state, and the commercial world had produced a different sort of creature entirely—humans less inclined to put myth over reality, more inclined to measure their beliefs by the standard of accuracy and practicality.

When anthropology and history moved closer together, so did their subjects of inquiry. Tribal people or nationalists, tellers of stories or keepers of account books, humans live in a world in which mental reality does not have to submit to narrow tests of accuracy.

To analyze how white Americans thought about the West, it helps to think anthropologically. One lesson of anthropology is the extraordinary power of cultural persistence; with American Indians, for instance, beliefs and values will persist even when the supporting economic and political structures have vanished. What holds for Indians holds as well for white Americans; the values they attached to westward expansion persist, in cheerful defiance of contrary evidence.

Among those persistent values, few have more power than the idea of innocence. The dominant motive for moving West was improvement and opportunity, not injury to others. Few white Americans went West intending to ruin the natives and despoil the continent. Even when they were trespassers, westering Americans were hardly, in their own eyes, criminals; rather, they were pioneers. The ends abundantly justified the means; personal interest in the acquisition of property coincided with national interest in the acquisition of territory, and those interests overlapped in turn with the mission to extend the domain of Christian civilization. Innocence of intention placed the course of events in a bright and positive light; only over time would the shadows compete for our attention.

One might expect John Wesley Hardin, the Texan mass murderer and outlaw, to forswear the role of innocent. But this is an assumption to be made with caution in Western history. Hardin was, after all, of innocent stock, the son of a preacher who named his son John Wesley, after the founder of Methodism. "In prison," a recent editor of Hardin's autobiography notes, "Hardin read the Bible and many books on theology. There he was appointed superintendent of the Sunday schools." If one read Hardin's autobiography with no knowledge of the author's later career, one might mistake the tone for that of a model citizen and pillar of the community. "Our parents taught us from infancy to be honest, truthful, and brave," he said, going on to provide further evidence of his good character: "I always tried to excel in my studies, and generally stood at the head," and if that was not enough, " I was always a very child of nature, and her ways and moods were my study."[1]

To be sure, Hardin fought a lot, but this was consonant with parental instructions that honor and the willingness to defend that honor came in the same package. When he was fifteen, he shot and killed a black man. This was to Hardin's mind not a loss of innocence, but a defense of it. The Negro, he said, had tried to bully him; the year was 1868, and Texas was at the mercy of postwar Reconstruction, bullied by "Yankee soldiers," "carpet-baggers and bureau-agents," blacks, and "renegades"—all of them "inveterate enemies of the South." And so, Hardin said, "unwillingly, I became a fugitive, not from justice be it known, but from the injustice and misrule of the people who had subjugated the South." Hardin did go on to kill twenty or more men, but he appears never to have wavered from his chosen role: the gunfighter as Western injured innocent, with a strong Southern accent.[2]

The idea of the innocent victim retains extraordinary power, and no situation made a stronger symbolic statement of this than that of the white woman murdered by Indians. Here was surely a clear case of victimization, villainy, and betrayed innocence. But few deaths of this kind occurred in American history with such purity; they were instead embedded in the complex dynamics of race relations, in which neither concept—villain or victim—did much to illuminate history.

Narcissa Prentiss Whitman made a very unlikely villain. Deeply moved by the thought of Western Indians living without knowledge of Christianity, Narcissa Prentiss wrote her mission board in 1835, "I now offer myself to the American Board to be employed in their service among the heathen. . . ."[3] In 1836, she left her home in New York to rescue the Indians in Oregon. An unattached female could hardly be a missionary, and before her departure Narcissa Prentiss hastily married another Oregon volunteer, Marcus Whitman. The Whitmans and Henry and Eliza Spalding set off to cross the country. Pioneers on the overland trail, they faced stiff challenges from nature and some from human nature. The fur trappers and traders with whom they traveled resented the delays and sermons that came with missionary companionship. The missionaries themselves presented less than a united front. They had the strong, contentious personalities of self-appointed agents of God. They also had a history; Henry Spalding had courted Narcissa, and lost. Anyone who thinks of the nineteenth-century West as a land of fresh starts and new beginnings might think of Henry Spalding and Narcissa Whitman and the memories they took with them to Oregon.

Arrived in the Oregon country, the missionaries—like salesmen dividing up markets—divided up tribes and locations. The Whitmans set to work on the Cayuse Indians. Narcissa Whitman's life in Oregon provides little support for the image of life in the West as free, adventurous, and romantic. Most of the time, she labored. She had one child of her own; she adopted many others—mixed-blood children of fur trappers, and orphans from the overland trail. "My health has been so poor," she wrote her sister in 1846, "and my family has increased so rapidly, that it has been impossible. You will be astonished to know that we have eleven children in our family, and not one of them our own by birth, but so it is. Seven orphans were brought to our door in Oct., 1844, whose parents both died on the way to this country. Destitute and friendless, there was no other alternative—we must take them in or they must perish."[4]

Depending on one's point of view, the Whitman mission had a lucky or an unlucky location—along the Oregon Trail, where exhausted travelers arrived desperate for food, rest, and help. Narcissa Whitman's small home served as kitchen, dining hall, dormitory and church building, while she longed for privacy and rest. She often cooked three meals a day for twenty people. For five years, she had no stove and cooked in an open fireplace.

In the midst of crowds, she was lonely, writing nostalgic letters to friends and family in the East who seemed to answer infrequently; she went as long as two years without a letter from home. Separated by distance and sometimes by quarrels, Narcissa and the other missionary wives in Oregon tried for a time to organize a nineteenth-century version of a woman's support group; at a certain hour every day, they would pause in their work, think of each other, and pray for strength to be proper mothers to their children in the wilderness.

Direct tragedy added to loneliness, overwork, and frustration. The Whitmans' only child, two years old, drowned while playing alone near a stream. Providence was testing Narcissa Whitman's faith in every imaginable way.

Then, in November of 1847, after eleven years with the missionaries among them, when the white or mixed-blood mission population had grown to twenty men, ten women, and forty-four children, the Cayuse Indians rose in rebellion and killed fourteen people—including Marcus and Narcissa Whitman.

Was Narcissa Whitman an innocent victim of brutality and ingratitude? What possessed the Cayuses?

One skill essential to the writing of Western American history is a capacity to deal with multiple points of view. It is as if one were a lawyer at a trial designed on the principle of the Mad Hatter's tea party—as soon as one begins to understand and empathize with the plaintiff's case, it is time to move over and empathize with the defendant. Seldom are there only two parties or only two points of view. Taking into account division within groups—

intertribal conflict and factions within tribes and, in Oregon, settlers against missionaries, Protestants against Catholics, British Hudson's Bay Company traders against Americans—it is taxing simply to keep track of the points of view.

Why did the Cayuses kill the Whitmans? The chain of events bringing the Whitmans to the Northwest was an odd and arbitrary one. In a recent book, the historian Christopher Miller explains that the Whitman mission was hardly the first crisis to hit the Columbia Plateau and its natives. A "three hundred year cold spell," a "result of the Little Ice Age," had shaken the environment, apparently reducing food sources. Moreover, the effects of European presence in North America began reaching the plateau even before the Europeans themselves arrived. The "conjunction of sickness, with the coming of horses, guns, climatic deterioration, and near constant war" added up to an "eighteenth-century crisis." Punctuated by a disturbing and perplexing ash fall from a volcanic explosion, the changes brought many of the Plateau Indians to the conviction that the world was in trouble. They were thus receptive to a new set of prophecies from religious leaders. A central element of this new worldview came in the reported words of the man known as the Spokan Prophet, words spoken around 1790: "Soon there will come from the rising sun a different kind of man from any you have yet seen, who will bring with them a book and will teach you everything, after that the world will fall to pieces," opening the way to a restored and better world. Groups of Indians therefore began to welcome whites, since learning from these newcomers was to be an essential stage in the route to a new future.[5]

In 1831, a small party of Nez Percé and Flathead Indians journeyed to St. Louis, Missouri. For years, Western historians said that these Indians had heard of Jesuits through contacts with fur traders and had come to ask for their own "Black Robes." That confident claim aside, Christopher Miller has recently written that it is still a "mystery how it all came to pass." Nonetheless, he argues persuasively that the Northwest Indians went to St. Louis pursuing religious fulfillment according to the plateau millennial tradition; it was their unlikely fate to be misunderstood by the equally millennial Christians who heard the story of the visit. A Protestant man named William Walker wrote a letter about the meetings in St. Louis, and the letter was circulated in church newspapers and read at church meetings, leaving the impression that the Indians of Oregon were begging for Christianity.[6]

And so, in this chain of circumstances "so bizarre as to seem providential," in Miller's words, the Cayuses got the Whitmans, who had responded to the furor provoked by the letter. Irritations began to pile up. The Whitmans set out to transform the Cayuses from hunters, fishers, and gatherers to farmers, from heathens to Presbyterians. As the place became a way station for the Oregon Trail, the mission began to look like an agency for the service of white people. This was not, in fact, too far from the founder's view of his organization. "It does not concern me so much what is to become of any particular set of Indians," Marcus Whitman wrote his parents, "as to give them

the offer of salvation through the gospel and the opportunity of civilization. . . . I have no doubt our greatest work is to be to aid the white settlement
of this country and help to found its religious institutions."[7]

The Cayuses began to suffer from white people's diseases, to which they
had no immunity. Finally, in 1847, they were devastated by measles. While
the white people at the mission seldom died from measles, the Indians noticed that an infected Cayuse nearly always died. It was an Indian conviction
that disease was "the result of either malevolence or spiritual transgression";
either way, the evidence pointed at the missionaries. When the Cayuses finally turned on the Whitmans, they were giving up "the shared prophetic vision" that these newcomers would teach a lesson essential to reshaping the
world.[8] The Cayuses were, in other words, acting in and responding to currents of history of which Narcissa Whitman was not a primary determinant.

Descending on the Cayuses, determined to bring light to the "benighted
ones" living in "the thick darkness of heathenism," Narcissa Whitman was
an intolerant invader. If she was not a villain, neither was she an innocent
victim. Her story is melancholy but on the whole predictable, one of many
similar stories in Western history that trigger an interventionist's urge.
"Watch out, Narcissa," one finds oneself thinking, 140 years too late, "you
think you are doing good works, but you are getting yourself—and others—
into deep trouble." Given the inability of Cayuses to understand Presbyterians, and the inability of Presbyterians to understand Cayuses, the trouble
could only escalate. Narcissa Whitman would not have imagined that there
was anything to understand; where the Cayuses had religion, social networks, a thriving trade in horses, and a full culture, Whitman would have
seen vacancy or, worse, heathenism.

Narcissa Whitman knew she was volunteering for risk; her willingness to
take on those risks is, however, easier to understand because it was based on
religion. Irrational faith is its own explanation; one can analyze its components, but the fact remains that extraordinary faith leads to extraordinary action. The mystery is not that Narcissa Whitman risked all for the demands of
the deity but that so many others risked all for the demands of the profit motive.

II

Missionaries may be an extreme case, but the pattern they represent had
parallels in other Western occupations. Whether the target resource was
gold, farmland, or Indian souls, white Americans went west convinced that
their purposes were as commonplace as they were innocent. The pursuit of
improved fortunes, the acquisition of property, even the desire for adventure
seemed so self-evident that they needed neither explanation nor justification.

If the motives were innocent, episodes of frustration and defeat seemed
inexplicable, undeserved, and arbitrary. Squatters defied the boundaries of
Indian territory and then were aggrieved to find themselves harassed and

attacked by Indians. Similarly, prospectors and miners went where the minerals were, regardless of Indian territorial claims, only to be outraged by threats to their lives and supply lines. Preemptors who traveled ahead of government surveys later complained of insecure land titles. After the Civil War, farmers expanded onto the Great Plains, past the line of semi-aridity, and then felt betrayed when the rains proved inadequate.

Western immigrants understood not just that they were taking risks but also that risks led to rewards. When nature or natives interrupted the progression from risk to reward, the Westerner felt aggrieved. Most telling were the incidents in which a rush of individuals—each pursuing a claim to a limited resource—produced their own collective frustration. In resource rushes, people hoping for exclusive opportunity often arrived to find a crowd already in place, blanketing the region with prior claims, constricting individual opportunity, and producing all the problems of food supply, housing, sanitation, and social order that one would expect in a growing city, but not in a wilderness.

If one pursues a valuable item and finds a crowd already assembled, one's complicity in the situation is obvious. The crowd has, after all, resulted from a number of individual choices very much like one's own. But frustration cuts off reflection on this irony; in resource rushes in which the sum of the participants' activities created the dilemma, each individual could still feel himself the innocent victim of constricting opportunity.

Contrary to all of the West's associations with self-reliance and individual responsibility, misfortune has usually caused white Westerners to cast themselves in the role of the innocent victim. One large group was composed of those who felt injured at the hands of nature. They had trusted nature, and when nature behaved according to its own rules and not theirs, they felt betrayed. The basic plot played itself out with a thousand variations.

Miners resented the wasted effort of excavating sites that had looked promising and proved barren. Cattlemen overgrazed the grasslands and then resented nature's failure to rebound. Farmers on the Southern Plains used mechanized agriculture to break up the land and weaken the ground cover, then unhappily watched the crop of dust they harvested. City dwellers accumulated automobiles, gas stations, and freeways, and then cursed the inversion patterns and enclosing mountains that kept the automobile effluvia before their eyes and noses. Homeowners purchased houses on steep slopes and in precarious canyons, then felt betrayed when the earth's surface continued to do what it has done for millennia: move around from time to time. And, in one of the most widespread and serious versions, people moved to arid and semiarid regions, secure in the faith that water would somehow be made available, then found the prospect of water scarcity both surprising and unfair.

In many ways, the most telling case studies concern plants. When, in the 1850s, white farmers arrived in Island County, Washington, they had a clear sense of their intentions: "to get the land subdued and the wilde nature out of it," as one of them put it. They would uproot the useless native plants and replace them with valuable crops, transforming wilderness to garden. On one count, nature did not cooperate—certain new plants, including corn, tomatoes, and wheat, could not adapt to the local climate and soil. On another count, nature proved all too cooperative. Among the plants introduced by white farmers, weeds frequently did better than crops. "Weeds," Richard White notes, "are an inevitable result of any human attempt to restrict large areas of land to a single plant." Laboring to introduce valued plants, the farmer came up against "his almost total inability to prevent the entry of unwanted invaders." Mixed with crop seeds, exotic plants like the Canadian thistle prospered in the plowed fields prepared for them, and then moved into the pastures cleared by overgrazing. The thistle was of no interest to sheep: "once it had replaced domesticated grasses the land became incapable of supporting livestock."[9]

A similar development took place between the Rockies and the Sierras and Cascades. There, as well, "species foreign to the region, brought accidentally by the settlers, came to occupy these sites to the virtual exclusion of the native colonizers." With the introduction of wheat, "entry via adulterated seed lots of the weeds of wheat . . . was inevitable." One particular species—cheatgrass—took over vast territories, displacing the native bunch grasses and plaguing farmers in their wheatfields. There is no more effective way to feel authentically victimized than to plant a crop and then to see it besieged by weeds. Farmers thus had their own, complicated position as injured innocents, plagued by a pattern in nature that their own actions had created.[10]

Yet another category of injured innocents were those who had believed and acted upon the promises of promoters and boomers. Prospective miners were particularly susceptible to reading reports of the gold strikes, leaping into action, and then cursing the distortions and exaggerations that had misled them into risking so much for so little reward. The pattern was common because resource rushes created a mood of such fevered optimism that trust came easily; people wanted so much to believe that their normal skepticism dropped away.

The authenticity of the sense of victimization was unquestionable. Still, there was never any indication that repeated episodes of victimization would reduce the pool of volunteers. Bedrock factors kept promoters and boomers supplied with believers: there *were* resources in the West, and the reports might be true; furthermore, the physical fact of Western distances meant, first, that decision making would have to rely on a chain of information stretched thin by the expanse of the continent and, second, that the truth of the reports and promises could not be tested without a substantial investment of time and money simply in getting to the site. One might well consume one's nest egg merely in reaching the place of expected reward.

Blaming nature or blaming human beings, those looking for a scapegoat had a third, increasingly popular target: the federal government. Since it was the government's responsibility to control the Indians and, in a number of ways increasing into the twentieth century, to control nature, Westerners found it easy to shift the direction of their resentment. Attacked by Indians or threatened by nature, aggrieved Westerners took to pointing accusingly at the federal government. In effect, Westerners centralized their resentments much more efficiently than the federal government centralized its powers.

Oregon's situation was a classic example of this transition. The earliest settlers were rewarded with Congress's Oregon Donation Act of 1850. Settlers arriving by a certain year were entitled to a generous land grant. This act had the considerable disadvantage of encouraging white settlement without benefit of treaties and land cessions from Oregon Indians. The Donation Act thus invited American settlers to spread into territory that had not been cleared for their occupation. It was an offer that clearly infringed on the rights of the Indians and that caused the government to stretch its powers thin. After the California gold rush, when prospectors spread north into the Oregon interior, a multifront Indian war began. Surely, the white miners and settlers said, it is now the obligation of the federal government to protect us and our property.[11]

At this point, a quirk of historical casting brought an unusual man named General John Wool into the picture. As the head of the Army's Pacific Division, General Wool was charged with cleaning up the mess that Oregon development had created. He was to control the Indians, protect the settlers, and end the wars. Here Wool's unusual character emerged: assessing this situation, he decided—and said bluntly—that the wars were the results of settler intrusion; he went so far as to propose a moratorium on further settlement in the Oregon interior, a proposal that outraged the sensitive settlers. Wool's personality did not make this difference of opinion more amicable. He was, in fact, something of a prig in pictures, the symmetrical and carefully waxed curls at his temples suggest that he and the Oregon pioneers might have been at odds without the troubles of Indian policy.[12]

Denounced by both the Oregon and the Washington legislatures, Wool's blunt approach did not result in a new direction in Indian affairs. The wars were prosecuted to their conclusions; the Indians, compelled to yield territory. But the Oregon settlers in 1857 knew what they thought of Wool. He was a supposed agent of the federal government, an agent turned inexplicably into a friend of the Indians and an enemy of the Americans.

It was not the first or the last time that white Americans would suspect the federal government and Indians of being in an unholy alliance. To the degree that the federal government fulfilled its treaty and statutory obligations to protect the Indians and their land, it would then appear to be not only soft on Indians but even in active opposition to its own citizens.

One other elemental pattern of their thought allowed Westerners to slide smoothly from blaming Indians to blaming the federal government. The idea of captivity organized much of Western sentiment. Actual white men, women, and children were at times taken captive by Indians, and narratives of those captivities were, from colonial times on, a popular form of literature.

tone! of anger + irony,

It was an easy transition of thought to move from the idea of humans held in an unjust and resented captivity to the idea of land and natural resources held in Indian captivity—in fact, a kind of monopoly in which very few Indians kept immense resources to themselves, refusing to let the large numbers of willing and eager white Americans make what they could of those resources. Land and natural resources, to the Anglo-American mind, were meant for development; when the Indians held control, the excluded whites took up the familiar role of injured innocents. The West, in the most common figure of speech, had to be "opened"—a metaphor based on the assumption that the virgin West was "closed," locked up, held captive by Indians.

As the federal government took over Indian territory, either as an addition to the public domain or as reservations under the government's guardianship, white Westerners kept the same sense of themselves as frustrated innocents, shut out by monopoly, but they shifted the blame. Released from Indian captivity, many Western resources, it seemed to white Americans, had merely moved into a federal captivity.

In 1979, the Nevada state legislature, without any constitutional authority, passed a law seizing from the federal government 49 million acres from the public domain within the state. This empty but symbolic act was the first scene in the media event known as the Sagebrush Rebellion, in which Western businessmen lamented their victimization at the hands of the federal government and pleaded for the release of the public domain from its federal captivity. Ceded to the states, the land that once belonged to all the people of the United States would at last be at the disposal of those whom the Sagebrush Rebels considered to be the *right* people—namely, themselves.[13]

Like many rebellions, this one foundered with success: the election of Ronald Reagan in 1980 and the appointment of James Watt as secretary of the interior meant that the much-hated federal government was now in the hands of two Sagebrush Rebels. It was not at all clear what the proper rebel response to the situation should be. In any case, the rebel claim to victimization had lost whatever validity it had ever had.

Reciting the catalog of their injuries, sufferings, and deprivations at the hands of federal officials, the rebels at least convinced Western historians of the relevance of their expertise. It was a most familiar song; the Western historian could recognize every note. Decades of expansion left this motif of victimization entrenched in Western thinking. It was second nature to see misfortune as the doings of an outside force, preying on innocence and vulnerability, refusing to play by the rules of fairness. By assigning responsibility elsewhere, one eliminated the need to consider one's own participation in courting misfortune. There was something odd and amusing about the late-twentieth-century businessmen adopting for themselves the role that might have suited Narcissa Whitman—that of the martyred innocents, trying to go about their business in the face of cruel and arbitrary opposition.

Even if the Sagebrush Rebels had to back off for a time, that did not mean idleness for the innocent's role. In 1982, Governor Richard Lamm of

Colorado and his coauthor, Michael McCarthy, published a book defending the West—"a vulnerable land"—from the assault of development. "A new Manifest Destiny," they said, "has overtaken America. The economic imperative has forever changed the spiritual refuge that was the West." The notion of a time in Western history when "the economic imperative" had not been a dominant factor was a quaint and wishful thought, but more important, Lamm and McCarthy thought, some Westerners now "refused" to submit to this change. "They—we—are the new Indians," Lamm and McCarthy concluded. "And they—we—will not be herded to the new reservations."[14]

In this breakthrough in the strategy of injured innocence, Lamm and McCarthy chose the most historically qualified innocent victims—the Indians facing invasion, fighting to defend their homelands—and appropriated their identity for the majority whites who had moved to the West for the good life, for open space and freedom of movement, and who were beginning to find their desires frustrated. Reborn as the "new Indians," Lamm's constituency had traveled an extraordinary, circular route. Yesterday's villains were now to be taken as today's victims; they were now the invaded, no longer the invaders. In keeping with this change, the *old* Indians received little attention in the book; as capacious as the category "injured innocent" had proven itself to be, the line had to be drawn somewhere.

Occasionally, continuities in American history almost bowl one over. What does Colorado's utterly twentieth-century governor have in common with the East Coast's colonial elite in the eighteenth century? "Having practically destroyed the aboriginal population and enslaved the Africans," one colonial historian has said, "the white inhabitants of English America began to conceive of themselves as the victims, not the agents, of Old World colonialism." "The victims, not the agents"—the changes and differences are enormous, but for a moment, if one looks from Revolutionary leaders, who held black slaves as well as the conviction that they were themselves enslaved by Great Britain, to Governor Richard Lamm, proclaiming himself and his people to be the new Indians, American history appears to be composed of one, continuous fabric, a fabric in which the figure of the innocent victim is the dominant motif.[15]

III

Of all the possible candidates, the long-suffering white female pioneer seemed to be the closest thing to an authentic innocent victim. Torn from family and civilization, overworked and lonely, disoriented by an unfamiliar landscape, frontierswomen could seem to be tragic martyrs to their husbands' willful ambitions.

But what relation did these sufferers bear to the actual white women in the West? Did their experiences genuinely support the image? Where in Western history did women fit? By the 1970s, it was commonly recognized that Turner-style history simply left women out. How, then, to address the oversight? Was it the sort of error that one could easily correct—revise the shopping list, retrace one's steps, put the forgotten item in the grocery cart, and then proceed with one's usual routine? Or was the inclusion of women a more consequential process of revision that would make it impossible to resume old habits and routines?

✗   We can best answer the question by considering the Western women apparently at the opposite end of the spectrum from Narcissa Whitman—the women who came West not to uplift men but to cater to their baser needs. The prostitute was as much a creature of Western stereotype as the martyred missionary, and in many ways a more appealing one. But while the colorful dance hall girl held sway in the movies, Western historians either looked discreetly away from this service industry or stayed within the stereotypes of a colorful if naughty subject.

When professional scholars finally took up the subject, their investigations disclosed the grim lives led by the majority of Western prostitutes. With few jobs open to women, prostitution provided a route to income, though it seldom led past subsistence. A few well-rewarded mistresses of rich men and a few madams skilled in a complicated kind of management may have prospered, but most prostitutes did well to keep revenue a fraction ahead of overhead costs—rent, clothing, food, payoffs to law officers. A woman might work independently, renting her own quarters and conducting her own solicitation, or she might try for security (shelter, food, and a degree of protection from violence) by working in a brothel. At the bottom ranks, even those unappealing alternatives disappeared; vagrant women at the farthest margins of society, or Chinese women controlled as virtual slaves, had little choice open to them. Western prostitution was, in other words, a very stratified operation: the adventuress of doubtful morality and the respectable married woman, though in different spheres, were both far removed from the down-and-out cribworker, without even a brothel to call home.

When prostitutes tried to find stability in marriage, they found their partners in an unpromising pool of saloon owners, pimps, and criminals, men who were often violent and who were neither inclined nor able to rescue their spouses from their rough lives. When prostitutes bore children, as they often did, their occupations made child care an extraordinary challenge and the children stood scant chance of rising to reputability. Many daughters of prostitutes followed their mothers into the business. Many factors—the sense of entrapment, the recognition that age was sure to reduce a woman's marketability, financial troubles—drove prostitutes to suicide. "Suicide," the historian Anne Butler has noted, "emerged as the most commonly employed means to retire from prostitution."[16] Excluded from much of society, prostitutes could not even expect to find comradeship with their colleagues; the intrinsic competition of the business put them at odds, and this rivalry, often unleashed by alcohol, led to frequent quarrels and even physical fights.

A study of Western prostitution leaves certain general lessons for Western history at large. First and foremost, one learns that the creature known as "the pioneer woman" is a generic concept imposed on a diverse reality. White, black, Hispanic, Chinese, and Indian women composed the work force of prostitution, scattered across a wide range of incomes. Moreover, anyone inclined to project a sentimentalized hope for women's essential solidarity into the past need only consider the case of Julia Bulette, a prostitute murdered in Virginia City in 1867. John Milleain was convicted of her murder after items stolen from Bulette were found in his possession. But he had murdered a prostitute, and this engaged the sympathy and support of some of the town's respectable ladies. "Respectable women," Marion S. Goldman has reported, "circulated a petition to the governor to commute Milleain's sentence from death to life imprisonment, visited him in jail, and made sure that he drank wine and ate omelettes during the days following his conviction." Just before his execution, Milleain offered his gratitude: "I also thank the ladies of Virginia who came to see me in my cell and brought with them consolation that only they could find for the circumstances."[17]

This curious sympathy pointed to the larger pattern: the elevation of respectable women rested on the downgrading of the disreputable. Fallen women could initiate young men into sexual activity and thus allow respectable young women to avoid the fall. Prostitutes offered men an outlet that enabled wives to hold on to the role of pure creatures set above human biological compulsions. Most of all, prostitution was an unending reminder of the advantages of conventional female domestic roles. The benefits of marriage never appeared more attractive than in contrast to the grim and unprotected struggle for subsistence of the prostitute. Accordingly, few Western communities tried to eliminate prostitution; instead, they tried to regulate and contain it. In towns dependent on mining, cattle, or military posts, with a substantial population of male workers, prostitution was essential to the town's prosperity. The whole exercise of regulating prostitution, beyond the economic benefits, "emphasiz[ed] the respectable community's behavioral boundaries, and heighten[ed] solidarity among respectable women."[18]

Second, the history of prostitutes also serves to break up an apparently purposeful monolith: white society under the compulsions of Manifest Destiny. If women were victims of oppression, who were their oppressors? In a mining town like Nevada City, the prostitute's most frequent patrons were wageworkers, miners who risked their lives daily in hard underground labor. The miners, as Marion Goldman has suggested, were themselves "treated like objects rather than individuals" and were thus conditioned to "think of themselves and others that way."[19] The economic elite of the towns often owned the real estate in which prostitution took place; vice districts were among the more rewarding Western investment opportunities. And the official representatives of the law took their cut of the enterprise in regular payoffs to prevent arbitrary arrests. In the broad sweep of Western history, it may look as if a united social unit called "white people" swept Indians off their lands; that group, as the history of prostitution shows, was not a monolith at all but a complex swirl of people as adept at preying on each other as at preying on Indians.

Third, the history of prostitution restores the participants of Western history to a gritty, recognizably physical reality. Testifying as a witness in a Nevada case in 1878, Belle West was asked to identify her occupation. "I go to bed with men for money," she said.[20] A century later, Belle West's frankness will not let us take refuge in sentimental and nostalgic images of the Western past. Acknowledge the human reality of Western prostitutes, and you have taken a major step toward removing Western history from the domain of myth and symbol and restoring it to actuality. Exclude women from Western history, and unreality sets in. Restore them, and the Western drama gains a fully human cast of characters—males and females whose urges, needs, failings, and conflicts we can recognize and even share.

It appears to be an insult and a disservice to place the murdered Narcissa Whitman and the murdered Julia Bulette in the same chapter. But women who in their own times would have fled each other's company turn out to teach similar historical lessons. It is the odd obligation of the historian to reunite women who would have refused to occupy the same room. Examine the actual experiences of white women in the West, at any level of respectability, and the stereotypes are left in tatters.

Consider Mrs. Amelia Stewart Knight. In 1853, she, her husband, and seven children went overland to Oregon and met the usual hazards—a grueling struggle through the muddy Midwestern prairies, difficult river crossings, dangerous alkali water, failing livestock. Mrs. Knight did occasionally record a bout of poor health, but frailty did not afflict women to the exclusion of men. "Still in camp," she wrote one day early in the journey, "husband and myself being sick. . . ."[21]

Supervising seven children elicited few complaints from Mrs. Knight. One simply has to imagine what some of her terse entries meant in practice: "Sunday, May 1st Still fine weather; wash and scrub all the children." The older children evidently helped out in caring for the younger ones; even with the best management, though, misadventures took place. The youngest child, Chatfield, seemed most ill-fated: "Chat has been sick all day with fever, partly caused by mosquitoe bites. . . . Here Chat fell out of the wagon but did not get hurt much. . . . [And then just five days later] Here Chat had a very narrow escape from being run over. Just as we were all getting ready to start, Chatfield the rascal, came around the forward wheel to get into the wagon and at that moment the cattle started and he fell under the wagon. Somehow he kept from under the wheels and escaped with only a good or I should say, a bad scare. I never was so frightened in my life."[22]

In the days just before they left the trail and headed for the Columbia River, a trying road through forests forced Mrs. Knight and the children to walk. "I was obliged to take care of myself and little ones as best I could," she wrote, and they spent their days "winding around the fallen timber and brush, climbing over logs creeping under fallen timber, sometimes lifting and carrying Chat."[23]

And then, near the end of the journey, Mrs. Knight had her eighth child. She had throughout this trip been in the later stages of pregnancy, and, in that final phase of walking, she had been at full term.

In endurance and stamina, Mrs. Knight was clearly the equal—if not the better—of the Kit Carsons and the Jedediah Smiths. The tone of her diary suggests few complaints and no self-glorification. It seems illogical to feel sorry for her, when she appears not to have felt sorry for herself.

The developing pictures of Western women's history suggest that Mrs. Knight, while perhaps braver than most women (and men), was no anomaly. Far from revealing weak creatures held captive to stronger wills, new studies show female Western settlers as full and vigorous participants in history. A recent close study of homesteading in northeastern Colorado demonstrates that single women took advantage of the spinster's and widow's right to claim land under the Homestead Act. In two counties, claim entries by women were 12 percent of the whole and, later in the process, as high as 18 percent. Many wives, though not entitled to claims of their own, nonetheless acted as genuine partners in the homestead, contributing equal labor and taking part in decisions.[24] While individuals may have conformed to the image of the passive, suffering female pioneer, the majority were too busy for such self-dramatization. Cooking, cleaning, washing, caring for children, planting gardens—any number of activities took priority over brooding.

One measure of independence and freedom in Western male settlers was the capacity to scorn others—to see oneself as being a superior sort of creature, placed above others. On that and many other counts, white women were active self-determiners. Downgrading Indians, Hispanics, Mormons, immoral men, or fallen women, many white women made it clear that the disorientation of migration had not stolen their confident ability to sort and rank humanity from best to worst.

In the record of their words and actions, the women of Western history have made a clear statement that they do not deserve or need special handling by historians. There is no more point in downgrading them as vulnerable victims than in elevating them as saintly civilizers. The same woman could be both inspirational in her loyalty to her family's welfare and disheartening in her hatred of Indians. Those two attributes were not contradictory; they were two sides to the same coin. We cannot emphasize one side at the expense of the other, without fracturing a whole, living person into disconnected abstractions.

Our inability to categorize the murdered Narcissa Whitman, or the murdered Julia Bulette, teaches us a vital lesson about Western history. Prostitutes were not consistently and exclusively sinners, nor were wives and mothers consistently and exclusively saints. Male or female, white Westerners were both sinned against and sinning. One person's reward often meant another person's loss; white opportunity meant Indian dispossession. Real

Westerners, contrary to the old divisions between good guys and bad guys, combined the roles of victim and villain.

Acknowledging the moral complexity of Western history does not require us to surrender the mythic power traditionally associated with the region's story. On the contrary, moral complexity provides the base for parables and tales of greater and deeper meaning. Myths resting on tragedy and on unforeseen consequences, the ancient Greeks certainly knew, have far more power than stories of simple triumphs and victories. In movies and novels, as well as in histories, the stories of men and women who both entered and created a moral wilderness have begun to replace the simple contests of savagery and civilization, cowboys and Indians, white hats and black hats. By questioning the Westerner's traditional stance as innocent victim, we do not debunk Western history but enrich it.

NOTES

[1] John Wesley Hardin, *The Life of John Wesley Hardin,* ed. Robert G. McCubbin (Norman: Univ. of Oklahoma Press, 1961), xvii, 6–7.

[2] Ibid., 13, 14.

[3] Clifford Drury, ed., *First White Women over the Rockies,* vol. 1 (Glendale, Calif.: Arthur H. Clark, 1963), 29.

[4] Ibid., 152.

[5] Christopher L. Miller, *Prophetic Worlds: Indians and Whites on the Columbia Plateau* (New Brunswick: Rutgers Univ. Press, 1985), 23, 25, 33, Spokan Prophet quoted on 45.

[6] Ibid., 60.

[7] Ibid., 1; Marcus Whitman quoted in Robert V. Hine and Edwin R. Bingham, eds., *The American Frontier: Readings and Documents* (Boston: Little, Brown, 1972), 162.

[8] Miller, *Prophetic Worlds,* 105, 117.

[9] Richard White, *Land Use, Environment, and Social Change: The Shaping of Island County, Washington* (Seattle: Univ. of Washington Press, 1980), 46, 68, Walter Crockett quoted on 35.

[10] Richard N. Mack, "Invaders at Home on the Range," *Natural History,* February 1984, 43.

[11] Dorothy O. Johansen and C. M. Gates, *Empire of the Columbia: A History of the Pacific Northwest,* 2d ed. (New York: Harper & Row, 1967), 250, 252.

[12] Robert Utley, *Frontiersmen in Blue: The United States Army and the Indian, 1848–1865* (1967; Lincoln: Univ. of Nebraska Press, 1981), 178–200.

[13] "The Angry West vs. the Rest," *Newsweek,* September 17, 1979, 31–40; "West Senses Victory in Sagebrush Rebellion," *U.S. News and World Report,* December 1, 1980, 29, 30.

[14] Richard D. Lamm and Michael McCarthy, *The Angry West: A Vulnerable Land and Its Future* (Boston: Houghton Mifflin, 1982), 4.

[15] Carole Shammas, "English-Born and Creole Elites in Turn-of-the-Century Virginia," in Thad Tate and David Ammerman, eds., *The Chesapeake in the Seventeenth Century: Essays on Anglo-American Society and Politics* (New York: W. W. Norton, 1979), 274.

[16] Anne M. Butler, *Daughters of Joy, Sisters of Mercy: Prostitutes in the American West, 1865–1890* (Urbana: Univ. of Illinois Press, 1985), 68.

[17] Marion S. Goldman, *Gold Diggers and Silver Miners: Prostitution and Social Life on the Comstock Lode* (Ann Arbor: Univ. of Michigan Press, 1981), 144, John Milleain quoted on 144.

[18] Ibid., 137.

[19] Ibid., 158.

[20] Ibid., 108.

[21] Amelia Stewart Knight, "Diary, 1853," in Lillian Schlissel, ed., *Women's Diaries of the Westward Journey* (New York: Schocken Books, 1982), 206.

[22] Ibid., 203, 208, 209, 210.

[23] Ibid., 215.

[24] Katherine Llewellyn Hill Harris, "Women and Families on Northeastern Colorado Homesteads, 1873–1920" (Ph.D. diss., Univ. of Colorado, 1983).

· · · · · · · · · · · ·

QUESTIONS FOR A SECOND READING

1. This selection, the opening chapter of Limerick's book *The Legacy of Conquest*, offers a view of history as both an area of research, and something written, a writer's account of past events. In it, Limerick offers criticism and advice, an account of the problems of constructing a history of the American West. As you reread, look for passages that define the problems and the possible solutions for historians. The question, then, is not what Limerick says about the American West but what she says about reading and writing history.

2. It is possible to read this chapter as addressed to a general public, not simply to professional historians. As you reread, think about how and why Limerick tries to define or constitute her audience. Why might the general reading public, in the 1980s and '90s, read this book? What, specifically, do you find to let you answer this question in Limerick's terms?

ASSIGNMENTS FOR WRITING

1. One way to work on Limerick's selection is to take the challenge and write history—to write the kind of history, that is, that takes into account the problems she defines: the problems of myth, point of view, fixed ideas. You are not a professional historian, you are probably not using this book in a history course, and you probably don't have the time to produce a carefully researched history, one that covers all the bases, but you can think of this as an exercise in history writing, a minihistory, a place to start. Here are two options:

   a. Go to your college library or, perhaps, the local historical society and find two or three first-person accounts of a single place, person, or event in your community. (This does not have to be a history of the American West.) Try to work with original documents. The more varied the accounts, the better. Then, working with these texts as your primary sources, write a history, one that you can offer as a response to Limerick's selection.

   b. While you can find materials in a library, you can also work with records that are closer to home. Imagine, for example, that you are going to write a family or neighborhood history. You have your own memories and experiences to work from, but for this to be a history (and not a "personal essay"), you will need to turn to other sources as well: interviews, old photos, newspaper clippings, letters, diaries—whatever you can find. After gathering your materials, write a family or neighborhood history, one that you can offer as a response to Limerick's work.

Choose one of the two projects. When you are done, write a quick one-page memo to Limerick. What can you tell her about the experience of a novice historian that she might find useful or interesting?

2. It is possible to see this selection as addressed to the general public, not just to professional historians. Limerick seems to write for a wide audience; she seems to believe that what she has to say about the West (and about history) has bearing on public issues, on our public imagination. What might a general public find important in Limerick's work? How might it be helpful to the present? What are the points of connection between what she says and, for example, your home or college community? What does she say that might be important to that community?

You could imagine that you stand in a position between Limerick and the community. Drawing on what you have read, or taking these selections as your beginning, write an essay that might be published on the op-ed page of your local (or school) newspaper, or as a review essay for a local magazine. Write a piece that introduces Limerick's work to your community or that places Limerick's project and concerns in the context of a local issue.

MAKING CONNECTIONS

1. Like Limerick, both Stephen Greenblatt in "Marvelous Possessions" (p. 268) and Jane Tompkins in "Indians" (p. 618) deal with historical materials, and both, to varying degrees, discuss the problems of reading and writing history. Greenblatt and Tompkins, however, are not historians, at least not in the strict, disciplinary sense of the word. They work in literature departments not history departments; in this sense, their commitments to and understandings of history are, perhaps, a bit different.

Reread these three selections as a set, as part of a single project investigating the problems of writing history and understanding the past. Mark sections you might use as examples. Write an essay in which you discuss these three approaches to history. While it is possible to chart the similarities in these essays, focus on the differences. How is the work of each different from the others? What concerns or methods belong to each? Is it useful to see Greenblatt and Tompkins as different from Limerick in ways that might be traced to their professional preparation?

2. While John Edgar Wideman is not writing a history in "Our Time" (p. 652), at least in the strict sense of the term, he *is* writing history—he is trying to recover and understand the story of his brother Robby, his family, and their neighborhood. He is trying to recover all those factors that might be said to have led to or produced his brother's present situation.

It is interesting to read "Our Time" and Limerick's chapter as alternate ways of thinking about and writing history. As you reread these selections, mark passages you might use to illustrate the styles, methods, and/or concerns of each writer. You should reread the essays as a pair, as part of a single project investigating the problems of writing about other people and about the past. With Limerick's selection as a point of reference, what do Wideman's methods allow him to do and prevent him from knowing/learning/doing? With Wideman's selection as a point of reference, what about Limerick's methods—what do they allow her to do and prevent her from knowing/learning/doing?

As a way of thinking about writing and history, write an essay in which you present your examples from each selection and discuss these two approaches to writing about the past.

LEWIS
NORDAN

L EWIS "BUDDY" NORDAN (b. 1940) grew up in Itta Bena, Mississippi, the real-life equivalent of Arrow Catcher, Mississippi, the fictional location of all his novels. The selections below are from his third book, Music of the Swamp *(1991). As you read through these stories, you will probably notice that Nordan changes the point of view, slipping from third-person stories about Sugar Mecklin to first-person narratives in which the narrator speaks about his child self, growing up in the fictional Arrow Catcher, Mississippi, inside Sugar's family. At the end of "OWLS," the last story, we find out that the narrator is telling these stories to the woman he loves as an adult in the present. The shifts in perspective are significant over the course of all his novels and stories. Nordan, perhaps, is working and reworking memory and imagination together, engaged in a process of what Adrienne Rich would call writing as re-vision, a re-seeing of the past and the construction of narratives of it to enable a livable present and a hopeful future.*

Nordan's work has been labeled by critics as "magical realism," a genre that has come into literary being largely since World War II. (The South American writer Gabriel García Márquez and U.S. author Toni Morrison are also considered magical realists.) Within this form, what both readers and writers might consider realistic characters, places, and events, are subtly mixed with improbable, poetic, and sometimes dreamlike instances and visions of horror and wonder. Both the visions and the instances—like the mermaid that Sugar Mecklin sees and hears singing in the swamp in his dream—are mixed with realistic details of everyday life—like Elvis Presley's voice on the radio, a gospel choir on Sunday morning, and a dead body floating in a lake—to give the stories the kind of resonance and complexity usually reserved for poetry.

Magical realism also often uses sudden twists into not just dreamlike and horrific moments but moments of wry humor as well. As in "real" life, both humor and wonder appear as unexpectedly as the horrific, with the unexpectedness itself contributing to our reactions to it. In "How Bob Steele Broke My Father's Heart," Nordan narrates a frightening scene of a father's attempt at drunken, self-pitying suicide and twists it into a story of redemption and loss revolving around an improbable TV cowboy, Bob Steele. Bob Steele had "no wife, no white hat, no good-looking horse, no Indian sidekick, nothing." And yet, he was "pure hope," he was, the narrator says, "what my father drank to become, and what I later drank to become." Bob Steele rides into town, into the middle of a shoot-out and asks "the only question there is," as the narrator's father says, "What's going on here?" The stories we tell in our attempts to answer that question, as Nordan elegantly demonstrates, make all the difference in our lives.

Music of the Swamp (1991) won the 1992 Mississippi Institute of Arts and Letters Award for literature (an award also given to Walker Percy) and was selected by the American Library Association's Notable Books Council as one of the twelve best fiction books of 1991. Nordan's other books include Welcome to the Arrow Catcher Fair (1983), The All-Girl Football Team (1986), and Wolf Whistle (1993), which won the Southern Book Critics and the Mississippi Author's awards for fiction. Both collections of Nordan's stories, Welcome to the Arrow Catcher Fair and The All-Girl Football Team, have been reprinted in the Vintage Contemporary Series. His latest book, The Sharpshooter: A Novel, was published in 1995.

Music of the Swamp

Music of the Swamp

The instant Sugar Mecklin opened his eyes on that Sunday morning, he believed that this was a special day and that something new and completely different from anything he had ever known before was about to jump out at him from somewhere unexpected, a willow shade, a beehive, a bird's nest, the bream beds in Roebuck Lake, a watermelon patch, the bray of the iceman's mule, the cry of herons in the swamp, he did not know from where, but wherever it came from he believed it would be transforming, it would open up worlds to him that before today had been closed. In fact, worlds seemed already to be opening to him.

When he later came into the kitchen and sat down to his Sunday breakfast of chocolate milk and homemade bread, toasted and smeared with sweet butter and fresh cinnamon, his mother noticed a difference in Sugar and placed her hand against his forehead and said, "Are you running a fever?"

And then when Sugar's father came into the room, Sugar leaped up out of his chair and did what he had never done before, he grabbed his father suddenly around the neck and hugged him and said, "I love you, Daddy."

This is the kind of day it was. This is the way Sugar Mecklin's summer morning started out.

First there were the mice. Sugar was still asleep when he heard them singing. Sugar was dreaming that he was standing alone in the shade of tupelo gums and cypress and chinaberry and weeping willow and mimosa and that the water of Roebuck Lake was exactly as it was in real life, slick and opaque as a black mirror, with the trees and high clouds reflected perfectly in the surface. He dreamed that he walked out to the end of a short pier, the one that in real life he had built, and saw a beautiful creature of some kind, a mermaid maybe, rise up from the water. Her breasts were bare, and she was singing directly to him as she combed her long hair with a comb the color of bone, and in the other hand held a mirror as dark and fathomless as the mirror-surface of Roebuck Lake.

He believed that this creature could foretell his future, or endow him with power and knowledge. There seemed little wonder to Sugar Mecklin, waking up to such thoughts, that this day should turn out to be special.

And then once he was awake, there was Elvis. Until this very morning Sugar Mecklin had never before heard the name of Elvis Presley. And now here he was, this Elvis person, in full uh-huh complaint on Sugar's Philco radio, and he seemed truly to be singing about the dream that Sugar Mecklin had just dreamed. Elvis told Sugar *you'll be so lonely you could die.*

It was as if the mermaid's song had come to him first through the sweet voices of the mice in his mattress and then from WMC in Memphis.

These were the reasons Sugar Mecklin astonished his father at the breakfast table by grabbing him suddenly and holding onto him for all he was worth and almost actually saying, pleading, Don't ever leave me, Daddy, I'll be so lonely I will die.

He did not actually say these words, he said only, "I love you, Daddy!" in a bright voice, and his father struggled and finally muttered, "Good luck on your travels through life," and then went out to the garage to get paint buckets and brushes and dropcloths and a stepladder to paint the bathroom, which had needed painting for a long time, probably.

And then after breakfast, while Sugar Mecklin's father spread paint and Sugar Mecklin's mother ran cold water through a colander full of figs to be put up in paraffin-sealed Mason jars as purpley preserves, Sugar Mecklin thought it might not be a bad idea at all to comb his hair with Wildroot Cream Oil and put on his hightop tennies and take a walk right down the middle of Lonely Street and stand along the shore of dark, wooded Roebuck Lake and look across its waters in search of barebreasted women. It was a day in which such a thing might happen, he believed.

His mother said, "Are you going to Sunday school this morning, Sugar?"

Sugar Mecklin said, "Haven't decided."

His mother said, "I wish you would put on a clean shirt and go to Sunday school once in a while."

Not today. Today was a Sunday, this was a whole summer, in fact, in which magic might prove once and for all to be true. It was a summer in which Sugar Mecklin noticed many things, as if they had not been there before, like the mice in his mattress, like Elvis Presley on the Philco. This summer Sugar Mecklin heard the high soothing music of the swamp, the irrigation pumps in the rice paddies, the long whine and complaint, he heard the wheezy, breathy asthma of the compress, the suck and bump and clatter like great lungs as the air was squashed out and the cotton was wrapped in burlap and bound with steel bands into six-hundred-pound bales, he heard the operatic voice of the cotton gin separating fibers from seeds, he heard a rat bark, he heard a child singing arias in a cabbage patch, he heard a parrot make a sound like a cash register, he heard the jungle rains fill up the Delta outside his window, he heard the wump-wump-wump-wump-wump of biplanes strafing the fields with poison and defoliants, he read a road sign that said WALNUT GROVE IS RADAR PATROLLED and heard poetry in the language, he heard mourning doves in the walnut trees.

And for a moment, when he arrived at the edge of the water, Sugar Mecklin almost believed that he had found whatever magical thing he had come looking for.

When he looked across the water to the spot where in his dream he had seen the woman admiring her own reflection in a black mirror, he heard clear sweet tuneful voices raised in plaintive anthems to God in heaven.

There was a cow, a brown-and-white heifer with horns, standing chest-deep in the water directly across the lake. The cow was not supposed to be there, it had only wandered there and could not be coaxed out of the water in time, and so it only stood and once or twice flicked its tail against invisible insects that may have been flying in the morning air.

All about the cow were men and women in white robes—black persons, colored people, Negroes, whatever they were called—and they too, like the cow, were standing chest-deep in the water, and it was their voices that Sugar Mecklin heard in song.

It was a baptizing. *I come to the garden alone* the voices said, in complaint as profound as Elvis Presley's uh-huh *and the voice I hear falling on my ear* the singers sang, speaking of Jesus, who would take away loneliness.

The song went on, and then when it finished there were other songs, questions—*shall we gather at the river,* the singers wanted to know *the beautiful, the beautiful river*—and in a way all of the songs were about loneliness, and the defeat of loneliness, and the heartbreak if it could not be defeated, as probably it never could *you'll be so lonely you could die.*

And so this was the happiest moment Sugar Mecklin had ever felt in his life. He was almost delirious with strong feeling. His face was flushed and

438

even in the Mississippi heat he was almost cold, almost shivering with emotion. The sweat beads on his arms were like a thin film of ice.

And then another child showed up.

Sugar Mecklin was startled. It was Sweet Austin. Where had Sweet Austin come from, so unexpectedly? Sugar Mecklin thought Sweet Austin looked a little like he had seen a ghost.

Sweet said, "Hey, Sugar Mecklin."

Sugar said, "Hey, Sweet Austin."

Sweet Austin walked out onto the narrow pier and stood behind Sugar, and for a minute or two neither of them said anything. Sugar and Sweet were the only two completely white-haired, blue-eyed, freckle-faced, skinny-assed boys in their whole class. People thought it was funny that they looked so much alike and their names were almost the same, Sugar and Sweet.

They only stood and watched the baptizing. *oh what needless pain we bear* sang the choir on the other side of the lake.

Sugar Mecklin said, "You know about a singer name of Elvis Presley?"

Sweet Austin said, "Hey, Sugar . . ."

Sugar Mecklin said, "He sings this song about Heartbreak Hotel."

Sweet Austin said, "Hey, Sugar, listen . . ."

Sugar Mecklin said, "His voice, this guy Elvis Presley's voice . . ." Sugar didn't know exactly what he was going to say about Elvis Presley's voice. That it made you visible to yourself and invisible to others.

Sweet Austin said, "I've got to show you something. Something bad."

Something was definitely wrong with Sweet Austin. Sweet Austin had definitely seen a ghost.

Across the lake the choir had a friend in Jesus. God's grace was amazing, they said, and sweet. There was a church in the wildwood, they said, and their voices floated across the lake to the pier where Sugar and Sweet were standing and the voices reached them like angels' voices and invited them to come to the church in the wildwood, come to the church in the dell, whatever a dell was, it might be like a swamp, mightn't it, or a bog, or a quicksand pit, what the hell was a dell, anyway?

Just then the brown-and-white cow decided it was time to leave the water and, as the choir sang a final song—*oh I'm tired and so weary but I must travel on*—the cow, as if it had been waiting for just this moment in the music, opened its amazing and sweet old cow-mouth and hollered one long heartbreaking bellow and moan, one incredible tenor note in perfect tune and time with the rest of the choir, as if to impart some message about hope, or maybe hopelessness and loneliness, who could tell the difference, or maybe just to say goodbye I've had enough of this, these horseflies and this sentimental music are driving me crazy, and then turned and slogged its way past the robed communicants and out of the water and up the muddy bank and into the pasture towards a barn.

there'll be no sadness, the choir sang, *no sorrow, no trouble* . . . and Sugar knew that when you say these things what you really mean is that sadness and sorrow are all there is and all there ever will be. And then somebody, a young woman in a white robe, waded forth, chest-deep in the black water, and allowed herself to be dunked backwards, out of sight, by a white-haired Negro woman, who held her hand over the young woman's face in the name of the Father and the Son and the Holy Ghost and held that young woman beneath the water for a long time while catfish and cottonmouths and snapping turtles joined with Christ Our Lord to wash away all her sins in the dear sweet magical blood of the Lamb while the choir sang songs.

Sweet Austin said, "I was running trotlines and found it. You've got to come with me."

Sweet Austin had come here in a boat. That was how he had appeared so unexpectedly behind Sugar Mecklin on the pier. When they had walked down the lake bank for a few yards, Sugar saw the boat pulled up in the weeds in a clear spot between the cypress knees. They crawled into the boat, first Sugar Mecklin, up front, and then Sweet Austin in back. Sugar looked out across the lake at the shanties and pulpwood along the ridge on Runnymeade plantation, where the Negroes lived.

Sweet Austin struck a Feather paddle into the gummy leaf-moldy bottom of the lake and used the paddle like a raft pole to shove the boat away from the bank and to ease them out into the deeper water.

Sweet Austin said to Sugar Mecklin, "I don't know what to do, tell me what to do, Sugar. If I had a daddy I would know what to do."

For one second, when Sugar Mecklin spotted the bare feet and legs sticking up out of the water, he managed to believe that Sweet Austin had brought him here to see the mermaid. He knew better, of course. He knew this was a dead person.

They were far down the lake now. White cranes stood in small gossipy groups along the shallow water near the Runnymeade side of the shore. Turkey vultures sailed like hopeful prayers above them in the wide blue sky and then settled into the empty branches of white-trunked leafless trees. Deep in the water there were fish everywhere, invisible to Sugar Mecklin, no one could know how many of them, bream and perch and bass, silver and gold and blue, and for the first time in his life the thought of hidden fish and all their familiar coloration and feathery gills and lidless eyes terrified Sugar, he could not say why.

It was a body, of course, snagged upside down in a drift of brush.

Now here is the oddest thing. When Sugar Mecklin saw the naked legs poking up out of the water, he thought first of his daddy in speckled overalls back at the house, standing on the fourth rung of a stepladder and holding a bucket and brush and smearing paint over the bathroom ceiling.

Sugar Mecklin said, "Turn the boat around, Sweet Austin. We got to tell somebody. We got to call Big Boy Chisholm."

The body was an old man, it turned out, who may have had a seizure of some kind before he went into the water. Later on, his boat was found with a fishing rod and baited hooks in the floorboards. There were two catfish still alive on a stringer hooked to the side of the boat. The old man had been missing for a couple of days—he lived on Runnymeade with his daughter. The daughter, the *Greenwood Commonwealth* reported, had told her father not to go out on the lake by himself, because he had "spells."

Sweet Austin and Sugar Mecklin did not know all this yet. They only knew that there were legs and feet sticking up out of the drift, and so they did the only thing they could do. Sweet Austin dragged the paddle behind the boat in a sculling motion and turned them in the direction of a camplanding a little farther on, near the town dump where the rats were as big as yellow dogs and howled all night at the moon. Sweet Austin dipped the paddle deep into Roebuck and caused the boat beneath them to move steadily across the lake to Raney's fish camp, where somebody would let them use the telephone to call Big Boy Chisholm, the lawman.

When they docked at the fish camp, Mr. Raney made the call for them, though it took him a while to find his glasses and even after he did find them he dialed the wrong number four times. Each time he said, "I. Godfrey," and then dialed again. He said, "Y'all just get yourself a Co-Cola out of the ice-box." He said, "Are y'all boys all right now?"

Sugar Mecklin and Sweet Austin said that they thought so, they thought they were all right. They looked at one another to decide whether this was true.

Mr. Raney said, "Y'all boys look enough alike to be sisters." This was Mr. Raney's kind way of making a dead man in the swamp a little less horrible idea than it actually was.

Mr. Raney was the last man in Arrow Catcher, Mississippi, who could spit into a brass spittoon from a long distance. He did this now. Ptooey! Pting! He did this as a way of thinking things out. Or maybe only to make a joke, nobody knew which. Ptooey! Pting!

A young man named Hydro—it was Mr. Raney's own son, his only child—who had a big head on his shoulders and a peach pie in his lap, sat down in Mr. Raney's high-backed rocker and rocked so far backwards he turned the pie upside down and nearly turned himself over in the chair, and said, "Shit far and save matches!" Hydro often chased cars and howled when the firetruck turned on the siren and had to be given ice cream so that he would stop.

Then several more times, Mr. Raney spat in rapid succession, ptooey pting! ptooey pting! ptooey pting! while Sugar Mecklin and Sweet Austin shifted from one foot to the other and listened to somebody pull the crank rope on an old Evinrude and start up the rattly little engine down by the dock, where it idled for now, smelling of gasoline and warm oil, and waiting for Big Boy Chisholm to show up so somebody could help steady him while he got into the boat and then lead him down Roebuck Lake to the brush pile where he would collect the corpse.

Mr. Raney said, "Hydro, get your lazy no-count ass out of my rocking chair, or I'll pistol-whip you within an inch of your worthless life."

Hydro was eating his mama's peach pie with a big steel spoon—he had gotten the deep dish turned upright again and had not lost much of the pie—and he did not hear his daddy just then, so Mr. Raney just blew his nose hard into a red bandana and said, "I. Godfrey," and let the matter drop, what good did it do to argue, what difference did it make anyway.

To Sugar Mecklin and Sweet Austin, Mr. Raney said, "We're all going to be a little edgy for a while, it don't mean nothing. It's normal after you find a floater."

Sweet Austin did not go to his own home that night. He couldn't do that. Sweet Austin's mama would be working late behind the bar at the American Legion Hut. She would turn on the switch that caused the Miller High Life sign to revolve. She would scatter sawdust on the little hardwood dance floor for whoever might want to take a turn to the music. She would reach into the cooler for long-necked beers in dark bottles, maybe Pabst Blue Ribbon, or Falstaff, or Jax, or even Pearl, and crack them open with a church key and say to men wearing bunion pads on their feet and Vitalis in their hair, "You don't want no glass with that, do you, loverboy?"

She might take a shot of Early Times herself and chase it down with a swig from one of those men's long-neck bottles, and then peel the label for him. She might belch real loud and make all the men in the Legion Hut laugh and make all the women think she was common. She might sing a song, too, if anybody asked her. She might sing "Honeycomb" if she felt like it, she might sing *honeycomb won't you be my baby oh honeycomb be my own just a hank of hair and a piece of bone my honeycomb* Her arms would be tired and cold and maybe numb from the ice chest and from weariness and loneliness because her man was dead, or she hoped he was anyway, and her apron would smell like the stale beer and cigarettes and her fingers would be crinkly from being wet all night, when she got home and finally found the light switch in the hall and scared the cockroaches off the counters and back up into the kitchen cabinets where they belonged, and staggered a little in the hallway, where she finally propped herself up and took off her shoes.

She might go into the room where her son slept on an army cot and wake up Sweet Austin and tell him what a no-count scoundrel his daddy was, and always had been, and she might tell Sweet Austin he was just like his daddy, just ee-zackly like him, and then she might crawl in right alongside Sweet Austin on the army cot and fall asleep and wake up full of regrets and no energy to apologize to her boy or to anybody else.

Or she might not come home at all that night, that was surely a possibility, a distinct possibility she herself might say, not if Al the Boogie Woogie Piano Player, who had two gold teeth in the front of his mouth and silver taps on his shoes, asked her to go somewhere with him after they turned off the lights of the Legion Hut and unplugged the slot machines and washed the last beer glasses and re-bagged the last of the pretzels and beernuts, especially if he asked her to go riding with him in his Oldsmobile, with the rag top down on this warm summer night and maybe kiss a few hard, whiskey-breathed kisses beneath the Confederate memorial.

She might sleep that night in Al the Boogie Woogie Piano Player's bed where he lived for now in a damp room of the Arrow Hotel, and she might feel just so damn awful after she got there and got her stockings off at long last, that she couldn't sleep and so she might ask Al to sing her a baby lullaby to help her drift off, she might ask him to sing a song she remembered from her own girlhood, on a record that she sneaked around to play on a wind-up Victrola, a song called "Let These Red Lips Kiss Your Blues Away," and Al might actually know the song, since he knew every song in this bad world, but he would be too tired to sing it, and so Sweet Austin's mama might have to go to sleep without it, it didn't matter, she had gone to sleep sick and lonely plenty of times before, what difference would one more time make, none, it wouldn't make any difference at all to anybody, why should it.

And so Big Boy Chisholm dropped the two boys off at Sugar Mecklin's house. Big Boy didn't turn on the siren today—the whistle, he always called it—or the revolving light on top of the car, though normally he did when he gave a child a ride home. Today he only drove them from the fish camp and stopped the car out by the iron fence in front of Sugar's house and said, "I'm sorry y'all boys had to bear witness to that floater, I truly am sorry." He waited until the two boys had left the car and slammed their doors good and were clear of the road and out of harm's way and up under the catalpa trees, which were covered in locust husks, and past the iron hitching posts in the shape of black horses, and then Big Boy Chisholm drove away in his car, real slow, down Lake Front Road.

It was late in the afternoon now. Bessie Smith was on the phonograph, so that meant that Sugar Mecklin's daddy was already drunk. Sugar Mecklin's daddy called his Bessie Smith records his wrist-cutting music. It was Bessie Smith singing a long time ago when Gilbert Mecklin stuck the ice pick in his chest. *my mama says I'm reckless* Bessie Smith had sung that day, and he knew just what she meant too, he was reckless too. *my daddy says I'm wild* Bessie Smith sang. Nobody knew better than Gilbert Mecklin what it meant to be reckless and wild. Nobody in this world. *I ain't good looking* she sang *but I'm somebody's angel child* Bessie Smith had been singing that day before Sugar Mecklin was even born. In a way that was the good old days, Gilbert Mecklin remembered them fondly, that day long time ago when he had let the record play to its end and then jammed an ice pick straight into his breast bone.

Sugar Mecklin had heard all about it, and he couldn't help wishing that Bessie Smith was not on the phonograph on this particular day. He wished instead that his daddy had waited until after Sugar had had time to come home and say, "Me and Sweet found a dead man. Can Sweet sleep over tonight?" before he started playing wrist-cutting music.

And, if the truth be knew—this was a phrase that Gilbert Mecklin used and drove Sugar's mama straight out of her last and only mind, "if the truth be knew"—Gilbert Mecklin was just this minute saying to himself, he his ownself would have preferred not to be drunk this afternoon. If the truth be knew, Gilbert Mecklin was sitting there in his chair thinking, Now I wonder how this happened again, just when I didn't want it to happen, how did it come to pass that I am sitting here unintentionally drunk on my ass with wrist-cutting music playing on the record player when I have great need to comfort two children who have lost so much and seen too much death in their little lives? The alcohol made Gilbert Mecklin groggy. He felt a little like he had been hit over the head and covered with a heavy blanket.

On the phonograph now there was a trombone. It started way down low, and it could have been the voice of a Texas longhorn cow at first, or an alligator in a swamp quartet singing bass, it was so low. Gilbert Mecklin listened to it. He had to. Nobody else knew how to listen to it. He wife sure hell didn't know how to listen to music. She didn't appreciate music. The trombone note was rising now, rising up and up. Listen to that clear note rise up from the muddy waters of the Delta!

Sugar Mecklin and Sweet Austin were standing in the doorway of Gilbert's bedroom, trying to tell him about the body.

Gilbert already knew about the body. Big Boy Chisholm had called him from the fish camp, had told him Sweet Austin was coming to spend the night. He didn't need to hear about the body.

Sugar said, "Hey, Daddy."

Well, the thing was, after the trombone note got up in the air high enough, it started to blend in with another horn, a trumpet maybe, that took up the note and brought it up even higher, headed up to the moon, until another note got inside these two, a clarinet, so high it was a squeak, like the sound at the tail end of a long crying spell, and then, well, Gilbert Mecklin couldn't very well say hey to Sugar right this very minute, because now Bessie Smith was right there in the room with him, talking to him about his whole life.

Dixie moonlight, Shawnee shore Bessie Smith said to Gilbert Mecklin. She seemed to be sitting right there on the bed beside his two boys. She had only one leg, she lost the other leg in Clarksdale, the night she was killed. Oh those sad brass horns, like a crying child. Bessie Smith said she was *headed homebound just once more* she said she was going to her Missy-Sippy Delta home. The trumpet was still there, but now it had a mute on it, and it was weeping real tears. Oh yes, it was a good thing Sugar Mecklin's mama had thrown that ice pick up under the house all those years ago, this was a song that took a man back to better days.

Sugar said, "Me and Sweet Austin found a dead man, Daddy."

Gilbert Mecklin said, "Hush, hush up, Sugar. Listen to this song."

Gilbert had not meant to say this. The last thing in the world he meant to do was tell his boy to hush up. What he meant to say was that there was just so much death in the Delta, it was everywhere, he didn't know how a child could stand all of it. He meant to tell Sweet Austin that he had known

Sweet's daddy—if Curtis Austin really was Sweet's daddy, who knows about this kind of thing, who can ever really know for sure—he had known Curtis well and one time watched him play semi-pro ball for the Greenwood Dodgers, a farm team for Brooklyn, where he played second base and got three hits that night under the lights. He meant to say that Sweet Austin's daddy was not an evil man, not completely, and was still alive, Gilbert knew this, and believed in his heart that he was doing the right thing by staying out of Sweet and his mama's life.

Sweet Austin said, "Hey, Mr. Mecklin."

Gilbert Mecklin said, "Hush up, Sweet Austin. Listen here, listen to this here song."

The music played, and Bessie Smith sang on, and the Delta was bad, bad, she was saying, and it was magic, it hypnotized you, you couldn't resist it even if you tried, and now it was calling her back. *I hear those breezes awhispering* she complained *I hear those breezes a-whispering come on back to me*

Gilbert Mecklin wanted to tell these two boys, one of them his own boy, and the other one, well God knows, Sweet Austin, only God knows—so, Lord, anyway, he wanted to tell them that there are worse things in this world than bodies in the swamp, and worse things than having a daddy who died there, or who ran off and left you, or didn't run off but just left you anyhow, there are worse things than being so lonely you could die. If you were real unlucky you could turn into one of those daddies who left.

Sugar Mecklin said, "Daddy, we saw the feet and legs." Sugar and Sweet were sitting on the edge of Gilbert Mecklin's bed, right next to Bessie Smith. Though Bessie Smith was black and a long time dead and had only one leg, the three of them looked enough alike to be wild and frightened sisters.

Sweet Austin said, "Lodged up in a drift. I was running trotlines, I didn't know what to do."

In a way it was a good thing that Gilbert Mecklin was so drunk right now, really it was, it wasn't a completely bad thing to be so drunk if you looked at it in the right light. Drunk like this, he didn't have to tell these two scared boys what it meant to have chickens in his back yard, Plymouth Rocks and Rhode Island Reds, the layers and bantams and the blue Andalusian rooster. He didn't have to say that when he walked out there and scattered shelled and fragrant corn from an enameled dishpan, one slow handful at a time, he could forget his own father, who spent all his family's pennies for shoes made of kangaroo leather and for Havana cigars and then beat him and his brother with fists and sticks and straps and then, worst of all, went blind for spite and had to be waited on hand and foot for the rest of his life.

And so Bessie Smith just kept on singing about the Delta. In fact she was singing about Arrow Catcher, Mississippi. She was singing about Roebuck Lake, right near where she died that rain-swole-up Delta summer in a crash on the highway and lost one of her legs. *muddy water 'round my feet* Bessie Smith was saying, and right now all of a sudden it wasn't Gilbert Mecklin she was singing to, it was Sweet Austin, who didn't know she didn't have feet, only one foot, there on the edge of the bed, like it was the edge of a cliff and he might fall off.

Bessie Smith was telling him what he already knew. You are trapped here, Sweet Austin, we all are. It don't help to have a daddy, you're trapped anyway, daddies will always leave, always die, always be somebody you don't know. Daddies ain't your trouble, Sweet Austin. Your trouble is the geography. You better learn to like it. Bessie Smith said there was *muddy water 'round my feet muddy water in the street* She said *just God's own shelter down on the Delta*

Sweet Austin knew about Sugar Mecklin's daddy and the ice pick. He said, "Mr. Mecklin, how come you want to listen to wrist-cutting music?"

Bessie Smith said *muddy water in my shoes*

Gilbert Mecklin looked and saw that Bessie Smith was not really sitting on the bed beside the two boys. Well, that was good anyway.

Way back behind Bessie Smith was a slow piano. Just one chord, and then her strong sad voice and then another chord, like punctuation. Sweet Austin thought of Al the Boogie Woogie Piano Player, he thought of the Oldsmobile and his mama's hair blowing in the Delta breeze. There was a one-note clarinet back there too, as slow as the piano, like an old, old, one-trick pony. Yikes! the clarinet said, like a sad swamp bird, and yes yes yes.

Sugar Mecklin's mama came into the room now. She said, "Gilbert, don't fill these boys' heads with drunk-talk. They're worth more than that."

Sugar Mecklin loved his mama's hairbrushes and bobby pins and facial creams, he loved her clean underwear in a drawer. He was glad she wasn't a floozie like Sweet Austin's mama, he was glad he didn't have to come home at night and wonder if she was sharing a room with Al the Boogie Woogie Piano Player at the Arrow Hotel, he was glad she never slipped into bed beside him and slept drunk all night.

Bessie Smith said *muddy water in my shoes, rocking in them lowdown blues* The piano, the squeaky old-fashioned one-trick-pony clarinet, and now one low and rising note from the trombone, like a good memory. And just then Sugar Mecklin started to know something that he had not quite known before. He knew that he was not all alone in the world after all, as he had for so long believed.

There was his mama, who always seemed sane in comparison with his daddy who was not sane at all. She was out of her mind with old grief, old loss, her own tyrannical father, her fat brother who could not get out of his bed for fear of lightning. She hated music, she secretly broke and threw away Gilbert's favorite records, one at a time while he was drunk, especially "Summertime," which seemed to Mrs. Mecklin an affront to everything decent— those first three high-squealing notes of self-pity and false sentiment—and which Sugar found in a million ragged pieces of plastic out by the chickenyard fence. She dreamed of trains crossing frozen landscapes, she made up stories of escape, using models in the Sears, Roebuck catalog for characters to represent herself and her fictional friends, she pretended she grew up as a serving girl in Canada and that for spare pennies she made beaded bags, huddled over her georgette-stretched beading frame, her fingers feeding beads and thread to her crochet needle like lightning.

And there beside him was Sweet Austin, who looked enough like himself to be his sister, and who looked enough like Gilbert Mecklin to be his, his, well, God only knows what. The world was not what Sugar Mecklin wanted it to be, but he was not alone, he would never be alone.

Bessie Smith said *I don't care, it's muddy there, but it's still my home*

Sweet Austin said, "What was so bad, Mr. Mecklin, was, like, I seen them bare legs poking up out of the water and I thought it was my daddy. I knowed it wont, but I thought it was."

Bessie Smith was wailing now, weeping in song *I don't care, I don't care, it's still my home* The muted trumpet was back and it was crying like a baby.

Gilbert said, "Naw, Sweetness, it wont your daddy." The alcohol was beginning to wear off a little. Gilbert Mecklin felt a little less bushwhacked than before. Maybe he better have one more drink, just so he don't get sick. Maybe he would, maybe he wouldn't.

Mrs. Mecklin sat down on the bed beside Sweet Austin and put her arms around his neck, and Sweet Austin leaned into her shoulder and started to cry. Sweet Austin was a big boy, a little taller than Sugar and maybe a little broader shouldered. When did that happen, Sugar wondered, when did he start to outgrow me? Sugar Mecklin felt funny sitting there and looking at this young man holding his mama and his mama holding him tighter than he himself had ever been held. They rocked back and forth to Sweet Austin's crying and to the sad old bluesy sentimental music.

Bessie Smith said *got my toes turned Dixie way*

Mrs. Mecklin said, "You just cry now, Sweetness, you just go right on and cry."

Bessie Smith said *'round the Delta let me lay*

Sweet Austin was really going at it now. He was boo-hooing flat out. Boo hoo, boo hoo, boo-fucking-hoo, man. He was getting snot in Mrs. Mecklin's hair. It didn't matter. It didn't matter to anybody, not even Sugar.

Mrs. Mecklin said, "Your mama loves you to death, Sweet Austin. And so does your daddy."

Gilbert Mecklin was wondering if he might risk getting up just this minute and easing into the kitchen for another nip of that Old Crow, just to settle his stomach.

Sweet Austin and Mrs. Mecklin were rocking and reeling now, slow, slow. Mrs. Mecklin was whispering like a mama. She said, "And me and Gilbert love you too, Sweetness. We love you like you was our own boy."

Yessir, no doubt about it, Gilbert Mecklin could certainly use another drink.

So that's what he did. He stood up and steadied himself beside his chair and then eased on out towards the kitchen, just so he didn't mess around and get sick from having an empty stomach. Maybe a beer would settle him down some. The carbonation, the food value. Maybe a shot of Old Crow would taste good with it.

Sweet Austin cried. Mrs. Mecklin sang him a soft baby lullaby. Sugar Mecklin believed he was a part of a family, and this filled him with love.

The world was not the way Sugar Mecklin wanted it to be, but he had to admit, this particular day had turned out even better than he had expected when he woke up to the sound of mice and Elvis Presley and the voice of a barebreasted woman singing into a black mirror.

Bessie Smith said *my heart cries out for muddy water*

Porpoises and Romance

After the hurricane, beach houses along the Gulf coast rented for a song, and so that was when my daddy got the idea of taking my mama on a second honeymoon. My mama said she never had a honeymoon in the first place, what did she want with a second one.

Daddy said they would take long walks and watch the sun rise and eat crabs and rent bicycles and browse in shops. He said they would put the zip back in their marriage.

Mama said, "Crabs! No way, José."

Daddy said it would be like having their own private beach.

Mama said, "I don't know why you want to be riding on a bicycle."

He said, "Come on, baby. Let's fall in love all over again."

Mama said, "Well, all right. Can Sugar go along?"

Daddy said, "On our second honeymoon?"

I said, "I ain't studying no second honeymoon."

Mama said, "I'm not going on no second honeymoon less Sugar comes along."

Daddy said, "It don't seem right, falling in love all over again right in front of your own boy."

Daddy was right about one thing anyway. The beach was deserted. It was worse than deserted. The hurricane had blown most of the sand five miles inland, not to mention the hotels. The beaches were mud, the hotels were hideouts for murderers and swamp-midgets. Daddy said, "Well, wouldn't you think they'd have got this place cleaned up a little by now?"

We were standing on the beach, which was filled with dead fish and other animal carcasses, including a whale full of buzzards.

I said, "I'm scared, I want to go home."

Daddy said, "That whale smells like Korea."

Mama said, "Hush up, both of you. Are both of you boys trying to spoil my one and only second honeymoon?"

Daddy looked at me like: duh.

The little coastal village where Mama and Daddy rented the house was a ghost town. Everything was full of sand from the hurricane, even the trees, the ones that were left standing. And you couldn't go barefoot on account of broken glass, you might step on a piece and cut the living daylights out of yourself. It's hard to clean up after a hurricane. Buzzards flew up out of the whale like bats out of a cave.

The shops were all closed, of course, and so were most of the restaurants. One restaurant still had a palm tree, roots and all, sticking through the busted-out front window. There was a coffee shop where we tried to have breakfast one morning, but the woman behind the counter slammed cups and saucers around like she was mad at us. Daddy whispered to Mama, "I hope she ain't expecting the full ten percent tip."

Even the parking meters had been stripped from their posts and stored away somewhere. Bicycle rental was out of the question, of course. And at night the house we were staying in, which was olive green with muscular mildew and alive with one million crickets in the kitchen cabinets and in the furniture and bathroom and light fixtures, foreign crickets blown in from Tahiti or Cuba on the hurricane, and fungi possibly from other planets, had buzzards roosting on the chimney like a gang of sea gulls gone bad, and it was the only place along the beach with any lights on. We were a lonely lighthouse, we were a ship lost at sea, we were an outpost in Indian Territory. We were one of the few places with a roof.

Mama said, "It's so quiet."

Daddy said, "Yeah." His voice was soft and a little frightened sounding. He said, "It's definitely a quiet little place."

Mock it down: My parents were not falling in love all over again.

It's not that they weren't trying to fall in love. They were trying until they turned blue in the face. It was embarrassing to watch them, Daddy was right about that too.

They said soft things (I just stayed out of their way, I just watched, I just slunk around and spied on them), they brought iced tea to bed with flowers on a tray, they ate dinner by candlelight on the front porch. Picture my daddy, with thirty-five years of housepaint under his fingernails and housepaint on the freckled, veined lids of his eyes, varnish permanent in the pigmentation of his skin, his hair, the color of his eyes, my daddy, with webbed toes on his feet and not one white tooth in his mouth, lighting candles for dinner for the first time in his entire life! It would break your heart to watch him, he was trying so hard to be in love, so desperate now that he knew he was not.

Daddy said, "Listen to the deep voice of the sea tonight." He actually said this, this man who scarcely said hello on all the other days of the year, and the sound of his own voice speaking language near to poetry, near to passion, scared my daddy so bad that he actually leaped straight up off the floor in fear and ran out of the room and flung himself on the bed and cried for a full minute at the shock of it.

Whenever I long for the return of my own innocence, I imagine becoming the person that my strange daddy was in that sixty seconds of his life, and then I have to admit that I was never so innocent, even as a child, no one on this earth ever was so innocent except him. My parents walked on the beach in the moonlight, stepping over strange things they could not see, they agreed on many things, including autumn as their favorite season of the year, and the smell of salt in the sea air. My mother was even beginning to be convinced that this might work, this second honeymoon in search of love.

But then love is cruel, I mean why lie about it.

The second honeymoon was not romantic. It was not working. It had nothing to do with the dead whale, or the other bodies that were beginning to wash up.

So they tried harder.

They played a couple of fantasy games. Daddy had read about sexual fantasies in a magazine called *Connections*. *Connections* was a magazine for people who wanted to put the zip back in their marriage. I had read the fantasies too. I found the magazine in Daddy's room before we ever left home, in the drawer of his bedside table, while I was stealing rubbers to lend to a child who could stretch a condom over his head. I read them while sitting with my pants down around my ankles on the hardwood floor of my room, beating away. It's one of my special childhood memories, sitting bare-assed on wood and holding my life in my hands.

I didn't see my parents play these games, of course, but I know it happened. Daddy tied Mama to the bed posts with four silk ties he had brought along, just for the purpose. Yikes. I found the ties still dangling there like dogs with their tongues hanging out, one morning. One of them had a hand-painted horse's head on it.

Well, I mean, you know. Suicide was one of the thoughts I had.

Mama said all the right things, I suppose, all the words that *Connections* magazine recommended. "Fuck me, master, I'm your slave," and like that. It's embarrassing to think of your mama saying she's a sex slave, you know, but it's not the end of the world. That's the way I thought of it at the time.

Connections had some other good ideas, too. *Connections* said that the concerned couple could pretend to be a young boy and his stern high school science teacher. They could use an electric vibrator as a part of the boy's high school science project.

Maybe they did this, maybe not. I looked for something that might be a vibrator, but I'm not sure. I found a device in the back of one of my daddy's dresser drawers, along with a bottle of Four Roses whiskey and a bag of peppermint candy. It might have been a vibrator, or it might have been a curling iron. Who knows? Some things about your parents you can never be sure of.

The thing is, sex was not the only area that *Connections* magazine had suggestions for. It had suggestions in areas far more fantastic than mere sexual playfulness, though that must have been foreign enough to my father.

Connections magazine had recommendations for metaphor and romance. It said, "Find a metaphor for romance, and pursue it with all your heart. If your first choice of metaphor fails, keep trying others until you hit upon just the right one for you and your partner."

I actually saw my father sitting on the side of his bed in his room at home reading this particular article. He had no shoes on, he was just home from a long day on an extension ladder, and so he worked his webbed toes against the floor as he read. I stood in the doorway and watched.

He finished the article and shook his head and sighed. He read the article a second time.

At last he looked up from the magazine and saw me. I had already read the article and understood it as little as my daddy did.

I heard a voice say, "What's a queer?"

It was my own voice, of course. What did I mean by asking such a question? It was a question I had often wanted the answer to, but why now, suddenly?

My daddy looked at me with a blank face.

Neither of us said anything for a long time.

Finally he said, "What? What did you say, Sugar?"

I said, "What's a queer?"

Daddy looked back down at *Connections* magazine and read again a part of the article he had just read. He looked back up at me.

I said, "Roy Dale Conroy is such a queer." Roy Dale, the white-trash child, my best friend, the one whose youngest brother could stretch condoms over his head.

Daddy said, "So you are asking me what's a queer, is that it, is that what you are asking?"

I said, "Right."

He sighed and looked down at the article and then back up at me. He said, "Don't say queer, Sugar. Queer is dirty. Roy Dale's not a queer just because his brother can do that trick with the condoms. And a very dangerous trick at that, I might add."

He looked back down at *Connections* magazine and read some more, the same paragraph, over and over.

I said, "Queer is dirty?"

Daddy didn't answer.

I said, "I thought queer meant odd. I thought queer meant Roy Dale is a jerk."

He looked up. He said, "What do you suppose this word means?" He held out the magazine to me and pointed to the page. I walked over to the bed and looked. He was pointing to the word *metaphor*. He said, "It must mean like a sign, a signal of some kind."

I said, "Like from outer space?"

He said, "Yes."

I said, "Like from God?"

He said, "I don't know."

We looked at the word *metaphor* for a long time. Neither of us dared to try to pronounce it. It lay there on the white page being itself, like a signal from outer space.

Daddy tested the word now, mostly to himself. "A mumpty-mump for romance," he mumbled over the word. "A sign from God of romance." He looked up at me, relieved. "Yeah, that's what it means! A sign from God. Right!"

He was very happy. His face was bright. He squinched his webbed toes joyfully on the wood floor.

I didn't know what to say. I said, "What's a queer?"

He said, "Do you know anything about cocksuckers?"

I said, "Some."

He said, "It's the same deal."

I said, "Thanks."

He said, "No problem, don't sweat it, glad to be of help."

Sunrises. That was the metaphor my daddy chose. Sunrises and romance, he said—that was it, that was just the ticket, sunrises. Now he had looked up the word *metaphor* in the dictionary and was pronouncing it all over the place. Metaphor this, metaphor that, even metaphorical a couple of times. "Sunrises all right with you, honey?" he said to my mother many times. "For a metaphor, I mean? I hope the sunrise metaphor for romance is all right with you. As a metaphor, it's the first metaphor that popped into my head. I mean, what could be more metaphorical than a sunrise, honey, I mean tell the truth? Sunrises are meta-fucking-phorical!"

Mama said, "Don't get carried away, Gilbert."

He said, "Scuse my French!"

Possibly this was one of the happiest days of my daddy's life.

Well, the thing is, sunrises didn't work. My daddy still wasn't falling in love all over again with my mother. And besides, he was always too sleepy and cranky at that time of the morning for anything to have worked.

And then maybe this is where things started to change. My daddy got it into his head that if he could spot a porpoise, then the love that he and Mama had once shared and now had lost would have swum back to them, alive and renewed in its gentleness.

To be fair to my daddy, the porpoise notion was not as arbitrary as it might sound. Once, a long time ago, before I was ever born, Daddy and some woman—maybe Mama, maybe not, depending on how drunk Daddy was when he told the story—took the ferry to Ship Island one night and stood on the deck with the Gulf breeze in their faces and watched a pair of dolphins follow the ship.

452

Sometimes when he was very drunk, he would tell me about the lights along that channel, the kerosene smell of the ship's engine, the salt sea air and the porpoises playful in the wake.

So my daddy started to look for porpoises in the dangerous, hurricane-ruined Gulf of Mexico, with blown-out hotels and littered mud beaches and roving gangs of violent teenagers in the abandoned shopping centers and ospreys and oyster-beds and Cajun knife-throwers and swamp-elves in the dark saltwater marshes at his back. He dedicated himself to seeing a porpoise, a metaphor for romance.

I said, "I want to go home. I cut my foot on a piece of glass. They's dead things on the beach. They's a dead man on the beach, washed up there. I don't want to be on a second honeymoon."

He said, "This is the world we live in, Sugar-man. This is the only second honeymoon we'll ever have as a family."

So every morning now Daddy was standing beside the blue Gulf of Mexico in the ruins of southern Mississippi, scanning the horizon and all the breaking waves for some sign of a porpoise.

Always I was awake first, and always I was either with my daddy or behind him, nearby, watching in fear of what all, or any, of this meant.

At times there were other people on the beach. Once there was an old guy surf fishing, and daddy talked to him about porpoises for a while. The old guy baited his dangerous-looking hooks with something slimy from a plastic bucket.

Daddy said, "Do you ever see porpoises out here?"

The old guy said, "I'm thinking about writing a book."

Daddy said, "I read mostly magazines. I'm reading one right now about how to put the zip back in your marriage."

The old guy's pants legs were rolled up and he was barefoot, despite the danger. The tip of his rod bent slightly toward the pull of the waves.

The old guy said, "I've already got a title for it. For this book I'm thinking about writing."

Daddy said, "This magazine, it's called *Connections*. It tells you all about metaphors."

The old guy said, "I'm going to call it *Fun Sex Facts about Animals*."

Daddy said, "Porpoises is my metaphor right now. I'm pursuing porpoises with all my heart, like the magazine says."

The old guy said, "You're actually talking about dolphins. Dolphins are what you see around here. They're bigger than porpoises. The dorsal fin is a little different. And of course they have the beak."

Daddy said, "I haven't had a drink of whiskey since me and my wife and boy left the Delta. No d.t.'s, no hallucinations, nothing."

The old guy said, "The calf is born tail first. That's the fun sex fact about dolphins. That's what I would say about dolphins if I was to write this book I'm telling you about."

Daddy said, "Well, good luck," and started to walk up the filthy beach.

The old guy called after Daddy. He said, "Whale penises are twenty feet long." This is what the old guy shouted to my daddy in the ruins. He shouted, "And bent in the middle."

Daddy waved back in his direction and shrugged as if he could not hear. I was running along trying to catch up now, but I had to be careful of glass in the muddy sand.

The old guy was not finished calling out. He hollered, "Whale vaginas are on the side. That's why the penises are bent, so they can reach around." Ospreys carried silvery fish to their nests in the cypress trees, bodies washed ashore, teenagers drank warm wine in the shopping centers, and God knows what dangerous creatures with scales lay beneath the Gulf waters.

The next day the ocean seemed paved with silver cobblestones. If love cannot be summoned by magic or a power of personal will, then at least love's metaphors can be. My mama and my daddy and I were there, wearing our leather shoes and swimsuits on the terrible beach. The pavement of silver in the Gulf was an enormous school of bluefish. There must have been a million of them, literally a million fish, directly on the surface of the water.

And then the porpoises themselves. The sweet hooked fins, the sleek backs and oily humps. My daddy had summoned a school of dolphins. My parents held hands and looked at each other with awe and astonishment.

The dolphins blew like whales. They rolled like wheels. Daddy counted them, but there were too many to count. They bounded, they arched, one of them left the water altogether, and the belly was so white in the sunshine that I wanted to say it was blue.

My daddy looked at my mama with gratitude that amounted to reverence, to religion itself. Porpoises were a perfect metaphor after all. *Connections* magazine did not lie.

The porpoises were close to the shore. The explosive exhalations of their breath! The squeaking and clicking of their voices! Mama and Daddy left me behind and ran together down the corpse-strewn beach, holding hands like movie-star lovers.

It was a porpoise infestation. The incredible school of bluefish had attracted a hundred or more dolphins, two hundred maybe. There were too many to count. They were crazed. Maybe still psychotic from the effects of the hurricane. I picked my way down the beach, and I could see what my parents saw.

The carnage was spectacular. There were dead fish everywhere. Large fish, small fish, parts of fish, fish heads and fish tails and fish guts, fish shit no doubt, washing up onto the beach on every incoming wave.

The porpoises were frightening, there were so many of them, they were so fierce, so large, so mechanical and maniacal in their feeding. They were strong and swift and ruthless and intelligent. The bluefish were hysterical with fear. They were stupid. They were cattle. They were too frightened to dive. They could not get away. They cluttered the surface of the sea.

Now the porpoises could be seen in all their enormity. They were huge. They were eight feet long, nine feet, some of them. They broke the surface, they leaped, they blew spray in spumes from their blowholes. They had a jillion teeth, sharp and dangerous. Their eyes were as hard and as tiny as the eyes of grizzly bears. That is what this was like. Like seeing a hundred, two hundred hungry bears tearing into some frightened frantic grouping of small stupid trapped animals.

Mama said, "What does it mean? What does it mean?"

Daddy said, "Don't look. Let's don't look."

She turned and he held her in his arms.

She said, "I love you."

He said, "I love you."

She said, "Really?"

Now he looked at her.

She had a new red plastic barrette in her hair, and she was sunburned, and she looked like a child.

She said, "Don't tell me you love me if you don't really love me."

I knew I should leave but I did not. I picked up pieces of broken window glass and Coke bottles and sidearmed them at huge dead sea turtles in the sand.

Daddy looked back out at the porpoises.

He said. "Do you love me?"

She said, "Yes. I mean, no. I mean, I don't know. Don't make me answer this." She said, "I can't do this any more. Second honeymoons are just too hard on a girl."

She turned and walked away, up towards the beach house.

Daddy called out to her, angry, hopeless. "Look at this beach!" he said. "Look at it! Porpoises was the best I could do! Porpoises was the best metaphor I could think of!"

My mother kept walking up the filthy sand.

Daddy called, "Jesus Christ, honey! I can't do no better! Maybe if we lived near a better beach!"

That's not the end of the story. It seems like it could be, since it's just the kind of thing I'm always hearing myself say these days: If the world were different, I would be different, I would be more in love.

But it's not the end. There is one more thing to tell.

We did not drive back to the Delta that day. We stayed on the coast the whole month. Federal grant money came through while we were still staying at the beach house, and so the bulldozers started up. Cranes with steel balls swung into the walls of buildings and finished the collapse the hurricane had begun. Politicians stumped around making speeches, billboards with clever sayings went up: THE SOUTH SHALL RISE AGAIN. Pumper barges and dredges cleared the Gulf channels and pumped new white sand up onto the beaches. Dead fish and turtles were hauled off in garbage scows, the whale full of buzzards was dragged out to sea by a tugboat. The red lights of ambulances and police cars flashed all night, as the last bodies were carted away to funeral homes. Plate glass in windows was replaced, fallen trees were chainsawed into firewood and stacked in ricks. The ospreys and the swamp creatures lay quiet, quiet in the Mississippi darkness. The knife-throwers went back to New Orleans, the swamp-midgets got work in the construction industry.

My parents and I took long drives in the car and watched the reconstruction. The Gulf coast slowly became beautiful again.

One day as we drove along we realized we had left the state of Mississippi altogether and were actually speeding down a Florida highway, and this made all of us happy, but for some reason it also frightened us, and so Daddy turned the car around and we drove back in the direction of Biloxi and Symbol City and Pass Christian and Gulfport and Pascagoula.

Daddy looked longingly out the car window at house painters on high ladders, brightening the walls and corners of big houses that the hurricane had stripped of paint. He spoke wistfully of possibly moving here, where work was so plentiful, and where the land was so beautiful and the Gulf waters smelled like flowers on the islands beyond the reef.

We kept all the windows of the car rolled down and Mama's hair was beautiful when the wind blew it. Daddy's face got sunburned and his freckles stood out like copper pennies. I found *Connections* magazine in the trash one day, and so I took it out to the dumpster with the shells of shrimp we had peeled and eaten together the night before.

There was no more talk of love or of romance or of metaphors, though this seemed to be a good thing, not bad. My parents talked more, I would say, and kissed less, and this seemed to make both of them happy, though I cannot say why. We spent less time on the beach and more time in the car, driving, driving, driving along the Gulf of Mexico.

Daddy said, "Symbol City is a funny name for a town."

Mama said, "Mississippi was never a subtle state."

Daddy said, "It's funny how you end up somewhere, and then that's your life."

Mama said, "I guess."

Daddy said, "I think I would like to read more books. I used to always be reading a book when I was in the army."

Mama said, "I guess."

Daddy said, "I met this guy who was writing a book. He was a writer, that's what he told me."

Mama said, "Is that right? I heard John Dillinger the gangster used to drive down this very highway."

Daddy said, "What has that got to do with a writer?"

We were in the car with the windows down. I was in the backseat thinking about cocksuckers.

I said, "Daddy."

Daddy said, "What is it, Sugar-man?" Then he said, "I could have given this writer a few tips for his book, if I'd of thought of it."

Mama said, "Tell the truth."

I said, "What if I wanted to grow up to be a cocksucker?"

Daddy said, "Sex facts about animals, that's what the book was about, see. He was collecting sex facts about animals."

Mama said, "I know one. I know a good one."

Daddy said, "You do? You know a good sex fact about animals?"

Mama said, "The common opossum has a forked penis. That's one, that's the one sex fact about animals that I know."

I got real quiet in the backseat. I had never heard my mother talk about sex before. It was stranger than seeing the silk ties on the bed posts.

Daddy said, "A *forked* one?"

Mama said, "That's it."

Daddy said, "Woo-ee."

Mama said, "In case they want to boink up the nose, I guess, I don't know."

The two of them laughed quietly at the joke. The wind was whipping through the car and stirring up dust devils in the backseat. The Gulf skies were blue, blue. It would have been an excellent time to be sitting on a hardwood floor instead of in the backseat of a car, I was thinking.

We drove along for a while and didn't talk.

Daddy said, "In the army I was stationed in Sarasota for a while." He said, "Friend of mine was with the circus. He was a swordswallower."

He seemed to be talking to me. I wondered if this was an answer to my question about cocksucking.

I said, "The circus?"

He said, "The winter circus. It's in Venice, near Sarasota. If we had an extra day or two we could drive down there. I wonder if he's still alive. He could take eighteen inches right down his throat."

Mama said, "It's so far to Sarasota, honey, and we're so comfortable here."

Daddy said, "Okay, all right, it was just a thought." He looked at Mama. He scrunched down in the driver's seat and looked through the steering wheel at the highway. He said, "I'm John Dillinger, rolling through, balling the jack, watch out, po-lice, watch out law-abiding citizens, watch out all you possums and cocksuckers!"

She said, "You're John Dillinger all right. You *think* you're John Dillinger." My mama was blushing and laughing, and she was flushed with excitement and joy.

He said, "You're my moll, bebby. You're a dangerous woman. You're the Lady in Red. You're my pistol-packing mama."

He gunned the engine and we sped along laughing like a bunch of wild Indians down the long bad coastal highway of the Gulf of Mexico.

Daddy said, "Git on down the damn road! Yeah!"

How Bob Steele Broke
My Father's Heart

Naughty demons accompanied my father wherever he went. All misery did not seem to be of his own making. In his home, the telephone often rang with no one on the line. Hoses broke on the Maytag. Pipes froze in the spring. Pets came down with diseases they had been inoculated against. Wrestling and "The Love Boat" appeared on television at unscheduled times. Lightning struck our house and sent a fireball across the floor. He was the only man in Mississippi to buy a bottle of Tylenol that actually had a cyanide capsule in it. He went to only two high school baseball games in his life and was beaned by a foul ball at each of them. A homeless person died on his back stoop. When he walked down the street bluejays chased after him and pecked at his face. He was allergic to the dye in his underwear. He mistakenly accepted a collect obscene phone call.

This sounds like a joke or an exaggeration, but I swear it is not. There was something magical about the amount of benign bad luck that, on a daily basis, swept through my father's life like weather and judgment.

After the separation my mother was suspicious of the outcome of any reunion with my father. He had quit drinking, it was true. And I was home on furlough from the army to lend her moral support, that was true as well. But even if she could have forgiven the incident with the knife, there was some chance, at least, that a reconciliation could lead to busted plumbing or bad wiring.

I should say more about the incident with the knife.

A year earlier, just before I went into the army, my parents had one of their usual fights.

My mother: "You, you, you!"

My father: "But, but, but . . ."

My mother: "You never, you always!"

My father: "But, but, but . . ."

My father was drunk, of course. I went upstairs to hide, as I always did.

I turned on my father's small black-and-white television and watched part of a "National Geographic Special" about whales. Japanese whalers shot harpoons into whales and the whales dragged boatloads of people in raingear through bloody water. A cartoon special was scheduled, but the whales came on instead. My father's portable television set.

Later wrestling came on, though "The Cowboy Bob Steele Film Festival" was scheduled.

The fight was over, so that was good.

I got out of bed and started downstairs to take a leak.

I walked past the kitchen just in time to see my father take a butcher knife from the sink and stab himself in the stomach. He was wearing only a light cotton robe, which was open in front. My mother had already gone to bed.

Then he stabbed himself again, and this time the knife sank two or three inches into his stomach.

For a second I was stone, and then I said "Daddy!" and rushed to hold him in case he should fall. I said, "Oh my God! Oh Jesus, Daddy!" I had my hands on his shoulders, and I tried to lead him to the sofa.

He drew the knife out of his stomach and dropped it on the kitchen table. Blood spilled down out of him, down his belly, down into the hair between his legs, down his thighs, onto the floor.

All I could say was, "Oh Jesus, oh Jesus."

My father said, "Hand me one of those cup towels from the rack. Watch that rack don't fall off the wall."

He took a clean dish towel and held it against the wound.

I said, "I'll wake Mama."

He said, "Don't do that, Sugar. She's had a rough night. Let the pore woman get some sleep."

I said, "I'll drive you, then." To the hospital, I meant.

He said, "Well, but somebody's going to have to clean up this mess."

So that was that. I stayed behind to wipe up the blood with a sponge and wash it down the kitchen sink.

I heard the car start up in the driveway—it was a Pinto he had bought from Runt Conroy, my friend Roy Dale Conroy's daddy, the car that later would actually explode, but tonight it started on the first try and there was no fire. I saw the lights come on, and then I watched out the window as my father backed the car out and drove up the street towards the highway and on to the hospital in Leflore, ten miles across the Delta.

After this incident my mother had had enough. She told him he would have to leave.

He said, "I'm going to make this up to you. I'm going to become a new man, you wait and see. I'm going to change my luck."

It was when I was on leave from the army, sometime in the spring of the following year, that my father came back to our house to beg to be taken back. That's what I thought he had come to do, anyway.

It was hard to deny that he was different. He had stopped drinking, for one thing. He went to meetings that he called his Don't Drink meetings, and to tell the truth, I had never seen him more in the flush of good health. It had been almost a whole year since he had a drink.

I had a brand new stripe on my dress greens and a spit shine on my shoes, and my mother seemed more at ease with herself than I had ever known her to be. Now here was my father going to his meetings and saying he might have his teeth fixed.

So when my father told me in confidence that he was planning to ask my mother's forgiveness for all his years of drunkenness, well, it didn't seem impossible to me that something very good might come of it.

My mother was not completely unaware of what might be in the offing. My father had called her and had asked, in his gentlest way, to be allowed to speak with her about matters of a personal nature. He said he was working a "step" of some kind for his D.D. meetings and would appreciate my mother's cooperation. This was the way he phrased his request, and so in my mother's mind it could mean nothing else except that he wanted to be taken back.

I need not go into the details of why she might oppose a complete reunion. Her life was moving along well enough, she had adapted to the small town gossip about the separation and the suicide attempt and my father's embarrassing Don't Drink meetings. She must still have harbored some grudge about the final scene at the house, the stabbing.

But in fact there was an irresistible quality about my father's particular doom. It did not seem entirely related to alcoholism. It seemed more cosmic, as if there were demons other than rum that did not care for my father at all.

The appointed day and hour arrived. I was home on leave, as I said. "You'll want to talk privately," I said to my mother, in an effort to get away from the house.

My mother insisted that I stay. "I need you here," she said. "If he asks to come back I'll need you here beside me."

I said, "What will you say?"

She said, "I'll say no. If he says, 'I'm sorry,' I'll say, 'I forgive you.' If he says, 'Take me back,' I'll say, 'No, I can't, it's too dangerous.' But you have to be here. If you are not here I might say yes."

So we waited for him.

My mother said, "I'll straighten up the kitchen."

She straightened it up, she more than straightened it up. She mopped the floor, she unloaded the dishwater, she put new dishtowels on the rack, she scrubbed the sink, she put Drano in the pipes, she scoured the range and sprayed the oven with Oven Off, she cleaned the venetian blinds and swept a cloth-covered broom over the cobwebs in the ceiling corners.

She said, "Do you know how to put up wallpaper?"

I said, "Mama, he'll be here soon."

She said, "I didn't mean I'd hang the paper right this minute!"

I said, "Why on earth would you say yes?" I wanted her to say yes.

She took off her rubber gloves and sat in a kitchen chair. She mopped sweat off her forehead with the back of her forearm.

She said, "He's just so helpless, Sugar. When all those bad things happen to him, I just can't keep from wanting to help him."

I said, "But do you love him?"

She said, "I don't even ask myself that question any more. It doesn't even matter any more."

At last my father's car appeared in front of the house. It was the Pinto. The car was just out of the shop for electrical and fuel pump problems, as usual. My father did not seem to mind paying large sums to have the car repaired. He expected mechanical failure.

Here is what I know now. When he came to the house on this day, my father had no intention of talking my mother into taking him back. His only purpose in coming was to say to my mother, "I have treated you badly. I am so very sorry."

My mother and I watched him out the front window. He sat for a few moments in his car. I thought his doors might have become accidentally locked, but I looked more closely and saw that his eyes were closed and his lips were moving. I think my father might have been saying a prayer. I think he might have been praying, "Keep the demons away from me while I do this thing." Who knows what he might have been doing. The key was probably stuck in the ignition, or the seat belt would not come unbuckled.

My mother said, "Jesus!" as if he had just done something awkward or unusual.

I said, "Poor Dad."

She said, "Oh, poor Dad, my foot! I am so sick and tired of hearing Poor Dad!"

The door opened and my father stepped out of the car. For a moment he stood beside the car and mopped his forehead with his handkerchief. He also seemed to be sniffing the air. Testing the air, maybe. For a fragrance of spring flowers? For a fragrance of fresh paint from a back-yard fence nearby? For the ripeness of possibilities, or something to do with his car, maybe, a flooded carburetor? It was impossible to tell.

My mother said, "What is that fool doing now?"

I said, "Mama, it hurts me for you to talk like that. He's not doing anything."

She said, "He's bringing his bad luck with him. He's going to infect me with his bad luck again."

I said, "You are in love with him. That's why you're so scared of him."

She said, "I'm not letting him move back into this house. He can have a minute to talk, but that's all. That's all he's going to get from me."

My mother opened the door and allowed my father to come into the living room.

She said, "You might as well sit down."

My father eased himself down onto the sofa, where he had once accidentally sat on the cat and broken its neck. He was careful to sit on nothing but cushions.

My mother said, "Sugar, you sit down too."

I sat on the other end of the sofa and made myself otherwise invisible. I looked steadfastly out the window and except for polite greetings said nothing.

My father was not an articulate man. He scarcely noticed my presence.

His face was pinched with concern for what he was about to say. *I'm sorry.* That's all he meant. I was beginning to understand that now. All he would have to do was say this and be gone.

Now my mother sat down as well. She was in the bentwood rocker. Not rocking but perched there, fragile as a bird on a twig.

This was it. My father was here to make amends.

Nothing happened. My father sat for a very long time and did not speak. His face was moving, his eyes, his jaw muscles, his ears and nose. There was even a wormy movement of his lips. He may have been speaking in there somewhere, he may have been carrying on conversations far back there in the silence. We didn't know. All my mother or I could know was that he was not speaking in the world in which we lived. He seemed to be carrying on a conversation in some other realm, where only he and the demons resided.

My mother kept waiting. Nothing happened.

My father put his hands on his knees. This may have been a gesture of decisiveness, it was hard to tell.

Some of my mother's anger had faded, or been stuffed out of sight somewhere. She was trying to help my father speak. "Can I come back, will you have me?" she believed he was trying to say from his weird silence.

She leaned forward in the rocker, as if to encourage him.

Still he said nothing.

My mother looked at me for help in jarring loose the words. I offered nothing. I fixed my eyes on the tree outside our front window.

My mother looked back at him. Truly demons inhabited whatever space he occupied.

I wanted to say it for him. *I'm sorry. I didn't mean to hurt you.*

My mother wanted to say it for him. *Take me back. I can't live without you.*

Nothing.

My mother said, "Was there something you came to tell me, Gilbert?"

My father was sweating now. He wiped sweat from his face with the back of his arm. Then, immediately, he wiped his face with the other arm. His underarms were big full moons of sweat stains.

I thought, If he could have a drink of whiskey he could do this. Sobriety has killed this moment, this marriage.

My mother said, "Gilbert?"

He said, "Yes, please, thank you. I wonder if you could, if you might—I wonder if you would please give me a drink."

My mother said, "A drink?"

He said, "Tap water is fine, yes."

She said, "Water?"

I was already out of my seat. I filled a glass with ice cubes and ran water into it from the tap.

He drank the water and crunched up all the ice cubes.

He said, "There were eight of us."

My mother sat back in her chair, and allowed it to rock slightly for the first time since my father arrived in the house.

My father was talking about his own poor family in Canada. His brothers and sisters, his parents. He told about his father, who was blinded in the mines by coal dust.

My mother was very irritated now. She said, "Your father was not blinded by coal dust. Your father had cancer of the eyes."

He said, "Six children. Guided through life by a blind man and a crazy woman. Dishes were forever piled up in the blackened sink. My mother was odd. Now you would say she was depressed. Then she was only odd. Some days she couldn't move out of her chair. The table was never cleared. The oil-cloth was stained with congealed foods. My father couldn't see it anyway, he was blind, but I could see it."

My mother said, "Gilbert, will you please get to the point?"

He said, "There was no telling what you might find on the breakfast table."

My mother had had enough. She said, "Gilbert, thank you for coming over."

He did not stop. He said, "A shoe, dirty clothing . . ."

Mother said to me, "Sugar, will you please . . ."

Father said, "A dead cat, once. Can you imagine that? A dead cat on the breakfast table."

Mother said, "I can imagine it all too well."

He said, "It was frozen, for some reason. Honestly, I can't think why."

She said, "I don't know what to say."

He said, "All I mean is . . ."

It was then that I heard the first sound. It was a sound like *wump*.

My father did not seem to hear the sound, but he did not finish his sentence either.

It was odd that he could not tell my mother he was sorry for their sadness together. He had apologized a million times in his life. On this occasion, though, when I suppose his words were genuinely important for the first time ever, he could say not a word that made sense.

Then the second time, this sound. *wump*. Small, distant, unreal. A cozy sound, I would say.

I continued to look out the window at the magnolia tree, as my father sat mute before my mother and me. My mother, in her anger, seemed to soften to the hope of hearing something sensible come out of my father's mouth. If he could have said, "I am sorry," she would have said, "I forgive you," and she would have meant it. If he had said, "I love you," she would have said, "I have always loved you," and this would have been true as well.

Out the window I saw the trees coming into leaf. Pecan and chinaberry and black walnut. I thought that those leaf-buds were almost voices. I thought that those new leaves, gold-green, were almost words, almost something being said. I believed, in this family silence, that I could hear the voices of the leaf-buds as a sound of their new growth. They were not just poised there, I watched them relax and spread. I believed that their greenness was a kind of grief.

My father said, "We ate cold canned spaghetti, dates, Post Toasties, Ovaltine, candy bars, soda water with cocaine in it, condensed milk by the teaspoonful. The contents of overstuffed drawers hung down to the floor like sad cold animals."

My mother moved from her chair and sat on the floor by my father's feet and held his hand as he talked.

I was embarrassed. I stood and walked to the window and looked out.

He said, "I hated my pap for going blind. He beat me and my sisters. He tore us up as fine as cat hair."

Mother said, "I know, baby, I know."

Now that I was at the window and could see the street I knew what the sound outside had been. Hearthlike, had been one of my thoughts when I first heard this cozy sound. My father's car had exploded and was burning in full flame. There was a third sound of *wump*, and now a crackling and a sound of air rushing and being sucked somewhere.

I said, "Dad, you car is on fire."

He said, "I'm not trying to make excuses."

She said, "I know, I know."

He said, "It might sound self-pitying."

She said, "No, baby, no it doesn't."

I said, "Uh, excuse me. Dad, your car is, you know, on fire."

He said, "My house gets robbed, my TV picks up programs that are no longer aired, people I don't know call me up on the telephone."

Mother said, "We never should have let that white cat sleep on a white couch in the first place."

I said, "I'll just call the fire department."

He said, "I'm just so sorry for everything. For the way things turned out."

She said, "Learn to love yourself, Gilbert. For once in your life, learn to love yourself."

We could hear the sirens now. The Arrow Catcher Volunteer Fire Department was on the move.

The Pinto looked like a forest fire. It would not be long before the gas tank blew and rocked the neighborhood. The black smoke from the tires looked like a tornado.

Now the three of us stood at the window together and watched the flames rise, and we were happy together when the Arrow Catcher pumper truck turned the corner at the Methodist church and banged to a halt in front of our house.

I wish this story ended more happily than it actually does. All this happened a long time ago, and now I'm middle-aged and have been going to Don't Drink meetings for a good long while myself. There is a good deal of wreckage in my own past, a family I hurt in the same way my father hurt me, and the same way his father hurt him. I tore my children up as fine as cat hair, you might say.

And I wish I could tell you that my father died a happy man, or at least a sober man. But the truth is he died a dozen years later underneath a blanket of fish. That, however, is another story. His skin was as yellow as a traffic light. These were hard times for all of us, especially for my mother.

But the night my father came over to the house and made amends to my mother and blew up his car, none of this sadness seemed possible. And for that blindness to the future I will always be grateful.

That night my father and my mother slept together in their bed in their house, for the first time since he stabbed himself. I imagine that she looked at the scar on his stomach for the first time ever. I imagine that she ran her fingers over it and maybe kissed it as a part of their love-making that night.

I heard nothing, not even their quiet voices, and not the sound of their touching. But I know this fantasy must be true, this dream of romance. There was such hope in all of us then.

Let me tell you what did happen that night. I was lying in the same bed, in the same room with the slanted ceiling and luminous decals of stars and planets above me, where I had lain on the night of the stabbing. The same magnolia tree scratched at my window. The same peach-basket-size moon celebrated the width of the Mississippi sky. I watched the same black-and-white television set that I had watched that night.

This night I did not follow a light in the kitchen and find my father there with a knife. This night my father left my mother asleep in their bed and eased inside the door of my room and stood without speaking with his back leaned against the door frame.

I said, "Hey, Daddy."

I was waiting through a commercial for the beginning of "Petticoat Junction." I met a boy in the army who had been to Hollywood and had walked through Petticoat Junction and Mayberry and two islands, Gilligan's and Fantasy. Because of him I tried to watch these re-runs whenever they were listed in *TV Guide*.

But when the commercial was over "Petticoat Junction" didn't come on. An old Western movie came on instead. It was a movie called *The Rider from Laredo*, with an actor named Bob Steele.

My father said, "Bob Steele." He was standing there, just inside my door.

I said, "*TV Guide* says 'Petticoat Junction' is supposed to come on now."

He said, "Bob Steele don't understand Western symbolism."

I said, "This televison set is crazy. It never picks up what is supposed to be on."

He said, "He can't sing, either. Don't even try."

I said, "Bob Steele?"

We looked at the TV screen and watched a distant horseback rider come into view. There was a dust cloud behind his horse.

My father said, "No wife, no white hat, no good-looking horse, no Indian sidekick, nothing."

The rider was close enough to see now. My father was right. There was nothing to distinguish this rider from a messenger, or a bad guy, or a minor character. There was no way to tell this was the star, the hero of the movie.

My father said, "And no comical sidekick either. Andy Clyde, Smiley Burnett—those guys wouldn't give Bob Steele the time of day."

We watched the movie. Bob Steele was not a good horseback rider. The horse was a small brown nondescript beast that was jerking its head this way and that. Bob Steele was tired and hassled-looking from struggling with it. This was not part of the script.

There is a gunfight going on in town. Bob Steele finally cracks his horse over the head with his fist to make it settle down. He reins the creature to a halt and the horse's eyes are wild from fear of being punched out, blind-sided.

My father said, "Bob Steele don't take no shit from a horse."

It's a gunfight sure enough. On one side of the street are all the solid citizens, the ranchers and farmers and the parson and the church ladies in bonnets. On the other side of the street are the gamblers and the floozies and the real estate swindlers and the saloon guys in black hats.

My father said, "Watch this."

Bob Steele is not tall, is not handsome, has no bullwhip, or sidekick, no distinguishing features. He can't ride a horse, he can't sing. He is new in town, and what I begin to understand is that without any help at all, without even a white hat or an interesting horse, Bob Steele is pure gold. He is the believable de-symbolized, unromanticized version of what every man on earth wants to be. He is the magic that can be touched. He is what my father drank to become, and what I later drank to become. He is alone, he is pure hope, and complete.

Bob Steele jumps off his horse.

The two sides of the street are blazing away at each other. Men and women in violent conflict. Confined and victimized by their wardrobes, their unchangeable, unalterable representations of themselves and beyond themselves.

Bob Steele takes out his six-shooter and fires off several shots, first one way and then the other. The gun is smoking. And then Bob Steele speaks the first words of the movie.

He does not say, Stop in the name of the law. He is no lawman, no Texas Ranger. He does not say, Hold your fire, or I've got you covered. Here's what Bob Steele says. He says, "What's going on here?"

My father looked at me.

He said, "Do you see what I mean?"

I said, "I'm not sure. You mean, shoot first and ask questions later?"

My father said, "No, I mean ask the right question. Ask the same question over and over. Ask the only question there is."

I said, "Ask, 'What's going on here'?"
My father said, "Maybe, maybe that's the right question."

• • • • • • • • • • •

QUESTIONS FOR A SECOND READING

1. The stories in *Music of the Swamp* are about Sugar Mecklin's family and childhood. They are also about memory and writing, about the adult, or the voice of the adult in the stories, trying to remember and represent that childhood. As you reread, mark those passages where the adult makes his presence felt as a storyteller. Where does he appear? What does he say about storytelling?

2. At the end of "How Bob Steele Broke My Father's Heart," Sugar says, in reference to the mythic cowboy figure of Bob Steele:

> He does not say, Stop in the name of the law. He is no lawman, no Texas Ranger. He does not say, Hold your fire, or I've got you covered. Here's what Bob Steele says. He says, "What's going on here?"
>
> My father looked at me.
>
> He said, "Do you see what I mean?"
>
> I said, "I'm not sure. You mean, shoot first and ask questions later?"
>
> My father said, "No, I mean ask the right question. Ask the same question over and over. Ask the only question there is."
>
> I said, "Ask, 'What's going on here'?"
>
> My father said, "Maybe, maybe that's the right question." (pp. 466–67)

Earlier in this episode, Sugar describes Bob Steele as "pure gold. He is the believable de-symbolized, unromanticized version of what every man on earth wants to be. . . . He is what my father drank to become, and what I later drank to become" (p. 466).

As you reread, think about the progression of the stories. Imagine that they are moving toward "How Bob Steele Broke My Father's Heart." What is the order in these stories? "What's going on here?"

Note: Since you are thinking about the order of things, it might be interesting to know how the book ends. "How Bob Steele . . ." is the last long story in the book. It is followed by two shorter pieces. The first presents the scene of his father's death "under a blanket of fish." The second, an epilogue titled "OWLS," presents a grown Sugar, talking to his lover. He has told a story about his father and a magical moment he has either remembered or invented:

> I believed my clumsy drunken inexpert father, or my invention of him, had prepared me for this magic. The woman beside me said, "I love you."
>
> In that moment every good thing that I had expected, longed to feel with my father, I felt with her. And I also felt it with my father, and

I heard his voice speak those words of love, though he was already a long time dead. He was with me in a way he could not be in life.

For one second the woman and I seemed to be become twins, or closer than twins. . . . Maybe we said nothing. Maybe we only lay in the band of sunlight that fell across our bed. Or maybe together we said, "There is great pain in love but we don't care, it's worth it."

ASSIGNMENTS FOR WRITING

1. If you took the perspective that each of these stories is part of an argument, how would you characterize that argument? What is it? To whom is it addressed? How does it make its points? And where and why, for you, is it (or is it not) convincing? Write an essay in which you think about the stories as part of an argument. As you work on your essay, be sure to work from specific passages or examples or moments from the text. (You should imagine that your readers are familiar with Nordan's work but don't have the text in front of them.)

2. Taken together, Nordan's stories may be read as a way of thinking through (or about) a number of complex, interrelated issues: family, storytelling, memory, maturation. For this assignment, write an essay in which you discuss both what you think Nordan is saying about these issues (or two or three you select) *and* his use of fiction as a way of exploring ideas. If fiction is a way of thinking about the world, then what does one gain by writing fiction rather than writing essays?

3. The stories in *Music of the Swamp* are about Sugar Mecklin and his family. They are also about memory and storytelling. They have two points of view—the point of view of Sugar the boy inside the experience and the point of view of Sugar the adult thinking back on his life, perhaps remembering, perhaps inventing, trying to reconstruct and to understand what happened (or what maybe happened).

Try your hand at writing a Nordan-like story. You can imagine that you are writing fiction or you can imagine that you are writing a memoir, a section of your autobiography. Your goal should be to try to catch the rhythm and style of Nordan's sentences, to get a sense of the shape and purpose of the stories he tells, and to establish *both* the perspective you had as a child (or adolescent) and the one you have now, as the writer, working on your story and through it thinking back to the past.

MAKING CONNECTIONS

1. Susan Douglas's "Narcissism as Liberation" (p. 117) and Nordan's stories are quite different pieces of writing, yet each can be said to present a way of thinking through the experiences available to us. Douglas is interested in the effects of media advertising on the formation of women's identity or self. Nordan is interested in the effects of family and memory on the creation of a boy's identity or self. In this sense, both Douglas and Nordan can be said to

present two different ways of accounting for the formation of identity or the self.

What arguments do these two pieces of writing seem to be making about the construction of the self? What commonalities can you point to? what differences? And what would you be willing to attribute to gender? to habits or traditions? to culturally designed desires? or to other things such as memory? or experience? or the writing itself?

For this assignment, write an essay in which you discuss what you think Douglas and Nordan are saying about these issues that involve the formation of identity or the self. Be sure to work from what you see as the key passages in each selection. You will want to present your reader with a substantial set of examples from each text to frame or ground your discussion.

2. Imagine that both Nordan and Susan Griffin in "Our Secret" (p. 319) are telling stories about their images of manhood, about what it means to be a man, and about how male identities are formed. What do you think they are saying about manhood? What passages would you use to argue your case? What would you say the two passages share in common? And what seems unique to each?

Write an essay in which you discuss Nordan's stories and Griffin's essay as examples of writers telling stories about their images of manhood. How, in other words, does Nordan "see" manhood? And Griffin? How do their visions shift or change? What would you say accounts for these shifts?

3. While one is offered as "fiction" and the other is offered as "nonfiction," Nordan's stories from *Music of the Swamp* and John Edgar Wideman's "Our Time" (p. 652) both use narrative to recall and understand and take a position in relation to family, to identity, and to the past. Sugar Mecklin tries to understand his father. Wideman tried to understand his brother, Robby. Both Sugar and Wideman raise questions about who they are in relation to their families and as writers.

Let's put aside the usual importance given to the differences between fiction and nonfiction, and let's look at both of these selections as examples of writers at work. Reread them both looking for the ways, as texts, they represent the problems of memory, narrative, and the past.

Write an essay in which you discuss the different ways in which Wideman and Nordan, as writers, represent the past, themselves, and their families. What problems of memory and language do they negotiate? How do they address those problems?

4. It is interesting to read Nordan's set of stories next to Joyce Carol Oates's story, "Theft" (p. 471). Both, in a sense, are stories about adolescence, about growing up and coming to understand things in ways that are impossible to people who have limited experience. And the two stories are strongly marked in terms of gender—that is, one is a boy's story written by a man and one is a girl's story written by a woman. Write an essay comparing these representations of men's and women's experience. What arguments do these two stories seem to make about the differences between men and women? In what ways do these arguments seem right? wrong? biased? incomplete? surprising?

JOYCE CAROL
OATES

*J*OYCE CAROL OATES (b. 1938) began publishing her fiction as an undergraduate at Syracuse University, winning the Mademoiselle college fiction
award for her story "In the Old World" in 1959. She has since published over forty
books of fiction, poetry, and literary criticism—an extraordinary record. Along the
way, she completed an M.A. at the University of Wisconsin and began a career as a
teacher, teaching at the University of Detroit, the University of Windsor (Ontario),
and Princeton, among others. She once said, "I'm always working. . . . Writing is
much more interesting to me than eating or sleeping." In Oates's case, one is inclined to believe that this may be true.

Even though the evidence might indicate that writing comes naturally to her,
Oates has said that failure is what writing continually teaches: "The writer, however
battered a veteran, can't have any real faith . . . in his stamina (let alone his theoretical 'gift') to get through the ordeal. . . . One is frequently asked whether the process
becomes easier with the passage of time, and the reply is obvious—Nothing gets easier with the passage of time, not even the passing of time." Oates writes, she says, in
"flurries" and then works and reworks her stories into shape. This process of revision
sometimes goes on even after a work has been published. The version of "Theft"
Oates offered for this volume, for example, differs from the version we first read in
Northwest Review. And the story reappears, with minor additional changes, as

Chapter 6 of her novel Marya: A Life *(1986). "The pleasure is the rewriting," Oates has said. "The first sentence can't be written until the final sentence is written. . . . The completion of any work automatically necessitates its revisioning. The same is true with reading, of course." About the revision of* Marya, *Oates has written, "It was not until I wrote the sentence 'Marya this is going to cut your life in two' on the novel's final page that I fully understood Marya's story, and was then in a position to begin again and to recast it as a single work of prose fiction. As I recall now how obsessively certain pages of the novel were written and rewritten, it seems to me miraculous that the novel was ever completed at all."*

Oates is currently Roger S. Berlind Distinguished Professor in the Humanities at Princeton University. Her recent work includes (Woman) Writer: Occasions and Opportunities *(1988), her fifth collection of essays;* Will You Always Love Me? and Other Stories *(1996); and three novels:* Zombie *(1995),* You Can't Catch Me *(1995), and* What I Lived For *(1994).*

Theft

The semester Marya became acquainted with Imogene Skillman, a thief suddenly appeared in Maynard House, where Marya was rooming in her sophomore year at Port Oriskany: striking at odd, inspired, daring hours, sometimes in the early morning when a girl was out of her room and showering in the bathroom just down the corridor, sometimes late at night when some of the girls sat in the kitchen, drinking coffee, their voices kept low so that the resident adviser would not hear. (The kitchen was supposed to close officially at midnight. Maynard House itself "closed" at midnight—there were curfews in those days, in the women's residences.) A wristwatch stolen from one room, seven dollars from another, a physics textbook from yet another . . . the thief was clearly one of the residents, one of the twenty-six girls who roomed in the house, but no one knew who it was; no one wanted to speculate too freely. Naturally there were wild rumors, cruel rumors. Marya once heard the tail end of a conversation in which her own name— "Knauer"—was mentioned. She had brushed by, her expression neutral, stony. She wanted the girls to know she had heard—she scorned even confronting them.

One Saturday morning in November Marya returned to her room after having been gone less than five minutes—she'd run downstairs to check the mail, though she rarely received letters—to see, with a sickening pang, that the door was ajar.

Her wallet had been taken from her leather bag, which she'd left carelessly in sight, tossed on top of her bed.

Her lips shaped empty, angry prayers—Oh God please *no*—but of course it was too late. She felt faint, sickened. She had just cashed a check for forty-five dollars—a week's part-time wages from the university library—and she'd had time to spend only a few dollars; she needed the money badly. "No," she said aloud, baffled, chagrined. "God damn it, *no*."

Someone stood in the opened doorway behind her saying Marya? Is something wrong? but Marya paid her no notice. She was opening the drawers of her bureau one by one; she saw, disgusted, frightened, that the thief had been there too—rooting around in Marya's woolen socks and sweaters and frayed underwear. And her fountain pen was gone. She kept it in the top drawer of the bureau, a prize of her own, a handsome black Parker pen with a thick nub . . . now it was gone.

She had to resist the impulse to yank the drawer out and throw it to the floor—to yank all the drawers out—to give herself up to rage. A flame seemed to pass through her, white-hot, scalding. It was so unfair: she needed that money, every penny of that money, she'd worked in the library in that flickering fluorescent light until she staggered with exhaustion, and even then she'd been forced to beg her supervisor to allow her a few more hours. Her scholarships were only for tuition; she needed that money. And the pen—she could never replace the pen.

It was too much: something in her chest gave way: she burst into tears like an overgrown child. She had never heard such great gulping ugly sobs. And the girl in the doorway—Phyllis, whose room was across the hall—shy, timid, sweet-faced Phyllis—actually tried to hold her in her arms and comfort her. It's so unfair, it's so unfair, Marya wept, what am I going to *do*. . . .

Eventually the wallet was returned to Marya, having been found in a trash can up the street. Nothing was missing but the money, as it turned out: nothing but the money! Marya thought savagely. The wallet itself—simulated crocodile, black, with a fancy brass snap—now looked despoiled, worn, contemptible. It had been a present from Emmett two years before and she supposed she'd had it long enough.

She examined it critically inside and out. She wondered what the thief had thought. Marya Knauer's things, Marya Knauer's "personal" possessions: were they worth stealing, really?

For weeks afterward Marya dreaded returning to her room. Though she was careful to lock the door all the time now it always seemed, when she stepped inside, that someone had been there . . . that something was out of place. Sometimes when she was halfway up the long steep hill to Stafford Hall she turned impulsively and ran back to her dormitory seven blocks away, to see if she'd remembered to lock the door. You're breaking down, aren't you, she mocked herself as she ran, her heart pumping, perspiration itching beneath her arms,—this is how it begins, isn't it: cracking up.

In the early years of the century Maynard House must have been impressive: a small Victorian mansion with high handsome windows, a wide veranda rimmed with elaborate fretwork, a cupola, a half-dozen fireplaces, walnut paneling in several of the downstairs rooms. But now it had become dim and shabby. The outside needed painting; the wallpaper in most of the rooms was discolored. Because it was so far from the main campus, and because its rooms were so cramped (Marya could stand at her full height on only one side of her room, the ceiling on the other slanted so steeply) it was one of the lowest priced residences for women. The girls who roomed there were all scholarship students like Marya, and, like Marya, uneasily preoccupied with studies, grades, part-time employment, finances of a minute and degrading nature. They were perhaps not so humorless and unattractive as Maynard House's reputation would have it, but they did share a superficial family resemblance—they might have been cousins, grimly energetic, easily distracted, a little vain (for they *were* scholarship winners after all, competition for these scholarships was intense throughout the state), badly frightened at the prospect of failure. They were susceptible to tears at odd unprovoked moments, to eating binges, to outbursts of temper; several, including Marya, were capable of keeping their doors closed for days on end and speaking to no one when they did appear.

Before the theft Marya had rather liked Maynard House; she prized her cubbyhole of a room because it was *hers*; because in fact she could lock the door for days on end. The standard university furniture didn't displease her—the same minimal bed, desk, chair, bureau, bedside table, lamp in each room—and the sloped ceiling gave the room a cavelike, warmly intimate air, especially at night when only her desk lamp was burning. Though she couldn't really afford it Marya had bought a woven rug for the floor—Aztec colors, even more fierce than those in hers and Alice's rug at home—and a new lampshade edged with a festive gold braid; she had bought a Chagall print for ninety-eight cents (marked down because it was slightly shopworn) at the University Store. The walls were decorated with unframed charcoal drawings she had done, sketches of imaginary people, a few glowering self-portraits: when she was too tense or excited to sleep after hours of studying, or after having taken an exam, she took up a stick of charcoal and did whatever it seemed to wish to do—her fingers empowered with a curious sort of energy, twitchy, sporadic, often quite surprising. From the room's walls smudged and shadowy variants of her own sober face contemplated her. Strong cheekbones, dark eyes, thick dark censorious brows. . . . She had made the portraits uglier than she supposed she really was; that provided some comfort, it might be said to have been a reverse vanity. Who is *that*? one of the girls on the floor once asked, staring at Marya's own image,—is it a man?—a woman?

Marya prized her aloneness, her monastic isolation at the top of the house, tucked away in a corner. She could stay up all night if she wished, she could skip breakfast if she wished, she could fall into bed after her morning classes and sleep a heavy drugged sleep for much of the afternoon; and no one knew or cared. It seemed extraordinary to her now that for so many years—for all of her lifetime, in fact—she had had to submit to the routine schedule of Wilma's household: going to bed when she wasn't sleepy, getting up when the others did, eating meals with them, living her life as if it were nothing more than an extension of theirs. She loved to read for pleasure once her own assignments were completed: the reading she did late at night acquired an aura, a value, a mysterious sort of enchantment, that did not usually belong to daylight. It was illicit, precious beyond estimation. It seemed to her at such times that she was capable of slipping out of her own consciousness and into that of the writer's . . . into the very rhythms of another's prose. Bodiless, weightless, utterly absorbed, she traversed the landscape of another's mind and found it like her own yet totally unlike—surprising and jarring her, enticing her, leading her on. It was a secret process yet it was not criminal or forbidden—she made her way with the stealth of the thief, elated, subdued, through another's imagination, risking no harm, no punishment. The later the hour and the more exhausted she was, the greater, oddly, her powers of concentration; nothing in her resisted, nothing stood aside to doubt or ridicule; the books she read greedily seemed to take life through her, by way of her, with virtually no exertion of her own. It scarcely seemed to matter what she read, or whom—Nietzsche, William James, the Brontës, Wallace Stevens, Virginia Woolf, Stendhal, the early Greek philosophers—the experience of reading was electrifying, utterly mesmerizing, beyond anything she could recall from the past. She'd been, she thought severely, a superficial person in the past—how could anything that belonged to Innisfail, to those years, matter?

A writer's authentic self, she thought, lay in his writing and not in his life; it was the landscape of the imagination that endured, that was really real. Mere life was the husk, the actor's performance, negligible in the long run. . . . How could it be anything more than the vehicle by which certain works of art were transcribed . . . ? The thought frightened her, exhilarated her. She climbed out of her bed and leaned out her window as far as she could, her hair whipping in the wind. For long vacant minutes she stared at the sky; her vision absorbed without recording the illuminated water tower two miles north of the campus, the flickering red lights of a radio station, the passage of clouds blown livid across the moon. Standing in her bare feet, shivering, her head fairly ringing with fatigue and her eyes filling with tears, she thought her happiness almost too exquisite to be borne.

The first time Imogene Skillman climbed, uninvited, to Marya's room at the top of the old mansion, she stood in the doorway and exclaimed in her low throaty amused voice, "So *this* is where you hide out! . . . this depressing little hole."

Imogene was standing with her hands on her hips, her cheeks flushed, her eyes moving restlessly about. Why, Marya's room was a former maid's room, wasn't it, partitioned off from the others on the floor; and it had only that one window—no wonder the air was stale and close; and that insufferable Chagall print!—wasn't Marya aware that everyone on campus had one? And it was a poor reproduction at that. Then Imogene noticed the charcoal sketches; she came closer to investigate; she said, after a long moment, "At least these are interesting, I wouldn't mind owning one or two of them myself."

Marya had been taken by surprise, sitting at her desk, a book opened before her; she hadn't the presence of mind to invite Imogene in, or to tell her to go away.

"So this is where Marya Knauer lives," Imogene said slowly. Her eyes were a pellucid blue, blank and innocent as china. "All alone, of course. Who would *you* have roomed with—?"

The loss of the money and the Parker fountain pen was so upsetting to Marya, and so bitterly ironic, partly because Marya herself had become a casual thief.

She thought, I deserve this.

She thought, I will never steal anything again.

Alice had led her on silly little shoplifting expeditions in Woolworth's: plastic combs, spools of thread, lipsticks, useless items (hairnets, thumbtacks) pilfered for the sheer fun of it. Once, years ago, when she was visiting Bonnie Michalak, she made her way stealthily into Mrs. Michalak's bedroom and took—what had it been?—a button, a thimble, two or three pennies?—from the top of her dresser. A tube of much-used scarlet lipstick from the locker of a high school friend; a card-sized plastic calendar (an advertisement from a stationer's in town) from Mr. Schwilk's desk; stray nickels and dimes, quarters, fifty-cent pieces. . . . One of her prizes, acquired with great daring and trepidation, was a (fake) ruby ring belonging to someone's older sister, which Marya had found beneath carelessly folded clothing in a stall in the women's bathroom at Wolf's Head Lake, but had never dared to wear. The thefts were always impulsive and rather pointless. Marya saw her trembling hand dart out, saw the fingers close . . . and in that instant, wasn't the object hers?

There was a moment when an item passed over from belonging to another person to belonging to Marya; that moment interested her greatly. She felt excitement, near-panic, elation. A sense of having triumphed, in however petty a fashion.

(It had come to seem to her in retrospect that she'd stolen Father Shearing's wristwatch. She seemed to recall . . . unless it was a particularly vivid dream . . . she seemed to recall slipping the watch from his table into her bookbag, that old worn soiled bookbag she'd had for years. Father Shearing was asleep in his cranked-up bed. Though perhaps not . . . perhaps he was watching her all along through his eyelashes. Marya? Dear Marya? A common thief?)

Since coming to Port Oriskany she felt the impulse more frequently but she knew enough to resist. It was a childish habit, she thought, disgusted,—it wasn't even genuine theft, intelligently committed. Presumably she wanted to transgress; even to be punished; she *wanted* to be sinful.

Odd, Marya thought uneasily, that no one has ever caught me. When I haven't seemed to care. When I haven't seemed to have *tried*.

It happened that, in her classes, she found herself gazing at certain individuals, and at their belongings, day after day, week after week. What began as simple curiosity gradually shaded into intense interest. She might find herself, for instance, staring at a boy's spiral notebook in a lecture class . . . plotting a way to getting it for herself, leafing through it, seeing what he'd written. (For this boy, like Marya, was a daydreamer; an elaborate and tireless doodler, not without talent.) There was an antique opal ring belonging to a girl in her English literature class: the girl herself had waist-long brown hair, straight and coarse, and Marya couldn't judge whether she was striking, and very good-looking, or really quite repulsive. (Marya's own hair was growing long again—long and wavy and unruly—but it would never be that length again; the ends simply broke off.) Many of the students at Port Oriskany were from well-to-do families, evidently, judging from their clothes and belongings: Marya's eye moved upon handtooled leather bags, and boots, and wristwatches, and earrings, and coats (suede, leather, fur-trimmed, camel's hair) half in scorn and half in envy. She did not want to steal these items, she did not *want* these items, yet, still, her gaze drifted onto them time and again, helplessly. . . .

She studied faces too, when she could. Profiles. That blonde girl in her political science class, for instance: smooth clear creamy skin, china-blue mocking eyes, a flawless nose, mouth: long hair falling over one shoulder. Knee-high leather boots, kid gloves, a handsome camel's hair coat, a blue cashmere muffler that hadn't been cleaned in some time. An engagement ring with a large square-cut diamond. . . . But it was the girl's other pieces of jewelry that drew Marya's interest. Sometimes she wore a big silver ring with a turquoise stone; and a long sporty necklace made of copper coins; and a succession of earrings in her pierced ears—gold loops that swung and caught the light, tiny iridescent-black stones, ceramic disks in which gold-burnished reds and blues flashed. Marya stared and stared, her heart quickening with—was it envy?—but envy of precisely what? It could not have been these expensive trinkets she coveted.

Imogene Skillman was a theater arts major; she belonged to one of the sororities on Masefield Avenue; Marya had even been able to discover that she was from Laurel Park, Long Island, and that she was engaged to a law student who had graduated from Port Oriskany several years ago. After she became acquainted with Imogene she would have been deeply humiliated if Imogene had known how much Marya knew of her beforehand. Not only her background, and her interest in acting, but that big leather bag, those boots, the silver ring, the ceramic earrings. . . .

It might have been Imogene's presence in class that inspired Marya to speak as she frequently did; answering their professor's questions in such detail, in such self-consciously structured sentences. (Marya thought of herself as shy, but, as it turned out, she could often speak at length if required—she became, suddenly, articulate and emphatic—even somewhat combative. The tenor of her voice caused people to turn around in their seats and often surprised, when it did not disconcert, her professors.) It wasn't that she spoke her mind—she rarely offered opinions—it seemed to her necessary to consider as many sides of an issue as possible, as many relevant points, presenting her case slowly and clearly and forcefully, showing no sign of the nervousness she felt. It was not simply that most of her professors solicited serious discussion—gave evidence, in fact, of being greatly dependent upon it to fill up fifty minutes of class time—or even that (so Marya reasoned, calculated) her precious grade might depend upon such contributions; she really became caught up in the subjects themselves. Conflicting theories of representative democracy, property rights, civil disobedience . . . the ethics of propaganda . . . revolution and counterrevolution . . . whether in fact terrorism might ever be justified. . . . Even when it seemed, as it sometimes did, that Marya's concern for these issues went beyond that of the professor's, she made her point; she felt a grudging approval throughout the room; and Imogene Skillman turned languidly in her seat to stare at her.

One afternoon Imogene left behind a little handwoven purse that must have slipped out of her leather bag. Marya snatched it up as if it were a prize. She followed after Imogene—followed her out of the building—that tall blonde girl in the camel's hair coat—striding along, laughing, in a high-spirited conversation with her friends. Marya approached her and handed her the purse, saying only, "You dropped this," in a neutral voice; she turned away without waiting for Imogene's startled thanks.

Afterward she felt both elated and unaccountably fatigued. As if she had experienced some powerful drain on her energy. As if, having returned Imogene's little purse to her, she now regretted having done so; and wondered if she had been a fool.

Marya's friendship with Imogene Skillman began, as it was to end, with a puzzling abruptness.

One day Imogene simply appeared beside Marya on one of the campus paths, asking if she was walking this way?—and falling comfortably in step with her. It was done as easily and as effortlessly as if they were old friends; as if Imogene had been reading Marya's most secret thoughts.

She began by flattering her, telling her she said "interesting" things in class; that she seemed to be the only person their professor really listened to. Then, almost coyly: "I should confess that it's your voice that really intrigues me. What if—so I ask myself, I'm always trying things on other people!— what if *she* was playing Hedda—Hedda Gabler—with that remarkable voice—and not mine—*mine* is so reedy—I've heard myself on tape and can barely stop from gagging. And there's something about your manner too— also your chin—when you speak—it looks as if you're gritting your teeth but you *are* making yourself perfectly audible, don't be offended! The thing is, I'm doing Hedda myself, I can't help but be jealous of how you might do her in my place though it's all *my* imagination of course. Are you free for lunch? No? Yes? We could have it at my sorority—no, better out—it's not so claustrophobic, out. We'll have to hurry, though, Marya, is it?—I have a class at one I don't *dare* cut again."

It gave Marya a feeling of distinct uneasiness, afterward, to think that Imogene had pursued *her*. Or, rather, that Imogene must have imagined herself the pursuer; and kept up for weeks the more active, the more charitably outgoing and inquisitive, of their two roles. (During their first conversation, for instance, Marya found herself stammering and blushing as she tried to answer Imogene's questions—Where are you from, what are you studying, where do you live on campus, what do you *think* of this place, isn't it disappointing?—put in so candid and ingenuous a manner, with that wide blue-eyed stare, Marya felt compelled to reply. She also felt vaguely criminal, guilty—as if she'd somehow drawn Imogene to her by the very intensity of her own interest, without Imogene's conscious knowledge.)

If Imogene reached out in friendship, at the beginning, Marya naturally drew back. She shared the Knauers' peasant shrewdness, or was it mean-spiritedness: what does this person want from *me*, why on earth would this person seek out *me*? It was mysterious, puzzling, disconcerting. Imogene was so pretty, so popular and self-assured, a dominant campus personality; Marya had only a scattering of friends—friendly acquaintances, really. She hadn't, as she rather coolly explained to Imogene, time for "wasting" on people.

She also disapproved of Imogene's public manner, her air of flippancy, carelessness. In fact Imogene was quite intelligent—her swiftness of thought, her skill at repartee, made that clear—but she played at seeming otherwise, to Marya's surprise and annoyance. Imogene was always *Imogene*, always *on*. She was a master of sudden dramatic reversals: sunny warmth that shaded into chilling mockery; low-voiced serious conversations, on religion, perhaps (Imogene was an agnostic who feared, she said, lapsing into Anglicanism—it ran in her family), that deteriorated into wisecracks and bawdy jokes simply because one of her theatre friends appeared. While Marya was too reserved to ask Imogene about herself, Imogene was pitiless in her interrogation of Marya, once the formality of their first meeting was out of the way. Has your family *always* lived in that part of the state, do you mean your father was really a *miner*, how old were you when he died, how old were you when your mother died, do you keep in touch with your high school friends, are you happy here, are you in love with anyone, have you ever been in love, are you a virgin, do you have any plans for this summer, what will you do after graduation?—what do you think your *life* will be? Marya was dazed, disoriented. She answered as succinctly and curtly as she dared, never really telling the truth, yet not precisely lying; she had the idea that Imogene could detect a lie; she'd heard her challenge others when she doubted the sincerity of what they said. Half-truths went down very well, however. Half-truths, Marya had begun to think, were so much more reasonable—so much more convincing—than whole truths.

For surely brazen golden-haired Imogene Skillman didn't really want to know the truth about Marya's family—her father's death (of a heart attack, aged thirty-nine, wasn't that a possibility?—having had rheumatic fever, let's say, as a boy); her mother's disappearance that was, at least poetically, a kind of death too (automobile accident, Marya ten at the time, no one to blame). Marya was flattered, as who would not be, by Imogene's intense *interest* and *sympathy* ("You seem to have had such a hard life. . . .") but she was shrewd enough to know she must not push her friend's generosity of spirit too far: it was one thing to be moved, another thing to be repulsed.

So she was sparing with the truth. A little truth goes a long way, she thought, not knowing if the remark was an old folk saying, or something she'd coined herself.

She told herself that she resented Imogene's manner, her assumption of an easygoing informality that was all one-sided, or nearly; at the same time it couldn't be denied that Marya Knauer visibly brightened in Imogene Skillman's presence. She saw with satisfaction how Imogene's friends—meeting them in the student union, in the pub, in the restaurants and coffee shops along Fairfield Street—watched them with curiosity, and must have wondered who Imogene's new friend was.

Marya Knauer: but who is *she*?—where did Imogene pick up *her*?

Marya smiled cynically to herself, thinking that she understood at last the gratification a man must feel, in public, in the company of a beautiful woman. Better, really, than being the beautiful woman yourself.

They would have quarreled, everything would have gone abrasive and sour immediately, if Marya hadn't chosen (consciously, deliberately) to admire Imogene's boldness, rather than to be insulted by it. (*Are you happy, are you lonely, have you ever been in love, are you a virgin?*—no one had ever dared ask Marya such questions. The Knauers were reticent, prudish, about such things as personal feelings: Wilma might haul off and slap her, and call her a little shit, but she'd have been convulsed with embarrassment to ask Marya if she was happy or unhappy, if she loved anyone, if, maybe, she knew how Wilma loved *her*. Just as Lee and Everard might quarrel, and Lee might dare to tell his brawny hot-tempered father to go to hell, but he'd never have asked him—he'd never have even imagined asking him—how much money he made in a year, how much he had in the bank, what the property was worth, did he have a will, did he guess that, well, Lee sort of looked up to *him*, loved *him*, despite all these fights?)

Marya speculated that she'd come a great distance from Innisfail and the Canal Road—light-years, really, not two hundred miles—and she had to be careful, cautious, about speaking in the local idiom.

Imogene was nearly as tall as Marya, and her gold-gleaming hair and ebullient manner made her seem taller. Beside her, Marya knew herself shabby, undramatic, unattractive; it was not *her* prerogative to take offense, to recoil from her friend's extreme interest. After all—were so very many people interested in her, here in Port Oriskany? Did anyone really care if she lied, or told the truth, or invented ingenious half-truths . . . ? In any case, despite Imogene's high spirits, there was usually something harried about her. She hadn't studied enough for an exam, play rehearsals were going badly, she'd had an upsetting telephone call from home the night before, what in Christ's name was she to *do*? . . . Marya noted that beautiful white-toothed smile marred by tiny tics of vexation. Imogene was always turning the diamond ring round and round her finger, impatiently; she fussed with her earrings and hair; she was always late, always running—her coat unbuttoned and flapping about her, her tread heavy. Her eyes sometimes filled with tears that were, or were not, genuine.

Even her agitation, Marya saw, was enviable. There are certain modes of unhappiness with far more style than happiness.

Imogene insisted that Marya accompany her to a coffee shop on Fairfield—pretentiously called a coffee "house"—where all her friends gathered. These were her *real* friends, apart from her sorority sisters and her fraternity admirers. Marya steeled herself against their critical amused eyes; she didn't want to be one of their subjects for mimicry. (They did devastating imitations of their professors and even of one another—Marya had to admit, laughing, that they were really quite good. If only she'd known such people back in Innisfail!—in high school!—she might have been less singled out for disapproval; she might have been less lonely.)

Marya made certain that she gave her opinions in a quick flat unhesitating voice, since opinions tenuously offered were usually rejected. If she chose to talk with these people at all she made sure that she talked fast, so that she wouldn't be interrupted. (They were always interrupting one another, Imogene included.) With her excellent memory Marya could, if required, quote passages from the most difficult texts; her vocabulary blossomed wonderfully in the presence of a critical, slightly hostile audience she knew she *must* impress. (For Imogene prided herself on Marya Knauer's brilliance, Marya Knauer's knowledge and wit. Yes, that's right, she would murmur, laughing, nudging Marya in the ribs, go on, go *on*, you're absolutely right—you've got them now!) And Marya smoked cigarettes with the others, and drank endless cups of bitter black coffee, and flushed with pleasure when things went well . . . though she was wasting a great deal of time these days, wasn't she? ... and wasn't time the precious element that would carry her along to her salvation?

The coffee shop was several blocks from the University's great stone archway, a tunnellike place devoid of obvious charm, where tables were crowded together and framed photographs of old, vanished athletes lined the walls. Everyone—Imogene's "everyone"—drifted there to escape from their living residences, and to sit for hours, talking loudly and importantly, about Strindberg, or Whitman, or Yeats, or the surrealists, or Prufrock, or Artaud, or *Ulysses*, or the Grand Inquisitor; or campus politics (who was in, who was out); or the theatre department (comprised half of geniuses and saints, half of losers). Marya soon saw that several of the boys were in love with Imogene, however roughly they sometimes treated her. She didn't care to learn their names but of course she did anyway—Scott, and Andy, and Matthew (who took a nettlesome sort of dislike to Marya); there was a dark ferret-faced mathematics student named Brian whose manner was broadly theatrical and whose eyeglasses flashed with witty malice. The other girls in the group were attractive enough, in fact quite striking, but they were no match for Imogene when she was most herself.

Of course the love, even the puppyish affection, went unrequited. Imogene was engaged—the diamond ring was always in sight, glittering and winking; Imogene occasionally made reference to someone named Richard, whose opinion she seemed to value highly. (What is Imogene's fiancé like, Marya asked one of the girls, and was told he was "quiet"—"watchful"— that Imogene behaved a little differently around him; she was quieter herself.)

One wintry day when Marya should have been elsewhere she sat with Imogene's friends in a booth at the smoky rear of the coffee house, half-listening to their animated talk, wondering why Imogene cared so much for them. Her mind drifted loose; she found herself examining one of the photographs on the walls close by. It was sepia-tinted, and very old: the 1899 University rowing team. Beside it was a photograph of the 1902 football team. How young those smiling athletes must have felt, as the century turned, Marya thought. It must have seemed to them ... *theirs.*

She was too lazy to excuse herself and leave. She was too jealous of Imogene. No, it was simply that her head ached; she hadn't slept well the night before and wouldn't sleep tonight. . . . Another rowing team. Hopeful young men, standing so straight and tall; their costumes slightly comical; their haircuts bizarre. An air of team spirit, hearty optimism, doom. Marya swallowed hard, feeling suddenly strange. She really should leave ... She really shouldn't be here. . . .

Time had been a nourishing stream, a veritable sea, for those young men. Like fish they'd swum in it without questioning it—without knowing it was the element that sustained them and gave them life. And then it had unaccountably withdrawn and left them exposed ... Forever youthful in those old photographs, in their outdated costumes; long since aged, dead, disposed of.

Marya thought in a panic that she must leave; she must return to her room and lock the door.

But when she rose Imogene lay a hand on her arm and asked irritably what was wrong, why was she always jumping up and down: couldn't she for Christ's sake sit *still*?

The vehemence of Imogene's response struck them all, it was in such disproportion to Marya's behavior. Marya herself was too rushed, too frightened, to take offense. She murmured, "Good-bye, Imogene," without looking at her; and escaped.

It was that night, not long before curfew, that Imogene dropped by for the first time at Maynard House. She rapped on Marya's door, poked her head in, seemed to fill the doorway, chattering brightly as if nothing were wrong; as if they'd parted amiably. Of course she *was* rather rude about the room—Marya hadn't realized it must have been a maid's room, in the house's earliest incarnation—but her rudeness as always passed by rather casually, in a sort of golden blue. She looked so pretty, flushed with cold, her eyes inordinately damp. . . .

Tell me about these drawings, she said,—I didn't know you were an artist. These are *good*.

But Marya wasn't in a mood for idle conversation. She said indifferently that she *wasn't* an artist; she was a student.

But Imogene insisted she was an artist. Because the sketches were so rough, unfinished, yet they caught the eye, there was something unnerving about them. "Do you see yourself like this, though?—Marya?" Imogene asked almost wistfully. "So stern and ugly?—it *isn't* you, is it?"

"It isn't anyone," Marya said. "It's a few charcoal strokes on old paper."

She was highly excited that Imogene Skillman had come to her room: had anyone on the floor noticed?—had the girl downstairs at the desk, on telephone duty, noticed? At the same time she wished her gone, it was an intrusion into her privacy, insufferable. She had never invited Imogene to visit her—she never would.

"So this is where you live," Imogene said, drawing a deep breath. Her eyes darted mercilessly about; she would miss nothing, forget nothing. "You're alone and you don't mind, that's *just* like you. You have a whole other life, a sort of secret life, don't you," she said, with a queer pouting downward turn of her lips.

Friendship, Marya speculated in her journal,—the most enigmatic of all relationships.

In a sense it flourished unbidden; in another, it had to be cultivated, nurtured, sometimes even forced into existence. Though she was tirelessly active in most aspects of her life she'd always been quite passive when it came to friendship. She hadn't time, she told herself; she hadn't energy for something so . . . ephemeral.

Nothing was worthwhile, really worthwhile, except studying; getting high grades; and her own reading, her own work. Sometimes Marya found herself idly contemplating a young man—in one of her classes, in the library; sometimes, like most of her female classmates, she contemplated one or another of her male professors. But she didn't want a lover, not even a romance. To cultivate romance, Marya thought, you had to give over a great deal of time for daydreaming: she hadn't time to waste on *that*.

Since the first month of her freshman year Marya had acquired a reputation for being brilliant—the word wasn't hers but Imogene's: Do you know everyone thinks you're brilliant, everyone is afraid of you?—and it struck Marya as felicitous, a sort of glass barrier that would keep other people at a distance. . . . And then again she sometimes looked up from her reading, and noted that hours had passed; where was she and what was she doing to herself? (Had someone called her? Whispered her name? Marya, Marya. . . . You little savage, Marya. . . .) Suddenly she ached with the desire to see Wilma, and Everard; and her brothers; even Lee. She felt as if she must leave this airless little cubbyhole of a room—take a Greyhound bus to Innisfail—see that house on the Canal Road—sit at the kitchen table with the others—tell them she loved them, she loved them and couldn't help herself: what was happening?

Great handfuls of her life were being stolen from her and she would never be able to retrieve them.

To counteract Imogene Skillman's importance in her life, Marya made it a point to be friendly—if not, precisely, to *become friends*—with a number of Maynard House girls. She frequently ate meals with them in the dining hall a few blocks away, though she was inclined (yes, it was rude) to bring along a book or two just in case. And if the conversation went nowhere Marya would murmur, Do you mind?—I have so much reading to do.

Of course they didn't mind. Catherine or Phyllis or Sally or Diane. They too were scholarship students; they too were frightened, driven.

(Though Marya knew they discussed her behind her back. She was the only girl in the house with a straight-A average and they were waiting . . . were they perhaps hoping? . . . for her to slip down a notch or two. They were afraid of her sarcasm, her razorish wit. Then again, wasn't she sometimes very funny?—If you liked that sort of humor. As for the sorority girl Imogene Skillman: what did Marya see in *her*?—what did *she* see in Marya? It was also likely, wasn't it, that Marya was the house thief? For the thief still walked off with things sporadically. These were mean, pointless thefts—a letter from a mailbox, another textbook, a single angora glove, an inexpensive locket on a tarnished silver chain. Pack-rat sort of thievery, unworthy, in fact, of any girl who roomed in Maynard.)

When Marya told Imogene about the thief and the money she'd lost,

Imogene said indifferently that there was a great deal of stealing on campus, and worse things too (this, with a sly twist of her lips), but no one wanted to talk about it; the student newspaper (the editors were all friends of hers, she knew such things) was forever being censored. For instance, last year a girl committed suicide by slashing her wrists in one of the off-campus senior houses and the paper wasn't allowed to publish the news, not even to *hint* at it, and the local newspaper didn't run anything either, it was all a sort of totalitarian kindergarten state, the university. As for theft. "*I've* never stolen anything in my life," Imogene said, smiling, brooding, "because why would I want anything that somebody else has already had?—something second-hand, used?"

Your friend Imogene, people began to say.

Your friend Imogene: she dropped by at noon, left his note for you.

Marya's pulses rang with pleasure, simple gratitude. She was flattered but—well, rather doubtful. Did she even *like* Imogene? Were they really friends? In a sense she liked one or two of the girls in Maynard better than she liked Imogene. Phyllis, for instance, a mathematics major, very sharp, very bright, though almost painfully shy; and a chunky farm girl named Diane from a tiny settlement north of Shaheen Falls, precociously matronly, with thick glasses and a heavy tread on the stairs and a perpetual odor of unwashed flesh, ill-laundered clothes. . . . But Diane was bright, very bright; Marya thought privately that here was her real competition at Port Oriskany, encased in baby fat, blinking through those thick lenses. (The residence buzzed with the rumor, however, that Diane was doing mysteriously poorly in her courses, had she a secret grief?—an unstated terror?) Marya certainly liked Phyllis and Diane, she recognized them as superior individuals, really much nicer, much kinder, than Imogene. Yet she had to admit it would not have deeply troubled her if she never saw them again. And the loss of Imogene would have been a powerful blow.

She went twice to see the production of *Hedda Gabler* in which Imogene starred. For she really did star, it was a one-woman show. That hard slightly drawling slightly nasal voice, that mercurial manner (cruel, seductive, mock-sweet, languid, genuinely anguished by turns), certain odd tricks and mannerisms (the way she held her jaw, for instance: had she pilfered that from Marya?)—Imogene was *really* quite good; really a success. And they'd made her up to look even more beautiful on stage than she looked in life: her golden hair in a heavy Victorian twist, her cheeks subtly rouged, her eyes enormous. Only in the tense sparring scene with Judge Brack, when Hedda was forced to confront a personality as strong as her own, did Imogene's acting falter: her voice went strident, her manner became too broadly erotic.

Marya thought, slightly dazed,—Is she really talented? Is there some basis for her reputation, after all?

Backstage, Marya didn't care to compete for Imogene's attention; let the others hug and kiss her and shriek congratulations if they wished. It was all

exaggerated, florid, embarrassing . . . so much emotion, such a *display*. . . .
And Imogene looked wild, frenzied, her elaborate makeup now rather
clownish, seen at close quarters. "Here's Marya," she announced, "—Marya
will tell the truth—here's Marya—shut up, you idiots!—she'll tell the truth—
was I any good, Marya?—*was* I really Hedda?" She pushed past her friends
and gripped Marya's hands, staring at her with great shining painted eyes.
She smelled of greasepaint and powder and perspiration; it seemed to Marya
that Imogene towered over her.

"Of course you were good," Marya said flatly. "You know you were
good."

Imogene gripped her hands tighter, her manner was feverish, outsized.
"What are you saying?—you didn't care for the performance? It wasn't
right? I failed?"

"Don't be ridiculous," Marya said, embarrassed, trying to pull away.
"You don't need me to assess you, in any case. You *know* you were—"

"You didn't like it! Did you!"

"—you were perfect."

"*Perfect!*" Imogene said in hoarse stage voice, "—but that doesn't sound
like one of your words, Marya—you don't *mean* it."

It was some seconds before Marya, her face burning with embarrassment
and resentment, could extricate her hands from Imogene's desperate grip.
No, she couldn't come to the cast party; she had to get back to work. And
yes, yes, for Christ's sake, *yes*—Imogene had been "perfect": or nearly.

Friendship, Marya wrote in her journal, her heart pounding with rage,—
play-acting of an amateur type.

Friendship, she wrote,—a puzzle that demands too much of the imagination.

So she withdrew from Imogene, tried even to stop thinking about her,
looking for her on campus. (That blue muffler, that camel's hair coat. And
she had a new coat too: Icelandic shearling, with a black fur collar.) She
threw herself into her work with more passion than before. Exams were
upon her, papers were due, she felt the challenge with a sort of eager dread,
an actual greed, knowing she could do well even if she didn't work hard; and
she intended to work very, very hard. Even if she got sick, even if her eyes
went bad.

Hour after hour of reading, taking notes, writing, rewriting. In her room,
the lamp burning through the night; in one or another of her secret places in
the library; in a corner of an old brick mansion a quarter-mile away that had
been converted into the music school, where she might read and scribble
notes and daydream, her heartbeat underscored by the muffled sounds of pi-
anos, horns, violins, cellos, flutes, from the rows of practice rooms. The
sounds—the various musics—were all rather harmonious, heard like this, in
secret. Marya thought, closing her eyes: If you could only *be* music.

At the same time she had her job in the library, her ill-paid job, a drain on her time and spirit, a terrible necessity. She explained that she'd lost her entire paycheck—the money had been stolen out of her wallet—she *must* be allowed to work a little longer, to clock a few more hours each week. She intended (so she explained to her supervisor) to make up the loss she'd suffered by disciplining herself severely, spending no extra money if she could avoid it. She *must* be allowed a few hours extra work. . . . (The Parker pen could never be replaced, of course. As for the money: Marya washed her hair now once a week, and reasoned that she did not really need toothpaste, why did anyone *need* toothpaste?—she was sparing with her toiletries in general, and, if she could, used other girls', left in the third floor bathroom. She was always coming upon lost ballpoint pens, lost notebooks, even loose change; she could appropriate—lovely word, "appropriate"—cheap mimeograph paper from a supply room in the library; sometimes she even found half-empty packs of cigarettes—though her newest resolution was to stop smoking, since she resented every penny spent on so foolish a habit. Her puritan spirit blazed; she thought it an emblem of her purity, that the waistbands of her skirts were now too loose, her underwear was a size too large.)

After an evening of working in the library—her pay was approximately $1 an hour—she hurried home to Maynard, exhausted, yet exhilarated, eager to get to her schoolwork. Once she nearly fainted running up the stairs and Diane, who happened to be nearby, insisted that she come into her room for a few minutes. You look terrible, she said in awe—almost as bad as I do. But Marya brushed her aside, Marya hadn't time. She was lightheaded from the stairs, that was all.

One night Imogene telephoned just before the switchboard was to close. What the hell was wrong, Imogene demanded, was Marya angry at her? She hurried out of class before Imogene could say two words to her—she never came down to Fairfield Street any longer—was she secretly in love?—was she working longer hours at the library?—would she like to come to dinner sometime this week, at the sorority?—or next week, before Christmas break?

Yes, thought Marya, bathed in gratitude, in golden splendor, "No," she said aloud, quietly, chastely, "—but thank you very much."

Schopenhauer, Dickens, Marx, Euripides. Oscar Wilde. Henry Adams. Sir Thomas More. Thomas Hobbes. And Shakespeare—of course. She read, she took notes, she daydreamed. It sometimes disturbed her that virtually nothing of what she read had been written by women (except Jane Austen, dear perennial Jane, *so* feminine!) but in her arrogance she told herself *she* would change all that.

Is this how it begins, she wondered, half-amused. Breaking down. Cracking up.

Why breaking *down* . . . but cracking *up* . . . ?

Her long periods of intense concentration began to be punctuated by bouts of directionless daydreaming, sudden explosions of *feeling*. At such times Shakespeare was too dangerous to be read closely—Hamlet whispered truths too cruel to be borne, every word in *Lear* hooked in flesh and could not be dislodged. As for Wilde, Hobbes, Schopenhauer . . . even cynicism, Marya saw, can't save you.

At such times she went for walks along Masefield Avenue, past the enormous sorority and fraternity houses. They too were converted mansions but had retained much of their original glamor and stateliness. Imogene's, for instance, boasted pretentious white columns, four of them, in mock–Southern Colonial style. The cryptic Greek letters on the portico struck an especially garish and irrelevant note. What did such symbols mean, what did it mean (so Marya wondered, not quite bitterly) to be *clubbable*—? In the winter twilight, in the cold, these outsized houses appeared especially warm and secretive; every window of their several storeys blazed. Marya thought, Why don't I feel anything, can't I even feel envy . . . ? But the sororities were crudely discriminatory (one was exclusively for Catholic girls, another exclusively for Jewish girls, the sixteen others had quotas for Catholics and blackballed all Jews who dared cross their threshold: the procedure was that blunt, that childish). Dues and fees were absurdly high, beyond the inflated price for room and board; the meetings involved pseudoreligious "Greek" rituals (handshakes, secret passwords, special prayers). Imogene complained constantly, was always cutting activities and being fined ($10 fine for missing a singing rehearsal!—the very thought made Marya shiver in disbelief), always mocking the alumns, those well-to-do matrons with too much time on their hands. Such assholes, all of them, Imogene said loftily, such *pretentious* assholes. It was part of Imogene's charm that she could be both contemptuous of pretension and marvelously—shamelessly—pretentious herself.

Time is the element in which we exist, Marya noted solemnly in her journal,—We are either borne along by it, or drowned in it.

It occurred to her with a chilling certitude that *every moment not consciously devoted to her work* was an error, a blunder. As if you can kill time, Thoreau said, without injuring Eternity.

Lying drowsily and luxuriously in bed after she'd wakened . . . conversations with most people, or, indeed *all* people . . . spending too long in the shower, or cleaning her room, or staring out the window, or eating three meals a day (unless of course she brought along a book to read) . . . daydreaming and brooding about Innisfail, or the Canal Road, or that wretched little tarpaper-roofed shanty near Shaheen Falls that had been her parents' house . . . crying over the past (though in fact she rarely cried these days) as if the past were somehow present. In high school she had been quite an athlete, especially at basketball and field hockey; in college she hadn't time, hadn't the slightest interest. It pleased her that she always received grades of A but at the same time she wondered,—Are these *really* significant grades, do I *really* know anything?—or is Port Oriskany one of the backwaters of the world, where nothing, even "excellence," greatly matters? She needed high grades in order to get into graduate school, however; beyond that she didn't allow herself to think. Though perhaps she wouldn't go to graduate school at all . . . perhaps she would try to write . . . her great problem being not that she hadn't anything to write about but that she had too much.

Unwisely, once, she confided in Imogene that she halfway feared to write anything that wasn't academic or scholarly or firmly rooted in the real world: once she began she wouldn't be able to stop: she was afraid of sinking too deep into her own head, cracking up, becoming lost.

Imogene said it once that Marya was just the type to be excessive, she needed reining in. "I know the symptoms," she said severely. Anyway, what good would academic success—or any kind of success—do her, if she destroyed her health?

"*You're* concerned about my health?" Marya asked incredulously.

"Of course. Yes, I *am*. Why shouldn't I be," Imogene said, "—aren't I a friend of yours?"

Marya stared at her, unable to reply. It struck her as wildly incongruous that Imogene Skillman, with her own penchant for abusing her health (she drank too much at fraternity parties, she stayed up all night doing hectic last-minute work) should be worrying about Marya.

"Aren't I a friend of yours?" Imogene asked less certainly. "Don't I have the right . . . ?"

Marya turned away with an indifferent murmur, perhaps because she was so touched.

"My health isn't of any use to me," she said, "if I don't get anything accomplished. If I fail."

Of course it was possible, Marya saw, to ruin one's health and fail anyway.

Several of her fellow residents in Maynard House were doing poorly in their courses, despite their high intelligence and the goading terror that energized them. One of them was Phyllis, who was failing an advanced calculus class; another, a chronically withdrawn and depressed girl named Mary, a physics major, whose deeply shadowed eyes and pale grainy skin, as well as her very name, struck a superstitious chord of dread in Marya—she avoided her as much as possible, and had the idea that Mary avoided *her*.

The University piously preached an ethic of knowledge for its own sake—knowledge and beauty being identical—the "entire person" was to be educated, not simply the mind; but of course it acted swiftly and pragmatically upon another ethic entirely. Performance was all, the grade-point average *was* everything. Marya, no idealist, saw that this was sound and just; but she felt an impatient sort of pity for those who fell by the wayside, or who, like the scholarship girls, in not being *best*, were to be judged *worthless*, and sent back home. (Anything below a B was failing for them.) She wanted only to be best, to be outstanding, to be . . . defined to herself as extraordinary . . . for, apart from being extraordinary, had she any essence at all?

The second semester of her freshman year she had come close to losing her perfect grade-point average. Unwisely, she signed up for a course in religion, having been attracted to the books on the syllabus and the supplementary reading list (the *Upanishads;* the *Bhagavad-Gītā;* the *Bible;* the *Koran; Hymns of the Rigveda;* books on Gnosticism, and Taoism, and medieval Christianity, and the Christian heresies, and animism, magic, witchcraft, Renaissance ideas of Platonic love). It was all very promising, very heady stuff; quite the antidote to the catechismal Catholicism in which Marya no longer believed, and for which she had increasingly less tolerance. The professor, however, turned out to be an ebullient balding popinjay who lectured from old notes in a florid and self-dramatizing style, presenting ideas in a melange clearly thrown together from others' books and articles. He wanted nothing more than these ideas (which were fairly simple, not at all metaphysical or troubling) given back to him on papers and examinations; and he did not encourage questions from the class. Marya would surely have done well—she transcribed notes faultlessly, even when contemptuous of their content—but she could not resist sitting in stony silence and refusing to laugh when the professor embarked upon one or another of his jocular anecdotes. It was a classroom mannerism of his, almost a sort of tic, that each time he alluded to something female he lowered his voice and added, as if off the cuff, a wry observation, meant not so much to be insulting as to be mildly teasing. He was a popular lecturer, well-liked by most, not taken seriously by the better students; even the girls laughed at his jokes, being grateful, as students are, for something—anything—to laugh at. Marya alone sat with her arms folded, her brow furrowed, staring. It was not until some years later that she realized, uncomfortably, how she must have appeared to that silly perspiring man—a sort of gorgon in the midst of his amiable little sea of admirers.

So it happened that, though Marya's grades for the course were all A's, the grade posted for her final examination was C; and the final grade for the course—a humiliating B+.

Marya was stunned, Marya was sickened—she would have had to reach back to her childhood—or to the night of that going-away party—for an episode of equal mortification. That it was petty made it all the more mortifying.

I can forget this insult and forget him, Marya instructed herself,—or I can go to him and protest. To forget it seemed in a way noble, even Christian; to go the man's office and humble herself in trying to get the grade raised (for she knew very well she hadn't written a C exam) somehow childish, degrading.

Of course she ran up to his office, made an appointment to see him; and, after a few minutes' clucking and fretting (he pretended she had failed to answer the last question, she hadn't handed in both examination booklets, but there the second booklet was, at the bottom of a heap of papers—ah, what a surprise!), he consented to raise the grade to A. And smiled roguishly at her, as if she had been caught out in mischief, or some sort of deception; for which he was forgiving her. "You seem like a rather grim young woman," he said, "you never smile—you look so *preoccupied*." Marya stared at his swinging foot. He was a satyrish middle-aged man, red-brown tufts of hair in his ears, a paunch straining against his shirt front, a strangely vulnerable smile; a totally mediocre personality in every way—vain, uncertain, vindictive—yet Marya could see why others liked him; he was predictable, safe, probably decent enough. But she hated him. She simply wished him dead.

He continued as if not wanting to release her, waiting for her smile of blushing gratitude and her meek *thank you*—which assuredly was not going to come; he said again, teasing, "Are you *always* such an ungiving young woman, Miss Knauer?"—and Marya swallowed hard, and fixed her dark loathing stare on him, and said: "My mother is sick. She's been sick all semester. I know I shouldn't think about it so much . . . I shouldn't depress other people . . . but sometimes I can't help it. She isn't expected to live much longer, the cancer has metastasized to the brain. . . . I'm sorry if I offended you."

He stared at her; then began to stammer his apologies, rising from his desk, flushing deeply—the very image of chagrin and repentance. In an instant the entire atmosphere between them changed. He was sorry, he murmured, so very sorry . . . of course he couldn't have known. . . .

A minute later Marya was striding down the corridor, her pulses beating hot, in triumph. In her coat pocket was the black fountain pen she had lifted from the man's cluttered desk.

An expensive pen, as it turned out. A Parker, with a squarish blunt nub, and the engraved initials E. W. S.

Marya used the pen to take notes in her journal, signing her name repeatedly, hypnotically: *Marya, Marya Knauer, Marya Marya Marya Marya Knauer*, a name that eventually seemed to have been signed by someone else, a stranger.

The shame of having humbled herself before the ignorant man had been erased by the shame—what should have been shame—of theft.

So Marya speculated, thinking of that curious episode in her life. Eventually the pen ran out of ink and she didn't indulge herself in buying more—it was so old-fashioned a practice, a luxury she couldn't afford.

Phyllis began staying out late, violating curfew, returning to the residence drunk, disheveled, tearful, angry—she couldn't stand the four walls of her room any longer, she told Marya; she couldn't stand shutting the door upon herself.

One night she didn't return at all. It was said afterward that she had been picked up by Port Oriskany police, wandering downtown, miles away, dazed and only partly clothed in the bitter cold—the temperature had gone as low as −5°F. She was taken at once to the emergency room of the city hospital; her parents, who lived upstate, were called; they came immediately the next morning to take her back home. No one at Maynard House was ever to see her again.

All the girls in the residence talked of Phyllis, somewhat dazed themselves, frightened. How quickly it had happened—how quickly Phyllis had disappeared. Marya was plied with questions about Phyllis (how many subjects she was failing, who were the boys she'd gone out with) but Marya didn't know; Marya grew vague, sullen.

And then the waters close over your head.—This phrase ran through Marya's mind repeatedly.

They talked about Phyllis for two or three days, then forgot her.

The following Saturday, however, Phyllis's mother and older sister arrived to pack up her things, clean out her room, fill out a half-dozen university forms. The resident advisor accompanied them; they looked confused, nervous, rather lost. Both women had Phyllis's pale blond limp hair, her rather small, narrow face. How is Phyllis, some of the girls asked, smiling, cautious, and Mrs. Myer said without looking at anyone, Oh Phyllis is fine, resting and eating and sleeping right again, sleeping good hours, she said, half-reproachfully, as if sleeping right hadn't been possible in Maynard House; and they were all to blame. Marya asked whether she might be returning second semester. No, not that soon, Mrs. Myer said quickly. She and the silent older sister were emptying drawers, packing suitcases briskly. Marya helped with Phyllis's books and papers, which lay in an untidy heap on her desk and on the floor surrounding the desk. There were dust balls everywhere. A great cobweb in which the desiccated corpses of insects hung, including that of the spider itself. Stiffened crumpled Kleenex wadded into balls, everywhere underfoot. An odor of grime and despair. . . . Marya discovered a calculus bluebook slashed heavily in red with a grade of D; a five-page paper on a subject that made no sense to her—Ring theory?—with a blunt red grade of F. It seemed to Marya that Phyllis was far more real now, more present, than she had been in the past . . . even when she'd tried to comfort Marya by taking her in her arms.

Marya supposed she had been Phyllis's closest friend at Port Oriskany. Yet Phyllis's mother and sister hadn't known her name, had no message for her . . . clearly Phyllis had never mentioned her to them at all. It was disappointing, sobering.

And the waters close over your head, Marya thought.

Then something remarkable happened: Marya rose from Phyllis's closet, a pile of books in her arms, her hair in her face, when she happened to see Mrs. Myer dumping loose items out of a drawer into a suitcase: a comb, ballpoint pens, coins, loose pieces of jewelry,—and her black fountain pen. *The* pen, unmistakable.

My God, Marya whispered.

No one heard. Marya stood rooted to the spot, staring, watching as her prize disappeared into Phyllis's suitcase, hidden now by a miscellany of socks and underwear. *The* pen—the emblem of her humiliation and triumph—disappearing forever.

It wasn't until months later that someone in Maynard made the observation that the thefts seemed to have stopped.... Since Phyllis moved out.... And the rest of the girls (they were at breakfast, eight or ten of them at a table) took it up, amazed, reluctant, wondering. Was it possible ... *Phyllis ...* ?

Marya said quietly that they shouldn't say such things since it couldn't be proved; that constituted slander.

Wednesday dinner, a "formal" dinner, in Imogene's sorority house, and Marya is seated beside Imogene, self-conscious, unnaturally shy, eating her food without tasting it. She *can* appreciate the thick slabs of roast beef, the small perfectly cooked parsley potatoes, the handsome gilt-edged china, the white linen tablecloth ("Oh it's Portuguese—from Portugal"), the crystal water goblets, the numerous tall candles, the silvery-green silk wallpaper, the house mother's poised social chatter at the head table ... and the girls' stylized animation, their collective stylized beauty. For they *are* beautiful, without exception, as unlike the girls of Maynard House as one species is unlike another.

Imogene Skillman, in this dazzling context, isn't Marya's friend; she is clearly a sorority girl; even wearing her pin with its tiny diamonds and rubies just above her left breast. Her high delicate laughter echoes that of the others', . . . she isn't going to laugh coarsely here, or say anything witty and obscene ... she can be a little mischievous, just a little cutting, at best. Marya notes how refined her table manners have become for the occasion; how practiced she is at passing things about, summoning one of the houseboys for assistance without quite looking at him. (The houseboy in his white uniform!—one of a subdued and faintly embarrassed little squadron of four or five boys, he turns out to be an acquaintance of Marya's from her Shakespeare class, who resolutely avoids her eye throughout the prolonged meal.)

Marya makes little effort to take part in the table's conversation, which swings from campus topics to vacation plans—Miami Beach, Sarasota, Bermuda, the Barbados, Trinidad, Switzerland ("for skiing"). Where are you going, Imogene asks Marya brightly, and Marya, with a pinched little smile says she will spend a few days at home, then return to school; she has work to do that must be done here. And Imogene's friends gaze upon her with faint neutral smiles. Is this the one Imogene boasted of, who is so intelligent and so well-spoken ... ? So *witty* ... ?

For days Marya has been anticipating this dinner, half in dread and half in simple childish excitement. She feared being ravenous with hunger and eating too much out of anxiety; she feared having no appetite at all. But everything is remote, detached, impersonal. Everything is taking place at a little distance from her. A mistake, my coming here, she thinks, my being invited. But she doesn't feel any great nervousness or discomfort. Like the uniformed houseboys who stand with such unnatural stiffness near the doorway to the kitchen, Marya is simply waiting for the meal to end.

She finds herself thinking of friendship, in the past tense. Phyllis, and Diane, and one or two others at Maynard; and, back in Innisfail, Bonnie Michalak, Erma Dietz. She *might* have been a close friend to any of these girls but of course she wasn't, isn't. As for Imogene—she knows she is disappointing Imogene but she can't seem to force herself to care. She halfway resents Imogene for having invited her—for having made a fool out of *herself*, in bringing Marya Knauer to dinner.

How pretty you look, Imogene said, very nearly puzzled, when Marya arrived at six-thirty,—what have you *done* to yourself?

Marya flushed with annoyance; then laughed; with such exuberance that Imogene laughed with her. For it *was* amusing, wasn't it?—Marya Knauer with her hair attractively up in a sort of French twist; Marya Knauer with her lips reddened, and her eyebrows plucked ("pruned," she might have said), Marya Knauer in a green-striped jersey dress that fitted her almost perfectly. A formal dinner meant high heels and stockings, which Marya detested; but she was wearing them nonetheless. And all for Imogene.

Yet now, seated beside Imogene, she pays very little attention to her friend's chatter; she feels subdued, saddened; thinking instead of old friendships, old half-friendships, that year or so during which she'd imagined herself extraordinary, because it had seemed that Emmett Schroeder loved her. She had not loved him—she wasn't capable, she supposed, of loving anyone—but she had certainly basked in the sunny intensity of *his* love: she'd lapped it up eagerly, thirstily (so she very nearly saw herself, a dog lapping water) as if convinced that it had something to do with her. And now Imogene's friendship, which she knows she cannot keep for very long . . . Imogene who has a reputation for being as recklessly improvident with her female friends as with her male friends. . . . Why make the effort, Marya reasons, when all that matters in life is one's personal accomplishment? Work, success, that numbing grade-point average . . . that promise of a future, any future. . . .

While Imogene and several of the others are discussing (animatedly, severely) a sorority sister not present, Marya studies her face covertly; recalls an odd remark Imogene made some weeks ago. The measure of a person's love for you is the depth of his hurt at your betrayal, *that's* the only way you can know how much, or how little, you matter.

Imogene's face had fairly glowed in excited triumph, as she told Marya this bit of wisdom. Marya thought,—She knows from experience, the bitch. She knows her own value.

Imogene is telling a silly convoluted story about a dear friend of hers (it turns out to be Matthew, devoted Matthew) who "helped" her with her term paper on Chekhov: she'd given him a messy batch of notes, he was kind enough to "arrange" them and "expand upon them" and "shape them into an 'A' paper." He's a saint, Imogene says sighing, laughing,—so sweet and so patient; so pathetic, really. But now Imogene is worried ("terrified") that their professor will call her into his office and interrogate her on her own paper, which she hadn't the time to read in its entirety; it was thirty pages long and heavy with footnotes. The girls assure her that if he marked it "A" it *is* an "A"; he'd never ask to see it again. Yes, says Imogene, opening her eyes wide,—but wait until he reads my final exam, and I say these ridiculous things about Chekhov!

Part of this is play-acting, Marya knows, because Imogene is quite intelligent enough, on the subject of Chekhov or anything else connected with drama; so Marya says, though not loudly enough for the entire table to hear: "That wasn't a very kind thing for *you* to do, was it?—and not very honest either."

Imogene chooses not to hear the tone of Marya's remark; she says gaily: "Oh you mean leading poor Matt on? Making him think—? But otherwise he wouldn't have written so *well*, there wouldn't have been so many impressive *footnotes*."

Marya doesn't reply. Marya draws her thumbnail hard against the linen tablecloth, making a secret indentation.

Imogene says, making a joke of it: "Marya's such a puritan—I know better than to ask help of *her*."

Marya doesn't rise to the bait; the conversation shifts onto other topics; in another fifteen minutes the lengthy dinner is over.

"You aren't going home immediately, are you?" Imogene says, surprised, She is smiling but there are strain lines around her mouth. "Come upstairs to my room for a while. Come on, we haven't had a chance to talk."

"Thank you for everything," says Marya. "But I really have to leave. I'm pressed for time these days. . . ."

"You *are* angry?—about that silly Matthew?" Imogene says.

Marya shrugs her shoulders, turns indifferently away.

"Well—are *you* so honest?" Imogene cries.

Marya gets her coat from the closet, her face burning. (Are *you* so honest! *You!*) Imogene is apologizing, talking of other things, laughing, while Marya thinks calmly that she will never see Imogene Skillman again.

"There's no reason why you shouldn't take this coat, it's a perfectly good coat," Imogene said in her "serious" voice—frank, level, unemphatic. "I don't want it any longer because I have so many coats, I never get to wear it and it *is* perfectly lovely, it shouldn't just hang in the closet. . . . Anyway here it is; I think it would look wonderful on you."

Marya stared at the coat. It was the camel's hair she had long admired. Pleasantly scratchy beneath her fingers, belted in back, with a beautiful silky-beige lining: she estimated it would have cost $250 or more, new. And it was almost new.

(Marya's coat, bought two or three years before in Innisfail, had cost $45 on sale.)

Imogene insisted, and Marya tried on the coat, flicking her hair out from inside the collar, studying herself critically in Imogene's full-length mirror. Imogene was saying, "If you're worrying that people will know it's my coat—it *was* my coat—don't: camel's hair coats all look alike. Except they don't look like wool imitations."

Marya met Imogene's frank blue gaze in the mirror. "What about your parents, your mother?—won't someone wonder where the coat has gone?"

Imogene puckered her forehead quizzically. "What business is it of theirs?" she asked. "It's *my* coat. My things are mine, I do what I want with them."

Marya muttered that she just couldn't *take* the coat, and Imogene scolded her for talking with her jaw clenched, and Marya protested in a louder voice, yet still faintly, weakly. . . . "It's a beautiful coat," she said. She was thinking: It's too good for me, I can't accept and I can't refuse and I hate Imogene for this humiliation.

Imogene brought the episode to an end by saying rather coldly: "You'll hurt my feelings, Knauer, if you refuse it. If you're weighing your pride against mine, don't bother—mine is far, far more of a burden."

"So you are—Marya," Mrs. Skillman said in an ambiguous voice (warm? amused? doubtful?) in the drab front parlor of Maynard House, as Marya approached. She and Mr. Skillman and Imogene were taking Marya out to dinner, downtown at the Statler Chop House, one of the area's legendary good restaurants. "We've heard so much about you from Imogene," Mrs. Skillman said, "I think we were expecting someone more. . . ."

"Oh Mother, what on earth—!" Imogene laughed sharply.

". . . I was going to say *taller*, perhaps *older*," Mrs. Skillman said, clearly annoyed by her daughter's interruption.

Marya shook hands with both the Skillmans and saw to her relief that they appeared to be friendly well-intentioned people, attractive enough, surely, and very well-dressed, but nothing like their striking daughter. *She* might have been their daughter, brunette and subdued. (Except she hadn't dared wear the camel's hair coat, as Imogene had wanted. She was wearing her old plaid wool and her serviceable rubberized boots.)

In their presence Imogene was a subtly different person. Rather more disingenuous, childlike, sweet. Now and then at dinner Marya heard a certain self-mocking tone in her friend's voice ("am I playing this scene correctly?—how is it going down?") but neither of the Skillmans took notice; and perhaps it was Marya's imagination anyway.

Then, near the end of the meal, Imogene got suddenly high on white wine and said of her father's business: "It's a sophisticated form of theft."

She giggled, no one else laughed; Marya kept her expression carefully blank.

". . . I mean it *is*, you know . . . it's indirect. . . . 'Savings and Loans' . . . and half the clients blacks who want their Dee-troit cars financed," Imogene said.

"Imogene, you aren't funny," Mrs. Skillman said.

"She's just teasing," Mr. Skillman said. "My little girl likes to tease."

"I do like to tease, don't I?—Marya knows," Imogene said, nudging her. Then, as if returning to her earlier sobriety, she said: *"I never mean a word of what I say and everybody knows it."*

The subject leapt to Imogene's negligence about writing letters, or even telephoning home. "If we try to call," Mrs. Skillman said, "the line at the residence is busy for hours; and when we finally get through you aren't in; you're *never* in. And you never return our calls. . . ."

Imogene said carelessly that her sorority sisters were bad at taking down messages. Most of them were assholes, actually—

"Imogene!" Mrs. Skillman said.

"Oh Mother you know they *are*," Imogene said in a childlike voice.

After an awkward pause Mr. Skillman asked about Richard: Richard had evidently telephoned *them*, asking if something was wrong with Imogene because he couldn't get through to her either. "Your mother and I were hoping there wasn't some sort of . . . misunderstanding between you."

Imogene murmured that there weren't any misunderstandings at all between them.

"He seemed to think . . . to wonder . . ." Mrs. Skillman said. "That is, as long as we were driving up to visit. . . ."

Imogene finished off her glass of white wine and closed her eyes ecstatically. She said: "I really don't care to discuss my private matters in a restaurant.—Anyway Marya is here: why don't we talk about something lofty and intellectual? *She's* taking a philosophy course—if she can't tell us the meaning of life no one can."

"You and Richard haven't quarreled, have you?" Mrs. Skillman said.

Imogene raised her left hand and showed the diamond ring to her mother, saying, *"Please* don't worry, I haven't given it back, it's safe." To Marya she said lightly: "Mother would be mortified if Dickie demanded it back. It's somebody's old dead socialite *grandmother's.*"

"Imogene," Mr. Skillman said, his voice edged with impatience, "you really shouldn't tease so much. I've just read that teasing is a form of aggression . . . did you know that?"

"Not that I'd give it back if Dickie *did* demand it," Imogene laughed. "It's mine, I've earned it, let him *sue* to get it back—right, Marya?—he's going to be a hotshot lawyer after all. Let him *practice.*"

Everyone, including Marya, laughed as if Imogene had said something unusually witty; and Imogene, in the cool voice she used to summon the houseboys at her sorority, asked a passing waiter for more wine.

Richard.

"Dickie."

Am I jealous of someone called "Dickie," Marya wondered, lying sprawled and slovenly across her bed. She was doing rough, impatient charcoal sketches of imaginary faces—beetle-browed, glowering, defiantly ugly—that inevitably turned out to be forms of her own.

In Imogene's cluttered room on the second floor of the baronial sorority house Marya had come upon, to her astonishment, copies of *Bride* magazine. She leafed through them, jeering, while Imogene hid her face in laughing protestation. Wedding gowns! Satin and pearls! Veils made of antique lace! Orange blossoms! Shoes covered in white silk! And what is this, Marya said, flapping the pages in Imogene's direction,—a wedding-cake bridegroom to go with it all?—standing a little out of the range of the camera's focus, amiable and blurred.

"Ah, but you'll have to be a bridesmaid," Imogene said dryly. "Or a maid of honor."

Imogene showed her snapshots of the legendary Richard, flicking them like playing cards. Marya saw that, yes, Richard was a handsome young man—dark strong features, a slightly heavy chin, intelligent eyes. He was demanding, perhaps; an excellent match for Imogene. But it was difficult, Marya thought, to believe that the person in the snapshots—*this* person, standing with his hands on his hips, his hair lifting in the wind—would be capable of loving Imogene as much as she required being loved.

Imogene threw herself across her bed, lay on her back, let her long hair dangle to the floor. Her belly was stretched flat; her pelvic bones protruded. She smoothed her shirt across her abdomen with long nervous fingers. ". . . The first time I came with him," she said hesitantly, but with a breathy laugh, "it wasn't . . . you know . . . it wasn't with him inside me, the way you're supposed to . . . I was afraid of that then, I thought I might get pregnant. And he was so big, I thought he'd hurt me, they're *very* big compared to . . . compared to us. The first time it worked for me he was, well, you know, kissing me there . . . he'd gotten all crazy and wild and I couldn't stop him, and I never thought I would let anyone do that . . . I'd *heard* about that . . . because . . . oh Marya, am I embarrassing you? . . . because afterward," she said, laughing shrilly, "they only want to kiss you: and it's disgusting."

She rolled over amidst the tumble of things strewn on her bed and hid her face from Marya.

After a long time she said, her breath labored, her face still turned away: "Am I embarrassing you?"

Marya's throat and chest were so constricted, she couldn't reply.

A Marya Knauer anecdote, told by Imogene with peals of cruel ribald laughter. . . .

Imogene insisted that Marya accompany her on a date, yes a "date," an actual "date" (though it was generally thought that Marya shunned men because she imagined they weren't *serious* enough). Her escort was Matthew Fein, of all people—Matthew who had seemed to dislike Marya but who in fact (so Imogene revealed) had simply been afraid of her.

"Afraid of me?—you're being ridiculous," Marya said. She hardly knew whether to be hurt or flattered.

"Of course he's afraid of you, or was," Imogene said. "And my poor sorority sisters!—they told me afterward they'd never seen such eyes as yours—taking them all in and condemning them! *Those assholes!*"

It would be an ordinary evening, Imogene promised, no need to dress up, no *need* for the high-heels-stockings routine, though it was perfectly all right (so Imogene said innocently) if Marya wanted to comb her hair. Imogene's date for the evening was a senior in business administration and advertising whose name Marya never caught, or purposefully declined to hear. They drove out to a suburban mall to see a movie—in fact it was a pretentious French "film"—and then they went to a local Italian restaurant where everyone, excepting of course Marya, drank too much; and then they drove to the water-tower hill where numerous other cars were parked, their headlights off. Marya stiffened. Matthew had not yet touched her but she knew that he would be kissing her in another minute; and she had no idea of how to escape gracefully.

". . . Few minutes?" Imogene murmured from the front seat.

She was sending them away!—Marya saw with disbelief that, by the time she and Matthew climbed out of the car, Imogene and her date were locked in a ravenous embrace. One would have thought the two of them lovers; one would have thought them at least fond of each other. Marya's heart was beating frantically. That bitch! That bitch! Marya worried that she might suffocate—she couldn't seem to catch her breath.

Matthew took her cold unresisting hand. He slipped his arm around her shoulders.

They were meant to stroll for a few minutes along the darkened path, to contemplate, perhaps, the view of Port Oriskany below, all sparkling winking lights. A romantic sight, no doubt. Beautiful in its way. Matthew was saying something rather forced—making a joke of some kind—about the French movie?— about Imogene's reckless behavior?—but Marya interrupted. "Isn't she supposed to be engaged?" she asked. "Yes, I suppose so," Matthew said in resignation, "but she does this all the time. It's just Imogene." "She does this all the *time*?" Marya said, "but why—?" Matthew laughed uncomfortably. He was not quite Marya's height and his dark eyes shied away from hers. "I don't know," he said defensively, "—as I said, it's just Imogene, it's her business. Why shouldn't she do what she wants to do? Don't be angry with *me*."

He was nervous yet keenly excited; Marya sensed his sexual agitation. Behind them, parked along the graveled drive, were lovers' cars, one after another; from this distance, the car in which Imogene and her "date" were pawing at each other was undistinguishable from the others.

"You might not approve," Matthew said, his voice edged now with an air of authority, "—but Imogene is a free soul, she does what she wants, I don't suppose she actually *lies* to her fiancé. He'd have to allow her some freedom, you know, or she'd break off the engagement."

"You know a lot about her," Marya said.

"Imogene is a close friend of mine, we've worked together . . . I was stage manager for *Hedda Gabler*, don't you remember?"

"It's all so . . . trivial," Marya said slowly. "So degrading."

"What do you mean?"

"Oh—this."

"This—?"

Marya indicated the cars parked along the drive. Her expression was contemptuous.

"You take an awfully superior attitude, don't you," Matthew said, with an attempt at jocular irony. He tightened his arm around her shoulders; he drew nearer. Marya could hear his quickened breathing.

Is this idiot really going to kiss me, Marya wondered. Her heart was still beating heavily; she could see Imogene's profile, the cameo-clear outline of her face, illuminated for an instant as the headlights were extinguished. Then she moved into the young man's embrace, she kissed him, slid her arms around his neck. . . .

"Does she make love with them?" Marya asked.

"Them—?"

"Different boys. Men. One week after another."

"I don't know," Matthew said resentfully. "I suppose so—if she wants to."

"I thought *you* were in love with her," Marya said mockingly.

"We're just friends," Matthew said, offended.

"Oh no," said Marya, "—everyone knows you're in *love* with her."

Matthew drew away from Marya and walked beside her without speaking. There was nothing for them to do, suddenly; not a thing left to say. It was still March and quite cold. Their footsteps sounded dully on the crusted snow. Marya thought, The various ways we seek out our humiliations. . . .

After a few minutes Matthew said something conciliatory about the night, the stars, the city lights, "infinity," certain remarks of Pascal's; but Marya made no effort to listen. She kept seeing Imogene kissing that near-stranger, Imogene locking her arms about his neck *as if he mattered. As if they were lovers.*

She was going to observe aloud, cynically, that making love was as good a way as any of passing the time, if you hadn't anything better to do, when Matthew, brave Matthew, turned to her and took hold of her shoulders and tried to kiss her. It was a desperate gesture—his breath smelled of sweet red wine—but Marya would have none of it. She shoved him roughly in the chest.

"Marya, for Christ's sake grow up," Matthew said angrily. "You're a big girl now—"

"Why should you *kiss* me?" Marya said, equally angry, "—when you don't even *like* me? When you know I don't like you in the slightest, when we haven't anything to say to each other, when we're just waiting for the evening to get finished!—in fact we've been made fools of, both of us. And now you want to kiss me," she said, jeering, "—just for something to do."

He began to protest but Marya dismissed him with a derisory wave of her hand. She was going to walk back to the residence, she said; she was through with them all. Especially Imogene.

Matthew followed along behind her for a few minutes, trying to talk her into coming back to the car. It was almost midnight, he said; the campus was two miles away; what if something happened to her. . . . Marya ignored him and walked faster, descending the hill past a slow stream of cars that were ascending it, their headlights blinding her eyes. She lowered her head, tried to hide her face, her hands thrust deep in the pockets of her camel's hair coat. At first she was furious—almost sick with fury—her head rang with accusations against Imogene—but the cold still night air was so invigorating, so wonderfully cleansing, she felt quite good by the time she got to Maynard House, not very long after midnight. She felt *very* good.

Next day, Sunday, Imogene stood at the downstairs desk ringing Marya's buzzer repeatedly, one two three four, one two three four, and then one long rude ring, until Marya appeared at the top of the stairs, her hair in a towel. "Who the hell—?" she called down. She and Imogene stared at each other. Then Imogene said contemptuously, "Here's your purse, you left your purse in the car, Knauer. D'you know, Knauer, your behavior is getting eccentric; it isn't even amusing, just what if something had happened to you last night— walking back here all alone—a college girl, in some of those neighbor- hoods!—don't you think Lyle and Matt and I would feel responsible? But *you*," she said, her voice rising, "—*you* haven't the slightest sense of—of re- sponsibility to other people—"

"Just leave the purse," Marya said, leaning over the banister. "Leave it and go back to screwing what's-his-name—that's *your* responsibility—"

"Go screw yourself!" Imogene shouted. "Go fuck yourself!"

"Go fuck *yourself!*" Marya shouted.

As the stories sifted back to Marya, over a period of a week or ten days, they became increasingly disturbing, ugly.

In one version Marya Knauer had been almost attacked—that is, raped— in a black neighborhood near the foot of Tower Hill; and had run back to her residence hall, hysterical and sobbing. It was an even graver insult that her purse had been taken from her—her purse and all her money.

In another version, Marya was so panicked at being simply touched by her date (she was a virgin, she was frigid, she'd never been kissed before) that she ran from the car, hysterical and panting . . . ran all the way back to campus. The boy was a blind date, someone in drama, or maybe business ad- ministration, it was all a total surprise to him that Marya Knauer was so . . . crazy.

In a third improbable version it was Imogene Skillman's fiancé who of- fered to take Marya back to the residence, because she was so upset—having a breakdown of some kind—and when they were halfway there she threw herself on him in the car *while he was actually driving*. And then, ashamed, she opened the car door and jumped out *while the car was still in motion*.

"It's Imogene," Marya said, licking her numbed lips. "She's making these things up . . . Why is she *doing* this to me . . . !"

There were vague rumors too that Marya had borrowed small sums of money from Imogene. And items of clothing as well—the camel's hair coat, for instance. (Because she hadn't a coat of her own. Because her coat had literally gone to shreds. Because she was so *poor*, a scholarship student from the hills, practically a *hillbilly*. . . .) As far as she was concerned, Imogene was reported saying, Marya Knauer could keep the coat if she was that desperate. Imogene no longer wanted it back.

Marya telephoned Imogene and accused her of telling lies, of telling slanderous tales. "Do you think I don't know who's behind this?" Marya cried. But Imogene hung up at once: Imogene was too wise to reply.

Marya began to see how people watched her . . . smiling covertly as she passed. They were pitying her, yet merciless. They knew. Marya Knauer with all her pretensions, Marya Knauer who had made a fool of herself with another girl's fiancé, Marya Knauer who was cracking up. . . .

In the fluorescent-lit dining hall she sat alone in an alcove, eating quickly, her head bowed; it was too much trouble to remove her plates and glass of water from the tray. Two boys passed near and she heard them laugh softly. . . . *That* the one? There? one of them whispered. She turned back to her book (. . . *the thought of suicide is a strong consolation, one can get through many a bad night with it*) but the print danced crazily in her eyes.

"Do you think I don't know who's behind this,—who's responsible?" Marya asked aloud, in anguish, in the privacy of her room. She tried to lock her door from the inside—as if there were any danger of being interrupted, invaded—but the doors in Maynard, as in university housing generally, did not lock in that direction.

At about this time Marya was notified that a short story she had submitted to a national competition had placed first; and, not long afterward—within a week or ten days, in fact—she learned that another story, sent out blindly and naively to a distinguished literary magazine, was accepted for publication.

She thought of telephoning Wilma and Everard . . . she thought of telephoning Imogene . . . running along the corridors of Maynard House, knocking on doors, sharing her good news. But her elation was tempered almost at once by a kind of sickened dread—she was going to be unequal to the task of whatever it was (so her panicked thoughts raced, veered) she might be expected to do.

Lately her "serious" writing frightened her. Not just the content itself—though the content was often wild, disturbing, unanticipated—but the emotional and psychological strain it involved. She could write all night long, sprawled across her bed, taking notes, drafting out sketches and scenes, narrating a story she seemed to be hearing in a kind of trance; she could write until her hand ached and her eyes filled with tears and she felt that another pulsebeat would push her over the brink—into despair, into madness, into sheer extinction. Nothing is worth this, she told herself very early one morning, nothing can be worth this, she thought, staring at herself in the mirror of the third floor bathroom,—a ghastly hollowed-eyed death's head of a face, hardly recognizable as Marya, as a girl of nineteen.

Give up. Don't risk it. *Don't* risk it.

So she cautioned herself, so she gave and took warning. There was another kind of writing—highly conscious, cerebral, critical, discursive—which she found far easier; far less dangerous. She was praised for it lavishly, given the highest grades, the most splendid sort of encouragement. She should plan, her professors said, to go on to graduate school . . . they would advise her, help her get placed, help her make her way. . . . Don't risk this, she told herself, the waters will suck you down and close over your head: I know the symptoms.

And she did, she did. As if she had lived a previous life and could recall vividly the anguish of . . . whatever it was that might happen.

One windy morning at the end of March she saw Imogene Skillman walking with several of her friends. Imogene in sunglasses, her hair blowing wild, her laughter shrill and childish, Imogene in tight-fitting jeans and a bulky white ski sweater, overlong in the sleeves. That slatternly waifish affect. . . . Marya stood watching. Staring. Poor Marya Knauer, staring. Why did you lie about me! she wanted to cry. Why did you betray me! But she stood silent, paralyzed, watching. No doubt a figure of pathos—or of comedy—her snarled black hair blowing wild as Imogene's, her skin grainy and sallow.

Of course Imogene saw her; but Imogene's eyes were discreetly hidden by the dark-tinted glasses. No need for her to give any sign of recognition. No need.

Marya wrote Imogene a muddled little note, the first week of April.

Things aren't going well for me, I missed a philosophy exam & have no excuse & can't make myself lie. I don't know . . . am I unhappy (is it that simple?) Why don't you drop by & see me sometime . . . or I could come over there & see you. . . .

Yet she felt a revulsion for Imogene; she *really* disliked her. That lazy drunken dip of her head, her lipstick smeared across her face, sliding her arms around the neck of . . . whoever it had been: kissing open-mouthed, simulating passion. Would you two let us alone for a few minutes, Imogene drawled,—Would you two like to go for a stroll, for a few minutes?

I'll come over there, Marya wrote, *and strangle you with that pretentious braid of yours.*

In all she wrote a dozen notes, some by hand and some on the typewriter.

But she sent only the first ("why don't you drop by & see me sometime . . . or I could come over there & see you"), not expecting, and not receiving, an answer.

What is fictitious in a friendship, Marya pondered, and what is "real": the world outside the head, the world *inside*: but whose world?—from whose point of view?

If Imogene died. . . .

If Imogene were dying. . . .

She wouldn't lift a hand to prevent that death!—so she thought.

At the same time she quizzed herself about how to respond, should Imogene really ask her to be a bridesmaid. (She had declined being a bridesmaid at Alice's wedding; but then she had the excuse of schoolwork, distance.) Imogene's wedding was going to be a costly affair held in Long Beach, New York sometime the following year. The bridesmaid's dress, the shoes . . . the shoes alone . . . would be staggeringly expensive.

I can't afford it, Marya would say.

I can't afford *you*.

Though they hadn't any classes together this semester Marya learned that Imogene had been absent from one of her lectures for three days running. So she simply went, one rainy April afternoon, to Imogene's residence—to that absurd white-columned "house" on Masefield Avenue—and rapped hard on Imogene's door; and let herself in before Imogene could call out sleepily, who is it . . . ?

The shades were crookedly drawn. Clothes and towels and books were strewn about. Imogene lay half-dressed on the bed with the quilted spread pulled over her; the room smelled of something acrid and medicinal.

"Oh Marya," Imogene said guiltily.

"Are you sick?" Marya asked.

They had both spoken at the same time.

". . . a headache, cramps, nothing worth mentioning," Imogene said hoarsely. ". . . the tail-end of this shitty flu that's been going around."

Marya stood with her hands on her hips, regarding Imogene in bed. Imogene's skin looked oddly coarse, her hair lay in spent greasy tangles on the pillow, spilling off the edge of the bed; her body was flat, curiously immobile. Without makeup she looked both young and rather ravaged. "If you're really sick, if you need a doctor, your sorority sisters will see to it," Marya said half-mockingly.

"I'm not really sick," said Imogene at once. "I'm resting."

After a long pause Marya said, as if incidentally: "You told so many lies about me."

Imogene coughed feebly. "They weren't exactly *lies*, there was an essence. . . ."

"They were lies," Marya said. "I wanted to strangle you."

Imogene lay without moving, her hands flat on her stomach. She said in a childish voice: "Oh nobody believed anything, it was just . . . talk . . . spinning tales. . . . You know, thinking 'What if' . . . that sort of thing. Anyway there was an *essence* that was true."

Marya was pacing about the room, the balls of her feet springy, the tendons of her calves strained. "I don't intend to let you destroy me," she said softly. "I don't even intend to do poorly in my courses." She brushed her hair out of her face and half-smiled at Imogene—a flash of hatred. "You won't make me lose my perfect record," she said.

"Won't I," said Imogene.

Marya laughed. She said: "But why did you concoct a story about your fiancé and me?—you know I've never even met him; I don't have any interest in meeting him."

"Yes you do," Imogene said, a little sharply. "You're jealous of him—of him and me."

"You're angry that I'm not jealous *enough*," Marya said. "Do you think I'd want to sleep with your precious 'Dickie'?"

"You think so goddam fucking highly of yourself, don't you," Imogene said, sitting up, adjusting a pillow impatiently behind her. "*You* can't be cracked open, can you?—a nut that can't be cracked," she said, laughing, yawning. "A tight little virgin, I suppose. And Catholic too!—what a joke! Very very proud of yourself."

"Why didn't you talk to me on the phone, why didn't you answer my note?" Marya asked quietly.

"Why did you avoid me on campus?"

"Avoid you when?"

"Why do you always look the other way?"

"Look the other way *when*—?"

"*All the time.*"

Marya was striking her hands, her fists, lightly together. She drew a deep shaky breath. "As for the coat—you *gave* me the coat. Your precious Salvation Army gesture. You *gave* me the coat, you *forced* it on me."

"Oh Knauer, nobody forces anything on *you*," Imogene said, sneering. "What bullshit—!"

"I want to know why you've been spreading lies about me and ridiculing me behind my back," Marya said levelly.

Imogene pulled at her hair in a lazy, mawkishly theatrical gesture. "Hey. Did I tell you. I'm transferring out of here next year," she said. "I'm going to school somewhere in New York, N.Y.U. probably. The drama courses are too *restrained* here, there's too much crap about *tradition*. . . ."

"I said I want to know *why*."

"Oh for Christ's sweet sake what are you talking about!" Imogene cried. "I'm sick, my head is spinning, if you don't leave me alone I'm going to puke all over everything. I haven't been to a class in two weeks and I don't give a damn but I refuse to give *you* the satisfaction. . . . Transfer to New York, Marya, why don't you: you know you think you're too good for us *here*."

Marya stared at her, trembling. She had a vision of running at her friend and pummeling her with her fists—the two of them fighting, clawing, grunting in silence.

"Your jealousy, your morbid possessiveness. . . ." Imogene was saying wildly, her eyes wide, ". . . the way you sat in judgment of my parents . . . my poor father trying so hard to be *nice* to you, to be *kind*, because he felt *sorry* for you . . . and my mother too . . . 'Is she one of your strays and misfits?' Mother said, 'another one of that gang that will turn on you.' . . . As for my sorority sisters. . . ."

Marya said slowly, groping: "And what about you? You're spoiled, you're vicious. . . . And you don't even act that well: people here baby you, lie to you, tell you the kind of crap you want to hear."

At this Imogene threw herself back against the flattened pillows, laughing, half-sobbing. "Yes," she said. "Good. Now leave me alone."

"Do you think they tell you anything else?—anything else but crap?" Marya said carelessly, "—people who are in love with you? People who don't even know who you *are*?"

Imogene pawed at the bedspread and pulled it roughly over herself. She lay very still but Marya could hear her labored breath. ". . . I took some aspirin before you came in, I want to sleep, maybe you'd better let me alone. I think you'd better let me alone."

She closed her eyes, she waved Marya away with a languid gesture.

"Good-bye, Marya!" she whispered.

On the sidewalk outside the house Marya took out the earrings boldly to examine them.

The Aztec ones, the barbarian-princess ones, bronze and red and blue, burnished, gleaming. . . . Marya had seen her hand reach out to take them but she did not remember *taking* them from the room.

She tossed them in the palm of her hand as she strode along Masefield Avenue, smiling, grinning. No one, she thought in triumph, can keep me from my perfect record.

She went that day to an earring shop down on Fairfield Street; asked to have her ears pierced and Imogene's splendid earrings inserted. But the proprietor told her that wasn't the procedure; first, gold studs are inserted . . . then, after a few weeks, when the wounds are healed. . . .

No, Marya insisted, put in *these*. I don't have time to waste.

But there was the danger of infection, she was told. Everything has to be germ-free, antiseptic. . . .

"I don't give a damn about that," Marya said fiercely. "These earrings *are* gold. Put antiseptic on *them*. . . . Just pierce my ears and put them in and I'll pay you and that's all."

"Do you have five dollars?" the young man said curtly.

Crossing the quadrangle between Stafford Hall and the chapel one cold May afternoon, Marya caught sight of Imogene approaching her. It had been approximately two weeks since the theft of the earrings—two weeks during which Marya had worn the earrings everywhere, for everyone to see, to comment upon, to admire. She and Imogene had frequently noticed each other, usually at a distance, though once in rather close quarters on a crowded stairway; and Marya had been amused at Imogene's shocked expression; and the clumsy way she'd turned aside, pretending she hadn't seen Marya and Marya's new earrings.

Not a very good actress after all, Marya thought.

Now, however, Imogene was approaching her head-on, though her movements were rather forced, wooden. Marya didn't slacken her pace; she was headed for the library. She wore her raincoat half-unbuttoned, her head was bare, her hair loose, the earrings swung heavily as she walked, tugged at her earlobes. (Yes, her earlobes *were* sore. Probably infected, Marya thought indifferently, waking in the night to small stabs of pain.)

Imogene's face was dead white, and not very attractive. Something horsy about that face, after all, Marya thought. Her mouth was strained, and the tendons in her neck were clearly visible as, suddenly, she ran at Marya. She was screaming something about "hillbilly bitch"—"thief"—She grabbed at Marya's left ear, she would have ripped the earring out of Marya's flesh, but Marya was too quick for her: she knew instinctively what Imogene would try to do.

She struck Imogene's hand aside, and gave her a violent shove; Imogene slapped her hard across the face; Marya slapped *her*. "You bitch!" Imogene cried. "You won't get away with this! *I know you!*"

All their books had fallen to the sidewalk, Imogene's leather bag was tripping her up, passers-by stopped to stare, incredulous. What a sight, Imogene Skillman and Marya Knauer fighting, in front of the chapel,—both in blue jeans, both livid with rage. Marya was shouting, "Don't you touch me, you! What do you mean, touching *me*!" She was the better fighter, crouching with her knees bent, like a man, swinging at Imogene, striking her on the jaw. Not a slap but an actual punch: Marya's fist was unerring.

The blow was a powerful one, for Marya struck from the shoulder. Imogene's head snapped back—blood appeared on her mouth—she staggered backward and swayed, almost lost her balance. "Oh, Marya," she said.

Marya snatched up her things and turned away. Her long fast stride and the set of her shoulders, the set of her head, must have indicated confidence; angry assurance; but in fact she was badly shaken . . . it was some time before she could catch her breath. When she turned to look back Imogene was sitting on the ground and a small crowd had gathered around her. You'll be all right, Marya thought, someone will always take care of *you*.

After that, very little happened.

Marya kept the earrings, though her ears *were* infected and she had to give up wearing them; Imogene Skillman never approached her again, never pressed charges; nor did anyone dare bring the subject up to either of the girls.

Marya's record remained perfect but Imogene did poorly at the end of the semester, failing two subjects; and, in place of transferring to another university she quit college altogether.

That fall, Marya learned that Imogene was living in New York City. She had broken off her engagement over the summer; she had joined a troupe of semiprofessional actors, and lived in an apartment off St. Mark's Square. It was said that she had a small role in an off-Broadway play scheduled to open sometime that winter but Marya never learned the title of the play, or when, precisely, it opened; or how successful it was.

. . . .

QUESTIONS FOR A SECOND READING

1. Go back over the variety of thefts in this story (and not all of them Marya's): outright thefts, supposed or imagined thefts, and metaphoric thefts (in which something other than property could be said to have been "stolen"). If we are getting Marya's view of the world in this story, what is it? Why would "theft" be a good term for describing what goes on in that world? What can you conclude from this about Marya's sense of her relations to other people? about the way she sees the connections between people and things?

2. How would you explain the relationship between Marya and Imogene? Is there a difference between how you would explain it and how the story *would have you* explain it? That is, what does Oates offer as the key terms and key moments in the story, and what do *you* see as the key terms and key moments?

ASSIGNMENTS FOR WRITING

1. The narrator of this story says, "There was a moment when an item passed over from belonging to another person to belonging to Marya; that moment interested her greatly." Why do you suppose this moment interests Marya? How does this fit with your sense of her personality? And how, then, would

you explain why she steals? For this assignment, write an essay explaining why you think Marya steals. What's her problem, and how might you account for it?

2. Reading, for Marya, at times was "a secret process yet it was not criminal or forbidden—she made her way with the stealth of the thief, elated, subdued, through another's imagination, risking no harm, no punishment." Look back over the sections of the story that give you access to Marya's intellectual life and her success as a student. What connections can you make between her academic life and her life as a thief? In an essay, explore how her successful intellectual performance as a student could be related to her thievery. As you read the story, what are the points of the comparison?

3. One could describe Oates's technique as a storyteller in "Theft" as "fragmented" or circling back on itself. For instance, we encounter Imogene before knowing the details of how she and Marya met, and we learn that the girls' friendship ends abruptly long before that ending occurs in the story. While this technique might seem confusing, at least the first time through, Oates invites a reader to be involved with the characters and events and to think about how the sequence of memories, thoughts, and impressions may not necessarily be experienced as linear.

As you reread "Theft," note those sections of the story that were particularly significant or important as you began to form your understanding of a character or an event. What connections did you make between those sections? What did you notice about the details? dialogues? characters' thoughts? Would you describe those sections as "fragmented" or circling back on themselves? How might you explain the way they worked on you as a reader? and the way you worked on them?

Using the sections of the story that you identified as significant or important, write an essay in which you discuss the work that you had to do as a reader of this story.

MAKING CONNECTIONS

1. It is interesting to read Lewis Nordan's stories (p. 436) next to "Theft." Both writers offer accounts of adolescence, stories about growing up and moving toward adulthood. And the stories are strongly marked in terms of gender— on the one hand you have a story written by a man, on the other a story written by a woman. Write an essay comparing these representations of men's and women's experience. Read together, what arguments do these stories seem to make about the differences between the ways men and women are created in stories written by a man? in a story written by a woman? What seems to be the argument of the author? the point of view of the storyteller? In what ways do these arguments seem right? wrong? biased? incomplete? surprising?

2. Richard Rodriguez, in "The Achievement of Desire" (p. 567), talks about his schooling as the process of becoming a "scholarship boy." He borrows the term (or takes it, as he takes many things, from his teachers) and uses it to

analyze his experience as a student. If you look at Marya the way Rodriguez looks at himself, do you think the term (or its equivalent, "scholarship girl") applies to her? If you consider Rodriguez as a student like Marya, as a person fascinated with that "moment when an item passed over from belonging to another person to belonging" to him, a person not beyond stealing but not quite a thief either, what can you say to explain his relationship to others? to the culture around him? Write an essay in which you discuss Rodriguez and Marya as examples of people who have a similar response to the experience of growing up, entering the world, and becoming educated.

WALKER
PERCY

WALKER PERCY, *in his midforties, after a life of relative obscurity and after a career as, he said, a "failed physician," wrote his first novel,* The Movie-goer. *It won the National Book Award for fiction in 1962, and Percy emerged as one of this country's leading novelists. Little in his background would have predicted such a career.*

After graduating from Columbia University's medical school in 1941, Percy (b. 1916) went to work at Bellevue Hospital in New York City. He soon contracted tuberculosis from performing autopsies on derelicts and was sent to a sanitorium to recover, where, as he said, "I was in bed so much, alone so much, that I had nothing to do but read and think. I began to question everything I had once believed." He returned to medicine briefly but suffered a relapse and during his long recovery began "to make reading a full-time occupation." He left medicine, but not until 1954, almost a decade later, did he publish his first essay, "Symbol as Need."

The essays that followed, including "The Loss of the Creature," all dealt with the relationships between language and understanding or belief, and they were all published in obscure academic journals. In the later essays, Percy seemed to turn away from academic forms of argument and to depend more and more on stories or anecdotes from daily life—to write, in fact, as a storyteller and to be wary of abstraction or explanation. Robert Coles has said that it was Percy's failure to find a form that would reach a larger audience that led him to try his hand at a novel. You will notice in the essay that follows that Percy delights in piling example upon example; he never seems to settle down to a topic sentence, or any sentence for that matter that sums everything up and makes the examples superfluous.

In addition to The Moviegoer, *Percy has written five other novels, including* Lancelot *(1977),* Love in the Ruins *(1971), and* The Thanatos Syndrome *(1987). He has published two books of essays,* The Message in the Bottle: How Queer Man Is, How Queer Language Is, and What One Has to Do with the Other *(1975, from which "The Loss of the Creature" is taken), and* Lost in the Cosmos: The Last Self-help Book *(1983). Walker Percy died at his home in Covington, Louisiana, on May 10, 1990, leaving a considerable amount of unpublished work, some of which has been gathered into a posthumous collection,* Signposts in a Strange Land *(1991).*

The Loss of
the Creature

I

Every explorer names his island Formosa, beautiful. To him it is beautiful because, being first, he has access to it and can see it for what it is. But to no one else is it ever as beautiful—except the rare man who manages to recover it, who knows that it has to be recovered.

Garcia López de Cárdenas discovered the Grand Canyon and was amazed at the sight. It can be imagined: One crosses miles of desert, breaks through the mesquite, and there it is at one's feet. Later the government set the place aside as a national park, hoping to pass along to millions the experience of Cárdenas. Does not one see the same sight from the Bright Angel Lodge that Cárdenas saw?

The assumption is that the Grand Canyon is a remarkably interesting and beautiful place and that if it had a certain value P for Cárdenas, the same value P may be transmitted to any number of sightseers—just as Banting's discovery of insulin can be transmitted to any number of diabetics. A counterinfluence is at work, however, and it would be nearer the truth to say that if the place is seen by a million sightseers, a single sightseer does not receive value P but a millionth part of value P.

It is assumed that since the Grand Canyon has the fixed interest value P, tours can be organized for any number of people. A man in Boston decides to spend his vacation at the Grand Canyon. He visits his travel bureau, looks at the folder, signs up for a two-week tour. He and his family take the tour, see the Grand Canyon, and return to Boston. May we say that this man has seen the Grand Canyon? Possibly he has. But it is more likely that what he has done is the one sure way not to see the canyon.

Why is it almost impossible to gaze directly at the Grand Canyon under these circumstances and see it for what it is—as one picks up a strange object from one's back yard and gazes directly at it? It is almost impossible because the Grand Canyon, the thing as it is, has been appropriated by the symbolic complex which has already been formed in the sightseer's mind. Seeing the canyon under approved circumstances is seeing the symbolic complex head on. The thing is no longer the thing as it confronted the Spaniard; it is rather that which has already been formulated—by picture postcard, geography book, tourist folders, and the words *Grand Canyon*. As a result of this preformulation, the source of the sightseer's pleasure undergoes a shift. Where the wonder and delight of the Spaniard arose from his penetration of the thing itself, from a progressive discovery of depths, patterns, colors, shadows, etc., now the sightseer measures his satisfaction *by the degree to which the canyon conforms to the preformed complex.* If it does so, if it looks just like the postcard, he is pleased; he might even say, "Why it is every bit as beautiful as a picture postcard!" He feels he has not been cheated. But if it does not conform, if the colors are somber, he will not be able to see it directly; he will only be conscious of the disparity between what it is and what it is supposed to be. He will say later that he was unlucky in not being there at the right time. The highest point, the term of the sightseer's satisfaction, is not the sovereign discovery of the thing before him; it is rather the measuring up of the thing to the criterion of the preformed symbolic complex.

Seeing the canyon is made even more difficult by what the sightseer does when the moment arrives, when sovereign knower confronts the thing to be known. Instead of looking at it, he photographs it. There is no confrontation at all. At the end of forty years of preformulation and with the Grand Canyon yawning at his feet, what does he do? He waives his right of seeing and knowing and records symbols for the next forty years. For him there is no present; there is only the past of what has been formulated and seen and the future of what has been formulated and not seen. The present is surrendered to the past and the future.

The sightseer may be aware that something is wrong. He may simply be bored; or he may be conscious of the difficulty: that the great thing yawning at his feet somehow eludes him. The harder he looks at it, the less he can see. It eludes everybody. The tourist cannot see it; the bellboy at the Bright Angel Lodge cannot see it: for him it is only one side of the space he lives in, like one wall of a room; to the ranger it is a tissue of everyday signs relevant to his own prospects—the blue haze down there means that he will probably get rained on during the donkey ride.

How can the sightseer recover the Grand Canyon? He can recover it in any number of ways, all sharing in common the stratagem of avoiding the approved confrontation of the tour and the Park Service.

It may be recovered by leaving the beaten track. The tourist leaves the tour, camps in the back country. He arises before dawn and approaches the South Rim through a wild terrain where there are no trails and no railed-in lookout points. In other words, he sees the canyon by avoiding all the facilities for seeing the canyon. If the benevolent Park Service hears about this fellow and thinks he has a good idea and places the following notice in the Bright Angel Lodge: *Consult ranger for information on getting off the beaten track*—the end result will only be the closing of another access to the canyon.

It may be recovered by a dialectical movement which brings one back to the beaten track but at a level above it. For example, after a lifetime of avoiding the beaten track and guided tours, a man may deliberately seek out the most beaten track of all, the most commonplace tour imaginable: he may visit the canyon by a Greyhound tour in the company of a party from Terre Haute—just as a man who has lived in New York all his life may visit the Statue of Liberty. (Such dialectical savorings of the familiar as the familiar are, of course, a favorite stratagem of *The New Yorker* magazine.) The thing is recovered from familiarity by means of an exercise in familiarity. Our complex friend stands behind his fellow tourists at the Bright Angel Lodge and sees the canyon through them and their predicament, their picture taking and busy disregard. In a sense, he exploits his fellow tourists; he stands on their shoulders to see the canyon.

Such a man is far more advanced in the dialectic than the sightseer who is trying to get off the beaten track—getting up at dawn and approaching the canyon through the mesquite. This stratagem is, in fact, for our complex man the weariest, most beaten track of all.

It may be recovered as a consequence of a breakdown of the symbolic machinery by which the experts present the experience to the consumer. A family visits the canyon in the usual way. But shortly after their arrival, the park is closed by an outbreak of typhus in the south. They have the canyon to themselves. What do they mean when they tell the home folks of their good luck: "We had the whole place to ourselves"? How does one see the thing better when the others are absent? Is looking like sucking: the more lookers, the less there is to see? They could hardly answer, but by saying this they testify to a state of affairs which is considerably more complex than the simple statement of the schoolbook about the Spaniard and the millions who followed him. It is a state in which there is a complex distribution of sovereignty, of zoning.

It may be recovered in a time of national disaster. The Bright Angel Lodge is converted into a rest home, a function that has nothing to do with the canyon a few yards away. A wounded man is brought in. He regains consciousness; there outside his window is the canyon.

The most extreme case of access by privilege conferred by disaster is the Huxleyan novel of the adventures of the surviving remnant after the great wars of the twentieth century. An expedition from Australia lands in Southern California and heads east. They stumble across the Bright Angel Lodge, now fallen into ruins. The trails are grown over, the guard rails fallen away, the dime telescope at Battleship Point rusted. But there is the canyon, exposed at last. Exposed by what? By the decay of those facilities which were designed to help the sightseer.

This dialectic of sightseeing cannot be taken into account by planners, for the object of the dialectic is nothing other than the subversion of the efforts of the planners.

The dialectic is not known to objective theorists, psychologists, and the like. Yet it is quite well known in the fantasy-consciousness of the popular arts. The devices by which the museum exhibit, the Grand Canyon, the ordinary thing, is recovered have long since been stumbled upon. A movie shows a man visiting the Grand Canyon. But the movie maker knows something the planner does not know. He knows that one cannot take the sight frontally. The canyon must be approached by the stratagems we have mentioned: the Inside Track, the Familiar Revisited, the Accidental Encounter. Who is the stranger at the Bright Angel Lodge? Is he the ordinary tourist from Terre Haute that he makes himself out to be? He is not. He has another objective in mind, to revenge his wronged brother, counterespionage, etc. By virtue of the fact that he has other fish to fry, he may take a stroll along the rim after supper and then we can see the canyon through him. The movie accomplishes its purpose by concealing it. Overtly the characters (the American family marooned by typhus) and we the onlookers experience pity for the sufferers, and the family experience anxiety for themselves; covertly and in truth they are the happiest of people and we are happy through them, for we have the canyon to ourselves. The movie cashes in on the recovery of sovereignty through disaster. Not only is the canyon now accessible to the remnant: the members of the remnant are now accessible to each other, a whole new ensemble of relations becomes possible—friendship, love, hatred, clandestine sexual adventures. In a movie when a man sits next to a woman on a bus, it is necessary either that the bus break down or that the woman lose her memory. (The question occurs to one: Do you imagine there are sightseers who see sights just as they are supposed to? a family who live in Terre Haute, who decide to take the canyon tour, who go there, see it, enjoy it immensely, and go home content? a family who are entirely innocent of all the barriers, zones, losses of sovereignty I have been talking about? Wouldn't most people be sorry if Battleship Point fell into the canyon, carrying all one's fellow passengers to their death, leaving one alone on the South Rim? I cannot answer this. Perhaps there are such people. Certainly a great many American families would swear they had no such problems, that they came, saw, and went away happy. Yet it is just these families who would be happiest if they had gotten the Inside Track and been among the surviving remnant.)

It is now apparent that as between the many measures which may be taken to overcome the opacity, the boredom, of the direct confrontation of the thing or creature in its citadel of symbolic investiture, some are less authentic than others. That is to say, some stratagems obviously serve other purposes than that of providing access to being—for example, various unconscious motivations which it is not necessary to go into here.

Let us take an example in which the recovery of being is ambiguous, where it may under the same circumstances contain both authentic and unauthentic components. An American couple, we will say, drives down into Mexico. They see the usual sights and have a fair time of it. Yet they are never without the sense of missing something. Although Taxco and Cuernavaca are interesting and picturesque as advertised, they fall short of "it." What do the couple have in mind by "it"? What do they really hope for? What sort of experience could they have in Mexico so that upon their return, they would feel that "it" had happened? We have a clue: Their hope has something to do with their own role as tourists in a foreign country and the way in which they conceive this role. It has something to do with other American tourists. Certainly they feel that they are very far from "it" when, after traveling five thousand miles, they arrive at the plaza in Guanajuato only to find themselves surrounded by a dozen other couples from the Midwest.

Already we may distinguish authentic and unauthentic elements. First, we see the problem the couple faces and we understand their efforts to surmount it. The problem is to find an "unspoiled" place. "Unspoiled" does not mean only that a place is left physically intact; it means also that it is not encrusted by renown and by the familiar (as in Taxco), that it has not been discovered by others. We understand that the couple really want to get at the place and enjoy it. Yet at the same time we wonder if there is not something wrong in their dislike of their compatriots. Does access to the place require the exclusion of others?

Let us see what happens.

The couple decide to drive from Guanajuato to Mexico City. On the way they get lost. After hours on a rocky mountain road, they find themselves in a tiny valley not even marked on the map. There they discover an Indian village. Some sort of religious festival is going on. It is apparently a corn dance in supplication of the rain god.

The couple know at once that this is "it." They are entranced. They spend several days in the village, observing the Indians and being themselves observed with friendly curiosity.

Now may we not say that the sightseers have at last come face to face with an authentic sight, a sight which is charming, quaint, picturesque, unspoiled, and that they see the sight and come away rewarded? Possibly this may occur. Yet it is more likely that what happens is a far cry indeed from an immediate encounter with being, that the experience, while masquerading as such, is in truth a rather desperate impersonation. I use the word *desperate* advisedly to signify an actual loss of hope.

The clue to the spuriousness of their enjoyment of the village and the festival is a certain restiveness in the sightseers themselves. It is given expression by their repeated exclamations that "this is too good to be true," and by their anxiety that it may not prove to be so perfect, and finally by their downright relief at leaving the valley and having the experience in the bag, so to speak—that is, safely enbalmed in memory and movie film.

What is the source of their anxiety during the visit? Does it not mean that the couple are looking at the place with a certain standard of performance in mind? Are they like Fabre, who gazed at the world about him with wonder, letting it be what it is; or are they not like the overanxious mother who sees her child as one performing, now doing badly, now doing well? The village is their child and their love for it is an anxious love because they are afraid that at any moment it might fail them.

We have another clue in their subsequent remark to an ethnologist friend. "How we wished you had been there with us! What a perfect goldmine of folkways! Every minute we would say to each other, if only you were here! You must return with us." This surely testifies to a generosity of spirit, a willingness to share their experience with others, not at all like their feelings toward their fellow Iowans on the plaza at Guanajuato!

I am afraid this is not the case at all. It is true that they longed for their ethnologist friend, but it was for an entirely different reason. They wanted him, not to share their experience, but to certify their experience as genuine.

"This is it" and "Now we are really living" do not necessarily refer to the sovereign encounter of the person with the sight that enlivens the mind and gladdens the heart. It means that now at last we are having the acceptable experience. The present experience is always measured by a prototype, the "it" of their dreams. "Now I am really living" means that now I am filling the role of sightseer and the sight is living up to the prototype of sights. This quaint and picturesque village is measured by a Platonic ideal of the Quaint and the Picturesque.

Hence their anxiety during the encounter. For at any minute something could go wrong. A fellow Iowan might emerge from a 'dobe hut; the chief might show them his Sears catalog. (If the failures are "wrong" enough, as these are, they might still be turned to account as rueful conversation pieces. "There we were expecting the chief to bring us a churinga and he shows up with a Sears catalog!") They have snatched victory from disaster, but their experience always runs the danger of failure.

They need the ethnologist to certify their experience as genuine. This is borne out by their behavior when the three of them return for the next corn dance. During the dance, the couple do not watch the goings-on; instead they watch the ethnologist! Their highest hope is that their friend should find the dance interesting. And if he should show signs of true absorption, an interest in the goings-on so powerful that he becomes oblivious of his friends—then their cup is full. "Didn't we tell you?" they say at last. What they want from him is not ethnological explanations; all they want is his approval.

What has taken place is a radical loss of sovereignty over that which is as much theirs as it is the ethnologist's. The fault does not lie with the ethnologist. He has no wish to stake a claim to the village; in fact, he desires the opposite: he will bore his friends to death by telling them about the village and the meaning of the folkways. A degree of sovereignty has been surrendered by the couple. It is the nature of the loss, moreover, that they are not aware of the loss, beyond a certain uneasiness. (Even if they read this and admitted it, it would be very difficult for them to bridge the gap in their confrontation of the world. Their consciousness of the corn dance cannot escape their consciousness of their consciousness, so that with the onset of the first direct enjoyment, their higher consciousness pounces and certifies: "Now you are doing it! Now you are really living!" and, in certifying the experience, sets it at nought.)

Their basic placement in the world is such that they recognize a priority of title of the expert over his particular department of being. The whole horizon of being is staked out by "them," the experts. The highest satisfaction of the sightseer (not merely the tourist but any layman seer of sights) is that his sight should be certified as genuine. The worst of this impoverishment is that there is no sense of impoverishment. The surrender of title is so complete that it never even occurs to one to reassert title. A poor man may envy the rich man, but the sightseer does not envy the expert. When a caste system becomes absolute, envy disappears. Yet the caste of layman-expert is not the fault of the expert. It is due altogether to the eager surrender of sovereignty by the layman so that he may take up the role not of the person but of the consumer.

I do not refer only to the special relation of layman to theorist. I refer to the general situation in which sovereignty is surrendered to a class of privileged knowers, whether these be theorists or artists. A reader may surrender sovereignty over that which has been written about, just as a consumer may surrender sovereignty over a thing which has been theorized about. The consumer is content to receive an experience just as it has been presented to him by theorists and planners. The reader may also be content to judge life by whether it has or has not been formulated by those who know and write about life. A young man goes to France. He too has a fair time of it, sees the sights, enjoys the food. On his last day, in fact as he sits in a restaurant in Le Havre waiting for his boat, something happens. A group of French students in the restaurant get into an impassioned argument over a recent play. A riot takes place. Madame la concierge joins in, swinging her mop at the rioters. Our young American is transported. This is "it." And he had almost left France without seeing "it"!

But the young man's delight is ambiguous. On the one hand, it is a pleasure for him to encounter the same Gallic temperament he had heard about from Puccini and Rolland. But on the other hand, the source of his pleasure testifies to a certain alienation. For the young man is actually barred from a direct encounter with anything French excepting only that which has been set forth, authenticated by Puccini and Rolland—those who know. If he had encountered the restaurant scene without reading Hemingway, without knowing that the performance was so typically, charmingly French, he would not have been delighted. He would only have been anxious at seeing things get so out of hand. The source of his delight is the sanction of those who know.

This loss of sovereignty is not a marginal process, as might appear from my example of estranged sightseers. It is a generalized surrender of the horizon to those experts within whose competence a particular segment of the horizon is thought to lie. Kwakiutls are surrendered to Franz Boas; decaying Southern mansions are surrendered to Faulkner and Tennessee Williams. So that, although it is by no means the intention of the expert to expropriate sovereignty—in fact he would not even know what sovereignty meant in this context—the danger of theory and consumption is a seduction and deprivation of the consumer.

In the New Mexico desert, natives occasionally come across strange-looking artifacts which have fallen from the skies and which are stenciled: *Return to U.S. Experimental Project, Alamogordo. Reward.* The finder returns the object and is rewarded. He knows nothing of the nature of the object he has found and does not care to know. The sole role of the native, the highest role he can play, is that of finder and returner of the mysterious equipment.

The same is true of the laymen's relation to *natural* objects in a modern technical society. No matter what the object or event is, whether it is a star, a swallow, a Kwakiutl, a "psychological phenomenon," the layman who confronts it does not confront it as a sovereign person, as Crusoe confronts a seashell he finds on the beach. The highest role he can conceive himself as playing is to be able to recognize the title of the object, to return it to the appropriate expert and have it certified as a genuine find. He does not even permit himself to see the thing—as Gerard Hopkins could see a rock or a cloud or a field. If anyone asks him why he doesn't look, he may reply that he didn't take that subject in college (or he hasn't read Faulkner).

This loss of sovereignty extends even to oneself. There is the neurotic who asks nothing more of his doctor than that his symptoms should prove interesting. When all else fails, the poor fellow has nothing to offer but his own neurosis. But even this is sufficient if only the doctor will show interest when he says, "Last night I had a curious sort of dream; perhaps it will be significant to one who knows about such things. It seems I was standing in a sort of alley—" (I have nothing else to offer you but my own unhappiness. Please say that it, at least, measures up, that it is a *proper* sort of unhappiness.)

II

A young Falkland Islander walking along a beach and spying a dead dogfish and going to work on it with his jacknife has, in a fashion wholly unprovided in modern educational theory, a great advantage over the Scarsdale high-school pupil who finds the dogfish on his laboratory desk. Similarly the citizen of Huxley's *Brave New World* who stumbles across a volume of Shakespeare in some vine-grown ruins and squats on a potsherd to read it is in a fairer way of getting at a sonnet than the Harvard sophomore taking English Poetry II.

The educator whose business it is to teach students biology or poetry is unaware of a whole ensemble of relations which exist between the student and the dogfish and between the student and the Shakespeare sonnet. To put it bluntly: A student who has the desire to get at a dogfish or a Shakespeare sonnet may have the greatest difficulty in salvaging the creature itself from the educational package in which it is presented. The great difficulty is that he is not aware that there is a difficulty; surely, he thinks, in such a fine classroom, with such a fine textbook, the sonnet must come across! What's wrong with me?

The sonnet and the dogfish are obscured by two different processes. The sonnet is obscured by the symbolic package which is formulated not by the sonnet itself but by the *media* through which the sonnet is transmitted, the media which the educators believe for some reason to be transparent. The new textbook, the type, the smell of the page, the classroom, the aluminum windows and the winter sky, the personality of Miss Hawkins—these media which are supposed to transmit the sonnet may only succeed in transmitting themselves. It is only the hardiest and cleverest of students who can salvage the sonnet from this many-tissued package. It is only the rarest student who knows that the sonnet must be salvaged from the package. (The educator is well aware that something is wrong, that there is a fatal gap between the student's learning and the student's life: the student reads the poem, appears to understand it, and gives all the answers. But what does he recall if he should happen to read a Shakespeare sonnet twenty years later? Does he recall the poem or does he recall the smell of the page and the smell of Miss Hawkins?)

One might object, pointing out that Huxley's citizen reading his sonnet in the ruins and the Falkland Islander looking at his dogfish on the beach also receive them in a certain package. Yes, but the difference lies in the fundamental placement of the student in the world, a placement which makes it possible to extract the thing from the package. The pupil at Scarsdale High sees himself placed as a consumer receiving an experience-package; but the Falkland Islander exploring his dogfish is a person exercising the sovereign right of a person in his lordship and mastery of creation. He too could use an instructor and a book and a technique, but he would use them as his subordinates, just as he uses his jackknife. The biology student does not use his scalpel as an instrument, he uses it as a magic wand! Since it is a "scientific instrument," it should do "scientific things."

The dogfish is concealed in the same symbolic package as the sonnet. But the dogfish suffers an additional loss. As a consequence of this double deprivation, the Sarah Lawrence student who scores A in zoology is apt to know very little about a dogfish. She is twice removed from the dogfish, once by the symbolic complex by which the dogfish is concealed, once again by the spoliation of the dogfish by theory which renders it invisible. Through no fault of zoology instructors, it is nevertheless a fact that the zoology laboratory at Sarah Lawrence College is one of the few places in the world where it is all but impossible to see a dogfish.

The dogfish, the tree, the seashell, the American Negro, the dream, are rendered invisible by a shift of reality from concrete thing to theory which Whitehead has called the fallacy of misplaced concreteness. It is the mistaking of an idea, a principle, an abstraction, for the real. As a consequence of the shift, the "specimen" is seen as less real than the theory of the specimen. As Kierkegaard said, once a person is seen as a specimen of a race or a species, at that very moment he ceases to be an individual. Then there are no more individuals but only specimens.

To illustrate: A student enters a laboratory which, in the pragmatic view, offers the student the optimum conditions under which an educational experience may he had. In the existential view, however—that view of the student in which he is regarded not as a receptacle of experience but as a knowing being whose peculiar property it is to see himself as being in a certain situation—the modern laboratory could not have been more effectively designed to conceal the dogfish forever.

The student comes to his desk. On it, neatly arranged by his instructor, he finds his laboratory manual, a dissecting board, instruments, and a mimeographed list:

Exercise 22: Materials
1 dissecting board
1 scalpel
1 forceps
1 probe
1 bottle india ink and syringe
1 specimen of *Squalus acanthias*

The clue of the situation in which the student finds himself is to be found in the last item: 1 specimen of *Squalus acanthias*.

The phrase *specimen of* expresses in the most succinct way imaginable the radical character of the loss of being which has occurred under his very nose. To refer to the dogfish, the unique concrete existent before him, as a "specimen of *Squalas acanthias*" reveals by its grammar the spoliation of the dogfish by the theoretical method. This phrase, *specimen of*, example of, instance of, indicates the ontological status of the individual creature in the eyes of the theorist. The dogfish itself is seen as a rather shabby expression of an ideal reality, the species *Squalus acanthias*. The result is the radical devaluation of the individual dogfish. (The *reductio ad absurdum* of Whitehead's shift is Toynbee's employment of it in his historical method. If a gram of NaCl is referred to by the chemist as a "sample of" NaCl, one may think of it as such and not much is missed by the oversight of the act of being of this particular pinch of salt, but when the Jews and the Jewish religion are understood as—in Toynbee's favorite phrase—a "classical example of" such and such a kind of *Voelkerwanderung*, we begin to suspect that something is being left out.)

If we look into the ways in which the student can recover the dogfish (or the sonnet), we will see that they have in common the stratagem of avoiding the educator's direct presentation of the object as a lesson to be learned and restoring access to sonnet and dogfish as beings to be known, reasserting the sovereignty of knower over known.

In truth, the biography of scientists and poets is usually the story of the discovery of the indirect approach, the circumvention of the educator's presentation—the young man who was sent to the *Technikum* and on his way fell into the habit of loitering in book stores and reading poetry; or the young man dutifully attending law school who on the way became curious about the comings and goings of ants. One remembers the scene in *The Heart Is a Lonely Hunter* where the girl hides in the bushes to hear the Capehart in the big house play Beethoven. Perhaps she was the lucky one after all. Think of the unhappy souls inside, who see the record, worry about scratches, and most of all worry about whether they are *getting it*, whether they are bona fide music lovers. What is the best way to hear Beethoven: sitting in a proper silence around the Capehart or eavesdropping from an azalea bush?

However it may come about, we notice two traits of the second situation: (1) an openness of the thing before one—instead of being an exercise to be learned according to an approved mode, it is a garden of delights which beckons to one; (2) a sovereignty of the knower—instead of being a consumer of a prepared experience, I am a sovereign wayfarer, a wanderer in the neighborhood of being who stumbles into the garden.

One can think of two sorts of circumstances through which the thing may be restored to the person. (There is always, of course, the direct recovery: A student may simply be strong enough, brave enough, clever enough to take the dogfish and the sonnet by storm, to wrest control of it from the educators and the educational package.) First by ordeal: The Bomb falls; when the young man recovers consciousness in the shambles of the biology laboratory, there not ten inches from his nose lies the dogfish. Now all at once he can see it directly and without let, just as the exile or the prisoner or the sick man sees the sparrow at his window in all its inexhaustibility; just as the commuter who has had a heart attack sees his own hand for the first time. In these cases, the simulacrum of everydayness and of consumption has been destroyed by disaster; in the case of the bomb, literally destroyed. Secondly, by apprenticeship to a great man: one day a great biologist walks into the laboratory; he stops in front of our student's desk; he leans over, picks up the dogfish, and, ignoring instruments and procedure, probes with a broken fingernail into the little carcass. "Now here is a curious business," he says, ignoring also the proper jargon of the speciality. "Look here how this little duct reverses its direction and drops into the pelvis. Now if you would look into a coelacanth, you would see that it—" And all at once the student can see. The technician and the sophomore who loves his textbooks are always offended by the genuine research man because the latter is usually a little vague and always humble before the thing; he doesn't have much use for the equipment or the jargon. Whereas the technician is never vague and never humble before the thing; he holds the thing disposed of by the principle, the formula, the textbook outline; and he thinks a great deal of equipment and jargon.

But since neither of these methods of recovering the dogfish is pedagogically feasible—perhaps the great man even less so than the Bomb—I wish to propose the following educational technique which should prove equally effective for Harvard and Shreveport High School. I propose that English poetry and biology should be taught as usual, but that at irregular intervals, poetry students should find dogfishes on their desks and biology students should find Shakespeare sonnets on their dissection boards. I am serious in declaring that a Sarah Lawrence English major who began poking about in a dogfish with a bobby pin would learn more in thirty minutes than a biology major in a whole semester; and that the latter upon reading on her dissecting board

> That time of year Thou may'st in me behold
> When yellow leaves, or none, or few, do hang
> Upon those boughs which shake against the cold—
> Bare ruin'd choirs where late the sweet birds sang

might catch fire at the beauty of it.

The situation of the tourist at the Grand Canyon and the biology student are special cases of a predicament in which everyone finds himself in a modern technical society—a society, that is, in which there is a division between expert and layman, planner and consumer, in which experts and planners take special measures to teach and edify the consumer. The measures taken are measures appropriate to the consumer: the expert and the planner *know* and *plan*, but the consumer *needs* and *experiences*.

There is a double deprivation. First, the thing is lost through its packaging. The very means by which the thing is presented for consumption, the very techniques by which the thing is made available as an item of need-satisfaction, these very means operate to remove the thing from the sovereignty of the knower. A loss of title occurs. The measures which the museum curator takes to present the thing to the public are self-liquidating. The upshot of the curator's efforts are not that everyone can see the exhibit but that no one can see it. The curator protests: why are they so indifferent? Why do they even deface the exhibit? Don't they know it is theirs? But it is not theirs. It is his, the curator's. By the most exclusive sort of zoning, the museum exhibit, the park oak tree, is part of an ensemble, a package, which is almost impenetrable to them. The archaeologist who puts his find in a museum so that everyone can see it accomplishes the reverse of his expectations. The result of his action is that no one can see it now but the archeologist. He would have done better to keep it in his pocket and show it now and then to strangers.

The tourist who carves his initials in a public place, which is theoretically "his" in the first place, has good reasons for doing so, reasons which the exhibitor and planner know nothing about. He does so because in his role of consumer of an experience (a "recreational experience" to satisfy a "recreational need") he knows that he is disinherited. He is deprived of his title over being. He knows very well that he is in a very special sort of zone in which his only rights are the rights of a consumer. He moves like a ghost through schoolroom, city streets, trains, parks, movies. He carves his initials as a last desperate measure to escape his ghostly role of consumer. He is saying in effect: I am not a ghost after all; I am a sovereign person. And he establishes title the only way remaining to him, by staking his claim over one square inch of wood or stone.

Does this mean that we should get rid of museums? No, but it means that the sightseer should be prepared to enter into a struggle to recover a sight from a museum.

The second loss is the spoliation of the thing, the tree, the rock, the swallow, by the layman's misunderstanding of scientific theory. He believes that the thing is *disposed of* by theory, that it stands in the Platonic relation of being a *specimen* of such and such an underlying principle. In the transmission of scientific theory from theorist to layman, the expectation of the theorist is reversed. Instead of the marvels of the universe being made available to the public, the universe is disposed of by theory. The loss of sovereignty takes this form: as a result of the science of botany, trees are not made available to every man. On the contrary. The tree loses its proper density and mystery as a concrete existent and, as merely another *specimen* of a species, becomes itself nugatory.

Does this mean that there is no use taking biology at Harvard and Shreveport High? No, but it means that the student should know what a fight he has on his hands to rescue the specimen from the educational package. The educator is only partly to blame. For there is nothing the educator can do to provide for this need of the student. Everything the educator does only succeeds in becoming, for the student, part of the educational package. The highest role of the educator is the maieutic role of Socrates: to help the student come to himself not as a consumer of experience but as a sovereign individual.

The thing is twice lost to the consumer. First, sovereignty is lost: it is theirs, not his. Second, it is radically devalued by theory. This is a loss which has been brought about by science but through no fault of the scientist and through no fault of scientific theory. The loss has come about as a consequence of the seduction of the layman by science. The layman will be seduced as long as he regards beings as consumer items to be experienced rather than prizes to be won, and as long as he waives his sovereign rights as a person and accepts his role of consumer as the highest estate to which the layman can aspire.

As Mounier said, the person is not something one can study and provide for; he is something one struggles for. But unless he also struggles for himself, unless he knows that there is a struggle, he is going to be just what the planners think he is.

· · · · · · · · · · · ·

QUESTIONS FOR A SECOND READING

1. Percy's essay proceeds by adding example to example, one after another. If all the examples were meant to illustrate the same thing, the same general point or idea, then one would most likely have been enough. The rest would have been redundant. It makes sense, then, to assume that each example gives a different view of what Percy is saying, that each modifies the others, or qualifies them, or adds a piece that was otherwise lacking. It's as though Percy needed one more to get it right or to figure out what was missing along the way. As you read back through the essay, pay particular attention to the *differences* between the examples (between the various tourists going to the Grand Canyon, or between the tourists at the Grand Canyon and the tourists in Mexico). Also note the logic or system that leads from one to the next. What progress of thought is represented by the movement from one example to another, or from tourists to students?

2. The essay is filled with talk about "loss"—the loss of sovereignty, the loss of the creature—but it is resolutely ambiguous about what it is that we have lost. As you work your way back through, note the passages that describe what we are missing and why we should care. Áre we to believe, for example, that Cárdenas actually had it (whatever "it" is)—that he had no preconceived notions when he saw the Grand Canyon? Mightn't he have said, "I claim this for my queen" or "There I see the glory of God" or "This wilderness is not fit for man"? To whom, or in the name of what, is this loss that Percy chronicles such a matter of concern? If this is not just Percy's peculiar prejudice, if we are asked to share his concerns, whose interests or what interests are represented here?

3. The essay is made up of stories or anecdotes, all of them fanciful. Percy did not, in other words, turn to first-person accounts of visitors to the Grand Canyon or to statements by actual students or teachers. Why not, do you suppose? What does this choice say about his "method"—about what it can and can't do? As you reread the essay, look for sections you could use to talk about the power and limits of Percy's method.

ASSIGNMENTS FOR WRITING

1. Percy tells several stories—some of them quite good stories—but it is often hard to know just what he is getting at, just what point it is he is trying to make. If he's making an argument, it's not the sort of argument that is easy to summarize. And if the stories (or anecdotes) are meant to serve as examples, they are not the sort of examples that lead directly to a single, general conclusion or that serve to clarify a point or support an obvious thesis. In fact, at the very moment when you expect Percy to come forward and pull

things together, he offers yet another story, as though another example, rather than any general statement, would get you closer to what he is saying.

There are, at the same time, terms and phrases to suggest that this is an essay with a point to make. Percy talks, for example, about "the loss of sovereignty," "symbolic packages," "consumers of experience," and "dialectic," and it seems that these terms and phrases are meant to name or comment on key scenes, situations, or characters in the examples.

For this assignment, tell a story of your own, one that is suggested by the stories Percy tells—perhaps a story about a time you went looking for something or at something, or about a time when you did or did not find a dogfish in your Shakespeare class. You should imagine that you are carrying out a project that Walker Percy has begun, a project that has you looking back at your own experience through the lens of "The Loss of the Creature," noticing what Percy would notice and following the paths that he would find interesting. Try to bring the terms that Percy uses— like "sovereign," "consumer," "expert," and "dialectic"—to bear on the story you have to tell. Feel free to imitate Percy's style and method in your essay.

2. Percy charts several routes to the Grand Canyon: you can take the packaged tour, you can get off the beaten track, you can wait for a disaster, you can follow the "dialectical movement which brings one back to the beaten track but at a level above it." This last path (or stratagem), he says, is for the complex traveler.

> Our complex friend stands behind his fellow tourists at the Bright Angel Lodge and sees the canyon through them and their predicament, their picture taking and busy disregard. In a sense, he exploits his fellow tourists; he stands on their shoulders to see the canyon. (p. 513)

The complex traveler sees the Grand Canyon through the example of the common tourists with "their predicament, their picture taking and busy disregard." He "stands on their shoulders" to see the canyon. This distinction between complex and common approaches is an important one in the essay. It is interesting to imagine how the distinction could be put to work to define ways of reading.

Suppose that you read "The Loss of the Creature" as a common reader. What would you see? What would you identify as key sections of the text? What would you miss? What would you say about what you see?

If you think of yourself, now, as a complex reader, modeled after any of Percy's more complex tourists or students, what would you see? What would you identify as key sections of the text? What would you miss? What would you say about what you see?

For this assignment, write an essay with three sections. You may number them, if you choose. The first section should represent the work of a common reader with "The Loss of the Creature," and the second should represent the work of a complex reader. The third section should look back and comment on the previous two. In particular, you might address these questions: Why might a person prefer one reading over the other? What is to be gained or lost with both?

MAKING CONNECTIONS

1. In "The Loss of the Creature," Percy writes about tourists and the difficulty they have seeing that which lies before them. In "Deep Play: Notes on the Balinese Cockfight" (p. 228), Clifford Geertz tells the story of his travels in Bali. Anthropologists, properly speaking, are not tourists. There is a scholarly purpose to their travel and, presumably, they have learned or developed the strategies necessary to get beyond the preformed "symbolic complex" that would keep them from seeing the place or the people they have traveled to study. They are experts, in other words, not common sightseers.

   In his travels to Bali, Geertz seems to get just what he wants. He gets both the authentic experience and a complex understanding of that experience. If you read "Deep Play" from the perspective of Percy's essay, however, it is interesting to ask whether Percy would say that this was the case (whether Percy might say that Geertz has gone as far as one can go after Cárdenas), and it is interesting to ask how Percy would characterize the "strategies" that define Geertz's approach to his subject.

   Write an essay in which you place Geertz in the context of Percy's tourists (not all of them, but two of three whose stories seem most interesting when placed alongside Geertz's). The purpose of your essay is to offer a Percian reading of Geertz's essay—to study his text, that is, in light of the terms and methods Percy has established in "The Loss of the Creature."

2. But the difference lies in the fundamental placement of the student in the world. . . . (Walker Percy, p. 519)

   What I am about to say to you has taken me more than twenty years to admit: *A primary reason for my success in the classroom was that I couldn't forget that schooling was changing me and separating me from the life I enjoyed before becoming a student.* (Richard Rodriguez, pp. 568–69)

   Both Percy and Richard Rodriguez, in "The Achievement of Desire" (p. 567), write about students and how they are "placed" in the world by teachers and by the way schools characteristically represent knowledge, the novice, and the expert. And both tell stories to make their points, stories of characteristic students in characteristic situations. Write an essay in which you tell a story of your own, one meant to serve as a corrective or a supplement to the stories Percy and Rodriguez tell. You will want both to tell your story and to use it as a way of returning to and commenting on Percy and Rodriguez, and the arguments they make. Your authority can rest on the fact that you are a student and as a consequence have ways of understanding that position that they do not.

MARY LOUISE
PRATT

*M*ARY LOUISE PRATT (b. 1948) grew up in Listowel, Ontario, a small Canadian farm town. She got her B.A. at the University of Toronto and her Ph.D.
from Stanford University, where she is now a professor in the departments of comparative literature and Spanish and Portuguese. At Stanford, she was one of the cofounders of the new freshman culture program, a controversial series of required
courses that replaced the old Western civilization core courses. The course she is particularly associated with is called "Europe and the Americas"; it brings together European representations of the Americas with indigenous American texts. As you
might guess from the essay that follows, the new program at Stanford expands the
range of countries, languages, cultures, and texts that are seen as a necessary introduction to the world; it also, however, revises the very idea of culture that many of us
take for granted—particularly the idea that culture, at its best, expresses common
values in a common language.

    Pratt is the author of Toward a Speech Act Theory of Literary Discourse
(1977) and coauthor of Women, Culture, and Politics in Latin America *(1990),
the textbook* Linguistics for Students of Literature *(1980) and* Amour Brujo:
The Images and Culture of Love in the Andes *(1990). Her most recent work is*
Imperial Eyes: Studies in Travel Writing and Transculturation *(1992). The
essay that follows was revised to serve as the introduction to* Imperial Eyes, *which*

is particularly about European travel writing in the eighteenth and nineteenth centuries, when Europe was "discovering" Africa and the Americas. It argues that travel writing produced "the rest of the world" for European readers. It didn't "report" on Africa or South America; it produced an "Africa" or an "America" for European consumption. Travel writing produced places that could be thought of as barren, empty, undeveloped, inconceivable, needful of European influence and control, ready to serve European industrial, intellectual, and commercial interests. The reports of travelers or, later, scientists and anthropologists are part of a more general process by which the emerging industrial nations took possession of new territory.

The European understanding of Peru, for example, came through European accounts, not from attempts to understand or elicit responses from Andeans, Peruvian natives. When such a response was delivered, when an Andean, Guaman Poma, wrote to King Philip III of Spain, his letter was unreadable. Pratt is interested in just those moments of contact between peoples and cultures. She is interested in how King Philip read (or failed to read) a letter from Peru, but also in how someone like Guaman Poma prepared himself to write to the king of Spain. To fix these moments, she makes use of a phrase she coined, the "contact zone," which, she says,

> I use to refer to the space of colonial encounters, the space in which peoples geographically and historically separated come into contact with each other and establish ongoing relations, usually involving conditions of coercion, radical inequality, and intractable conflict. . . . By using the term "contact," I aim to foreground the interactive, improvisational dimensions of colonial encounters so easily ignored or suppressed by diffusionist accounts of conquest and domination. A "contact" perspective emphasizes how subjects are constituted in and by their relations to each other. It treats the relations among colonizers and colonized, or travelers and "travelees," not in terms of separateness or apartheid, but in terms of copresence, interaction, interlocking understandings and practices.

Like Adrienne Rich's "When We Dead Awaken: Writing as Re-Vision" (p. 549) (and, for that matter, Clifford Geertz's "Deep Play," p. 228, and Virginia Woolf's "A Room of One's Own," p. 719), "Arts of the Contact Zone" was first written as a lecture. It was delivered as a keynote address at the second Modern Language Association Literacy Conference, held in Pittsburgh, Pennsylvania, in 1990.

Arts of the Contact Zone

Whenever the subject of literacy comes up, what often pops first into my mind is a conversation I overheard eight years ago between my son Sam and his best friend, Willie, aged six and seven, respectively: "Why don't you trade me Many Trails for Carl Yats . . . Yesits . . . Ya-strum-scrum." "That's not how you say it, dummy, it's Carl Yes . . . Yes . . . oh, I don't know." Sam and Willie had just discovered baseball cards. Many Trails was their decoding, with the help of first-grade English phonics, of the name Manny Trillo. The name they were quite rightly stumped on was Carl Yastremski. That was the first time I remembered seeing them put their incipient literacy to their own use, and I was of course thrilled.

Sam and Willie learned a lot about phonics that year by trying to decipher surnames on baseball cards, and a lot about cities, states, heights, weights, places of birth, stages of life. In the years that followed, I watched Sam apply his arithmetic skills to working out batting averages and subtracting retirement years from rookie years; I watched him develop senses of patterning and order by arranging and rearranging his cards for hours on end, and aesthetic judgment by comparing different photos, different series, layouts, and color schemes. American geography and history took shape in his mind through baseball cards. Much of his social life revolved around trading them, and he learned about exchange, fairness, trust, the importance of processes as opposed to results, what it means to get cheated, taken advantage of, even robbed. Baseball cards were the medium of his economic life too. Nowhere better to learn the power and arbitrariness of money, the absolute divorce between use value and exchange value, notions of long- and short-term investment, the possibility of personal values that are independent of market values.

Baseball cards meant baseball card shows, where there was much to be learned about adult worlds as well. And baseball cards opened the door to baseball books, shelves and shelves of encyclopedias, magazines, histories, biographies, novels, books of jokes, anecdotes, cartoons, even poems. Sam learned the history of American racism and the struggle against it through baseball; he saw the Depression and two world wars from behind home plate. He learned the meaning of commodified labor, what it means for one's body and talents to be owned and dispensed by another. He knows something about Japan, Taiwan, Cuba, and Central America and how men and boys do things there. Through the history and experience of baseball stadiums he thought about architecture, light, wind, topography, meteorology, the dynamics of public space. He learned the meaning of expertise, of knowing about something well enough that you can start a conversation with a stranger and feel sure of holding your own. Even with an adult—especially with an adult. Throughout his preadolescent years, baseball history was Sam's luminous point of contact with grown-ups, his lifeline to caring. And, of course, all this time he was also playing baseball, struggling his way through the stages of the local Little League system, lucky enough to be a pretty good player, loving the game and coming to know deeply his strengths and weaknesses.

Literacy began for Sam with the newly pronounceable names on the picture cards and brought him what has been easily the broadest, most varied, most enduring, and most integrated experience of his thirteen-year life. Like many parents, I was delighted to see schooling give Sam the tools with which to find and open all these doors. At the same time I found it unforgivable that schooling itself gave him nothing remotely as meaningful to do, let alone anything that would actually take him beyond the referential, masculinist ethos of baseball and its lore.

However, I was not invited here to speak as a parent, nor as an expert on literacy. I was asked to speak as an MLA [Modern Language Association] member working in the elite academy. In that capacity my contribution is undoubtedly supposed to be abstract, irrelevant, and anchored outside the real world. I wouldn't dream of disappointing anyone. I propose immediately to head back several centuries to a text that has a few points in common with baseball cards and raises thoughts about what Tony Sarmiento, in his comments to the conference, called new visions of literacy. In 1908 a Peruvianist named Richard Pietschmann was exploring in the Danish Royal Archive in Copenhagen and came across a manuscript. It was dated in the city of Cuzco in Peru, in the year 1613, some forty years after the final fall of the Inca empire to the Spanish and signed with an unmistakably Andean indigenous name: Felipe Guaman Poma de Ayala. Written in a mixture of Quechua and ungrammatical, expressive Spanish, the manuscript was a letter addressed by an unknown but apparently literate Andean to King Philip III of Spain. What stunned Pietschmann was that the letter was twelve hundred pages long. There were almost eight hundred pages of written text and four hundred of captioned line drawings. It was titled *The First New Chronicle and Good Government.* No one knew (or knows) how the manuscript got to the library in Copenhagen or how long it had been there. No one, it appeared, had ever bothered to read it or figured out how. Quechua was not thought of as a written language in 1908, nor Andean culture as a literate culture.

Pietschmann prepared a paper on his find, which he presented in London in 1912, a year after the rediscovery of Machu Picchu by Hiram Bingham. Reception, by an international congress of Americanists, was apparently confused. It took twenty-five years for a facsimile edition of the work to appear in Paris. It was not till the late 1970s, as positivist reading habits gave way to interpretive studies and colonial elitisms to postcolonial pluralisms, that Western scholars found ways of reading Guaman Poma's *New Chronicle and Good Government* as the extraordinary intercultural tour de force that it was. The letter got there, only 350 years too late, a miracle and a terrible tragedy.

I propose to say a few more words about this erstwhile unreadable text, in order to lay out some thoughts about writing and literacy in what I like to call the *contact zones.* I use this term to refer to social spaces where cultures meet, clash, and grapple with each other, often in contexts of highly asymmetrical relations of power, such as colonialism, slavery, or their aftermaths as they are lived out in many parts of the world today. Eventually I will use the term to reconsider the models of community that many of us rely on in teaching and theorizing and that are under challenge today. But first a little more about Guaman Poma's giant letter to Philip III.

Insofar as anything is known about him at all, Guaman Poma exemplified the sociocultural complexities produced by conquest and empire. He was an indigenous Andean who claimed noble Inca descent and who had adopted (at least in some sense) Christianity. He may have worked in the Spanish colonial administration as an interpreter, scribe, or assistant to a Spanish tax collector—as a mediator, in short. He says he learned to write from his half brother, a mestizo whose Spanish father had given him access to religious education.

Guaman Poma's letter to the king is written in two languages (Spanish and Quechua) and two parts. The first is called the *Nueva corónica*, "New Chronicle." The title is important. The chronicle of course was the main writing apparatus through which the Spanish presented their American conquests to themselves. It constituted one of the main official discourses. In writing a "new chronicle," Guaman Poma took over the official Spanish genre for his own ends. Those ends were, roughly, to construct a new picture of the world, a picture of a Christian world with Andean rather than European peoples at the center of it—Cuzco, not Jerusalem. In the *New Chronicle* Guaman Poma begins by rewriting the Christian history of the world from Adam and Eve (fig. 1), incorporating the Amerindians into it as offspring of one of the sons of Noah. He identifies five ages of Christian history that he links in parallel with the five ages of canonical Andean history—separate but equal trajectories that diverge with Noah and reintersect not with Columbus but with Saint Bartholomew, claimed to have preceded Columbus in the Americas. In a couple of hundred pages, Guaman Poma constructs a veritable encyclopedia of Inca and pre-Inca history, customs, laws, social forms, public offices, and dynastic leaders. The depictions resemble European manners and customs description, but also reproduce the meticulous detail with which knowledge in Inca society was stored on *quipus* and in the oral memories of elders.

Guaman Poma's *New Chronicle* is an instance of what I have proposed to call an *autoethnographic* text, by which I mean a text in which people undertake to describe themselves in ways that engage with representations others have made of them. Thus if ethnographic texts are those in which European metropolitan subjects represent to themselves their others (usually their conquered others), autoethnographic texts are representations that the so-defined others construct *in response to* or in dialogue with those texts. Autoethnographic texts are not, then, what are usually thought of as autochthonous forms of expression or self-representation (as the Andean *quipus* were). Rather they involve a selective collaboration with and appropriation of idioms of the metropolis or the conqueror. These are merged or infiltrated to varying degrees with indigenous idioms to create self-representations intended to intervene in metropolitan modes of understanding. Autoethnographic works are often addressed to both metropolitan audiences and the speaker's own community. Their reception is thus highly indeterminate. Such texts often constitute a marginalized group's point of entry into the

Figure 1. Adam and Eve

dominant circuits of print culture. It is interesting to think, for example, of American slave autobiography in its autoethnographic dimensions, which in some respects distinguish it from Euramerican autobiographical tradition. The concept might help explain why some of the earliest published writing by Chicanas took the form of folkloric manners and customs sketches written in English and published in English-language newspapers or folklore magazines (see Treviño). Autoethnographic representation often involves concrete collaborations between people, as between literate ex-slaves and abolitionist intellectuals, or between Guaman Poma and the Inca elders who were his informants. Often, as in Guaman Poma, it involves more than one language. In recent decades autoethnography, critique, and resistance have reconnected with writing in a contemporary creation of the contact zone, the *testimonio.*

Guaman Poma's *New Chronicle* ends with a revisionist account of the Spanish conquest, which, he argues, should have been a peaceful encounter of equals with the potential for benefiting both, but for the mindless greed of the Spanish. He parodies Spanish history. Following contact with the Incas, he writes, "In all Castille, there was a great commotion. All day and at night in their dreams the Spaniards were saying, 'Yndias, yndias, oro, plata, oro, plata del Piru'" ("Indies, Indies, gold, silver, gold, silver from Peru") (fig. 2). The Spanish, he writes, brought nothing of value to share with the Andeans, nothing "but armor and guns con la codicia de oro, plata oro y plata, yndias, a las Yndias, Piru" ("with the lust for gold, silver, gold and silver, Indies, the Indies, Peru") (372). I quote these words as an example of a conquered subject using the conqueror's language to construct a parodic, oppositional representation of the conqueror's own speech. Guaman Poma mirrors back to the Spanish (in their language, which is alien to him) an image of themselves that they often suppress and will therefore surely recognize. Such are the dynamics of language, writing, and representation in contact zones.

The second half of the epistle continues the critique. It is titled *Buen gobierno y justicia,* "Good Government and Justice," and combines a description of colonial society in the Andean region with a passionate denunciation of Spanish exploitation and abuse. (These, at the time he was writing, were decimating the population of the Andes at a genocidal rate. In fact, the potential loss of the labor force became a main cause for reform of the system.) Guaman Poma's most implacable hostility is invoked by the clergy, followed by the dreaded *corregidores,* or colonial overseers (fig. 3). He also praises good works, Christian habits, and just men where he finds them, and offers at length his views as to what constitutes "good government and justice." The Indies, he argues, should be administered through a collaboration of Inca and Spanish elites. The epistle ends with an imaginary question-and-answer session in which, in a reversal of hierarchy, the king is depicted asking Guaman Poma questions about how to reform the empire—a dialogue imagined across the many lines that divide the Andean scribe from the imperial monarch, and in which the subordinated subject single-handedly gives himself authority in the colonizer's language and verbal repertoire. In a way, it worked—this extraordinary text did get written—but in a way it did not, for the letter never reached its addressee.

To grasp the import of Guaman Poma's project, one needs to keep in mind that the Incas had no system of writing. Their huge empire is said to be the only known instance of a full-blown bureaucratic state society built and administered without writing. Guaman Poma constructs his text by appropriating and adapting pieces of the representational repertoire of the invaders. He does not simply imitate or reproduce it; he selects and adapts it along Andean lines to express (bilingually, mind you) Andean interests and aspirations. Ethnographers have used the term *transculturation* to describe processes whereby members of subordinated or marginal groups select and invent from materials transmitted by a dominant or metropolitan culture. The term, originally coined by Cuban sociologist Fernando Ortiz in the 1940s, aimed to replace overly reductive concepts of acculturation and assimilation used to characterize culture under conquest. While subordinate peoples do not usually control what emanates from the dominant culture, they do

Figure 2. Conquista. Meeting of Spaniard and Inca. The Inca says in Quechua,
"You eat this gold?" Spaniard replies in Spanish, "We eat this gold."

determine to varying extents what gets absorbed into their own and what it
gets used for. Transculturation, like autoethnography, is a phenomenon of
the contact zone.

As scholars have realized only relatively recently, the transcultural character of Guaman Poma's text is intricately apparent in its visual as well as its
written component. The genre of the four hundred line drawings is European—there seems to have been no tradition of representational drawing
among the Incas—but in their execution they deploy specifically Andean systems of spatial symbolism that express Andean values and aspirations.[1]

In figure 1, for instance, Adam is depicted on the left-hand side below the
sun, while Eve is on the right-hand side below the moon, and slightly lower
than Adam. The two are divided by the diagonal of Adam's digging stick. In
Andean spatial symbolism, the diagonal descending from the sun marks the
basic line of power and authority dividing upper from lower, male from female, dominant from subordinate. In figure 2, the Inca appears in the same
position as Adam, with the Spaniard opposite, and the two at the same

Figure 3. Corregidor de minas. Catalog of Spanish abuses of indigenous labor force.

height. In figure 3, depicting Spanish abuses of power, the symbolic pattern is reversed. The Spaniard is in a high position indicating dominance, but on the "wrong" (right-hand) side. The diagonals of his lance and that of the servant doing the flogging mark out a line of illegitimate, though real, power. The Andean figures continue to occupy the left-hand side of the picture, but clearly as victims. Guaman Poma wrote that the Spanish conquest had produced *"un mundo al reves,"* "a world in reverse."

In sum, Guaman Poma's text is truly a product of the contact zone. If one thinks of cultures, or literatures, as discrete, coherently structured, monolingual edifices, Guaman Poma's text, and indeed any autoethnographic work, appears anomalous or chaotic—as it apparently did to the European scholars Pietschmann spoke to in 1912. If one does not think of cultures this way, then Guaman Poma's text is simply heterogeneous, as the Andean region was itself and remains today. Such a text is heterogeneous on the reception end as well as the production end: it will read very differently to people in different positions in the contact zone. Because it deploys European and Andean systems of meaning making, the letter necessarily means differently to bilingual Spanish-Quechua speakers and to monolingual speakers in either language; the drawings mean differently to monocultural readers, Spanish or Andean, and to bicultural readers responding to the Andean symbolic structures embodied in European genres.

In the Andes in the early 1600s there existed a literate public with considerable intercultural competence and degrees of bilingualism. Unfortunately, such a community did not exist in the Spanish court with which Guaman Poma was trying to make contact. It is interesting to note that in the same year Guaman Poma sent off his letter, a text by another Peruvian was adopted in official circles in Spain as the canonical Christian mediation between the Spanish conquest and Inca history. It was another huge encyclopedic work, titled the *Royal Commentaries of the Incas*, written, tellingly, by a mestizo, Inca Garcilaso de la Vega. Like the mestizo half brother who taught Guaman Poma to read and write, Inca Garcilaso was the son of an Inca princess and a Spanish official, and had lived in Spain since he was seventeen. Though he too spoke Quechua, his book is written in eloquent, standard Spanish, without illustrations. While Guaman Poma's life's work sat somewhere unread, the *Royal Commentaries* was edited and reedited in Spain and the New World, a mediation that coded the Andean past and present in ways thought unthreatening to colonial hierarchy.[2] The textual hierarchy persists; the *Royal Commentaries* today remains a staple item on Ph.D. reading lists in Spanish, while the *New Chronicle and Good Government*, despite the ready availability of several fine editions, is not. However, though Guaman Poma's text did not reach its destination, the transcultural currents of expression it exemplifies continued to evolve in the Andes, as they still do, less in writing than in storytelling, ritual, song, dance-drama, painting and sculpture, dress, textile art, forms of governance, religious belief, and many other vernacular art forms. All express the effects of long-term contact and intractable, unequal conflict.

Autoethnography, transculturation, critique, collaboration, bilingualism, mediation, parody, denunciation, imaginary dialogue, vernacular expression—these are some of the literate arts of the contact zone. Miscomprehension, incomprehension, dead letters, unread masterpieces, absolute heterogeneity of meaning—these are some of the perils of writing in the contact zone. They all live among us today in the transnationalized metropolis of the United States and are becoming more widely visible, more pressing, and, like Guaman Poma's text, more decipherable to those who once would have ignored them in defense of a stable, centered sense of knowledge and reality.

Contact and Community

The idea of the contact zone is intended in part to contrast with ideas of community that underlie much of the thinking about language, communication, and culture that gets done in the academy. A couple of years ago, thinking about the linguistic theories I knew, I tried to make sense of a utopian quality that often seemed to characterize social analyses of language by the academy. Languages were seen as living in "speech communities," and these tended to be theorized as discrete, self-defined, coherent entities, held together by a homogeneous competence or grammar shared identically and equally among all the members. This abstract idea of the speech community seemed to reflect, among other things, the utopian way modern nations conceive of themselves as what Benedict Anderson calls "imagined communities."[3] In a book of that title, Anderson observes that with the possible exception of what he calls "primordial villages," human communities exist as *imagined* entities in which people "will never know most of their fellow-members, meet them or even hear of them, yet in the mind of each lives the image of their communion." "Communities are distinguished," he goes on to say, "not by their falsity/genuineness, but by *the style in which they are imagined*" (15; emphasis mine). Anderson proposes three features that characterize the style in which the modern nation is imagined. First, it is imagined as *limited,* by "finite, if elastic, boundaries"; second, it is imagined as *sovereign;* and, third, it is imagined as *fraternal,* "a deep, horizontal comradeship" for which millions of people are prepared "not so much to kill as willingly to die" (15). As the image suggests, the nation-community is embodied metonymically in the finite, sovereign, fraternal figure of the citizen-soldier.

Anderson argues that European bourgeoisies were distinguished by their ability to "achieve solidarity on an essentially imagined basis" (74) on a scale far greater than that of elites of other times and places. Writing and literacy play a central role in this argument. Anderson maintains, as have others, that the main instrument that made bourgeois nation-building projects possible was print capitalism. The commercial circulation of books in the various European vernaculars, he argues, was what first created the invisible networks that would eventually constitute the literate elites and those they ruled as nations. (Estimates are that 180 million books were put into circulation in Europe between the years 1500 and 1600 alone.)

Now obviously this style of imagining of modern nations, as Anderson describes it, is strongly utopian, embodying values like equality, fraternity, liberty, which the societies often profess but systematically fail to realize. The prototype of the modern nation as imagined community was, it seemed to me, mirrored in ways people thought about language and the speech community. Many commentators have pointed out how modern views of language as code and competence assume a unified and homogeneous social world in which language exists as a shared patrimony—as a device, precisely, for imagining community. An image of a universally shared literacy is also part of the picture. The prototypical manifestation of language is generally taken to be the speech of individual adult native speakers face-to-face (as in Saussure's famous diagram) in monolingual, even monodialectal situations—in short, the most homogeneous case linguistically and socially. The same goes for written communication. Now one could certainly imagine a theory that assumed different things—that argued, for instance, that the most revealing speech situation for understanding language was one involving a gathering of people each of whom spoke two languages and understood a third and held only one language in common with any of the others. It depends on what workings of language you want to see or want to see first, on what you choose to define as normative.

In keeping with autonomous, fraternal models of community, analyses of language use commonly assume that principles of cooperation and shared understanding are normally in effect. Descriptions of interactions between people in conversation, classrooms, medical and bureaucratic settings, readily take it for granted that the situation is governed by a single set of rules or norms shared by all participants. The analysis focuses then on how those rules produce or fail to produce an orderly, coherent exchange. Models involving games and moves are often used to describe interactions. Despite whatever conflicts or systematic social differences might be in play, it is assumed that all participants are engaged in the same game and that the game is the same for all players. Often it is. But of course it often is not, as, for example, when speakers are from different classes or cultures, or one party is exercising authority and another is submitting to it or questioning it. Last year one of my children moved to a new elementary school that had more open classrooms and more flexible curricula than the conventional school he started out in. A few days into the term, we asked him what it was like at the new school. "Well," he said, "they're a lot nicer, and they have a lot less rules. But know *why* they're nicer?" "Why?" I asked. "So you'll obey all the rules they don't have," he replied. This is a very coherent analysis with considerable elegance and explanatory power, but probably not the one his teacher would have given.

When linguistic (or literate) interaction is described in terms of orderliness, games, moves, or scripts, usually only legitimate moves are actually named as part of the system, where legitimacy is defined from the point of view of the party in authority—regardless of what other parties might see themselves as doing. Teacher-pupil language, for example, tends to be described almost entirely from the point of view of the teacher and teaching, not from the point of view of pupils and pupiling (the word doesn't even exist, though the thing certainly does). If a classroom is analyzed as a social world unified and homogenized with respect to the teacher, whatever students do other than what the teacher specifies is invisible or anomalous to the analysis. This can be true in practice as well. On several occasions my fourth grader, the one busy obeying all the rules they didn't have, was given writing assignments that took the form of answering a series of questions to build up a paragraph. These questions often asked him to identify with the interests of those in power over him—parents, teachers, doctors, public authorities. He invariably sought ways to resist or subvert these assignments. One assignment, for instance, called for imagining "a helpful invention." The students were asked to write single-sentence responses to the following questions:

What kind of invention would help you?
How would it help you?
Why would you need it?
What would it look like?
Would other people be able to use it also?
What would be an invention to help your teacher?
What would be an invention to help your parents?

Manuel's reply read as follows:

A grate adventchin

Some inventchins are GRATE!!!!!!!!!!! My inventchin would be a shot that would put every thing you learn at school in your brain. It would help me by letting me graduate right now!! I would need it because it would let me play with my friends, go on vacachin and, do fun a lot more. It would look like a regular shot. Ather peaple would use to. This inventchin would help my teacher parents get away from a lot of work. I think a shot like this would be GRATE!

Despite the spelling, the assignment received the usual star to indicate the task had been fulfilled in an acceptable way. No recognition was available, however, of the humor, the attempt to be critical or contestatory, to parody the structures of authority. On that score, Manuel's luck was only slightly better than Guaman Poma's. What is the place of unsolicited oppositional discourse, parody, resistance, critique in the imagined classroom community? Are teachers supposed to feel that their teaching has been most successful when they have eliminated such things and unified the social world, probably in their own image? Who wins when we do that? Who loses?

Such questions may be hypothetical, because in the United States in the 1990s, many teachers find themselves less and less able to do that even if they want to. The composition of the national collectivity is changing and so are the styles, as Anderson put it, in which it is being imagined. In the 1980s in many nation-states, imagined national syntheses that had retained hegemonic force began to dissolve. Internal social groups with histories and lifeways different from the official ones began insisting on those histories and lifeways *as part of their citizenship,* as the very mode of their membership in the national collectivity. In their dialogues with dominant institutions, many groups began asserting a rhetoric of belonging that made demands beyond those of representation and basic rights granted from above. In universities we started to hear, "I don't just want you to let me be here, I want to belong here; this institution should belong to me as much as it does to anyone else." Institutions have responded with, among other things, rhetorics of diversity and multiculturalism whose import at this moment is up for grabs across the ideological spectrum.

These shifts are being lived out by everyone working in education today, and everyone is challenged by them in one way or another. Those of us committed to educational democracy are particularly challenged as that notion finds itself besieged on the public agenda. Many of those who govern us display, openly, their interest in a quiescent, ignorant, manipulable electorate. Even as an ideal, the concept of an enlightened citizenry seems to have disappeared from the national imagination. A couple of years ago the university where I work went through an intense and wrenching debate over a narrowly defined Western-culture requirement that had been instituted there in 1980. It kept boiling down to a debate over the ideas of national patrimony, cultural citizenship, and imagined community. In the end, the requirement was transformed into a much more broadly defined course called Cultures, Ideas, Values.[4] In the context of the change, a new course was designed that centered on the Americas and the multiple cultural histories (including European ones) that have intersected here. As you can imagine, the course attracted a very diverse student body. The classroom functioned not like a homogeneous community or a horizontal alliance but like a contact zone. Every single text we read stood in specific historical relationships to the students in the class, but the range and variety of historical relationships in play were enormous. Everybody had a stake in nearly everything we read, but the range and kind of stakes varied widely.

It was the most exciting teaching we had ever done, and also the hardest. We were struck, for example, at how anomalous the formal lecture became in a contact zone (who can forget Atahuallpa throwing down the Bible because it would not speak to him?). The lecturer's traditional (imagined) task—unifying the world in the class's eyes by means of a monologue that rings equally coherent, revealing, and true for all, forging an ad hoc community, homogeneous with respect to one's own words—this task became not only impossible but anomalous and unimaginable. Instead, one had to work in the knowledge that whatever one said was going to be systematically received in radically heterogeneous ways that we were neither able nor entitled to prescribe.

The very nature of the course put ideas and identities on the line. All the students in the class had the experience, for example, of hearing their culture discussed and objectified in ways that horrified them; all the students saw their roots traced back to legacies of both glory and shame; all the students experienced face-to-face the ignorance and incomprehension, and occasionally the hostility, of others. In the absence of community values and the hope of synthesis, it was easy to forget the positives; the fact, for instance, that kinds of marginalization once taken for granted were gone. Virtually every student was having the experience of seeing the world described with him or her in it. Along with rage, incomprehension, and pain, there were exhilarating moments of wonder and revelation, mutual understanding, and new wisdom—the joys of the contact zone. The sufferings and revelations were, at different moments to be sure, experienced by every student. No one was excluded, and no one was safe.

The fact that no one was safe made all of us involved in the course appreciate the importance of what we came to call "safe houses." We used the term to refer to social and intellectual spaces where groups can constitute themselves as horizontal, homogeneous, sovereign communities with high degrees of trust, shared understandings, temporary protection from legacies of oppression. This is why, as we realized, multicultural curricula should not seek to replace ethnic or women's studies, for example. Where there are legacies of subordination, groups need places for healing and mutual recognition, safe houses in which to construct shared understandings, knowledges, claims on the world that they can then bring into the contact zone.

Meanwhile, our job in the Americas course remains to figure out how to make that crossroads the best site for learning that it can be. We are looking for the pedagogical arts of the contact zone. These will include, we are sure, exercises in storytelling and in identifying with the ideas, interests, histories, and attitudes of others; experiments in transculturation and collaborative work and in the arts of critique, parody, and comparison (including unseemly comparisons between elite and vernacular cultural forms); the redemption of the oral; ways for people to engage with suppressed aspects of history (including their own histories), ways to move *into and out of* rhetorics of authenticity; ground rules for communication across lines of difference and hierarchy that go beyond politeness but maintain mutual respect; a systematic approach to the all-important concept of *cultural mediation*. These arts were in play in every room at the extraordinary Pittsburgh conference on literacy. I learned a lot about them there, and I am thankful.

WORKS CITED

Adorno, Rolena. *Guaman Poma de Ayala: Writing and Resistance in Colonial Peru.* Austin: U of Texas P, 1986.

Anderson, Benedict. *Imagined Communities: Reflections on the Origins and Spread of Nationalism.* London: Verso, 1984.

Garcilaso de la Vega, El Inca. *Royal Commentaries of the Incas.* 1613. Austin: U of Texas P, 1966.

Guaman Poma de Ayala, Felipe. *El primer nueva corónica y buen gobierno.* Manuscript. Ed. John Murra and Rolena Adorno. Mexico: Siglo XXI, 1980.

Pratt, Mary Louise. "Linguistic Utopias." *The Linguistics of Writing.* Ed. Nigel Fabb et al. Manchester: Manchester UP, 1987. 48–66.

Treviño, Gloria. "Cultural Ambivalence in Early Chicano Prose Fiction." Diss. Stanford U, 1985.

NOTES

[1] For an introduction in English to these and other aspects of Guaman Poma's work, see Rolena Adorno. Adorno and Mercedes Lopez-Baralt pioneered the study of Andean symbolic systems in Guaman Poma.

[2] It is far from clear that the *Royal Commentaries* was as benign as the Spanish seemed to

assume. The book certainly played a role in maintaining the identity and aspirations of indigenous elites in the Andes. In the mid–eighteenth century, a new edition of the *Royal Commentaries* was suppressed by Spanish authorities because its preface included a prophecy by Sir Walter Raleigh that the English would invade Peru and restore the Inca monarchy.

[3] The discussion of community here is summarized from my essay "Linguistic Utopias."

[4] For information about this program and the contents of courses taught in it, write Program in Cultures, Ideas, Values (CIV), Stanford Univ., Stanford, CA 94305.

·   ·   ·   ·   ·   ·   ·   ·   ·   ·   ·

QUESTIONS FOR A SECOND READING

1. Perhaps the most interesting question "Arts of the Contact Zone" raises for its readers is how to put together the pieces: the examples from Pratt's children, the discussion of Guaman Poma and the *New Chronicle and Good Government*, the brief history of European literacy, and the discussion of curriculum reform at Stanford. The terms that run through the sections are, among others, these: "contact," "community," "autoethnography," "transculturation." As you reread, mark those passages you might use to trace the general argument that cuts across these examples.

2. This essay was originally delivered as a lecture. Before you read her essay again, create a set of notes on what you remember as important, relevant, or worthwhile. Imagine yourself as part of her audience. Then reread the essay. Where would you want to interrupt her? What questions could you ask her that might make "Arts of the Contact Zone" more accessible to you?

3. This is an essay about reading and writing and teaching and learning, about the "literate arts" and the "pedagogical arts" of the contact zone. Surely the composition class, the first-year college English class, can be imagined as a contact zone. And it seems in the spirit of Pratt's essay to identify (as a student) with Guaman Poma. As you reread, think about how and where this essay might be said to speak directly to you about your education as a reader and writer in a contact zone.

4. There are some difficult terms in this essay: "autochthonous," "autoethnography," "transculturation." The last two are defined in the text; the first you will have to look up. (We did.) In some ways, the slipperiest of the key words in the essay is "culture." At one point Pratt says,

> If one thinks of cultures, or literatures, as discrete, coherently structured, monolingual edifices, Guaman Poma's text, and indeed any autoethnographic work, appears anomalous or chaotic—as it apparently did to the European scholars Pietschmann spoke to in 1912. If one does not think of cultures this way, then Guaman Poma's text is simply heterogeneous, as the Andean region was itself and remains today. Such a text is heterogeneous on the reception end as well as the production end: it will read very differently to people in different positions in the contact zone. (p. 535)

If one thinks of cultures as "coherently structured, monolingual edifices," the text appears one way; if one thinks otherwise the text is "simply heterogeneous." What might it mean to make this shift in the way one thinks of culture? Can you do it—that is, can you read the *New Chronicle* from both points of view, make the two points of view work in your own imagining? Can you, for example, think of a group that you participate in as a "community"? Then can you think of it as a "contact zone"? Which one seems "natural" to you? What does Pratt assume to be the dominant point of view now, for *her* readers?

As you reread, not only do you want to get a sense of how to explain these two attitudes toward culture, but you need to practice shifting your point of view from one to the other. Think, from inside the position of each, of the things you would be expected to say about Poma's text, Manuel's invention, and your classroom.

ASSIGNMENTS FOR WRITING

Here, briefly, are two descriptions of the writing one might find or expect in the "contact zone." They serve as an introduction to the three writing assignments.

> Autoethnography, transculturation, critique, collaboration, bilingualism, mediation, parody, denunciation, imaginary dialogue, vernacular expression—these are some of the literate arts of the contact zone. Miscomprehension, incomprehension, dead letters, unread masterpieces, absolute heterogeneity of meaning—these are some of the perils of writing in the contact zone. They all live among us today in the transnationalized metropolis of the United States and are becoming more widely visible, more pressing, and, like Guaman Poma's text, more decipherable to those who once would have ignored them in defense of a stable, centered sense of knowledge and reality. (p. 536)

> We are looking for the pedagogical arts of the contact zone. These will include, we are sure, exercises in storytelling and in identifying with the ideas, interests, histories, and attitudes of others; experiments in transculturation and collaborative work and in the arts of critique, parody, and comparison (including unseemly comparisons between elite and vernacular cultural forms); the redemption of the oral; ways for people to engage with suppressed aspects of history (including their own histories), ways to move *into and out of* rhetorics of authenticity; ground rules for communication across lines of difference and hierarchy that go beyond politeness but maintain mutual respect; a systematic approach to the all-important concept of *cultural mediation*. (p. 541)

1. One way of working with Pratt's essay, of extending its project, would be to conduct your own local inventory of writing from the contact zone. You might do this on your own or in teams with others from your class. You will want to gather several similar documents, your "archive," before you make your final selection. Think about how to make that choice. What makes one document stand out as representative? Here are two ways you might organize your search:

a. You could look for historical documents. A local historical society might have documents written by Native Americans ("Indians") to the white settlers. There may be documents written by slaves to masters or to northern whites explaining their experience with slavery. There may be documents by women (like suffragettes) trying to negotiate for public positions and rights. There may be documents from any of a number of racial or ethnic groups—Hispanic, Jewish, Irish, Italian, Polish, Swedish—trying to explain their positions to the mainstream culture. There may, perhaps at union halls, be documents written by workers to owners. Your own sense of the heritage of your area should direct your search.

b. Or you could look for contemporary documents in the print that is around you, things that you might otherwise overlook. Pratt refers to one of the characteristic genres of the Hispanic community, the *"testimonio."* You could look at the writing of any marginalized group, particularly writing intended, at least in part, to represent the experience of outsiders to the dominant culture (or to be in dialogue with that culture or to respond to that culture). These documents, if we follow Pratt's example, would encompass the work of young children or students, including college students.

Once you have completed your inventory, choose a document you would like to work with and present it carefully and in detail (perhaps in even greater detail than Pratt's presentation of the *New Chronicle*). You might imagine that you are presenting this to someone who would not have seen it and would not know how to read it, at least not as an example of the literate arts of the contact zone.

2. Another way of extending the project of Pratt's essay would be to write your own autoethnography. It should not be too hard to locate a setting or context in which you are the "other"—the one who speaks from outside rather than inside the dominant discourse. Pratt says that the position of the outsider is marked not only by differences of language and ways of thinking and speaking but also by differences in power, authority, status. In a sense, she argues, the only way those in power can understand you is in *their* terms. These are terms you will need to use to tell your story, but your goal is to describe your position in ways that "engage with representations others have made of [you]" without giving in or giving up or disappearing in their already formed sense of who you are.

This is an interesting challenge. One of the things that will make the writing difficult is that the autoethnographic or transcultural text calls upon skills not usually valued in American classrooms: bilingualism, parody, denunciation, imaginary dialogue, vernacular expression, storytelling, unseemly comparisons of high and low cultural forms—these are some of the terms Pratt offers. These do not fit easily with the traditional genres of the writing class (essay, term paper, summary, report) or its traditional values (unity, consistency, sincerity, clarity, correctness, decorum).

You will probably need to take this essay (or whatever it should be called) through several drafts. It might be best to begin as Pratt's student, using her description as a preliminary guide. Once you get a sense of your own project, you may find that you have terms or examples to add to her list of the literate arts of the contact zone.

3. Citing Benedict Anderson and what he calls "imagined communities," Pratt argues that our idea of community is "strongly utopian, embodying values like equality, fraternity, liberty, which the societies often profess but systematically fail to realize." Against this utopian vision of community, Pratt argues that we need to develop ways of understanding (even noticing) social and intellectual spaces that are not homogeneous, unified; we need to develop ways of understanding and valuing difference.

    Think of a community of which you are a member, a community that is important to you. And think about the utopian terms you are given to name and describe this community. Think, then, about this group in Pratt's terms—as a "contact zone." How would you name and describe this social space? Write an essay in which you present these alternate points of view on a single social group. You will need to present this discussion fully, so that someone who is not part of your group can follow what you say, and you should take time to think about the consequences (for you, for your group) of this shift in point of view, in terms.

MAKING CONNECTIONS

1. There are selections in *Ways of Reading* that might be said to represent the autoethnographic text: the chapters by Gloria Anzaldúa (p. 22), the slave narrative by Harriet Jacobs (p. 374), and the story by John Edgar Wideman (p. 652). Choose one of these and, using the example of Pratt's work with the *New Chronicle*, write an essay presenting a reading of it as an autoethnographic and/or transcultural text. You should think about not only how it might be read from this point of view but also how, from another view of culture, it might be misread or unread. This will allow you not only to put Pratt's ideas to work but to think about what is lost or gained through this alternative way of reading.

2. While Mary Louise Pratt does not write about Columbus in "Arts of the Contact Zone," she writes about moments of contact between Europe and the "New World." And she offers a theoretical account of how writing functions at those moments. Her interest is in the writing produced from the other side, from the side of the natives or those who are put into a subordinate position in relationship to a dominant culture. (If the Native Americans had written about or to Columbus, she would be interested in those documents.)

    Stephen Greenblatt, in "Marvelous Possessions (p. 268), is interested in texts written by Europeans about the New World and its inhabitants. And, in a sense, he also charts the "literate arts" of the contact zone. Using Pratt's theory (of contact zones) and her terms (like "autoethnography") as points of reference, write an essay in which you discuss one or two of the long passages quoted in Greenblatt (or perhaps some of the images included in his chapter). What are the key features in this writing? How might you describe its characteristic practices? its problems and its power? How does Greenblatt describe them?

3. Joyce Carol Oates's short story "Theft" (p. 471) looks at the relationship between characters on a college campus, a setting that could (in Pratt's terms) be thought of as a "contact zone." Pratt's essay looks at ways of writing and teaching in the contact zone. It does not, at least not directly, look at codes of behavior—the ways individuals relate, the ways they imagine their connections and obligations to others. Using Oates's representation of how college students act and how they imagine their relations to others (and drawing on your own experience in this setting), write an essay on the college campus as a contact zone.

A D R I E N N E
R I C H

*A*DRIENNE RICH *(b. 1929) once said that whatever she knows, she wants to "know it in [her] own nerves." As a writer, Rich found it necessary to acknowledge her anger at both the oppression of women and her immediate experience of that oppression. She needed to find the "anger that is creative." "Until I could tap into the very rich ocean," she said, "I think that my work was constrained in certain ways. There's this fear of anger in women, which is partly because we've been told it was always destructive, it was always unseemly, and unwomanly, and monstrous."*

 Rich's poetry combines passion and anger with a "yen for order." She wrote her first book of poems, A Change of World, *while an undergraduate at Radcliffe College. The book won the 1951 Yale Younger Poets Award and a generous introduction from W. H. Auden, who was one of the judges. In 1991 she won the Commonwealth Award in Literature and in 1992 the Robert Frost Medal from the Poetry Society of America for a lifetime of achievement in literature. Her other works, which include* The Diamond Cutters *(1955),* Snapshots of a Daughter-in-Law *(1963, 1967),* Necessities of Life *(1966),* Leaflets *(1969),* The Will to Change *(1970), and Diving into the Wreck *(1973), show an increasing concern for the political and psychological consequences of life in patriarchal society. When offered the National Book Award for* Diving into the Wreck, *Rich refused it as an individual but accepted it, in a statement written with two other nominees—Audre Lorde and Alice Walker* *(whose essay "In Search of Our Mothers' Gardens" appears on p. 639)—in the name of all women:*

> We . . . together accept this award in the name of all the women whose voices have gone and still go unheard in a patriarchal world, and in the name of those who, like us, have been tolerated as token women in this culture, often at great cost and in great pain. . . . We dedicate this occasion to the struggle for self-determination of all women, of every color, identification, or derived class, . . . the women who will understand what we are doing here and those who will not understand yet; the silent women whose voices have been denied us, the articulate women who have given us the strength to do our work.

After graduating from Radcliffe in 1951, Rich married and raised three sons. One of her prose collections, Of Woman Born: Motherhood as Experience and Institution *(1976), treats her experience as both mother and daughter with eloquence, even as it calls for the destruction of motherhood as an institution. In 1970 Rich left her marriage, and six years later she published a book of poems that explore a lesbian relationship. But the term "lesbian" for Rich referred to "nothing so simple and dismissible as the fact that two women might go to bed together." As she says in "It Is the Lesbian in Us," a speech reprinted in* On Lies, Secrets, and Silence: Selected Prose *(1979), it refers also to "a sense of desiring oneself; above all, of choosing oneself; it was also a primary intensity between women, an intensity which in the world at large was trivialized, caricatured, or invested with evil. . . . It is the lesbian in us who drives us to feel imaginatively, render in language, grasp, the full connection between woman and woman."*

Rich has published thirteen books of poetry and four collections of prose. In Blood, Bread and Poetry: Selected Prose *(1986), she offers a series of commencement speeches, reviews, lectures, and articles on feminism, gay and lesbian rights, racism, anti-Semitism, and the necessity for the artist, university, and state to find a commitment to social justice. Her most recent book of poems is* Dark Fields of the Republic: Poems 1991–1995 *(1995). In 1991, she published* An Atlas of the Difficult World: Poems, 1988–91, *which was awarded the 1992 Los Angeles Times Book Prize for poetry and was a finalist for both the National Book Award and the National Book Critics Circle Award. In 1993 she also published* Collected Early Poems: 1950–1970. *Rich has taught at Columbia, Brandeis, Cornell, Rutgers, and Stanford universities, Swarthmore College, and the City College of New York. Among her many awards and honors she has held two Guggenheim Fellowships and an Amy Lowell Traveling Fellowship. She has been a member of the department of literature of the American Academy and Institute of Arts and Letters since 1990. She lives in California.*

When We Dead Awaken: Writing as Re-Vision°

The Modern Language Association is both marketplace and funeral parlor for the professional study of Western literature in North America. Like all gatherings of the professions, it has been and remains a "procession of the sons of educated men" (Virginia Woolf): a congeries of old-boys' networks, academicians rehearsing their numb canons in sessions dedicated to the literature of white males, junior scholars under the lash of "publish or perish" delivering papers in the bizarrely lit drawing-rooms of immense hotels: a ritual competition veering between cynicism and desperation.

However, in the interstices of these gentlemanly rites (or, in Mary Daly's words, on the boundaries of this patriarchal space),[1] some feminist scholars, teachers, and graduate students, joined by feminist writers, editors, and publishers, have for a decade been creating more subversive occasions, challenging the sacredness of the gentlemanly canon, sharing the rediscovery of buried works by women, asking women's questions, bringing literary history and criticism back to life in both senses. The Commission of the Status of Women in the Profession was formed in 1969, and held its first public event in 1970. In 1971 the Commission asked Ellen Peck Killoh, Tillie Olsen, Elaine Reuben, and myself, with Elaine Hedges as moderator, to talk on "The Woman Writer in the Twentieth Century." The essay that follows was written for that forum, and later published, along with the other papers from the forum and workshops, in an issue of College English *edited by Elaine Hedges ("Women Writing and Teaching," vol. 34, no. 1, October 1972). With a few revisions, mainly updating, it was reprinted in* American Poets *in 1976, edited by William Heyen (New York: Bobbs-Merrill, 1976). That later text is the one published here.*

The challenge flung by feminists at the accepted literary canon, at the methods of teaching it, and at the biased and astigmatic view of male "literary scholarship," has not diminished in the decade since the first Women's Forum; it has become broadened and intensified more recently by the challenges of black and lesbian feminists pointing out that feminist literary criticism itself has overlooked or held back from examining the work of black women and lesbians. The dynamic between a political vision and the demand for a fresh vision of literature is clear: without a growing feminist movement, the first inroads of feminist scholarship could not have been made; without the sharpening of a black feminist consciousness, black

---

As Rich explains, this essay—written in 1971—was first published in 1972 and then included in her volume *On Lies, Secrets, and Silence* (1979). At that time she added the introductory note reprinted here, as well as some notes, identified as *"A.R., 1978."* [Editor's note in the Norton edition.]

women's writing would have been left in limbo between misogynist black
male critics and white feminists still struggling to unearth a white women's
tradition; without an articulate lesbian/feminist movement, lesbian writing
would still be lying in that closet where many of us used to sit reading forbidden books "in a bad light."

Much, much more is yet to be done; and university curricula have of
course changed very little as a result of all this. What *is* changing is the availability of knowledge, of vital texts, the visible effects on women's lives of seeing, hearing our wordless or negated experience affirmed and pursued further in language.

Ibsen's *When We Dead Awaken* is a play about the use that the male artist
and thinker—in the process of creating culture as we know it—has made of
women, in his life and in his work; and about a woman's slow struggling
awakening to the use to which her life has been put. Bernard Shaw wrote in
1900 of this play:

> [Ibsen] shows us that no degradation ever devised or permitted
> is as disastrous as this degradation; that through it women can
> die into luxuries for men and yet can kill them; that men and
> women are becoming conscious of this; and that what remains
> to be seen as perhaps the most interesting of all imminent so-
> cial developments is what will happen "when we dead
> awaken."[2]

It's exhilarating to be alive in a time of awakening consciousness; it can
also be confusing, disorienting, and painful. The awakening of dead or sleeping consciousness has already affected the lives of millions of women, even
those who don't know it yet. It is also affecting the lives of men, even those
who deny its claims upon them. The argument will go on whether an oppressive economic class system is responsible for the oppressive nature of
male/female relations, or whether, in fact, patriarchy—the domination of
males—is the original model of oppression on which all others are based. But
in the last few years the women's movement has drawn inescapable and illuminating connections between our sexual lives and our political institutions.
The sleepwalkers are coming awake, and for the first time this awakening
has a collective reality; it is no longer such a lonely thing to open one's eyes.

Re-vision—the act of looking back, of seeing with fresh eyes, of entering
an old text from a new critical direction—is for women more than a chapter
in cultural history: it is an act of survival. Until we can understand the assumptions in which we are drenched we cannot know ourselves. And this
drive to self-knowledge, for women, is more than a search for identity: it is
part of our refusal of the self-destructiveness of male-dominated society. A
radical critique of literature, feminist in its impulse, would take the work first
of all as a clue to how we live, how we have been living, how we have been

led to imagine ourselves, how our language has trapped as well as liberated us, how the very act of naming has been till now a male prerogative, and how we can begin to see and name—and therefore live—afresh. A change in the concept of sexual identity is essential if we are not going to see the old political order reassert itself in every new revolution. We need to know the writing of the past, and know it differently than we have ever known it; not to pass on a tradition but to break its hold over us.

For writers, and at this moment for women writers in particular, there is the challenge and promise of a whole new psychic geography to be explored. But there is also a difficult and dangerous walking on the ice, as we try to find language and images for the consciousness we are just coming into, and with little in the past to support us. I want to talk about some aspect of this difficulty and this danger.

Jane Harrison, the great classical anthropologist, wrote in 1914 in a letter to her friend Gilbert Murray:

> By and by, about "Women," it has bothered me often—why do women never want to write poetry about Man as a sex—why is Woman a dream and a terror to man and not the other way around? . . . Is it mere convention and propriety, or something deeper?[3]

I think Jane Harrison's question cuts deep into the myth-making tradition, the romantic tradition; deep into what women and men have been to each other; and deep into the psyche of the woman writer. Thinking about that question, I began thinking of the work of two twentieth-century women poets, Sylvia Plath and Diane Wakoski. It strikes me that in the work of both Man appears as, if not a dream, a fascination and a terror; and that the source of the fascination and the terror is, simply, Man's power—to dominate, tyrannize, choose, or reject the woman. The charisma of Man seems to come purely from his power over her and his control of the world by force, not from anything fertile or life-giving in him. And, in the work of both these poets, it is finally the woman's sense of *herself*—embattled, possessed—that gives the poetry its dynamic charge, its rhythms of struggle, need, will, and female energy. Until recently this female anger and this furious awareness of the Man's power over her were not available materials to the female poet, who tended to write of Love as the source of her suffering, and to view that victimization by Love as an almost inevitable fate. Or, like Marianne Moore and Elizabeth Bishop, she kept sexuality at a measured and chiseled distance in her poems.

One answer to Jane Harrison's question has to be that historically men and women have played very different parts in each others' lives. Where woman has been a luxury for man, and has served as the painter's model and the poet's muse, but also as comforter, nurse, cook, bearer of his seed, secretarial assistant, and copyist of manuscripts, man has played a quite different role for the female artist. Henry James repeats an incident which the writer Prosper Mérimée described, of how, while he was living with George Sand,

> he once opened his eyes, in the raw winter dawn, to see his companion, in a dressing-gown, on her knees before the domestic hearth, a candle-stick beside her and a red *madras* round her head, making bravely, with her own hands the fire that was to enable her to sit down betimes to urgent pen and paper. The story represents him as having felt that the spectacle chilled his ardor and tried his taste; her appearance was unfortunate, her occupation an inconsequence, and her industry a reproof—the result of all which was a lively irritation and an early rupture.[4]

The specter of this kind of male judgment, along with the misnaming and thwarting of her needs by a culture controlled by males, has created problems for the woman writer: problems of contact with herself, problems of language and style, problems of energy and survival.

In rereading Virginia Woolf's *A Room of One's Own* (1929) for the first time in some years, I was astonished at the sense of effort, of pains taken, of dogged tentativeness, in the tone of that essay. And I recognized that tone. I had heard it often enough, in myself and in other women. It is the tone of a woman almost in touch with her anger, who is determined not to appear angry, who is *willing* herself to be calm, detached, and even charming in a roomful of men where things have been said which are attacks on her very integrity. Virginia Woolf is addressing an audience of women, but she is acutely conscious—as she always was—of being overheard by men: by Morgan and Lytton and Maynard Keynes and for that matter by her father, Leslie Stephen.[5] She drew the language out into an exacerbated thread in her determination to have her own sensibility yet protect it from those masculine presences. Only at rare moments in that essay do you hear the passion in her voice; she was trying to sound as cool as Jane Austen, as Olympian as Shakespeare, because that is the way the men of the culture thought a writer should sound.

No male writer has written primarily or even largely for women, or with the sense of women's criticism as a consideration when he chooses his materials, his theme, his language. But to a lesser or greater extent, every woman writer has written for men even when, like Virginia Woolf, she was supposed to be addressing women. If we have come to the point when this balance might begin to change, when women can stop being haunted, not only by "convention and propriety" but by internalized fears of being and saying themselves, then it is an extraordinary moment for the woman writer—and reader.

I have hesitated to do what I am going to do now, which is to use myself as an illustration. For one thing, it's a lot easier and less dangerous to talk about other women writers. But there is something else. Like Virginia Woolf, _ironical_

boss = husband

I am aware of the women who are not with us here because they are washing the dishes and looking after the children. Nearly fifty years after she spoke, that fact remains largely unchanged. And I am thinking also of women whom she left out of the picture altogether—women who are washing other people's dishes and caring for other people's children, not to mention women who went on the streets last night in order to feed their children. We seem to be special women here, we have liked to think of ourselves as special, and we have known that men would tolerate, even romanticize us as special, as long as our words and actions didn't threaten their privilege of tolerating or rejecting us and our work according to _their_ ideas of what a special woman ought to be. An important insight of the radical women's movement has been how **divisive** and how ultimately destructive is this myth of the special woman, who is also the token woman. Every one of us here in this room has had great luck—we are teachers, writers, academicians; our own gifts could not have been enough, for we all know women whose gifts are buried or aborted. Our struggles can have meaning and our privileges—however precarious under patriarchy—can be justified only if they can help to change the lives of women whose gifts—and whose very being—continue to be thwarted and silenced.

My own luck was being born white and middle-class into a house full of books, with a father who encouraged me to read and write. So for about twenty years I wrote for a particular man, who criticized and praised me and made me feel I was indeed "special." The obverse side of this, of course, was that I tried for a long time to please him, or rather, not to displease him. And then of course there were other men—writers, teachers—the Man, who was not a terror or a dream but a literary master and a master in other ways less easy to acknowledge. And there were all those poems about women, written by men: it seemed to be a given that men wrote poems and women frequently inhabited them. These women were almost always beautiful, but threatened with the loss of beauty, the loss of youth—the fate worse than death. Or, they were beautiful and died young, like Lucy and Lenore. Or, the woman was like Maud Gonne, cruel and disastrously mistaken, and the poem reproached her because she had refused to become a luxury for the poet.

A lot is being said today about the influence that the myths and images of women have on all of us who are products of culture. I think it has been a peculiar confusion to the girl or woman who tries to write because she is peculiarly susceptible to language. She goes to poetry or fiction looking for _her_ way of being in the world, since she too has been putting words and images together; she is looking eagerly for guides, maps, possibilities; and over and over in the "words' masculine persuasive force" of literature she comes up against something that negates everything she is about: she meets the image of Woman in books written by men. She finds a terror and a dream, she finds a beautiful pale face, she finds La Belle Dame Sans Merci, she finds Juliet or

Woman Knowledge?

Tess or Salomé, but precisely what she does not find is that absorbed, drudging, puzzled, sometimes inspired creature, herself, who sits at a desk trying to put words together.

So what does she do? What did I do? I read the older women poets with their peculiar keenness and ambivalence: Sappho, Christina Rossetti, Emily Dickinson, Elinor Wylie, Edna Millay, H. D. I discovered that the woman poet most admired at the time (by men) was Marianne Moore, who was maidenly, elegant, intellectual, discreet. But even in reading these women I was looking in them for the same things I had found in the poetry of men, because I wanted women poets to be the equals of men, and to be equal was still confused with sounding the same.

I know that my style was formed first by male poets: by the men I was reading as an undergraduate—Frost, Dylan Thomas, Donne, Auden, MacNeice, Stevens, Yeats. What I chiefly learned from them was craft.[6] But poems are like dreams: in them you put what you don't know you know. Looking back at poems I wrote before I was twenty-one, I'm startled because beneath the conscious craft are glimpses of the split I even then experienced between the girl who wrote poems, who defined herself in writing poems, and the girl who was to define herself by her relationships with men. "Aunt Jennifer's Tigers" (1951), written while I was a student, looks with deliberate detachment at this split.

> Aunt Jennifer's tigers stride across a screen,
> Bright topaz denizens of a world of green.
> They do not fear the men beneath the tree;
> They pace in sleek chivalric certainty.
>
> Aunt Jennifer's fingers fluttering through her wool
> Find even the ivory needle hard to pull.
> The massive weight of Uncle's wedding band
> Sits heavily upon Aunt Jennifer's hand.
>
> When Aunt is dead, her terrified hands will lie
> Still ringed with ordeals she was mastered by.
> The tigers in the panel that she made
> Will go on striding, proud and unafraid.

In writing this poem, composed and apparently cool as it is, I thought I was creating a portrait of an imaginary woman. But this woman suffers from the opposition of her imagination, worked out in tapestry, and her lifestyle, "ringed with ordeals she was mastered by." It was important to me that Aunt Jennifer was a person as distinct from myself as possible—distanced by the formalism of the poem, by its objective, observant tone—even by putting the woman in a different generation.

In those years formalism was part of the strategy—like asbestos gloves, it allowed me to handle materials I couldn't pick up barehanded. A later strategy was to use the persona of a man, as I did in "The Loser" (1958):

A man thinks of the woman he once loved:
first, after her wedding, and then nearly a
decade later.

I

I kissed you, bride and lost, and went
home from that bourgeois sacrament,
your cheek still tasting cold upon
my lips that gave you benison
with all the swagger that they knew—
as losers somehow learn to do.

Your wedding made my eyes ache; soon
the world would be worse off for one
more golden apple dropped to ground
without the least protesting sound,
and you would windfall lie, and we
forget your shimmer on the tree.

Beauty is always wasted: if
not Mignon's song sung to the deaf,
at all events to the unmoved.
A face like yours cannot be loved
long or seriously enough.
Almost, we seem to hold it off.

II

Well, you are tougher than I thought.
Now when the wash with ice hangs taut
this morning of St. Valentine,
I see you strip the squeaking line,
your body weighed against the load,
and all my groans can do no good.

Because you still are beautiful,
though squared and stiffened by the pull
of what nine windy years have done.
You have three daughters, lost a son.
I see all your intelligence
flung into that unwearied stance.

My envy is of no avail.
I turn my head and wish him well
who chafed your beauty into use
and lives forever in a house
lit by the friction of your mind.
You stagger in against the wind.

I finished college, published my first book by a fluke, as it seemed to me, and broke off a love affair. I took a job, lived alone, went on writing, fell in love. I was young, full of energy, and the book seemed to mean that others agreed I was a poet. Because I was also determined to prove that as a woman poet I could also have what was then defined as a "full" woman's life, I plunged in my early twenties into marriage and had three children before I was thirty. There was nothing overt in the environment to warn me: these were the fifties, and in reaction to the earlier wave of feminism, middle-class women were making careers of domestic perfection, working to send their husbands through professional schools, then retiring to raise large families. People were moving out to the suburbs, technology was going to be the answer to everything, even sex; the family was in its glory. Life was extremely private; women were isolated from each other by the loyalties of marriage. I have a sense that women didn't talk to each other much in the fifties—not about their secret emptinesses, their frustrations. I went on trying to write; my second book and first child appeared in the same month. But by the time that book came out I was already dissatisfied with those poems, which seemed to me mere exercises for poems I hadn't written. The book was praised, however, for its "gracefulness"; I had a marriage and a child. If there were doubts, if there were periods of null depression or active despairing, these could only mean that I was ungrateful, insatiable, perhaps a monster.

About the time my third child was born, I felt that I had either to consider myself a failed woman and a failed poet, or to try to find some synthesis by which to understand what was happening to me. What frightened me most was the sense of drift, of being pulled along a current which called itself my destiny, but in which I seemed to be losing touch with whoever I had been, with the girl who had experienced her own will and energy almost ecstatically at times, walking around a city or riding a train at night or typing in a student room. In a poem about my grandmother I wrote (of myself): "A young girl, thought sleeping, is certified dead" "Halfway"). I was writing very little, partly from fatigue, that female fatigue of suppressed anger and loss of contact with my own being; partly from the discontinuity of female life with its attention to small chores, errands, work that others constantly undo, small children's constant needs. What I did write was unconvincing to me; my anger and frustration were hard to acknowledge in or out of poems because in fact I cared a great deal about my husband and my children. Trying to look back and understand that time I have tried to analyze the real nature of the conflict. Most, if not all, human lives are full of fantasy—passive day-dreaming which need not be acted on. But to write poetry or fiction, or even to think well, is not to fantasize, or to put fantasies on paper. For a poem to coalesce, for a character or an action to take shape, there has to be an imaginative transformation of reality which is in no way passive. And a certain freedom of the mind is needed—freedom to press on, to enter the currents of your thought like a glider pilot, knowing that your motion can be sustained, that the buoyancy of your attention will not be suddenly snatched away. Moreover, if the imagination is to transcend and transform experience it has to question, to challenge, to conceive of alternatives, perhaps to the very life you are living at that moment. You have to be free to play around with the notion that day might be night, love might be hate; nothing can be too sacred for the imagination to turn into its opposite or to call experimentally by another name. For writing is renaming. Now, to be maternally with small children all day in the old way, to be with a man in the old way of marriage, requires a holding-back, a putting-aside of that imaginative activity, and demands instead a kind of conservatism. I want to make it clear that I am *not* saying that in order to write well, or think well, it is necessary to become unavailable to others, or to become a devouring ego. This has been the myth of the masculine artist and thinker; and I do not accept it. But to be a female human being trying to fulfill traditional female functions in a traditional way *is* in direct conflict with the subversive function of the imagination. The word traditional is important here. There must be ways, and we will be finding out more and more about them, in which the energy of creation and the energy of relation can be united. But in those years I always felt the conflict as a failure of love in myself. I had thought I was choosing a full life; the life available to most men, in which sexuality, work, and parenthood could coexist. But I felt, at twenty-nine, guilt toward the people closest to me, and guilty toward my own being.

I wanted, then, more than anything, the one thing of which there was never enough: time to think, time to write. The fifties and early sixties were years of rapid revelations: the sit-ins and marches in the South, the Bay of Pigs, the early antiwar movement, raised large questions—questions for which the masculine world of the academy around me seemed to have expert and fluent answers. But I needed to think for myself—about pacifism and dissent and violence, about poetry and society, and about my own relationship to all these things. For about ten years I was reading in fierce snatches, scribbling in notebooks, writing poetry in fragments; I was looking desperately for clues, because if there were no clues then I thought I might be insane. I wrote in a notebook about this time:

> Paralyzed by the sense that there exists a mesh of relationships—e.g., between my anger at the children, my sensual life, pacifism, sex (I mean sex in its broadest significance, not merely sexual desire)—an interconnectedness which, if I could see it, make it valid, would give me back myself, make it possible to function lucidly and passionately. Yet I grope in and out among these dark webs.

I think I began at this point to feel that politics was not something "out there" but something "in here" and of the essence of my condition.

In the late fifties I was able to write, for the first time, directly about experiencing myself as a woman. The poem was jotted in fragments during children's naps, brief hours in a library, or at 3:00 A.M. after rising with a wakeful child. I despaired of doing any continuous work at this time. Yet I began to feel that my fragments and scraps had a common consciousness and a common theme, one which I would have been very unwilling to put on paper at an earlier time because I had been taught that poetry should be "universal," which meant, of course, nonfemale. Until then I had tried very much *not* to identify myself as a female poet. Over two years I wrote a ten-part poem called "Snapshots of a Daughter-in-Law" (1958–1960), in a longer looser mode than I'd ever trusted myself with before. It was an extraordinary relief to write that poem. It strikes me now as too literary, too dependent on allusion; I hadn't found the courage yet to do without authorities, or even to use the pronoun "I"—the woman in the poem is always "she." One section of it, No. 2, concerns a woman who thinks she is going mad; she is haunted by voices telling her to resist and rebel, voices which she can hear but not obey.

2.
Banging the coffee-pot into the sink
she hears the angels chiding, and looks out
past the raked gardens to the sloppy sky.
Only a week since They said: *Have no patience.*

The next time it was: *Be insatiable.*
Then: *Save yourself; others you cannot save.*
Sometimes she's let the tapstream scald her arm,
a match burn to her thumbnail,

or held her hand above the kettle's snout
right in the woolly steam. They are probably angels,
since nothing hurts her anymore, except
each morning's grit blowing into her eyes.

The poem "Orion," written five years later, is a poem of reconnection with a part of myself I had felt I was losing—the active principle, the energetic imagination, the "half-brother" whom I projected, as I had for many years, into the constellation Orion. It's no accident that the words "cold and egotistical" appear in this poem, and are applied to myself.

Far back when I went zig-zagging
through tamarack pastures
you were my genius, you
my cast-iron Viking, my helmed
lion-heart king in prison.
Years later now you're young

my fierce half-brother, staring
down from that simplified west
your breast open, your belt dragged down
by an oldfashioned thing, a sword
the last bravado you won't give over
though it weighs you down as you stride

and the stars in it are dim
and maybe have stopped burning.
But you burn, and I know it;

as I throw back my head to take you in
an old transfusion happens again:
divine astronomy is nothing to it.

Indoors I bruise and blunder,
break faith, leave ill enough
alone, a dead child born in the dark.
Night cracks up over the chimney,
pieces of time, frozen geodes
come showering down in the grate.

A man reaches behind my eyes
and finds them empty
a woman's head turns away
from my head in the mirror
children are dying my death
and eating crumbs of my life.

Pity is not your forte.
Calmly you ache up there
pinned aloft in your crow's nest,
my speechless pirate!
You take it all for granted
and when I look you back

it's with a starlike eye
shooting its cold and egotistical spear
where it can do least damage.
Breathe deep! No hurt, no pardon
out here in the cold with you
you with your back to the wall.

The choice still seemed to be between "love"—womanly, maternal love, altruistic love—a love defined and ruled by the weight of an entire culture; and
egotism—a force directed by men into creation, achievement, ambition, often
at the expense of others, but justifiably so. For weren't they men, and wasn't
that their destiny as womanly, selfless love was ours? We know now that the
alternatives are false ones—that the word "love" is itself in need of re-vision.

There is a companion poem to "Orion," written three years later, in which
at last the woman in the poem and the woman writing the poem become the
same person. It is called "Planetarium," and it was written after a visit to a
real planetarium, where I read an account of the work of Caroline Herschel,
the astronomer, who worked with her brother William, but whose name remained obscure, as his did not.

Thinking of Caroline Herschel, 1750–1848,
astronomer, sister of William; and others

A woman in the shape of a monster
a monster in the shape of a woman
the skies are full of them

a woman   'in the snow
among the Clocks and instruments
or measuring the ground with poles'

in her 98 years to discover
8 comets

she whom the moon ruled
like us
levitating into the night sky
riding the polished lenses

Galaxies of women, there
doing penance for impetuousness
ribs chilled
in those spaces   of the mind

An eye,

    'virile, precise and absolutely certain'
from the mad webs of Uranusborg

                        encountering the NOVA

every impulse of light exploding
from the core
as life flies out of us

        Tycho whispering at last
        'Let me not seem to have lived in vain'

What we see, we see
and seeing is changing

the light that shrivels a mountain
and leaves a man alive

Heartbeat of the pulsar
heart sweating through my body

The radio impulse
pouring in from Taurus

        I am bombarded yet   I stand

I have been standing all my life in the
direct path of a battery of signals
the most accurately transmitted most
untranslateable language in the universe
I am a galactic cloud so deep   so invo-
luted that a light wave could take 15
years to travel through me   And has
taken   I am an instrument in the shape
of a woman trying to translate pulsations
into images   for the relief of the body
and the reconstruction of the mind.

In closing I want to tell you about a dream I had last summer. I dreamed I was asked to read my poetry at a mass women's meeting, but when I began to read, what came out were the lyrics of a blues song. I share this dream with you because it seemed to me to say something about the problems and the future of the woman writer, and probably of women in general. The awakening of consciousness is not like the crossing of a frontier—one step and you are in another country. Much of woman's poetry has been of the nature of the blues song: a cry of pain, of victimization, or a lyric of seduction.[7] And today, much poetry by women—and prose for that matter—is charged with anger. I think we need to go through that anger, and we will betray our own reality if we try, as Virginia Woolf was trying, for an objectivity, a detachment, that would make us sound more like Jane Austen or Shakespeare. We know more than Jane Austen or Shakespeare knew: more than Jane Austen because our lives are more complex, more than Shakespeare because we know more about the lives of women—Jane Austen and Virginia Woolf included.

Both the victimization and the anger experienced by women are real, and have real sources, everywhere in the environment, built into society, language, the structures of thought. They will go on being trapped and explored by poets, among others. We can neither deny them, nor will we rest there. A new generation of women poets is already working out of the psychic energy released when women begin to move out towards what the feminist philosopher Mary Daly has described as the "new space" on the boundaries of patriarchy.[8] Women are speaking to and of women in these poems, out of a newly released courage to name, to love each other, to share risk and grief and celebration.

To the eye of a feminist, the work of Western male poets now writing reveals a deep, fatalistic pessimism as to the possibilities of change, whether societal or personal, along with a familiar and threadbare use of women (and nature) as redemptive on the one hand, threatening on the other; and a new tide of phallocentric sadism and overt woman-hating which matches the sexual brutality of recent films. "Political" poetry by men remains stranded amid the struggles for power among male groups; in condemning U.S. imperialism or the Chilean junta the poet can claim to speak for the oppressed while remaining, as male, part of a system of sexual oppression. The enemy is always outside the self, the struggle somewhere else. The mood of isolation, self-pity, and self-imitation that pervades "nonpolitical" poetry suggests that a profound change in masculine consciousness will have to precede any new male poetic—or other—inspiration. The creative energy of patriarchy is fast running out; what remains in its self-generating energy for destruction. As women, we have our work cut out for us.

NOTES

[1] Mary Daly, *Beyond God the Father* (Boston: Beacon, 1973), pp. 40–41.

[2] G. B. Shaw, *The Quintessence of Ibsenism* (New York: Hill & Wang, 1922), p. 139.

[3] J. G. Stewart, *Jane Ellen Harrison: A Portrait from Letters* (London: Merlin, 1959), p. 140.

[4] Henry James, "Notes on Novelists," in *Selected Literary Criticism of Henry James,* Morris Shapira, ed. (London: Heinemann, 1963), pp. 157–58.

[5] *A. R., 1978:* This intuition of mine was corroborated when, early in 1978, I read the correspondence between Woolf and Dame Ethel Smyth (Henry W. and Albert A. Berg Collection, The New York Public Library, Astor, Lenox and Tilden Foundations); in a letter dated June 8, 1933, Woolf speaks of having kept her own personality out of *A Room of One's Own* lest she not be taken seriously: ". . . how personal, so will they say, rubbing their hands with glee, women always are; *I even hear them as I write.*" (Italics mine.)

[6] *A. R., 1978:* Yet I spent months, at sixteen, memorizing and writing imitations of Millay's sonnets; and in notebooks of that period I find what are obviously attempts to imitate Dickinson's metrics and verbal compression. I knew H. D. only through anthologized lyrics; her epic poetry was not then available to me.

[7] *A. R., 1978:* When I dreamed that dream, was I wholly ignorant of the tradition of Bessie Smith and other women's blues lyrics which transcended victimization to sing of resistance and independence?

[8] Mary Daly, *Beyond God the Father: Towards a Philosophy of Women's Liberation* (Boston: Beacon, 1973).

• • • • • • • • • • • •

QUESTIONS FOR A SECOND READING

1. Rich says, "We need to know the writing of the past, and know it differently than we have ever known it; not to pass on a tradition but to break its hold over us." In what ways does this essay, as an example of a woman writing, both reproduce and revise the genre? As she is writing here, what does Rich *do* with the writing of the past—with the conventions of the essay or the public lecture? As you reread the essay, mark sections that illustrate the ways Rich is either reproducing or revising the conventions of the essay or the public lecture. Where and how does she revise the genre? Where and how does she not? Where does Rich resist tradition? Where does she conform? How might you account for the differences?

2. It is a rare pleasure to hear a poet talk in detail about her work. As you read back through the essay, pay particular attention to what Rich notices in her poems. What *does* she notice? What does she say about what she notices? What does this allow you to say about poems or the making of poems? What does it allow you to say about the responsibilities of a reader?

3. As Rich writes her essay, she refers to a number of literary figures like Morgan, Lytton, and Maynard Keynes, Lucy and Lenore and Maude Gonne, and Plath, Bishop, and Wakoski. Reading through her essay again, make a complete list of the names Rich draws into her discussion. Who are these people? To answer this question you will need to do some library investigation checking such sources as a biographical index, *Who's Who,* and literary texts, or consulting with a reference librarian on how to find such information.

   Once you've identified the names on your list, the next question to consider is how this knowledge influences your reading of Rich. What does each individual represent that merits her or his inclusion? To answer this question you will need to have located and read through at least one text by the individuals—one "primary source," that is—or one text about the individuals—a "secondary source"—you are researching. Why might Rich have chosen to include particular references at particular moments? What differences do they make in her arguments? in your reading of her arguments?

ASSIGNMENTS FOR WRITING

1. Rich says,

   > For a poem to coalesce, for a character or an action to take shape, there has to be an imaginative transformation of reality which is in no way passive. . . . Moreover, if the imagination is to transcend and transform experience it has to question, to challenge, to conceive of alternatives, perhaps to the very life you are living at that moment. You have to be free to play around with the notion that day might be night, love might be hate; nothing can be too sacred for the imagination to turn into its opposite or to call experimentally by another name. For writing is re-naming. (pp. 556–57)

   This is powerful language, and it is interesting to imagine how it might work for a person trying to read and understand one of Rich's poems. For this assignment, begin with a close reading of the quotation from Rich: What is your understanding of her term "imaginative transformation"? What does it allow a writer to do? And why might that be important? Then, as a way of testing Rich's term and your reading of it, choose one of the poems Rich includes in the essay and write an essay of your own that considers the poem as an act of "imaginative transformation." What is transformed into what? and to what end? or to what consequence? What can you say about the poem as an act of "renaming"? as a form of political action?

2. In "When We Dead Awaken: Writing as Re-Vision," Rich chooses five of her poems to represent stages in her history as a poet; however, it is a history not charted entirely (or mostly) by conscious decisions on her part as she tells us when she writes: "poems are like dreams: in them you put what you don't know you know." It is through the act of "re-vision"—of entering the old text of her poems from a new critical direction—that patterns in her work as a writer begin to emerge.

   Write an essay in which you explore Rich's term—"re-vision"—by describing what you consider to be a significant pattern of change in Rich's poems. As you do this work, you will want to attend closely to and quote from the language of her poems and what she has to say about them. You might want to consider such questions as: How does her explanation of herself as a poet inform your reading of her poems? What did she put into her poems that she didn't yet know on a conscious level? What does her poetry reveal about the evolution of Rich as a poet? as a woman?

3. I have hesitated to do what I am going to do now, which is to use myself as an illustration. For one thing, it's a lot easier and less dangerous to talk about other[s]. . . . (p. 552)

> Until we can understand the assumptions in which we are drenched
> we cannot know ourselves. (p. 550)

Although Rich tells a story of her own, she does so to provide an illustration of an even larger story—one about what it means to be a woman and a writer. Tell a story of your own about the ways you might be said to have been named or shaped or positioned by an established and powerful culture. Like Rich does (and perhaps with similar hesitation), use your own experience as an illustration, as a way of investigating both your own situation and the situation of people like you. You should imagine that this assignment is a way for you to use (and put to the test) some of Rich's terms, words like "revision," "renaming," and "structure." You might also want to consider defining key terms specific to your story (for Rich, for example, a defining term is "patriarchy").

4. Rich says, "We need to know the writing of the past, and know it differently than we have ever known it; not to pass on a tradition but to break its hold over us." That "us" includes you too. Look back over your own writing (perhaps the drafts and revisions you have written for this course), and think back over comments teachers have made, textbooks you've seen; think about what student writers do and what they are told to do, about the secrets students keep and the secrets teachers keep. You can assume, as Rich does, that there are ways of speaking about writing that are part of the culture of schooling and that they are designed to preserve certain ways of writing and thinking and to discourage others.

   One might argue, in other words, that there are traditions here. As you look at the evidence of the "past" in your own work, what are its significant features? What might you name this tradition (or these traditions)? How would you illustrate its hold on your work or the work of students generally? What might you have to do to begin to "know it differently," "to break its hold," or to revise? And, finally, why would someone want (or not want) to break its hold?

MAKING CONNECTIONS

1. There are striking parallels between Rich's essay and Virginia Woolf's "A Room of One's Own" (p. 719) but also some striking differences. If you think of Rich's essay as a revision of Woolf's—that is, if you imagine that Rich had, for whatever reason, to rewrite Woolf's essay for her own time and her own purposes—what would you notice in the differences between the two essays and what might you say about what you notice? Write an essay in which you discuss "When We Dead Awaken" as a demonstration of Rich's efforts to reread and rewrite the writing of the past.

2. Patricia J. Williams (p. 692), Susan Douglas (p. 115), and Gloria Anzaldúa (p. 21) all make strong statements about the situation of women—in relation to the past, to language, politics, and culture. The essays have certain similarities, but it is also interesting to consider their differences and what these dif-

ferences might be said to represent. Choose one selection to compare with "When We Dead Awaken," read the two together, marking passages you might use in a discussion, and write an essay in which you examine the interesting differences between these essays. Consider the essays as different forms or schools of feminist thought, different ways of thinking critically about the situations of women. Assume that there is more to say than "different people have different opinions," or "different people write about different subjects." How else might you account for these differences? their significance?

RICHARD
RODRIGUEZ

*R*ICHARD RODRIGUEZ, *the son of Mexican immigrants, was born in San Francisco in 1944. He grew up in Sacramento, where he attended Catholic schools before going on to Stanford University, Columbia University, the Warburg Institute in London, and the University of California at Berkeley, eventually completing a Ph.D. in English Renaissance literature. His essays have been published in* Saturday Review, The American Scholar, Change, *and elsewhere. He now lives in San Francisco and works as a lecturer, educational consultant, and freelance writer. He has published several books:* Days of Obligation: An Argument with My Mexican Father *(1992),* The Ethics of Change *(1992), and* Hunger of Memory *(1981).*

In Hunger of Memory, *a book of autobiographical essays that the* Christian Science Monitor *called "beautifully written, wrung from a sore heart," Rodriguez tells the story of his education, paying particular attention to both the meaning of his success as a student and, as he says, "its consequent price—the loss." Rodriguez's loss is represented most powerfully by his increased alienation from his parents and the decrease of intimate exchanges in family life. His parents' primary language was Spanish; his, once he became eager for success in school, was English. But the barrier was not only a language barrier. Rodriguez discovered that the interests he developed at school and through his reading were interests he did not share with those at* home—in fact, his desire to speak of them tended to threaten and humiliate his mother and father.

This separation, Rodriguez argues, is a necessary part of every person's development, even though not everyone experiences it so dramatically. We must leave home and familiar ways of speaking and understanding in order to participate in public life. On these grounds, Rodriguez has been a strong voice against bilingual education, arguing that classes conducted in Spanish will only reinforce Spanish-speaking students' separateness from mainstream American life. Rodriguez's book caused a great deal of controversy upon publication, particularly in the Hispanic community. As one critic argued, "It is indeed painful that Mr. Rodriguez has come to identify himself so completely with the majority culture that he must propagandize for a system of education which can only produce other deprived and impoverished souls like himself."

The selection that follows, Chapter 2 of Hunger of Memory, deals with Rodriguez's experiences in school. "If," he says, "because of my schooling I had grown culturally separated from my parents, my education finally had given me ways of speaking and caring about that fact." This essay is a record of how he came to understand the changes in his life. A reviewer writing in the Atlantic Monthly concluded that Hunger of Memory will survive in our literature "not because of some forgotten public issues that once bisected Richard Rodriguez's life, but because his history of that life has something to say about what it means to be American . . . and what it means to be human."

[handwritten: Just as thieving gave Marya ways of releasing her own.]

The Achievement of Desire

I stand in the ghetto classroom—"the guest speaker"—attempting to lecture on the mystery of the sounds of our words to rows of diffident students. "Don't you hear it? Listen! The music of our words. 'Sumer is icumen in. . . .' And songs on the car radio. We need Aretha Franklin's voice to fill plain words with music—her life." In the face of their empty stares, I try to create an enthusiasm. But the girls in the back row turn to watch some boy passing outside. There are flutters of smiles, waves. And someone's mouth elongates heavy, silent words through the barrier of glass. Silent words—the lips straining to shape each voiceless syllable: "Meet meee late errr." By the door, the instructor smiles at me, apparently hoping that I will be able to spark some enthusiasm in the class. But only one student seems to be listening. A girl, maybe fourteen. In this gray room her eyes shine with ambition. She keeps nodding and nodding at all that I say; she even takes notes. And each time I ask a question, she jerks up and down in her desk like a marionette, while her hand waves over the bowed heads of her classmates. It is myself (as a boy) I see as she faces me now (a man in my thirties).

The boy who first entered a classroom barely able to speak English, twenty years later concluded his studies in the stately quiet of the reading room in the British Museum. Thus with one sentence I can summarize my academic career. It will be harder to summarize what sort of life connects the boy to the man.

With every award, each graduation from one level of education to the next, people I'd meet would congratulate me. Their refrain always the same: "Your parents must be very proud." Sometimes then they'd ask me how I managed it—my "success." (How?) After a while, I had several quick answers to give in reply. I'd admit, for one thing, that I went to an excellent grammar school. (My earliest teachers, the nuns, made my success their ambition.) And my brother and both my sisters were very good students. (They often brought home the shiny school trophies I came to want.) And my mother and father always encouraged me. (At every graduation they were behind the stunning flash of the camera when I turned to look at the crowd.)

As important as these factors were, however, they account inadequately for my academic advance. Nor do they suggest what an odd success I managed. For although I was a very good student, I was also a very bad student. I was a "scholarship boy," a certain kind of scholarship boy. Always successful, I was always unconfident. Exhilarated by my progress. Sad. I became the prized student—anxious and eager to learn. Too eager, too anxious—an imitative and unoriginal pupil. My brother and two sisters enjoyed the advantages I did, and they grew to be as successful as I, but none of them ever seemed so anxious about their schooling. A second-grade student, I was the one who came home and corrected the "simple" grammatical mistakes of our parents. ("Two negatives make a positive.") Proudly I announced—to my family's startled silence—that a teacher had said I was losing all trace of a Spanish accent. I was oddly annoyed when I was unable to get parental help with a homework assignment. The night my father tried to help me with an arithmetic exercise, he kept reading the instructions, each time more deliberately, until I pried the textbook out of his hands, saying, "I'll try to figure it out some more by myself."

When I reached the third grade, I outgrew such behavior. I became more tactful, careful to keep separate the two very different worlds of my day. But then, with ever-increasing intensity, I devoted myself to my studies. I became bookish, puzzling to all my family. Ambition set me apart. When my brother saw me struggling home with stacks of library books, he would laugh, shouting: "Hey, Four Eyes!" My father opened a closet one day and was startled to find me inside, reading a novel. My mother would find me reading when I was supposed to be asleep or helping around the house or playing outside. In a voice angry or worried or just curious, she'd ask: "What do you see in your books?" It became the family's joke. When I was called and wouldn't reply, someone would say I must be hiding under my bed with a book.

(How did I manage my success?)

What I am about to say to you has taken me more than twenty years to admit: A *primary reason for my success in the classroom was that I couldn't forget that schooling was changing me and separating me from the life I enjoyed before becoming a student.* That simple realization! For years I never spoke to anyone about it. Never mentioned a thing to my family or my teachers or classmates. From a very early age, I understood enough, just enough about my classroom experiences to keep what I knew repressed, hidden beneath layers of embarrassment. Not until my last months as a graduate student, nearly thirty years old, was it possible for me to think much about the reasons for my academic success. Only then. At the end of my schooling, I needed to determine how far I had moved from my past. The adult finally confronted, and now must publicly say, what the child shuddered from knowing and could never admit to himself or to those many faces that smiled at his every success. ("Your parents must be very proud. . . .")

I

At the end, in the British Museum (too distracted to finish my dissertation) for weeks I read, speed-read, books by modern educational theorists, only to find infrequent and slight mention of students like me. (Much more is written about the more typical case, the lower-class student who barely is helped by his schooling.) Then one day, leafing through Richard Hoggart's *The Uses of Literacy,* I found, in his description of the scholarship boy, myself. For the first time I realized that there were other students like me, and so I was able to frame the meaning of my academic success, its consequent price—the loss.

Hoggart's description is distinguished, at least initially, by deep understanding. What he grasps very well is that the scholarship boy must move between environments, his home and the classroom, which are at cultural extremes, opposed. With his family, the boy has the intense pleasure of intimacy, the family's consolation in feeling public alienation. Lavish emotions texture home life. *Then,* at school, the instruction bids him to trust lonely reason primarily. Immediate needs set the pace of his parents' lives. From his mother and father the boy learns to trust spontaneity and nonrational ways of knowing. *Then,* at school, there is mental calm. Teachers emphasize the value of a reflectiveness that opens a space between thinking and immediate action.

Years of schooling must pass before the boy will be able to sketch the cultural differences in his day as abstractly as this. But he senses those differences early. Perhaps as early as the night he brings home an assignment from school and finds the house too noisy for study.

> He has to be more and more alone, if he is going to "get on."
> He will have, probably unconsciously, to oppose the ethos of
> the hearth, the intense gregariousness of the working-class
> family group. Since everything centres upon the living-room,

there is unlikely to be a room of his own; the bedrooms are cold and inhospitable, and to warm them or the front room, if there is one, would not only be expensive, but would require an imaginative leap—out of the tradition—which most families are not capable of making. There is a corner of the living-room table. On the other side Mother is ironing, the wireless is on, someone is singing a snatch of song or Father says intermittently whatever comes into his head. The boy has to cut himself off mentally, so as to do his homework, as well as he can.[1]

The next day, the lesson is as apparent at school. There are even rows of desks. Discussion is ordered. The boy must rehearse his thoughts and raise his hand before speaking out in a loud voice to an audience of classmates. And there is time enough, and silence, to think about ideas (big ideas) never considered at home by his parents.

Not for the working-class child alone is adjustment to the classroom difficult. Good schooling requires that any student alter early childhood habits. But the working-class child is usually least prepared for the change. And, unlike many middle-class children, he goes home and sees in his parents a way of life not only different but starkly opposed to that of the classroom. (He enters the house and hears his parents talking in ways his teachers discourage.)

Without extraordinary determination and the great assistance of others—at home and at school—there is little chance for success. Typically most working-class children are barely changed by the classroom. The exception succeeds. The relative few become scholarship students. Of these, Richard Hoggart estimates, most manage a fairly graceful transition. Somehow they learn to live in the two very different worlds of their day. There are some others, however, those Hoggart pejoratively terms "scholarship boys," for whom success comes with special anxiety. Scholarship boy: good student, troubled son. The child is "moderately endowed," intellectually mediocre, Hoggart supposes—though it may be more pertinent to note the special qualities of temperament in the child. High-strung child. Brooding. Sensitive. Haunted by the knowledge that one *chooses* to become a student. (Education is not an inevitable or natural step in growing up.) Here is a child who cannot forget that his academic success distances him from a life he loved, even from his own memory of himself.

Initially, he wavers, balances allegiance. ("The boy is himself [until he reaches, say, the upper forms] very much of *both* the worlds of home and school. He is enormously obedient to the dictates of the world of school, but emotionally still strongly wants to continue as part of the family circle.") Gradually, necessarily, the balance is lost. The boy needs to spend more and more time studying, each night enclosing himself in the silence permitted and required by intense concentration. He takes his first step toward academic success, away from his family.

From the very first days, through the years following, it will be with his parents—the figures of lost authority, the persons toward whom he feels deepest love—that the change will be most powerfully measured. A separation will unravel between them. Advancing in his studies, the boy notices that his mother and father have not changed as much as he. Rather, when he sees them, they often remind him of the person he once was and the life he earlier shared with them. He realizes what some Romantics also know when they praise the working class for the capacity for human closeness, qualities of passion and spontaneity, that the rest of us experience in like measure only in the earliest part of our youth. For the Romantic, this doesn't make working-class life childish. Working-class life challenges precisely because it is an *adult* way of life.

The scholarship boy reaches a different conclusion. He cannot afford to admire his parents. (How could he and still pursue such a contrary life?) He permits himself embarrassment at their lack of education. And to evade nostalgia for the life he has lost, he concentrates on the benefits education will bestow upon him. He becomes especially ambitious. Without the support of old certainties and consolations, almost mechanically, he assumes the procedures and doctrines of the classroom. The kind of allegiance the young student might have given his mother and father only days earlier, he transfers to the teacher, the new figure of authority. "[The scholarship boy] tends to make a father-figure of his form-master," Hoggart observes.

But Hoggart's calm prose only makes me recall the urgency with which I came to idolize my grammar school teachers. I began by imitating their accents, using their diction, trusting their every direction. The very first facts they dispensed, I grasped with awe. Any book they told me to read, I read—then waited for them to tell me which books I enjoyed. Their every casual opinion I came to adopt and to trumpet when I returned home. I stayed after school "to help"—to get my teacher's undivided attention. It was the nun's encouragement that mattered most to me. (She understood exactly what—my parents never seemed to appraise so well—all my achievements entailed.) Memory gently caressed each word of praise bestowed in the classroom so that compliments teachers paid me years ago come quickly to mind even today.

The enthusiasm I felt in second-grade classes I flaunted before both my parents. The docile, obedient student came home a shrill and precocious son who insisted on correcting and teaching his parents with the remark: "My teacher told us. . . ."

I intended to hurt my mother and father. I was still angry at them for having encouraged me toward classroom English. But gradually this anger was exhausted, replaced by guilt as school grew more and more attractive to me. I grew increasingly successful, a talkative student. My hand was raised in the classroom; I yearned to answer any question. At home, life was less noisy than it had been. (I spoke to classmates and teachers more often each day than to family members.) Quiet at home, I sat with my papers for hours each night. I never forgot that schooling had irretrievably changed my family's life. That knowledge, however, did not weaken ambition. Instead, it strengthened resolve. Those times I remembered the loss of my past with regret, I quickly reminded myself of all the things my teachers could give me. (They could make me an educated man.) I tightened my grip on pencil and books. I evaded nostalgia. Tried hard to forget. But one does not forget by trying to forget. One only remembers. I remembered too well that education had changed my family's life. I would not have become a scholarship boy had I not so often remembered.

Once she was sure that her children knew English, my mother would tell us, "You should keep up your Spanish." Voices playfully groaned in response. "¡Pochos!" my mother would tease. I listened silently.

After a while, I grew more calm at home. I developed tact. A fourth-grade student, I was no longer the show-off in front of my parents. I became a conventionally dutiful son, politely affectionate, cheerful enough, even—for reasons beyond choosing—my father's favorite. And much about my family life was easy then, comfortable, happy in the rhythm of our living together: hearing my father getting ready for work; eating the breakfast my mother had made me; looking up from a novel to hear my brother or one of my sisters playing with friends in the backyard; in winter, coming upon the house all lighted up after dark.

But withheld from my mother and father was any mention of what most mattered to me: the extraordinary experience of first-learning. Late afternoon: in the midst of preparing dinner, my mother would come up behind me while I was trying to read. Her head just over mine, her breath warmly scented with food. "What are you reading?" Or, "Tell me all about your new courses." I would barely respond, "Just the usual things, nothing special." (A half smile, then silence. Her head moving back in the silence. Silence! Instead of the flood of intimate sounds that had once flowed smoothly between us, there was this silence.) After dinner, I would rush to a bedroom with papers and books. As often as possible, I resisted parental pleas to "save lights" by coming to the kitchen to work. I kept so much, so often, to myself. Sad. Enthusiastic. Troubled by the excitement of coming upon new ideas. Eager. Fascinated by the promising texture of a brand-new book. I hoarded the pleasures of learning. Alone for hours. Enthralled. Nervous. I rarely looked away from my books—or back on my memories. Nights when relatives visited and the front rooms were warmed by Spanish sounds, I slipped quietly out of the house.

It mattered that education was changing me. It never ceased to matter. My brother and sisters would giggle at our mother's mispronounced words. They'd correct her gently. My mother laughed girlishly one night, trying not to pronounce *sheep* as *ship*. From a distance I listened sullenly. From that distance, pretending not to notice on another occasion, I saw my father looking at the title pages of my library books. That was the scene on my mind when I walked home with a fourth-grade companion and heard him say that his parents read to him every night. (A strange-sounding book—*Winnie the Pooh*.) Immediately, I wanted to know, "What is it like?" My companion, however, thought I wanted to know about the plot of the book. Another day, my mother surprised me by asking for a "nice" book to read. "Something not too hard you think I might like." Carefully I chose one, Willa Cather's *My Ántonia*. But when, several weeks later, I happened to see it next to her bed unread except for the first few pages, I was furious and suddenly wanted to cry. I grabbed up the book and took it back to my room and placed it in its place, alphabetically on my shelf.

"Your parents must be very proud of you." People began to say that to me about the time I was in sixth grade. To answer affirmatively, I'd smile. Shyly I'd smile, never betraying my sense of the irony: I was not proud of my mother and father. I was embarrassed by their lack of education. It was not that I ever thought they were stupid, though stupidly I took for granted their enormous native intelligence. Simply, what mattered to me was that they were not like my teachers.

But, "Why didn't you tell us about the award?" my mother demanded, her frown weakened by pride. At the grammar school ceremony several weeks after, her eyes were brighter than the trophy I'd won. Pushing back the hair from my forehead, she whispered that I had "shown" the *gringos*. A few minutes later, I heard my father speak to my teacher and felt ashamed of his labored, accented words. Then guilty for the shame. I felt such contrary feelings. (There is no simple road-map through the heart of the scholarship boy.) My teacher was so soft-spoken and her words were edged sharp and clean. I admired her until it seemed to me that she spoke too carefully. Sensing that she was condescending to them, I became nervous. Resentful. Protective. I tried to move my parents away. "You both must be very proud of Richard," the nun said. They responded quickly. (They were proud.) "We are proud of all our children." Then this afterthought: "They sure didn't get their brains from us." They all laughed. I smiled.

Tightening the irony into a knot was the knowledge that my parents were always behind me. They made success possible. They evened the path. They sent their children to parochial schools because the nuns "teach better." They paid a tuition they couldn't afford. They spoke English to us.

For their children my parents wanted chances they never had—an easier way. It saddened my mother to learn that some relatives forced their children to start working right after high school. To *her* children she would say, "Get all the education you can." In schooling she recognized the key to job advancement. And with the remark she remembered her past.

As a girl new to America my mother had been awarded a high school diploma by teachers too careless or busy to notice that she hardly spoke English. On her own, she determined to learn how to type. That skill got her jobs typing envelopes in letter shops, and it encouraged in her an optimism about the possibility of advancement. (Each morning when her sisters put on uniforms, she chose a bright-colored dress.) The years of young womanhood passed, and her typing speed increased. She also became an excellent speller of words she mispronounced. "And I've never been to college," she'd say, smiling, when her children asked her to spell words they were too lazy to look up in a dictionary.

Typing, however, was dead-end work. Finally frustrating. When her youngest child started high school, my mother got a full-time office job once again. (Her paycheck combined with my father's to make us—in fact—what we had already become in our imagination of ourselves—middle class.) She worked then for the (California) state government in numbered civil service positions secured by examinations. The old ambition of her youth was re-kindled. During the lunch hour, she consulted bulletin boards for announce-ments of openings. One day she saw mention of something called an "anti-poverty agency." A typing job. A glamorous job, part of the governor's staff. "A knowledge of Spanish required." Without hesitation she applied and be-came nervous only when the job was suddenly hers.

"Everyone comes to work all dressed up," she reported at night. And didn't need to say more than that her co-workers wouldn't let her answer the phones. She was only a typist, after all, albeit a very fast typist. And an excel-lent speller. One morning there was a letter to be sent to a Washington cabi-net officer. On the dictating tape, a voice referred to urban guerrillas. My mother typed (the wrong word, correctly): "gorillas." The mistake horrified the anti-poverty bureaucrats who shortly after arranged to have her returned to her previous position. She would go no further. So she willed her ambition to their children. "Get all the education you can; with an education you can do anything." (With a good education *she* could have done anything.)

When I was in high school, I admitted to my mother that I planned to be-come a teacher someday. That seemed to please her. But I never tried to ex-plain that it was not the occupation of teaching I yearned for as much as it was something more elusive: I wanted to *be* like my teachers, to possess their knowledge, to assume their authority, their confidence, even to assume a teacher's persona.

In contrast to my mother, my father never verbally encouraged his chil-dren's academic success. Nor did he often praise us. My mother had to re-mind him to "say something" to one of his children who scored some acade-mic success. But whereas my mother saw in education the opportunity for job advancement, my father recognized that education provided an even more startling possibility: it could enable a person to escape from a life of mere labor.

In Mexico, orphaned when he was eight, my father left school to work as an "apprentice" for an uncle. Twelve years later, he left Mexico in frustration and arrived in America. He had great expectations then of becoming an engi-neer. ("Work for my hands and my head.") He knew a Catholic priest who promised to get him money enough to study full time for a high school diploma. But the promises came to nothing. Instead there was a dark succes-sion of warehouse, cannery, and factory jobs. After work he went to night school along with my mother. A year, two passed. Nothing much changed, except that fatigue worked its way into the bone; then everything changed. He didn't talk anymore of becoming an engineer. He stayed outside on the steps of the school while my mother went inside to learn typing and shorthand.

By the time I was born, my father worked at "clean" jobs. For a time he was a janitor at a fancy department store. ("Easy work; the machines do it all.") Later he became a dental technician. ("Simple.") But by then he was pessimistic about the ultimate meaning of work and the possibility of ever escaping its claims. In some of my earliest memories of him, my father already seems aged by fatigue. (He has never really grown old like my mother.) From boyhood to manhood, I have remembered him in a single image: seated, asleep on the sofa, his head thrown back in a hideous corpse-like grin, the evening newspaper spread out before him. "But look at all you've accomplished," his best friend said to him once. My father said nothing. Only smiled.

It was my father who laughed when I claimed to be tired by reading and writing. It was he who teased me for having soft hands. (He seemed to sense that some great achievement of leisure was implied by my papers and books.) It was my father who became angry while watching on television some woman at the Miss America contest tell the announcer that she was going to college. ("Majoring in fine arts.") "College!" he snarled. He despised the trivialization of higher education, the inflated grades and cheapened diplomas, the half education that so often passed as mass education in my generation.

It was my father again who wondered why I didn't display my awards on the wall of my bedroom. He said he liked to go to doctors' offices and see their certificates and degrees on the wall. ("Nice.") My citations from school got left in closets at home. The gleaming figure astride one of my trophies was broken, wingless, after hitting the ground. My medals were placed in a jar of loose change. And when I lost my high school diploma, my father found it as it was about to be thrown out with the trash. Without telling me, he put it away with his own things for safekeeping.

These memories slammed together at the instant of hearing that refrain familiar to all scholarship students: "Your parents must be proud. . . ." Yes, my parents were proud. I knew it. But my parents regarded my progress with more than mere pride. They endured my early precocious behavior— but with what private anger and humiliation? As their children got older and would come home to challenge ideas both of them held, they argued before submitting to the force of logic or superior factual evidence with the disclaimer, "It's what we were taught in our time to believe." These discussions ended abruptly, though my mother remembered them on other occasions when she complained that our "big ideas" were going to our heads. More acute was her complaint that the family wasn't close anymore, like some others she knew. Why weren't we close, "more in the Mexican style"? Everyone is so private, she added. And she mimicked the yes and no answers she got in reply to her questions. Why didn't we talk more? (My father never asked.) I never said.

I was the first in my family who asked to leave home when it came time to go to college. I had been admitted to Stanford, one hundred miles away. My departure would only make physically apparent the separation that had occurred long before. But it was going too far. In the months preceding my leaving, I heard the question my mother never asked except indirectly. In the hot kitchen, tired at the end of her workday, she demanded to know, "Why aren't the colleges here in Sacramento good enough for you? They are for your brother and sister." In the middle of a car ride, not turning to face me, she wondered, "Why do you need to go so far away?" Late at night, ironing, she said with disgust, "Why do you have to put us through this big expense? You know your scholarship will never cover it all." But when September came there was a rush to get everything ready. In a bedroom that last night I packed the big brown valise, and my mother sat nearby sewing initials onto the clothes I would take. And she said no more about my leaving.

Months later, two weeks of Christmas vacation: the first hours home were the hardest. ("What's new?") My parents and I sat in the kitchen for a conversation. (But, lacking the same words to develop our sentences and to shape our interests, what was there to say? What could I tell them of the term paper I had just finished on the "universality of Shakespeare's appeal"?) I mentioned only small, obvious things: my dormitory life; weekend trips I had taken; random events. They responded with news of their own. (One was almost grateful for a family crisis about which there was much to discuss.) We tried to make our conversation seem like more than an interview.

II

From an early age I knew that my mother and father could read and write both Spanish and English. I had observed my father making his way through what, I now suppose, must have been income tax forms. On other occasions I waited apprehensively while my mother read onion-paper letters airmailed from Mexico with news of a relative's illness or death. For both my parents, however, reading was something done out of necessity and as quickly as possible. Never did I see either of them read an entire book. Nor did I see them read for pleasure. Their reading consisted of work manuals, prayer books, newspaper, recipes.

Richard Hoggart imagines how, at home,

> [the scholarship boy] sees strewn around, and reads regularly
> himself, magazines which are never mentioned at school,
> which seem not to belong to the world to which the school in-
> troduces him; at school he hears about and reads books never

mentioned at home. When he brings those books into the house they do not take their place with other books which the family are reading, for often there are none or almost none; his books look, rather, like strange tools.

In our house each school year would begin with my mother's careful instruction: "Don't write in your books so we can sell them at the end of the year." The remark was echoed in public by my teachers, but only in part: "Boys and girls, don't write in your books. You must learn to treat them with great care and respect."

OPEN THE DOORS OF YOUR MIND WITH BOOKS, read the red and white poster over the nun's desk in early September. It soon was apparent to me that reading was the classroom's central activity. Each course had its own book. And the information gathered from a book was unquestioned. READ TO LEARN, the sign on the wall advised in December. I privately wondered: What was the connection between reading and learning? Did one learn something only by reading it? Was an idea only an idea if it could be written down? In June, CONSIDER BOOKS YOUR BEST FRIENDS. Friends? Reading was, at best, only a chore. I needed to look up whole paragraphs of words in a dictionary. Lines of type were dizzying, the eye having to move slowly across the page, then down, and across. . . . The sentences of the first books I read were coolly impersonal. Toned hard. What most bothered me, however, was the isolation reading required. To console myself for the loneliness I'd feel when I read, I tried reading in a very soft voice. Until: "Who is doing all that talking to his neighbor?" Shortly after, remedial reading classes were arranged for me with a very old nun.

At the end of each school day, for nearly six months, I would meet with her in the tiny room that served as the school's library but was actually only a storeroom for used textbooks and a vast collection of *National Geographic*s. Everything about our sessions pleased me: the smallness of the room; the noise of the janitor's broom hitting the edge of the long hallway outside the door; the green of the sun, lighting the wall; and the old woman's face blurred white with a beard. Most of the time we took turns. I began with my elementary text. Sentences of astonishing simplicity seemed to me lifeless and drab: "The boys ran from the rain. . . . She wanted to sing. . . . The kite rose in the blue." Then the old nun would read from her favorite books, usually biographies of early American presidents. Playfully she ran through complex sentences, calling the words alive with her voice, making it seem that the author somehow was speaking directly to me. I smiled just to listen to her. I sat there and sensed for the very first time some possibility of fellowship between a reader and a writer, a communication, never *intimate* like that I heard spoken words at home convey, but one nonetheless *personal*.

One day the nun concluded a session by asking me why I was so reluctant to read by myself. I tried to explain; said something about the way written words made me feel all alone—almost, I wanted to add but didn't, as

577

when I spoke to myself in a room just emptied of furniture. She studied my face as I spoke; she seemed to be watching more than listening. In an uneventful voice she replied that I had nothing to fear. Didn't I realize that reading would open up whole new worlds? A book could open doors for me. It could introduce me to people and show me places I never imagined existed. She gestured toward the bookshelves. (Bare-breasted African women danced, and the shiny hubcaps of automobiles on the back covers of the *Geographic* gleamed in my mind.) I listened with respect. But her words were not very influential. I was thinking then of another consequence of literacy, one I was too shy to admit but nonetheless trusted. Books were going to make me "educated." *That* confidence enabled me, several months later, to overcome my fear of the silence.

In fourth grade I embarked upon a grandiose reading program. "Give me the names of important books," I would say to startled teachers. They soon found out that I had in mind "adult books." I ignored their suggestion of anything I suspected was written for children. (Not until I was in college, as a result, did I read *Huckleberry Finn* or *Alice's Adventures in Wonderland*.) Instead, I read *The Scarlet Letter* and Franklin's *Autobiography*. And whatever I read I read for extra credit. Each time I finished a book, I reported the achievement to a teacher and basked in the praise my effort earned. Despite my best efforts, however, there seemed to be more and more books I needed to read. At the library I would literally tremble as I came upon whole shelves of books I hadn't read. So I read and I read and I read: *Great Expectations;* all the short stories of Kipling; *The Babe Ruth Story;* the entire first volume of the *Encyclopedia Britannica* (A–ANSTEY); the *Iliad; Moby Dick; Gone with the Wind; The Good Earth; Ramona; Forever Amber; The Lives of the Saints; Crime and Punishment; The Pearl....* Librarians who initially frowned when I checked out the maximum ten books at a time started saving books they thought I might like. Teachers would say to the rest of the class, "I only wish the rest of you took reading as seriously as Richard obviously does."

But at home I would hear my mother wondering, "What do you see in your books?" (Was reading a hobby like her knitting? Was so much reading even healthy for a boy? Was it the sign of "brains"? Or was it just a convenient excuse for not helping about the house on Saturday mornings?) Always, "What do you see . . . ?"

What *did* I see in my books? I had the idea that they were crucial for my academic success, though I couldn't have said exactly how or why. In the sixth grade I simply concluded that what gave a book its value was some major idea or theme it contained. If that core essence could be mined and memorized, I would become learned like my teachers. I decided to record in a notebook the themes of the books that I read. After reading *Robinson Crusoe,* I wrote that its theme was "the value of learning to live by oneself." When I completed *Wuthering Heights,* I noted the danger of "letting emotions get out of control." Rereading these brief moralistic appraisals usually left me disheartened. I couldn't believe that they were really the source of reading's value. But for many more years, they constituted the only means I had of describing to myself the educational value of books.

In spite of my earnestness, I found reading a pleasurable activity. I came to enjoy the lonely good company of books. Early on weekday mornings, I'd read in my bed. I'd feel a mysterious comfort then, reading in the dawn quiet—the blue-gray silence interrupted by the occasional churning of the refrigerator motor a few rooms away or the more distant sounds of a city bus beginning its run. On weekends I'd go to the public library to read, surrounded by old men and women. Or, if the weather was fine, I would take my books to the park and read in the shade of a tree. A warm summer evening was my favorite reading time. Neighbors would leave for vacation and I would water their lawns. I would sit through the twilight on the front porches or in backyards, reading to the cool, whirling sounds of the sprinklers.

I also had favorite writers. But often those writers I enjoyed most I was least able to value. When I read William Saroyan's *The Human Comedy*, I was immediately pleased by the narrator's warmth and the charm of his story. But as quickly I became suspicious. A book so enjoyable to read couldn't be very "important." Another summer I determined to read all the novels of Dickens. Reading his fat novels, I loved the feeling I got—after the first hundred pages—of being at home in a fictional world where I knew the names of the characters and cared about what was going to happen to them. And it bothered me that I was forced away at the conclusion, when the fiction closed tight, like a fortune-teller's fist—the futures of all the major characters neatly resolved. I never knew how to take such feelings seriously, however. Nor did I suspect that these experiences could be part of a novel's meaning. Still, there were pleasures to sustain me after I'd finish my books. Carrying a volume back to the library, I would be pleased by its weight. I'd run my fingers along the edge of the pages and marvel at the breadth of my achievement. Around my room, growing stacks of paperback books reenforced my assurance.

I entered high school having read hundreds of books. My habit of reading made me a confident speaker and writer of English. Reading also enabled me to sense something of the shape, the major concerns, of Western thought. (I was able to say something about Dante and Descartes and Engels and James Baldwin in my high school term papers.) In these various ways, books brought me academic success as I hoped that they would. But I was not a good reader. Merely bookish, I lacked a point of view when I read. Rather, I read in order to acquire a point of view. I vacuumed books for epigrams, scraps of information, ideas, themes—anything to fill the hollow within me and make me feel educated. When one of my teachers suggested to his drowsy tenth-grade English class that a person could not have a "complicated idea" until he had read at least two thousand books, I heard the remark without detecting either its irony or its very complicated truth. I merely determined to compile a list of all the books I had ever read. Harsh with myself, I included only once a title I might have read several times. (How, after all, could one read a book more than once?) And I included only those books over a hundred pages in length. (Could anything shorter be a book?)

There was yet another high school list I compiled. One day I came across a newspaper article about the retirement of an English professor at a nearby state college. The article was accompanied by a list of the "hundred most important books of Western Civilization." "More than anything else in my life," the professor told the reporter with finality, "these books have made me all that I am." That was the kind of remark I couldn't ignore. I clipped out the list and kept it for the several months it took me to read all of the titles. Most books, of course, I barely understood. While reading Plato's *Republic,* for instance, I needed to keep looking at the book jacket comments to remind myself what the text was about. Nevertheless, with the special patience and superstition of a scholarship boy, I looked at every word of the text. And by the time I reached the last word, relieved, I convinced myself that I had read *The Republic.* In a ceremony of great pride, I solemnly crossed Plato off my list.

III

The scholarship boy pleases most when he is young—the working-class child struggling for academic success. To his teachers, he offers great satisfaction; his success is their proudest achievement. Many other persons offer to help him. A businessman learns the boy's story and promises to underwrite part of the cost of his college education. A woman leaves him her entire library of several hundred books when she moves. His progress is featured in a newspaper article. Many people seem happy for him. They marvel. "How did you manage so fast?" From all sides, there is lavish praise and encouragement.

In his grammar school classroom, however, the boy already makes students around him uneasy. They scorn his desire to succeed. They scorn him for constantly wanting the teacher's attention and praise. "Kiss Ass," they call him when his hand swings up in response to every question he hears. Later, when he makes it to college, no one will mock him aloud. But he detects annoyance on the faces of some students and even some teachers who watch him. It puzzles him often. In college, then in graduate school, he behaves much as he always has. If anything is different about him it is that he dares to anticipate the successful conclusion of his studies. At last he feels that he belongs in the classroom, and this is exactly the source of the dissatisfaction he causes. To many persons around him, he appears too much the academic. There may be some things about him that recall his beginnings—his shabby clothes; his persistent poverty; or his dark skin (in those cases when it symbolizes his parents' disadvantaged condition)—but they only make clear how far he has moved from his past. He has used education to re-make himself.

It bothers his fellow academics to face this. They will not say why exactly. (They sneer.) But their expectations become obvious when they are disappointed. They expect—they want—a student less changed by his schooling. If the scholarship boy, from a past so distant from the classroom, could remain in some basic way unchanged, he would be able to prove that it is possible for anyone to become educated without basically changing from the person one was.

Here is no fabulous hero, no idealized scholar-worker. The scholarship boy does not straddle, cannot reconcile, the two great opposing cultures of his life. His success is unromantic and plain. He sits in the classroom and offers those sitting beside him no calming reassurance about their own lives. He sits in the seminar room—a man with brown skin, the son of working-class Mexican immigrant parents. (Addressing the professor at the head of the table, his voice catches with nervousness.) There is no trace of his parents' in his speech. Instead he approximates the accents of teachers and classmates. Coming from *him* those sounds seem suddenly odd. Odd too is the effect produced when *he* uses academic jargon—bubbles at the tip of his tongue: "*Topos* . . . negative capability . . . vegetation imagery in Shakespearean comedy." He lifts an opinion from Coleridge, takes something else from Frye or Empson or Leavis. He even repeats exactly his professor's earlier comment. All his ideas are clearly borrowed. He seems to have no thought of his own. He chatters while his listeners smile—their look one of disdain.

When he is older and thus when so little of the person he was survives, the scholarship boy makes only too apparent his profound lack of *self*-confidence. This is the conventional assessment that even Richard Hoggart repeats:

> [The scholarship boy] tends to over-stress the importance of examinations, of the piling-up of knowledge and of received opinions. He discovers a technique of apparent learning, of the acquiring of facts rather than of the handling and use of facts. He learns how to receive a purely literate education, one using only a small part of the personality and challenging only a limited area of his being. He begins to see life as a ladder, as permanent examination with some praise and some further exhortation at each stage. He becomes an expert imbiber and doler-out; his competence will vary, but will rarely be accompanied by genuine enthusiasms. He rarely feels the reality of knowledge, of other men's thoughts and imaginings, on his own pulses. . . . He has something of the blinkered pony about him. . . .

But this is criticism more accurate than fair. The scholarship boy is a very bad student. He is the great mimic; a collector of thoughts, not a thinker; the very last person in class who ever feels obliged to have an opinion of his own. In large part, however, the reason he is such a bad student is because he realizes more often and more acutely than most other students—than Hoggart himself—that education requires radical self-reformation. As a very young boy, regarding his parents, as he struggles with an early homework assignment, he knows this too well. That is why he lacks self-assurance. He does not forget that the classroom is responsible for remaking him. He relies on his teacher, depends on all that he hears in the classroom and reads in his books. He becomes in every obvious way the worst student, a dummy mouthing the opinions of others. But he would not be so bad—nor would he become so successful, a *scholarship* boy—if he did not accurately perceive that the best synonym for primary "education" is "imitation."

Those who would take seriously the boy's success—and his failure—would be forced to realize how great is the change any academic undergoes, how far one must move from one's past. It is easiest to ignore such considerations. So little is said about the scholarship boy in pages and pages of educational literature. Nothing is said of the silence that comes to separate the boy from his parents. Instead, one hears proposals for increasing the self-esteem of students and encouraging early intellectual independence. Paragraphs glitter with a constellation of terms like *creativity* and *originality.* (Ignored altogether is the function of imitation in a student's life.) Radical educationalists meanwhile complain that ghetto schools "oppress" students by trying to mold them, stifling native characteristics. The truer critique would be just the reverse: not that schools change ghetto students too much, but that while they might promote the occasional scholarship student, they change most students barely at all.

From the story of the scholarship boy there is no specific pedagogy to glean. There is, however, a much larger lesson. His story makes clear that education is a long, unglamorous, even demeaning process—*a nurturing never natural to the person one was before one entered a classroom.* At once different from most other students, the scholarship boy is also the archetypal "good student." He exaggerates the difficulty of being a student, but his exaggeration reveals a general predicament. Others are changed by their schooling as much as he. They too must re-form themselves. They must develop the skill of memory long before they become truly critical thinkers. And when they read Plato for the first several times, it will be with awe more than deep comprehension.

The impact of schooling on the scholarship boy is only more apparent to the boy himself and to others. Finally, although he may be laughable—a blinkered pony—the boy will not let his critics forget their own change. He ends up too much like them. When he speaks, they hear themselves echoed. In his pedantry, they trace their own. His ambitions are theirs. If his failure were singular, they might readily pity him. But he is more troubling than that. They would not scorn him if this were not so.

IV

Like me, Hoggart's imagined scholarship boy spends most of his years in the classroom afraid to long for his past. Only at the very end of his schooling does the boy-man become nostalgic. In this sudden change of heart, Richard Hoggart notes:

> He longs for the membership he lost, "he pines for some Nameless Eden where he never was." The nostalgia is the stronger and the more ambiguous because he is really "in quest of his own absconded self yet scared to find it." He both wants to go back and yet thinks he has gone beyond his class, feels himself weighted with knowledge of his own and their situation, which hereafter forbids him the simpler pleasures of his father and mother. . . .

According to Hoggart, the scholarship boy grows nostalgic because he remains the uncertain scholar, bright enough to have moved from his past, yet unable to feel easy, a part of a community of academics.

This analysis, however, only partially suggests what happened to me in my last year as a graduate student. When I traveled to London to write a dissertation on English Renaissance literature, I was finally confident of membership in a "community of scholars." But the pleasure that confidence gave me faded rapidly. After only two or three months in the reading room of the British Museum, it became clear that I had joined a lonely community. Around me each day were dour faces eclipsed by large piles of books. There were the regulars, like the old couple who arrived every morning, each holding a loop of the shopping bag which contained all their notes. And there was the historian who chattered madly to herself. ("Oh dear! Oh! Now, what's this? What? Oh, my!") There were also the faces of young men and women worn by long study. And everywhere eyes turned away the moment our glance accidentally met. Some persons I sat beside day after day, yet we passed silently at the end of the day, strangers. Still, we were united by a common respect for the written word and for scholarship. We did form a union, though one in which we remained distant from one another.

More profound and unsettling was the bond I recognized with those writers whose books I consulted. Whenever I opened a text that hadn't been used for years, I realized that my special interests and skills united me to a mere handful of academics. We formed an exclusive—eccentric!—society, separated from others who would never care or be able to share our concerns. (The pages I turned were stiff like layers of dead skin.) I began to wonder: Who, beside my dissertation director and a few faculty members, would ever read what I wrote? And: Was my dissertation much more than an act of social withdrawal? These questions went unanswered in the silence of the Museum reading room. They remained to trouble me after I'd leave the library each afternoon and feel myself shy—unsteady, speaking simple sentences at the grocer's or the butcher's on my way back to my bed-sitter.

Meanwhile my file cards accumulated. A professional, I knew exactly how to search a book for pertinent information. I could quickly assess and summarize the usability of the many books I consulted. But whenever I started to write, I knew too much (and not enough) to be able to write anything but sentences that were overly cautious, timid, strained brittle under the heavy weight of footnotes and qualifications. I seemed unable to dare a passionate statement. I felt drawn by professionalism to the edge of sterility, capable of no more than pedantic, lifeless, unassailable prose.

Then nostalgia began.

After years spent unwilling to admit its attractions, I gestured nostalgically toward the past. I yearned for that time when I had not been so alone. I became impatient with books. I wanted experience more immediate. I feared the library's silence. I silently scorned the gray, timid faces around me. I grew to hate the growing pages of my dissertation on genre and Renaissance literature. (In my mind I heard relatives laughing as they tried to make sense of its title.) I wanted something—I couldn't say exactly what. I told myself that I wanted a more passionate life. And a life less thoughtful. And above all, I wanted to be less alone. One day I heard some Spanish academics whispering back and forth to each other, and their sounds seemed ghostly voices recalling my life. Yearning became preoccupation then. Boyhood memories beckoned, flooded my mind. (Laughing intimate voices. Bounding up the front steps of the porch. A sudden embrace inside the door.)

For weeks after, I turned to books by educational experts. I needed to learn how far I had moved from my past—to determine how fast I would be able to recover something of it once again. But I found little. Only a chapter in a book by Richard Hoggart. . . . I left the reading room and the circle of faces.

I came home. After the year in England, I spent three summer months living with my mother and father, relieved by how easy it was to be home. It no longer seemed very important to me that we had little to say. I felt easy sitting and eating and walking with them. I watched them, nevertheless, looking for evidence of those elastic, sturdy strands that bind generations in a web of inheritance. I thought as I watched my mother one night: of course a friend had been right when she told me that I gestured and laughed just like my mother. Another time I saw for myself: my father's eyes were much like my own, constantly watchful.

But after the early relief, this return, came suspicion, nagging until I realized that I had not neatly sidestepped the impact of schooling. My desire to do so was precisely the measure of how much I remained an academic. *Negatively* (for that is how this idea first occurred to me): my need to think so much and so abstractly about my parents and our relationship was in itself an indication of my long education. My father and mother did not pass their thinking about the cultural meanings of their experience. It was I who described their daily lives with airy ideas. And yet, *positively:* the ability to consider experience so abstractly allowed me to shape into desire what would otherwise have remained indefinite, meaningless longing in the British Museum. If, because of my schooling, I had grown culturally separated from my parents, my education finally had given me ways of speaking and caring about that fact.

My best teachers in college and graduate school, years before, had tried to prepare me for this conclusion, I think, when they discussed texts of aristocratic pastoral literature. Faithfully, I wrote down all that they said. I memorized it: "The praise of the unlettered by the highly educated is one of the primary themes of 'elitist' literature." But, "the importance of the praise given the unsolitary, richly passionate and spontaneous life is that it simultaneously reflects the value of a reflective life." I heard it all. But there was no way for any of it to mean very much to me. I was a scholarship boy at the time, busily laddering my way up the rungs of education. To pass an examination, I copied down exactly what my teachers told me. It would require many more years of schooling (an inevitable miseducation) in which I came to trust the silence of reading and the habit of abstracting from immediate experience—moving away from a life of closeness and immediacy I remembered with my parents, growing older—before I turned unafraid to desire the past, and thereby achieved what had eluded me for so long—the end of education.

NOTE
<hr>

[1] All quotations in this essay are from Richard Hoggart, *The Uses of Literacy* (London: Chatto and Windus, 1957), chapter 10. [Author's note]

• • • • • • • • • • • •

QUESTIONS FOR A SECOND READING

1. In *Hunger of Memory,* the book from which "The Achievement of Desire" is drawn, Rodriguez says several times that the story he tells, although it is very much his story, is also a story of our common experience—growing up, leaving home, becoming educated, entering the world. When you reread this essay, look particularly for sections or passages you might bring forward as evidence that this is, in fact, an essay which can give you a way of looking at your own life, and not just his. And look for sections that defy universal application. To what degree *is* his story the story of our common experience? Why might he (or his readers) want to insist that his story is everyone's story?

2. At the end of the essay, Rodriguez says

> It would require many more years of schooling (an inevitable miseducation) in which I came to trust the silence of reading and the habit of abstracting from immediate experience—moving away from a life of closeness and immediacy I remembered with my parents, growing older—before I turned unafraid to desire the past, and thereby achieved what had eluded me for so long—the end of education.

What do you think, as you reread this essay, is the "end of education"? And what does that end (that goal? stopping point?) have to do with "miseducation," "the silence of reading," "the habit of abstracting from immediate experience," and "desiring the past"?

ASSIGNMENTS FOR WRITING

1. You could look at the relationship between Richard Rodriguez and Richard Hoggart as a case study of the relation of a reader to a writer or a student to a teacher. Look closely at Rodriguez's references to Hoggart's book, *The Uses of Literacy,* and at the way Rodriguez made use of that book to name and describe his own experience as a student. What did he find in the book? How did he use it? How does he use it in his own writing?

   Write an essay in which you discuss Rodriguez's use of Hoggart's *The Uses of Literacy.* How, for example, would you compare Rodriguez's version of the "scholarship boy" with Hoggart's? (At one point, Rodriguez says that Hoggart's account is "more accurate than fair." What might he have meant by that?) And what kind of reader is the Rodriguez who is writing "The Achievement of Desire"—is he still a "scholarship boy," or is that description no longer appropriate?

   Note: You might begin your research with what may seem to be a purely technical matter, examining how Rodriguez handles quotations and works Hoggart's words into paragraphs of his own. On the basis of Rodriguez's use of quoted passages, how would you describe the relationship between Hoggart's words and Rodriguez's? Who has the greater authority? Who is the expert, and under what conditions? What "rules" might Rodriguez be said to follow or to break? Do you see any change in the course of the essay in how Rodriguez uses block quotations? in how he comments on them?

2. Rodriguez insists that his story is also everyone's story. Take an episode from your life, one that seems in some way similar to one of the episodes in "The Achievement of Desire," and cast it into a shorter version of Rodriguez's essay. Your job here is to look at your experience in Rodriguez's terms, which means thinking the way he does, noticing what he would notice, interpreting details in a similar fashion, using his key terms, seeing through his point of view; it could also mean imitating his style of writing, doing whatever it is you see him doing characteristically while he writes. Imitation, Rodriguez argues, is not necessarily a bad thing; it can, in fact, be one of the powerful ways in which a person learns.

   Note: This assignment can also be used to read against "The Achievement of Desire." Rodriguez insists on the universality of his experience leaving home and community and joining the larger public life. You could high-light the differences between your experience and his. You should begin by imitating Rodriguez's method; you do not have to arrive at his conclusions, however.

3.   What I am about to say to you has taken me more than twenty years to admit: *A primary reason for my success in the classroom was that I couldn't forget that schooling was changing me and separating me from the life I en-joyed before becoming a student.* (pp. 568–69)

If, because of my schooling, I had grown culturally separated from my parents, my education finally had given me ways of speaking and car-ing about that fact. (p. 585)

As you reread Rodriguez's essay, what would you say are his "ways of speaking and caring"? One way to think about this question is to trace how the lessons he learned about reading, education, language, family, culture, and class shifted as he moved from elementary school through college and graduate school to his career as a teacher and a writer. What scholarly abili-ties did he learn that provided him with "ways of speaking and caring" val-ued in the academic community? Where and how do you see him using them in his essay?

Write an essay in which you discuss how Rodriguez reads (reviews, summarizes, interprets) his family, his teachers, his schooling, himself, and his books. What differences can you say such reading makes to those ways of speaking and caring that you locate in the text?

MAKING CONNECTIONS

1. Paulo Freire, in "The 'Banking' Concept of Education" (p. 212), discusses the political implications of the relations between teachers and students. Some forms of schooling, he says, can give students control over their lives, but most schooling teaches students only to submit to domination by others. If you look closely at the history of Rodriguez's schooling from the perspective of Freire's essay, what do you see? Write an essay describing how Freire might analyze Rodriguez's education. How would he see the process as it unfolds throughout Rodriguez's experience, as a student, from his early schooling (including the study he did on his own at home), through his col-lege and graduate studies, to the position he takes, finally, as the writer of "The Achievement of Desire?"

2. Patricia J. Williams, in "And We Are Not Married" (p. 694), argues that her identity as a black woman is "socially constructed." As a part of her argu-ment, she tells a number of stories to serve as examples of social construction as it could be said to mold or shape people's thinking. As you read through her essay, mark those moments that you could use to present her notions of social construction. What does she mean, for example, when she says that the raciality of black women and men is socially constructed? What example would you turn to from her essay to explain the way she thinks social con-struction works and what its elements might be?

Once you've read Williams's essay and you have created a set of notes toward representing her notions of social construction, reread "The Achievement of Desire" by Richard Rodriguez from Williams's perspective on social construction. Imagine that Rodriguez's identity could also be said to have been socially constructed by school, by particular groups of people, by his family, and, as Williams would argue, by his perceptions of himself. What examples from Rodriguez's essay would you turn to to argue that, like Williams's identity, Rodriguez's identity could also be said to be socially constructed? How would Williams's notion apply to Rodriguez? What would be similar? different?

Write an essay in which you use Williams's notions of the social construction as a set of critical ideas to resee or reimagine one of Rodriguez's examples or stories.

JAMES
SCHUYLER

*JAMES SCHUYLER (1924–1991) won the Pulitzer Prize for poetry for his
fourth book,* The Morning of the Poem *(1980). The poem below is the title
piece from his fifth book,* A Few Days *(1985). This poem is unusually long and de-
ceptively simple. Schuyler writes as we might expect him to paint if he were a
painter. His desire is "merely," as he says in the poem, "to say, to see and to say,
things / as they are." He notices the ordinary and extraordinary equally, shifting
from playful to serious, from contemplative to funny, as the world he lives in evokes
these different sensibilities.*

*The few months of time that the poem chronicles are rendered subtly as both "a
few days in the life of James Schuyler" and as the last days of his aging mother, in a
powerful elegiac form that builds quietly as the poem progresses. It is also a poem
that overwhelms on first reading, not just because of its length, but because the number of places, people, things, and ideas drawn into the story is vast. Schuyler travels
literally from his Manhattan apartment to Buffalo, New York, to visit his mother and
then back again. He also travels in his memories to times, places, and events in his
past. He recalls friends and their conversations, their attitudes, their relationships to
him and each other, their lives and sometimes their deaths, along with the poets he
reveres, the art he loves, the wonderful architecture of Italy, and the geographical
places that are dear to him, all in an intricately woven tapestry of a life thoughtfully*

lived. All of the moments of this long poem can be read as small stories layered onto one another like scenes in a complex painting.

Schuyler also talks so much about the seemingly mundane details of daily life that it is often hard during a first reading to feel and appreciate the complex linguistic rhythms of the lines that help to define the work. His language offers us a way to read and write that's more akin to linguistic collage, a Schuyleresque vision we might call it, than to a logic of argumentation or a predictable chronology of story.

Schuyler spent much of his adult life in New York City purposefully situated on the edges of the literary scene and the gay community. He was hospitalized several times for suicide attempts and psychological breakdowns. These experiences became subject matter for his poetry. Like Anne Sexton, Sylvia Plath, Robert Lowell, and John Berryman—to name a few of our modern poets—Schuyler was also a poet-chronicler of breakdown and recovery.

Because of its scope and musicality, his work has been called Whitmanesque by critics who situate him firmly within an American poetic tradition that dates back nearly a century and a half. However, his vision is darker than Whitman's, sadder perhaps, for having been influenced by the sparse lines and objectivist sensibilities of the modernist era. Like many modernist poets, Schuyler is very conscious of language as that which constructs the world for us; his poems, then, are visions of the worlds they create. As one critic, Lawrence Joseph, has said of another of his long poems, "The Morning of the Poem":

> what is undeniable is the subtle force by which the poem's language is projected into form, into an object of felt expression. Call it collage; call it projected verse; call it inscape. What you actually see, hear and feel, at bottom, is the form and language of the poem itself, what it perceptually embodies.

Joseph's comment prompts a useful question: What does the language of a long Schuyler poem perceptually embody? "The Morning of the Poem" could be thought of as an earlier companion to "A Few Days." It is, perhaps, a poem in which Schuyler most successfully shaped his desires to write long, collagelike poems. He had worked on the long poem in his earlier books Hymn to Life and The Crystal Lithium, but "The Morning of the Poem" pulls together this past work in a way that marks a transition in his writing. It might be helpful to imagine Schuyler sitting down each morning and writing sections of his poem, the way some people read the newspaper, and doing it day after day after day; and to think then, of "A Few Days," the poem included here, as a more recent offspring of this earlier, even longer, and equally astonishing poem.

Schuyler's long poems, like "A Few Days," engage readers with dramatic visual re-presentations of the things Schuyler notices, and the things he notices give us, as readers (and writers), a vision of the world on the page that is smart, funny, compassionate, and quirky. It's a vision that allows us to see both the ordinary and the extraordinary differently. And that's a rare thing whether it happens in paintings or stories or essays or poems.

Schuyler died in 1991 a week after suffering a stroke. His works include seven collections of poetry: Freely Espousing *(1969),* The Crystal Lithium *(1972),* Hymn to Life *(1974),* The Morning of the Poem *(1980),* A Few Days (1985), Selected Poems *(1988), and* Collected Poems *(1993). He also published three novels:* Alfred and Guinevere *(1958),* A Nest of Ninnies *(1976, with John Ashbery), and* What's for Dinner? *(1978). He also published* The Home Book *(1977), a work in prose and verse, edited by Trevor Winkfield.*

A Few Days

are all we have. So count them as they pass. They pass
    too quickly
out of breath: don't dwell on the grave, which yawns for
    one and all.
Will you be buried in the yard? Sorry, it's against
    the law. You can only
lie in an authorized plot but you won't be there to
    know it so why worry
about it? Here I am at my brother's house in western
    New York: I came
here yesterday on the Empire State Express, eight hours
    of boredom on the train.
A pretty blond child sat next to me for a while. She
    had a winning smile,
but I couldn't talk to her, beyond "What happened to
    your shoes?" "I put them under the seat." And
so she had. She pressed the button that released the
    seat back and sank
back like an old woman. Outside, the purple loosestrife
    bloomed in swathes
that turned the railway ditch and fields into a
    sunset-reflecting lake.
And there was goldenrod and tattered Queen Anne's lace
    and the noble Hudson
on which just one sailboat sailed, billowing, on a
    weekday afternoon.
A tug towed some scows. Sandy red earth and cows,
    the calves like
big dogs. With Fresca and ham and cheese on a roll the
    eight hours somehow passed.
My sister-in-law met me at the Buffalo Central Station
    and drove me out to their house.

Hilde is just back from a visit home to Augsburg,
    where she was born
not too long ago. She taught herself to speak English, which
    she does extremely well.
My mother now lives with them in the house my brother built
    himself. She's old: almost eighty-nine
and her sight is failing. She has little to do but sit and
    listen to the TV rumble.
When I came in she said, "I can't see you but I know your
    voice."
"Some corner of a garden where the soul sinks down under
    its own weight. . . ."
But this isn't about my family, although I wish it were. My
    niece Peggy is at
camp in the Adirondacks so I am staying in her room.
    It's essence of teenage
girl: soft lilac walls, colored photographs of rock stars,
    nosegays of artificial flowers,
signs on the door: THIS ROOM IS A DISASTER AREA, and
    GARBAGEDUMP.
"Some ashcan at the world's end . . ." but this is not
    my family's story, nor
is it Molly's: the coon hound pleading silently for table
    scraps. The temperature
last night dipped into the forties: a record for August
    14th. There is a German
down pouff on the bed and I was glad to wriggle under
    it and sleep the sleep
of the just. Today is a perfection of blue: the leaves
    go lisp in the breeze.
I wish I were a better traveler; I love new places, the
    arrival in a station
after the ennui of a trip. On the train across the aisle
    from me there was a young couple.
He read while she stroked the flank of his chest in a
    circular motion, motherly,
covetous. They kissed. What is lovelier than young love?
    Will it only lead
to barren years of a sour marriage? They were perfect
    together. I wish
them well. This coffee is cold. The eighteen-cup pot
    like most inventions
doesn't work so well. A few days: how to celebrate them?
    It's today I want
to memorialize but how can I? What is there to it?
    Cold coffee and
a ham-salad sandwich? A skinny peach tree holds no
    peaches. Molly howls

at the children who come to the door. What did they
    want? It's the wrong
time of year for Girl Scout cookies.
My mother can't find her hair net. She nurses a cup of
    coffee substitute, since
her religion (Christian Science) forbids the use
    of stimulants. On this
desk, a vase of dried blue flowers, a vase of artificial
    roses, a bottle with
a dog for stopper, a lamp, two plush lions that hug
    affectionately, a bright
red travel clock, a Remington Rand, my Olivetti, the
    ashtray and the coffee cup.
Moonlight Serenade:
                Moon, shine in my yard,
                let the grass blades
                cast shadows on themselves.
                Harbinger of dreams,
                let me sleep in your
                eternal glow.
That was last night. Today, the color of a buttercup,
    winds on the spool
of time, an opaque snapshot. Today is better than yesterday,
    which was too cold for
August. Still, it had its majesty of tumultuous cloud wrack.
    Here and there a sunbeam
struggled through. Like the picture in my grandmother's Bible
    of Judgment Day:
Rembrandtesque beams of spotlights through cloud cities on a
    desolate landscape. I
used to feel frightened when I saw that effect in the sky. The
    August coolness:
a winter's-coming autumn feeling of it's time to pull our
    horns in and snuggle
down for winter. The radio, the anodyne of the lonely, speaks
    or rather sings:
                I love you only
                don't want to be lonely
delectable, deleterious trash. Three in the afternoon, when
    time stands still.
Is your watch right? Rest after labor doth greatly ease. There is
    no place to put
anything. These squandered minutes, hours, days. A few days, spend
    them riotously. There
is no occasion for riot. I haven't had a drink in years, begging
    a few glasses of
wine. I dream at night about liquor: I was mad at Fairfield because
    he invited people

to dinner and all he bought for them to drink was a pint of rum.
    I poured some for Anne
in a crumbling eggshell. And what does all that mean? I'm no
    good at interpreting
dreams. Hands fumble with clothes, and just at the delirious
    moment I wake up:
Is a wet dream too much to ask for? Time for a cigarette. Why are
    pleasures bad for you?
But how good the tobacco smoke tastes. Uhm. Blow smoke rings
    if you can. Or
blow me: I could do with a little carnal relief. The yard slopes
    down to a swampy bit,
then fields rise up where cows are pastured. They do nothing
    all day but eat:
filling their faces so they'll have a cud to chew on. I'm not uncowlike
    myself: life as a
continuous snack. Another ham-salad sandwich and then goodbye.
    Will you say no to a
stack of waffles? I need a new pastime: photography turned out to
    be just too expensive. I
miss it though, stalking the motif, closing in on a flower, my
    photograph of Katherine Koch
laughing and leaning back in a porch that blazed with sunlight.
    You went off to Naropa
in Boulder, Colorado, and I have a postcard to prove it.
    I think about your
lesbian love for your roommate. You're a modern miss and I like
    you as you are.
Today is tomorrow, it's that dead time again: three in the afternoon
    under scumbled clouds,
livid, that censor the sun and withhold the rain: impotent as
    an old man ("an
old man's penis: limp as a rabbit's ear"). It's cool
    for August and I
can't nail the days down. They go by like escalators, each alike,
    each with its own
message of tears and laughter. I could go pick beans only Hilde
    beat me to it.
The drive to the village: a whole generation younger than I
    seem to rule the
roost. Where Sipprell the photographer used to live and work
    is someone else's
now. He was a kind and gentle man. I knew his sons. The one I
    knew best is dead
and gone now, as he is himself. Life sends us struggling forth
    like "the green vine
angering for life" and rewards us with a plate of popovers
    labeled "your death."

Where is mine waiting? What will it be like when there's no
        more tomorrow? I
can't quite escape the feeling of death as a sleep
        from which we awaken
refreshed, in eternity. But when the chips are down I plunk
        them on nothingness;
my faith ran out years ago. It may come back, but I doubt it.
        "Rest in peace"
is all I have to say on the subject. I drink too much strong
        German coffee and
can't sleep at night. Last night I woke up laughing from
        a beautiful sensual
dream: a man who looked like a handsome woman who looked like
        a man. He told
me I should read in the sun to get a better color. But oh, the
        delicate touchings!
Venison stew, rank and gamey. Choke it down. Have a dumpling.
        Once again it's
another day, a gray day, damp as a dog's mouth, this unlikely
        August. In the vegetable
plot the squash are ripening, and tomatoes. Perhaps there are
        nematodes: cucumbers
won't grow here. They start to produce and then the plants die
        back. In the garden
(the flower garden) edelweiss thrives and so do China asters.
        Here, at home, I'm
lonelier than alone in my New York digs. There is no one to talk
        to, nothing to talk
about. "Tell me the story of your life," in great detail. Your first
        memory, the scariest thing
that ever happened: travels and food, the works. "Are you really
        interested?" "Passionately."
When you rest your head like that you suddenly look like an
        old woman, the old
woman you may one day become. Struggle into the shower to wash
        your hair, then crimp
it in rollers. You have a corrugated head. Can't you throw
        caution to the winds
and buy a little of some decent scent? Scent is one of the great
        amenities. Smelling like
a whore's dream. The dream shop and the dram shop. Dram shops
        in Amsterdam, old and cozy
enclosing the small fires of marvelous *ginevra*. It burns
        my throat and my eyes water;
so good to be free in the mid-afternoon, free to be a slightly
        drunk tourist, eyeing
the man-made wonders along the Amstel. Go to Naples to buy
        striped socks off a barrow.

Besides the dram shops there is the Pleasure Chest, with its
          edifying displays: pleasure takes
          many forms: keep it
simple is the best bet. I especially hate the picture of two
          Scotties with pink bows
on their heads. Sentimentality can go further than the door to
          the cellar and the
braid of garlic. Guess I'm ready for lunch: ready as I'll
          ever be, that is.
Lunch was good: now to move my bowels. That was good too:
          "Oh shit," she said,
"I stepped in some doggy pooh." Worse things could happen
          to you. Meeting a
man-eating tiger in the street, for instance. A little
          trembling worthless
thing: a mobile. It balances five angels and I lie in bed
          and throw puffs of
breath at it. It does its shimmering dance. Sunday, "the
          worst day," and we
all sit snowbound in drifts of Sunday paper. No news is
          good news but it
sure makes Jack a dull boy. "I can't get in there: my grades
          aren't good enough."
My nephew Mike came home at two in the morning from his
          hitchhiking trip in the Middle West. He
liked Springfield, Mo., the best. I can't make out why: a
          girl perhaps. He's
sixteen and smokes, which makes my brother see red. I wanted
          to ask him if he ever
smokes pot, but a sudden shyness came over me, the way
          the white sky overcame
this bluest of mornings. A sound of rolling peas:
          traffic goes by.
"Is Fred your uncle?" my mother asked out of the dimness
          of time. "No: he's
my kid brother." "Oh, I see." It's time for Hilde
          to brush and comb
her hair, a glory of white. She sits all day, a monument
          to patience, almost eighty-nine
if she's a day. We talk, but nothing comes of it. Minnesota
          winters when the sleighs
whirled over the snow-covered fences and jokes were
          made about the Scandinavians.
Exhilaration: one night we took the toboggan and went
          to Emery Park, where
there was a long, long slide, on which we sped
          into the night. "I'll
wash your face in the snow!" "Get away from me, you
          punk rock rabbit."

I just sat outside with my mother: my one good deed
    of the day.
That day passed like any other and I took the train from
    Buffalo to New York.
Buffalo, the city God forgot. Not even the Pope is going
    to visit it,
and he should: it's the largest Polish city in the world.
    Now I'm back
in New York on West Twenty-third Street with the buses farting
    past. And the one
dog that barks its head off at two or three in the morning.
    I hate to miss
the country fall. I think with longing of my years in
    Southampton, leaf-turning
trips to cool Vermont. Things should get better as you
    grow older, but that
is not the way. The way is inscrutable and hard to handle.
    Here it is
the Labor Day weekend and all my friends are out of town:
    just me and some
millions of others, to whom I have not yet been introduced.
    A walk in the
streets is not the same as a walk on the beach, by
    preference, a beach
emptied by winter winds. A few days, and friends will
    trickle back to
town. Dinner parties, my favorite form of entertainment.
    Though in these
inflationary times you're lucky to get chicken in
    place of steak.
What I save on meals I spend on taxis. Lately a lot
    of cabs have
signs: NO SMOKING, PLEASE, or NO SMOKING DRIVER ALLERGIC.
    A quiet smoke in
a taxi is my idea of bliss. Yes, everything gets more
    restricted, less free.
Yet I am free, one of the lucky ones who does not
    have to show up
Monday morning at some boring desk. I remember the years
    at NBC, looking
discontentedly out at grimy Sixth Avenue, waiting for
    the time to pass.
It did. Pass, I mean, and I took ship for Europe. A
    pleasant interlude
on the whole, despite my operation. I miss Rino, my
    Roman lover, and
often wonder how he is and what he's up to. Probably
    a grandfather by
now. Good day, Signor Oscari: are you still a grocer

by trade? Did
your uncle die and leave you his shop in the *periferia?*
    Italy seems so
far away (just a few hours by plane), and, you see,
    since I was there
I fell in love with an island in Maine, now out of
    bounds. I'd like to
find a new place, somewhere where there are friends and
    not too many
houses. This summer has passed like a dream. On the last
    day of August
I feel much better than I felt in June, heaven be praised.
    Who said, "Only
health is beautiful"? There's truth in the old saw. I
    have always been
more interested in truth than in imagination: I
    wonder if that's
true? I have one secret, which I sometimes have an almost
    overwhelming desire
to blurt out; but I won't. Actually, I have told it to
    my shrink, so it's
not an absolute secret anymore. Too bad. Are secrets a
    way of telling lies,
I wonder? Yes, they are. So, let it be. I don't drink
    anymore, still, I
just had four double cocktails: margaritas. At least I
    stopped there. I
like not drinking. Hangovers were too horrible. I MEAN THAT.
    Really mean it.
Tomorrow is another day, but no better than today if
    you only realize it.
Let's love today, the what we have now, this day, not
    today or tomorrow or
yesterday, but this passing moment, that will
    not come again.
Now tomorrow is today, the day before Labor Day,
    1979. I want to
live to see the new century come: but perhaps it's
    bad luck to
say so. To live to be seventy-six: is that so much
    to ask? My father
died in his forties, but his mother lived to be ninety,
    as my mother seems
likely to. In what rubbishy old folks' home will I
    pass my sunset years?
A house on the edge of a small town, private but
    convenient, is my
wish. I won't say no to Vermont or Maine, not that
    I want to spend

my old age shoveling snow. I spent my youth doing
    that. Our drive
was cut into the side of a hill and no sooner
    was it cleared
than the wind would drift it full again. Monotonous
    days, daydreaming
of any place but there. It rained earlier today: I
    lay on the bed
and watched the beads it formed on the foliage of
    my balcony balustrade
drop of their own weight. I remember the night the
    house in Maine
was struck by lightning. It was attracted to a
    metal flue
and coursed harmlessly down to the wood-burning
    stove that heated
the bath water for my end of the house. I could
    write a book about
the island, but I don't want to. I want to write
more novels. I've made more false starts than anyone
    since Homer was a
pup. Now it's dinner time: time to feed the inner man. I
    wish I could go
on a diet of water for a few days: to reduce the outer
    man to weigh what
he should weigh. A letter from Joe Brainard: he's
    my favorite pen pal.
Joe decides what he's going to do, then he does it.
    This summer it's
been sunbathing and reading Dickens and Henry James.
    And he sends a poem:
        "Ah! the good old days!"
        "If gobbled then—digested now.
        (Clarified by time—romanticised by mind.)
        For today's repast remembered."
            and:
        "Reminds me of you—Jimmy—out in
        Southampton in the big Porter House in your
        little room of many books it takes game-
        board strategy to relocate now, as then."
            and:
        "Out trekking up South Main Street
        you are:
        a pair of thick white legs
        sporting Bermuda shorts
        (of a *most* unusual length)
        and plain blue sneakers so 'you'
        they are."
I tripped and fell the other night and struck the curb

with my head,
face forward. I went to the emergency at St. Vincent's.
          They put stitches
in my chin: I look like "The Masque of the Red Death."
          Feel like it, too.
I wish this humid unsunny day would get its act together
          and take it on the road.
It's no day for writing poems. Or for writing, period.
          So I didn't.
Write, that is. The bruises on my face have gone, just
          a thin scab on
the chin where they put the stitches. I'm back on Antabuse:
          what a drag. I
really love drinking, but once I'm sailing I can't seem
          to stop. So, pills
are once again the answer. It must have been horrible
          to live before
the days of modern medicine—all those great artists going
          off their chump
from syphilis or coughing their lungs out with TB. But
          they still haven't
found a live-forever pill. But soon. Across the street
          sunlight falls like
a shadow on the Palladian office building. This room
          faces north, which
usually I don't like, but the French doors to the
          balcony make it light
enough. I ought to buy a plant, but plants are too much
          like pets: suppose
you want to go away (and I do), someone has to take care
          of it. So I waste my
money on cut flowers. I'm spoiled: I'm used to gathering
          flowers for the house,
not buying them. Thirty-five dollars for a dozen roses,
          Sterling Silver:
not today. Always thinking about what things cost: well,
          I have to, except
when a cab comes in my view: then I flag it down.
          I'd be scared to
figure up how much I spend a year on chauffeur-driven
          comfort. I'd like to spend
          part of this lovely
day in a darkened movie theater: only there's nothing I
          want to see. Fellini's
Orchestra Rehearsal was too much like *Alice in Orchestralia.*
          Perhaps a good
walk is more what's called for. I could tool down to
          Dave's Pot Belly

and have a butterscotch sundae: eating on the pounds I
    walked off. Or
I could go shopping: I need cologne. Taylor's Eau de Portugal
    for choice. In the
country you can take a walk without spending money. In
    the city it isn't
easy. This soft September sun makes the air fizzy like
    soda water: Perrier
in the odd-shaped bottle from France. I dreamed last
    night about autumn
trees: orange, red, yellow, and the oaks dark green. I
    wish there were
something besides ginkgos and plane trees to see short
    of Central Park.
"It does wonders for your back . . ." The radio is on:
    perhaps this will
be a lucky day and they'll play something besides the
    New World Symphony
or Telemann. I could call Ruth and chat, only it isn't
    noon so she
isn't up yet. It still isn't noon: it's tomorrow
    morning. The risen
sun almost comes in the north windows: I see it lie
    along the balcony,
cut into shapes by the wrought-iron balustrade, a
    design of crazy
chrysanthemums and willow leaves. This old hotel is
    well built: if
you hold your breath and make a wish you'll meet Virgil
    Thomson in the elevator
or a member of a punk rock band. I still want to go to
    a movie but
there isn't any. A month ago when I wasn't in the
    mood there were lots:
Flying Down to Rio, Million Dollar Legs, Blonde Bombshell
    or do I date myself?
A red, pink and blue slip on my desk tells me that
    I am going to
spend forty dollars to have a jacket relined. A child
    of the thirties,
that seems to me what you spend for a new suit. More
    money! I got that
cologne: sixteen twenty. Think I'll splash some on
    right now. Uhm. Feels good.
    I think I'll take a shower.
No. That would mean taking my clothes off and putting
    them on again. I
haven't got the energy for that. And the waste of hot water!

And I should wash my hair.
But that would mean putting my shoes on and a tromp around
        the corner to the
drugstore that isn't open yet. Or I could wash it with plain
        cucumber soap and
rinse it with lime juice (I think there is a lime). I
        think I'll leave it matted
and get it cut—oh—tomorrow. For a while I let it get
        really long, I
looked like Buffalo Bill's mother. Ruth says, "Oh, Jimmy,
        you look much better
with short hair." "Graciousness, part of the Japanese
        character." The radio
is still on. "It's time for one of our classical hits:
        you'll recognize this
one." But I don't. Good grief, it's "Greensleeves." I'm
        a real music lover!
I'd rather listen to rock, but if I tune WNCN out I
        can never find it
again. Last night they played the Brahms Second Piano
        Concerto, which sent
me off contentedly to bye-bye land. The sleeping pills
        I scoffed helped too.
It used to be when I checked out a medicine chest there
        would be lots of
amphetamines. No more. Doctors won't prescribe them.
        I heard a rumor
about a diet doctor in Queens who will. Must find out
        his address. But
Queens seems awfully far to give the day a gentle lift.
        I can do it with
coffee, only that much coffee gives me sour stomach. Urp.
        Belch. Guess I'll
make a cup of Taster's Choice. My sister-in-law and
        Donald Droll both use
that brand. Not bad. *The Burning Mystery of Anna in 1951:*
        I prefer the genteel wackiness
of John Ashbery's *As We Know.* A poem written in two
        columns, supposed to
be read simultaneously: John is devoted to the impossible.
        The sunlight still
sits on my balcony, invitingly. I decline the invitation:
        out there, it gives
me vertigo. People who come here say, "Oooh, you have a
        balcony," as though I
spent my days out there surveying Twenty-third Street:
        Chelsea Sewing Center,
Carla Hair Salon. Twenty-third Street hasn't got much

   going for it, unless
you love the YMCA. I once did. I remember Christmas '41.
   I was in the shower
when a hunk walked in. I got a hard-on just like that.
   He dropped his soap
to get a view of it and in no time we were in bed in
   his room. Sure was
a change from West Virginia. When I told Alex Katz I
   went to college in West
Virginia, he said in that way of his, "Nah,
   you're Harvard." Wish I
were, but I'm a lot more panhandle than I am Cambridge,
   Mass. Which reminds
me, I saw in the *Times* that my old friend Professor Billy
   Vinson died of the
heart condition he knew he had. Billy was the Navy officer
   who, when he was
getting fucked by an apelike sailor, lifted his head out of
   the pillow and
said, "I order you back to your ship." His camp name was
   Miss Williemae.
He was a virologist who detected two new viruses, which he
   named for Chester
Kallman and me: *Fiordiligi* and *Dorabella.* If anybody called
   me by my camp name
nowadays I'd sock them—I like to think. I remember how
   I felt when Chester
dedicated his book to me and wrote the poem in "camp": "Wearing
   a garden hat her mother
wore . . ." Bitch. Chester's gone now, and so are Wystan, Billy Vinson,
   Brian Howard, Bill Aalto and Brian's
friend, the red-haired boy whose name I can't remember.
   Chester was a martyr
to the dry martini. So, in his way, was Wystan. Brian
   committed suicide:
Why do people do that? For fun? Brian was the most
   bored and boring man
I ever met. He was what the French call *épatant:* he told
   an American officer
that he was a clandestine homosexual. The officer knocked
   him to the barroom floor.
Brian looked up and said, "That proves it." I could tell
   a thousand Brian
stories, the way some people can reel off limericks. For
   a great poet, Wystan
Auden's dirty limericks are singularly uninspired. Sorry
   I can't remember any
to quote you. *The Platonic Blow* gives me hives. Funny porn

I guess is a gift,
like any other. Who wrote:
          "Lil tried shunts and double-shunts
          And all tricks known to common cunts . . . "?
A tired newspaperman? A gifted coal miner in West
          Virginia? The morning
passes like an elephant in no stampede. The morning passes like
          Salome's veil. Famous last
lines: "I am still alive!" and "Kill that woman!" Fast
          curtain. The morning
passes too slowly. I want it to be seven forty-five in the evening,
          when I'm invited
to dine on delectables chez John Ashbery. I wonder if the
          cuisine will be
Indian? The little minx took a course in it, after all
          those years in France.
Tall Doug and blond Frank will be there: I wonder about
          David Kermani of the
shoe-button eyes? Lately whenever I've gone there he's
          been out on some
important errand: is he avoiding me? I hope not. I like
          him. What a
devil he is for work. I hope his boss, Tibor, values him
          at his true worth.
The sun is off the balcony. The sun is off: a scrim of
          cloud obscures the
sky. Yesterday was such a heaven day: blue, warm, breezy.
          When I cabbed up to Barbara's
I found the park full of joggers: men and women whose
          breasts and buttocks
went jounce, jounce. Uhm: a shave and a splash of Eau
          de Portugal,
Taylor's best. I mustn't use it up too fast: think what
          it cost. The only trouble
with it is that it doesn't hang on: I like a cologne that
          makes people say, "You
smell good," like Guerlain's Impériale. Paco
          really hangs on:
people who say "You smell so good" look as though
          they're going to retch.
I threw caution to the winds and threw it out. I
          would like to go
in the bathroom and swizzle on some of Taylor's best,
          but the maid is in
there stinking up the house with household ammonia.
          "Is that girl who
comes and takes care of you your niece?" she asked me.
          No, Eileen Myles is

my assistant: she comes and makes my breakfast and
    lunch, runs errands
to the grocery store, the p.o., the bank, mails letters,
    and always arrives with
that morning's *Times*. I lie in bed and read the obituaries
    and smell the French
toast frying. Served with applesass. I think I'll
    let her take the laundry
out; she needs the exercise. The sun is off the balcony,
    the air is cool
as one of Barbara's kisses, which don't make me feel
    I turn her on.
Her husband won't give her money to pay the cleaning
    woman and they
have a huge co-op. It is all neat and tidy. Barbara is
    very organized
for a literary lady. She loaned me a book about Natalie
    Barney I thought
would be fascinating but the writing is much too coy,
    "Amazon" instead of
dyke or Lesbian. I always think I can read anything
    but some things turn me off:
like trying to read jellied gasoline. I could almost
    put a sweater on
the air from the French doors is so cool. But I think
    I like to live
cold, like George Montgomery and Frank O'Hara wearing
    chinos and sneakers
in the snow at Harvard. It was the thing to do. "I'd like
    to kiss Jimmy," said
a dope who came to the door. Frank made a grand gesture at
    me lying reading on
the couch and said, "Help yourself." So he did. I wonder
    what I was reading?
I should keep a reading diary of all the books and mags
    I read, but what
would be the use? I can't remember what I read. I read
    Graham Greene's *A*
Sort of Life and a week later reread it without remembering
    anything, except his
playing Russian roulette. It's a lovely book, the writing
    is so concrete. I
have a foible for books of family life, like Gwen Raverat's
    Period Piece and
Frances Marshall's *A Pacifist's War*. I went out to post
    some letters (Chemical
Bank, Denver Art Museum, Richard Savitsky, my lawyer) and
    the sun was hot. In

the shadows it was cool but when you stepped into a sun-
        spot you felt the heat.
It's a beautiful day, the gray nimbus devoured itself. No
        clouds at all.
I bought the *Post*. More mothers killing their babies be-
        cause they're mad
at their husbands. What kind of sense does that make? Maybe
        they wanted to have
abortions and their husbands wouldn't let them. How
        does that grab you?
Eileen took the double-breasted blazer Joe Hazan
        gave me to have
the sleeves shortened half an inch. It came from Hunts-
        man! I used to have a
Huntsman hacking raincoat. In Alex Katz's painting
        Incident you can see
me wearing it, flanked by Ada Katz in a hat and Rudi
        Burckhardt with a
camera. That was a long time ago. I wonder if they still
        have their Teddy Wilson
record? The Alicia de Larrocha of the hot piano.
        A few days! I
started this poem in August and here it is September
        nineteenth. September
is almost my favorite month, barring October and May.
        November, my natal
month, is too damn wintry, I don't like it but I like
        my birthstone, the topaz.
In Venice I saw a pair of cufflinks, square topazes
        edged with paste
diamonds—sixty-five bucks, but Arthur, who was
        picking up the check,
wouldn't buy them for me. Cheap is cheap. It was funny
        having no money of
my own. Every time I went out sightseeing I would see
        a black-and-red knitted
tie I wanted passionately to own. Last weekend I spent
        at Barbara's in
Water Mill: a funny turreted house, commodious within
        (this coffee is too strong),
all the woodwork very nineteen-hundred, dark wood balusters
        and cream walls,
Barbara's pictures: Paul Georges, Robert Goodenough, Fairfield
        Porter. We went
to call on Anne Porter, who is selling the house at 49 South
        Main, where I used
to live. The library was void of books: it made me sad, the
        way it did when

my mother sold her house. That one back room in the ell was
    my room. I could
lie in the four-poster on the horsehair mattress and stare
    at Fairfield's color
lithograph of Sixth Avenue and the Waverly Theater en-
    tranced by its magic.
The cover of *Hymn to Life* is Fairfield's version of the
    view from my
south window: the wondrous pear tree in white bloom. Did
    you know that you
can force pears to bloom? Go out in the snow and cut a
    few knobbly twigs
with buds. Soak them overnight in water, put them in a vase
    and hold your breath:
a Chinese print is what you have. A haircut: Breck's
    Shampoo for Normal Hair.
I looked for the *New York Review of Books,* which has a
    review in it of my novel
by Stephen Spender. Couldn't find it. Damn. It's funny,
    having a review come
out a whole year later. Everyone on the street was wearing
    sweaters. There was a
man lying on the sidewalk, one shoe off, his shirt un-
    buttoned down to his
navel. Passersby looked at him coldly; nobody offered
    to help him. I
curbed my Good Samaritan instincts. Poor guy: once he was
    a little boy. How
do you degenerate that way? There aren't any novels about
    blindstiffs these
days: *Tramping on Life* and Jim Tully. Joe Hazan, who lives
    in a Fifth Avenue penthouse,
went on the bum when he was young. I'm thinking about D. D.
    Ryan and her "mothwing" eyebrows.
She says they grew that way, but in a bright light I
    wondered.
She never appears until her face is on. Her boys, Beau and Drew, are
    match-happy. I went
outside and there in the autumn leaves was a circle of flame.
    We managed to stamp
it out. It was right by the house: Kenward's little cottage
    reduced to ashes! Almost.
D. D.'s Vuitton cosmetic trunk that weighed a ton. When we
    stopped at a diner
in Rutland I saw a stark-naked man in the john. He dashed
    into a stall and hid
himself. "I really hate to do this," D. D. said, passing a
    car on the right

at ninety miles an hour. *"On ne voit pas le rivage de la
     mort deux fois, D. D.,"*
as Racine said. When we got to New York Kenward and I
     went to Casey's
and got hysterical with laughter.
Blossoming afternoon, what can I tell you? You tell me that
     my hair is clean and cut.
Breck's Shampoo for Normal Hair, 40¢ off. It's nice and
     gloopy. I'd like to
take a bubble bath but I haven't got the stuff. Bath oil
     is risky business:
it coats the tub with slime and taking a shower is a perilous
     stunt. Help! my Eau
de Portugal is half empty. I've been slathering it on. I
     love it. I ought to
get a Caswell-Massey sampler and see what smells best. Patchouli.
     Vetiver (ugh). September
evening, what have you to say to me? Tell me the time. Still
     two and three-quarter hours
until John's. I'm reading Osbert Sitwell's autobiography
     stitched in brocade. I
read a page, then rush back to my poem. I would once have
     thought that Sitwell
was "influencing" me. I'm too me for that. Poor trembling
     Osbert, suffering from
Parkinson's disease. I met him at a party Wystan gave for
     them. John was
dashing tears from his eyes: "What's wrong?" "I just met
     Edith Sitwell." Tender
heart. Edith looked less like her photographs. She was
     creased and had that
famous nose. September day, how shall I color you? In blue
     and white and airy tones.
September evening, you give your benediction. Ruth is
     in love with a priest
(an Episcopalian) who smokes grass. Ruth can convert from
     Judaism and wear a
hat in church. "The Overture to *Zampa* led by Leonard Bernstein
     with the New York
Philharmonic." The radio is such a pleasure. A Hand in
     a Glove: a vase
you couldn't believe. "Price includes round-trip air fare."
     Oh, the radio! I
can't live without it. Yes, I must put a sweater on. Brrr.
     September, how fickle you are,
there is the shadow of a flapping flag. The Plaza Hotel
     was flying a Japanese
flag: who was staying there? I have on a George Schneeman
     T-shirt, a plaid

shirt on a coat hanger. Useless gas. Here is my Blue-Cross/
    Blue Shield number: 11223677

Ho8. I don't know my social security number. It's in two
    names: James Ridenour

and James Schuyler. Ridenour was my stepfather's name,
    and when I went to

Europe in 1947 I found my name had never legally been
    changed. Sometimes someone

comes up to me and says, "Aren't you Jimmy Ridenour?" I
    plotz. It's good to

have your own name. Ask me, I'll tell you. It's pink!
    the light I mean

shining from the west on the office building. The sunset.
    That's the trouble with

a north view: you can't see the sunset. North is kinda dreary.
    Will it be dark

when I set out for John Ashbery's? It spooks me. His
    apartment is so nice:

full of French antiques and oriental rugs and collectibles.
    An angel wing begonia

and wandering Jew, peperomia. He has willowware china
    which reminds me of

the Willow tea room, where I used to eat in eighth grade.
    Salisbury steak. Chop suey.

There were motifs from the willowware painted on the walls.
    It's Wednesday morning, but

later than I got up yesterday: the sun is off the balcony.
    There's a chill in the air,

I put on a Jaeger sweater, sand color. The dinner was
    nice: cold soup, veal

collops with a brown sauce, broccoli, noodles, pineapple
    upside-down cake, whipped cream.

The latter had rum in it and I ate it rather nervously but
    it didn't activate the Antabuse.

Rather nervously describes the way I was all evening: just
    sat and drank Perrier

and smoked. Didn't say a word, even when someone spoke to
    me. I meant to say

to John, "Is there any coffee in the house?" Instead I said,
    "Is there any liquor in

the house?" He looked astounded. I faced it out, didn't tell
    him what I really

meant. I have a sleeping-pill hangover; my head feels like
    Venetian glass. I

only took two pills, not three, which puts me to sleep but
    makes me feel crappy.

The *Times* says there's a vogue for pumps: Eileen and I did
    the galleries and I

watched the women's feet: they were all wearing sandals,

very chic, especially
a black chick who had on a stylish suit. I thought I could
    beat the starting gun
by taking my pills at seven: seven Sleepeze, two Nembutal,
    the scoffed pills, three
antidepressant pills, a red pill that controls the side
    effects of the antidepressants.
I went to sleep like a babe, and here I am wide awake at
    eleven. Anne Dunn is here.
She can't see me until Saturday lunch. I wanted to have
    dinner with her tonight.
Christ, I feel shitty. I took two more sleeping pills and
    what I feel like. Creamed
shit. I lay in bed for an hour; it was torture. It's the
    witching hour of night.
I feel great. This is the morning; it's wonderful. I can't
    tell you about it.
It's a grand day. I feel cold and I
    mailed letters today:
Denver Art Museum, Chemical Bank (that should bring in
    money), Savitsky, my lawyer: he pays my bills, like
the rent ($550). I went back to bed and slept some after
    all. Eleven hours
all told. Not bad
but I still have the old sleeping-pill hangover. "He brought
    it on himself."
I know I'm going to regret it but still I do it—take that
    one extra pill at
the wrong time. I could kick myself around the block. It's
    getting light out
not sunlight, just morning gray. It looks the way it feels—
    chill. THE LAW FIRM
OF RICHARD D. SAVITSKY, a card says. I wonder if I trust him?
    There's no reason why
I shouldn't. I wonder how they broke the news to him. "There's
    this guy who keeps
having nervous breakdowns and he can't pay the hospital
    bills—state hospitals being of course out of the
question." Bellevue is proof of that: the scary patients,
    the nothing to do, the
insolent staff (that one nice girl), the egg for breakfast,
    One morning I had a bowl of cream of wheat, the black guy
sitting next to me said, "Hunh, putting sugar on
    grits," so this is
what grits are, people stealing cigarettes out of your pajama
    pocket while you sleep,
patients who will share a cigarette with you, you have to
    be an enforced abstainer

to know you'll never give up smoking, Christ I'm cold,
the up in the air TV you can't see, just a blur, the ennui,
     the doctor: "If there's anymore
smoking on this side smoking privileges will be taken away,"
     that's when you know
you'll never give up smoking. When I was in you could
     only smoke if you had money to buy the cigarettes.
I didn't have any money and had to depend on the charity of
     others. It was surprising
how many there were who were charitable. I swore I'd never
     give up smoking. I
did though. It turned me into a fiend. I took up the costly
     cigar. My first cigarette
tasted good. I talk big: I have a pain in my chest and
     worry about lung cancer.
Better make an appointment with the doc. I don't like my
     doctors, except the dentist and my shrink. "Come on
in, Jim." "What are you thinking about?" "Nothing." Not
     true: you're always thinking something.
I'm thinking about this poem. How to make it good, really
     good. I'm proud of my poems.
I wrote a poem about Ruth Kligman in which
     every line began "Ruth"—
talk about maddening. Ruth claimed to like it. When I
     told her it was a
stinker she said, "I didn't think it was one of your best."
     I've got to find that
notebook and tear it up, when I'm dead some creep will
     publish it in a thin
volume called *Uncollected Verse*. It will be a collector's
     item. I hate to think
of the contents of that volume. "Dorabella's Hat," "They
     Two Are Drifting Uptown on a
Bus." Bill Berkson asked me to send him any writings I had
     so I sent him "They Two." He didn't publish it. It's
very funny. The two are Frank and Larry. It's not a poem.
     It's a playlet. I used
to write lots of playlets. "Presenting Jane" is lost.
     It was produced. By
Herbert Machiz. It was horrible thanks to Herbert. When
     I first met Herbert
he said, "A nice-looking boy like you shouldn't have
     dirty fingernails." I blanched. I looked at my
nails: I felt creepy. "I work in a bookstore," I
     extenuated. "Is it
a second-hand bookstore?" he demanded. "No,
     it specializes in
English books." "English dirt." I recounted this to Frank,

who broke out laughing!
"Jimmy, Herbert is a wit." Herbert dropped dead, on a
      rug? John Latouche
fell down a flight of stairs in a small gray clapboard cottage
      at Apple Hill
among the leaves at Calais (pronounced callous), Vermont.
      Wystan died in his sleep
in a hotel in ring-streeted Vienna not far from his
      country home in verdant
southern Austria: Austria utterly turns me off: the
      goldenesdachtel at Innsbruck
is the worst thing, except for the dragon of Klagenfurt,
      Egg-am-Fackersee. The train
through torrent-torn needle-clad (I mean trees like
      spruce, pines and firs)
mountains and granite-boulders, then you're in Italy
      among the lemon
lamps and *"Permesso,"* which means "Move or I will mow you
      down with this dolly of
bricks." Then there's *"Ti da fastidio?"* which means "If
      I smoke will it give you the fastids?"
Then one day
the telephone:
it's Hilde:
"Mother passed on
in her sleep
last night. No,
you needn't
come, it's not that
kind of a ceremony.
Fred is seeing
to it all right
now. The last
three months were
pretty grim."
And so I won't be
there to see my Maney
enearthed beside
my stepfather:
once when I was
home a while ago
I said I realized
that in his way he
loved me. "He did
not," my mother said.
"Burton hated you."
The old truth-teller!
She was so proud

in her last dim
years (ninety years
are still
a few days) to be
longest-lived of
the Slaters: for-
getting her mother
was the Slater, she
a Connor:
Margaret Daisy Connor Schuyler Ridenour,
rest well,
the weary journey done.

• • • • • • • • • • • •

QUESTIONS FOR A SECOND READING

1. Schuyler's poem might be thought of as the work of a writer gathering and thinking through his materials. As you reread the poem, mark and note those moments where you become aware of patterns in the ways Schuyler works. What are his materials? What are his characteristic ways of presenting them? of thinking through them? And what would you say his purpose or purposes might be? How might you use his characteristic ways of working, his methods, to draw conclusions about his purposes in writing?

2. If Schuyler's poem might be read as an argument, what would you say that argument is? He touches on numerous subjects, including his writing, as he creates this poem, seemingly over a specific period with segues back and forth in time. He thinks out loud on the page, offering a plenitude of opinions. Which of these writerly devices might guide you to bring forward an argument you imagine he is making? As you reread, mark three or four passages that seem useful to your work in viewing this poem as an argument. What would you say that argument is? And what guides you to it in your reading of the poem?

3. What makes "A Few Days" a poem? To be sure, Schuyler presents "A Few Days" as a poem (it was the title poem in his fifth book of poetry), and the piece certainly looks like a poem; but if you imagine "poemness" as something enacted in the work itself, as a sense of writing represented in a poet's work, what would you say it is in "A Few Days"? As you reread, mark those moments (even obvious ones like the line breaks) that would allow you to talk about this poem *as* a poem. How does Schuyler, in "A Few Days," define the work of the poet? What does the poem allow him to do as a writer? How does he define the text as a poem for his readers? What assumptions about poetry does he frustrate or satisfy?

4. **Part I.** As Schuyler writes his long poem, he refers to a number of women

and men—individuals, artists of various sorts, and literary figures, such as Fairfield Porter, Joe Brainard, John Ashbery, Alex Katz, Wystan Auden, Frank O'Hara, George Montgomery, and Edith Sitwell. Reading through his poem again, make a complete list of the names Schuyler draws into his poem. Who are these people? To answer this question, you will need to do some library investigation checking such sources as a biographical index, *Who's Who,* and literary texts, or consulting with a reference librarian on how to find such information. After you have taken an initial pass at researching the names on your list, identifying as many as you can, choose a handful that interest you, that you'd like to do further research on.

Once you've identified a handful of names on your list that you'd like to research further, the next question to consider is how this knowledge of them influences your reading of Schuyler. What does each individual represent that merits her or his inclusion in the poem? To answer this question you will need to have located and read through or looked at (in the case of artists) at least a handful of works by the individuals you research. (You needn't, for example, read a whole book of poems by Frank O'Hara, although you might decide to, but you do need to read at least a few of his poems, or look at some reproductions of Fairfield Porter's paintings, to be able to write about what they might represent to Schuyler.) After you've completed your research, go back to Schuyler's poem: how do you now think of him as an artist working in relation to these other artists and writers? Why, given your reading of his poem, would he be interested in these artists and literary figures?

Part II. Schuyler also refers to many other people in his poem, people like his sister-in-law Hilde, his niece Peggy, his nephew Mike, his ex-lover Rino, the grocer Signor Oscari, the filmmaker Fellini, authors he had read or is reading, and composers. Some of these people you may have researched; others will emerge as simply authors he has read or composers whose music he has listened to (and, for example, whose music you might want to sample); others you will not find in a biographical index, because they're friends and relatives. Once you have completed the first part of this assignment, go back and make a second list (or perhaps even a third) of the different kinds of people Schuyler refers to. Who are *these* people? What bearing do they have on his poem? What status do they have in relation to the artists and literary figures he knows or seems to know, or whom he seems to work in relation to? And, finally, how do they figure into his work? That is, what do they stand for in relation to the other artistic or literary figures he mentions?

ASSIGNMENTS FOR WRITING

1. Schuyler's poem may be read as a way of thinking through or about a number of complex, interrelated issues: family, poetry, relationships, objects in the world, places, storytelling, and memory, to name some of the more obvious ones.

    For this assignment, write an essay in which you discuss what you think

Schuyler is saying both about these issues (or ones you select) that attract your attention *and* about his use of poetry as a way of exploring ideas. If poetry is a way of thinking about the world, then what does one gain by writing poems rather than writing essays or stories? What might one lose? And how might one's thinking change because of its being written as a poem?

2. "A Few Days" gives poetic representation to the processes of memory, observation, and reflection. It is a poem that figures things out, things that seem quite ordinary, even unremarkable, and things that seem at moments quite extraordinary (or that are defined as extraordinary). In this sense, the poem (and its sentences, its rhythms, its use of the line as a unit of composition) is an interesting device for thinking—in particular, thinking like a poet rather than an essayist or a writer of prose.

   Write a poem of your own based on Schuyler's. This is both an invitation to dramatize yourself as a writer using Schuyler as your model and an invitation to write a certain kind of verse. Whether to cast yourself as a Schuyler-like character or not is a decision to consider. It is important, however, to think of this assignment as an exercise in writing his kind of line or sentence, his kind of stanza, his way of organizing or thinking through places and scenes and people. Your poem, in other words, should look and sound like his.

   After you have written your poem, step back from it, and in a separate assignment, write a two-page essay in which you suggest how your poem might be read as Schuyleresque. How would you describe the work you did to construct a poem that articulates a Schuyler kind of celebration? What are its subjects, methods, and effects?

3. Early in the poem, Schuyler writes:

   > A few days: how to celebrate them?
   > It's today I want
   > to memorialize but how can I? What is there to it?
   > Cold coffee and
   > a ham-salad sandwich? (p. 592)

   What is there to it? What is there to Schuyler's celebrating the few days that he puts down on paper? From a certain point of view, the poem does not seem like a celebration at all. The language can be fairly flat (it does not try to be beautiful), the lives not noble or heroic, the details determinedly ordinary and mundane.

   Write an essay in which you explain or challenge "A Few Days" as a poem of celebration.

MAKING CONNECTIONS

1. Placing Susan Griffin's essay "Our Secret" (p. 319) alongside Schuyler's "A Few Days" provides two examples of quite different works by writers. If you imagine that each work is a representation of each writer's characteristic ways of thinking and working, how would you describe those habits and patterns of thinking? How, for instance, do they gather their materials? How do they present them to readers? What devices do they use to direct readers?

And what attracts their attention as writers? What, that is, do they notice and make commitments to in their writing?

Write an essay in which you use Schuyler and Griffin to talk about the work of writing. Here you have the example of two writers, both considered important contemporary writers, both experimenting with their genres, neither "famous," or universally accepted. What does their work allow you to say about the work of writing at the present time? What is at stake? Why, given what you understand of their work, would an adult commit to writing as a vocation? What are the problems of writing that seem important to writers like Schuyler and Griffin? What are the problems of reading? How might one think of this work as work?

2. James Schuyler's "A Few Days" and Gloria Anzaldúa's "Entering into the Serpent" seem to be very different works by very different writers. Yet, if we listen to what Anzaldúa has to say about her work elsewhere in her book, it bears a strange resemblance to what one might say about Schuyler's poem.

> I see a mosaic pattern (Aztec-like) emerging, a weaving pattern, thin here, thick there. . . . This almost finished product seems an assemblage, a montage, a beaded work with several leitmotifs and with a central core, now appearing, now disappearing in a crazy dance. The whole thing has a mind of its own, escaping me and insisting on putting together the pieces of its own puzzle with minimal direction from my will. . . . Though it is a flawed thing—clumsy, complex, groping, blind thing, for me it is alive, infused with spirit. I talk to it; it talks to me.

Write a piece of your own that is "an assemblage, a montage, a beaded work with several leitmotifs and with a central core, now appearing, now disappearing in a crazy dance." With Anzaldúa, the invitation is to write a piece that mixes poetry and prose (and that alludes to or uses the words of other writers). You should think of your work as a way of reading and honoring these two writers, Anzaldúa and Schuyler.

3. Even though Joan Didion in "Sentimental Journeys" (p. 79) and James Schuyler produce quite different kinds of writing, both writers can be thought of as presenting ways of studying the world—ways of reflecting on people and places, on events and their consequences.

As you read through each selection a second time, think about them as accounts of current events. Think about each writer as someone who could be said to be studying, analyzing, and reflecting on the events of the day. How does each work? What does each writer notice? What counts as important? What are the problems of understanding? What is the author's relationship to subject matter? How might the subjects be said to be working on the writers? Who do they imagine as readers? What work do they invite readers to do?

Write an essay in which you present Didion and Schuyler as writers who are studying, analyzing, and reflecting on events.

JANE
TOMPKINS

JANE TOMPKINS (b. 1940) received her B.A. from Bryn Mawr and completed both and M.A. and a Ph.D. at Yale. She has taught at Temple University, Connecticut College, and Duke University. Among her publications are two books: Sensational Designs: The Cultural Work of American Fiction, 1790–1860 *(1985) and* West of Everything: The Inner Life of Westerns *(1992). She is also editor of* Reader-Response Criticism: From Formalism to Post-Structuralism *(1980).*

In Sensational Designs *Tompkins suggest that novels and short stories ought to be studied "not because they manage to escape the limitations of their particular time and place, but because they offer powerful examples of the way a culture thinks about itself, articulating and proposing solutions for the problems that shape a particular historical moment." This perspective leads Tompkins to conclude that the study of literature ought to focus not merely on those texts we call masterpieces but also on the texts of popular or best-selling authors. By studying these popular texts, Tompkins believes we can learn more of the "work" of novels and short stories, the influence they exert over the society in which they have been produced.*

"Indians" was first published in 1986 in the influential journal of literacy criticism Critical Inquiry. *It is an unusual essay in many ways, not the least of which is how it turns, as Tompkins's work often does, to anecdote and personal example. This is a surprising essay, perhaps even more surprising to faculty than to*

undergraduates. It is as though Tompkins was not willing to hide the "limitation of [her] particular time and place," limitations most scholars are more than happy to hide. In fact, Tompkins's selection could be said to take the reader behind the scenes of the respectable drama of academic research, offering a powerful example of how contemporary academic culture thinks about itself, articulating and proposing solutions for the problems that shape its particular historical moment. If individual interpretations are made and not found; if, for that matter, the "truths" of history or the background to American literature are made and not found, then there is every reason to acknowledge the circumstances of their making. And this is what Tompkins does. "Indians" is both a report on Tompkins's research and a reflection on the ways knowledge is produced, defended, and revised in academic life.

"Indians": Textualism, Morality, and the Problem of History

When I was growing up in New York City, my parents used to take me to an event in Inwood Park at which Indians—real American Indians dressed in feathers and blankets—could be seen and touched by children like me. This event was always a disappointment. It was more fun to imagine that you *were* an Indian in one of the caves in Inwood Park than to shake the hand of an old man in a headdress who was not overwhelmed at the opportunity of meeting you. After staring at the Indians for a while, we would take a walk in the woods where the caves were, and once I asked my mother if the remains of a fire I had seen in one of them might have been left by the original inhabitants. After that, wandering up some stone steps cut into the side of the hill, I imagined I was a princess in a rude castle. My Indians, like my princesses, were creatures totally of the imagination, and I did not care to have any real exemplars interfering with what I already knew.

I already knew about Indians from having read about them in school. Over and over we were told the story of how Peter Minuit had bought Manhattan Island from the Indians for twenty-four dollars' worth of glass beads. And it was a story we didn't mind hearing because it gave us the rare pleasure of having someone to feel superior to, since the poor Indians had not known (as we eight-year-olds did) how valuable a piece of property Manhattan Island would become. Generally, much was made of the Indian presence in Manhattan; a poem in one of our readers began: "Where we walk to school today / Indian children used to play," and we were encouraged to write poetry on this topic ourselves. So I had a fairly rich relationship with Indians before I ever met the unprepossessing people in Inwood Park. I felt that I had a lot in common with them. They, too, liked animals (they were often named after animals); they, too, made mistakes—they liked the brightly colored trinkets of little value that the white men were always offering them; they were handsome, warlike, and brave and had led an exciting, romantic life in the forest long ago, a life such as I dreamed of leading myself. I felt lucky to be living in one of the places where they had definitely been. Never mind where they were or what they were doing now.

My story stands for the relationship most non-Indians have to the people who first populated this continent, a relationship characterized by narcissistic fantasies of freedom and adventure, of a life lived closer to nature and to spirit than the life we lead now. As Vine Deloria, Jr., has pointed out, the American Indian Movement in the early seventies couldn't get people to pay attention to what was happening to Indians who were alive in the present, so powerful was this country's infatuation with people who wore loincloths, lived in tepees, and roamed the plains and forest long ago.[1] The present essay, like these fantasies, doesn't have much to do with actual Indians, though its subject matter is the histories of European-Indian relations in seventeenth-century New England. In a sense, my encounter with Indians as an adult doing "research" replicates the childhood one, for while I started out to learn more about Indians, I ended up preoccupied with a problem of my own.

This essay enacts a particular instance of the challenge poststructuralism poses to the study of history. In simpler language, it concerns the difference that point of view makes when people are giving accounts of events, whether at first or second hand. The problem is that if all accounts of events are determined through and through by the observer's frame of reference, then one will never know, if any given case, what really happened.

I encountered this problem in concrete terms while preparing to teach a course in colonial American literature. I'd set out to learn what I could about the Puritans' relations with American Indians. All I wanted was a general idea of what happened between the English settlers and the natives in seventeenth-century New England; poststructuralism and its dilemmas were the furthest thing from my mind. I began, more or less automatically, with Perry Miller, who hardly mentions the Indians at all, then proceeded to the work of historians who had dealt exclusively with the European-Indian encounter. At first, it was a question of deciding which of these authors to believe, for it quickly became apparent that there was no unanimity on the subject. As I read on, however, I discovered that the problem was more complicated than deciding whose version of events was correct. Some of the conflicting accounts were not simply contradictory, they were completely incommensurable, in that their assumptions about what counted as a valid approach to the subject, and what the subject itself was, diverged in fundamental ways. Faced with an array of mutually irreconcilable points of view, points of view which determined what was being discussed as well as the terms of the discussion, I decided to turn to primary sources for clarification, only to discover that the primary sources reproduced the problem all over again. I found myself, in other words, in an epistemological quandary, not only unable to decide among conflicting versions of events but also unable to believe that any such decision could, in principle, be made. It was a moral quandary as well. Knowledge of what really happened when the Europeans and the Indians first met seemed particularly important, since the result of that encounter was virtual genocide. This was the kind of past "mistake" which, presumably, we studied history in order to avoid repeating. If studying history couldn't put us in touch with actual events and their causes, then what was to prevent such atrocities from happening again?

For a while, I remained at this impasse. But through analyzing the process by which I had reached it, I eventually arrived at an understanding which seemed to offer a way out. This essay records the concrete experience of meeting and solving the difficulty I have just described (as an abstract problem, I thought I had solved it long ago). My purpose is not to throw new light on antifoundationalist epistemology—the solution I reached is not a new one—but to dramatize and expose the troubles antifoundationalism gets you into when you meet it, so to speak, in the road.

My research began with Perry Miller. Early in the preface to *Errand into the Wilderness*, while explaining how he came to write his history of the New England mind, Miller writes a sentence that stopped me dead. He says that what fascinated him as a young man about his country's history was "the massive narrative of the movement of European culture into the vacant wilderness of America."[2] "Vacant?" Miller, writing in 1956, doesn't pause over the word "vacant," but to people who read his preface thirty years later, the word is shocking. In what circumstances could someone proposing to write a history of colonial New England *not* take account of the Indian presence there?

The rest of Miller's preface supplies an answer to this question, if one takes the trouble to piece together its details. Miller explains that as a young man, jealous of older compatriots who had had the luck to fight in World War I, he had gone to Africa in search of adventure. "The adventures that Africa afforded," he writes, "were tawdry enough, but it became the setting for a sudden epiphany" (p. vii). "It was given to me," he writes, "disconsolate on the edge of a jungle of central Africa, to have thrust upon me the mission of expounding what I took to be the innermost propulsion of the United States, while supervising, in that barbaric topic, the unloading of drums of case oil flowing out of the inexhaustible wilderness of America" (p. viii). Miller's picture of himself on the banks of the Congo furnishes a key to the kind of history he will write and to his mental image of a vacant wilderness; it explains why it was just there, under precisely these conditions, that he should have had his epiphany.

The fuel drums stand, in Miller's mind, for the popular misconception of what this country is about. They are "tangible symbols of [America's] appalling power," a power that everyone but Miller takes for the ultimate reality (p. ix). To Miller, "the mind of man is the basic factor in human history," and he will plead, all unaccommodated as he is among the fuel drums, for the intellect—the intellect for which his fellow historians, with their chapters on "stoves or bathtubs, or tax laws," "the Wilmot Proviso" and "the chain store," "have so little respect" (p. viii, ix). His preface seethes with a hatred of the merely physical and mechanical, and this hatred, which is really a form of moral outrage, explains not only the contempt with which he mentions the stoves and bathtubs but also the nature of his experience in Africa and its relationship to the "massive narrative" he will write.

Miller's experiences in Africa are "tawdry," his tropic is barbaric because the jungle he stands on the edge of means nothing to him, no more, indeed something less, than the case oil. It is the nothingness of Africa that precipitates his vision. It is the barbarity of the "dark continent," the obvious (but superficial) parallelism between the jungle at Matadi and America's "vacant wilderness" that releases in Miller the desire to define and vindicate his country's cultural identity. To the young Miller, colonial Africa and colonial America are—but for the history he will bring to light—mirror images of one another. And what he fails to see in the one landscape is the same thing he overlooks in the other: the human beings who people it. As Miller stood with his back to the jungle, thinking about the role of mind in human history, his failure to see that the land into which European culture had moved was not vacant but already occupied by a varied and numerous population, is of a piece with his failure, in his portrait of himself at Matadi, to notice *who* was carrying the fuel drums he was supervising the unloading of.

The point is crucial because it suggests that what is invisible to the historian in his own historical moment remains invisible when he turns his gaze to the past. It isn't that Miller didn't "see" the black men, in a literal sense, any more than it's the case that when he looked back he didn't "see" the Indians, in the sense of not realizing they were there. Rather, it's that neither the Indians nor the blacks *counted* for him, in a fundamental way. The way in which Indians can be seen but not counted is illustrated by an entry in Governor John Winthrop's journal, three hundred years before, when he recorded that there had been a great storm with high winds "yet through God's great mercy it did no hurt, but only killed one Indian with the fall of a tree."[3] The juxtaposition suggests that Miller shared with Winthrop a certain colonial point of view, a point of view from which Indians, though present, do not finally matter.

A book entitled *New England Frontier: Puritans and Indians, 1620–1675*, written by Alden Vaughan and published in 1965, promised to rectify Miller's omission. In the outpouring of work on the European-Indian encounter that began in the early sixties, this book is the first major landmark, and to a neophyte it seems definitive. Vaughan acknowledges the absence of

Indian sources and emphasizes his use of materials which catch the Puritans "off guard."[4] His announced conclusion that "the New England Puritans followed a remarkably humane, considerate, and just policy in their dealings with the Indians" seems supported by the scope, documentation, and methodicalness of his project (*NEF*, p. vii). The author's fair-mindedness and equanimity seem everywhere apparent, so that when he asserts "the history of interracial relations from the arrival of the Pilgrims to the outbreak of King Philip's War is a credit to the integrity of both peoples," one is positively reassured (*NEF*, p. viii).

But these impressions do not survive an admission that comes late in the book, when, in the course of explaining why works like Helen Hunt Jackson's *Century of Dishonor* had spread misconceptions about Puritan treatment of the Indians, Vaughan finally lays his own cards on the table.

> The root of the misunderstanding [about Puritans and Indians] . . . lies[s] in a failure to recognize the nature of the two societies that met in seventeenth century New England. One was unified, visionary, disciplined, and dynamic. The other was divided, self-satisfied, undisciplined, and static. It would be unreasonable to expect that such societies could live side by side indefinitely with no penetration of the more fragmented and passive by the more consolidated and active. What resulted, then, was not—as many have held—a clash of dissimilar ways of life, but rather the expansion of one into the areas in which the other was lacking. [*NEF*, p. 323]

From our present vantage point, these remarks seem culturally biased to an incredible degree, not to mention inaccurate: Was Puritan society unified? If so, how does one account for its internal dissensions and obsessive need to cast out deviants? Is "unity" necessarily a positive culture trait? From what standpoint can one say that American Indians were neither disciplined nor visionary, when both these characteristics loom so large in the ethnographies? Is it an accident that ways of describing cultural strength and weakness coincide with gender stereotypes—active/passive, and so on? Why is one culture said to "penetrate" the other? Why is the "other" described in terms of "lack"?

Vaughan's fundamental categories of apprehension and judgment will not withstand even the most cursory inspection. For what looked like evenhandedness when he was writing *New England Frontier* does not look that way anymore. In his introduction to *New Directions in American Intellectual History*, John Higham writes that by the end of the sixties

> the entire conceptual foundation on which [this sort of work] rested [had] crumbled away. . . . Simultaneously, in sociology, anthropology, and history, two working assumptions . . . came under withering attack: first, the assumption that societies tend to be integrated, and second, that a shared culture maintains

that integration.... By the late 1960s all claims issued in the name of an "American mind"... were subject to drastic skepticism.[5]

"Clearly," Higham continues, "the sociocultural upheaval of the sixties created the occasion" for this reaction.[6] Vaughan's book, it seemed, could only have been written before the events of the sixties had sensitized scholars to questions of race and ethnicity. It came as no surprise, therefore, that ten years later there appeared a study of European-Indian relations which reflected the new awareness of social issues the sixties had engendered. And it offered an entirely different picture of the European-Indian encounter.

Francis Jennings's *The Invasion of America* (1975) rips wide open the idea that the Puritans were humane and considerate in their dealings with the Indians. In Jennings's account, even more massively documented than Vaughan's, the early settlers lied to the Indians, stole from them, murdered them, scalped them, captured them, tortured them, raped them, sold them into slavery, confiscated their land, destroyed their crops, burned their homes, scattered their possessions, gave them alcohol, undermined their systems of belief, and infected them with diseases that wiped out 90 percent of their numbers within the first hundred years after contact.[7]

Jennings mounts an all-out attack on the essential decency of the Puritan leadership and their apologists in the twentieth century. The Pequot War, which previous historians had described as an attempt on the part of Massachusetts Bay to protect itself from the fiercest of the New England tribes, becomes, in Jennings's painstakingly researched account, a deliberate war of extermination, waged by whites against Indians. It starts with trumped-up charges, is carried on through a series of increasingly bloody reprisals, and ends in the massacre of scores of Indian men, women, and children, all so that Massachusetts Bay could gain political and economic control of the southern Connecticut Valley. When one reads this and then turns over the page and sees a reproduction of the Bay Colony seal, which depicts an Indian from whose mouth issue the words "Come over and help us," the effect is shattering.[8]

But even so powerful an argument as Jennings's did not remain unshaken by subsequent work. Reading on, I discovered that if the events of the sixties had revolutionized the study of European-Indian relations, the events of the seventies produced yet another transformation. The American Indian Movement, and in particular the founding of the Native American Rights Fund in 1971 to finance Indian litigation, and a court decision in 1975 which gave the tribes the right to seek redress for past injustices in federal court, created a climate within which historians began to focus on the Indians themselves. "Almost simultaneously," writes James Axtell, "frontier and colonial historians began to discover the necessity of considering the American natives as real determinants of history and the utility of ethnohistory as a way of ensuring parity of focus and impartiality of judgment."[9] In Miller,

Indians had been simply beneath notice; in Vaughan, they belonged to an inferior culture; and in Jennings, they were the more or less innocent prey of power-hungry whites. But in the most original and provocative of the ethnohistories, Calvin Martin's *Keepers of the Game*, Indians became complicated, purposeful human beings, whose lives were spiritually motivated to a high degree.[10] Their relationship to the animals they hunted, to the natural environment, and to the whites with whom they traded became intelligible within a system of beliefs that formed the basis for an entirely new perspective on the European-Indian encounter.

Within the broader question of why European contact had such a devastating effect on the Indians, Martin's specific aim is to determine why Indians participated in the fur trade which ultimately led them to the brink of annihilation. The standard answer to this question had always been that once the Indian was introduced to European guns, copper kettles, woolen blankets, and the like, he literally couldn't keep his hands off them. In order to acquire these coveted items, he decimated the animal populations on which his survival depended. In short, the Indian's motivation in participating in the fur trade was assumed to be the same as the white European's—a desire to accumulate material goods. In direct opposition to this thesis, Martin argues that the reason why Indians ruthlessly exploited their own resources had nothing to do with supply and demand, but stemmed rather from a breakdown of the cosmic worldview that tied them to the game they killed in a spiritual relationship of parity and mutual obligation.

The hunt, according to Martin, was conceived not primarily as a physical activity but as a spiritual quest, in which the spirit of the hunter must overmaster the spirit of the game animal before the kill can take place. The animal, in effect, *allows* itself to be found and killed, once the hunter has mastered its spirit. The hunter prepared himself through rituals of fasting, sweating, or dreaming which revealed the identity of his prey and where he can find it. The physical act of killing is the least important element in the process. Once the animal is killed, eaten, and its parts used for clothing or implements, its remains must be disposed of in ritually prescribed fashion, or the game boss, the "keeper" of that species, will not permit more animals to be killed. The relationship between Indians and animals, then, is contractual; each side must hold up its end of the bargain, or no further transactions can occur.

What happened, according to Martin, was that as a result of diseases introduced into the animal population by Europeans, the game suddenly disappeared, began to act in inexplicable ways, or sickened and died in plain view, and communicated their diseases to the Indians. The Indians, consequently, believed that their compact with the animals had been broken and that the keepers of the game, the tutelary spirits of each animal species whom they had been so careful to propitiate, had betrayed them. And when missionization, wars with the Europeans, and displacement from their tribal lands had further weakened Indian society and its belief structure, the

Indians, no longer restrained by religious sanctions, in effect, turned on the animals in a holy war of revenge.

Whether or not Martin's specific claim about the "holy war" was correct, his analysis made it clear to me that, given the Indians' understanding of economic, religious, and physical processes, an Indian account of what transpired when the European settlers arrived here would look nothing like our own. Their (potential, unwritten) history of the conflict could bear only a marginal resemblance to Eurocentric views. I began to think that the key to understanding European-Indian relations was to see them as an encounter between wholly disparate cultures, and that therefore either defending or attacking the colonists was beside the point since, given the cultural disparity between the two groups, conflict was inevitable and in large part a product of mutual misunderstanding.

But three years after Martin's book appeared, Shepard Krech III edited a collection of seven essays called *Indians, Animals, and the Fur Trade*, attacking Martin's entire project. Here the authors argued that we don't need an ideological or religious explanation for the fur trade. As Charles Hudson writes,

> The Southeastern Indians slaughtered deer (and were prompted to enslave and kill each other) because of their position on the outer fringes of an expanding modern world-system. . . . In the modern world-system there is a core region which establishes *economic* relations with its colonial periphery. . . . If the Indians could not produce commodities, they were on the road to cultural extinction. . . . To maximize his chances for survival, an eighteenth-century Southeastern Indian had to . . . live in the interior, out of range of European cattle, forestry, and agriculture. . . . He had to produce a commodity which was valuable enough to earn him some protection from English slavers.[11]

Though we are talking here about Southeastern Indians, rather than the subarctic and Northeastern tribes Martin studied, what really accounts for these divergent explanations of why Indians slaughtered the game are the assumptions that underlie them. Martin believes that the Indians acted on the basis of perceptions made available to them by their own cosmology; that is, he explains their behavior as the Indians themselves would have explained it (insofar as he can), using a logic and a set of values that are not Eurocentric but derived from within Amerindian culture. Hudson, on the other hand, insists that the Indians' own beliefs are irrelevant to an explanation of how they acted, which can only be understood, as far as he is concerned, in the terms of a Western materialist economic and political analysis. Martin and Hudson, in short, don't agree on what counts as an explanation, and this disagreement sheds light on the preceding accounts as well. From this standpoint, we can see that Vaughan, who thought that the Puritans were superior to the Indians, and Jennings, who thought the reverse, are both, like Hudson, using Eurocentric criteria of description and evaluation. While all three critics (Vaughan, Jennings and Hudson) acknowledge that Indians and Europeans behave differently from one another, the behavior differs, as it were, within the order of the same: all three assume, though only Hudson makes the assumption explicit, that an understanding of relations between the Europeans and the Indians must be elaborated in European terms. In Martin's analysis, however, what we have are not only two different sets of behavior but two incommensurable ways of describing and assigning meaning to events. This difference at the level of explanation calls into question the possibility of obtaining any theory-independent account of interaction between Indians and Europeans. mAy Be wAAT she is looking for

At this point, dismayed and confused by the wildly divergent views of colonial history the twentieth-century historians had provided, I decided to look at some primary materials. I thought, perhaps, if I looked at some firsthand accounts and at some scholars looking at those accounts, it would be possible to decide which experts were right and which were wrong by comparing their views with the evidence. Captivity narratives seemed a good place to begin, since it was logical to suppose that the records left by whites who had been captured by Indians would furnish the sort of firsthand information I wanted.

I began with two fascinating essays based on these materials written by the ethnohistorian James Axtell, "The White Indians of Colonial America" and "The Scholastic Philosophy of the Wilderness."[12] These essays suggest that it would have been a privilege to be captured by North American Indians and taken off to Canada to dwell in a wigwam for the rest of one's life. Axtell's reconstruction of the process by which Indians taught European captives to feel comfortable in the wilderness, first taking their shoes away and giving them moccasins, carrying the children on their backs, sharing the scanty food supply equally, ceremonially cleansing them of their old identities, giving them Indian clothes and jewelry, assiduously teaching them the Indian language, finally adopting them into their families, and even visiting them after many years if, as sometimes happened, they were restored to white society—all of this creates a compelling portrait of Indian culture and helps to explain the extraordinary attraction that Indian culture apparently exercised over Europeans.

But, as I had by now come to expect, this beguiling portrait of the Indians' superior humanity is called into question by other writings on Indian captivity—for example, Norman Heard's *White into Red*, whose summation of the comparative treatment of captive children east and west of the Mississippi seems to contradict some of Axtell's conclusions:

> The treatment of captive children seems to have been similar in initial stages. . . . Most children were treated brutally at the time of capture. Babies and toddlers usually were killed

immediately and other small children would be dispatched during the rapid retreat to the Indian villages if they cried, failed to keep the pace, or otherwise indicated a lack of fortitude needed to become a worthy member of the tribe. Upon reaching the village, the child might face such ordeals as running the gauntlet or dancing in the center of a throng of threatening Indians. The prisoner might be so seriously injured at this time that he would no longer be acceptable for adoption.[13]

One account which Heard reprints in particularly arresting. A young girl captured by the Comanches who had not been adopted into the family but used as a slave had been peculiarly mistreated. When they wanted to wake her up the family she belonged to would take a burning brand from the fire and touch it to her nose. When she was returned to her parents, the flesh of her nose was completely burned away, exposing the bone.[14]

Since the pictures drawn by Heard and Axtell were in certain respects irreconcilable, it made sense to turn to a firsthand account to see how the Indians treated their captives in a particular instance. Mary Rowlandson's "The Soveraignty and Goodness of God," published in Boston around 1680, suggested itself because it was so widely read and had set the pattern for later narratives. Rowlandson interprets her captivity as God's punishment on her for failing to keep the Sabbath properly on several occasions. She sees everything that happens to her as a sign from God. When the Indians are kind to her, she attributes her good fortune to Divine Providence; when they are cruel, she blames her captors. But beyond the question of how Rowlandson interprets events is the question of what she saw in the first place and what she considered worth reporting. The following passage, with its abrupt shifts of focus and peculiar emphases, makes it hard to see her testimony as evidence of anything other than the Puritan point of view:

> Then my heart began to fail: and I fell weeping, which was the first time to my remembrance, that I wept before them. Although I had met with so much Affliction, and my heart was many times ready to break, yet could I not shed one tear in their sight: but rather had been all this while in a maze, and like one astonished: but not I may say as, Psal. 137.1. *By the Rivers of Babylon, there we sate down; yea, we wept when we remembered Zion.* There one of them asked me, why I wept, I could hardly tell what to say: yet I answered, they would kill me: No, said he, none will hurt you. Then came one of them and gave me two spoon-fulls of Meal to comfort me, and another gave me half a pint of Pease; which was more worth than many Bushels at another time. Then I went to see King Philip, he bade me come in and sit down, and asked me whether I woold smoke it (a usual Complement nowadayes among Saints and Sinners) but this no way suited me. For though I had formerly used Tobacco, yet I had left it ever since I was first taken. It seems to be a Bait, the Devil layes to make men loose their

precious time: I remember with shame, how formerly, when I had taken two or three pipes, I was presently ready for another, such a bewitching thing it is: But I thank God, he has now given me power over it; surely there are many who may be better imployed than to ly sucking a stinking Tobacco-pipe.[15]

Anyone who has ever tried to give up smoking has to sympathize with Rowlandson, but it is nonetheless remarkable, first, that a passage which begins with her weeping openly in front of her captors, and comparing herself to Israel in Babylon, should end with her railing against the vice of tobacco; and, second, that it has not a word to say about King Philip, the leader of the Indians who captured her and mastermind of the campaign that devastated the white population of the English colonies. The fact that Rowlandson has just been introduced to the chief of chiefs makes hardly any impression on her at all. What excites her is a moral issue which was being hotly debated in the seventeenth century: to smoke or not to smoke (Puritans frowned on it, apparently, because it wasted time and presented a fire hazard). What seem to us the peculiar emphases in Rowlandson's relation are not the result of her having *screened out* evidence she couldn't handle, but of her way of constructing the world. She saw what her seventeenth-century English Separatist background made visible. It is when one realizes that the biases of twentieth-century historians like Vaughan or Axtell cannot be corrected for simply by consulting the primary materials, since the primary materials are constructed according to *their* authors' biases, that one begins to envy Miller his vision at Matadi. Not for what he didn't see—the Indian and the black—but for his epistemological confidence.

Since captivity narratives made a poor source of evidence for the nature of European-Indian relations in early New England because they were so relentlessly pietistic, my hope was that a better source of evidence might be writings designed simply to tell Englishmen what the American natives were like. These authors could be presumed to be less severely biased, since they hadn't seem their loved ones killed by Indians or been made to endure the hardships of captivity, and because they weren't writing propaganda calculated to prove that God had delivered his chosen people from the hands of Satan's emissaries.

The problem was that these texts were written with aims no less specific than those of the captivity narrative, though the aims were of a different sort. Here is a passage from William Wood's *New England's Prospect*, published in London in 1634.

> To enter into a serious discourse concerning the natural conditions of these Indians might procure admiration from the people of any civilized nations, in regard of their civility and good natures. . . . These Indians are of affable, courteous and well disposed natures, ready to communicate the best of their wealth to the mutual good of one another; . . . so . . . perspicuous is their

> love . . . that they are as willing to part with a mite in poverty as
> treasure in plenty. . . . If it were possible to recount the courte-
> sies they have showed the English, since their first arrival in
> those parts, it would not only steady belief, that they are a loving
> people, but also win the love of those that never saw them, and
> wipe off that needless fear that is too deeply rooted in the con-
> ceits of many who think them envious and of such rancorous
> and inhumane dispositions, that they will one day make an end
> of their English inmates.[16]

However, in a pamphlet published twenty-one years earlier, Alexander
Whitaker of Virginia has this to say of the natives:

> These naked slaves . . . serve the divell for feare, after a most
> base manner, sacrificing sometimes (as I have heere heard)
> their own Children to him. . . . They live naked in bodie, as if
> their shame of their sinne deserved no covering: Their names
> are as naked as their bodie: They esteem it a virtue to lie, de-
> ceive and steale as their master the divell teacheth to them.[17]

According to Robert Berkhofer in *The White Man's Indian,* these divergent
reports can be explained by looking at the authors' motives. A favorable report like Wood's, intended to encourage new emigrants to America, naturally represented Indians as loving and courteous, civilized and generous, in
order to allay the fears of prospective colonists. Whitaker, on the other hand,
a minister who wishes to convince his readers that the Indians are in need of
conversion, paints them as benighted agents of the devil. Berkhofer's commentary constantly implies that white men were to blame for having represented the Indians in the image of their own desires and needs.[18] But the evidence supplied by Rowlandson's narrative, and by the accounts left by early
reporters such as Wood and Whitaker, suggests something rather different.
Though it is probably true that in certain cases Europeans did consciously
tamper with the evidence, in most cases there is no reason to suppose that
they did not record faithfully what they saw. And what they saw was not an
illusion, was not determined by selfish motives in any narrow sense, but was
there by virtue of a *way* of seeing which they could no more consciously manipulate than they could choose not to have been born. At this point, it
seemed to me, the ethnocentric bias of the firsthand observers invited an investigation of the cultural situation they spoke from. Karen Kupperman's
Settling with the Indians (1980) supplied just such an analysis.

Kupperman argues that Englishmen inevitably looked at Indians in exactly the same way that they looked at other Englishmen. For instance, if they
looked down on Indians and saw them as people to be exploited, it was not
because of racial prejudice or antique notions about savagery, it was because
they looked down on ordinary English men and women and saw them as
subjects for exploitation as well.[19] According to Kupperman, what concerned
these writers most when they described the Indians were the insignia of

social class, of rank, and of prestige. Indian faces are virtually never described in the earliest accounts, but clothes and hairstyles, tattoos and jewelry, posture and skin color are. "Early modern Englishmen believed that people can create their own identity, and that therefore one communicates to the world through signals such as dress and other forms of decoration who one is, what group or category one belongs to."[20]

Kupperman's book marks a watershed in writings on European-Indian relations, for it reverses the strategy employed by Martin two years before. Whereas Martin had performed an ethnographic analysis of Indian cosmology in order to explain, from within, the Indians' motives for engaging in the fur trade, Kupperman performs an ethnographic study of seventeenth-century England in order to explain, from within, what motivated Englishmen's behavior. The sympathy and understanding that Martin, Axtell, and others extend to the Indians are extended in Kupperman's work to the English themselves. Rather than giving an account of "what happened" between Indians and Europeans, like Martin, she reconstructs the worldview that gave the experience of one group its context. With her study, scholarship on European-Indian relations comes full circle.

It may well seem to you at this point that, given the tremendous variation among the historical accounts, I had no choice but to end in relativism. If the experience of encountering conflicting versions of the "same" events suggests anything certain it is that the attitude a historian takes up in relation to a given event, the way in which he or she judges and even describes "it"— and the "it" has to go in quotation marks because, depending on the perspective, that event either did or did not occur—this stance, these judgments and descriptions are a function of the historian's position in relation to the subject. Miller, standing on the banks of the Congo, couldn't see the black men he was supervising because of his background, his assumptions, values, experiences, goals. Jennings, intent on exposing the distortions introduced into the historical record by Vaughan and his predecessors stretching all the way back to Winthrop, couldn't see that Winthrop and his peers were not racists but only Englishmen who looked at other cultures in the way their own culture had taught them to see one another. The historian can never escape the limitations of his or her own position in history and so inevitably gives an account that is an extension of the circumstances from which it springs. But it seems to me that when one is confronted with this particular succession of stories, cultural and historical relativism is not a position that one can comfortably assume. The phenomena to which these histories testify—conquest, massacre, and genocide, on the one hand; torture, slavery, and murder on the other—cry out for judgment. When faced with claims and counterclaims of this magnitude one feels obligated to reach an understanding of what actually did occur. The dilemma posed by the study of European-Indian relations in early America is that the highly charged nature of the materials demands a moral decisiveness which the succession of conflicting accounts effectively precludes. That is the dilemma I found myself in at the end of this course of reading, and which I eventually came to resolve as follows.

After a while it began to seem to me that there was something wrong with the way I formulated the problem. The statement that the materials on European-Indian relations were so highly charged that they demanded moral judgment, but that the judgment couldn't be made because all possible descriptions of what happened were biased, seemed to contain an internal contradiction. The statement implied that in order to make a moral judgment about something, you have to know something else first—namely, the facts of the case you're being call upon to judge. My complaint was that their perspectival nature would disqualify any facts I might encounter and that therefore I couldn't judge. But to say as I did that the materials I had read were "highly charged" and therefore demanded judgment suggests both that I was reacting to something real—to some facts—*and* that I judged them. Perhaps I wasn't so much in the lurch morally or epistemologically as I had thought. If you—or I—react with horror to the story of the girl captured and enslaved by Comanches who touched a firebrand to her nose every time they wanted to wake her up, it's because we read this as a story about cruelty and suffering, and not as a story about the conventions of prisoner exchange or the economics of Comanche life. The *seeing* of the story as a cause for alarm rather than a droll anecdote or a piece of curious information is evidence of values we already hold, of judgments already made, of facts already perceived as facts.

My problem presupposed that I couldn't judge because I didn't know what the facts were. All I had, or could have, was a series of different perspectives, and so nothing that would count as an authoritative source on which moral judgments could be based. But, as I have just shown, I did judge, and that is because, as I now think, I did have some facts. I seemed to accept as facts that ninety percent of the native American population of New England died after the first hundred years of contact, that tribes in eastern Canada and the northeastern United States had a compact with the game they killed, that Comanches had subjected a captive girl to casual cruelty, that King Philip smoked a pipe, and so on. It was only where different versions of the same event came into conflict that I doubted the text was a record of something real. And even then, there was no question about certain major catastrophes. I believed that four hundred Pequots were killed near Saybrook, that Winthrop was the Governor of the Massachusetts Bay Colony when it happened, and so on. My sense that certain events, such as the Pequot War, did occur in no way reflected the indecisiveness that overtook me when I tried to choose among the various historical versions. I fact, the need I felt to make up my mind was impelled by the conviction that certain things *had* happened that shouldn't have happened. Hence it was never the case that "what happened" was completely unknowable or unavailable. It's rather that in the process of reading so many different approaches to the same phenomenon I became aware of the difference in the attitudes that informed these approaches. The awareness of the interests motivating each version cast suspicion over everything, in retrospect, and I ended by claiming that there was nothing I could know. This, I now see, was never really the case. But how did it happen?

Someone else, confronted with the same materials, could have decided that one of these historical accounts was correct. Still another person might have decided that more evidence was needed in order to decide among them. Why did I conclude that none of the accounts was accurate because they were all produced from some particular angle of vision? Presumably there was something in my background that enabled me to see the problem in this way. That something, very likely, was poststructuralist theory. I let my discovery that Vaughan was a product of the fifties, Jennings of the sixties, Rowlandson of a Puritan worldview, and so on lead me to the conclusion that all facts are theory dependent because that conclusion was already a thinkable one for me. My inability to come up with a true account was not the product of being situated nowhere; it was the product of certitude that existed *somewhere else,* namely, in contemporary literary theory. Hence, the level at which my indecision came into play was a function of particular beliefs I held. I was never in a position of epistemological indeterminacy, I was never *en abyme.* The idea that all accounts are perspectival seemed to me a superior standpoint from which to view all the versions of "what happened," and to regard with sympathetic condescension any person so old-fashioned and benighted as to believe that there really was some way of arriving at the truth. But this skeptical standpoint was just as firm as any other. The fact that it was also seriously disabling—it prevented me from coming to any conclusion about what I had read—did not render it any less definite.

At this point something is beginning to show itself that has up to now been hidden. The notion that all facts are only facts within a perspective has the effect of emptying statements of their content. Once I had Miller and Vaughan and Jennings, Martin and Hudson, Axtell and Heard, Rowlandson and Wood and Whitaker, and Kupperman; I had Europeans and Indians, ships and canoes, wigwams and log cabins, bows and arrows and muskets, wigs and tattoos, whiskey and corn, rivers and forts, treaties and battles, fire and blood—and then suddenly all I had was a metastatement about perspectives. The effect of bringing perspectivism to bear on history was to wipe out completely the subject matter of history. And it follows that bringing perspectivism to bear in this way on any subject matter would have a similar effect; everything is wiped out and you are left with nothing but a single idea—perspectivism itself.

But—and it is a crucial but—all this is true only if you believe that there is an alternative. As long as you think that there are or should be facts that exist outside of any perspective, then the notion that facts are perspectival will have this disappearing effect on whatever it touches. But if you are convinced that the alternative does not exist, that there really are no facts except as they are embedded in some particular way of seeing the world, then the argument that a set of facts derives from some particular worldview is no longer an argument against that set of facts. If all facts share this characteristic, to say that any one fact is perspectival doesn't change its factual nature in the slightest. It merely reiterates it.

This doesn't mean that you have to accept just anybody's facts. You can show that what someone else asserts to be a fact is false. But it does mean that you can't argue that someone else's facts are not facts *because they are only the product of a perspective,* since this will be true of the facts that you perceive as well. What this means then is that arguments about "what happened" have to proceed much as they did before poststructuralism broke in with all its talk about language-based reality and culturally produced knowledge. Reasons must be given, evidence adduced, authorities cited, analogies drawn. Being aware that all facts are motivated, believing that people are always operating inside some particular interpretive framework or other is a pertinent argument when what is under discussion is the way beliefs are grounded. But it doesn't give one any leverage on the facts of a particular case.[21]

What this means for the problem I've been addressing is that I must piece together the story of European-Indian relations as best I can, believing this version up to a point, that version not at all, another almost entirely, according to what seems reasonable and plausible, given everything else that I know. And this, as I've shown, is what I was already doing in the back of my mind without realizing it, because there was nothing else I *could* do. If the accounts don't fit together neatly, that is not a reason for rejecting them all in favor of a metadiscourse about epistemology; on the contrary, one encounters contradictory facts and divergent points of view in practically every phase of life, from deciding whom to marry to choosing the right brand of cat food, and one decides as best one can given the evidence available. It is only the nature of the academic situation which makes it appear that one can linger on the threshold of decision in the name of an epistemological principle. What has really happened in such a case is that the subject of debate has changed from the question of what happened in a particular instance to the question of how knowledge is arrived at. The absence of pressure to decide what happened creates the possibility for this change of venue.

The change of venue, however, is itself an action taken. In diverting attention from the original problem and placing it where Miller did, on "the mind of man," it once again ignores what happened and still is happening to American Indians. The moral problem that confronts me now is not that I can never have any facts to go on, but that the work I do is not directed toward solving the kinds of problems that studying the history of European-Indian relations has awakened me to.

NOTES

[1] See Vine Deloria, Jr., *God is Red* (New York, 1973), pp. 39–56.

[2] Perry Miller, *Errand into the Wilderness* (Cambridge, Mass., 1964), p. vii; all further references will be included in the text.

[3] This passage from John Winthrop's *Journal* is excerpted by Perry Miller in his anthology *The American Puritans: Their Prose and Poetry* (Garden City, N.Y., 1956), p. 43. In his headnote to the selections from the *Journal,* Miller speaks of Winthrop's "characteristic objectivity" (p. 37).

[4] Alden T. Vaughan, *New England Frontier: Puritans and Indians, 1620–1675* (Boston, 1965), pp. vi–vii; all further references to this work, abbreviated *NEF,* will be included in the text.

[5] John Higham, intro. to *New Directions in American Intellectual History,* ed. Higham and Paul K. Conkin (Baltimore, 1979), p. xii.

[6] Ibid.

[7] See Francis Jennings, *The Invasion of America: Indians, Colonialism, and the Cant of Conquest* (New York, 1975), pp. 3–31. Jennings writes: "The so-called settlement of America was a *re*settlement, reoccupation of a land made waste by the diseases and demoralization introduced by the newcomers. Although the source data pertaining to populations have never been compiled, one careful scholar, Henry D. Dobyns, has provided a relatively conservative and meticulously reasoned estimate conforming to the known effects of conquest catastrophe. Dobyns has calculated a total aboriginal population for the western hemisphere within the range of 90 to 112 million, of which 10 to 12 million lived north of the Rio Grande" (p. 30).

[8] Jennings, fig. 7, p. 229; and see pp. 186–229.

[9] James Axtell, *The European and the Indian: Essays in the Ethnohistory of Colonial North America* (Oxford, 1981), p. viii.

[10] See Calvin Martin, *Keepers of the Game: Indian-Animal Relationships and the Fur Trade* (Berkeley and Los Angeles, 1978).

[11] See the essay by Charles Hudson in *Indians, Animals, and the Fur Trade: A Critique of "Keepers of the Game,"* ed. Shepard Krech III (Athens, Ga., 1981), pp. 167–69.

[12] See Axtell, "The White Indians of Colonial America" and "The Scholastic Philosophy of the Wilderness," *The European and the Indian,* pp. 168–206 and 131–67.

[13] J. Norman Heard, *White into Red: A Study of the Assimilation of White Persons Captured by Indians* (Metuchen, N.J., 1973), p. 97.

[14] See ibid., p. 98.

[15] Mary Rowlandson, "The Soveraignty and Goodness of God, Together with the Faithfulness of His Promises Displayed; Being a Narrative of the Captivity and Restauration of Mrs. Mary Rowlandson (1676)," in *Held Captive by Indians: Selected Narratives, 1642–1836,* ed. Richard VanDerBeets (Knoxville, Tenn., 1973), pp. 57–58.

[16] William Wood, *New England's Prospect,* ed. Vaughan (Amherst, Mass., 1977), pp. 88–89.

[17] Alexander Whitaker, *Goode Newes from Virginia* (1613), quoted in Robert F. Berkhofer, Jr., *The White Man's Indian: Images of the American Indian from Columbus to the Present* (New York, 1978), p. 19.

[18] See, for example, Berkhofer's discussion of the passages he quotes from Whitaker (*The White Man's Indian,* pp. 19, 20).

[19] See Karen Ordahl Kupperman, *Settling with the Indians: The Meeting of English and Indian Cultures in America, 1580–1640* (Totowa, N.J., 1980), pp. 3, 4.

[20] Ibid., p. 35.

[21] The position I've been outlining is a version of neopragmatism. For an exposition, see *Against Theory: Literary Studies and the New Pragmatism,* ed. W. J. T. Mitchell (Chicago, 1985).

. . . .

QUESTIONS FOR A SECOND READING

1. Tompkins's essay can be divided into three parts: the account of her childhood understanding of Indians; the account of her research into scholarly and first-person accounts of the relations between the Indians and the settlers in New England; and a final conclusion (beginning on p. 631). The conclusion, in many ways, is the hardest part of the essay to understand. Like the conclusion to Clifford Geertz's "Deep Play: Notes on the Balinese Cockfight" (p. 228), it assumes not only that you have followed a chain of reasoning but that you have access to the larger philosophical questions that have preoccupied the academic community. In this sense the conclusion presents special problems for a student reader. Why might one be dissatisfied with "metadiscourse"? What kind of work is Tompkins talking about, for example, when she says, "The moral problem that confronts me now is . . . that the work I do is not directed toward solving the kinds of problems that studying the history of European-Indian relations has awakened me to"?

   As you reread the essay, look to see how the first two sections might be seen as a preparation for the conclusion. And as you reread the concluding section (which you may have to do several times), try to imagine the larger, unspoken issues it poses for those who teach American literature or who are professionally involved in reading and researching the past.

2. One of the things to notice about Tompkins's essay is how neatly all the pieces fit together in her narrative. If you wanted to read against this essay, you might say that they fit together *too* neatly. The seemingly "natural" progression from book to book or step to step in this account of her research and her thinking could be said to reveal the degree to which the story was shaped or made, constructed for the occasion. Real experience is never quite so tidy.

   As you reread the essay, be aware of the narrative as something made and ask yourself, How does she do that? What is she leaving out? Where is she working hard to get her material to fit? This is partly a matter of watching how Tompkins does her work—looking at paragraphs, for instance, and seeing how they represent her material and her reading of that material. It is also a matter of looking for what is not there, for seams that indicate necessary or unconscious omissions (as though while writing this essay, too, she "did not care to have any real exemplars interfering with what I already knew").

ASSIGNMENTS FOR WRITING

1. Tompkins's essay tells the story of a research project. It also, however, "reads" that narrative—that is, not only does Tompkins describe what she did, or what other people said, but she reflects on what her actions or the

work of others might be said to represent. She writes about "point of view" or "frame of reference" and the ways they might be said to determine how people act, what they write, and what they know.

Write an essay that tells a similar story, one of your own, using Tompkins's essay as a model. There are two ways you might do this:

a. You could tell the story of a research project, a paper (most likely a term paper) you prepared for school. This does not have to be a pious or dutiful account. Tompkins, after all, is writing against what she takes to be the predictable or expected account of research as the disinterested pursuit of truth—in which a student would go to the library to "find" the truth about the Indians and the settlers. And she writes in a style that is not solemnly academic. Like Tompkins, you can tell what you take to be the untold story of term-paper research, you can reflect on the "problem" of such research by turning to your own account.

Your account should begin well before your work in the library—that is, you too will want to show the "prehistory" of your project, the possible connections between school work and your life outside school. It should also tell the story of your work with other people's writing. The purpose of all this is to reflect on how knowledge is constructed and how you, as a student, have been expected to participate (and how you have, in fact, participated) in that process.

b. You could tell the story of a discovery that did not involve reading or library research; in fact, you could tell the story of a discovery that did not involve school at all. In this sense you would be working in response to the first section of Tompkins's essay, in which what she knows about Indians is constructed from a combination of cultural models and personal desire.

2. In her essay Tompkins offers her experience as a representative case. Her story is meant to highlight a problem central to teaching, learning, and research—central, that is, to academic life. As a student, you can read this essay as a way of looking in on the work and concerns of your faculty (a group represented not only by Tompkins but by those against whom she is arguing). Write an essay directed to someone who has not read "Indians," someone who will be entering your school as a first-year student next semester. Your job is to introduce an incoming freshman to the academy, using Tompkins as your guide. You will need to present her argument and her conclusion in such a way as to make clear the consequences of what she says for someone about to begin an undergraduate education. Remember, you are writing to an incoming student; you will want to capture that audience's attention.

MAKING CONNECTIONS

1. As Tompkins reviews the books she gathered in her project, she presents each in terms of its point of view, the "aims" with which it was written. She sees these books, that is, not as sources of truth but as representations of In-

dians and settlers, representations shaped by a theory, an agenda, or the cultural-historical situation of the scholar. The differences between the sources are not matters of right and wrong, nor are they simply matters of individual style.

In a parallel way, take two essays from *Ways of Reading* that deal with a single subject and treat them as cases of different points of view or frames of reference. "When We Dead Awaken: Writing as Re-Vision" by Adrieinne Rich (p. 549) or "A Room of One's Own" by Virginia Woolf (p. 719) are particularly suggestive for a project like this. They both deal with the situation of women writers. In fact, Rich's essay makes specific reference to Woolf and her work. One sign of Rich's difference from Woolf, then, will be the way she reads Woolf.

Write an essay in which you look at the differences between Rich's essay and Woolf's (or two others of your choice) and speculate on how those differences might reflect different times (different frames of reference) and different agendas (different points of view), even though they deal with a common topic and could easily be said to make a similar argument.

2. In "Our Time" (p. 652), John Edgar Wideman writes about the problems he has "knowing" and writing about his brother Robby. In this sense, both "Our Time" and "Indians" are about the problems of understanding, about the different relationship between "real exemplars" and what we know. Write an essay in which you compare these two selections, looking in particular at the differences in the ways each author represents this problem and its possible solutions. Although you are working from only two sources, you could imagine that your essay is a way of investigating the differences between the work of a "creative" writer and that of a scholar.

ALICE
WALKER

A LICE WALKER, *the youngest of eight children in a sharecropping family, was born in 1944 in Eatonton, Georgia. She is now one of the most widely read contemporary American novelists. In her work, she frequently returns to scenes of family life—some violent, some peaceful. "I was curious to know," she writes, "why people of families (specifically black families) are often cruel to each other and how much of this cruelty is caused by outside forces. . . . Family relationships are sacred. No amount of outside pressure and injustice should make us lose sight of that fact." In her nonfiction, Walker has helped to define a historical context for the contemporary black artist, a legacy that has had to be recovered from libraries and archives. The essay that follows, "In Search of Our Mothers' Gardens," defines black history as a family matter. It begins by charting the violence done to women who "died with their real gifts stifled within them" and concludes with Walker's recollection of her own mother, a recollection that enables her to imagine generations of black women handing on a "creative spark" to those who follow.*

In addition to In Search of Our Mothers' Gardens *(1983), Walker has written novels, including* The Third Life of Grange Copeland *(1970) and* The Color Purple *(1982), which won the Pulitzer Prize; collections of poems, including* Revolutionary Petunias *(1973) and* Good Night, Willie Lee, I'll See You in the Morning *(1979); two collections of short stories,* In Love and Trouble *(1973) and*

You Can't Keep a Good Woman Down *(1981), and a biography of Langston Hughes. She has also served as an editor at* Ms. *magazine. After graduating from Sarah Lawrence College in 1965, she taught at a number of colleges and universities, including Wellesley College and Yale University. She has held a Guggenheim Fellowship and a National Endowment for the Arts fellowship. She lives in San Francisco and teaches at the University of California at Berkeley.*

While pursuing her own career as a writer, Walker has fought to win recognition for the work of Zora Neale Hurston, a black woman author and anthropologist whose best-known work is the novel Their Eyes Were Watching God *(1937). Hurston died penniless in a Florida welfare home. Walker's most recent work includes* Living by the Word *(1988), a collection of essays, letters, journal entries, lectures, and poems on the themes of race, gender, sexuality, and political freedom;* To Hell with Dying *(1988), a children's picture book;* The Temple of My Familiar *(1989), and* Possessing the Secret of Joy *(1992), both novels; and* Her Blue Body Everything We Know: Earthling Poems, 1965–1990 *(1991), a collection of poems. Walker has also co-written, with Michael Meade, the introduction to a sound recording by Sobonfu Some entitled* We Have No Word for Sex *(1994), an African oral tale.*

In Search of
Our Mothers' Gardens

> I described her own nature and temperament. Told how they needed a larger life for their expression. . . . I pointed out that in lieu of proper channels, her emotions had overflowed into paths that dissipated them. I talked, beautifully I thought, about an art that would be born, an art that would open the way for women the likes of her. I asked her to hope, and build up an inner life against the coming of that day. . . . I sang, with a strange quiver in my voice, a promise song.
>
> — "AVEY," JEAN TOOMER, *Cane*
> *The poet speaking to a prostitute who falls*
> *asleep while he's talking*

When the poet Jean Toomer walked through the South in the early twenties, he discovered a curious thing: black women whose spirituality was so intense, so deep, so *unconscious,* they were themselves unaware of the richness they held. They stumbled blindly through their lives: creatures so abused and mutilated in body, so dimmed and confused by pain, that they considered themselves unworthy even of hope. In the selfless abstractions their bodies became to the men who used them, they became more than "sexual objects," more even than mere women: they became "Saints." Instead of being perceived as whole persons, their bodies became shrines: what was thought to be their minds became temples suitable for worship. These crazy Saints stared out at the world, wildly, like lunatics—or quietly, like suicides; and the "God" that was in their gaze was as mute as a great stone.

Who were these Saints? These crazy, loony, pitiful women?

Some of them, without a doubt, were our mothers and grandmothers.

In the still heat of the post-Reconstruction South, this is how they seemed to Jean Toomer: exquisite butterflies trapped in an evil honey, toiling away their lives in an era, a century, that did not acknowledge them, except as "the *mule* of the world." They dreamed dreams that no one knew—not even themselves, in any coherent fashion—and saw visions no one could understand. They wandered or sat about the countryside crooning lullabies to ghosts, and drawing the mother of Christ in charcoal on courthouse walls.

They forced their minds to desert their bodies and their striving spirits sought to rise, like frail whirlwinds from the hard red clay. And when those frail whirlwinds fell, in scattered particles, upon the ground, no one mourned. Instead, men lit candles to celebrate the emptiness that remained, as people do who enter a beautiful but vacant space to resurrect a God.

Our mothers and grandmothers, some of them: moving to music not yet written. And they waited.

They waited for a day when the unknown thing that was in them would be made known; but guessed, somehow in their darkness, that on the day of their revelation, they would be long dead. Therefore to Toomer they walked, and even ran, in slow motion. For they were going nowhere immediate, and the future was not yet within their grasp. And men took our mothers and grandmothers, "but got no pleasure from it." So complex was their passion and their calm.

To Toomer, they lay vacant and fallow as autumn fields, with harvest time never in sight; and he saw them enter loveless marriages, without joy; and become prostitutes, without resistance; and become mothers of children, without fulfillment.

For these grandmothers and mothers of ours were not Saints, but Artists; driven to a numb and bleeding madness by the springs of creativity in them for which there was no release. They were Creators, who lived lives of spiritual waste, because they were so rich in spirituality—which is the basis of Art—that the strain of enduring their unused and unwanted talent drove them insane. Throwing away this spirituality was their pathetic attempt to lighten the soul to a weight their work-worn, sexually abused bodies could bear.

What did it mean for a black woman to be an artist in our grandmothers' time? In our great-grandmothers' day? It is a question with an answer cruel enough to stop the blood.

Did you have a genius of a great-great-grandmother who died under some ignorant and depraved white overseer's lash? Or was she required to

why is not done – no there

bake biscuits for a lazy backwater tramp, when she cried out in her soul to paint watercolors of sunsets, or the rain falling on the green and peaceful pasturelands? Or was her body broken and forced to bear children (who were more often than not sold away from her)—eight, ten, fifteen, twenty children—when her one joy was the thought of modeling heroic figures of rebellion, in stone or clay?

How was the creativity of the black woman kept alive, year after year and century after century, when for most of the years black people have been in America, it was a punishable crime for a black person to read or write? And the freedom to paint, to sculpt, to expand the mind with action did not exist. Consider, if you can bear to imagine it, which might have been the result if singing, too, had been forbidden by law. Listen to the voices of Bessie Smith, Billie Holiday, Nina Simone, Roberta Flack, and Aretha Franklin, among others, and imagine those voices muzzled for life. Then you may begin to comprehend the lives of our "crazy," "Sainted" mothers and grandmothers. The agony of the lives of women who might have been poets, Novelists, Essayists, and Short-Story Writers (over a period of centuries), who died with their real gifts stifled within them.

And, if this were the end of the story, we would have cause to cry out in my paraphrase of Okot p'Bitek's great poem:

> O, my clanswomen
> Let us all cry together!
> Come,
> Let us mourn the death of our mother,
> The death of a Queen
> The ash that was produced
> By a great fire!
> O, this homestead is utterly dead
> Close the gates
> With *lacari* thorns,
> For our mother
> The creator of the Stool is lost!
> And all the young women
> Have perished in the wilderness!

But this is not the end of the story, for all the young women—our mothers and grandmothers, *ourselves*—have not perished in the wilderness. And if we ask ourselves why, and search for and find the answer, we will know beyond all efforts to erase it from our minds, just exactly who, and of what, we black American women are.

One example, perhaps the most pathetic, most misunderstood one, can provide a backdrop for our mothers' work: Phillis Wheatley, a slave in the 1700s.

Virginia Woolf, in her book *A Room of One's Own,* wrote that in order for a woman to write fiction she must have two things, certainly; a room of her own (with key and lock) and enough money to support herself.

What then are we to make of Phillis Wheatley, a slave, who owned not even herself? This sickly, frail black girl who required a servant of her own at times—her health was so precarious—and who, had she been white, would have been easily considered the intellectual superior of all the women and most of the men in the society of her day.

Virginia Woolf wrote further, speaking of course not of our Phillis, that "any woman born with a great gift in the sixteenth century [insert "eighteenth century," insert "black woman," insert "born or made a slave"] would certainly have gone crazed, shot herself, or ended her days in some lonely cottage outside the village, half witch, half wizard [insert "Saint"], feared and mocked at. For it needs little skill and psychology to be sure that a highly gifted girl who had tried to use her gift of poetry would have been so thwarted and hindered by contrary instincts [add "chains, guns, the lash, the ownership of one's body by someone else, submission to an alien religion"], that she must have lost her health and sanity to a certainty."

The key words, as they relate to Phillis, are "contrary instincts." For when we read the poetry of Phillis Wheatley—as when we read the novels of Nella Larsen or the oddly false-sounding autobiography of that freest of all black women writers, Zora Hurston—evidence of "contrary instincts" is everywhere. Her loyalties were completely divided, as was, without question, her mind.

But how could this be otherwise? Captured at seven, a slave of wealthy, doting whites who instilled in her the "savagery" of the Africa they "rescued" her from . . . one wonders if she was even able to remember her homeland as she had known it, or as it really was.

Yet, because she did try to use her gift for poetry in a world that made her a slave, she was "so thwarted and hindered by . . . contrary instincts, that she . . . lost her health. . . ." In the last years of her brief life, burdened not only with the need to express her gift but also with a penniless, friendless "freedom" and several small children for whom she was forced to do strenuous work to feed, she lost her health, certainly. Suffering from malnutrition and neglect and who knows what mental agonies, Phillis Wheatley died.

So torn by "contrary instincts" was black, kidnapped, enslaved Phillis that her description of "the Goddess"—as she poetically called the Liberty she did not have—is ironically, cruelly humorous. And, in fact, has held Phillis up to ridicule for more than a century. It is usually read prior to hanging Phillis's memory as that of a fool. She wrote:

> The Goddess comes, she moves divinely fair,
> Olive and laurel binds her *golden* hair.
> Wherever shines this native of the skies,
> Unnumber'd charms and recent graces rise. [My italics]

It is obvious that Phillis, the slave, combed the "Goddess's" hair every morning, prior, perhaps, to bringing in the milk, or fixing her mistress's lunch. She took her imagery from the one thing she saw elevated above all others.

With the benefit of hindsight we ask, "How could she?"

But at last, Phillis, we understand. No more snickering when your stiff, struggling, ambivalent lines are forced on us. We know now that you were not an idiot or a traitor; only a sickly little black girl, snatched from your home and country and made a slave; a woman who still struggled to sing the song that was your gift, although in a land of barbarians who praised you for your bewildered tongue. It is not so much what you sang, as that you kept alive, in so many of our ancestors, *the notion of song.*

Black women are called, in the folklore that so aptly identified one's status in society, "the *mule* of the world," because we have been handed the burdens that everyone else—*everyone* else—refused to carry. We have also been called "Matriarchs," "Superwomen," and "Mean and Evil Bitches." Not to mention "Castraters" and "Sapphire's Mama." When we have pleaded for understanding, our character has been distorted; when we have asked for simple caring, we have been handed empty inspirational appellations, then stuck in the farthest corner. When we have asked for love, we have been given children. In short, even our plainer gifts, our labors of fidelity and love, have been knocked down our throats. To be an artist and a black woman, even today, lowers our status in many respects, rather than raises it: and yet, artists we will be.

Therefore we must fearlessly pull out of ourselves and look at and identify with our lives the living creativity some of our great-grandmothers were not allowed to know. I stress *some* of them because it is well known that the majority of our great-grandmothers knew, even without "knowing" it, the reality of their spirituality, even if they didn't recognize it beyond what happened in the singing at church—and they never had any intention of giving it up.

How they did it—those millions of black women who were not Phillis Wheatley, or Lucy Terry or Frances Harper or Zora Hurston or Nella Larsen or Bessie Smith; or Elizabeth Catlett, or Katherine Dunham, either—brings me to the title of this essay, "In Search of Our Mothers' Gardens," which is a personal account that is yet shared, in its theme and its meaning, by all of us. I found, while thinking about the far-reaching world of the creative black woman, that often the truest answer to a question that really matters can be found very close.

In the late 1920s my mother ran away from home to marry my father. Marriage, if not running away, was expected of seventeen-year-old girls. By the time she was twenty, she had two children and was pregnant with a third. Five children later, I was born. And this is how I came to know my mother: she seemed a large, soft, loving-eyed woman who was rarely impatient in our home. Her quick, violent temper was on view only a few times a year, when she battled with the white landlord who had the misfortune to suggest to her that her children did not need to go to school.

She made all the clothes we wore, even my brothers' overalls. She made all the towels and sheets we used. She spent the summers canning vegetables and fruits. She spent the winter evenings making quilts enough to cover all our beds.

During the "working" day, she labored beside—not behind—my father in the fields. Her day began before sunup, and did not end until late at night. There was never a moment for her to sit down, undisturbed, to unravel her own private thoughts; never a time free from interruption—by work or the noisy inquiries of her many children. And yet, it is to my mother—and all our mothers who were not famous—that I went in search of the secret of what has fed that muzzled and often mutilated, but vibrant, creative spirit that the black woman has inherited, and that pops out in wild and unlikely places to this day.

But when, you will ask, did my overworked mother have time to know or care about feeding the creative spirit?

The answer is so simple that many of us have spent years discovering it. We have constantly looked high, when we should have looked high—and low.

For example: in the Smithsonian Institution in Washington, D.C., there hangs a quilt unlike any other in the world. In fanciful, inspired, and yet simple and identifiable figures, it portrays the story of the Crucifixion. It is considered rare, beyond price. Though it follows no known pattern of quilt-making, and though it is made of bits and pieces of worthless rags, it is obviously the work of a person of powerful imagination and deep spiritual feeling. Below this quilt I saw a note that says it was made by "an anonymous black woman in Alabama, a hundred years ago."

If we could locate this "anonymous" black woman from Alabama, she would turn out to be one of our grandmothers—an artist who left her mark in the only materials she could afford, and in the only medium her position in society allowed her to use.

As Virginia Woolf wrote further, in *A Room of One's Own:*

> Yet genius of a sort must have existed among women as it must have existed among the working class. [Change this to "slaves" and the "wives and daughters of sharecroppers."] Now and again an Emily Brontë or a Robert Burns [change this to "a Zora Hurston or a Richard Wright"] blazes out and proves its presence. But certainly it never got itself on to paper. When, however, one reads of a witch being ducked, of a woman possessed by devils [or "Sainthood"], of a wise woman selling herbs [our root workers], or even a very remarkable man who had a mother, then I think we are on the track of a lost novelist,

a suppressed poet, or some mute and inglorious Jane Austen. . . . Indeed, I would venture to guess that Anon, who wrote so many poems without singing them, was often a woman. . . .

And so our mothers and grandmothers have, more often than not anonymously, handed on the creative spark, the seed of the flower they themselves never hoped to see: or like a sealed letter they could not plainly read.

And so it is, certainly, with my own mother. Unlike "Ma" Rainey's songs, which retained their creator's name even while blasting forth from Bessie Smith's mouth, no song or poem will bear my mother's name. Yet so many of the stories that I write, that we all write, are my mother's stories. Only recently did I fully realize this: that through years of listening to my mother's stories of her life, I have absorbed not only the stories themselves, but something of the manner in which she spoke, something of the urgency that involves the knowledge that her stories—like her life—must be recorded. It is probably for this reason that so much of what I have written is about characters whose counterparts in real life are so much older than I am.

But the telling of these stories, which came from my mother's lips as naturally as breathing, was not the only way my mother showed herself as an artist. For stories, too, were subject to being distracted, to dying without conclusion. Dinners must be started, and cotton must be gathered before the big rains. The artist that was and is my mother showed itself to me only after many years. This is what I finally noticed.

Like Mem, a character in *The Third Life of Grange Copeland*, my mother adorned with flowers whatever shabby house we were forced to live in. And not just your typical straggly country stand of zinnias, either. She planted ambitious gardens—and still does—with over fifty different varieties of plants that bloom profusely from early March until late November. Before she left home for the fields, she watered her flowers, chopped up the grass, and laid out new beds. When she returned from the fields she might divide clumps of bulbs, dig a cold pit, uproot and replant roses, or prune branches from her taller bushes or trees—until night came and it was too dark to see.

Whatever she planted grew as if by magic, and her fame as a grower of flowers spread over three counties. Because of her creativity with her flowers, even my memories of poverty are seen through a screen of blooms—sunflowers, petunias, roses, dahlias, forsythia, spirea, delphiniums, verbena . . . and on and on.

And I remember people coming to my mother's yard to be given cuttings from her flowers; I hear again the praise showered on her because whatever rocky soil she landed on, she turned into a garden. A garden so brilliant with colors, so original in its design, so magnificent with life and creativity, that to this day people drive by our house in Georgia—perfect strangers and imperfect strangers—and ask to stand or walk among my mother's art.

I notice that it is only when my mother is working in her flowers that she is radiant, almost to the point of being invisible—except as Creator: hand and eye. She is involved in work her soul must have. Ordering the universe in the image of her personal conception of Beauty.

Her face, as she prepares the Art that is her gift, is a legacy of respect she leaves to me, for all that illuminates and cherishes life. She has handed down respect for the possibilities—and the will to grasp them.

For her, so hindered and intruded upon in so many ways, being an artist has still been a daily part of her life. This ability to hold on, even in very simple ways, is work black women have done for a very long time.

This poem is not enough, but it is something, for the woman who literally covered the holes in our walls with sunflowers.

> They were women then
> My mama's generation
> Husky of voice—Stout of
> Step
> With fists as well as
> Hands
> How they battered down
> Doors
> And ironed
> Starched white
> Shirts
> How they led
> Armies
> Headragged Generals
> Across mined
> Fields
> Booby-trapped
> Kitchens
> To discover books
> Desks
> A place for us
> How they knew what we
> *Must* know
> Without knowing a page
> Of it
> Themselves

Guided by my heritage of a love of beauty and a respect for strength—in search of my mother's garden, I found my own.

And perhaps in Africa over two hundred years ago, there was just such a mother; perhaps she painted vivid and daring decorations in oranges and yellows and greens on the walls of her hut; perhaps she sang—in a voice like Roberta Flack's—*sweetly* over the compounds of her village; perhaps she wove the most stunning mats or told the most ingenious stories of all the village storytellers. Perhaps she was herself a poet—although only her daughter's name is signed to the poems that we know.

Perhaps Phillis Wheatley's mother was also an artist.

Perhaps in more than Phillis Wheatley's biological life is her mother's signature made clear.

• • • • • • • • • • •

QUESTIONS FOR A SECOND READING

1. In the essay, Walker develops the interesting notion of "contrary instincts," particularly when she discusses Phillis Wheatley. The problem for Walker (and others) is that Wheatley would idolize a fair-haired white woman as a goddess of liberty rather than turn to herself as a model, or to the black women who struggled mightily for their identities and liberty. Walker asks, "How could she?" As you reread the essay, pay attention to the sections in which Walker discusses "contrary instincts." How would you define this term? What kind of answers does this essay make possible to the question "How could she?"

2. Bessie Smith, Roberta Flack, Phillis Wheatley, Zora Neale Hurston—Walker's essay is filled with allusions to black women artists; in fact, the essay serves as a kind of book list or reader's guide; it suggests a program of reading. Jean Toomer, however, is a man, and Virginia Woolf, a white woman; the references aren't strictly to black women. As you reread this essay, pay attention to the names (go to the library and track down some you don't know; you can use the bibliographical index in a good dictionary or ask a reference librarian to help you look up the information). What can you make of the collection of writers, poets, singers, and artists Walker sets down as a heritage? What use does she make of them?

3. As you reread the essay, note the sections in which Walker talks about herself. How does she feel about her mother, the history of black women in America, and "contrary instincts"? How would you describe Walker's feelings and attitudes toward herself, the past, and the pressures of living in a predominantly white culture? In considering these questions, don't settle for big words like "honest," "sensitive," or "compassionate." They are accurate, to be sure, but they are imprecise and don't do justice to Walker's seriousness and individuality.

ASSIGNMENTS FOR WRITING

1. Walker's essay poses a number of questions about the history of African American women in America, including how their "creative spirit" survived in the face of oppressive working and living conditions. At one point, Walker describes her mother's life in the late 1920s, after she ran away from home to marry Walker's father. Her mother's difficult life was filled with unrelenting work, yet she managed to keep a "vibrant, creative spirit" alive. At another

point, Walker writes, "Our mothers and grandmothers, some of them: moving to music not yet written. And they waited . . . for a day when the unknown thing that was in them would be made known; but guessed, somehow in their darkness, that on the day of their revelation they would be long dead" (p. 640).

Walker uses Virginia Woolf's term "contrary instincts" as a way to imagine this legacy of the creative spirit in the face of oppressive conditions, revising it, making it her own to fit the situations she's discussing as she weaves it into her writing. How would you say that Walker puts this term, "contrary instincts," to use in her own project? How do you understand Walker's rewriting of *A Room of One's Own?* What does Walker's use of the term allow her to understand about the creative spirit of African American women, including Phillis Wheatley and her own mother? How might Walker's essay itself stand as a response to this tradition?

Write an essay in which you discuss Walker's project as a creative endeavor, one in which she reconceives, or rewrites, texts from the past. What would you say, in other words, that Walker creates as she writes her essay?

2. In her essay Walker raises the question of what it meant (and what it still means) to be a black woman and an artist, and her response proceeds from examples that take her mother and herself, among others, into account. As you read her essay, observe Walker's methods of working. How does she build her arguments? Where does her evidence come from? her authority? To whom is she appealing? What do her methods allow her to see (and say) and not to see? And, finally, how might her conclusions be related to her methods?

Write a paper in which you examine Walker's essay in terms of the methods by which it proceeds. Consider the connections among her arguments, evidence, supposed audience, and conclusions, and feel free to invent names and descriptions for what you would call her characteristic ways of working. Remember that your job is to invent a way of describing how Walker works and how her methods—her ways of gathering materials, of thinking them through, of presenting herself and her thoughts, of imagining a world of speakers and listeners—might be related to the issues she raises and the conclusions she draws.

MAKING CONNECTIONS

1. Throughout "Our Time" (p. 652) by John Edgar Wideman, Robby talks about his contrary instincts, his ambivalent feelings toward making it in the "square" world. How can you consider Robby in light of Walker's observations about contrary instincts and the way black women lived in the past? Write an essay in which you explore how Wideman's understanding of his brother Robby's contrary instincts is different from Walker's understanding of her mother's contrary instincts.

2. At key points in her essay, Alice Walker refers to Virginia Woolf's *A Room of One's Own* (p. 719). Not only does she cite passages, but she revises them in order to bring them to bear on her experience or to make them serve her ar-

gument. There is a similar moment in Ralph Ellison's "An Extravagance of Laughter," (p. 140) where he cites and revises W. B. Yeats's argument on masks.

Use these examples to think about the relationship between African American writers and a white European intellectual heritage. Why do these writers do what they do with these passages? Work closely with the changes they make in the texts, and think about the writers' possible intentions. (Why, for example, wouldn't they avoid such moments?) And think about differences as well as similarities—in what ways might Walker and Ellison be said to be working toward different ends or different effects?

3. Alice Walker's essay raises questions about what it means to be a black woman and an artist. She refers to the "contrary instincts" that have "thwarted and hindered" the artistic endeavors of black women. She says,

> For when we read the poetry of Phillis Wheatley—as when we read the novels of Nella Larsen or the oddly false-sounding autobiography of that freest of all black women writers, Zora Hurston—evidence of "contrary instincts" is everywhere. Her loyalties were completely divided, as was, without question, her mind. (p. 642)

In her essay "And We Are Not Married" (p. 694), Patricia J. Williams takes up a similar argument about the contradictions that trap black professional women. In one passage, where she writes about her mother's insistence that she present herself professionally, she says that

> when I am fully dressed, my face is hung with contradictions; I try not to wear all my contradictions at the same time. I pick and choose among them; like jewelry, I hunt for this set of expectations that will go best with that obligation. (p. 705)

And a moment later, when she refers to the breakdown of Judge Maxine Thomas, she writes that "Thomas's job as black female judge was to wear all the contradictions at the same time—to wear them well and reconcile them" (p. 705).

Write an essay in which you discuss these two essays and their accounts of African American women. And, as an exercise (one designed to resist the temptation to see all accounts of experience as common), write an essay in which you look for differences—differences in attitude and point of view, differences in theory and argument, differences in example and testimony. Think of Williams and Walker as offering different positions on the question of race, gender, and identity, perhaps subtle differences, but differences nonetheless. You can assume that your reader is familiar with the issues raised in these essays but has not read the essays.

JOHN EDGAR
WIDEMAN

*J*OHN EDGAR WIDEMAN *was born in 1941 in Washington, D.C., but spent most of his youth in Homewood, a neighborhood in Pittsburgh. He earned a B.A. from the University of Pennsylvania, taught at the University of Wyoming, and is currently a professor of English at the University of Massachusetts at Amherst. In addition to the nonfiction work* Brothers and Keepers *(1984), from which this selection is drawn, Wideman has published a number of critically acclaimed works of fiction, including* The Lynchers, Reuben, Philadelphia Fire: A Novel, Fever: Twelve Stories, *and a series of novels set in Homewood:* Damballah, Hiding Place, *and* Sent for You Yesterday *(which won the 1984 PEN/Faulkner Award). The latter novels have been reissued as a set, titled* The Homewood Trilogy. *In 1994, Wideman published another work of nonfiction,* Fatheralong: A Meditation on Fathers and Sons, Race and Society.*

In the preface to this collection, Wideman writes,

> The value of black life in America is judged, as life generally in this country is judged, by external, material signs of success. Urban ghettoes are dangerous, broken-down, economically marginal pockets of real estate infected with drugs, poverty, violence, crime, and since black life is seen as rooted in the ghetto, black people are identified with the ugliness, danger, and deterioration surrounding them. This logic is simpleminded and devastating, its hold on the American

*imagination as old as slavery; in fact, it recycles the classic justifica-
tion for slavery, blaming the cause and consequences of oppression on
the oppressed. Instead of launching a preemptive strike at the flawed
assumptions that perpetuate racist thinking, blacks and whites are
doomed to battle endlessly with the symptoms of racism.*

*In these three books again bound as one I have set myself to the
task of making concrete those invisible planes of existence that bear
witness to the fact that black life, for all its material impoverishment,
continues to thrive, to generate alternative styles, redemptive strategies, people who hope and cope. But more than attempting to prove a
"humanity," which should be self-evident anyway to those not
blinded by racism, my goal is to celebrate and affirm.* Where did I
come from? Who am I? Where am I going?

Brothers and Keepers *is a family story; it is about Wideman and his brother
Robby. John went to Oxford as a Rhodes scholar, and Robby went to prison for his
role in a robbery and a murder. In the section that follows, "Our Time," Wideman
tries to understand his brother, their relationship, where they came from, where they
are going. In this account, you will hear the voices of Robby, John, and people from
the neighborhood, but also the voice of the writer, speaking about the difficulty of
writing and the dangers of explaining away Robby's life.*

Brothers and Keepers *is not the first time Wideman has written to or about his
brother. The first of the Homewood series,* Damballah *(1981), is dedicated to Robby.
The dedication reads:*

*Stories are letters. Letters sent to anybody or everybody. But the best
kind are meant to be read by a specific somebody. When you read that
kind you know you are eavesdropping. You know a real person somewhere will read the same words you are reading and the story is that
person's business and you are a ghost listening in.*

*Remember. I think it was Geral I first heard call a watermelon a
letter from home. After all these years I understand a little better what
she meant. She was saying the melon is a letter addressed to us. A
story for us from down home. Down Home being everywhere we've
never been, the rural South, the old days, slavery, Africa. That juicy,
striped message with red meat and seeds, which always looked like
roaches to me, was blackness as cross and celebration, a history we
could taste and chew. And it was meant for us. Addressed to us. We
were meant to slit it open and take care of business.*

*Consider all these stories as letters from home. I never liked wa-
termelon as a kid. I think I remember you did. You weren't afraid of
becoming instant nigger, of sitting barefoot and goggle-eyed and
Day-Glo black and drippy-lipped on massa's fence if you took one bite
of the forbidden fruit. I was too scared to enjoy watermelon. Too self-
conscious. I let people rob me of a simple pleasure. Watermelon's still
tainted for me. But I know better now. I can play with the idea even if
I can't get down and have a natural ball eating a real one.*

*Anyway . . . these stories are letters. Long overdue letters from
me to you. I wish they could tear down the walls. I wish they could
snatch you away from where you are.*

Our Time

You remember what we were saying about young black men in the street-world life. And trying to understand why the "square world" becomes completely unattractive to them. It has to do with the fact that their world is the GHETTO and in that world all the glamour, all the praise and attention is given to the slick guy, the gangster especially, the ones that get over in the "life." And it's because we can't help but feel some satisfaction seeing a brother, a black man, get over on these people, on their system without playing by their rules. No matter how much we have incorporated these rules as our own, we know that they were forced on us by people who did not have our best interests at heart. So this hip guy, this gangster or player or whatever label you give these brothers that we like to shun because of the poison that they spread, we, black people, still look at them with some sense of pride and admiration, our children openly, us adults somewhere deep inside. We know they represent rebellion—what little is left in us. Well, having lived in the "life," it becomes very hard— almost impossible—to find any contentment in joining the status quo. Too hard to go back to being nobody in a world that hates you. Even if I had struck it rich in the life, I would have managed to throw it down the fast lane. Or have lost it on a revolutionary whim. Hopefully the latter.

I have always burned up in my fervent passions of desire and want. My senses at times tingle and itch with my romantic, idealistic outlook on life, which has always made me keep my distance from reality, reality that was a constant insult to my world, to my dream of happiness and peace, to my people-for-people kind of world, my easy-cars-for-a-nickel-or-a-dime sorta world. And these driving passions, this sensitivity to the love and good in people, also turned on me because I used it to play on people and their feelings. These aspirations of love and desire turned on me when I wasn't able to live up to this sweet-self morality, so I began to self-destruct, burning up in my sensitivity, losing direction, because nowhere could I find this world of truth and love and harmony.

In the real world, the world left for me, it was unacceptable to be "good," it was square to be smart in school, it was jive to show respect to people outside the street world, it was cool to be cold to your woman and the people that loved you. The things we liked we called "bad." "Man, that was a bad girl." The world of the angry black kid growing up in the sixties was a world in which to be in was to be out—out of touch with the square world and all of its rules on what's right and wrong. The thing was to make your own rules, do your own thing, but make sure it's contrary to what society says or is.

I SHALL ALWAYS PRAY

I

Garth looked bad. Real bad. Ichabod Crane anyway, but now he was a skeleton. Lying there in the bed with his bones poking through his skin, it made you want to cry. Garth's barely able to talk, his smooth, medium-brown skin yellow as pee. Ichabod legs and long hands and long feet, Garth could make you laugh just walking down the street. On the set you'd see him coming a far way off. Three-quarters leg so you knew it had to be Garth the way he was split up higher in the crotch than anybody else. Wilt the Stilt with a lean bird body perched on top his high waist. Size-fifteen shoes. Hands could palm a basketball easy as holding a pool cue. Fingers long enough to wrap round a basketball, but Garth couldn't play a lick. Never could get all that lankiness together on the court. You'd look at him sometimes as he was trucking down Homewood Avenue and think that nigger ain't walking, he's trying to remember how to walk. Awkward as a pigeon on roller skates. Knobby joints out of whack, arms and legs flailing, going their separate ways, his body jerking to keep them from going too far. Moving down the street like that wouldn't work, didn't make sense if you stood back and watched, if you pretended you hadn't seen Garth get where he was going a million times before. Nothing funny now, though. White hospital sheets pulled to his chest. Garth's head always looked small as a tennis ball way up there on his shoulders. Now it's a yellow, shrunken skull.

Ever since Robby had entered the ward, he'd wanted to reach over and hide his friend's arm under the covers. For two weeks Gar had been wasting away in the bed. Bad enough knowing Gar was dying. Didn't need that pitiful stick arm reminding him how close to nothing his main man had fallen. So fast. It could happen so fast. If Robby tried to raise that arm it would come off in his hand. As gentle as he could would not be gentle enough. The arm would disintegrate, like a long ash off the end of a cigarette.

Time to leave. No sense in sitting any longer. Garth not talking, no way of telling whether he was listening either. And Robby has nothing more to say. Choked up the way he gets inside hospitals. Hospital smell and quiet, the bare halls and bare floors, the echoes, something about all that he can't name, wouldn't try to name, rises in him and chills him. Like his teeth are chattering the whole time he's inside a hospital. Like his entire body is trembling uncontrollably, only nobody can see it or hear it but him. Shaking because he can't breathe the stuffy air. Hot and cold at the same time. He's been aching to leave since he entered the ward. Aching to get up and bust through the big glass front doors. Aching to pounce on that spidery arm flung back behind Gar's head. The arm too wasted to belong to his friend. He wants to grab it and hurl it away.

Robby pulls on tight white gloves the undertaker had dealt out to him and the rest of the pallbearers. His brown skin shows through the thin material, turns the white dingy. He's remembering that last time in Garth's ward. The hospital stink. Hot, chilly air. A bare arm protruding from the sleeve of the hospital gown, more dried-up toothpick than arm, a withered twig, with Garth's fingers like a bunch of skinny brown bananas drooping from the knobby tip.

Robby had studied the metal guts of the hospital bed, the black scuff marks swirling around the chair's legs. When he'd finally risen to go, his chair scraping against the vinyl floor broke a long silence. The noise must have roused Garth's attention. He'd spoken again.

You're good, man. Don't ever forget, Rob. You're the best.

Garth's first words since the little banter back and forth when Robby had entered the ward and dragged a chair to the side of Gar's bed. A whisper scarcely audible now that Robby was standing. Garth had tried to grin. The best he could manage was a pained adjustment of the bones of his face, no more than a shadow scudding across the yellow skull, but Robby had seen the famous smile. He hesitated, stopped rushing toward the door long enough to smile back. Because that was Gar. That was the way Gar was. He always had a smile and a good word for his cut buddies. Garth's grin was money in the bank. You could count on it like you could count on a good word from him. Something in his face would tell you you were alright, better than alright, that he believed in you, that you were, as he'd just whispered, "the best." You could depend on Garth to say something to make you feel good, even though you knew he was lying. With that grin greasing the lie you had to believe it, even though you knew better. Garth was the gang's dreamer. When he talked, you could see his dreams. That's why Robby had believed it, seen the grin, the bright shadow lighting Garth's face an instant. Out of nothing, out of pain, fear, the certainty of death gripping them both, Garth's voice had manufactured the grin.

Now they had to bury Garth. A few days after the visit to the hospital the phone rang and it was Garth's mother with the news of her son's death. Not really news. Robby had known it was just a matter of time. Of waiting for the moment when somebody else's voice would pronounce the words he'd said to himself a hundred times. *He's gone. Gar's dead.* Long gone before the telephone rang. Gar was gone when they stuck him up in the hospital bed. By the time they'd figured out what ailed him and admitted him to the hospital, it was too late. The disease had turned him to a skeleton. Nothing left of Garth to treat. They hid his messy death under white sheets, perfumed it with disinfectant, pumped him full of drugs so he wouldn't disturb his neighbors.

The others had squeezed into their pallbearers' gloves. Cheap white cotton gloves so you could use them once and throw them away like the rubber ones doctors wear when they stick their fingers up your ass. Michael, Cecil, and Sowell were pallbearers, too. With Robby and two men from Garth's family they would carry the coffin from Gaines Funeral Parlor to the hearse. Garth had been the dreamer for the gang. Robby counted four black fingers in the white glove. Garth was the thumb. The hand would be clumsy, wouldn't work right without him. Garth was different. But everybody else was different, too. Mike, the ice man, supercool. Cecil indifferent, ready to do most anything or nothing and couldn't care less which it was. Sowell wasn't really part of the gang; he didn't hang with them, didn't like to take the risks that were part of the "life." Sowell kept a good job. The "life" for him was just a way to make quick money. He didn't shoot up; he thought of himself as a businessman, an investor not a partner in their schemes. They knew Sowell mostly through Garth. Perhaps things would change now. The four survivors closer after they shared the burden of Gar's coffin, after they hoisted it and slid it on steel rollers into the back of Gaines's Cadillac hearse.

Robby was grateful for the gloves. He'd never been able to touch anything dead. He'd taken a beating once from his father rather than touch the bloody mousetrap his mother had nudged to the back door with her toe and ordered him to empty. The brass handle of the coffin felt damp through the glove. He gripped tighter to stop the flow of blood or sweat, whatever it was leaking from him or seeping from the metal. Garth had melted down to nothing by the end so it couldn't be him nearly yanking off Robby's shoulder when the box shifted and its weight shot forward. Felt like a coffin full of bricks. Robby stared across at Mike but Mike was a soldier, eyes front, riveted to the yawning rear door of the hearse. Mike's eyes wouldn't admit it, but they'd almost lost the coffin. They were rookie pallbearers and maneuvering down the carpeted front steps of Gaines Funeral Parlor they'd almost let Garth fly out their hands. They needed somebody who knew what he was doing. An old, steady head to show them the way. They needed Garth. But Garth was long gone. Ashes inside the steel box.

They began drinking later that afternoon in Garth's people's house. Women and food in one room, men hitting the whiskey hard in another. It was a typical project apartment. The kind everybody had stayed in or visited one time or another. Small, shabby, featureless. Not a place to live. No matter what you did to it, how clean you kept it or what kind of furniture you loaded it with, the walls and ceilings were not meant to be home for anybody. A place you passed through. Not yours, because the people who'd been there before you left their indelible marks everywhere and you couldn't help adding your bruises and knots for the next tenants. You could rent a kitchen and bedroom and a bathroom and a living room, the project flats were laid out so you had a room for each of the things people did in houses. Problem was, every corner was cut. Living cramped is one thing and people can get cozy in the closest quarters. It's another thing to live in a place designed to be just a little less than adequate. No slack, no space to personalize, to stamp the flat with what's peculiar to your style. Like a man sitting on a toilet seat that's too small and the toilet too close to the bathtub so his knees shove against the enamel edge. He can move his bowels that way and plenty of people in the world have a lot less but he'll never enjoy sitting there, never feel the deep down comfort of belonging where he must squat.

Anyway, the whiskey started flowing in that little project apartment. Robby listened, for Garth's sake, as long as he could to old people reminiscing about funerals they'd attended, about all the friends and relatives they'd escorted to the edge of Jordan, old folks sipping good whiskey and moaning and groaning till it seemed a sin to be left behind on this side of the river after so many saints had crossed over. He listened to people express their grief, tell sad, familiar stories. As he got high he listened less closely to the words. Faces and gestures revealed more than enough. When he split with Mike and Cecil and their ladies, Sowell tagged along. By then the tacky, low-ceilinged rooms of the flat were packed. Loud talk, laughter, storytellers competing for audiences. Robby half expected the door he pushed shut behind himself to pop open again, waited for bottled-up noise to explode into the funky hallway.

Nobody thinking about cemeteries now. Nobody else needs to be buried today, so it was time to get it on. Some people had been getting close to rowdy. Some people had been getting mad. Mad at one of the guests in the apartment, mad at doctors and hospitals and whites in general who had the whole world in their hands but didn't have the slightest idea what to do with it. A short, dark man, bubble-eyed, immaculately dressed in a three-piece, wool, herringbone suit, had railed about the callousness, the ignorance of white witch doctors who, by misdiagnosing Garth's illness, had sealed his doom. His harangue had drawn a crowd. He wasn't just talking, he was testifying, and a hush had fallen over half the room as he dissected the dirty tricks of white folks. If somebody ran to the hospital and snatched a white-coated doctor and threw him into the circle surrounding the little fish-eyed man, the mourners would tear the pale-faced devil apart. Robby wished he could feed them one. Remembered Garth weak and helpless in the bed and the doctors and nurses flitting around in the halls, jiving the other patients, ignoring Gar like he wasn't there. Garth was dead because he had believed them. Dead because he had nowhere else to turn when the pain in his gut and the headaches grew worse and worse. Not that he trusted the doctors or believed they gave a flying fuck about him. He'd just run out of choices and had to put himself in their hands. They told him jaundice was his problem, and while his liver rotted away and pain cooked him dizzy Garth assured anyone who asked that it was just a matter of giving the medicine time to work. To kill the pain he blew weed as long as he had strength to hold a joint between his lips. Take a whole bunch of smoke to cool me out these days. Puffing like a chimney till he lost it and fell back and Robby scrambling to grab the joint before Garth torched hisself.

When you thought about it, Garth's dying made no sense. And the more you thought the more you dug that nothing else did neither. The world's a stone bitch. Nothing true if that's not true. The man had you coming and going. He owned everything worth owning and all you'd ever get was what he didn't want anymore, what he'd chewed and spit out and left in the gutter for niggers to fight over. Garth had pointed to the street and said, If we ever make it, it got to come from there, from the curb. We got to melt that rock till we get us some money. He grinned then, Ain't no big thing. We'll make it, brother man. We got what it takes. It's our time.

Something had crawled in Garth's belly. The man said it wasn't nothing. Sold him some aspirins and said he'd be alright in no time. The man killed Garth. Couldn't kill him no deader with a .357 magnum slug, but ain't no crime been committed. Just one those things. You know, everybody makes mistakes. And a dead nigger ain't really such a big mistake when you think about it. Matter of fact you mize well forget the whole thing. Nigger wasn't going nowhere, nohow. I mean he wasn't no brain surgeon or astronaut, no movie star or big-time athlete. Probably a dope fiend or gangster. Wind up killing some innocent person or wasting another nigger. Shucks. That doctor ought to get a medal.

Hey, man. Robby caught Mike's eye. Then Cecil and Sowell turned to him. They knew he was speaking to everybody. Late now. Ten, eleven, because it had been dark outside for hours. Quiet now. Too quiet in his pad. And too much smoke and drink since the funeral. From a bare bulb in the kitchen ceiling light seeped down the hallway and hovered dimly in the doorway of the room where they sat. Robby wondered if the others felt as bad as he did. If the cemetery clothes itched their skin. If they could smell grave dust on their shoes. He hoped they'd finish this last jug of wine and let the day be over. He needed sleep, downtime to get the terrible weight of Garth's death off his mind. He'd been grateful for the darkness. For the company of his cut buddies after the funeral. For the Sun Ra tape until it ended and plunged them into a deeper silence than any he'd ever known. Garth was gone. In a few days people would stop talking about him. He was in the ground. Stone-cold dead. Robby had held a chunk of crumbly ground in his white-gloved fingers and mashed it and dropped the dust into the hole. Now the ground had closed over Garth and what did it mean? Here one day and gone the next and that was that. They'd bury somebody else out of Gaines tomorrow. People would dress up and cry and get drunk and tell lies and next day it'd be somebody else's turn to die. Which one of the shadows in this black room would go first? What did it matter? Who cared? Who would remember their names; they were ghosts already. Dead as Garth already. Only difference was, Garth didn't have it to worry about no more. Garth didn't have to pretend he was going anywhere cause he was there. He'd made it to the place they all were headed fast as their legs could carry them. Every step was a step closer to the stone-cold ground, the pitch-black hole where they'd dropped Garth's body.

Hey, youall. We got to drink to Garth one last time.

They clinked glasses in the darkness. Robby searched for something to say. The right words wouldn't come. He knew there was something proper and precise that needed to be said. Because the exact words eluded him, because only the right words would do, he swallowed his gulp of heavy, sweet wine in silence.

He knew he'd let Garth down. If it had been one of the others dead, Michael or Cecil or Sowell or him, Garth wouldn't let it slide by like this, wouldn't let it end like so many other nights had ended, the fellows nodding off one by one, stupefied by smoke and drink, each one beginning to shop around in his mind, trying to figure whether or not he should turn in or if there was a lady somewhere who'd welcome him in her bed. No. Garth would have figured a way to make it special. They wouldn't be hiding in the bushes. They'd be knights in shining armor around a big table. They'd raise their giant, silver cups to honor the fallen comrade. Like in the olden days. Clean, brave dudes with gold rings and gold chains. They'd draw their blades. Razor-edged swords that gleam in the light with jewels sparkling in the handles. They'd make a roof over the table when they stood and raised their swords and the points touched in the sky. A silver dagger on a satin pillow in the middle of the table. Everybody roll up their sleeves and prick a vein and go round, each one touching everybody else so the blood runs together and we're brothers forever, brothers as long as blood flows in anybody's arm. We'd ride off and do unbelievable shit. The dead one always with us cause we'd do it all for him. Swear we'd never let him down.

It's our time now. We can't let Garth down. Let's drink this last one for him and promise him we'll do what he said we could. We'll be the best. We'll make it to the top for him. We'll do it for Garth.

Glasses rattled together again. Robby empties his and thinks about smashing it against a wall. He'd seen it done that way in movies but it was late at night and these crazy niggers might not know when to stop throwing things. A battlefield of broken glass for him to creep through when he gets out of bed in the morning. He doesn't toss the empty glass. Can't see a solid place anyway where it would strike clean and shatter to a million points of light.

My brother had said something about a guy named Garth during one of my visits to the prison. Just a name mentioned in passing. *Garth* or *Gar*. I'd asked Robby to spell it for me. Garth had been a friend of Robby's, about Robby's age, who died one summer of a mysterious disease. Later when Robby chose to begin the story of the robbery and killing by saying, "It all started with Gar dying," I remembered that first casual mention and remembered a conversation with my mother. My mom and I were in the kitchen of the house on Tokay Street. My recollection of details was vague at first but something about the conversation had made a lasting impression because, six years later, hearing Robby say the name *Garth* brought back my mother's words.

My mother worried about Robby all the time. Whenever I visited home, sooner or later I'd find myself alone with Mom and she'd pour out her fears about Robby's *wildness*, the deep trouble he was bound for, the web of entanglements and intrigues and bad company he was weaving around himself with a maddening disregard for the inevitable consequences.

I don't know. I just don't know how to reach him. He won't listen. He's doing wrong and he knows it but nothing I say makes any difference. He's not like the rest of youall. You'd misbehave but I could talk to you or smack you if I had to and you'd straighten up. With Robby it's like talking to a wall.

I'd listen and get angry at my brother because I registered not so much the danger he was bringing on himself, but the effect of his escapades on the woman who'd brought us both into the world. After all, Robby was no baby. If he wanted to mess up, nobody could stop him. Also Robby was my brother, meaning that his wildness was just a stage, a chaotic phase of his life that would only last till he got his head together and decided to start doing right. Doing as the rest of us did. He was my brother. He couldn't fall too far. His brushes with the law (I'd had some, too), the time he'd spent in jail, were serious but temporary setbacks. I viewed his troubles, when I thought about them at all, as a form of protracted juvenile delinquency, and fully expected Robby would learn his lesson sooner or later and return to the fold, the prodigal son, chastened, perhaps a better person for the experience. In the meantime the most serious consequence of his wildness was Mom's devastating unhappiness. She couldn't sustain the detachment, the laissez-faire optimism I had talked myself into. Because I was two thousand miles away, in Wyoming, I didn't have to deal with the day-to-day evidence of Robby's trouble. The syringe Mom found under his bed. The twenty-dollar bill missing from her purse. The times he'd cruise in higher than a kite, his pupils reduced to pinpricks, with his crew and they'd raid the refrigerator and make a loud, sloppy feast, all of them feeling so good they couldn't imagine anybody not up there on cloud nine with them enjoying the time of their lives. Cruising in, then disappearing just as abruptly, leaving their dishes and pans and mess behind. Robby covering Mom with kisses and smiles and drowning her in babytalk hootchey-coo as he staggers through the front door. Her alone in the ravaged, silent kitchen, listening as doors slam and a car squeals off on the cobblestones of Tokay, wondering where they're headed next, wishing, praying Robby will return and eat and eat and eat till he falls asleep at the table so she can carry him upstairs and tuck him in and kiss his forehead and shut the door gently on his sleep.

I wasn't around for all that. Didn't want to know how bad things were for him. Worrying about my mother was tough enough. I could identify with her grief, I could blame my brother. An awful situation, but simple too. My role, my responsibilities and loyalties were clear. The *wildness* was to blame, and it was a passing thing, so I just had to help my mother survive the worst of it, then everything would be alright. I'd steel myself for the moments alone with her when she'd tell me the worst. In the kitchen, usually, over a cup of coffee with the radio playing. When my mother was alone in the house on Tokay, either the TV or a radio or both were always on. Atop the kitchen table a small clock radio turned to WAMO, one of Pittsburgh's soul stations, would background with scratchy gospel music whatever we said in the morning in the kitchen. On a morning like that in 1975, while I drank a cup of coffee and part of me, still half-asleep, hidden, swayed to the soft beat of gospel, my mother had explained how upset Robby was over the death of his friend, Garth.

It was a terrible thing. I've known Garth's mother for years. He was a good boy. No saint for sure, but deep down a good boy. Like your brother. Not a mean bone in his body. Out there in the street doing wrong, but that's where most of them are. What else can they do, John? Sometimes I can't blame them. No jobs, no money in their pockets. How they supposed to feel like men? Garth did better than most. Whatever else he was into, he kept that little job over at Westinghouse and helped out his mother. A big, playful kid. Always smiling. I think that's why him and Robby were so tight. Neither one had good sense. Giggled and acted like fools. Garth no wider than my finger. Straight up and down. A stringbean if I ever saw one. When Robby lived here in the house with me, Garth was always around. I know how bad Robby feels. He hasn't said a word but I know. When Robby's quiet, you know something's wrong. Soon as his eyes pop open in the morning he's looking for the party. First thing in the morning he's chipper and chattering. Looking for the party. That's your brother. He had a match in Garth.

Shame the way they did that boy. He'd been down to the clinic two or three times but they sent him home. Said he had an infection and it would take care of itself. Something like that anyway. You know how they are down there. Have to be spitting blood to get attention. Then all they give you is a Band-Aid. He went back two times, but they kept telling him the same dumb thing. Anybody who knew Garth could see something awful was wrong. Circles under his eyes. Sallow look to his skin. Losing weight. And the poor thing didn't have any weight to lose. Last time I saw him I was shocked. Just about shocked out my shoes. Wasn't Garth standing in front of me. Not the boy I knew.

Well, to make a long story short, they finally took him in the hospital but it was too late. They let him walk the streets till he was dead. It was wrong. Worse than wrong how they did him, but that's how those dogs do us every day God sends here. Garth's gone, so nothing nobody can say will do any good. I feel so sorry for his mother. She lived for that boy. I called her and tried to talk but what can you say? I prayed for her and prayed for Garth and prayed for Robby. A thing like that tears people up. It's worse if you keep it inside. And that's your brother's way. He'll let it eat him up and then go out and do something crazy.

Until she told me Garth's story I guess I hadn't realized how much my mother had begun to change. She had always seemed to me to exemplify the tolerance, the patience, the long view epitomized in her father. John French's favorite saying was, Give 'em the benefit of the doubt. She could get as ruffled, as evil as the rest of us, cry and scream or tear around the house fit to be tied. She had her grudges and quarrels. Mom could let it all hang out, yet most of the time she radiated a deep calm. She reacted strongly to things but at the same time held judgment in abeyance. Events, personalities always deserved a second, slower appraisal, an evaluation outside the sphere of everyday hassles and vexations. You gave people the benefit of the doubt. You attempted to remove your ego, acknowledge the limitations of your individual view of things. You consulted as far as you were equipped by temperament and intelligence a broader, more abiding set of relationships and connections. You tried on the other person's point of view. You sought the other, better person in yourself who might talk you into relinquishing for a moment your selfish interest in whatever was at issue. You stopped and considered the long view, possibilities other than the one that momentarily was leading you by the nose. You gave yourself and other people the benefit of the doubt.

My mother had that capacity. I'd admired, envied, and benefited infinitely from its presence. As she related the story of Garth's death and my brother's anger and remorse, her tone was uncompromisingly bitter. No slack, no margin of doubt was being granted to the forces that destroyed Garth and still pursued her son. She had exhausted her reserves of understanding and compassion. The long view supplied the same ugly picture as the short. She had an enemy now. It was that revealed truth that had given the conversation its edge, its impact. *They* had killed Garth, and his dying had killed part of her son; so the battle lines were drawn. Irreconcilably. Absolutely. The backside of John French's motto had come into play. Giving someone the benefit of the doubt was also giving him enough rope to hang himself. If a person takes advantage of the benefit of the doubt and keeps on taking and taking, one day the rope plays out. The piper must be paid. If you've been the one giving, it becomes incumbent on you to grip your end tight and take away. You turn the other cheek, but slowly, cautiously, and keep your fist balled up at your side. If your antagonist decides to smack rather than kiss you or leave you alone, you make sure you get in the first blow. And make sure it's hard enough to knock him down.

Before she told Garth's story, my mother had already changed, but it took years for me to realize how profoundly she hated what had been done to Garth and then Robby. The gentleness of my grandfather, like his fair skin and good French hair, had been passed down to my mother. Gentleness styled the way she thought, spoke, and moved in the world. Her easy disposition and sociability masked the intensity of her feelings. Her attitude to authority of any kind, doctors, clerks, police, bill collectors, newscasters, whites in general partook of her constitutional gentleness. She wasn't docile or cowed. The power other people possessed or believed they possessed didn't frighten her; she accommodated herself, offered something they could accept as deference but that was in fact the same resigned, alert attention she paid to roaches or weather or poverty, any of the givens outside herself that she couldn't do much about. She never engaged in public tests of will, never pushed herself or her point of view on people she didn't know. Social awkwardness embarrassed her. Like most Americans she didn't like paying taxes, was suspicious of politicians, resented the disparity between big and little people in our society and the double standard that allowed big shots to get away with murder. She paid particular attention to news stories that reinforced her basic political assumption that power corrupts. On the other hand she knew the world was a vale of tears and one's strength, granted by God to deal with life's inevitable calamities, should not be squandered on small stuff.

In spite of all her temperamental and philosophic resistance to extremes, my mother would be radicalized. What the demonstrations, protest marches, and slogans of the sixties had not effected would be accomplished by Garth's death and my brother's troubles. She would become an aggressive, acid critic of the status quo in all its forms: from the President ("If it wasn't for that rat I'd have a storm door to go with the storm windows but he cut the program") on down to bank tellers ("I go there every Friday and I'm one of the few black faces she sees all day and she knows me as well as she knows that wart on her cheek but she'll still make me show my license before she'll cash my check"). A son she loved would be pursued, captured, tried, and imprisoned by the forces of law and order. Throughout the ordeal her love for him wouldn't change, couldn't change. His crime tested her love and also tested the nature, the intent of the forces arrayed against her son. She had to make a choice. On one side were the stark facts of his crime: robbery, murder, flight; her son an outlaw, a fugitive; then a prisoner. On the other side the guardians of society, the laws, courts, police, judges, and keepers who were responsible for punishing her son's transgression.

She didn't invent the two sides and initially didn't believe there couldn't be a middle ground. She extended the benefit of the doubt. Tried to situate herself somewhere in between, acknowledging the evil of her son's crime while simultaneously holding on to the fact that he existed as a human being before, after, and during the crime he'd committed. He'd done wrong but he was still Robby and she'd always be his mother. Strangely, on the dark side, the side of the crime and its terrible consequences, she would find room to exercise her love. As negative as the elements were, a life taken, the grief of the survivors, suffering, waste, guilt, remorse, the scale was human; she could apply her sense of right and wrong. Her life to that point had equipped her with values, with tools for sorting out and coping with disaster. So she would choose to make her fight there, on treacherous yet familiar ground—familiar since her son was there—and she could place herself, a woman, a mother, a grieving, bereaved human being, there beside him.

Nothing like that was possible on the other side. The legitimacy of the other side was grounded not in her experience of life, but in a set of rules seemingly framed to sidestep, ignore, or replace her sense of reality. Accepting the version of reality encoded in *their* rules would be like stepping into a cage and locking herself in. Definitions of her son, herself, of need and frailty and mercy, of blackness and redemption and justice had all been neatly formulated. No need here for her questions, her uncertainty, her fear, her love. Everything was clean and clear. No room for her sense that things like good and evil, right and wrong bleed into each other and create a dreadful margin of ambiguity no one could name but could only enter, enter at the risk of everything because everything is at stake and no one on earth knows what it means to enter or what will happen if and when the testing of the margin is over.

She could love her son, accept his guilt, accept the necessity of punishment, suffer with him, grow with him past the stage of blaming everyone but himself for his troubles, grieve with him when true penitence began to exact its toll. Though she might wish penance and absolution could be achieved in private, without the intervention of a prison sentence, she understood dues must be paid. He was her son but he was also a man who had committed a robbery in the course of which another woman's son had been killed. What would appall her and what finally turned her against the forces of law and order was the incapacity of the legal system to grant her son's humanity. "Fair" was the word she used—a John French word. She expected them to treat Robby fair. Fairness was what made her willing to give him up to punishment even though her love screamed no and her hands clung to his shoulders. Fairness was what she expected from the other side in their dealings with her and her son.

She could see their side, but they steadfastly refused to see hers. And when she realized fairness was not forthcoming, she began to hate. In the lack of reciprocity, in the failure to grant that Robby was first a man, then a man who had done wrong, the institutions and individuals who took over control of his life denied not only his humanity but the very existence of the world that had nurtured him and nurtured her—the world of touching, laughing, suffering black people that established Robby's claim to something more than a number.

Mom expects the worst now. She's peeped their hole card. She understands they have a master plan that leaves little to accident, that most of the ugliest things happening to black people are not accidental but the predictable results of the working of the plan. What she learned about authority, about law and order didn't make sense at first. It went against her instincts, what she wanted to believe, against the generosity she'd observed in her father's interactions with other Homewood people. He was fair. He'd pick up the egg rolls he loved from the back kitchen door of Mr. Wong's restaurant and not blame Wong, his old talking buddy and card-playing crony, for not serving black people in his restaurant. Wong had a family and depended on white folks to feed them, so Wong didn't have any choice and neither did John French if he wanted those incredible egg rolls. He treated everyone, high and low, the same. He said what he meant and meant what he said. John French expected no more from other people than he expected from himself. And he'd been known to mess up many a time, but that was him, that was John French, no better, no worse than any man who pulls on his britches one leg at a time. He needed a little slack, needed the benefit of that blind eye people who love, or people who want to get along with other people, must learn to cast. John French was grateful for the slack, so was quick to extend it to others. Till they crossed him.

My mother had been raised in Homewood. The old Homewood. Her relations with people in that close-knit, homogeneous community were based on trust, mutual respect, common spiritual and material concerns. Face-to-face contact, shared language and values, a large fund of communal experience rendered individual lives extremely visible in Homewood. Both a person's self-identity ("You know who you are") and accountability ("Other people know who you are") were firmly established.

If one of the Homewood people said, "That's the French girl" or, "There goes John French's daughter," a portrait with subtle shading and complex resonance was painted by the words. If the listener addressed was also a Homewood resident, the speaker's voice located the young woman passing innocently down Tioga Street in a world invisible to outsiders. A French girl was somebody who lived in Cassina Way, somebody you didn't fool with or talk nasty to. Didn't speak to at all except in certain places or on certain occasions. French girls were church girls, Homewood African Methodist Episcopal Zion Sunday-school-picnic and social-event young ladies. You wouldn't find them hanging around anywhere without escorts or chaperones. French girls had that fair, light, bright, almost white redbone complexion and fine blown hair and nice big legs but all that was to be appreciated from a distance because they were nice girls and because they had this crazy daddy who wore a big brown country hat and gambled and drank wine and once ran a man out of town, ran him away without ever laying a hand on him or making a bad-mouthed threat, just cut his eyes a certain way when he said the man's name and the word went out and the man who had cheated a drunk John French with loaded dice was gone. Just like that. And there was the time Elias Brown was cleaning his shotgun in his backyard. Brown had his double-barreled shotgun across his knees and a jug of Dago Red on the ground beside him and it was a Saturday and hot and Brown was sweating through his BVD undershirt and paying more attention to the wine than he was to the gun. Next thing you know, *Boom!* Off it goes and buckshot sprayed down Cassina Way, and it's Saturday and summer like I said, so chillens playing everywhere but God watches over fools and babies so nobody hit bad. Nobody hit at all except the little French girl, Geraldine, playing out there in the alley and she got nicked in her knee. Barely drew blood. A sliver of that buckshot musta ricocheted off the cobblestones and cut her knee. Thank Jesus she the only one hit and she ain't hit bad. Poor Elias Brown don't quite know what done happened till some the mens run over in his yard and snatch the gun and shake the wine out his head. What you doing, fool? Don't you know no better all those children running round here? Coulda killed one these babies. Elias stone drunk and don't hear nothing, see nothing till one the men say French girl. Nicked the little French girl, Geraldine. Then Elias woke up real quick. His knees, his dusty butt, everything he got starts to trembling and his eyes get big as dinner plates. Then he's gone like a turkey through the corn. Nobody seen Elias for a week. He's in Ohio at his sister's next time anybody hear anything about Elias. He's cross there in Ohio and still shaking till he git word John French ain't after him. It took three men gon over there telling the same story to get Elias back to Homewood. John French ain't mad. He *was* mad but he ain't mad now. Little girl just nicked is all and French ain't studying you, Brown.

You heard things like that in Homewood names. Rules of etiquette, thumbnail character sketches, a history of the community. A dire warning to get back could be coded into the saying of a person's name, and a further inflection of the speaker's voice could tell you to ignore the facts, forget what he's just reminded you to remember and go on. Try your luck.

Because Homewood was self-contained and possessed such a strong personality, because its people depended less on outsiders than they did on each other for so many of their most basic satisfactions, they didn't notice the net settling over their community until it was already firmly in place. Even though the strands of the net—racial discrimination, economic exploitation, white hate and fear—had existed time out of mind, what people didn't notice or chose not to notice was that the net was being drawn tighter, that ruthless people outside the community had the power to choke the life out of Homewood, and as soon as it served their interests would do just that. During the final stages, as the net closed like a fist around Homewood, my mother couldn't pretend it wasn't there. But instead of setting her free, the truth trapped her in a cage as tangible as the iron bars of Robby's cell.

Some signs were subtle, gradual. The A & P started to die. Nobody mopped filth from the floors. Nobody bothered to restock empty shelves. Fewer and fewer white faces among the shoppers. A plate-glass display window gets broken and stays broken. When they finally close the store, they paste the going-out-of-business notice over the jagged, taped crack. Other signs as blatant, as sudden as fire engines and patrol cars breaking your sleep, screaming through the dark Homewood streets. First Garth's death, then Robby's troubles brought it all home. My mother realized her personal unhappiness and grief were inseparable from what was happening *out there*. Out there had never been further away than the thousand insults and humiliations she had disciplined herself to ignore. What she had deemed petty, not worth bothering about, were strings of the net just as necessary, as effective as the most dramatic intrusions into her life. She decided to stop letting things go by. No more benefit of the doubt. Doubt had been cruelly excised. She decided to train herself to be as wary, as unforgiving as she'd once been ready to live and let live. My mother wouldn't become paranoid, not even overtly prickly or bristling. That would have been too contrary to her style, to what her blood and upbringing had instilled. The change was inside. What she thought of people. How she judged situations. Things she'd say or do startled me, set me back on my heels because I didn't recognize my mother in them. I couldn't account for the stare of pure unadulterated hatred she directed at the prison guard when he turned away from her to answer the phone before handing her the rest-room key she'd requested, the vehemence with which she had cussed Richard Nixon for paying no taxes when she, scraping by on an income of less than four thousand dollars a year, owed the IRS three hundred dollars.

Garth's death and Robby's troubles were at the center of her new vision. Like a prism, they caught the light, transformed it so she could trace the seemingly random inconveniences and impositions coloring her life to their source in a master plan.

I first heard Garth's story in the summer of 1975, the summer my wife carried our daughter Jamila in her belly, the summer before the robbery and killing. The story contained all the clues I'm trying to decipher now. Sitting in the kitchen vaguely distracted by gospel music from the little clock radio atop the table, listening as my mother expressed her sorrow, her indignation at the way Garth was treated, her fears for my brother, I was hearing a new voice. Something about the voice struck me then, but I missed what was novel and crucial. I'd lost my Homewood ear. Missed all the things unsaid that invested her words with special urgency. People in Homewood often ask: You said that to say what? The impacted quality of an utterance either buries a point too obscurely or insists on a point so strongly that the listener wants the meat of the message repeated, wants it restated clearly so it stands alone on its own two feet. If I'd been alert enough to ask that question, to dig down to the root and core of Garth's story after my mother told it, I might have understood sooner how desperate and dangerous Homewood had become. Six years later my brother was in prison, and when he began the story of his troubles with Garth's death, a circle completed itself; Robby was talking to me, but I was still on the outside, looking in.

That day six years later, I talked with Robby three hours, the maximum allotted for weekday visits with a prisoner. It was the first time in life we'd ever talked that long. Probably two and a half hours longer than the longest, unbroken, private conversation we'd ever had. And it had taken guards, locks, and bars to bring us together. The ironies of the situation, the irony of that fact, escaped neither of us.

I listened mostly, interrupting my brother's story a few times to clarify dates or names. Much of what he related was familiar. The people, the places. Even the voice, the words he chose were mine in a way. We're so alike, I kept thinking, anticipating what he would say next, how he would say it, filling in naturally, easily with my words what he left unsaid. Trouble was our minds weren't interchangeable. No more than our bodies. The guards wouldn't have allowed me to stay in my brother's place. He was the criminal. I was the visitor from outside. Different as night and day. As Robby talked I let myself forget that difference. Paid too much attention to myself listening and lost some of what he was saying. What I missed would have helped define the difference. But I missed it. It was easy to half listen. For both of us to pretend to be closer than we were. We needed the closeness. We were brothers. In the prison visiting lounge I acted toward my brother the way I'd been acting toward him all my life, heard what I wanted to hear, rejected the rest.

When Robby talked, the similarity of his Homewood and mine was a trap. I could believe I knew exactly what he was describing. I could relax into his story, walk down Dunfermline or Tioga, see my crippled grandmother sitting on the porch of the house on Finance, all the color her pale face had lost blooming in the rosebush beneath her in the yard, see Robby in the downstairs hall of the house on Marchand, rapping with his girl on the phone, which sat on a three-legged stand just inside the front door. I'd slip unaware out of his story into one of my own. I'd be following him, an obedient shadow, then a cloud would blot the sun and I'd be gone, unchained, a dark form still skulking behind him but no longer in tow.

The hardest habit to break, since it was the habit of a lifetime, would be listening to myself listen to him. That habit would destroy any chance of seeing my brother on his terms; and seeing him in his terms, learning his terms, seemed the whole point of learning his story. However numerous and comforting the similarities, we were different. The world had seized on the difference, allowed me room to thrive, while he'd been forced into a cage. Why did it work out that way? What was the nature of the difference? Why did it haunt me? Temporarily at least, to answer these questions, I had to root my fiction-writing self out of our exchanges. I had to teach myself to listen. Start fresh, clear the pipes, resist too facile an identification, tame the urge to take off with Robby's story and make it my own.

I understood all that, but could I break the habit? And even if I did learn to listen, wouldn't there be a point at which I'd have to take over the telling? Wasn't there something fundamental in my writing, in my capacity to function, that depended on flight, on escape? Wasn't another person's skin a hiding place, a place to work out anxiety, to face threats too intimidating to handle in any other fashion? Wasn't writing about people a way of exploiting them?

A stranger's gait, or eyes, or a piece of clothing can rivet my attention. Then it's like falling down to the center of the earth. Not exactly fear or panic but an uneasy, uncontrollable momentum, a sense of being swallowed, engulfed in blackness that has no dimensions, no fixed points. That boundless, incarcerating black hole is another person. The detail grabbing me functions as a door and it swings open and I'm drawn, sucked, pulled in head over heels till suddenly I'm righted again, on track again and the peculiarity, the ordinariness of the detail that usurped my attention becomes a window, a way of seeing out of another person's eyes, just as for a second it had been my way in. I'm scooting along on short, stubby legs and the legs are not anybody else's and certainly not mine, but I feel for a second what it's like to motor through the world atop these peculiar duck thighs and foreshortened calves and I know how wobbly the earth feels under those run-over-at-the-heel, split-seamed penny loafers. Then just as suddenly I'm back. I'm me again, slightly embarrassed, guilty because I've been trespassing and don't know how long I've been gone or if anybody noticed me violating somebody else's turf.

Do I write to escape, to make a fiction of my life? If I can't be trusted with the story of my own life, how could I ask my brother to trust me with his?

•   •   •

The business of making a book together was new for both of us. Difficult. Awkward. Another book could be constructed about a writer who goes to a prison to interview his brother but comes away with his own story. The conversations with his brother would provide a stage for dramatizing the writer's tortured relationship to other people, himself, his craft. The writer's motives, the issue of exploitation, the inevitable conflict between his role as detached observer and his responsibility as a brother would be at the center of such a book. When I stopped hearing Robby and listened to myself listening, that kind of book shouldered its way into my consciousness. I didn't like the feeling. That book compromised the intimacy I wanted to achieve with my brother. It was as obtrusive as the Wearever pen in my hand, the little yellow sheets of Yard Count paper begged from the pad of the guard in charge of overseeing the visiting lounge. The borrowed pen and paper (I was not permitted into the lounge with my own) were necessary props. I couldn't rely on memory to get my brother's story down and the keepers had refused my request to use a tape recorder, so there I was. Jimmy Olson, cub reporter, poised on the edge of my seat, pen and paper at ready, asking to be treated as a brother.

We were both rookies. Neither of us had learned very much about sharing our feelings with other family members. At home it had been assumed that each family member possessed deep, powerful feelings and that very little or nothing at all needed to be said about these feelings because we all were stuck with them and talk wouldn't change them. Your particular feelings were a private matter and family was a protective fence around everybody's privacy. Inside the perimeter of the fence each family member resided in his or her own quarters. What transpired in each dwelling was mainly the business of its inhabitant as long as nothing generated within an individual unit threatened the peace or safety of the whole. None of us knew how traditional West African families were organized or what values the circular shape of their villages embodied, but the living arrangements we had worked out among ourselves resembled the ancient African patterns. You were granted emotional privacy, independence, and space to commune with your feelings. You were encouraged to deal with as much as you could on your own, yet you never felt alone. The high wall of the family, the collective, communal reality of other souls, other huts like yours eliminated some of the dread, the isolation experienced when you turned inside and tried to make sense out of the chaos of your individual feelings. No matter how grown you thought you were or how far you believed you'd strayed, you knew you could cry *Mama* in the depths of the night and somebody would tend to you. Arms would wrap round you, a soft soothing voice lend its support. If not a flesh-and-blood mother then a mother in the form of song or story or a surrogate, Aunt Geral, Aunt Martha, drawn from the network of family numbers.

Privacy was a bridge between you and the rest of the family. But you had to learn to control the traffic. You had to keep it uncluttered, resist the temptation to cry wolf. Privacy in our family was a birthright, a union card granted with family membership. The card said you're one of us but also certified your separateness, your obligation to keep much of what defined your separateness to yourself.

An almost aesthetic consideration's involved. Okay, let's live together. Let's each build a hut and for security we'll arrange the individual dwellings in a circle and then build an outer ring to enclose the whole village. Now your hut is your own business, but let's in general agree on certain outward forms. Since we all benefit from the larger pattern, let's compromise, conform to some degree on the materials, the shape of each unit. Because symmetry and harmony please the eye. Let's adopt a style, one that won't crimp anybody's individuality, one that will buttress and enhance each member's image of what a living place should be.

So Robby and I faced each other in the prison visiting lounge as familiar strangers, linked by blood and time. But how do you begin talking about blood, about time? He's been inside his privacy and I've been inside mine, and neither of us in thirty-odd years had felt the need to exchange more than social calls. We shared the common history, values, and style developed within the tall stockade of family, and that was enough to make us care about each other, enough to insure a profound depth of mutual regard, but the feelings were undifferentiated. They'd seldom been tested specifically, concretely. His privacy and mine had been exclusive, sanctioned by family traditions. Don't get too close. Don't ask too many questions or give too many answers. Don't pry. Don't let what's inside slop out on the people around you.

The stories I'd sent to Robby were an attempt to reveal what I thought about certain matters crucial to us both. Our shared roots and destinies. I wanted him to know what I'd been thinking and how that thinking was drawing me closer to him. I was banging on the door of his privacy. I believed I'd shed some of my own.

We were ready to talk. It was easy to begin. Impossible. We were neophytes, rookies. I was a double rookie. A beginner at this kind of intimacy, a beginner at trying to record it. My double awkwardness kept getting in the way. I'd hidden the borrowed pen by dropping my hand below the level of the table where we sat. Now when in hell would be the right moment to raise it? To use it? I had to depend on my brother's instincts, his generosity. I had to listen, listen.

Luckily there was catching up to do. He asked me about my kids, about his son, Omar, about the new nieces and nephews he'd never seen. That helped. Reminded us we were brothers. We got on with it. Conditions in the prisons. Robby's state of mind. The atmosphere behind the prison walls had been particularly tense for over a year. A group of new, younger guards had instituted a get-tough policy. More strip searches, cell shakedowns, strict enforcement of penny-ante rules and regulations. Grown men treated like children by other grown men. Inmates yanked out of line and punished because a button is undone or hair uncombed. What politicians demanded in the free world was being acted out inside the prison. A crusade, a war on crime waged by a gang of gung-ho guards against men who were already certified casualties, prisoners of war. The walking wounded being beaten and shot up again because they're easy targets. Robby's closest friends, including Cecil and Mike, are in the hole. Others who were considered potential troublemakers had been transferred to harsher prisons. Robby was warned by a guard. We ain't caught you in the shit yet, but we will. We know what you're thinking and we'll catch you in it. Or put you in it. Got your buddies and we'll get you.

The previous summer, 1980, a prisoner, Leon Patterson, had been asphyxiated in his cell. He was an asthma sufferer, a convicted murderer who depended on medication to survive the most severe attacks of his illness. On a hot August afternoon when the pollution index had reached its highest count of the summer, Patterson was locked in his cell in a cell block without windows and little air. At four o'clock, two hours after he'd been confined to the range, he began to call for help. Other prisoners raised the traditional distress signal, rattling tin cups against the bars of their cells. Patterson's cries for help became screams, and his fellow inmates beat on the bars and shouted with him. Over an hour passed before any guards arrived. They carted away Patterson's limp body. He never revived and was pronounced dead at 10:45 that evening. His death epitomized the polarization in the prison. Patterson was seen as one more victim of the guards' inhumanity. A series of incidents followed in the ensuing year, hunger strikes, melees between guards and prisoners, culminating in a near massacre when the dog days of August hung once more over the prison.

One of the favorite tactics of the militant guards was grabbing a man from the line as the prisoners moved single-file through an archway dividing the recreation yard from the main cell blocks. No reason was given or needed. It was a simple show of force, a reminder of the guards' absolute power, their right to treat the inmates any way they chose, and do it with impunity. A sit-down strike in the prison auditorium followed one of the more violent attacks on an inmate. The prisoner who had resisted an arbitrary seizure and strip search was smacked in the face. He punched back and the guards jumped him, knocked him to the ground with their fists and sticks. The incident took place in plain view of over a hundred prisoners and it was the last straw. The victim had been provoked, assaulted, and surely would be punished for attempting to protect himself, for doing what any man would and should do in similar circumstances. The prisoner would suffer again. In addition to the physical beating they'd administered, the guards would attack the man's record. He'd be written up. A kangaroo court would take away his *good time,* thereby lengthening the period he'd have to wait before becoming eligible for probation or parole. Finally, on the basis of the guards' testimony he'd probably get a sixty-day sojourn in the hole. The prisoners realized it was time to take a stand. What had happened to one could happen to any of them. They rushed into the auditorium and locked themselves in. The prisoners held out till armed state troopers and prison guards in riot gear surrounded the building. Given the mood of that past year and the unmistakable threat in the new warden's voice as he repeated through a loudspeaker his refusal to meet with the prisoners and discuss their grievances, everybody inside the building knew that the authorities meant business, that the forces of law and order would love nothing better than an excuse to turn the auditorium into a shooting gallery. The strike was broken. The men filed out. A point was driven home again. Prisoners have no rights the keepers are bound to respect.

That was how the summer had gone. Summer was bad enough in the penitentiary in the best of times. Warm weather stirred the prisoners' blood. The siren call of the streets intensified. Circus time. The street blooming again after the long, cold winter. People outdoors. On their stoops. On the corners. In bright summer clothes or hardly any clothes at all. The free-world sounds and sights more real as the weather heats up. Confinement a torture. Each cell a hotbox. The keepers take advantage of every excuse to keep you out of the yard, to deprive you of the simple pleasure of a breeze, the blue sky. Why? So that the pleasant weather can be used as a tool, a boon to be withheld. So punishment has a sharper edge. By a perverse turn of the screw something good becomes something bad. Summer a bitch at best, but this past summer as the young turks among the guards ran roughshod over the prisoners, the prison had come close to blowing, to exploding like a piece of rotten fruit in the sun. And if the lid blew, my brother knew he'd be one of the first to die. During any large-scale uprising, in the first violent, chaotic seconds no board of inquiry would ever be able to reconstruct, scores would be settled. A bullet in the back of the brain would get rid of troublemakers, remove potential leaders, uncontrollable prisoners the guards hated and feared. You were supremely eligible for a bullet if the guards couldn't press your button. If they hadn't learned how to manipulate you, if you couldn't be bought or sold, if you weren't into drug and sex games, if you weren't cowed or depraved, then you were a threat.

Robby understood that he was sentenced to die. That all sentences were death sentences. If he didn't buckle under, the guards would do everything in their power to kill him. If he succumbed to the pressure to surrender dignity, self-respect, control over his own mind and body, then he'd become a beast, and what was good in him would die. The death sentence was unambiguous. The question for him became: How long could he survive in spite of the death sentence? Nothing he did would guarantee his safety. A disturbance in a cell block halfway across the prison could provide an excuse for shooting him and dumping him with the other victims. Anytime he was ordered to go with guards out of sight of other prisoners, his escorts could claim he attacked them, or attempted to escape. Since the flimsiest pretext would make murdering him acceptable, he had no means of protecting himself. Yet to maintain sanity, to minimize their opportunities to destroy him, he had to be constantly vigilant. He had to discipline himself to avoid confrontations, he had to weigh in terms of life and death every decision he made; he had to listen and obey his keepers' orders, but he also had to determine in certain threatening situations whether it was better to say no and keep himself out of a trap or take his chances that this particular summons was not the one inviting him to his doom. Of course to say no perpetuated his reputation as one who couldn't be controlled, a bad guy, a guy you never turn your back on, one of the prisoners out to get the guards. That rap made you more dangerous in the keepers' eyes and therefore increased the likelihood they'd be frightened into striking first. Saying no put you in no less jeopardy than going along with the program. Because the program was contrived to kill you. Directly or indirectly, you knew where you were headed. What you didn't know was the schedule. Tomorrow. Next week. A month. A minute. When would one of them get itchy, get beyond waiting a second longer? Would there be a plan, a contrived incident, a conspiracy they'd talk about and set up as they drank coffee in the guards' room or would it be the hair-trigger impulse of one of them who held a grudge, harbored an antipathy so elemental, so irrational that it could express itself only in a burst of pure, unrestrained violence?

If you're Robby and have the will to survive, these are the possibilities you must constantly entertain. Vigilance is the price of survival. Beneath the vigilance, however, is a gnawing awareness boiling in the pit of your stomach. You can be as vigilant as you're able, you can keep fighting the good fight to survive, and still your fate is out of your hands. If they decide to come for you in the morning, that's it. Your ass is grass and those minutes, and hours, days and years you painfully stitched together to put off the final reckoning won't matter at all. So the choice, difficult beyond words, to say yes or say no is made in light of the knowledge that in the end neither your yes nor your no matters. Your life is not in your hands.

The events, the atmosphere of the summer had brought home to Robby the futility of resistance. Power was absurdly apportioned all on one side. To pretend you could control your own destiny was a joke. You learned to laugh at your puniness, as you laughed at the stink of your farts lighting up your cell. Like you laughed at the seriousness of the masturbation ritual that romanticized, cloaked in darkness and secrecy, the simple, hungry shaking of your penis in your fist. You had no choice, but you always had to decide to go on or stop. It had been a stuttering, stop, start, maybe, fuck it, bitch of a summer, and now, for better or worse, we were starting up something else. Robby backtracks his story from Garth to another beginning, the house on Copeland Street in Shadyside where we lived when he was born.

I know that had something to do with it. Living in Shadyside with only white people around. You remember how it was. Except for us and them couple other families it was a all-white neighborhood. I got a thing about black. See, black was like the forbidden fruit. Even when we went to Freed's in Homewood, Geraldine and them never let me go no farther than the end of the block. All them times I stayed over there I didn't go past Mr. Conrad's house by the vacant lot or the other corner where Billy Shields and them stayed. Started to wondering what was so different about a black neighborhood. I was just a little kid and I was curious. I really wanted to know why they didn't want me finding out what was over there. Be playing with the kids next door to Freed, you know, Sonny and Gumpy and them, but all the time I'm wondering what's round the corner, what's up the street. Didn't care if it was *bad* or good or dangerous or what, I had to find out. If it's something bad I figured they would have told me, tried to scare me off. But nobody said nothing except, No. Don't you go no farther than the corner. Then back home in Shadyside nothing but white people so I couldn't ask nobody what was special about black. Black was a mystery and in my mind I decided I'd find out what it was all about. Didn't care if it killed me, I was going to find out.

One time, it was later, I was close to starting high school, I overheard Mommy and Geraldine and Sissy talking in Freed's kitchen. They was talking about us moving from Shadyside back to Homewood. The biggest thing they was worried about was me. How would it be for me being in Homewood and going to Westinghouse? I could tell they was scared. Specially Mom. You know know she is. She didn't want to move. Homewood scared her. Not so much the place but how I'd act if I got out there in the middle of it. She already knew I was wild, hard to handle. There'd be too much mess for me to get into in Homewood. She could see trouble coming.

And she was right. Me and trouble hooked up. See, it was a question of being somebody. Being my own person. Like youns had sports and good grades sewed up. Wasn't nothing I could do in school or sports that youns hadn't done already. People said, Here comes another Wideman. He's gon be a good student like his brothers and sister. That's the way it was spozed to be. I was another Wideman, the last one, the baby, and everybody knew how I was spozed to act. But something inside me said no. Didn't want to be like the rest of youns. Me, I had to be a rebel. Had to get out from under youns' good grades and do. Way back then I decided I wanted to be a star. I wanted to make it big. My way. I wanted the glamour. I wanted to sit high up.

Figured out school and sports wasn't the way. I got to thinking my brothers and sister was squares. Loved youall but wasn't no room left for me. Had to figure out a new territory. I had to be a rebel.

Along about junior high I discovered Garfield. I started hanging out up on Garfield Hill. You know, partying and stuff in Garfield cause that's where the niggers was. Garfield was black, and I finally found what I'd been looking for. That place they was trying to hide from me. It was heaven. You know. Hanging out with the fellows. Drinking wine and trying anything else we could get our hands on. And the ladies. Always a party on the weekends.

Had me plenty sweet little soft-leg Garfield ladies. Niggers run my butt off that hill more than a couple times behind messing with somebody's piece but I'd be back next weekend. Cause I'd found heaven. Looking back now, wasn't much to Garfield. Just a rinky-dink ghetto up on a hill, but it was the street. I'd found my place.

Having a little bit of a taste behind me I couldn't wait to get to Homewood. In a way I got mad with Mommy and the rest of them. Seemed to me like they was trying to hold me back from a good time. Seemed like they just didn't want me to have no fun. That's when I decided I'd go on about my own business. Do it my way. Cause I wasn't getting no slack at home. They still expected me to be like my sister and brothers. They didn't know I thought youns was squares. Yeah. I knew I was hipper and groovier than youns ever thought of being. Streetwise, into something. Had my own territory and I was bad. I was a rebel. Wasn't following in nobody's footsteps but my own. And I was a hip cookie, you better believe it. Wasn't a hipper thing out there than your brother, Rob. I couldn't wait for them to turn me loose in Homewood.

Me being the youngest and all, the baby in the family, people always said, ain't he cute. That Robby gon be a ladykiller. Been hearing that mess since day one so ain't no surprise I started to believing it. Youns had me pegged as a lady's man so that's what I was. The girls be talking the same trash everybody else did. Ain't he cute. Be petting me and spoiling me like I'm still the baby of the family and I sure ain't gon tell them stop. Thought I was cute as the girls be telling me. Thought sure enough, I'm gon be a star. I loved to get up and show my behind. Must have been good at it too cause the teacher used to call me up in front of the class to perform. The kids'd get real quiet. That's probably why the teacher got me up. Keep the class quiet while she nods off. Cause they'd listen to me. Sure nuff pay attention.

Performing always come natural to me. Wasn't nervous or nothing. Just get up and do my thing. They liked for me to do impressions. I could mimic anybody. You remember how I'd do that silly stuff around the house. Anybody I'd see on TV or hear on a record I could mimic to a T. Bob Hope, Nixon, Smokey Robinson, Ed Sullivan. White or black. I could talk just like them or sing a song just like they did. The class yell out a famous name and I'd do the one they wanted to hear. If things had gone another way I've always believed I could have made it big in show business. If you could keep them little frisky kids in Liberty School quiet you could handle any audience. Always could sing and do impressions. You remember Mom asking me to do them for you when you came home from college.

I still be performing. Read poetry in the hole. The other fellows get real quiet and listen. Sing down in there too. Nothing else to do, so we entertain each other. They always asking me to sing or read. "Hey, Wideman. C'mon man and do something." Then it gets quiet while they waiting for me to start. Quiet and it's already dark. You in your own cell and can't see nobody else. Barely enough light to read by. The other fellows can hear you but it's just you and them walls so it feels like being alone much as it feels like you're singing or reading to somebody else.

Yeah. I read my own poems sometimes. Other times I just start in on whatever book I happen to be reading. One the books you sent me, maybe. Fellows like my poems. They say I write about the things they be thinking. Say it's like listening to their own self thinking. That's cause we all down there together. What else you gonna do but think of the people on the outside. Your woman. Your kids or folks, if you got any. Just the same old sad shit we all be thinking all the time. That's what I write and the fellows like to hear it.

Funny how things go around like that. Go round and round and keep coming back to the same place. Teacher used to get me up to pacify the class and I'm doing the same thing in prison. You said your teachers called on you to tell stories, didn't they? Yeah. It's funny how much we're alike. In spite of everything I always believed that. Inside. The feeling side. I always believed we was the most alike out of all the kids. I see stuff in your books. The kinds of things I be thinking or feeling.

Your teachers got you up, too. To tell stories. That's funny, ain't it.

I listen to my brother Robby. He unravels my voice. I sit with him in the darkness of the Behavioral Adjustment Unit. My imagination creates something like a giant seashell, enfolding, enclosing us. Its inner surface is velvet-soft and black. A curving mirror doubling the darkness. Poems are Jean Toomer's petals of dusk, petals of dawn. I want to stop. Savor the sweet, solitary pleasure, the time stolen from time in the hole. But the image I'm creating is a trick of the glass. The mirror that would swallow Robby and then chime to me: You're the fairest of them all. The voice I hear issues from a crack in the glass. I'm two or three steps ahead of my brother, making fiction out of his words. Somebody needs to snatch me by the neck and say, Stop. Stop and listen, listen to him.

The Behavioral Adjustment Unit is, as one guard put it, "a maximum-security prison within a maximum-security prison." The "Restricted Housing Unit" or "hole" or "Home Block" is a squat, two-story cement building containing thirty-five six-by-eight-foot cells. The governor of Pennsylvania closed the area in 1972 because of "inhumane conditions," but within a year the hole was reopened. For at least twenty-three hours a day the prisoners are confined to their cells. An hour of outdoor exercise is permitted only on days the guards choose to supervise it. Two meals are served three hours apart, then nothing except coffee and bread for the next twenty-one. The regulation that limits the time an inmate can serve in the BAU for a single offense is routinely sidestepped by the keepers. "Administrative custody" is a provision allowing officials to cage men in the BAU indefinitely. Hunger strikes are one means the prisoners have employed to protest the harsh conditions of the penal unit. Hearings prompted by the strikes have produced no major changes in the way the hole operates. Law, due process, the rights of the prisoners are irrelevant to the functioning of this prison within a prison. Robby was sentenced to six months in the BAU because a guard suspected he was involved in an attempted escape. The fact that a hearing, held six months later, established Robby's innocence, was small consolation since he'd already served his time in the hole.

Robby tells me about the other side of being the youngest: Okay, you're everybody's pet and that's boss, but on the other hand you sometimes feel you're the least important. Always last. Always bringing up the rear. You learn to do stuff on your own because the older kids are always busy, off doing their things, and you're too young, left behind because you don't fit, or just because they forget you're back here, at the end, bringing up the rear. But when orders are given out, you sure get your share. "John's coming home this weekend. Clean up your room." Robby remembers being forced to get a haircut on the occasion of one of my visits. Honor thy brother. Get your hair cut, your room rid up, and put on clean clothes. He'll be here with his family and I don't want the house looking like a pigpen.

I have to laugh at the image of myself as somebody to get a haircut for. Robby must have been fit to be tied.

Yeah, I was hot. I mean, you was doing well and all that, but shit, you were my brother. And it was my head. What's my head got to do with you? But you know how Mommy is. Ain't no talking to her when her mind gets set. Anything I tried to say was "talking *back*," so I just went ahead to the man and got my ears lowered.

I was trying to be a rebel but back then the most important thing still was what the grown-ups thought about me. How they felt meant everything. Everything. Me and Tish and Dave were the ones at home then. You was gone and Gene was gone so it was the three of us fighting for attention. And we fought. Every crumb, everytime something got cut up or parceled out or it was Christmas or Easter, we so busy checking out what the other one got wasn't hardly no time to enjoy our own. Like a dogfight or cat fight all the time. And being the youngest I'm steady losing ground most the time. Seemed like to me, Tish, and Dave the ones everybody talked about. Seemed like my time would never come. That ain't the way it really was, I know. I had my share cause I was the baby and ain't he cute and lots of times I know I got away with outrageous stuff or got my way cause I could play that baby mess to the hilt. Still it seemed like Dave and Tish was the ones really mattered. Mommy and Daddy and Sis and Geral and Big Otie and Ernie always slipping some change in their pockets or taking them to the store or letting them stay over all night in Homewood. I was a jealous little rascal. Sometimes I thought everybody thought I was just a spoiled brat. I'd say damn all youall. I'd think, Go on and love those square turkeys, but one day I'll be the one coming back with a suitcase full of money and a Cadillac. Go on and love them good grades. Robby gon do it his own way.

See, in my mind I was Superfly. I'd drive up slow to the curb. My hog be half a block long and these fine foxes in the back. Everybody looking when I ease out the door clean and mean. Got a check in my pocket to give to Mom. Buy her a new house with everything in it new. Pay her back for the hard times. I could see that happening as real as I can see your face right now. Wasn't no way it wasn't gon happen. Rob was gon make it big. I'd be at the door, smiling with the check in my hand and Mommy'd be so happy she'd be crying.

Well, it's a different story ain't it. Turned out different from how I used to think it would. The worst thing I did, the thing I feel most guilty behind is stealing Mom's life. It's like I stole her youth. Can't nothing change that. I can't give back what's gone. Robbing white people didn't cause me to lose no sleep back then. Couldn't feel but so bad about that. How you gon feel sorry when society's so corrupt, when everybody got their hand out or got their hand in somebody else's pocket and ain't no rules nobody listens to if they can get away with breaking them? How you gon apply the rules? It was dog eat dog out there, so how was I spozed to feel sorry if I was doing what everybody else doing. I just got caught is all. I'm sorry about that, and damned sorry that guy Stavros got killed, but as far as what I did, as far as robbing white people, ain't no way I was gon torture myself over that one.

I tried to write Mom a letter. Not too long ago. Should say I did write the letter and put it in an envelope and sent it cause that's what I did, but I be crying so much trying to write it I don't know what wound up in that letter. I wanted Mom to know I knew what I'd done. In a way I wanted to say I was sorry for spoiling her life. After all she did for me I turned around and made her life miserable. That's the wrongest thing I've done and I wanted to say I was sorry but I kept seeing her face while I was writing the letter. I'd see her face and it would get older while I was looking. She'd get this old woman's face all lined and wrinkled and tired about the eyes. Wasn't nothing I could do but watch. Cause I'd done it and knew I done it and all the letters in the world ain't gon change her face. I sit and think about stuff like that all the time. It's better now. I think about other things too. You know like trying to figure what's really right and wrong, but there be days the guilt don't never go away.

I'm the one made her tired, John. And that's my greatest sorrow. All the love that's in me she created. Then I went and let her down.

When you in prison you got plenty of time to think, that's for damned sure. Too much time. I've gone over and over my life. Every moment. Every little thing again and again. I lay down on my bed and watch it happening over and over. Like a movie. I get it all broke down in pieces then I break up the pieces then I take the pieces of the pieces and run them through my hands so I remember every word a person said to me or what I said to them and weigh the words till I think I know what each and every one meant. Then I try to put it back together. Try to understand where I been. Why I did what I did. You got time for that in here. Time's all you got in here.

Going over and over things sometimes you can make sense. You know.

Like the chinky-chinky Chinaman sittin' on the fence. You put it together and you think, yes. That's why I did thus and so. Yeah. That's why I lost that job or lost that woman or broke that one's heart. You stop thinking in terms of something being good or being evil, you just try to say this happened because that happened because something else came first. You can spend days trying to figure out just one little thing you did. People out there in the world walk around in a daze cause they ain't got time to think. When I was out there, I wasn't no different. Had this Superfly thing and that was the whole bit. Nobody could tell me nothing.

Seems like I should start the story back in Shadyside. In the house on Copeland Street. Nothing but white kids around. Them little white kids had everything, too. That's what I thought, anyway. Nice houses, nice clothes. They could buy pop and comic books and candy when they wanted to. We wasn't that bad off, but compared to what them little white kids had I always felt like I didn't have nothing. It made me kinda quiet and shy around them. Me knowing all the time I wanted what they had. Wanted it bad. There was them white kids with everything and there was the black world Mommy and them was holding back from me. No place to turn, in a way. I guess you could say I was stuck in the middle. Couldn't have what the white kids in Shadyside had, and I wasn't allowed to look around the corner for something else. So I'd start the story with Shadyside, the house on Copeland.

Another place to start could be December 29, 1950—the date of Robby's birth. For some reason—maybe my mother and father were feuding, maybe we just happened to be visiting my grandmother's house when my mother's time came—the trip to the hospital to have Robby began from Finance Street, from the house beside the railroad tracks in Homewood. What I remember is the bustle, people rushing around, yelling up and down the stairwell, doors slammed, drawers being opened and shut. A cold winter day so lots of coats and scarves and galoshes. My mother's face was very pale above the dark cloth coat that made her look even bigger than she was, carrying Robby the ninth month. On the way out the front door she stopped and stared back over her shoulder like she'd forgotten something. People just about shoving her out the house. Lots of bustle and noise getting her through the crowded hallway into the vestibule. Somebody opened the front door and December rattled the glass panes. Wind gusting and whistling, everybody calling out last-minute instructions, arrangements, goodbyes, blessings, prayers. My mother's white face calm, hovering a moment above it all as she turned back toward the hall, the stairs where I was planted, halfway to the top. She didn't find me, wasn't looking for me. A thought had crossed her mind and carried her far away. She didn't know why so many hands were rushing her out the door. She didn't hear the swirl of words, the icy blast of wind. Wrapped in a navy-blue coat, either Aunt Aida's or an old one of my grandmother's, which didn't have all its black buttons but stretched double over her big belly, my mother was wondering whether or not she'd turned off the water in the bathroom sink and deciding whether or not she should return up the stairs to check. Something like that crossing her mind, freeing her an instant before she got down to the business of pushing my brother into the world.

Both my grandfathers died on December 28. My grandmother died just after dawn on December 29. My sister lost a baby early in January. The end of the year has become associated with mournings, funerals; New Year's Day arrives burdened by a sense of loss, bereavement. Robby's birthday became tainted. To be born close to Christmas is bad enough in and of itself. Your birthday celebration gets upstaged by the orgy of gift giving on Christmas Day. No matter how many presents you receive on December 29, they seem a trickle after the Christmas flood. Plus there's too much excitement in too brief a period. Parents and relatives are exhausted, broke, still hung over from the Christmas rush, so there just isn't very much left to work with if your birthday comes four short days after Jesus'. Almost like not having a birthday. Or even worse, like sharing it with your brothers and sister instead of having the private oasis of your very own special day. So Robby cried a lot on his birthdays. And it certainly wasn't a happy time for my mother. Her father, John French, died the year after Robby was born, one day before Robby's birthday. Fifteen years and a day later Mom would lose her mother. The death of the baby my sister was carrying was a final, cruel blow, scaring my mother, jinxing the end of the year eternally. She dreaded the holiday season, expected it to bring dire tidings. She had attempted at one point to consecrate the sad days, employ them as a period of reflection, quietly, privately memorialize the passing of the two people who'd loved her most in the world. But the death of my father's father, then the miscarriage within this jinxed span of days burst the fragile truce my mother had effected with the year's end. She withdraws into herself, anticipates the worse as soon as Christmas decorations begin appearing. In 1975, the year of the robbery and murder, Robby was on the run when his birthday fell. My mother was sure he wouldn't survive the deadly close of the year.

Robby's birthday is smack dab in the middle of the hard time. Planted like a flag to let you know the bad time's arrived. His adult life, the manhood of my mother's last child, begins as she is orphaned, as she starts to become nobody's child.

I named Robby. Before the women hustled my mother out the door into a taxi, I jumped down the stairs, tugged on her coattail, and reminded her she'd promised it'd be Robby. No doubt in my mind she'd bring me home a baby brother. Don't ask me why I was certain. I just was. I hadn't even considered names for a girl. Robby it would be. Robert Douglas. Where the Douglas came from is another story, but the Robert came from me because I liked the sound. Robert was formal, dignified, important. Robert. And that was nearly as nice as the chance I'd have to call my little brother Rob and Robby.

He weighed seven pounds, fourteen ounces. He was born in Allegheny Hospital at 6:30 in the evening, December 29, 1950. His fingers and toes were intact and quite long. He was a plump baby. My grandfather, high on Dago

Red, tramped into the maternity ward just minutes after Robby was delivered. John French was delighted with the new baby. Called him Red. A big fat little red nigger.

December always been a bad month for me. One the worst days of my life was in December. It's still one the worst days in my life even after all this other mess. Jail. Running. The whole bit. Been waiting to tell you this a long time. Ain't no reason to hold it back no longer. We into this telling-the-truth thing so mize well tell it all. I'm still shamed, but there it is. You know that TV of youall's got stolen from Mommy's. Well, I did it. Was me and Henry took youall's TV that time and set the house up to look like a robbery. We did it. Took my own brother's TV. Couldn't hardly look you in the face for a long time after we done it. Was pretty sure youall never knowed it was me, but I felt real bad round youns anyway. No way I was gon confess though. Too shamed. A junkie stealing from his own family. See. Used to bullshit myself. Say I ain't like them other guys. They stone junkies, they hooked. Do anything for a hit. But me, I'm Robby. I'm cool. I be believing that shit, too. Fooling myself. You got to bullshit yourself when you falling. Got to do it to live wit yourself. See but where it's at is you be doing any goddam thing for dope. You hooked and that's all's to it. You a stone junkie just like the rest.
Always wondered if you knew I took it.

Mom was suspicious. She knew more than we did then. About the dope. The seriousness of it. Money disappearing from her purse when nobody in the house but the two of you. Finding a syringe on the third floor. Stuff like that she hadn't talked about to us yet. So your stealing the TV was a possibility that came up. But to me it was just one of many. One of the things that could have happened along with a whole lot of other possibilities we sat around talking about. An unlikely possibility as far as I was concerned. Nobody wanted to believe it was you. Mom tried to tell us how it *could* be but in my mind you weren't the one. Haven't thought about it much since then. Except as one of those things that make me worry about Mom living in the house alone. One of those things making Homewood dangerous, tearing it down.

I'm glad I'm finally getting to tell you. I never could get it out. Didn't want you to think I'd steal from my own brother. Specially since all youall done to help me out. You and Judy and the kids. Stealing youall's TV. Don't make no sense, does it? But if we gon get the story down mize well get it all down.
It was a while ago. Do you remember the year?
Nineteen seventy-one was Greens. When we robbed Greens and got in big trouble so it had to be the year before that, 1970. That's when it had to be. Youns was home for Christmas. Mommy and them was having a big party. A reunion kinda cause all the family was together. Everybody home for the

first time in a long time. Tish in from Detroit. David back from Philly. Youns in town. My birthday, too. Party spozed to celebrate my birthday too, since it came right along in there after Christmas. Maybe that's why I was feeling so bad. Knowing I had a birthday coming and knowing at the same time how fucked up I was.

Sat in a chair all day. I was hooked for the first time. Good and hooked. Didn't know how low you could feel till that day. Cold and snowing outside. And I got the stone miseries inside. Couldn't move. Weak and sick. Henry too. He was wit me in the house feeling bad as I was. We was two desperate dudes. Didn't have no money and that Jones down on us.

Mommy kept asking, What's wrong with you two? She was on my case all day. What ails you, Robby? Got to be about three o'clock. She come in the room again: You better get up and get some decent clothes on. We're leaving for Geral's soon. See cause it was the day of the big Christmas party. Geral had baked a cake for me. Everybody was together and they'd be singing Happy Birthday Robby and do. The whole bit an I'm spozed to be guest of honor and can't even move out the chair. Here I go again disappointing everybody. Everybody be at Geral's looking for me and Geral had a cake and everything. Where's Robby? He's home dying cause he can't get no dope.

 Feeling real sorry for myself but I'm hating me too. Wrapped up in a blanket like some damned Indin. Shivering and wondering how the hell Ima go out in this cold and hustle up some money. Wind be howling. Snow pitching a bitch. There we is. Stuck in the house. Two pitiful junkies. Scheming how we gon get over. Some sorry-assed dudes. But it's comical in a way too, when you look back. To get well we need to get money. And no way we gon get money less we go outside and get sicker than we already is. Mom peeking in the room, getting on my case. Get up out that chair, boy. What are you waiting for? We're leaving in two minutes.

So I says, Go on. I ain't ready. Youns go on. I'll catch up with youns at Geral's.

Mommy standing in the doorway. She can't say too much, cause youns is home and you ain't hip to what's happening. C'mon now. We can't wait any longer for you. Please get up. Geral baked a cake for you. Everybody's looking forward to seeing you.

Seem like she stands there a hour begging me to come. She ain't mad no more. She's begging. Just about ready to cry. Youall in the other room. You can hear what she's saying but you can't see her eyes and they tearing me up. Her eyes begging me to get out the chair and it's tearing me up to see her hurting so bad, but ain't nothing I can do. Jones sitting on my chest and ain't no getup in me.

Youns go head, Mommy. I'll be over in a little while. Be there to blow them candles out and cut the cake.

She knew better. Knew if I didn't come right then, chances was I wasn't coming at all. She knew but wasn't nothing she could do. Guess I knew I was lying too. Nothing in my mind cept copping that dope. Yeah, Mom. Be there to light them candles. I'm grinning but she ain't smiling back. She knows I'm in trouble, deep trouble. I can see her today standing in the doorway begging me to come with youns.

But it ain't meant to be. Me and Henry thought we come up with a idea. Henry's old man had some pistols. We was gon steal em and hock em. Take the money and score. Then we be better. Wouldn't be no big thing to hustle some money, get the guns outa hock. Sneak the pistols back in Henry's house, everything be alright. Wouldn't even exactly be stealing from his old man. Like we just borrowing the pistols till we score and take care business. Henry's old man wouldn't even know his pistols missing. Slick. Sick as we was, thinking we slick.

A hundred times. Mom musta poked her head in the room a hundred times.

What's wrong with you?

Like a drum beating in my head. What's wrong with you? But the other thing is stronger. The dope talking to me louder. It says get you some. It says you ain't never gon get better less you cop.

We waited long as we could but it didn't turn no better outside. Still snowing. Wind shaking the whole house. How we gon walk to Henry's and steal them pistols? Henry live way up on the hill. And the way up Tokay then you still got a long way to go over into the projects. Can't make it. No way we gon climb Tokay. So then what? Everybody's left for Geral's. Then I remembers the TV youns brought. A little portable Sony black-and-white, right? You and Judy sleeping in Mom's room and she has her TV already in there, so the Sony ain't unpacked. Saw it sitting with youall's suitcases over by the dresser. On top the dresser in a box. Remembered it and soon's I did I knew we had to have it. Sick as I was that TV had to go. Wouldn't really be stealing. Borrow it instead of borrowing the pistols. Pawn it. Get straight. Steal some money and buy it back. Just borrowing youall's TV.

Won't take me and Henry no time to rob something and buy back the TV. We stone thieves. Just had to get well first so we could operate. So we took youns TV and set the house up to look like a robbery.

I'm remembering the day. Wondering why it had slipped completely from my mind. I feel like a stranger. Yet as Robby talks, my memory confirms details of his recollection. I admit, yes. I was there. That's the way it was. But *where* was I? Who was I? How did I miss so much?

His confessions make me uncomfortable. Instead of concentrating on what he's revealing, I'm pushed into considering all the things I could be confessing, should be confessing but haven't and probably won't ever. I feel hypocritical. Why should I allow my brother to repose a confidence in me when it's beyond my power to reciprocate? Shouldn't I confess that first? My embarrassment, my uneasiness, the clinical, analytic coldness settling over me when I catch on to what's about to happen.

I have a lot to hide. Places inside myself where truth hurts, where incriminating secrets are hidden, places I avoid, or deny most of the time. Pulling one piece of that debris to the surface, airing it in the light of day doesn't accomplish much, doesn't clarify the rest of what's buried down there. What I feel when I delve deeply into myself is chaos. Chaos and contradiction. So how up front can I get? I'm moved by Robby's secrets. The heart I have is breaking. But what that heart is and where it is I can't say. I can't depend on it, so he shouldn't. Part of me goes out to him. Heartbreak is the sound of ice cracking. Deep. Layers and layers muffling the sound.

I listen but I can't trust myself. I have no desire to tell everything about myself so I resist his attempt to be up front with me. The chaos at my core must be in his. His confession pushes me to think of all the stuff I should lay on him. And that scares the shit out of me. I don't like to feel dirty, but that's how I feel when people try to come clean with me.

Very complicated and very simple too. The fact is I don't believe in clean. What I know best is myself and, knowing what I know about myself, clean seems impossible. A dream. One of those better selves occasionally in the driver's seat but nothing more. Nothing to be depended upon. A self no more or less in control than the countless other selves who each, for a time, seem to be running things.

Chaos is what he's addressing. What his candor, his frankness, his confession echo against. Chaos and time and circumstances and the old news, the bad news that we still walk in circles, each of us trapped in his own little world. Behind bars. Locked in our cells.

But my heart can break, does break listening to my brother's pain. I just remember differently. Different parts of the incident he's describing come back. Strange thing is my recollections return through the door he opened. My memories needed his. Maybe the fact that we recall different things is crucial. Maybe they are foreground and background, propping each other up. He holds on to this or that scrap of the past and I listen to what he's saved and it's not mine, not what I saw or heard or felt. The pressure's on me then. If his version of the past is real, then what's mine? Where does it fit? As he stitches his memories together they bridge a vast emptiness. The time lost enveloping us all. Everything. And hearing him talk, listening to him try to make something of the nothing, challenges me. My sense of the emptiness playing around his words, any words, is intensified. Words are nothing and everything. If I don't speak I have no past. Except the nothing, the emptiness. My brother's memories are not mine, so I have to break into the silence with my own version of the past. My words. My whistling in the dark. His story freeing me, because if forces me to tell my own.

I'm sorry you took so long to forgive yourself. I forgave you a long time ago, in advance for a sin I didn't even know you'd committed. You lied to me. You stole from me. I'm in prison now listening because we committed those sins against each other countless times. I want your forgiveness. Talking about debts you owe me makes me awkward, uneasy. We remember different things. They set us apart. They bring us together searching for what is lost, for the meaning of difference, of distance.

For instance, the Sony TV. It was a present from Mort, Judy's dad. When we told him about the break-in and robbery at Mom's house, he bought us another Sony. Later we discovered the stolen TV was covered by our home-owner's policy even though we'd lost it in Pittsburgh. A claim was filed and eventually we collected around a hundred bucks. Not enough to buy a new Sony but a good portion of the purchase price. Seemed a lark when the check arrived. Pennies from heaven. One hundred dollars free and clear since we already had the new TV Mort had surprised us with. About a year later one of us, Judy or I, was telling the story of the robbery and how well we came out of it. Not until that very moment when I caught a glimpse of Mort's face out of the corner of my eye did I realize what we'd done. Judy remembers urging me to send Mort that insurance check and she probably did, but I have no recollection of an argument. In my mind there had never been an issue. Why shouldn't we keep the money? But when I saw the look of sur-prise and hurt flash across Mort's face, I knew the insurance check should have gone directly to him. He's a generous man and probably would have re-fused to accept it, but we'd taken advantage of his generosity by not offering the check as soon as we received it. Clearly the money belonged to him. Unasked, he'd replaced the lost TV. I had treated him like an institution, one of those faceless corporate entities like the gas company or IRS. By then, by the time I saw the surprise in Mort's face and understood how selfishly, thoughtlessly, even corruptly I'd behaved, it was too late. Offering Mort a hundred dollars at that point would have been insulting. Anything I could think of saying sounded hopelessly lame, inept. I'd fucked up. I'd injured someone who'd been nothing but kind and generous to me. Not intention-ally, consciously, but that only made the whole business worse in a way be-cause I'd failed him instinctively. The failure was a measure of who I was. What I'd unthinkingly done revealed something about my relationship to Mort I'm sure he'd rather not have discovered. No way I could take my ac-tion back, make it up. It reflected a truth about who I was.

That memory pops right up. Compromising, ugly. Ironically, it's also about stealing from a relative. Not to buy dope, but to feed a habit just as self-destructive. The habit of taking good fortune for granted, the habit of blind self-absorption that allows us to believe the world owes us everything and we are not responsible for giving anything in return. Spoiled children. The good coming our way taken as our due. No strings attached.

Lots of other recollections were triggered as Robby spoke of that winter and the lost TV. The shock of walking into a burgled house. How it makes you feel unclean. How quickly you lose the sense of privacy and security a house, any place you call home, is supposed to provide. It's a form of rape. Forced entry, violation, brutal hands defiling what's personal, and pre-cious. The aftershock of seeing your possessions strewn about, broken. Fear gnawing at you because what you thought was safe isn't safe at all. The worst has happened and can happen again. Your sanctuary has been destroyed. Any time you walk in your door you may be greeted by the same scene. Or worse. You may stumble upon the thieves themselves. The symbolic rape of your dwelling place enacted on your actual body. Real screams. Real blood. A knife at your throat. A stranger's weight bearing down.

Mom put it in different words but she was as shaken as I was when we walked into her house after Geral's party. Given what I know now, she must have been even more profoundly disturbed than I imagined. A double bind. Bad enough to be ripped off by anonymous thieves. How much worse if the thief is your son? For Mom the robbery was proof Robby was gone. Somebody else walking round in his skin. Mom was wounded in ways I hadn't begun to guess at. At the root of her pain were your troubles, the troubles stealing you away from her, from all of us. The troubles thick in the air as that snow you are remembering, the troubles falling on your head and mine, troubles I refused to see. . . .

Snowing and the hawk kicking my ass but I got to have it. TV's in a box under my arm and me and Henry walking down Bennett to Homewood Avenue. Need thirty dollars. Thirty dollars buy us two spoons. Looking for One-Arm Ralph, the fence. Looking for him or that big white Cadillac he drives.

Wind blowing snow all up in my face. Thought I's bout to die out there. Nobody on the avenue. Even the junkies and dealers inside today. Wouldn't put no dog out in weather like that. So cold my teeth is chattering, talking to me. No feeling in my hands but I got to hold on to that TV. Henry took it for a little while so's I could put both my hands in my pockets. Henry lookin bad as I'm feeling. Thought I was gon puke. But it's too goddamn cold to puke.

Nobody in sight. Shit and double shit's what I'm thinking. They got to be somewhere. Twenty-four hours a day, seven days a week somebody doing business. Finally we seen One-Arm Ralph come out the Hi Hat.

This TV, man, Lemme hold thirty dollars on it.

Ralph ain't goin for it. Twenty-five the best he say he can do. Twenty-five don't do us no good. It's fifteen each for a spoon. One spoon ain't enough. We begging the dude now. We got to have it, man. Got to get well. We good for the money. Need thirty dollars for two hits. You get your money back.

Too cold to be standing around arguing. The dude go in his pocket and give us the thirty. He been knowing us. He know we good for it. I'm telling him don't sell the TV right away. Hold it till tomorrow we have his money. He say, You don't come back tonight you blow it. Ralph a hard motherfucker and don't want him changing his mind again about the thirty so I say, We'll have the money tonight. Hold the TV till tonight, you get your money.

Now all we got to do is find Goose. Goose always be hanging on the set. Ain't nobody else dealing, Goose be out there for his people. Goose an alright dude, but even Goose ain't out in the street on no day like this. I know the cat stays over the barbershop on Homewood Avenue. Across from Murphy's

five-and-ten. I goes round to the side entrance, the alleyway tween Homewood and Kelly. That's how you get to his place. Goose lets me in and I cop.
For some reason I turn up the alley and go toward Kelly instead of back to
Homewood the way I came in. Don't know why I did it. Being slick. Being
scared. Henry's waiting on the avenue for me so I go round the long way just
in case somebody pinned him. I can check out the scene before I come back
up the avenue. That's probably what I'm thinking. But soon's I turn the corner of Kelly, Bam. Up pops the devil.
   Up against the wall, Squirrel.
   It's Simon and Garfunkel, two jive undercover cops. We call them that,
you dig. Lemme tell you what kind of undercover cops these niggers was.
Both of em wearing Big Apple hats and jackets like people be wearing then
but they both got on police shoes. Police brogans you could spot a mile away.
But they think they slick. They disguised, see. Apple hats and hippy-dip
jackets. Everybody knew them chumps was cops. Ride around in a big Continental. Going for bad. Everybody hated them cause everybody knew they in
the dope business. They bust a junkie, take his shit and sell it. One them had
a cousin. Biggest dealer on the Hill. You know where he getting half his
dope. Be selling again what Simon and Garfunkel stole from junkies. Some
rotten dudes. Liked to beat on people too. Wasn't bad enough they robbing
people. They whipped heads too.
   Soon's I turn the corner they got me. Bams me up against the wall. They
so lame they think they got Squirrel. Think I'm Squirrel and they gon make a
big bust. We got you, Squirrel. They happy, see, cause Squirrel dealing heavy
then. Thought they caught them a whole shopping bag of dope.
   Wearing my double-breasted pea coat. Used to be sharp but it's raggedy
now. Ain't worth shit in cold weather like that. Pockets got holes and the
dope dropped down in the lining so they don't find nothing the first time
they search me. Can tell they mad. Thought they into something big and
don't find shit. Looking at each other like, What the fuck's going on here? We
big-time undercover supercops. This ain't spozed to be happening to us.
They roughing me up too. Pulling my clothes off and shit. Hands all down in
my pockets again. It's freezing and I'm shivering but these fools don't give a
fuck. Rip my goddamn pea coat off me. Shaking it. Tearing it up. Find the
two packs of dope inside the lining this time. Ain't what they wanted but
they pissed off now. Take what they can get now.
   What's this, Squirrel? Got your ass now.
   Slinging me down the alley. I'm stone sick now. Begging these cats for
mercy. Youall got me. You got your bust. Lemme snort some the dope, man.
Little bit out each bag. You still got your bust. I'm dying. Little taste fore you
lock me up.
   Rotten motherfuckers ain't going for it. They see I'm sick as a dog. They
know what's happening. Cold as it is, the sweat pouring out me. It's sweat
but it's like ice. Like knives cutting me. They ain't give back my coat.
Snowing on me and I'm shaking and sweating and sick. They can see all this.

They know what's happening but ain't no mercy in these dudes. Henry's cross the street watching them bust me. Tears in his eyes. Ain't nothing he can do. The street's empty. Henry's bout froze too. Watching them sling my ass in their Continental. Never forget how Henry looked that day. All alone on the avenue. Tears froze in his eyes. Seeing him like that was a sad thing. Last thing I saw was him standing there across Homewood Avenue before they slammed me up in the car. Like I was in two places. That's me standing there in the snow. That's me so sick and cold I'm crying in the empty street and ain't a damn thing I can do about it.

By the time they get me down to the Police Station, down to No. 5 in East Liberty, I ain't no more good, sure nuff. Puking. Begging them punks not to bust me. Just bout out my mind. Must have been a pitiful sight. Then's when Henry went to Geral's house and scratched on the window and called David out on the porch. That's when youall found out I was in trouble and had to come down and get me. Right in the middle of the party and everything. Henry's sick too and he been walking round Homewood in the cold didn't know what to do. But he's my man. He got to Geral's so youall could come down and help me. Shamed to go in so he scratched on the window to get Dave on the porch.

Party's over and youns go to Mommy's and on top everything else find the house broke in and the TV gone. All the stuff's going through my mind. I'm on the bottom now. Low as you can go. Had me in a cell and I was lying cross the cot staring at the ceiling. Bars all round. Up cross the ceiling too. Like in a cage in the zoo. Miserable as I could be. All the shit staring me in the face. You're a dope fiend. You stole your brother's TV. You're hurting Mommy again. Hurting everybody. You're sick. You're nothing. Looking up at the bars on the ceiling and wondering if I could tie my belt there. Stick my neck in it. I wanted to be dead.

Tied my belt to the ceiling. Then this guard checking on me he starts to hollering.

What you doing? Hey, Joe. This guy's trying to commit suicide.

They take my clothes. Leave me nothing but my shorts. I'm lying there shivering in my underwear and that's the end. In a cage naked like some goddamn animal. Shaking like a leaf. Thinking maybe I can beat my head against the bars or maybe jump down off the bed head first on the concrete and bust my brains open. Dead already. Nothing already. Low as I can go.

Must have passed out or gone to sleep or something, cause it gets blurry round in here. Don't remember much but they gave back my clothes and took me Downtown and there was a arraignment next morning.

Mommy told me later, one the cops advised her not to pay my bond. Said the best thing for him be to stay in jail awhile. Let him see how it is inside. Scare im. But I be steady beggin. Please, please get me out here. Youns got soft-hearted. Got the money together and paid the bond.

What would have happened if you left me to rot in there till my hearing? Damned if I know. I probably woulda went crazy, for one thing. I do know that. Know I was sick and scared and cried like a baby for Mommy and them to get me out. Don't think it really do no good letting them keep me in there. I mean the jail's a terrible place. You can get everything in jail you get in the street. No different. Cept in jail it's more dangerous cause you got a whole bunch of crazies locked up in one little space. Worse than the street. Less you got buddies in there they tear you up. Got to learn to survive quick. Cause jail be the stone jungle. Call prison the House of Knowledge cause you learns how to be a sure nuff criminal. Come in lame you leave knowing all kinds of evil shit. You learn quick or they eats you up. That's where it's at. So you leave a person in there, chances are they gets worse. Or gets wasted.

But Mom has that soft heart anyway and she ain't leaving her baby boy in no miserable jail. Right or wrong, she ain't leaving me in no place like that. Daddy been talking to Simon and Garfunkel. Daddy's hip, see. He been out there in the street all his life and he knows what's to it. Knows those guys and knows how rotten they is. Ain't no big thing they catch one pitiful little junkie holding two spoons. They wants dealers. They wants to look good Downtown. They wants to bust dealers and cop beaucoup dope so's they can steal it and get rich. Daddy makes a deal with them rats. Says if they drop the charges he'll make me set up Goose. Finger Goose and then stay off Homewood Avenue. Daddy says I'll do that so they let me go.

No way Ima squeal on Goose but I said okay, it's a deal. Soon's I was loose I warned Goose. Pretend like I'm trying to set him up so the cops get off my ass but Goose see me coming know the cops is watching. Helped him, really. Like a lookout. Them dumb motherfuckers got tired playing me. Simon got greedy. Somebody set him up. He got busted for drugs. Still see Garfunkel riding round in his Continental but they took him off the avenue. Too dangerous. Everybody hated them guys.

My lowest day. Didn't know till then I was strung out. That's the first time I was hooked. Started shooting up with Squirrel and Bugs Johnson when Squirrel be coming over to Mom's sometimes. Get up in the morning, go up to the third floor, and shoot up. They was like my teachers. Bugs goes way back. He started with Uncle Carl. Been shooting ever since. Dude's old now. Call him King of the Junkies, he been round so long. Bugs seen it all. You know junkies don't hardly be getting old. Have their day then they gone. Don't see em no more. They in jail or dead. Junkie just don't have no long life. Fast life but your average dopehead ain't round long. Bugs different. He was a pal of Uncle Carl's back in the fifties. Shot up together way back then. Now here he is wit Squirrel and me, still doing this thing. Everybody knows Bugs. He the King.

Let me shoot up wit em but they wouldn't let me go out in the street and hustle wit em. Said I was too young. Too green.

Learning from the King, see. That's how I started the heavy stuff. Me and Squirrel and Bugs first thing in the morning when I got out of bed. Mom was gone to work. They getting themselves ready to hit the street. Make that money. Just like a job. Wasn't no time before I was out there, too. On my own learning to get money for dope. Me and my little mob. We was ready. Didn't take us no time fore we was gangsters. Gon be the next Bugs Johnson. Gon make it to the top.

Don't take long. One day you the King. Next day dope got you and it's the King. You ain't nothing. You lying there naked bout to die and it don't take but a minute. You fall and you gone in a minute. That's the life. That's how it is. And I was out there. I know. Now they got me jammed up in the slammer. That's the way it is. But nobody could tell me nothing then. Hard head. You know. Got to find out for myself. Nobody could tell me nothing. Just out of high school and my life's over and I didn't even know it. Too dumb. Too hardheaded. I was gon do it my way. Youns was square. Youns didn't know nothing. Me, I was gon make mine from the curb. Hammer that rock till I was a supergangster. Be the one dealing the shit. Be the one running the junkies. That's all I knew. Street smarts. Stop being a chump. Forget that nickel-dime hoodlum bag. Be a star. Rise to the top.

You know where that got me. You heard that story. Here I sit today behind that story. Nobody to blame but my ownself. I know that now. But things was fucked up in the streets. You could fall in them streets, Brother. Low. Them streets could snatch you bald-headed and turn you around and wring you inside out. Streets was a bitch. Wake up some mornings and you think you in hell. Think you died and went straight to hell. I know cause I been there. Be days I wished I was dead. Be days worser than that.

• • • • • • • • • • •

QUESTIONS FOR A SECOND READING

1. Wideman frequently interrupts this narrative to talk about the problems he is having as a writer. He says, for example, "The hardest habit to break, since it was the habit of a lifetime, would be listening to myself listen to him. That habit would destroy any chance of seeing my brother on his terms; and seeing him in his terms, learning his terms, seemed the whole point of learning his story" (p. 667). What might Wideman mean by this—listening to himself listen? As you reread "Our Time," note the sections in which Wideman speaks to you directly as a writer. What is he saying? Where and how are you surprised by what he says?

   Wideman calls attention to the problems he faces. How does he try to solve them? Are you sympathetic? Do the solutions work, so far as you are concerned?

2. Wideman says that his mother had a remarkable capacity for "[trying] on the other person's point of view." Wideman tries on another point of view himself, speaking to us in the voice of his brother Robby. As you reread this selection, note the passages spoken in Robby's voice and try to infer Robby's point of view from them. If you look at the differences between John and

Robby as evidenced by the ways they use language to understand and represent the world, what do you notice?

3. Wideman talks about three ways he could start Robby's story: with Garth's death, with the house in Shadyside, and with the day of Robby's birth. What difference would it make in each case if he chose one and not the others? What's the point of presenting all three?

ASSIGNMENTS FOR WRITING

1. At several points in the essay, Wideman discusses his position as a writer, telling Robby's story, and he describes the problems he faces in writing this piece (or in "reading" the text of his brother's life). You could read this selection, in other words, as an essay about reading and writing.

   Why do you think Wideman talks about these problems here? Why not keep quiet and hope that no one notices? Choose three or four passages in which Wideman refers directly or indirectly to his work as a writer, and write an essay defining the problems Wideman faces and explaining why you think he raises them as he does. Finally, what might this have to do with your work as a writer—or as a student in this writing class?

2. Wideman tells Robby's story in this excerpt, but he also tells the story of his neighborhood, Homewood; of his mother; and of his grandfather John French. Write an essay retelling one of these stories and explaining what it might have to do with Robby and John's.

3. "Our Time" is a family history, but it is also a meditation on the problems of writing family histories—or, more generally, the problems of writing about the "real" world. There are sections in "Our Time" where Wideman speaks directly about the problems he faces as a writer. And the unusual features in the prose stand as examples of how he tried to solve these problems—at certain points Wideman writes as an essayist, at others like a storyteller; at certain points he switches voices and/or typeface; the piece breaks up into sections, it doesn't move from introduction to conclusion. Think of these as part of Wideman's method, as his way of working on the problems of writing as practical problems, where he is trying to figure out how to do justice to his brother and his story.

   As you prepare to write this assignment, read back through the selection to think about it as a way of doing one's work, as a project, as a way of writing. What are the selection's key features? What is its shape or design? How does Wideman, the writer, do what he does? And you might ask: What would it take to learn to write like this? How is this writing related to the writing taught in school? Where and how might it serve you as a student?

   Once you have developed a sense of Wideman's method, write a Wideman-like piece of your own, one that has the rhythm and the moves, the shape and the design of "Our Time." As far as subject matter is concerned, let Wideman's text stand as an invitation (inviting you to write about family and neighborhood) but don't feel compelled to follow his lead. You can write about anything you want. The key is to follow the essay as an example of a *way* of writing—moving slowly, turning this way and that, combining stories and reflection, working outside of a rigid structure of thesis and proof.

MAKING CONNECTIONS

1. Various selections in this book can be said to be "experimental" in their use of nonfiction prose. These are essays that don't do what essays are supposed to do. They break the rules. They surprise. The writers work differently than most writers. They imagine a different project (or they imagine their project differently).

   Although any number of the other selections might be read alongside "Our Time," here are some that have seemed interesting to our students: Patricia J. Williams, "And We Are Not Married" (p. 694); Virginia Woolf, "A Room of One's Own" (p. 719); Susan Griffin, "Our Secret" (p. 319); and the essays by Gloria Anzaldúa (p. 22).

   Choose one selection to compare with Wideman's, and write an essay in which you both explain and explore the projects represented by the two pieces of writing. What do they do? (You should assume that you are presenting this information to someone who has not seen the essays. You will need, that is, to be careful in choosing and presenting examples.) And what is to be gained (or what is at stake) in writing this way? (Would you, for example, argue that these forms of writing should be taught in college?)

2. Both Harriet Jacobs, in "Incidents in the Life of a Slave Girl" (p. 374), and Wideman speak directly to the reader. They seem to feel that there are problems of understanding in the stories they have to tell and in their relations to their subjects and audiences. Look back over both stories and mark the passages in which the authors address you as a reader. Ask yourself why the authors might do this. What do they reveal about their work as writers at such moments? How would you describe the relationship each writer has with her or his subject matter? As a reader of each of these stories, how would you describe the relationship between the authors and yourself as the "audience"?

   After you have completed this preliminary research, write an essay in which you discuss these two acts of writing *as* acts of writing—that is, as stories in which the writers are self-conscious about their work as writers and make their audience aware of their self-consciousness. What differences or connections exist between you, the authors, and their subject matter? How do these differences or connections influence you as a reader?

PATRICIA J.
WILLIAMS

*P*ATRICIA J. WILLIAMS (b. 1951) *is a law professor at Columbia University.*
She was an undergraduate at Wellesley College, received her J.D. from Har-
vard University, and was a fellow in the prestigious School of Criticism and Theory
at Dartmouth College. Williams is one of a group of young legal scholars who bring
to the law arguments about interpretation and authority drawn from literary theory.
She is, in a sense, a lawyer who has also learned to think like a literary critic.
Williams has written widely on legal issues and on race. She is a contributing editor
to The Nation, *a popular political magazine, and has written for popular publica-*
tions such as Ms., *but what brought her to national attention was her remarkable*
book, The Alchemy of Race and Rights *(1990). Williams's new book,* The
Rooster's Egg: On the Persistence of Prejudice, *was published in 1995.*

Williams's work challenges the way identity, including racial identity, is repre-
sented in traditional legal thinking. What makes her work so remarkable is the way
its arguments are enacted in its prose, a prose where questions about identity, and
the person, continually intrude upon the solidities of the law and the security of a
system of thought that relies on generalization, where one case must stand for many.
Williams demonstrates how deeply ways of thinking are rooted in ways of writing;
any serious attempt to reconceive traditional habits of thought requires experiments
with the conventions of prose. In this sense, Williams can be read along with the

other powerful American prose stylists, including Ralph Waldo Emerson, Gertrude Stein, Toni Morrison, Adrienne Rich, and John Edgar Wideman.

Barbara Johnson, Mellon Professor of the Humanities at Harvard, has said,

> Williams has invented a whole new genre of writing. Not autobiography, or legal theory, or editorial, or allegory, it partakes of all of these. It seeks to restore texture and connection to the social fabric, not to draw up "sides."

And Henry Louis Gates, Jr., head of the African American studies department at Harvard, has said about The Alchemy of Race and Rights,

> Williams's book crisscrosses so many boundaries that you forget where they used to be. Which part is "theory," which "autobiography"? Which is the example, which the proposition? You might argue, in fact, that Alchemy is first and foremost a meditation on example. For good reason: Case law is all about example. It's founded on the legal doctrine of stare decisis ("Let the decision stand"), of respecting precedent, of leaving well enough alone.
>
> "Most of us," she writes, "were taught that our heartfelt instincts would subvert the law and defeat the security of a well-ordered civilization; but faithful adherence to the word of law, to stare decisis and clearly stated authority, would lead as a matter of course to a bright clear world in which those heartfelt instincts would, like the Wizard of Oz, be waiting." Williams's problem is that she can't help wondering about things she's been instructed to pay no attention to. Who is that man behind the curtain anyway, she wants to know.

Williams combines her professional knowledge of the law, its standard examples and standard interpretations, with examples drawn from newspapers and from her experience as an African American, someone often caught in a variety of competing roles or "subject positions." She is acutely aware of the impossible positions she is sometimes put in because she is an African American woman in a professional world dominated by white men, where one can think of a lawyer or a woman or an African American, but never all at once, never as a single identity. Williams questions the assumptions that underlie the legal system's "rules" about what counts as evidence, legitimacy, a "right." She is, in this sense, a poststructuralist thinker: someone who looks at a system of thought and questions the conditions of its possibility.

The essay that follows was one of several such essays that Williams drew upon for The Alchemy of Race and Rights. *It is offered as a series of journal entries, but these are journal entries with footnotes, as the prose also turns to more formal and public modes of discussion. As you read this selection, you will find yourself in the midst of stories, arguments, and "musings," some coming one on top of another, and in no predictable order, all of them unwilling to be read easily, quickly summed up, or filed away in a proper category. Each case, for Williams, begs to be mulled over, considered this way and that. It is prose that thinks about what it is doing, about the "ideology of style," and it invites a similar form of reflection from its readers.*

And We Are Not Married

A Journal of Musings upon Legal Language and the Ideology of Style

This, after my skin will have been peeled off; but I would behold God from my flesh.

— Job 19:26

Journal Entry of 28 May 1988
(The Phantom Room)

I am at a conference on race/gender/class and critical legal thought. The discussion topic is Harvard Law School Professor Derrick Bell's new book, *And We Are Not Saved.*[1] The chapter being discussed is entitled "The Race-Charged Relationship of Black Men and Black Women." The chapter deals generally with the social construction of antimiscegenation laws; forced sterilization and castration; the structure of the black family; teenage pregnancy; and the disproportionate number of black men in U.S. prisons. But the precise subject within the chapter which has caught everyone's attention is a surprising little parable entitled "The Chronicle of the Twenty-seventh-Year Syndrome." The chronicle is structured as an interiorized dream had by Professor Bell; he then tells it to an exteriorized dream-vision-anima figure named Geneva Crenshaw. In the dream, Twenty-seventh-Year Syndrome is an affliction affecting only young black professional women: if they are not married to, or have not yet received a marriage proposal from, a black man by their twenty-seventh year, they fall into a deep coma from which they awaken only after several weeks, physically intact but having lost all their professional skills.

This story has scared everyone in the room, including me, to death. The conversation is very, very anxious and abstract.

The discussion rages around my ears. Big words rush through the air, careening dangerously close to my head. Defining feminism. Undefining feminism. Women/men. Blackwoe/men. Black/white. Biology/social construction. Male creation/control of sexuality. Challenge/structure. Post–legal realist feminist/feminist. Identify/define/understand. Privilege of white womanhood/self-flagellation. Problematic/useful. Critique of patriarchy/pervasive abstracted universal wholeness. Actual/historical pathways to possibility and/or of perversion. And the cabbage head of hegemony.

I/me am sitting quietly in the vortex, trying to recall the last time I heard such definitional embattlement; suddenly a sharp voice cuts through all the rest and asks: "All this stuff about black people being socially constructed—I don't *experience* them as socially constructed. Who the hell does?" I think about that for a while; the memory that comes to me is the following:

About two years ago, New York merchants started installing buzzers and locks on the doors of their stores. Favored particularly by smaller stores and boutiques, the buzzer systems were rationalized as screening devices to reduce the incidence of robbery. When the buzzer sounds, if the face at the door looks "desirable," the door is unlocked. If the face is that of an "undesirable," the door stays locked.

The installation of these buzzers happened very swiftly in New York; stores that had always had their doors wide open suddenly became "exclusive" or received people "by appointment only." I discovered them and their meaning one Saturday in 1986. I was shopping in Soho and saw in the window of Benetton's, of all places, a sweater that I wanted to purchase for my mother. I pressed my round brown face to the store window and my finger to the buzzer, seeking admittance. A narrow-eyed white youth glared at me, evaluating me. After about five seconds, he mouthed, "We're closed" and turned his back on me. It was two Saturdays before Christmas; it was one o'clock in the afternoon; there were several white people in the store who appeared to be shopping for things for *their* mothers.

I was enraged. At that moment I wanted to break all of the windows in the store and *take* lots of sweaters for my mother. In the flicker of his judgmental gray eyes, that saleschild had reduced my brightly sentimental, joy-to-the-world, pre-Christmas spree to a shambles. He had snuffed my sense of humanitarian catholicity, and there was nothing I could do to snuff his, without simply making a spectacle of myself. His refusal to let me into the store was an outward manifestation of his never having let someone like me into the realm of his reality. He had no connection, no reference to me, and no desire to acknowledge me even at the estranged level of arm's-length transactor.

The violence of my desire to burst into Benetton's is probably quite apparent. I often wonder if the violence and the exclusionary hatred are equally apparent in the repeated public urgings that blacks understand the buzzer system by putting themselves in the shoes of white store owners[2]—that, in effect, blacks look into the mirror of frightened white faces for the reality of their undesirability, and that then blacks would "just as surely conclude that [they] would not let [themselves] in under similar circumstances."[3]

When this happened to me, I turned to a form of catharsis I have always found quite healing: I typed up as much of the story as I have just reiterated, made a big poster of it, put a nice colorful border around it, and, after Benetton's was truly closed, I stuck it to their big sweater-filled window. I exercised my First Amendment rights to place my business with them right out in the street. (I call this aspect of my literary endeavors *guerrilla writing*. I mark the spots at which I observe some racial or other indignity. In instances in which I am reduced to anonymity,[4] I do it anonymously;[5] and I always use a little piece of gum rubber with which to attach the posters so that they are easily removable without causing the slightest property damage.)

Anyway, that was the first telling of this story. The second telling came a few months later at a symposium on excluded voices sponsored by the University of Miami Law Review for which I was invited to submit an article. I sat down and wrote an essay summing up my feelings about being excluded from Benetton's and analyzing "how the rhetoric of increased privatization, in response to racial issues, functions as the rationalizing agent of public unaccountability, and ultimately, irresponsibility."[6] Weeks later, I received the first edit. From the first page to the last, my fury had been carefully carved out. My rushing, run-on rage had been reduced to simple declarative sentences. The active personal had been inverted in favor of the passive impersonal. My words were different; they spoke to me upside down. I was afraid to read too much of it at a time—meanings rose up at me oddly, stolen and strange.

A week and a half later, I received the second edit. All reference to Benetton's had been deleted because, according to the editors and the faculty advisor, it was "defamatory"; they feared "harassment and liability"; they said printing it would be "irresponsible."[7] I called them and offered to supply a footnote attesting to this as my personal experience at one particular location and of a buzzer system not limited to Benetton's; the editors told me that they were not in the habit of publishing things that were "unverifiable." (I could not help but wonder, in this refusal even to let me file an affidavit, what it would take to make my experience "verifiable." The testimony of an independent white bystander?—a requirement in fact imposed in U.S. Supreme Court holdings through the first part of the century.[8])

Two days *after* the piece was sent to press, I received copies of the final page proofs. All reference to my race had been eliminated because "we have concluded that . . . [it] is inconsistent with our editorial policy" to permit descriptions of physiognomy. "I realize," wrote one editor, "that this was a very personal experience, but any reader will know what you must have looked like when standing at that window."[9] In a telephone conversation with them, I ranted on wildly about the significance of such an omission. "It's irrelevant," another editor explained in a voice gummy with soothing and patience; "It's nice and poetic," but it doesn't "advance the discussion of any principle. . . . This is a law review, after all."[10] Frustrated, I accused him of censorship; calmly, he assured me it was not. "This is just a matter of style," he said with firmness and finality.[11]

Ultimately, I did convince them that mention of my race was a central force in making sense of all the subsequent text; that my whole story became one of extreme paranoia without the knowledge that I am black; or that it became one in which the reader had to fill in the gap by assumption, presumption, prejudgment, prejudice. What was most interesting to me in this experience was how the blind application of principles of neutrality, through the device of omission, acted either to make me look crazy or to make the reader participate in the mental habits of cultural bias.[12]

That was the second telling of my story. The third telling came last April when I was invited to participate in a conference on equality and difference sponsored by the University of West Virginia Law School. I retold my sad tale of exclusion from Soho's most glitzy and colorful boutique, focusing, in this version, on the characterization of Miami's editing process as a consequence of an ideology of style rooted in a social text of neutrality. I opined:

> Law and legal writing aspire to formalized, color-blind, liberal ideals. Neutrality is the standard for assuring these ideals; yet the adherence to it is often determined by reference to an aesthetic of uniformity, in which difference is simply omitted. For example, when segregation was eradicated from the American lexicon, its omission led many actually to believe that racism therefore no longer existed. Race neutrality in law has become the presumed antidote for race bias in real life. With the entrenchment of the notion of race neutrality came attacks on the concept of affirmative action and the rise of reverse discrimination suits. Blacks, for so many generations deprived of jobs based on the color of our skin, are now told that we ought to find it demeaning to be *hired* based on the color of our skin. Such is the silliness of simplistic either-or inversions as remedies to complex problems.
>
> What *is* truly demeaning in this era of double-speak-no-evil is going on interviews and not getting hired because someone doesn't think *we'll* be comfortable. It is demeaning not to get promoted because we're judged "too weak," then putting in a lot of energy the next time and getting fired because we're "too strong." It is demeaning to be told what we find demeaning. It is very demeaning to stand on street corners unemployed and begging. It is downright demeaning to have to explain why we haven't been employed for months and then watch the job go to someone who is "more experienced." It is outrageously demeaning that none of this can be called racism, even if it happens only to, or to large numbers of, black people; as long as it's done with a smile, a handshake, and a shrug; as long as the phantom word *race* is never used.
>
> The image of *race* as a phantom word came to me after I moved into my late godmother's home. In an attempt to make it my own, I cleared the bedroom for painting. The following morning the room asserted itself, came rushing and raging at me through the emptiness, exactly as it had been for twenty-five years: one day filled with profuse and overwhelming complexity; the next day filled with persistently recurring memories. The shape of the past came to haunt me, the shape of the emptiness confronted me each time I was about to enter the

room. The force of its spirit drifts like an odor throughout the house.

The power of that room, I have thought since, is very like the power of racism as status quo: it is deep, angry, eradicated from view, but strong enough to make everyone who enters the room walk around the bed that isn't there, avoiding the phantom as they did the substance, for fear of bodily harm. They do not even know they are avoiding; they defer to the unseen shapes of things with subtle responsiveness, guided by an impulsive awareness of nothingness and the deep knowledge and denial of witchcraft at work.

The phantom room is to me symbolic of the emptiness of formal equal opportunity, particularly as propounded by President Reagan and his Civil Rights Commission. Blindly formalized constructions of equal opportunity are the creation of a space that is filled in by a meandering stream of unguided hopes, dreams, fantasies, fears, recollections. They are the presence of the past in imaginary, imagistic form—the phantom-roomed exile of our longing.

It is thus that I strongly believe in the efficacy of programs and paradigms like affirmative action. Blacks are the objects of a constitutional omission that has been incorporated into a theory of neutrality. It is thus that omission is really a form of expression, as oxymoronic as that sounds: racial omission is a literal part of original intent; it is the fixed, reiterated prophecy of the Founding Fathers. It is thus that affirmative action *is* an affirmation; the affirmative act of hiring—or hearing—blacks is a recognition of individuality that replaces blacks as a social statistic, that is profoundly interconnective to the fate of blacks and whites either as subgroups or as one group. In this sense, affirmative action is as mystical and beyond the self as an initiation ceremony. It is an act of verification and of vision. It is an act of social as well as professional responsibility.[13]

Thus spake I to the assembled faculty and students of the University of West Virginia.

The following morning, I opened the *Dominion Post*, the Morgantown local newspaper, to find that the event of my speech had commanded two columns on the front page of the "Metro" section. I quote only the opening lines: "Affirmative action promotes prejudice by denying the status of women and blacks, instead of affirming them as its name suggests. So said New York City attorney Patricia Williams to an audience Wednesday."[14]

[Here end my journal notes for 28 May 1988. In the margin, there is a note to myself from myself: eventually, it says, I should try to pull all these threads together into yet another law review article. The problem, of course, will be that in the hierarchy of law review citation, the article in the *Dominion Post* will have more authoritative weight about me, as a so-called "primary resource" on me, than I will have; it will take precedence over my own citation of the "unverifiable" testimony of my speech.]

Journal Entry of 29 May 1988
(The Men's Room)

Back at the Critical Legal Studies conference. For the second day in a row, the question about black women and men as social constructions hangs in the air like a fuzzy gray cloud. I think: I have always known that my raciality is socially constructed, and I experience it as such. I feel my black self as an eddy of conflicted meanings—and meaninglessness—in which my self can get lost; in which agency and consent are hopelessly relativized as a matter of constant motion. This is how I experience social constructions of race. This sense of motion, this constant windy sound of manipulation whistling in my ears is a reminder of society's constant construction, and reconstruction, of my blackness.

Somewhere at the center, my heart gets lost. I transfigure the undesirability of my racial ambiguity into the necessity of deference, the accommodation of condescension. It is very painful when I permit myself to see all this. It is terrifying when this truth announces itself to me. I shield myself from it, wherever possible. Indeed, at the conference it feels too dangerous to say any of this aloud, so I continue to muse to myself, pretending to doze. I am awakened suddenly and completely to a still and deadly serious room: someone has asked me to comment upon the rape of black women and the death of our children.

Unprepared and slightly dazed, I finessed the question with statistics and forgotten words; what actually comes to my mind, however, is one of the most tragically powerful embodiments of my ambiguous, tenuous, social positioning: the case of Tawana Brawley, a fifteen-year-old black girl from Wappinger Falls, New York. In late November 1987, after a four-day disappearance, she was found in a vacant lot, clothed only in a shirt and a plastic garbage bag into which she had apparently crawled; she was in a dazed state, responding neither to noise, cold, nor ammonia; there was urine-soaked cotton stuffed in her nose and ears; her hair had been chopped off; there were cigarette burns over one-third of her body; the words *KKK* and *nigger* had been inscribed on her torso; and her body was smeared with dog feces.[15] This much is certain—*certain* because there were objective third persons to testify as to her condition in that foundling state (and independent "objective" testimony is apparently what is required before experience gets to be labeled *truth*);[16] and this much is certainly worth the conviction that she has been the victim of some unspeakable crime. No matter how she got there. No matter who did it to her—and even if she did it to herself. Her condition was clearly the expression of some crime against her—some tremendous violence, some great violation that challenges comprehension.

It is this much that I grieve about, all told. The rest of the story is lost or irrelevant in the worst of all possible ways.

But there is a second version of this story. On 14 July 1988, New York State Attorney General Robert Abrams stated "There may not have been any crime committed here."[17] A local television call-in poll showed that the vast majority of New Yorkers—the vast majority of any potential jury pool in other words—agreed with him. Most people, according to the poll, felt either that if she were raped it was "consensual" (as cruel an oxymoron as ever was) or that she "did it to herself" (as though self-mutilation and attempted suicide are just free enterprise, privatized matters of no social consequence, with reference to which the concern of others is an invasion of privacy, an imprisoning of choice).[18] It was a surprise to no one, therefore, when a New York grand jury concluded that Tawana Brawley had made the whole thing up.[19] It is instructive to examine some of the circumstances that surround these conflicting interpretations.

When Tawana Brawley was finally able to tell her story—she remained curled in a fetal position for several days after she was found—she indicated, by nodding or shaking her head to questions posed by police, that she had been kidnapped and raped by six white men.[20] The white men she implicated included the district attorney of Wappinger Falls, a highway patrolman, and a local police officer. This accusation was not only the first, but also the last, public statement Tawana Brawley ever made.[21]

What replaced Tawana's story was a thunderous amount of media brouhaha, public offerings of a thousand and one other stories, fables, legends, and myths. A sample of these enticing distractions includes:

- Tawana's mother, Glenda Brawley (who fled to the sanctuary of a church to avoid arrest for failing to testify before a grand jury and to protest the failure of the same grand jury to subpoena the men named by her daughter);[22]
- Tawana's stepfather (with whom she was reportedly disaffected; from whom she had allegedly run away on prior occasions; by whom she had allegedly been beaten many times before; and who served seven years for manslaughter in the death of his first wife, whom he stabbed fourteen times, and while awaiting trial for that much, then shot and killed);[23]
- Tawana's boyfriend (who was serving time on drug charges in an upstate "facility" and whom she had gone to visit shortly before her disappearance);[24]
- Tawana's lawyers, civil rights activists Alton Maddox and C. Vernon Mason (who advised their client not to cooperate with investigating authorities until an independent prosecutor was appointed to handle the case);[25]
- Tawana's spiritual counselor, the Reverend Al Sharpton (described variously as a "minister without a congregation,"[26] a drug informant for the FBI,[27] a man who had a long and well-publicized history of involvement

in the wiretapping of civil rights leaders,[28] yet, *mirabile dictu*, a sudden but "trusted advisor" to the Brawley family.[29] Al Sharpton, tumbling off the stage in a bout of fisticuffs with Roy Innis on the neoconservative Morton Downey television program, brought to you Live! from the Apollo Theater.[30] Al Sharpton, railing against the court order holding Glenda Brawley in contempt, saying to the television cameras, "Their arms are too short to box with God").

It was Al Sharpton who proceeded to weave the story where Tawana left off. It was Al Sharpton who proceeded to implicate the Irish Republican Army, a man with a missing finger, and the Mafia. And it was Al Sharpton who spirited Tawana Brawley off into hiding shortly after the police officer whom Tawana Brawley implicated in her rape committed suicide.

Al Sharpton led Tawana Brawley off into hiding. More hiding. As though it were a metareenactment of her kidnap; as though it were a metametareenactment of her disappearing into the middle of her own case. It was like watching the Pied Piper of Harlem, this slowly replayed television spectacle of Tawana led off by the hand, put in a car, and driven to "a secret location"; this dance into thin air which could be accounted for by nothing less than sheer enchantment. I had a terrible premonition, as I watched, that Tawana Brawley would never be heard from again.

Tawana Brawley has not been heard from again. From time to time there are missives from her advisors to the world: Tawana is adjusting well to her new school; Tawana wants to be a model; Tawana approves of the actions of her advisors; and, most poignantly, Tawana is "depressed," so her advisors are throwing her a *party*.

But the stories in the newspapers are no longer about Tawana anyway. They are all about black manhood and white justice—a contest of wills among her attorneys, the black community, and the New York State prosecutor's office. Since Tawana's statement implicated a prosecutor, an issue was the propriety of her case being handled through the usual channels rather than having a special unit set up to handle this and other allegations of racial violence. But even this issue was not able to hold center stage with all the thunder and smoke of raucous male outcry, curdling warrior accusations, the clash and flash of political swords and shields—typified by Governor Cuomo's gratuitous offer to talk to Tawana personally; by Al Sharpton's particularly gratuitous statement that Tawana might show up at her mother's contempt hearing because "Most children want to be in court to say good-bye to their mothers before they go to jail";[31] by television personality Phil Donahue's interview with Glenda Brawley which he began with "No one wants to jump on your bones and suggest that you are not an honorable person but"; by the enlistment of the support of the Reverend Louis Farrakhan and a good deal of other anti-Semitic insinuation; by the mishandling and loss of key evidence by investigating authorities; by the commissioning of a self-styled Black Army to encircle Glenda Brawley on the courthouse steps; by the refusal of the New

York Attorney General's office to take seriously the request for an independent prosecutor; and by the testimony of an associate of Sharpton's, a former police officer named Perry McKinnon, that neither Mason, Maddox, nor Sharpton believe Tawana's story. (On television, I hear this latter story reported in at least three different forms: McKinnon says Tawana lied; McKinnon says Sharpton lied about believing Tawana's story; and/or McKinnon says that Mason and Maddox made up the whole thing in order to advance their own political careers. Like a contest or a lottery with some drunken solomonic gameshow host at the helm, the truth gets sorted out by a call-in poll: Channel 7, the local ABC affiliate, puts the issue to its viewers. Do you believe Sharpton? Or do you believe McKinnon? I forgot to listen to the eleven o'clock news, when the winner and the weather were to have been announced.)

To me, the most ironic thing about this whole bad business—as well as the thread of wisdom which runs at the heart of the decision not to have Tawana Brawley testify—is that were she to have come out of her hiding and pursued trial in the conventional manner, I have no doubt that she would have undergone exactly what she did go through, in the courts and in the media; it's just that without her, the script unfolded at a particularly abstract and fantastical level. But the story would be the same: wild black girl who loves to lie, who is no innocent,[32] and whose wiles are the downfall of innocent, jaded, desperate white men; this whore-lette, the symbolic consort of rapacious, saber-rattling, buffoonish black men asserting their manhood, whether her jailbird boyfriend, her smooth-headed FBI drug-buster informant of a spiritual advisor; her grand-standing, pretending-to-be-professional unethically boisterous, so-called lawyers who have yet to establish "a *single* cognizable legal claim,"[33] and so forth.

Tawana's awful story has every black woman's worst fears and experiences wrapped into it. Few will believe a black woman who has been raped by a white man.[34] If they believe that a white man even wanted her, no one will believe that she is not a whore. (White women are prostitutes; black women are whores. White women sell themselves because they are jaded and desperate; black women *whore,* as a way of being, as an innateness of sootiness and contamination, as a sticky-sweet inherency of black womanhood persistently imaged as overripe fruit [e.g., melons]; so they whore, according to this fantasy script, as easily as they will cut your throat or slit open said ripe melon for said deep sweet fruit, spitting out afterward a predictable stream of blood and seeds and casual curses.) Black women whore because it is sensual and lazy and vengeful. How can such a one be raped? Or so the story goes.

It is not any easier when a black woman is raped by a black man (many of the newspapers have spun eager nets of suspicion around Tawana's stepfather[35] and/or a boyfriend); black-on-black rape is not merely the violation of one woman by one man: it is a sociological event, a circus of stereotypification.[36] It is a trial of the universalized black man against the lusty black female. The intimacy of rape becomes a public display full of passion, pain, and gutsy blues.

702

Tawana Brawley herself remains absent from all this. She is a shape, a hollow, an emptiness at the center.[37]

There is no respect or wonder for her silence. The world that created her oppression now literally countenances it, filling the suffering of her void with sacrilegious noise, clashing color, serial tableaux of lurid possibility. Truth, like a fad, takes on a life of its own, independent of action and limited only by the imagination of a plurality of self-proclaimed visionaries; untruth becomes truth through belief, and disbelief untruths the truth. The world turns upside down; the quiet, terrible, nearly invisible story of her suffering may never emerge from the boiling noise that overtook the quest for "what happened" and polarized it into the bizarre and undecidable litigation of "something happened" *versus* "nothing happened."

In the face of all this, there is some part of me that wants this child to stay in hiding, some part of me that understands the instinct to bury her rather than expound. Exposure is the equivalent of metarape, as hiding with Al Sharpton is the equivalent of metakidnap. It feels as though there are no options other than hiding or exposing. There is danger everywhere for her. There is no shelter, no protection. There is no medicine circle for her, no healing society, no stable place to testify and be heard, as the unburdening of one heart.

Journal Entry of 30 May 1988
(The Women's Room)

The world is full of black women who have never been heard from again. Take Maxine, for example. According to one version, Los Angeles Municipal Court Judge Maxine Thomas's nervous breakdown was inexplicable.[38] She was as strong a black woman as ever conjured; a celebrated, savvy judge who presided over hundreds of mostly white male judges. Yet one day she just snapped and had to be carted from her chambers, helpless as a baby.[39]

Another version has it that Judge Thomas was overcommitted. She had bitten off more than she could chew; she had too many irons in the fire; and she just was not competent or skillful enough to handle it all.[40]

Some said that she was manic-depressive and that her endless politicking was nothing less than shamelessly irresponsible self-promotion, which is clearly the sign of an unbalanced black woman.[41]

Others said she was a woman who, like many women, thought of herself *through* other people. A woman who drained others in search of herself. A woman who criticized others into conformity; a woman who used others as substitutes for herself, as self-extenders, as personality enhancers, as screens, as crutches, and as statements. A woman who was nothing without others.[42]

A woman who had forgotten her roots.[43]
A woman who exploited her blackness.[44]
A woman who was too individualistic.[45]

A woman who could not think for herself.[46]
A woman who had the perfect marriage.[47]
A woman who overpowered her men and assaulted their manhood.[48]
A woman who was too emotional.[49]
A woman who needed to loosen up.[50]
A woman who took her profession too seriously.[51]
A woman who did not take her profession seriously enough.[52]

My mother's most consistent message to me, growing up, was that I must become a "professional woman." My only alterative, as she presented it, was to "die in the gutter." There was for me no in between. My mother was a gritty realist, a chess player always on the verge of checkmate, cagey, wary, penultimately protective. And so I became a professional woman.

According to all the best statistics available, I am the perfect average black professional woman. Single. Never married. Having bred a statistically negligible number of children.[53] I suppose I should be miserable, but in fact it is not the end of the world. The very existence of such a statistical category is against all the odds, is company enough for me. I feel like my life is a long graceful miracle, a gentle golden space through which I float on silken phoenix wings. I do not feel any inclination to marry myself off just because I am single. I like being single. (Yet as a social statistic, sometimes I feel less like I am single than socially widowed. Sometimes when I walk down the street and see some poor black man lying over a heating vent, I feel as though I am looking into the face of my companion social statistic, my lost mate—so passionate, original, creative, fine-boned, greedy, and glorious—lying in the gutter [as my mother envisioned] lost, tired, drunk, and howling.) Nor do I feel the obligation to have children just because engineering social statisticians tell me I am "better able" to parent than the vast majority of black women who, being lower class, are purportedly "least able" to parent. (Yet sometimes I wonder what denial of the death all around me, what insistence on the Holy Grail of a certain promised form of life keeps me from taking into my arms the companions to my sorrow—real orphans, black and brown children who languish in institutional abundance and abandon, children born of desperate caring, unions of explosive love, but lives complicated at a more intimate level than I can know by guttered hopes and homelessness.)

It is early morning, the day after the Critical Legal Studies conference. Next door, as I write, my mother, who is visiting me, rises and prepares to greet the day. She makes lots of little trips to the bathroom, in developing stages of undress then dress. Back and forth, from bedroom to bath, seeking and delivering small things: washcloths, eyeliners, stockings, lipstick. The last trip to the bathroom is always the longest. It is then that she does her face and hair. Next door, I can hear the anxiety of her preparations: the creaking of the floorboards as she stands closer then farther from the mirror; the lifting and placing of infinite bottles and jars on the shelves, in the cabinets; the click of her closing a compact of blush; the running of water over her hairbrush; an anonymous fidgety frequency of sounds. She is in a constancy of small motions, like clatters, soft rattles, and bumps. When she leaves the bathroom at last, she makes one final quick trip to the bedroom, then goes downstairs, completely composed, with small brave steps.

When I get up in the morning I stare in the mirror and stick on my roles: I brush my teeth with my responsibility to my community. I buff my nails with paving the way for my race. I comb my hair in the spirit of pulling myself up by my bootstraps. I dab astringent on my pores that I might be a role model upon whom all may gaze with pride. I mascara my eyelashes that I may be "different" from all the rest. I glaze my lips with the commitment to deny pain and "rise above" racism.

I gaze in the mirror and realize that I am very close to being Maxine. When I am fully dressed, my face is hung with contradictions; I try not to wear all my contradictions at the same time. I pick and choose among them; like jewelry, I hunt for this set of expectations that will go best with that obligation. I am just this close.

Judge Maxine Thomas's job as black female judge was to wear all the contradictions at the same time—to wear them well and reconcile them. She stretched wide and reconciled them all. She swallowed all the stories, all the roles; she opened wide to all the expectations.

Standing before the mirror, I understand the logic of her wild despair, the rationality of her unbounded rage. I understand the break she made as necessary and immediate; I understand her impatient self-protection as the incantation of an ancient and incomprehensible restlessness. Knowing she was to be devoured by life, she made herself inedible, full of thorns and sharp edges.

She split at the seams. She returned to the womb. She lay huddled in a wilderness of meaning, lost, a speechless child again, her accommodative language heard as babble, the legacy of *KKK* and *nigger* spilling from her heart, words and explanations dribbling, seeping, bursting from her. Giving birth to a thousand possibilities, she exploded, leaking fragments of intelligence and scattered wisdom.

Her clerk found her curled into a fetal position, crying in her chambers. She was singing her small songs, her magic words, her soothsayings of comfort and the inky juice of cuttlefish. She was singing the songs of meadow saffron and of arbor vitae, of eel serum and of marking nut; snowberry, rue, bitterwort, and yew. She had—without knowing, yet feeling the way of power always—invoked sea onion, shepherd's purse, red clover. In her desperation, she had called upon divinations larger than herself: pinkroot, aguilegia, jambol seeds, thorn apple, and hedge hyssop.

Her bailiff turned her in. (He, the taskmaster of the threshold world. He, the marker of the order of things. The tall protector of the way that things must be, a fierce border guard, bulldog-tough in his guarding of the gate, whose reward was not the slung scrap of salary but the satisfaction—the deep, solid warmth that comes from making-safe. How betrayed he must have felt when this creamy-brown woman rose over her needled rim and rebuked him; told him, in her golden madness, above all to mix, mix, mix it all up. Dangerously. Such conscientious, sacrilegious mockery of protective manhood.)

Once over the edge, once into the threshold world, another sober archangel, her attorney and spokesperson, announced to the public that not only was it unlikely she would ever be able to rejoin the ranks of the judiciary, she would probably never be able to rejoin the ranks of practicing lawyers.[54] Needing so badly to be loved and lacking the professionalism to intercede on behalf of those less fortunate than she, it is unlikely she will ever be heard from again.[55]

Entry of 31 May 1988
(The Living Room)

It is two days after the Critical Legal Studies conference, and I am finally able to think directly about Professor Bell's Chronicle of the Twenty-seventh-Year Syndrome—this thorn of a story, this remarkable gauntlet cast into sadness and confusion.

Here, finally, are my thoughts on the matter: giving it every benefit of the doubt, Professor Bell's story is about gender relations as a political issue. The issue in the twenty-seventh year is not only the behavior or lack of political black mates; the issue is also the hidden, unmentionable secret among us: the historic white master-mate. Romantic love is the fantasy bridge across this gap, this silent chasm. The wider the chasm, the more desperately passionate the structuring of our compensatory vision.

The deep sleep into which the women of the twenty-seventh year fall is an intellectual castration—they are cut off from the black community as well as from all their knowledge and talent and training. The acquisition of professionalism is sexualized: its assertion masculinizes as well as whitens. Professionalism, according to this construction, is one of several ways to get marooned in an uncomprehending white and patriarchal society; thus it sets women up to be cut off and then lost in the profundity of that world's misunderstanding and shortcoming.

The blackness of black people in this society has always represented the blemish, the uncleanliness, the barrier separating individual and society. Castration from blackness thus becomes the initiatory tunnel, the portal through which black people must pass if they are not to fall on their faces in the presence of society, of paternity, of hierarchy. Once castrated, they have shed their horrid mortality, the rapacious lust of lower manhood, the raucous, mother-witted passion of lower womanhood, and opened themselves up to participation in the pseudocelestial white community. Intellectual castration is thus for blacks a sign of suffering for the Larger Society's love as well as a sign to others, as in the Chronicle of the Twenty-seventh-Year Syndrome, of membership in the tribe of those who must, who need to be loved best.

For most blacks, however, this passage from closure to openness turns out not to be a passage from mortality to divine revelation but openness in the opposite extreme direction: openness as profane revelation. Not communion, but exposure, vulnerability, the collapse of boundary in the most assaultive way. White society is the place of the blinding glory of Abraham's God. Pharaoh, not Yahweh.

Another thought I have about this chronicle is Professor Bell's "use" of the imaginary Geneva Crenshaw: throughout the whole book *And We Are Not Saved*, Geneva Crenshaw, this witchy, dream-filled wishing woman, is his instrument by which to attack the monolithism of white patriarchal legal discourse. She is an anti–Founding Father, wandering across time to the Constitutional Convention and back again, a source of aboriginal wisdom and intent. She is the word-creation by which he legitimizes his own critique, as he delegitimizes the limits of the larger body of law's literature. She is the fiction who speaks from across the threshold to the powerful unfiction of the legal order; he argues with her, but he owns her, this destroyer of the rational order. Yet the Chronicle of the Twenty-seventh Year is the one chronicle in the entire series of chronicles in *And We Are Not Saved* which is not of her telling, which Bell owns by himself. In a reversal of roles, she receives *his* story and critiques it; from this "outside position," it is easy to forget that Geneva Crenshaw is not a "real, objective" third person, but part of Bell. She is an extension of Bell, no less than the doctrines of precedent and of narrow constructionism are extensions of the judges who employ them. She is an opinion, no less than any judge's opinion, an invention of her author; an outgrowth of the text; a phantom.

As I think about this, I remember that my father would use my sister and me in that way. He would write poems of extraordinary beauty and interest; he really wanted to publish them, but did not. He gave them to us instead. In so doing, he could resolve his need for audience in safety; with his daughters as judges, he was assured a kind and gloating reception. Fears of failure or of success or of exposure motivated him I suppose; however, it placed my sister and me—or me, in any event—in a remarkably authoritative position. I was powerful. I knew what I was expected to say, and I did my duty. The fact that I meant it did not matter. What I did was a lie, regardless of how much I believed or not in the talent of his poetry. My power was in living the lie that I was all audiences. My power was in the temptation to dissemble, either out of love or disaffection. This is blacks' and women's power, I used to think: this power to lie while existing in the realm of someone else's fantasy. This power to refrain from exerting the real, to shift illusion, while serving as someone else's weaponry, nemesis, language club.

After meeting my new sisters, these inventions of Professor Bell's mind, however, I began to wonder what would happen if I told my father the truth.

What would happen, I wonder, if I were to cut through the fantasy and really let him know that I am not an extension of his pen; what if I were to tell him that I like his writing (or not), but in my own words and on my own terms.

By the same token, what would happen, I wonder, if the victims of Twenty-seventh-Year Syndrome were to awaken from their comatose repose, no longer merely derivative of the black or white male experience, but sharper-tongued than ever. Whose legitimacy would be at risk? theirs? Professor Bell's? Geneva Crenshaw's? the twenty-seven-year-olds who cannot shake the sleep from their eyes?

Or is there any risk at all?

[An undated entry in the unbounded body of sometime after May 1988: A dream. I am in an amphitheater, creeping around the back wall. I am not supposed to be there—it is after-hours, the theater is not open to the general public. On the stage, dead center, surrounded by a circle of friends, spotlighted in the quiet dark of the theater, is a vision, a version of myself. My hair is in an exaggerated beehive (a style I affected, only once, fresh from an application of the hot-comb, at the age of twelve), and I am wearing a sequined low-cut red dress (a dress I actually wore, again once, at the liberated age of twenty-three). There I am with that hair and that ridiculous cowgirl dress: it is an eye scorcher of a sparkling evening gown, my small breasts stuffed into it and uplifted in a way that resembles cleavage.

The me-that-is-on-stage is laughing loudly and long. She is extremely vivacious, the center of attention. She is, just as I have always dreamed of being, fascinating. She is showy yet deeply intelligent. She is not beautiful in any traditional sense, as I am not in real life—her mouth and teeth are very large, her nose very long, like a claymation model of myself—but her features are riveting. And she is so radiantly, splendidly good-natured. She is lovely in the oddest possible combination of ways. I sit down in the small circle of friends-around-myself, to watch myself, this sparkling homely woman, dressed like a moment lost in time. I hear myself speaking: *"Voices lost in the chasm speak from the slow eloquent fact of the chasm. They speak and speak and speak, like flowing water."*

From this dream, into a complicated world, a propagation of me's awakens, strong, single-hearted, and completely refreshed.]

NOTES

[1] (New York: Basic Books, 1987.)

[2] Gross, "When 'By Appointment' Means Keep Out," *New York Times,* 17 December 1986, p. B1, col. 3.

[3] Letter to the Editor from Michael Levin and Marguerita Levin, *New York Times,* 11 January 1987, p. E32, col. 3.

[4] My experience was based on his treating me as a generality; the person whom he excluded was not me, but the universal me; she was both everybody and nobody.

[5] Although even then I always reclaim it through some other form of my writing, as

now; or as in the letters I wrote to Benetton's headquarters (in New York and Italy) and to the *New York Times*. (Nothing ever came of them.)

[6] P. Williams, *Spirit-Murdering the Messenger: The Discourse of Fingerpointing as the Law's Response to Racism*, 42 *U. of Miami L. Rev.* 127, 129 (1987).

[7] Letters of 8 October and 13 October, on file at City University of New York Law School.

[8] See generally, Blyew v. United States, 80 U.S. 581 (1871) upholding a state's right to forbid blacks to testify against whites.

[9] Letter of 5 November 1987, on file at City University of New York Law School.

[10] Affidavit of P. Williams (conversation with Rick Bendremer, 7 November 1987) on file at City University of New York Law School.

[11] Ibid.

[12] Professor Charles Ogletree has done research showing how the elimination of the race of defendants in criminal cases, like Mapp v. Ohio and Terry v. Ohio, changes one's relation to the outcome; a defendant acting "suspiciously" while walking down a public street is a perception one accepts or not based on one's knowledge of pervasive social acquiescence in theories of "inherent" suspiciousness that black as opposed to white defendants bring to bear.

[13] P. Williams, *The Obliging Shell*, 87 *U. of Mich. L. Rev* 2128 (1989).

[14] Matesa, "Attorney Says Affirmative Action Denies Racism, Sexism," *Dominion Post*, 8 April 1988, p. B1, col. 1–2.

[15] E. Diamond, "The Brawley Fiasco," *New York Magazine*, 18 July 1988, p. 22, col. 2.

[16] Even this much certainty was persistently recast as nothing at all in the subsequent months: by September, the *New York Times* was reporting that "her ears and nose were *protected* by cotton wads" [emphasis added]; that it was not her *own* hair that was cut, but rather hair extensions "woven into her own short hair" which had either been torn or cut out; that only her clothes and not her body had been burned; that, from the moment she was found, "*seemingly* dazed and degraded, [she] assumed the mantle of victim" [emphasis added]; and that her dazed condition was "ephemeral" because, in the emergency room, after resisting efforts to physically pull open her eyes, "Dr. Pena concluded that Tawana was not unconscious and was aware of what was going on around her. . . . In a moment of quiet drama, Dr. Pena confronted Miss Brawley: 'I know you can hear me so open your eyes,' she commanded. Tawana opened her eyes and was able to move them in all directions by following Pena's finger." "Evidence Points to Deceit by Brawley," *New York Times*, 27 September 1988, p. A17, col. 1–3.

[17] M. Cottman, "Abrams' Brawley Update: There Might Be No Crime," *New York Newsday*, 15 July 1988, p. 5, col. 3.

[18] Diamond, "The Brawley Fiasco," p. 22.

[19] R. McFadden, "Brawley Made Up Story of Assault, Grand Jury Finds," *New York Times*, 7 October 1988, p. 1, col. 1.

[20] "Nodding or shaking her head to questions, . . . Miss Brawley gave contradictory answers. She indicated that she had been subjected to acts of oral sex, and after first indicating she had not been raped, she suggested she had been assaulted by three white men . . . Asked who assaulted her, she grabbed the silver badge on his uniform but did not respond when he asked if the badge she saw was like his. He then gave her his notebook and she wrote 'white cop.' Asked where, she wrote 'woods.' He then asked her if she had been raped, and she wrote: 'a lot' and drew an arrow to 'white cop.' . . . This response was the closest Miss Brawley ever came to asserting to authorities that she had been raped; her family and advisors, however, asserted many times that she was raped, sodomized, and subjected to other abuse." "Evidence Points to Deceit by Brawley," p. A17, col. 3.

[21] One may well question why she, being a minor, was ever put in the position of making public statements at all: "What first signaled to me that a black girl was about to become a public victim was hearing the *name* of an alleged rape victim—Tawana Brawley—given on a local radio news show. Since when does the press give the name of any rape victim,

much less one who is underage? Obviously when the victim is black, and thus not worthy of the same respect and protection that would be given a white child. A few days later we had another demeaning first: television cameras invading the Brawley home to zoom in for a close-up of Tawana lying on a couch, looking brutalized, disoriented, almost comatose. Later, there would be published police evidence photographs showing Tawana Brawley as she looked when she was first brought by ambulance to a hospital following her rape: unconscious, dirty, half-naked, a 'censorship band' on the pictures covering only the nipples on her otherwise exposed breasts." A. Edwards, "The Rape of Tawana Brawley," *Essence*, November 1988, p. 79, 80.

As NAACP attorney Conrad Lynn observed, moreover, "[s]tate law provides that if a child appears to have been sexually molested, then the Child Protective Services Agency is supposed to take jurisdiction and custody of that child. Now, Tawana Brawley was fifteen at the time of the incident. If that had been done, as I proposed early on, the agency would have given her psychiatric attention and preserved evidence, if there were evidence. . . . But there was a state decision that the agency shouldn't be involved." "What Happened to Tawana Brawley's Case—And to Attitudes About Race and Justice," *New York Times*, 9 October 1988, p. E8, col. 1.

[22] Diamond, "The Brawley Fiasco," p. 22.

[23] "Evidence Points to Deceit by Brawley," p. A17, col. 2; Diamond, "The Brawley Fiasco," p. 22, col. 2.

[24] "Evidence Points to Deceit by Brawley," p. A17, col. 1.

[25] Diamond, "The Brawley Fiasco," p. 22.

[26] "Mr. Sharpton, who is still a member of the Washington Temple Church of God in Christ, does not serve as the pastor of any church. 'My total time is civil rights,' he said. 'It's kind of hard to do both.'" E. R. Shipp, "A Flamboyant Leader of Protests," *New York Times*, 21 January 1988, p. B6, col. 3–4.

[27] "The Rev. Al Sharpton, a Brooklyn minister who has organized civil disobedience demonstrations and has frequently criticized the city's predominantly white political leadership, assisted law-enforcement officials in at least one recent criminal investigation of black community groups, Government sources said.

"He also allowed investigators to wiretap a telephone in his home, the sources said." M. Farber, "Protest Figure Reported to be a U.S. Informant," *New York Times*, 21 January 1988, p. B1, col. 5–6. "Mr. Sharpton said that he—not investigators—had put a recording device on his phone, but only to serve as a 'hot line' for people turning in crack dealers." Ibid., p. B6, col. 4.

[28] "[S]enior New York City police officials said they had learned a year ago that Mr. Sharpton was an informer for the FBI—'that's the word that was used,' one official said. "A Federal official said Mr. Sharpton had been 'introduced' to federal prosecutors for the Eastern District of New York by another law-enforcement agency more than a year ago." M. Farber, "Protest Figure Reported to be a U.S. Informant," p. B1, col. 5–6.

[29] Diamond, "The Brawley Fiasco," p. 22.

[30] "Conservative black leader Roy Innis toppled Tawana Brawley advisor Al Sharpton while taping a TV program on black leadership, and the two civil rights gadflies vowed yesterday to settle their dispute in a boxing ring. . . . 'He tried to "Bogart" me in the middle of my statement,' said Innis. . . . 'I said no dice. . . . We stood up and the body language was not good. So I acted to protect myself. I pushed him and he went down.'. . . As the rotund preacher tumbled backward, Downey and several bodyguards jumped between the pair. Neither man was hurt. . . . Sharpton said he hoped boxing promoter Don King would help organize a Sharpton-Innis charity boxing match. . . . but said he would promote it himself if necessary. . . . The best part is that we will be giving a very positive lesson to young black people in this city about conflict resolution—but not on the street with guns and knives,' Innis said. 'It will be an honest, clean and honorable contest.'" "Roy Innis Pushes Al Sharpton: Fracas at 'Downey Show' Taping; Boxing Match Planned," *Washington Post*, 11 August 1988, p. D4, col. 1.

[31] A. Bollinger, "Tawana's Mom to Get 'Black Army' Escort," *New York Post,* 3 June 1988, p. 7, col. 2.

[32] In New York, television newcasters inadvertently, but repeatedly, referred to her as the "defendant."

[33] H. Kurtz, "New York Moves Against Brawley Lawyers," *Washington Post,* 7 October 1988, p. A1, col. 1.

[34] In one of the more appallingly straightforward statements to this effect, Pete Hamill, while excoriating the "racist hustlers" Sharpton, Mason, and Maddox for talking "about 'whites' as if they were a monolith," asked, "After Tawana Brawley, who will believe the next black woman who says she was raped by white men? or the one after her?" P. Hamill, "Black Media Should Tell the Truth," *New York Post,* 29 September 1988, p.5, col. 5. A slightly more highbrow version of the same sentiment was put forth in an editorial in the *New York Times:* "How can anyone know the depths of cynicism and distrust engendered by an escapade like this? Ask the next black person who is truly victimized—and meets skepticism and disbelief. Ask the next skeptic, white or black." "The Victims of the Brawley Case," *New York Times,* 28 September 1988, p. A22, col. 2.

[35] "One witness said Mr. King 'would watch her exercise' and talked to the girl 'in a real sexual way,' sometimes describing her as a 'fine fox.'" "Evidence Points to Deceit by Brawley," p. A16, col. 3.

[36] "Then it was off to the airport cafeteria for a strategy session and some cheeseburgers with advisors Alton Maddox, C. Vernon Mason, and the Rev. Al Sharpton. 'The fat one, he ate the most,' said Carmen, the cashier. 'He and the skinny one [an aide] bought about $50 or $60 of cheeseburgers, orange juice, chocolate cake, pasta salad and pie,' she added." J. Nolan, "Traveling Circus has 'Em Rollin' in Aisles," *New York Post,* 29 September 1988, p. 4, col. 5; p. 5, col. 1.

[37] "There is a silence that cannot speak.

"There is a silence that will not speak.

"Beneath the grass the speaking dreams and beneath the dreams is a sensate sea. The speech that frees comes forth from that amniotic deep. To attend its voice, I can hear it say, is to embrace its absence. But I fail the task. The word is stone.

"I admit it.

"I hate the stillness. I hate the stone. I hate the sealed vault with its cold icon. I hate the staring into the night. The questions thinning into space. The sky swallowing the echoes.

"Unless the stone bursts with telling, unless the seed flowers with speech, there is in my life no living word. The sound I hear is only sound. White sound. Words, when they fall, are pock marks on the earth. They are hailstones seeking an underground stream.

"If I could follow the stream down and down to the hidden voice, would I come at last to the freeing word? I ask the night sky but the silence is steadfast. There is no reply." J. Kogawa, *Obasan* (Boston: David R. Godine, 1981), 1.

[38] "'I thought Maxine was a lady of unlimited potential,' said Reginald Dunn, of the Los Angeles city attorney's office." R. Arnold and T. Pristin, "The Rise and Fall of Maxine Thomas," *Los Angeles Times,* 6 May 1988, p. 1, col. 1.

[39] "Clerk Richard Haines found Thomas—the first black woman to head the Municipal Court and role model for young blacks in Los Angeles—slumped in her leather chair. The 40-year-old judge's head was bowed, and she wept uncontrollably." Ibid.

[40] "'She's a small, frail person,' said Johnnie L. Cochran Jr., a prominent attorney and longtime Thomas friend. 'A human being breaks. . . . All these things turned in on her.'" Ibid., col. 3.

[41] "Pampered, emotionally immature and unforgiving on one hand, she could also be seductively charming, selflessly kind. In public, she could inspire children with her speeches on how to succeed. In private, faced with disappointment or dissension, she could resort to temper tantrums." Ibid., p. 3, col. 1.

[42] "'I think that all along there was a perception of her by a not unsubstantial group of people that there was more form than substance, that there was a lot of razzle-dazzle and

not a lot to back it up,' said one of [her] critics. Like several others, this judge asked not to be identified to avoid further rancor on the court." Ibid.

[43] "The only child of a janitor and a sometime domestic worker, Thomas grew up in the heart of south-central Los Angeles in a nondescript frame house near 47th Street and Hooper Avenue. She was adored as a child, coddled as an adult.... 'Maxine never had to do anything. She wasn't the type of girl who ever had to clean up her room,' said actress Shirley Washington, Thomas's closest friend and confidante for the past 16 years." Ibid.

[44] "Attorney Cochran, who now represents Thomas, characterizes her as having 'reached almost heroine status in the black community.'

"For Thomas, it was all according to plan."

"'She was a very friendly young lawyer with a great future,' said Atty. Gen. John K. Van de Kamp, who first met Thomas in the early 1970s. 'It was a time for strong and able black women.'" Ibid., col. 2–3.

[45] "'I think she thought the job carried a certain power it just doesn't carry,' said retired Municipal Judge Xenophon Lang Sr. 'You're certainly not the boss of other judges.... You're not a king of anything or queen of anything.'" Ibid., col. 4.

[46] "'She wasn't able to function very well,' said Justice Joan Dempsey Klein, who reviewed Thomas's performance."

[47] "Her career in chaos, Thomas focused on her private life and a new romantic interest. He was Donald Ware, a never-married cardiologist who admired her 'fighting spirit.' It seemed the perfect match, and after only a few months, Ware bought her a 4-carat diamond engagement ring.

"The pair planned a lavish May wedding, complete with 40 attendants, the bridesmaids garbed in lilac, the ushers in top hats and tails. The wedding party rode in a motorcade of Rolls-Royces, stretch limousines and vintage automobiles, and there were four soloists including Thelma Houston, Linda Hopkins and Scherrie Payne....

"After the nuptials, about 1,000 guests attended a reception at the Four Seasons Hotel in Beverly Hills, where they feasted on a five-tiered wedding cake iced in lavender and white....

"There was only one glitch in the fairy tale scenario. The wedding wasn't legal. The couple weren't married.

"They had no valid marriage license, and for that Ware blames Thomas. Thomas blames Ware." Ibid., p. 3, col. 5–6.

[48] "In all, the honeymoon trip lasted three weeks, the volcanic 'marriage' about four.

"'The girl wanted everything, my money and my income,' Ware said afterward. 'Our personal life has been a tragedy. She's got a lot of problems and wanted to give me problems.'" Ibid., p. 3, col. 6.

[49] "'She wasn't professional,' said one judge who observed Thomas at work. 'I remember her clapping her hands when there was a settlement.... The way she would exclaim her glee was not very judgelike.'" Ibid., p. 3, col. 5.

[50] "'People were afraid, truly afraid to confront her ... because of a reputation, right or wrong, of vindictiveness,' one judge said. 'She probably came on the court with more political power than probably any of the other judges.'" Ibid., p. 3, col. 4.

[51] "'Here's a girl who was basically a straight-A student all her life, who never knew what rejection was, never knew what failure was until she decided to run for Superior Court,' Washington said. 'After the election, I went over there and had to pull her out of bed. All she was saying, 'It isn't fair; it's not fair.'" Ibid., p. 3, col. 5.

[52] "She launched a night version of small claims court and then joined her judicial colleague Richard Adler in promoting a program to process short civil cases at night and in opening a special small claims court for visitors to the 1984 Olympics. Thomas was written up in the newspapers, not part of the routine for most Municipal Court judges.

"There was rumbling among some of the judges, and in private the more critical of them began deriding her, questioning where she was trying to go with her splashy programs and complaining that she was neglecting the nitty-gritty work of the court." Ibid., p. 3, col. 3.

[53] Despite persistent public images to the contrary, "[b]lack birth rates have declined from 153.5 per 1000 women in 1960, to 81.4 per 1000 women in 1984." T. B. Edsell, "Race in Politics," *New York Review of Books,* 22 December 1988, p. 24, col. 1.

[54] "For now, doctors say, Thomas should not even consider a return to law, much less to the courts.

"'I think right now the doctors are saying not in the near future,' Green said. 'I'm not a doctor, but my personal view would be never.'" Arnold, "Rise and Fall," col. 7.

[55] "Did you ever . . . ,
wear a certain kind of silk dress
and just by accident,
so inconsequential you barely notice it,
your fingers graze that dress
and you hear the sound of a knife cutting paper,
you see it too
and you realize how that image
is simply the extension of another image,
that your own life is a chain of words
that will one day snap."
–Ai, "Conversation," in *Sin* (Boston: Houghton Mifflin, 1986), 17.

•   •   •   •   •   •   •   •   •   •   •   •   •

QUESTIONS FOR A SECOND READING

1. As you reread Williams's essay, create a set of notes on her examples. She tells a number of stories about her experiences and the experiences of others. She relates a racist incident she experienced at Benetton, the editing of a law journal article of hers, the case of Tawana Brawley, the breakdown of Judge Maxine Thomas, and a story about her mother. She tells all of these after she hears a story titled "the Twenty-seventh-Year Syndrome" at a conference. How would you explain the connections among these various stories to her initial story? What links them? How are they ordered? Where do they lead?

2. One way of reading the essay is as a meditation on social construction—"All this stuff about black people being socially constructed." Williams is alluding to a wide-ranging and difficult set of arguments, drawn from many books and authors and argued again and again on the floors of professional meetings and conferences. These arguments have shaped the way a variety of professionals talk about the relations between the individual and culture, society or history. In a sense, you are listening in on these arguments as you read the essay. What can you make of them? What might this phrase "social construction" mean? How is it used? by whom and to what end? What's at stake?

   And what is Williams's reading of those arguments? As you reread, mark sentences you could use to work on these questions. (As an exercise, you might take some of those sentences and work on them by first writing out a paraphrase, then translating them for someone new to Williams and her work.)

3. The subtitle to the essay refers to the "ideology of style." In her essay, Williams comments on the ideology of the style of academic/legal writing. (You might mark those passages as you reread.) But her essay has its own distinctive style; in fact, it seems to be a distinctive mix of styles. In its writing, it *enacts* an argument with what we might call an "official" style. Or, it creates within its pages a conversation between styles. What are the distinctive stylistic features in Williams's writing? What is she doing *as a writer* in this essay? How does the writing do its work? (Or, what work is it able to do?) Note: Don't forget the endnotes—something is going on there as well.

ASSIGNMENTS FOR WRITING

1. Early in her essay, Williams writes,

> I have always known that my raciality is socially constructed, and I experience it as such. I feel my black self as an eddy of conflicted meanings—and meaninglessness—in which my self can get lost; in which agency and consent are hopelessly relativized as a matter of constant motion. This is how I experience social constructions of race. This sense of motion, this constant windy sound of manipulation whistling in my ears is a reminder of society's constant construction, and reconstruction, of my blackness. (p. 699)

The social construction of raciality is an important idea for Williams, yet it is not at all an easy concept to understand in this essay. As you reread, identify one of Williams's examples or stories that you think best represents her notions of the social construction of raciality. What definition of social construction do you derive from the example? How does she (and how might you) use the example to think about identity, for example, and experience?

Write an essay in which you use this example to explain Williams's position. (You should imagine that your reader has not yet read the article.) Then—perhaps as an extension or in a later draft—reflect on the rest of Williams's essay. What do the other examples say about the range of her interests or concerns? Where does her argument lead—or, how does it serve to direct her attention or define a project? What is at stake in this for her? What about for you?

2. Williams subtitles her essay "A Journal of Musings upon Legal Language and the Ideology of Style," and in the essay she relates a specific incident concerning the editing of a paper she had submitted to the *University of Miami Law Review*. She argues that the editors tried to erase her raciality by claiming that their editing was neutral, that it was just a neutral style of editing. She claimed the style represented an ideology. What do you think she means by this? How does their "style" represent an ideology? What would that ideology be? And, if you think of style broadly, more broadly than just an editing style, as something people could be said to possess or exhibit, what other of Williams's stories could serve as representations of the

ideology of style? What would that style be? And what ideology would you say it represents?

Write an essay in which you use two examples from Williams's essay, including the law review example, to explain what you think Williams means by the term "ideology of style." How would you identify or define the styles in question? And what ideology would you say they represent?

3. Williams's essay makes a powerful and distinctive argument. It is also a powerful and distinctive piece of writing. The preceding questions have asked you to write *about* Williams's essay. In this assignment, we'd like you to consider writing *like* Williams—whatever that might mean for you, or however best you might make such an exercise work. Think of the essay as a method—as a way of thinking things through, of doing one's work. It is this, as well as a way of addressing others or getting a point across.

Perhaps the best way to begin is to reread the essay, making an inventory of its distinctive features. (See the third "Question for a Second Reading.") Traditionally, you might look at organization, at sentences, at the "voice" or "voices" at work in the essay. You might also look at how Williams presents her material, or at how she imagines what her "material" might be. You might think about genre. The piece opens as a "journal entry"—but what kind of journal has endnotes?

Then you need to begin gathering materials. The invitation of the essay is to work on a set of issues (stories, documents, positions) that have bearing on you. (In this sense, Williams's essay "begins" when Derrick Bell provokes her with a comment on unmarried black women.)

Note: Williams's essay is both layered (one thing next to another) and cumulative (one thing after another). These effects can be produced by revision—where a second or third draft adds another section or another layer. You don't have to imagine—in fact, it is probably wrong to imagine—that Williams wrote her essay all at once.

MAKING CONNECTIONS

1. In "And We Are Not Married," Patricia Williams argues that her identity as a black woman is "socially constructed." As a part of her argument, she claims also that black women and men are socially constructed, and she tells a number of stories to serve as examples of social construction as it could be said to mold or shape people's perceptions. As you read through her essay, mark those moments that you could use to present her notions of social construction. What does she mean, for example, when she says that the raciality of black women and men is socially constructed? What example would you turn to from her essay to explain the way she thinks social construction works and what its elements might be?

Once you've read Williams's essay and you have created a set of notes representing her notions of social construction, read "The Achievement of Desire" by Richard Rodriguez (p. 567) from Williams's perspective on social construction. Imagine that Rodriguez's identity could also be said to have been socially constructed by school, by particular groups of people, by his family, and, as Williams would argue, by his perceptions of himself. What examples from Rodriguez's essay would you turn to to argue that, like Williams's identity, Rodriguez's identity could also be said to be socially constructed? How would Williams's notion apply to Rodriguez? Which aspects would be similar? which different?

Write an essay in which you use Williams's notions of the social construction as a set of critical ideas to resee or reimagine one of Rodriguez's examples or stories.

2. Various selections in this textbook can be said to be "experimental" in their use of nonfiction prose. These are essays that don't do what essays are supposed to do. They break the rules. They surprise. The writers work differently than most writers. They imagine a different project (or they imagine their project differently).

Although any of the selections might be read alongside "And We Are Not Married," here are some that have seemed interesting to our students: John Wideman, "Our Time" (p. 652); Virginia Woolf, "A Room of One's Own" (p. 719); Susan Griffin, "Our Secret" (p. 319); and the essays by Gloria Anzaldúa (p. 22).

Choose one selection to pair with Williams's and write an essay in which you both explain and explore the projects represented by the two pieces of writing. What do they do? (You should assume that you are presenting this information to someone who has not seen the essays. You will need, that is, to be careful in choosing and presenting examples.) And what is to be gained (or what is at stake) in writing this way? Would you, for example, argue that these forms of writing should be taught in the schools?

3. Adrienne Rich (p. 547), Susan Douglas (p. 115), and Gloria Anzaldúa (p. 21) all make strong statements about the situation of women—in relation to the past, to language, politics, and culture. The essays have certain similarities, but it is also interesting to consider their differences and what these differences might be said to represent. Choose one selection to compare with "And We Are Not Married," read the two together, marking passages you might use in a discussion, and write an essay in which you examine the interesting differences between these essays. Consider the essays as different forms or schools of feminist thought, different ways of thinking critically about the situations of women. Assume that there is more to say than "different people have different opinions," or "different people write about different subjects." How else might you account for these differences? What is their significance?

VIRGINIA
WOOLF

*V*IRGINIA WOOLF *is generally considered one of the twentieth century's major British writers. Born in London in 1882, Woolf was the daughter of prominent figures in London artistic circles, and her parents encouraged the young girl in her intellectual pursuits. But even as a child Woolf was made aware of the different expectations her culture held for men and women. For, while the female children of the household were taught at home by their mother and a series of tutors and governesses, the boys were sent away to school. Later in her life Woolf expressed her bitterness over the inequities of this system of education, a system shared by most Victorian families.*

Woolf began her literary career studying Greek, reading in her father's library, and meeting in her parents' home some of the leading figures of British arts and letters. After her father's death in 1904, Woolf and her sister and two brothers moved to Bloomsbury, where their home became a center for young writers and intellectuals trying to shake free from the restrictions of Victorian life and culture. Woolf began teaching in a working women's college in South London and writing reviews for the prestigious Times Literary Supplement.

Woolf's first review, published in 1904, when she was twenty-two, was the beginning of a distinguished career which ultimately encompassed six volumes of essays and reviews, two biographies, two book-length essays, several volumes of letters and diaries, nine novels, and two collections of short stories. In addition to being one of the cofounders (with her husband, Leonard) of the Hogarth Press, a publishing company which produced editions of the work of the poet T. S. Eliot, short story writer Katherine Mansfield, and English translations of the work of Sigmund Freud, Woolf is considered one of the finest literary critics of her time and arguably one of the most innovative novelists of the twentieth century. Her novels include Mrs. Dalloway (1925), To the Lighthouse (1927), Orlando (1928), and The Waves (1931). Orlando is the imaginary biography of a character who lives for four hundred years and changes from male to female in the late seventeenth century. It has been called the companion piece to A Room of One's Own.

The following selection is the first and last chapters of Woolf's extended essay A Room of One's Own, a revised version of two papers she read at the women's colleges at Oxford, Girton and Newnham. The two chapters here frame Woolf's lecture on the topic "women and fiction." Because the final chapter alludes to what has come before, it is useful to have a brief sketch of the middle chapters.

In these chapters Woolf surveys what men have said about women, and she looks over the history of women's writing, from Renaissance England to the early twentieth century. In Chapter 3 she imagines what might have happened if Shakespeare had had a sister. This young woman, Judith, might have been

> as adventurous, as imaginative, as agog to see the world as [her brother] was. But she was not sent to school. She had no chance of learning grammar and logic, let alone of reading Horace and Virgil. She picked up a book now and then. . . . But then her parents came in and told her to mend the stockings or mind the stew and not moon about with books and papers. They would have spoken sharply but kindly, for they were substantial people who knew the conditions of life for a woman and loved their daughter—indeed, more likely than not she was the apple of her father's eye.

Finally, the young girl is promised in marriage to a man she does not desire, and she runs away to London to try her fortune in the theater.

> What is true . . . , so it seemed to me, reviewing the story of Shakespeare's sister as I had made it, is that any woman born with a great gift in the sixteenth century would certainly have gone crazed, shot herself, or ended her days in some lonely cottage outside the village, half witch, half wizard, feared and mocked at. For it needs little skill in psychology to be sure that a highly gifted girl who had tried to use her gift for poetry would have been so thwarted and hindered by other people, so tortured and pulled asunder by her own contrary instincts, that she must have lost her health and sanity to a certainty. No girl could have walked to London and stood at a stage door and forced her way into the presence of actor-managers without doing herself a violence and suffering an anguish which may have been irrational—for chastity may be a fetish invented by certain societies for unknown reasons—but were none the less inevitable. . . . To have lived a free life in London in the sixteenth century would have meant for a

woman who was poet and playwright a nervous stress and dilemma which might well have killed her. Had she survived, whatever she had written would have been twisted and deformed, issuing from a strained and morbid imagination. And undoubtedly, I thought, looking at the shelf where there are no plays by women, her work would have gone unsigned.

Chapters 1 and 6 establish Woolf's project and her way of addressing her audience. They are marked by a strong and distinctive style. For one thing, Woolf delivers most of the lecture through the voice of a character ("call me Mary Beton, Mary Seton, Mary Carmichael, or by any name you please—it is not a matter of any importance"). In a letter to a friend, Dame Ethel Smyth, Woolf once said, "I didn't write A Room without considerable feeling . . . ; I'm not cool on the subject. And I forced myself to keep my own figure fictitious, legendary. If I had said, 'Look here, I am uneducated because my brothers used the family funds'—which is the fact—'well,'" they'd have said, 'she has an axe to grind'; and no one would have taken me seriously." Although this essay is "signed," Woolf leaves open some questions about the status and the presence of its author. As you read, you will want to think about the ways this essay might be seen as an example of the problems and possibilities for a woman's writing.

A Room of One's Own

Chapter One

But, you may say, we asked you to speak about women and fiction—what has that got to do with a room of one's own? I will try to explain. When you asked me to speak about women and fiction I sat down on the banks of a river and began to wonder what the words meant. They might mean simply a few remarks about Fanny Burney; a few more about Jane Austen; a tribute to the Brontës and a sketch of Haworth Parsonage under snow; some witticisms if possible about Miss Mitford; a respectful allusion to George Eliot; a reference to Mrs. Gaskell and one would have done. But at second sight the words seemed not so simple. The title women and fiction might mean, and you may have meant it to mean, women and what they are like; or it might mean women and the fiction that they write; or it might mean women and the fiction that is written about them; or it might mean that somehow all three are inextricably mixed together and you want me to consider them in that light. But when I began to consider the subject in this last way, which seemed the most interesting, I soon saw that it had one fatal drawback. I should never be able to come to a conclusion. I should never be able to fulfill what is, I understand, the first duty of a lecturer—to hand you after an hour's discourse a nugget of pure truth to wrap up between the pages of your note-books and keep on the mantelpiece for ever. All I could do was to offer you an opinion upon one minor point—a woman must have money and a room of her own if she is to write fiction; and that, as you will see, leaves the great problem of the true nature of woman and the true nature of fiction unsolved. I have shirked the duty of coming to a conclusion upon these two ques-tions—women and fiction remain, so far as I am concerned, unsolved prob-lems. But in order to make some amends I am going to do what I can to show you how I arrived at this opinion about the room and the money. I am going to develop in your presence as fully and freely as I can the train of thought which led me to think this. Perhaps if I lay bare the ideas, the prejudices, that lie behind this statement you will find that they have some bearing upon women and some upon fiction. At any rate, when a subject is highly contro-versial—and any question about sex is that—one cannot hope to tell the truth. One can only show how one came to hold whatever opinion one does hold. One can only give one's audience the chance of drawing their own con-clusions as they observe the limitations, the prejudices, the idiosyncrasies of the speaker. Fiction here is likely to contain more truth than fact. Therefore I propose, making use of all the liberties and licenses of a novelist, to tell you the story of the two days that preceded my coming here—how, bowed down by the weight of the subject which you have laid upon my shoulders, I pon-dered it, and made it work in and out of my daily life. I need not say that what I am about to describe has no existence; Oxbridge is an invention; so is Fernham; "I" is only a convenient term for somebody who has no real being. Lies will flow from my lips, but there may perhaps be some truth mixed up with them; it is for you to seek out this truth and decide whether any part of it is worth keeping. If not, you will of course throw the whole of it into the wastepaper basket and forget all about it.

Here then was I (call me Mary Beton, Mary Seton, Mary Carmichael, or by any name you please—it is not a matter of any importance) sitting on the banks of a river a week or two ago in fine October weather, lost in thought. That collar I have spoken of, women and fiction, the need of coming to some conclusion on a subject that raises all sorts of prejudices and passions, bowed my head to the ground. To the right and left bushes of some sort, golden and crimson, glowed with the color, even it seemed burnt with the heat, of fire. On the further bank the willows wept in perpetual lamentation, their hair about their shoulders. The river reflected whatever it chose of sky and bridge and burning tree, and when the undergraduate had oared his boat through the reflections they closed again, completely, as if he had never been. There one might have sat the clock round lost in thought. Thought—to call it by a prouder name than it deserved—had let its line down into the stream. It swayed, minute after minute, hither and thither among the reflections and the weeds, letting the water lift it and sink it, until—you know the little tug—the sudden conglomeration of an idea at the end of one's line: and then the cautious hauling of it in, and the careful laying of it out? Alas, laid on the grass how small, how insignificant this thought of mine looked; the sort of fish that a good fisherman puts back into the water so that it may grow fatter and be one day worth cooking and eating. I will not trouble you with that thought now, though if you look carefully you may find it for yourselves in the course of what I am going to say.

But however small it was, it had, nevertheless, the mysterious property of its kind—put back into the mind, it became at once very exciting, and important; and as it darted and sank, and flashed hither and thither, set up such a wash and tumult of ideas that it was impossible to sit still. It was thus that I found myself walking with extreme rapidity across a grass plot. Instantly a man's figure rose to intercept me. Nor did I at first understand that the gesticulations of a curious-looking object, in a cutaway coat and evening shirt, were aimed at me. His face expressed horror and indignation. Instinct rather than reason came to my help; he was a Beadle; I was a woman. This was the turf; there was the path. Only the Fellows and Scholars are allowed here; the gravel is the place for me. Such thoughts were the work of a moment. As I regained the path the arms of the Beadle sank, his face assumed its usual repose, and though turf is better walking than gravel, no very great harm was done. The only charge I could bring against the Fellows and Scholars of whatever the college might happen to be was that in protection of their turf, which has been rolled for three hundred years in succession, they had sent my little fish into hiding.

What idea it had been that had sent me so audaciously trespassing I could not now remember. The spirit of peace descended like a cloud from heaven, for if the spirit of peace dwells anywhere, it is in the courts and quadrangles of Oxbridge on a fine October morning. Strolling through those colleges past those ancient halls the roughness of the present seemed smoothed away; the body seemed contained in a miraculous glass cabinet through which no sound could penetrate, and the mind, freed from any contact with facts (unless one trespassed on the turf again), was at liberty to settle down upon whatever meditation was in harmony with the moment. As chance would have it, some stray memory of some old essay about revisiting Oxbridge in the long vacation brought Charles Lamb to mind—Saint Charles, said Thackeray, putting a letter of Lamb's to his forehead. Indeed, among all the dead (I give you my thoughts as they came to me), Lamb is one of the most congenial; one to whom one would have liked to say, Tell me then how you wrote your essays? For his essays are superior even to Max Beerbohm's, I thought, with all their perfection, because of that wild flash of imagination, that lightning crack of genius in the middle of them which leaves them flawed and imperfect, but starred with poetry. Lamb then came to Oxbridge perhaps a hundred years ago. Certainly he wrote an essay—the name escapes me—about the manuscript of one of Milton's poems which he saw here. It was *Lycidas* perhaps, and Lamb wrote how it shocked him to think it possible that any word in *Lycidas* could have been different from what it is. To think of Milton changing the words in that poem seemed to him a sort of sacrilege. This led me to remember what I could of *Lycidas* and to amuse myself with guessing which word it could have been that Milton had altered, and why. It then occurred to me that the very manuscript itself which Lamb had looked at was only a few hundred yards away, so that one could follow Lamb's footsteps across the quadrangle to that famous library where the treasure is kept. Moreover, I recollected, as I put this plan into execution, it is in this famous library that the manuscript of Thackeray's *Esmond* is also preserved. The critics often say that *Esmond* is Thackeray's most perfect novel. But the affectation of the style, with its imitation of the eighteenth century, hampers one, so far as I remember; unless indeed the eigtheenth-century style was natural to Thackeray—a fact that one might prove by looking at the manuscript and seeing whether the alterations were for the benefit of the style or of the sense. But then one would have to decide what is style and what is meaning, a question which—but here I was actually at the door which leads into the library itself. I must have opened it, for instantly there issued, like a guardian angel barring the way with a flutter of black gown instead of white wings, a deprecating, silvery, kindly gentleman, who regretted in a low voice as he waved me back that ladies are only admitted to the library if accompanied by a Fellow of the College or furnished with a letter of introduction.

That a famous library has been cursed by a woman is a matter of complete indifference to a famous library. Venerable and calm, with all its treasures safe locked within its breast, it sleeps complacently and will, so far as I am concerned, so sleep forever. Never will I wake those echoes, never will I ask for that hospitality again, I vowed as I descended the steps in anger. Still an hour remained before luncheon, and what was one to do? Stroll on the meadows? sit by the river? Certainly it was a lovely autumn morning; the leaves were fluttering red to the ground; there was no great hardship in doing either. But the sound of music reached my ear. Some service or celebration was going forward. The organ complained magnificently as I passed the chapel door. Even the sorrow of Christianity sounded in that serene air more like the recollection of sorrow than sorrow itself; even the groanings of the ancient organ seemed lapped in peace. I had no wish to enter had I the right, and this time the verger might have stopped me, demanding perhaps my baptismal certificate, or a letter of introduction from the Dean. But the outside of these magnificent buildings is often as beautiful as the inside. Moreover, it was amusing enough to watch the congregation assembling, coming in and going out again, busying themselves at the door of the chapel like bees at the mouth of a hive. Many were in cap and gown; some had tufts of fur on their shoulders; others were wheeled in bath chairs; others, though not past middle age, seemed creased and crushed into shapes so singular that one was reminded of those giant crabs and crayfish who heave with difficulty across the sand of an aquarium. As I leant against the wall the University indeed seemed a sanctuary in which are preserved rare types which would soon be obsolete if left to fight for existence on the pavement of the

Strand. Old stories of old deans and old dons came back to mind, but before I had summoned up courage to whistle—it used to be said that at the sound of a whistle old Professor ——— instantly broke into a gallop—the venerable congregation had gone inside. The outside of the chapel remained. As you know, its high domes and pinnacles can be seen, like a sailing ship always voyaging never arriving, lit up at night and visible for miles, far away across the hills. Once, presumably, this quadrangle with its smooth lawns, its massive buildings, and the chapel itself was marsh too, where the grasses waved and the swine rooted. Teams of horses and oxen, I thought, must have hauled the stone in wagons from far countries, and then with infinite labor the gray blocks in whose shade I was now standing were poised in order one on top of another, and then the painters brought their glass for the windows, and the masons were busy for centuries up on that roof with putty and cement, spade and trowel. Every Saturday somebody must have poured gold and silver out of a leathern purse into their ancient fists, for they had their beer and skittles presumably of an evening. An unending stream of gold and silver, I thought, must have flowed into this court perpetually to keep the stones coming and the masons working; to level, to ditch, to dig, and to drain. But it was then the age of faith, and money was poured liberally to set these stones on a deep foundation, and when the stones were raised, still more money was poured in from the coffers of kings and queens and great nobles to ensure that hymns should be sung here and scholars taught. Lands were granted; tithes were paid. And when the age of faith was over and the age of reason had come, still the same flow of gold and silver went on; fellowships were founded; lectureships endowed; only the gold and silver flowed now, not from the coffers of the king, but from the chests of merchants and manufacturers, from the purses of men who had made, say, a fortune from industry, and returned, in their wills, a bounteous share of it to endow more chairs, more lectureships, more fellowships in the university where they had learnt their craft. Hence the libraries and laboratories; the observatories; the splendid equipment of costly and delicate instruments which now stands on glass shelves, where centuries ago the grasses waved and the swine rooted. Certainly, as I strolled round the court, the foundation of gold and silver seemed deep enough; the pavement laid solidly over the wild grasses. Men with trays on their heads went busily from staircase to staircase. Gaudy blossoms flowered in window boxes. The strains of the gramophone blared out from the rooms within. It was impossible not to reflect—the reflection whatever it may have been was cut short. The clock struck. It was time to find one's way to luncheon.

It is a curious fact that novelists have a way of making us believe that luncheon parties are invariably memorable for something very witty that was said, or for something very wise that was done. But they seldom spare a word for what was eaten. It is part of the novelist's convention not to mention soup and salmon and ducklings, as if soup and salmon and ducklings were of no importance whatsoever, as if nobody ever smoked a cigar or drank a glass of wine. Here, however, I shall take the liberty to defy that convention and to tell you that the lunch on this occasion began with soles, sunk in a deep dish, over which the college cook had spread a counterpane of the whitest cream, save that it was branded here and there with brown spots like the spots on the flanks of a doe. After that came the partridges, but if this suggests a couple of bald, brown birds on a plate you are mistaken. The partridges, many and various, came with all their retinue of sauces and salads, the sharp and the sweet, each in its order; their potatoes, thin as coins but not so hard; their sprouts, foliated as rosebuds but more succulent. And no sooner had the roast and its retinue been done with than the silent serving man, the Beadle himself perhaps in a milder manifestation, set before us, wreathed in napkins, a confection which rose all sugar from the waves. To call it pudding and so relate it to rice and tapioca would be an insult. Meanwhile the wineglasses had flushed yellow and flushed crimson; had been emptied; had been filled. And thus by degrees was lit, halfway down the spine, which is the seat of the soul, not that hard little electric light which we call brilliance, as it pops in and out upon our lips, but the more profound, subtle, and subterranean glow, which is the rich yellow flame of rational intercourse. No need to hurry. No need to sparkle. No need to be anybody but oneself. We are all going to heaven and Vandyck is of the company—in other words, how good life seemed, how sweet its rewards, how trivial this grudge or that grievance, how admirable friendship and the society of one's kind, as, lighting a good cigarette, one sunk among the cushions in the window seat.

If by good luck there had been an ashtray handy, if one had not knocked the ash out of the window in default, if things had been a little different from what they were, one would not have seen, presumably, a cat without a tail. The sight of that abrupt and truncated animal padding softly across the quadrangle changed by some fluke of the subconscious intelligence the emotional light for me. It was as if some one had let fall a shade. Perhaps the excellent hock was relinquishing its hold. Certainly, as I watched the Manx cat pause in the middle of the lawn as if it too questioned the universe, something seemed lacking, something seemed different. But what was lacking, what was different, I asked myself, listening to the talk. And to answer that question I had to think myself out of the room, back into the past, before the war indeed, and to set before my eyes the model of another luncheon party held in rooms not very far distant from these; but different. Everything was different. Meanwhile the talk went on among the guests, who were many and young, some of this sex, some of that; it went on swimmingly, it went on agreeably, freely, amusingly. And as it went on I set it against the background of that other talk, and as I matched the two together I had no doubt that one was the descendant, the legitimate heir of the other. Nothing was changed; nothing was different save only—here I listened with all my ears not entirely to what was being said, but to the murmur or current behind it. Yet, that was it—the change was there. Before the war at a luncheon party like this people would have said precisely the same things but they would have sounded different, because in those days they were accompanied by a sort of humming noise, not articulate, but musical, exciting, which changed the value of the words themselves. Could one set that humming noise to words? Perhaps with the help of the poets one could. A book lay beside me and, opening it, I turned casually enough to Tennyson. And here I found Tennyson was singing:

> There has fallen a splendid tear
>   From the passion-flower at the gate.
> She is coming, my dove, my dear;
>   She is coming, my life, my fate;
> The red rose cries, "She is near, she is near";
>   And the white rose weeps, "She is late";
> The larkspur listens, "I hear, I hear";
>   And the lily whispers, "I wait."

Was that what men hummed at luncheon parties before the war? And the women?

> My heart is like a singing bird
>   Whose nest is in a water'd shoot;
> My heart is like an apple tree
>   Whose boughs are bent with thick-set fruit;
> My heart is like a rainbow shell
>   That paddles in a halcyon sea;
> My heart is gladder than all these
>   Because my love is come to me.

Was that what women hummed at luncheon parties before the war?

There was something so ludicrous in thinking of people humming such things even under their breath at luncheon parties before the war that I burst out laughing, and had to explain my laughter by pointing at the Manx cat, who did look a little absurd, poor beast, without a tail, in the middle of the lawn. Was he really born so, or had he lost his tail in an accident? The tailless cat, though some are said to exist in the Isle of Man, is rarer than one thinks. It is a queer animal, quaint rather than beautiful. It is strange what a difference a tail makes—you know the sort of things one says as a lunch party breaks up and people are finding their coats and hats.

This one, thanks to the hospitality of the host, had lasted far into the afternoon. The beautiful October day was fading and the leaves were falling from the trees in the avenue as I walked through it. Gate after gate seemed to close with gentle finality behind me. Innumerable beadles were fitting innumerable keys into well-oiled locks; the treasure house was being made secure for another night. After the avenue one comes out upon a road—I forget its name—which leads you, if you take the right turning, along to Fernham. But there was plenty of time. Dinner was not till half past seven. One could almost do without dinner after such a luncheon. It is strange how a scrap of poetry works in the mind and makes the legs move in time to it along the road. Those words—

> There has fallen a splendid tear
>> From the passion-flower at the gate.
> She is coming, my dove, my dear—

sang in my blood as I stepped quickly along towards Headingley. And then, switching off into the other measure, I sang, where the waters are churned up by the weir:

> My heart is like a singing bird
>> Whose nest is in a water'd shoot;
> My heart is like an apple tree . . .

What poets, I cried aloud, as one does in the dusk, what poets they were!

In a sort of jealousy, I suppose, for our own age, silly and absurd though these comparisons are, I went on to wonder if honestly one could name two living poets now as great as Tennyson and Christina Rossetti were then. Obviously it is impossible, I thought, looking into those foaming waters, to compare them. The very reason why the poetry excites one to such abandonment, such rapture, is that it celebrates some feeling that one used to have (at luncheon parties before the war perhaps), so that one responds easily, familiarly, without troubling to check the feeling, or to compare it with any that one has now. But the living poets express a feeling that is actually being made and torn out of us at the moment. One does not recognize it in the first place; often for some reason one fears it; one watches it with keenness and compares it jealously and suspiciously with the old feeling that one knew. Hence the difficulty of modern poetry; and it is because of this difficulty that one cannot remember more than two consecutive lines of any good modern poet. For this reason—that my memory failed me—the argument flagged for want of material. But why, I continued, moving on towards Headingley, have we stopped humming under our breath at luncheon parties? Why has Alfred ceased to sing

> She is coming, my dove, my dear?

Why has Christina ceased to respond

> My heart is gladder than all these
> Because my love is come to me?

Shall we lay the blame on the war? When the guns fired in August 1914, did the faces of men and women show so plain in each other's eyes that romance was killed? Certainly it was a shock (to women in particular with their illusions about education, and so on) to see the faces of our rulers in the light of the shell fire. So ugly they looked—German, English, French—so stupid. But lay the blame where one will, on whom one will, the illusion which inspired Tennyson and Christina Rossetti to sing so passionately about the coming of their loves is far rarer now than then. One has only to read, to look, to listen, to remember. But why say "blame"? Why, if it was an illusion, not praise the catastrophe, whatever it was, that destroyed illusion and put truth in its place? For truth ... those dots mark the spot where, in search of truth, I missed the turning up to Fernham. Yes indeed, which was truth about these houses, for example, dim and festive now with their red windows in the dusk, but raw and red and squalid, with their sweets and their bootlaces, at nine o'clock in the morning? And the willows and the river and the gardens that run down to the river, vague now with the mist stealing over them, but gold and red in the sunlight—which was the truth, which was the illusion about them? I spare you the twists and turns of my cogitations, for no conclusion was found on the road to Headingley, and I ask you to suppose that I soon found my mistake about the turning and retraced my steps to Fernham.

As I have said already that it was an October day, I dare not forfeit your respect and imperil the fair name of fiction by changing the season and describing lilacs hanging over garden walls, crocuses, tulips, and other flowers of spring. Fiction must stick to facts, and the truer the facts the better the fiction—so we are told. Therefore it was still autumn and the leaves were still yellow and falling, if anything, a little faster than before, because it was now evening (seven twenty-three to be precise) and a breeze (from the southwest to be exact) had risen. But for all that there was something odd at work:

> My heart is like a singing bird
> Whose nest is in a water'd shoot;
> My heart is like an apple tree
> Whose boughs are bent with thick-set fruit—

perhaps the words of Christina Rossetti were partly responsible for the folly of the fancy—it was nothing of course but a fancy—that the lilac was shaking its flowers over the garden walls, and the brimstone butterflies were scudding hither and thither, and the dust of the pollen was in the air. A wind blew, from what quarter I know not, but it lifted the half-grown leaves so that there was a flash of silver gray in the air. It was the time between the lights when colors undergo their intensification and purples and golds burn in windowpanes like the beat of an excitable heart; when for some reason the beauty of the world revealed and yet soon to perish (here I pushed into the garden, for, unwisely, the door was left open and no beadles seemed about), the beauty of the world which is so soon to perish, has two edges, one of laughter, one of anguish, cutting the heart asunder. The gardens of Fernham lay before me in the spring twilight, wild and open, and in the long grass, sprinkled and carelessly flung, were daffodils and bluebells, not orderly perhaps at the best of times, and now windblown and waving as they tugged at their roots. The windows of the building, curved like ships' windows among generous waves of red brick, changed from lemon to silver under the flight of the quick spring clouds. Somebody was in a hammock, somebody, but in this light they were phantoms only, half guessed, half seen, raced across the grass—would no one stop her?—and then on the terrace, as if popping out to breathe the air, to glance at the garden, came a bent figure, formidable yet humble, with her great forehead and her shabby dress—could it be the famous scholar, could it be J—— H—— herself? All was dim, yet intense too, as if the scarf which the dusk had flung over the garden were torn asunder by star or sword—the flash of some terrible reality leaping, as its way is, out of the heart of the spring. For youth————

Here was my soup. Dinner was being served in the great dining hall. Far from being spring it was in fact an evening in October. Everybody was assembled in the big dining room. Dinner was ready. Here was the soup. It was a plain gravy soup. There was nothing to stir the fancy in that. One could have seen through the transparent liquid any pattern that there might have been on the plate itself. But there was no pattern. The plate was plain. Next came beef with its attendant greens and potatoes—a homely trinity, suggesting the rumps of cattle in a muddy market, and sprouts curled and yellowed at the edge, and bargaining and cheapening, and women with string bags on Monday morning. There was no reason to complain of human nature's daily food, seeing that the supply was sufficient and coal miners doubtless were sitting down to less. Prunes and custard followed. And if any one complains that prunes, even when mitigated by custard, are an uncharitable vegetable (fruit they are not), stringy as a miser's heart, and exuding a fluid such as might run in miser's veins who have denied themselves wine and warmth for eighty years and yet not given to the poor, he should reflect that there are people whose charity embraces even the prune. Biscuits and cheese came next, and here the water jug was liberally passed round, for it is the nature of biscuits to be dry, and these were biscuits to the core. That was all. The meal was over. Everybody scraped their chairs back; the swing doors swung violently to and fro; soon the hall was emptied of every sign of food and made ready no doubt for breakfast next morning. Down corridors and up staircases the youth of England went banging and singing. And was it for a guest, a stranger (for I had no more right here in Fernham than in Trinity or Somerville or Girton or Newnham or Christchurch), to say, "The dinner was not good," or to say (we were now, Mary Seton and I, in her sitting room), "Could we not have dined up here alone?" for if I had said anything of the kind I should have been prying and searching into the secret economies of a house which to the stranger wears so fine a front of gaiety and courage. No, one could say nothing of the sort. Indeed, conversation for a moment flagged. The human frame being what it is, heart, body, and brain all mixed together, and not contained in separate compartments as they will be no doubt in another million years, a good dinner is of great importance to good talk. One cannot think well, love well, sleep well, if one has not dined well. The lamp in the spine does not light on beef and prunes. We are all *probably* going to heaven, and Vandyck is, we *hope*, to meet us round the next corner—that is the dubious and qualifying state of mind that beef and prunes at the end of the day's work breed between them. Happily my friend, who taught science, had a cupboard where there was a squat bottle and little glasses—(but there should have been sole and partridge to begin with)—so that we were able to draw up to the fire and repair some of the damages of the day's living. In a minute or so we were slipping freely in and out among all those objects of curiosity and interest which form in the mind in the absence of a particular person, and are naturally to be discussed on coming together again—how somebody has married, another has not; one thinks this, another that; one has improved out of all knowledge, the other most amazingly gone to the bad—with all those speculations upon human nature and the character of the amazing world we live in which spring naturally from such beginnings. While these things were being said, however, I became shamefacedly aware of a current setting in of its own accord and carrying everything forward to an end of its own. One might be talking of Spain or Portugal, of book or racehorse, but the real interest of whatever was said was none of those things, but a scene of masons on a high roof some five centuries ago. Kings and nobles brought treasure in huge sacks and poured it under the earth. This scene was forever coming alive in my mind and placing itself by another of lean cows and a muddy market and withered greens and the stringy hearts of old men—these two pictures, disjointed and disconnected and nonsensical as they were, were forever coming together and combating each other and had me entirely at their mercy. The best course, unless the whole talk was to be distorted, was to expose what was in my mind to the air, when with good luck it would fade and crumble like the head of the dead king when they opened the coffin at Windsor. Briefly, then, I told Miss Seton about the masons who had been all those years on the roof of the chapel, and about the kings and queens and nobles bearing sacks of gold and silver on their shoulders, which they shoveled into the earth; and then how the great financial magnates of our own time came and laid checks and bonds, I suppose, where the others had laid ingots and rough lumps of gold. All that lies beneath the colleges down there, I said; but this college, where we are now sitting, what lies beneath its gallant red brick and the wild unkempt grasses of the garden? What force is behind the plain china off which we dined, and (here it popped out of my mouth before I could stop it) the beef, the custard, and the prunes?

Well, said Mary Seton, about the year 1860—Oh, but you know the story, she said, bored, I suppose, by the recital. And she told me—rooms were hired. Committees met. Envelopes were addressed. Circulars were drawn up. Meetings were held; letters were read out; so-and-so has promised so much; on the contrary, Mr. ——— won't give a penny. The *Saturday Review* has been very rude. How can we raise a fund to pay for offices? Shall we hold a bazaar? Can't we find a pretty girl to sit in the front row? Let us look up what John Stuart Mill said on the subject. Can anyone persuade the editor of the ——— to print a letter? Can we get Lady ——— to sign it? Lady ——— is out of town. That was the way it was done, presumably, sixty years ago, and it was a prodigious effort, and a great deal of time was spent on it. And it was only after a long struggle and with the utmost difficulty that they got thirty thousand pounds together.[1] So obviously we cannot have wine and partridges and servants carrying tin dishes on their heads, she said. We cannot have sofas and separate rooms. "The amenities," she said, quoting from some book or other, "will have to wait."[2]

At the thought of all those women working year after year and finding it hard to get two thousand pounds together, and as much as they could do to get thirty thousand pounds, we burst out in scorn at the reprehensible poverty of our sex. What had our mothers been doing then that they had no wealth to leave us? powdering their noses? looking in at shop windows? flaunting in the sun at Monte Carlo? There were some photographs on the mantelpiece. Mary's mother—if that was her picture—may have been a wastrel in her spare time (she had thirteen children by a minister of the church), but if so her gay and dissipated life had left too few traces of its pleasures on her face. She was a homely body; an old lady in a plaid shawl which was fastened by a large cameo; and she sat in a basket chair, encouraging a spaniel to look at the camera, with the amused, yet strained expression of one who is sure that the dog will move directly the bulb is pressed. Now if she had gone into business; had become a manufacturer of artificial silk or a magnate on the Stock Exchange; if she had left two or three thousand pounds to Fernham, we could have been sitting at our ease tonight and the subject of our talk might have been archaeology, botany, anthropology, physics, the nature of the atom, mathematics, astronomy, relativity, geography. If only Mrs. Seton and her mother and her mother before her had learnt the great art of making money and had left their money, like their fathers and their grandfathers before them, to found fellowships and lectureships and prizes and scholarships appropriated to the use of their own sex, we might have dined very tolerably up here alone off a bird and a bottle of wine; we might have looked forward without undue confidence to a pleasant and honorable lifetime spent in the shelter of one of the liberally endowed professions. We might have been exploring or writing; mooning about the venerable places of the earth; sitting contemplative on the steps of the Parthenon, or going at ten to an office and coming home comfortably at half past four to write a little poetry. Only, if Mrs. Seton and her like had gone into business at the age of fifteen, there would have been—that was the snag in the argument—no Mary. What, I asked, did Mary think of that? There between the curtains was the October night, calm and lovely, with a star or two caught in the yellowing trees. Was she ready to resign her share of it and her memories (for they had been a happy family, though a large one) of games and quarrels up in Scotland, which she is never tired of praising for the fineness of its air and the quality of its cakes, in order that Fernham might have been endowed with fifty thousand pounds or so by a stroke of the pen? For, to endow a college would necessitate the suppression of families altogether. Making a fortune and bearing thirteen children—no human being could stand it. Consider the facts, we said. First there are nine months before the baby is born. Then the baby is born. Then there are three or four months spent in feeding the baby. After the baby is fed there are certainly five years spent in playing with the baby. You cannot, it seems, let children run about the streets. People who have seen them running wild in Russia say that the sight is not a pleasant one. People say, too, that human nature takes its shape in the years between one and five. If Mrs. Seton, I said, had been making money, what sort of memories would you have had of games and quarrels? What would you have known of Scotland, and its fine air and cakes and all the rest of it? But it is useless to ask these questions, because you would never have come into existence at all. Moreover, it is equally useless to ask what might have happened if Mrs. Seton and her mother and her mother before her had amassed great wealth and laid it under the foundations of college and library, because, in the first place, to earn money was impossible for them, and in the second, had it been possible, the law denied them the right to possess what money they earned. It is only for the last forty-eight years that Mrs. Seton has had a penny of her own. For all the centuries before that it would have been her husband's property—a thought which, perhaps, may have had its share in keeping Mrs. Seton and her mothers off the Stock Exchange. Every penny I earn, they may have said, will be taken from me and disposed of according to my husband's wisdom—perhaps to found a scholarship or to endow a fellowship in Balliol or Kings, so that to earn money, even if I could earn money, is not a matter that interests me very greatly. I had better leave it to my husband.

At any rate, whether or not the blame rested on the old lady who was looking at the spaniel, there could be no doubt that for some reason or other our mothers had mismanaged their affairs very gravely. Not a penny could be spared for "amenities"; for partridges and wine, beadles and turf, books and cigars, libraries and leisure. To raise bare walls out of the bare earth was the utmost they could do.

So we talked standing at the window and looking, as so many thousands look every night, down on the domes and towers of the famous city beneath us. It was very beautiful, very mysterious in the autumn moonlight. The old stone looked very white and venerable. One thought of all the books that were assembled down there; of the pictures of old prelates and worthies hanging in the paneled rooms; of the painted windows that would be throwing strange globes and crescents on the pavement; of the tablets and memorials and inscriptions; of the fountains and the grass; of the quiet rooms looking across the quiet quadrangles. And (pardon me the thought) I thought, too, of the admirable smoke and drink and the deep armchairs and the pleasant carpets: of the urbanity, the geniality, the dignity which are the offspring of luxury and privacy and space. Certainly our mothers had not provided us with anything comparable to all this—our mothers who found it difficult to scrape together thirty thousand pounds, our mothers who bore thirteen children to ministers of religion at St. Andrews.

So I went back to my inn, and as I walked through the dark streets I pondered this and that, as one does at the end of the day's work. I pondered why it was that Mrs. Seton had no money to leave us; and what effect poverty has on the mind; and what effect wealth has on the mind; and I thought of the queer old gentlemen I had seen that morning with tufts of fur upon their shoulders; and I remembered how if one whistled one of them ran; and I thought of the organ booming in the chapel and of the shut doors of the library; and I thought how unpleasant it is to be locked out; and I thought how it is worse perhaps to be locked in; and, thinking of the safety and prosperity of the one sex and of the poverty and insecurity of the other and of the effect of tradition and of the lack of tradition upon the mind of a writer, I thought at last that it was time to roll up the crumpled skin of the day, with its arguments and its impressions and its anger and its laughter, and cast it into the hedge. A thousand stars were flashing across the blue wastes of the sky. One seemed alone with an inscrutable society. All human beings were laid asleep—prone, horizontal, dumb. Nobody seemed stirring in the streets of Oxbridge. Even the door of the hotel sprang open at the touch of an invisible hand—not a boots was sitting up to light me to bed, it was so late.

Chapter Six

Next day the light of the October morning was falling in dusty shafts through the uncurtained windows, and the hum of traffic rose from the street. London then was winding itself up again; the factory was astir; the machines were beginning. It was tempting, after all this reading, to look out of the window and see what London was doing on the morning of the twenty-sixth of October 1928. And what was London doing? Nobody, it seemed, was reading *Antony and Cleopatra*. London was wholly indifferent, it appeared, to Shakespeare's plays. Nobody cared a straw—and I do not blame them—for the future of fiction, the death of poetry, or the development by the average woman of a prose style completely expressive of her mind. If opinions upon any of these matters had been chalked on the pavement, nobody would have stooped to read them. The nonchalance of the hurrying feet would have rubbed them out in half an hour. Here came an errand boy; here a woman with a dog on a lead. The fascination of the London street is that no two people are ever alike; each seems bound on some private affair of his own. There were the businesslike, with their little bags; there were the drifters rattling sticks upon area railings; there were affable characters to whom the streets serve for clubroom, hailing men in carts and giving information without being asked for it. Also there were funerals to which men, thus suddenly reminded of the passing of their own bodies, lifted their hats. And then a very distinguished gentleman came slowly down a doorstep and paused to avoid collision with a bustling lady who had, by some means or other, acquired a splendid fur coat and a bunch of Parma violets. They all seemed separate, self-absorbed, on business of their own.

At this moment, as so often happens in London, there was a complete lull and suspension of traffic. Nothing came down the street; nobody passed. A single leaf detached itself from the plane tree at the end of the street, and in that pause and suspension fell. Somehow it was like a signal falling, a signal pointing to a force in things which one had overlooked. It seemed to point to a river, which flowed past, invisibly, round the corner, down the street, and took people and eddied them along, as the stream at Oxbridge had taken the undergraduate in his boat and the dead leaves. Now it was bringing from one side of the street to the other diagonally a girl in patent leather boots, and then a young man in a maroon overcoat; it was also bringing a taxicab; and it brought all three together at a point directly beneath my window; where the taxi stopped; and the girl and the young man stopped; and they got into the taxi; and then the cab glided off as if it were swept on by the current elsewhere.

The sight was ordinary enough; what was strange was the rhythmical order with which my imagination had invested it; and the fact that the ordinary sight of two people getting into a cab had the power to communicate something of their own seeming satisfaction. The sight of two people coming down the street and meeting at the corner seems to ease the mind of some strain, I thought, watching the taxi turn and make off. Perhaps to think, as I had been thinking these two days, of one sex as distinct from the other is an effort. It interferes with the unity of the mind. Now that effort had ceased and that unity had been restored by seeing two people come together and get into a taxicab. The mind is certainly a very mysterious organ, I reflected, drawing my head in from the window, about which nothing whatever is known, though we depend upon it so completely. Why do I feel that there are severances and oppositions in the mind, as there are strains from obvious causes on the body? What does one mean by "the unity of the mind," I pondered, for clearly the mind has so great a power of concentrating at any point at any moment that it seems to have no single state of being. It can separate itself from the people in the street, for example, and think of itself as apart from them, at an upper window looking down on them. Or it can think with other people spontaneously, as, for instance, in a crowd waiting to hear some piece of news read out. It can think back through its fathers or through its mothers, as I have said that a woman writing thinks back through her mothers. Again if one is a woman one is often surprised by a sudden splitting off of consciousness, say in walking down Whitehall, when from being the natural inheritor of that civilization, she becomes, on the contrary, outside of it, alien and critical. Clearly the mind is always altering its focus, and bringing the world into different perspectives. But some of these states of mind seem, even if adopted spontaneously, to be less comfortable than others. In order to keep oneself continuing in them one is unconsciously holding something back, and gradually the repression becomes an effort. But there may be some state of mind in which one could continue without effort because nothing is required to be held back. And this perhaps, I thought, coming in from the window, is one of them. For certainly when I saw the couple get into the taxicab the mind felt as if, after being divided, it had come together again in a natural fusion. The obvious reason would be that it is natural for the sexes to cooperate. One has a profound, if irrational, instinct in favor of the theory that the union of man and woman makes for the greatest satisfaction, the most complete happiness. But the sight of the two people getting into the taxi and the satisfaction it gave me made me also ask whether there are two sexes in the mind corresponding to the two sexes in the body, and whether they also require to be united in order to get complete satisfaction and happiness. And I went on amateurishly to sketch a plan of the soul so that in each of us two powers preside, one male, one female; and in the man's brain, the man predominates over the woman, and in the woman's brain, the woman predominates over the man. The normal and comfortable state of being is that when the two live in harmony together, spiritually cooperating. If one is a man, still the woman part of the brain must have effect; and a woman also must have intercourse with the man in her. Coleridge perhaps meant this when he said that a great mind is androgynous. It is when this fusion takes place that the mind is fully fertilized and uses all its faculties. Perhaps a mind that is purely masculine cannot create, any more than a mind that is purely feminine, I thought. But it would be well to test what one meant by man-womanly, and conversely by woman-manly, by pausing and looking at a book or two.

Coleridge certainly did not mean, when he said that a great mind is androgynous, that it is a mind that has any special sympathy with women; a mind that takes up their cause or devotes itself to their interpretation. Perhaps the androgynous mind is less apt to make these distinctions than the single-sexed mind. He meant, perhaps, that the androgynous mind is resonant and porous; that it transmits emotion without impediment; that it is naturally creative, incandescent, and undivided. In fact one goes back to Shakespeare's mind as the type of the androgynous, of the man-womanly mind, though it would be impossible to say what Shakespeare thought of women. And if it be true that it is one of the tokens of the fully developed mind that it does not think specially or separately of sex, how much harder it is to attain that condition now than ever before. Here I came to the books by living writers, and there paused and wondered if this fact were not at the root of something that had long puzzled me. No age can ever have been as stridently sex-conscious as our own; those innumerable books by men about women in the British Museum are a proof of it. The Suffrage campaign was no doubt to blame. It must have roused in men an extraordinary desire for self-assertion; it must have made them lay emphasis upon their own sex and its characteristics which they would not have troubled to think about had they not been challenged. And when one is challenged, even by a few women in black bonnets, one retaliates, if one has never been challenged before, rather excessively. That perhaps accounts for some of the characteristics that I remember to have found here, I thought, taking down a new novel by Mr. A, who is in the prime of life and very well thought of, apparently, by the reviewers. I opened it. Indeed, it was delightful to read a man's writing again. It was so

direct, so straightforward after the writing of women. It indicated such freedom of mind, such liberty of person, such a confidence in himself. One had a
sense of physical well-being in the presence of this well-nourished, well-
educated, free mind, which had never been thwarted, or opposed, but had
had full liberty from birth to stretch itself in whatever way it liked. All this
was admirable. But after reading a chapter or two a shadow seemed to lie
across the page. It was a straight dark bar, a shadow shaped something like
the letter "I." One began dodging this way and that to catch a glimpse of the
landscape behind it. Whether that was indeed a tree or a woman walking I
was not quite sure. Back one was always hailed to the letter "I." One began to
be tired of "I." Not but what this "I" was a most respectable "I"; honest and
logical; as hard as a nut, and polished for centuries by good teaching and
good feeding. I respect and admire that "I" from the bottom of my heart.
But—here I turned a page or two, looking for something or other—the worst
of it is that in the shadow of the letter "I" all is shapeless as mist. Is that a
tree? No, it is a woman. But . . . she has not a bone in her body, I thought,
watching Phoebe, for that was her name, coming across the beach. Then Alan
got up and the shadow of Alan at once obliterated Phoebe. For Alan had
views and Phoebe was quenched in the flood of his views. And then Alan, I
thought, has passions; and here I turned page after page very fast, feeling
that the crisis was approaching, and so it was. It took place on the beach
under the sun. It was done very openly. It was done very vigorously. Nothing could have been more indecent. But . . . I had said "but" too often. One
cannot go on saying "but." One must finish the sentence somehow. I rebuked
myself. Shall I finish it. "But—I am bored!" But why was I bored? Partly because of the dominance of the letter "I" and the aridity, which, like the giant
beech tree, it casts within its shade. Nothing will grow there. And partly for
some more obscure reason. There seemed to be some obstacle, some impediment of Mr. A's mind which blocked the fountain of creative energy and
shored it within narrow limits. And remembering the lunch party at
Oxbridge, and the cigarette ash and the Manx cat and Tennyson and
Christina Rossetti all in a bunch, it seemed possible that the impediment lay
there. As he no longer hums under his breath, "There has fallen a splendid
tear from the passion-flower at the gate," when Phoebe crosses the beach,
and she no longer replies, "My heart is like a singing bird whose nest is in a
water'd shoot," when Alan approaches what can he do? Being honest as the
day and logical as the sun, there is only one thing he can do. And that he
does, to do him justice, over and over (I said, turning the pages) and over
again. And that, I added, aware of the awful nature of the confession, seems
somehow dull. Shakespeare's indecency uproots a thousand other things in
one's mind, and is far from being dull. But Shakespeare does it for pleasure;
Mr. A, as the nurses say, does it on purpose. He does it in protest. He is
protesting against the equality of the other sex by asserting his own superiority. He is therefore impeded and inhibited and self-conscious as Shakespeare
might have been if he too had known Miss Clough and Miss Davies. Doubt-

less Elizabethan literature would have been very different from what it is if the woman's movement had begun in the sixteenth century and not in the nineteenth.

What, then, it amounts to, if this theory of the two sides of the mind holds good, is that virility has now become self-conscious—men, that is to say, are now writing only with the male side of their brains. It is a mistake for a woman to read them, for she will inevitably look for something that she will not find. It is the power of suggestion that one most misses, I thought, taking Mr. B the critic in my hand and reading, very carefully and very dutifully, his remarks upon the art of poetry. Very able they were, acute and full of learning; but the trouble was, that his feelings no longer communicated; his mind seemed separated into different chambers; not a sound carried from one to the other. Thus, when one takes a sentence of Mr. B into the mind it falls plump to the ground—dead; but when one takes a sentence of Coleridge into the mind, it explodes and gives birth to all kinds of other ideas, and that is the only sort of writing of which one can say that it has the secret of perpetual life.

But whatever the reason may be, it is a fact that one must deplore. For it means—here I had come to rows of books by Mr. Galsworthy and Mr. Kipling—that some of the finest works of our greatest living writers fall upon deaf ears. Do what she will a woman cannot find in them that fountain of perpetual life which the critics assure her is there. It is not only that they celebrate male virtues, enforce male values, and describe the world of men; it is that the emotion with which these books are permeated is to a woman incomprehensible. It is coming, it is gathering, it is about to burst on one's head, one begins saying long before the end. That picture will fall on old Jolyon's head; he will die of the shock; the old clerk will speak over him two or three obituary words; and all the swans on the Thames will simultaneously burst out singing. But one will rush away before that happens and hide in the gooseberry bushes, for the emotion which is so deep, so subtle, so symbolical to a man moves a woman to wonder. So with Mr. Kipling's officers who turn their backs; and his Sowers who sow the Seed; and his Men who are alone with their Work; and the Flag—one blushes at all these capital letters as if one had been caught eavesdropping at some purely masculine orgy. The fact is that neither Mr. Galsworthy nor Mr. Kipling has a spark of the woman in him. Thus all their qualities seem to a woman, if one may generalize, crude and immature. They lack suggestive power. And when a book lacks suggestive power, however hard it hits the surface of the mind it cannot penetrate within.

And in that restless mood in which one takes books out and puts them back again without looking at them I began to envisage an age to come of pure, of self-assertive virility, such as the letters of professors (take Sir Walter Raleigh's letters, for instance) seem to forbode, and the rulers of Italy had already brought into being. For one can hardly fail to be impressed in Rome by the sense of unmitigated masculinity; and whatever the value of unmitigated masculinity upon the state, one may question the effect of it upon the art of poetry. At any rate, according to the newspapers, there is a certain anxiety about fiction in Italy. There has been a meeting of academicians whose object it is "to develop the Italian novel." "Men famous by birth, or in finance, industry, or the Fascist corporations" came together the other day and discussed the matter, and a telegram was sent to the Duce expressing the hope "that the Fascist era would soon give birth to a poet worthy of it." We may all join in that pious hope, but it is doubtful whether poetry can come out of an incubator. Poetry ought to have a mother as well as a father. The Fascist poem, one may fear, will be a horrid little abortion such as one sees in a glass jar in the museum of some county town. Such monsters never live long, it is said; one has never seen a prodigy of that sort cropping grass in a field. Two heads on one body do not make for the length of life.

However, the blame for all this, if one is anxious to lay blame, rests no more upon one sex than upon the other. All seducers and reformers are responsible, Lady Bessborough when she lied to Lord Granville; Miss Davies when she told the truth to Mr. Greg. All who have brought about a state of sex-consciousness are to blame, and it is they who drive me, when I want to stretch my faculties on a book, to seek it in that happy age, before Miss Davies and Miss Clough were born, when the writer used both sides of his mind equally. One must turn back to Shakespeare then, for Shakespeare was androgynous; and so was Keats and Sterne and Cowper and Lamb and Coleridge. Shelley perhaps was sexless. Milton and Ben Johnson had a dash too much of the male in them. So had Wordsworth and Tolstoi. In our time Proust was wholly androgynous, if not perhaps a little too much of a woman. But that failing is too rare for one to complain of it, since without some mixture of the kind the intellect seems to predominate and the other faculties of the mind harden and become barren. However, I consoled myself with the reflection that this is perhaps a passing phase; much of what I have said in obedience to my promise to give you the course of my thoughts will seem out of date; much of what flames in my eyes will seem dubious to you who have not yet come of age.

Even so, the very first sentence that I would write here, I said, crossing over to the writing table and taking up the page headed Women and Fiction, is that it is fatal for any one who writes to think of their sex. It is fatal to be a man or woman pure and simple; one must be woman-manly or man-womanly. It is fatal for a woman to lay the least stress on any grievance; to plead even with justice any cause; in any way to speak consciously as a woman. And fatal is no figure of speech; for anything written with that conscious bias is doomed to death. It ceases to be fertilized. Brilliant and effective, powerful and masterly, as it may appear for a day or two, it must wither at nightfall; it cannot grow in the minds of others. Some collaboration has to take place in the mind between the woman and the man before the act of creation can be accomplished. Some marriage of opposites has to be consummated. The whole of the mind must lie wide open if we are to get the sense that the writer is communicating his experience with perfect fullness. There must be freedom and there must be peace. Not a wheel must grate, not a light glimmer. The curtains must be close drawn. The writer, I thought, once his experience is over, must lie back and let his mind celebrate its nuptials in darkness. He must not look or question what is being done. Rather, he must pluck the petals from a rose or watch the swans float calmly down the river. And I saw again the current which took the boat and the undergraduate and the dead leaves; and the taxi took the man and the woman, I thought, seeing them come together across the street, and the current swept them away, I thought, hearing far off the roar of London's traffic, into that tremendous stream.

Here, then, Mary Beton ceases to speak. She has told you how she reached the conclusion—the prosaic conclusion—that it is necessary to have five hundred a year and a room with a lock on the door if you are to write fiction or poetry. She has tried to lay bare the thoughts and impressions that led her to think this. She has asked you to follow her flying into the arms of a Beadle, lunching here, dining there, drawing pictures in the British Museum, taking books from the shelf, looking out of the window. While she has been doing all these things, you no doubt have been observing her failings and foibles and deciding what effect they have had on her opinions. You have been contradicting her and making whatever additions and deductions seem good to you. That is all as it should be, for in a question like this truth is only to be had by laying together many varieties of error. And I will end now in my own person by anticipating two criticisms, so obvious that you can hardly fail to make them.

No opinion has been expressed, you may say, upon the comparative merits of the sexes even as writers. That was done purposely, because, even if the time had come for such a valuation—and it is far more important at the moment to know how much money women had and how many rooms than to theorize about their capacities—even if the time had come I do not believe that gifts, whether of mind or character, can be weighed like sugar and butter, not even in Cambridge, where they are so adept at putting people into classes and fixing caps on their heads and letters after their names. I do not believe that even the Table of Precedency which you will find in Whitaker's *Almanac* represents a final order of values, or that there is any sound reason to suppose that a Commander of the Bath will ultimately walk in to dinner behind a Master in Lunacy. All this pitting of sex against sex, of quality against quality; all this claiming of superiority and imputing of inferiority, belong to the private-school stage of human existence where there are "sides," and it is necessary for one side to beat another side, and of the utmost importance to walk up to a platform and receive from the hands of the Headmaster himself a highly ornamental pot. As people mature they cease to believe in sides or in Headmasters or in highly ornamental pots. At any rate, where books are concerned, it is notoriously difficult to fix labels of merit in such a way that they do not come off. Are not reviews of current literature a perpetual illustration of the difficulty of judgment? "This great book," "this worthless book," the same book is called by both names. Praise and blame alike mean nothing. No, delightful as the pastime of measuring may be, it is the most futile of all occupations, and to submit to the decrees of the measurers the most servile of attitudes. So long as you write what you wish to write, that is all that matters; and whether it matters for ages or only for hours, nobody can say. But to sacrifice a hair of the head of your vision, a shade of its color, in deference to some Headmaster with a silver pot in his hand or to some professor with a measuring rod up his sleeve, is the most abject treachery, and the sacrifice of wealth and chastity which used to be said to be the greatest of human disasters, a mere flea bite in comparison.

Next I think that you may object that in all this I have made too much of the importance of material things. Even allowing a generous margin for symbolism, that five hundred a year stands for the power to contemplate, that a lock on the door means the power to think for oneself, still you may say that the mind should rise above such things; and that great poets have often been poor men. Let me then quote to you the words of your own Professor of Literature, who knows better than I do what goes to the making of a poet. Sir Arthur Quiller-Couch writes:[3]

> What are the great poetical names of the last hundred years or so? Coleridge, Wordsworth, Byron, Shelley, Landor, Keats, Tennyson, Browning, Arnold, Morris, Rossetti, Swinburne— we may stop there. Of these, all but Keats, Browning, Rossetti were University men; and of these three, Keats, who died young, cut off in his prime, was the only one not fairly well to do. It may seem a brutal thing to say, and it is a sad thing to say: but, as a matter of hard fact, the theory that poetical genius bloweth where it listeth, and equally in poor and rich, holds little truth. As a matter of hard fact, nine out of those twelve were University men: which means that somehow or other they procured the means to get the best education England can give. As a matter of hard fact, of the remaining three you know that Browning was well to do, and I challenge you that, if he had not been well to do, he would no more have attained to write *Saul* or *The Ring and the Book* than Ruskin would have attained to writing *Modern Painters* if his father had not dealt prosperously in business. Rossetti had a small private income; and, moreover, he painted. There remains but Keats; whom Atropos slew young, as she slew John Clare in a madhouse, and James Thomson by the laudanum he took to drug disappointment. These are dreadful facts, but let us face them. It is—however dishonoring to us as a nation—certain that, by some fault in our commonwealth, the poor poet had not in these days, nor has had for two hundred years, a dog's chance. Believe me— and I have spent a great part of ten years in watching some three hundred and twenty elementary schools—we may prate

of democracy, but actually, a poor child in England has little more hope than had the son of an Athenian slave to be emancipated into that intellectual freedom of which great writings are born.

Nobody could put the point more plainly. "The poor poet has not in these days, nor has had for two hundred years, a dog's chance . . . a poor child in England has little more hope than had the son of an Athenian slave to be emancipated into that intellectual freedom of which great writings are born." That is it. Intellectual freedom depends upon material things. Poetry depends upon intellectual freedom. And women have always been poor, not for two hundred years merely, but from the beginning of time. Women have had less intellectual freedom than the sons of Athenian slaves. Women, then, have not had a dog's chance of writing poetry. That is why I have laid so much stress on money and a room of one's own. However, thanks to the toils of those obscure women in the past, of whom I wish we knew more, thanks, curiously enough, to two wars, the Crimean which let Florence Nightingale out of her drawing room, and the European War which opened the doors to the average woman some sixty years later, these evils are in the way to be bettered. Otherwise you would not be here tonight, and your chance of earning five hundred pounds a year, precarious as I am afraid that it still is, would be minute in the extreme.

Still, you may object, why do you attach so much importance to this writing of books by women when, according to you, it requires so much effort, leads perhaps to the murder of one's aunts, will make one almost certainly late for luncheon, and may bring one into very grave disputes with certain very good fellows? My motives, let me admit, are partly selfish. Like most uneducated Englishwomen, I like reading—I like reading books in the bulk. Lately my diet has become a trifle monotonous; history is too much about wars; biography too much about great men; poetry has shown, I think, a tendency to sterility, and fiction—but I have sufficiently exposed my disabilities as a critic of modern fiction and will say no more about it. Therefore I would ask you to write all kinds of books, hesitating at no subject however trivial or however vast. By hook or by crook, I hope that you will possess yourselves of money enough to travel and to idle, to contemplate the future or the past of the world, to dream over books and loiter at street corners and let the line of thought dip deep into the stream. For I am by no means confining you to fiction. If you would please me—and there are thousands like me—you would write books of travel and adventure, and research and scholarship, and history and biography, and criticism and philosophy and science. By so doing you will certainly profit the art of fiction. For books have a way of influencing each other. Fiction will be much better for standing cheek by jowl with poetry and philosophy. Moreover, if you consider any great figure of the past, like Sappho, like the Lady Murasaki, like Emily Brontë, you will find that she is an inheritor as well as an originator, and has come into existence because women have come to have the habit of writing naturally; so that even as a prelude to poetry such activity on your part would be invaluable.

But when I look back through these notes and criticize my own train of thought as I made them, I find that my motives were not altogether selfish. There runs through these comments and discursions the conviction—or is it the instinct?—that good books are desirable and that good writers, even if they show every variety of human depravity, are still good human beings. Thus when I ask you to write more books I am urging you to do what will be for your good and for the good of the world at large. How to justify this instinct or belief I do not know, for philosophic words, if one has not been educated at a university, are apt to play one false. What is meant by "reality"? It would seem to be something very erratic, very undependable—now to be found in a dusty road, now in a scrap of newspaper in the street, now in a daffodil in the sun. It lights up a group in a room and stamps some casual saying. It overwhelms one walking home beneath the stars and makes the silent world more real than the world of speech—and then there it is again in an omnibus in the uproar of Piccadilly. Sometimes, too, it seems to dwell in shapes too far away for us to discern what their nature is. But whatever it touches, it fixes and makes permanent. That is what remains over when the skin of the day has been cast into the hedge; that is what is left of past time and of our loves and hates. Now the writer, as I think, has the chance to live more than other people in the presence of this reality. It is his business to find it and collect it and communicate it to the rest of us. So at least I infer from reading *Lear* or *Emma* or *La recherche du temps perdu*. For the reading of these books seems to perform a curious couching operation on the senses; one sees more intensely afterwards; the world seems bared of its covering and given an intenser life. Those are the enviable people who live at enmity with unreality; and those are the pitiable who are knocked on the head by the thing done without knowing or caring. So that when I ask you to earn money and have a room of your own, I am asking you to live in the presence of reality, an invigorating life, it would appear, whether one can impart it or not.

Here I would stop, but the pressure of convention decrees that every speech must end with a peroration. And a peroration addressed to women should have something, you will agree, particularly exalting and ennobling about it. I should implore you to remember your responsibilities, to be higher, more spiritual; I should remind you how much depends upon you, and what an influence you can exert upon the future. But those exhortations can safely, I think, be left to the other sex, who will put them, and indeed have put them, with far greater eloquence than I can compass. When I rummage in my own mind I find no noble sentiments about being companions and equals and influencing the world to higher ends. I find myself saying briefly and prosaically that it is much more important to be oneself than anything else. Do not dream of influencing other people, I would say, if I knew how to make it sound exalted. Think of things in themselves.

And again I am reminded by dipping into newspapers and novels and biographies that when a woman speaks to women she should have something very unpleasant up her sleeve. Women are hard on women. Women dislike women. Women—but are you not sick to death of the word? I can assure you that I am. Let us agree, then, that a paper read by a woman to women should end with something particularly disagreeable.

But how does it go? What can I think of? The truth is, I often like women. I like their unconventionality. I like their subtlety. I like their anonymity. I like—but I must not run on in this way. That cupboard there,—you say it holds clean table napkins only; but what if Sir Archibald Bodkin were concealed among them? Let me then adopt a sterner tone. Have I, in the preceding words, conveyed to you sufficiently the warnings and reprobation of mankind? I have told you the very low opinion in which you were held by Mr. Oscar Browning. I have indicated what Napoleon once thought of you and what Mussolini thinks now. Then, in case any of you aspire to fiction, I have copied out for your benefit the advice of the critic about courageously acknowledging the limitations of your sex. I have referred to Professor X and given prominence to his statement that women are intellectually, morally, and physically inferior to men. I have handed on all that has come my way without going in search of it, and here is a final warning—from Mr. John Langdon Davies.[4] Mr. John Langdon Davies warns women "that when children cease to be altogether desirable, women cease to be altogether necessary." I hope you will make a note of it.

How can I further encourage you to go about the business of life? Young women, I would say, and please attend, for the peroration is beginning, you are, in my opinion, disgracefully ignorant. You have never made a discovery of any sort of importance. You have never shaken an empire or led an army into battle. The plays of Shakespeare are not by you, and you have never introduced a barbarous race to the blessings of civilization. What is your excuse? It is all very well for you to say, pointing to the streets and squares and forests of the globe swarming with black and white and coffee-colored inhabitants, all busily engaged in traffic and enterprise and lovemaking, we have had other work on our hands. Without our doing, those seas would be unsailed and those fertile lands a desert. We have borne and bred and washed and taught, perhaps to the age of six or seven years, the one thousand six hundred and twenty-three million human beings who are, according to statistics, at present in existence, and that, allowing that some had help, takes time.

There is truth in what you say—I will not deny it. But at the same time may I remind you that there have been at least two colleges for women in existence in England since the year 1866; that after the year of 1880 a married woman was allowed by law to possess her own property; and that in 1919—which is a whole nine years ago—she was given a vote? May I also remind you that the most of the professions have been open to you for close on ten years now? When you reflect upon these immense privileges and the length of time during which they have been enjoyed, and the fact that there must be at this moment some two thousand women capable of earning over five hundred a year in one way or another, you will agree that the excuse of lack of opportunity, training, encouragement, leisure, and money no longer holds good. Moreover, the economists are telling us that Mrs. Seton has had too many children. You must, of course, go on bearing children, but, so they say, in twos and threes, not in tens and twelves.

Thus, with some time on your hands and with some book learning in your brains—you have had enough of the other kind, and are sent to college partly, I suspect, to be uneducated—surely you should embark upon another stage of your very long, very laborious, and highly obscure career. A thousand pens are ready to suggest what you should do and what effect you will have. My own suggestion is a little fantastic, I admit; I prefer, therefore, to put it in the form of fiction.

I told you in the course of this paper that Shakespeare had a sister; but do not look for her in Sir Sidney Lee's life of the poet. She died young—alas, she never wrote a word. She lies buried where the omnibuses now stop, opposite the Elephant and Castle. Now my belief is that this poet who never wrote a word and was buried at the crossroads still lives. She lives in you and in me, and in many other women who are not here tonight, for they are washing up the dishes and putting the children to bed. But she lives; for great poets do not die; they are continuing presences; they need only the opportunity to walk among us in the flesh. This opportunity, as I think, it is now coming within your power to give her. For my belief is that if we live another century or so—I am talking of the common life which is the real life and not of the little separate lives which we live as individuals—and have five hundred a year each of us and rooms of our own; if we have the habit of freedom and the courage to write exactly what we think; if we escape a little from the common sitting room and see human beings not always in their relation to each other but in relation to reality; and the sky, too, and the trees or whatever it may be in themselves; if we look past Milton's bogey, for no human being should shut out the view; if we face the fact, for it is a fact, that there is no arm to cling to, but that we go alone and that our relation is to the world of reality and not only to the world of men and women, then the opportunity will come and the dead poet who was Shakespeare's sister will put on the body which she has so often laid down. Drawing her life from the lives of the unknown who were her forerunners, as her brother did before her, she will be born. As for her coming without that preparation, without that effort on our part, without that determination that when she is born again she shall find it possible to live and write her poetry, that we cannot expect, for that would be impossible. But I maintain that she would come if we worked for her, and that so to work, even in poverty and obscurity, is worth while.

NOTES

[1] "We are told that we ought to ask for £30,000 at least. .... It is not a large sum, considering that there is to be but one college of this sort for Great Britain, Ireland, and the Colonies, and considering how easy it is to raise immense sums for boys' schools. But considering how few people really wish women to be educated, it is a good deal."—Lady Stephen, *Life of Miss Emily Davies*.

[2] Every penny which could be scraped together was set aside for building, and the amenities had to be postponed.—R. Strachey, *The Cause*.

[3] *The Art of Writing*, by Sir Arthur Quiller-Couch.

[4] *A Short History of Women*, by John Langdon Davies.

• • • • • • • • • • •

QUESTIONS FOR A SECOND READING

1. One of the difficulties in reading "A Room of One's Own" is getting a feel for the tone of voice on the page—or, more properly, the tones of voice. Not only are there different voices speaking to you, but they speak as though they *were* speaking—that is, they rely on inflection and context to give you a sense of how a sentence is to be taken. How, for example, are you to read a line like this one near the conclusion of the final chapter: "Young women, I would say, and please attend, for the peroration is beginning, you are, in my opinion, disgracefully ignorant"? Who is speaking here? Or in whose voice is the speaker speaking? and to whom? That is, what kind of listener is imagined here? As you reread the essay, think about how its lines might be delivered and pay attention to shifts in tone of voice. You will need to do this not only to pick up the fine grain of the argument but also to see the argument about women's writing that is being *enacted* in this prose.

2. There are many unusual gestures and surprises in Woolf's prose. And these could be thought of as part of her argument about women's writing—that is, it is possible to see the writing in the essay as an enactment of her argument about the place of a woman writer in the context of a genre representing the voices and habits of men. The opening word of the book, for example, is "but," itself a bit of a surprise. "But, you may say, we asked you to speak about women and fiction—what has that got to do with a room of one's own?" From the very beginning, the text stands contrary to conventional expectations about style, subject, and presentation.

   As you reread the chapters, mark sections or places that break what you take to be the conventions of the essay, particularly the essay as it could be said to be a masculine genre. And as you mark them, think about what these moments might be said to represent. If they are resisting or revising the genre, why? to what end? with what possible intention?

3. As you read these two chapters you have the sense that you have been taken into someone else's thoughts as they are being developed. A sentence is broken, for example, when the speaker misses a turn in the road. Behind this fiction of spontaneous utterance, however, is a writer at work, not walking

down the street but sitting somewhere and writing, constructing this moment that you will experience at some other time and place. *This* writer is hard to find, however, behind the "I" of the speaker and the "I" of Mary Seton. At one point, in fact, Woolf says that the "I" in these sentences "is only a convenient term for somebody who has no real being."

As you reread these chapters, mark sections you could use to talk about their strategies of presentation and how these strategies are consistent (or inconsistent) with the argument the text makes about women's writing.

ASSIGNMENTS FOR WRITING

1. The title page of the original edition of *A Room of One's Own* said, "This essay is based upon two papers read to the Arts Society at Newnham and the Odtaa at Girton in October 1928. The papers were too long to be read in full, and have since been altered and expanded." As either an essay or the text of a public lecture, *A Room of One's Own* is full of surprises. It doesn't sound like the usual lecture; it doesn't do what essays usually do. At many places and in many ways it takes liberties with the conventions of the genre, with the essay's or the lecture's characteristic ways of addressing the audience, gathering information, and presenting an argument.

   As you reread these chapters and prepare to write about them, make note of the ways Woolf (the writer writing the text) constructs a space for speaker and audience, a kind of imaginary place where a woman can do her work, find a way of speaking, think as she might like to think, and prepare others to listen. Look for interesting and potentially significant ways she defies or transforms what you take to be the conventions of the essay. (See the second "Question for a Second Reading.") You might especially want to look at those places where Woolf seems to be saying, "I know what I should be doing here, but I won't. I'll do this instead."

   Choose four such moments and write an essay in which you discuss Woolf's chapters as a performance, a demonstration of a way of writing that pushes against the usual ways of manipulating words. While there is certainly an argument *in* Woolf's essay, your paper will be about the argument represented *by* the essay, an argument enacted in a way of writing. What is Woolf doing? How might you explain what she is doing and why? In what ways might her essay be seen as an example of someone working on the problems of writing? of a woman's writing? And what might this have to do with you, a student in a writing class?

2. In the opening of her essay, Woolf says that the "I" of her text "is only a convenient term for somebody who has no real being." And at the beginning of the last chapter (in reference to a new novel by "Mr. A"), she says,

   > But after reading a chapter or two a shadow seemed to lie across the page. It was a straight dark bar, a shadow shaped something like the letter "I." One began dodging this way and that to catch a glimpse of the landscape behind it. Whether that was indeed a tree or a woman walking I was not quite sure. Back one was always hailed to the letter "I." One began to be tired of "I." (p. 735)

It's hard to know what to make of this, as an argument about either the position of women or writing. Read back through Woolf's essay, noting sections you could use to investigate the ways an "I" is or is not present in this text and to investigate the argument that text makes about a writer's (or speaker's) presence. (See the third "Question for a Second Reading.")

Write an essay in which you examine the ways Woolf, a writer, is and is not present in this piece of writing. Where and how does she hide? And why? Whom do you find in her place? How might this difficulty over the presence of the writer be said to be a part of Woolf's argument about women and writing? And what might this have to do with you and the writing you are doing, either in this class or in school generally?

MAKING CONNECTIONS

1. In a section of the book not included here, Woolf talks about sentences. She says that one of the problems women writers face is that the sentences available to them are men's sentences, unsuitable for a woman's use: "The weight, the pace, the stride of a man's mind are too unlike her own for her to lift anything substantial from him successfully." Moreover, she says, "a book is not made of sentences laid end to end, but of sentences built, if an image helps, into arcades or domes. And this shape too has been made by men out of their own needs for their own uses."

   Sentences, and sentences built into shapes—let's take Woolf's line of thought seriously and inquire into the characteristic shapes of some writing that seems "manly" or "womanly." You will need to begin by gathering interesting specimens—sentences, paragraphs, whatever "shapes" seem significant and manageable. Begin with Woolf's essay and turn to two others in this book—one that seems more manly than womanly and one that seems more womanly than manly. You will need to gather sentences, paragraphs, or passages from these essays as well. (Keep in mind that these types of prose are not necessarily determined by the sex of the writer.) Write an essay in which you present and discuss these pieces of writing as representative ways of gathering material, of thinking it through, of presenting oneself and one's thoughts, of imagining a world of speakers and listeners.

2. In "When We Dead Awaken: Writing as Re-Vision" (p. 549), Adrienne Rich says the following of Woolf's prose:

   > In rereading Virginia Woolf's *A Room of One's Own* (1929) for the first time in some years, I was astonished at the sense of effort, of pains taken, of dogged tentativeness, in the tone of that essay. And I recognized that tone. I had heard it often enough, in myself and in other women. It is the tone of a woman almost in touch with her anger, who is determined not to appear angry, who is *willing* herself to be calm, detached, and even charming in a roomful of men where things have been said which are attacks on her very integrity. Virginia Woolf is addressing an audience of women, but she is acutely conscious—as she always was—of being overheard by men: by Morgan and Lytton and Maynard Keynes and for that matter by her father, Leslie Stephen. She drew the language out into an exacerbated thread in her determination

to have her own sensibility yet protect it from those masculine presences. Only at rare moments in that essay do you hear the passion in her voice; she was trying to sound as cool as Jane Austen, as Olympian as Shakespeare, because that is the way the men of the culture thought a writer should sound. (p. 552)

Let's assume that this is a way of reading *A Room of One's Own*, but not the last word. It can be seen as opening a space for a response, for a conversation. Write an essay in which you offer a response to Rich, one rooted in your own experience reading (or rereading) these chapters.

Before you begin writing, you should reread the chapters, paying particular attention to tone and voice, looking for passages you can use in forming a response to Rich. You should also reread Rich's essay, not only for what she says about Woolf but for the examples she offers of tone and voice, of a woman writing, conscious, as Rich is too, of the context provided by the men of the culture. You can offer your reading not only of Woolf's prose but of Rich's prose as well.

Assignment
Sequences

WORKING WITH ASSIGNMENT SEQUENCES

*T*HE *ASSIGNMENT SEQUENCES* that follow are different from the single writing assignments at the end of each essay. The single writing assignments are designed to give you a way back into the works you have read. They define the way you, the reader, can work on an essay by writing about it—testing its assumptions, probing its examples, applying its way of thinking to a new setting or to new material. A single assignment might ask you to read what Paulo Freire has to say about education and then, as a writer, to use Freire's terms and methods to analyze a moment from your own schooling. The single assignments are designed to demonstrate how a student might work on an essay, particularly an essay that is long or complex, and they are designed to show how pieces that might seem daunting are open, manageable, and managed best by writing.

The assignment sequences have a similar function, but with one important difference. Instead of writing one paper, or working on one or two selections from the book, you will be writing several essays and reading several selections. Your work will be sequential as well as cumulative. The work you do on Freire, for example, will give you a way of beginning with Mary Louise Pratt, or Adrienne Rich. It will give you an angle of vision. You won't be a newcomer to such discussions. Your previous reading will make the new essay rich with association. Passages or examples will jump out, as if magnetized, and demand your attention. And by reading these essays in context, you will see each writer as a single voice in a larger discussion. Neither Freire, nor Pratt, nor Rich, after all, has had the last word on the subject of education. It is not as though, by working on one of the essays, you have wrapped the subject up, ready to be put on the shelf.

The sequences are designed, then, so that you will be working not only on essays but on a subject, like education (or history, or culture, or the autobiography), a subject that can be examined, probed, and understood through the various frames provided by your reading. Each essay becomes a way of seeing a problem or a subject; it becomes a tool for thinking, an example of how a mind might work, a way of using language to make a subject rich and alive. In the assignment sequences, your reading is not random. Each sequence provides a set of readings that can be pulled together into a single project.

The sequences allow you to participate in an extended academic project, one with several texts and several weeks' worth of writing. You are not just adding one essay to another (Freire + Pratt = ?) but trying out an approach to a subject by revising it, looking at new examples, hearing what someone else has to say, and beginning again to take a position of your own. Projects like these take time. It is not at all uncommon for professional writers to devote weeks or even months to a single essay, and the essay they write marks not the end of their thinking on the subject, but only one stage. Similarly, when readers are working on a project, the pieces they read accumulate on their desks and in their minds and become part of an extended conversation with several speakers, each voice offering a point of view on a subject, a new set of examples, or a new way of talking that resonates with echoes from earlier reading.

A student may read many books, take several courses, write many papers; ideally each experience becomes part of something larger, an education. The work of understanding, in other words, requires time and repeated effort. The power that comes from understanding cannot be acquired quickly—by reading one essay or working for a few hours. A student, finally, is a person who choreographs such experiences, not someone who passes one test only to move on to another. And the assignment sequences are designed to reproduce, although in a condensed period of time, the rhythm and texture of academic life. They invite you to try on its characteristic ways of seeing, thinking, and writing. The work you do in one week will not be lost when it has bearing on the work you do in the next. If an essay by Virginia Woolf has value for you, it is not because you proved to a teacher that you read it, but because you have put it to work and made it a part of your vocabulary as a student.

Working with a Sequence

Here is what you can expect as you work with a sequence. You begin by working with a single story or essay. You will need to read each piece twice, the second time with the "Questions for a Second Reading" and the assignment sequence in mind. Before rereading the selection, in other words, you should read through the assignments to get a sense of where you will be headed. And you should read the questions at the end of each selection. (You can use those questions to help frame questions of your own.) The purpose of all these questions, in a sense, is to prepare the text to speak—to bring it to life and insist that it respond to your attention, answer your questions. If you think of the authors as people you can talk to, if you think of their pages as occasions for dialogue (as places where you get to ask questions and insist on responses)—if you prepare your return to those pages in these ways, you are opening up the essays or stories (not closing them down or finishing them off) and creating a scene where you get to step forward as a performer.

While each sequence moves from selection to selection in *Ways of Reading*, the most significant movement in the sequence is defined by the essays you write. Your essays provide the other major text for the course. In fact, when we teach these sequences, we seldom have any discussion of the assigned readings before our students have had a chance to write. When we talk as a group about Rich's "When We Dead Awaken: Writing as Re-Vision," for example, we begin by reproducing one or two student essays, handing them out to the class, and using them as the basis for discussion. We want to start, in other words, by looking at ways of reading Rich's essay—not at her essay alone.

The essays you write for each assignment in a sequence might be thought of as work-in-progress. Your instructor will tell you the degree to which each essay should be finished—that is, the degree to which it should be revised and copy-edited and worked into a finished performance. In our classes, most writing assignments go through at least one revision. After we have had a chance to see a draft (or after a draft has been seen by others in the class), and after we have had some discussion of sample student essays we ask students to read the assigned essay or story one more time and to rework their essays to bring their work one step further—not necessarily to finish the essays (as though there would be nothing else to say) but to finish up this stage in their work and to feel their achievement in a way a writer simply cannot the first time through. Each assignment, then, really functions as two assignments in the schedule for the course. As a consequence, we don't "cover" as many essays in a semester as students might in another class. But coverage is not our goal. In a sense, we are teaching our students how to read slowly and closely, to return to a text rather than set it aside, to take the time to reread and rewrite and to reflect on what these activities entail. Some of these sequences, then, contain more readings or more writing assignments than you can address in a quarter or semester. Different courses work at different paces. It is important, however, to preserve time for rereading and rewriting. The sequences were written with the assumption that they would be revised to meet the needs of teachers, students, and programs. As you look at your syllabus, you may find, then, that reading or writing assignments have been changed, added, or dropped.

You will be writing papers that can be thought of as single essays. But you will also be working on a project, something bigger than its individual parts. From the perspective of the project, each piece you write is part of a larger body of work that evolves over the term. You might think of each sequence as a revision exercise, where the revision looks forward to what comes next as well as backward to what you have done. This form of revision asks you to do more than complete a single paper; it invites you to resee a subject or reimagine what you might say about it from a new point of view. You should feel free, then, to draw on your earlier essays when you work on one of the later assignments. There is every reason for you to reuse ideas, phrases, sentences, even paragraphs as your work builds from one week to the next. The advantage of work-in-progress is that you are not starting over completely every time you sit down to write. You've been over this territory before. You've developed some expertise in your subject. There is a body of work behind you.

Most of the sequences bring together several essays from the text and ask you to imagine them as an extended conversation, one with several speakers. The assignments are designed to give you a voice in the conversation as well, to allow you to speak in turn and to take your place in the company of other writers. This is the final purpose of the assignment sequence: after several weeks' work on the essays and on the subject that draws them together, you will begin to establish your own point of view. You will develop a position from which you can speak with authority, drawing strength from the work you have done as well as from your familiarity with the people who surround you.

This book brings together some of the most powerful voices of our culture. They speak in a manner that asks for response. The assignments at the end of each selection and, with a wider range of reference, the assignment sequences here at the end of the book demonstrate that there is no reason for a student, in such company, to remain silent.

The Aims of Education

Paulo Freire

Adrienne Rich

Mary Louise Pratt

Susan Griffin

*Y*OU HAVE BEEN in school for several years, long enough for your experiences in the classroom to seem natural, inevitable. The purpose of this
sequence is to invite you to step outside a world you may have begun to take
for granted, to look at the ways you have been taught and at the unspoken
assumptions behind your education. The eight assignments that follow bring
together four essays that discuss how people (and particularly students) become trapped inside habits of thought. These habits of thought (they are
sometimes referred to as "structures" of thought; Adrienne Rich calls them
the "assumptions in which we are drenched") become invisible (or seem natural) because of the ways our schools work or because of the ways we have
traditionally learned to use language when we speak, read, or write.

The essays brought together in this sequence provide powerful critiques
of the usual accounts of education. The first two (by Paulo Freire and Adrienne Rich) argue that there are, or should be, ways of using language that
can enable a person to break free from limited or limiting ways of thinking.
The next, by Mary Louise Pratt, examines the classroom as an imagined community and discusses the nature of a student's participation in that community. The last reading in this sequence, the selection from Susan Griffin's
A Chorus of Stones, is presented as an example of an alternative intellectual or

academic project, one driven by a desire to know and understand the past but written outside the usual conventions of history or the social sciences. The writing assignments that accompany the readings provide an opportunity for you to test the arguments in the individual essays by weighing them against scenes and episodes from your own schooling. Some ask you to work within a specific argument (Rich's account of patriarchy, for example), and some ask you to experiment with the conventions of academic prose. (In some classes, students may be asked to work with a selection of these assignments.) The final assignment provides an occasion for you to draw material from all the essays you have written for this sequence into a final and more comprehensive statement on schools and schooling.

• • • • • • • • • • • •

ASSIGNMENT 1

Applying Freire to Your Own Experience as a Student [Freire]

> The teacher talks about reality as if it were motionless, static, compartmentalized, and predictable. Or else he expounds on a topic completely alien to the existential experience of the students. His task is to "fill" the students with the contents of his narration—contents which are detached from reality, disconnected from the totality that engendered them and could give them significance. Words are emptied of their concreteness and become a hollow, alienated, and alienating verbosity. (p. 212)
>
> — PAULO FREIRE
> *The "Banking" Concept of Education*

Surely, anyone who has made it through twelve years of formal education can think of a class, or an occasion outside of class, to serve as a quick example of what Freire calls the "banking" concept of education, where students are turned into "containers" to be "filled" by their teachers. If Freire is to be useful to you, however, he must do more than call up quick examples. He should allow you to say more than that a teacher once treated you like a container (or that a teacher once gave you your freedom).

Write an essay that focuses on a rich and illustrative incident from your own educational experience and read it (that is, interpret it) as Freire would. You will need to provide careful detail: things that were said and done, perhaps the exact wording of an assignment, a textbook, or a teacher's comments. And you will need to turn to the language of Freire's argument, to take key phrases and passages from his argument and see how they might be used to investigate your case.

To do this you will need to read your account as not simply the story of you and your teacher, since Freire is not writing about individual personalities (an innocent student and a mean teacher, a rude teacher, or a thoughtless teacher) but about the roles we are cast in, whether we choose to be or not, by our culture and its institutions. The key question, then, is not who you were or who your teacher was but what roles you played and how those roles can lead you to better understand the larger narrative or drama of Education (an organized attempt to "regulate the way the world 'enters into' the students").

Note: Freire would not want you to work passively or mechanically, as though you were merely following orders. He would want you to make your own mark on the work he has begun. Use your example, in other words, as a way of testing and examining what Freire says, particularly those passages that you find difficult or obscure.

．　．　．　．　．　．　．　．　．　．　．　．

ASSIGNMENT 2

Studying Rich as a Case in Point
[Freire, Rich]

The truth is, however, that the oppressed are not "marginals," are not men living "outside" society. They have always been "inside"—inside the structure which made them "beings for others." The solution is not to "integrate" them into the structure of oppression, but to transform that structure so that they can become "beings for themselves." Such transformation, of course, would undermine the oppressors' purposes. (pp. 214–15)

− PAULO FREIRE
The "Banking" Concept of Education

For a poem to coalesce, for a character or an action to take shape, there has to be an imaginative transformation of reality which is in no way passive. . . . Moreover, if the imagination is to transcend and transform experience it has to question, to challenge, to conceive of alternatives, perhaps to the very life you are living at that moment. You have to be free to play around with the notion that day might be night, love might be hate; nothing can be too sacred for the imagination to turn into its opposite or to call experimentally by another name. For writing is renaming. (pp. 556–57)

— ADRIENNE RICH
When We Dead Awaken: Writing as Re-Vision

Both Freire and Rich talk repeatedly about transformations—about transforming structures, transforming the world, transforming the way language is used, transforming the relations between people. In fact, the changes in Rich's poetry might be seen as evidence of her transforming the structures from within which she worked. And, when Freire takes a situation we think of as "natural" (teachers talking and students sitting silent) and names it "banking education," he makes it possible for students and their teachers to question, challenge, conceive of alternatives, and transform experience. Each, in other words, can be framed as an example in the language of the other—Freire in Rich's terms, Rich in Freire's. For both, this act of transformation is something that takes place within and through the use of language.

Rich's essay could be read as a statement about the aims of education, particularly if the changes in her work are taken as evidence of something the poet learned to do. Rich talks about teachers, about people who helped her to reimagine her situation as a woman and a poet, and about the work she had to do on her own.

For this assignment, take three of the poems Rich offers as examples of change in her writing—"Aunt Jennifer's Tigers," the section from "Snapshots of a Daughter-in-Law," and "Planetarium"—and use them as a way of talking about revision. What, to your mind, are the key differences between these poems? What might the movement they mark be said to represent? And what do these poems, as examples, have to do with the argument about writing, culture, and gender in the rest of the essay?

As you prepare to write, you might also ask some questions in Freire's name. For example: What problems did Rich pose for herself? How might this be taken as an example of a problem-posing education? In what ways might Rich be said to have been having a "dialogue" with her own work? Who was the teacher (or the teachers) here and what did the poet learn to do?

You are not alone as you read these poems, in other words. In fact, Rich provides her own commentary on the three poems, noting what for her are key changes and what they represent. You will want to acknowledge what Rich has to say, to be sure, but you should not be bound by it. You, too, are a person with a point of view on this issue. Rich (with Freire) provides a powerful language for talking about change, but you want to be sure to carve out space where you have the opportunity to speak as well.

• • • • • • • • • • •

ASSIGNMENT **3**

Tradition and the Writing of the Past [Rich]

> We need to know the writing of the past, and know it differ-
> ently than we have ever known it; not to pass on a tradition but
> to break its hold over us. (p. 551)
> — ADRIENNE RICH
> *When We Dead Awaken: Writing as Re-Vision*

"We need to know the writing of the past," Rich says. The "we" of that sentence can be read as an invitation to you. Look back over your own writing (perhaps the drafts and revisions you have written for this course), and think back over comments teachers have made, textbooks you have seen; think about what student writers do and what they are told to do, about the secrets students keep and the secrets teachers keep. You can assume, as Rich does, that there are ways of speaking about writing that are part of the culture of schooling and that they are designed to preserve certain ways of writing and thinking and to discourage others. Write an essay in which you reflect on the writing of the past and its presence in your own work as a writer.

One might argue, in other words, that there are ways of writing that are part of schooling. There are traditions here, too. As you look at the evidence of the "past" in your own work, what are its significant features: What might you name this tradition (or these traditions)? What are the "official" names? What do these names tell us? What do they hide? What difference might it make to name tradition in terms of gender and call it "patriarchal"?

How would you illustrate the hold this tradition has on your work or the work of students generally? What might you have to do to begin to "know it differently," "to break its hold," or to revise? And, finally, why would someone want (or not want) to make such a break?

759

• • • • • • • • • • • •

ASSIGNMENT 4

The Contact Zone [Pratt]

> The idea of the contact zone is intended in part to contrast with ideas of community that underlie much of the thinking about language, communication, and culture that gets done in the academy. (p. 536)
>
> — MARY LOUISE PRATT
> *Arts of the Contact Zone*

Citing Benedict Anderson and what he calls "imagined communities," Pratt argues that our idea of community is "strongly utopian, embodying values like equality, fraternity, liberty, which the societies often profess but systematically fail to realize." Against this utopian vision of community, Pratt argues that we need to develop ways of understanding (even noticing) social and intellectual spaces that are not homogeneous, unified; we need to develop ways of understanding and valuing difference. And, for Pratt, the argument extends to schooling. "What is the place," she asks,

> of unsolicited oppositional discourse, parody, resistance, cri-
> tique in the imagined classroom community? Are teachers sup-
> posed to feel that their teaching has been most successful when
> they have eliminated such things and unified the social world,
> probably in their own image? Who wins when we do that?
> Who loses? (p. 539)

Such questions, she says, "may be hypothetical, because in the United States in the 1990s, many teachers find themselves less and less able to do that even if they want to."

"In the United States in the 1990s." "The imagined classroom." From your experience, what scenes might be used to represent schooling in the 1990s? How are they usually imagined (idealized, represented, interpreted, valued)? What are the implications of Pratt's argument?

Write an essay in which you use Pratt's terms to examine a representa-tive scene from your own experience with schools and schooling. What ex-amples, stories, or images best represent your experience? How might they be interpreted as examples of community? as examples of "contact zones"? As you prepare your essay, you will want to set the scene as carefully as you can, so that someone who was not there can see it fully. Think about how someone who has not read Pratt might interpret the scene. And think through the various ways *you* might interpret your example. And you should also think about your position in an argument about school as a "contact zone." What do you (or people like you) stand to gain or lose when you adopt Pratt's point of view?

* * * * * * * * * * * *

ASSIGNMENT 5

The Pedagogical Arts of the Contact Zone [Pratt]

> Meanwhile, our job in the Americas course remains to figure out how to make that crossroads the best site for learning that it can be. We are looking for the pedagogical arts of the contact zone. These will include, we are sure, exercises in storytelling and in identifying with the ideas, interests, histories, and attitudes of others; experiments in transculturation and collaborative work and in the arts of critique, parody, and comparison (including unseemly comparisons between elite and vernacular cultural forms); the redemption of the oral; ways for people to engage with suppressed aspects of history (including their own histories), ways to move *into and out of* rhetorics of authenticity; ground rules for communication across lines of difference and hierarchy that go beyond politeness but maintain mutual respect; a systematic approach to the all-important concept of *cultural mediation*. (p. 541)

> — MARY LOUISE PRATT
> *Arts of the Contact Zone*

Pratt writes generally about culture and history, but also about reading and writing and teaching and learning, about the "literate" and "pedagogical" arts of this place she calls the "contact zone." Think about the class you are in—its position in the curriculum, in the institution. Think about its official goals (and its unofficial goals). Think about the positions represented by the students, the teacher. Think about how to think about the class, in Pratt's terms, as a "contact zone."

And think about the unusual exercises represented by her list: "storytelling," "experiments in transculturation," "critique," "parody," "unseemly comparisons," moving into and out of "rhetorics of authenticity"—these are some of them. Take one of these suggested exercises, explain what you take it to mean, and then go on to discuss how it might be put into practice in a writing class. What would students do? to what end? How would their work be evaluated? What place would the exercise have in the larger sequence of assignments over the term, quarter, or semester? In your terms, and from your point of view, what might you learn from such an exercise?

Or you could think of the question this way: What comments would a teacher make on one of the papers you have written so far in order that its revision might stand as one of these exercises? How would the revision be different from what you are used to doing?

Write an essay in which you present and discuss an exercise designed to serve the writing class as a "contact zone."

. . . .

ASSIGNMENT 6

Writing against the Grain [Griffin]

As you reread "Our Secret," think of Griffin's prose as experimental, as deliberate and crafted. She is trying to do something that she can't do in the "usual" essay form. She wants to make a different kind of argument and engage her reader in a different manner. And so she mixes personal and academic writing. She assembles fragments and juxtaposes seemingly unrelated material in surprising and suggestive relationships. She breaks the "plane" of the page with italicized inter-sections. She organizes her material, that is, but not in the usual mode of thesis-example-conclusion. The arrangement is not nearly so linear. At one point, when she seems to be prepared to argue that German child-rearing practices produced the Holocaust, she quickly says:

> Of course there cannot be one answer to such a monumental riddle, nor does any event in history have a single cause. Rather a field exists, like a field of gravity that is created by the movements of many bodies. Each life is influenced and it in turn becomes an influence. Whatever is a cause is also an effect. Childhood experience is just one element in the determining field. (p. 324)

Her prose serves to create a "field," one where many bodies are set in relationship.

It is useful, then, to think about Griffin's prose as the enactment of a method, as a way of doing a certain kind of intellectual work. One way to study this, to feel its effects, is to imitate it, to take it as a model. For this assignment, write a Griffin-like essay, one similar in its methods or organization and argument. You will need to think about the stories you might tell, about the stories and texts you might gather (stories and texts not your own).

As you write, you will want to think carefully about arrangement and about commentary (about where, that is, you will speak to your reader *as* the writer of the piece). You should not feel bound to Griffin's subject matter, but you should feel that you are working in her spirit.

• • • • • • • • • • •

ASSIGNMENT 7

The Task of Attention [Griffin]

I am looking now at the etching called *Poverty*, made in 1897. Near the center, calling my attention, a woman holds her head in her hands. (p. 328)

— SUSAN GRIFFIN
Our Secret

This is one of the many moments where Griffin speaks to us as though in the midst of her work. The point of this assignment is to think about that work—what it is, how she does it, and what it might have to do with schools and schooling. She is, after all, doing much of the traditional work of scholars—going to the archive, studying old materials, traveling and interviewing subjects, learning and writing history.

And yet this is not the kind of prose you would expect to find in a textbook for a history course. Even if the project is not what we usually think of as a "research" project, Griffin is a careful researcher. Griffin knows what she is doing. Having experimented with a Griffin-like essay, go back now to look again (this time with a writer's eye) at both the features of Griffin's prose and the way she characterizes her work as a scholar, gathering and studying her materials.

Write an essay in which you present an account of *how* Griffin does her work. You should use her words and examples from the text, but you should also feel that it is your job to explain what you present and to comment on it from the point of view of a student. As you reread, look to those sections where Griffin seems to be speaking to her readers about her work—about how she reads and how she writes, about how she gathers her materials and how she studies them. What is she doing? What is at stake in adopting such methods? How might they be taught? Where in the curriculum might (should?) such lessons be featured?

· · · · · · · · · · · ·

ASSIGNMENT 8

Putting Things Together
[Freire, Rich, Pratt, Griffin]

This is the final assignment of this sequence, and it is the occasion for you to step back and take stock of all that you have done. Perhaps the best way for you to do this is by making a statement of your own about the role of reading and writing in an undergraduate education. You might, for example, write a document for students who will be entering your school for the first time, telling them what they should expect or what they should know about reading and writing if they want to make the most of their education. Or this might be an essay written for an alumni magazine or a paper for a faculty committee charged with reviewing undergraduate education. Or you might want to think of this essay as primarily autobiographical, as that chapter of your autobiography where you think through your experiences with schooling.

You should feel free to draw as much as you can from the papers you have already written, making your points through examples you have already examined, perhaps using your own work with these assignments as an example of what students might be expected to do.

SEQUENCE TWO

The Arts of the
Contact Zone

Mary Louise Pratt
Gloria Anzaldúa
Harriet Jacobs
Stephen Greenblatt

*T*HIS SEQUENCE allows you to work closely with the argument of Mary Louise Pratt's "Arts of the Contact Zone," not so much through summary (repeating the argument) as through extension (working under its influence, applying its terms and protocols). In particular, you are asked to try your hand at those ways of reading and writing Pratt defines as part of the "literate arts of the contact zone," ways of reading and writing that have not historically been taught or valued in American schools.

Pratt is one of the country's most influential cultural critics. In "Arts of the Contact Zone," she makes the argument that our usual ways of reading and writing assume identification—that is, we learn to read and write the texts that express our own position and point of view. As a result, texts that reproduce different ways of thinking, texts that allude to different cultural systems, seem flawed, wrong, or inscrutable. As a counterposition, Pratt asks us to imagine scenes of reading, writing, teaching, and learning as "contact zones," places of contact between people who can't or don't or won't necessarily identify with one another.

In the first assignment, you are asked to search for or produce a document to exemplify the arts of the contact zone, working in library archives, searching the streets, or writing an "autoethnography." This is a big job, and probably new to most students; it is a project you will want to come back to and revise. The next assignments ask you to look at three selections in *Ways of Reading* that exemplify or present movements of cultural contact: Gloria Anzaldúa's *Borderlands/La frontera,* a text that announces itself as the product of a mixed, *mestiza* cultural position; Harriet Jacobs's "Incidents in the Life of a Slave Girl," a slave narrative (or "autoethnography"); and Stephen Greenblatt's reading of Columbus's journals in "Marvelous Possessions." The final assignment asks you to think back over both Pratt's argument and your work to make a more general statement about the arts of the contact zone.

• • • • • • • • • • •

ASSIGNMENT 1

The Literate Arts of the Contact Zone [Pratt]

Here, briefly, are two descriptions of the writing one might find or expect in the "contact zone":

> Autoethnography, transculturation, critique, collaboration, bilingualism, mediation, parody, denunciation, imaginary dialogue, vernacular expression—these are some of the literate arts of the contact zone. Miscomprehension, incomprehension, dead letters, unread masterpieces, absolute heterogeneity of meaning—these are some of the perils of writing in the contact zone. They all live among us today in the transnationalized metropolis of the United States and are becoming more widely visible, more pressing, and, like Guaman Poma's text, more decipherable to those who once would have ignored them in defense of a stable, centered sense of knowledge and reality. (p. 536)

> We are looking for the pedagogical arts of the contact zone. These will include, we are sure, exercises in storytelling and in identifying with the ideas, interests, histories, and attitudes of others; experiments in transculturation and collaborative work and in the arts of critique, parody, and comparison (including unseemly comparisons between elite and vernacular cultural forms); the redemption of the oral; ways for people to engage with suppressed aspects of history (including their own histories), ways to move *into and out of* rhetorics of authenticity; ground rules for communication across lines of difference and

hierarchy that go beyond politeness but maintain mutual respect; a systematic approach to the all-important concept of *cultural mediation*. (p. 541)

Here are two ways of working on Pratt's idea of the "contact zone." Choose one.

1. One way of working with Pratt's essay, of extending its project, would be to conduct your own local inventory of writing from the contact zone. You might do this on your own or in teams, with others from your class. You will want to gather several similar documents, your "archive," before you make a final selection. Think about how to make that choice. What makes one document stand out as representative? Here are two ways you might organize your search:

   a. You could look for historical documents. A local historical society might have documents written by Native Americans ("Indians") to the white settlers. There may be documents written by slaves to masters or to northern whites explaining their experience. There may be documents written by women (suffragettes, for example) trying to negotiate for public positions or rights. There may be documents from any of a number of racial or ethnic groups—Hispanic, Jewish, Irish, Italian, Polish, Swedish—trying to explain their positions to the mainstream culture. There may, perhaps at union halls, be documents written by workers to owners. Your own sense of the heritage of your area should direct your search.

   b. Or you could look at contemporary documents in the print that is around you, texts that you might otherwise overlook. Pratt refers to one of the characteristic genres of the Hispanic community, the *"testimonio."* You could look for songs, testimonies, manifestos, statements by groups on campus, stories, autobiographies, interviews, letters to the editor. You could look at the writing of any marginalized group, particularly writing intended, at least in part, to represent the experience of outsiders to the dominant culture (or to be in dialogue with that culture or to respond to that culture). These documents, if we follow Pratt's example, would encompass the work of young children or students, including college students.

   Once you have completed your inventory, choose a document you would like to work with and write an essay that presents it carefully and in detail (perhaps in even greater detail than Pratt's presentation of the *New Chronicle*). You will, in other words, need to set the scene, summarize, explain, and work block quotations into your essay. You might imagine that you are presenting this to someone who would not have seen it and would not know how to read it, at least not as an example of the literate arts of the contact zone.

2. Another way of extending the project of Pratt's essay would be to write your own autoethnography. It should not be too hard to locate a setting or context in which you are the "other"—the one who speaks from outside rather than inside the dominant discourse. Pratt says that the position of the outsider is marked not only by differences of language and ways of thinking and speaking but also by differences in power, authority, status. In a sense, she argues, the only way those in power can understand you is in *their* terms. These are terms you will need to use to tell your story, but your goal is to describe your position in ways that "engage with representations others have made of [you]" without giving in or giving up or disappearing in their already formed sense of who you are.

   This is an interesting challenge. One of the things that will make the writing difficult is that the autoethnographic or transcultural text calls upon skills not usually valued in American classrooms: bilingualism, parody, denunciation, imaginary dialogue, vernacular expression, storytelling, unseemly comparisons of high and low cultural forms—these are some of the terms Pratt offers. These do not fit easily with the traditional genres of the writing class (essay, term paper, summary, report) or its traditional values (unity, consistency, sincerity, clarity, correctness, decorum).

   You will probably need to take this essay (or whatever it should be called) through several drafts. (In fact, you might revise this essay after you have completed assignments 2 and 3.) It might be best to begin as Pratt's student, using her description as a preliminary guide. Once you get a sense of your own project, you may find that you have terms or examples to add to her list of the literate arts of the contact zone.

· · · · · · · · · · · ·

ASSIGNMENT 2

Borderlands [Pratt, Anzaldúa]

In "Arts of the Contact Zone," Pratt talks about the "autoethnographic" text, "a text in which people undertake to describe themselves in ways that engage with representations others have made of them," and about "transculturation," the "processes whereby members of subordinated or marginal groups select and invent from the materials transmitted by a dominant or metropolitan culture."

Write an essay in which you present a reading of *Borderlands/La frontera* as an example of an autoethnographic and/or transcultural text. You should imagine that you are writing to someone who is not familiar with either

Pratt's argument or Anzaldúa's thinking. Part of your work, then, is to present Anzaldúa's text to readers who don't have it in front of them. You have the example of Pratt's reading of Guaman Poma's *New Chronicle and Good Government.* And you have her discussion of the "literate arts of the contact zone." Think about how Anzaldúa's text might be similarly read, and about how her text does and doesn't fit Pratt's description. Your goal should be to add an example to Pratt's discussion and to qualify it, to alter or reframe what she has said now that you have had a chance to look at an additional example.

•   •   •   •   •   •   •   •   •   •   •

ASSIGNMENT 3

Autoethnography [Pratt, Jacobs]

Here is Mary Louise Pratt on the "autoethnographic" text:

> Guaman Poma's *New Chronicle* is an instance of what I have proposed to call an *autoethnographic* text, by which I mean a text in which people undertake to describe themselves in ways that engage with representations others have made of them. Thus, if ethnographic texts are those in which European metropolitan subjects represent to themselves their others (usually their conquered others), autoethnographic texts are representations that the so-defined others construct *in response to* or in dialogue with those texts. . . . they involve a selective collaboration with an appropriation of idioms of the metropolis or the conqueror. These are merged or infiltrated to varying degrees with indigenous idioms to create self-representations intended to intervene in metropolitan modes of understanding. Autoethnographic works are often addressed to both metropolitan audiences and the speaker's own community. Their reception is thus highly indeterminate. Such texts often constitute a marginalized group's point of entry into the dominant circuits of print culture. It is interesting to think, for example, of American slave autobiography in its autoethnographic dimensions, which in some respects distinguish it from Euramerican autobiographical tradition. (pp. 531–32)

Reread Harriet Jacobs's "Incidents in the Life of a Slave Girl" after reading Pratt's essay. Using the example of Pratt's work with the *New Chronicle,* write an essay presenting a reading of Jacobs's text as an autoethnographic and/or transcultural text. You should think about not only how it might be read from this point of view but also how, without this perspective, it might (in Pratt's terms) be misread or unread. Imagine that you are working to put Pratt's ideas to the test but also to see what you can say on your own about "Incidents" as a text, as something written and read.

. . . .

ASSIGNMENT 4

Writing America [Greenblatt]

While Mary Louise Pratt does not write about Columbus in "Arts of the Contact Zone," she writes about the aftermath of the European conquest of the Americas, about ensuing moments of contact between Europe and the "New World." And she offers a theoretical account of how writing functions for native Americans at those moments. Her interest is in the writing produced from the other side, from the side of the natives or those who are put into a subordinate position in relationship to a dominant culture. (If the native Americans had written about or to Columbus, for example, she would study those documents.)

Stephen Greenblatt, in "Marvelous Possessions," is interested in texts written by Europeans about the New World and its inhabitants. And, in a sense, he also charts the "literate arts" of the contact zone. Here, however, he is charting the ways of writing (the "discursive actions") that best served those in power. Using Pratt's theory of contact zones, and using her description of the "arts of the contact zone" as points of reference, write an essay in which you discuss one or two of the long passages quoted in Greenblatt (or perhaps some of the images included in his chapter). In a sense, you will be describing the arts belonging to the other side at these moments of contact. What are the key features in this writing? As a reader of Pratt, how might you describe its characteristic practices? its effects? its problems? its power? How does Greenblatt describe them?

• • • • • • • • • • •

Writing the Other [Greenblatt]

Greenblatt offers a powerful lesson in how to read the past. You feel this in his command of the material and in the range of examples available to him. You also feel it in the demonstrations he provides, in the careful, close readings of long passages from Columbus's letters and journals and from the texts that surround his work. He is arguing that Europeans took possession of the New World through acts of language, through writing. He shows how to read a text, a text whose meaning seems at first glance to be obvious; he shows how to read that text as both strange or noteworthy and as a discursive act, as a complex way of working on the world.

Go back to the essay to look closely both at the ways Greenblatt talks about language and at one or two examples of his work with passages. (The "Questions for a Second Reading" might be useful for this.) Then, to see if you can make a similar (or a contradictory) argument by performing a similar kind of reading, write an essay in which you take as your primary text one of the following:

1. Any text, including a recent one, that stands as an attempt by someone (or some group) to bring experience under control by writing (perhaps to "grasp the radical otherness" of people and/or places).
2. The following section of Columbus's journals:

    > Sunday, Oct. 21st [1492]. At 10 o'clock, we arrived at a cape of the island, and anchored, the other vessels in company. After having dispatched a meal, I went ashore, and found no habitation save a single house, and that without an occupant; we had no doubt that the people had fled in terror at our approach, as the house was completely furnished. I suffered nothing to be touched, and went with my captains and some of the crew to view the country. This island even exceeds the others in beauty and fertility. Groves of lofty and flourishing trees are abundant, and also large lakes, surrounded and overhung by foliage, in a most enchanting manner. Everything looked as green as in April in Andalusia. The melody of the birds was so exquisite that one was never willing to part from the spot, and the flocks of parrots obscured the heavens. The diversity in the appearance of the feathered tribe from those of our country is extremely curious. A thousand different sorts of trees, with their fruit were to be met with, and of a wonderfully delicious odour. It was a great affliction to me to be ignorant of their

natures, for I am very certain they are all valuable; specimens of them and of the plants I have preserved. Going round one of these lakes, I saw a snake, which we killed, and I have kept the skin for your Highnesses; upon being discovered he took to the water; whither we followed him, as it was not deep, and dispatched him with our lances; he was seven spans in length; I think there are many more such about here. I discovered also the aloe tree, and am determined to take on board the ship tomorrow, ten quintals of it, as I am told it is valuable. While we were in search of some good water, we came upon a village of the natives about half a league from the place where the ships lay; the inhabitants on discovering us abandoned their houses, and took to flight, carrying off their goods to the mountain. I ordered that nothing which they had left should be taken, not even the value of a pin. Presently we saw several of the natives advancing towards our party, and one of them came up to us, to whom we gave some hawk's bells and glass beads, with which he was delighted. We asked him in return, for water, and after I had gone on board the ship, the natives came down to the shore with their calabashes full, and showed great pleasure in presenting us with it. I ordered more glass beads to be given them, and they promised to return the next day. It is my wish to fill all the water casks of the ships at this place, which being executed, I shall depart immediately, if the weather serve, and sail round the island, till I succeed in meeting with the king, in order to see if I can acquire any of the gold, which I hear he possesses. Afterwards I shall set sail for another very large island which I believe to be *Cipango,* according to the indications I receive from the Indians on board. They call the Island *Colba,* and say there are many large ships, and sailors there. This other island they name *Bosio,* and inform me that it is very large; the others which like in our course, I shall examine on the passage, and according as I find gold or spices in abundance, I shall determine what to do; at all events I am determined to proceed on to the continent, and visit the city of *Guisay* where I shall deliver the letters of your Highnesses to the *Great Can,* and demand an answer, with which I shall return.

> — from *The Heath Anthology of American Literature,*
> ed. Paul Lauter et al. (1990), 1:70–71

3. The following essay, written by a college student when asked to write about other people and other places:

> A few summers ago, I accompanied my church youth group on a mission trip to St. Croix, in the Virgin Islands. We were to clean up damage from a hurricane which passed through the summer before. To tell you the truth, I really wasn't looking forward to working, but rather I was excited to visit the Virgin

Islands. But, by the end of my trip, I would not have traded my experience for anything in the world.

Our group flew from Philadelphia to Puerto Rico, and then to St. Croix. After arriving from a long plane trip we were driven to the place which for the next couple of weeks we would call home. We stayed on an old plantation which was located in the lower-class part of St. Croix. The plantation was surrounded by a 15-foot-high stone wall, but on the other side of the wall were the slums. As we entered the driveway leading to the plantation, adults as well as children lined up. They all watched carefully, probably trying to figure out why we were on their island.

On the first day of our journey, we started by picking up trash and tree limbs which had fallen to the ground from the hurricane the year before. It was so incredible how much damage was done and how it appeared that the hurricane had just passed. This task took several days to accomplish, even in a small area. There were just so many things covering the ground it was just unbelievable.

From day to day, we came in contact with lots of people who had lived on the island for many years. Quickly, we learned how many of the islanders felt about people from the "States." Once, while we were working, a group of islanders approached us and inquired why we were there. They asked why we were intruding on their land when we had a land of our own which was better. It was almost as if they were afraid that we were trying to take their island from them. I could tell by their voice of inquiry that they felt threatened. Even after we tried to explain that we were trying to help them in a time of need, they still wanted to know what we expected in return. At this point in time, I felt shut out. They would not accept that the only reason that we were there was to help them.

Over the weeks we accomplished several tasks. These tasks included digging up 5-foot-diameter tree stumps, rebuilding roofs of homes which were blown off, picking up trash, and helping run a coffee shop for the homeless and less fortunate. All of these tasks were time consuming and entailed much work. As we went to the different locations, I found the chance to talk to a lot of the islanders. They seemed very anxious to know my reasons for helping them. I explained that all my work was volunteer and that I liked to help others. Slowly they started to accept the fact that I, as well as the others, just wanted to befriend them. I witnessed their feelings starting to change toward us and soon they appreciated the work we had done.

As our time of service came to an end, I looked back on the huge difference which we had made on the island. After these several weeks, the islanders came to realize that we did not expect anything in return for our work, except their friendship. In the beginning, this concept was hard for them to understand, but as they watched the changes occur, they learned to appreciate our help. In fact, by the end, the many people who at one time had questioned our existence were the ones to tell us how sad they were to see us leave. They graciously thanked us over and over for our help. Their appreciation was unbelievable. They just constantly asked how they could pay us back. They praised the work which we had done and expressed their undying gratitude.

This change in our position in such a short amount of time was incredible. We went from being the unacceptable in their community to the heroes of the community. We were once looked down and frowned upon, but after working hard to prove our position we were more than accepted. Our efforts proved to change our position in that particular society, and we became well-respected guests on the island.

• • • • • • • • • • • •

A S S I G N M E N T 6

On Culture
[Pratt, Anzaldúa, Jacobs, Greenblatt]

In some ways, the slipperiest of the key words in Pratt's essay "Arts of the Contact Zone" is "culture." At one point Pratt says,

> If one thinks of cultures, or literatures, as discrete, coherently structured, monolingual edifices, Guaman Poma's text, and indeed any autoethnographic work, appears anomalous or chaotic—as it apparently did to the European scholars Pietschmann spoke to in 1912. If one does not think of cultures this way, then Guaman Poma's text is simply heterogeneous; as the Andean region was itself and remains today. Such a text is heterogeneous on the reception end as well as the production end: it will read very differently by people in different positions in the contact zone. (p. 535)

If one thinks of cultures as "coherent structures, monolingual edifices" the text appears one way; if one thinks otherwise the text is "simply heterogeneous." What might it mean to make this shift in the way one thinks of culture? Can you do it—that is, can you read the *New Chronicle* (or its excerpts) from both points of view? What about your own culture? Can you, for example, think of a group that you participate in as a "community"? Then can you think of it as a "contact zone"? Which one seems "natural" to you? What does Pratt assume to be the dominant point of view now, for her readers?

The assignments in this sequence have been an exercise in reading texts as heterogeneous, as contact zones. As a way of reflecting back over your work in this sequence, write an essay in which you explain the work you have been doing to someone who is not in the course, someone who is interested in reading and writing and learning, but who has not read Pratt or Anzaldúa or Jacobs or Greenblatt.

SEQUENCE THREE

Autobiographical Explorations

Ralph Ellison
Richard Rodriguez
Lewis Nordan
Jane Tompkins

*A*UTOBIOGRAPHICAL WRITING has been a regular feature of writing courses since the nineteenth century, when writing courses were introduced to the undergraduate curriculum. There are a variety of reasons for the prevalence of autobiography, not the least of which is the pleasure students take in thinking about and writing about their lives and their world. There is also a long tradition of published autobiographical writing, particularly in the United States. The title of this sequence puts a particular spin on that tradition, since it points to a more specialized use of autobiography, phrased here as "exploration." What is suggested by the title is a use of writing (and the example of one's experience, including intellectual experience) to investigate, question, explore, inquire. Often the genre is not used for these purposes at all. Autobiographical writing is often used for purposes of display or self-promotion, or to further (rather than question) an argument (about success, about how to live a good or proper or fulfilling life).

There are two threads to this sequence. The first is to invite you to experiment with the genre of "autobiographical exploration." The second is to foreground the relationship between your work and the work of others, to think about how and why and where you are prepared to write autobiographically (prepared not only by the lessons you've learned in school but by the culture and the way it invites you to tell—and live—the story of your life). And, if you are working inside a conventional field, a predictable way of writing, the sequence asks where and how you might make your mark or assert your position—your identity as a person (a character in a life story) and as a writer (someone working with the conventions of life-writing).

The first four assignments ask you to write from within the example of some of the most distinctive and influential writers of our time: Ralph Ellison, Richard Rodriguez, Lewis Nordan, and Jane Tompkins. One of the difficulties, for a student, of an extended project like this is finding a way of writing differently. An autobiographical project *without* the readings (where, in a sense, you were writing on your own) might well produce each week only more of the same, the same story written in the same style. Our goal is to make you aware of the options available to you as a writer as you think about, write, and represent your life. You should think of these assignments as asking not for mere or mechanical imitation, but as invitations to think about areas of your life as these authors have and to imagine the problems and potential of life-writing through the example of their prose, its style and methods.

The last assignment in the sequence is a retrospective assignment. Here you are asked to think back over what you have done and to write a "Preface" to your work, a short essay to prepare other readers to understand what you have been working on and best appreciate the problems and achievements of your work. We will be asking you to think of yourself as an author, to read what you have written and to write about your texts, as, perhaps, you have sometimes been asked to write *about* the works of other authors.

This sequence is accompanied by a minisequence titled "Autobiographical Explorations (II)." This alternative sequence provides similar assignments but with different readings. They can be substituted for assignments in the first "Autobiographical Explorations" sequence or added to those assignments.

•   •   •   •   •   •   •   •   •   •   •

ASSIGNMENT 1

Autobiographical Exploration [Ellison]

Early in his essay, Ellison refers to "An Extravagance of Laughter" as an "autobiographical exploration." He is writing from his past and from memory, but he is also engaged, as a writer, in a process of exploration. For Ellison, this essay represents a *way* of writing, a method, one that combines autobiography with a desire to analyze and to explore (to think about experience, not just recount it) and, at least in Ellison's case, to also think broadly about ideas and issues (about W. B. Yeats and masks, about humor, about race relations in the North and South in the 1930s).

As you prepare to write this assignment, read through the essay again thinking about it as a way of doing one's work, as a project, as a way of writing. What are its key features? What is its shape or design? How does Ellison, the writer, do what he does? And, you might ask: What would it take to learn to write like this? How is this writing related to the writing taught in school? Where and how might it serve you as a student? (The third "Questions for a Second Reading" following the essay is designed to prompt this kind of reflection.)

Once you have developed a sense of Ellison's method, write an autobiographical exploration of your own, one that has the rhythm and the moves, the shape and the design of "An Extravagance of Laughter." As far as subject matter is concerned, let Ellison's text stand as an invitation (inviting you to write about race or difference or region or travel or difficult moments), but don't feel compelled to follow his lead. You can write about anything you want (but you would be wise, we've learned, to stay away from childhood experiences and to stick with more adult experiences). The key is to follow the essay as an example of a *way* of writing—moving slowly, turning this way and that, combining stories and reflection, working outside of more predictable forms—either straightforward chronological narrative (first this, then that) or a rigid structure of thesis and proof.

. . . .

ASSIGNMENT 2

Desire, Reading, and the Past
[Rodriguez]

In "The Achievement of Desire," Richard Rodriguez tells stories of home but also stories of reading, of moments when things he read allowed him a way of reconsidering or revising ("framing," he calls it) the stories he would tell himself about himself. It is a very particular account of neighborhood, family, ethnicity, and schooling.

At the same time, Rodriguez insists that his story is also everyone's story—that his experience is universal. Take an episode from your life, one that seems in some ways similar to one of the episodes in "The Achievement of Desire," and cast it into a shorter version of Rodriguez's essay. Try to make use of your reading in ways similar to his. Think about what you have read lately in school, perhaps in this anthology.

In general, however, your job in this assignment is to look at your experience in Rodriguez's terms, which means thinking the way he does, noticing what he would notice, interpreting details in a similar fashion, using his key terms, seeing through his point of view; it could mean imitating his style of writing, doing whatever it is you see him doing characteristically when he writes. Imitation, Rodriguez argues, is not necessarily a bad thing; it can, he argues, be one of the powerful ways a person learns. Let this assignment serve as an exercise.

•   •   •   •   •   •   •   •   •   •   •

Point of View [Nordan]

The stories in *Music of the Swamp* are about Sugar Mecklin and his family. They are also about memory and storytelling. They have two points of view—the point of view of Sugar the boy inside the experience, and the point of view of Sugar the adult thinking back on his life, perhaps remembering, perhaps inventing, trying to reconstruct and to understand what happened (or what maybe happened).

Try your hand at writing a Nordan-like story. You can imagine that you are writing fiction, or you can imagine that you are writing a memoir, a section of your autobiography. Your goal should be to try to catch the rhythm and style of Nordan's sentences, to get a sense of the shape and purpose of the stories he tells, and to establish *both* the perspective of yourself as a child (or adolescent) and yourself now, as the writer, working on your story and, through it, thinking back to the past.

• • • • • • • • • • •

ASSIGNMENT 4

Personal Experience as Intellectual Experience [Tompkins]

Jane Tompkins's essay "Indians" tells the story of a research project, one undertaken as a professor prepares to teach a course, but with reference to its own prehistory, way back to the author's childhood in New York City. Tompkins provides an example of how personal experience is not simply action in the world but also (and often) intellectual experience, a narrative defined by books read, courses taken, changes of mind, new understandings.

Using Tompkins's essay as a model, write a personal essay that tells a similar story, one drawing on your own experiences. You could tell the story of a research project, a paper (most likely a term paper) you prepared for school. This does not have to be a pious or dutiful account. Tompkins, after all, is writing *against* what she takes to be the predictable or expected account of research as the disinterested pursuit of truth—in which a student would go to the library to "find" the truth about the Indians and the settlers. And she writes in a style that is not solemnly academic. Like Tompkins, you can tell what you take to be the untold story of term-paper research, you can reflect on the problem of such research as a story of learning. Or you could tell the story of any important experience you have had as a student or, out of school, as a person who observes, reads, and thinks. Your goal should be to think of your story *as* a story, with characters and scenes (and, perhaps, dialogue), with action, suspense, and surprises.

• • • • • • • • • • •

ASSIGNMENT 5

The "I" of the Personal Essay [Ellison, Rodriguez, Nordan, Tompkins]

The assignments in this sequence have been designed to prompt autobiographical writing. They have been invitations for you to tell your story and to think about the ways stories represent a person and a life. They have also, of course, been exercises in imitation, in writing "like" Ellison, Rodriguez, Nordan, and Tompkins, in casting your story in their terms. These exercises highlight the ways in which your story is never just your own but also written through our culture's sense of what it means to be a person, to live, grow, change, learn, experience. No writer simply gets to invent childhood. Childhood, like adulthood, is a category already determined by hundreds of thousands of representations of life—in books, in songs, on TV, in paintings, in the stories we tell ourselves about ourselves. As you have written these four personal narratives, you have, of course, been "telling the truth," just as you have also, of course, been creating a character, setting scenes, providing certain representations that provide a version of (but that don't begin to sum up) your life.

Read back over the four essays you have written (and perhaps revised). As you read, look for examples of where you feel you were doing your best work, where you are proud of the writing and interested in what it allows you to see or to think (where the "investigations" seem most worthwhile).

And think about what is *not* contained in these essays. What experiences are missing? What point of view? What ways of speaking or thinking or writing? If you were to go back to assemble these pieces into a longer essay, what would you keep and what would you add or change? What are the problems facing a writer, like you, trying to write a life, to take experience and represent it in sentences?

With these questions in mind, reread the four essays you have written and write a "Preface," a short piece introducing a reader to what you have written (to your work—and perhaps work you may do on these essays in the future).

SEQUENCE FOUR

Autobiographical Explorations (II)

Adrienne Rich
James Schuyler
John Wideman

THIS SEQUENCE provides an alternative set of readings for Sequence Three. All of these can be used to represent personal narrative as a writing problem, as something risky, even dangerous, as something to work on and to work on carefully, not as something simple or easy or to be taken for granted.

. . . .

ASSIGNMENT 1

A Moment of Hesitation [Rich]

> I have hesitated to do what I am going to do now, which is to use myself as an illustration. For one thing, it's a lot easier and less dangerous to talk about other[s]. . . . (p. 552)

Until we can understand the assumptions in which we are drenched we cannot know ourselves. (p. 550)
— ADRIENNE RICH
When We Dead Awaken: Writing as Re-Vision

Write an essay in which you, like Rich (and perhaps with similar hesitation), use your experience as an illustration, as a way of investigating not just your situation but the situations of people like you. Tell a story from your recent past and use it to talk about the ways you might be said to have been shaped or named or positioned by an established and powerful culture. You could imagine that this assignment is a way for you to use (and put to the test) some of Rich's key terms, words like "re-vision," "renaming," "structure," and "patriarchy."

• • • • • • • • • • •

A S S I G N M E N T **2**

"A Few Days" [Schuyler]

"A Few Days" gives poetic representation to the processes of memory, observation, and reflection. It is a poem that figures things out, things that seem quite ordinary, even unremarkable, and things that seem at moments quite extraordinary (or that are defined as extraordinary). In this sense, the poem (and its sentences, its rhythms, its use of the line as a unit of composition) is an interesting device for thinking—thinking like a poet rather than an essayist or a writer of prose.

Write a poem of your own based on Schuyler's. On the one hand this is an invitation to dramatize yourself as a writer using Schuyler as your model; on the other, it is an invitation to write a certain kind of verse. Whether you cast yourself as a Schuyler-like character or not is a decision to consider. It is important, however, that you think of this assignment as an exercise in writing *his* kind of line or sentence, his kind of stanza, his way of organizing or thinking through places and scenes and people. Your poem, in other words, should look and sound like his.

• • • • • • • • • • • •

Old Habits [Wideman]

Wideman frequently interrupts the narrative in "Our Time" to talk about the problems he is having as a writer. He says, for example, "The hardest habit to break, since it was the habit of a lifetime, would be listening to myself listen to him. That habit would destroy any chance of seeing my brother on his terms; and seeing him in his terms, learning his terms, seemed the whole point of learning his story" (p. 667).

Wideman gives you the sense of a writer who is aware from the inside, while writing, of the problems inherent in the personal narrative. This genre always shades and deflects; it is always partial and biased; in its very attempts to be complete, to understand totally, it reduces its subject in ways that are unacceptable. And so you can see Wideman's efforts to overcome these problems—he writes in Robby's voice; he starts his story three different times, first with Garth, later with the neighborhood, hoping that a variety of perspectives will overcome the limits inherent in each; he stops and speaks to us not as the storyteller but as the writer, thinking about what he is doing and not doing.

Let Wideman's essay provide a kind of writing lesson. It highlights problems; it suggests alternatives. Using Wideman, then, as your writing teacher, write a family history of your own. Yours will most likely be shorter than Wideman's, but let its writing be the occasion for you also to work on a personal narrative as a writing problem, an interesting problem that forces a writer to think about the limits of representation and point of view (about who gets to speak and in whose terms, about who sums things up and what is left out in this accounting).

SEQUENCE FIVE

Experimental Readings and Writings

Susan Griffin

Patricia J. Williams

James Schuyler

Gloria Anzaldúa

*T*HIS SEQUENCE offers you opportunities to work with selections that are striking both for what they have to say and for the ways they use writing. In each case the writer is experimenting, pushing against or stepping outside of conventional ways of writing and thinking. The sequence is an opportunity to learn about these experimental ways of writing from the inside, as a practitioner, as someone who learns from doing the very thing that he or she is studying. You will be asked to try out the kinds of writing you've read in the course. For example, the first assignment asks you to step into Susan Griffin's shoes, to mix personal and academic writing, and in doing so, you are challenged to do a kind of intellectual work on subject matter to which you feel strong (though maybe contrary and paradoxical) ties.

The second assignment challenges you to work on a set of issues in a manner similar to Patricia J. Williams's in her essay "And We Are Not Married." The third assignment asks you to study Griffin's and Williams's essays as examples of methods, as ways of doing intellectual work. With Williams's argument in mind, it asks you to think about the "ideology of style."

In assignment 4, you're asked to think about poetry as a way of thinking (through James Schuyler's poem, "A Few Days"). Assignment 5 then moves you to the most unconventional text in the series, chapters from Gloria Anzaldúa's mixed-language book, *Borderlands/La frontera*. She describes her writing as "a crazy dance," "an assemblage, a montage, a beaded work." And here, again, you are asked to work from inside of this unconventional project, with its unconventional style. The sixth and final assignment asks you to step back and study the experimental work you have completed. It is also an occasion for you to think through the relationship of experimental writing and the writing you learn in school. You are invited to comment on what might be gained or lost from doing this kind of experimental work.

•　•　•　•　•　•　•　•　•　•　•

ASSIGNMENT **1**

A Mix of Personal and Academic Writing [Griffin]

> To tell a story, or to hear a story told, is not a simple transmission of information. Something else in the telling is given too, so that, once hearing, what one has heard becomes a part of oneself. (p. 346)

> I have come to believe that every life bears in some way on every other. The motion of cause and effect is like the motion of a wave in water, continuous, within and not without the matrix of being, so that all consequences, whether we know them or not, are intimately embedded in our experience. (p. 339)
>
> — SUSAN GRIFFIN
> *Our Secret*

It is useful to think of Griffin's prose as experimental. She is trying to do something that she can't do in the "usual" essay form. She wants to make a different kind of argument or engage her reader in a different manner. And so she mixes personal and academic writing. She assembles fragments and puts seemingly unrelated material into surprising and suggestive relationships. She breaks the "plane" of the page with italicized inter-sections. She organizes her material, that is, but not in the usual mode of thesis-example-conclusion. Nor does she only represent people's stories, including her own. The arrangement is not nearly so linear. At one point, when she seems to be prepared to argue that German child-rearing practices produced the Holocaust, she quickly says:

786

Of course there cannot be one answer to such a monumental riddle, nor does any event in history have a single cause. Rather a field exists, like a field of gravity that is created by the movements of many bodies. Each life is influenced and it in turn becomes an influence. Whatever is a cause is also an effect. Childhood experience is just one element in the determining field. (p. 324)

Her prose serves to create a "field," one where many bodies are set in relationship.

It is useful, then, to think about Griffin's prose as the enactment of a method, as a way of doing a certain kind of intellectual work, a work to which she has strong personal and emotional ties. One way to study this, to feel its effects, is to imitate it, to take it as a model. For this assignment, write a Griffin-like essay, one similar to "Our Secret" in its methods of organization and argument. You will need to think about the stories you might tell, about the stories and texts you might gather (stories and texts not your own), stories to which you are drawn by an emotional and intellectual curiosity. As you write, you will want to think carefully about arrangement and about commentary (about where, that is, you will speak to your reader *as* the writer of the piece). You should not feel bound to Griffin's subject matter, but you should feel that you are working in her spirit with subjects that matter to you.

•   •   •   •   •   •   •   •   •   •   •

ASSIGNMENT 2

Layered and Cumulative Writing [Williams]

I hate the stillness. I hate the stone. I hate the sealed vault with its cold icon. I hate the staring into the night. The questions thinning into space. The sky swallowing the echoes.

Unless the stone bursts with telling, unless the seed flowers with speech, there is in my life no living word. The sound I hear is only sound. White sound. Words, when they fall, are pock marks on the earth. They are hailstones seeking an underground stream. (p. 711n)

— J. KOGAWA, from *Obasan*, quoted by
Patricia J. Williams in *And We Are Not Married*

Patricia J. Williams's essay, "And We Are Not Married," makes a powerful and distinctive argument. It is also a powerful and distinctive piece of writing. In this assignment, we'd like you to consider writing like Williams—whatever that might mean for you, or however you might make such an exercise work best. Think of the essay as a method—as a way of thinking things through, as a way of doing one's work. It is this, as well as a way of addressing others or getting points across.

Perhaps the best way to begin is to reread the essay, making an inventory of its distinctive features. (See the third "Question for a Second Reading" on p. 714 following Williams's essay on how you might do this.) Traditionally, you might look at organization, at sentences, at the "voice" or "voices" at work in the essay. You might also look at how Williams presents her materials. Or at how she imagines what her "material" might be. You might think about genre (or how she thinks about and mixes genres). The piece opens as a "journal entry," for instance, but what kind of journal has endnotes?

Then you need to begin gathering your materials. The invitation of this assignment is to work on a set of issues (stories, documents, positions) that have bearing on you. (In this sense, Williams's essay "begins" when Derrick Bell provokes her with a comment on unmarried black women.)

Note: Williams's essay is both layered (one thing next to another) and cumulative (one thing after another). These effects can be produced by revision—where a second or third draft adds another section or another layer. You don't have to imagine—in fact, it is probably wrong to imagine—that Williams wrote her essay all at once.

• • • • • • • • • • • •

ASSIGNMENT 3

Thinking about Method
[Griffin, Williams]

One of the obvious questions that a reader might ask of Patricia J. Williams's essay "And We Are Not Married" has to do with her methods of thinking, writing, and working. Her work is challenging in part because she enacts in her writing a particular response to oppressive conditions, and her methods are part and parcel of the issues she is writing about—race, gender, identity, and writing itself. What, one might ask, are her characteristic ways of gathering materials, of thinking them through, of presenting them to readers? As you work back through her text, think about the writing as an example of method and intention (or, as she might say, the traits of a method that purposely stands against "formalized, color-blind, liberal ideals"). You might also ask yourself, for instance, questions about the kinds of readers her work requires. What does she assume of her readers? How does she teach readers to read?

The same questions can be asked of Susan Griffin's essay "Our Secret." What are her characteristic ways of gathering materials, thinking them through, presenting them to readers? How would you describe her methods? Her intentions? And what does she assume of her readers? How does she teach readers to read?

Write an essay in which you use Griffin and Williams to talk about writers, their methods, and their projects. Be sure to work closely from examples from each. And look for differences as well as similarities. See, in your essay, if you can move out from your discussion of their examples to think more generally about the problems of writing. You might ask, what is it that writers like Griffin and Williams work on when they work on their writing? What are the problems of writing that seem important to them? What did you work on in assignments 1 and 2? What problems seem important to you now as you reread the pieces you wrote for assignments 1 and 2? What might a writer learn by using Griffin and Williams as examples? What did *you* learn?

· · · · · · · · · · · ·

ASSIGNMENT 4

What Is There to It? [Schuyler]

> A few days: how to celebrate them?
> It's today I want
> to memorialize but how can I? What is there to it?
> Cold coffee and
> a ham-salad sandwich? (p. 592)
>
> — JAMES SCHUYLER
> *A Few Days*

"A Few Days" gives poetic representation to the processes of memory, observation, and reflection. It is a poem that figures things out, things that seem quite ordinary, even unremarkable, and things that seem at moments quite extraordinary (or that are defined as extraordinary). In this sense, the poem (and its sentences, its rhythms, its use of the line as a unit of composition) is an interesting device for thinking—for thinking like a poet rather than an essayist or a writer of prose.

Write a poem of your own based on Schuyler's. On the one hand this is an invitation to dramatize yourself as a writer using Schuyler as your model; on the other, it is an invitation to write a certain kind of verse. Whether you cast yourself as a Schuyler-like character or not is a decision to consider. It is important, however, that you think of this assignment as an exercise in writing his kind of line or sentence, his kind of stanza, his way of organizing or thinking through places and scenes and people. Your poem, in other words, should look and sound like his.

. . . .

ASSIGNMENT 5

A Crazy Dance [Anzaldúa]

In looking at this book that I'm almost finished writing, I see a mosaic pattern (Aztec-like) emerging, a weaving pattern, thin here, thick there. . . . This almost finished product seems an assemblage, a montage, a beaded work with several leitmotifs and with a central core, now appearing, now disappearing in a crazy dance. The whole thing has had a mind of its own, escaping me and insisting on putting together the pieces of its own puzzle with minimal direction from my will. It is a rebellious, willful entity, a precocious girl-child forced to grow up too quickly, rough, unyielding, with pieces of feather sticking out here and there, fur, twigs, clay. My child, but not for much longer. This female being is angry, sad, joyful, is Coatlicue, dove, horse, serpent, cactus. Though it is a flawed thing— clumsy, complex, groping blind thing, for me it is alive, infused with spirit. I talk to it; it talks to me.

— GLORIA ANZALDÚA
Borderlands / La frontera

Gloria Anzaldúa has described her text in *Borderlands/La frontera* as a kind of crazy dance; it is, she says, a text with a mind of its own, "putting together the pieces of its own puzzle with minimal direction from my will." Hers is a prose full of variety and seeming contradictions; it is a writing that could be said to represent the cultural "crossroads" which is her experience/sensibility.

As an experiment whose goal is the development of an alternate (in Anzaldúa's terms, a mixed or *mestiza*) understanding, write an autobiographical text whose shape and motives could be described in her terms: a mosaic, woven, with numerous overlays; a montage, a beaded work, a crazy dance, drawing upon the various ways of thinking, speaking, understanding that might be said to be part of your own mixed cultural position, your mixed sensibility.

To prepare for this essay, think about the different positions you could be said to occupy, the different voices that are part of your background or present, the competing ways of thinking that make up your points of view. Imagine that your goal is to present your world and your experience to those who are not necessarily prepared to be sympathetic or to understand. And, following Anzaldúa, you should work to construct a mixed text, not a single unified one. This will be hard, since you will be writing what might be called a "forbidden" text, one you have not been prepared to write.

· · · · · · · · · · ·

ASSIGNMENT 6

Writing and Schooling
[Griffin, Williams, Schuyler, Anzaldúa]

You have written five assignments so far, and all of them, with perhaps the exception of the third—the one in which you were asked to write about Griffin's and Williams's methods—could be described as experimental. (It might be worth asking: Did you write a conventional essay for the third? Did you have a choice?)

The selections you took as your models, writing by Griffin, Williams, Schuyler, and Anzaldúa, certainly did not follow the usual guidelines for school writing. They broke some rules. They pushed the limits. They didn't do what essays or poems are supposed to do, at least by certain standards. They were frustrated by the limits of the usual ways of doing things with words. In a sense, they saw "good" writing as a problem, a problem they could work on as writers. Most likely, the same things could be said about your writing in this sequence. You did things that stood outside of (or that stood against) the forms of writing most often taught in school.

Read over your work. What were you able to do that you wouldn't, or couldn't, have done if you had written in a more conventional style? Be as precise as you can. How and where does this writing differ from the writing you have been taught in school? Again, be as precise as you can—go to old papers, textbooks, or syllabi to look for examples of "good writing" and the standard advice to young writers. Given what you have seen, where and how might more experimental writing be used in the schools (or in schooling)? What role might it play in courses that are not writing courses? What role might it play in a young writer's education?

Write an essay in which you use the example of your work in this sequence to think about writing and the teaching of writing in our schools.

SEQUENCE SIX

Experts and Expertise

Joan Didion
Adrienne Rich
Clifford Geertz
John Edgar Wideman
Walker Percy

THE FIRST FOUR ASSIGNMENTS in this sequence give you the chance to think about familiar settings or experiences through the imaginations of thinkers who have had a profound effect on contemporary culture: Joan Didion, Adrienne Rich, Clifford Geertz, and John Edgar Wideman.

In "Sentimental Journeys," Didion asks her readers to think about the newspaper and media accounts of violence in New York City in the 1980s as narratives with stock characters and predictable outcomes. She calls these master narratives. You may be asked to study recent news stories that could be said to reproduce master narratives. To gather material for her argument about the relations between an individual and culture, Rich brings poems and personal narrative into her essay. You may be asked to experiment similarly with the conventions of the essay. Geertz, in "Deep Play: Notes on the Balinese Cockfight," argues that the Balinese cockfight is a story the Balinese tell themselves about themselves. With Geertz as a model, you may be given the opportunity to interpret a characteristic scene from the culture around you. And Wideman, in his attempts to understand and represent his brother's life and thoughts, provides an example of the kind of interpretive expertise that stands outside usual academic conventions for investigation and report.

In each case, you will be given the opportunity to work alongside these thinkers as an apprentice, carrying out work they have begun. The final assignment in the sequence will ask you to look back on what you have done, to take stock, and to draw some conclusions about the potential and consequences of this kind of intellectual apprenticeship.

. . . .

A S S I G N M E N T 1

Master Narratives in the News
[Didion]

> The imposition of a sentimental, or false, narrative on the disparate and often random experience that constitutes the life of a city or a country means, necessarily, that much of what happens in that city or country will be rendered merely illustrative, a series of set pieces or performance opportunities. (p. 100)
>
> — JOAN DIDION
> *Sentimental Journeys*

"Sentimental Journeys" can be taken as a lesson in how to read the news. The essay can be read, that is, as an exemplary project. Didion follows a news story, reads its key accounts closely (looking for the master narrative that gives them shape and meaning), and she reads it against other stories, stories that become "meaningless" or back-page material in the face of the dominance of the key story. Didion shows a reader how to read the news as a text, she shows how to read the news as more than just "the news," and she shows how to write out such readings. Her essay provides a fine example of how a writer takes large blocks of text (the block quotations in this essay) and works with them through the medium of the paragraph.

For this assignment, follow Didion's lead and provide a similar reading of a local or national news story. You should look for a "front-page" story of some duration—one, that is, that stayed in the news for several weeks. You will need to present the event and its accounts so that a reader can follow both the story as it evolves in the media and the story as it serves your line of thinking. Following Didion, you will need to read those accounts for evidence of the master narrative they represent (perhaps a "sentimental" narrative), and you will need to think about whose interests are served in its production and reception.

Note: It would probably be useful to work with a relatively recent story.

Your library will have back issues of local and national newspapers. You will need a current or breaking story if you want to work with TV news. (It would be a different assignment and a different challenge to deal with a historical event as represented in the news.)

.   .   .   .

ASSIGNMENT 2

Looking Back [Rich]

> Re-vision—the act of looking back, of seeing with fresh eyes, of entering an old text from a new critical direction—is for women more than a chapter in cultural history: it is an act of survival. Until we can understand the assumptions in which we are drenched we cannot know ourselves. (p. 550)
>
> I have hesitated to do what I am going to do now, which is to use myself as an illustration. For one thing, it's a lot easier and less dangerous to talk about other[s]. . . . (p. 552)
> — ADRIENNE RICH
> *When We Dead Awaken: Writing as Re-Vision*

In "When We Dead Awaken," Rich is writing not to tell her story but to tell a collective story, the story of women or women writers, a story in which she figures only as a representative example. In fact, the focus on individual experience might be said to run against the argument she has to make about the shaping forces of culture and history, in whose context knowing oneself means knowing the assumptions in which one is "drenched."

Yet Rich tells her story—offering poems, anecdotes, details from her life. Write an essay in which you too (and perhaps with similar hesitation) use your own experience as an illustration, as a way of investigating not just your situation but the situation of people like you. (Think about what materials you might have to offer in place of her poems.) Tell a story of your own and use it to talk about the ways you might be said to have been shaped or named or positioned by an established and powerful culture. You should imagine that this assignment is a way for you to use (and put to the test) some of Rich's key terms, words like "re-vision," "renaming," "structure," and "patriarchy."

. . . .

A S S I G N M E N T   3

Seeing Your World through
Geertz's Eyes [Geertz]

> The culture of a people is an ensemble of texts, themselves en-
> sembles, which the anthropologist strains to read over the
> shoulders of those to whom they properly belong. (p. 255)
> — CLIFFORD GEERTZ
> *Deep Play: Notes on the Balinese Cockfight*

Geertz talks about "reading" a culture while peering over the shoulders of those to whom it properly belongs. In "Deep Play," he "reads" the cockfight over the shoulders of the Balinese. But the cockfight is not a single event to be described in isolation. It is itself a "text," one that must be understood in context. Or, as Geertz says, the cockfight is a "Balinese reading of Balinese experience; a story they tell themselves about themselves."

The job of the anthropologist, Geertz says, is "formulating sociological principles, not . . . promoting or appreciating cockfights." And the question for the anthropologist is this: "What does one learn about such principles from examining culture as an assemblage of texts?" Societies, he says, "like lives, contain their own interpretations. One has only to learn how to gain access to them."

Anthropologists are experts at gaining access to cultures and at performing this kind of complex reading. One of the interesting things about being a student is that you get to (or you have to) act like an expert even though, properly speaking, you are not. Write an essay in which you prepare a Geertzian "reading" of some part of our culture you know well (sorority rush, window shopping in a shopping mall, slam dancing, studying in the library, decorating a dorm room, tailgate parties at the football game, whatever). Ideally, you should go out and observe the behavior you are studying, looking at the players and taking notes with your project in mind. You should imagine that you are working in Geertz's spirit, imitating his method and style and carrying out work that he has begun.

. . . .

ASSIGNMENT 4

Wideman as a Case in Point
[Wideman]

The hardest habit to break, since it was the habit of a lifetime, would be listening to myself listen to him. That habit would destroy any chance of seeing my brother on his terms; and seeing him in his terms, learning his terms, seemed the whole point of learning his story. However numerous and comforting the similarities, we were different. The world had seized on the difference, allowed me room to thrive, while he'd been forced into a cage. (p. 667)

– JOHN EDGAR WIDEMAN
Our Time

At several points in this selection, Wideman discusses his position as a writer, researching and telling Robby's story, and he describes the problems he faces in writing this piece (and in "reading" the text of his brother's life). You could read this excerpt, in other words, as an essay on reading and writing.

Why do you think Wideman brings himself and these problems into the text? Why not keep quiet and hope no one notices? Choose three or four passages where Wideman refers directly or indirectly to the work he is doing as he writes this piece, and write an essay describing this work and why you think Wideman refers to it as he does. If he confronts problems, what are they and how does he go about solving them? If Wideman is an expert, how might you describe his expertise? And what might his example say to you as you think about your work as a student? as a writer?

. . . .

ASSIGNMENT 5

On Experts and Expertise
[Didion, Rich, Geertz, Wideman, Percy]

The whole horizon of being is staked out by "them," the experts. The highest satisfaction of the sightseer (not merely the tourist but any layman seer of sights) is that his sight should be certified as genuine. The worst of this impoverishment is that there is no sense of impoverishment. (p. 517)

I refer to the general situation in which sovereignty is surrendered to a class of privileged knowers, whether these be theorists or artists. A reader may surrender sovereignty over that which has been written about, just as a consumer may surrender sovereignty over a thing which has been theorized about. The consumer is content to receive an experience just as it has been presented to him by theorists and planners. The reader may also be content to judge life by whether it has or has not been formulated by those who know and write about life. (p. 517)

— WALKER PERCY
The Loss of the Creature

In the last four assignments you were asked to try on other writers' ways of seeing the world. You looked at what you had read or done, and at scenes from your own life, casting your experience in the terms of others.

Percy, in "The Loss of the Creature," offers what might be taken as a critique of such activity. "A reader," he says, "may surrender sovereignty over that which has been written about, just as a consumer may surrender sovereignty over a thing which has been theorized about." Didion, Rich, Geertz, and Wideman have all been presented to you as, in a sense, "privileged knowers." You have been asked to model your own work on their examples.

It seems safe to say that, at least so far as Percy is concerned, surrendering sovereignty is not a good thing to do. If Percy were to read over your work in these assignments, how do you think he would describe what you have done? If he were to take your work as an example in his essay, where might he place it? And how would his reading of your work fit with your sense of what you have done? Would Percy's assessment be accurate, or is there something he would be missing, something he would fail to see?

Write an essay in which you describe and comment on your work in this sequence, looking at it both from Percy's point of view and from your own, but viewing that work as an example of an educational practice, a way of reading (and writing) that may or may not have benefits for the reader.

Note: You will need to review carefully those earlier papers and mark sections that you feel might serve as interesting examples in your discussion. You want to base your conclusions on the best evidence you can. When you begin writing, it might be useful to refer to the writer of those earlier papers as a "he" or a "she" who played certain roles and performed his or her work in certain characteristic ways. You can save the first person, the "I," for the person who is writing this assignment and looking back on those texts.

History and Ethnography: Reading the Lives of Others

Clifford Geertz

Patricia Nelson Limerick

John Edgar Wideman

Mary Louise Pratt

*W*RITING REMAINS one of the most powerful tools we have for preserving and understanding the past and the present. This is simple to say. What good writing is, and what writing is good for—these questions are constantly debated by writers and academics. There are big philosophical questions here (what is the borderline between the truth and fiction, between what is there and what is a product of imagination or point of view?). There are practical questions (how do you learn to write history or ethnography? how do you revise it to make it better?). And both the philosophical questions and the practical questions have bearing on the work a student performs in the undergraduate curriculum, where students are constantly called upon to read and write textual accounts of human experience. This sequence is designed to give you a chance to do the work firsthand, to write a history or ethnography, and to think about and revise that work through the work of critics and theorists.

The first two assignments ask you to prepare first drafts of an ethnography and a history, written in response to the examples of Clifford Geertz (an anthropologist) and Patricia Nelson Limerick (a historian). The third assignment asks you to read "Our Time," by John Edgar Wideman. Wideman, in professional terms, is neither an anthropologist nor a historian. He is, rather, a fiction writer who has turned his hand to nonfiction, to write about African American culture and his family. With Wideman as a lever for thinking about issues of representation, you are asked to turn to all three essays to prepare a guide for writers, and, in the fourth assignment, you are asked to revise one of your earlier essays. The next assignment takes an additional theoretical step, looking (through Mary Louise Pratt's essay "Arts of the Contact Zone") at problems of representation as they are rooted more generally in culture, history, and ideology (and not just in the work of an individual writer and his or her text). The last assignment is an opportunity for a further revision, one that includes a section of reflection on the work you have done.

* * * * * * * * * * *

ASSIGNMENT 1

Ethnography [Geertz]

> As in more familiar exercises in close reading, one can start anywhere in a culture's repertoire of forms and end up anywhere else. One can stay, as I have here, within a single, more or less bounded form and circle steadily within it. One can move between forms in search of broader unities or informing contrasts. One can even compare forms from different cultures to define their character in reciprocal relief. But whatever the level at which one operates, and however intricately, the guiding principle is the same: societies, like lives, contain their own interpretations. One has only to learn how to gain access to them. (p. 255)
>
> — CLIFFORD GEERTZ
> *Deep Play: Notes on the Balinese Cockfight*

Geertz says that "the culture of a people is an ensemble of texts, themselves ensembles, which the anthropologist strains to read over the shoulders of those to whom they properly belong." Anthropologists are expert at "reading" in this way; they are trained to do it.

One of the interesting things about being a student is that you get to (or you have to) act like an expert even though you are not "officially" credentialed. Write an essay in which you prepare a Geertzian "reading" of the activities of some subgroup or some part of our culture you know well. Ideally, you should go out and observe the behavior you are studying ("straining to read over the shoulders" of those to whom this "text" properly belongs), examining it and taking notes with your project in mind. You should imagine that you are working in Geertz's spirit, imitating his method and style and carrying out work that he has begun. (It might be wise, however, to focus more locally than he does. He writes about a national culture—the Balinese cockfight as a key to Bali. You should probably not set out to write about "America" but about something more local. And you should write about some group of which you are not already a part, a group which you can imagine as "foreign," different, other.)

. . . .

ASSIGNMENT 2

History [Limerick]

One skill essential to the writing of Western American history is a capacity to deal with multiple points of view. It is as if one were a lawyer at a trial designed on the principle of the Mad Hatter's tea party—as soon as one begins to understand and empathize with the plaintiff's case, it is time to move over and empathize with the defendant. Seldom are there only two parties or only two points of view. (p. 419)

– PATRICIA NELSON LIMERICK
Empire of Innocence

One way to work on Limerick's selection is to take the challenge and write history—to write the kind of history, that is, that takes into account the problems she defines: the problems of myth, point of view, fixed ideas. You are not a professional historian, you are probably not using this book in a history course, and you probably don't have the time to produce a carefully researched history, one that covers all the bases, but you can think of this as an exercise in history writing, a minihistory, a place to start. Here are two possible starting points:

1. Go to your college library or, perhaps, the local historical society and find two or three first-person accounts of a single place, person, or event in your community. (This does not have to be a history of the American West.) Try to work with original documents. The more varied the accounts, the better. Then, working with these texts as your primary sources, write a history, one that you can offer as a response to Limerick's selection.

2. While you can find materials in a library, you can also work with records that are closer to home. Imagine, for example, that you are going to write

a family or a neighborhood history. You have your own memories and experiences to work from, but for this to be a history (and not a "personal essay"), you will need to turn to other sources as well: interviews, old photos, newspaper clippings, letters, diaries—whatever you can find. After gathering your materials, write a family or neighborhood history, one that you can offer as a response to Limerick's work.

Choose one of the two projects. When you are done, write a short one-page memo to Limerick. What can you tell her about the experience of a novice historian that she might find useful or interesting?

• • • • • • • • • •

ASSIGNMENT 3

A Writer's Guide
[Wideman, Geertz, Limerick]

While John Edgar Wideman is not writing history or ethnography in "Our Time," at least not in the strict sense of the terms, he is writing about others and about the past—he is trying to recover, represent, and understand the story of his brother Robby, his family, and their neighborhood. He is trying to recover all those factors that might be said to have led to or produced his brother's present situation.

It is interesting to read "Our Time," Geertz's "Deep Play," and Limerick's "Empire of Innocence" as alternate ways of thinking about the problems of history and ethnography. As you reread these selections, mark passages you might use to illustrate the styles, methods, and/or concerns of each writer. You should reread the essays as a group, as part of a single project investigating the problems of writing about other people and about the past. Each essay could be read as both a reflection on writing and a practical guide for those who follow. What do they say about method? What tips do they offer, directly or through their examples? What cautions?

Write an essay in which you present, as though for a textbook or manual, a "Practical Guide for the Writer of History and Ethnography," drawn from the work of Wideman, Geertz, and Limerick.

ASSIGNMENT **4**

Revision
[Geertz, Limerick, Wideman]

Go back to the first two essays you wrote for this sequence, the ethnography and the history, and choose one to revise. As always with revision, you should select the best essay, the one you care about the most. Your goal in revising this paper should be to take it on to its next step, not necessarily to fix it or clean it up or finish it, but to see how you can open up and add to what you have begun. As you prepare, you should consider the guidelines you wrote in assignment 3.

ASSIGNMENT **5**

Reading Others [Pratt]

Pratt, in "Arts of the Contact Zone," makes the case for the difficulties of reading, as well as writing, the "other":

> Autoethnography, transculturation, critique, collaboration, bilingualism, mediation, parody, denunciation, imaginary dialogue, vernacular expression—these are some of the literate arts of the contact zone. Miscomprehension, incomprehension, dead letters, unread masterpieces, absolute heterogeneity of meaning—these are some of the perils of writing in the contact zone. They all live among us today in the transnationalized metropolis of the United States and are becoming more widely visible, more pressing, and, like Guaman Poma's text, more decipherable to those who once would have ignored them in defense of a stable, centered sense of knowledge and reality. (p. 536)
>
> We are looking for the pedagogical arts of the contact zone. These will include, we are sure, exercises in storytelling and in identifying with the ideas, interests, histories, and attitudes of others; experiments in transculturation, and collaborative work

> and in the arts of critique, parody, and comparison (including unseemly comparisons between elite and vernacular cultural forms); the redemption of the oral; ways for people to engage with suppressed aspects of history (including their own histories), ways to move *into and out of* rhetorics of authenticity; ground rules for communication across lines of difference and hierarchy that go beyond politeness but maintain mutual respect; a systematic approach to the all-important concept of *cultural mediation.* (p. 541)

One way of working with Pratt's essay, of extending its project, would be to conduct your own local inventory of writing from the contact zone. You might do this on your own or in teams, with others from your class. Here are two ways you might organize your search:

1. You could look for historical documents. A local historical society might have documents written by Native Americans ("Indians") to the white settlers. There may be documents written by slaves to masters or to northern whites. There may be documents written by women to men (written by the suffragettes, for example) negotiating public positions or rights. There may be documents from any of a number of racial or ethnic groups—Hispanic, Jewish, Irish, Italian, Polish, Swedish—trying to explain their positions to the mainstream culture. There may, perhaps at union halls, be documents written by workers to owners. Your own sense of the heritage of your area should direct your search.

2. Or you could look at contemporary documents in the print that is around you, texts that you might otherwise overlook. Pratt refers to one of the characteristic genres of the Hispanic community, the *"testimonio."* You could look for songs, testimonies, manifestos, statements by groups on campus, stories, autobiographies, interviews, letters to the editor. You could look at the writing of any marginalized group, particularly writing intended, at least in part, to represent the experience of outsiders to the dominant culture (or to be in dialogue with that culture or to respond to that culture). These documents, if we follow Pratt's example, would include the work of young children or students, including college students.

Once you have completed your inventory, choose a document you would like to work with and present it carefully and in detail (perhaps in even greater detail than Pratt's presentation of the *New Chronicle*). You might imagine that you are presenting this to someone who would not have seen it and would not know how to read it, at least not as an example of the literate arts of the contact zone.

• • • • • • • • • • •

ASSIGNMENT **6**

Revision (Again)
[Geertz, Limerick, Wideman, Pratt]

Pratt has provided a way to think about the problems of writing about the past or present as they are rooted in culture, history, and ideology (and not simply in the work of an individual writer on his or her text). You can't escape your position in the scene of contact, she argues—there is, in other words, no place outside of history or culture that is pure or free, offering a clear view of the past or others. This does not mean, however, that there is nothing to do. Behind Pratt's essay is a clear concern for improving the "literate arts" of the contact zone, for improving reading or writing.

Go back to the revision you prepared in assignment 4 and take it through one more revision. For the purposes of this sequence, it is a final draft, although few writers ever assume that their work is "finished." For this draft, your goal should be to bring your work to some provisional close. You want to make it as elegant and eloquent (and nicely produced) as you can. You also want to make it as thoughtful and responsible as it can be—that is, you want to show, in your practice, that you are conscious of the problems inherent in writing ethnography or history.

For this draft, whether you are writing an ethnography or a history, you should also add a short final reflective section (like Geertz's "Saying Something of Something"), in which you think about your work in the essay, reflecting not so much on what you have learned as on what you have done. This is a space where you can step out of your role as historian or ethnographer to think about the writing and your work as a writer.

SEQUENCE EIGHT

The Problems of Difficulty

Virginia Woolf
Michel Foucault
John Edgar Wideman
Patricia J. Williams

*T*HE FIVE ASSIGNMENTS in this sequence invite you to consider the nature of difficult texts and how the problems they pose might be said to belong simultaneously to language, to readers, and to writers. The sequence presents four difficult essays. The assumption the sequence makes is that they are difficult for all readers, not just students, and that the difficulty is necessary, strategic, not a mistake or evidence of a writer's failure.

The first assignment asks you to look closely at Virginia Woolf's "A Room of One's Own" in order to discuss the position in which she puts you, the reader, as she makes her argument. The second asks you to look at Michel Foucault's "Panopticism," particularly as it could be said to present an argument that is at once eloquent yet hard to understand. The third and fourth assignments ask you to look at texts with unusual modes of development (John Edgar Wideman's "Our Time" and Patricia J. Williams's "And We Are Not Married"). Both of these texts argue that just as writers need to write differently at times, so do readers need to learn to read differently. The assignments ask you to consider how and why. And the last assignment is a retrospective. It asks you to read back over your work and to pull together what you've learned into a "theory of difficulty."

• • • • • • • • • • • •

ASSIGNMENT 1

I Will Try to Explain [Woolf]

The first chapter of *A Room of One's Own* begins: "But, you may say, we asked you to speak about women and fiction— what has that got to do with a room of one's own? I will try to explain." There are many unusual gestures and turns in Woolf's prose. And these could be thought of as part of her argument about women's writing—that is, it is possible to see the writing in the essay as an enactment of her argument about the place of a woman writer in the context of a genre representing the voices and habits of men. The opening word of the book, for example, is "but," itself a bit of a surprise. And the explanation that follows moves in several directions, but never straight to the finish. From the very beginning, the text stands contrary to conventional expectations about style, subject, and presentation.

As you reread these chapters and prepare to write about them, make note of the ways Woolf (the writer writing the text) constructs a space for speaker and audience, a kind of imaginary place where a woman can do her work, find a way of speaking, think as she might like to think, and prepare others to listen. Look for interesting and potentially significant ways she defies or transforms what you take to be the conventions of the essay. You might especially want to take a look at those places where Woolf seems to be saying, "I know what I should be doing here, but I won't. I'll do this instead."

Choose four such moments and write an essay in which you discuss Woolf's chapters as a performance, a demonstration of a way of writing that pushes against the usual ways of manipulating words. While there is certainly an argument *in* Woolf's essay, your paper will be about the argument represented *by* the essay, an argument enacted in a way of writing. What is Woolf doing? How might you explain her motives? the effects of her prose? What does she assume of her readers? In what ways might her essay be seen as an example of someone working on the problems of writing? of a woman's writing? And what might this have to do with you, a student in a writing class?

• • • • • • • • • • • •

Foucault's Fabrication [Foucault]

About three quarters of the way into "Panopticism," Foucault says,

> Our society is one not of spectacle, but of surveillance; under
> the surface of images, one invests bodies in depth; behind the
> great abstraction of exchange, there continues the meticulous,
> concrete training of useful forces; the circuits of communication
> are the supports of an accumulation and a centralization of
> knowledge; the play of signs defines the anchorages of power;
> it is not that the beautiful totality of the individual is ampu-
> tated, repressed, altered by our social order, it is rather that the
> individual is carefully fabricated in it, according to a whole
> technique of forces and bodies. (pp. 197–98)

This prose is eloquent and insists on its importance to our moment and our
society; it is also very hard to read or to paraphrase. Who is doing what to
whom? How do we think about the individual being carefully fabricated in
the social order?

Take this selection as a problem to solve. What is it about? What are its
key arguments, its examples and conclusions? Write an essay that summarizes "Panopticism." Imagine that you are writing for readers who have read
the chapter (although they won't have the pages in front of them) and who
are at sea as to its argument. You will need to take time to present and discuss examples from the text. Your job is to help your readers figure out what
it says. You get the chance to take the lead and be the teacher. In addition,
you should feel free to acknowledge that you don't understand certain section even as you write about them.

So how do you write about something you don't completely understand?
Here's a suggestion. When you have completed your summary, read it over
and treat it as a draft. Ask questions like these: What have I left out? What
was I tempted to ignore or finesse? Go back to those sections of the chapter
that you ignored and bring them into your essay. Revise by adding discussions of some of the very sections you don't understand. You can write about
what you think Foucault might be saying—you can, that is, be cautious and
tentative; you can admit that the text is what it is, hard to read. You
don't have to master this text. You do, however, need to see what you can
make of it.

. . . .

ASSIGNMENT 3

A Story of Reading [Wideman]

At several points in "Our Time," Wideman interrupts the narrative to discuss his position as a writer telling Robby's story. He describes the problems he faces in writing this piece (or in "reading" the text of his brother's life). You could read this selection, in other words, as an essay about reading and writing. It is Wideman's account of his work.

And, as a narrative, "Our Time" is made up of sections, fragments, different voices. It is left to the reader, in a sense, to put the pieces together and complete the story. There is work for a reader to do, in other words, and one way to account for that work is to call it "practice" or "training." Wideman wants to force a reader's attention by offering a text that makes unusual demands, a text that teaches a reader to read differently. If you think of your experience with the text, of how you negotiated its terrain, what is the story of reading you might tell? In what way do your difficulties parallel Wideman's—at least those he tells us about when he stops to talk about the problems he faces as a writer?

Write an essay in which you tell the story of what it was like to read "Our Time" and compare your experience working with this text with Wideman's account of his own.

A story of reading—this is not a usual school exercise. Usually you are asked what texts mean, not what it was like to read them. As you prepare for this assignment, think back as closely as you can to your experience the first time through. And you will want to reread, looking for how and where Wideman seems to be deliberately working on his reader, defying expectation and directing response. You want to tell a story that is rich in detail, precise in accounting for moments in the text. You want to bring forward the features that can make your story a good story to read—suspense, action, context, drama. Since this is your story, you are one of the characters. You will want to refer to yourself as you were at the moment of reading while also reserving a space for you to speak from your present position, as a person thinking about what it was like to read the text, and as a person thinking about Wideman and about reading. You are telling a story, but you will need to break the narrative (as Wideman breaks his) to account in more general terms for the demands Wideman makes on readers. What habits does he assume a reader will bring to this text? How and why does he want to break them?

• • • • • • • • • • •

Distinctive Styles [Williams]

One challenge Williams's writing presents is its unusual style, mixing conference reports, anecdote, musings, legal theory, and personal essay. Her prose is hard to classify. To prepare this assignment, begin by rereading Williams's "And We Are Not Married" and marking sections you could use to identify the distinctive (and peculiar) features of her style. What might they be said to represent?

The subtitle of Williams's essay refers to the "ideology of style." She argues that style is not simply a matter of personal taste but a critical response to conventional ways of reading and writing, ways that serve certain social and political interests even when they masquerade as "neutral." But her essay has its own distinctive style; in fact, it seems to be a distinctive mix of styles. In its writing, it enacts an argument with what we might call an "official" style—or it creates within its pages a conversation between styles. What are the distinctive stylistic features in Williams's writing? What is she doing as a writer in this essay? How does the writing do its work—or what work is it able to do? Why would anyone want to write this way?

Write an essay in which you tell a story of writing, the story of the writer in "And We Are Not Married," the story, that is, of a writer working against (and within) conventional ways of writing (and reading).

• • • • • • • • • • •

A Theory of Difficulty
[Woolf, Foucault, Wideman, Williams]

Now that you have worked with these four texts, you are in a good position to review what you have written about each of them in order to say something more general about difficulty—difficulty in writing, difficulty in reading.

Write an essay in which you present a theory of difficulty, a kind of guide, something that might be useful to students who are regularly asked to confront difficult assignments. You will want to work from your previous essays—pulling out sections, revising, reworking examples for this new essay. Don't let your earlier work go unacknowledged. But, at the same time, feel free to move out from these readings to other materials, examples, or situations.

SEQUENCE NINE

Reading Culture

John Berger
Susan Douglas
Joan Didion

IN THIS SEQUENCE, you will be reading and writing about culture. Not Culture, something you get if you go to the museum or a concert on Sunday, but culture—the images, words, and sounds that pervade our lives and organize and represent our common experience. This sequence invites your reflection on the ways culture "works" in and through the lives of individual consumers.

The difficulty of this sequence lies in the way it asks you to imagine that you are not a sovereign individual, making your own choices and charting the course of your life. This is conceptually difficult, but it can also be distasteful, since we learn at an early age to put great stock in imagining our own freedom. Most of the readings that follow ask you to imagine that you are the product of your culture; that your ideas, feelings, and actions, your ways of thinking and being, are constructed for you by a large, organized, pervasive force (sometimes called history, sometimes called culture, sometimes called ideology). You don't feel this to be the case, but that is part of the power of culture, or so the argument goes. These forces hide themselves. They lead you to believe that their constructions are naturally, inevitably there, that things are the way they are because that is just "the way things are." The assignments in this sequence ask you to read against your common sense. You will be expected to try on the role of the critic—to see how and where it might be useful to recognize complex motives in ordinary expressions.

The authors in this sequence all write as though, through great effort, they could step outside culture to see and criticize its workings. The assignments in this sequence will ask you both to reflect on this type of criticism and to participate in it. The first assignment is an exercise in the kind of historical reading represented by the work of John Berger, a reading designed to take a painting from the context of The Museum or High Culture and to put it back (Berger would say) into the context of history and of the images that dominate daily life. The second assignment draws on Susan Douglas's essay "Narcissism as Liberation." As Berger questions the status of "high art," Douglas turns critical scrutiny toward advertising and popular culture. The final assignments turn to journalism and media and the "master narratives" which shape our understanding of public life.

. . . .

ASSIGNMENT 1

Looking at Pictures [Berger]

> Original paintings are silent and still in a sense that information never is. Even a reproduction hung on the wall is not comparable in this respect for in the original the silence and stillness permeate the actual material, the paint, in which one follows the traces of the painter's immediate gestures. This has the effect of closing the distance in time between the painting of the picture and one's own act of looking at it. . . . What we make of that painted moment when it is before our eyes depends upon what we expect of art, and that in turn depends today upon how we have already experienced the meaning of paintings through reproductions. (pp. 70–71)
>
> — JOHN BERGER
> *Ways of Seeing*

While Berger describes original paintings as silent in this passage, it is clear that these paintings begin to speak if one approaches them properly, if one learns to ask "the right questions of the past." Berger demonstrates one route of approach, for example, in his reading of the Hals paintings, where he asks questions about the people and objects and their relationship to the painter and the viewer. What the paintings might be made to say, however, depends upon the viewer's expectations, his or her sense of the questions that seem appropriate or possible. Berger argues that, because of the way art is currently displayed, discussed, and reproduced, the viewer expects only to be mystified.

For this assignment, imagine that you are working against the silence and mystification Berger describes. Go to a museum—or, if that is not possible, to a large-format book of reproductions in the library (or, if that is not possible, to the reproductions in "Ways of Seeing")—and select a painting that seems silent and still, yet invites conversation. Your job is to figure out what sorts of questions to ask, to interrogate the painting, to get it to speak, to engage with the past in some form of dialogue. Write an essay in which you record this process and what you have learned from it. Somewhere in your essay, perhaps at the end, turn back to Berger's chapter to talk about how this process has or hasn't confirmed what you take to be Berger's expectations.

Note: If possible, include with your essay a reproduction of the painting you select. (Check the postcards at the museum gift shop.) In any event, you want to make sure that you describe the painting in sufficient detail for your readers to follow what you say.

• • • • • • • • • • •

ASSIGNMENT 2

Reading the '90s [Douglas]

One way of working along with Douglas is to see what it is like to read as she does. For this assignment, imagine that you are accepting the challenge of Douglas's essay (or following in her footsteps). Write an essay in which you extend her project to a set of related advertisements of your choosing. These could be the "next generation" of ads directed at women. They could be ads directed at men—or, for that matter, at any representative group. (Copy or clip the ads and include them with your essay.)

Your goal should be to begin with and to test (to engage with, perhaps to argue with) Douglas's critical frame. You will need to "read" and present your ads closely and carefully, as she does, and to use them to think about the forces of power and influence in American popular culture. You should find yourself moving toward making your own statements about the '90s.

. . . .

ASSIGNMENT 3

"The Upper Thigh Thus Became Freighted with Meaning" [Douglas]

Douglas's prose is written to reach and place a large audience; even so, behind it is a fairly specialized training. You can see traces of this in her vocabulary (references to "the male code," to "sites of resistance," to "deconstruction," to "capitalism" and its ability to "co-opt and domesticate opposition"). And you can see it in her essay's larger ambitions, connecting ads in "women's magazines" to American history and American political life (to the '80s, the '90s, and the "age of Reagan").

Douglas is both making an argument about the effects of popular culture and offering her readers a lesson in how to read—in particular, a lesson in how to read materials like magazine advertisements that seem to be so naturally and inevitably a part of the cultural landscape that they don't need to be "read at all." "Ads are ads," we can imagine ourselves saying, "so what's the fuss? What else is there to say?" Plenty, if we take Douglas as a guide.

Douglas's work, like John Berger's, is designed to make the obvious seem strange and arbitrary, part of a design that has been hidden from us. So what is this design? who is the designer? According to Douglas, who is doing what to whom, and why? And what about John Berger—is his argument similar or different? Both Douglas and Berger are interested in correcting the way images are read. Both are concerned with the ways in which images serve the interests of power and money. Both are writing to get the attention of a general audience and to teach readers how and why they should pay a different kind of attention to the images around them.

Write an essay in which you consider the two essays as examples of an ongoing project. Berger's essay precedes Douglas's by at least a quarter century. If you look closely at one or two of their examples, and if you look at the larger concerns in their arguments, are they saying the same thing? doing the same work? If so, why? Why is such work still necessary? If not, how do their projects differ? And how might you account for those differences?

. . . .

Reading the News [Didion]

Didion asks a reader to think about the newspaper and media accounts in "Sentimental Journeys" as stories, as narratives with stock characters and predictable outcomes. She assumes that they are standard fare in the American imaginary, so standard that they have become invisible—we take them for granted.

"Sentimental Journeys" can be taken as a lesson in how to read the news, one that stands as a corrective to what Didion assumes to be common practice. The essay can be read, that is, as an exemplary project. Didion follows a news story, reads its key accounts closely (looking for the master narrative that gives them shape and meaning), and she reads it against other stories, stories that become "meaningless" or back-page material in the face of the dominance of the key story. Didion shows a reader how to read the news as a text, she shows how to read the news as more than just "the news," and she shows how to write out such readings. Her essay provides a fine example of how a writer takes large blocks of texts (the block quotations in this essay) and works with them through the medium of the paragraph.

For this assignment, follow Didion's lead and provide a similar reading of a local or national news story. You should look for a "front-page" story of some duration—one, that is, that stayed in the news for several weeks. You will need to present the event and its accounts so that a reader can follow both the story as it evolves in the media and the story as it serves your line of thinking. Following Didion, you will need to read those accounts for evidence of the master narrative they represent (perhaps a "sentimental" narrative), and you will need to think about whose interests are served in its production and reception.

Note: It would probably be useful to work with a relatively recent story. Your library will have back issues of local and national newspapers. You will need a current or breaking story if you want to work with TV news. (It would be a different assignment and a different challenge to deal with a historical event as represented in the news.)

· · · · · · · · · · · ·

ASSIGNMENT 5

Life in the '90s
[Berger, Douglas, Didion]

You have spent several assignments working inside the arguments of noted contemporary cultural critics. This assignment is a chance for you to stop, now that you have gotten a feel for this kind of argument, and to think about *your* story. Write an autobiographical essay, one that can reflect or illustrate (and then, perhaps, challenge) the arguments of these critics. (There are autobiographical moments in Douglas's essay. You need not feel compelled to imitate her style, but it might be useful to reread her essay in order to get a feel for the way she tells her story.)

You can think of your essay as a response to what you have been reading, one where you turn to your experience as a participant or consumer in some area of contemporary American culture, perhaps including the ways you might be said to be a product of your culture. This is your chance to represent yourself as a character in the story of American TV, movies, print, and rock and roll. Your story should be rich and detailed—a good story, that is. But a careful reader should also be able to hear echoes and allusions to the pieces you have been reading.

Working with the Past

Richard Rodriguez
Joyce Carol Oates
Harriet Jacobs
Alice Walker

THIS SEQUENCE takes a close and extended look at the relations between a writer and the past, including that part of the past which is represented by other books and by tradition and convention. The point of the sequence is to examine instances where authors directly or indirectly work under the influence of others. Much of the usual talk about "creativity" and "originality" hides the ways in which all texts allude to others, the ways all draw upon (and sometimes, revise) the work of the past. By erasing the past, readers give undue attention to an author's "genius" or independence, losing sight of the larger cultural and historical field within which (and sometimes against which) a writer works. (And, while this connection is not highlighted in the sequence, it is possible for you to see your own work with *Ways of Reading* mirrored in the work of these other writers. As you write in response to their work, they write in response to others'.)

The first assignment gives precise, material definition to the past, representing it in an extended passage from Richard Hoggart's *The Uses of Literacy*. Hoggart is a British cultural critic, the son of working-class parents, who writes in the section included here about "the scholarship boy"—that is, the working-class boy in a more elite educational environment. Richard Rodriguez, in "The Achievement of Desire," alludes to and quotes from this section of Hoggart's book. The assignment asks you to look at the larger text from which Rodriguez drew in order to ask questions about what he missed, what he left out, and how he read.

The next two assignments place the questions of the uses of prior texts in the context of education, through an examination of Joyce Carol Oates's short story, "Theft," and through a story you will write about your own education. The final three assignments work with Harriet Jacobs's autobiographical narrative, "Incidents in the Life of a Slave Girl," and Alice Walker's "In Search of Our Mothers' Gardens." Readers are often tempted to read the Jacobs narrative as, in a sense, coming from nowhere, since the stereotypical figure of the slave is of someone who cannot read and write. It is hard for readers to place Jacobs in relation to either slave culture or the culture of American literacy. These assignments ask you to imagine both Jacobs's representation of her own past through the collection of "incidents" that make up her narrative and her relationship to other texts, represented by the assumptions she makes about her readers and the way they will read. With Walker, we return to a more direct discussion of tradition and legacy, this time with particular reference to the legacy of African American women's writing. This sequence is accompanied by a minisequence, "Working with the Past (II)" (p. 834). This alternative sequence provides similar assignments but with different readings. They can be substituted for assignments in the opening sequence.

. . . .

ASSIGNMENT 1

The Scholarship Boy [Rodriguez]

At the end of this assignment, you will find an extended section from Richard Hoggart's *The Uses of Literacy*. This is the book Rodriguez found in the British Museum, the book he used, he says, to "frame the meaning of my academic success." The section here is the one that surrounds the passages Rodriguez cites in "The Achievement of Desire." Read the Hoggart excerpt and think about these questions: How might you compare Rodriguez's version of the "scholarship boy" with Hoggart's? How might you explain the importance of Hoggart's book to Rodriguez? What kind of reader is the Rodriguez who is writing "The Achievement of Desire"—is he still a "scholarship boy" or is that description no longer appropriate?

You could look at the relationship between Rodriguez and Hoggart as a case study in the possible relations between a writer and a prior text or between a student and a teacher. Read the two together, taking notes to assist such a comparative reading. As you read Rodriguez's discussion of Hoggart's book, pay attention to both the terms and passages Rodriguez selects and those he ignores, and pay attention to what Rodriguez *does* with what he selects. Look closely at how Rodriguez reads and presents Hoggart's text.

As you read Hoggart's account of the scholarship boy, try to read from outside Rodriguez's point of view. How else might these passages be read? In what ways might Hoggart be said to be saying what Rodriguez says he is saying? In what ways might he be said to be saying something else, something Rodriguez misses or ignores? In what ways might Hoggart be said to be making a different argument, telling a different story? What position or point of view or set of beliefs would authorize this other reading, the reading from outside Rodriguez's point of view? And, if you can establish this "alternative" reading, what does that tell you about the position or point of view or set of beliefs that authorize Rodriguez's use of the text?

As you prepare to write about Rodriguez's use of Hoggart, think about how you will describe his performance. What, for example, might you attribute to strategy, to Rodriguez's intent? What might you attribute to blindness (a failure to see or notice something in the text)? What might you attribute to the unconscious (a fear of the text, a form of repression, a desire to transform the text into something else)? These are conventional ways of telling the story of reading. What use are they to your project? Can you imagine others?

Write an essay in which you discuss Rodriguez as an example of a reader and writer working with a prior text. Your goal should be to understand Rodriguez and "The Achievement of Desire" better but also to think about the implications of his "case" for readers and writers in the undergraduate curriculum.

A. Scholarship Boy

> For my part I am very sorry for him. It is an uneasy lot at best, to be what we call highly taught and yet not to enjoy: to be present at this great spectacle of life and never to be liberated from a small hungry shivering self.
>
> — GEORGE ELIOT

This is a difficult chapter to write, though one that should be written. As in other chapters, I shall be isolating a group of related trends: but the consequent dangers of over-emphasis are here especially acute. The three immediately preceding chapters have discussed attitudes which could from one point of view appear to represent a kind of poise. But the people most affected by the attitudes now to be examined—the "anxious and the uprooted"—are to be recognised primarily by their lack of poise, by their uncertainty. About the self-indulgences which seem to satisfy many in their class they tend to be unhappily superior: they are much affected by the cynicism which affects almost everyone, but this is likely to increase their lack of purpose rather than tempt them to "cash in" or to react into further indulgence.

In part they have a sense of loss which affects some in all groups. With them the sense of loss is increased precisely because they are emotionally uprooted from their class, often under the stimulus of a stronger critical intelligence or imagination, qualities which can lead them into an unusual self-consciousness before their own situation (and make it easy for a sympathiser to dramatise their *"Angst"*). Involved with this may be a physical uprooting from their class through the medium of the scholarship system. A great many seem to me to be affected in this way, though only a very small proportion badly; at one boundary the group includes psychotics; at the other, people leading apparently normal lives but never without an underlying sense of some unease.

It will be convenient to speak first of the nature of the uprooting which some scholarship boys experience. I have in mind those who, for a number of years, perhaps for a very long time, have a sense of no longer really belonging to any group. We all know that many do find a poise in their new situations. There are "declassed" experts and specialists who go into their own spheres after the long scholarship climb has led them to a Ph.D. There are brilliant individuals who become fine administrators and officials, and find themselves thoroughly at home. There are some, not necessarily so gifted, who reach a kind of poise which is yet not a passivity nor even a failure in awareness, who are at ease in their new group without any ostentatious adoption of the protective colouring of that group, and who have an easy relationship with their working-class relatives, based not on a form of patronage but on a just respect. Almost every working-class boy who goes through the process of further education by scholarships finds himself chafing against his environment during adolescence. He is at the friction-point of two cultures; the test of his real education lies in his ability, by about the age of twenty-five, to smile at his father with his whole face and to respect his flighty young sister and his slower brother. I shall be concerned with those for whom the uprooting is particularly troublesome, not because I underestimate the gains which this kind of selection gives, nor because I wish to stress the more depressing features in contemporary life, but because the difficulties of some people illuminate much in the wider discussion of cultural change. Like transplanted stock, they react to a widespread drought earlier than those who have been left in their original soil.

I am sometimes inclined to think that the problem of self-adjustment is, in general, especially difficult for those working-class boys who are only moderately endowed, who have talent sufficient to separate them from the majority of their working-class contemporaries, but not to go much farther. I am not implying a correlation between intelligence and lack of unease; intellectual people have their own troubles: but this kind of anxiety often seems most to afflict those in the working-classes who have been pulled one stage away from their original culture and yet have not the intellectual equipment which would then cause them to move on to join the "declassed" profession-als and experts. In one sense, it is true, no one is ever "declassed"; and it is in-teresting to see how this occasionally obtrudes (particularly today, when ex-working-class boys move in all the managing areas of society)—in the touch of insecurity, which often appears as an undue concern to establish "pres-ence" in an otherwise quite professional professor, in the intermittent rough homeliness of an important executive and committee-man, in the tendency to vertigo which betrays a lurking sense of uncertainty in a successful journalist.

But I am chiefly concerned with those who are self-conscious and yet not self-aware in any full sense, who are as a result uncertain, dissatisfied, and gnawed by self-doubt. Sometimes they lack will, though they have intelli-gence, and "it takes will to cross this waste." More often perhaps, though they have as much will as the majority, they have not sufficient to resolve the complex tensions which their uprooting, the peculiar problems of their par-ticular domestic settings, and the uncertainties common to the time create.

As childhood gives way to adolescence and that to manhood, this kind of boy tends to be progressively cut off from the ordinary life of his group. He is marked out early: and here I am thinking not so much of his teachers in the "elementary" school as of fellow-members of his family. " 'E's got brains," or " 'E's bright," he hears constantly; and in part the tone is one of pride and ad-miration. He is in a way cut off by his parents as much as by his talent which urges him to break away from his group. Yet on their side this is not alto-gether from admiration: " 'E's got brains," yes, and he is expected to follow the trail that opens. But there can also be a limiting quality in the tone with which the phrase is used; character counts more. Still, he has brains—a mark of pride and almost a brand; he is heading for a different world, a different sort of job.

He has to be more and more alone, if he is going to "get on." He will have, probably unconsciously, to oppose the ethos of the hearth, the intense gregariousness of the working-class family group. Since everything centres upon the living-room, there is unlikely to be a room of his own; the bed-rooms are cold and inhospitable, and to warm them or the front room, if there is one, would not only be expensive, but would require an imaginative leap—out of the tradition—which most families are not capable of making. There is a corner of the living-room table. On the other side Mother is iron-ing, the wireless is on, someone is singing a snatch of song, or Father says in-termittently whatever comes into his head. The boy has to cut himself off mentally, so as to do his homework, as well as he can. In summer, matters can be easier; bedrooms are warm enough to work in: but only a few boys, in my experience, take advantage of this. For the boy is himself (until he reaches, say, the upper forms) very much of *both* the worlds of home and school. He is enormously obedient to the dictates of the world of school, but emotionally still strongly wants to continue as part of the family circle.

So the first big step is taken in the progress towards membership of a different sort of group or to isolation, when such a boy has to resist the central domestic quality of working-class life. This is true, perhaps particularly true, if he belongs to a happy home, because the happy homes are often the more gregarious. Quite early the stress on solitariness, the encouragement towards strong self-concern, is felt; and this can make it more difficult for him to belong to another group later.

At his "elementary" school, from as early as the age of eight, he is likely to be in some degree set apart, though this may not happen if his school is in an area which each year provides a couple of dozen boys from "the scholarship form" for the grammar-schools. But probably he is in an area predominantly working-class and his school takes up only a few scholarships a year. The situation is altering as the number of scholarships increases, but in any case human adjustments do not come as abruptly as administrative changes.

He is similarly likely to be separated from the boys' groups outside the home, is no longer a full member of the gang which clusters round the lamp-posts in the evenings; there is homework to be done. But these are the male groups among which others in his generation grew up, and his detachment from them is emotionally linked with one more aspect of his home situation—that he now tends to be closer to the women of the house than to the men. This is true, even if his father is not the kind who dismisses books and reading as "a woman's game." The boy spends a large part of his time at the physical centre of the home, where the woman's spirit rules, quietly getting on with his work whilst his mother gets on with her jobs—the father not yet back from work or out for a drink with his mates. The man and the boy's brothers are outside, in the world of men; the boy sits in the women's world. Perhaps this partly explains why many authors from the working-classes, when they write about their childhood, give the women in it so tender and central a place. There is bound to be occasional friction, of course—when they wonder whether the boy is "getting above himself," or when he feels a strong reluctance to break off and do one of the odd jobs a boy is expected to do. But predominantly the atmosphere is likely to be intimate, gentle, and attractive. With one ear he hears the women discussing their worries and ailments and hopes, and he tells them at intervals about his school and the work and what the master said. He usually receives boundless uncomprehending sympathy: he knows they do not understand, but still he tells them; he would like to link the two environments.

This description simplifies and overstresses the break; in each individual case there will be many qualifications. But in presenting the isolation in its most emphatic form the description epitomises what is very frequently found. For such a boy is between two worlds, the worlds of school and home; and they meet at few points. Once at the grammar-school, he quickly learns to make use of a pair of different accents, perhaps even two different apparent characters and differing standards of value. Think of his reading-material, for example: at home he sees strewn around and reads regularly himself, magazines which are never mentioned at school, which seem not to belong to the world to which the school introduces him; at school he hears about and reads books never mentioned at home. When he brings those books into the house they do not take their place with other books which the family are reading, for often there are none or almost none; his books look, rather, like strange tools.

He will perhaps, especially today, escape the worst immediate difficulties of his new environment, the stigma of cheaper clothes, of not being able to afford to go on school-holiday trips, of parents who turn up for the grammar-school play looking shamefully working-class. But as a grammar-school boy, he is likely to be anxious to do well, to be accepted or even to catch the eye as he caught the eye, because of his brains, at the "elementary" school. For brains are the currency by which he has bought his way, and increasingly brains seem to be the currency that tells. He tends to make his schoolmasters over-important, since they are the cashiers in the new world of brain-currency. In his home-world his father is still his father; in the other world of school his father can have little place: he tends to make a father-figure of his form-master.

Consequently, even though his family may push him very little, he will probably push himself harder than he should. He begins to see life, for as far as he can envisage it, as a series of hurdle-jumps, the hurdles of scholarships which are won by learning how to amass and manipulate the new currency. He tends to over-stress the importance of examinations, of the piling-up of knowledge and of received opinions. He discovers a technique of apparent learning, of acquiring of facts rather than of the handling and use of facts. He learns how to receive a purely literate education, one using only a small part of the personality and challenging only a limited area of his being. He begins to see life as a ladder, as a permanent examination with some praise and some further exhortation at each stage. He becomes an expert imbiber and doler-out; his competence will vary, but will rarely be accompanied by genuine enthusiasms. He rarely feels the reality of knowledge, of other men's thoughts and imaginings, on his own pulses; he rarely discovers an author for himself and on his own. In this half of his life he can respond only if there is a direct connection with the system of training. He has something of the blinkered pony about him; sometimes he is trained by those who have been through the same regimen, who are hardly unblinkered themselves, and who praise him in the degree to which he takes comfortably to their blinkers. Though there is a powerful, unidealistic, unwarmed realism about his attitude at bottom, that is his chief form of initiative; of other forms—the freely-ranging mind, the bold flying of mental kites, the courage to reject some "lines" even though they are officially as important as all the rest—of these he probably has little, and his training does not often encourage them. This is not a new problem; Herbert Spencer spoke of it fifty years ago: but it still exists: "The established systems of education, whatever their matter may be, are fundamentally vicious in their manner. They encourage *submissive receptivity* instead of *independent activity*."

There is too little stress on action, on personal will and decision; too much goes on in the head, with the rather-better-than-normal intellectual machine which has brought him to his grammar-school. And because so often the "good" boy, the boy who does well, is the one who with his conscientious passivity meets the main demand of his new environment, he gradually loses spontaneity so as to acquire examination-passing reliability. He can snap his fingers at no one and nothing; he seems set to make an adequate, reliable, and unjoyous kind of clerk. He has been too long "afraid of all that has to be obeyed." Hazlitt, writing at the beginning of the nineteenth century, made a wider and more impassioned judgment on trends in his society; but it has some relevance here and now:

> Men do not become what by nature they are meant to be, but what society makes them. The generous feelings, and high propensities of the soul are, as it were, shrunk up, seared, violently wrenched, and amputated, to fit us for our intercourse with the world, something in the manner that beggars maim and mutilate their children, to make them fit for their future situation in life.

Such a scholarship boy has lost some of the resilience and some of the vitality of his cousins who are still knocking about the streets. In an earlier generation, as one of the quicker-witted persons born into the working-classes, he would in all probability have had those wits developed in the jungle of the slums, where wit had to ally itself to energy and initiative. He plays little on the streets; he does not run round delivering newspapers: his sexual growth is perhaps delayed. He loses something of the gamin's resilience and carelessness, of his readiness to take a chance, of his perkiness and boldness, and he does not acquire the unconscious confidence of many a public-school-trained child of the middle-classes. He has been trained like a circus-horse, for scholarship winning.

As a result, when he comes to the end of the series of set-pieces, when he is at last put out to raise his eyes to a world of tangible and unaccommodating things, of elusive and disconcerting human beings, he finds himself with little inner momentum. The driving-belt hangs loosely, disconnected from the only machine it has so far served, the examination-passing machine. He finds difficulty in choosing a direction in the world where there is no longer a master to please, a toffee-apple at the end of each stage, a certificate, a place in the upper half of the assessable world. He is unhappy in a society which presents largely a picture of disorder, which is huge and sprawling, not limited, ordered, and centrally-heated; in which the toffee-apples are not accurately given to those who work hardest nor even to the most intelligent: but in which disturbing imponderables like "character," "pure luck," "ability to mix" and "boldness" have a way of tipping the scales.

His condition is made worse because the whole trend of his previous training has made him care too much for marked and ticketed success. This world, too, cares much for recognisable success, but does not distribute it along the lines on which he has been trained to win it. He would be happier if he cared less, if he could blow the gaff for himself on the world's success values. But they too closely resemble the values of school; to reject them he would have first to escape the inner prison in which the school's tabulated rules for success have immured him.

He does not wish to accept the world's criterion—get on at any price (though he has an acute sense of the importance of money). But he has been equipped for hurdle-jumping; so he merely dreams of getting-on, but some-how not in the world's way. He has neither the comforts of simply accepting the big world's values, nor the recompense of feeling firmly critical towards them.

He has moved away from his "lower" origins, and may move farther. If so, he is likely to be nagged underneath by a sense of how far he has come, by the fear and shame of a possible falling-back. And this increases his inability to leave himself alone. Sometimes the kind of job he gets only increases this slightly dizzy sense of still being on the ladder; unhappy on it, but also proud and, in the nature of his condition, usually incapable of jumping-off, of pulling-out of that particular race:

> Pale, shabby, tightly strung, he had advanced from post to post in his insurance office with the bearing of a man about to be discharged. . . . Brains had only meant that he must work harder in the elementary school than those born free of them. At night he could still hear the malicious chorus telling him that he was a favourite of the master. . . . Brains, like a fierce heat, had turned the world to a desert round him, and across the sands in the occasional mirage he saw the stupid crowds, playing, laughing, and without thought enjoying the tender-ness, the compassion, the companionship of love.

That is over-dramatised, not applicable to all or even to most—but in some way affecting many. It affects also that larger group, to which I now turn, of those who in some ways ask questions of themselves about their society, who are because of this, even though they may never have been to grammar-schools, "between two worlds, one dead, the other powerless to be born." They are the "private faces in public places" among the working-classes; they are Koestler's "thoughtful corporals"; they are among those, though not the whole of those, who take up many kinds of self-improvement. They may be performing any kind of work, from manual labour to teaching; but my own experience suggests that they are to be found frequently among minor clerks and similarly black-coated workers, and among elementary school-teachers, especially in the big cities. Often their earnestness for improvement shows itself as an urge to act like some people in the middle-classes; but this is not a political betrayal: it is much nearer to a mistaken idealism.

• • •

This kind of person, and we have seen that this is his first great loss, belongs now to no class, usually not even to what is called, loosely enough, the "classless intelligentsia." He cannot face squarely his own working-class, for that, since the intuitive links have gone, would require a greater command in facing himself than he is capable of. Sometimes he is ashamed of his origins; he has learned to "turn up his nose," to be a bit superior about much in working-class manners. He is often not at ease about his own physical appearance which speaks too clearly of his birth; he feels uncertain or angry inside when he realises that that, and a hundred habits of speech and manners, can "give him away" daily. He tends to visit his own sense of inadequacy upon the group which fathered him; and he provides himself with a mantle of defensive attitudes. Thus he may exhibit an unconvincing pride in his own gaucheness at practical things— "brain-workers" are never "good with their hands." Underneath he knows that his compensatory claim to possess finer weapons, to be able to handle "book-knowledge," is insecurely based. He tries to read all the good books, but they do not give him that power of speech and command over experience which he seeks. He is as gauche there as with the craftsman's tools.

He cannot go back; with one part of himself he does not want to go back to a homeliness which was often narrow: with another part he longs for the membership he has lost, "he pines for some Nameless Eden where he never was." The nostalgia is the stronger and the more ambiguous because he is really "in quest of his own absconded self yet scared to find it." He both wants to go back and yet thinks he has gone beyond his class, feels himself weighted with knowledge of his own and their situation, which hereafter forbids him the simpler pleasures of his father and mother. And this is only one of his temptations to self-dramatisation.

If he tries to be "pally" with working-class people, to show that he is one of them, they "smell it a mile off." They are less at ease with him than with some in other classes. With them they can establish and are prepared to honour, seriously or as a kind of rather ironical game, a formal relationship; they "know where they are with them." But they can immediately detect the uncertainty in his attitudes, that he belongs neither to them nor to one of the groups with which they are used to performing a hierarchical play of relations; the odd man out is still the odd man out.

He has left his class, at least in spirit, by being in certain ways unusual; and he is still unusual in another class, too tense and overwound. Sometimes the working-classes and the middle-classes can laugh together. He rarely laughs; he smiles constrainedly with the corner of his mouth. He is usually ill at ease with the middle-classes because with one side of himself he does not want them to accept him; he mistrusts or even a little despises them. He is divided here as in so many other ways. With one part of himself he admires much he finds in them: a play of intelligence, a breadth of outlook, a kind of style. He would like to be a citizen of that well-polished, prosperous, cool, book-lined, and magazine-discussing world of the successful intelligent middle-class which he glimpses through doorways or feels awkward among on short visits, aware of his grubby finger-nails. With another part of himself he develops an asperity towards that world: he turns up his nose at its self-satisfactions, its earnest social concern, its intelligent coffee-parties, its suave sons at Oxford, and its Mrs. Miniverish or Mrs. Ramseyish cultural pretensions. He is rather over-ready to notice anything which can be regarded as pretentious or fanciful, anything which allows him to say that these people do not know what life is really like. He wavers between scorn and longing.

> — RICHARD HOGGART
> *The Uses of Literacy* (1957)

• • • • • • • • • • •

ASSIGNMENT 2

Theft [Rodriguez, Oates]

Rodriguez, in "The Achievement of Desire," talks about his schooling as the process of becoming a "scholarship boy," a term he borrows from Richard Hoggart's *The Uses of Literacy*. Reading Hoggart allowed Rodriguez to reread his experience as a student; his account of Hoggart's work could, in a variety of ways, be described as a revision (or re-vision) of that text. The character Marya in Oates's short story, "Theft" (like the other girls in her dorm) is a scholarship student; she is fascinated with that "moment when an item passed over from belonging to another person to belonging" to her. Oates, like Rodriguez, is interested in the ways education places the individual in relationship to others.

Write an essay in which you reconsider Rodriguez's experience as a student through the frame established in Oates's short story, "Theft." How are Rodriguez (the figure in the narrative) and Marya defined as "scholarship students"? How does each narrative think through the experience of the scholarship student? Where and in what ways might Rodriguez and Marya pose arguments counter to each other? What arguments are Oates and Rodriguez (the writer of the narrative) making about education and class, knowledge and identity?

• • • • • • • • • • •

ASSIGNMENT 3

Telling a Story of Education
[Rodriguez, Oates]

You have read Rodriguez's and Oates's accounts of education. What about yours? As a student you have something in common with Rodriguez and Marya, and you can think about your differences from them. What might you offer as a representative story of your college experience? What use might you make of their stories in imagining or understanding your own? As you think about your story, what aspects won't stay within the terms and patterns established by Rodriguez's and Oates's narratives? Why won't they fit? If your story is not a version of theirs, what prior narratives, what stories about growing up or about education might it be said to allude to?

With careful attention to scene, dialogue, and detail, tell a story that might stand as one way of representing your college experience. And, as a frame for that story, consider it in relation to the stories offered by Rodriguez and Oates.

• • • • • • • • • • •

ASSIGNMENT 4

A Life Story [Jacobs]

By creating a narrator who presents her private sexual history as a subject of public political concern, Jacobs moves her book out of the world of conventional nineteenth-century polite discourse. In and through her creation of Linda Brent, who yokes her success story as a heroic slave mother to her confession as a woman who mourns that she is not a storybook heroine, Jacobs articulates her struggle to assert her womanhood and projects a new kind of female hero.

           — JEAN FAGIN YELLIN
           "Introduction," *Incidents in the Life of a Slave Girl*

In an essay titled "The Voice of the Southern Slave," literary critic Houston Baker says,

The voice of the unwritten self, once it is subjected to the linguistic codes, literary conventions, and audience expectations of a literate population, is perhaps never again the authentic voice of black American slavery. It is, rather, the voice of a self transformed by an autobiographical act into a sharer in the general public discourse about slavery.

This voice shares not only in the general public discourse about slavery but also in the general public discourse representing family, growing up, love, marriage, virtue, childbirth. It shares in the discourse of "normal" life—that is, life outside of slavery. For a slave, the self and its relations to others had a different public construction. A slave was property. A mother didn't have the right to her children, a woman to her body. While some may say that this was true generally of women in the nineteenth century (and the twentieth), slavery enacted and enforced the most extreme social reservations about a woman's rights and selfhood.

The passage from Baker's essay allows us to highlight the gap between a life and a narrative, between a person (Harriet Jacobs) and a person rendered on the page (Linda Brent), between the experience of slavery and the conventional ways of telling the story of life, between experience and the ways experience is shaped by a writer, readers, and a culture.

Write an essay in which you examine Jacobs's work as a writer. Consider the ways she works on her reader (a figure she both imagines and constructs) and also the ways she works on her material (a set of experiences but also a language and the story and conventional ways of representing a young woman's life). Where *is* Jacobs in this text? What is her work? What can you say about the sources of her work, the models or conventions it draws upon, deploys, or transforms? The narrative was written in retrospect when Jacobs was older and free, as a series of incidents. You can read the text as a writer's reconstruction of the past. What can you say about the ways Jacobs, as a writer, works with the past?

· · · · · · · · · · ·

ASSIGNMENT 5

Working with the Past [Walker]

In her essay "In Search of Our Mothers' Gardens," Walker views the "creative spirit" of African American women as a legacy passed down from generation to generation, in spite of societal barriers: "Our mothers and grandmothers, some of them: moving to music not yet written. And they waited . . . for a day when the unknown thing that was in them would be made known; but guessed, somehow in their darkness, that on the day of their revelation they would be long dead" (p. 640).

Walker (much like Rodriguez, who "borrows" from Hoggart) uses Virginia Woolf's term "contrary instincts" to explain this legacy. And her essay is filled with passages from other texts. How does she use these? Why? What is the relationship of the "creative spirit" to the work of the past, at least as that relationship is both argued and represented in Walker's prose?

Write an essay in which you discuss Walker's project as a "creative" endeavor. What work does she do when she borrows the term "contrary instincts" from Woolf? What about the other allusions to the past, to texts written and unwritten? How might you characterize this work? Taking Walker's position as an African American artist of today into consideration, how might this essay be read as part of the tradition of creativity she charts? How might it be read as part of a tradition? How might it be read as an example of "creativity"? Or, to pose the question in different terms, what might you say Walker "creates" as she writes this essay?

. . . .

ASSIGNMENT 6

Legacies [Walker, Jacobs]

Walker's reading of the history of African American women focuses on the "creative spirit" of these women in the face of oppression. Of her mother, Walker writes:

> Her face, as she prepares the Art that is her gift, is a legacy of respect she leaves to me, for all that illuminates and cherishes life. She has handed down respect for the possibilities—and the will to grasp them. (p. 646)

And to the poet Phillis Wheatley, she writes,

> But at last, Phillis, we understand. No more snickering when your stiff, struggling, ambivalent lines are forced on us. We know now that you were not an idiot or a traitor; only a sickly little black girl, snatched from your home and country and made a slave; a woman who still struggled to sing the song that was your gift, although in a land of barbarians who praised you for your bewildered tongue. It is not so much what you sang, as that you kept alive, in so many of our ancestors, *the notion of song*. (p. 643).

Although Walker chooses to focus on artists other than Harriet Jacobs in her essay, one could imagine ways in which Jacobs's example is appropriate to Walker's discussion of African American women's creativity.

Write an essay in which you extend Walker's project by considering how and where Jacobs's work as a writer would or would not serve Walker's argument. You can draw on the essays you wrote for assignments 4 and 5 for this essay, but you should treat them as material for a revision. You should reread Jacobs, and you should reread your essay with a mind to sections that you can rework. What legacy might Jacobs be said to create? What kind of example might she provide? How would it serve or alter Walker's argument? Why might Jacobs be overlooked?

SEQUENCE ELEVEN

Working with the Past (II)

Virginia Woolf
Alice Walker
Ralph Ellison
Susan Griffin

*T*HIS SEQUENCE provides a variation on sequence ten. For a full description of the rationale behind the sequence, see the introduction to sequence ten, page 819.

This sequence begins with our selection from *A Room of One's Own*, chapters that can be seen as a rewriting of a tradition of essayist literature. After examining Woolf's revision of the texts of the past, you are asked to look at Walker's rewriting of Woolf and to think about what this contemporary African American writer has changed and what she has preserved in turning to a text written by a British woman in the early twentieth century. The next assignment looks at a similar moment in Ralph Ellison's "An Extravagance of Laughter." Like Walker, he rewrites the words of a key figure in British literature, W. B. Yeats. And, more generally, his essay, like Susan Griffin's (which follows) can be read as both a meditation on history and a reworking of the conventions of the prose essay. A final assignment asks you to reflect on the work you have done with these materials.

• • • • • • • • • • •

Reading the Past [Woolf]

The title page of the original edition of *A Room of One's Own* said, "This essay is based upon two papers read to the Arts Society of Newnham and the Odtaa at Girton in October 1928. The papers were too long to be read in full, and have since been altered and expanded." As either an essay or the text of a public lecture, *A Room of One's Own* is full of surprises. It doesn't sound like the usual lecture; it doesn't do what essays usually do. At many places and in many ways it takes liberties with the conventions of the genre, with the essay's or the lecture's characteristic ways of addressing the audience, gathering information, and presenting an argument.

As you reread these chapters and prepare to write about them, make note of the ways Woolf (the writer writing the text) constructs a space for speaker and audience, a kind of imaginary place where a woman can do her work, find a way of speaking, think as she might like to think, and prepare others to listen. Look for interesting and potentially significant ways she defies or transforms what you take to be the conventions of the essay. You might especially want to take a look at those places where Woolf seems to be saying, "I know what I should be doing here, but I won't. I'll do this instead."

Choose four such moments and write an essay in which you discuss Woolf's chapters as a performance, a demonstration of a way of writing that pushes against the usual ways of manipulating words. While there is certainly an argument *in* Woolf's essay, your paper will be about the argument represented *by* the essay, an argument enacted in a way of writing. What is Woolf doing? How might you explain what she is doing and why? In what ways might her essay be seen as an example of someone working with the writing of the past? with the figure of the woman writer? with the textual spaces available to women? What does she preserve? What does she revise? How might you define her attitude to the past?

• • • • • • • • • • •

•

Rewriting "A Room of One's Own" [Walker]

On page 641, Walker invokes and then rewrites a passage from Woolf's *A Room of One's Own*. The passage she cites comes from chapter 3, not included in our selections from Woolf's text, in which Woolf imagines what might have happened if Shakespeare had had a sister. (See the headnote to our selections from *A Room of One's Own*, p. 717, for a discussion of this chapter and the context of the passage Walker cites.)

Read closely to see how, where, and why Walker invokes and then rewrites Woolf. Write an essay in which you describe and explain the translation or transformation Walker makes. What does she change? Why? What, from this, can we infer about Walker's attitude toward Woolf? her way of reading Woolf? her sense of the uses of the past? And how might you connect what Walker does as a writer with the argument of her essay, an argument about legacy? Does Walker honor Woolf? And why choose Woolf, a British woman, white, the daughter of privilege? How might you explain the role Woolf plays in Walker's text?

• • • • • • • • • • •

Rewriting Yeats [Ellison]

In the middle of "An Extravagance of Laughter," Ellison cites W. B. Yeats, the Irish poet, on "masks" in a passage that concludes with the (perhaps surprising) assertion that "active virtue . . . is the wearing of a mask." And then, to make Yeats's words work for him, Ellison has to imagine a revision of the passage, adapting it as a concept that can be used to think about African American experience. As you reread, let the opening of the essay lead you to that passage. Then, when you get there, take a moment to work out the Ellison revision of Yeats: What does it say once the substitutions are made? And, from that, how do you read the rest of the essay, an essay that could be said to rework the standard accounts of the civil rights movement and to revise the conventions of the essay? Write an essay in which you represent Ellison's use of the past in "An Extravagance of Laughter." If the essay recounts (and offers) a lesson in thinking about change and thinking about the past, what is it? How might it speak to you or to your generation?

• • • • • • • • • • •

A S S I G N M E N T **4**

Writing History [Griffin]

At several points in her essay, Griffin argues that we—all of us, especially all of us who read her essay—are part of a complex web of connections. She asks, for example,

> Who are we? The question is not simple. What we call the self is part of a larger matrix of relationship and society. Had we been born to a different family, in a different time, to a different world, we would not be the same. All the lives that surround us are in us. (pp. 355–56)

Later she asks, "Is there any one of us who can count ourselves outside the circle circumscribed by our common past?" (p. 365). At another point she speaks of a "field,"

> like a field of gravity that is created by the movements of many bodies. Each life is influenced and it in turn becomes an influence. Whatever is a cause is also an effect. Childhood experience is just one element in the determining field. (p. 324)

One way of thinking about this concept of the self (and of interrelatedness), at least to think about it under Griffin's guidance, is to work on the connections implied and asserted in her text. In her essay, Griffin writes *about* the past—how we can know it, what its relation is to the present, why we should care. In the way she writes, however, she is also making an argument about how we can know and understand the past—in, for example, the way she represents key figures, like Himmler, or minor figures, like Leo.

As you reread the selection, look for powerful and surprising juxtapositions, for fragments that stand together in interesting and suggestive ways. Think about the arguments represented by the blank space between those sections. (And look for Griffin's written statements about "relatedness.")

Look for connections that seem important to the text (and to you) and representative of Griffin's thinking (and yours).

Write an essay in which you use these examples to think through your understanding of Griffin's claims for this "larger matrix," the "determining field," or our "common past."

. . . .

ASSIGNMENT 5

On Reading the Past
[Woolf, Walker, Ellison, Griffin]

You have written about Virginia Woolf, and her use of the tradition of the essay (the roles it allows the writer, its ways of thinking and presenting examples, its methods of address), and you have written about Alice Walker and her use of Woolf. You've also written about Susan Griffin and Ralph Ellison. All these writers, it is safe to say, write with a desire to clear a space for other writers, to make it possible for writers (like you) to do what they have not been prepared to do, to do what they may have believed to be impossible or forbidden.

In your own education, both directly and indirectly, you have been given lessons in how and why to read the texts of the past. You have been instructed in the "proper" ways to use books, or any prior text, in papers that you write—most likely in the form of term papers but perhaps in other forms as well. Think about the ways you have been prepared to work with the past. Consider a variety of examples, including your best moments in school, when you felt you had done something powerful or important or interesting or exciting or useful. Write an essay in which, through these examples from your education, and through the examples provided by your reading, you discuss the ways your education (and American schooling generally) prepares and/or fails to prepare its students to use and understand the works of the past.

SEQUENCE TWELVE

Writing History

Patricia Nelson Limerick
Jane Tompkins

*T*HIS SHORT SEQUENCE has two goals: to present two views of the "problem of history" (the problem of representing and understanding the past) and to use these accounts as an introduction to academic life (or to the forms of theorizing particular to that branch of the academy preoccupied by the problems of understanding the past). The first two assignments ask you to translate articles by Patricia Nelson Limerick and Jane Tompkins for an audience of beginning undergraduates. Your goal is to teach your audience something about the essays but also to use the essays as an introduction to the ways academics think and work. The final assignment asks you to write a short history (a local, family, or neighborhood history) and to think about your work in the context of problems of method presented by Limerick and Tompkins. You are working as a novice; they are working as professionals. The questions the sequence ends with are these: what would Limerick and Tompkins have to say to you about your work? What do you have to say to them about theirs?

This sequence is accompanied by a minisequence, "Writing History (II)" (p. 842). This alternative sequence provides similar assignments but with different readings. They can be substituted for assignments in the opening sequence or added to those assignments. Greenblatt offers another example of a significant figure in the academy's struggle to represent and understand the past. Like Limerick and Tompkins, Susan Griffin writes from a sense of the problems of historical understanding as writing problems.

• • • • • • • • • • • •

ASSIGNMENT 1

The Legacy of Conquest [Limerick]

"Empire of Innocence" is a chapter from Patricia Limerick's book, *The Legacy of Conquest.* It both presents episodes from the history of the American West and thinks out loud about history as something written (about the problems of history as reading and writing problems). In it, Limerick offers criticism and advice, an account of the problems of Western history and how they might be addressed (concerns about "point of view" and about "myth," for example). As you reread, look for passages that define both the problems and the possible solutions for those who read and write about the past.

Write an essay in which you present Limerick's account of the problems of history to a novice, someone new to Limerick and new to the academy. You should assume that your reader has not read the selection in this textbook—you will, that is, need to set the scene, to summarize, paraphrase, quote, and explain. Your goal is to give your reader not only a sense of what Limerick says but an idea of why it might be important to a student in the early stages of a college or university career.

• • • • • • • • • • • •

ASSIGNMENT 2

"Indians" [Tompkins]

In "Indians," Tompkins offers her experience researching and writing about Native Americans in colonial America as a representative case. Her story is meant to highlight a problem central to teaching, learning, and research—central, that is, to academic life. As a student, you can read this essay as a way of looking in on the work and concerns of your faculty (a group represented not only by Tompkins but by those against whom she is arguing). Write an essay directed to someone who has not read "Indians," someone who will be entering your school as a first-year student next semester. Your job is to introduce an incoming freshman to the academy, using Tompkins as your guide. (Since you've already written about Limerick, and since you can assume that the same readers will read both essays, you can bring Limerick in as a point of reference or comparison.) You will need to present Tompkins's argument and her conclusion in such a way as to make clear the consequences of what she says for someone about to begin an undergraduate education.

•   •   •   •   •   •   •   •   •   •   •   •

Writing History [Limerick, Tompkins]

One way to work on these selections is to take the challenge and write history—to write the kind of history, that is, that takes into account the problems defined by Limerick and Tompkins: the problems of myth, point of view, fixed ideas, facts and perspective, morality. You are not a professional historian, you are probably not using this book in a history course, and you probably don't have the time to produce a carefully researched history, one that covers all the bases, but you can think of this as an exercise in history writing, a minihistory, a place to start. Here are two options:

1. Go to your college library or, perhaps, the local historical society and find two or three first-person accounts of a single place, person, or event in your community. Try to work with original documents. The more varied the accounts, the better. Then, working with these texts as your primary sources, write a history, one that you can offer as a response to Limerick and Tompkins.

2. While you can find materials in a library, you can also work with records that are closer to home. Imagine, for example, that you are going to write a family or a neighborhood history. You have your own memories and experiences to work from, but for this to be a history (and not a "personal essay"), you will need to turn to other sources as well: interviews, old photos, newspaper clippings, letters, diaries—whatever you can find. After gathering your materials, write a family or neighborhood history, one that you can offer as a response to Limerick and Tompkins.

Choose one of the two projects. When you are done, write a quick one-page memo to the experts, Limerick and Tompkins. What can you tell them about the experience of a novice historian that they might find useful or interesting?

o—o—o—o—o—o—o—o—o—o—o—o—o—o—o—o

Writing History (II)

Stephen Greenblatt
Susan Griffin

*T*HE ASSIGNMENTS here are meant to supplement the assignments in "Writing History" (p. 839). They can be added to the sequence or substituted. Stephen Greenblatt's "Marvelous Possessions" stands as an example of the application of "close reading" to historical documents. He is one of the leading figures in the "new historicism." Like Jane Tompkins, he is working on the problem of history from the position of literary studies and literary criticism. Susan Griffin's work in *A Chorus of Stones* is offered as an alternative to more conventional historical writing. She is a careful and serious researcher. Her work is not, however, "a historian's history." She said, "What's in it is true, but I think of it as a book that verges on myth and legend, because those are the ways we find the deepest meanings and significance of events." These comments bring to mind Patricia Nelson Limerick's comments on the "mythic" power of the history of the American West.

. . . .

Reading and Writing America [Greenblatt]

In "Marvelous Possessions," Greenblatt argues that Europeans used conventional intellectual and organization structures to take possession of the New World. He writes at length about the "discourse of the marvelous." What is this discourse? What are its interests and its effects? Who uses it—when, why, and to what end?

But what about Greenblatt? What about Greenblatt's writing on Columbus and the New World? Hasn't he made these texts into something "marvelous"? Doesn't he "discover" them and take possession? What is Greenblatt doing to Columbus and the New World in this text? In what ways might you define and locate his writing as discursive action? Can you imagine (or can you provide examples of) any other way of working with the past?

Write an essay in which you explain Greenblatt's account of the discourse of the marvelous. You should assume that you are writing to someone who has not read "Marvelous Possessions," and who does not have the text close at hand. And see if you can use this discussion of the "marvelous" as a way of thinking back on this text, its aims and intentions, and on Greenblatt as a writer.

. . . .

Secrets [Griffin]

At several points in her essay, Griffin argues that we—all of us, especially all of us who read her essay—are part of a complex web of connections. She asks, for example,

> Who are we? The question is not simple. What we call the self is part of a larger matrix of relationship and society. Had we been born to a different family, in a different time, to a different world, we would not be the same. All the lives that surround us are in us. (pp. 355–56)

Later she asks, "Is there any one of us who can count ourselves outside the circle circumscribed by our common past?" (p. 365). At another point she speaks of a "field,"

> like a field of gravity that is created by the movements of many bodies. Each life is influenced and it in turn becomes an influence. Whatever is a cause is also an effect. Childhood experience is just one element in the determining field. (p. 324)

One way of thinking about this concept of the self (and of interrelatedness), at least to think about it under Griffin's guidance, is to work on the connections implied and asserted in her text. In her essay, Griffin writes *about* the past—how we can know it, what its relation is to the present, why we should care. In the *way* she writes, she is also making an argument about how we can know and understand the past, for example, in the way she represents key figures like Himmler or minor figures like Leo.

As you reread the selection, look for powerful and surprising juxtapositions, fragments that stand together in interesting and suggestive ways. Think about the arguments represented by the blank space between those sections. (And look for Griffin's written statements about "relatedness.") Look for connections that seem important to the text (and to you) and representative of Griffin's thinking (and yours).

Write an essay in which you use these examples to think through your understanding of Griffin's project, one that represents the past and an understanding of the past, but not necessarily as this would be done by a historian. Hers, she said, is "not a historian's history." How does she do her work? What does she work on when she works on her writing? What are the problems of writing that seem important to her? What might a writer learn (what did you learn?) from her example?

Writing and "Real" Life

Joyce Carol Oates
Lewis Nordan
John Edgar Wideman

YOU HAVE BEEN living with stories for a large part of your life. The purpose of this sequence is to invite you to examine the borderlines between what we conventionally call "fiction" and "fact." The five assignments that follow bring together two short stories that could be called "realistic" and a work of nonfiction that questions its powers to represent the "real." The first three assignments lead you to consider the "contact zones" between what we have learned to refer to as fiction and nonfiction and to think about how readers and writers face the problems associated with representing or constructing the "real" world. After telling a story of your own, one that blurs the line between fact and fiction, you are invited to step back and re-examine the essays you have written on writing the stories of real life.

. . . .

Imagining Landscapes [Oates]

> A writer's authentic self, she thought, lay in his writing and not in his life; it was the landscape of the imagination that endured, that was really real. Mere life was the husk, the actor's performance, negligible in the long run. . . . How could it be anything more than the vehicle by which certain works of art were transcribed . . . ? (p. 474)
>
> — JOYCE CAROL OATES
> *Theft*

It is fair to say that readers are tempted to think of the scenes and characters in Oates's short story, "Theft," as real. It is a realistic story; its "storyness" disappears once we enter the fiction. It takes a special effort to think of it as something Oates made up, something crafted. As part of a larger project, one in which you will examine the boundaries between fact and fiction, reread "Theft," measuring the story against the "real" world of college life as you know it. Read it as though it were an account of a real person's experience, as though Marya were telling her own story, not Oates, as though the "story" here were like the stories real people tell one another about their real experience. If you read it as "real," what does Oates get right? What did she miss? What has she failed to see or understand? Where does she stretch the boundaries of truth? Where, if anywhere, is the frame of the "real" broken?

Write an essay in which you discuss "Theft" as a realistic account of college life, measuring it against your own sense of what that life is like.

When you are done, write an additional one-page "coda" in which you take a different position and talk about the story as fiction, something made up, in which the text is not simply a mirror held up to real life. From this position, which is Oates doing in the story—making an argument? trying to influence you in some way? fantasizing? idealizing? offering an alternative to "real life"? Who would want to believe that "Theft" is a true story? Why? And what, then, might "true" mean?

• • • • • • • • • • • •

ASSIGNMENT **2**

Using Stories [Nordan]

Music of the Swamp ends with two shorter stories. The first presents the death of Sugar Mecklin's father "under a blanket of fish." The second, an epilogue titled "OWLS," is narrated by a grown Sugar. Having just told his lover a story about his father, he begins to reflect on a magical moment he has either remembered or invented:

> I believed my clumsy drunken inexpert father, or my invention of him, had prepared me for this magic. The woman beside me said, "I love you."
>
> In that moment every good thing that I had expected, longed to feel with my father, I felt with her. And I also felt it with my father, and I heard his voice speak those words of love, though he was already a long time dead. He was with me in a way he could not be in life.
>
> For one second the woman and I seemed to become twins, or closer than twins. . . . Maybe we said nothing. Maybe we only lay in the band of sunlight that fell across our bed. Or maybe together we said, "There is great pain in love, but we don't care, it's worth it."

As you consider the borderline between fact and fiction, it can be helpful to think about how readers make use of stories they read and tell. Most readers, for example, are tempted to read Nordan's story as true, as the "true" account of the author's experience with his family. In this case, Nordan is revealing intimate details about his family and childhood. Read back through the story, thinking of it as true, as real life. What do you notice? What use is it to you? What use might it be to Nordan?

Now read back through the story again and think of it as fiction, as something made up—as one more version of the familiar tale about an innocent child in a difficult situation and the triumph of love. In this case, Nordan is casting himself and his family in an old story, as a kind of Huck Finn, or a Cinderella, with a difficult parent. Now what happens? What use is this story to you? to him?

Write an essay in which you present and discuss these two views of Nordan's stories from *Music of the Swamp.* You could imagine that you are thinking through responses to questions Nordan raises in the passage quoted above: Why did he tell these stories? Or why did he invent them?

. . . .

Studying Fact and Fiction [Wideman]

The hardest habit to break, since it was the habit of a lifetime, would be listening to myself listen to him. That habit would destroy any chance of seeing my brother on his terms; and seeing him in his terms, learning his terms, seemed the whole point of learning his story. However numerous and comforting the similarities, we were different. The world had seized on the difference, allowed me room to thrive, while he'd been forced into a cage. Why did it work out that way? What was the nature of the difference? Why did it haunt me? Temporarily at least, to answer these questions, I had to root my fiction-writing self out of our exchanges. I had to teach myself to listen. Start fresh, clear the pipes, resist too facile an identification, tame the urge to take off with Robby's story and make it my own. (p. 667)

I couldn't rely on memory to get my brother's story down and the keepers had refused my request to use a tape recorder, so there I was. Jimmy Olsen, cub reporter, poised on the edge of my seat, pen and paper at ready, asking to be treated as a brother. (p. 668)

— JOHN EDGAR WIDEMAN
Our Time

At several points in "Our Time," Wideman discusses his position as a fiction writer writing nonfiction, and the difficulties he faces in writing about his brother and his family and their past (or in "reading" the text of his brother's life). At one point he says, "I had to root my fiction-writing self out of our exchanges. I had to teach myself to listen. Start fresh, clear the pipes, resist too facile an identification, tame the urge to take off with Robby's story and make it my own." What might Wideman mean by this—rooting out his "fiction-writing self"? resisting "too facile an identification"? making Robby's story his own? You have here the example of a fiction writer thinking through many of the questions that have been yours in this sequence.

As you reread "Our Time," note and mark the sections where Wideman speaks directly about his work as a writer. And note those sections where indirectly, in practice, through methods and devices, he seems to be working out the problems of writing on the borderline between fiction and fact.

Which sections seem to best represent the "real"? Which sections seem con-trived, fictional? What convinces you that the "real" scenes are real? What convinces Wideman?

Choose three or four passages from "Our Time" you can discuss in detail and write an essay in which you take Wideman the writer and "Our Time" as a case study of the relationships between writing, fiction, and fact.

• • • • • • • • • • • •

ASSIGNMENT **4**

Writing Your Own Story
[Oates, Nordan, Wideman]

Bodiless, weightless, utterly absorbed, she traversed the land-scape of another's mind and found it like her own yet totally unlike—surprising and jarring her, enticing her, leading her on. It was a secret process yet it was not criminal or forbid-den—she made her way with the stealth of the thief, elated, subdued, through another's imagination, risking no harm, no punishment. (p. 474)

— JOYCE CAROL OATES
Theft

I said, "Mother, do you remember the time Dad took me fishing and it made me so sad to see the fish die?"

She said, "Your daddy never took you fishing, Sugar. I begged him a hundred times to take you, but he never did."

I said, "No, I'm sure he took me once. He caught silvery-looking fish and I finally caught one, well, a catfish I suppose, an ugly monstrous old creature of a fish. It looked nothing like the fish he was catching."

She said, "You must have dreamed it, Sugar-man. It never happened. Your daddy never took you fishing."

— LEWIS NORDAN, from "Creatures with Shining Scales"
in *Music of the Swamp*

The detail grabbing me functions as a door and it swings open and I'm drawn, sucked, pulled in head over heels till suddenly I'm righted again, on track again and the peculiarity, the ordi-

nariness of the detail that usurped my attention becomes a
window, a way of seeing out of another person's eyes, just as
for a second it had been my way in. (p. 667)

— JOHN EDGAR WIDEMAN
Our Time

Now it is time for you to try your hand at this. Write a story that will be
read as "real" in which you combine fact and fiction, real scenes and scenes
that you make up. Make this a story, with scenes, characters, dialogue, details, and make it a story worth telling and worth reading, not simply an
exercise.

You have before you three examples of storytelling—Oates's, Nordan's,
and Wideman's. You should turn to them as you prepare and feel free to
model what you do on what they have done, singly or as a group. They
should also help you to ask the "writerly" questions: Can you rely on memory? What are the alternatives? Where do you get details and dialogue? How
will you get into someone else's head? What is the line between a "character"
and a "person"? How does the "fiction" serve the "real"? How does the
"real" serve the "fiction"? Where will you go for the shape of your narrative—its beginning, middle, and end? Who and what do you identify with?
Whose story is this?

•   •   •   •   •   •   •   •   •   •   •

ASSIGNMENT **5**

Writing and "Real" Life
[Oates, Nordan, Wideman]

This is the final assignment in the sequence. It is a chance for you to reflect on the work you have done. Take your story from assignment 4 as a
place to begin, and take the questions that stood at the end of assignment 4:

> Can you rely on memory? What are the alternatives? Where do
> you get details and dialogue? How will you get into someone
> else's head? What is the line between a "character" and a "per-
> son"? How does the "fiction" serve the "real"? How does the
> "real" serve the "fiction"? Where will you go for the shape of
> your narrative—its beginning, middle, and end? Who and
> what do you identify with? Whose story is this?

Write an essay in which you talk about your story, perhaps its reception by others in your class, about your work as a writer, and, through that work, about the general question of the relationship between writing and the "real" world. You could think of your essay as a kind of extended introduction or afterword to your story, something a reader might read to look into your work as a writer. You might also think of your essay as a chance to allude back to "Theft," the stories from *Music of the Swamp*, and "Our Time." You might bring those works back into the conversation.

ACKNOWLEDGMENTS

(continued from p. iv)

Susan Douglas, "Narcissism as Liberation." From *Where the Girls Are: Growing Up Female with the Mass Media* by Susan J. Douglas. Copyright © 1994 by Susan J. Douglas. Reprinted by permission of Times Books, a division of Random House, Inc. *Biotherm: The Cellulite Solution* (advertisement) reprinted by permission of Cosmair, Inc.

Ralph Ellison, "An Extravagance of Laughter." From *Going to the Territory* by Ralph Ellison. Copyright © 1986 by Ralph Ellison. Reprinted by permission of Random House, Inc.

Michel Foucault, "Panopticism." From *Discipline and Punish: The Birth of the Prison.* Copyright © 1975 by Éditions Gallimard. Translation copyright © 1977 by Alan Sheridan. Reprinted by permission of Georges Borchardt, Inc. *L'Art d'écrire* engraved by Prévost, from *L'Encyclopédie,* 1763. Reprinted by permission of l'Institut National de Recherche Pédagogique, Musée National de l'Education. Jeremy Bentham, *Plan of the Panopticon* from *The Works of Jeremy Bentham,* edited by Bowring, 1843. Reprinted by permission of Oxford University Press.

Paulo Freire, "The 'Banking' Concept of Education." From Ch. 2 of *Pedagogy of the Oppressed* by Paulo Freire. Copyright © 1970 by the author. Reprinted by permission of the Continuum Publishing Group.

Clifford Geertz, "Deep Play: Notes on the Balinese Cockfight." Reprinted by permission of *Daedalus,* Journal of the American Academy of Arts and Sciences, from the issue entitled, "Myth, Symbol, and Culture," Winter 1972, vol. 101, no. 1.

Stephen Greenblatt, "Marvelous Possessions." Ch. 3 in *Marvelous Possessions* by Stephen Greenblatt. Copyright © Stephen Greenblatt 1991. All rights reserved. Reprinted by permission of the University of Chicago Press and the author. *The Tupinamba greeting ritual* from Jean de Léry, *Histoire d'un voyage fait en la terre du Brasil, dite Amerique,* Vignon, 1600. *Lienzo de Tlaxcala* from Alfredo Chavero, *Antiquedades Mexicanas,* 1892. *Signs of Possession* from Theodor de Bry, *America,* Part I (1591), pl. VIII. *The Spanish "thirst" for gold quenched* from Theodor de Bry, *America,* Part IV (1592), pl. XX. *The gift of necessities* from Theodor de Bry, *America,* Parts VII and VIII (1599). Reprinted by permission of Bancroft Library, University of California, Berkeley. *Algonquian child holding an English doll* by John White, #G6837. Reprinted by permission of The British Library. *The map in a fool's cap* from *Douce Portfolio* 142(92). Reprinted by permission of the Bodleian Library. *The Marvels of the East* from *Mandeville's Travels,* Alcala, 1547. Reprinted by permission of the Department of Printing and Graphic Arts, The Houghton Library, Harvard University. *T-Q Map* from Isidore of Seville, *Etymologiae,* Augsburg, 1472. Photo courtesy of The Newberry Library. Early German woodcut reprinted by permission of The Spencer Collection, New York Public Library, Astor, Lenox, and Tilden Foundations.

Susan Griffin, "Our Secret." From *A Chorus of Stones* by Susan Griffin. Copyright © 1992 by Susan Griffin. Used by permission of Doubleday, a division of Bantam Doubleday Dell Publishing Group, Inc.

Patricia Nelson Limerick, "Empire of Innocence." Reprinted from *The Legacy of Conquest: The Unbroken Past of the American West* by Patricia Nelson Limerick, with the permission of W. W. Norton & Company, Inc. Copyright © 1987 by Patricia Nelson Limerick.

Lewis Nordan, "Music of the Swamp," "Porpoises and Romance," and "How Bob Steele Broke My Father's Heart." From *Music of the Swamp* by Lewis Nordan. Copyright © 1991 by Lewis Nordan. Reprinted by permission of Algonquin Books of Chapel Hill, a division of Workman Publishing Co., New York, NY. Excerpts from "Muddy Water" by Harry Richman, Peter DeRose, and Jo Trent. Copyright © 1926 (renewed) Sony/ATV Tunes LLC/Music Sales Corp/Broadway Music Corp. All rights on behalf of Sony/ATV Tunes LLC administered by Sony/ATV Music Publishing, 8 Music Square West, Nashville, TN 37203. All rights reserved. Used by permission.

Joyce Carol Oates, "Theft." From *Marya: A Life* by Joyce Carol Oates. Copyright © Ontario Review, Inc., 1989. Reprinted by permission of the author.

Walker Percy, "The Loss of the Creature." From *The Message in the Bottle* by Walker Percy. Copyright © 1975 by Walker Percy. Reprinted by permission of Farrar, Straus & Giroux, Inc.

Mary Louise Pratt, "Arts of the Contact Zone." From *Profession 91.* Copyright © 1991. Reprinted by permission of the Modern Language Association of America.

Adrienne Rich, "When We Dead Awaken: Writing as Re-Vision." Reprinted from *On Lies, Secrets, and Silence: Selected Prose 1966–1978* by Adrienne Rich, by permission of the author and W. W. Norton & Company, Inc. Copyright © 1979 by W. W. Norton & Company, Inc.

Richard Rodriguez, "The Achievement of Desire." From *Hunger of Memory* by Richard Rodriguez. Copyright © 1982 by Richard Rodriguez. Reprinted by permission of David R. Godine, Publisher, Inc. Richard Hoggart excerpts appearing in "The Achievement of Desire" by Richard Rodriguez from *The Uses of Literacy* by Richard Hoggart. Copyright 1957. Reprinted by permission of Oxford University Press and Random House UK Limited.

James Schuyler, "A Few Days." From *Collected Poems* by James Schuyler. Copyright © 1993 by the Estate of James Schuyler. Reprinted by permission of Farrar, Straus & Giroux, Inc.

Jane Tompkins, "'Indians': Textualism, Morality, and the Problem of History." From *Critical Inquiry,* vol. 13, no. 1 (Autumn 1986). Reprinted in Henry Louis Gates, ed., *Race, Writing, and Difference* (1986), pp. 101–19. © 1986 The University of Chicago. All rights reserved. Reprinted by permission of the publisher.

Alice Walker, "In Search of Our Mothers' Gardens." From *In Search of Our Mothers' Gardens: Womanist Prose,* copyright © 1974 by Alice Walker. Reprinted by permission of Harcourt Brace & Company.

"Women" (internal poem) from *Revolutionary Petunias and Other Poems,* copyright © 1970 by A Walker. Reprinted by permission of Harcourt Brace & Company.

John Edgar Wideman, "Our Time." From *Brothers and Keepers* by John Edgar Wideman. Copyright 1984 by John Edgar Wideman. Reprinted by permission of Henry Holt and Co., Inc.

Patricia J. Williams, "And We Are Not Married: A Journal of Musings upon Legal Language and the Id. ology of Style." From *Consequences of Theory,* Jonathan Arac and Barbara Johnson, eds., Johns Hop kins Press. Reprinted by permission of the author.

Virginia Woolf, "A Room of One's Own." Chs. 1 and 6 from *A Room of One's Own* by Virginia Woolf. Copyright 1929 by Harcourt Brace & Company and renewed 1957 by Leonard Woolf. Reprinted by permission of the publisher.

ice

©